D1299656

American Casebook Series
Hornbook Series and Basic Legal Texts
Nutshell Series

of

WEST PUBLISHING COMPANY
P.O. Box 43526
St. Paul, Minnesota 55164
June, 1984

ACCOUNTING

Faris' Law and Accounting in a Nutshell, 377 pages, 1984 (Text)

Fiflis, Kripke and Foster's Teaching Materials on Accounting for Business Lawyers, 3rd Ed., 838 pages, 1984 (Casebook)

Siegel and Siegel's Accounting and Financial Disclosure: A Guide to Basic Concepts, 259 pages, 1983 (Text)

ADMINISTRATIVE LAW

Davis' Cases, Text and Problems on Administrative Law, 6th Ed., 683 pages, 1977 (Casebook)

Davis' Basic Text on Administrative Law, 3rd Ed., 617 pages, 1972 (Text)

Davis' Police Discretion, 176 pages, 1975 (Text)

Gellhorn and Boyer's Administrative Law and Process in a Nutshell, 2nd Ed., 445 pages, 1981 (Text)

Mashaw and Merrill's Introduction to the American Public Law System, 1095 pages, 1975, with 1980 Supplement (Casebook)

Robinson, Gellhorn and Bruff's The Administrative Process, 2nd Ed., 959 pages, 1980, with 1983 Supplement (Casebook)

ADMIRALTY

Healy and Sharpe's Cases and Materials on Admiralty, 875 pages, 1974 (Casebook)

Maraist's Admiralty in a Nutshell, 390 pages, 1983 (Text)

Sohn and Gustafson's Law of the Sea in a Nutshell, 264 pages, 1984 (Text)

AGENCY—PARTNERSHIP

Fessler's Alternatives to Incorporation for Persons in Quest of Profit, 258 pages, 1980 (Casebook)

AGENCY—PARTNERSHIP—Continued

Henn's Cases and Materials on Agency, Partnership and Other Unincorporated Business Enterprises, 2nd Ed., approximately 400 pages, 1985 (Casebook)

Reuschlein and Gregory's Hornbook on the Law of Agency and Partnership, 625 pages, 1979, with 1981 pocket part (Text)

Seavey, Reuschlein and Hall's Cases on Agency and Partnership, 599 pages, 1962 (Casebook)

Selected Corporation and Partnership Statutes and Forms, 556 pages, 1982

Steffen and Kerr's Cases and Materials on Agency-Partnership, 4th Ed., 859 pages, 1980 (Casebook)

Steffen's Agency-Partnership in a Nutshell, 364 pages, 1977 (Text)

AMERICAN INDIAN LAW

Canby's American Indian Law in a Nutshell, 288 pages, 1981 (Text)

Getches, Rosenfelt and Wilkinson's Cases on Federal Indian Law, 660 pages, 1979, with 1983 Supplement (Casebook)

ANTITRUST LAW

Gellhorn's Antitrust Law and Economics in a Nutshell, 2nd Ed., 425 pages, 1981 (Text)

Gifford and Raskind's Cases and Materials on Antitrust, 694 pages, 1983 (Casebook)

Hovenkamp's Economics and Federal Antitrust Law, Student Ed., approximately 375 pages, 1985 (Text)

Oppenheim, Weston and McCarthy's Cases and Comments on Federal Antitrust Laws, 4th Ed., 1168 pages, 1981 (Casebook)

Posner and Easterbrook's Cases and Economic Notes on Antitrust, 2nd Ed., 1077 pages, 1981, with 1984–85 Supplement (Casebook)

ANTITRUST LAW—Continued

Sullivan's Hornbook of the Law of Antitrust, 886 pages, 1977 (Text)

See also Regulated Industries, Trade Regulation

ART LAW

DuBoff's Art Law in a Nutshell, 335 pages, 1984 (Text)

BANKING LAW

Lovett's Banking and Financial Institutions in a Nutshell, 409 pages, 1984 (Text)

Symons and White's Teaching Materials on Banking Law, 2nd Ed., approximately 943 pages, 1984 (Casebook)

BUSINESS PLANNING

Epstein and Scheinfeld's Teaching Materials on Business Reorganization Under the Bankruptcy Code, 216 pages, 1980 (Casebook)

Painter's Problems and Materials in Business Planning, 2nd Ed., 1008 pages, 1984 (Casebook)

Selected Securities and Business Planning Statutes, Rules and Forms, 485 pages, 1982

CIVIL PROCEDURE

Casad's Res Judicata in a Nutshell, 310 pages, 1976 (text)

Cound, Friedenthal and Miller's Cases and Materials on Civil Procedure, 3rd Ed., 1147 pages, 1980 with 1984 Supplement (Casebook)

Ehrenzweig, Louisell and Hazard's Jurisdiction in a Nutshell, 4th Ed., 232 pages, 1980 (Text)

Federal Rules of Civil-Appellate-Criminal Procedure—West Law School Edition, approximately 477 pages, 1984

Hodges, Jones and Elliott's Cases and Materials on Texas Trial and Appellate Procedure, 2nd Ed., 745 pages, 1974 (Casebook)

Hodges, Jones and Elliott's Cases and Materials on the Judicial Process Prior to Trial in Texas, 2nd Ed., 871 pages, 1977 (Casebook)

Kane's Civil Procedure in a Nutshell, 271 pages, 1979 (Text)

Karlen's Procedure Before Trial in a Nutshell, 258 pages, 1972 (Text)

Karlen, Meisenholder, Stevens and Vestal's Cases on Civil Procedure, 923 pages, 1975 (Casebook)

Koffler and Reppy's Hornbook on Common Law Pleading, 663 pages, 1969 (Text)

Park's Computer-Aided Exercises on Civil Procedure, 2nd Ed., 167 pages, 1983 (Coursebook)

CIVIL PROCEDURE—Continued

Siegel's Hornbook on New York Practice, 1011 pages, 1978 with 1981–82 Pocket Part (Text)

See also Federal Jurisdiction and Procedure

CIVIL RIGHTS

Abernathy's Cases and Materials on Civil Rights, 660 pages, 1980 (Casebook)

Cohen's Cases on the Law of Deprivation of Liberty: A Study in Social Control, 755 pages, 1980 (Casebook)

Lockhart, Kamisar and Choper's Cases on Constitutional Rights and Liberties, 5th Ed., 1298 pages plus Appendix, 1981, with 1984 Supplement (Casebook)—reprint from Lockhart, et al. Cases on Constitutional Law, 5th Ed., 1980

Vieira's Civil Rights in a Nutshell, 279 pages, 1978 (Text)

COMMERCIAL LAW

Bailey's Secured Transactions in a Nutshell, 2nd Ed., 391 pages, 1981 (Text)

Epstein and Martin's Basic Uniform Commercial Code Teaching Materials, 2nd Ed., 667 pages, 1983 (Casebook)

Henson's Hornbook on Secured Transactions Under the U.C.C., 2nd Ed., 504 pages, 1979 with 1979 P.P. (Text)

Murray's Commercial Law, Problems and Materials, 366 pages, 1975 (Coursebook)

Nordstrom and Clovis' Problems and Materials on Commercial Paper, 458 pages, 1972 (Casebook)

Nordstrom and Lattin's Problems and Materials on Sales and Secured Transactions, 809 pages, 1968 (Casebook)

Nordstrom, Murray and Clovis' Problems and Materials on Sales, 515 pages, 1982 (Casebook)

Nordstrom's Hornbook on Sales, 600 pages, 1970 (Text)

Selected Commercial Statutes, 1379 pages, 1983

Speidel, Summers and White's Teaching Materials on Commercial and Consumer Law, 3rd Ed., 1490 pages, 1981 (Casebook)

Stockton's Sales in a Nutshell, 2nd Ed., 370 pages, 1981 (Text)

Stone's Uniform Commercial Code in a Nutshell, 2nd Ed., approximately 500 pages, 1984 (Text)

Uniform Commercial Code, Official Text with Comments, 994 pages, 1978

UCC Article 9, Reprint from 1962 Code, 128 pages, 1976

UCC Article 9, 1972 Amendments, 304 pages, 1978

Weber and Speidel's Commercial Paper in a Nutshell, 3rd Ed., 404 pages, 1982 (Text)

COMMERCIAL LAW—Continued

White and Summers' Hornbook on the Uniform Commercial Code, 2nd Ed., 1250 pages, 1980 (Text)

COMMUNITY PROPERTY

Mennell's Community Property in a Nutshell, 447 pages, 1982 (Text)

Verrall and Bird's Cases and Materials on California Community Property, 4th Ed., 549 pages, 1983 (Casebook)

COMPARATIVE LAW

Barton, Gibbs, Li and Merryman's Law in Radically Different Cultures, 960 pages, 1983 (Casebook)

Glendon, Gordon, and Osakwe's Comparative Legal Traditions in a Nutshell, 402 pages, 1982 (Text)

Langbein's Comparative Criminal Procedure: Germany, 172 pages, 1977 (Casebook)

COMPUTERS AND LAW

Mason's An Introduction to the Use of Computers in Law, 223 pages, 1984 (Text)

CONFLICT OF LAWS

Cramton, Currie and Kay's Cases-Comments-Questions on Conflict of Laws, 3rd Ed., 1026 pages, 1981 (Casebook)

Scoles and Hay's Hornbook on Conflict of Laws, Student Ed., 1085 pages, 1982 (Text)

Scoles and Weintraub's Cases and Materials on Conflict of Laws, 2nd Ed., 966 pages, 1972, with 1978 Supplement (Casebook)

Siegel's Conflicts in a Nutshell, 469 pages, 1982 (Text)

CONSTITUTIONAL LAW

Engdahl's Constitutional Power in a Nutshell: Federal and State, 411 pages, 1974 (Text)

Lockhart, Kamisar and Choper's Cases-Comments-Questions on Constitutional Law, 5th Ed., 1705 pages plus Appendix, 1980, with 1984 Supplement (Casebook)

Lockhart, Kamisar and Choper's Cases-Comments-Questions on the American Constitution, 5th Ed., 1185 pages plus Appendix, 1981, with 1984 Supplement (Casebook)—reprint from Lockhart, et al. Cases on Constitutional Law, 5th Ed., 1980

Manning's The Law of Church-State Relations in a Nutshell, 305 pages, 1981 (Text)

Miller's Presidential Power in a Nutshell, 328 pages, 1977 (Text)

CONSTITUTIONAL LAW—Continued

Nowak, Rotunda and Young's Hornbook on Constitutional Law, 2nd Ed., Student Ed., 1172 pages, 1983 (Text)

Rotunda's Modern Constitutional Law: Cases and Notes, 1034 pages, 1981, with 1984 Supplement (Casebook)

Williams' Constitutional Analysis in a Nutshell, 388 pages, 1979 (Text)

See also Civil Rights

CONSUMER LAW

Epstein and Nickles' Consumer Law in a Nutshell, 2nd Ed., 418 pages, 1981 (Text)

McCall's Consumer Protection, Cases, Notes and Materials, 594 pages, 1977, with 1977 Statutory Supplement (Casebook)

Selected Commercial Statutes, 1379 pages, 1983

Spanogle and Rohner's Cases and Materials on Consumer Law, 693 pages, 1979, with 1982 Supplement (Casebook)

See also Commercial Law

CONTRACTS

Calamari & Perillo's Cases and Problems on Contracts, 1061 pages, 1978 (Casebook)

Calamari and Perillo's Hornbook on Contracts, 2nd Ed., 878 pages, 1977 (Text)

Corbin's Text on Contracts, One Volume Student Edition, 1224 pages, 1952 (Text)

Fessler and Loiseaux's Cases and Materials on Contracts, 837 pages, 1982 (Casebook)

Freedman's Cases and Materials on Contracts, 658 pages, 1973 (Casebook)

Friedman's Contract Remedies in a Nutshell, 323 pages, 1981 (Text)

Fuller and Eisenberg's Cases on Basic Contract Law, 4th Ed., 1203 pages, 1981 (Casebook)

Hamilton, Rau and Weintraub's Cases and Materials on Contracts, 830 pages, 1984 (Casebook)

Jackson and Bollinger's Cases on Contract Law in Modern Society, 2nd Ed., 1329 pages, 1980 (Casebook)

Keyes' Government Contracts in a Nutshell, 423 pages, 1979 (Text)

Reitz's Cases on Contracts as Basic Commercial Law, 763 pages, 1975 (Casebook)

Schaber and Rohwer's Contracts in a Nutshell, 2nd Ed., 425 pages, 1984 (Text)

COPYRIGHT

See Patent and Copyright Law

CORPORATIONS

Hamilton's Cases on Corporations—Including Partnerships and Limited Partnerships, 2nd Ed., 1108 pages, 1981, with 1981 Statutory Supplement and 1984 Supplement (Casebook)

CORPORATIONS—Continued

Hamilton's Law of Corporations in a Nutshell, 379 pages, 1980 (Text)

Henn's Cases on Corporations, 1279 pages, 1974, with 1980 Supplement (Casebook)

Henn and Alexander's Hornbook on Corporations, 3rd Ed., Student Ed., 1371 pages, 1983 (Text)

Jennings and Buxbaum's Cases and Materials on Corporations, 5th Ed., 1180 pages, 1979 (Casebook)

Selected Corporation and Partnership Statutes, Regulations and Forms, 556 pages, 1982

Solomon, Stevenson and Schwartz' Materials and Problems on the Law and Policies on Corporations, 1172 pages, 1982 with 1984 Supplement (Casebook)

CORPORATE FINANCE

Hamilton's Cases and Materials on Corporate Finance, 895 pages, 1984 (Casebook)

CORRECTIONS

Krantz's Cases and Materials on the Law of Corrections and Prisoners' Rights, 2nd Ed., 735 pages, 1981, with 1982 Supplement (Casebook)

Krantz's Law of Corrections and Prisoners' Rights in a Nutshell, 2nd Ed., 384 pages, 1983 (Text)

Popper's Post-Conviction Remedies in a Nutshell, 360 pages, 1978 (Text)

Robbins' Cases and Materials on Post Conviction Remedies, 506 pages, 1982 (Casebook)

Rubin's Law of Criminal Corrections, 2nd Ed., 873 pages, 1973, with 1978 Supplement (Text)

CREDITOR'S RIGHTS

Bankruptcy Code and Rules, Law School Ed., 438 pages, 1984

Epstein's Debtor-Creditor Law in a Nutshell, 2nd Ed., 324 pages, 1980 (Text)

Epstein and Landers' Debtors and Creditors: Cases and Materials, 2nd Ed., 689 pages, 1982 (Casebook)

Epstein and Sheinfeld's Teaching Materials on Business Reorganization Under the Bankruptcy Code, 216 pages, 1980 (Casebook)

Riesenfeld's Cases and Materials on Creditors' Remedies and Debtors' Protection, 3rd Ed., 810 pages, 1979 with 1979 Statutory Supplement and 1981 Case Supplement (Casebook)

CRIMINAL LAW AND CRIMINAL PROCEDURE

Cohen and Gobert's Problems in Criminal Law, 297 pages, 1976 (Problem book)

CRIMINAL LAW AND CRIMINAL PROCEDURE—Continued

Davis' Police Discretion, 176 pages, 1975 (Text)

Dix and Sharlot's Cases and Materials on Criminal Law, 2nd Ed., 771 pages, 1979 (Casebook)

Federal Rules of Civil-Appellate-Criminal Procedure—West Law School Edition, approximately 477 pages, 1984

Grano's Problems in Criminal Procedure, 2nd Ed., 176 pages, 1981 (Problem book)

Israel and LaFave's Criminal Procedure in a Nutshell, 3rd Ed., 438 pages, 1980 (Text)

Johnson's Cases, Materials and Text on Substantive Criminal Law in its Procedural Context, 2nd Ed., 956 pages, 1980 (Casebook)

Kamisar, LaFave and Israel's Cases, Comments and Questions on Modern Criminal Procedure, 5th ed., 1635 pages plus Appendix, 1980 with 1984 Supplement (Casebook)

Kamisar, LaFave and Israel's Cases, Comments and Questions on Basic Criminal Procedure, 5th Ed., 869 pages, 1980 with 1984 Supplement (Casebook)—reprint from Kamisar, et al. Modern Criminal Procedure, 5th ed., 1980

LaFave's Modern Criminal Law: Cases, Comments and Questions, 789 pages, 1978 (Casebook)

LaFave and Israel's Hornbook on Criminal Procedure, Student Ed., approximately 1300 pages, 1985 (Text)

LaFave and Scott's Hornbook on Criminal Law, 763 pages, 1972 (Text)

Langbein's Comparative Criminal Procedure: Germany, 172 pages, 1977 (Casebook)

Loewy's Criminal Law in a Nutshell, 302 pages, 1975 (Text)

Saltzburg's American Criminal Procedure, Cases and Commentary, 2nd Ed., 1193 pages, 1984 with 1984 Supplement (Casebook)

Uviller's The Processes of Criminal Justice: Investigation and Adjudication, 2nd Ed., 1384 pages, 1979 with 1979 Statutory Supplement and 1983 Update (Casebook)

Uviller's The Processes of Criminal Justice: Adjudication, 2nd Ed., 730 pages, 1979. Soft-cover reprint from Uviller's The Processes of Criminal Justice: Investigation and Adjudication, 2nd Ed. (Casebook)

Uviller's The Processes of Criminal Justice: Investigation, 2nd Ed., 655 pages, 1979. Soft-cover reprint from Uviller's The Processes of Criminal Justice: Investigation and Adjudication, 2nd Ed. (Casebook)

CRIMINAL LAW AND CRIMINAL PROCEDURE—Continued

Vorenberg's Cases on Criminal Law and Procedure, 2nd Ed., 1088 pages, 1981 (Casebook)

See also Corrections, Juvenile Justice

DECEDENTS ESTATES

See Trusts and Estates

DOMESTIC RELATIONS

Clark's Cases and Problems on Domestic Relations, 3rd Ed., 1153 pages, 1980 (Casebook)

Clark's Hornbook on Domestic Relations, 754 pages, 1968 (Text)

Krause's Cases and Materials on Family Law, 2nd Ed., 1221 pages, 1983 (Casebook)

Krause's Family Law in a Nutshell, 400 pages, 1977 (Text)

Krauskopf's Cases on Property Division at Marriage Dissolution, 250 pages, 1984 (Casebook)

ECONOMICS, LAW AND

Goetz' Cases and Materials on Law and Economics, 547 pages, 1984 (Casebook)

Manne's The Economics of Legal Relationships—Readings in the Theory of Property Rights, 660 pages, 1975 (Text)

See also Antitrust, Regulated Industries

EDUCATION LAW

Alexander and Alexander's The Law of Schools, Students and Teachers in a Nutshell, 409 pages, 1984 (Text)

Morris' The Constitution and American Education, 2nd Ed., 992 pages, 1980 (Casebook)

EMPLOYMENT DISCRIMINATION

Player's Cases and Materials on Employment Discrimination Law, 2nd Ed., 782 pages, 1984 (Casebook)

Player's Federal Law of Employment Discrimination in a Nutshell, 2nd Ed., 402 pages, 1981 (Text)

See also Women and the Law

ENERGY AND NATURAL RESOURCES LAW

Rodgers' Cases and Materials on Energy and Natural Resources Law, 2nd Ed., 877 pages, 1983 (Casebook)

Selected Environmental Law Statutes, 758 pages, 1984

Tomain's Energy Law in a Nutshell, 338 pages, 1981 (Text)

See also Environmental Law, Oil and Gas, Water Law

ENVIRONMENTAL LAW

Bonine and McGarity's Cases and Materials on the Law of Environment and Pollution, 1076 pages, 1984 (Casebook)

Findley and Farber's Cases and Materials on Environmental Law, 738 pages, 1981, with 1983 Supplement (Casebook)

Findley and Farber's Environmental Law in a Nutshell, 343 pages, 1983 (Text)

Rodgers' Hornbook on Environmental Law, 956 pages, 1977 (Text)

Selected Environmental Law Statutes, 758 pages, 1984

See also Energy and Natural Resources Law, Water Law

EQUITY

See Remedies

ESTATES

See Trusts and Estates

ESTATE PLANNING

Kurtz' Cases, Materials and Problems on Family Estate Planning, 853 pages, 1983 (Casebook)

Lynn's Introduction to Estate Planning, in a Nutshell, 3rd Ed., 370 pages, 1983 (Text)

See also Taxation

EVIDENCE

Broun and Meisenholder's Problems in Evidence, 2nd Ed., 304 pages, 1981 (Problem book)

Cleary and Strong's Cases, Materials and Problems on Evidence, 3rd Ed., 1143 pages, 1981 (Casebook)

Federal Rules of Evidence for United States Courts and Magistrates, approximately 325 pages, 1984

Graham's Federal Rules of Evidence in a Nutshell, 429 pages, 1981 (Text)

Kimball's Programmed Materials on Problems in Evidence, 380 pages, 1978 (Problem book)

Lempert and Saltzburg's A Modern Approach to Evidence: Text, Problems, Transcripts and Cases, 2nd Ed., 1296 pages, 1983 (Casebook)

Lilly's Introduction to the Law of Evidence, 486 pages, 1978 (Text)

McCormick, Elliott and Sutton's Cases and Materials on Evidence, 5th Ed., 1212 pages, 1981 (Casebook)

McCormick's Hornbook on Evidence, 3rd Ed., Student Ed., 1155 pages, 1984 (Text)

Rothstein's Evidence, State and Federal Rules in a Nutshell, 2nd Ed., 514 pages, 1981 (Text)

EVIDENCE—Continued

Saltzburg's Evidence Supplement: Rules, Statutes, Commentary, 245 pages, 1980 (Casebook Supplement)

FEDERAL JURISDICTION AND PROCEDURE

Currie's Cases and Materials on Federal Courts, 3rd Ed., 1042 pages, 1982 (Casebook)

Currie's Federal Jurisdiction in a Nutshell, 2nd Ed., 258 pages, 1981 (Text)

Federal Rules of Civil-Appellate-Criminal Procedure—West Law School Edition, approximately 477 pages, 1984

Forrester and Moye's Cases and Materials on Federal Jurisdiction and Procedure, 3rd Ed., 917 pages, 1977 with 1981 Supplement (Casebook)

Redish's Cases, Comments and Questions on Federal Courts, 878 pages, 1983 (Casebook)

Vetri and Merrill's Federal Courts, Problems and Materials, 2nd Ed., 232 pages, 1984

Wright's Hornbook on Federal Courts, 4th Ed., Student Ed., 870 pages, 1983 (Text)

FUTURE INTERESTS

See Trusts and Estates

IMMIGRATION LAW

Weissbrodt's Immigration Law and Procedure in a Nutshell, 345 pages, 1984 (Text)

INDIAN LAW

See American Indian Law

INSURANCE

Dobbyn's Insurance Law in a Nutshell, 281 pages, 1981 (Text)

Keeton's Cases on Basic Insurance Law, 2nd Ed., 1086 pages, 1977

Keeton's Basic Text on Insurance Law, 712 pages, 1971 (Text)

Keeton's Case Supplement to Keeton's Basic Text on Insurance Law, 334 pages, 1978 (Casebook)

Keeton's Programmed Problems in Insurance Law, 243 pages, 1972 (Text Supplement)

York and Whelan's Cases, Materials and Problems on Insurance Law, 715 pages, 1982 (Casebook)

INTERNATIONAL LAW

Henkin, Pugh, Schachter and Smit's Cases and Materials on International Law, 2nd Ed., 1152 pages, 1980, with Documents Supplement (Casebook)

INTERNATIONAL LAW—Continued

Jackson's Legal Problems of International Economic Relations, 1097 pages, 1977, with Documents Supplement (Casebook)

Kirgis' International Organizations in Their Legal Setting, 1016 pages, 1977, with 1981 Supplement (Casebook)

Weston, Falk and D'Amato's International Law and World Order—A Problem Oriented Coursebook, 1195 pages, 1980, with Documents Supplement (Casebook)

Wilson's International Business Transactions in a Nutshell, 2nd Ed., 476 pages, 1984 (Text)

INTERVIEWING AND COUNSELING

Binder and Price's Interviewing and Counseling, 232 pages, 1977 (Text)

Shaffer's Interviewing and Counseling in a Nutshell, 353 pages, 1976 (Text)

INTRODUCTION TO LAW

Dobbyn's So You Want to go to Law School, Revised First Edition, 206 pages, 1976 (Text)

Hegland's Introduction to the Study and Practice of Law in a Nutshell, 418 pages, 1983 (Text)

Kinyon's Introduction to Law Study and Law Examinations in a Nutshell, 389 pages, 1971 (Text)

See also Legal Method and Legal System

JUDICIAL ADMINISTRATION

Carrington, Meador and Rosenberg's Justice on Appeal, 263 pages, 1976 (Casebook)

Nelson's Cases and Materials on Judicial Administration and the Administration of Justice, 1032 pages, 1974 (Casebook)

JURISPRUDENCE

Christie's Text and Readings on Jurisprudence—The Philosophy of Law, 1056 pages, 1973 (Casebook)

JUVENILE JUSTICE

Fox's Cases and Materials on Modern Juvenile Justice, 2nd Ed., 960 pages, 1981 (Casebook)

Fox's Juvenile Courts in a Nutshell, 3rd Ed., 291 pages, 1984 (Text)

LABOR LAW

Gorman's Basic Text on Labor Law—Unionization and Collective Bargaining, 914 pages, 1976 (Text)

Leslie's Labor Law in a Nutshell, 403 pages, 1979 (Text)

Nolan's Labor Arbitration Law and Practice in a Nutshell, 358 pages, 1979 (Text)

LABOR LAW—Continued

Oberer, Hanslowe and Andersen's Cases and Materials on Labor Law—Collective Bargaining in a Free Society, 2nd Ed., 1168 pages, 1979, with 1979 Statutory Supplement and 1982 Case Supplement (Casebook)

See also Employment Discrimination, Social Legislation

LAND FINANCE

See Real Estate Transactions

LAND USE

Hagman's Cases on Public Planning and Control of Urban and Land Development, 2nd Ed., 1301 pages, 1980 (Casebook)

Hagman's Hornbook on Urban Planning and Land Development Control Law, 706 pages, 1971 (Text)

Wright and Gitelman's Cases and Materials on Land Use, 3rd Ed., 1300 pages, 1982 (Casebook)

Wright and Webber's Land Use in a Nutshell, 316 pages, 1978 (Text)

LEGAL HISTORY

Presser and Zainaldin's Cases on Law and American History, 855 pages, 1980 (Casebook)

See also Legal Method and Legal System

LEGAL METHOD AND LEGAL SYSTEM

Aldisert's Readings, Materials and Cases in the Judicial Process, 948 pages, 1976 (Casebook)

Bodenheimer, Oakley and Love's Readings and Cases on an Introduction to the Anglo-American Legal System, 161 pages, 1980 (Casebook)

Davies and Lawry's Institutions and Methods of the Law—Introductory Teaching Materials, 547 pages, 1982 (Casebook)

Dvorkin, Himmelstein and Lesnick's Becoming a Lawyer: A Humanistic Perspective on Legal Education and Professionalism, 211 pages, 1981 (Text)

Fryer and Orentlicher's Cases and Materials on Legal Method and Legal System, 1043 pages, 1967 (Casebook)

Greenberg's Judicial Process and Social Change, 666 pages, 1977 (Coursebook)

Kelso and Kelso's Studying Law: An Introduction, 587 pages, 1984 (Coursebook)

Kempin's Historical Introduction to Anglo-American Law in a Nutshell, 2nd Ed., 280 pages, 1973 (Text)

Kimball's Historical Introduction to the Legal System, 610 pages, 1966 (Casebook)

Mashaw and Merrill's Introduction to the American Public Law System, 1095 pages, 1975, with 1980 Supplement (Casebook)

LEGAL METHOD AND LEGAL SYSTEM—Continued

Murphy's Cases and Materials on Introduction to Law—Legal Process and Procedure, 772 pages, 1977 (Casebook)

Reynolds' Judicial Process in a Nutshell, 292 pages, 1980 (Text)

See also Legal Research and Writing

LEGAL PROFESSION

Aronson's Problems in Professional Responsibility, 280 pages, 1978 (Problem book)

Aronson and Weckstein's Professional Responsibility in a Nutshell, 399 pages, 1980 (Text)

Mellinkoff's The Conscience of a Lawyer, 304 pages, 1973 (Text)

Mellinkoff's Lawyers and the System of Justice, 983 pages, 1976 (Casebook)

Pirsig and Kirwin's Cases and Materials on Professional Responsibility, 4th Ed., approximately 650 pages, 1984 (Casebook)

Schwartz and Wydick's Problems in Legal Ethics, 285 pages, 1983 (Casebook)

Selected Statutes, Rules and Standards on the Legal Profession, approximately 260 pages, Revised 1984

Smith's Preventing Legal Malpractice, 142 pages, 1981 (Text)

LEGAL RESEARCH AND WRITING

Cohen's Legal Research in a Nutshell, 4th Ed., approximately 425 pages, 1984 (Text)

Cohen and Berring's How to Find the Law, 8th Ed., 790 pages, 1983. Problem book by Foster and Kelly available (Casebook)

Cohen and Berring's Finding the Law, 8th Ed., Abridged Ed., 556 pages, 1984 (Casebook)

Dickerson's Materials on Legal Drafting, 425 pages, 1981 (Casebook)

Felsenfeld and Siegel's Writing Contracts in Plain English, 290 pages, 1981 (Text)

Gopen's Writing From a Legal Perspective, 225 pages, 1981 (Text)

Mellinkoff's Legal Writing—Sense and Nonsense, 242 pages, 1982 (Text)

Rombauer's Legal Problem Solving—Analysis, Research and Writing, 4th Ed., 424 pages, 1983 (Coursebook)

Squires and Rombauer's Legal Writing in a Nutshell, 294 pages, 1982 (Text)

Statsky's Legal Research, Writing and Analysis, 2nd Ed., 167 pages, 1982 (Coursebook)

Statsky's Legislative Analysis: How to Use Statutes and Regulations, 2nd Ed., 217 pages, 1984 (Text)

Statsky and Wernet's Case Analysis and Fundamentals of Legal Writing, 2nd Ed., 441 pages, 1984 (Text)

LEGAL RESEARCH AND WRITING—Continued

Teply's Programmed Materials on Legal Research and Citation, 334 pages, 1982. Student Library Exercises available (Coursebook)

Weihofen's Legal Writing Style, 2nd Ed., 332 pages, 1980 (Text)

LEGISLATION

Davies' Legislative Law and Process in a Nutshell, 279 pages, 1975 (Text)

Nutting and Dickerson's Cases and Materials on Legislation, 5th Ed., 744 pages, 1978 (Casebook)

Statsky's Legislative Analysis: How to Use Statutes and Regulations, 2nd Ed., 217 pages, 1984 (Text)

LOCAL GOVERNMENT

McCarthy's Local Government Law in a Nutshell, 2nd Ed., 404 pages, 1983 (Text)

Michelman and Sandalow's Cases-Comments-Questions on Government in Urban Areas, 1216 pages, 1970, with 1972 Supplement (Casebook)

Reynolds' Hornbook on Local Government Law, 860 pages, 1982 (Text)

Valente's Cases and Materials on Local Government Law, 2nd Ed., 980 pages, 1980 with 1982 Supplement (Casebook)

MASS COMMUNICATION LAW

Gillmor and Barron's Cases and Comment on Mass Communication Law, 4th Ed., 1076 pages, 1984 (Casebook)

Ginsburg's Regulation of Broadcasting: Law and Policy Towards Radio, Television and Cable Communications, 741 pages, 1979, with 1983 Supplement (Casebook)

Zuckman and Gayne's Mass Communications Law in a Nutshell, 2nd Ed., 473 pages, 1983 (Text)

MEDICINE, LAW AND

King's The Law of Medical Malpractice in a Nutshell, 340 pages, 1977 (Text)

Shapiro and Spece's Problems, Cases and Materials on Bioethics and Law, 892 pages, 1981 (Casebook)

Sharpe, Fiscina and Head's Cases on Law and Medicine, 882 pages, 1978 (Casebook)

MILITARY LAW

Shanor and Terrell's Military Law in a Nutshell, 378 pages, 1980 (Text)

MORTGAGES

See Real Estate Transactions

NATURAL RESOURCES LAW

See Energy and Natural Resources Law, Environmental Law, Oil and Gas, Water Law

NEGOTIATION

Edwards and White's Problems, Readings and Materials on the Lawyer as a Negotiator, 484 pages, 1977 (Casebook)

Williams' Legal Negotiation and Settlement, 207 pages, 1983 (Coursebook)

OFFICE PRACTICE

Hegland's Trial and Practice Skills in a Nutshell, 346 pages, 1978 (Text)

Strong and Clark's Law Office Management, 424 pages, 1974 (Casebook)

See also Computers and Law, Interviewing and Counseling, Negotiation

OIL AND GAS

Hemingway's Hornbook on Oil and Gas, 2nd Ed., Student Ed., 543 pages, 1983 (Text)

Huie, Woodward and Smith's Cases and Materials on Oil and Gas, 2nd Ed., 955 pages, 1972 (Casebook)

Lowe's Oil and Gas Law in a Nutshell, 443 pages, 1983 (Text)

See also Energy and Natural Resources Law

PARTNERSHIP

See Agency—Partnership

PATENT AND COPYRIGHT LAW

Choate and Francis' Cases and Materials on Patent Law, 2nd Ed., 1110 pages, 1981 (Casebook)

Miller and Davis' Intellectual Property—Patents, Trademarks and Copyright in a Nutshell, 428 pages, 1983 (Text)

Nimmer's Cases on Copyright and Other Aspects of Law Pertaining to Literary, Musical and Artistic Works, 2nd Ed., 1023 pages, 1979 (Casebook)

POVERTY LAW

Brudno's Poverty, Inequality, and the Law: Cases-Commentary-Analysis, 934 pages, 1976 (Casebook)

LaFrance, Schroeder, Bennett and Boyd's Hornbook on Law of the Poor, 558 pages, 1973 (Text)

See also Social Legislation

PRODUCTS LIABILITY

Noel and Phillips' Cases on Products Liability, 2nd Ed., 821 pages, 1982 (Casebook)

Noel and Phillips' Products Liability in a Nutshell, 2nd Ed., 341 pages, 1981 (Text)

PROPERTY

Aigler, Smith and Tefft's Cases on Property, 2 volumes, 1339 pages, 1960 (Casebook)

Bernhardt's Real Property in a Nutshell, 2nd Ed., 448 pages, 1981 (Text)

Boyer's Survey of the Law of Property, 766 pages, 1981 (Text)

LAW SCHOOL PUBLICATIONS—Continued

PROPERTY—Continued

Browder, Cunningham and Smith's Cases on Basic Property Law, 4th Ed., 1431 pages, 1984 (Casebook)

Bruce, Ely and Bostick's Cases and Materials on Modern Property Law, 1004 pages, 1984 (Casebook)

Burby's Hornbook on Real Property, 3rd Ed., 490 pages, 1965 (Text)

Burke's Personal Property in a Nutshell, 322 pages, 1983 (Text)

Chused's A Modern Approach to Property: Cases-Notes-Materials, 1069 pages, 1978 with 1980 Supplement (Casebook)

Cohen's Materials for a Basic Course in Property, 526 pages, 1978 (Casebook)

Cunningham, Whitman and Stoebuck's Hornbook on the Law of Property, Student Ed., 916 pages, 1984 (Text)

Donahue, Kauper and Martin's Cases on Property, 2nd Ed., 1362 pages, 1983 (Casebook)

Hill's Landlord and Tenant Law in a Nutshell, 319 pages, 1979 (Text)

Moynihan's Introduction to Real Property, 254 pages, 1962 (Text)

Phipps' Titles in a Nutshell, 277 pages, 1968 (Text)

Uniform Land Transactions Act, Uniform Simplification of Land Transfers Act, Uniform Condominium Act, 1977 Official Text with Comments, 462 pages, 1978

See also Real Estate Transactions, Land Use

REAL ESTATE TRANSACTIONS

Bruce's Real Estate Finance in a Nutshell, 2nd Ed., approximately 300 pages, 1985 (Text)

Maxwell, Riesenfeld, Hetland and Warren's Cases on California Security Transactions in Land, 3rd Ed., 728 pages, 1984 (Casebook)

Nelson and Whitman's Cases on Real Estate Transfer, Finance and Development, 2nd Ed., 1114 pages, 1981, with 1983 Supplement (Casebook)

Osborne's Cases and Materials on Secured Transactions, 559 pages, 1967 (Casebook)

Osborne, Nelson and Whitman's Hornbook on Real Estate Finance Law, 3rd Ed., 885 pages, 1979 (Text)

REGULATED INDUSTRIES

Gellhorn and Pierce's Regulated Industries in a Nutshell, 394 pages, 1982 (Text)

Morgan's Cases and Materials on Economic Regulation of Business, 830 pages, 1976, with 1978 Supplement (Casebook)

REGULATED INDUSTRIES—Continued

Pozen's Financial Institutions: Cases, Materials and Problems on Investment Management, 844 pages, 1978 (Casebook)

See also Mass Communication Law, Banking Law

REMEDIES

Dobbs' Hornbook on Remedies, 1067 pages, 1973 (Text)

Dobbs' Problems in Remedies, 137 pages, 1974 (Problem book)

Dobbyn's Injunctions in a Nutshell, 264 pages, 1974 (Text)

Friedman's Contract Remedies in a Nutshell, 323 pages, 1981 (Text)

Leavell, Love and Nelson's Cases and Materials on Equitable Remedies and Restitution, 3rd Ed., 704 pages, 1980 (Casebook)

McCormick's Hornbook on Damages, 811 pages, 1935 (Text)

O'Connell's Remedies in a Nutshell, 2nd Ed., approximately 330 pages, 1984 (Text)

York and Bauman's Cases and Materials on Remedies, 4th Ed., approximately 1200 pages, 1985 (Casebook)

REVIEW MATERIALS

Ballantine's Problems

Black Letter Series

Smith's Review Series

West's Review Covering Multistate Subjects

SECURITIES REGULATION

Hazen's Hornbook on The Law of Securities Regulation, approximately 520 pages, 1984 (Text)

Ratner's Securities Regulation: Materials for a Basic Course, 2nd Ed., 1050 pages, 1980 with 1982 Supplement (Casebook)

Ratner's Securities Regulation in a Nutshell, 2nd Ed., 322 pages, 1982 (Text)

Selected Securities and Business Planning Statutes, Rules and Forms, 485 pages, 1982

SOCIAL LEGISLATION

Hood and Hardy's Workers' Compensation and Employee Protection Laws in a Nutshell, 274 pages, 1984 (Text)

LaFrance's Welfare Law: Structure and Entitlement in a Nutshell, 455 pages, 1979 (Text)

Malone, Plant and Little's Cases on Workers' Compensation and Employment Rights, 2nd Ed., 951 pages, 1980 (Casebook)

See also Poverty Law

TAXATION

Dodge's Federal Taxation of Estates, Trusts and Gifts: Principles and Planning, 771 pages, 1981 with 1982 Supplement (Casebook)

TAXATION—Continued

Garbis and Struntz' Cases and Materials on Tax Procedure and Tax Fraud, 829 pages, 1982 with 1984 Supplement (Casebook)

Gunn's Cases and Materials on Federal Income Taxation of Individuals, 785 pages, 1981 with 1983 Supplement (Casebook)

Hellerstein and Hellerstein's Cases on State and Local Taxation, 4th Ed., 1041 pages, 1978 with 1982 Supplement (Casebook)

Kahn's Handbook on Basic Corporate Taxation, 3rd Ed., Student Ed., 614 pages, 1981 with 1983 Supplement (Text)

Kahn and Gann's Corporate Taxation and Taxation of Partnerships and Partners, 2nd Ed., approximately 1300 pages, 1984 (Casebook)

Kragen and McNulty's Cases and Materials on Federal Income Taxation, Vol. I: Taxation of Individuals, 3rd Ed., 1283 pages, 1979 with 1983 Supplement (Casebook)

Kragen and McNulty's Cases and Materials on Federal Income Taxation, Vol. II: Taxation of Corporations, Shareholders, Partnerships and Partners, 3rd Ed., 989 pages, 1981 with 1983 Supplement (Casebook)

McNulty's Federal Estate and Gift Taxation in a Nutshell, 3rd Ed., 509 pages, 1983 (Text)

McNulty's Federal Income Taxation of Individuals in a Nutshell, 3rd Ed., 487 pages, 1983 (Text)

Posin's Hornbook on Federal Income Taxation of Individuals, Student Ed., 491 pages, 1983 (Text)

Rice and Solomon's Problems and Materials in Federal Income Taxation, 3rd Ed., 670 pages, 1979 (Casebook)

Rose and Raskind's Advanced Federal Income Taxation: Corporate Transactions—Cases, Materials and Problems, 955 pages, 1978 (Casebook)

Selected Federal Taxation Statutes and Regulations, 1255 pages, 1983

Sobeloff and Weidenbruch's Federal Income Taxation of Corporations and Stockholders in a Nutshell, 362 pages, 1981 (Text)

TORTS

Christie's Cases and Materials on the Law of Torts, 1264 pages, 1983 (Casebook)

Green, Pedrick, Rahl, Thode, Hawkins, Smith and Treece's Cases and Materials on Torts, 2nd Ed., 1360 pages, 1977 (Casebook)

Green, Pedrick, Rahl, Thode, Hawkins, Smith, and Treece's Advanced Torts: Injuries to Business, Political and Family Interests, 2nd Ed., 544 pages, 1977 (Casebook)—reprint from Green, et al. Cases and Materials on Torts, 2nd Ed., 1977

TORTS—Continued

Keeton, Keeton, Sargentich and Steiner's Cases and Materials on Torts, and Accident Law, 1360 pages, 1983 (Casebook)

Kionka's Torts in a Nutshell: Injuries to Persons and Property, 434 pages, 1977 (Text)

Malone's Torts in a Nutshell: Injuries to Family, Social and Trade Relations, 358 pages, 1979 (Text)

Prosser and Keeton's Hornbook on Torts, 5th Ed., Student Ed., 1286 pages, 1984 (Text)

Shapo's Cases on Tort and Compensation Law, 1244 pages, 1976 (Casebook)

See also Products Liability

TRADE REGULATION

McManis' Unfair Trade Practices in a Nutshell, 444 pages, 1982 (Text)

Oppenheim, Weston, Maggs and Schechter's Cases and Materials on Unfair Trade Practices and Consumer Protection, 4th Ed., 1038 pages, 1983 (Casebook)

See also Antitrust, Regulated Industries

TRIAL AND APPELLATE ADVOCACY

Appellate Advocacy, Handbook of, 249 pages, 1980 (Text)

Bergman's Trial Advocacy in a Nutshell, 402 pages, 1979 (Text)

Binder and Bergman's Fact Investigation: From Hypothesis to Proof, 354 pages, 1984 (Coursebook)

Goldberg's The First Trial (Where Do I Sit?, What Do I Say?) in a Nutshell, 396 pages, 1982 (Text)

Hegland's Trial and Practice Skills in a Nutshell, 346 pages, 1978 (Text)

Hornstein's Appellate Advocacy in a Nutshell, 325 pages, 1984 (Text)

Jeans' Handbook on Trial Advocacy, Student Ed., 473 pages, 1975 (Text)

McElhaney's Effective Litigation, 457 pages, 1974 (Casebook)

Nolan's Cases and Materials on Trial Practice, 518 pages, 1981 (Casebook)

Parnell and Shellhaas' Cases, Exercises and Problems for Trial Advocacy, 171 pages, 1982 (Coursebook)

Sonsteng, Haydock and Boyd's The Trialbook: A Total System for Preparation and Presentation of a Case, Student Ed., approximately 400 pages, 1984 (Coursebook)

TRUSTS AND ESTATES

Atkinson's Hornbook on Wills, 2nd Ed., 975 pages, 1953 (Text)

Averill's Uniform Probate Code in a Nutshell, 425 pages, 1978 (Text)

Bogert's Hornbook on Trusts, 5th Ed., 726 pages, 1973 (Text)

Clark, Lusky and Murphy's Cases and Materials on Gratuitous Transfers, 2nd Ed., 1102 pages, 1977 (Casebook)

TRUSTS AND ESTATES—Continued

Gulliver's Cases and Materials on Future Interests, 624 pages, 1959 (Casebook)

Gulliver's Introduction to the Law of Future Interests, 87 pages, 1959 (Casebook)—reprint from Gulliver's Cases and Materials on Future Interests, 1959

McGovern's Cases and Materials on Wills, Trusts and Future Interests: An Introduction to Estate Planning, 750 pages, 1983 (Casebook)

Mennell's Cases and Materials on California Decedent's Estates, 566 pages, 1973 (Casebook)

Mennell's Wills and Trusts in a Nutshell, 392 pages, 1979 (Text)

Powell's The Law of Future Interests in California, 91 pages, 1980 (Text)

Simes' Hornbook on Future Interests, 2nd Ed., 355 pages, 1966 (Text)

Turrentine's Cases and Text on Wills and Administration, 2nd Ed., 483 pages, 1962 (Casebook)

Uniform Probate Code, 5th Ed., Official Text With Comments, 384 pages, 1977

Waggoner's Future Interests in a Nutshell, 361 pages, 1981 (Text)

WATER LAW

Getches' Water Law in a Nutshell, 439 pages, 1984 (Text)

Trelease's Cases and Materials on Water Law, 3rd Ed., 833 pages, 1979, with 1984 Supplement (Casebook)

See also Energy and Natural Resources Law, Environmental Law

WILLS

See Trusts and Estates

WOMEN AND THE LAW

Kay's Text, Cases and Materials on Sex-Based Discrimination, 2nd Ed., 1045 pages, 1981, with 1983 Supplement (Casebook)

Thomas' Sex Discrimination in a Nutshell, 399 pages, 1982 (Text)

See also Employment Discrimination

WORKERS' COMPENSATION

See Social Legislation

HOW TO FIND THE LAW

EIGHTH EDITION

MORRIS L. COHEN
Librarian and Professor of Law
Yale Law School

ROBERT C. BERRING
Librarian and Professor of Law
Boalt Hall,
University of California,
Berkeley, School of Law

ST. PAUL, MINN.
WEST PUBLISHING CO.
1983

50 West Kellogg Boulevard
P.O. Box 3526
St. Paul, Minnesota 55165

Printed in the United States of America

Library of Congress Cataloging in Publication Data

Cohen, Morris L., 1927–
How to find the law.

(American casebook series)
Includes bibliographies and index.
1. Legal research—United States. I. Berring, Robert C. II. Title. III. Series.
KF240.C538 1983 340'.072073 83-12510

ISBN 0-314-74304-9

How to Find the Law 8th Ed. ACB
1st Reprint—1984

Dedicated to our parents:

Robert C. and Rita P. Berring

and

Emanuel and Anna Cohen

*

PREFACE

Does the world need another treatise on the sources and methods of legal research? Despite the continued availability of such popular texts as *Effective Legal Research, Fundamentals of Legal Research,* and *Legal Research in a Nutshell,* and the recent appearance of several new, less conventional guides, we found substantial reason for a new edition of the venerable *How to Find the Law.* Each of the existing treatises approaches legal literature in a different way and each has developed its own appeal and style. For many teachers and students, *How to Find the Law* represents the middle way—a comprehensive approach to the basic elements of legal bibliography, full coverage of *new* materials and *new* techniques of legal research, extensive use of illustrative exhibits, but an avoidance of encumbering minutiae.

Along with the proliferation of new legal publications, there have been significant changes in emphasis in legal education and in the practice of law, and increased use of computers in legal research. These developments alone call for a fresh approach in describing legal literature and law-finding and that has been our goal in this new edition.

Instruction in legal research remains an essential part of legal education and yet it still struggles for time, attention and effectiveness in the law school curriculum. This extensive revision of *How to Find the Law,* like its predecessors, is designed as a teaching tool rather than a reference book. However, it incorporates sufficient detail to guide the student beyond the first year of training and to support advanced study in legal research as well. While the basic text provides an introduction for the beginning law student, the footnote references and suggested readings at the end of most chapters open the way to further exploration.

We believe that effective training in legal research requires the prompt application of the information which has been transmitted by reading and class participation. This is best achieved by actual problems or exercises done by the student in the law library. Only there can the published materials be seen, examined, and tested in use. For this reason, we urge that such application take place as soon as possible after the readings are assigned. A completely new problem book for *How to Find the Law* has been prepared for this purpose by Elizabeth Slusser Kelly and Lynn Foster of the Southern Illinois University School of Law. Learning legal bibliography and legal research involves a unity of theory and practice. We hope that this latest edition of *How to Find the Law* will provide the theory and that use of the new problem book will facilitate the practice.

PREFACE

In addition to updating of bibliographic information throughout the text, most chapters have been completely rewritten and many have been expanded. Among the major changes are new separate chapters covering Introduction to Court Reports; Annotated Reports; Constitutions; Court Rules; Research Approaches and Strategies; and four bibliographic Appendices. In view of the recent proliferation of excellent texts and manuals on legal writing, that subject is omitted from this edition.

Viewed from a research point of view, American law today does seem to be a seamless web. As treated by courts and other lawmaking bodies, the sources of law are functionally inter-related and are rarely meaningful and useable in isolation. To understand a statute, one needs the decisions which have interpreted it; to understand a court's decision, one needs the statute which it has applied; to understand an administrative regulation, one must see the statute by which it was authorized; even to read a legal periodical article or a treatise, one needs access to all of the primary sources it cites and discusses.

Therefore, the study of legal literature requires a similar integrative approach. Each chapter of this book should be considered in relation to what has gone before and what will follow. Legal bibliography should not be fragmented, although the use of separate chapters to cover individual forms of law may be necessary for description. The totality of this literature is often complex in its relationships and sometimes even beautiful in its harmony. The increasing versatility of many finding tools, with their varied cross-references, facilitates the integration of legal sources in research. The functional unity of legal bibliography is difficult to project in a text such as this, but the reader should be aware of its underlying presence and the teacher should emphasize its pervasiveness.

MORRIS L. COHEN
ROBERT C. BERRING

June 1983

ACKNOWLEDGEMENTS

The authors wish to thank the family of the late Professor Edwin G. Schuck for permission to include his Chapter I, *Analysis of the Problem,* revised from the 7th edition; Emeritus Professor Vaclav Mostecky for his revised Chapter XXI, *International Law*; Scott Burson, Esq. for his work on Chapter XVIII, *Research in the Social Sciences*; Professor Kathy Shimpock and Diane Teeple for their respective work on Chapter XIX, *English and Canadian Materials*; and Terry Swanlund of the Harvard Law School Library staff for his Appendix, *Sources of Federal Regulatory Agency Rules, Regulations and Adjudications.* We are also grateful for the assistance of our many colleagues at the libraries of the Harvard Law School, University of California at Berkeley School of Law, University of Washington Law School, and Yale Law School, and for their bibliographic assistance.

Bob Berring extends further thanks to Valerie Wedin, Lynn Matis and Kathleen Vanden Heuvel for their assistance and advice in the preparation of the manuscript. Each played a crucial role in seeing the project successfully to its end. No end would have been reached without the aid of Vickie Moor and Patti Castelli, whose typing, organization and suggestions were indispensable. The many colleagues and students who have shaped my thinking on this subject deserve the credit for inspiration and example, but since they include among their number the authors of competing texts, I will let discretion guide me.

Morris Cohen acknowledges the assistance of Kay Webb, Stephen R. Hildrich, Laura Praglin, Carl Lamers, in the preparation of several Chapters, and Wes Daniels for his helpful advice and assistance throughout. Thanks are also extended to Irene Ayres, Betsy J. Collins, Susan Johnsen, and Ethel Moriarty for their typing services often rendered under pressured circumstances. The indexes were prepared by Sara Robbins and Laura Praglin, and their help is gratefully acknowledged.

We both wish to thank the following publishers for permission to reproduce illustrations from their respective publications: ABC-Clio Press; American Association of Law Libraries; American Law Institute; Bancroft-Whitney Company; R. R. Bowker Co.; Bureau of National Affairs, Inc.; Butterworth & Company Publishers, Ltd.; Canada Law Book, Ltd.; Capitol Services, Inc.; Carswell Co., Ltd.; Columbia Books, Inc.; Commerce Clearing House, Inc.; Congressional Information Service, Inc.; Gale Research Co.; Information Access Corp.; Institute for Scientific Information Press; Lawyers Co-operative Publishing Company; Martindale-Hubbell, Inc.; Mead Data Central; MIT Press; Oceana Publications, Inc.; Fred B. Rothman Co.; Shepard's/ McGraw Hill; Sweet & Maxwell, Ltd.; West Publishing Company; H. W. Wilson Company.

ACKNOWLEDGEMENTS

This volume derives from what we ourselves have learned. For that, we owe a debt to all the teachers of legal bibliography and legal research—those who taught us, those with whom we now teach, and those who will teach its readers.

MORRIS L. COHEN
ROBERT C. BERRING

June 1983

SUMMARY OF CONTENTS

*

TABLE OF CONTENTS

TABLE OF CONTENTS

Chapter 11. Administrative and Executive Publications—Cont'd

Chapter 15. Treatises, Restatements, Dictionaries, etc.—Cont'd

HOW TO FIND THE LAW

EIGHTH EDITION

*

Chapter 1

ANALYSIS OF THE PROBLEM [1]

A. INTRODUCTION

As you examine the law school library, you will note the volume, variety and apparent complexity of the scholarly apparatus it contains. You will see a legal collection developed to meet wide-ranging teaching and research needs. The collection is extensive, and, by the very nature of legal bibliography, it must grow continuously if it is to retain its integrity as a resource for learning and research.

You may be overwhelmed by the sheer immensity of the law library; you may also be wondering how you can possibly be expected, in the short space of three years, to become master of all the information contained in such a vast collection. You may set your mind at ease, at least in this single respect. You will never know all the law contained in the volumes the law library holds, even after a lifetime

1. This Chapter was originally written for the 7th edition of *How to Find the Law* by the late Professor Edwin G. Schuck, then Librarian of the Columbia University School of Law. It is retained in this edition, with some modification, for its continuing relevancy to the study of legal research and for its effectiveness in introducing that discipline.

of practice. It is a well-kept professional secret that no lawyer knows more than a relatively infinitesimal part of the law, nor does any judge. Professional education, however, in addition to fostering the disciplined, pragmatic and critical intellectual process known as "thinking like a lawyer," must equip the law student, by instruction in the techniques of legal research, to *find* the law in volumes you have examined.

B. FACTORS DETERMINING THE METHODS OF LEGAL RESEARCH

1. CHARACTERISTICS OF LAW

Before you can begin to understand the necessity for the methods employed in legal research, you must know something about the characteristics of two major elements which shape those methods. One of these elements is the organizational structure of published legal materials. The form in which such research sources are published results, in turn, from three readily discernible characteristics of American law.

a. Constant Change

The first of these, perhaps more clearly apparent in recent years than in any earlier period of our history, is that law is constantly changing. It has been estimated that our legislatures, both Federal and State, are enacting statutes, one of the primary sources of our law, at the approximate rate of 15,000 annually. It has also been estimated that judicial opinions, another primary source of law, are being published at the rate of 55,000 each year; adding these to the estimated 3,000,000 judicial opinions already extant and noting that many of these judicial opinions are concerned with the interpretation and application of statutes, one begins to understand the necessity for the large number of volumes brought together in the law library, and the reasons for the constant growth of that collection.

b. Stability v. Progress

A second characteristic of our law is its manifestation of constant interplay between the desire to maintain certainty and stability and the need for flexibility in regulating the broad spectrum of activities in which human beings engage. Certainty and stability are basic requirements, for law is the most significant single means by which society is ordered and the rights and obligations of its members are defined. Without more, however, these qualities would be an inadequate foundation for the institutions of governing which make civilized life possible, for the law must also be capable of change if it is to satisfy the fresh aspirations and expectations which are constantly generated by a dynamic society. In short, the law must provide stability, yet apparently paradoxically, it must not stagnate. It is, then, the function of law to meet and satisfy changing and often conflicting societal needs without endangering the social order, and it is this function which results in the constant change we have already noted.

c. Multiplicity of Sources

Finally, it is characteristic of American law that it is derived from a multitude of sources. Our governmental organization includes a federal system, consisting of a legislature, a hierarchy of courts, and an executive department, all having law-making functions. In addition, there are fifty states (plus the District of Columbia) each of which has its legislature, its hierarchy of courts, and its executive agencies, all of which produce "law." Within the state jurisdictions, moreover, there are lesser political subdivisions, cities, counties, and other entities, also having courts, ordinance-making bodies, and administrators. The output of all of these various agencies of government results in the tremendous volume of statutes and judicial opinions published annually, as well as in the ever-burgeoning body of administrative regulations and adjudications which constitute the third primary source of United States law. All these constitute the grist of the lawyer's mill.

2. CHARACTERISTICS OF THE PRIMARY SOURCES

From what has already been said, you now know that there are three primary sources of law—statutes, judicial opinions and administrative regulations and adjudications. For the remainder of this chapter, it will simplify our analysis if we consider administrative regulations to be subsumed within the statutory category (for the reason that they are normally promulgated pursuant to statute, and because, like statutes, they are binding upon the people to whom they apply, administrative regulations are said to be quasi-legislative instruments). We will also consider that the term "judicial opinions" includes administrative adjudications (because both judicial decisions and administrative rulings are binding upon the parties to the controversies from which they result, and both are the result of adversary proceedings before a decision-making body, administrative rulings are called quasi-judicial). For our present practical purposes, then, the primary legal materials in the law library consist of statutes and judicial opinions.

a. Chronological Publication

It is characteristic of both these primary sources that they are published chronologically, so that in any volume of reports, an opinion on a criminal appeal may be followed by an opinion in an antitrust matter, which in turn may be followed by an opinion in a civil rights controversy. Similarly, a legislature enacts statutes on a variety of subjects during any given legislative session. These, the *session laws*, are published in the order of their enactment, without regard to their substance, so that any volume of *session laws*, like any volume of judicial opinions, consists of an undifferentiated mass of documents having no relationship to each other except that they appear in the volume in the chronological order in which they became law.

b. Need for Subject Access

Cases and statutes so arranged are of little use to the lawyer, who is faced with a specific problem involving a specific set of facts, in a specific legal area. One must, therefore, have *subject* access to the cases and statutes, that is, we must have some means of finding, among the chronologically published statutes and opinions, those which deal with the legal subject or with the legally significant facts in which we are interested. This need is met by a variety of "finding tools," a term which includes codes, digests, encyclopedias, catalogs, indexes, tables, and computers, all of which are housed in the law library, and with which the legal researcher must be familiar.

c. Official and Unofficial Publication

It is another characteristic of the primary sources that in most states they are published both officially *and* unofficially. In legal documents, it is always necessary to cite the official publication, and if the unofficial version is also cited, the official citation must come first. The required order of citation, however, is not an index of the relative popularity enjoyed by the two kinds of publications. The commercial versions are by far the more popular among practitioners and scholars, for they appear much more promptly than do the official texts, and they include a wide range of annotations, tables and other aids to legal research which are conspicuously absent in official publications.

3. THE LEGAL SYSTEM

Why is all this complicated research necessary? Why must one delve into the cases decided in the past in order to solve a present problem? Surely, one expects, any controversy can be finally adjudicated by the intelligent application to it of moral, ethical and philosophical considerations, so that the dispute is disposed of, and substantial justice is done to the parties, without reference to the manner in which similar controversies may have been resolved in the past.

a. Stare Decisis

These questions bring to the fore the second major element, mentioned earlier, which shapes the techniques of legal research. That element, fundamental to our legal system, is *stare decisis*, the doctrine that precedents should be followed. The doctrine embraces a basic concept of fairness, the feeling that people similarly situated should be similarly dealt with, and that judgments should be consistent, rather than arbitrary, so that one may predict the consequences of contemplated conduct by reference to the treatment afforded similar conduct in the past.

This concept is the theoretical and practical basis for the doctrine of *stare decisis*, and it explains the lawyer's need for access to the decided cases. It follows from the doctrine that a rule of law announced by an appellate court in any given judicial hierarchy is binding on all lower courts in that jurisdiction; that is, the lower courts are *bound* to follow that rule in similar cases which come before them. When you begin research into judicial opinions, therefore, you will be looking for:

A prior case, as nearly the same as possible on its material facts to the case now before you, decided in the highest possible court in your jurisdiction, dealing with the issue presented by your own case, which has not been overruled or modified.

When you have found such a case, commonly called a "case on all fours," or a "case in point," [2] the rule of that case will be binding on the lower court considering your own case. The doctrine of *stare decisis* will therefore require the court to apply to your case the rule of law provided by the earlier case, and the objective of your research has been achieved. This is, of course, a vast oversimplification of the research process, which is usually complicated by the presence of several legal issues, rather than a single issue, by the fact that no two cases are ever exactly the same on their material facts, by the possibility that the passage of time has generated new social circumstances and interests, consideration of which might lead to a quite different result from that reached earlier, and by other similar factors.

It is entirely possible that you will find no "case in point" in your own jurisdiction, for the reason that a controversy embodying a similar factual situation, and presenting identical legal issues, has never before been decided in that jurisdiction. In such circumstances, you will necessarily extend your search for such a case to the judicial opinions rendered in other jurisdictions. Such a case, when found, would not be binding on a court in your own jurisdiction under the doctrine of *stare decisis*, but it might be *persuasive* to that court, that is, in the absence of precedents of its own, your court might adopt the rule of law announced in the out-of-state case, depending on the reputation of that court and on the quality of the particular opinion involved.

It is important to note here that most areas of the law are now governed by statute, and that statutes generally have no effect—not even persuasive effect—outside the jurisdiction which enacted them. If the "case on all fours" found in another jurisdiction than your own involves the application or interpretation of a statute, therefore, or if the facts of your own case are governed by a statute, the sister-state case will probably be of little or no use to you in your own jurisdiction, even though the courts of your jurisdiction have established no

2. The terms "case on all fours" and "case in point" seem to have essentially the same meaning, and are frequently used interchangeably. If there is a difference in their meanings, it may lie in the differing degrees of similarity of the facts of the cases involved, the greater degree of similarity being characterized, in general usage, by the "all fours" designation.

precedents to guide them in the resolution of the controversy with which you are concerned. A noteworthy exception to this general caveat lies in the existence of "uniform" laws which have been adopted by several states (e.g., The Uniform Commercial Code; The Uniform Partnership Act; The Model Business Corporations Act, and others). The decisions of the courts of another state construing a provision of such a statute could well be persuasive to a court required to interpret the same provision in its own law for the first time.

The fact that much of our law is embodied in statutes raises still another *caveat*. It follows from this circumstance that your research into any legal problem will usually begin with a search for an applicable statute. When, by use of the methods treated in subsequent chapters of this book, you have found a statute which appears by its terms to cover your case, your research is far from finished. It is a peculiarity of American statutes that they are prolix and specific, for the drafters of legislation usually attempt to enumerate in a statute all of the foreseeable situations to which they wish it to apply, in order that rights and obligations established by the legislation may be explicitly defined, and the consequences of contemplated conduct clearly perceived. Perhaps because of this very prolixity and specificity, or perhaps simply because language is at best only an inadequate means for the communication of ideas or because under our adversary system of justice lawyers strive to create ambiguity where ambiguity would not otherwise appear, it has usually been necessary for the courts to interpret, clarify and explain statutory language in the course of resolving legal controversies.

Research, therefore, cannot be completed with only the text of a statute applicable to one's problem; it must include the judicial opinions which have interpreted and applied the statute, in order to ascertain the court's understanding of the statute's terms. It is the court's interpretation of the statute, rather than the naked statutory language, which is binding under the doctrine of *stare decisis*. Even at this point, research into the effect of a statute is not complete, for, as we shall shortly see, it is then necessary to insure that the statute has not been amended subsequent to the court's analysis. The finding tools which will enable you to perform all of the research functions mentioned only briefly here will be treated fully and in detail in the subsequent chapters of this volume.

As you will learn from your reading of the cases, as well as from the discussion which immediately follows, judges enjoy great freedom of expression in writing their opinions, and this free literary style permits the lawyer, as well as the judge, to express the meaning of a case in a variety of ways, all equally correct. In reading a statute, however, there is no such license. The law as embodied in a statute is the exclusive expression of the legislature's will, and the specificity which characterizes statutory language is intended to define the reach of law with the utmost clarity and certainty. Every word in the statutory text, therefore, is important. Consequently, if the facts of your case do not fall squarely within the strict terms of the statutory language, it is unlikely that the statute will serve your purpose.

b. The Ratio Decidendi of a Case

Having found a prior case, or cases, which provide a rule of law applicable to the facts of the controversy which is before you, it then becomes necessary to identify more exactly the rule of law, usually called the "holding" of a case, or its *ratio decidendi,* which is the elusive end-product of case-law research. Under the doctrine of *stare decisis,* that holding will govern other cases in which the facts and issues are substantially similar to those of the case which generated the rule of law.

The holding, or *ratio decidendi* of a case can usually be summed up in a single declaratory sentence; everything else in the court's opinion is *dictum,* or *obiter dictum,* that is, something "said by the way." The importance of the distinction between holding and *dictum* lies in the fact that only the holding of the court is authoritative, only the holding is binding in like cases under the doctrine of precedent. The reason for the distinction, as it has been described for beginning law students by Professor Arthur Murphy,[3] lies in the adversary system which is central to our legal process. That system assumes that both parties to a legal controversy will be represented by competent counsel, that counsel will each produce the best possible arguments for the resolution of disputed issues in his favor, that in the cross-fire of argument on the disputed issues, lapses in the legal reasoning espoused by either party will become apparent, and a right result will be reached. Crucial to this theory is the term "disputed," for under the adversary system, it is assumed that the court is competent to decide only those issues which were in controversy, and which were therefore argued before it. The issues in dispute, of course, are the issues which the court is required to resolve in order to decide the controversy between the parties. Accordingly, Murphy and other authoritative legal writers generally limit the concept of "holding" to that part of the court's opinion which sets forth its decision, plus the facts which were necessary, or material, to the court's arriving at the decision. All else is *dictum,* and therefore not binding.

With this definition in mind, how does the lawyer distill, from a forty-page judicial opinion, the concise holding of the court? Finding the court's decision is a simple enough matter—it will be announced in the opinion. But how does one ascertain which are the material facts? The court will, of course, recite in its opinion the facts which it regards as material to its decision of the case, but it may also recite a great many other facts which may or may not be material. Even if there were a convention pursuant to which judges were to exclude from their opinions all the facts except those which the court considered material to its judgment, its own recital of the facts would not

3. See Murphy, "An Analysis of Holding and Dictum," in Dowling, Patterson and Powell, *Materials for Legal Method* (2d ed., 1952) at p. 153.

be definitive, for we are concerned not with what the court believed to be material to its decision, but with what a later court will decide was material in the earlier case.

That later court, in considering a similar case, is faced with two fact situations, that of the case before it, and that of the prior case. In this situation, the court is in a position to profit from prior judicial wisdom by following the precedent established by the earlier court, or by extending the scope of the prior holding to embrace a fact situation more distantly related to the facts which generated the earlier decision. Alternatively, the court may limit or even reject what it regards as earlier judicial error or folly, by "distinguishing" the earlier case from the case now before it, that is, by pointing out differences or distinctions between the factual circumstances of the two cases which, in its view, render the holding of the earlier case inapplicable to the later case. This process of distinguishing an earlier case on its facts may, indeed, be carried to the point where the later court limits the earlier rule of law to "the particular facts" of the case, thereby effectively eliminating its precedential value. Since to do so might tend to undermine the integrity of the judicial process, courts are usually unwilling to overrule a prior decision in explicit terms, and ordinarily will not resort to this ultimate measure unless it is impossible, without manifestly straining the credulity of the reader, to reach a just result otherwise.

How, then, does the lawyer proceed to extract a general rule of law from the court's opinion in a case? The question is a crucial one, for the lawyer's initial function, whether in counseling or advocacy, is to predict, from the holdings of prior cases, what today's court will hold in case now before it.

To do this, one must be able to move from the narrow rule of law based on the peculiar facts of an earlier case to a more general rule which will cover another case which is similar, but not identical in its facts. There is no magic formula which will enable you to perform this critical professional task. The process is an art, rather than a science, and increasing sophistication in its exercise will be achieved as you read and analyze many judicial opinions. A hypothetical example, however, may afford some insights into the nature of the intellectual process involved.

Assume that on a hot day in July, Ms. Jones bought a can of chilled soup at the supermarket, and served it to her father for lunch. Shortly after consuming the soup, Mr. Jones, a retired policeman, experienced nausea, dizziness and other symptoms of serious illness. When he became partially paralyzed, his doctor removed him to a hospital, where he died shortly after admission. An autopsy revealed that his death resulted from botulism poisoning, for which there is no cure, and the botulism was traced to the soup.

Investigation revealed that the soup was part of a batch canned by the Supercaloric Foods Company, that the company's technician responsible for insuring compliance with high sanitary canning standards had been absent from work on the day the soup was produced, and that therefore no one had insured that this lot of soup was heated to a sufficiently high temperature to destroy the botulism-producing organism. The trial court awarded Ms. Jones damages, and the appellate court affirmed.

What are the significant or material facts upon which the appellate court necessarily relied in arriving at its determination of liability in this case, and which facts are not material to that determination, so that they may be disregarded in arriving at the holding of Supercaloric Foods v. Jones? Your common sense tells you that certainly neither the names of the parties nor the state of the weather nor Jones' status as a retired policeman are material. It seems clear, too, that it is not material that Jones died quickly rather than slowly, or that he died at the hospital rather than at home. Nothing which occurred between his consumption of the soup and his death could be relevant to the case, since there is no cure for the poisoning which killed him.

It is significant, however, that the soup was the cause of Jones' death, and that its poisonous state was the result of Supercaloric's omission of steps in its manufacture which has been devised to prevent that very condition. This omission, of course, smacks of negligence, a term with which you are already acquainted from your early reading in Torts. Reason and logic tell us, moreover, that the court's decision did not turn upon the fact that soup was involved; surely the result would have been the same if any kind of food had been the deadly agent.

We could now perhaps formulate the *ratio decidendi* (the narrow rule of law arising from this case), ignoring the immaterial facts, somewhat like this: *A manufacturer of food is liable for negligently poisoning his product if his negligence results in the death of a person who consumes the product.*

In formulating this rule, we have already begun the process of establishing the holding of a case, the process of moving from the specific facts in that case to more general terms. We have enlarged the scope of the rule to cover the general term food, rather than only a single example of that category, soup. Surely, however, we can accomplish more by way of generalization to reach a more inclusive, and therefore more useful holding.

Is it crucial to the rule of law in this case, for example, that food was involved? Should not a manufacturer be held to a high standard of care in preparing other items meant for human ingestion, such as drugs or medicines? Was it necessary to the decision in the *Supercaloric* case that the result of the manufacturer's negligence was a poison? Should he not be equally liable for any disease-causing negligence? Would the outcome of the case have been different if the victim had suffered only temporary injury, rather than death? Let us, then, again moving from specific facts to more general terms, reformulate our rule of law: *A manufacturer of a product meant for human consumption is liable for negligently introducing a disease-causing agent into it, if his negligence results in injury to a person who consumes it.*

Can we reasonably extend our generalizations to encompass a later case in which the injury is not a disease, but some other physical damage? Will the rule of this case cover the broken tooth caused by a loose bolt which fell from the canning machine into the chili, or the perforated intestine caused by the pin which fell from a factory employee's apron into the applesauce? If we changed "disease-producing" to the more general term "harmful," would we not cover these cases, and still remain well within the reason of the rule established by *Supercaloric*? The holding now appears to be: *A manufacturer of a product intended for human consumption is liable for negligently introducing a harmful substance into it, if his negligence results in injury to a consumer of his product.*

We could continue to extend this holding, to include, for example, injury to any living animal, rather than the narrower category of humans. We could eliminate the need to prove negligence on the part of the manufacturer by deleting the entire concept of negligence from the rule, thus making the manufacturer strictly liable for any injury resulting from the use of his product. How far *should* we proceed with our generalizing process?

From this hypothetical case, and from the questions raised by our ringing the changes on its particular facts, it seems that there are no outer limits to the degree of generalization to which one may progress from specific to general, other than the limits imposed by one's own imagination and sense of proportion. The lawyer's purpose in establishing the holdings of decided cases, however, is to predict what view a later court will take of an earlier court's rule of law. At what point, then, does one halt in this process of devising increasingly general categories of facts from particular circumstances? Your own knowledge of the law will be helpful to some degree in answering this question. Common sense is also a factor in arriving at that determination. The language employed by the court in explaining and clarifying its decision will certainly assist you to ascertain the court's own intention regarding the narrowness or breadth of its holding, so no competent lawyer ever totally ignores *dictum*. A later court, however, is not bound by that *dictum*, and may not be receptive to its rationale. For any of a variety of reasons, a court may see fit to reject an earlier court's view of its own holding. While *dictum* cannot be ignored, then, it cannot be relied upon. It should be noted, however, that occasionally a court will take it upon itself, in deciding a case, to clarify its views on an important legal question not necessarily before it in that case, in anticipation that the question will arise in the future. It should never be forgotten, therefore, that a well-considered *dictum* may be more persuasive—and therefore more significant—than an outworn holding.

The reading of a whole series of opinions, especially recent opinions, in cases factually related to your own, provides the only reliable source of clues as to how far you may safely generalize from the particular facts of cases to arrive at a rule of law. Such reading will help you to develop a sense of the direction in which the law has been moving and of the direction in which it is likely to progress, that is, a sense of the degree to which the courts are prepared, at any given time, to diminish the law's stability in the interest of desirable change or to slow the pace of change in the interest of stability. Only by extensive reading, therefore, will you be able to perfect the fine art of recognizing where, at a particular point in the law's development, you have gone too far from the particular to the general in abstracting the *ratio decidendi* of a case.

4. ORGANIZATION OF THE FINDING TOOLS

We have now seen that the doctrine of *stare decisis,* central to our legal system, requires that the lawyer have access to the decided cases, and we have focussed our attention briefly upon the techniques by which the holdings of such cases may be extracted. We have seen also that the need for access to prior cases is not served by the form of publication in which those cases are contained, because the primary sources of law are published chronologically. The need, then, for subject access to the primary sources is readily apparent, for the lawyer's research is directed toward the cases and statutes affecting a particular legal problem or a particular fact situation. This need is met by an array of digests, codes, indexes, encyclopedias, computers, and other tools, and the lawyer's research methods are necessarily determined by the structure of those tools. The use of each of the "finding tools" will be discussed in detail in the subsequent chapters of this book.

a. Case Finders

The need for subject access to judicial opinions is met by the *Digest,* a device which imposes on the recorded cases an alphabetically arranged subject classification, and by several other research tools. The most comprehensive case digest, both for the extensiveness of its coverage and the intensiveness of its internal structure, is the West Publishing Company's digest system with its unique key number arrangement.

The annotated reporters, typified by the *American Law Reports* (published by the Lawyers Cooperative Publishing Company, and usually referred to as *A.L.R.*) are an important alternative to the West Digest System. Legal encyclopedias are also useful as case finders. Computer based research systems are a recent, and very effective addition to the list of case-finding aids.

Many lawyers and legal scholars begin their research by first reading an article in a legal periodical or a treatise (these are called secondary materials) on the general area of law in which they are interested. This approach may not only provide the names of cases, but also citations to other textual treatments which themselves will provide additional research leads.

It is important to note at this point in our discussion, that digests, like computers, are neither primary nor secondary authority; they are not authoritative in any sense, and are never cited. They are merely tools devised for the sole purpose of enabling you to find primary authority. When by these means, or any other means, you have found the cases which appear to be relevant to your problem, it then is necessary for you to read the cases themselves, exercising your own analytical skills in formulating their holdings, and exercising your own professional judgment, through the techniques described earlier in this chapter, in determining their applicability to your case. The lawyer who relies upon someone else's analysis of the case is not only acting unprofessionally, but is courting disaster in the legal forum. This is true for practical, as well as ethical reasons, since most case-finding tools yield many cases which are relevant to your problem in their *dicta*, not in their actual holdings.

Most of what has been said here applies also to encyclopedias. These are, indeed, sometimes cited by lawyers and even courts, as authority. It is much better practice, however, to cite instead the cases upon which the encyclopedia text relies for its statement of the law, *after* you have read the cases and satisfied yourself with regard to their holdings. For the reasons just alluded to, as well as because they are updated infrequently, encyclopedias should be used exclusively as finding tools, and should neither be cited nor relied upon for their analyses of the cases.

b. Statute Finders

We have thus far concerned ourselves with judicial opinions, one of the primary sources of law, and with the organization of the tools designed to provide subject access to the cases. Statutes, the other primary source of American law, present problems in legal research comparable to those offered by judicial opinions, and for the same reason. For like opinions, statutes are published chronologically. Consequently, an examination of the successive statutes found in any volume of the laws enacted during a legislative session[4] will reveal no substantive nexus; the statutes appear in the order in which they were enacted, and while each volume of session laws will contain a subject index of the statutes contained in that volume, there is no cumulative index to all the session laws of a given jurisdiction.

The lawyer therefore needs subject access to statutory materials, as in the case of judicial opinions, for the lawyer is interested in the solution of a specific problem, rather than in the day-by-day history of the activities of the legislative body. The importance of access to statutes is illuminated by the fact that virtually every case decided by the Supreme Court of the United States in recent years has involved some statutory question.

4. Hence the name "Session Laws." The title of the official edition of the session laws may vary from jurisdiction to jurisdiction, e.g., *Statutes at Large* (for the U.S.); *Laws of New York*; *Acts and Resolves of Massachusetts*, etc.

Subject access to statutes is provided not by digests, but by codes. A code is a subject compilation of the current public general statutes of a given jurisdiction, enabling you, by the judicious use of an index to find the statutory provisions affecting a particular legal problem, quickly and efficiently. Most statutory codes are unofficial codes, that is, they are commercially published, although some states do publish official codes. The most sophisticated and widely used editions, however, are those published commercially. The great attraction of these codes, aside from the promptness with which they appear and the regularity with which they are supplemented, lies in the annotations they provide. Such editions bring to the researcher not only the text of relevant statutes, as an official code would, but also abstracts of the judicial opinions which have interpreted, construed or applied each section of the code, together with citations to the texts of those opinions. They will be dealt with in greater detail in Chapter 7 below.

c. Authority Finders

When you have found the statute which governs your legal problem, and the cases which have interpreted and applied that statute, one further task remains before your research may be considered complete. You must now ascertain the *current authority* of your statute and cases, that is, you must assure yourself that the statutory language upon which you propose to rely has not been amended by the legislature since it was enacted in the form in which you found it, and that its most recent construction by the courts is consistent with your prior judicial interpretation of its language. Similarly, whether or not a statute is involved, you must be sure that the holdings of the case upon which your legal argument will be based have not been modified or overruled by subsequent opinions, so that they no longer support your legal position. Nothing can be more devastating to a lawyer's case—and professional reputation—than to have opposing counsel inform the court that a statute cited has been repealed or adversely construed, or that the cases relied upon have been overruled, limited, or otherwise so treated by subsequent opinions that they no longer constitute authority for the argument stated.

Such a disaster is avoided by the use of a tool called *Shepard's Citations*, a set of volumes which, for statutes, indicates every modification effected by the legislature, and cites every judicial opinion which has construed, applied, or even mentioned it. *Shepard's* performs a similar function for judicial opinions, citing every case which has in any way commented upon a prior case, and indicating the effect of each such subsequent opinion upon the precedential authority of the cited case. In "Shepardizing" a judicial opinion, it is important to remember that even though the cases upon which you rely do not indicate the existence of a relevant statute, legislatures frequently enact statutes for the sole purpose of changing, or even nullifying, the legal impact of judicial opinion. *Shepard's Citations* do not indicate the effect of statutes on judicial opinions, as they do that of judicial opinions on statutes. It is always necessary, therefore, to investigate, independently of the citators, whether a statute enacted subsequent to the promulgation of a legal opinion has affected the authority of that opinion. *Shepard's Citations* and other citators are treated in detail in Chapter 9.

C. SECONDARY SOURCES

Under the doctrine of *stare decisis,* only statutes and judicial opinions are authoritative, in that they are binding within the jurisdictions in which they apply. Secondary sources, which include treatises, legal periodicals and other textual treatments of the law, do not have the same primary authority as statutes and judicial decisions. A secondary source may be said to have authority, however, within the ordinary meaning of the word, to the extent that its well-reasoned statements of the law, as these have been distilled from the cases, may be persuasive. The authority of a treatise or periodical article, moreover, may be buttressed by the scholarly reputation of its author.[5] Certainly no court is bound by any author's analysis or conclusions, yet the continued citation by judges of such authors as Prosser, Wigmore and Williston indicates quite clearly that the force of their legal analyses has remained persuasive over the years. Legal arguments based upon the primary sources of law, therefore, may be strengthened and supported by the citation of secondary materials. These will be more fully discussed in Chapters 15 and 16 of this book.

D. NONLEGAL RESEARCH SOURCES

In 19th and the early 20th century American judicial opinions typically cited only legal authorities in support of their conclusions. The neglect of nonlegal sources of information thus manifested was not fortuitous. The tradition, inherited from the English courts, was nourished by the establishment of separate schools for the study of law in the early nineteenth century. Prior to that separation, law had been only one of several university subjects the study of which was thought necessary to a broadly based education. Thereafter, however, the study of law developed independently, until it existed in almost complete isolation from the other academic disciplines. The separation had at least one unfortunate side effect; it tended to diminish, in the minds of lawyers and judges, the concept of law as a dynamic societal force.

With increasing sophistication, we have come to see that the very nature of the lawyer's function includes the capacity to influence the direction of social change. That perception is reflected in judicial opinions which articulate quite clearly the social, economic, political and even psychological consequences with which they are concerned. Recent studies have noted the marked increase in the volume of non-

5. This feature is lacking in the case of legal encyclopedias which, as was indicated earlier, are sometimes cited as authority in memoranda and opinions, although they are best used only as research aids.

legal sources cited by the courts. Lawyers must increasingly do research in the literature of disciplines in the periphery of, or even remotely removed from law, for law has become in fact an interdisciplinary study. A treatment of research in such materials is included in Chapters 17 and 18.

A chapter of this kind should not end without a brief discussion of the lawyer's only tool, *i.e.*, words. Professional facility in the use of that tool will depend not only on superior skill in reading and writing the English language, but upon your developing special skills in the use of the language which is peculiar to the law.

Much of the legal terminology in current use is our heritage from days long past. Latin, law French, and later, the stylized language employed by early Anglo-American lawyers has given us a miscellany of terms which must be clearly understood if you are to read legal materials intelligently. Many of these terms will be completely unfamiliar to you; some you will have encountered before, but in an entirely different context, for many terms in common English use have quite different meanings when used in law. You cannot, as you might in reading a science fiction novel, simply skip over unfamiliar terms when you read a case. You must understand the case in all its complexity; the unfamiliar terms must be looked up, and their meaning clearly understood, if your reading is to serve its purpose. For that reason, a law dictionary should be readily available to you whenever you are reading legal materials. Specific titles are suggested in Chapter 15.

The use of proper citation form is an essential skill of the legal researcher. Poor citations can confuse, mislead and exasperate the reader of legal writing and can be avoided with the exercise of care. The most widely accepted guide to legal citation practice is the *Uniform System of Citation*,[6] generally known as "the blue book" from its blue covers. In addition to its value for citations, it contains other useful aids to legal research and writing.

E. SUMMARY

It has been the purpose of this chapter not only to introduce you to the kinds of resources and tools you will deal with in the later chapters of this book, as well as in your entire professional career, but to attempt to show the relationship of the nature of law and the structure of legal literature to the methods necessarily employed in legal research. As you have by now gathered, the methods are cumbersome, largely because they must be adequate to deal in meticulous fashion with a large and ever-burgeoning mass of chronologically arranged materials. Though cumbersome, however, the methods are effective. Practice will result in increased facility on your part in dealing with the complex fact situations which frequently surround legal controversies and will enable you quickly and efficiently to rec-

6. Harvard Law Review Association, 13th edition, 1981.

ognize the material and relevant, while discarding the legally insignificant. It can thereby reduce the time you must spend in this arduous, but intellectually rewarding task. More important, however, than the techniques taught and the insights afforded by the methods of legal research is the training that can be derived from its critical and pragmatic thought processes. It is the creative function of legal research and legal reasoning to draw upon the knowledge of all of the sciences, using that knowledge to test the claims of competing interests critically and rigorously, in order to reach a reasoned decision and just result, in view of all the facts and circumstances of a case.

F. ADDITIONAL READING

E.H. Levi, *An Introduction to Legal Reasoning* (University of Chicago Press, 1963).

K.N. Llewellyn, *The Bramble Bush* (Oceana Publications, 1969).

T.B. Marvell, *Appellate Courts and Lawyers, Information Gathering in the Adversary System* (Greenwood Press, 1978).

D. Mellinkoff, *The Language of the Law* (Little, Brown, 1963).

G.L. Williams, *Learning the Law*, 11th ed. (Stevens, 1982).

Chapter 2

INTRODUCTION TO COURT REPORTS

A. Introduction: Issues of Law and Issues of Fact.
B. Publication of Cases.
C. Forms of Published Decisions.
D. Components of a Decision.
  1. Caption.
  2. Docket Number.
  3. Attorneys.
  4. Syllabus and Headnotes.
  5. Opinion.
  6. Holding and Dicta.
E. Summary.
F. Additional Reading.

A. INTRODUCTION: ISSUES OF LAW AND ISSUES OF FACT

American law, both in its popular manifestations and in the minds of many of its practitioners focuses upon "case law." Law students are educated by the case method, lawyers portrayed in the media are almost always working on cases, and the American legal system, along with the common law generally, is most easily distinguished from other legal systems by its heavy reliance on the precedential value of cases. Traditionally, legal research courses and texts have given considerable attention to cases, their forms of publication, and finding tools. This emphasis was justified not only by the idiosyncratic method of early case reporting and the complicated modern systems of case publication and digesting, but also because of the commonly shared assumption that mastering case law research was the most important and the necessary first step in approaching legal research.

With the increasing growth of legislation and administrative law, there is now reason to moderate that assumption. Most commentators would admit statutory law plays a far more important role than case law in the day-to-day life of individuals in the United States, and an even stronger argument could be made for the pervasive influence of administrative law. Although the role of the courts in law-making and law reform has fluctuated in this country,[1] the importance of judicial decisions as a major source of American law cannot be doubted. It is impossible to conduct systematic research without a complete understanding of cases, their components, their systems of publication, and the means of access to them. This chapter will concentrate on these questions.

Before proceeding further it is important to understand what is meant when the term "case law" is used. Essential to this understanding is awareness of the basic structure of the American judicial system. Illustration A presents a simple diagram that can be used as a paradigm for the court system of each of the 51 jurisdictions (fifty states, plus the federal system) that comprise the courts of the United States. The titles given to the various levels of courts here are generic and the actual names of the courts at each level, in each state, will differ, but every jurisdiction will have judicial bodies that serve those functions. A brief examination of each of the three levels may be useful.

COURT OF LAST RESORT

INTERMEDIATE APPELLATE COURT

TRIAL COURTS

(sometimes organized into separate or different types of trial and jurisdictional subdivisions)

Illustration A

The *Trial Court* level is the first level in the court system. In operation it may have numerous subdivisions and special branches (e.g., probate, family court, small claims court, etc.), but every jurisdiction has a trial court of general jurisdiction at which most disputes, both civil and criminal, are initially adjudicated. Here persons who wish to litigate civil matters can bring before a trier of fact (a judge or jury) the issues in their case. It is also at this level that most criminal cases are brought to trial. It should be noted that in a few exceptional situations, both in the state and federal systems, a case can begin at the Appellate Court level, and, even more rarely, at the Court of Last Resort level.

To illustrate the difference between the trial of a case and an appeal, let us take the following hypothetical situation and see how it would progress from trial to appeal.[2]

1. See, for example, J.W. Hurst, *The Growth of American Law: The Law Makers* (Little, Brown, 1950) at pp. 185–189.

2. For a more detailed description, see M.A. Franklin, *The Biography of a Law Dispute* (Foundation Press, 1968).

Mr. R. Colavito is crossing the street in Cleveland when he is struck by an automobile operated by Mr. B. Sipe. Mr. Colavito claims that Mr. Sipe was operating his vehicle in an unsafe manner, was in excess of the existing speed limit, and went through a red light. Mr. Sipe claims that Mr. Colavito was too inebriated to notice the light was against him, and that he, Mr. Sipe, had been driving prudently and was passing through the intersection while the light was green, when Mr. Colavito stumbled out in front of him. There are several issues of fact posed by these two versions of the event. Was Mr. Sipe operating his car in an unsafe manner in excess of the speed limit? Was Mr. Colavito inebriated? What color was the light? All of these are matters that can be settled by a trier of fact in an initial trial court forum. Either a jury or a judge will answer these factual questions, and those answers will be fixed for the balance of the litigation, unless some irregularity of procedure or bias can be shown in the fact-finding process. That is to say once the trial court determines the light was red for oncoming traffic, that fact is determined and cannot be appealed. There is, however, another kind of issue that can arise at the trial court level—an issue of "law." Let us hypothesize, for example, that Mr. Colavito's attorney attempted to introduce testimony from a witness who claimed that Mr. Sipe's mother had informed him that Mr. Sipe had admitted to her that he had in fact been speeding at the time of the accident. Mr. Sipe's attorney might have objected that such testimony should not be admitted into evidence because of the *hearsay rule,* which governs what secondhand testimony is admissible at trial. A question concerning the admissibility of evidence is an issue of law, and must be determined by the judge.

The trial judge's ruling on an issue of law *can* be appealed to a higher level of court. If, in fact, there was a valid evidentiary question posed, and if it was an issue that was appealable under the rules of the existing court system, then the court at the intermediate level on the diagram, the Appellate Level, would decide whether or not the trial court was correct in its ruling on the admission of evidence. If this occurs, the attorneys for each party file and exchange written briefs setting forth their respective positions with the Appellate Court, and an oral argument may be held. Probably that court would consist of more than one judge, but even if only one heard the case, he or she, in making the ruling on this issue of law might write an opinion summarizing the question, stating the determination (or holding), and setting forth the reasoning behind it. The written resolution of such issues of law constitute the decision of the case. *"Cases," as we will use the term in this text, represent those decisions, or the written determination of issues of law.*

Because judicial decisions resolve issues of law, most are generated from the upper two levels of the court diagram. Few states publish decisions from their Trial Court level [3] and, although the U.S. Dis-

3. Decisions of the New York State trial courts, for example, are reported officially in New York *Miscellaneous Reports,* and unofficially in the West Publishing Company's *New York Supplement.* Both are selective reporters, pub-

trict Courts (the Trial Court level in the federal system) do produce some opinions on questions of law, they represent only a small percentage of reported cases. Even though most trial court proceedings do not result in, or produce a written opinion, those proceedings do generate some kind of record. Trial records and pre-trial proceedings in every action are filed with the clerk of the court, but are not usually published. The absence of a written or published opinion often confuses novice researchers who expect to find a report of every "case". One may read in the newspaper about an important new "case" but can find no opinion. In fact, there usually is no judicial opinion written in most trials.

In some cases, after the determination of an appeal in the intermediate appeal court, a second appeal may be taken, this time from the appellate court to the high court. Thus, there may be one or two decisions reported in the same case, on the same issues of law. However, since the sets of published decisions for intermediate appellate courts, like those for trial courts, are selective, not all of even the *appeal* decisions are published. Virtually all decisions of the highest courts for all fifty states and the federal system are reported in full, however.

B. PUBLICATION OF CASES

During the Colonial period and the early years of Independence, the decisions of American courts were not published. American lawyers and judges relied for precedents on the decisions of the British courts, but only a limited number of those volumes were available here.[4] The first volumes of American court decisions were not published until 1789,[5] thirteen years after Independence. Publication of domestic reports developed slowly and the courts of many of the new states operated for decades without published decisions. There were several reasons that undoubtedly spurred the movement for publication.

First, the patriotic feeling that it was important to construct an American system of jurisprudence. Now that the country had freed itself from British rule, it should no longer be subject to British case law. This is apparent from the "reception" statutes passed by many state legislatures which frequently limited the "reception" of British law to those cases decided before the date of Independence, and further limited even such cases to those which were not repugnant to

lishing only about 10% of written opinions at that level.

4. For a detailed study of the availability of English lawbooks generally in America in this period, see H.A. Johnson, *Imported Eighteenth-Century Law Treatises in American Libraries, 1700–1799* (Univ. of Tennessee Press, 1978).

5. In that year, Ephraim Kirby's *Reports* for Connecticut and Francis Hopkinson's *Judgements in the Admiralty of Pennsylvania* were published. Some later reports included cases decided earlier than those in Kirby and Hopkinson, but these two were the first to be published.

the law of the newly independent states.[6] Second, revolutionary times produced a general distrust of judges. Being generally wary of unrepresentative authority, the citizens of the new republic felt that judges should be accountable for the decisions which they made. Written decisions and their publication would facilitate that accountability. Third, the doctrine of precedent, which was discussed in Chapter 1, created a need for the publication of decisions. The underlying rationale for the importance of precedent was equally significant in requiring that decisions be recorded and published. Since case law affected the rights and responsibilities of those subject to it, that law must be known. Individuals should be able to expect to be treated as others in like circumstances had been treated before, and should not be held accountable for developments in the law to which they did not have easy access. If judges rendered decisions which created new rights and responsibilities and changed the common law, those decisions should be recorded and made available to the public. These three themes and others led to the growth of domestic case reporting.

In its early period, American case reporting was a private enterprise, and Ephraim Kirby in the introduction to his 1789 volume stated his reasons for such publication.[7] Kirby's statement reflects the underlying rationale for case reports, as described above:

> "The uncertainty and contradiction attending the judicial decisions in this state, have long been subjects of complaint. The source of this complaint is easily discovered. When our ancestors emigrated here, they brought with them the notions of jurisprudence which prevailed in the country from whence they came. The riches, luxury, and extensive commerce of that country, contrasted with the equal distribution of property, simplicity of manners, and agricultural habits and employments of this, rendered a deviation from the English laws, in many instances, highly necessary. This was observed—and the intricate and prolix practice of the English courts was rejected, and a mode of practice more simple, and better accommodated to an easy and speedy administration of justice, adopted. Our courts were still in a state of embarrassment, sensible that the common law of England, 'though a highly improved system,' was not fully applicable to our situation; but no provision being made to preserve and publish proper histories of their adjudications, every attempt of the judges, to run the line of distinction, between what was applicable and what not, proved abortive; for the principles of their decisions were soon forgot, or misunderstood, or erroneously reported from memory. Hence arose a confusion in the determination of our courts: the

6. For example, the Vermont reception statute (Laws, 1782) stated:

> "Be it enacted, etc. that so much of the common law of England, as is not repugnant to the Constitution or to any act of the legislature of this State, be, and is hereby adopted, and shall be, and continue to be, law within this state."

7. *Reports of cases adjudged in the . . . State of Connecticut . . .* (Litchfield: Printed by Collier & Adam, 1789).

rules of property became uncertain, and litigation proportionably increased.

In this situation, some legislative exertion was found necessary; and in the year 1785 an act passed, requiring the Judges of the Superior Court, to render written reasons for their decisions, in cases where the pleadings closed in an issue of law. This was a great advance toward improvement; still it left the business of reformation but half performed: For the arguments of the Judges, without a history of the whole case, would not always be intelligible; and they would become known to but few persons; and being written on loose paper, were exposed to be mislaid, and soon sink into total oblivion. Besides, very many important matters are determined on motions of various kinds, where no written reasons are rendered, and so are liable to be forever lost.

Hence it became obvious to everyone, that should histories of important causes be carefully taken and published, in which the whole process should appear, showing the true grounds and principles of the decision, it would in time produce a permanent system of common law. But the court being ambulatory through the state, the undertaking would be attended with considerable expense and interruption of other business, without any prospect of private advantage; therefore, no gentleman of the profession seemed willing to make so great a sacrifice: I had entered upon this business in a partial manner, for private use; which came to the knowledge of several gentlemen of distinction. I was urged to pursue it more extensively; and being persuaded that an attempt of the kind (however imperfect) might be made in some degree subservient to the great object, I compiled the Volume of Reports which is now presented to the public. Could any effort of mine induce government to provide for the prosecution of so necessary a work by a more able hand, my wishes would be gratified, and my labour in accomplishing this amply repaid . . ."

These early volumes of court decisions differ markedly from the sophisticated case reporters of today. The individual reporter compiled the decisions (often from his own observation and notes, rather than from texts submitted by the judges), summarized the oral arguments, and often added his own analysis. Many of the early reports were quite unsystematic—they often contained decisions from several courts, and sometimes even from several jurisdictions. Alexander Dallas' first volume of the *United States Reports* contains only Pennsylvania decisions, and none of the U.S. Supreme Court. His second and third volumes contain cases from both Pennsylvania and the U.S. Supreme Court, as does his fourth volume which adds decisions from Delaware and New Hampshire. Many of these early case reports were reviewed much as treatises would be reviewed today.[8] It was not until the second half of the 19th century that, as litigation grew more complex, the need for systematic publication became clear, and

8. Such reviews are cited in T.J. Young, "A look at American law reporting in the 19th century," 68 *Law Library J.* 294 (1975).

the individual reporter became outmoded. Reporting had never been a lucrative enterprise, and when a U.S. Supreme Court decision in 1834 held that the reporter could not hold a copyright in the text of the decisions,[9] the days of unofficial individual reporters were numbered.

As seen in Kirby's introduction to his *Reports*, there was an early belief that the states should assume the responsibility of publishing their court decisions. State-appointed reporters and officially sanctioned publication of decisions developed slowly, however. Statutes for this purpose were passed in Massachusetts (1803), in New York and Kentucky (1804), and New Jersey (1806). The reporter of the Supreme Court of the United States did not have official status until 1817.[10]

Systematic official publication of judicial decisions was needed to bring order to reporting. The early individual reporters, known as "nominatives" because they were cited by the name of the reporter, gave way to officially published sets which became known and cited as the states' reports. Subsequently, some states renumbered their reports, incorporating the volumes of the early nominative reporters as the first numbered volumes in the official set. In other states, particularly those which were among the early colonies, there are large numbers of nominative volumes, and tables of state reports like that in Appendix B, at the end of this book, must be used to determine where particular citations can be found.

The story of American case reporting does not end with the official reports, which represented only the second phase of a three-stage development. In the 19th century, as the population grew and the country expanded and became industrialized, the volume of litigation increased rapidly and the official reporting system became overburdened with the proliferation of judicial decisions. Furthermore, since the reporter in many states became a political position and publication became subject to the uncertainties of legislative appropriation, the reports were often inaccurate and frequently slow in appearing. In 1876, in response to the need for improved and more rapid publication, an entrepreneur in Minnesota, John B. West, started a private reporting system, beginning with selected decisions of the Minnesota Supreme Court in an eight page weekly leaflet called, *The Syllabi*.[11] *The Syllabi* gradually expanded, adding decisions from the federal courts in Minnesota, from lower state courts, and abstracts of decisions from other states. The venture proved so successful that in 1879, West incorporated full decisions from five surrounding states in a new publication, the present *Northwestern Reporter*. West's thriving business quickly drew competition from a rival series employing the regional concept, and the following reporters appeared briefly: *Central Reporter* (1886–1888, in 12 vols.), *New England Reporter*

9. Wheaton, et al. v. Peters, et al., 33 U.S. (8 Peters) 591 (1834).

10. By Act of March 3, 1817 (3 *Stat.* 376).

11. *West Law Finder* (1982 ed.) p. 5.

(1885–1888, in 6 vols.), *Western Reporter* (1885–1888, in 14 vols.), and there were others.

West responded to the growing competition by establishing a national system that included all states and promised comprehensive coverage through seven regional reporters. By focusing on comprehensive reporting and accuracy, West achieved great success. In only a few years its National Reporter System absorbed some of the competing reporters, while others folded, and West became the dominant publisher of law reports. Appendix C lists the present names of the National Reporter System's regional reporters and the state reports covered by each of them.

These regional reporters offered several unique features. By grouping states, West collected enough cases to publish an advance sheet or pamphlet form of decisions on a monthly or bi-weekly basis. Bound volumes also appeared with greater frequency and the decisions of all the states in a region were reported more quickly. West could fairly claim to publish more decisions than the official reporters and to publish them faster.

In addition, West created a headnoting and digesting system, known as the *Key Number System,* which added a case-finding feature to its reporters. This scheme will be described in Chapter 5. West's unofficial publications of state court decisions have proven so effective that over one-third of the states have discontinued their own official publications, leaving one of West's regional reporters or another unofficial reporter, as the only source for their decisions. Appendix B indicates which states no longer publish official reports and which reporter, if any, has official status in each state. Since the federal government does not publish official reports of the decisions of its trial courts and of its intermediary appellate courts, researchers must rely for these cases on several unofficial West reporters which are discussed in Chapter 3 following.

To extend its marketing, West also began to spin off from its regional reporters collections of the decisions of individual states and reissue them in separate state reporters. Thus one found the decisions of the Texas appellate courts not only in the *Southwestern Reporter*, but also in a set called *Texas Cases.* Such reprint reporters are now available for thirty-three states, and they allow the practitioner in one state to purchase a smaller set in the usual West format, but containing only the decisions of that jurisdiction. The pagination in these sets is usually irregular, reflecting the omission of decisions from the other states contained in the regional reporter from which the reprint edition is derived.

The majority of states, however, still publish their own reports, and the general practice is to require that cases cited in briefs be designated by their official citation. Although it is customary to add unofficial citations, the official report, if one exists, *must* be cited. Because of the slower publication of official reports and the continuing trend of states ending their official reports, however, the unofficial citation is frequently the only one available. Parallel tables provided by the National Reporter System publishers make it a simple matter to obtain state report citations.

There are other commercial publishers that publish federal and state decisions selectively and these will be described in the next chapter. Particularly important are the selective, *annotated* reports produced by the Lawyers' Cooperative Publishing Company, which will be treated more fully in Chapter 4. A brief summary of the early development and predecessors is appropriate here, however.

When West began his first publications, another commercial approach to reporting was already underway. This was a selective, rather than comprehensive, system which published a limited number of important decisions of general interest from courts in many states.[12] These decisions were annotated, however, to reflect the state of the law throughout the country on the issues covered by those cases. The first three of these reporters became known as the "Trinity Series" and included: *American Reports* (published from 1871 to 1888 in 60 volumes, covering 1868 to 1887); *American Decisions* (1878 to 1888 in 100 volumes, covering earlier decisions from the Colonial period down to 1868); and *American State Reports* (1887 to 1911 in 140 volumes, covering roughly those years). These were followed by *American and English Annotated Cases* (1906 to 1911 in 21 vols.) which merged with *American Annotated Cases* (1912 to 1918 in 32 vols.). Partially overlapping these reports was *Lawyers' Reports Annotated* (1st series, 1888–1905 in 70 vols.; *New Series*, 1905–1914 in 52 vols.; and the last series of dated volumes, 1914–1918 in 24 vols.), which led directly to *American Law Reports Annotated* (known as *A.L.R.*), the modern successor of this system. *A.L.R.* will be the main focus of Chapter 4.

C. FORMS OF PUBLISHED DECISIONS

Judicial decisions are published successively in three different formats. The first appearance of most decisions is the official "slip opinion", usually a separate pamphlet publication of a single decision (or decisions, if there are concurring or dissenting opinions) in one case. It is individually paginated and contains the full text of the court's decision, sometimes with an official syllabus, or summary. Slip opinions are issued by the court itself, and in some jurisdictions are distributed on a subscription basis. Lawyers rarely subscribe to the slip opinions, however, because of their expense, their slow distribution, and the difficulty of organizing them for retrieval by subject.

The first form of publication that is distributed widely is the *advance sheet*, a pamphlet which contains the full text of a number of the court's decisions, arranged chronologically, and page-numbered in a continuous sequence. The *advance sheet* usually contains the syllabus, headnotes, digests, index and tables which appear in the perma-

12. For more on the controversy between comprehensive and selective reporting, see Chapter 4, at pp. 71–72.

nent form of publication, the bound volume. However, *advance sheets* are preliminary in form, and judges may revise the text of their opinions between that publication and its final form in the bound volume. Most *advance sheets* contain the pagination that will appear in the bound volume, but occasionally there are minor variations. Illustrations B and C show a decision of the Supreme Court of the United States, first in its official slip opinion form, and then in its *advance sheet* publication, called the *preliminary print* of the official *United States Reports.* Advance sheets are published for most official reporters, for all West reporters, and for some other unofficial reporters.

The third stage of publication is the bound case reporter volume. The bound volumes consolidate several *advance sheets* and contain a large number of decisions arranged chronologically in the same sequence as they appeared in the *advance sheets.* They usually contain subject indexes, alphabetical lists of the cases reported therein, and often lists of words defined, statutes construed, and earlier cases cited. The volumes are numbered in a consecutive series, although some publishers periodically begin a second series, starting at volume one again. This is done at an arbitrary time convenient for publication or sales purposes. The second or third series of a reporter does not replace the prior series, but merely continues it with a new numbering sequence. The notation of a series other than the first must always be included in the citation to a case.

D. COMPONENTS OF A DECISION

To further describe the publication of decisions and to facilitate research in case law, we now examine the components of a typical case. References in this section are keyed to the pages that comprise Illustration D, the official report of a decision of the Supreme Court of the United States.

1. CAPTION

The caption or *style of cause* of a case sets forth the names of the parties involved. The normal form is X v. Y. Note that the caption (#1) of the case in Illustration D is *New York Times Company v. United States.* The party which appears first in the caption is usually the plaintiff, the second party the defendant. There are other names by which these parties can be designated. If it is a case on appeal, as is often the situation, some jurisdictions will call the first party the appellant and the second party the appellee. In certain types of actions, some jurisdictions will refer to the first party as the petitioner and the second party as the respondent. In some matters concerning the disposition of an estate or litigation over a particular piece of property, the caption *In re* may be used, followed by the name of the person, estate, or a description of the property which is the subject of the action. In a criminal prosecution, since the State brings the action, the first party will often be the jurisdiction itself,

(Slip Opinion)

NOTE: Where it is feasible, a syllabus (headnote) will be released, as is being done in connection with this case, at the time the opinion is issued. The syllabus constitutes no part of the opinion of the Court but has been prepared by the Reporter of Decisions for the convenience of the reader. See *United States* v. *Detroit Lumber Co.*, 200 U.S. 321, 337.

SUPREME COURT OF THE UNITED STATES

Syllabus

WATT, SECRETARY OF THE INTERIOR, ET AL. *v.* ALASKA

CERTIORARI TO THE UNITED STATES COURT OF APPEALS FOR THE NINTH CIRCUIT

No. 79–1890. Argued January 13, 1981—Decided April 21, 1981*

The Kenai National Moose Range was created in 1941 as a national wildlife refuge by withdrawing acreage from public lands in Alaska. Commercially significant quantities of oil underlie the Range, and the Secretary of the Interior issued oil and gas leases for the Range, beginning in the 1950's. The Secretary has distributed revenues from these leases according to the formula provided in § 35 of the Mineral Leasing Act of 1920, whereby 90% of the revenues are paid to Alaska and 10% to the United States Treasury. In 1964, § 401 (a) of the Wildlife Refuge Revenue Sharing Act was amended so as to add the word "minerals" to the list of refuge resources, the revenues from which were to be distributed according to the formula provided in § 401 (c) of that Act, whereby 25% of the revenues are paid to counties in which the wildlife refuge lies, and the remaining funds are used by the Department of the Interior for public purposes. The Department's Solicitor then made a determination, in which the Comptroller General concurred, that the amended § 401 (a) superseded § 35 of the Mineral Leasing Act of 1920, with the result that the formula under § 401 (c) was to be applied to oil and gas lease revenues from wildlife refuges. Petitioner Kenai Peninsula Borough, a "county" within which Moose Range lies, thereafter brought suit in Federal District Court, seeking a declaration that the amended § 401 (a) governed the distribution of oil and gas revenues from the Range. Alaska also filed suit in the same court, seeking a declaration that § 35 still governed such distribution, and the suits were consolidated. The District Court granted summary judgment for Alaska, and the Court of Appeals affirmed.

---

*Together with No. 79–1904, *Kenai Peninsula Borough* v. *Alaska et al.*, also on certiorari to the same court.

I

Illustration B

Opening page of an official slip opinion of the Supreme Court of the United States.

Syllabus

WATT, SECRETARY OF THE INTERIOR, ET AL. *v.* ALASKA

CERTIORARI TO THE UNITED STATES COURT OF APPEALS FOR THE NINTH CIRCUIT

No. 79-1890. Argued January 13, 1981—Decided April 21, 1981*

The Kenai National Moose Range was created in 1941 as a national wildlife refuge by withdrawing acreage from public lands in Alaska. Commercially significant quantities of oil underlie the Range, and the Secretary of the Interior issued oil and gas leases for the Range, beginning in the 1950's. The Secretary has distributed revenues from these leases according to the formula provided in § 35 of the Mineral Leasing Act of 1920, whereby 90% of the revenues are paid to Alaska and 10% to the United States Treasury. In 1964, § 401 (a) of the Wildlife Refuge Revenue Sharing Act was amended so as to add the word "minerals" to the list of refuge resources, the revenues from which were to be distributed according to the formula provided in § 401 (c) of that Act, whereby 25% of the revenues are paid to counties in which the wildlife refuge lies, and the remaining funds are used by the Department of the Interior for public purposes. The Department's Solicitor then made a determination, in which the Comptroller General concurred, that the amended § 401 (a) superseded § 35 of the Mineral Leasing Act of 1920, with the result that the formula under § 401 (c) was to be applied to oil and gas lease revenues from wildlife refuges. Petitioner Kenai Peninsula Borough, the "county" within which Moose Range lies, thereafter brought suit in Federal District Court, seeking a declaration that the amended § 401 (a) governed the distribution of oil and gas revenues from the Range. Alaska also filed suit in the same court, seeking a declaration that § 35 still governed such distribution, and the suits were consolidated. The District Court granted summary judgment for Alaska, and the Court of Appeals affirmed.

Held: Revenues generated by oil and gas leases on federal wildlife refuges consisting of reserved public lands, as here, must be distributed according to the formula provided in § 35 of the Mineral Leasing Act of 1920. Absent any expression of congressional intention to repeal

---

*Together with No. 79-1904, *Kenai Peninsula Borough* v. *Alaska et al.*, also on certiorari to the same court.

Illustration C

Opening page of an opinion of the U.S. Supreme Court in its official advance sheet, the *preliminary print.*

e.g., *United States,* or *Commonwealth of Massachusetts,* or *People of the State of New York.* You will recall from the court diagram in Illustration A, that cases may go through several levels. As a case is appealed, the parties may change places, and the plaintiff at the trial level becomes the respondent at an appellate level. Thus it is important to check the name of the parties in both positions when searching for a case.[13] The availability of both Plaintiff-Defendant tables and Defendant-Plaintiff tables in most Digests facilitates searching for decisions by case name.

2. DOCKET NUMBER

The docket number is the number assigned by the court clerk to the case when it is filed initially for the court's consideration. In the case shown in Illustration D, the docket number (at #2) is 1873. The docket number is useful in following the case on the court's calendar before it is decided; in identifying slip opinions, which are often filed and cited by their docket number; and in locating the appeal record and briefs of a case, an increasingly valuable source of information on important and complex decisions. Records and briefs will be discussed later in Chapter 15, below.

3. ATTORNEYS

The names of the attorneys who represented the parties to an action usually appear after the syllabus and before the opinion in the case report. In Illustration D, they are designated #3. Identifying the attorneys in the case can be important because they may provide further information about the litigation or its outcome. At one time reported decisions regularly carried excerpts or summaries of the arguments of the attorneys. This information is no longer provided in most reporters.

4. SYLLABUS AND HEADNOTES

Labelled #4 in the illustration is the *syllabus,* sometimes called the *headnote.* In the official reports of some jurisdictions, the syllabus is prepared by the court itself. The syllabus is a summary or digest of a point of law decided by the court.[14] Many actions contain more than one question of law, and a court may dispose of two, three or more individual legal questions in a single opinion. It is also common for the reporter to prepare headnotes describing the various points decided by the court. Although the official reporter is appointed by the Court, the headnotes are not an "official" part of the

13. For example, the case of San Antonio Independent School District v. Rodriguez, 411 U.S. 1 (1973), was designated Rodriguez v. San Antonio Independent School District, in the lower court at 337 F.Supp. 280 (1971).

14. Ohio is unusual in providing that the syllabus, which is prepared by the court, is the official statement of the law of the case. In fact, if there is an inconsistency between the syllabus and the opinion, the syllabus governs.

Syllabus

NEW YORK TIMES CO. *v.* UNITED STATES ← Caption (1)

CERTIORARI TO THE UNITED STATES COURT OF APPEALS FOR THE SECOND CIRCUIT

(2) Docket Number → No. 1873. Argued June 26, 1971—Decided June 30, 1971*

The United States, which brought these actions to enjoin publication in the New York Times and in the Washington Post of certain classified material, has not met the "heavy burden of showing justification for the enforcement of such a [prior] restraint." ← (4) Syllabus

No. 1873, 444 F. 2d 544, reversed and remanded; No. 1885, — U. S. App. D. C. —, 446 F. 2d 1327, affirmed.

Alexander M. Bickel argued the cause for petitioner in No. 1873. With him on the brief were *William E. Hegarty* and *Lawrence J. McKay.*

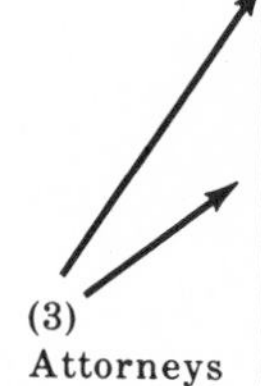

Solicitor General Griswold argued the cause for the United States in both cases. With him on the brief were *Assistant Attorney General Mardian* and *Daniel M. Friedman.*

William R. Glendon argued the cause for respondents in No. 1885. With him on the brief were *Roger A. Clark, Anthony F. Essaye, Leo P. Larkin, Jr.,* and *Stanley Godofsky.*

Briefs of *amici curiae* were filed by *Bob Eckhardt* and *Thomas I. Emerson* for Twenty-Seven Members of Congress; by *Norman Dorsen, Melvin L. Wulf, Burt Neuborne, Bruce J. Ennis, Osmond K. Fraenkel,* and *Marvin M. Karpatkin* for the American Civil Liberties Union; and by *Victor Rabinowitz* for the National Emergency Civil Liberties Committee.

---

*Together with No. 1885, *United States* v. *Washington Post Co. et al.,* on certiorari to the United States Court of Appeals for the District of Columbia Circuit.

Illustration D

Opening page of a decision in the official *United States Reports.*

decision. The opinion itself gives the holding, although it is often not expressly designated as such, and if the syllabus or the headnotes are inconsistent with the Court's opinion, the opinion governs. The headnote may still serve as a useful guide to what is discussed in the case. Many official reporters prepare only the briefest of summaries, and in those states that have discontinued their official reports, none may be officially prepared. The commercial publishers of case reports assign their *own* editors to read and digest each decision which they report. These editors prepare their own headnotes, which are usually more extensive than those of the official reporter. They are specifically designed to aid the researcher in locating relevant material in the opinion, and, in the West reporting system, are part of a larger system of digesting and case finding. Illustration E shows the West report of the decision in *New York Times Co. v. United States,* appearing in its *Supreme Court Reporter.* Arrows in that illustration designate the headnotes prepared by West's editors.

Since the Lawyers' Cooperative Publishing Company publishes its own reporter for the United States Supreme Court, called *Lawyers' Edition of the U.S. Supreme Court Reports,* it may be helpful to contrast *their* editors' headnotes for the same opinion, as shown in Illustration F. Since each publisher offers the same text of the decision as the official *U.S. Reports,* the differences in the headnotes of the two unofficial reporters simply reflect different editorial judgment and phrasing. In using unofficial reports, it is essential to remember that the headnotes are not prepared by the court or the official reporter, but by an editor working for a commercial publisher. Thus the headnotes in unofficial reporters are not authoritative, and should not be relied upon or cited.

5. OPINION

The name of the judge writing the opinion appears at the beginning of the opinion. At the second and third levels of the court system in any jurisdiction, it is likely that more than one judge will hear the appeal. In the court of last resort, there will usually be a bench of five, seven or nine judges, while at the appellate level three or five judges are common. The decision thus may be the product of discussion and compromise among several judges. When it is impossible to achieve unanimity among them, more than one decision may result. The decision of the court, reflecting at least a majority of the vote (although occasionally only a plurality) appears first. It can be assumed that all other judges subscribed to the first opinion, unless they have written or expressly joined in either a concurring or dissenting opinion. A concurring opinion is written when one or more judges agree with the result reached by the majority of the court, but do not agree with the reasoning used to reach that result or with the opinion written for the majority. In some decisions, there are more than one concurring opinion.

Cite as 91 S.Ct. 2140 (1971)

burden of showing justification for imposition of restraint on publication of the contents of the study.

Judgment of the Court of Appeals for the District of Columbia Circuit affirmed; order of the Court of Appeals for the Second Circuit reversed and case remanded with directions.

Mr. Justice Black filed concurring opinion in which Mr. Justice Douglas joined; Mr. Justice Douglas filed concurring opinion in which Mr. Justice Black joined; Mr. Justice Brennan filed concurring opinion; Mr. Justice Stewart filed concurring opinion in which Mr. Justice White joined; Mr. Justice White filed concurring opinion in which Mr. Justice Stewart joined; Mr. Justice Marshall filed concurring opinion; Mr. Chief Justice Burger dissented and filed opinion; Mr. Justice Harlan dissented and filed opinion in which The Chief Justice and Mr. Justice Blackmun joined; and Mr. Justice Blackmun dissented and filed opinion.

Headnote → **1. Constitutional Law ⚷90**

Any system of prior restraints of expression bears heavy presumption against its constitutional validity, and Government carries heavy burden of showing justification for imposition of such a restraint.

Headnote → **2. Injunction ⚷128**

In cases in which the Government sought to enjoin newspapers from publishing contents of classified study on the "History of U. S. Decision-Making Process on Viet Nam Policy", Government failed to meet its burden of showing justification for imposition of such restraint.

Sol. Gen. Erwin N. Griswold, for the United States.

Alexander M. Bickel, New Haven, Conn., for the New York Times.

William R. Glendon, Washington, D. C., for the Washington Post Co.

⊥PER CURIAM. ⊥714

We granted certiorari, 403 U.S. 942, 943, 91 S.Ct. 2270, 2271, 29 L.Ed.2d 853 (1971) in these cases in which the United States seeks to enjoin the New York Times and the Washington Post from publishing the contents of a classified study entitled "History of U. S. Decision-Making Process on Viet Nam Policy."

[1, 2] "Any system of prior restraints of expression comes to this Court bearing a heavy presumption against its constitutional validity." Bantam Books, Inc. v. Sullivan, 372 U.S. 58, 70, 83 S.Ct. 631, 639, 9 L.Ed.2d 584 (1963); see also Near v. Minnesota ex rel. Olson, 283 U.S. 697, 51 S.Ct. 625, 75 L.Ed. 1357 (1931). The Government "thus carries a heavy burden of showing justification for the imposition of such a restraint." Organization for a Better Austin v. Keefe, 402 U.S. 415, 419, 91 S.Ct. 1575, 1578, 29 L.Ed.2d 1 (1971). The District Court for the Southern District of New York in the *New York Times* case, 328 F.Supp. 324, and the District Court for the District of Columbia and the Court of Appeals for the District of Columbia Circuit, 446 F.2d 1327, in the *Washington Post* case held that the Government had not met that burden. We agree.

The judgment of the Court of Appeals for the District of Columbia Circuit is therefore affirmed. The order of the Court of Appeals for the Second Circuit is reversed, 444 F.2d 544, and the case is remanded with directions to enter a judgment affirming the judgment of the District Court for the Southern District of New York. The stays entered June 25, 1971, by the Court are vacated. The judgments shall issue forthwith.

So ordered.

Judgment of the Court of Appeals for the District of Columbia Circuit affirmed; order of the Court of Appeals

Illustration E

West's headnotes in the *Supreme Court Reporter.*

Headnote

Headnote

HEADNOTES

Classified to U. S. Supreme Court Digest, Annotated

Appeal and Error § 1289 — prior restraint on expression — presumption of invalidity

1. Any system of prior restraints of expression comes to the United States Supreme Court bearing a heavy presumption against its constitutional validity, and a party who seeks to have such a restraint upheld thus carries a heavy burden of showing justification for the imposition of such a restraint.

Constitutional Law § 928 — freedom of press — prior restraint

2. The United States government will be denied an injunction against the publication by newspapers of the contents of a classified study entitled "History of U. S. Decision-Making Process on Viet Nam Policy," where the government has not met its burden of showing justification for the imposition of a prior restraint of expression.

APPEARANCES OF COUNSEL

Solicitor General **Erwin N. Griswold** argued the cause for the United States.

Alexander M. Bickel argued the cause for the New York Times.

William R. Glendon argued the cause for the Washington Post Company.

Briefs of Counsel, p 1104, infra.

OPINION OF THE COURT

[403 US 714]

Per Curiam.

We granted certiorari in these cases in which the United States seeks to enjoin the New York Times and the Washington Post from publishing the contents of a classified study entitled "History of U. S. Decision-Making Process on Viet Nam Policy." Post, 942, 943, 29 L Ed 2d 853, 91 S Ct 2270, 2271 (1971).

[1, 2] "Any system of prior restraints of expression comes to this Court bearing a heavy presumption against its constitutional validity." Bantam Books, Inc. v Sullivan, 372 US 58, 70, 9 L Ed 2d 584, 593, 83

TOTAL CLIENT-SERVICE LIBRARY® REFERENCES

16 AM JUR 2d, Constitutional Law §§ 343, 344; 42 AM JUR 2d, Injunctions § 34

US L ED DIGEST, Appeal and Error § 1289; Constitutional Law § 928

ALR DIGESTS, Constitutional Law § 791

L ED INDEX TO ANNO, Constitutional Law

ALR QUICK INDEX, Freedom of Speech and Press

FEDERAL QUICK INDEX, Freedom of Speech and Press

ANNOTATION REFERENCE

The Supreme Court and the right of free speech and press. 93 L Ed 1151, 2 L Ed 2d 1706, 11 L Ed 2d 1116, 16 L Ed 2d 1053, 21 L Ed 2d 976.

Illustration F

Headnotes and beginning of opinion in *Lawyers' Edition of the U.S. Supreme Court Reports.*

Following the concurring opinion, there may be one or more dissenting opinions. Dissenting opinions reflect the views of judges who cannot agree with the result reached by the majority of the court. Sometimes judges will simply note their dissent, but often they find it necessary to set forth their reasons. Although ordinarily dissenting opinions carry no force as precedent, they are on occasion cited by counsel or judges who disagree with the majority ruling. In some cases, earlier dissents have been cited in support of changes in the law. Some opinions will feature a dizzying array of concurrences and dissents, and some justices may concur in part and dissent in part.[15] This unfortunate atomization of opinion is not uncommon among the justices of the Supreme Court of the United States.

Another type of decision that should be noted is the "*per curiam*" decision, represented by Illustrations D, E and F. The *per curiam* decision represents the entire court speaking with one voice, but not attributing authorship to any individual justice. *Per curiam* decisions are generally short, and cover points of law that the court either feels are so obvious as not to need elaboration, or represent decisions that the court does not want to treat so specially as to create precedential problems in the future. *Per curiam* opinions, however, carry the weight of precedent.

Although they do not qualify as opinions, it is appropriate at this point to mention orders by the court. Very often appellate courts will simply affirm or reject the appeal from the trial court by order. This may mean adopting the reasoning of the lower court's opinion, or refusing, for other reasons, to discuss the case specifically. By refusing to hear an appeal the court may actually decide the issue, but without an opinion. Frequently newspapers will carry articles concerning such a "decision" of a court, where no opinion was actually written and consequently no report of the case produced. This confuses researchers, but is quite common.

6. HOLDING AND DICTA

To evaluate the authority, or the precedential weight of a case, it is important to distinguish between the court's "holding," that is, the *ratio decidendi* described in Chapter 1, and "dicta", which are gratuitous remarks or reasoning offered by the court in their opinion. Judges may comment in their opinions on any number of extraneous

15. In Regents of the University of California v. Bakke, 438 U.S. 265 (1978), Justice Powell wrote the majority opinion, and each of the other eight judges concurred in part and dissented in part, in different combinations on different issues. The Court described the opinions in that case, as follows:

> "Powell, J., announced the Court's judgment and filed an opinion expressing his views of the case, in Parts I, III–A, and V–C of which White, J., joined; and Parts I and V–C of which Brennan, Marshall, and Blackmun, JJ., joined. Brennan, White, Marshall, and Blackmun, JJ., filed an opinion concurring in the judgment in part and dissenting in part, *post*, p. 324. White, J., *post*, p. 379, Marshall, J., *post*, p. 387, and Blackmun, J., *post*, p. 402, filed separate opinions. Stevens, J., filed an opinion concurring in the judgment in part and dissenting in part, in which Burger, C.J., and Stewart and Rehnquist, JJ., joined, *post*, p. 408." (p. 26)

issues, or enlarge on their reasoning, or speculate about possibilities which are not material to the resolution of the immediate controversy. Chapter 1 described the process of determining the ruling or holding on the material facts of a case. Although strictly speaking, only the actual "holding" has binding authority or precedential value, the court's dicta may be persuasive in a later case. Dicta should not be cited, however, as the holding of a case, nor should a case be cited, without explanation, as authority for a proposition, merely on the basis of its dicta.

E. SUMMARY

This chapter has examined what cases are, how they come to be published, what form their publication takes, and what are the components of a case report. This discussion should be related to the preceding chapter which discussed the role of precedent and authority in American law. The next chapter will describe the specific published case reports at the federal and state levels.

F. ADDITIONAL READING

F.R. Aumann, "American law reports: yesterday and today", 4 *Ohio State L.J.* 331 (1938).

F.C. Hicks, *Materials and Methods of Legal Research*, 3d revised ed. (Lawyers' Co-operative Publishing Co., 1942) Chapters VI and VIII.

K.N. Llewellyn, *The Bramble Bush* (Oceana Publications, 1960) Chapters II, III and IV.

E.C. Surrency, "Law reports in the United States", 25 *Amer. J. of Legal History* 48 (1981).

T.J. Young, Jr., "A look at American law reporting in the 19th century", 68 *Law Library J.* 294 (1975).

Chapter 3

PUBLISHED CASES

A. INTRODUCTION

The preceding chapter introduced case law and case reporting in general terms. This chapter will describe the existing sets of reported decisions that the researcher will encounter in working with American case materials. Because of the increasing emphasis placed on federal research, much of the chapter will be devoted to the reports of federal court decisions. The second part of the chapter will describe the sets which report cases at the state level. The annotated reports will be treated separately in Chapter 4.

B. SUPREME COURT OF THE UNITED STATES

The structure of the federal court system follows closely the paradigm of a court system set forth in Illustration A of Chapter 2. In this paradigm, the United States Supreme Court corresponds to the court of last resort level. The United States Supreme Court serves as the final level of appeal in any federal dispute, although it is not required to accept the responsibility of determining all points of law that are appealed to it. Indeed only a small percentage of the cases appealed to the Supreme Court are accepted for consideration. In most instances the Court will decline to review the decision of the courts below or will dispose of the matter through an order of the Court. The process of determining what matters the Court will consider is a complex one and beyond the scope of this chapter. There *are* some situations in which the United States Supreme Court because of constitutional provision or legislative mandate must take a matter "on appeal," and there even are circumstances in which the Supreme Court serves as the first forum for a dispute. In the end, however, the Court typically writes opinions in less than 150 cases per term.

The decisions of the United States Supreme Court are widely reported. The history of their publication corresponds to the brief history of American law reporting described in the last chapter. The first reports were compiled by individuals and were known as "nominative" reporters. Even after the federal government began to officially sanction the reports, they were still private ventures of the individual reporters. Thus the first 90 volumes of the *U.S. Reports* are still cited as "nominative" reporters and designated by the name of the individual reporter. The following list describes these early nominative reporters, their nominative and *U.S. Reports* citations, and the dates covered:

Reporter	**Nominative Citation**	**U.S. Reports Citation**	**Dates**
Dallas	1–4 Dallas	1–4 *U.S.*	1790 – 1800
Cranch	1–9 Cranch	5–13 *U.S.*	1801 – 1815
Wheaton	1–12 Wheaton	14–25 *U.S.*	1816 – 1827
Peters	1–16 Peters	26–41 *U.S.*	1828 – 1842
Howard	1–24 Howard	42–65 *U.S.*	1843 – 1860
Black	1–2 Black	66–67 *U.S.*	1861 – 1862
Wallace	1–23 Wallace	68–90 *U.S.*	1863 – 1874

Later sets, including current reprints, simply have incorporated these nominatives into the general numbering scheme of the *U.S. Reports*. Thus one might find a case cited in 5 *U.S.* (1 *Cranch*) which means that the case, originally in volume 1 of *Cranch's Reports* is now in volume 5 of the renumbered set. Those working with older collections may find mixed into their sets some of the various recompilations that were attempted during the 19th and 20th centuries. These recompilations were attempts to reprint earlier cases in a smaller and less expensive edition.[1] These reprints are no longer used much, but are still found on the shelves of many law libraries and are occasionally needed to trace citations to them in older works.

1. Perhaps the best known of early reprint editions are those of Richard Peters (*Peters' Condensed Reports*, covering 1 – 25 *U.S.*, 1791–1827 in 4 vols.) and Benjamin Curtis (*Curtis' Reports of Decisions*, covering 2–58 *U.S.*, 1790–1854 in 22 vols.).

1. U.S. REPORTS

The official reporter for the Supreme Court of the United States, is the *United States Reports* (abbreviated for citation purposes as *U.S.*). Although there are still individual reporters preparing the current volumes, they are now employees of the Court and their names are no longer used to designate their volumes.

The Supreme Court's annual term runs from October to July, and several volumes of *U.S. Reports* are added every year. Following the general pattern of publication, the decisions appear first in slip opinion form, followed by an official advance sheet (called the "preliminary print"), and finally appear in the bound *U.S. Reports* volume. Illustration A presents the beginning page of a case in the *U.S. Reports.* Note that the offical court reporter has prefaced the text of decisions with a syllabus (the preliminary paragraph summarizing the case) and "headnotes" (the numbered statements of what the Court held).

The *U.S. Reports* is an accurate, well-indexed compilation of the full official text of all decisions of the Supreme Court of the United States. At first glance it might seem that it should provide quite adequately for the needs of researchers. Unfortunately, as with many official publications, the advance sheets and volumes of the *U.S. Reports* tend to appear quite slowly. Currently, more than a year passes between the decision of the case and the appearance of the published decision in the advance sheet, and even longer in the bound volume. Because of the importance of Supreme Court opinions, this slow pace of reporting is inadequate for practising attorneys. In response to the need for more timely publication, commercial publishers produce a variety of unofficial compilations of these decisions. Commercial case reporters are published and distributed much more quickly than the official set and also offer special interpretative tools and digesting that make their editions more useful to the legal researcher. More than half a dozen versions of the full text of every United States Supreme Court decisions are issued unofficially, in a variety of formats. Because of the importance of these Supreme Court opinions, each of these publications is discussed below.

2. WEST'S SUPREME COURT REPORTER

This publication prints the full text of all United States Supreme Court decisions, beginning in 1882 with its first volume corresponding to volume 106 of the *U.S. Reports.* It appears first in advance sheets, then as a bound volume, with the same pagination in each format. The set is numbered seriatim, with one numbered volume appearing each year. In years in which two physical volumes have been needed to include all cases, West has issued both the numbered volume, and a supplement designated with an "A" (*e.g.*, volumes 97 and 97A cover the October Term of 1976).

FIRST NATIONAL BANK OF BOSTON *v.* BELLOTTI 765

Syllabus

FIRST NATIONAL BANK OF BOSTON ET AL. *v.* BELLOTTI, ATTORNEY GENERAL OF MASSACHUSETTS

APPEAL FROM THE SUPREME JUDICIAL COURT OF MASSACHUSETTS

No. 76–1172. Argued November 9, 1977—Decided April 26, 1978

Syllabus

Appellants, national banking associations and business corporations, wanted to spend money to publicize their views opposing a referendum proposal to amend the Massachusetts Constitution to authorize the legislature to enact a graduated personal income tax. They brought this action challenging the constitutionality of a Massachusetts criminal statute that prohibited them and other specified business corporations from making contributions or expenditures "for the purpose of . . . influencing or affecting the vote on any question submitted to the voters, other than one materially affecting any of the property, business or assets of the corporation." The statute specified that "[n]o question submitted to the voters solely concerning the taxation of the income, property or transactions of individuals shall be deemed materially to affect the property, business or assets of the corporation." On April 26, 1976, the case was submitted to a single Justice of the Supreme Judicial Court of Massachusetts on an expedited basis and upon agreed facts. Judgment was reserved and the case was referred to the full court. On September 22, 1976, the court directed entry of a judgment for appellee and issued its opinion upholding the constitutionality of the statute after the referendum, at which the proposal was rejected. *Held:*

Headnotes

1. The case is not rendered moot by the fact that the 1976 referendum has been held and the proposal for a constitutional amendment defeated. The 18-month interval between legislative authorization of placement of the proposal on the ballot and its submission to the voters was too short for appellants to obtain complete judicial review, and likely would be too short in any future challenge to the statute; and in view of the number of times that such a proposal has been submitted to the electorate, there is reasonable expectation that appellants again will be subjected to the threat of prosecution under the statute. *Weinstein* v. *Bradford,* 423 U. S. 147, 149. Pp. 774–775.

2. The portion of the Massachusetts statute at issue violates the First Amendment as made applicable to the States by the Fourteenth. Pp. 775–795.

Illustration A

The first page of a decision in the official *U.S. Reports.*

What makes these unofficial editions commercially viable? Why would a library or an attorney buy the unofficial set when the official edition was available, and at a lower price? In the case of the West *Supreme Court Reporter* there are several reasons.

First, the *Supreme Court Reporter* appears much more quickly than the *U.S. Reports.* Its advance sheet pamphlet appears within a few weeks of the appearance of the decision—a significant improvement on the *U.S. Reports'* performance.

Second, the West Publishing Company provides a variety of research aids in each advance sheet and bound volume that are designed to aid the researcher. In addition to the full report of each decision, the West editors prepare their own headnotes that often are more detailed than those done by the official compiler. Illustration B shows the *Supreme Court Reporter* headnotes. Tables of cases reported, of statutes construed, and of words and phrases defined, also are included in each advance sheet and bound volume of the *Supreme Court Reporter.* The advance sheets and bound volumes also contain an Index-Digest of the headnotes of all of the cases reported in the text. This provides subject access to the contents of the reporter. These features are all of great use to the researcher, but are now also included in most current reporters. It is a third feature that is unique to West's *Supreme Court Reporter.*

This third feature, West's system of abstracting and digesting the points of law in each opinion, integrates the *Supreme Court Reporter* into West's comprehensive subject digest system and with many of West's other publications. This abstracting structure, with its "key number" classification scheme, will be explained in Chapter 5 on Case Finding. For now, note the topic and key number designations assigned to each headnote in Illustration B.

It should be noted here that in its early years the *Supreme Court Reporter* and other West reporters benefited from the reputation for accuracy in case reporting gained by the West Publishing Company. In the early days of American reporting, complaints about inaccuracies in published decisions were common. Each of the reporters described in this chapter is generally reliable as to accuracy of text, and errors in reporting are rare.

3. UNITED STATES SUPREME COURT REPORTS, LAWYERS' EDITION

This series, published by the Lawyers Cooperative Publishing Company (hereafter called simply, Lawyers Co-op), also prints the full text of all Supreme Court opinions. The set, popularly known as the "*Lawyers' Edition,*" includes Supreme Court decisions back to the earliest cases. Although it consists of far fewer physical volumes than the official edition, it reprints all of the decisions of the *United States Reports.* After reaching volume 100, the

FIRST NAT. BANK OF BOSTON v. BELLOTTI 1407

435 U.S. 765 Cite as 98 S.Ct. 1407 (1978)

"Star Paging"

435 U.S. 765, 55 L.Ed.2d 707

FIRST NATIONAL BANK OF BOSTON et al., Appellants,

v.

Francis X. BELLOTTI, etc.

No. 76–1172.

Argued Nov. 9, 1977.

Decided April 26, 1978.

Rehearing Denied June 26, 1978.

See 438 U.S. 907, 98 S.Ct. 3126.

West syllabus

National banking associations and business corporations brought action to challenge the constitutionality of a Massachusetts criminal statute that prohibited them and other business corporations from making contributions or expenditures to influence the outcome of a vote on any question submitted to voters other than questions materially affecting the property, business or assets of the corporation. The case was submitted to a single justice of the Supreme Judicial Court of Massachusetts. Judgment was reserved and the case referred to the full court which upheld the constitutionality of the statute, 371 Mass. 773, 359 N.E.2d 1262. The corporations appealed, and the Supreme Court, Mr. Justice Powell, held that: (1) because the case fell within the class of controversies capable of repetition but evading review, the questions were not rendered moot by the fact that the referendum in connection with which plaintiffs sought to publicize their views had been held; (2) there was no support in the Constitution for the proposition that expression of views on issues of public importance loses First Amendment protection simply because its source is a corporation that cannot prove that the issues materially affect the corporation's business; (3) the statute could not be justified by the asserted interest in protecting the role of the individual citizen in the electoral process and preventing diminution of confidence in government; (4) the statute was both under-inclusive and over-inclusive with respect to the asserted purpose of protecting rights of corporate shareholders, and (5) the Massachusetts statute prohibiting corporate expenditures regarding individual income tax referenda violated the First Amendment as made applicable to the states by the Fourteenth.

Reversed.

Mr. Chief Justice Burger filed a concurring opinion.

Mr. Justice White filed a dissenting opinion in which Mr. Justice Brennan and Mr. Justice Marshall joined.

Mr. Justice Rehnquist filed a dissenting opinion.

West headnotes

1. Constitutional Law ⚷46(1)

Suit wherein certain corporations sought to have declared unconstitutional a Massachusetts criminal statute forbidding expenditures by banks and business corporations for the purpose of influencing the vote on any question other than one materially affecting the property, business or assets of the corporation, including questions of individual income taxation, was not moot by reason of the fact that the referendum with respect to which plaintiffs sought to publicize their views had been held where, under no reasonably foreseeable circumstances could plenary review of the issue presented be obtained in advance of a similar referendum and there was a reasonable expectation that plaintiffs would again be subject to the threat of prosecution under the challenged statute. M.G.L.A. c. 55 § 8.

2. Constitutional Law ⚷82(1)

The Constitution often protects interests broader than those of the party seeking their vindication; the First Amendment, in particular, serves significant societal interests. U.S.C.A.Const. Amend. 1.

3. Constitutional Law ⚷90(1)

For purpose of determining whether proposed speech is within the protection of the First Amendment, the inherent worth of the speech in terms of its capacity for informing the public does not depend on the identity of its source, whether corporation, association, union or individual. U.S.C.A. Const. Amend. 1.

4. Banks and Banking ⚷232

National banks are creatures of federal law and instrumentalities of the federal

Illustration B

The first page of a decision in West's *Supreme Court Reporter*.

publisher of *Lawyers' Edition* began a second series, known as *Lawyers' Edition 2d*, which continues today. As with most reporters, the bound volumes of *Lawyers' Edition 2d* are preceded by advance sheet pamphlets.

Illustrations C–1 to C–3 show the same decision which appeared in Illustration B, but now in its *Lawyers' Edition* format.

What features does *Lawyers' Edition* offer that distinguish it from both the official *U.S. Reports* and its commercial competitor, *Supreme Court Reporter*?

In comparison with the official set, *Lawyers' Edition* offers speed of publication. Like the *Supreme Court Reporter*, it puts decisions in the researchers' hands in a matter of weeks, not months. In addition, the editors at Lawyers Co-op prepare both a "summary" of each case, cross references to their other publications on the same subject, and their own headnotes. Note these features in Illustrations C–1 to C–3, and contrast the *Lawyers' Edition* headnotes in Illustration C–3 with those of the *Supreme Court Reporter* in Illustration B.

The fact that the editors of these two commercial publications formulate different statements of the points of law in the same case demonstrates the subjectivity of legal research. It also underscores the fact that headnotes are a secondary source. Each volume of *Lawyers' Edition 2d* has essentially the same helpful lists and tables as are found in *Supreme Court Reporter*. In addition to these features, each volume of *Lawyers' Edition* has several special aids.

First, *Lawyers' Edition 2d* provides short summaries of the briefs of counsel. These permit study of the line of argument presented by each party and offer a new perspective on the Court's decision. Many early reporters carried such summaries, but *Lawyers' Edition* is the only commercial reporter that still does so.[2] Second, the publisher includes Annotations on a few of the more important cases in each volume. These Annotations analyze in considerable detail one or more of the points of law covered in the case and present other primary authorities on the same topic. Note, however, that *Lawyers' Edition* contains annotations for only a few of the decisions it publishes, unlike its companion reporters, *A.L.R.* and *A.L.R. Federal*, which annotate every decision they publish. A set of volumes entitled *Later Case Service* keeps up to date the Annotations in volumes 1–32 of *Lawyers' Edition 2d*. Since volume 32, each volume includes internal supplementation by an annual pocket part. Chapter 4, Annotated Law Reports, will discuss more fully the subject of these Annotations and their use.

Lawyers' Edition is part of the "Total Client-Service Library," a tradename for the research system developed by Lawyers Co-op to link all of its various publications. Like the West system of interrelated publications, this "library" includes a wide range of primary

2. Unfortunately, summaries of briefs are now included for only a few of the cases in *Lawyers' Edition*.

[435 US 765]

FIRST NATIONAL BANK OF BOSTON et al., Appellants,

v

FRANCIS X. BELLOTTI, etc.,

435 US 765, 55 L Ed 2d 707, 98 S Ct 1407, reh den (US), 57 L Ed 2d 1150, 98 S Ct 3126

[No. 76–1172]

Argued November 9, 1977. Decided April 26, 1978.

SUMMARY

On an expedited basis and upon agreed facts, certain national banking associations and business corporations brought an action before the Supreme Judicial Court of Massachusetts challenging the constitutionality of a state statute which forbids certain expenditures by banks and certain business corporations for the purpose of influencing the vote on referendum proposals, other than ones materially affecting any of the property, business, or assets of the corporation. The court directed the entry of a judgment upholding the constitutionality of the statute, holding that only when a general political issue materially affected a corporation's business, property, or assets could that corporation claim First Amendment protection for its speech or other activities entitling it to communicate its position on that issue to the general public (359 NE2d 1262).

On appeal, the United States Supreme Court reversed. In an opinion by Powell, J., joined by Burger, Ch. J., and Stewart, Blackmun, and Stevens, JJ., it was held that the state statute abridged freedom of speech in violation of the First and Fourteenth Amendments, and that the abridgment was not justified by (1) the state's interest in sustaining the active role of the individual citizen in the electoral process and thereby preventing diminution of the citizen's confidence in government, since there was no showing that the relative voice of corporations had been overwhelming or even significant in influencing state referenda, or that there had been any threats to the confidence of the citizenry in government, or by (2) the state's interest in protecting the rights of shareholders whose views differed from those expressed by management on behalf of the corporation, since there was no substantially relevant correlation between the governmental interest and the state's effort to prohibit the corporations from speaking.

Briefs of Counsel, p 967, infra.

Illustration C–1

The first page of a decision in *Lawyers' Edition*, showing its editor's summary.

U.S. SUPREME COURT REPORTS 55 L Ed 2d

BURGER, Ch. J., concurred, expressing the view that the First Amendment did not belong to any definable category of persons, but belonged to all who exercised its freedoms.

WHITE, J., joined by BRENNAN and MARSHALL, JJ., dissenting, stated that the state statute was constitutional and that the First Amendment did not forbid state interference with managerial decisions to use corporate funds to circulate fact and opinion irrelevant to the corporation's business and necessarily representing the managers' own personal or collective views about political and social questions.

REHNQUIST, J., dissented, expressing the view that business corporations did not have a constitutionally protected liberty to engage in political activity with regard to matters having no material effect on their business.

HEADNOTES

Classified to U. S. Supreme Court Digest, Lawyers' Edition

Constitutional Law § 935.5 — freedom of speech — corporations — state statutory restriction

1a, 1b, 1c. A state statute which forbids certain expenditures by banks and certain business corporations for the purpose of influencing the vote on referendum proposals, other than ones mate-

TOTAL CLIENT-SERVICE LIBRARY® REFERENCES

16 Am Jur 2d, Constitutional Law §§ 341–350

7 Am Jur Pl & Pr Forms (Rev), Constitutional Law, Forms 11, 24

USCS; Constitution, 1st and 14th Amendments

US L Ed Digest, Constitutional Law § 935.5

ALR Digests, Constitutional Law § 794

L Ed Index to Annos, Freedom of Speech, Press, Religion, and Assembly

ALR Quick Index, Freedom of Speech and Press

Federal Quick Index, Freedom of Speech and Press

ANNOTATION REFERENCES

Right to free speech and press as including right to refuse to foster, repeat, advertise, or disseminate views, messages, statements, or slogans repugnant to one's moral, religious, or political beliefs. 51 L Ed 2d 924.

What circumstances render civil case, or issues arising therein, moot so as to preclude Supreme Court's consideration of their merits. 44 L Ed 2d 745.

Applicability to advertisements of First Amendment's guaranty of free speech and press. 37 L Ed 2d 1124.

The Supreme Court and the right of free speech and press. 93 L Ed 1151, 2 L Ed 2d 1706, 11 L Ed 2d 1116, 16 L Ed 2d 1053, 21 L Ed 2d 976.

708

Illustration C–2

The second page of a *Lawyers' Edition* decision, showing cross-references.

FIRST NATIONAL BANK OF BOSTON v BELLOTTI

435 US 765, 55 L Ed 2d 707, 98 S Ct 1407

rially affecting any of the property, business, or assets of the corporation, abridges freedom of speech in violation of the First and Fourteenth Amendments; the abridgment of freedom of speech by the statute is not justified by (1) the state's interest in sustaining the active role of the individual citizen in the electoral process and thereby preventing diminution of the citizen's confidence in government, where there is no showing that the relative voice of corporations has been overwhelming or even significant in influencing state referenda, or that there has been any threat to the confidence of the citizenry in government, or by (2) the state's interest in protecting the rights of shareholders whose views differ from those expressed by management on behalf of the corporation, where there is no substantially relevant correlation between the governmental interest and the state's effort to prohibit the corporations from speaking. (White, Brennan, Marshall, and Rehnquist, JJ., dissented from this holding.)

Appeal and Error § 1662 — moot case — holding of referendum

2. An appeal to the United States Supreme Court of a state court decision upholding the constitutionality of a state statute which forbids certain expenditures by banks and certain business corporations for the purpose of influencing the vote on referendum proposals, other than ones materially affecting any of the property, business, or assets of the corporation, is not moot, even though the referendum contested by the corporations has been held, and the proposed amendment of the state constitution, which is the subject of the referendum, has been defeated, where (1) under no reasonably forseeable circumstances could the corporations obtain full review by the Supreme Court of the constitutionality of the statute in advance of a referendum on a similar constitutional amendment, and (2) there is no serious doubt that there is a reasonable expectation that the corporations again will be subject to the threat of prosecution under the state statute.

Constitutional Law § 935.5 — freedom of speech — state referendum

3. A state referendum on a proposal to amend the state constitution to authorize the legislature to enact a graduated personal income tax falls within the scope of issues about which information is needed or appropriate to enable the members of society to cope with the exigencies of their period, fully entitled to protection under the First Amendment.

Constitutional Law § 925 — freedom of speech and press — matters of public concern

4. The freedom of speech and of the press guaranteed by the United States Constitution embraces at the least the liberty to discuss publicly and truthfully all matters of public concern without previous restraint or fear of subsequent prosecution.

Constitutional Law § 925 — freedom of speech — scope

5. Freedom of discussion embraces all issues about which information is needed or appropriate to enable members of society to cope with the exigencies of their period.

Constitutional Law § 925 — freedom of speech — purpose

6. A major purpose of the First Amendment is to protect the free discussion of governmental affairs.

Constitutional Law § 935.5 — freedom of speech — state referendum

7. For First Amendment purposes, speech concerning the issues in a referendum on a state constitutional amendment is the type of speech indispensible to decisionmaking in a democracy, even where the speech comes from a corporation rather than an individual; the inherent worth of the speech in terms of its capacity for informing the public does not depend upon the identity of the source, whether corporation, association, union, or individual.

709

Illustration C-3

The third page of a *Lawyers' Edition* decision showing its headnotes.

and secondary sources. Each Lawyers Co-op publication will refer the researcher to other Co-op products that deal with the same issue. As with the West system, the Total Client-Service Library enhances the utility of each of its constituent parts.

A final advantage of *Lawyers' Edition* is the availability of its companion set, *U.S. Supreme Court Digest, Lawyer's Edition*, which contains a topical arrangement of abstracts of the points of law covered in all U.S. Supreme Court opinions. The two sets are designed to be used together. As with the West system of "key-numbering," a fuller description of the features and uses of this digest will be provided in Chapter 5, "Case Finding."

The three case reporters described above, *U.S. Reports, Supreme Court Reporter*, and *Lawyers' Edition*, provide the full text of every opinion of the U.S. Supreme Court in a traditional case reporter format. The next examples are not of case reporters, but of other forms of legal publication in which the text of these decisions can also be found.

4. UNITED STATES LAW WEEK

United States Law Week is a two-volume looseleaf service, published by another commercial publisher, the Bureau of National Affairs. It reproduces, in a looseleaf format, the full text of every opinion of the United States Supreme Court. The unique value of *U.S. Law Week* is the speed with which it prints and distributes these opinions. Because even the fastest advance sheet of the *Supreme Court Reporter* or *Lawyers' Edition 2d* will not arrive for several weeks after the rendering of a decision, there is a need for a service that provides faster access to these important decisions. To answer this need, *U.S. Law Week* photographically reproduces the text of the decision from the slip opinion, adding no headnotes or editorial comment. The decisions in the weekly issues of *U.S. Law Week* reach subscribers within a few days of their issuance by the Supreme Court. During the Supreme Court term, it often publishes extra issues in busy weeks. This coverage and prompt service has made *U.S. Law Week* one of the most popular legal publications.

The *Supreme Court* volume of *U.S. Law Week* also contains additional sections that provide news of the U.S. Supreme Court, chronicle its proceedings, and list all cases docketed, argued, and otherwise treated by the Court. A second volume, called *General Law*, contains news and abstracts of important opinions from other federal courts and from the state courts, and, very selectively, reports of new legislation and administrative law development. *U.S. Law Week* will be discussed further in Chapter 13, Looseleaf Services.

5. SUPREME COURT BULLETIN

This looseleaf publication of Commerce Clearing House contains many of the same features as the *Supreme Court* volume of *U.S. Law Week*. It also prints and distributes the full text of all United

States Supreme Court opinions on a weekly basis. The *Supreme Court Bulletin* also reports the calendars, proceedings and orders of the Court, but does not contain a general law section like that in *U.S. Law Week*.

Both *U.S. Law Week* and the *Supreme Court Bulletin* are useful for locating the text of recently written decisions. Neither has accompanying headnotes, nor are they integrated into larger research systems. Once a decision has appeared in the advance sheets or bound volumes of one of the standard reporters (*U.S. Reports, Supreme Court Reporter*, or *Lawyers' Edition*) that text and citation of the case should be used. Until then, a citation to one of these looseleaf services is completely acceptable.

6. LEXIS AND WESTLAW

These two on-line computer data bases provide machine access to the text of the decisions of the United States Supreme Court. The operation of these search services are more fully described in Chapter 22, New Media in Legal Research. Neither provides complete historical coverage of past Supreme Court decisions, but both are constantly extending their data bases retrospectively. The data bases normally contain the text of opinions well before the publication of advance sheets. Both WESTLAW and LEXIS have pledged to have the full text of all U.S. Supreme Court opinions in their data bases within 72 hours of decision, which would make them faster than even *U.S. Law Week* or *Supreme Court Bulletin,* for subscribers to those looseleaf services. Because most large research law libraries and many law firms contain terminals for one of these two computer systems, they offer another source of United States Supreme Court opinions.

Each of the sources of Supreme Court opinions offer its own advantages. For detailed analysis and headnoting, *Supreme Court Reporter* and *Lawyers' Edition* are best; for the official citation, the *U.S. Reports* is needed; for speed of access, one of the computer data bases or looseleaf services may be most appropriate. The sophisticated retrieval capability of LEXIS and WESTLAW will be discussed in Chapter 22.

7. NEWSPAPER ACCOUNTS

Copies of decisions, as they are issued, are distributed to the press at the Supreme Court, and are similarly available to anyone at the Court in Washington, D.C. National newspapers, such as the *New York Times* and the *Washington Post,* assign reporters to the Supreme Court who follow and report on its activities. Frequently, the day after the decisions are rendered articles in these papers discuss the most important decisions, and a side bar on an inside page summarizes actions of the Court. While this does not provide any material that would be cited in a legal brief, it enables lawyers and researchers to follow major cases. On occasion even docket numbers are included in these accounts. If a decision is of major national impact, excerpts from the text may be found.

8. OTHER LOOSELEAF SERVICES

A number of secondary sources also reprint selected United States Supreme Court opinions. Chief among these are the looseleaf services that concentrate on special subject areas. When a United States Supreme Court decision in one of those subject areas is rendered, it will be reprinted in the looseleaf service as part of its regular service to subscribers. These subject-oriented looseleaf services are combinations of primary sources and secondary materials. As will be discussed in Chapter 13 on Looseleaf Services, one should monitor those services in one's fields of special interest for quick access to the latest primary sources and for the analytical discussions the services also provide.

C. LOWER FEDERAL COURTS

The two lower levels of the federal court system, the U.S. Courts of Appeals and the U.S. District Courts, correspond to the second and third steps of the court diagram in Illustration A of Chapter 2 (p. 18). It is a surprising fact that no *official* case reporter publishes the decisions of these lower federal courts. Although records on each case before those courts are kept on file with the clerk of each individual court, there is no official publication of the decisions of those courts, other than their slip opinions. The slip opinions are not widely distributed, and these decisions can be obtained effectively only through their selective publication in unofficial reporters.

Until the advent of computerized research the only comprehensive source of decisions of the lower federal courts was in the publications of the West Publishing Company. *A.L.R.* and later, *A.L.R. Federal,* published only very few such decisions. These are discussed in Chapter 4, *Annotated Law Reports.* A brief survey of the reporting of lower federal cases in the West system follows here.

1. FEDERAL CASES

During the 19th century a number of individual "nominative" reporters published decisions of the many lower federal courts. To complicate matters even further, the structure of the lower federal courts changed several times in the 19th century. Congress has the power to restructure these courts and on several occasions has done so. Over two hundred separate reporters, most covering but a single court, published decisions from various federal courts during the 19th century.[3] Chaos thus attended any attempt to retrieve federal cases, and in some instances these private reporters presented varying texts

3. A list of these reporters appears in the first volume of West's *Federal Cases.*

for the same decision. Only a few libraries throughout the country had any significant number of these reporters.

This troublesome situation was resolved by the West Publishing Company, which collected the decisions from all of the various nominative reporters and compiled them into a single closed set entitled, *Federal Cases*. *Federal Cases* arranged the more than 20,000 cases in alphabetical order by case name and assigned a number to each individual case. The resulting thirty volume set, published from 1894 to 1897, contains all available lower federal court case law up to 1882. If the only available citation is from one of the original nominative reporters, the researcher can consult a volume accompanying this set that converts citations from original nominative reporters to the case's new location in *Federal Cases*, though the alphabetic arrangement is usually the quickest approach. Thus, *Federal Cases* provides access to any federal court decision by (1) names of the parties, (2) citation from the nominative reporter through the conversion table, or (3) the case number assigned by the West Publishing Company.

The U.S. Courts of Appeals now consists of thirteen judicial circuits, the 11th Circuit having been added in 1980 (94 Stat. 1994, 28 U.S.C. 41, 1980) and the Federal Circuit having been added in 1982 (96 Stat. 25, 28 U.S.C. 41, 1982). The jurisdictional coverage of these circuits is shown on the map on the following page.

2. FEDERAL REPORTER AND FEDERAL SUPPLEMENT

To cover the decisions following those reported in *Federal Cases*, the West Publishing Company began, in 1880, a new set entitled *Federal Reporter*. *Federal Reporter* systematically published decisions from both the appellate and trial court levels of the United States federal court system. Many researchers labor under the mistaken impression that *all* cases considered by the federal courts during the relevant period were represented by decisions published in *Federal Reporter*. In fact, only a small percentage of the matters that came before the courts actually resulted in written opinions. Initially, all opinions that were issued by the U.S. Courts of Appeals (formerly called the U.S. Circuit Courts of Appeals) did appear in this set, but even from the beginning only a selection of U.S. District Court decisions were published in *Federal Reporter*.

The explosion of federal litigation that occurred in the early part of this century accelerated rapidly in the 1920's and 1930's and led West to divide the *Federal Reporter* into two parts. Beginning with the October term of 1932, a new West reporter, *Federal Supplement* published a selection of U.S. District Court decisions, and *Federal Reporter* continued the publication of the appellate level decisions from the U.S. Court of Appeals.

In addition to their respective publication of U.S. Courts of Appeals and U.S. District Court decisions, as described above, *Federal*

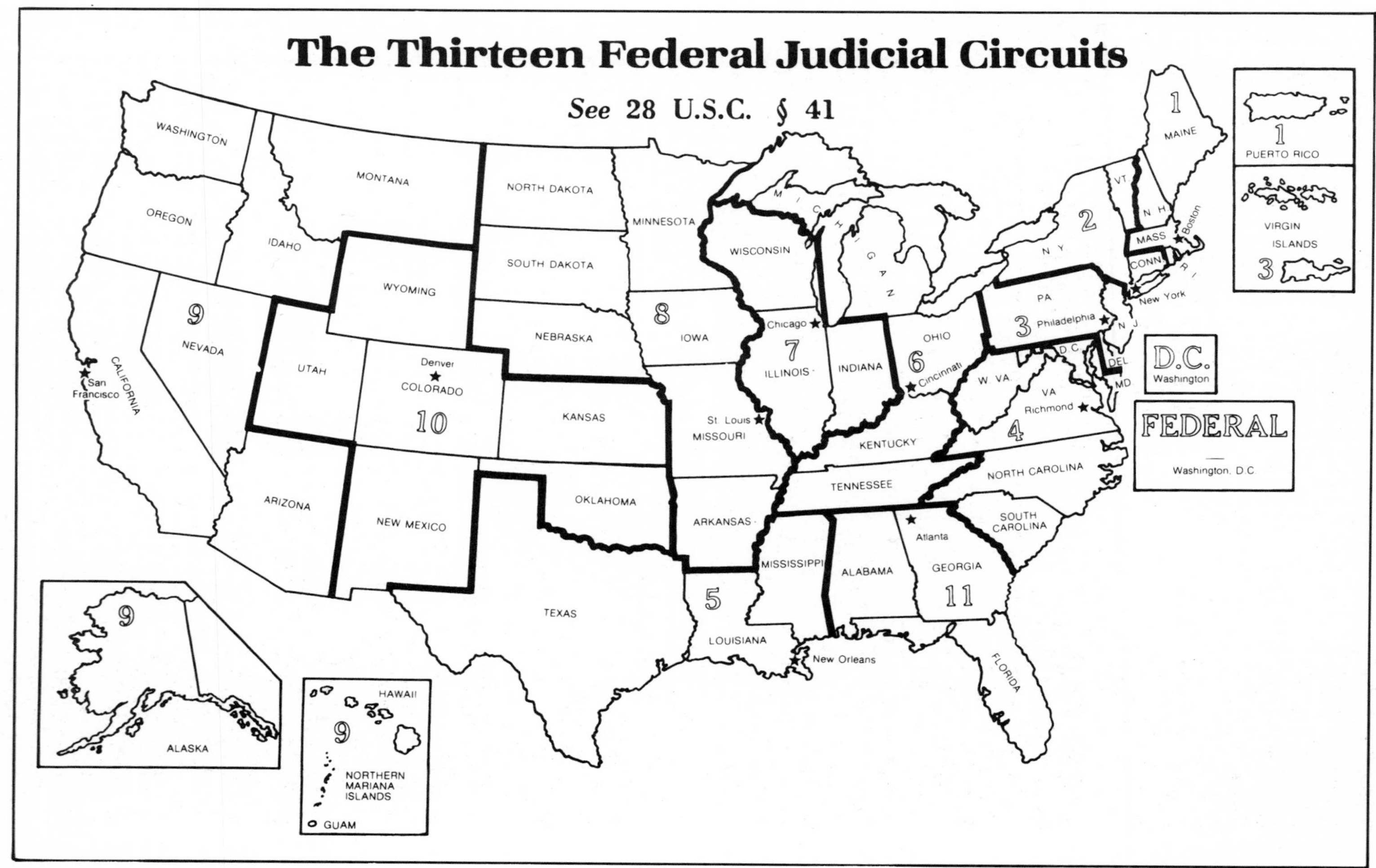
The Thirteen Federal Judicial Circuits
See 28 U.S.C. § 41
WASHINGTON
OREGON
IDAHO
MONTANA
NORTH DAKOTA
SOUTH DAKOTA
MINNESOTA
WYOMING
NEBRASKA
9
NEVADA
CALIFORNIA
San Francisco
UTAH
Denver
COLORADO
10
KANSAS
8
IOWA
St. Louis
MISSOURI
ARIZONA
NEW MEXICO
OKLAHOMA
ARKANSAS
TEXAS
5
LOUISIANA
New Orleans
MISSISSIPPI
ALABAMA
Atlanta
GEORGIA
11
FLORIDA
SOUTH CAROLINA
NORTH CAROLINA
TENNESSEE
KENTUCKY
WISCONSIN
M I C H I G A N
Chicago
7
ILLINOIS
INDIANA
OHIO
6
Cincinnati
W. VA.
VA
Richmond
4
PA
3
Philadelphia
D.C.
DEL
MD
N J
N Y
2
New York
CONN
R I
MASS
Boston
VT
N H
1
MAINE
D.C.
Washington
FEDERAL
Washington, D.C.
1
PUERTO RICO
VIRGIN ISLANDS
3
9
ALASKA
HAWAII
9
NORTHERN MARIANA ISLANDS
GUAM

Reporter and *Federal Supplement* have also published, in varying patterns, the decisions of several specialized federal courts, such as the U.S. Court of Claims, the U.S. Court of Customs and Patent Appeals, the U.S. Emergency Court of Appeals, the Temporary Emergency Court of Appeals, and the U.S. Customs Court (now called the U.S. Court of International Trade). Their current coverage is as follows: *Federal Reporter* now reports the U.S. Courts of Appeals; the U.S. Court of Claims; the U.S. Court of Customs and Patent Appeals; and the Temporary Emergency Court of Appeals. *Federal Supplement* reports the U.S. District Courts; the U.S. Court of International Trade; the Special Court under the Regional Rail Reorganization Act; and the rulings of the Judicial Panel on Multi-District Litigation. These two publications continue today to be the most comprehensive and systematic source of lower federal court opinions,[4] although, as will be noted below, West has also added several more reporters of federal decisions, focusing on specific subject areas.

The explosive growth in the number of cases being decided by the federal courts by the 1960's caused increasing concern that *too many* cases were being published. The cost of maintaining the existing reporters and the burden of research in the multitude of routine and repetitive decisions led the individual U.S. Courts of Appeals to develop their own programs to limit publication and to establish criteria for determining what cases should be published. These programs have had some success and each of the Courts has now established rules for this purpose.[5] A recent commentator has estimated that by the 1978–79 term *Federal Reporter, 2d Series* published an average of only 38.3% of the U.S Court of Appeals decisions throughout the country, ranging from a low of 18.1% for the 3rd Circuit to a high of 68.2% for the 8th Circuit.[6] It has also been estimated that *Federal Supplement* now publishes only 10 to 15% of the U.S. District Court decisions. This, however, has not resulted in diminished growth of the *Federal Reporter 2d* or the *Federal Supplement.* In fact, despite all efforts at stemming the tide of published cases, both sets find their rate of growth still accelerating. This is due to the constant increase in the number of cases filed in the various federal courts, the increased number of judges, and the continuing proliferation of written opinions.

Despite efforts by the federal judiciary to limit the number of decisions being published, the growth of *Federal Reporter* and *Federal*

4. However, a computerized research service, LEXIS, offers access to many federal court decisions which are not published in *Federal Reporter 2d* or *Federal Supplement,* and many of the looseleaf services also contain some federal decisions in specialized subject fields that are not in the West reporters.

5. W.L. Reynolds & W.M. Richman, "The non-precedential precedent—limited publication and no-citation rules in the United States Courts of Appeals," 78 *Columbia L.R.* 1167 (1978) and L.F. Chanin, "A survey of the writing and publication of opinions in federal and state appellate courts," 67 *Law Library J.* 362 (1974). For a more critical view of the limitation on publication of decisions, see D.N. Hoffman, "Nonpublication of federal appellate court opinions," 6 *Justice System J.* 405 (1981).

6. W.L. Reynolds and W.M. Richman, "An evaluation of limited publication in the United States Courts of Appeals: The price of reform", 48 *U. of Chicago L.R.* 573 (1981).

Supplement remains staggering. One solution being attempted by West is the creation of topical reporters to draw off decisions in certain specialized fields and offer them separately to researchers primarily interested in those subjects. In recent years, West has spun off several topical reporters of this kind from the *Federal Reporter, 2d* and *Federal Supplement.* The first was *Federal Rules Decisions,* begun in 1940. It includes selective opinions of the U.S. District Courts on matters related to the Federal Rules of Criminal and Civil Procedure and the Rules of Evidence. This reporter contains not only the text of decisions but also, from time to time, proceedings of judicial conferences, speeches, and articles on federal procedural law.

3. SPECIAL WEST REPORTERS

Then in 1977 the *Military Justice Reporter* was initiated, covering decisions from the U.S. Court of Military Appeals and the Courts of Military Review for the Army, Navy-Marine, Air Force, and Coast Guard. In 1979 another topical reporter, West's *Bankruptcy Reporter,* began publication of decisions from the U.S. Bankruptcy Courts, as well as cases from all levels of the federal court system that deal with bankruptcy matters. In 1982 West's *Education Law Reporter* was issued, including selected federal and state court decisions on education law topics, and some articles in that field. The most recent, West's *Social Security Reporter,* is due for publication in 1983.

Each of these subject-oriented reporters contains the standard West research aids, including the key-number digesting system, and represents a response to the flood of case law and the need of specialists to have access to primary materials in their own fields. If these are successful, more topical reporters of this kind are likely. The diagram on the following page shows graphically the development of West's federal and topical reporters.

Through the *Supreme Court Reporter, Federal Reporter, 2d Series, Federal Supplement* and the special reporters just discussed, the West Publishing Company covers a wide range of federal court decisions. At one time it could have been said that the three main West federal series were the only significant reporters of federal decisions. Now, however, there are several other sources of thse decisions. The annotated reporting system of Lawyers Co-op has, since 1969, included *American Law Reports-Federal,* which will be described in Chapter 4. In addition, looseleaf services, a number of topical reporters in special subject fields, and the computerized legal research systems, all provide substantial access to federal decisions, many of which are not published in the West system.

4. LOOSELEAF SERVICES AND TOPICAL REPORTERS

Looseleaf services will be discussed more fully in Chapter 13, but require mention here, both for their own inclusion of federal court

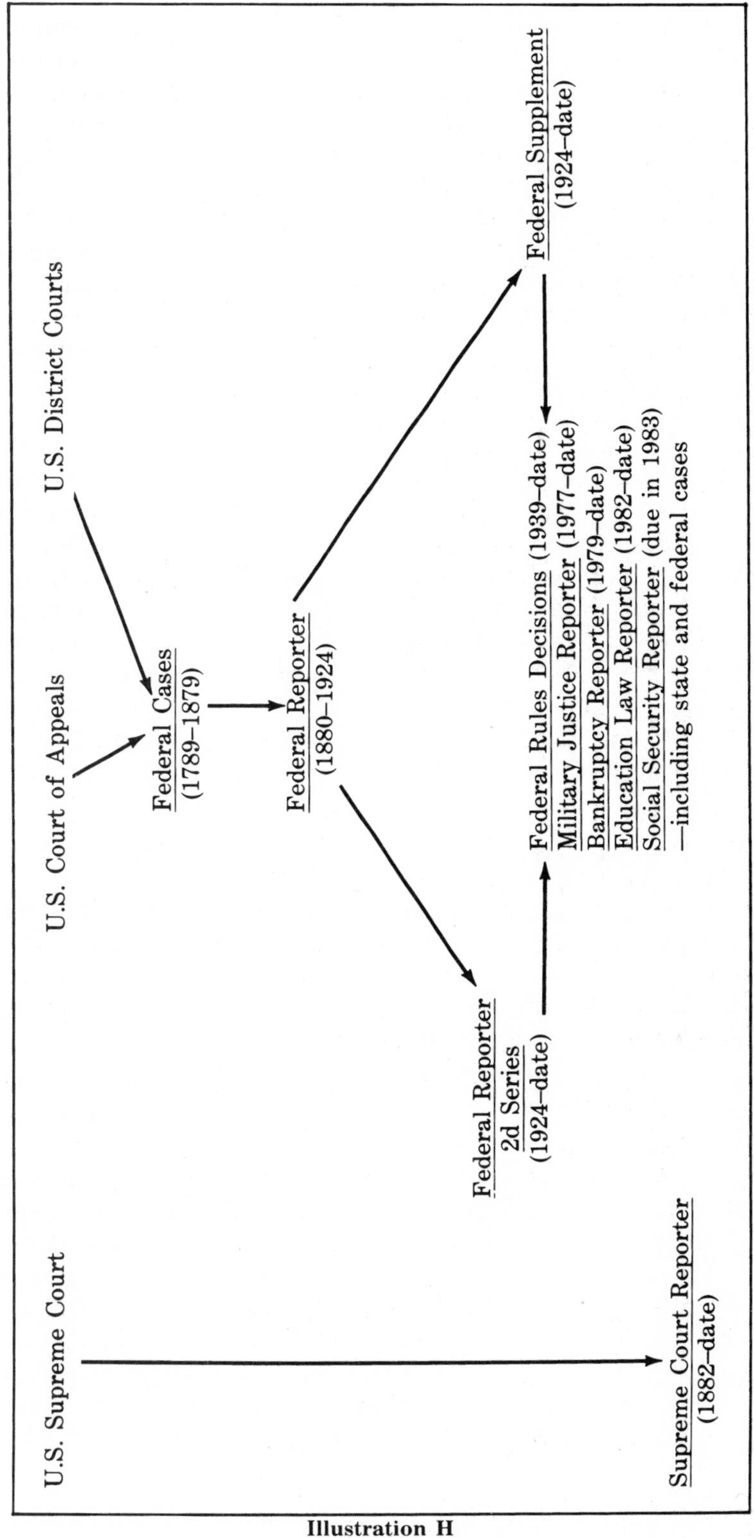

Illustration H

Development of West's federal reporting system with dates covered by each reporter.

decisions in the subject fields they cover, and for their role in issuing permanent bound volumes of decisions as adjunct series to their own publication.

Looseleaf services typically bring together all of the major types of legal publications on one subject, frequently with weekly supplementation, several indexing approaches, and explanatory text material. A very comprehensive looseleaf service may include federal and state court decisions, federal and state statutes, and federal and state administrative regulations and rulings, all in the particular subject field of the service. Sometimes the decisions appear only as abstracts, but most of the major services in public law fields provide the full text of at least the federal court decisions, including many lower federal court decisions which do not appear in the West reporters described above. Because of their weekly supplementation, these decisions are often published faster than they are in the West advance sheets.

In recent years, the three largest publishers of looseleaf services, Commerce Clearing House, Prentice-Hall, and Bureau of National Affairs, have also issued bound volume series of the full text of federal court decisions in their selected subject areas. Several also include state court decisions, and some offer administrative agency decisions as well. In some fields, the court and agency decisions are published in separate series, and in some the federal and state decisions are published separately. A few join all four categories in one series. However structured, these topical reporters give a more permanent form to decisions which have already appeared in the looseleaf service, and sometimes include additional decisions in full text which may not have appeared in the looseleaf service or may have appeared only in a digested form.

There are also a number of older topical reporters which are not issued in conjunction with looseleaf services. Some of these also include state court and administrative agency decisions. Examples of these independent reporters include *American Maritime Cases, Public Utilities Reported Annotated,* and *U.S. Aviation Cases.*

5. LEXIS AND WESTLAW

Another source of federal decisions are two computerized legal research services which are becoming increasingly popular. LEXIS and WESTLAW will be treated in more detail in Chapter 22, but we must mention here that they provide full text coverage of all federal court cases that appear in print in the various West reporters. These decisions are often available via the computer terminals before they appear in advance sheets. Furthermore, the LEXIS legal research service enters into its data-base many slip opinions from the U.S. Courts of Appeals and District Courts that are never published in a West reporter. Although most court rules limiting the number of published decisions provide that "unreported" decisions are not to be cited as precedent, some courts have permitted citations to such decisions when a copy is served on all parties and the court.

The availability of computerized data bases is already creating a disadvantage for the practitioner who does not have access to computerized research tools, and who must compete with government agencies and law firms that have such terminals at their disposal. This inequity is not being alleviated by the limited number of public or shared terminals available. This situation is not essentially different than the problem of inequality in access to research facilities between large firms and single practitioners, between urban and rural practitioners, and in fact between representation for the rich and poor generally in our society, but the computer is certainly increasing these inequities. It is thus creating a problem in legal research for the future which must be faced by the courts, the legal profession, and society as a whole.

Finally, to illustrate some of the forms of publication of lower federal court decisions, the next series of Illustrations show a single case, *Brody v. President & Fellows of Harvard College*, as it appears in the following different forms:

Illustration D—The official slip opinion.

Illustration E—West's *Federal Reporter 2d.*

Illustration F—CCH College & University Reporter (looseleaf; now discontinued).

Illustration G—The LEXIS printout.

Illustration H—The WESTLAW printout.

D. STATE REPORTS

The decisions of the courts of the fifty states have traditionally been published in both official and unofficial reporters. While an increasing number of states have discontinued their official reports,[7] the number and variety of unofficial reports have been growing. For the approximately twenty-four states which still publish their own reporters, that publication is the authoritative text of decisions and must be cited in briefs, arguments and memoranda to the courts. Beyond that, most professional research is actually conducted in one or another of the unofficial reporters covering decisions of that state—usually one of the reporters in West's comprehensive National Reporter System, referred to earlier. The other major reporting scheme is the selective, but annotated series, *American Law Reports* (generally called *ALR* and now in its 4th series). *ALR* will be discussed fully in Chapter 4. There are now several other unofficial sources for state decisions, including the two computer research systems (LEXIS and WESTLAW), the looseleaf services in some subject fields, and a number of specialized topic reporters, issued by a number of different publishers.

7. See Appendix B at the end of this book for a complete listing of the available reports, including designation of those with official status, for all of the states.

United States Court of Appeals
For the First Circuit

Nos. 80-1595
80-1685

LEON H. BRODY,
PLAINTIFF, APPELLANT,

v.

PRESIDENT & FELLOWS OF HARVARD COLLEGE,
DEFENDANT, APPELLEE.

APPEALS FROM THE UNITED STATES DISTRICT COURT
FOR THE DISTRICT OF MASSACHUSETTS
[HON. A. DAVID MAZZONE, *U.S. District Judge*]

Before
COFFIN, *Chief Judge*,
CAMPBELL and BOWNES, *Circuit Judges*.

Leon H. Brody, on brief pro se.
Richard P. Ward, *Eleanor D. Acheson*, and *Ropes & Gray* on memorandum in support of motion from summary disposition for appellee.

November 16, 1981

Per Curiam. Appellant Leon Brody was denied employment as a librarian in defendant's library system. Claiming that age discrimination was the basis for his rejection, he retained an attorney and ultimately sued in the district court under the Age Discrimination in Employment Act. After a trial without a jury, the court entered judgment for defendant. Plaintiff brings this appeal *pro se*.

Appellant's first and principal point is that the district judge, who graduated from defendant Harvard College, was disqualified by 28 U.S.C. § 455(a), which provides that a judge recuse himself if "his impartiality might reasonably be questioned." Appellant acknowledges that the judge disclosed his

Illustration D

The official slip opinion.

[6] We comment on only one other matter in this area, defendant's attempt to say that the prosecutor stated there was additional unfavorable evidence beyond what he had introduced, citing *Ginsberg v. United States*, 5 Cir., 1958, 257 F.2d 950, 954–55. This is an improper construction. When defendant, during trial, came up with an unexpected defense, the court gave the government a day and a half recess to meet it, during which interval the government unearthed considerable rebuttal. In the course of discussing this rebuttal the prosecutor stated, "[W]e had a day and a half, ladies and gentlemen, from the time this whole story came up. And I submit to you if we had more time, we would have been able to come up with more evidence." This was patently argument and not a statement of fact, and, we add, not unfair. The government had discovered enough holes in the story ("a giant Swiss cheese") to warrant the inference that there might well be more discovered if time permitted. In no way was it an impermissible statement of fact.

Defendant is grasping at straws. We find nothing in the prosecutor's extensive—and cogent—summation to criticize.

Affirmed.

Leon H. BRODY, Plaintiff, Appellant,

v.

PRESIDENT & FELLOWS OF HARVARD COLLEGE, Defendant, Appellee.

Nos. 80–1595, 80–1685.

United States Court of Appeals, First Circuit.

Submitted Nov. 2, 1981.

Decided Nov. 16, 1981.

Applicant for employment at university library brought age discrimination suit against university. The United States District Court for the District of Massachusetts, A. David Mazzone, J., rendered judgment for the university and applicant appealed. The Court of Appeals held that the judge's having attended or graduated from the defendant university, without more, was not a reasonable basis for questioning his impartiality and did not require his recusal.

Affirmed.

1. Judges ⚷49(1)

Judge's having attended or graduated from university which was party to case, without more, was not reasonable basis for questioning his impartiality and was not ground for recusal. 28 U.S.C.A. § 455(e).

2. Judges ⚷49(1)

Reasonable suspicion of judicial bias will usually arise only in the presence of factors such as financial or strong personal interest in one of the litigants. 28 U.S.C.A. § 455(e).

3. Judges ⚷49(1)

All judges come to bench with background of experiences, associations and viewpoints and this background alone is seldom sufficient in itself to provide reasonable basis for recusal. 28 U.S.C.A. § 455(e).

4. Attorney and Client ⚷91

Litigant was bound by his attorney's waiver of motion to disqualify judge. 28 U.S.C.A. § 455(e).

5. Attorney and Client ⚷88

Civil litigants are ordinarily bound by their attorneys' tactical decisions.

6. Federal Courts ⚷893

In action against university, fact that judge's disclosure of fact that he was graduate of defendant university was made at unrecorded conference was not prejudicial, since judge's disclosure did not, without more, require his recusal. 28 U.S.C.A. § 455(e).

Illustration E

West's *Federal Reporter 2d.*

¶ 21,061 BANKER'S MBA EXPENSES WERE NOT DEDUCTIBLE

Back reference: ¶ 6512.

James E. and Jean Carey v. Commissioner, U. S. Tax Court, Dkt. No. 1002-78, CCH Dec. 38,493(M), T. C. Memo. 1981-708, December 17, 1981.

A taxpayer who took a two-year, nine-month leave of absence from his position in a bank's credit training program in order to obtain a Master of Business Administration degree could not deduct the educational expenses incurred in attaining that degree, the U. S. Tax Court has ruled. The Court said that the taxpayer was not engaged in a trade or business at the time the expenses were incurred, and, following graduation, he obtained employment at another bank as an associate investment banker, a position that required an individual with at least an MBA degree.

On redetermination of the disallowed deduction for the post-graduate educational expenses incurred during the leave of absence, the Court held that the act of the taxpayer's first employer in placing him on a leave of absence did not prove that he remained in the trade or business of being a lending analyst trainee for the period he spent in obtaining his MBA degree. In addition, the Court said that it was far from clear whether the taxpayer intended to remain in the same trade since he enrolled in a program in which he sought a joint degree in architecture and business. Furthermore, the Court noted that the taxpayer obtained new employment, with a different employer, which required an MBA degree as a minimum condition of employment. Therefore, the Commissioner of Internal Revenue's disallowance of the claimed deductions was upheld.

¶ 21,062 JUDGE MAY HEAR JOB BIAS CASE INVOLVING HIS ALMA MATER

Back reference: ¶ 7795.

Leon H. Brody v. President and Fellows of Harvard College, U. S. Court of Appeals, First Circuit, 27 EPD ¶ 32,215, Dkt. Nos. 80-1595, 80-1685, November 16, 1981; affirming U. S. District Court, District of Massachusetts.

The dismissal of an age discrimination suit against a university was not subject to reversal merely because the federal trial court judge who heard the case had been a student at the university, the federal court of appeals in Boston has ruled. The court said that matriculation from a school of higher education does not prejudice an individual's judgment regarding one of its personnel decisions.

This action was initiated by an individual who was denied employment as a librarian in a university library system. He claimed that age bias was the basis for this rejection and sued the school under federal age bias in employment law. After a trial without a jury, the court entered judgment for the university. On appeal, the complainant argued that this decision should be reversed since the district court judge, who graduated from the university being sued, should have been disqualified from the case.

The court held that merely contending that a judge's having attended or graduated from a school that is a party in a suit affected his impartiality was not reasonable. The mere association of a judge with a party to a suit, without any indication that the judge stood to benefit from a particular outcome, was insufficient to mandate disqualification. Also, where the interest asserted bears only a tangential relationship to the subject matter of the suit, the alleged bias is even further attenuated, the court said. Finally, the court noted that the judge disclosed his alumnus status at a pre-trial conference and that the complainant's attorney explicitly assented to the judge's continuing with the case. Civil litigants are ordinarily bound by their attorney's tactical decisions, the court pointed out.

Illustration F

CCH College & University Reporter (looseleaf). Published and copyrighted by Commerce Clearing House, Inc., Chicago, Il. 60646, and reproduced with their permission. This publication has recently been discontinued.

Fed.2d Citation

Topical Reporter Citations

LEVEL 1 - 1 OF 1 CASE

LEON H. BRODY, PLAINTIFF, APPELLANT, v. PRESIDENT & FELLOWS OF HARVARD COLLEGE, DEFENDANT, APPELLEE.

Nos. 80-1595, 80-1685

United States Court of Appeals For the First Circuit

664 F.2d 10; 27 EPD P32,215; 27 FEP Cases 500

November 16, 1981

APPEAL-STATEMENT:
APPEALS FROM THE UNITED STATES DISTRICT COURT FOR THE DISTRICT OF MASSACHUSETTS [HON. A. DAVID MAZZONE, U.S. District Judge]

COUNSEL:
Leon H. Brody , on brief pro se.

Richard P. Ward, Eleanor D. Acheson , and Ropes & Gray on memorandum in support of motion from summary disposition for appellee.

664 F.2d 10; 27 EPD P32,215; 27 FEP Cases 500

Text of Decision

OPINION:
Before COFFIN, Chief Judge ,

CAMPBELL and BOWNES, Circuit Judges .

Per Curiam . Appellant Leon Brody was denied employment as a librarian in defendant's library system. Claiming that age discrimination was the basis for his rejection, he retained an attorney and ultimately sued in the district court under the Age Discrimination in Employment Act. After a trial without a jury, the court entered judgment for defendant. Plaintiff brings this appeal pro se .

Appellant's first and principal point is that the district judge, who graduated from defendant Harvard College, was disqualified by 28 U.S.C. § 455(a), which provides that a judge recuse himself if "his impartiality might reasonably be questioned." Appellant acknowledges that the judge disclosed his alumnus status at a pre-trial conference and that his attorney explicitly assented to the judge's continuing with the case. He maintains that his attorney's agreement did not amount to a waiver under section 455(e) since appellant was not present. He also argues that the judge's disclosure was insufficient since it was not "on the record," id ., as the conference was not recorded. Appellant also maintains that the disclosure was not "full" in that the judge did not disclaim such matters as any possible prior contact with

Illustration G

The LEXIS printout.

```
                         COPR. (C) WEST 1983 NO CLAIM TO ORIG. U.S. GOVT. WORKS
Citation                    Rank(R)            Page(P)          Database   Mode
664 F.2d 10                 R 1 OF 1           P 1 OF 12        FED        T
                   Leon H. BRODY, Plaintiff, Appellant.
                                 v.
      PRESIDENT & FELLOWS OF HARVARD COLLEGE. Defendant, Appellee.
                        Nos. 80-1595, 80-1685.
                      United States Court of Appeals,
                            First Circuit.
                        Submitted Nov. 2, 1981.
                        Decided Nov. 16, 1981.
 Applicant for employment at university library brought age discrimination suit
against university.  The United States District Court for the District of
Massachusetts, A. David Mazzone, J., rendered judgment for the university and
applicant appealed.  The Court of Appeals held that the judge's having attended
or graduated from the defendant university, without more, was not a reasonable
basis for questioning his impartiality and did not require his recusal.
 Affirmed.
```

Fed.2d citation

Summary of decision

```
                         COPR. (C) WEST 1983 NO CLAIM TO ORIG. U.S. GOVT. WORKS
664 F.2d 10                 R 1 OF 1           P 8 OF 12        FED        P
 Leon H. Brody, pro se.
 Richard P. Ward, Eleanor D. Acheson, and Ropes & Gray, Boston, Mass., on
memorandum in support of motion from summary disposition for defendant,
appellee.

 Before COFFIN, Chief Judge, CAMPBELL and BOWNES, Circuit Judges.

 PER CURIAM.
 Appellant Leon Brody was denied employment as a librarian in defendant's
library system.  Claiming that age discrimination was the basis for his
rejection, he retained an attorney and ultimately sued in the district court
under the Age Discrimination in Employment Act.  After a trial without a jury,
the court entered judgment for defendant.  Plaintiff brings this appeal pro se.
 Appellant's first and principal point is that the district judge, who
graduated from defendant Harvard College, was disqualified by 28 U.S.C. s
455(a), which provides that a judge recuse himself if "his impartiality might
reasonably be questioned."  Appellant acknowledges that the judge disclosed his
alumnus status at a pre-trial conference and that his attorney explicitly
assented to the judge's continuing with the case.  He maintains that his
attorney's agreement did not amount to a waiver under section 455(e) since
appellant was not present.  He also argues that the judge's disclosure was
insufficient since it was not "on the record," id., as the conference was not
```

Text of decision

```
                         COPR. (C) WEST 1983 NO CLAIM TO ORIG. U.S. GOVT. WORKS
664 F.2d 10                 R 1 OF 1           P 2 OF 12        FED        P
 (1)
 227k49(1)
 JUDGES
 k. In general.
 C.A.Mass. 1981.
 Judge's having attended or graduated from university which was party to case,
 without more, was not reasonable basis for questioning his impartiality and was
 not ground for recusal.  28 U.S.C.A. s 455(e).
 Brody v. President & Fellows of Harvard College
 664 F.2d 10
```

West topic & key number

West Headnote

Illustration H

The WESTLAW printout.

This section will describe these various reporters *briefly,* since most of their general characteristics have been set out previously in Sections B and C, above, on the U.S. Supreme Court and the lower federal courts.

1. OFFICIAL REPORTS

The most striking features of the official reports today are almost all negative—the trend of their discontinuance; the long delays in their publication; the relative lack of auxiliary research aids in most of them (as compared to their commercial counterparts); and the failure of many to provide preliminary access to their decisions by advance sheets. Their positive aspects should in fairness be stated: many are still well prepared and a few offer useful research features like headnotes; summaries; tables; internal, non-cumulative indexing and digesting; and changes in court rules. They are the authoritative sources for their decisions and, as such, must be cited. It is sad to note, however, that the long and often distinguished history of official reporting, which succeeded the early nominative reporters, is now waning.

The ultimate indignity, the physical deterioration of the books themselves because of the high acid content of book paper since the industrial revolution, has been partially offset, however, by their preservation on microfilm. The Trans-Media Publishing Company offers a microfilm edition of the official state reports which pre-date the National Reporter System, and many of the later reports are becoming available as well in microform.

Most of the states which have discontinued their official reports, have since designated a West reporter as the official report for that state. These are either the West regional reporter which includes the decisions of that state's courts, or a separately published reporter for that state. These single state West reporters are of two kinds—some like those for Alabama, Arizona, Idaho and New Mexico, are true reporters, succeeding the official reporters. The others are West offprint reporters, simply reproducing consecutive pages from the West regional reporter in separate volumes, and thereby creating a new state reporter with its own volume numbering sequence, but with pages derived from the regional reporter.

Most of the surviving official state reports include *only* the decisions of the highest court in the state, usually (but not always) called the Supreme Court. A few of the more populous (and hence more litigious) states publish more than one official report, the second set usually reporting decisions from the intermediate appellate court. These include California, Illinois, Massachusetts, New York, Ohio, Pennsylvania, and a few less heavily populated states. New York is one of the few states to issue three official reporters (*New York Reports* for its highest court, the Court of Appeals; *Appellate Division Reports* for the Appellate Division of its Supreme Court; and *Miscellaneous Reports,* containing a selection of lower court decisions).

Slip opinions in individual cases are issued by at least the highest court in most states, but these are usually not widely distributed. As noted above, advance sheets for the official reports are available in only some of the states.

2. WEST REGIONAL REPORTER SYSTEM

The origin of West's National Reporter System has already been described in Chapter 2. It publishes more decisions—now approximately 55,000 each year—than any other reporting system in the world. The decisions appear rapidly in their advance sheets, which are published for each of the seven regional reporters comprising the system, and for each of fourteen major state reporters therein—*West's California Reporter, West's Illinois Decisions, West's Texas Cases, West's Louisiana Cases, West's Florida Cases, West's North Carolina Reporter, West's Missouri Cases, West's Colorado Cases, West's Indiana Cases, West's Ohio Cases, West's Massachusetts Decisions, West's Georgia Cases, West's Wisconsin Reporter* and *New York Supplement.* They are linked, along with the West federal and specialized reporters, described above, by the key number indexing and digesting system. The finding aids in each advance sheet and bound volume are those described above in Sections B and C. They simplify the use of these reporters and facilitate legal research in other ways. An ultra-fiche edition of the first series of the regional reporters and Federal Reporter is now available, reducing each volume to a single 4″ × 6″ sheet of microfilm, with a very high reduction ratio.

The seven regions represented by the West regional reporters are shown in Illustration I.

The regional reporters are Atlantic, Pacific, North Eastern, South Eastern, North Western, South Western and Southern. Each covers the appellate courts of the States in their respective region as shown on the map in Illustration I and each is now in a second series. Appendix C at the end of this volume shows the state reports contained in each regional reporter and their dates of inception. These reporters are augmented by separate reporters for three large and legally active states: *West's California Reporter, West's Illinois Decisions,* and *New York Supplement.* These include selected decisions from the lower courts in those States.

The ten reporters for the state level, together with West's various federal court reporters and new specialized topical reporters comprise a unified system in which the West topics and key numbers provide a mechanism for comprehensive indexing and digesting. This case finding aspect of the West reporters will be described in Chapter 5 below.

Parallel citations from the official state report to the unofficial regional reporter are provided in several ways, and from the unoffi-

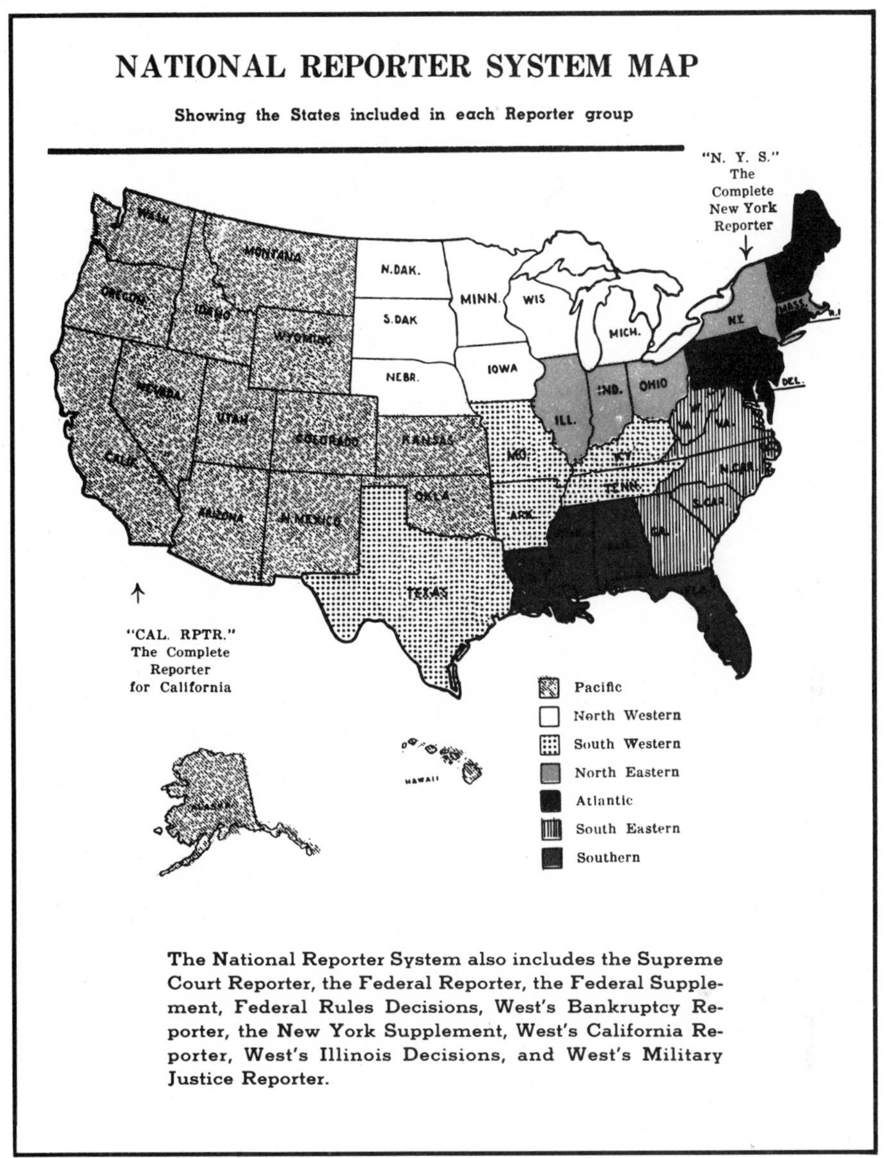
NATIONAL REPORTER SYSTEM MAP
Showing the States included in each Reporter group
"N. Y. S." The Complete New York Reporter
N.DAK.
S.DAK
NEBR.
MINN.
WIS
IOWA
MICH.
ILL.
OHIO
TEXAS
"CAL. RPTR." The Complete Reporter for California
Pacific
North Western
South Western
North Eastern
Atlantic
South Eastern
Southern
The National Reporter System also includes the Supreme Court Reporter, the Federal Reporter, the Federal Supplement, Federal Rules Decisions, West's Bankruptcy Reporter, the New York Supplement, West's California Reporter, West's Illinois Decisions, and West's Military Justice Reporter.

Illustration I

Map showing states included in each regional reporter.

cial reporter to the official report in slightly different ways. A researcher will frequently have a citation to one form of publication and will need the other, either to complete a citation to the case or to examine the alternative form. The following methods can be used for each procedure:

(1) From the official state report to the unofficial reporter:

(a) National Reporter Blue Book, issued by West for this purpose, as shown below:

52 NEW YORK REPORTS, SECOND SERIES

N.Y.2d	N.Y.S.2d		N.E.2d	
Page	Vol.	Page	Vol.	Page
1	436	196	417	490
9	436	199	417	493
24	436	207	417	501
37	436	213	417	507
58	436	224	417	518
72	436	231	417	525
82	436	236	417	530
88	436	239	417	533
105	436	247	417	541
114	436	251	417	545
139	436	850	418	365
148	436	853	418	368
157	436	858	418	373
170	436	862	418	377
179	437	57	418	650
193	437	63	418	656
200	437	66	418	659
208	437	270	418	1289
214	437	272	418	1291
228	437	279	418	1298
236	437	283	418	1302
242	437	286	418	1305
253	437	291	418	1310
268	437	643	419	321
276	437	646	419	324
291	437	654	419	332
302	437	961	419	864
309	438	242	420	40
322	438	247	420	45
333	438	253	420	51
341	438	257	420	55
350	438	261	420	59
363	438	266	420	64

N.Y.2d	N.Y.S.2d		N.E.2d	
Page	Vol.	Page	Vol.	Page
754	436	272	417	565
756	436	277	417	571
758	436	277	417	571
759	436	612	417	1000
760	436	621	417	1009
763	436	612	417	1000
766	436	614	417	1002
768	436	614	417	1002
771	436	616	417	1004
773	436	621	417	1009
775	436	617	417	1005
777	436	621	417	1009
777	439	918	422	578
778	439	918	422	578
779	436	618	417	1006
779	439	918	422	578
781	436	620	417	1008
783	436	621	417	1009
784	436	622	417	1010
785	436	622	417	1010
785	436	623	417	1011
786	436	624	417	1012
787	436	624	417	1012
787	439	918	422	578
788	436	702	417	1243
790	436	703	417	1244
793	436	707	417	1248
794	436	707	417	1248
796	436	707	417	1248
798	436	704	417	1245
801	436	878	418	393
802	436	867	418	382
809	436	871	418	386

N.Y.2d	N.Y.S.2d		N.E.2d	
Page	Vol.	Page	Vol.	Page
918	437	663	419	341
920	437	663	419	341
921	437	664	419	342
923	437	668	419	346
925	437	668	419	346
927	437	669	419	347
929	437	665	419	343
931	437	669	419	347
932	437	666	419	344
935	437	669	419	347
936	437	669	419	347
937	437	670	419	348
938	437	967	419	870
939	437	967	419	870
941	437	967	419	870
943	437	967	419	870
945	437	968	419	871
947	437	964	419	867
947	437	965	419	868
948	437	968	419	871
950	437	968	419	871
954	437	968	419	871
956	437	966	419	869
957	437	969	419	872
959	437	969	419	872
962	437	969	419	872
963	437	969	419	872
968	437	971	419	874
968	437	972	419	875
969	437	972	419	875
970	438	282	420	80
972	438	79	419	1078
974	438	283	420	81

(b) *Shepard's state citators*—the first citation in the listing of each case refers to the citation of that case in the unofficial regional reporter. That citation is usually given in parentheses.

(2) From the unofficial reporter to the official state report:

(a) State Blue and White books, currently issued by West for 26 states, provide parallel citations from the official state reports to the West regional reporters. White pages in those volumes also carry citation tables from the unofficial reporter to the official state reports. Their arrangement is similar to that in National Reporter Blue Book, shown above, but with the references reversed. See Illustration on page 66 below.

(b) *Shepard's regional reporter citators*—the first citation listed, usually in parentheses, is to the same case in the official state report, reversing the process shown above under 1(b).

(c) The official citation is also given at the beginning of the decision reported in the regional reporter, if it is available at the time the regional reporter goes to press. This is becoming less frequent because of the long delays in the publication of the official reporter.

When either the actual name of the case or its popular name is known, the tables of cases in the various West digests, or the Shepard's Table, Acts and cases by Popular can be used to get all citations to case—official, regional reporter, and annotated report. This process is more fully described in Sections B–3–a and D–2 of Chapter 5 below.

Vol. 438 NEW YORK SUPPLEMENT, 2d SERIES (Court of Appeals Cases)

- 261 -
(52NY350)
(420NE59)
s423S2d975
j438S2d745
d442S2d[1]142
442S2d[2]143
j442S2d144
e443S2d[2]935
444S2d[2]930
448S2d[2]546
523FS1208

- 266 -
(52NY363)
(420NE64)
s423S2d580
s426S2d517
s433S2d388
s434S2d46
439S2d[1]378
f443S2d[3]1018
443S2d [10]1019
j448S2d169
e450S2d[2]626

- 282 -
(52NY970)
(420NE80)
s425S2d438
439S2d[2]700
441S2d438
441S2d[2]666

- 283 -
(52NY974)
(420NE81)
s422S2d116

- 284 -
(52NY976)
(420NE82)
s419S2d614

- 287 -
Case 1
(52NY982)
(420NE85)
s420S2d347
s424S2d933
cc449S2d112
439S2d290
447S2d[1]389
j449S2d453

- 287 -
Case 2
(52NY990)
(420NE85)
s417S2d95

- 288 -
(52NY991)
(420NE86)
US cert den
s350S2d974
s374S2d569
s423S2d453
s439S2d1030
442S2d440
e447S2d[1]1020

- 289 -
(52NY995)
(420NE87)

s428S2d272
450S2d242

- 290 -
(52NY1000)
(420NE88)
s421S2d605

- 291 -
(52NY1002)
(420NE89)
s421S2d387
443S2d[3]426
452S2d[2]680

- 292 -
(52NY1004)
(420NE90)
s415S2d687

- 293 -
(52NY1006)
(420NE91)
s407S2d106
s426S2d1008
441S2d[1]332
e445S2d[1]644
450S2d975

- 294 -
Case 1
(52NY1008)
(420NE92)
s428S2d762

- 294 -
Case 2
(52NY1010)
(420NE92)
s416S2d591

- 295 -
(52NY1013)
(420NE93)
s429S2d299

- 296 -
(52NY1019)
(420NE94)
s422S2d272
s440S2d1028

- 297 -
(52NY1020)
(420NE95)
US cert den
s427S2d125
s440S2d583
442S2d[2]285
444S2d380

- 298 -
(52NY1023)
(420NE96)
s420S2d807
s421S2d553
s423S2d458
438S2d[1]298
442S2d[1]285

- 299 -
Case 1
(52NY1025)
(420NE97)
s417S2d864

- 299 -
Case 2
(52NY1027)
(420NE97)
s424S2d484
441S2d[1]414
442S2d[1]571
444S2d[1]898
j445S2d805
447S2d[1]235
533FS[1]262

- 301 -
Case 1
(52NY1015)
(420NE99)
s440S2d1028

- 301 -
Case 2
(52NY1015)
(420NE99)
s422S2d271

- 301 -
Case 3
(52NY1015)
(420NE99)
s433S2d453

- 301 -
Case 4
(52NY1016)
(420NE99)

- 301 -
Case 5
(52NY1016)
(420NE99)
s409S2d660
s431S2d33

- 302 -
Case 1
(52NY1016)
(420NE100)
s433S2d789
s439S2d1030
j449S2d102

- 302 -
Case 2
(52NY1017)
(420NE100)

- 302 -
Case 3
(52NY1017)
(420NE100)
s419S2d182

- 302 -
Case 4
(52NY1022)
(420NE100)
s431S2d55

- 302 -
Case 5
(52NY1026)
(420NE101)
s427S2d522
440S2d773

- 303 -
Case 1
(52NY1030)
(420NE101)
s431S2d678

- 303 -
Case 2
(52NY1030)
(420NE101)
s433S2d116

- 303 -
Case 3
(52NY1030)
(420NE101)
s433S2d502

- 303 -
Case 4
(52NY1030)
(420NE102)
s428S2d283

- 304 -
Case 1
(52NY1031)
(420NE102)

- 304 -
Case 2
(52NY1031)
(420NE102)

- 304 -
Case 3
(52NY1031)
(420NE102)
s434S2d932

- 482 -
(52NY394)
(420NE363)
s430S2d275
448S2d[4]810
448S2d[5]810
453S2d[5]473
682F2d[3]387
682F2d[4]387
j682F2d394
522FS1279
d530FS[6]1338
17BRW[6]798

- 490 -
(52NY410)
(420NE371)
s429S2d519
s431S2d826
441S2d231
452S2d10

- 496 -
(52NY422)
(420NE377)
s422S2d552
s425S2d101
cc397S2d943
439S2d353
453S2d490

- 504 -
Case 1
(52NY1032)
(420NE385)
s419S2d689

- 504 -
Case 2
(52NY1036)
(420NE385)
s423S2d51

- 505 -
(52NY1038)
(420NE386)
s405S2d199
s438S2d397

- 509 -
(52NY1046)
(420NE390)
s419S2d4

- 514 -
(52NY1055)
(420NE395)
s427S2d994
450S2d[1]923

- 515 -
(52NY1059)
(420NE396)
s420S2d433

- 516 -
Case 1
(52NY1062)
(420NE397)
s425S2d903

- 516 -
Case 2
(52NY1064)
(420NE397)
s425S2d874
s439S2d1030

- 519 -
Case 1
(52NY1034)
(420NE400)
s429S2d741
s433S2d20
s440S2d1028
s441S2d59
447S2d54
452S2d831

- 519 -
Case 2
(52NY1045)
(420NE400)
449S2d992

- 519 -
Case 3
(52NY1053)
(420NE400)
s414S2d791

- 519 -
Case 4
(52NY1057)
(420NE400)
s429S2d659
s440S2d226
j452S2d895

- 520 -
Case 1
(52NY1061)
(420NE401)
s428S2d293

- 520 -
Case 2
(52NY1067)
(420NE401)
s409S2d445

- 520 -
Case 3
(52NY1069)
(420NE401)
US cert den
s433S2d166

- 737 -
(52NY440)
(420NE929)
s419S2d851
s425S2d904
cc444S2d381

- 741 -
(52NY454)
(420NE933)
s404S2d935
s408S2d1037
s411S2d303
s424S2d402
442S2d[3]143
d451S2d897
452S2d[2]764
670F2d[3]979

- 746 -
(52NY463)
(420NE938)
s429S2d336
s429S2d339
s430S2d909
cc422S2d549
438S2d325
j439S2d779
440S2d540
440S2d[2]598
443S2d[2]576
444S2d[3]350
e444S2d[3]559
449S2d[3]506
450S2d839
451S2d770

- 753 -
(52NY479)
(420NE945)
s437S2d920
s449S2d239
449S2d[1]106
451S2d[1]454

- 754 -
(52NY483)
(420NE946)
s429S2d872
442S2d[8]585
451S2d146

- 761 -
(52NY496)
(420NE953)
s423S2d324
cc228S2d120
cc344S2d270
cc358S2d367
cc382S2d407
cc417S2d537
e442S2d[8]109
442S2d[2]490
443S2d460
443S2d[2]463
443S2d[14]897
444S2d[3]915
444S2d[6]915
445S2d[3]115
448S2d207
448S2d[14]671
452S2d[2]14
681F2d158

- 774 -
(53NY618)
(420NE966)
s422S2d1014
j447S2d480

- 775 -
(53NY619)
(420NE967)
s421S2d78
j441S2d67

- 776 -
(53NY621)
(420NE968)
s425S2d516
450S2d[1]114

- 777 -
(53NY623)
(420NE969)
s412S2d641
s429S2d910
443S2d[1]894

- 778 -
(53NY625)
(420NE970)
s422S2d179
446S2d[1]840

- 779 -
(53NY627)
(420NE971)
s418S2d27
j445S2d7

- 780 -
Case 1
(53NY629)
(420NE972)
s423S2d200
439S2d[1]171

- 780 -
Case 2
(53NY631)
(420NE972)
s424S2d296
s429S2d247
d447S2d[2]431
j447S2d432

- 782 -
Case 1
(53NY633)
(420NE974)
s428S2d758

- 782 -
Case 2
(53NY635)
(420NE974)
s422S2d98

- 783 -
(53NY639)
(420NE975)
s427S2d639

- 786 -
Case 1
(53NY613)
(420NE978)
s426S2d102
446S2d870

- 786 -
Case 2
(53NY615)
(420NE978)
s412S2d395
s430S2d636

- 786 -
Case 3
(53NY616)
(420NE978)
s423S2d85
e440S2d136
440S2d789

- 786 -
Case 4
(53NY637)
(420NE978)
s429S2d87
442S2d384

- 787 -
Case 1
(53NY641)
(420NE979)

- 787 -
Case 2
(53NY641)
(420NE979)
s437S2d952

- 787 -
Case 3
(53NY642)
(420NE979)
s444S2d961
s452S2d333

- 787 -
Case 4
(53NY642)
(420NE979)
s430S2d339

- 787 -
Case 5
(53NY642)
(420NE980)
s429S2d340
s437S2d304

- 989 -
(52NY523)
(421NE109)
s429S2d874
439S2d[3]962

STATE REPORT REFERENCES FOR NEW YORK SUPPLEMENT CASES 229

438 N.Y. SUPPLEMENT 2d

Supp. Page	Other Report	Supp. Page	Other Report	Supp. Page	Other Report	Supp. Page	Other Report
1	81 A.D.2d 521	152	81 A.D.2d 753	342	80 A.D.2d 326	544	80 A.D.2d 186
3	80 A.D.2d 109	153	81 A.D.2d 753	343	81 A.D.2d 673	577	81 A.D.2d 674
6	81 A.D.2d 620	154	101 Misc.2d 375	344 [1]	81 A.D.2d 673	579	80 A.D.2d 184
8	81 A.D.2d 615	156	108 Misc.2d 994	344 [2]	81 A.D.2d 673	580	80 A.D.2d 170
9	81 A.D.2d 614	160	108 Misc.2d 606	345	81 A.D.2d 673	587	80 A.D.2d 261
11	81 A.D.2d 607	162	107 Misc.2d 124	346	81 A.D.2d 672	593	81 A.D.2d 820
13	81 A.D.2d 956	164	107 Misc.2d 135	347	81 A.D.2d 672	594	81 A.D.2d 821
16	80 A.D.2d 958	170	107 Misc.2d 239	348	81 A.D.2d 671	596	81 A.D.2d 823
18	80 A.D.2d 954	171	108 Misc.2d 626	349	81 A.D.2d 670	597	81 A.D.2d 824
21	80 A.D.2d 951	172	107 Misc.2d 241	351	81 A.D.2d 668	599	81 A.D.2d 824
22	80 A.D.2d 949	174	108 Misc.2d 986	353 [1]	81 A.D.2d 668	600	81 A.D.2d 825
25	80 A.D.2d 946	180	110 Misc.2d 193	353 [2]	81 A.D.2d 667	601	81 A.D.2d 825
26	80 A.D.2d 945	182	107 Misc.2d 244	354	81 A.D.2d 666	602	81 A.D.2d 826
28	80 A.D.2d 945	184	107 Misc.2d 248	356	81 A.D.2d 665	603	80 A.D.2d 980
29	80 A.D.2d 942	187	108 Misc.2d 603	357	81 A.D.2d 665	605	80 A.D.2d 979
32	80 A.D.2d 943	189	108 Misc.2d 485	359	81 A.D.2d 663	606	80 A.D.2d 977
34	80 A.D.2d 947	193	108 Misc.2d 587	361	81 A.D.2d 663	609	80 A.D.2d 975
37	80 A.D.2d 952	195	— Misc.2d —	362	81 A.D.2d 662	611	80 A.D.2d 974
38	80 A.D.2d 953	196	108 Misc.2d 583	363	81 A.D.2d 661	612	80 A.D.2d 973
40	80 A.D.2d 952	199	109 Misc.2d 341	365	81 A.D.2d 661	614	80 A.D.2d 973
41	81 A.D.2d 679	207	108 Misc.2d 622	366	81 A.D.2d 661	615 [1]	80 A.D.2d 972
43	79 A.D.2d 186	209	109 Misc.2d 354	367	81 A.D.2d 660	615 [2]	80 A.D.2d 972
47	108 Misc.2d 581	215	109 Misc.2d 80	368	81 A.D.2d 658	617	80 A.D.2d 971
48	108 Misc.2d 555	220	108 Misc.2d 610	370	81 A.D.2d 658	618	80 A.D.2d 970
50	107 Misc.2d 71	224–241	Mem. Dec.	371	81 A.D.2d 657	619	80 A.D.2d 970
52	107 Misc.2d 114	242	52 N.Y.2d 309	372	81 A.D.2d 656	621	80 A.D.2d 969
54	107 Misc.2d 88	247	52 N.Y.2d 322	374	81 A.D.2d 655	622	80 A.D.2d 968
57	107 Misc.2d 938	253	52 N.Y.2d 333	377	81 A.D.2d 653	624	80 A.D.2d 966
59	108 Misc.2d 562	257	52 N.Y.2d 341	379	81 A.D.2d 651	626	80 A.D.2d 965
62	108 Misc.2d 558	261	52 N.Y.2d 350	381	81 A.D.2d 650	627	80 A.D.2d 966
65	108 Misc.2d 980	266	52 N.Y.2d 363	383	81 A.D.2d 650	628	80 A.D.2d 976
68	108 Misc.2d 565	282	52 N.Y.2d 970	384	81 A.D.2d 648	629	81 A.D.2d 695
71	108 Misc.2d 579	283	52 N.Y.2d 974	386	79 A.D.2d 415	631	81 A.D.2d 694
72	108 Misc.2d 598	284	52 N.Y.2d 976	389	80 A.D.2d 68	633	81 A.D.2d 692

State Blue and White Book for New York.

3. LEXIS AND WESTLAW

State court decisions are a major component of the data bases in the two computer research services, LEXIS and WESTLAW. The periods of coverage vary between the two systems, from state to state. The extent of coverage in both systems, however, has been increasing retrospectively and they are growing in importance as retrieval sources for state court decisions. The use of these computer services is discussed in more detail in Section F of Chapter 5 and in Chapter 16.

4. LOOSELEAF SERVICES AND TOPICAL REPORTERS

Some of the looseleaf services and topical reporters of court decisions described in Section 3 and 4 above also contain state court decisions. The use and availability of looseleaf services and their related topical case reporters are treated in more detail in Chapter 12, Looseleaf Services.

5. VERDICT REPORTERS AND LEGAL NEWSPAPERS

A relatively new phenomenon, the verdict reporter, provides information on trial results and damages awarded, primarily in tort cases. This type of service, of which the *Personal Injury Valuation Handbooks* (8 vol., looseleaf) of Jury Verdict Research Inc., is perhaps the best example, do not contain actual opinions of the courts in-

NORTHEASTERN REPORTER, 2d SERIES **Vol. 420**

– 890 –
(66OA31)
(20Op3d76)

– 895 –
(66M7)
(20Op3d86)

– 897 –
(84Il2d469)
(50IlD629)

– 899 –
(84Il2d446)
(50IlD631)
s398NE1064
421NE1033

– 906 –
(84Il2d400)
(50IlD638)
s403NE708
s413NE1389
419NE[1]278
420NE[1]186
421NE[1]1026
f422NE[1]255
423NE[1]1359
d424NE[1]45
f424NE[1]100
424NE[1]833
e424NE[1]937
f424NE[1]991

– 909 –
(84Il2d406)
(50IlD641)
s402NE819
f424NE78
f424NE[1]78

– 913 –
(84Il2d390)
(50IlD645)
s404NE1065
f424NE[4]1284

– 918 –
(84Il2d461)
(50IlD650)
s405NE855
s405NE859
f419NE[1]1239
e424NE[1]1284

– 921 –
(91IlA655)
(50IlD653)

– 924 –
(94IlA361)
(50IlD656)
s352NE427
s391NE29

– 935 –
(95IlA185)
(50IlD667)
424NE[1]29

– 940 –
(95IlA191)
(50IlD672)

– 947 –
(95IlA199)
(50IlD679)

– 951 –
(95IlA204)
(50IlD683)
cc414NE543
cc419NE729

– 956 –
(95IlA181)
(50IlD688)

– 960 –
(95IlA215)
(50IlD692)

– 969 –
s375NE203

– 973 –
425NE[4]644

– 999 –
s423NE673
421NE[1]744
425NE[1]668

– 1004 –
421NE[1]1136
421NE[2]1136

– 1015 –
422NE[2]308

– 1021 –
m422NE399

– 1024 –
s424NE1064

– 1049 –
420NE[1]357

– 1052 –
f419NE860

– 1069 –
421NE[1]463

– 1075 –
421NE[2]781

– 1078 –
Case 1
(52NY972)
(438S2d79)
s425S2d852

– 1078 –
Case 2
(52NY984)
(438S2d79)
s426S2d778

– 1078 –
Case 3
(52NY986)
(438S2d79)
s422NE596
s428S2d102

– 1078 –
Case 4
(52NY988)
(438S2d79)
s422S2d232

– 1079 –
Case 1
(52NY994)
(438S2d80)
s425S2d115

– 1079 –
Case 2
(52NY997)
(438S2d80)
s426S2d768
651F2d138

– 1079 –
Case 3
(52NY999)
(438S2d80)
s433S2d274

– 1079 –
Case 4
(52NY999)
(438S2d80)
s432S2d656

– 1081 –
(66OS45)
(20Op3d38)

– 1084 –
(66OS51)
(20Op3d41)

– 1086 –
(66OS53)
(20Op3d43)

– 1087 –
(66OS54)
(20Op3d44)
423NE[1]481

– 1089 –
(66OS57)
(20Op3d45)
j424NE582

– 1094 –
(66OS74)
(20Op3d64)
j424NE582

– 1102 –
(66OS113)
(20Op3d100)

– 1104 –
(66OS116)
(20Op3d102)

– 1108 –
(66OA79)
(20Op3d142)

– 1112 –
(66OA72)
(20Op3d138)

– 1117 –
(66OA65)
(20Op3d134)

– 1121 –
(66OA55)
(20Op3d128)

– 1128 –
(66OA17)
(20Op3d49)

– 1138 –
(66M1)
(20Op3d82)

– 1141 –
(66M23)
(20Op3d148)

– 1145 –
(84Il2d480)
(50IlD696)
s401NE323

– 1150 –
(84Il2d493)
(50IlD701)
s402NE790
425NE[3]999

– 1159 –
(84Il2d538)
(50IlD710)
j421NE196

– 1165 –
(84Il2d474)
(50IlD716)
s403NE1285

– 1167 –
(84Il2d512)
(50IlD718)
420NE[7]1168
e424NE[1]806

– 1181 –
(95IlA62)
(50IlD732)

– 1188 –
(95IlA115)
(50IlD739)
s326NE737

– 1205 –
(95IlA254)
(50IlD756)

– 1212 –
(95IlA46)
(50IlD763)

– 1223 –
(95IlA243)
(50IlD774)

– 1227 –
(95IlA235)
(50IlD778)

– 1230 –
(95IlA230)
(50IlD781)

– 1233 –
(95IlA248)
(50IlD784)

– 1237 –
(95IlA238)
(50IlD788)

– 1240 –
(95IlA283)

– 1246 –
(95IlA262)
(50IlD797)
s356NE350

– 1253 –
(95IlA223)
(50IlD804)

– 1257 –
(95IlA272)
(50IlD808)
423NE[3]564

– 1262 –
(95IlA291)
(50IlD813)
421NE1346

– 1267 –
(95IlA228)
(50IlD818)
s409NE95

– 1276 –
(95IlA280)
(50IlD827)

– 1279 –
425NE[13]188

– 1302 –
421NE1116

– 1308 –
f421NE[5]710
421NE711
425NE[5]172

– 1318 –
423NE[1]729

– 1326 –
422NE[2]1263
422NE[4]1263

– 1332 –
422NE[1]308

– 1355 –
421NE[1]17

– 1358 –
423NE[3]03

– 1372 –
420NE[2]300

– 1378 –
425NE[4]283
425NE[4]289
425NE[4]291
d425NE[3]310
425NE385

– 1384 –
422NE[1]1383

Vol. 420

– 1 –
425NE[7]370

– 8 –
d421NE[8]786

– 18 –
422NE785

– 40 –
(52NY309)
(438S2d242)
s421NE848
s422NE596
s425S2d936
441S2d262
j441S2d264

– 45 –
(52NY322)
(438S2d247)
423NE[2]373
j423NE378
439S2d[7]322
440S2d[3]615
440S2d[6]896
j440S2d901
441S2d520
442S2d286
442S2d642
e442S2d661

– 51 –
(52NY333)
(438S2d253)
s431S2d547

– 55 –
(52NY341)
(438S2d257)
s425S2d351
cc372S2d304
421NE[4]503
439S2d[4]103
d441S2d182

– 59 –
(52NY350)
(438S2d261)
d442S2d142
j442S2d144

– 64 –
(52NY363)
(438S2d266)
s423S2d580
s426S2d517
s433S2d388
s434S2d46

– 80 –
(52NY970)
(438S2d282)
424NE[2]553
441S2d438
441S2d[2]666

– 81 –
(52NY974)
(438S2d283)
s422S2d116

– 82 –
(52NY976)
(438S2d284)
s419S2d614

– 85 –
Case 1
(52NY982)
(438S2d287)
s424S2d933

– 85 –
Case 2
(52NY990)
(438S2d287)
s417S2d95

– 86 –
(52NY991)
(438S2d288)
s422NE596
s350S2d974
s374S2d569
s423S2d453
425NE828
442S2d440

– 87 –
(52NY995)
(438S2d289)
s428S2d272

– 88 –
(52NY1000)
(438S2d290)
s421S2d605

– 89 –
(52NY1002)
(438S2d291)
s421S2d387

– 90 –
(52NY1004)
(438S2d292)
s415S2d687

– 91 –
(52NY1006)
(438S2d293)
s407S2d106
s426S2d1008

– 92 –
Case 1
(52NY1008)
(438S2d294)
s428S2d762

– 92 –
Case 2
(52NY1010)
(438S2d294)
s416S2d591

– 93 –
(52NY1013)
(438S2d295)
s429S2d299

– 94 –
(52NY1019)
(438S2d296)
s423NE415

– 95 –
(52NY1020)
(438S2d297)
s427S2d125
s440S2d583
441S2d890
442S2d285

– 96 –
(52NY1023)
(438S2d298)
s420S2d807
s421S2d553
s423S2d458
420NE[1]95
438S2d[1]298
441S2d890
442S2d285

– 97 –
Case 1
(52NY1025)
(438S2d299)
s417S2d864

– 97 –
Case 2
(52NY1027)
(438S2d299)
s424S2d484
441S2d414
442S2d571

– 99 –
Case 1
(52NY1015)
(438S2d301)
s423NE415

– 99 –
Case 2
(52NY1015)
(438S2d301)

– 99 –
Case 3
(52NY1015)
(438S2d301)

– 99 –
Case 4
(52NY1016)
(438S2d301)
s409S2d660
s438S2d301

– 99 –
Case 5
(52NY1016)
(438S2d301)
s431S2d33

– 100 –
Case 1
(52NY1016)
(438S2d302)
s422NE596
s433S2d789

– 100 –
Case 2
(52NY1017)
(438S2d302)

*Illinois Appellate Court Cases when Certiorari or Appeal Denied or Dismissed

volved, but merely the trial verdicts and damages awarded, usually for different classes of tort litigation. Another recent service of this kind is *Verdicts and Settlements* (1981–date), published by the Litigation Research Group in San Francisco.

A few of the legal newspapers published in the large cities often report the decisions of lower courts which do not appear in the standard state court reports. These elusive decisions are generally accessible only through the indexes included periodically in some of the newspapers. New York, however, has a digest specifically designed for this purpose—*Clark's Digest,* which covers decisions published in the *New York Law Journal.*

E. SUMMARY

The variety and overwhelming detail of the various published reports described herein should not obscure the literary quality and the multi-faceted significance of the decisions they contain. The style of judicial opinions range from mundane prose and legalese to the clear, sharp texts of masters like Learned Hand and Oliver Wendell Holmes, and the sometimes poetic humanism of Benjamin Nathan Cardozo.[8] One can be moved by the human drama reflected in opinions which struggle to resolve the disputes arising between ordinary people and the tensions and conflicts besetting groups in society, or which judge the individual who has broken the law. The published cases also reflect the great social, economic and political changes which have affected our world. We usually confront these movements as impersonal, abstract forces—in the microcosm of the law reports, however, they can be seen more vividly. One can trace, in decisions on the law of property, for example, the evolution from feudalism to mercantilism to capitalism, and then through the industrial revolution, the welfare state, and what some call the modern post-industrial society. There are more than headnotes, citations, and holdings in these volumes.

F. ADDITIONAL READINGS

R.A. Leflar, *Appellate Judicial Opinions* (West Publishing Co., 1974). An anthology of short excerpts on various aspects of judicial opinions.

R.A. Leflar, "Sources of Judge-Made Law," 24 *Oklahoma L.Rev.* 319 (1971).

K.N. Llewellyn, "Case Law," in *Encyclopedia of the Social Sciences* (Macmillan, 1930) v. 3, pp. 249–251. (*Not* in the revised *International Encyclopedia of Social Sciences.*)

8. On legal style in general, see D. Mellinkoff, *The Language of the Law* (Little, Brown, 1963) and J.B. White, *The Legal Imagination, Studies in the Nature of Legal Thought and Expression* (Little, Brown, 1973).

K.N. Llewellyn, *The Common Law Tradition, Deciding Appeals* (Little, Brown, 1960). A classic jurisprudential study of appellate law.

A. Vestal, "A Survey of Federal District Court Opinions: West Publishing Company Reports," 20 *Southwestern L.J.* 63 (1966); "Reported Federal District Court Opinions, Fiscal 1962," 4 *Houston L.Rev.* 185 (1966); "Reported Opinions of the Federal District Courts: Analysis and Suggestions," 52 *Iowa L.Rev.* 379 (1966); "Publishing District Court Opinions in the 1970's," 17 *Loyola L.Rev.* 673 (1971). Several critiques of modern law reporting of federal decisions.

J.W. Wallace, "Remarks Upon the Value of Observations Concerning the Reporters," in *The Reporters, Chronologically Arranged: With Occasional Remarks Upon Their Respective Merits* . . . 4th ed. (Philadelphia, 1882), pp. 1–58. An analysis of critical standards for evaluation of law reports, primarily based on the English reports.

Chapter 4

ANNOTATED LAW REPORTS

A. INTRODUCTION

Chapters 2 and 3 discussed the genesis of American case reporting, traced its development through the nominative and official reporters, the emergence of commercially published reports, and finally described the current status of published cases, including the establishment of West's National Reporter System. It was noted that, at the time of the creation of the National Reporter System, a variety of regional reporters were issued by other publishers, only to be absorbed by West or discontinued. These were not the only competitors to the West system. Another form of case reporting was already developing when West began his first publications. These reports, briefly described in Chapter 2, were based on the concept of selective reporting with annotations appended to each decision. This Chapter is devoted to the development and current forms of publication of those annotated law reports.

B. THE ORIGIN OF THE ANNOTATED REPORTS

By the late 19th Century, practitioners were already being overwhelmed by the proliferation of judicial decisions. The American lawyer's research burden had changed from the simpler days of Daniel Webster, when a practitioner could read virtually all of the published appellate decisions from at least one state and the federal courts, and master them. Lawyers were concerned about access to the increasing number of decisions being reported and the vast corpus of case law which was accumulating.[1] The West Publishing Company's approach to handling the volume of cases was to publish the decisions comprehensively, but to facilitate access by providing a subject classification in a digest format, so that the practitioner or researcher could locate relevant cases in the mass of judicial opinions. There was another publication approach, however. The company now represented by the Lawyers Cooperative/Bancroft-Whitney group employed a scheme of "selective" publication of leading cases, some of which were then annotated. This publisher assumed that most of the cases being decided and published did not state new doctrine, and added little, if anything, to the existing body of law. If publication of these many redundant cases could be eliminated, and only those cases that dealt with important points of law, or illuminated new areas, were published, they believed that a much more manageable system of law reporting could be developed, which would compete effectively with West's comprehensive reporting approach. This system began with the "Trinity Series" described in Chapter 2 at p. 25, and gradually developed into the modern annotated report system, represented by *American Law Reports (ALR).*

The controversy between comprehensive reporting and selective, annotated reporting, is reflected in the exchange published in a symposium carried in 1889 in volume 23 of the *American Law Review.*[2] The editors of that review asked leading law publishers to comment upon the most effective system of publishing cases. Of the several respondents, James Briggs of Lawyers Co-op and John B. West of the West Publishing Company were the main proponents of the selectivist and comprehensivist approaches, respectively. It was one of the rare occasions on which these early law publishers articulated their views. West described his position as follows:

> "I believe it to be the principle business of American law publishers, to enable the legal profession to examine the American case law on any given subject, as easily, exhaustively, and economically as possible. It is a remarkable fact that until within the last few years there has been no successful attempt to handle systematically and comprehensively, the current decisions of the courts of

1. This concern is reflected in "Reports, Reporters and Reporting," 5 *So. Law Rev.* 53 (1880) and J.L. High, "What Shall Be Done with the Reports," 16 *Amer.L.Rev.* 429 (1882).

2. 23 *Amer.L.Rev.* 396, 407–408 (1889).

last resort, which are constantly developing and modifying the law in every subject . . . "

Briggs, writing for Lawyers Co-op set forth the opposing viewpoint:

> "There is a generally felt and frequently expressed regret, on the part of the bench and bar here and in England, for the unlimited production of law books, whether of reports or textbooks which, instead of simplifying and facilitating a knowledge of the present state of the law on any given question, complicate and embarrass it by the very quantity of matter presented for examination and reconciliation.
>
> It is a fact that no one, working industriously ten hours a day, could simply read all the published opinions—hence, the publisher's duty to render them quickly accessible. . . .
>
> In America the multiplicity of jurisdictions, and their independence of each other, rendering it a much more serious question, would seem to devolve it upon volunteers, in whom the profession might have confidence, and whose names and reputation are a guarantee of intelligent and conscientious work, to make this examination and selection in publication for their countrymen, which the Committee of the Incorporated Law Society of England performs for Englishmen.
>
> This work is undertaken by this Company in its Digest and *Lawyers Reports Annotated* . . . "

Briggs set forth the English system of case reporting as a model in his argument for the Lawyers Co-op approach of winnowing the precedential wheat from the chaff.

Both systems flourish today and are represented by West's National Reporter System and the *American Law Reports* (successor to *Lawyers Reports Annotated*). The development of the annotated reports in this country included the following series, prior to *American Law Reports:*

	Period Covered
Trinity Series	
American Decisions (Am.Dec.) 100 vols.	1760–1868
American Reports (Am.Rep.) 60 vols.	1868–1887
American State Reports (Am.St.Rep.) 140 vols.	1887–1911
Annotated Cases	
American & English Annotated Cases (A. & E. Ann.Cas.) 21 vols., merging into:	1906–1911
American Annotated Cases (Ann.Cas.) 32 vols.	1912–1918
Lawyers Reports Annotated	
Lawyers Reports Annotated, First Series, (L.R.A.) 70 vols.	1888–1905
Lawyers Reports Annotated, New Series, (L.R.A.,N.S.) 52 vols.	1905–1914
Lawyers Reports Annotated, Dated Series (L.R.A., 1915 etc.) 24 vols.	1914–1918

A further rationale of the annotated reporter, and its primary justification today, is the effectiveness of the annotation in providing a broad statement of the law applicable in all jurisdictions. The researcher is assured that every case relevant to the topic of the annotation has been gathered and analyzed. Thus the annotation extends the precedential relevance of the case and its consequent research value. Although originally the cases selected for publication were "leading cases", important in their own right and often of national significance, today the reported cases are no longer of any special interest themselves, but are selected for their convenience and timing as a take-off point for substantial and relevant annotations. In the early series, the case report was the primary feature of the annotated reporters and the annotations a secondary benefit, but now the reverse is true. The annotations are the main attraction of *ALR* and *ALR Federal* and the cases reported are secondary and often unread by the researcher, unless they are jurisdictionally relevant. This difference is reflected in the fact that only *some* of the cases in the early annotated reporters were in fact annotated (even into the first series of *ALR*), while every case in *ALR* and *ALR Federal* today is annotated.

Unlike the other annotated reporters, the Lawyers Co-op reporter for the U.S. Supreme Court, called *Lawyers Edition,* provides annotations for only a few of the cases it reports. This departure is probably due, at least in part, to the time required to prepare the annotations and the unwillingness of lawyers to wait that long for the current decisions of the U.S. Supreme Court. Similar reasoning undoubtedly explains why advance sheets are *not* prepared for *ALR* and *ALR Federal,* but *are* prepared for *Lawyers Edition.* The advance sheets for *Lawyers Edition* do not include the few annotations that are prepared for the bound volumes of that reporter.

At its inception, the annotated reporters were promoted and sold as a complete substitute for the National Reporter System. Because truly leading cases were reported, the argument could be made that a lawyer need only subscribe to the selective reporter, and other reporters would rarely be needed for most research. Today, the cases selected for *ALR* and *ALR Federal* are no longer necessarily the most important decisions and the sets are generally used as adjuncts to a comprehensive collection of other reporters. It is difficult to imagine effective research based only on the annotated reports, even when used in conjunction with the other publications of the Lawyers Co-op "Total Client-Service Library".[3] However, *ALR* remains a popular reporter because of the quality of its annotations and its value as a research aid and case-finding tool. The annotations provide an extensive survey of the legal issues dealt with in the reported cases, tracing their development and their judicial treatment in all jurisdictions. They provide numerous citations to other decisions, to statutes where relevant, and to a variety of secondary sources published by Lawyers Co-op. The annotations range in length, depending on the complexity

3. The "Total Client Service Library" is a promotional designation used by Lawyers Co-op to describe its inter-related system of publications (annotated reporters, encyclopedias, formbooks, statutory codes, digests, treatises, etc.) which contain helpful cross-references to each other.

of the issues, from short articles of a few pages to extensive treatises of hundreds of pages.

C. CURRENT COMPONENTS OF THE ANNOTATED REPORTING SYSTEM

The modern *ALR* annotated system of reports, following the earlier annotated reporters described above, now includes these several series:

1. AMERICAN LAW REPORTS

A.L.R. (First Series) 1919 to 1948 (175 vols.)

A.L.R.2d (Second Series) 1948 to 1965 (100 vols.)

A.L.R.3d (Third Series) 1965 to 1980 (100 vols.)

A.L.R.4th (Fourth Series) 1980 to date (current)

The first two series included decisions from both the state courts and the federal courts, the latter primarily from the U.S. Courts of Appeals. In the 3d series, coverage focused on state court decisions, and *ALR* became virtually a state reporter when *ALR Federal* was created to provide a parallel reporter for federal court decisions. The finding aids and updating mechanisms for *ALR* have varied from series to series, and are more fully described in sections E and F below.

2. ALR FEDERAL

Beginning in 1969, Lawyers Co-op began a new series, *American Law Reports—Federal,* with a format and research aids similar to those being used in *ALR3d. ALR Federal* continues to annotate all decisions reported in its volumes and now serves as a companion series to *ALR4th,* which includes state court decisions. It is currently accessible through its own index, the *Federal Quick Index,* described below in Section E–2C, and through other Lawyers Co-op publications.

3. LAWYERS' EDITION

Begun in 1882, the Lawyers Co-op reporter for the decisions of the Supreme Court of the United States is designated by the long title, *United States Supreme Court Reports, Lawyers' Edition,* but is popularly called *Lawyers' Edition.* It includes retrospective coverage going back to the first volume of the *U.S. Reports* (1 Dallas), 1790, and thus constitutes a complete, but more compact reporter of all U.S. Supreme Court decisions. The early volumes of *Lawyers' Edition,* in fact, contained many decisions not reported in the first volumes of the official reports, and later volumes even included, as did West's *Supreme Court Reporter,* some per curiam decisions and decisions of Supreme Court justices sitting as Circuit Court judges which were not officially reported in the *U.S. Reports. Lawyers' Edition* includes several special features such as star-paging (indicating the pagination of the *official* report, in the text of *Lawyers' Edition*, so that one can cite to the official report, while actually using *Lawyers' Edition*) and summaries of the briefs of counsel in a few of the important cases in each volume. Unlike *ALR* and *ALR Federal*, however, *Lawyers' Edition* reports all decisions of the Supreme Court, but *unlike* its companion reporters it annotates only a very few of the decisions it reports.[4] Thus, *Lawyers' Edition* is not a fully *annotated* reporter. It therefore can issue an advance sheet which delivers current decisions to its subscribers within weeks of their announcement.

After volume 100 (1956), *Lawyers' Edition* instituted a second series, beginning with the decisions appearing in volume 350 *U.S. Reports*.

There are many other special research aids in *Lawyers' Edition*,[5] including a *Lawyers' Edition 2d Desk Book* which contains a variety of reference features relating to the Supreme Court of the United States and a number of finding tables to that set.

D. THE STRUCTURE OF AN ANNOTATED REPORT

This section will examine an *ALR* annotation and describe its component parts, using one from *ALR4th* as an example.[6] The annotations in the recent series of *ALR* are quite different from those in *ALR1st* series. The current annotations are the result of a process of development and tend to be longer, more sophisticated in their research aids, and more extensive in their coverage.

1. THE CASE REPORT

Each annotation is preceded by the report of a selected court decision, the subject of which is used as the theme of the annotation which follows the decision. Illustrations A–1 to A–4 show such a decision, *Pope v. State of Maryland*, decided by the Court of Appeals of Maryland, and also reported at 396 *A.2d* 1054. Note that the National Reporter System citation appears at the top of the Illustration A–1, followed by a summary of the decision, prepared by the Lawyers Co-op editorial staff. Not shown in the Illustration, but following are Lawyers Co-op headnotes and then the text of the opinion of the court. To this point, *ALR* has functions like any other reporter.

2. THE ANNOTATION FORMAT

Following the decision, Illustration A–2 shows the beginning of the Annotation itself, with the title of the Annotation, the name of its author (usually a member of the publisher's editorial staff and a law-

4. The selective annotations and summaries of briefs now appear in a separate section at the back of each volume; previously, they had appeared with the appropriate decisions.

5. See *The Living Law* (1982) pp. 78–89.

6. 1 *ALR4th* 38 (1980), appended to the decision in *Pope v. State of Maryland*.

SUBJECT OF ANNOTATION

Validity and construction of penal statute prohibiting child abuse

Joyce Lillian POPE

v

STATE of Maryland

Court of Appeals of Maryland
January 19, 1979
396 A2d 1054, 1 ALR4th 1

SUMMARY OF DECISION

The Circuit Court, Montgomery County, Maryland, Philip M. Fairbanks, J., entered judgment of conviction against defendant for child abuse and misprision of felony. The evidence adduced at trial established that a three-month-old child died as a result of physical injuries inflicted by his mother over a period of several hours at defendant's home and in defendant's presence. Two days earlier, defendant and the child's mother returned with the child from a church service. The mother seemed "caught up in a religious frenzy" and declared that she was God. The mother and child remained at defendant's home and defendant stayed up with the baby while the mother slept. The next day, the mother lapsed in and out of the frenzied episodes. That night, defendant again stayed up with the child while the mother slept. On the following day the mother's episodes of changing to God became more pronounced. The mother called out that Satan had hidden in the body of her son, and began to verbally exorcise the spirit and physically abuse the child by punching and poking him repeatedly about the stomach, chest and privates. The mother beat the child about the head and began to squeeze him. The child was wrapped in a towel and taken to church. En route to the church the mother and defendant passed several hospitals, police stations and rescue squads. At the church the child was given to the reverend and it was discovered that the child was dead. When questioned by the police, defendant at first said that she had not seen the mother strike the baby, but the next day gave the police full details. On direct appeal the Court of Special Appeals, Thomas Lowe, J., reversed the judgment entered on the child abuse

1

Illustration A–1

Beginning of case report, *Pope v. State of Maryland* in *ALR4th.*

ANNOTATION

VALIDITY AND CONSTRUCTION OF PENAL STATUTE PROHIBITING CHILD ABUSE

by

Milton Roberts, J.D.

TOTAL CLIENT-SERVICE LIBRARY® REFERENCES

42 Am Jur 2d, Infants § 16; 59 Am Jur 2d, Parent and Child § 24

Annotations: See the related matters listed in the annotation, infra.

2 Am Jur Proof of Facts 2d 365, Child Abuse—The Battered Child Syndrome

ALR Digests, Infants § 16

L Ed Index to Annos, Children and Minors; Medical Treatment or Care; Statutes

ALR Quick Index, Battered Child Cases; Children; Medical Treatment or Care; Parent and Child; Statutes

Federal Quick Index, Child Abuse and Neglect; Children and Minors; Constitutional Law; Construction and Interpretation; Statutes

Consult POCKET PART in this volume for later cases

38

Illustration A–2

Annotation title and cross references following *Pope v. State of Maryland.*

1 ALR4th PENAL STATUTES PROHIBITING CHILD ABUSE
1 ALR4th 38

Validity and construction of penal statute prohibiting child abuse

39

Illustration A-3

Outline of Annotation Contents to *Pope v. State of Maryland.*

INDEX

Illustration A–4

Beginning of Index of Annotation to *Pope v. State of Maryland.*

yer), and then a box containing cross references to relevant sections of other units in the Total Client-Service Library. As noted above, this is the name of the Lawyers Co-op research system, which links all of the publications. These cross references, appearing only in *ALR3d & 4th* and *ALR Federal,* enable a researcher who has found a relevant Annotation, to get access to other parts of that system on the same topic.

a. Finding Aids

Before the text of the Annotation itself, there are a series of finding aids which help the reader identify and locate its most relevant sections for the problem being researched. These include an outline or table of contents of the Annotation (Illustration A–3), a detailed Subject Index of the Annotation (Illustration A–4), and a Table of Jurisdictions Represented in the text of the Annotation (Illustration A–5). Both the Index and the Table of Jurisdictions Represented give specific references to the sections and subsections in which the relevant material for the researcher's problem can be found. The latter Table arranges alphabetically, by state, all citations to the Annotation's sections referring to the particular jurisdiction. The researcher who is interested only in the material of a specific jurisdiction can thus locate directly all relevant references to that jurisdiction. These indexes and tables are effectively designed to expedite and focus one's research.

b. Body of the Annotation

Illustrations A–5 and A–6 show the beginning of the text of the Annotation itself. Sections 1 and 2 of all *ALR* annotations now follow the same format. Section 1(a) describes the "Scope" of the Annotation, setting out in detail what it covers. Section (b) discusses "Related Matters." This directs the researcher to other *ALR* Annotations related to the same topic, but not on the same precise point. Section 2 provides a "Summary and Comment." This section always begins with a general overview of what is contained in the Annotation, followed by a subsection called "Practice Pointers" which describes practical and procedural aspects of litigation under that topic. The Annotation, from which the pages shown in these Illustrations were drawn, covers 66 pages, almost twice the number of pages in the actual opinion reported. The difference in length, at least in this instance, indicates the relative importance of the reported decision and the Annotation in the current series of *ALR.*

Two questions remain: how to find a relevant annotation and how can the annotation be updated to get current references and citations since its publication?

TABLE OF JURISDICTIONS REPRESENTED
Consult POCKET PART in this volume for later cases

US: §§ 4[a], 5, 11[a, b], 21[a, b]
Ala: §§ 4[a, b], 17[a]
Cal: §§ 2[b], 4[a], 5, 7, 8[a], 9[a], 11[b], 12[a, b], 13[c], 14[a], 15[b, c], 17[a, b], 18, 20, 22
Colo: §§ 4[a, b], 11[a], 14[b]
Conn: §§ 13[b], 15[c], 17[a]
DC: §§ 11[a], 22
Fla: §§ 4[a], 10[b], 11[a], 12[b], 13[c], 17[a], 18
Ga: §§ 2[b], 4[a], 8[b], 10[d], 11[a, c], 12[c], 13[c], 14[a], 15[c], 17[a], 22
Ill: §§ 4[a], 8[a], 10[a], 11[a], 13[c], 14[b], 15[c], 17[a]
Ind: §§ 4[a], 11[b], 12[a], 17[a], 20, 22
Kan: §§ 4[a, b]
La: §§ 4[a], 9[b], 14[a, b], 21[b]
Md: §§ 4[a], 9[a], 10[c, d], 11[b, c], 13[a], 14[a], 17[a, b], 21[a, b]
Mich: §§ 13[a, b], 14[a], 16, 17[a, b], 22
Mo: §§ 10[c], 13[c], 17[a]
NJ: §§ 2[b], 6[a, b], 11[b], 12[a], 14[b], 16, 17[a], 19
NM: §§ 3, 4[a], 5, 11[b], 12[a, b], 17[a], 21[a]
NY: §§ 2[b], 4[a], 9[a], 12[b], 13[a], 14[b], 16, 19, 21[a]
NC: §§ 3, 4[a], 6[a], 22
Ohio: §§ 4[a], 11[a-c], 13[c], 14[a], 15[a], 17[a, b], 20
Okla: §§ 4[a], 5, 10[c], 14[a], 17[a]
Or: §§ 4[a], 13[a]
Pa: §§ 17[a]
Tex: §§ 4[a], 10[d], 13[c], 14[a]
Va: §§ 10[d]
Wis: §§ 3, 4[a], 11[b], 13[a], 14[a], 22
Wyo: §§ 4[b]

I. Preliminary matters

§ 1. Introduction

[a] Scope

This annotation[1] collects and analyzes the cases in which the courts have determined or discussed the validity of, or have interpreted or applied provisions of a penal statute prohibiting child abuse—[2] that is, prohibiting cruel treatment of, or intentional or willful infliction of actual or potential harm on, a child, or like treatment. Cases involving statutes prohibiting excessive "punishment" of a "person" are also included if the victim is a child, since the term "punishment" would seem to indicate that the "person" intended to be protected by the statute is a child. Cases involving a child abuse statute, as described above, are included even if the crime charged under the statute is injury to a child resulting from the accused's neglect or omission to act. Similarly, if child neglect is included in the statutory definition of child abuse, cases under such a statute involving child neglect are also treated herein. However, cases involving a prosecution under a provision of a penal statute which in terms prohibits child neglect, without relating it to

1. For cases within the scope of the present annotation, the reader no longer need consult the annotation at 89 ALR2d 396, §§ 8, 15, 21.

2. Cases in which the court merely quotes, recites, or paraphrases the language of a child abuse statute, without determining its validity, construing it, or applying it to particular facts, or in which the court affirms or reverses a conviction on the facts without detailing the evidence relied on, are not treated herein.

Illustration A–5

"Table of Jurisdictions Represented" and "Scope Note" in Annotation to *Pope v. State of Maryland.*

child abuse, are not included. Also excluded are cases involving prosecutions under criminal statutes of general application, such as those proscribing murder, manslaughter, or assault and battery, even if the victim was a child, unless a child abuse statute is also involved.[3]

The validity issues treated herein are those involving a claimed conflict between the statute in question and a federal or state constitutional provision. However, validity issues equally applicable to any statute, such as those relating to the manner of promulgation, conformity of the statutory object to the title, and the like, are excluded. Only the constitutionality of the charging part of the statute is considered herein and not, for example, the validity of the sentence provided by the statute.

Since relevant statutes are included only to the extent that they are reflected in the reported cases within the scope of this annotation, the reader is advised to consult the latest enactments of pertinent jurisdictions.

[b] Related matters

Who has custody or control of child within terms of penal statute punishing cruelty or neglect by one having custody or control. 75 ALR3d 933.

Physical abuse of the child by parent as ground for termination of parent's right to child. 53 ALR3d 605.

Application, to illegimate children, of criminal statutes relating to abandonment, neglect, and nonsupport of children. 99 ALR2d 746.

Criminal liability for excessive or improper punishment inflicted on child by parent, teacher, or one in loco parentis. 89 ALR2d 396.

Mistreatment of the children as ground for divorce. 82 ALR2d 1361.

Liability of a truant or attendance officer for assault and battery. 62 ALR2d 1328.

Civil liability of a teacher for administering corporal punishment to a pupil. 43 ALR2d 469.

Civil liability of a parent or person in loco parentis for a personal tort against a minor child. 19 ALR2d 423.

Failure to provide medical attention for child as criminal neglect. 12 ALR2d 1047.

Administration of corporal punishment in public school system as cruel and unusual punishment under Eighth Amendment. 25 ALR Fed 431

◆

Child Abuse Symposium, 54 Chi-Kent L Rev 635 (1978).

§ 2. Summary and comment

[a] Generally

Enactment of a penal statute prohibiting child abuse has been held to be within the police power of the state.[4] Moreover, many courts before whom the question has arisen have upheld the validity of such statutes against contentions that they, as an entirety, or that particular terms contained therein were unconstitutionally vague or overbroad and thus constituted a deprivation of due process,[5] or that the statute was discriminatory, involved a denial of equal protection of the laws, or constituted class legis-

3. The subject of who has custody or control of a child under a penal statute punishing cruelty to a child by one having "custody" or "control," without using the qualifying word "legal," is discussed in the annotation at 75 ALR3d 933, and, therefore, is not treated in the present annotation.

4. § 3, infra.

5. § 4[a], infra.

Illustration A-6

"Related Matters" and "Summary and Comment" in Annotation to *Pope v. State of Maryland.*

E. FINDING ANNOTATIONS

1. EARLY ALR DIGESTS AND WORD INDEXES

Each series of *ALR* has its own finding tools, and their respective formats have changed from series to series. For historical purposes, it should be noted that the first and second series of *ALR* each had its own digest, somewhat similar to the West digests, but of course not using West's proprietary classification scheme of topics and key numbers. The *ALR* digests did, however, employ a subject classification of topics and numbered subtopics. Though these digests are rarely used today, the Tables of Cases for the *ALR1st* and *2d* series are still helpful and are contained in the last volume of their respective digests. The Tables of Cases are the means of locating decisions in all *ALR* series and are the most direct means of case finding when the *name* of the case being sought is known to the researcher.

Another means of locating *ALR* Annotations are the *Word Indexes* to *ALR1st* and *2d.* Although no longer supplemented, these indexes, which are similar to the West *Descriptive Word Indexes,* are still useful for searches in the *1st* and *2d* series of *ALR* since they are somewhat more detailed than their successors, the *Quick Indexes.*

2. ALR QUICK INDEXES

a. Quick Indexes to ALR1st and 2d

The recommended subject approach to *ALR1st* and *2d* is through the *Quick Indexes* to those series. Although they are much faster than the old cumbersome digests and more current than the old *Word Indexes,* they lack the specificity of the latter. The *Quick Indexes* are, however, an effective means of subject access to the Annotations. They contain an alphabetical list of subject terms, both factual and legal, with subtopics, and provide references to relevant cases and citations to their Annotations. If the Annotations have been superseded by later Annotations in subsequent series, that fact is indicated with a reference to the later Annotation, but these Indexes have not been kept current and the updating references are not continued past their last publication. There are now other means of supplementation which will be described in Section F below. Illustration B shows a sample page from the *Quick Index to ALR1st.*

ALR2d also has its own *Quick Index,* covering that closed series and hence not being currently updated. Its format and function are similar to those of the *ALR1st Quick Index.* Neither of these two *Quick Indexes* provide cross references to the other publications of the Lawyers Co-op Total Client-Service Library. That practice began in the later *Quick Indexes.*

Illustration B

Quick Index to ALR1st.

b. Quick Index to ALR3d and 4th

The finding tool for the *3d* and *4th* series of *ALR* is a one volume *Quick Index* to both series. Since *ALR4th* is a continuing series, this *Quick Index* is supplemented by a pocket part located in the front of that volume which updates references in the main section. Both the volume and the pocket part contain "Tables of Cases Reported". The *Quick Index to ALR3d and 4th* also contains references to *ALR Federal* (in italics) and to other units of the Total Client-Service Library, as shown in Illustration C.

c. Federal Quick Index and Fed Tables

ALR Federal also has its own *Quick Index* (now in its 3d edition) which is kept up to date with pocket parts. In addition to references to *ALR Federal,* the *Federal Quick Index* (as shown in Illustration D) also contains citations to federal sources in the other units in the Total Client-Service Library, including the *United States Supreme Court Reports, Lawyers' Edition,* which has its own Annotations to some of the cases it reports. However, *Federal Quick Index* references to cases in *Lawyers' Edition* are not always to *annotated* cases. See section E.3 below for the *Lawyers' Edition* equivalent to a *Quick Index,* called *Index to Annotations.*

Another finding aid for *ALR Federal* is the volume called *Fed Tables,* which includes a "Table of Cases Reported in *ALR Federal*" and the very helpful "Table of Laws and Regulations Cited in *ALR Federal*".

3. REFERENCES FROM OTHER PUBLICATIONS

Several legal research tools provide references to the Annotations in *ALR* and the other annotated reporters. The most important of these are the various units of the Lawyers Co-op Total Client-Service Library, and citators published by Shepard's Citations.

Am.Jur.2d, the Lawyers Co-op legal encyclopedia (to be described in Chapter 14 below), provides, in the footnotes to its various articles, numerous citations to the several annotated reporters. These enable the researcher to move from the *Am.Jur.2d* article to more extensive discussions in the Annotations of *ALR, ALR Federal,* and *Lawyers' Edition.* These references sometimes also serve to update *Am.Jur. 2d,* by providing citations to Annotations written subsequently to the *Am.Jur.2d* article, as shown by the *Am.Jur.2d* pocket part in Illustration E.

Lawyers' Edition has two indexes prepared in a format similar to that of the *Quick Indexes,* but known by other names, i.e., *Index to Annotations* and the *Lawyers' Edition Desk Book.* These aids refer to Annotations in *ALR Federal* and *Lawyers' Edition.* Lawyers Co-

QUICK INDEX **Children**

nal case of blood alcohol test where blood was taken despite defendant's objection or refusal to submit to test, 14 ALR4th 690

CHEMICAL WEAPONS

Products liability: firearms, ammunition, and chemical weapons, 15 ALR4th 909

CHEST

Excessiveness or adequacy of damages awarded for injuries to trunk or torso, or internal injuries, 16 ALR4th 238

CHILDREN

§ 1. Generally.

Handicapped children: when does change in "educational placement" occur for purposes of § 615(b)(1)(C) of the Education for All Handicapped Children Act of 1975 (20 USCS § 1415(b)(1)(C)), requiring notice to parents prior to such change, 54 ALR Fed 570

References to *ALR Federal* in italics.

Joint custody: propriety of awarding joint custody of children, 17 ALR4th 1013

Marital status of prospective adopting parents as factor in adoption proceedings, 2 ALR4th 555

Modification of child support: removal by custodial parents of child from jurisdiction in violation of court order as justifying termination, suspension, or reduction of child support payments, 8 ALR4th 1231

Poor and poor laws: income tax refund as income or resource to be considered in determining eligibility for benefits under aid to families with dependent children program, 3 ALR4th 1074

School attendance: conditions at school as excusing or justifying nonattendance, 9 ALR4th 122

Truancy as indicative of delinquency or incorrigibility, justifying commitment of infant or juvenile, 5 ALR4th 1212

§ 2. Status as to capacities, privileges and rights.

Divorce and separation: effect of trial court giving consideration to needs of children in making property division—modern status, 19 ALR4th 239

Grandchildren: right of illegitimate grandchildren to take under testamentary gift to "grandchildren", 17 ALR4th 1292

Insurance: unborn child as insured or injured person within meaning of insurance policy, 15 ALR4th 548

Social security: denial of social security benefits to adopted children who are neither natural children nor stepchildren of eligible individual and who do not meet dependency requirements, under § 202(d)(8) of the Social Security Act, as amended (42 USCS § 402(d)(8)), 57 ALR Fed 942

Standing: right of illegitimate child to maintain action to determine paternity, 19 ALR4th 1082

Witnesses

Reference to Annotation of *Pope v. State of Maryland* under entry, CHILDREN, subdivision PROTECTION.

§ 3. Protection.

Abuse: validity and construction of penal statute prohibiting child abuse, 1 ALR4th 38

Medical treatment: circumstances warranting court-ordered medical treatment of minors, 24 Am Jur POF2d, pp 169–210

Stepparent: award of custody of child where contest is between natural parent and stepparent, 10 ALR4th 767

§ 5. Tort liability.

Parental injury: child's right of action for loss of support, training, parental attention, or the like, against a third person negligently injuring parent, 11 ALR4th 549

§ 6. —Injuries to children.

Elevators: products liability, 7 ALR4th 852

Glue and other adhesive products: products liability, 7 ALR4th 155

Police custody, wrongful death while in, 28 Am Jur Trials, p

Reference to *Am.Jur. Trials*, another Total Client-Service Library publication.

§ 7. Criminal ma

Adult children: admissibility of evidence discov-

Consult QUICK INDEX volumes for earlier annotations 41

Illustration C

Annual Update of *Quick Index to ALR3d & 4th,* showing reference to Annotation of *Pope v. Maryland.*

op also offers an excellent digest for *Lawyers' Edition,* which is now called *U.S. Supreme Court Digest, Lawyers' Edition.* In addition to a number of other useful functions, it is the primary case finder for *Lawyers' Edition.* This digest, quite different than West's *U.S. Supreme Court Digest,* is more fully described in Section C.1 of Chapter 5.

Another important tool that refers one to *ALR* Annotations are the various units of the Shepard's Citations system, described below more fully in Chapter 9, Citators. When Shepardizing a case or statute, the appearance of an *ALR* citation enables the researcher to locate an Annotation which may provide useful analysis of the case in question and references to many more relevant authorities.

Similarly, references to *ALR* and *ALR Federal* in *any* secondary sources, such as treatises, periodical articles, or looseleaf services, provide the same potentially valuable Annotations.

F. UPDATING ANNOTATIONS

One concern that inevitably faces the user of a research tool like *ALR,* that claims to "gather every case on point", is determining whether and how the service is kept current. As soon as an Annotation is published, new cases are published, old cases are overruled, and the law summarized in the text may change. One can view the various series of *ALR* as increasingly sophisticated attempts to deal with this problem. Since the methods of updating *ALR* have changed several times, it is necessary to examine each series separately.

1. ALR1st: BLUE BOOK OF SUPPLEMENTAL DECISIONS

Because of the proliferation of new decisions issued every year, the Annotations of *ALR* would be obsolete immediately after their publication unless some means of supplementation were provided. For the first series of *ALR,* the method chosen was the *ALR Blue Book of Supplemental Decisions.* This updating service was arranged by the volume and page citations of each annotation in *ALR.* Following those references were citations to new cases that dealt with the statements and topics of that Annotation. Illustration F shows a typical page in this service. Note that it is a simple list of new citations relevant to the subject of the annotation.

Five successive, permanent volumes of the Blue Book were issued as follows: the first covering the period 1919–1946; the second, 1946–1952; the third, 1952–1958; the fourth, 1959–1967; and the fifth, 1968–1975. A sixth volume in paperback is revised and reissued annually continuing the supplementation from 1976 to date. This form of supplementation proved cumbersome for the researcher. It required use of several volumes and, once found, the bare citation to the later case did not indicate the subject, holding,

QUICK INDEX — CUSTOMER, ETC.

CROSS-EXAMINATION—Cont'd

Inconsistent statements: cross-examination of accused at murder trial in state court regarding inconsistency between his direct testimony and testimony of police officer, held not violative of due process, 65 L Ed 2d 222

Miranda warnings: state prosecutor's cross-examination of defendant as to post-arrest silence, held not violative of Fourteenth Amendment due process in absence of Miranda warning assurances, 71 L Ed 2d 490

Opinion evidence: attacking or supporting credibility of witness by evidence in form of opinion or reputation, under Rule 608(a) of Federal Rules of Evidence, 52 ALR Fed 440

Rape victim: constitutionality of "rape shield" statute restricting use of evidence of victim's sexual experiences, 1 ALR4th 283

Self-incrimination privilege: propriety of court's failure or refusal to strike direct testimony of government witness who refuses, on grounds of self-incrimination, to answer questions on cross-examination, 55 ALR Fed 742

Silence: use of accused's prearrest silence to impeach credibility on cross-examination in state prosecution, held not violative of Fifth and Fourteenth Amendments, 65 L Ed 2d 86

Witnesses, Fed Proc, L Ed §§ 80:43 et seq.

CRUDE OIL

Windfall profits tax on domestic crude oil, 26 USCS §§ 4986 et seq.

CRUEL AND UNUSUAL PUNISHMENT

Drugs and narcotics: sentence of two consecutive 20-year prison terms and two fines of $10,000 for convictions of possession and distribution of 9 ounces of marijuana, held not to constitute cruel and unusual punishment under Eighth Amendment, 70 L Ed 2d 556

Habitual criminals
- life sentence imposed upon defendant under Texas recidivism law for being thrice convicted of property-related felonies, held not to constitute cruel and unusual punishment under Eighth Amendment, 63 L Ed 2d 382
- validity and construction of statute or ordinance mandating imprisonment for habitual or repeated traffic offender, 2 ALR4th 618

CRUEL AND UNUSUAL PUNISHMENT —Cont'd

Housing two inmates in single cell in maximum-security state prison held not to constitute cruel and unusual punishment under Eighth and Fourteenth Amendments, 69 L Ed 2d 59

Mitigation of penalty: state trial judge's refusal to consider defendant's family history and emotional disturbance in mitigation of death penalty sentencing hearing, held violative of Eighth and Fourteenth Amendments, 71 L Ed 2d 1

Prison conditions amounting to, generally, 60 Am Jur 2d Penal Inst §§ 44.5 (supp); 7 Am Jur Pl & Pr Forms (Rev ed), Const L, Form 5

Violent crimes: validity of statutes prohibiting or restricting parole, probation, or suspension of sentence in cases of violent crimes, 100 ALR3d 431

CUSTODY OF CHILDREN

Assistance of counsel: refusal to appoint counsel for indigent parent in parental status termination proceeding, held not violative of due process clause of Fourteenth Amendment, 68 L Ed 2d 640

Habeas corpus: availability of federal habeas corpus relief, under 28 USCS §§ 2241 and 2254, in child custody cases, 49 ALR Fed 674

Race as factor in custody award or proceedings, 10 ALR4th 796

CUSTODY OF PERSON

Acquittal: validity of conditions imposed when releasing person committed to institution as consequence of acquittal of crime on ground of insanity, 2 ALR4th 934

CUSTOM AND USAGE

Admissibility of evidence of habit or routine practice under Rule 406, Federal Rules of Evidence, 53 ALR Fed 703

Evidence, generally, Fed Proc, L Ed §§ 33:143 et seq.

CUSTOMER BANK COMMUNICATION TERMINALS

What is a "branch" under 12 USCS § 36(f) which a national banking association may retain, establish, or operate, 52 ALR Fed 649

Consult FEDERAL QUICK INDEX (3d Ed) Volume for earlier references **85**

Illustration D

Federal Quick Index.

(front pocket part)

NTS INFANTS § 16

§ 8. Generally

Practice Aids: Wilkins, Children's Rights: Removing The Parental Consent Barrier to Medical Treatment of Minors. 1975 Ariz St LJ 31, 1975.

Right of minor to have abortion performed without parental consent. 42 ALR3d 1406.

Glantz et al., Scientific Research with Children: Legal Incapacity and Proxy Consent. XI Fam LQ 253, Fall, 1977.

Brown & Truitt, The Right of Minors to Medical Treatment. 28 De … 1979.

Garvey, Children and … ment. 57 Tex LR 321, 197…

§ 9. Progressive capacity

Practice Aids: Monsees, The Sometimes-Person: Legal Autonomy and the Child. 6 Ohio No U LR 570, 1979.

§ 11. Right to repudiate compromise or settlement

Practice Aids: Covenant not to sue—By parents—Claim of minor child. 16 AM JUR LEGAL FORMS 2d 223:18.

Release of claims for accidental injuries to minor. 16 AM JUR LEGAL FORMS 2d 223:65.

§ 14. Generally

Practice Aids: Symposium, Family law. Brigham Young U L Rev 605, 1976.

p 20, n 20—

The power of a state to control the conduct of children reaches beyond the scope of its authority over adults, even where there is an invasion of constitutionally protected freedoms; the well-being of its children is a subject within a state's constitutional power to regulate. Ginsberg v N… 88 S Ct … 887, 88…

Reference to Section of Main Volume.

§ 15. L…

Practice Aids: Supreme Court's views as to validity of laws restricting or prohibiting sale or distribution to minors of particular types of goods or services otherwise available to adults. 52 L Ed 2d 882.

§ 16. Protection from neglect, ill-treatment, abuse, or danger to health or morals

For later cases involving prosecution for molesting child, see § 17.5.

For a discussion of the right of a person, or someone in his or her behalf to refuse medical care necessary to sustain life, see Am Jur 2d New Topic Service, Right to Die; Wrongful Life.

Practice Aids: Symposium, Child Abuse. 8 Creighton L Rev 729 et seq., June, 1975.

[42 Am Jur 2d Supp]

Katz et al, Child Neglect Laws in America. 9 Family LQ 1, Spring, 1975.

Areen, Intervention Between Parent and Child: A Reappraisal of the State's Role in Child Neglect and Abuse Cases. 63 Georgetown LJ 887, March, 1975.

Goodpaster and Angel, Child Abuse and the Law: The California System. 26 Hastings LJ 1081, March, 1975.

Isaacson, Child Abuse Reporting Statutes: The Case for Holding Physicians Civilly Lia… …ort. 12 San Diego L…

Reference to Annotated report of *Pope Case* in *ALR 4th.*

… FACTS 2d 265, CHILD … ical care. 14 J Family …

Who has custody or control of child within terms of penal statute punishing cruelty or neglect by one having custody or control. 75 ALR3d 933.

Validity and construction of penal statute prohibiting child abuse. 1 ALR4th 38.

Circumstances warranting court-ordered medical treatment of minors. 24 AM JUR PROOF OF FACTS 2d 169.

p 21, n 18—Daly, Willful Child Abuse and State Reporting Statutes. 23 Miami L Rev 283.

—*Delete reference to* PARENT AND CHILD (1st ed §§ 102–121) *and insert:* DESERTION AND NONSUPPORT §§ 56–70.

p 22, n 19—*Delete reference to* PARENT AND CHILD (1st ed § 102) *and insert:* DESERTION AND NONSUPPORT § 64.

Custody or control of a child within meaning of penal statute punishing cruelty and neglect by one having such custody and control is not restricted in its application to those having legal custody; thus, jury question was presented whether a stepfather, standing in loco parentis, had custody of a child within meaning of the statute. Lovis v Commonwealth, 212 Va 848, 188 SE2d 206, cert den 407 US 922, 32 L Ed 2d 808, 92 S Ct 2469.

p 22, n 2—

See Re Green, 448 Pa 338, 292 A2d 387, 52 ALR3d 1106, later app 452 Pa 373, 307 A2d 279, holding, in an action seeking a declaration that a minor was a neglected child, that, as between a parent and the state, the state does not have an interest of sufficient magnitude outweighing a parent's religious beliefs when the child's life is not immediately imperiled by his physical condition.

Annotation: 52 ALR3d 1118 (superseding 30 ALR2d 1138).

p 22, n 3—

Annotation: Transplantation: power of parent, guardian, or committee to consent to surgical invasion of ward's person for benefit of another. 35 ALR3d 692.

p 22, n 6—People v Vandiver, 51 Ill 2d 525, 283 NE2d 681.

[42 Am Jur 2d Supp]

Statutes:

Child abuse prevention and treatment, see 42 USCS §§ 5101–5106.

Additional case authorities for section:

Court had power to order blood transfusion for infant where, although there was only incidental danger to life, there was, to reasonable medical certainty, immediate danger of irreparable brain damage and concomitant severe mental retardation if transfusion was withheld, notwithstanding that the child's parents, who were devout Jehovah's Witnesses, refused to permit such transfusion on religious grounds. Muhlenberg Hospital v Patterson, 128 NJ Super 498, 320 A2d 518.

A child abuse statute using the words "or inflicts unjustifiable physical pain or mental suffering . . . in a manner which is not ordinary and reasonable discipline and punishment" was unconstitutionally vague. State v Ballard (Ala Crim) 341 So 2d 957.

Where school doctor found oldest of three children to be suffering from hernia, cavities, and "fractured teeth" and where mother refused to permit medical or dental care of child or to permit medical or dental examination of other children on grounds of religious beliefs, court found neglect and ordered mental and dental examination of each child with further action be taken by court upon recipt of examinations. Re S, 85 Misc 2d 846, 380 NYS2d 620.

An order of the trial court assigning custody of five children ages 4 through 12 to a state family services agency as neglected children was supported by evidence showing that the children had been subject to beatings and had been forced to view sexual activity. Re State in interest of Young (La App) 342 So 2d 1205.

In action against mother for neglect of children in which court ordered medical examination, mother's refusal to permit medical or dental care for child with hernia, cavities, and fractured teeth was not constitutionally privileged despite mother's sincere religious belief that God would help children without assistance of doctors or dentists. Matter of Gregory F. (Misc) 380 NYS2d 620.

Under a state statute making it an offense for anyone having the care or custody of a child to place it in such situation that its person or health is endangered, the word "child" was not intended to refer to an unborn child. Accordingly, a pregnant woman who continued using heroin during the final two months of pregnancy and failed to seek prenatal care, despite warnings of a public health nurse that such conduct would endanger her unborn child, did not violate the statute even though the twin boys born to her were addicted to heroin and suffered withdrawal. The requirement of the statute that the offender must be a person "having the care or custody or [a] child," presupposes the existence of a living child susceptible to care or custody. Moreover, when the Legislature has intended to include a fetus or unborn child within the protection of a penal

15

Illustration E

Reference in *Am.Jur.2d* pocket part to annotated report of *Pope v. State of Maryland.*

or possible usefulness, of the new decision. Furthermore, the listing of all later citations under the Annotation's first page number did not help one who was interested in only one part of the Annotation's coverage.

There was an additional problem, this one involving the text of the annotations themselves. Because the text became inaccurate as the law changed, it was necessary to issue supplementary and superseding annotations. The *supplementary* annotation was written when new developments had rendered the original annotation incomplete or partially out-of-date. This *supplementary* annotation was to be read with the original Annotation to provide full coverage of the subject. A *superseding* annotation was written when the Annotation

457 **SUPPLEMENTAL DECISIONS** **130 ALR**

130 ALR 94–103

U. S.—**Prudential Ins. Co. v L. (DC Ala) 306 F Supp 1177**
Fla.—**Bannerman v B. (App) 204 So 2d 234**
Ga.—**Riley v R. 157 SE2d 285**
Ind.—S. ex rel. Knowles v E. C. C. 268 NE2d 79
La.—Tannehill v T. (App) 226 So 2d 185
N. M.—Davey v D. 422 P2d 38
N. Y.—Bohm v B. 37 App Div 2d 958, 326 NYS2d 534
N. C.—Little v L. (App) 183 SE 2d 278
Vt.—Gerdell v G. 313 A2d 8 (citing anno)

130 ALR 107–110

U. S.—Rochester Liederkranz, Inc. v U. S. (CA NY) 456 F2d 152
Augusta Golf Ass'n, Inc. v U. S. (DC Ga) 338 F Supp 272
Pittsburgh Press Club v U. S. (DC Pa) 388 Supp 1269

130 ALR 113–120

Superseded 63 ALR3d 780✦

130 ALR 130–134

La.—Mailhos v O. (App) 201 So 2d 108
Wis.—S. ex rel. Warren v N. 59 Wis 2d 391, 208 NW2d 780

130 ALR 139–147

Superseded 63 ALR2d 911✦

130 ALR 164–178

Supplemented 81 ALR2d 733✦

130 ALR 198–204

Supplemented 166 ALR 641✦

130 ALR 212–225

U. S.—Nash v U. S. 398 US 1, 26 L Ed 2d 1, 90 S Ct 1550.
Gustin v C. I.R. (CA6) 412 F2d 803
Farmers' and Merchants' Bank v U. S. (CA W Va) 476 F2d 406
Loventhal v U. S. (CA Tenn) 478 F2d 311
Riss v C. I. R. (CA8) 478 F2d 1160
Stratmore v U. S. (DC NJ) 292 F Supp 59

130 ALR 231–234

Cal.—Redke v S. (App) 93 Cal Rptr 898

130 ALR 239–245

Ark.—Southwestern Bell Tel. Co. v T. I. C. 479 SW2d 232

130 ALR 250–265

Supplemented 75 ALR2d 591✦

130 ALR 272–286

Supplemented in 132 ALR 1443✦

130 ALR 291–310

U. S.—Williams v W. (DC Tenn) 346 F Supp 1377
Ill.—Burnett v C. 7 Ill App 3d 266, 285 NE2d 619

Ind.—Moster v B. (App) 286 NE 2d 419
Mich.—P. v Thomas, 14 Mich App 642, 165 NW2d 879 (citing anno)
Pa.—Thompson v C. of P. (Super) 294 A2d 826

130 ALR 316–323

Cal.—City of Orange v V. 37 CA 3d 240, 112 Cal Rptr 379
Del.—M. v State, 293 A2d 287
Fla.—Henley v C. of C. C. (App) 292 So 2d 410
Coral Gables v W. (App) 305 So 2d 261
Ga.—Rhodes v B. (App) 156 SE 2d 545
Ill.—Schmeisser v N. (App) 251 NE2d 784
La.—Reed v A. (App) 212 So 2d 286
Department of Highways v C. (App) 298 So 2d 94
Me.—S. v Rush, 324 A2d 748
Md.—Richmond Corp. v B. of C. C. 255 A2d 398
Mass.—Shoppers' World, Inc. v B. T. R., Inc. 228 NE2d 446
C. v Protami, 236 NE2d 649
Mich.—Zrenchik v Z. B. of A. 15 Mich App 53, 166 NW2d 59
O'Keefe v Z. B. of A. 35 Mich App 583, 192 NW2d 509
Miss.—Yates v M. and C. of J. 244 So 2d 724
Mo.—**City of Kansas City v H. C. 499 SW2d 449**
Mont.—S. ex rel. Russell Center v C. of M. 533 P2d 1087
N. H.—**Scott v M. 242 A2d 58**
N. J.—J. D. Const. Corp. v B. of F. 119 NJ Super 140, 290 A2d 452
Kirylad v M. & C. of B. of E. (Super L) 131 NJ Super 461, 330 A2d 395
S. v Kligerman, 128 NJ Super 531, 320 A2d 536
N. Y.—Overhill Bldg. Co. v D. 28 NY2d 449, 322 NYS2d 696, 271 NE2d 537
Off Shore Rest. Corp. v L. 30 NY2d 160, 331 NYS2d 397, 282 NE2d 299
North Shore Steak House, Inc. v B. of A. 30 NY2d 238, 331 NYS2d 645, 282 NE2d 606
Suddell v Z. B. of A. 36 NY2d 312, 367 NYS2d 766, 327 NE2d 809
Tape Vee Corp. v T. B. of H. 55 Misc 2d 989, 287 NYS2d 590
Brush v Z. B. of A. 57 Misc 2d 751, 293 NYS2d 387
Comparato v K. 61 Misc 2d 245, 305 NYS2d 640
P. v G. N. I., Inc. 63 Misc 2d 583, 312 NYS2d 826
Ohio—12701 Shaker Blvd. Co. v C. 31 Ohio App 2d 199, 60 Ohio Ops 2d 324, 287 NE2d 814
Pa.—Gaebel v Z. H. B. of T. T. (Cmwlth) 285 A2d 218
Bidwell v Z. B. of A. (Cmwlth) 286 A2d 471
Goettler v Z. Bd. of A. of C. of B. (Cmwlth) 321 A2d 401
R. I.—Goodman v Z. Bd. of R. 254 A2d 743
Tex.—City of Spring Valley v S. B. T. Co. 484 SW2d 579
Wis.—Madison v M. 171 NW2d 426
Dane County v M. 198 NW2d 667

130 ALR 327–341

U. S.—See v S. 387 US 541, 18 L ed 2d 943, 87 S Ct 1737
First Nat. Bank v C. S. Co. 391 US 253, 20 L Ed 2d 569, 88 S Ct 1575
Southern Ry. Co. v L. (CA Ga) 403 F2d 119
Hartford Acc. & Indem. Co. v H. (DC Ga) 275 F Supp 610
Mich.—Cowles v E.-R. L. Co. (App) 176 NW2d 412
Mo.—S. ex rel. R. W. Filkey, Inc. v S. (App) 407 SW2d 79
Ohio—Mason v R. 35 Ohio App 2d 29, 64 Ohio Ops 2d 160, 300 NE2d 211 (citing anno)
Tex.—McGregor v G. 442 SW2d 751 (citing anno)

130 ALR 352–369

Supplemented 75 ALR2d 833✦

130 ALR 374–402

Supplemented 140 ALR 797✦

130 ALR 408–416

Supplemented 143 ALR 230, 144 ALR 1337 and 167 ALR 554✦

130 ALR 423–428

Cal.—A. A. Baxter Corp. v H. O. & L. 7 Cal App 3d 725, 86 Cal Rptr 854
E. D. McGillicuddy Constr. Co. v K. R. Asso. 31 Cal App 3d 891, 107 Cal Rptr 899
Associated Sand & Gravel Co. v D. P. 8 Wash App 938, 509 P2d 1020 (citing anno)
N. Y.—Country Village Heights Condominium (Group I) v M. B., Inc. 79 Misc 2d 1088, 363 NYS2d 501

130 ALR 436

Supplemented 7 ALR Fed 707✦

130 ALR 440–486

U. S.—**Jefferson-Travis, Inc. v G. E. M., Inc. (CA Pa) 393 F2d 426**
Bott v A. H. C. (CA Tex) 441 F2d 896
Prather v N. P., I. (CA Fla) 446 F2d 338
Duisen v F. S. H. No. 1 (DC Mo) 332 F Supp 125
Ala.—Hunter v S. 293 Ala 226, 301 So 2d 541
Ariz.—Re Bedwell's Estate, 454 P2d 985
Russell v I. C. 456 P2d 918
Enyart v I. C. (App) 458 P2d 514
Cal.—San Francisco v W. C. A. B. (Cal App) 77 Cal Rptr 427
Conn.—Morrisette v A. 31 Conn Supp 302, 329 A2d 622
Fla.—Houston v F. G. T. Co. (App) 192 So 2d 540
Walker v W. (App) 254 So 2d 832
Ga.—Webb v L. 133 Ga App 18, 209 SE2d 712
Hawaii—**Acoustic, Insulation & Drywall, Inc. v L. & I. R. A. Bd. 459 P2d 541**
Idaho—**Shell v S. O. Co. 461 P2d 265**
Ill.—Conness v C. (App) 236 NE 2d 753
Edwards v W. 313 NE2d 529 (citing anno)
Beletz v I. C. 246 NE2d 262

✦When Supplemented see later Note and Blue Book under caption of later Note

Illustration F

Sample page in *ALR Bluebook of Supplemental Decisions.*

had become so obsolete that an entirely new approach to the problem was needed. It then became necessary to warn researchers who were approaching the original Annotation that it had been supplemented or superseded. There was little point in using a *superseded* annotation, and to use one that had been supplemented could be quite misleading. The existence of a later supplementing or superseding Annotation is indicated in each Blue Book volume and in the annual paperback supplement.

2. ALR2d: LATER CASE SERVICE

The cumbersome nature of the *Blue Books* convinced the publisher that a better method of supplementation was needed for the new *ALR2d* series, which began in 1948. The *Blue Books* for *ALR1st* continue to be supplemented since *ALR1st* is still used occasionally, but a new supplementing device was created for *ALR2d,* the *Later Case Service.* Like the *ALR1st Blue Books,* the *Later Case Service* is a separate series of successive volumes, also arranged by volume and page of the Annotations, and providing citations to later cases and textual changes. The *Later Case Service,* however, instead of simply listing all new cases under the original Annotation's volume and page number, designates the later citations to particular sections of the original Annotation. It also includes a brief description of new case's holding, enabling one to determine if the new case is really relevant to the researcher's problem and to what section of the Annotation it relates. The *Later Case Service* indicates when the earlier Annotation has been supplemented or superseded. The service is now supplemented by annual pocket parts in the back of each volume. Illustration G shows a typical page in the *Later Case Service.*

3. ALR3d AND 4th: SUPPLEMENTS (POCKET PARTS)

While the *Later Case Service* represented a significant improvement over the *Blue Books,* it still forced the researcher to consult a separate set of books for supplementation, the volumes of which might be off the shelf when needed. For this reason, when *ALR3d* was started in 1965, another supplementing device was adopted. This approach continued to key the new cases to particular sections within the Annotation and to provide brief summaries of the cases' holdings but, instead of relying upon separate sets like the *Blue Books* or *Later Case Service* to convey this information, it substituted the pocket part method of supplementation. An annually revised pocket part in each volume of *ALR3d and 4th* supplements the contents of that volume. Now the researcher who locates an Annotation need only turn to the pocket part at the back of the volume to find new cases keyed to that Annotation. Illustration H shows the opening page from a pocket part in *ALR4th.*

son. Robertson v Devereaux, 32 **Mich** App 85, 188 NW2d 209.

94 ALR2d 1161–1165

Preferential treatment as respects seniority of replacement or nonstriking employees, or returning strikers, as unfair labor practice.

§ 2. Conduct held unfair labor practice, p. 1162.

If, after the conclusion of a strike, the employer refuses to reinstate striking employees, the effect is to discourage employees from exercising their rights to organize and strike guaranteed by §§ 7 and 13 of the amended National Labor Relations Act (29 USC §§ 157 and 163); hence, unless an employer who refuses to reinstate strikers can show that his action was due to legitimate and substantial business justifications, he is guilty of an unfair labor practice. NLRB v Fleetwood Trailer Co. 389 **US** 375, 19 L Ed 2d 614, 88 S Ct 543, holding further that the right of unreplaced economic strikers to reinstatement does not expire on the day they first apply for reinstatement, but continues until they have obtained other regular and substantially equivalent employment, absent the employer's showing legitimate and substantial business justification for refusing reinstatement.

Insistence by employer during bargaining negotiations followed by strike on superseniority provision for replacement of strikers to point of impasse constituted unfair labor practice. Philip Carey Mfg. Co., Miami Cabinet Div. v NLRB (CA6) 331 **F2d** 720, cert den 379 **US** 888, 13 L Ed 2d 92, 85 S Ct 159.

Superseniority provisions imposed by company after settlement of strike, giving preference to replacements and employees who worked during strike, were discriminatory on their face and constituted unfair labor practice, even though they were embodied in collective agreements entered into by union and employer after strike. Great Lakes Carbon Corp. v NLRB (CA4) 360 **F2d** 19.

An offer of reinstatement which excluded seniority rights where the proposal was to create "new jobs" for returning employees, thus making it clear that the employees would have to return as new employees, is not an offer of substantially equivalent employment and is an unfair labor practice and hence strikers entitled to back pay from day after offers to return to work were received by employer until day of reinstatement or day work made available to them. NLRB v Hilton Mobile Homes (CA8) 387 **F2d** 7.

Refusal of employer to reinstate returning female strikers as knitters, thereby placing them at bottom of seniority list, constituted unfair labor practice, as did failure to assign certain strikers to preferential work they had previously done and which had always been awarded on basis of seniority. Oneita Knitting Mills, Inc. v NLRB (CA4) 375 **F2d** 385.

Offer of superseniority to strike replacement workers was unfair labor practice and had aspects of continuing inducement, but such offer could be effectively withdrawn and its original effect completely dissipated as unlawful influence on an election. NLRB v Lawrence Typographical Union No. 570 (CA10) 402 **F2d** 452.

Failure to accord returning strikers full and complete reinstatement was discriminatory and unlawful where employer in effect treated them as new employees by informing them that because of "new law," they would have to fill out application forms, would not be covered by insurance for 30 days, and would lose seniority and vacation benefits. C. H. Guenther & Son, Inc. v NLRB (CA5 Tex) 427 **F2d** 983, cert den 400 **US** 942, 27 L Ed 2d 246, 91 S Ct 240.

Strikers recalled as "temporary" employees, but assigned same jobs under same conditions they held before strike, were, in absence of any substantial business justification by employer for considering them temporary, regular employees and were entitled to full reinstatement rights, including seniority. NLRB v Duncan Foundry & Machine Works, Inc. (CA7 Ill) 435 **F2d** 612.

Employer's practice of laying off reinstated economic strikers as a group ahead of replacements was unfair labor practice; reinstated strikers could not be treated as new employees. NLRB v Transport Co. of Texas (CA5) 438 **F2d** 258.

Employer's insistence upon super-seniority for strike replacements constituted refusal to bargain and converted existing economic strike into unfair labor practice strike. Rogers Mfg. Co. v NLRB (CA6) 486 **F2d** 644, cert den 416 **US** 937, 40 L Ed 2d 288, 94 S Ct 1937.

Employer violated § 8(a)(3) of NLRA by rehiring two economic strikers, who had been replaced during strike, as new employees, meaning that they lost their pre-strike seniority. NLRB v Anvil Products, Inc. (CA5 Tex) 496 **F2d** 94.

Where 18 employees repeatedly engaged in illegal picketing during strike they forfeited

Illustration G

Sample page from *Later Case Service* to *ALR2d.*

AMERICAN LAW REPORTS

FOURTH SERIES

1982 Supplement

VOLUME 1 ALR4th

1 ALR4th 38–104

§ 4. Vagueness, indefiniteness, or overbreadth; due process:

[a] Validity upheld

Also holding penal statute prohibiting child abuse not to be unconstitutionally vague or indefinite, or overbroad:

Colo—People v Taggart (1981, Colo) 621 P2d 1375.

Fla—Mahaun v State (1979, Fla) 377 So 2d 1158.

Ohio—State v Daniels (1980) 61 Ohio St 2d 220, 15 Ohio Ops 3d 232, 400 NE2d 399, cert den (US) 66 L Ed 2d 63, 101 S Ct 142.

Statute prohibiting child abuse by contributing to delinquency or dependency of minors is not unconstitutionally vague and overbroad. Purvis v State (1979, **Fla**) 377 So 2d 674.

§ 5. Equal protection; discrimination; class legislation:

Legislative classification of child abuse as crime more serious in penalty than offense of criminally negligent homicide was neither arbitrary nor unreasonable and did not violate right to equal protection of laws where child abuse statute proscribed conduct particularly abusive to children and negligent homicide statute proscribed in general terms gross carelessness that causes death to any individual. People v Taggart (1981, **Colo**) 621 P2d 1375.

§ 8. —Particular terms:

[b] —As determined by age and other criteria

Under child molesting statute which explicitly provided accused a defense if he or she reasonably believed that child was 16 years of age or older at time of conduct, evidence was sufficient to support finding that defendant did not reasonably believe 12-year-old victim was 16 years of age or older where defense was misidentification and defendant failed to introduce any evidence concerning belief by him that victim was 16 years of age or older, and where victim appeared in court and testified, her appearance in itself evidence that trier of fact could weigh as determinative of such issue. Neblett v State (1979, **Ind** App) 396 NE2d 930.

§ 11. Necessity or materiality of wrongful mental attitude:

[a] Required

Also holding that a wrongful mental attitude was required to sustain a conviction for child abuse under the penal statutes involved:

Ga—Brewer v State (1980) 156 Ga App 468, 274 SE2d 817 ("wilfulness").

[b] Not required

Also holding or implying that it was not necessary, to sustain a conviction under the child abuse statute involved, to show that the accused's acts were done with a wrongful mental attitude:

Colo—People v Hoehl (1980, Colo App) 629 P2d 1083.

§ 12. Conduct prohibited by statute—generally:

[a] Intentional or nonaccidental abuse

Defendant's conduct constituted "intentional or criminally negligent mistreatment" of her child where evidence showed that defendant either deliberately filled bathtub with hot water and then held her son in tub to punish him, or that she carelessly allowed water to become scalding and then held him in tub, and defendant's conviction for cruelty

3

Illustration H

Supplement to 1 *ALR4th* (pocket part) showing updating of Annotation to *Pope v. State of Maryland.*

4. ANNOTATION HISTORY TABLE

The new method of pocket part supplementation did not solve the problem of keeping track of changes in the text of Annotations by later supplementing or superseding Annotations. A new device, the *Annotation History Table,* appears in the *ALR3d and 4th Quick Index* and, for *ALR Federal,* has recently been added to the pocket part of the *ALR Federal Tables* volume. The *Annotation History Table* provides updating information about the annotations contained in *ALR2d, 3d, 4th* and *ALR Federal.* It directs the researcher to Annotations which supersede or supplement those in the designated series. The pocket part of this *Quick Index* supplements both the *Annotation History Table,* and the *Index.* Before reading *any* annotation in *ALR,* particularly one in the earlier series, one should check this Table to be certain the annotation has not been superseded or supplemented. To find supplementing or superseding Annotations for those in *ALR1st,* unfortunately one must still use the *ALR Blue Book of Supplemental Decisions.* Illustration I shows a typical page from an *Annotation History Table.*

The Index to Annotations in *Lawyers' Edition* has an *Annotation History Table* for annotations in that reporter for the U.S. Supreme Court.

G. SUMMARY

The annotated reports system of Lawyers Co-op in its various series can be a very useful research tool for many legal problems. However, their annotations are not law, but only secondary source material. Annotations therefore should not be cited as authority and, in giving the citation to a case, the annotated report citation should *follow* the official citation. It is generally inadvisable to quote from the text of an *ALR* Annotation in a brief or argument, because it is not considered an authoritative text. The annotations are, however, usually well done and reliable, and do provide many references to primary source material and a synthesis of cases in its narrative text. For many researchers it is a preferred tool for case finding, more thorough than an encyclopedia article and more readable than a digest. However, not every topic is covered by an Annotation and therein lies one of the shortcomings of that system.

Illustration J, which follows on pages 96–97, graphically summarizes the primary components of the annotated reporting system.

HISTORICAL TABLE

92 ALR2d 421–459
§ 21 superseded 80 ALR3d 1280

93 ALR2d 313–333
Superseded 89 ALR3d 32

94 ALR2d 221–266
§§ 9–13 Superseded 97 ALR3d 1270

94 ALR2d 1087–1099
Superseded 63 ALR3d 311
Superseded 83 ALR3d 749
Superseded 83 ALR3d 777

94 ALR2d 1237–1241
§ 3 Superseded 97 ALR3d 347

94 ALR2d 1417–1422
Superseded 27 ALR Fed 780

94 ALR2d 1431–1450
§§ 5, 8 Superseded 95 ALR3d 203

95 ALR2d 1217–1226
Superseded 12 ALR3d 1064

97 ALR2d 1125–1135
§ 5 Superseded 94 ALR3d 63

97 ALR2d 1283–1314
§ 8 superseded 57 ALR3d 172

98 ALR2d 488–503
§§ 2–6 superseded 44 ALR3d 797

98 ALR2d 527–530
Superseded 87 ALR3d 571

98 ALR2d 537–538
Superseded 94 ALR3d 1188

99 ALR2d 599–627
§ 14[a, b,] superseded 94 ALR3d 317

99 ALR2d 1016–1060
§ 29 Superseded 35 ALR Fed 481
§§ 16, 21–23, and 30–31 Superseded 36 ALR Fed 240

99 ALR2d 1016–1060
§ 20 Superseded 46 ALR Fed 24
Superseded 37 ALR Fed 537

100 ALR2d 177–217
Superseded 44 ALR Fed 363
Superseded 97 ALR3d 96 & 44 ALR Fed 468

100 ALR2d 1057–1063
Superseded 95 ALR3d 449

2 ALR3d 1151–1202
§ 9 superseded 23 ALR3d 932

5 ALR3d 1214–1235
§ 3[d] Superseded 93 ALR3d 297

7 ALR3d 591–600
Superseded 99 ALR3d 37

7 ALR3d 732–741
Superseded 29 ALR Fed 353

8 ALR3d 916–924
Superseded 93 ALR3d 472

11 ALR3d 1231–1240
Superseded 30 ALR3d 9

13 ALR3d 1057–1103
§ 10[e] superseded 52 ALR3d 121
§ 11 superseded 46 ALR3d 240

14 ALR3d 330–355
§ 5 superseded 46 ALR Fed 657

15 ALR3d 992–1007
Superseded 84 ALR3d 411

15 ALR3d 1428–1431
Superseded 92 ALR3d 9

17 ALR3d 1010–1149
§ 14 Superseded 91 ALR3d 1237
§ 16 Superseded 96 ALR3d 1275
§ 26 superseded 73 ALR3d 248
§ 29.2 superseded 66 ALR3d 190
§ 36[a] Superseded 90 ALR3d 1141
§ 37 Superseded 98 ALR3d 586
§ 40[a] Superseded 98 ALR3d 1183
§ 46 Superseded 96 ALR3d 299
§ 58 superseded 93 ALR3d 584
§ 59[c] Superseded 88 ALR3d 416
§§ 59(e) & 59(f) Superseded 97 ALR3d 908

18 ALR3d 1376–1402
§ 11(b) Superseded 97 ALR3d 714

21 ALR3d 964
§ 3[a] Superseded 88 ALR3d 949

22 ALR3d 1112–1127
§§ 6 and 8 superseded 71 ALR3d 1000
Superseded 83 ALR3d 15

22 ALR3d 1441–1448
Superseded 83 ALR3d 15

23 ALR3d 932–1013
§ 11 superseded 97 ALR3d 798

§ 23 superseded 97 ALR3d 1114
§ 29[a–c] superseded 78 ALR3d 1020
§§ 32b and 35 superseded 67 ALR3d 144
Superseded 88 ALR3d 1100

29 ALR3d 1407–1415
§ 3 superseded 24 ALR Fed 808
Superseded 96 ALR3d 195 & 24 ALR Fed 808
§§ 3[a], 3[b], 3[g], 3[i] superseded 100 ALR3d 1205

29 ALR3d 1425–1430
§§ 3[a], 3[b], 3[g], 3[i] Superseded 100 ALR3d 1205

30 ALR3d 9–120
§ 6 superseded 76 ALR3d 11
§ 19[c] Superseded 99 ALR3d 807 & 99 ALR3d 1080
§ 29 superseded 69 ALR3d 1162

30 ALR3d 203–283
§ 18 superseded 46 ALR3d 900

42 ALR3d 560–588
§ 8 Superseded 96 ALR3d 265

47 ALR3d 1286–1288
Superseded 81 ALR3d 1119
Superseded 83 ALR3d 777
Superseded 83 ALR3d 749

49 ALR3d 915–924
Superseded 97 ALR3d 294

53 ALR3d 1285–1290
Superseded 97 ALR3d 528

55 ALR3d 581–614
§ 9[c,d] Superseded 86 ALR3d 1116

62 ALR3d 1243–1265
Superseded 88 ALR3d 1064
§ 19[d] Superseded 100 ALR3d 10
§ 16 Superseded 100 ALR3d 940

67 ALR3d 308–323
§ 19[d] Superseded 100 ALR3d 10
§ 16 Superseded 100 ALR3d A940

75 ALR3d 751–754
Superseded 77 ALR3d 1349

75 ALR3d 1000–1016
Superseded 77 ALR3d 1363

Consult POCKET PART for later history **1433**

Illustration I

Sample page of "Annotation Historical Table" in ALR3d and 4th Quick Index volume.

THE ANNOTATED

	UNITED STATES SUPREME COURT REPORTS LAWYERS' EDITION		AMERIC
LAW FINDERS	Federal Quick Index, Third Edition Alternates: US L Ed Index to Annotations - 1 vol. US L Ed Digest - 20 vols. (34 books) USCS Am Jur 2d Fed Proc, L Ed	US L Ed 2d Desk Book Auto-Cite	ALR Quick Index Alternates: Word Index - 4 vols. Digest - 12 vols. Am Jur 2d
THE LAW	US L Ed UNITED STATES SUPREME COURT REPORTS LAWYERS' EDITION First Series 1789–1956 Vols. 1–100	US L Ed 2d Second Series 1956–Present Vols. 1–	ALR AMERICAN First Series 1919–1948 Vols. 1–175
UPDATING TOOLS	US L Ed Annotation History Table located in back of US L Ed Index to Annotations		ALR 3d, AL
	US L Ed First Series Annotations supplemented as required only through later annotations	Vols. 1–31 of US L Ed 2d supplemented by single Later Case Service volume which itself is supplemented annually; Vols. 32 et seq, annually supplemented by pocket parts for each volume	ALR Blue Book of Supplemental Decisions 5 Volumes plus Paperback Supp. published annually

Law School Department
THE LAWYERS CO-OPERATIVE PUBLISHING CO.
BANCROFT-WHITNEY CO.
Rochester, New York 14694

Illustration J

REPORTS SYSTEM

AN LAW REPORTS ANNOTATED (ALR)

A Quick Command Of All Case Law in Point
With Additional References To Law Reviews And Other Legal Authority

ALR 2d Quick Index	ALR 3d-4th Quick Index (Supplemented by Paperback in hardbound ALR 3d Quick Index Volume)		Federal Quick Index, Third Edition (Supplemented by Paperback from vol. 48–)
Alternates: ALR 2d Word Index – 3 vols. ALR 2d Digest – 7 vols. Am Jur 2d Fed Proc, L Ed Auto-Cite	Alternates: Am Jur 2d Fed Proc, L Ed Auto-Cite	Alternates: Am Jur 2d Fed Proc, L Ed Auto-Cite	Alternates: Am Jur 2d Fed Proc, L Ed L Ed 2d Desk Book Auto-Cite
ALR 2d	ALR 3d	ALR 4th	ALR Fed

LAW REPORTS ANNOTATED

Since the publication in 1969 of 1 ALR Fed, annotations based on questions of Federal law are covered in ALR Federal. Prior to this, such annotations are covered in ALR, ALR 2d and vols 1 thru 27 of ALR 3d.

Second Series 1948–1965 Vols. 1–100	Third Series 1965–1980 Vols. 1–100	Fourth Series 1980–Present Vols. 1–	ALR Federal 1969–Present Vols. 1–
Annotation History Table for ALR, ALR 2d, R 4th, ALR Fed (located in the back of ALR 3d-4th Quick Index)			Separate Annotation History Table for ALR Fed located in ALR Fed Tables Volume
ALR 2d Later Case Service 21 Volumes Supplemented on an annual basis by pocket parts	ALR 3d Pocket Part Supps. Published annually for each volume	ALR 4th Pocket Part Supps. Published annually for each volume	ALR Fed Pocket Part Supps. Published annually for each volume

January 1983

Illustration J (continued)

Chapter 5

CASE FINDING

- A. Introduction.
- B. West Digests.
  - 1. American Digest System: Overview.
    - a. *General Digest.*
    - b. *Decennial Digests.*
    - c. *Century Digest.*
  - 2. West's Jurisdictional Digests.
    - a. *U.S. Supreme Court Digest.*
    - b. Federal Digests.
    - c. Regional Digests.
    - d. State Digests.
    - e. Specialized Digests.
  - 3. Locating Cases in the West Digests.
    - a. Starting With a Case.
    - b. The Index Search.
    - c. The Topic Method.
    - d. Caveats.
- C. Case Finding in Annotated Reports.
  - 1. *U.S. Supreme Court Digest, Lawyers' Edition.*
  - 2. *A.L.R. Digests.*
  - 3. *Quick Indexes.*
  - 4. The Annotation.
- D. Other Case Finding Tools.
  - 1. *Words and Phrases.*
  - 2. Popular Name Tables.
  - 3. Annotated Statutes.
  - 4. Shepard's.
    - a. Citators as Case Finders.
    - b. Shepard's Locators.
- E. Secondary Materials.
  - 1. Encyclopedias.
  - 2. Treatises and Periodicals.
  - 3. Looseleaf Services.
- F. Computer Research Services.
  - 1. Contents.
  - 2. Search Strategy.
  - 3. Integrating Manual and Computerized Research.
- G. Summary.

A. INTRODUCTION

Having described in Chapters 2 to 4 court reports and their varied forms of publication, we turn now to the several research methods and tools actually employed in locating judicial decisions, a process generally called *case-finding*. It is the purpose of this chapter to describe how the researcher can identify decisions relevant to a particular legal issue, or locate a specific case by its name, subject, or points of law. Since much of legal research involves the search for relevant judicial precedents, case-finding is a very important research skill.

The classic movie "Anatomy of a Murder" features a scene in which one of the defense attorneys, who is hoping to bolster an insanity defense in a murder trial, paces excitedly around a law library, then spins on his heel and snatches a book from a shelf, seemingly guided only by instinct. Opening it, he finds a case in point, and exclaims in joy. This apparently casual approach may be possible in searching for a crucial case, but when one considers that there are over three million reported decisions available for perusal, with some 50,000 new decisions being added every year to the corpus of American law,[1] the use of more systematic search techniques is clearly necessary.

Fortunately, the research apparatus of American law includes a finely developed, wide-ranging infrastructure of research tools specifically designed for case-finding, and a variety of other sources which can also be used for this purpose. There are at least three major approaches for locating decisions by subject or name. The first of these is the traditional case digest method with all of its sub-systems and related publications; the second are the computerized legal research systems; and the third approach is the use of secondary source materials. This chapter will explore the traditional case finding methods in some detail. It will also treat the use of computer data bases and secondary sources more briefly, since these methods will be explained in other chapters of the book.

It must be emphasized at the outset that there are a great variety of case-finding methods and that no *one* approach can be recommended for *all* situations. Some are clearly preferable for certain types of searches, while for other searches one can reasonably choose from a number of alternative approaches, or utilize a combination of these alternatives.

1. The 1980 Annual Report of the Director of the Administrative Office of the United States Courts shows that, at the end of the 1979–1980 reporting year, there were 20,252 appeals pending in the U.S. Courts of Appeals alone, and that 168,789 civil cases had been commenced in the District Courts in the preceding twelve months.

B. WEST DIGESTS

1. AMERICAN DIGEST SYSTEM: OVERVIEW

The most well-developed and probably still the most widely used method of case location is the one developed by the West Publishing Company.

John West's research scheme did not end with the systematic reporting of appellate court decisions from all jurisdictions, as described in Chapters 2 and 3. In order to facilitate access to the growing volume of reported decisions, he devised a digesting system which was based on a subject classification of the legal and factual issues dealt with in the published decisions. Although the decades have seen modifications in approach and style, a general characterization of the system can be stated quite simply.

West divided all foreseeable legal situations into seven major categories: Persons; Property; Contracts; Torts; Crimes; Remedies; and Government. These seven areas were then subdivided into more than 400 individual legal topics. Each of the topics was then further subdivided into sub-topics, and even narrower refinement, with each of the resulting sub-topics assigned a classification number, which West called a "key number". Some of the larger or more complex topics had thousands of key numbers for their numerous sub-topics and finer subdivisions, while smaller topics had only a few. West thereby created a subject framework that sought to provide a particular topic and a key number subdivision to cover *every* conceivable legal situation that could be treated in a case. To some observers, this was an impressive effort of enormous intellectual import for American jurisprudence, while to others it represented an oversimplification and potential distortion of the legal universe.

Illustrations A and A–1 show the seven major divisions and their logical breakdown into the more than 400 individual topics. Another list in each West digest provides a complete alphabetical arrangement of the major topics. The topics vary widely in scope (e.g. from the very broad "Criminal Law" to the relatively narrow "Fish") and in current importance (e.g. from "Blasphemy" to "Social Security and Public Welfare"). The test of any system is its utility, and the fact is that the subject structure created by West around the turn of the century not only survives, but is still relatively effective and is widely used today. West periodically adds new subdivisions within a topic and creates new topics, as needed, but for the most part West's original divisions have been maintained.[2] Illustration B shows a preliminary page in the first volume of the *8th Decennial Digest* listing the new and revised topics in that unit of the American Digest System.

2. Although West continues to adapt this scheme to the changing law, some claim the changes are too slow and too cautious. Since the issuance of the last Decennial Digest (8th) in 1976, 25 new or revised topics have been added to the structure. Obviously changes cannot be made casually or too frequently in a system so large and complex.

OUTLINE OF THE LAW

Digest Topics arranged for your convenience by Seven Main Divisions of Law

1. PERSONS
2. PROPERTY
3. CONTRACTS
4. TORTS
5. CRIMES
6. REMEDIES
7. GOVERNMENT

1. PERSONS

RELATING TO NATURAL PERSONS IN GENERAL

Civil Rights
Dead Bodies
Death
Domicile
Drugs and Narcotics
Food
Health and Environment
Holidays
Intoxicating Liquors
Names
Poisons
Seals
Signatures
Sunday
Time
Weapons

PARTICULAR CLASSES OF NATURAL PERSONS

Absentees
Aliens
Chemical Dependents
Citizens
Convicts
Illegitimate Children
Indians
Infants
Mental Health
Paupers
Slaves
Spendthrifts

PERSONAL RELATIONS

Adoption
Attorney and Client
Employers' Liability
Executors and Administrators
Guardian and Ward
Husband and Wife
Labor Relations
Marriage
Master and Servant
Parent and Child
Principal and Agent
Workers' Compensation

ASSOCIATED AND ARTIFICIAL PERSONS

Associations
Beneficial Associations
Building and Loan Associations
Clubs
Colleges and Universities
Corporations
Exchanges
Joint-Stock Companies and Business Trusts
Partnership
Religious Societies

PARTICULAR OCCUPATIONS

Accountants
Agriculture
Auctions and Auctioneers
Aviation
Banks and Banking
Bridges
Brokers
Canals
Carriers
Commerce
Consumer Credit
Consumer Protection
Credit Reporting Agencies
Detectives
Electricity
Explosives
Factors
Ferries
Gas
Hawkers and Peddlers
Innkeepers
Insurance
Licenses
Manufactures
Monopolies
Physicians and Surgeons
Pilots
Railroads
Seamen
Shipping
Steam
Telecommunications
Theaters and Shows
Towage
Turnpikes and Toll Roads
Urban Railroads
Warehousemen
Wharves

2. PROPERTY

NATURE, SUBJECTS, AND INCIDENTS OF OWNERSHIP IN GENERAL

Abandoned and Lost Property
Accession
Adjoining Landowners
Confusion of Goods
Improvements
Property

PARTICULAR SUBJECTS AND INCIDENTS OF OWNERSHIP

Animals
Annuities
Automobiles
Boundaries
Cemeteries
Common Lands
Copyrights and Intellectual Property
Crops
Fences
Fish
Fixtures
Franchises
Game
Good Will
Logs and Logging
Mines and Minerals
Navigable Waters
Party Walls
Patents
Public Lands
Trade Regulation
Waters and Water Courses
Woods and Forests

PARTICULAR CLASSES OF ESTATES OR INTERESTS IN PROPERTY

Charities
Condominium
Dower and Curtesy
Easements
Estates in Property
Joint Tenancy
Landlord and Tenant
Life Estates
Perpetuities
Powers
Remainders
Reversions
Tenancy in Common
Trusts

PARTICULAR MODES OF ACQUIRING OR TRANSFERRING PROPERTY

Abstracts of Title
Adverse Possession
Alteration of Instruments
Assignments
Chattel Mortgages
Conversion
Dedication
Deeds
Descent and Distribution
Escheat
Fraudulent Conveyances
Gifts
Lost Instruments
Mortgages
Pledges
Secured Transactions
Wills

3. CONTRACTS

NATURE, REQUISITES, AND INCIDENTS OF AGREEMENTS IN GENERAL

Contracts
Customs and Usages
Frauds, Statute of
Interest
Usury

PARTICULAR CLASSES OF AGREEMENTS

Bailment
Bills and Notes
Bonds
Breach of Marriage Promise
Champerty and Maintenance
Compromise and Settlement
Covenants
Deposits and Escrows
Exchange of Property
Gaming
Guaranty
Implied and Constructive Contracts
Indemnity
Joint Adventures
Lotteries
Principal and Surety
Rewards
Sales
Subscriptions
Vendor and Purchaser

PARTICULAR CLASSES OF IMPLIED OR CONSTRUCTIVE CONTRACTS OR QUASI CONTRACTS

Account Stated
Contribution

PARTICULAR MODES OF DISCHARGING CONTRACTS

Novation
Payment
Release
Subrogation
Tender

4. TORTS

Assault and Battery
Collision
Conspiracy
False Imprisonment
Forcible Entry and Detainer

Illustration A

Fraud
Libel and Slander
Malicious Prosecution
Negligence
Nuisance
Products Liability
Seduction
Torts
Trespass
Trover and Conversion
Waste

5. CRIMES

Abduction
Abortion and Birth Control
Adulteration
Adultery
Affray
Arson
Bigamy
Blasphemy
Breach of the Peace
Bribery
Burglary
Common Scold
Compounding Offenses
Counterfeiting
Criminal Law
Disorderly Conduct
Disorderly House
Disturbance of Public Assemblage
Dueling
Embezzlement
Embracery
Escape
Extortion and Threats
False Personation
False Pretenses
Fires
Forgery
Fornication
Homicide
Incest
Insurrection and Sedition
Kidnapping
Larceny
Lewdness
Malicious Mischief
Mayhem
Miscegenation
Neutrality Laws
Obscenity
Obstructing Justice
Perjury
Piracy
Prize Fighting
Prostitution
Rape
Receiving Stolen Goods
Rescue
Riot
Robbery
Sodomy
Suicide
Treason
Unlawful Assembly
Vagrancy

6. REMEDIES

REMEDIES BY ACT OR AGREEMENT OF PARTIES

Accord and Satisfaction
Arbitration
Submission of Controversy

REMEDIES BY POSSESSION OR NOTICE

Liens
Lis Pendens
Maritime Liens
Mechanics' Liens
Notice
Salvage

MEANS AND METHODS OF PROOF

Acknowledgment
Affidavits
Estoppel
Evidence
Oath
Records
Witnesses

CIVIL ACTIONS IN GENERAL

Action
Declaratory Judgment
Election of Remedies
Limitation of Actions
Parties
Set-Off and Counterclaim
Venue

PARTICULAR PROCEEDINGS IN CIVIL ACTIONS

Abatement and Revival
Appearance
Costs
Damages
Execution
Exemptions
Homestead
Judgment
Jury
Motions
Pleading
Process
Reference
Stipulations
Trial

PARTICULAR REMEDIES INCIDENT TO CIVIL ACTIONS

Arrest
Assistance, Writ of
Attachment
Bail
Deposits in Court
Garnishment
Injunction
Judicial Sales
Ne Exeat
Pretrial Procedure
Receivers
Recognizances
Sequestration
Undertakings

PARTICULAR MODES OF REVIEW IN CIVIL ACTIONS

Appeal and Error
Audita Querela
Certiorari
Exceptions, Bill of
New Trial
Review

ACTIONS TO ESTABLISH OWNERSHIP OR RECOVER POSSESSION OF SPECIFIC PROPERTY

Detinue
Ejectment
Entry, Writ of
Interpleader
Possessory Warrant
Quieting Title
Real Actions
Replevin
Trespass to Try Title

FORMS OF ACTIONS FOR DEBTS OR DAMAGES

Account, Action on
Action on the Case
Assumpsit, Action of
Covenant, Action of
Debt, Action of

ACTIONS FOR PARTICULAR FORMS OR SPECIAL RELIEF

Account
Cancellation of Instruments
Debtor and Creditor
Divorce
Partition
Reformation of Instruments
Specific Performance

CIVIL PROCEEDINGS OTHER THAN ACTIONS

Habeas Corpus
Mandamus
Prohibition
Quo Warranto
Scire Facias
Supersedeas

SPECIAL CIVIL JURISDICTIONS AND PROCEDURE THEREIN

Admiralty
Bankruptcy
Equity
Federal Civil Procedure

PROCEEDINGS PECULIAR TO CRIMINAL CASES

Extradition and Detainers
Fines
Forfeitures
Grand Jury
Indictment and Information
Pardon and Parole
Penalties
Searches and Seizures

7. GOVERNMENT

POLITICAL BODIES AND DIVISIONS

Counties
District of Columbia
Municipal Corporations
States
Territories
Towns
United States

SYSTEMS AND SOURCES OF LAW

Administrative Law and Procedure
Common Law
Constitutional Law
International Law
Parliamentary Law
Statutes
Treaties

LEGISLATIVE AND EXECUTIVE POWERS AND FUNCTIONS

Bounties
Census
Customs Duties
Drains
Eminent Domain
Highways
Inspection
Internal Revenue
Levees and Flood Control
Pensions
Post Office
Private Roads
Public Contracts
Public Service Commissions
Schools
Securities Regulation
Social Security and Public Welfare
Taxation
Weights and Measures
Zoning and Planning

JUDICIAL POWERS AND FUNCTIONS, AND COURTS AND THEIR OFFICERS

Amicus Curiae
Clerks of Courts
Contempt
Court Commissioners
Courts
Federal Courts
Judges
Justices of the Peace
Removal of Cases
Reports
United States Magistrates

CIVIL SERVICE, OFFICERS, AND INSTITUTIONS

Ambassadors and Consuls
Asylums
Attorney General
Coroners
District and Prosecuting Attorneys
Elections
Hospitals
Newspapers
Notaries
Officers and Public Employees
Prisons
Reformatories
Registers of Deeds
Sheriffs and Constables
United States Marshals

MILITARY AND NAVAL SERVICE AND WAR

Armed Services
Military Justice
Militia
War and National Emergency

Illustration A–1

WEST'S
EIGHTH DECENNIAL DIGEST

This is the eighth unit of the American Digest System employing the unique KEY NUMBER classification, universally recognized as the standard classification of American case law.

The period covered by this Decennial has seen many important additions to the ever-expanding body of decisional law.

The result of this growth has been the continued refinement of the KEY NUMBER classification system by the editorial development of numerous expanded key lines to accommodate the volume of new material and changes in case law. In addition, the following new and revised topics have been developed and are included in this Eighth Decennial Digest:

ARBITRATION
CIVIL RIGHTS
DRUGS AND NARCOTICS
FEDERAL COURTS
PRETRIAL PROCEDURE
PRODUCTS LIABILITY
PUBLIC CONTRACTS
SECURITIES REGULATION
SOCIAL SECURITY AND PUBLIC WELFARE
TAXATION

Research is facilitated by references to **Corpus Juris Secundum,** America's great law encyclopedia, which appear under those KEY NUMBERS for which the decade produced no case references, and which direct the researcher to a comprehensive discussion of the subject.

A **Descriptive Word Index,** the "starting point of research," is included in West's Eighth Decennial Digest. It indexes the facts as well as the law of the cases covered by this digest, and is an indispensable guide to cases dealing with similar facts and legal principles.

The **Table of Cases** lists all decisions reported during the period, showing the title and citation, as well as the Digest topic and KEY NUMBER for each point of law drawn from the opinion. Additionally, the **Table of Cases** includes the case history of each decision, where such information was available at the time the Table was prepared, enabling the researcher to determine at a glance any action affecting the decision taken by the Courts subsequent to its rendition. Subsequent case history information will be set out in the Table of Cases Affirmed, Reversed or Modified, of the General Digest, Fifth Series.

THE PUBLISHER

February, 1977

III *

Illustration B

List of topics added or revised in the 8th *Decennial Digest.*

Thus, West has produced and continues to publish two interlocking, comprehensive services: a system of case reporting which contains the full text of appellate decisions from state and federal courts, and a digest structure providing for the classification, and later retrieval, by subject, of the points of law determined in judicial decisions reported by West. The combination theoretically allows a researcher to locate the text of published decisions from any American jurisdiction on any topic.

The digest system is most easily understood by examining how it is constructed.

The decisions to be published are collected by West, and read by its editorial staff. *Each* of the legal issues treated by the decisions is identified, summarized, and assigned a topic and sub-topic key number from the West classification system. These summaries or abstracts, with their topics and key numbers, are then placed in separate headnotes printed at the beginning of the published opinions. As discussed in an earlier chapter, a syllabus and headnotes, prepared either by the official court reporter or by an editor at a commercial publisher, appear in many reporters. Each of the West headnotes is assigned a West topic and key number, for later incorporation into the West digest system. By having the points of law in each published decision classified into the same subject scheme, a highly effective case finding mechanism is created, spanning decades in time and covering all American federal and state jurisdictions. When a researcher locates a case in which a relevant point of law is discussed, the West headnotes in that published decision can be scanned to identify the topic and key numbers assigned to that point of law. These topics and key numbers can then be used as locators in the appropriate West digest to find other decisions from all West reporters on the same issues. Illustration C contains examples of headnotes written by West's editors for one of its published decisions. Note that each headnote has a topic and key number assigned to it.

West first publishes its reported decisions in an advance sheet for each reporter series. These advance sheets contain a section entitled "Key Number Digests", which arranges the headnote abstracts of each of the cases included, by the topics and key numbers assigned to them in the West report. Each West advance sheet thus contains a mini-digest in which one can find, by topic and key number, the cases published therein which cover a particular point of law. The advance sheets are later compiled into a bound volume reporter, which carries a similar digest section. Of course, many topics and key numbers do not appear in any particular advance sheet or bound volume. Illustration D shows a typical page from the Key Number Digest of a bound volume of the *Federal Reporter 2d*, showing the headnote abstracts from the decision in Illustration C.

396 680 FEDERAL REPORTER, 2d SERIES

UNITED STATES of America, Plaintiff-Appellee,

v.

6,162.78 ACRES OF LAND, More or Less, SITUATED IN CONCORDIA PARISH, STATE OF LOUISIANA, Defendants,

and

Ida Hoagland Yakey, et al., Defendants-Appellants.

No. 81-3183.

United States Court of Appeals, Fifth Circuit.

July 14, 1982.

Landowners appealed from a judgment of the United States District Court for the Western District of Louisiana, Nauman S. Scott, Chief Judge, awarding just compensation in an eminent domain proceeding. The Court of Appeals, Gee, Circuit Judge, held that: (1) jury verdict was within range of evidence; (2) claim that United States engaged in bad faith by requiring appraisers to meet predetermined value for land was not supported by record; and (3) district court did not err in refusing to allow landowners to present evidence of bad faith to jury since question of bad faith was for court.

Affirmed.

1. Eminent Domain ⚷262(4)

Weighing of evidence in condemnation proceeding is within sole purview of fact finder, and it is not for Court of Appeals to reweigh evidence; rather, Court of Appeals must determine whether verdict was within range of evidence.

2. Federal Courts ⚷847

Jury finding based on sharply conflicting evidence is conclusively binding in Court of Appeals.

3. Eminent Domain ⚷149(1)

In condemnation proceeding, jury verdict of $2,071,973 in just compensation was within range of evidence where landowners' appraisals went from high of $3,220,000 to low of $3,052,193 and Government's appraisals ranged from high of $1,891,973 to low of $1,704,700.

4. Eminent Domain ⚷131

In condemnation proceeding, landowners' claim that United States acted in bad faith by requiring its appraisers to meet predetermined value for land was not supported by record which showed that appraisals relied on at trial were done by independent appraisers who were not given information from United States outside of maps and hydrology.

5. Evidence ⚷142(1)

In condemnation proceeding, United States did not engage in bad faith by refusing to instruct its appraisers to consider award made for adjacent property where adjacent property was superior in quality to subject tract.

6. Evidence ⚷142(1)

In condemnation proceeding, United States did not engage in bad faith by using sales that were not comparable because of circumstances under which they were negotiated since question of how comparable sales were was for jury.

7. Eminent Domain ⚷223

In condemnation proceeding, jury verdict did not improperly deny landowners separate award of severance damages for loss of access to their remainder tract as result of the taking where jury was properly charged to award severance damages as it thought proper and thus jury verdict included any severance damages jury felt were warranted.

8. Eminent Domain ⚷221

Question of government's bad faith in eminent domain proceedings is not jury question. Fed.Rules Civ.Proc. Rule 71A(h), 28 U.S.C.A.

9. Eminent Domain ⚷201

In condemnation proceeding, trial court did not err in allowing landowners to present evidence of bad faith to jury and in

Illustration C

A decision in a West reporter with headnotes indicating relevant topics and key numbers.

a. General Digest

Periodically, when the amount of material warrants, West cumulates all of the headnote abstracts (sometimes called "squibs") which have been written for decisions published in all West case reporters for a given time period, and publishes them, arranged by topic and key number, in a bound volume of a set known as the *General Digest.* (Ten such *General Digest* volumes appeared during 1982.) These volumes are, in effect, "advance sheets" for an even larger cumulation called a *Decennial Digest* (see section b, below).

In addition to the abstracts arranged by topic and key number, each *General Digest* volume contains a "Descriptive Word Index", which provides detailed subject references to the topics and key numbers contained in that volume; a "Table of Cases", in which names of all cases digested in the volume are arranged alphabetically by plaintiffs' or appellants' (but not defendants') names; and a "Table of Cases Affirmed, Reversed, etc." by the decisions abstracted in that *General Digest* volume.

The abstracts appearing in each *General Digest* volume are not cumulated again until the publication of the next *Decennial Digest.* For each ten volumes of the *General Digest,* however, cumulative "Descriptive Word Indexes" and "Tables of Cases Affirmed, Reversed, etc." are published. (Previously issued as separate volumes, these cumulative indexes are now printed in the *General Digest* volumes themselves.) Also included are cumulative "Tables of Key Numbers," which are lists of all topic-key number combinations appearing in the previous ten digest volumes, with references to those *General Digest* volumes which actually contain abstracts under those key numbers. This can be useful since not all topics and key numbers appear in every *General Digest* volume, and fruitless consultation of numerous digest volumes can thereby be avoided. Illustration E shows a sample page from one of those "Tables of Key Numbers".

The *General Digest* is currently in its sixth series, which began in 1981. It will eventually be entirely superseded by the *Ninth Decennial Digest,* Part I (see section b, below).

b. Decennial Digests

The *Decennial Digests* contain all headnotes assigned to cases during a ten-year period, arranged in topic and key numbers order according to the original West subject structure. The First *Decennial Digest* appeared in 1896 and West issued them for ten-year periods thereafter, through the *Eighth Decennial* covering 1966–1976. The number of cases digested had become so large that the *Eighth Decennial* numbered fifty volumes and was not completed until 1979. As a result, West has now begun cumulating the *General Digest* volumes every five years. The *Ninth Decennial Digest* will appear in two parts: Part 1 (which began to appear in 1982) will cover 1976–1981, and Part 2 will digest cases for 1981–1986.

⚷11.2(2) ELECTRICITY

1944, § 5, 16 U.S.C.A. § 825s; 28 U.S.C.A. § 1491.—City of Fulton v. U. S., 680 F.2d 115.

EMINENT DOMAIN

I. NATURE, EXTENT, AND DELEGATION OF POWER.

⚷2(1.1). Particular acts and regulations.

Ct.Cl. 1982. Extinguishment by Alaska Native Claims Settlement Act of claims by Eskimo tribe for trespasses committed by third parties under authority of temporary federal land patents and temporary state leases did not amount to taking by United States for which tribe was entitled to just compensation where Settlement Act extinguished aboriginal title of tribe retroactively to date of the patents and leases, in that subsequent entries thereunder thus necessarily were not trespasses upon any protectible interest Eskimos had; furthermore, validity of trespasses was litigated in prior case and was binding by collateral estoppel on tribe's claim for just compensation for taking of their claims for trespass based upon entries pursuant to federal patents and state leases. Alaska Native Claims Settlement Act, § 4(a), 43 U.S.C.A. § 1603(a).—Inupiat Community of Arctic Slope v. U. S., 680 F.2d 122.

Extinguishment by Alaska Native Claims Settlement Act of claims of Eskimo tribe based upon trespasses by third parties to the land did not amount to a taking by United States which required just compensation where claim for taking was based upon tribe's unrecognized aboriginal title to the land, in that Eskimos' presence on and use of the land, and scope, measure, and form of protection of that presence and use were matters within exclusive authority and discretion of Congress. Alaska Native Claims Settlement Act, § 4(c), 43 U.S.C.A. § 1603(c).—Id.

Extinguishment by Alaska Native Claims Settlement Act of claims by Eskimo tribe against United States for various alleged breaches of Government's fiduciary duties to Eskimos did not constitute a taking for which tribe was entitled to just compensation, in that such claim for taking was based upon tribe's unrecognized aboriginal title which was within exclusive authority and discretion of Congress, and statutes upon which Eskimos relied to prove their claim were only regulatory provisions which did not waive Government's sovereign immunity. Alaska Native Claims Settlement Act, §§ 2–31, 4, 43 U.S.C.A. §§ 1601–1628, 1603; Act May 17, 1884, ch. 53, § 8, 23 Stat. 24; Act March 3, 1891, ch. 561, § 14, 26 Stat. 1095; Act May 14, 1898, ch. 299, § 7, 30 Stat. 409; Act June 6, 1900, ch. 786, § 27, 31 Stat. 321; 25 U.S.C.A. § 177; 28 U.S.C.A. §§ 1346, 1491.—Id.

II. COMPENSATION.

(B) TAKING OR INJURING PROPERTY AS GROUND FOR COMPENSATION.

⚷82. —— Real property in general.

Ct.Cl. 1982. Aboriginal title is a right of occupancy based on possession from time immemorial, and such title may be recognized or unrecognized; if recognized, its extinction is compensable, but taking of unrecognized title is not compensable.—Inupiat Community of Arctic Slope v. U. S., 680 F.2d 122.

⚷96. —— Taking part of tract.

C.A.Tex. 1982. A "partial taking" generally refers to an appropriation in fee of a portion of a larger tract.—U. S. v. 8.41 Acres of Land, More or Less, Situated in Orange County, State of Tex., 680 F.2d 388, rehearing denied 685 F.2d 1385, U. S. v. 5.00 Acres of Land, More or Less, Situated in Orange County, State of Tex., 685 F.2d 1386 and U. S. 6.90 Acres of Land, More or Less, Situated in Orange County, State of Tex., 685 F.2d 1386.

(C) MEASURE AND AMOUNT.

⚷124. Time with reference to which compensation to be made.

C.A.Tex. 1982. Value of condemned land is to be ascertained as of date of taking.—U. S. v. 8.41 Acres of Land, More or Less, Situated in Orange County, State of Tex., 680 F.2d 388, rehearing denied 685 F.2d 1385, U. S. v. 5.00 Acres of Land, More or Less, Situated in Orange County, State of Tex., 685 F.2d 1386 and U. S. 6.90 Acres of Land, More or Less, Situated in Orange County, State of Tex., 685 F.2d 1386.

⚷131. —— Value of land.

C.A.La. 1982. In condemnation proceeding, landowners' claim that United States acted in bad faith by requiring its appraisers to meet predetermined value for land was not supported by record which showed that appraisals relied on at trial were done by independent appraisers who were not given information from United States outside of maps and hydrology.—U. S. v. 6,162.78 Acres of Land, More or Less, Situated in Concordia Parish, State of La., 680 F.2d 396.

C.A.Tex. 1982. An owner of lands to be condemned is entitled to their market value fairly determined.—U. S. v. 8.41 Acres of Land, More or Less, Situated in Orange County, State of Tex., 680 F.2d 388, rehearing denied 685 F.2d 1385, U. S. v. 5.00 Acres of Land, More or Less, Situated in Orange County, State of Tex., 685 F.2d 1386 and U. S. 6.90 Acres of Land, More or Less, Situated in Orange County, State of Tex., 685 F.2d 1386.

In determining market value of condemned land, value of separate interests in land cannot exceed worth of whole.—Id.

⚷134. —— Value for special use.

C.A.Tex. 1982. In determining market value of condemned land, court must look not only at present use of property, but also at highest and best use for which property is adaptable and needed.—U. S. v. 8.41 Acres of Land, More or Less, Situated in Orange County, State of Tex., 680 F.2d 388, rehearing denied 685 F.2d 1385, U. S. v. 5.00 Acres of Land, More or Less, Situated in Orange County, State of Tex., 685 F.2d 1386 and U. S. 6.90 Acres of Land, More or Less, Situated in Orange County, State of Tex., 685 F.2d 1386.

In determining market value of condemned land, district court must value property as a whole rather than as the sum of various uses to which it has been placed.—Id.

⚷136. —— In general.

C.A.Tex. 1982. Under Texas law, compensation in partial taking cases is determined by awarding fair market value of strip actually taken, plus damages for any diminution in value of landowner's remaining property by virtue of severance or use to which strip taken is to be put.—U. S. v. 8.41 Acres of Land, More or Less, Situated in Orange County, State of Tex., 680 F.2d 388, rehearing denied 685 F.2d 1385, U. S. v. 5.00 Acres of Land, More or Less, Situated in

(38)

Illustration D

Key Number Digest in a volume of West's *Federal Reporter 2d.*

Key No Tbl—58

ELECTIONS—Cont'd

305(6)—22, 23, 31
305(7)—23, 30
307—25
308—23
309—22, 25, 28, 32
311—21, 22, 23, 24, 25, 26, 28, 29, 30, 31, 32, 33
311.1—21, 27, 28, 31, 32, 33
311.2(1)—22, 24, 27, 29
312—22
313—28
316—24, 29, 31
317—22, 23, 24, 25, 26, 27, 28, 29, 30, 31, 32, 33
318—23
323—27, 29
326—21
328(1)—30
329—22, 24, 28
330—24
332—23

ELECTRICITY

1—21, 22, 23, 24, 25, 27, 28, 29, 30, 31
2—32
8—27
8.1(1)—21, 24, 25
8.1(2)—21, 22, 23, 27, 28, 29, 33
8.1(3)—22, 27, 29
8.1(4)—23, 25, 27, 29, 33
8.4—21, 23, 24, 25, 27, 29, 31, 32, 33
8.5—26
8.5(1)—21, 27, 30, 32
8.5(2)—23, 24, 30, 31, 33
9—21
9(1)—21, 22, 23, 24, 26, 27, 28, 29, 31, 32, 33
9(2)—21, 22, 24, 26, 28, 29, 33
9(3)—27
9(5)—27, 33
10—27
11(2)—22, 23
11(3)—22, 28, 29
11.1(1)—23, 25, 27, 28, 29, 30, 31
11.1(2)—25
11.1(3)—25, 29
11.2(1)—21, 24
11.2(2)—21, 24
11.2(3)—32
11.3(1)—21, 22, 23, 24, 25, 27, 28, 29, 30, 32
11.3(2)—23, 25, 26, 28, 29, 30, 32, 33
11.3(3)—23, 32
11.3(4)—21, 22, 23, 24, 25, 26, 27, 28, 30
11.3(5)—22, 23, 24, 25, 27, 28, 29, 32, 33
11.3(6)—21, 22, 23, 24, 25, 27, 28, 29, 31, 32, 33
11.3(7)—21, 22, 23, 24, 25, 27, 28, 29, 30, 31, 32, 33
11.4—22, 24, 25, 26, 27, 28, 29, 30, 32
11.5(1)—22, 23, 24, 25, 26, 27, 28, 29, 31, 32
11.5(2)—23
13—21, 22, 23, 26, 27, 30
14(1)—22, 23, 24, 26, 27, 28, 29, 30, 32, 33

ELECTRICITY—Cont'd

15(1)—31, 32
15(2)—32
16(1)—22, 23, 27, 28, 29, 30, 31, 32, 33
16(2)—21, 22, 23, 30, 31
16(5)—33
16(7)—23
17—22, 30
18(1)—22, 23, 29, 30, 31, 33
18(3)—24
18(4)—22
19(3)—24, 26, 27, 32
19(4)—21, 31
19(5)—22, 23, 24, 26, 29, 31
19(6)—21, 22, 24, 26, 27, 30, 32
19(12)—22, 24, 25
19(13)—21, 30, 32
21—25, 29, 31

EMBEZZLEMENT

1—22, 24, 27, 28, 29, 30, 31, 33
2—21, 23, 24, 27, 28, 29, 30, 33
4—21, 22, 23, 25, 27, 28
5—21, 22, 23, 24, 26, 27, 28, 29, 33
6—23, 26, 28, 29, 30
7—30
8—22, 25, 26, 28, 30, 31, 33
9—24, 26
10—21, 22, 25, 26
11(1)—23, 24, 26, 27, 28, 29, 30, 31, 33
11(2)—26
14—23, 25, 33
20—28, 30
21—28, 30
23—22, 24, 25, 30
24—22
26—25, 26, 27, 30
27—22, 26
30—33
32—26
35—23, 25, 27, 30
36—23, 25, 27, 28, 33
38—22, 23, 25, 26, 28, 29, 30, 33
39—28
42—22, 31
43—32
44(1)—21, 22, 23, 24, 25, 26, 27, 28, 29, 30, 31, 32, 33
44(2)—23, 28, 29, 30
44(4)—28
44(5)—24, 26, 28
44(6)—28
47—21, 22, 24, 29, 30, 33
48(1)—21, 22, 25, 29, 30, 31
48(2)—21, 22, 23, 26
48(3)—21, 22
48(4)—26
49—29, 30
52—21, 26, 28, 30

EMBRACERY

1—33

EMINENT DOMAIN

1—22, 23, 25, 29, 32
2—21, 22, 23, 24, 26, 27, 28, 29, 30, 32, 33

EMINENT DOMAIN —Cont'd

2(1)—21, 22, 23, 24, 25, 26, 27, 28, 29, 30, 31, 32, 33
2(1.1)—21, 22, 23, 24, 25, 26, 27, 28, 29, 30, 31, 32, 33
2(1.2)—21, 22, 23, 24, 25, 26, 27, 28, 29, 30, 31, 32, 33
2(3)—22
2(4)—26, 31
2(5)—23, 28
2(6)—21, 22, 23, 24, 26
2(7)—22, 24, 25, 27, 29, 30, 33
2(9)—29, 31
2(10)—21, 22, 23, 24, 25, 26, 28, 29, 30, 32
2(11)—21, 22, 23, 24, 25, 26, 28, 29, 31
3—21, 22, 23, 24, 29
5—29
6—21, 22
7—23, 27, 29
8—21, 22, 24, 32
9—22, 31, 32
10(1)—21, 29
10(3)—28
13—21, 22, 23, 25, 26, 28, 29, 30, 31, 32, 33
17—21, 22, 23, 26, 29, 32
18—28
18.5—22, 29
19—21, 23, 28, 32
20(1)—23, 26
28—21
29—28
31—24
34—24
35—25, 33
41—26
45—22, 23, 24, 26, 27, 29, 32
46—26
47(1)—25, 26, 28, 31
47(7)—22, 26, 28, 31
49—28
50—23, 28, 29
55—22, 25, 26, 27, 28, 31, 32
56—22, 23, 25, 26, 27, 29, 31, 33
57—23, 25, 30, 32
58—21, 22, 23, 26, 27, 29, 31, 32
61—24, 25, 28, 29, 32, 33
63—22, 24, 25, 26, 27, 28
64—25
66—21, 22, 23, 25, 26, 28, 29, 30, 31, 32
67—21, 23, 29
68—23, 26, 31
69—22, 23, 24, 26, 27, 31
70—29
71—29, 30
74—28
75—30
76—22, 28
81—22, 24, 25, 29, 30, 31
82—22, 23, 24, 25, 26, 28, 31, 32
83—30
84—28
85—21, 22, 23, 24, 26, 28, 29, 30, 33
87—28
90—24
91—28, 31
93—23, 24, 28, 33
95—23, 24, 26, 27, 28, 29, 30, 31, 33

EMINENT DOMAIN —Cont'd

96—21, 22, 23, 24, 25, 26, 27, 28, 31, 32, 33
97—24
98—26, 28
100(6)—24, 28
101(1)—21
102—24, 30
104—24, 26
106—21, 22, 23, 24, 25, 26, 27, 28, 29, 30, 32, 33
107—21, 22, 23, 24, 25, 26, 31, 32
109—24, 26
112—21, 24, 30
113—21, 24, 26
116—24, 28
118—27
121—33
122—21, 23, 24, 26, 27, 28, 29, 30, 31, 32, 33
123—24
124—21, 22, 24, 25, 26, 28, 29, 30, 31, 33
126(1)—30
130—30, 31, 32
131—21, 22, 23, 24, 26, 27, 28, 29, 30, 31, 32, 33
132—31
133—21, 22, 23, 25, 27, 29, 30, 31, 32, 33
134—21, 22, 23, 24, 25, 26, 28, 29, 30, 31, 32, 33
136—21, 22, 23, 24, 25, 26, 27, 29, 30, 31, 32, 33
137—21, 26
138—21, 22, 23, 24, 26, 27, 28, 29, 30, 31, 32, 33
140—26, 28
142—23, 28
143—24
145(1)—23, 28, 29, 31
145(4)—22
146—22, 28, 33
147—21, 22, 23, 24, 25, 26, 28, 29, 31, 32, 33
148—22, 24, 25, 26, 28, 29, 30, 31
149(1)—21, 22, 23, 24, 28, 29, 30, 31, 32, 33
149(2)—21, 30, 31
149(3)—25
149(4)—27, 28
149(5)—21, 23, 24, 25, 26, 27, 29
149(7)—22, 23, 24, 26, 29, 30, 32, 33
150—24, 26, 27, 28, 29, 30, 31, 32, 33
152(1)—22, 23, 28
153—28
154—21, 22
155—22, 26, 28, 30, 31, 33
157—21, 22, 23, 25, 26, 27, 30, 33
158—21, 22
160—33
164—22
165—21, 22, 26, 29, 30
166—21, 22, 24, 27, 28, 29, 31
167(1)—22
167(2)—22, 24, 29
167(3)—22, 28
167(4)—21, 28, 30

Illustration E

"Table of Key Numbers" in a volume of the *General Digest*.

Within a *Decennial Digest* it is likely that every topic and most key numbers will be represented by at least one headnote, and some of the more common topics and key numbers may include thousands of digested cases. Each decision will be represented, as it was in the Digest of the advance sheet, the bound case reporter, and the volumes of the *General Digest*, by a reprinting of the *original* headnote abstract, followed by the citation to the decision, so that one may easily locate (and then read) the full text of the case. These *Decennial Digests* are massive tools offering subject access to all American jurisdictions for ten-year periods. If one knows the relevant topic and key number, one can find headnotes and citations for all cases published by West during that time period.

In summary, the digesting process consists of the following stages:

1. Editor prepares abstracts from the decision, for headnotes.
2. Editor assigns topic and key number to each abstract.
3. Headnote appears in topic and key number sequence at the beginning of the reported decision.
4. Headnote appears in topic and key number sequence in the Key Number Digest of the advance sheet, and then the bound reporter.
5. Headnote appears in topic and key number sequence in the *General Digest.*
6. Headnote appears in topic and key number sequence in *Decennial Digest.*
7. Headnote appears in the appropriate jurisdictional and subject digests, as well as in other annotated West publications.

Illustration F–1 to F–4 shows examples, respectively, of the headnote in a West report (step 3), in the Digest section of the bound reporter (step 4), in the *General Digest* (step 5), and in a jurisdictional digest, West's *Federal Practice Digest 2d* (step 7).

c. Century Digest

To provide retrospective coverage of cases predating 1896, when the *First Decennial Digest* began publication, West compiled a fifty-volume set, entitled *Century Digest,* which included reported cases from 1658 to 1896. The *Century Digest* unfortunately does *not* use the same topic and key number system as the subsequent *Decennial Digest.* The researcher can easily convert a modern topic and key number reference to one used in the *Century Digest* by consulting the cross references in the *First* and *Second Decennial Digests.* To convert a *Century Digest* number to its equivalent key number in the *Decennials,* one uses the pink page tables in volume 21 of the *First Decennial.* With that minor adjustment in topic and key number, one can locate decisions on a particular legal point from 1658 to the current year, by searching the *Century Digest,* eight *Decennial Digests,* and the volumes of the *General Digest, 6th Series.*

Lord is the very same song as He's So Fine with different words,[13] and Harrison had access to He's So Fine. This is, under the law, infringement of copyright, and is no less so even though subconsciously accomplished. *Sheldon v. Metro-Goldwyn Pictures Corp.*, 81 F.2d 49, 54 (2d Cir. 1936); *Northern Music Corp. v. Pacemaker Music Co., Inc.*, 147 U.S.P.Q. 358, 359 (S.D.N.Y. 1965).

Given the foregoing, I find for the plaintiff on the issue of plagiarism, and set the action down for trial on November 8, 1976 on the issue of damages and other relief as to which the plaintiff may be entitled. The foregoing constitutes the Court's findings of fact and conclusions of law.

So Ordered.

EQUAL EMPLOYMENT OPPORTUNITY COMMISSION, Plaintiff,

v.

AMERICAN NATIONAL BANK, Defendant.

Civ. A. No. 76–26–N.

United States District Court,
E. D. Virginia,
Norfolk Division.

Aug. 31, 1976.

Equal Employment Opportunity Commission brought Civil Rights Act suit complaining that branch of defendant bank was guilty of discriminatory employment practices. Defendant moved for summary judgment. The District Court, Clarke, J., held that an administrative agency such as the EEOC, even in the absence of specific statutory time limits, may not postpone enforcement indefinitely without excuse to prejudice of a defendant, that absent special circumstances, mere existence of a burdensome work load does not justify undue delays, that mere fact of six and one-half-year delay between filing of initial charges and bringing of action was insufficient to establish a defense in the nature of laches but that defense was good since defendant established prejudice in that, among other things, vital witness was presently 72 years of age and neither such witness nor two other witnesses of importance were currently employed by the bank and claimant herself could not remember having filed an employment application with subject branch of defendant bank.

Motion granted.

1. Civil Rights ⚷**40**

Although Equal Employment Opportunity Commission is not bound by any strict statutory time limit in bringing discriminatory employment practices suits, either state or federal, a limitation on EEOC enforcement powers may be found in traditional notions of equity and in provision of Administrative Procedure Act authorizing a reviewing court to compel agency action unlawfully withheld or unreasonably delayed. Civil Rights Act of 1964, § 701 et seq. as amended 42 U.S.C.A. § 2000e et seq.; 5 U.S.C.A. §§ 706, 706(1).

2. United States ⚷**133**

Although general principle is that doctrine of laches may not be imputed against the United States to bar its actions in court, the government is not universally immune from claims of delay and resulting prejudice. 5 U.S.C.A. §§ 706, 706(1).

3. Civil Rights ⚷**38**

In order to file suit against employers or others to vindicate the public interest, the Equal Employment Opportunity Com-

13. Harrison himself acknowledged on the stand that the two songs were substantially similar. This same conclusion was obviously reached by a recording group called the "Belmonts" who recorded My Sweet Lord at a later time. With "tongue in cheek" they used the words from *both* He's So Fine and My Sweet Lord interchangeably at certain points.

Illustration F–1

Headnotes in the report of a decision in West's *Federal Supplement.*

CIVIL RIGHTS ⚷43

D.C.Va. 1976. Equal Employment Opportunity Commission's "letter of determination," containing EEOC's findings on multiple employment discrimination claims of five charging parties and ending with invitation to conciliation rather than dismissal of even those claims found unmeritorious, did not begin running of 90-day period within which charging parties could bring action in district court. Civil Rights Act, § 706(e) as amended 42 U.S.C.A. § 2000e-5(f)(1).—Askins v. Imperial Reading Corp., 420 F.Supp. 413.

Period of limitation under Title VII began to run only when employees received "right to sue" letters from Equal Employment Opportunity Commission, and not upon their receipt of "failure of conciliation" notices. Civil Rights Act, § 706(e) as amended 42 U.S.C.A. § 2000e-5(f)(1). —Id.

Equal Employment Opportunity Commission's delay in conciliation proceedings could not serve as basis for dismissal of employment discrimination action on grounds of laches. Civil Rights Act, § 701 et seq. as amended 42 U.S.C.A. § 2000e et seq.—Id.

D.C.Va. 1976. Two-year limitation period applicable to claims arising under Civil Rights Act of 1870 and 180-day limitation period of Title VII of Civil Rights Act of 1964 are not operative when person challenges continuous discriminatory conduct rather than any single discriminatory act. Civil Rights Act of 1964, § 701 et seq. as amended 42 U.S.C.A. § 2000e et seq.; 42 U.S.C.A. § 1981.—Woodard v. Virginia Bd. of Bar Examiners, 420 F.Supp. 211.

Claim of black citizen who failed to pass Virginia bar examination, to effect that Virginia Board of Bar Examiners engaged in allegedly racially discriminatory practices which deprived black applicants of equal opportunity to become practicing attorneys at law in Virginia, was timely even though filed more than 180 days after claimant learned of results of his examination, since both allegedly illegal practice and its effects upon claimant were presently continuing. Civil Rights Act of 1964, § 701 et seq. as amended 42 U.S.C.A. § 2000e et seq.—Id.

→ **D.C.Va. 1976.** Although Equal Employment Opportunity Commission is not bound by any strict statutory time limit in bringing discriminatory employment practices suits, either state or federal, a limitation on EEOC enforcement powers may be found in traditional notions of equity and in provision of Administrative Procedure Act authorizing a reviewing court to compel agency action unlawfully withheld or unreasonably delayed. Civil Rights Act of 1964, § 701 et seq. as amended 42 U.S.C.A. § 2000e et seq.; 5 U.S.C.A. §§ 706, 706(1).—Equal Employment Opportunity Commission v. Bank, 420 F.Supp. 181.

Fundamental fairness requires reasonably prompt action by the government when seeking to impose a substantial penalty on parties charged with discrimination; unreasonable delay in proceedings, such as under discriminatory employment practice provisions of Civil Rights Act, not only disserves the policy of any discrimination while leaving the alleged victim without relief but also the parties charged are left in the Damoclean situation of never knowing when an old charge may spring into life as a basis of a lawsuit. Civil Rights Act of 1964, § 701 et seq., as amended 42 U.S.C.A. § 2000e et seq.; 5 U.S.C.A. §§ 706, 706(1).—Id.

Elements of affirmative defense, denominated as "in the nature of laches," to a charge of discrimination in employment are unreasonable or unexplained delay in bringing proceedings and resulting prejudice to the defendant. Civil Rights Act of 1964, § 701 et seq. as amended 42 U.S.C.A. § 2000e et seq.; 5 U.S.C.A. §§ 706, 706(1).—Id.

Release of Equal Employment Opportunity Commission from inflexible time restraints on bringing discriminatory employment practices suits is no authorization for investigations of indefinite duration or limitless postponement on initiation of suit following failure of conciliation. Civil Rights Act of 1964, §§ 701 et seq., 706 as amended 42 U.S.C.A. §§ 2000e et seq., 2000e-5; 5 U.S.C.A. § 706(1).—Id.

Mere fact of six and one-half-year delay between filing of charges of discriminatory employment practices and Equal Employment Opportunity Commission's filing of action based thereon was insufficient to establish affirmative defense in the nature of laches; however, there was sufficient prejudice to make the defense good where neither vital witness, who was now 72 years of age, nor two other witnesses of importance were currently employed by defendant bank and complainant herself stated that she was unable to produce any records pertaining to any charge that she might have filed against the bank and, in fact, could not remember whether she applied at the subject branch. Civil Rights Act of 1964, §§ 701 et seq., 706 as amended 42 U.S.C.A. §§ 2000e et seq., 2000e-5; 5 U.S.C.A. § 706(1).—Id.

Absent special circumstances, mere existence of burdensome work load did not justify six and one-half-year delay between filing of initial charges of discriminatory employment practices and bringing of action by Equal Employment Opportunity Commission based on such charges, specially since suit was not particularly involved. Civil Rights Act of 1964, §§ 701 et seq., 706 as amended 42 U.S.C.A. §§ 2000e et seq., 2000e-5; 5 U.S.C.A. § 706(1).—Id.

⚷41. —— Parties.

D.C.Pa. 1976. Those complainants in civil rights suit against employer who failed to timely file charges with Equal Employment Opportunity Commission, or who failed to timely file suit against employer after receipt of "right to sue" letters, failed to comply with jurisdictional prerequisites of Civil Rights Act of 1964, and would therefore be dismissed as named plaintiffs. Civil Rights Act of 1964, § 706(d, e) as amended 42 U.S.C.A. § 2000e-5(e), (b)(1); Fed.Rules Civ. Proc. rule 8(f), 28 U.S.C.A.—Bates v. Western Elec., 420 F.Supp. 521.

D.C.Va. 1976. Virginia Board of Bar Examiners was agent of state for purpose of judging whether statutory definition of employer found in Title VII of Civil Rights Act of 1964 was satisfied. Civil Rights Act of 1964, § 701(b) as amended 42 U.S.C.A. § 2000e(b); Code Va.1950, § 54-53 et seq.—Woodard v. Virginia Bd. of Bar Examiners, 420 F.Supp. 211.

⚷43. —— Evidence in general.

D.C.Mass. 1976. Employer may not successfully rebut prima facie case of employment discrimination merely by showing that it subsequently hired other minority members although such a showing is relevant and has a tendency to bolster reliability of other evidence of nondiscriminatory reasons for refusal to hire. Civil Rights Act of 1964, § 701 et seq. as amended 42 U.S.C.A. § 2000e et seq.—Townsend v. Exxon Co., U. S. A., 420 F.Supp. 189.

D.C.Mo. 1976. Where by reason of an employer's past policies of racial or sex discrimination,

(19)

Illustration F-2

Headnote abstract appearing under topic and key number in Key Number Digest of bound *Federal Supplement* volume.

275 **CIVIL RIGHTS ⚷40**

his timely filed suit with proper service, his claim for back pay likewise came too late. LSA–C.C. arts. 2315, 3536; 42 U.S.C.A. §§ 1981, 1988.—Id.

D.C.La. 1976. Limitation period for claims under Title VII of Civil Rights Act of 1964 tolled with filing of charge with Equal Employment Opportunity Commission. Civil Rights Act of 1964, § 701 et seq. as amended 42 U.S.C.A. § 2000e et seq.—Johnson v. Shreveport Garment Co., 422 F.Supp. 526.

Limitation period with respect to claims of employment discrimination under Civil Rights Acts of 1870 and 1871 tolled with claimants' filing of lawsuit against employers. 42 U.S. C.A.

West's

GENERAL DIGEST

FIFTH SERIES

aware that his claim for reemployment was rejected by both employer and union, claim was untimely and district court did not have jurisdiction. Civil Rights Act of 1964, § 706(d) as amended 42 U.S.C.A. § 2000e–5(e).—Stewart v. Marquette Tool & Die Co., Inc., 420 F.Supp. 478, affirmed 527 F.2d 127.

D.C.Neb. 1976. Employee, who within one month of his discharge sought aid of local agency with authority to grant or seek relief from discriminatory employment practices, thereby became entitled to statutory extension of time in which to file his complaint with Equal Employment Opportunity Commission and thus his complaint in subsequently filed employment discrimination suit was timely. Civil Rights Act of 1964, § 706(a–d) as amended 42 U.S.C.A. §§ 2000e–5(a–e).—St. Aubin v. Transcon Lines, Inc., 420 F.Supp. 972.

D.C.Pa. 1976. Personnel who have allegedly been aggrieved by unlawful employment practices which occurred prior to amendment to Civil Rights Act of 1964, requiring filing of charges with Equal Employment Opportunity Commission within 180 days of occurrence of alleged unlawful employment practice, and who had no charge pending with Commission at time of amendment, are subject to original time limits of Act requiring filing within 90 days of alleged unlawful employment practice. Civil Rights Act of 1964, § 706(d, e) as amended 42 U.S.C.A. § 2000e–5(e), (f)(1).—Bates v. Western Elec., 420 F.Supp. 521.

Where, within 90 days of alleged unlawful employment practice, claimant filed charge against employer with Equal Employment Opportunity Commission, and claimant filed civil action against employer within 90 days of receipt from Commission of "right to sue" letter, claimant was altogether timely and his suit would not be dismissed. Fed.Rules Civ. Proc. rule 8(f), 28 U.S.C.A.; Civil Rights Act of 1964, § 701 et seq. as amended 42 U.S. C.A. § 2000e et seq.—Id.

Claimant who waited 462 days to file employment discrimination charge with Equal Employment Opportunity Commission was precluded from bringing employment discrimination suit against employer, notwithstanding that delay had been occasioned by administrative determination of claimant's union grievance. Civil Rights Act of 1964, § 706(d, e) as amended 42 U.S.C.A. § 2000e–5(e), (b)(1).—Id.

D.C.Pa. 1976. Where underlying wrong affecting plaintiff was not alleged operation of racially discriminatory seniority system but of racially discriminatory hiring system, and her complaint therefore hinged on continuing ef-

Period of limitation under Title VII began to run only when employees received "right to sue" letters from Equal Employment Opportunity Commission, and not upon their receipt of "failure of conciliation" notices. Civil Rights Act, § 706(e) as amended 42 U.S.C.A. § 2000e–5(f)(1).—Id.

Equal Employment Opportunity Commission's delay in conciliation proceedings could not serve as basis for dismissal of employment discrimination action on grounds of laches. Civil Rights Act, § 701 et seq. as amended 42 U.S.C.A. § 2000e et seq.—Id.

D.C.Va. 1976. Two-year limitation period applicable to claims arising under Civil Rights Act of 1870 and 180-day limitation period of Title VII of Civil Rights Act of 1964 are not operative when person challenges continuous discriminatory conduct rather than any single discriminatory act. Civil Rights Act of 1964, § 701 et seq. as amended 42 U.S.C.A. § 2000e et seq.; 42 U.S.C.A. § 1981.—Woodard v. Virginia Bd. of Bar Examiners, 420 F.Supp. 211.

Claim of black citizen who failed to pass Virginia bar examination, to effect that Virginia Board of Bar Examiners engaged in allegedly racially discriminatory practices which deprived black applicants of equal opportunity to become practicing attorneys at law in Virginia, was timely even though filed more than 180 days after claimant learned of results of his examination, since both allegedly illegal practice and its effects upon claimant were presently continuing. Civil Rights Act of 1964, § 701 et seq. as amended 42 U.S.C.A. § 2000e et seq.—Id.

D.C.Va. 1976. Although Equal Employment Opportunity Commission is not bound by any strict statutory time limit in bringing discriminatory employment practices suits, either state or federal, a limitation on EEOC enforcement powers may be found in traditional notions of equity and in provision of Administrative Procedure Act authorizing a reviewing court to compel agency action unlawfully withheld or unreasonably delayed. Civil Rights Act of 1964, § 701 et seq. as amended 42 U.S. C.A. § 2000e et seq.; 5 U.S.C.A. §§ 706, 706(1).—Equal Employment Opportunity Commission v. Bank, 420 F.Supp. 181.

Fundamental fairness requires reasonably prompt action by the government when seeking to impose a substantial penalty on parties charged with discrimination; unreasonable delay in proceedings, such as under discriminatory employment practice provisions of Civil Rights Act, not only disserves the policy of any discrimination while leaving the alleged victim without relief but also the parties charged are

Mere fact of six and one-half-year delay between filing of charges of discriminatory employment practices and Equal Employment Opportunity Commission's filing of action based thereon was insufficient to establish affirmative defense in the nature of laches; however, there was sufficient prejudice to make the defense good where neither vital witness, who was now 72 years of age, nor two other witnesses of importance were currently employed by defendant bank and complainant herself stated that she was unable to produce any records pertaining to any charge that she might have filed against the bank and, in fact, could not remember whether she applied at the subject branch. Civil Rights Act of 1964, §§ 701 et seq., 706 as amended 42 U.S.C.A. §§ 2000e et seq., 2000e–5; 5 U.S.C.A. § 706(1).—Id.

Absent special circumstances, mere existence of burdensome work load did not justify six and one-half-year delay between filing of initial charges of discriminatory employment practices and bringing of action by Equal Employment Opportunity Commission based on such charges, specially since suit was not particularly involved. Civil Rights Act of 1964, §§ 701 et seq., 706 as amended 42 U.S.C.A. §§ 2000e et seq., 2000e–5; 5 U.S.C.A. § 706(1).—Id.

D.C.W.Va. 1976. Where alleged discriminatory act complained of was a completed act more than a year prior to the time plaintiff had filed charge with the Equal Employment Opportunity Commission, failure to file within 90 days of the act precluded court's jurisdiction of civil action for sex discrimination, notwithstanding claim that the discrimination was a continuing violation, and since plaintiff's civil action was predicated on identical factual situation involved in her previously unsuccessful litigation which was dismissed for lack of jurisdiction, doctrine of collateral estoppel applied to bar subsequent action as well. Civil Rights Act § 701 et seq. as amended 42

see Table of Cases Affirmed, Reversed or Modified

Illustration F–3

Headnote abstract appearing in the *General Digest.*

⚷40 CIVIL RIGHTS 9A F P D 2d—208

For later cases see same Topic and Key Number in Pocket Part

discriminatory employment practices in federal government mandates that person file action in district court within 30 days of receipt of notice of final action taken by department or agency; failure to comply with such provision will result in dismissal of action. Civil Rights Act of 1964, §§ 706(d), 717, 717(b, c) as amended 42 U.S.C.A. §§ 2000e–5(e), 2000e–16, 2000e–16(b, c).

Adams v. Bailar, 426 F.Supp. 263.

"Continuing discrimination" doctrine was inapplicable and would not toll limitations period as to complaint filed by postal service employee alleging sexually discriminatory job evaluation and reclassification where discriminatory conduct of which employee complained

Period of limitation under Title VII began to run only when employees received "right to sue" letters from Equal Employment Opportunity Commission, and not upon their receipt of "failure of conciliation" notices. Civil Rights Act, § 706(e) as amended 42 U.S.C.A. § 2000e–5(f)(1).

Askins v. Imperial Reading Corp., 420 F.Supp. 413.

Equal Employment Opportunity Commission's delay in conciliation proceedings could not serve as basis for dismissal of employment discrimination action on grounds of laches. Civil Rights Act, § 701 et seq. as amended 42 U.S.C.A. § 2000e et seq.

Askins v. Imperial Reading Corp., 420

WEST'S FEDERAL PRACTICE DIGEST 2d

hearing on complaint, employee candidly admitted that she was aware that certain time limitations were applicable to claims brought under Title VII of Civil Rights Act of 1964 but that she was hesitant to pursue her claims through formal litigation because she viewed herself as "company person" and thought that any such action would be futile. Civil Rights Act of 1964, §§ 701 et seq., 717 as amended 42 U.S.C.A. §§ 2000e et seq., 2000e–16; 39 U.S.C.A. § 101 et seq.

Adams v. Bailar, 426 F.Supp. 263.

Attempted "in-house" resolution of legal disputes does not toll applicable limitations period for actions brought under Title VII of Civil Rights Act of 1964. Civil Rights Act of 1964, §§ 701 et seq., 717 as amended 42 U.S.C.A. §§ 2000e et seq., 2000e–16; 39 U.S.C.A. § 101 et seq.

Adams v. Bailar, 426 F.Supp. 263.

D.C.Va. 1976. Equal Employment Opportunity Commission's "letter of determination," containing EEOC's findings on multiple employment discrimination claims of five charging parties and ending with invitation to conciliation rather than dismissal of even those claims found unmeritorious, did not begin running of 90-day period within which charging parties could bring action in district court. Civil Rights Act, § 706(e) as amended 42 U.S.C.A. § 2000e–5(f)(1).

Askins v. Imperial Reading Corp., 420 F.Supp. 413.

Claim of black citizen who failed to pass Virginia bar examination, to effect that Virginia Board of Bar Examiners engaged in allegedly racially discriminatory practices which deprived black applicants of equal opportunity to become practicing attorneys at law in Virginia, was timely even though filed more than 180 days after claimant learned of results of his examination, since both allegedly illegal practice and its effects upon claimant were presently continuing. Civil Rights Act of 1964, § 701 et seq. as amended 42 U.S.C.A. § 2000e et seq.

Woodard v. Virginia Bd. of Bar Examiners, 420 F.Supp. 211.

D.C.Va. 1976. Although Equal Employment Opportunity Commission is not bound by any strict statutory time limit in bringing discriminatory employment practices suits, either state or federal, a limitation on EEOC enforcement powers may be found in traditional notions of equity and in provision of Administrative Procedure Act authorizing a reviewing court to compel agency action unlawfully withheld or unreasonably delayed. Civil Rights Act of 1964, § 701 et seq. as amended 42 U.S.C.A. § 2000e et seq.; 5 U.S.C.A. §§ 706, 706(1).

Equal Employment Opportunity Commission v. American Nat. Bank, 420 F.Supp. 181, vacated 574 F.2d 1173, certiorari denied 99 S.Ct. 213.

Fundamental fairness requires reasonably prompt action by the government when seek-

For cited U.S.C.A. sections and legislative history

Illustration F–4

Headnote abstract appearing in West's *Federal Practice Digest 2d.*

The following sequence traces in chronological order the present components of the American Digest System:

Years Covered	Digest Unit	No. of Volumes
1658–1896	Century Digest	50
1897–1906	First Decennial	25
1907–1916	Second Decennial	24
1916–1926	Third Decennial	29
1926-1936	Fourth Decennial	34
1936–1946	Fifth Decennial	49
1946–1956	Sixth Decennial	36
1956–1966	Seventh Decennial	38
1966–1976	Eighth Decennial	42
1976–1981	Ninth Decennial, Part 1	38
1981–date	General Digest, 6th Series	In progress

Each of these units contains two finding aids [3]: a "Table of Cases", listing alphabetically the name of every case appearing in the unit, and a "Descriptive Word Index" which serves as the basic subject finding tool in all West digests. The "Tables of Cases" are Plaintiff-Defendant tables only. Although most other West digests also include a reverse Defendant-Plaintiff table, those in the American Digest System are listed only by the Plaintiff's name. These finding aids will be discussed in more detail in Section B. 3 below.

It should be emphasized that these Digests do not constitute legal authority and contain no substantive narrative texts. They are effective for identifying and locating relevant cases, but those cases must be read and evaluated (and then Shepardized and evaluated again) before being cited in a brief, argument, or memorandum. Each case is decided on its own facts, and, although its listing under a particular digest topic and key number may be accurate, its relevancy and authority for the researcher's immediate purpose must still be determined.

2. WEST'S JURISDICTIONAL DIGESTS

The amazing chronological and jurisdictional breadth of the whole American Digest System may often prove counterproductive. It is quite rare that one will want to locate *all* cases from *all* jurisdictions on a particular topic. Most searches are more specific, focusing on either the federal level or one state, and sometimes even on the decisions of one court. Since the *Decennial Digests* cover all jurisdictions and do not cumulate decisions beyond their designated time periods, it is inefficient to search the digests described above if one's research problem concerns federal law only, or the law of a particular state.

For this reason and for obvious marketing purposes, West has created a number of narrower digests utilizing the same topics and key numbers, the same finding aids, and the same format as the De-

3. The *Century Digest* and the *First Decennial Digest,* however, share one combined "Table of Cases", located in volumes 21 to 25 of the First Decennial, and both the *First* and *Second Decennials,* and the *Third* and *Fourth Decennials,* respectively, share combined "Descriptive Word Indexes".

cennial Digests of the American Digest System. These more specific digests contain abstracts of decisions (identical in form and content to those in the Decennials) only from the particular court, region, or jurisdiction covered by that digest. All of those abstracts also appear in the Decennial Digest for the appropriate period in which the case was decided.

The following lists indicate the current jurisdictional digests published by West, which will be described below:

(1) State Key Numbers Digests

Alabama Digest
Alaska Digest
Arizona Digest
Arkansas Digest
California Digest [4]
Colorado Digest
Connecticut Digest
Dakota Digest
District of Columbia Digest
Florida Digest
Georgia Digest
Hawaii Digest
Idaho Digest
Illinois Digest [4]
Indiana Digest
Iowa Digest
Kansas Digest
Kentucky Digest
Louisiana Digest
Maine Digest
Maryland Digest
Massachusetts Digest
Michigan Digest
Minnesota Digest
Mississippi Digest
Missouri Digest
Montana Digest
Nebraska Digest
New Hampshire Digest
New Jersey Digest
New Mexico Digest
New York (Abbott) Digest [5]
North Carolina Digest
Ohio Digest
Oklahoma Digest
Oregon Digest
Pennsylvania (Vale) Digest[4]
Rhode Island Digest
South Carolina Digest
Tennessee Digest
Texas Digest [4]
Vermont Digest
Virginia & West Virginia Digest
Washington Digest
Wisconsin Digest
Wyoming Digest

4. Now in two series.

5. Now in three series.

(2) Regional Reporter Key Number Digests

Key Number Digests are published for the following Regional Reporters:

Atlantic Digest
North Western Digest
Pacific Digest
South Eastern Digest
Southern Digest

Each of these digests is an index to all of the cases published in the particular Reporter. Some of them index cases published in the states of the Reporter area prior to the commencement of the Reporter. All of the above Reporters began between 1879 and 1887.

(3) Key Number Digests for Certain Courts

U.S. Supreme Court Digest
Federal Digest
Modern Federal Practice Digest
West's Federal Practice Digest, 2nd
West's Bankruptcy Digest
West's Military Justice Digest
U.S. Court of Claims Digest

The United States Supreme Court Digest is a complete index to the decisions of the United States Supreme Court. The Federal Digest, West's Modern Federal Practice Digest and West's Federal

Practice Digest, 2nd, cover the decisions of all federal courts, including the U.S. Supreme Court. West's Bankruptcy Digest indexes all cases reported in West's Bankruptcy Reporter. A new cumulative digest is published and mailed with each bound volume of West's Bankruptcy Reporter. West's Military Justice Digest indexes the decisions of the United States Court of Military Appeals and the Courts of Military Review for the Army, Navy, Air Force and Coast Guard. The Court of Claims Digest indexes the cases of the former U.S. Court of Claims. United States Claims Court Digest pamphlets index the cases from the new United States Claims Court.

a. U.S. Supreme Court Digest

When searching for a decision of the Supreme Court of the United States, whether by case name or subject, the *U.S. Supreme Court Digest* is the appropriate West digest. Its format is the same as that of all other West digests: headnote abstracts for U.S. Supreme Court decisions (from West's *Supreme Court Reporter*), arranged by West topics and key numbers. Accompanying the set are volumes containing the usual "Descriptive Word Index" and "Table of Cases". A "Defendant-Plaintiff Table" is also available (reversing the order of names in the "Table of Cases") to provide access if only the name of the defendant is known.

Because the number of decisions digested is so much smaller, this source is much less cumbersome than the *Decennial* and *General Digests*. The *U.S. Supreme Court Digest* volumes, along with their annual pocket parts, are totally cumulative. This means that once the researcher has identified the proper topic and key number, all relevant Supreme Court cases may be located by looking in only two places: the bound volume containing the topic and key number, and that volume's pocket part. There is no need to search several chronologically divided sets of volumes. Remember, however, that a key number search for Supreme Court cases may be updated even further by consulting the "Key Number Digest" sections in the advance sheets and bound volumes of West's *Supreme Court Reporter*.

b. Federal Digests

West also provides a series of three federal digests, each of which covers together decisions from the U.S. Supreme Court (thereby duplicating the U.S. Supreme Court Digest), the U.S. Courts of Appeals, the U.S. District Courts, and several other specialized federal courts. These digests are in fact three successive series of the same digest which was originally and sensibly called the *Federal Digest* (covering cases through 1939), but underwent name changes to *Modern Federal Practice Digest* (covering cases from 1940 to 1960) and *Federal Practice Digest, 2d* (covering cases from 1961 to date), in its second and third series respectively. Each uses the same key number digest format as in all other West digests, and the current volumes are updated by annual pocket parts. One hopes that when another series is required, the whole work will be recompiled under one title, or, if a separate new series, *must* be added, that it be called simply *Federal Digest 4th.* In libraries where the volumes have not been rebound because of their heavy use, the series can be distinguished by their original colors: *Federal Digest,* red; *Modern Federal Practice Digest,* green; and *Federal Practice Digest, 2d,* blue. For comprehensive searches of federal decisions in all periods, all three series must be used.

c. Regional Digests

West currently publishes five regional digests, which parallel its regional reporters. The *Atlantic, North Western,* and *South Eastern Digests* are each currently being published in a second series, and the *Pacific Digest* is in four series. As with the federal digests the divisions are chronological, and all components (including pocket parts) must be searched to assure comprehensive coverage, unless the researcher knows that a relevant case could have been decided only after (or before) a certain date. West's *Southern Digest* is totally cumulative in one series. Digests are no longer being published for the North Eastern and South Western regions, and individual state digests for the states in those regions must be consulted.

Some of the regional digests also index cases published in the states of the region prior to the publication of the West regional reporter.

d. State Digests

Forty-six state digests are currently being published by West (see list above on p. 115), including one for the District of Columbia. The *Dakota Digest* and *Virginia & West Virginia Digest* each cover two states. Only Delaware, Nevada and Utah lack individualized coverage, and cases from those states must be located through the corresponding regional digests. Most of the state digests are cumulated in one series. The exceptions are New York, for which there are now three chronologically distinct digest series and California, Illinois and Texas which each have two series.

With one exception (again, New York), West's state digests cover not only state court cases but also the decisions of the federal courts sitting in the state, and the U.S. Court of Appeals and U.S. Supreme Court decisions in cases arising from that state.

Among the added features found in state digests are summaries of legal periodical articles and of opinions of the state's Attorney General.

Some of West's state digests carry the name of a prior publisher in the title (*Vale's Pennsylvania Digest,* for example), and this may be confusing.

There are, however, a few additional state digests currently being issued by publishers other than West. Examples include the *California Digest of Official Reports, Third Series* from Bancroft-Whitney, and the *Illinois Digest, Third Edition* published by Callaghan.

These publications, of course, are not organized by West's copyrighted key number system, but according to alternative classification schemes devised by those digests' publishers.

e. Specialized Digests

West also issues a number of digests for specialized courts or subject areas.

West's Bankruptcy Digest indexes all cases reported in *West's Bankruptcy Reporter,* which began publication in 1979.

West's Military Justice Digest covers the decisions of the U.S. Court of Military Appeals and the Courts of Military Review for the Army, Navy, Air Force and Coast Guard.

United States Claims Court Digest pamphlets index all cases reported in United States Claims Court Reporter. Cases from the former U.S. Court of Claims are indexed in the U.S. Court of Claims Digest.

3. LOCATING CASES IN THE WEST DIGESTS

Having described the structure and forms of publication of the various West digests, we turn now to the actual search procedures employed in their use. How does one find cases in these digests? There are three basic approaches: by case name, by subject searching in indexes, and by topical analysis.

a. Starting With a Case

At each stage of the digesting process, West provides case tables, as noted above. These are alphabetical listings of the names of the cases covered in the publication. Each *Decennial Digest* has an alphabetical listing of all decisions from all jurisdictions published by the West Publishing Company, for the ten year period covered by that *Decennial.* Each of the *General Digest* volumes contains alphabetical listings of cases in that volume and there are also cumulative tables of cases for every ten volumes of the *General Digest.*

Every one of West's jurisdictional and specialized digests contains its own table of cases, as well as a Defendant-Plaintiff table. Updating these digest tables, there are similar tables in each advance sheet and bound volume of the various West reporters, listing the cases published within them. These case tables allow researchers to locate decisions quickly if the case name, and either the approximate year of publication or the jurisdiction, is known. Illustration G shows a page from one of the "Tables of Cases".

Notice that following the name of the case and the citation to its location in a published reporter are the topics and key numbers under which the headnote abstracts for the points of law decided in the case can be found in the digest. Consultation of those key numbers may reveal additional cases on the same points of law.

49-8th D—1137

NEW YORK

References are to Digest Topics and Key Numbers

New York State Thruway Authority v. Hurd, NYSup, 290 NYS2d 777, aff 294 NYS2d 357, aff 303 NYS 2d 51, 250 NE2d 335—States 132; Statut 212.1, 223.2(16).

New York State Thruway Authority v. Maislin Bros Transport Ltd, NYAD4th, 315 NYS2d 954—Bridges 27; Forfeit 2; Penalties 2.

New York State Thruway Authority v. State 22 NY2d 509, 293 NYS2d 311, 239 NE2d 904—States 191(1.1, 1.22).

New York State Thruway Authority v. State, NYAD3d, 298 NYS2d 204 —States 171, 184.44, 191(1.22).

New York State Thruway Authority v. State, CtCl, 272 NYS2d 657, aff 282 NYS2d 476, mod 293 NYS2d 314, 239 NE2d 904, rearg den 295 NYS 2d 62, 242 NE2d 95—States 184.30, 191(1.1, 1.22); Statut 221.

New York State Thruway Authority v. State, CtCl, 274 NYS2d 631—Courts 70, 472.1; States 184.2.

New York State Thruway Authority v. State, NYCtCl, 294 NYS2d 729, mod 298 NYS2d 204, rev 303 NYS2d 374, 250 NE2d 469—State 171, 191 (1.22).

New York State Urban Development Corp, Petition of, DCPa, 346 FSupp 1323. See Penn Cent Transp Co, In re.

New York State Urban Development Corp, Petition of, DCPa, 346 FSupp 1333. See Penn Cent Transp Co, In re.

New York State Urban Development Corp v. Goldfeld, NYAD4th, 376 N YS2d 763—Em Dom 262(4), 263.

New York State Urban Development Corp v. Memphis Const, Inc, NY Sup, 368 NYS2d 765—States 84.

New York State Water Resources Commission v. City of Oswego, NY Sup, 270 NYS2d 544—Waters 190, 196.

New York State Water Resources Commission v. Liberman, NYAD3d, 326 NYS2d 284, appeal dism 330 NYS2d 63, 280 NE2d 889—Em Dom 2(10); Nav Wat 1(6), 2, 36(1), 38, 39(2); States 201; Statut 263.

New York State Waterways Ass'n, Inc v. Diamond, CANY, 469 F2d 419—Adm 1(2), 7; Fed Cts 32, 65, 175, 194, 218, 992, 998.

New York Stock Exchange v. Pickard & Co, DelCh, 274 A2d 148—Brok 6, 24(1), 25; Receivers 67.

New York Stock Exchange v. Pickard & Co, DelCh, 282 A2d 651—Courts 489(1).

New York Stock Exchange v. Pickard & Co, Inc, DelCh, 296 A2d 143—Bankr 345.4(2); Const Law 306; Contracts 187(1); Corp 544(1), 565 (1), 566(1, 3, 4).

New York Stock Exchange, Inc v. Goodbody & Co, NYAD1st, 345 NYS 2d 58—Courts 489(1, 8).

New York Stock Exchange, Inc v. New York State Division of Human Rights 37 AD2d 941, 325 NYS2d 778—Civil R 9.10, 68.

New York Stock Exchange, Inc v. Sloan, DCNY, 391 FSupp 530—Exchanges 4, 5(1); Fed Civ Proc 2511; Partners 357.

New York Stock Exchange, Inc v. Sloan, DCNY, 394 FSupp 1303—Contracts 187(1); Fed Civ Proc 2463; Sec Reg 54, 105.

New York Stock Exchange, Inc v. Smith, DCDC, 404 FSupp 1091—Admin Law 701, 704; Banks 235, 217; Decl Judgm 294.

N Y Stoomv Maats Nederland v. Jarka Corp of Baltimore, DCMd, 43 FRD 374. See Banks v. Hanover S S Corp.

New York Tel Co v. Alvord and Swift, NYAD1st, 372 NYS2d 671—Arbit 7.3.

New York Tel Co v. Board of Trustees of Village of Lynbrook, NY Sup, 334 NYS2d 462—Discov 31, 39, 46; Tax 438.

New York Tel Co v. City of Binghamton 18 NY2d 152, 272 NYS2d 359, 219 NE2d 184—Mun Corp 688.

New York Tel Co v. City of New York, NYAD2d, 323 NYS2d 722. See Brooklyn Union Gas Co v. City of New York.

New York Tel Co v. City School Dist of City of Binghamton 17 NY2d 294, 270 NYS2d 601, 217 NE2d 656—Tel 309.

New York Tel Co v. Commissioner of New York State Dept of Transp, NYSup, 307 NYS2d 945—Decl Judgm 121; High 95(1), 99¼; Tel 77.

New York Tel Co v. Communications Workers of America, AFL-CIO, CA NY, 445 F2d 39—Fed Cts 562, 573, 576, 598; Inj 231; Labor 887, 975, 1029, 1032; Stip 14(12).

New York Tel Co v. County Asphalt, Inc, NYSup, 382 NYS2d 211—Lim of Act 129.

New York Tel Co v. Grandcom, Inc, NYAD1st, 384 NYS2d 165—Tel 127.

New York Tel Co v. Holden, NYAD 2d, 317 NYS2d 201, appeal dism 320 NYS2d 755, 269 NE2d 413—Em Dom 57, 253(1); Judgm 729.

New York Tel Co v. New York City Transp Administration, NYAD1st, 355 NYS2d 6—App & E 654; Evid 48; Inj 163(1).

New York Tel Co v. Public Service Commission 29 NY2d 164, 324 NYS 2d 53, 272 NE2d 554—Pub Serv Com 7.4, 7.10; Tel 335.

New York Tel Co v. Public Service Commission, NYAD3d, 320 NYS2d 280—Const Law 316, 318(1); Inj 136(3), 137(1, 4); Pub Serv Com 2, 7.3, 17, 24; Tel 330, 340, 343.

New York Tel Co v. Public Service Commission, NYSup, 315 NYS2d 327 rev 320 NYS2d 280, mod 324 NYS 2d 53, 272 NE2d 554—Tel 344.

New York Tel Co v. Secord Bros, Inc, NYSup, 309 NYS2d 814—Contracts 187(1); Mun Corp 861, 873.

New York Tel Co v. Teichner, NY DistCt, 329 NYS2d 689—Contracts 4, 5, 15, 177, 188; Divorce 313; Hus & W 4, 17, 19(1, 14).

New York Tel Co v. Telesystems Corp, NYAD3d, 277 NYS2d 481—Judgm 181(1); Tel 110, 127.

New York Tel Co v. Torrington Const Co, NYAD3d, 284 NYS2d 738. See American Mut Liability Ins Co v. Niagara Mohawk Power Corp.

New York Tel Co v. Torrington Const Co, NYSup, 274 NYS2d 198. See American Mut Liability Ins Co v. Niagara Mohawk Power Corp.

New York Tel Co v. Town of North Hempstead, NYSup, 385 NYS2d 436 aff 385 NYS2d 505—Em Dom 2(1), 8, 35, 45, 48, 86; Judgm 181(14); Tel 110, 337.

New York Tel Co v. Wethers 36 AD 2d 541, 317 NYS2d 119, aff 334 NYS2d 896, 286 NE2d 273—Civil R 62, 64, 67.

New York Thruway Authority v. State, 25 NY2d 210, 303 NYS2d 374, 250 NE2d 469—App & E 358; States 171, 184.44, 191(1.22).

New York Times, In re, NYSup, 370 NYS2d 1007. See People v. Monroe.

New York Times Co v. City of New York Commission on Human Rights, NYAD1st, 374 NYS2d 9—Civil R 9.10.

New York Times Co v. City of New York Commission on Human Rights, NYSup, 349 NYS2d 940—Civil R 66; Const Law 90.1(8); Prohib 3(1), 10(1).

New York Times Co v. City of New York, Commission on Human Rights, NYSup, 362 NYS2d 321, aff 374 NYS2d 9—Civil R 9.10, 62; Const Law 90.1(8), 274.1(2); States 4.12.

New York Times Co v. Connor, CAAla, 365 F2d 567—Const Law 90.1(5), 305(6); Corp 668(14); Libel 50, 51 (5), 101(1), 112(2).

New York Times Co v. Givens, NY City CivCt, 305 NYS2d 164—Tel 266.

New York Times Co v. New York Typographical Union No 6, NYAD 1st, 350 NYS2d 676, rev 354 NYS 2d 940, 310 NE2d 537, cert dism 94 SCt 3190—Arbit 1.1; Labor 261.

New York Times Co v. New York Typographical Union No 6, NYSup, 353 NYS2d 594, rev 350 NYS2d 676, rev 354 NYS2d 940, 310 NE2d 537 —Labor 261.

New York Times Co v. Starkey, NY AD2d, 380 NYS2d 239—Const Law 82, 90(1), 90.1(3), 268(7); Crim Law 633(1), 635; Mand 61.

New York Times Co v. U S, USNY, 91 SCt 2140—Const Law 90(1); Inj 128(9).

New York Trap Rock Corp v. Incorporated Village of Roslyn, NY Sup, 320 NYS2d 584—Mun Corp 607.

New York Trap Rock Corp v. National Bank of Far Rockaway 260 AD 1035, 24 NYS2d 426—Pub Contr 30.

New York Trap Rock Corp v. National Bank of Far Rockaway 177 Misc 954, 32 NYS2d 443—Pub Contr 26, 29.

New York Trap Rock Corp v. Tug Devon, CANY, 371 F2d 430—Adm 118.6(1); Towage 15(2).

New York Underwriters Ins Co v. Civil Service Emp Ins Co, Ariz, 456 P2d 914. See New York Underwriters Ins Co v. Superior Court In and For Maricopa County.

New York Underwriters Ins Co v. Friedland, CANev, 439 F2d 350—Evid 434(13); Insurance 255.

New York Underwriters Ins Co v. Michigan Consolidated Gas Co, Mich App, 143 NW2d 801. See St Paul Fire & Marine Ins Co v. Michigan Consolidated Gas Co.

New York Underwriters Ins Co v. Royals Farm Supply, Inc, FlaApp, 186 So2d 317. See Employers' Liability Assur Corp v. Royals Farm Supply, Inc.

New York Underwriters Ins Co v. Spiller, Ariz, 504 P2d 932—Insurance 435.18(2), 512.1(4).

New York Underwriters Ins Co v. Superior Court In and For Maricopa County, Ariz, 456 P2d 914—Insurance 435(1), 435.18(2).

New York Underwriters Ins Co v. Union Const Co, CAKan, 432 F2d 182—Fed Civ Proc 2416; Insurance 156(3), 435.2(6).

New York Underwriters Ins Co v. Union Const Co, DCKan, 285 FSupp 868—Fed Civ Proc 1245, 1600.1; Witn 199(1), 201(1), 204(1), 206.

New York University v. Dormitory Authority, NYADist, 349 NYS2d 716, aff 361 NYS2d 651, 320 NE2d 281—Colleges 6(1).

New York University v. N L R B, DCNY, 364 FSupp 160—Decl Judgm 272; Dismissal 55, 65; Fed Cts 201, 1135; Labor 202, 203, 206, 665, 968.

New York University v. New York State Division of Human Rights, NYSup, 378 NYS2d 842, aff 373 NYS2d 719—Civil R 9, 62; Colleges 9.

New York University v. Reichman, NYSup, 313 NYS2d 173, aff 319 NY S2d 804—Land & Ten 278.6.

New York University v. Taylor 251 AD 444, 296 NYS 848—Tax 1265.

New York Urban League v. Speer, N YAD2d, 336 NYS2d 395—Civil R 63.

New York World's Fair 1964-1965 Corp v. DeRijdt, NYAD2d, 294 NY S2d 80—Corp 626.

New York World-Telegram Corp v. McGoldrick 298 NY 11, 80 NE2d 61—Tax 1236.

Note references to topics and key numbers.

Illustration G

A typical page from the "Table of Cases" in a West Digest.

Another variation of the case name approach is possible. Throughout this text the strategy of finding "one good case" will be stressed as a potential lead to other relevant cases. If one has such a case, you can isolate the part of the case that is relevant to your research and locate the headnotes for that issue. With the topic and key number assigned to this headnote in a West publication of the decision, one has a tool for locating other relevant cases. The topic and key number can be used to search for cases in one's own jurisdiction, in a neighboring jurisdiction, or to make a general search through the *Decennial Digests.* A more difficult problem arises when one does not already have "one good case". Most of the balance of this Chapter will deal with the search for cases by subject or topic, initially focusing on subject searching in digests but then moving on to other case finding techniques.

b. The Index Search

Each of the components in West's American Digest System, beginning with the *General Digest,* and each of the West jurisdictional digests have a "Descriptive Word Index". Those indexes are minutely constructed listings of the subjects covered by the cases indexed within that unit, with references to the specific topics and key numbers under which decisions on that subject have been abstracted in the digest. The "Descriptive Word Indexes" are simply detailed subject indexes to the contents of the digests. In the case of the *Decennial Digests* and the jurisdictional digests, the indexes will be quite large, and their indexing will be quite specific. Illustration H reproduces a page from the "Descriptive Word Index" that accompanies the *Eighth Decennial Digest.*

West suggests that before consulting a "Descriptive Word Index", the researcher analyze the problem to be searched, and draw from it very specific search words or phrases by breaking the problem down into the following general categories: Parties; Places and Things; Basis of Action or Issue; Defense; and Relief Sought. This method is more fully described in West's instructional manual, the *West Law Finder,* at pages 21 to 24.

Research by means of a "Descriptive Word Index" can best be illustrated by an example. Let us assume a client named Fallon is visiting a large supermarket and, while searching for the perfect avocado, she slips on a lettuce leaf lying on the floor of the vegetable section and injures herself. The client seeks damages for her injury, and you wish to determine the supermarket's liability. If one had no way of locating a relevant case, one could begin one's search in the digest unit for the state in which the accident occurred, by going directly to the "Descriptive Word Index" for that digest. In this case, an analysis of the problem might yield search words such as Negligence, Slip, Fall, Supermarket, Lettuce, etc. As a general rule, one should use the most specific search words, since general words are likely to have too many references, covering an enormous number of

46-8th D—959 **DOGS**

DOCUMENTARY EVIDENCE—Cont'd
Rape, paper containing discourse on how to commit in automobile, finding on defendant, admissibility. **Rape 42**
Records—
Business records, authentication by employee not head bookkeeper. **Evid 376(9)**
Hospital records—
Physician-patient communication privilege. **Witn 212**
Regular course of business, treatment of patient. **Evid 351**
Police report, automobile accident, admissibility as business records. **Evid 333(1)**
Review of rulings. **Fed Cts 854**
Searches and seizures, arrest without warrant. **Crim Law 394.4(13)**
Telegrams—
Admission into evidence, prerequisite. **Crim Law 444**
Unemployment compensation cases, see this index **Unemployment Compensation**
Weather reports of neighboring airfield, absence of snow when visitor injured in fall. **Trial 9(1)**
X-ray pictures. **Evid 380**
Absence from courtroom, physician unable to give prognosis testimony without X-rays—
App & E 1048(1)
Evid 555
Radiologist not present to testify, doctor's opinion testimony. **App & E 1053(3)**

DOCUMENTARY STAMP TAX
Execution of deed in satisfaction and discharge of mortgage debt. **Tax 105½**

DOCUMENTS
Attorneys—
Arguing existence before reviewing court, nonexistent document purportedly in record. **Atty & C 32**
Papers of clients not returned after request. **Atty & C 58**
Retainer contract, validity of provision giving lien to secure fee payment. **Atty & C 176**
Attorney preparing false document and threat of criminal prosecution to enforce claim, ethical code violation. **Atty & C 32**
Broker, misrepresentation, necessity of finding damages to signers in order to revoke license. **Brok 3**
Complaint, variance from attached documents, parties to breached contracts. **Plead 312**
Convicts, regulation requiring storage of legal papers in writ room. **Civil R 13.13(3)**
Draft card burning, freedom of speech. **Armed S 20.1(2)**
Extradition—
Sufficiency to support. **Extrad 34**
Hearsay, documents containing admissions by licensee contesting revocation of license. **Evid 215(1)**
Income tax evasion prosecution, seizure of papers relating to income—
Crim Law 394.4(5)
Int Rev 2222
Landowner option assertion, specific terms, option language absent. **Ven & Pur 3(4)**
News media, order enjoining disclosure of other indictments against accused, entry without notice. **Inj 204**
Photostatic copy shipper's memoranda, banker's blanket bond. **Insurance 430(4)**
President of United States, custody of former president's documents. **Records 13, 14**
Removal of government documents, statutory proscription, permissibility of photocopying. **Records 21**
Searches and seizures, papers not immune. **Searches 7(10)**
Secret law, administrative agency, freedom of information. **Records 14**

DOCUMENTS—Cont'd
Seizure, without warrant, plainly visible on rear floor of automobile. **Searches 3.3(4)**
Substantial interests in land, preparation of documents without attorney's aid. **Atty & C 11(3)**
United States senator, documents taken from files, action for conversion. **Trover 2**

DODGERS
Permit, city distribution. **Mun Corp 591**

DODGING
Automobiles, drag racing, offense. **Autos 331**

DOE PLEADING
Permissibility of practice. **Fed Civ Proc 388**

DOG BITE
Automobile service station customer, leased premises, lessor oil company liability. **Land & Ten 167(8)**

DOG BITES
Cause of action. **Anim 74(1)**
Combination of damages action with medical expense action of mother found contributorily negligent. **App & E 171(1)**
Common law remedy, statutory repeal. **Anim 68**
Homeowner insurer without coverage paying claim, subrogation against automobile insurer having coverage. **Insurance 606(5)**
Minor petting growling dog, verdict for dog owner despite evidence of previous bitings. **Anim 74(5)**

DOG INJURY STATUTE
Cause of action. **Anim 74(1)**
Limitation of actions. **Lim of Act 31, 127(18)**

DOG KENNELS
Nuisance, interference with neighboring landowners. **Nuis 3(10)**
Operators as indispensable parties, action to enjoin kennel operations. **Inj 114(3)**
Special five-year use permit, agricultural area, discretion. **Zoning 384**

DOG RACES
Spectator injury, shoe caught in expansion joint crack. **Theaters 6(17)**

DOG RACING
Arbitration, labor disputes, jurisdiction. **Labor 54, 436**
Taxes, pari-mutuel pools, validity of proposed statute originating in senate. **Statut 6**
Vote to rescind not permitted. **Theaters 2**

DOG REPELLANT
Search warrant authorizing seizure of canisters of noxious material, not vague or lacking particularity—
Crim Law 394.4(8)
Searches 3.7

DOG SLEDS
Incorporation, borough, surface access limited to dog teams and snow machines. **Mun Corp 6**

DOGHOUSE
Accused emerging from hiding, arrest, probable cause. **Arrest 63.4(16)**

DOGS
Absolute liability, owner, dog biting without provocation. **Anim 68**
Absolute liability, owner of dog running into path of motorcyclist losing control. **Autos 178**
Actions—
Damages, personal property inflicted by dog, negligence allegation. **Anim 74(2)**
Air carrier, limitation of liability, failure of shipper to declare value. **Carr 218(1)**

DOGS—Cont'd
Airline employee bitten by dog crated for shipment, liability of airline and owner of dog—
Anim 72
Mast & S 99
Annual inoculation exemption, continuous confinement. **Anim 29**
Armed robbery, dog accompanying accused into victim's bedroom. **Rob 24.1(3)**
Arrest, releasing police dogs on robbery suspect, resisting with pistol, probable cause. **Arrest 63(3)**
Assistant dog warden, discharge without hearing. **Const Law 318(2)**
Attack or injury by, owner's liability. **Anim 74(2)**
Attractive nuisance, dogs not qualifying as. **Neglig 39**
Automobile insurance, dog biting passenger. **Insurance 435.16**
Automobile service, station selling oil company's gasoline, agency relationship, lessee's dog biting patron's son. **Princ & A 23(5)**
Automobiles—
Collision, attempt to avoid dog running across street, lease law breached. **Judgm 185.3(21)**
Emergency, sudden appearance of dog in roadway, motorist subsequently striking another vehicle. **Autos 244(5)**
Guest bitten by owner's dog during ride, obligation to defend. **Insurance 435.16**
Instructions, intervening-superseding cause, permitting dog to run at large, rear-end collision. **Autos 246(22)**
Power pole hit, driver losing control due to escaped dog running into street. **Autos 178**
Proximate cause of injury to person. **Judgm 181(33)**
Pursuit as evidence of viciousness. **Anim 68**
Stopping to avoid hitting dog, contributory negligence. **Autos 245(81)**
Barking, regulation making it offense to allow, vagueness. **Dist of Col 19**
Barking dogs, nuisance. **Nuis 3(3), 19, 73**
Barking dogs, private nuisance, sufficiency of complaint. **Nuis 48**
Bicycle, rider falling from while being chased, cause jury question. **Anim 74(8)**
Bicyclist, attack on, landowner's duty to warn. **Anim 74(8)**
Bicyclist riding in street, dog biting, assumption of risk instruction. **Trial 252(8)**
Bite—
Boy under six screaming dog bit him, res gestae. **Evid 123(10)**
Controlling statute of limitations. **Lim of Act 31**
Inflammatory evidence of dog's prior behavior—
Anim 74(4)
App & E 1050.1(7)
Presumption of owner's fault, evidence not rebutting. **Anim 74(3)**
Three year old boy, absolute liability of owner showing dog at fair. **Anim 68**
Bite cases, summary judgment. **Judgm 181(33), 185.3(21)**
Bites, board of health hearing. **Anim**
Biting, owner's knowledge of dog's propensity to bite. **Anim 74(5)**
Biting, owner's knowledge of vicious propensities of dog. **Anim 74(3)**
Biting breeder and trainer accompanying owner, contributory negligence. **Anim 71**
Biting child—
Anim 74(5)
Parent & C 7(9)
Biting dog—
Liability for injuries. **Anim 68**
Bloodhounds, identification of defendant, admissibility. **Crim Law 386**

Illustration H

A typical page in a "Descriptive Word Index".

irrelevant cases. Thus, a search word like "Negligence" would be too broad and lead to many unrelated cases. "Supermarket," "Slip" and "Fall" are more likely to be useful, and a term as specific as "lettuce" might be effective. The broader the search, the more irrelevant information will be retrieved, and the more time-consuming it will be to pinpoint useful cases.

Illustrations I–1 to I–4, respectively, show only some of the entries under Lettuce, Slipping, Fall, and Supermarket in the "Descriptive Word Index" of the *Eighth Decennial Digest.* Note the variety of topics and key numbers to which one is directed. Note also that "lettuce" was *not* an effective search term, but that the other words *were* helpful, particularly when relevant subheadings of the primary search word were used.

One of the faults of the problems assigned in legal research courses, is that they encourage the belief that for every hypothetical problem, there is a perfectly-designed case abstract waiting to be found. In practice one seldom finds a precedent in which an identical fact situation raised the exact legal issues and resulted in the same decision. What one realistically hopes to find is a precedent that involves *similar* facts and the same legal issues. One must usually analogize from similar situations. "Descriptive Word Indexes" can be quite effective, but they rarely produce the research equivalent of a golfer's "hole in one".

c. The Topic Method

A generally less effective approach to the digests is through one of the more than 400 topics by which West's digests are classified. By scanning the topics in the front of the digests (or by knowing beforehand which topic is most relevant), one can focus on an appropriate topic for searching. One then studies the scope note and analysis which precedes each topic in the body of the digest to determine the most relevant key number subdivisions of that topic. In a small, specific topic, with relatively few subdivisions, like that shown in Illustration J, the approach might work. However, choosing the correct topic is quite chancy and the process of scanning the subdivisions for the relevant key numbers may be very time-consuming. This is usually an extremely ineffective means of research, and generally inferior to the index method. However, if the "Descriptive Word Index" yields nothing, a topic search may be worth trying, as a last resort.

d. Caveats

There are several dangers and disadvantages in using the digests which should be recognized by the researcher. Because digests serve as case finders, leading researchers to summaries of, and citations to, court decisions, the temptation exists to treat them as primary

Illustration I-1

From the "Descriptive Word Index" for the *Eighth Decennial Digest.*

47–8th D—1026

SLEEPLESSNESS
Workmen's compensation, arising out of employment, evidence. **Work Comp 1552**

SLEEPWALKING
Homicide, defenses. **Homic 254**

SLEEVES
Border inspection, persons entering required to roll up sleeves for arm inspection. **Cust Dut 126**

SLICK FLOOR
Store patron fall, excess oil, evidence. **Neglig 134(5, 7)**

SLIDE
Assumption of risk, father not wanting children to think him "chicken." **Neglig 105**

SLIDE DEVICES
Res ipsa loquitur, amusement slide, drinking patron disregarding warning signs. **Theaters 6(39)**

SLIDE RULES
Interscholastic league, director barring slide rule from contest. **Monop 28 (1.7)**

SLIDER RECLINER HARDWARE UNITS
Preliminary injunction, competitor using units to solicit sales for own hardware. **Trade Reg 613**

SLIDES
Children and minors, injuries from defective slide. **Neglig 134(4)**
City's liability for injuries to minor in park. **Mun Corp 851**
Fall, claim notice asserting slide defective, negligence and breach of warranty. **Schools 112**
Swimming pool, club erecting slide, seller's liability to injured club member. **Prod Liab 60**
Television station's preparation for advertiser—
Constituting sale. **Licens 15.1(5)**
Sales tax. **Licens 15.1(5)**
Wounds, etc., on murder victim's body, evidence, premeditation—
Crim Law 438(6)
Homic 142(8)

SLIDING BOARD
Contributory negligence of motel guests. **Inn 10.7**

SLIDING DOORS
Business invitee, using doors for support, injury. **Neglig 136(24)**

SLIDING GLASS DOORS
Church, negligence, child falling through. **Relig Soc 30**
Manufacturer guaranteeing water tightness, water entering during hurricane, damages. **Sales 442(6, 8)**
Stores, safety glass. **Neglig 136(22)**

SLING
Rating information, necessity for warning ultimate users a jury question. **Neglig 136(24)**

SLINGERS
Trademarks, jeans, similarity to Singer for textile piece goods. **Trade Reg 196**

SLINGSHOT
Infants—
Hunting companion—
Assumption of risk. **Weap 18 (2)**
Minor, purchasing at church bazaar, subsequent eye injury. **Insurance 435.22(2, 4)**

SLIP AND FALL
Basketball player, water puddle resulting from auditorium roof leak. **Neglig 32(1), 119(1), 122(1), 136(22)**
Dark colored scatter rug on light colored floor. **Neglig 136(22)**
Diving board, city swimming pool. **Mun Corp 857**

SLIP AND FALL—Cont'd
Foreign objects on floor, liability of owner of establishment. **Neglig 44, 48**
Grocery store customer, string bean on floor. **Neglig 121(1)**
Guest, on steps at rear of residence. **Neglig 136(22)**
Hotel restaurant, hotel employees' knowledge of alleged extraneous substance on floor. **Inn 10.12**
Negligence, question for jury. **Judgm 185.3(21)**
Store entranceway, water tracked in by customers on rainy day. **Neglig 44, 50**

SLIP CASTING
Green ceramic ware, production method, patentability. **Pat 18**

SLIP OF THE TONGUE
District attorney, inaccurate statement that accused plead guilty. **Crim Law 730(2)**
Instructions to jury, defendant's failure to testify, prejudice. **Crim Law 1172.2**

SLIPPERY ROAD
Rear-end collision, rush hour traffic. **Autos 172(7)**

SLIPPING
Admiralty, jurisdiction, merchant vessel moored as visitor attraction. **Adm 20**
Automobiles slipping off jack, driver's liability for failure to release brakes—
Autos 245(9)
Evid 201, 265(2)
Bank customer falling on water-slick floor, bank's knowledge of danger **Neglig 111(1, 2)**
Bill collector slipping on linoleum, action against housing authority. **Neglig 122(1)**
Caterer serving food at wedding banquet—
Injuries by fall on dance floor by slipping on food. **Neglig 134(5), 136(22)**
Court's decision dependent on peculiar facts of case. **Courts 89**
Dry cleaning deliveryman, injuries—
Ice covered stairway. **Neglig 136 (22)**
Evidence, other falls or near falls attributable to same conditions. **Neglig 125**
Expert testimony, foot will slide on dry cement, sand, and gravel on floor—
App & E 1050.1(12)
Evid 506
Flying bridge, debris left by antenna insulator installer, contribution. **Ship 85**
Greasy substance, store floor, customer slipping. **Neglig 134(5)**
Lathe, attempt to step over exposed worm gear, contributory negligence. **Corp 306**
Pizza vendor's constructive knowledge of slippery floor, customers eating in aisles. **Neglig 48**
Plastic pin, store aisle, fact question of storeowner's knowledge. **Neglig 136(16)**
Policeman, lower back injury, service connected disability. **Mun Corp 187 (10)**
Railroad's liability for injuries to student switchman slipping on oil on engine step, question for jury. **Mast & S 285(7)**
Restaurant patron, liability for maintaining floor similar in color to catsup. **Neglig 44**
Sand, third-parties placing on city sidewalk, pedestrian slipping. **Indem 15 (6)**
Seaworthiness, oil or grease on deck or bilge, noncrew member marine worker slipping. **Ship 84(3¼)**
Separate grounds of recovery, failure to remove dangerous condition, failure to warn. **Neglig 50, 52**

47–8th D—1027

SLIPPING—Cont'd
Store customer—
Mopped and damp floor—
Contributory negligence. **Neglig 82**
Store customer on floor with sawdust—
Contributory negligence. **Neglig 66 (1)**
Supermarket, patron on melted ice cream on floor. **Damag 132(3)**
Trespassing boy, injuries—
Slipping from rock platform into pond. **Neglig 85(4)**
Throw rug, obvious peril, social visitor. **Neglig 32(1)**
Workmens compensation—
Emotional problems, initial injury from slip on employer's floor. **Work Comp 597**
Garbage collector, slip or fall down knoll, causal connection with disability. **Work Comp 1593**
Jack during repair of automobile causing death—
Course of employment. **Work Comp 1559**
Nurse, hospital floor, pelvic traction. **Work Comp 1637**
Waiter leaving after finishing job, fall on sidewalk of employer's leased premises. **Work Comp 732**

SLITTER MACHINES
Unexpected activation, assumption of risk by employee attempting to adjust machine. **Torts 28**

SLOGANS
Contempt, shouting "All power to the people" in court. **Contempt 7**
Hair color so natural only her hairdresser knows for sure, registrability as trademark. **Trade Reg 165**
Radio stations, call letters, infringement of slogan by radio station with similar call letters. **Trade Reg 587, 596, 598**

SLOT MACHINE REPAIRMAN
Admission to gambling establishment supervisors, admission in evidence. **Crim Law 406(2)**

SLOT MACHINES
Amusement devices, coin operated, sales tax liability. **Licens 15.1(5)**
Bailment, compensation limit to 50 percent of gross receipts, validity of statute. **Licens 7(1)**
Booby-trap, dynamite charge, child killed while engaged in theft—
Death 21
Neglig 47
Car wash business, police power to regulate—
Const Law 296(1)
Mun Corp 611
Cheating device, demonstrative evidence, admissibility. **Crim Law 650**
Console and pinball machines, free plays for replay or merchandise. **Gaming 68(3)**
Contracts, five-year term, supplier permitted to modify, repair, or replace, validity. **Contracts 10(7)**
Customs duties, plastic article resembling slot machine properly classified as toy. **Cust Dut 37(15)**
Free-play pinball machines, state law permitting, federal forfeiture for nonregistration. **Gaming 58**
Gambling—
Criminal responsibility—
Search and forfeiture, machines designed and manufactured for—
Const Law 258
Gaming 52
Forfeitures, unregistered claimant engaged in business sought to be regulated. **Const Law 319**
Searches and seizures—
Seizure without warrant specifying. **Crim Law 394.4(8)**
Stamp dispensing machine resembling slot machine. **Gaming 87 (1)**
Gambling device test, element of chance, validity of statute prescribing test. **Gaming 63(1)**

Illustration I–2

From the "Descriptive Word Index" for the *Eighth Decennial Digest.*

46–8th D—1176

FALL—Cont'd

States, water trickling down embankment, claimant falling on sidewalk. **States 184.24**

Statute of limitation, tolling, praecipe for writ of summons filed. **Lim of Act 119(2)**

Step constructed instead of ramp, expert testimony charging bad practice. **Evid 507**

Step-down at end of exit ramp, construction safety standards, evidence. **Neglig 124(1)**

Step-in-the-dark rule, conflicting evidence disproving voluntary, deliberate step into unknown darkness presenting question for jury. **Neglig 136(10)**

Stepping from sidewalk by pedestrian—
- Abutting owners, liability for injuries. **Mun Corp 808(1)**

Stepping stone, close juxtaposition to walk leading to house, duty to warn of existence. **Neglig 52**

Steps, deterioration of nonslip surface, liability. **Neglig 31**

Stone masons, ladder rung collapsing, homeowner's policy exclusion of persons on premises for business services. **Insurance 467.4**

Store—
- Manager patrolling area every ten minutes, porters cleaning up debris half hourly. **Neglig 50**
- Nonfeasance of manager, sufficiency of petition. **Neglig 54**
- Remodeling subcontractor spreading slippery substance on floor, owner's vicarious liability. **Mast & S 316(2)**
- Running youths knocking down customer. **Neglig 134(7)**

Store aisle, customer stepping on floor polisher attachment, clerk observing other person using attachment to skate in aisles. **Neglig 134(5)**

Store customer—
- Broken jar of mayonnaise. **Neglig 136(22)**
- Contributory negligence. **Neglig 82**
- Gentle sloping asphalt surface. **Neglig 134(5)**
- Pool of liquid on floor. **Neglig 134(5)**
- Slippery condition of floor, constructive notice. **Neglig 48, 121(1)**

Store customer, sawdust on floor—
- Contributory negligence. **Neglig 66(1)**

Store entrance, icy condition, contributory negligence of customer. **Neglig 66(1)**

Store employee's conflicting testimony about cleaning floor. **Neglig 134(5)**

Store invitee, presence of water, mud or snow on floor. **Neglig 32(1), 121(3)**

Storekeeper failing to place mat inside door in rainy weather, slip and fall plaintiff, burden of proving knowledge of dangerous condition. **Neglig 134(8)**

Storekeepers, interior arrangements of store representing circumstances likely to deceive reasonable man, jury question. **Neglig 136(22)**

Store patron—
- Escalator—
  - Knowledge of popcorn and other debris. **Carr 293, 318(3)**
- Slippery substance on floor. **Judgm 185.3(21)**
- Slipping in puddle, assumption of risk defense. **Neglig 136(2)**

Stores, res ipsa loquitur. **Neglig 121(3)**

Stores and storekeepers—
- Customer slipping in passageway in front, cashiers busy and not sweeping. **Neglig 50**
- Floor freshly waxed, jury question whether negligently maintained. **Neglig 136(22)**
- Knowledge of substance on floor, no direct evidence. **Neglig 48**

46–8th D—1177

FALL—Cont'd

Stores and storekeepers—Cont'd
- Slippery substance creating unreasonable hazard, time on floor not shown. **Neglig 134(7)**
- Unexplained grape on floor of produce department. **Neglig 121(3)**
- Water or foreign substance, normal accumulation from customers tracking in. **Neglig 44**

Stormy day, risk to invitees from way entry arranged, necessity for instruction—
- **App & E 1067**
- **Neglig 138(3)**

Strangulation, fog room, child falling while wearing jacket tied to crib spring. **Phys 15(8), 16, 18.80(2)**

Stream of water, attempt to avoid when stepping onto dock area. **Neglig 135(1)**

Streetcar, motorman's miscalculation requiring sudden stop, passenger falling. **Carr 318(4)**

Street pavement defect, judgment non obstante veredicto, negligence not shown. **Judgm 199(3.15)**

Strict liability, lessor, hotel lessee's employee falling from defective duck board. **Land & Ten 165(1)**

Stringbean, store customer slipping on, time laying on floor not shown, employee not causing presence. **Neglig 44, 48**

Strip mine shovel, status as structure. **Neglig 31**

Structural engineer, climbing horizontal steel members instead of ladder, fall due to electric shock. **Electricity 19(12)**

Structural work, general contractor's status as one having charge of work, jury question. **Mast & S 332(3)**

Structural work, instruction using direct cause instead of proximate cause. **App & E 1064.1(7)**

Stump, child running from football game on adjoining lot. **Neglig 33(3)**

Subcontractors—
- Employee—

Subcontractor's employee, contractor not reporting to insurer for almost two years. **Insurance 539.12(4)**
- Hazardous condition causing fall through roof self-created. **Mast & S 319**
- Hole created by crew of subcontractor, general contractor not liable. **Neglig 55**
  - Platform chain hoist giving way, evidence, prime contractor negligence. **Neglig 134(1, 8)**
- Lessee's employee, operation of forklift truck—
  - **App & E 1067**
  - **Land & Ten 169(10)**
- President of general building construction contractor not liable. **Corp 306**

Subcontractor's employee, supervisors knowing of hole, contractor's duty to warn. **Neglig 55**

Subcontractor's workman, contractor's scaffolding device lacking safety rail. **Indem 8(4)**

Subfloor giving way, floor load limits violation not shown to be cause. **Neglig 134(5, 11)**

Sublet hall for wedding reception, lessee not obliged to inspect after reception started. **Land & Ten 167(1, 8)**

Substance on store floor, duration and placement by employees, customer unable to prove. **Neglig 136(22)**

Sub-subcontractor's employee, hole in floor, demolition work. **Mast & S 318(1)**

Substance on store floor 15–20 minutes beforehand. **Neglig 48**

Subway station, substance on stairs hard and dirty. **Carr 318(2)**

Subway station stairs, patron, assumption of disputed fact. **Trial 382**

Sugar on floor of supermarket, aisles of store swept morning, afternoon and night. **Neglig 44**

FALL—Cont'd

Summary judgment—
- Condition on adjoining private property exposing sidewalk users to substantial risk. **Judgm 185.3(21)**
- Tomato near produce section, store customer slipping. **Judgm 185.3(21)**

Summary proceedings—
- Judgment, continuance, plaintiff lacking time to get witness' affidavit. **Judgm 186**

Summary proceedings, judgment, store patron carrying grocery bags obstructing vision, stepping in driveway hole. **Judgm 185.3(21)**

Sunken living room, prospective purchaser tripping while entering, model home. **Neglig 136(22)**

Supermarket—
- Child falling from shopping cart on parking lot during nonbusiness hours, summary judgment precluded. **Judgm 181(33)**
- Customer tripping and falling against stack of beer cases. **Neglig 44, 56(2), 82**
- Evidence not showing cause was substance on floor or known dangerous condition. **Neglig 134(11)**
- Patron turning after conversation with employee holding icy packages. **Neglig 134(5)**
- Patron's slip on melted ice cream on floor. **Damag 132(3)**
- Wet floor. **Neglig 136(26)**
- Whipped cream-covered pumpkin pie sample on floor. **Neglig 44, 50**

Supermarket aisle, debris on floor causing, res ipsa loquitur. **Neglig 121(3)**

Supermarket customer, candy wrapper on sidewalk outside supermarket, summary judgment not granted. **Judgm 181(33)**

Super market customer, tripping and falling over flour bag. **Neglig 135(4)**

Supermarket customer tripping over check-out boy activating automatic door, contributory negligence. **Neglig 66(1)**

Supermarket invitee, supermarket's comprehension of danger, jury instruction. **Neglig 139(6)**
- Merchandise attractively displayed, customer's duty of due care. **Neglig 67**

Supermarket parking lot, lessee with right to make repairs and deduct cost from rent, liability for injuries sustained by customer. **Land & Ten 167(5)**

Supermarket sidewalk, operator's third-party complaint against owner, common-law indemnity. **Indem 15(6)**

Supervised church group outing, charitable immunity doctrine. **Char 45(2)**

Swimmer, push from behind while standing on diving platform, municipality's liability. **Theaters 6(9)**

Swimming pool, absence of self-latching and closing gate, infant falling in **Prod Liab 62**

Swimming pool excavation, minor falling into in own yard, contractor's liability. **Neglig 136(15)**

Swimming pool slide, failure to re-anchor slide legs. **Neglig 134(11)**

Swing, child injured by collapse, town employees not carefully assembling. **Towns 79**

Swing, unreasonable risk to children, knowledge of defendant, fact question. **Neglig 136(16)**

Synthetic swimming pool, small amount of water, nine year old trespasser breaking elbow. **Neglig 33(3)**

Tailgate, mounting to direct backing, driver causing truck to jerk, last clear chance. **Autos 227(3)**

Tarpaulin covering new paving, walking over in dark. **Neglig 67**

Tavern—
- Intoxicated patron, wrongful death. **Int Liq 295**

Illustration I–3

From the "Descriptive Word Index" for the *Eighth Decennial Digest.*

SUNKEN VESSELS OR CARGO

47–8th D—1138

SUNKEN VESSELS OR CARGO
Abandonment, divesture of title. **Ship 213**
Continental shelf, wreck outside territorial waters, government's jurisdiction—
  Salv 4
  U S 2
Diving and salvage operations, enjoining within state territorial waters. **Nav Wat 36(5)**
Navigable waters, removal. **Nav Wat 26(2)**

SUNLIGHT
Automobiles, sun impairing vision, duty of care. **Autos 211**
Blinding motorist, stopping within assured clear distance ahead. **Autos 168(1)**
Blinding motorist, striking pedestrian. **Autos 244(34)**

SUNRISE AND SUNSET
Time charts, admissibility. **Evid 361**

SUNSHINE LAW
Jurisdiction of court. **Courts 206(16)**

SUNSHINE LIST
Bank charter applications, notice only to listed persons. **Banks 6**

SUNTAN LOTION
Advertisement, toddler with bare bottom, offensive sexual material. **Obscen 5**

SUPER BOWL
Television policy, class suit attacking, standing to maintain. **Fed Civ Proc 181, 187**

SUPER CONTRACT
Police, step and longevity pay, ordinance not providing due to wage freeze. **Mun Corp 889**

SUPER LITE
Safety, federal statute, preemption of state regulation, automobiles. **States 4.13**

SUPERENFRANCHISEMENT
Weighted voting plan, county government, smaller units superenfranchised. **Counties 38**

SUPERFECTA WAGERS
Tickets not representing winning selection, bets on winning selection refused. **Gaming 25**

SUPERFICIARY HOUSE
Adverse possession. **Adv Poss 60(1)**

SUPERINTENDENT OF SCHOOLS
Suspension with salary for duration of contract without hearing, due process. **Const Law 318(2)**

SUPERINTENDENTS
Attorney fees, successful challenge to discharge by school district. **Civil R 13.17**
County superintendent of education, Voting Rights Act, applicability. **Elections 12**
Insurance, see this index **Insurance Commissioner or Superintendent**
Labor relations board, counsel for general counsel remarking about superintendent's national origin—
  Const Law 318(4)
  Labor 727
Public instruction, validity of constitutional amendments deleting office. **Const Law 9(1)**
Public Works—
  Conservation law authorizing direction to removal or reconstruct for improving water in natural stream or water course, construction. **Waters 37**
  Mandamus, court of claims as without jurisdiction to issue mandamus to require approval of final estimate and final payment under contract. **Mand 141**
School districts, board selecting superintendent without consulting community groups. **Schools 63(1)**

SUPERINTENDENTS—Cont'd
School districts, termination of contract, discretion. **Schools 53(5), 63(1)**
Schools—
  Absence of order and fairness in removal hearing. **School 48(4, 7)**
  Administrative and teaching certificates of, revocation. **Schools 61**
  Attorneys' services utilized as legal advisers for school officers. **Atty & C 11(2)**
  Boundaries, amending record. **Schools 63(3)**
  Discharge of teacher, hearing. **Schools 141(5)**
  Disciplinary hearing, majority group also comprising investigative or prosecutorial body. **Const Law 318(2)**
  Exemption from increased minimum requirements, office holders and persons serving one term. **Schools 46**
  Libel and slander, defamatory statements made at school board meeting. **Libel 50**
  Removal by county board, reversal without notice of appeal. **Schools 48(4)**
  Removal from office, quorum. **Schools 48(4)**
  Termination of employment, board acting in executive session. **Schools 56**
  Unused annual leave, judgment obtained for compensation, attorney fees. **Costs 173(1)**
State police, county court appeals involving, attorney general to appear. **Atty Gen 4**
Town highways, trespass. **High 96(1)**

SUPERINTENDENTS OF RECREATION
City park, duty to provide. **Mun Corp 851**

SUPERINTENDING CONTROL
Order of court, authority to issue to prosecutor and assistants. **Const Law 72**

SUPERIOR COURTS
Appellate jurisdiction—
  Kentucky. **Courts 223(2)**
  Pennsylvania. **Courts 242(3)**
Attorney's fees, application, treatment as having been made in appellate division. **Costs 252**
Class suits, aggregation of claims to meet jurisdictional amount. **Courts 121(4)**
Hearing, jurisdiction to conduct, waiver of infant's right to hearing on transfer to adult status. **Infants 68**
Judge, habeas corpus writ on grounds prior to affirmance of conviction judgment. **Hab Corp 4**
Judicial notice, transfer of judges from one department to another. **Evid 5(2)**
Public utilities commission order closing city street, review jurisdiction absent. **R R 94(2)**

SUPERIOR EQUITIES DOCTRINE
Stolen automobile, good-faith buyer owning corporation, liability to insurer. **Sales 234(6)**

SUPERIOR KNOWLEDGE
Element of res ipsa loquitur. **Neglig 121.2(4)**

SUPERIOR KNOWLEDGE PRINCIPLE
Sovereign acts defense, independence of knowledge principle. **U S 70(24)**

SUPERMARKET LEASE
Shopping center, execution violating supermarket lease. **Land & Ten 44(1)**

SUPERMARKET PYLON
Defective engineering design, collapse, patron injuries. **Neglig 136(22, 25)**

SUPERMARKETS
Amusement ride—
  Splitting profits—
    Joint adventures. **Joint Adv 1.12**
Amusement rides, child injury. **Theaters 6(27)**
Burglary, entry without authority element. **Burg 4**
Collective bargaining—
  Unit representation. **Labor 205**
Covenant in lease precluding construction, injunction—
  Inj 62(2), 113
  Land & Ten 44(1)
Customer slipping and falling on sugar on floor, aisles swept morning, afternoon and night. **Neglig 44**
Customer tripping and falling over bag of flour. **Neglig 135(4)**
Door in entryway, controlled during repairs. **Neglig 134(5)**
Fall—
  Child from shopping cart on parking lot during nonbusiness hours, summary judgment precluded. **Judgm 181(33)**
  Customer slipping on candy wrapper on sidewalk outside supermarket, summary judgment not granted. **Judgm 181(33)**
  Owner-operator allowing continued use of old, frayed runner or mat. **Neglig 48**
  Transparent oil substance on floor. **Neglig 67**
  Whipped creamed-covered pumpkin pie sample on floor. **Neglig 44, 50**
Fires—
  Cigarettes. **Neglig 134(2)**
Fruit on floor causing fall, negligence. **Neglig 136(16)**
Injuries to pedestrian by fall of board, lessee's liability, res ipsa loquitur. **Land & Ten 169(4)**
Labor contract, change of ownership terminating employee rights. **Labor 262**
Leases, sprinkler system installation, tenant obligations. **Land & Ten 157(1)**
Lotteries, enforcement. **Lotteries 3**
Lotteries, promotional drawings. **Lotteries 21**
Malicious prosecution, patron arrested as common thief. **Mal Pros 68**
Managers, heart attack, workmen's compensation. **Work Comp 1536**
Prices, inducing discriminatory price from suppliers. **Trade Reg 923**
Product picketing, use of lighted candles by picketers enjoined. **Labor 843**
Res ipsa loquitur—
  Debris on floor causing fall. **Neglig 121(3)**
  Falling board striking pedestrian. **Land & Ten 169(4)**
Retail grocer, promotional drawings. **Lotteries 21**
Robbery, employee's and customer's testimony, corroboration of accomplice. **Crim Law 511(5)**
Robbery, evidence. **Rob 24(1)**
Self-service by customers, judicial notice. **Evid 20(1)**
Shopping cart, falling object. **Neglig 121(3)**
Tax exemption, industrial incentive program. **Tax 220**
3.2 beer, off premises license, arbitrary denial of application. **Int Liq 71**
Town, validity of bylaws forbidding food and beverage sales between specfied hours. **Const Law 296(1)**
Unfair trade practices—
  Chain stores, price cutting, particular location destroying competition. **Trade Reg 928**
Union label grapes and lettuce, enjoining picketing and leaflet distribution to induce limitation of amount and quantity of lettuce and grapes sold. **Labor 836**
Union organization, supervisors attempted undermining, good faith refusal to bargain. **Labor 394**

Illustration I–4

From the "Descriptive Word Index" for the *Eighth Decennial Digest.*

18–9th D Pt 1—664

FISH

SUBJECTS INCLUDED

Animals inhabiting the water
Regulations for their preservation
Nature and incidents of rights of fishery

SUBJECTS EXCLUDED AND COVERED BY OTHER TOPICS

Sunday, fishing on, see SUNDAY

For detailed references to other topics, see Descriptive-Word Index

Analysis

1. Nature of property.
2. What is fish.
3. Fish in public waters.
4. Seal fisheries.
5. Private rights of fishery.
   (1). Nature, acquisition, and extent.
   (2). Conveyances and contracts respecting fishery rights.
   (3). Civil liability for invasion of private rights.
6. Injury to or destruction of fish.
7. Oyster and clam beds.
   (1). In general.
   (2). Grant, allotment, or lease by public authorities.
   (3). Invasion of private rights.
8. Power to protect and regulate.
9. Constitutional and statutory provisions.
10. Licenses.
   (1). In general.
   (2). Fishing locations.
11. Fish wardens and other officers.
12. Preservation and propagation.
13. Offenses.
   (1). In general.
   (2). Use of nets or other devices.
   (3). Offenses as to oysters, clams, and other shellfish.
14. Penalties for violations of regulations.
15. Criminal prosecutions.
16. Searches, seizures, and forfeitures.
17. Rights of property and contracts as to fish illegally taken.

For detailed references to other topics, see Descriptive-Word Index

Illustration J

Scope and analysis of a short topic in the *Ninth Decennial Digest.*

source material. As noted above, a case should not be cited merely on the basis of its abstract. The actual decision must be read to verify its holding and its relevancy, and then Shepardized to determine its current authority.

The universal nature of the structure of topics and key numbers in the West digest system sometimes leads researchers to the following misconceptions. Some assume that the subject and topic breakdown created by the West system is the only possible means of classifying legal situations. Other digesting systems exist that divide legal subjects in very different ways. An unsuccessful search in the digests does not preclude more favorable results in another system. Researchers may think that the West digest system is the only available case finding device. The next sections describe a variety of alternative approaches.

Among the disadvantages of the digests, we can note the following characteristics: (1) They contain no narrative text or explanatory comment, but frequently only a long, undifferentiated series of abstracts which the researcher must then synthesize. (2) They do not reflect change in the law very well, and do not clearly indicate when cases are later overruled, questioned, or criticized. (3) They reflect statutory law, which is central to our legal system, only incidentally and without reflecting its importance in analyzing many cases and issues. (4) They do not effectively distinguish between dicta and holding, and for safety sake tend to over-abstract most cases, thereby rendering their use cumbersome and time-consuming. (5) The rigidity of their subject structure does not always allow for the variations which exist in some jurisdictions.

Despite its shortcomings, the digest remains an ingenious and essential part of our research apparatus. While a digest is sometimes a poor choice as an initial search mechanism, it is often a very effective tool in research involving the use and manipulation of case law. However, the computerized research systems, described in Section F below and later in Chapter 22, will increasingly be favored over the digests, at least for those who can afford and arrange access to them.

C. CASE FINDING IN ANNOTATED REPORTS

West's digest system is so comprehensive, and has become so traditional a feature of legal research, that it is easy to overlook the availability and utility of other digests and case finding tools. Among these are the various search tools associated with the annotated reporting system of Lawyers Co-op.

1. U.S. SUPREME COURT DIGEST, LAWYERS' EDITION

For access to the decisions of the U.S. Supreme Court, there is an alternative to the West digest, namely the *United States Supreme Court Digest, Lawyers' Edition,* published in approximately thirty volumes by Lawyers Co-operative/Bancroft Whitney.[6] This digest divides the legal issues covered by the decisions of the U.S. Supreme Court into some 400 topics and numerous subdivisions of those topics. These topics and subtopics are, however, different from those used by West, and some claim that, because the *Lawyers' Edition* digest is designed specifically around Supreme Court decisions, it can accommodate them better than the West scheme, which has to be general enough to cover *all* jurisdictions. In any case, this different arrangement is keyed to the headnotes and annotations in the Lawyers' Co-op *United States Supreme Court Reports, Lawyers' Edition.* It can be accessed in essentially the same three ways as has been described above for the West digests, but without the same versatility for use in other digests as the West topics and key numbers. Like other Lawyers Co-op publications, it is tied by cross references to *ALR* and *ALR Federal,* as well as to the *Lawyers' Edition* itself. The digest also includes several useful volumes of court rules and rules of evidence for the federal courts. All volumes of the digest are updated annually by pocket part supplementation.

6. This publication has previously been called *Digest of United States Supreme Court Reports* and *United States Supreme Court Digest, Annotated.*

2. A.L.R. DIGESTS

As described more extensively in Chapter 4, there are now four series of *A.L.R.*, as well as a separate reporter, *A.L.R. Federal,* for selected federal court decisions. The finding tools developed by Lawyers Co-op for *A.L.R.* have changed over time. One of the early forms was the *A.L.R. Digest,* which was organized to function like a West digest, but with a different classification scheme. There are two such digests: one for *A.L.R.1st,* the other for *A.L.R.2d.* There are no digests for *A.L.R.3d* or *4th,* or for *A.L.R. Federal.* To find cases by subject in these later series, the appropriate *Quick Index* should be consulted.

3. QUICK INDEXES

The preferred method of finding cases and annotations in the *A.L.R.* system is the use of alphabetical subject indexes called *Quick Indexes.* Four such indexes exist, corresponding to the *A.L.R.1st, A.L.R.2d, A.L.R.3d & 4th* (covering all volumes of *A.L.R.3d* plus all volumes of *A.L.R.4th* issued to date), and *A.L.R. Federal.*

The *A.L.R.3d & 4th Quick Index* contains references not only to annotations in those series, but also to *A.L.R. Federal* annotations and to two other Lawyers Co-op publications, *Am.Jur. Proof of Facts* and *Am.Jur. Trials.* The *Federal Quick Index, 3d Edition,* in two volumes, indexes all federal matters contained in the other publications of Lawyers Co-op, including *A.L.R. Federal* annotations.

Pocket supplements are issued for both currently-published *Quick Indexes,* and are located (unusually) inside the *front* cover of the bound volumes. They are cumulatively updated and replaced with every odd-numbered volume of *A.L.R.4th* and *A.L.R. Federal,* and should be consulted to update one's research.

4. THE ANNOTATION

As seen in Chapter 4, the various *A.L.R.* series are designed to report significant court decisions selectively, and to append to them exhaustive analyses of the points of law discussed in those decisions. Since these analyses attempt to incorporate references to other important American court decisions dealing with the legal issues decided in the cases being annotated, *A.L.R.* annotations can often be used effectively as case finding tools.

Included with each annotation is a "Table of Jurisdictions Represented" or, in *A.L.R. Federal,* a "Table of Courts and Circuits." The texts of the annotations are organized by sections, and the tables refer to those sections in which cases from other jurisdictions are discussed or cited. If the case being annotated in *A.L.R.* discusses the relevant point of law being researched but was decided by a court other than one which is of concern to the researcher, references to relevant case law in the researcher's jurisdiction of interest may be uncovered through these jurisdictional tables.

D. OTHER CASE FINDING TOOLS

1. WORDS AND PHRASES

Since many cases turn on the definition or interpretation of a particular word or phrase, case finding often involves the search for decisions containing such interpretations. For this purpose, West has compiled *Words and Phrases,* a specialized digest of definitions of thousands of legally significant words and phrases, abstracted from court decisions. Sometimes viewed as a judicial dictionary, *Words and Phrases* consists of forty-six volumes of case abstracts which are drawn from West reporters and are identical to the abstracts appearing in West digests and annotated codes. Here the abstracts are presented under the alphabetically arranged words and phrases which they define, interpret or construe. No text synthesis or evaluation is provided, and the set is more of a digest than a dictionary. In any event, it is a useful, specialized case finder and is faster and more efficient than other digests when the search concerns the meaning or judicial interpretation of a word or phrase. When the number of abstracts under a particular word or phrase warrants it, an index to those abstracts is provided. Cross references to related terms are also used. Each abstract includes the full citation of the decision from which it is derived, so that the decision can be read in full, evaluated, and, if relevant, then Shepardized. As with other digests, the decisions should not be cited merely on the basis of the abstract.

Words and Phrases is supplemented by annual pocket parts in each of its volumes, and by tables of words and phrases which are included in the advance sheets and bound volumes of all West reporters.

Illustration K shows a typical page in *Words and Phrases.*

2. POPULAR NAME TABLES

Judicial decisions are sometimes referred to by their "popular" names. These designations may be quite famous, e.g., the "Dred Scott Case" or they may be quite obscure, "popular" only in the broadest sense of that term. (See, for example, some of those in Illustration L.) Fortunately, there is a tool, *Shepard's Acts and Cases by Popular Names,* which serves as a guide in either situation. Covering both the federal and state levels, this volume lists many popular names in alphabetical order, and provides full citations for them. A bound volume now in its second edition, is updated by a cumulative pamphlet supplement. Illustration L presents a page from this useful publication.

Similar popular name tables were formerly published as part of some West digests, but these tables have now been discontinued. Since the Shepard's table does not duplicate entirely those in the West digests, the latter may still be useful for older cases.

FISCAL YEAR

"Fiscal year" within contract for cultivation of land in citrus grove authorizing owner of grove to take possession thereof at any time prior to expiration of contract on payment of all amounts then due and payment in advance for cultivation of grove for balance of current "fiscal year," commenced on date when parties began to execute contract according to terms and conditions of letter written by owner transferring contract to land other than that described in original contract rather than on date of original contract. Bishop v. Orange Belt Securities Co., 174 So. 1, 2, 127 Fla. 709.

Where corporation had no accounting period which ended on last day of month except by accident, it had no fiscal year within meaning of Revenue Act 1918, § 212(b), 40 Stat. 1064, directing manner in which net income to be returned shall be computed, and together with section 200, 40 Stat. 1058, laying down a rule with reference to accounting periods and defining term "fiscal year," and requiring computation of net income on basis of calendar year where taxpayer's annual accounting is other than fiscal year, or in case taxpayer has no annual accounting period, or does not keep books. Swift & Co. v. U. S., Ct.Cl., 38 F.2d 365, 376.

Since V.A.M.S.Const. art. 10, § 12, limiting the extent to which a county, city, or town may incur an indebtedness in any year does not use the words "fiscal year," and since the word "year" as used therein means a calendar year as a basis from which to determine the amount of debt which may be contracted for that year, and that basis must be taken both by counties and cities for the purpose indicated, the words "fiscal year," as used in Rev.St.1919, § 8275, V.A.M.S. § 95.350, Laws 1893, p. 77, § 70, authorizing a municipality to incur a bonded indebtedness not to exceed one-half of the amount of revenue for the fiscal year, means calendar year, the use of the word "fiscal" not sufficing within section 7058, V.A.M.S. § 1.020 et seq. to show a contrary meaning; "fiscal" meaning financial year, at the end of which accounts are balanced. Union Trust & Savings Bank v. City of Sedalia, 254 S.W. 28, 30, 300 Mo. 399.

FISH

Index to sub-groups

Cross References

Anadromous
Animal
Fast Fish
Feræ Naturæ
Food Fish
Fresh Fish
Royal Fishes
Seining of Fish for Commercial Purposes
Soft Fish
Splitting Fish
Taking Fish

Cross references to related terms

In general

"Fish" are feræ naturæ. Columbia River Fishermen's Protective Union v. City of St. Helens, 87 P.2d 195, 198, 160 Or. 654; Van Clief v. Comptroller of State of Md., 126 A.2d 865, 867, 211 Md. 191.

Fish, before they are taken, are property of no one. Fuller v. Fuller, 24 A. 946, 84 Me. 475, 479.

Crabs are fish, and the law applicable to fish is applicable to crabs. State v. Savage, 184 P. 567, 570, 96 Or. 53.

Escallops are fish within the regulations of the State Fisheries Commission Board and of the statute creating it. State v. Dudley, 109 S.E. 63, 65, 182 N.C. 822.

Fish themselves are feræ naturæ—the common property of the public or of the state—in this country. State v. Theriault, 41 A. 1030, 1032, 70 Vt. 617, 43 L.R.A. 290, 67 Am.St.Rep. 695.

"The common law has always recognized the right of the riparian owner to take fish in the waters running over his own soil and appropriate them to his own use, but, the fish being the common property of the people, the owner has never had the right to obstruct their passage from that portion of the river which flows over his land, nor has he the right to destroy the fish, and thus deprive the community of their right to, and ownership in, the fish." Parker v. People, 111 Ill. 581, 603, 53 Am.Rep. 643.

Under provision of Motor Carrier Act exempting from operation of the act motor

128

Illustration K

A typical page in *Words and Phrases.*

Door Case
51 Cal2d 558, 334 P2d 881

Dope Peddler Entrapment Case
198 F2d 760

Dorado Case
62 Cal2d 338, 42 CaR 169, 398 P2d 361

Double Jeopardy Cases
429 US 1, 50 LE2d 1, 97 SC 24
429 US 5, 50 LE2d 5, 97 SC 26
429 US 14, 50 LE2d 17, 97 SC 20
430 US 564, 51 LE2d 642, 97 SC 1349
57 LE2d 1, 98 SC 2141

Dougherty Case
54 F2d 721

Dover Case
39 NJL 173

Dover Church Case
(Del) 74 At 841

Downe's Estate Case
2 TCt 967

Down's Case
336 F2d 988

Doyle Case
234 AppDiv 613, 251 NYSupp 802, 867, 868; 234 AppDiv 614, 251 NYSupp 868; 257 NY 244, 177 NE 489; 257 NY 545, 178 NE 788; 141 Misc 141, 252 NYSupp 387; 234 AppDiv 843, 253 NYSupp 1065; 258 NY 437, 180 NE 110

Draft Cases (World War II)
36 FS 915
120 F2d 236
131 F2d 818
318 US 749, 87 LE 1125, 63 SC 758
319 US 33, 87 LE 1194, 63 SC 912
319 US 785, 87 LE 1728, 63 SC 1323
132 F2d 348
318 US 754, 87 LE 1129, 63 SC 980
319 US 484, 87 LE 1534, 63 SC 1206

Drainage Commission Case
49 LaAnn 1199, 22 So 623

Draining Company Case
11 LaAnn 338

Drake Bakeries Case
370 US 254, 8 LE2d 474, 82 SC 1346; 287 F2d 155; 294 F2d 399; 196 FS 148

Dram Shop Case
9 IllApp2d 96, 132 NE2d 427

Draper Case
145 F2d 199

Dravo Case
16 FS 527; 301 US 665, 81 LE 1331, 57 SC 787; 301 US 672, 57 SC 947; 302 US 134, 82 LE 155, 58 SC 208; 114 F2d 242; 312 US 678, 85 LE 1117, 61 SC 450; 312 US 714, 85 LE 1144, 61 SC 620

Dred Scott Case
60 US 393, 15 LE 691

Drinkhouse Gambling Case
15 Misc2d 425, 183 NYSupp2d 679

Drive-It-Yourself Case
144 Md 223, 125 At 69

Driven-Well Cases
8 Fed 269
15 Fed 109; 122 US 40, 30 LE 1064, 7 SC 1073
16 Fed 387; 123 US 267, 31 LE 160, 8 SC 101; 124 US 694, 31 LE 557, 8 SC 676
FC No. 371

Driver's License Revocation Case
(Cal) 187 P2d 421; 32 Cal2d 226, 195 P2d 792

Dr. Miles Case
164 Fed 803, 90 CCA 579; 212 US 575, 53 LE 657, 29 SC 683; 220 US 373, 55 LE 502, 31 SC 376

Dr. Mudd's Case
FC No. 9,899

Drover's Pass Cases
84 US 357, 21 LE 627
95 US 655, 24 LE 535
67 Fed 209, 14 CCA 368
73 Fed 519, 19 CCA 551
200 Fed 197, 118 CCA 383
40 Ark 298
6 Del 469
160 Ill 40, 43 NE 809; 57 IllApp 538
174 Ill 13, 50 NE 1019; 69 IllApp 363
184 Ill 294, 56 NE 331; 81 IllApp 137
47 Ind 471
71 Ind 271
139 Mich 590, 102 NW 1037
88 Mo 239
24 NY 222
29 Barb 132
78 Hun 387; 149 NY 610, 44 NE 1120
19 OhioSt 1
51 PaSt 315
208 PaSt 623, 57 At 1125
13 Utah 275, 44 P 932; 15 Utah 334, 49 P 646
122 Wis 423, 99 NW 1034

Illustration L

A sample page from the case section of *Shepard's Acts and Cases by Popular Names.*

3. ANNOTATED STATUTES

Since many cases and many research problems involve the application or interpretation of statutes, the use of annotated statutory codes (to be described in Chapter 7) is frequently the best initial case finding approach for such problems. The annotated codes provide, following each statutory section, annotations containing headnote abstracts to decisions which have applied or interpreted that section. These abstracts are composed like those in the West digest, and, in the many states for which West has published such a code, the annotations are the same as those used in the West digests. When the number of annotations requires it, indexes to them are provided, just preceding the annotations. The annotations, like the statutes themselves, are updated by annual pocket parts, and, even more currently, by "Tables of Statutes Construed" in the advance sheets and bound volumes of every West reporter.

Case finding by this method has the added advantage of saving research steps—one not only has the benefit of the case abstracts in the annotations, but also has the statutory text needed for the problem, along with the other notes and cross references which are usually provided in the codes. Illustration M shows these features in a West annotated code, *U.S.C.A.*

4. SHEPARD'S

a. Citators as Case Finders

In addition to their primary functions of verifying the authority of judicial decisions and tracing their subsequent judicial history and treatment, the various case units of Shepard's citators are also widely used as case finders. Shepard's Citations, and their structure and use, are described in Chapter 9, Citators, below. Shepard's provides case citators for every state, for the various federal courts, for the District of Columbia and Puerto Rico, for the various West regional reporters, and for many administrative agencies. It is sufficient to note their case finding function here and refer the reader to Section C of Chapter 9 for a fuller discussion of this use.

b. Shepard's Locators

Shepard's has also published finding tools called locators which provide references to a variety of primary and secondary sources. The most successful and most relevant here is their *Federal Tax Locator,* a six volume set originally published from 1974 to 1978, and kept current by quarterly pocket parts. Arranged alphabetically by subjects in the tax field, it directs the researcher to a wide range of sources on each subject—statutes, regulations, rulings, periodicals, and judicial decisions. It can thus be used effectively as a case finder in that broad area. Although it does not contain the actual decisions, the references to cases do include a very brief squib of the main point of the decision. Illustration N shows a typical page from the Shepard's *Federal Tax Locator.*

Ch. 29 ELECTIONS; POLITICAL ACTIVITIES **18 § 597**

Statutory text

§ 597. Expenditures to influence voting

Whoever makes or offers to make an expenditure to any person, either to vote or withhold his vote, or to vote for or against any candidate; and

Whoever solicits, accepts, or receives any such expenditure in consideration of his vote or the withholding of his vote—

Shall be fined not more than $1,000 or imprisoned not more than one year, or both; and if the violation was willful, shall be fined not more than $10,000 or imprisoned not more than two years, or both.

June 25, 1948, c. 645, 62 Stat. 721.

Notes

Historical and Revision Notes

Reviser's Note. Based on sections 250, 252, of Title 2, U.S.C., 1940 ed., The Congress (Feb. 28, 1925, c. 368, Title III, §§ 311, 314, 43 Stat. 1073, 1074).

This section consolidates the provisions of sections 250 and 252 of Title 2, U.S.C., 1940 ed., The Congress.

Reference to persons causing or procuring was omitted as unnecessary in view of definition of "principal" in section 2 of this title.

The punishment provisions of section 252 of Title 2, U.S.C., 1940 ed., The Congress, were incorporated at end of section upon authority of reference in such section making them applicable to this section.

Words "or both" were added to conform to the almost universal formula of the punishment provisions of this title.

Changes were made in phraseology.

Cross References

Cross References

Definitions of terms applicable to this section, see section 591 of this title.
Minor offenses tried by United States magistrates as excluding offenses punishable under this section, see section 3401 of this title.

References to other West publications

Library References

Elections ⚷317. C.J.S. Elections §§ 329, 356.

West's Federal Forms

Indictment, see prec. 7101 Comment.
Sentence and fine, see § 7531 et seq.

Index to Annotations

Notes of Decisions

Constitutionality 1
Construction 2
Disbarment from practice 9
Grand jury investigation 6
Indictment 8
Jurisdiction 7
Law governing 3
Mandamus 10
Perjury 5
Time of expenditure 4

Annotations

1. Constitutionality

In determining the constitutionality of this section, the U.S.C.A.Const. Amend. 1 rights of corporations and labor unions must be weighed against the substantial governmental interests in preserving the integrity of the electoral process, in preventing corporate and union officials from using corporate assets or general union dues to promote political parties and candidates without the consent of stockholders or union members with differing political views, and in protecting individuals who may refuse to contribute to campaign funds against reprisals; the need for such safeguards is particularly acute in the labor field where labor union membership can be condition of employment. U. S. v. Chestnut, D.C.N.Y. 1975, 394 F.Supp. 581.

This section did not violate U.S.C.A. Const. Amend. 1 rights of corporations

311

Illustration M

A section of U.S.C.A., showing the statutory text, notes, cross references, index to annotations, and the annotations to decisions under that section.

LAW OR FACT

LAW OR FACT

See **QUESTION OF LAW OR FACT**

LAW PARTNERSHIPS

See **PROFESSIONAL PRACTITIONERS**

LAW SCHOOL

EDUCATIONAL EXPENSES
accountant attending law school Condit, James J 329 F2d 153 (I-1964-6 Cir) s 39 TC 1123; Huene, Herbert A 247 FS 564 (I-1965-NY); Taubman, Morton S 60 TC 814 (I-1973); O'Donnell, Patrick L 62 TC 781 (I-1974)

Reference to court decision

aerospace engineer Bakken, Lawrence H 51 TC 603 (I-1969)
attorney attending university to take courses in tax law Booth, Joseph T III 35 TC 1144 (I-1961)
construction company employee Baker, N Kent 51 TC 243 (I-1968)
discussed 39 SJLR 249
electronics teacher Bodley, David N 56 TC 1357 (I-1971)
foreign degree, required law course to enable holder of to qualify for state's bar examination not deductible business expenses (I) Rev Rul 75-412, IRB 1975-39, 6
high school teacher Bradley, Burke W Jr 54 TC 216 (I-1970)
immigrant lawyer, Horodysky, Yaroslaw 54 TC 490 (I-1970)
IRS agent
–field auditing, attending law school to qualify for Melnik, John 521 F2d 1065 (I-1975-9 Cir)
–leaving service after passing state bar examination Welsh, Martin J 210 FS 597 (I-1962-Oh) a 329 F2d 145; Weiler, Jeffrey L 54 TC 398 (I-1970)
LLB degrees discussed 39 SJLR 249
patent agent becoming patent attorney as qualifying for new trade or business Weiszmann, Ronald F 483 F2d 817 (I-1973-10 Cir)
patent examiner Martin, John C Jr 363 F2d 35 (I-1966-4 Cir) s 44 TC 864; Weiszmann, Ronald 52 TC 1106 (I-1969) a 443 F2d 29
patent trainee, engineer employed as Weiszmann, Ronald F 52 TC 1106 (I-1969) a 443 F2d 29; Lamb, Owen L 46 TC 539 (I-1966)
police officer Carroll, James A 418 F2d 91 (I-1969-7 Cir)
post-graduate course in taxation Johnson 332 FS 906 (I-1971-La)
practicing law institute Bistline, Anne 145 FS 802 (I-1956-Id) a 260 F2d 80

ELECTRONICS TEACHER, nondeductibility of expenses for attending Bodley, David N 56 TC 1357 (I-1971)

GOVERNMENT AGENCY, amounts agency pays to job related law courses includable in employee's gross income depending upon whether course leads to entitling employee to sit for bar examinations (I) Rev Rul 76-62, IRB 1976-9, 6

INDIGENT DEFENDANT'S REPRESENTATION, gross income, fees received by faculty members and students and turned over to the university not includable in recipient's gross income (I) Rev Rul 74-581, IRB 1974-49, 6

PATENT TRAINEE, taxpayer not entitled to deduct expenses incurred in attending while part time patent clerk and patent trainee Weiszmann, Ronald F 443 F2d 29 (I-1971-9 Cir)

LAWTHERS, ROBERT J

BASIC PLANNING PRINCIPLES IN QUALIFYING LIFE INSURANCE FOR THE MARITAL DEDUCTION 5 TCQ 79

FRAGILE BARK OF THE SMALL CORPORATION 2v1 TCQ 97

224

Illustration N

A type page in the Shepard's *Federal Tax Locator*.

E. SECONDARY MATERIALS

Virtually every secondary source material in law provides citations to judicial decisions, either to support its text and the positions taken or the statements made therein, or to provide references to the various primary sources of law as part of its informational function. Thus, these materials can be used as case finders by locating the relevant text or other part of the work, and noting the citations to the decisions referred to therein. In addition to the decisions so found, one also has the benefit of the text or other features of those secondary sources.

1. ENCYCLOPEDIAS

The two national legal encyclopedias, *Corpus Juris Secundum* and *Am.Jur.2d,* and the several state encyclopedias, all of which will be discussed in detail in Chapter 14 below, are particularly good examples of the use of secondary sources as case finders. Being well indexed, the relevant articles in these encyclopedias are easy to locate. The text may be useful itself, but the footnote citations provide a case finding mechanism which may equal that of a digest. West purports to cite in the footnotes to *Corpus Juris Secundum* virtually all of the significant decisions relevant to its text. It illustrates again the *comprehensive* approach used by that publisher. *Am.Jur.2d,* following the *selective* approach favored by Lawyers' Co-op, cites to fewer cases in its footnotes. However, many of those are in annotated reporters and hence may lead one to Annotations which contain many more useful citations, as well as an expanded text synthesis of the topics covered. Both of these encyclopedias also contain numerous cross references to other research tools of their respective publishers.

2. TREATISES AND PERIODICALS

Legal treatises, whether broad in scope or narrow in focus, *and* articles in legal periodicals, provide access to citations of cases which relate to or support their text. Their case finding use is similar to that of encyclopedias, i.e. find and read the relevant part of the text, then search the footnotes for citations to decisions which seem to relate to your problem. It may be a mundane aspect of great scholarly writing, but it is an effective research approach and should not be overlooked. The researcher can, of course, also derive whatever benefit may be had from the text itself, and the author may get his or her glory from the more sublime aspects of the work. Tables of cases in many treatises and the tables of cases in periodical indexes enable one to reverse the process, and locate explanatory discussions of decisions which have already been identified as of interest.

These and other aspects of legal treatises and of the *Restatements of the Law* (which also have case finding potential) are presented in Chapter 15. Periodicals, their indexes, and uses, are discussed in Chapter 16.

3. LOOSELEAF SERVICES

One of the great research values of looseleaf services is their effectiveness in bringing together several forms of law in one set of volumes, with prompt supplementation and both integrated and varied indexing approaches. For the subject field it covers, a typical looseleaf service will provide the texts of statutes; the texts, either full or abstracted, of judicial and administrative decisions; administrative rules and regulations; and an explanatory discussion of the legal topics in that field. Many of the services have also added a topical case reporter which preserves the decisions in the field in a permanent format, with their own finding aids. These finding aids, both in the looseleaf service and the topical reporter volumes invariably include tables of cases and subject indexing, and sometimes also include case digests and citators. Since these finding tools and indexes are usually designed specifically for that subject field, they often provide the most efficient and most effective access to the subject covered.

Looseleaf services and their special features are described in Chapter 13 below. They are noted here only briefly because of their relevance to case finding. Before beginning research on a particular problem, one should always determine whether a looseleaf service is available in that field and examine it for potential use. Details as to how one discovers what services exist are set forth in Chapter 13.

F. COMPUTER RESEARCH SERVICES

The legal community has been blessed by the development, within the last decade, of two competing computerized research services, each of which provides the full texts of judicial opinions and effective search mechanisms for retrieving them in a variety of ways. Today, both of these systems, LEXIS, a product of Mead Data Central, and WESTLAW, created by the West Publishing Company, offer more than just cases. Each has expanded rapidly into the realm of administrative law, and ancillary data bases of secondary sources are being added to both. The Shepard's citator system is now available on-line through both systems. Court decisions, however, remain the primary focus of both LEXIS and WESTLAW, and the systems are potentially dynamic case finding tools.

While there are differences in coverage and in the search techniques used in each system, in concept and design they are quite similar. We offer here only a brief description of the contents of these data bases for case finding, as well as some advice on structuring searching and on incorporating them into a comprehensive research approach. Chapter 22, dealing with New Media in Legal Research, will contain a more detailed treatment of both systems.

1. CONTENTS

Both systems contain full texts of opinions from the federal courts and from all fifty states. Retrospective coverage varies, and both systems are expanding this coverage. There also are current cases being entered into LEXIS that do not appear in either the printed edition of West's National Reporter System or in the WESTLAW computer data base. In general, these are decisions from the lower federal courts which the courts for various reasons have decided not to release for publication. These "phantom" cases generally have little precedential value, and many courts have rules limiting their use. Some courts, however, do allow attorneys to cite them, as long as copies are furnished to the opposing attorneys. It remains to be seen whether the increased availability of LEXIS will result in changes in the rules governing the use of "unpublished" opinions.

One major difference in the cases which appear in the two systems is that those in WESTLAW, but not those in LEXIS, contain the West synopses, headnotes and key numbers, and hence can be searched through those additional access points.

2. SEARCH STRATEGY

Both systems enable the researcher to search the full text of opinions for any words or phrases the researcher believes may appear in relevant cases. Through the use of Boolean searching techniques, which make it possible to retrieve words and phrases in specified combinations, the researcher can construct search requests at increasing levels of precision and sophistication.

To return to the earlier hypothetical situation in which Ms. Fallon slipped on a lettuce leaf in a supermarket and wants to sue, one could find all cases within a predetermined set (chosen by jurisdiction, judge, date, etc.) that contain the words "lettuce," "supermarket" and "fall". Such a search would be quite imprecise, and one would need to frame it more carefully to find desired precedents. Most searches will require modification and adjustment, and the interactive nature of on-line computer systems makes it feasible to accomplish this quickly and efficiently.

Since there is no intervening editor, one must try to frame a search request to match the terms that will be used by judges in relevant opinions. This is an art that can be learned only through a familiarity both with the legal terminology of the subject area and the potentials of the computer. The computer's searching capacity is indeed impressive, but it is circumscribed by the skill of the operator who frames and modifies the request. Preliminary planning of a search by analysis of the problem and careful selection of search words and their connectors is essential.

WESTLAW offers the added flexibility of searching by West topics and key numbers, either alone or in combination with words or phrases chosen by the researcher. The West synopsis, which summarizes the case and which is searchable in WESTLAW, may contain terminology descriptive of the legal or factual issues involved, in terms not used by the judge. This may allow the researcher to locate relevant cases which may have been missed in a search of the text of the opinion alone.

3. INTEGRATING MANUAL AND COMPUTERIZED RESEARCH

The key to efficient use of the data bases is to remember that they are case finding mechanisms, not case reporters. The terminal should be used to frame searches, skim highlights, and obtain citations. The efficient researcher should then look for decisions in the standard case reporters. While many law schools have arrangements with LEXIS and WESTLAW that allow use of the terminals for a flat, discounted fee, the normal method of charging is by the minute. Sloppiness in searching or reading whole cases on the terminal thus becomes very expensive.

A second danger is that of becoming too dependent on the terminal. If one allows standard research skills to atrophy, one may pay a high price. The data bases are still limited and one or more of the many other research alternatives are often preferable, and sometimes indispensable. Both services are most effective when used in conjunction with other research sources and tools.

LEXIS and WESTLAW both offer new opportunities for fruitful searching of primary legal sources. The computer can add great flexibility and incredible speed to the process of case finding. As part of a carefully developed research strategy, they can aid the researcher, but they are a means, not an end, and their results are often only the beginning of one's research effort.

G. SUMMARY

A recurring theme of this book is that the key to success in a research effort is to find one relevant primary source, which can be used to widen one's search to other sources. Through the use of the various tools described above, the relevant case can provide references to other cases, to relevant statutes, administrative rules and regulations, and secondary sources.

The enormous body of published decisions in American law is accessible through the varied research tools described above. The traditional case digests, represented by the many units of the West digest system, can be of help in finding cases from any period or jurisdiction. Annotations in the Lawyers Co-op annotated report system, encyclopedias, citators, treatises, periodicals, and looseleaf services, all have their own advantages and shortcomings for case finding. Annotated statutory codes are most useful when one's problem involves a statute. *Words and Phrases* can be used when the search focuses on a legally significant word or phrase. The development of LEXIS and WESTLAW has opened new vistas in case finding and in legal research generally. Secondary sources often remain the simplest way to find cases by subject, and provide useful analysis which may enrich one's search in other respects.

The wise researcher will learn all of these approaches, test them, use them, and develop individual preferences for particular types of problems. Flexibility, multiple approaches, and the use of several in combination will often be the most effective procedure.

Chapter 6

CONSTITUTIONS

A. INTRODUCTION

The constitution is the organic document of a political entity and of its legal system. Constitutions set the parameters for governmental action; they allocate power and responsibility among the branches of government and between the central government and its political subdivisions. In addition, they describe the fundamental rules by which the system functions, and, in some jurisdictions, they also define the basic rights of individuals. Constitutions can take any of a number of forms, ranging from relatively brief and general statements (the United States Constitution can be easily printed in ten pages) to quite lengthy documents of considerable specificity (the

Texas constitution, covers 138 pages [1]). A constitution need not even be a single written document, as the British Constitution demonstrates.

The Constitution of the United States defines its own primacy in our legal system. Article VI of the Constitution states: "This Constitution, and the laws of the United States which shall be made in pursuance thereof; . . . shall be the supreme law of the land; . . ." Research in constitutional law in the United States is shaped by our concept of judicial review, which was derived in part from that clause of Article VI. This doctrine, established by Chief Justice Marshall's opinion in *Marbury v. Madison*,[2] established the power of the judicial branch to review actions of the executive and legislature and to rule on their constitutionality. The power has, of course, been extensively used during various periods in our history both at the federal and state levels, and has greatly increased litigation over constitutional issues. Occasionally, it has also created political crises.

Because of the frequent judicial interpretation and application of constitutional provisions, and the vast secondary literature which has been written and will undoubtedly continue to be produced on the Constitution, only a small part of constitutional law research relates to locating relevant constitutional provisions. The related historical background, judicial interpretations, legislative actions, and scholarly commentaries are a major focus of most research problems. The relationship of federal and state constitutional issues, and the conflict between federal and state jurisdiction and prerogatives introduces further complications in constitutional research. In any event, the constitutional documents of the United States and of the fifty states represent a separate and distinct literature and require their own research procedures and tools.[3]

B. HISTORICAL BACKGROUND OF THE FEDERAL CONSTITUTION

1. PRIOR HISTORY AND ADOPTION

The Constitution of the United States was drafted in Philadelphia in 1787, and ratified by the states between 1787 and 1790. The Constitutional Convention was called to address deficiencies in the Articles of Confederation which had been in force from 1781 to 1789. The first ten amendments to the Constitution, which are known as the Bill of Rights, were proposed in 1789 and ratified in 1791. Many other amendments to the Constitution have been proposed, but, at present, the Constitution contains only twenty-six amendments.

1. *Vernon's Annotated Texas Constitution.*

2. 1 Cranch 137 (1803).

3. For a full bibliographic survey of this literature, see K.L. Hall, *Complete Bibliography of American Constitutional and Legal History* (Kraus International, 1983).

Although the Constitutional Convention did not issue an official record of its proceedings, the following sources provide useful documentary background to the drafting and adoption of the Constitution:

J. Elliot, *The Debates, Resolutions and Other Proceedings, in Convention, on the Adoption of the Federal Constitution, . . .* (Washington, 1827–1830) 4v.

William F. Swindler, *Sources and Documents of U.S. Constitutions* (Oceana, 1982–19__) New Series, "National Documents." Although the first ten volumes of this set covered state constitutions (see Section D.1 below), the recently inaugurated "New Series" covers National Documents.

U.S. Bureau of Rolls and Library of the Department of State, *Documentary History of the Constitution of the United States of America, 1786–1870* (U.S. Govt. Printing Office, 1894–1905).

U.S. Library of Congress. Legislative Reference Service, *Documents Illustrative of the Formation of the Union of the American States,* H.Doc.R. No. 398, 69th Cong., 1st Sess., compiled by C.C. Tansill (U.S. Govt. Printing Office, 1927).

M. Farrand, *The Records of the Federal Convention of 1787* (Yale Univ. Press, 1937, reprinted in paperback 1967) 4v.

The Federalist, containing the essays of James Madison, John Jay and Alexander Hamilton in support of the adoption of the Constitution, has been issued in many editions since its first collected publication in 1788, and remains an indispensable work for the study of the Constitution.

2. RATIFICATION BY THE STATES

The debates concerning ratification of the federal Constitution by the state constitutional conventions are recorded in a variety of sources, including J. Elliot's *Debates in the Several State Conventions on the Adoption of the Federal Constitution* (Washington, 1836–1845, reprinted 1937). M. Jensen's multi-volume set, *Documentary History of the Ratification of the Constitution* (State Historical Society of Wisconsin, 1976–19__) 4 vols. to date, will be, when completed, the most thorough and up-to-date compilation of documents on the ratification of the Constitution by the states.

An older useful source is Paul L. Ford's *Bibliography and Reference List of the History and Literature Relating to the Adoption of the Constitution of the United States 1787–8* (Brooklyn, N.Y., 1896).

3. AMENDMENTS

Information on the Bill of Rights and other proposed or enacted amendments to the federal Constitution can be found in the following sources:

Ames, H.V. *Proposed Amendments to the Constitution during the first century of its history* [with bibliography]. (In American Historical Association Rept., 1896, v. 2; 54th Congress, 2nd session. House Document No. 353, pt. 2).

U.S. Library of Congess. Legislative Reference Service. *Proposed amendments to the Constitution of the U.S. introduced in Congress from December 4, 1889 to July 2, 1926* (U.S. Govt. Printing Office, 1926).

U.S. Congress, Senate Library, *Proposed Amendments to the Constitution of the U.S. of America, introduced in Congress from the 69th Congress, 2d Session through the 87th Congress, 2d Session, December 6, 1926 to January 3, 1963* . . . (U.S. Govt. Printing Office, 1963) with supplement covering 1963 to 1969 (1969).

The Declaration of Independence and the Constitution of the U.S. of America, 92nd Congress, House Document, No. 328, (U.S. Govt. Printing Office, reprinted 1972). (Lists proposed amendments not ratified by the states, under names and subjects. Also gives historical notes on each adopted constitutional amendment.)

In addition, a particularly useful guide to research sources on the early legislative history of the Constitution is Chapter VI, "Sources for Constitutional Provisions", of G. Folsom's *Legislative History: Research for the Interpretation of Laws.*[4]

C. RESEARCH IN THE FEDERAL CONSTITUTION

1. SIMPLE TEXT

The Constitution of the United States is usually considered to be the oldest constitutional document in continuous force in the world today. It provides the authority for all federal legislation (*i.e.,* treaties, acts, joint resolutions, and interstate compacts). The text of the Constitution can be found in a variety of sources. It appears in many pamphlet editions, in standard reference works, and in most state and federal statutory compilations. Because its text is infrequently amended, it is not difficult to obtain a current version. Perhaps the most easily accessible version is the one included in the *U.S. Code.*

Most research into problems of constitutional law requires extrinsic aids, beyond the text of the Constitution. The researcher therefore needs, in addition to the simple text, access to interpretive judicial decisions and the scholarly analysis of commentators. The next sections describe the research tools available for such access—annotated editions of the Constitution, digests, indexes, citators, and secondary sources.

4. University Press of Virginia, 1972; reprinted by Fred B. Rothman, 1979.

2. ANNOTATED CODE TEXTS: *USCA* AND *USCS*.

An annotated edition of the U.S. Constitution is one that provides annotations to judicial decisions which have applied or interpreted it. There are three such "annotated" texts of the constitution in common use.

Two of these three are part of the unofficial, annotated editions of the *U.S. Code:* the "Constitution" volumes of the *United States Code Annotated* (West) and of the *United States Code Service* (Lawyers Co-op/Bancroft-Whitney). The format and use of these sets is similar and will be described in Chapter 7, Statutes and Related Materials. They contain multi-volume printings of the U.S. Constitution that set forth, after each article and amendment, brief abstracts of the relevant cases decided under those provisions, with citations to their published reports.

a. USCA

United States Code Annotated, following the traditional West approach, provides "comprehensive" coverage by including annotations to both federal *and* state decisions that concern each article or amendment of the U.S. Constitution. As a result, the ten page text of the Constitution, when annotated in *USCA,* requires fifteen volumes (including six bound supplements). The annotations to the Fifth Amendment alone fill two separate *USCA* volumes. The volumes are kept up to date with annual pocket parts and up to four interim pamphlets. As part of the West research system, the "Constitution" volumes of the *USCA* also include relevant key numbers indicating digest reference points, not only to Supreme Court cases, but also to relevant lower federal court and state court decisions; cross references to other West publications; citations to articles in periodicals, Attorneys General opinions, Executive Orders, etc. Since some of the *USCA* Constitution volumes were issued years ago, the more relevant cross references will be found in the pocket parts. The annotations to each article and amendment have separate indexes located just before the annotations themselves, and a separate set of index volumes are provided for the whole work, with pocket part supplementation. Illustration A shows the first two pages from the bound volume of the *USCA* containing the Fifth Amendment.

b. USCS

The "Constitution" volumes of the *United States Code Service* serve many of the same functions as those of the *USCA,* described above. Published originally as *Federal Code Annotated,* the approach of *USCS* differs somewhat in that it includes fewer annotations, so that the Constitution and its amendments, with annotations and indexes, are contained in only two volumes. The *USCS* annotations, however, contain slightly longer abstracts of each decision than

Amend. 5 CONSTITUTION

AMENDMENT V—CAPITAL CRIMES; DOUBLE JEOPARDY; SELF-INCRIMINATION; DUE PROCESS; JUST COMPENSATION FOR PROPERTY

No person shall be held to answer for a capital, or otherwise infamous crime, unless on a presentment or indictment of a Grand Jury, except in cases arising in the land or naval forces, or in the Militia, when in actual service in time of War or public danger; nor shall any person be subject for the same offence to be twice put in jeopardy of life or limb; nor shall be compelled in any criminal case to be a witness against himself, nor be deprived of life, liberty, or property, without due process of law; nor shall private property be taken for public use, without just compensation.

Historical Note

Proposal and Ratification. The first ten amendments to the Constitution were proposed to the Legislatures of the several States by the First Congress on September 25, 1789, and were ratified on December 15, 1791. For the States which ratified these amendments, and the dates of ratification, see notes preceding Amendment I.

Amendment V. Grand Jury Indictment For Capital Crimes

No person shall be held to answer for a capital, or otherwise infamous crime, unless on a presentment or indictment of a Grand Jury, except in cases arising in the land or naval forces, or in the Militia, when in actual service in time of War or public danger; * * *

Notes of Decisions

4

Illustration A

Amendment V in *USCA*, with index to annotations.

I. GENERALLY

Subdivision Index

1. Common law

The requirement of this amendment of indictment or presentment does not preclude, as essential to the validity of the indictment, inclusion of requisites which did not exist at common law. U. S. v. Cox, C.A.Miss.1965, 342 F.2d 167, certiorari denied 85 S.Ct. 1767, 381 U.S. 935, 14 L.Ed.2d 700.

This amendment adopted the grand jury as it existed at common law and thereby made grand jury a part of the fundamental law of the United States for the prosecution of crime. In re April 1956 Term Grand Jury, C.A.Ill.1956, 239 F.2d 263, certiorari denied 77 S.Ct. 552, 352 U.S. 998, 1 L.Ed.2d 544.

The grand jury in federal Government is same as at common law and as common law existed at time this amendment was adopted. U. S. v. Owen, D.C.Mo.1951, 11 F.R.D. 371.

Illustration A—Continued.

the West edition. These volumes are also indexed, arrange the annotations by subject, and include annual supplementation by pocket parts. The *USCS* volumes on the Constitution also provide cross references to Annotations and the texts in other Lawyers Co-op/Bancroft-Whitney publications, and to law review articles. Illustration B shows the Fifth Amendment in the Constitution volumes of *USCS.*

Despite their usefulness as case finders for decisions under particular clauses of the Constitution, some researchers find these two annotated editions of the U.S. Constitution too massive and cumbersome for effective use, and prefer the following more compact version.

3. THE LIBRARY OF CONGRESS EDITION

The third annotated edition of the U.S. Constitution is that prepared by the Congressional Research Service of the Library of Congress, *The Constitution of the United States of America; Analysis and Interpretation.*[5] This one-volume work, with too-infrequent pocket part supplementation, was first issued in 1953, having been prepared initially by the distinguished constitutional law scholar, Edward S. Corwin. A revised edition by Lester S. Jayson was published in 1964, and the current text, also edited by Jayson, was issued in 1973. With the pattern of ten-year revisions, a new edition is expected shortly.

The current version includes the text of the Constitution interspersed with extensive commentary, historical background, legal analysis, and summaries of judicial interpretation of each clause of the Constitution. The major constitutional decisions are discussed in detail, and the footnotes include numerous citations to other relevant cases and scholarly interpretations. The various amendments are similarly treated. The volume is well indexed and contains a case table, tables of amendments that were proposed but not ratified, and lists of state and federal acts that have been held unconstitutional.

The major shortcoming of this otherwise-superb work is its infrequent supplementation. The last supplement appeared in 1976, and, in a field subject to such rapid change as constitutional law, the lack of regular supplementation is a serious detriment. The volume must therefore be used with some caution. Illustrations C–1 and C–2 show the opening pages of text on the Fifth Amendment, and Illustration D shows the updating text in the 1976 pocket part supplementation. The several important decisions of the Supreme Court on this Amendment rendered since 1976 are, of course, not reflected here.

4. SHEPARDIZING THE U.S. CONSTITUTION

The statutes volume of *Shepard's United States Citations* provides references to federal court decisions which have applied or in-

5. U.S. Govt. Printing Office, 1973; with 1976 supplement.

CONSTITUTION

of the

UNITED STATES OF AMERICA

AMENDMENT 5

Criminal actions—Provisions concerning—Due process of law and just compensation clauses.

No person shall be held to answer for a capital, or otherwise infamous crime, unless on a presentment or indictment of a Grand Jury, except in cases arising in the land or naval forces, or in the Militia, when in actual service in time of War or public danger; nor shall any person be subject for the same offence to be twice put in jeopardy of life or limb; nor shall be compelled in any criminal case to be a witness against himself, nor be deprived of life, liberty, or property, without due process of law; nor shall private property be taken for public use, without just compensation.

CROSS REFERENCES

Constitutional right to be informed of nature and cause of accusation, generally, Constitution, Amendment 6.

Prohibition against state's denial of due process or equal protection, Constitution, Amendment 14.

Grand jury procedure, generally, Rule 6 of Federal Rules of Criminal Procedure.

Procedure as to indictment and information, generally, Rule 7 of Federal Rules of Criminal Procedure.

RESEARCH GUIDE

Am Jur:

16 Am Jur 2d, Constitutional Law §§ 332–334, 361–381, 542–584.

21 Am Jur 2d, Criminal Law §§ 165–216, 220–228, 349–368.

26 Am Jur 2d, Eminent Domain §§ 1 et seq.

38 Am Jur 2d, Grand Jury § 3.

77 Am Jur 2d, United States §§ 35, 92, 93, 114.

Annotations:

Supreme Court's views as to the federal legal aspects of the right of privacy. 43 L Ed 2d 871.

1

Illustration B

Amendment V in *USCS.*

RIGHTS OF PERSONS

FIFTH AMENDMENT

No person shall be held to answer for a capital, or otherwise infamous crime, unless on a presentment or indictment of a Grand Jury, except in cases arising in the land or naval forces, or in the Militia, when in actual service in time of War or public danger; nor shall any person be subject for the same offence to be twice put in jeopardy of life or limb; nor shall be compelled in any criminal case to be a witness against himself, nor be deprived of life, liberty, or property, without due process of law; nor shall private property be taken for public use, without just compensation.

INDICTMENT BY GRAND JURY

The history of the grand jury is rooted in the common and civil law, extending back to Athens, pre-Norman England, and the Assize of Clarendon promulgated by Henry II.[1] The right seems to have been first mentioned in the colonies in the Charter of Liberties and Privileges of 1683, which was passed by the first assembly permitted to be elected in the colony of New York.[2] Included from the first in Madison's introduced draft of the Bill of Rights, the provision elicited no recorded debate and no opposition. "The grand jury is an English institution, brought to this country by the early colonists and incorporated in the Constitution by the Founders. There is every reason to believe that our constitutional grand jury was intended to operate substantially like its English progenitor. The basic purpose of the English grand jury was to provide a fair method for instituting

[1] Morse, "A Survey of the Grand Jury System," 10 Ore. L. Rev. 101 (1931).

[2] 1 B. Schwartz, *The Bill of Rights: A Documentary History* (New York: 1971), 162, 166. The provision read: "That in all Cases Capitall or Criminall there shall be a grand Inquest who shall first present the offence . . . ."

1089

Illustration C–1

The text on the Fifth Amendment in the 1973 edition of *The Constitution of the U.S.; Analysis and Interpretation.*

criminal proceedings against persons believed to have committed crimes. Grand jurors were selected from the body of the people and their work was not hampered by rigid procedural or evidential rules. In fact, grand jurors could act on their own knowledge and were free to make their presentments or indictments on such information as they deemed satisfactory. Despite its broad power to institute criminal proceedings the grand jury grew in popular favor with the years. It acquired an independence in England free from control by the Crown or judges. Its adoption in our Constitution as the sole method for preferring charges in serious criminal cases shows the high place it held as an instrument of justice. And in this country as in England of old the grand jury has convened as a body of laymen, free from technical rules, acting in secret, pledged to indict no one because of prejudice and to free no one because of special favor." [3]

The prescribed constitutional function of grand juries in federal courts [4] is to return criminal indictments, but the juries serve a considerably broader series of purposes as well. Principle among these is the investigative function, which is served through the fact that grand juries may summon witnesses by process and compel testimony and the production of evidence generally. Operating in secret, under the direction but not control of a prosecutor, unbound by a number of evidentiary and constitutional restrictions, such juries may examine witnesses in the absence of their counsel and without informing them of the object of the investigation or the place of the witnesses in it.[5] Besides indictments, grand juries may issue as well reports which may indicate

---

[3] *Costello* v. *United States*, 350 U.S. 359, 362 (1956).

[4] This provision applies only in federal courts and is not applicable to the States either as an element of due process or as a command of the Fourteenth Amendment imposing the command directly. *Hurtado* v. *California*, 110 U.S. 516 (1884) ; *Palko* v. *Connecticut*, 302 U.S. 319, 323 (1937).

[5] *Cf. United States* v. *Scully*, 225 F. 2d 113, 116 (C.A. 2), *cert. den.*, 350 U.S. 897 (1955). The privilege against self-incrimination must be observed by the grand jury, *Blau* v. *United States*, 340 U.S. 159 (1950) ; *Hoffman* v. *United States*, 341 U.S. 479 (1951), as well apparently as the Fourth Amendment protection against unreasonable searches and seizures. *Silverthorne Lumber Co.* v. *United States*, 251 U.S. 385 (1920) ; *Hale* v. *Henkel*, 201 U.S. 43, 76–77 (1906) ; *cf. In re Dionisio*, 442 F. 2d 276 (C.A 7, 1971), and *Mara* v. *United States*, 454 F. 2d 580 (C.A. 7, 1971) (Fourth Amendment limitations on compelled production of voice exemplars and handwriting samples). Additionally, the husband-wife privilege, *Blau* v. *United States*, 340 U.S. 332 (1951), and the attorney-client privilege, *Alexander* v. *United States*, 138 U.S. 353 (1891), may be asserted before a grand jury. The Court has interpreted a provision of federal wiretap law, 18 U.S.C. § 2515, to prohibit utilization of unlawful wiretap information as a basis for questioning witnesses before grand juries. *Gelbard* v. *United States*, 408 U.S. 41 (1972). The traditional secrecy of grand jury proceedings has been relaxed a degree to permit a limited discovery of testimony. Compare *Pittsburgh Plate Glass Co.* v. *United States*, 360 U.S. 395 (1959), with *Dennis* v. *United States*, 384 U.S. 855 (1966). There is no constitutional right to counsel before grand juries,

Illustration C–2

The text on the Fifth Amendment, continued.

AMENDMENT 5—RIGHTS OF PERSONS

Indictment by Grand Jury

[P. 1090, in text following N. 5, add:]

The investigatory powers of grand juries were substantially extended by the Court in recent decisions. It was held that the exclusionary rule was inapplicable in grand jury proceedings with the result that a witness called before a grand jury could be questioned on the basis of knowledge obtained through the use of illegally-seized evidence.[1.5] In thus allowing the use of evidence obtained in violation of the Fourth Amendment, the Court nonetheless restated the principle that, while free of many rules of evidence that bind trial courts, grand juries are not unrestrained by constitutional considerations.[2.5] A witness called before a grand jury is not entitled to be informed that he may be indicted for the offense under inquiry [3.5] and the commission of perjury by a witness before the grand jury is punishable, irrespective of the nature of the warning given him when he appears and regardless of the fact that he may be a putative defendant already when he is called.[4.5]

[1.5] *United States* v. *Calandra*, 414 U.S. 338 (1975). Justices Brennan, Douglas, and Marshall dissented, id., 355.

[2.5] "Of course, the grand jury's subpoena is not unlimited. It may consider incompetent evidence, but it may not itself violate a valid privilege, whether established by the Constitution, statutes, or the common law. . . . Although, for example, an indictment based on evidence obtained in violation of a defendant's Fifth Amendment privilege is nevertheless valid . . . the grand jury may not force a witness to answer questions in violation of that constitutional guarantee. . . . Similarly, a grand jury may not compel a person to produce books and papers that would incriminate him. . . . The grand jury is also without power to invade a legitimate privacy interest protected by the Fourth Amendment. A grand jury's subpoena duces tecum will be disallowed if it is 'far too sweeping in its terms to be regarded as reasonable under the Fourth Amendment.' *Hale* v. *Henkel*, 201 U.S. 43, 76 (1906). Judicial supervision is properly exercised in such cases to prevent the wrong before it occurs." Id., 346. See also *United States* v. *Dionisio*, 410 U.S. 1, 11–12 (1973).

[3.5] *United States* v. *Washington*, 431 U.S. 181 (1977). Justices Brennan and Marshall dissented. Id., 191. Because defendant when he appeared before the grand jury was warned of his rights to decline to answer questions on the basis of self-incrimination, the decision was framed in terms of those warnings, but the Court twice noted that it had not decided, and was not deciding, "whether any Fifth Amendment warnings whatever are consitutionally required for grand jury witnesses. . . ." Id., 186, 190.

[4.5] *United States* v. *Mandujano*, 425 U.S. 564 (1976) ; *United States* v. *Wong*, 431 U.S. 174 (1977). Mandujano had been told of his right to assert the privilege against self-incrimination, of the consequences of perjury, and of his right to

S160

Illustration D

The updating text on the Fifth Amendment in the 1976 supplement.

terpreted the various provisions of the United States Constitution. It also includes references to federal legislation, treaties, and to Annotations in *ALR, ALR Federal,* and *Lawyers' Edition.* Illustration E–1 from Shepard's instructional pamphlet, *How to Use Shepard's Citations,* describes this coverage. Illustration E–2 shows a typical page from an advance sheet to *Shepard's States Citations,* covering the U.S. Constitution.

Most Shepard's state citators also use the U.S. Constitution as cited material and provide references thereunder to decisions of that state's courts and statutes.

5. FEDERAL COURT INTERPRETATIONS BY DIGESTS

West's *United States Supreme Court Digest,* contains abstracts of decisions of the U.S. Supreme Court, arranged in classified order by West topic and key numbers. Many of these decisions involve provisions of the U.S. Constitution, and the Digest can thus be used topically to find cases relating to various constitutional provisions and issues. The usual "Descriptive Word Index" and "Table of Cases" provide access to the Digest by subject and case name, respectively. The set is kept up to date by annual pocket parts, quarterly supplements, and, for the U.S. Constitution, by the tables of statutes construed in the bound volumes and advance sheets of the various West reporters. Illustration F shows a typical page from West's *U.S. Supreme Court Digest.*

The several West federal digests (*Federal Digest, Modern Federal Practice Digest,* and *Federal Practice Digest 2d*) also provide access to decisions involving constitutional interpretation. These include all of the decisions abstracted in West's *U.S. Supreme Court Digest,* as well as decisions of the *lower* federal courts. Although the annotated codes are more effective starting points for constitutional research, the digests can serve as an alternative approach to the same decisions.

United States Supreme Court Digest, Lawyers' Edition (Lawyers Co-op), as described above in Chapter 5, can be used to find cases on constitutional law, through its references to U.S. Supreme Court decisions appearing in *Lawyers' Edition.* Two other features of this Digest give more direct references to Supreme Court decisions, by the specific constitutional provisions which were applied or interpreted in those decisions.

Volume 14 of this Digest formerly included a citator for the U.S. Constitution, referring to *Lawyers' Edition* decisions under each of the provisions of the Constitution. This was discontinued when the volume was revised in 1972. However, in 1978, when the *Lawyers' Edition Desk Book* was published, it included a "Table of Federal Laws, Rules and Regulations Cited and Construed." That table contains references to decisions in *Lawyers' Edition* which deal with provisions of the U.S. Constitution. Illustration G shows typical entries in that table for Articles of the Constitution.

CONSTITUTIONS

Amend. 17
415US721
424US269
426US841
39LE712
46LE830
49LE251
94SC1322
96SC750
96SC2469
368FS1341
376FS240
400FS1013
417FS840
59ABA
[1149
27ARF33n

FEDERAL:

Citations to the United States Constitution (Preamble, Articles and Amendments) are listed in Shepard's United States Citations, Statutes. (A sample is shown at the left.) The sources of citations in this publication are as follows:

United States Supreme Court Reports
Lawyers' Edition, United States Supreme Court Reports
Supreme Court Reporter
Federal Reporter
Federal Supplement
Federal Rules Decisions
United States Statutes at Large
United States Treaties and Other International Acts Series
American Bar Association Journal

and in annotations of

Lawyers' Edition, United States Supreme Court Reports
American Law Reports
American Law Reports, Federal

Amend. 17
89HLR695
60MnL1127
50NYL552
27StnL618
75WLR440

Additional citations may be found in Shepard's Federal Law in Selected Law Reviews. (A sample at the left) Here you will find quick access to the thinking of the scholars.

Amend. 17
140Min220
156Min270
184Min236
190Min342
208Min592
243Min98
167NW481
194NW631
238NW498
251NW531
296NW32
66NW610
42AGNo76

To obtain citations to the United States constitution by the state courts the researcher should turn to the statute section of his state citator. (Sample at the left is from Shepard's Minnesota Citations.)

STATE:

Citations to the constitution of each state are included in each of the various state editions of Shepard's. The sources of such citations are presented on the half-title page preceding the listings of citations in each state edition.

Illustration E–1

Coverage of the U.S. Constitution in *Shepard's United States Citations* (from *How to Use Shepard's Citations*).

Amend. 4 UNITED STATES CONSTITUTION

685F2d1218
685F2d1280
686F2d86
686F2d97
686F2d187
686F2d236
686F2d357
686F2d756
686F2d859
686F2d1188
687F2d46
687F2d151
687F2d177
687F2d205
687F2d253
687F2d265
687F2d292
687F2d331
687F2d535
687F2d751
687F2d888
687F2d1041
687F2d1097
687F2d1138
687F2d1214
688F2d61
688F2d583
688F2d654
688F2d1046
688F2d1142
689F2d14
689F2d168
542FS219
542FS359
542FS489
542FS613
542FS710
542FS830
542FS858
542FS913
542FS929
542FS1269
542FS1314
543FS57
543FS331
543FS511
543FS696
543FS887
543FS926
543FS932
543FS1009
543FS1076
544FS57
544FS151
544FS411
544FS469
544FS540
544FS655
544FS707
544FS722
544FS785
545FS44
545FS106
545FS181
545FS660
545FS730
545FS805
545FS827
545FS1089
545FS1092
546FS302
546FS460
546FS503
546FS613
546FS933
546FS1126
546FS1223
547FS30
547FS100
547FS187
13MJ448
13MJ953
13MJ955
13MJ981
14MJ520

Amend. 5

454US221
454US922
454US1019
454US1048
454US1068
72LE795
73LE80
73LE209
73LE238
73LE319
73LE359
73LE423
73LE523
73LE612
73LE717
73LE757
73LE886
73LE925
73LE1197
73LE1295
682F2d216
682F2d475
682F2d507
682F2d598
682F2d671
682F2d802
682F2d855
682F2d861
682F2d934
682F2d983
682F2d1021
682F2d1028
682F2d1079
682F2d1107
682F2d1277
682F2d1311
683F2d67
683F2d77
683F2d86
683F2d103
683F2d124
683F2d263
683F2d390
683F2d412
683F2d457
683F2d589
683F2d770
683F2d818
683F2d881
683F2d946
683F2d954
683F2d995
683F2d1077
683F2d1160
683F2d1223
683F2d1233
683F2d1348
684F2d19
684F2d153
684F2d158
684F2d207
684F2d259
684F2d278
684F2d301
684F2d346
684F2d536
684F2d545
684F2d563
684F2d637
684F2d667
684F2d732
684F2d797
684F2d922
684F2d953
684F2d1016
684F2d1070
684F2d1130
684F2d1150
684F2d1196
684F2d1296
684F2d1308
684F2d1343
685F2d89
685F2d157
685F2d252
685F2d323
685F2d371
685F2d387
685F2d551
685F2d941
685F2d1015
685F2d1043
685F2d1067
685F2d1136
685F2d1190
685F2d1217
685F2d1297
686F2d32
686F2d39
686F2d105
686F2d126
686F2d199
686F2d302
686F2d343
686F2d349
686F2d364
686F2d755
686F2d835
686F2d1020
686F2d1089
686F2d1159
686F2d1169
686F2d1328
686F2d1330
687F2d19
687F2d54
687F2d151
687F2d240
687F2d253
687F2d265
687F2d303
687F2d333
687F2d373
687F2d609
687F2d624
687F2d648
687F2d704
687F2d890
687F2d954
687F2d1095
687F2d1138
687F2d1225
687F2d1233
687F2d1274
687F2d1354
688F2d55
688F2d58
688F2d83
688F2d91
688F2d126
688F2d198
688F2d226
688F2d274
688F2d449
688F2d473
688F2d484
688F2d575
688F2d589
688F2d604
688F2d659
688F2d684
688F2d780
688F2d937
688F2d963
688F2d1116
688F2d1179
689F2d14
689F2d25
689F2d101
689F2d129
689F2d146
689F2d164
542FS226
542FS452
542FS485
542FS608
542FS697
542FS710
542FS770
542FS799
542FS916
542FS929
542FS1109
542FS1265
542FS1269
542FS1334
543FS7
543FS182
543FS337
543FS339
543FS452
543FS727
543FS818
543FS884
543FS929
543FS942
543FS985
543FS997
543FS1017
543FS1038
543FS1046
543FS1076
543FS1119
543FS1272
544FS57
544FS411
544FS483
544FS538
544FS570
544FS632
544FS665
544FS722
544FS785
544FS833
544FS984
544FS1012
544FS1019
544FS1043
544FS1175
545FS91
545FS106
545FS139
545FS181
545FS546
545FS570
545FS578
545FS593
545FS802
545FS827
545FS1089
545FS1260
545FS1275
545FS1284
546FS43
546FS237
546FS273
546FS302
546FS407
546FS460
546FS521
546FS703
546FS854
546FS862
546FS896
546FS1005
546FS1127
546FS1223
546FS1255
546FS1371
547FS30
547FS40
547FS48
547FS100
547FS126
547FS188
94FRD454
94FRD569
21BRW576
22BRW246
13MJ421
13MJ448
13MJ976
14MJ75
14MJ538
14MJ544
14MJ568

Amend. 6

454US1
454US989
454US1007
72LE796
73LE253
73LE323
73LE495
73LE758
73LE1197
682F2d216
682F2d287
682F2d373
682F2d508
682F2d579
682F2d692
682F2d706
682F2d748
682F2d879
682F2d1020
682F2d1079
682F2d1361
683F2d60
683F2d98
683F2d218
683F2d881
683F2d1058
683F2d1165
683F2d1348
683F2d1391
684F2d301
684F2d345
684F2d487
684F2d535
684F2d673
684F2d689
684F2d788
684F2d796
684F2d1130
684F2d1196
684F2d1296
684F2d1338
685F2d328
685F2d375
685F2d387
685F2d807
685F2d868
685F2d1019
685F2d1166
685F2d1234
686F2d105
686F2d380
686F2d529
686F2d658
686F2d755
686F2d828
686F2d838
686F2d871
686F2d1089
686F2d1187
686F2d1378
686F2d1383
687F2d66
687F2d236
687F2d253
687F2d332
687F2d662
687F2d947
687F2d954
687F2d973
687F2d1013
687F2d1028
687F2d1065
687F2d1142
687F2d1236
687F2d1274
688F2d21
688F2d226
688F2d274
688F2d498
688F2d604
688F2d661
688F2d727
688F2d738
688F2d959
688F2d1182
689F2d63
689F2d130
542FS219
542FS226
542FS330
542FS411
542FS591
542FS831
542FS977
542FS1265
543FS108
543FS182
543FS412
543FS765
544FS318
544FS411
544FS540
544FS570
544FS592
545FS44
545FS666
545FS680
545FS802
545FS827
545FS1273
546FS37
546FS244
546FS365
546FS649
546FS703
546FS825
546FS933
546FS1223
22BRW246
13MJ440
13MJ971
14MJ75
14MJ526
14MJ538

Amend. 7

454US1066
682F2d325
682F2d486
682F2d1192
684F2d282
685F2d742
686F2d750
687F2d265
687F2d1010
688F2d192
688F2d424
688F2d724
688F2d977
542FS657
543FS1246
544FS257
94FRD337
94FRD565
22BRW213

Amend. 8

453US930
454US908
454US1038
71LE5
73LE34
73LE214
73LE495
73LE1145
73LE1322
73LE1360
682F2d752
682F2d1245
683F2d267
683F2d1165
683F2d1315
684F2d8
684F2d447
684F2d584
684F2d714
684F2d798
685F2d140
685F2d152
685F2d323
685F2d1233
686F2d302
686F2d1167
687F2d265
687F2d618
687F2d1000
687F2d1022
688F2d28
688F2d486
689F2d57
542FS594
542FS710
542FS883
543FS272
543FS295
543FS387
543FS926
544FS57
544FS151
544FS347
544FS411
544FS598
544FS773
544FS785
545FS827
545FS995
545FS1048
546FS212
546FS503
546FS521
546FS729
546FS782
546FS1339
547FS30
547FS194
13MJ421

Amend. 9

687F2d265
688F2d732
689F2d146
543FS7
544FS57
544FS411
545FS441
545FS827
546FS1063
546FS1223

Amend. 10

685F2d1001
686F2d1251
686F2d1364
687F2d265
542FS278
543FS1196
543FS1203
544FS551
545FS48
546FS907
546FS1208
21BRW802
21BRW998
22BRW581

Amend. 11

453US931
454US129
72LE698
72LE757
73LE187
73LE576
73LE1010
73LE1061
682F2d654
682F2d1346
683F2d71

Continued

See note on first page of this division. See prior volumes, Statute Edition for earlier citations

12

Illustration E–2

A typical page in a *Shepard's United States Citations advance sheet,* showing the U.S. Constitution as *cited* matter.

⚷½ CONSTITUTIONAL LAW

5 S Ct D—14

For later cases see same Topic and Key Number in Pocket Part

I. ESTABLISHMENT AND AMENDMENT OF CONSTITUTIONS.

⚷½.

See ⚷1.

⚷1. Nature, authority, and adoption.

Library references

C.J.S. Constitutional Law § 1 et seq.

Pa. 1798. The constitution of the United States is the constitution of Pennsylvania, having been ratified and adopted by the sovereign act of the people in convention, December 12, 1787. They made it irrevocably their own by their entering into a solemn compact with the peoples of their sister states—binding them for all time—unalterable in any other mode than that pointed out by its own terms; and the government of the United States is a part of the government of this and of every other state in the Union.

Respublica v. Cobbet, 3 U.S. 467, 3 Dall. 467, 1 L.Ed. 683, 2 Yeates 352.

U.S.Md. 1819. The constitution of the United States is to be considered as emanating from the people and not as the act of sovereign and independent states.

McCulloch v. State of Md., 17 U.S. 316, 4 Wheat. 316, 4 L.Ed. 579.

U.S.Pa. 1821. The constitution of the United States was made for the whole people of the union and is equally binding upon all the courts and all citizens.

Farmers' & Mechanics' Bank of Pa. v. Smith, 19 U.S. 131, 6 Wheat. 131, 5 L. Ed. 224.

U.S.R.I. 1830. The federal Constitution was not intended to furnish a corrective for every abuse of power which may be committed by state governments.

Providence Bank v. Billings, 29 U.S. 514, 4 Pet. 514, 7 L.Ed. 939.

U.S.Ala. 1845. All constitutional laws are binding on the people in new states or old states whether they consent to be bound by them or not.

Pollard v. Hagen, 44 U.S. 212, 3 How. 212, 11 L.Ed. 565.

Every constitutional congressional act is passed by the will of the people, expressed through their representatives, and becomes the supreme law of the land, operating by its own force on the subject matter in whatever state or territory it may happen to be.

Pollard v. Hagen, 44 U.S. 212, 3 How. 212, 11 L.Ed. 565.

U.S.Ariz. 1921. A purpose of the Constitution was to protect the fundamental rights of the individual against experiments by the government.

Truax v. Corrigan, 42 S.Ct. 124, 257 U.S. 312, 66 L.Ed. 254, 27 A.L.R. 375.

U.S.Ky. 1936. Beneficent aims however great or well directed can never serve in lieu of constitutional power.

Carter v. Carter Coal Co., 56 S.Ct. 855, 298 U.S. 238, 80 L.Ed. 1160.

U.S.Neb. 1941. The Federal Constitution is the "supreme law of the land," and the obligation to guard and enforce every right secured by that constitution rests on the state courts equally with the federal courts.

Smith v. O'Grady, 61 S.Ct. 572, 312 U.S. 329, 85 L.Ed. 859.

U.S.N.J. 1942. The Constitution is intended to preserve practical and substantial rights, not to maintain theories.

Faitoute Iron & Steel Co. v. City of Asbury Park, N. J., 62 S.Ct. 1129, 316 U.S. 502, 86 L.Ed. 1629.

U.S.N.Y. 1942. The New York Decedent Estate Law which provides in effect that, except as otherwise directed by the decedent's will, the burden of any federal death taxes paid by personal representative shall be spread proportionately among the distributees or beneficiaries of the estate does not contravene the "supremacy" clause of the Federal Constitution, since it is not in conflict with the federal estate tax law. Decedent Estate Law, N. Y., § 124; 26 U.S.C.A. (I.R.C.1939) § 800 et seq.; U.S.C.A.Const. art. 6, cl. 2.

Riggs v. Del Drago, 63 S.Ct. 109, 317 U.S. 95, 87 L.Ed. 106, 142 A.L.R. 1131, reversed 38 N.E.2d 131, 287 N.Y. 61, reargument denied 40 N.E.2d 46, 287 N.Y. 764.

U.S.Pa. 1944. The purpose of the supremacy clause in the Constitution was to avoid the disparities, confusions and conflicts that would follow if the federal government's general authority were subject to local controls. U.S.C.A.Const. art. 6, cl. 2.

U. S. v. Allegheny County, Pa., 64 S.Ct. 908, 322 U.S. 174, 88 L.Ed. 1209.

U.S.R.I. 1946. The United States Constitution and the laws passed pursuant to it are the supreme laws of the land, binding alike upon states, courts, and the people, anything in the Constitution or laws of any state to the contrary notwithstanding. U.S.C.A.Const. art. 6, § 2.

Testa v. Katt, 67 S.Ct. 810, 330 U.S. 386, 91 L.Ed. 967, 172 A.L.R. 225.

U.S.Cal. & Dist. Col. 1963. The federal Constitution is a law for rulers and people, equally in war and in peace, and covers with

Illustration F

A typical page on the U.S. Constitution from West's *U.S. Supreme Court Digest.*

III.

TABLE OF FEDERAL LAWS, RULES, AND REGULATIONS CITED AND CONSTRUED[1]

The table which follows contains citations to decisions of the United States Supreme Court found in volumes 1–50 of the United States Supreme Court Reports, Lawyers' Edition, Second Series, which have cited or construed, in some *meaningful* way, various federal laws, rules, and regulations.

The table is arranged so that citations to various portions of the United States Constitution are included first, followed by citations to federal statutes found in the United States Code Service; Statutes at Large; Admiralty Rules; Federal Rules of Appellate Procedure; Federal Rules of Civil Procedure; Federal Rules of Criminal Procedure; Federal Rules of Evidence; Rules of the Supreme Court of the United States; Administrative Rules and Regulations; and rules and regulations found in the Code of Federal Regulations.

Thus, for example, by looking up Rule 56(c) of the Federal Rules of Civil Procedure, you will find that this Rule has been meaningfully construed by the Supreme Court in three cases found at 3 L Ed 2d 368; 8 L Ed 2d 176; and 26 L Ed 2d 142.

Please do not forget to consult the annual pocket supplement to this volume when it is issued.

CONSTITUTION

	Vol. and page
Art I	1 L Ed 2d 601; 11 L Ed 2d 481; 41 L Ed 2d 1039
Art I § 2	37 L Ed 2d 298, 314, 335
Art I § 2 cl 1	11 L Ed 2d 481; 22 L Ed 2d 519, 535; 23 L Ed 2d 491; 27 L Ed 2d 272
Art I § 2 cl 2	12 L Ed 2d 222
Art I § 2 cl 3	4 L Ed 2d 1158
Art I § 2 cl 5	15 L Ed 2d 494; 26 L Ed 2d 100
Art I § 3 cl 3	12 L Ed 2d 222
Art I § 3 cl 6	15 L Ed 2d 494; 26 L Ed 2d 100
Art I § 4 cl 1	11 L Ed 2d 481; 27 L Ed 2d 272; 31 L Ed 2d
Art I § 5 cl 1	23 L Ed 2d 491; 31 L Ed 2d 1; 46 L Ed 2d 659
Art I § 5 cl 2	23 L Ed 2d 491
Art I § 6	1 L Ed 2d 601; 40 L Ed 2d 90
Art I § 6 cl 1	10 L Ed 2d 778; 15 L Ed 2d

1. CREDITS: The Table of Federal Laws, Rules, and Regulations Cited and Construed is a recompiled, modified, and combined version of similar tables found in each of the 50 individual bound volumes of **UNITED STATES SUPREME COURT REPORTS, LAWYERS' EDITION, SECOND SERIES,** copyrighted © 1956, 1957, 1958, 1959, 1960, 1961, 1962, 1963, 1964, 1965, 1966, 1967, 1968, 1969, 1970, 1971, 1972, 1973, 1974, 1975, 1976, and 1977, by **The Lawyers Co-operative Publishing Company,** Rochester, New York 14603, and **Bancroft-Whitney Company,** San Francisco, California 94107.

133

Illustration G

"Table of Federal Laws, etc." in *Lawyers' Edition Desk Book,* with references to the U.S. Constitution.

In Volume 17 of the *U.S. Supreme Court Digest, Lawyers' Edition,* the text of the United States Constitution is set out with references to sections of that Digest covering each provision of the Constitution. See Exhibit H for a page from that section.

6. STATE COURT INTERPRETATIONS

Since state courts frequently apply and interpret the United States Constitution, their decisions are often relevant to research on constitutional problems, particularly on issues arising in subsequent state litigation or in cases reaching the federal courts from the state courts. As noted above, the annotations under the provisions of the U.S. Constitution in *USCA* and *USCS* include abstracts of state court decisions, as well as those of the federal courts. The following additional research aids may also be helpful in locating state court decisions.

a. Digests

West's American Digest System, its regional digests and state digests, all use the topic, "Constitutional Law" and provide abstracts of all state court decisions published in West reporters on various aspects of that topic. By use of the "Descriptive Word Indexes" and other finding aids described in Chapter 5, one can locate state decisions interpreting the U.S. Constitution, in addition to those interpreting the state constitutions.

b. Annotated State Statutory Codes

Most state annotated statutory codes contain the U.S. Constitution, in addition to the Constitution of that state. While all of the codes annotate the state constitution, a few of these codes also annotate the U.S. Constitution with abstracts of decisions of the courts of that state, thereby providing another means of access to such decisions. Although the state codes published by West do not generally provide such annotations, those issued by Lawyers Co-op do include them.

c. Annotations in ALR Federal and Lawyers' Edition

Many of the Annotations to decisions in *ALR Federal* and *Lawyers' Edition* contain extensive discussion of federal constitutional issues and include citations to state court decisions where they are relevant. These annotated reporters and the methods of access to them are discussed in Chapters 4 and 5, above.

d. Shepard's Citators

As noted below, the U.S. Constitution appears as cited material in the various Shepard's state statutory citators. Those citators can, therefore, be used to locate *state* court decisions applying and interpreting the U.S. Constitution.

Amendment 3

No Soldier shall, in time of peace be quartered in any house, without the consent of the Owner, nor in time of war, but in a manner to be prescribed by law.

Amendment 4

The right of the people to be secure in their persons, houses, papers, and effects, against unreasonable searches and seizures, shall not be violated, and no Warrants shall issue, but upon probable cause, supported by Oath or affirmation, and particularly describing the place to be searched, and the persons or things to be seized.

Digest Reference: Search and Seizure, §§ 1–16.

Amendment 5

No person shall be held to answer for a capital, or otherwise infamous crime, unless on a presentment or indictment of a Grand Jury, except in cases arising in the land or naval forces, or in the Militia, when in actual service in time of War or public danger; nor shall any person be subject for the same offence to be twice put in jeopardy of life or limb; nor shall be compelled in any criminal case to be a witness against himself, nor be deprived of life, liberty, or property, without due process of law; nor shall private property be taken for public use, without just compensation.

Cross References: Deprivation of due process by state, see Amendments, Art. XIV, § 1. Rights of accused, see also Amendments, Art. VI.

Digest References: Constitutional Law, §§ 513–854; Criminal Law, §§ 22–40; Eminent Domain, §§ 1–114; Indictment, etc., §§ 8–12; Witnesses, §§ 72–94.

Amendment 6

In all criminal prosecutions, the accused shall enjoy the right to a speedy and public trial, by an impartial jury of the State and district wherein the crime shall have been committed, which district shall have been previously ascertained by law, and to be informed of the nature and cause of the accusation; to be confronted with the witnesses against him; to have compulsory process for obtaining witnesses in his favor, and to have the Assistance of Counsel for his defence.

Cross Reference: Rights of accused, see also Amendments, Art. V.

Digest References: Criminal Law, §§ 46–53; Jury, §§ 17, 33, 34; Indictment, etc., §§ 8–12.

Illustration H

Typical page from U.S. Constitution, with cross references, in volume 17 of *U.S. Supreme Court Digest, Lawyers' Edition.*

e. Federal Quick Index

The *Federal Quick Index* to the Lawyers Co-op annotated reports offers the researcher access to constitutional annotations in the *ALR Federal* and *Lawyers' Edition.* Illustration I shows a sample page from this Index.

7. SECONDARY SOURCES

The extensive literature of secondary sources in encyclopedias, treatises, periodicals, and looseleaf services, contains coverage of constitutional law. Research on federal constitutional problems is often aided by the commentary and analysis of legal scholars. In addition to the many standard treatises on constitutional law, the periodical literature is rich in articles that approach the Constitution from both historical and contemporary viewpoints. While Chapters 15 and 16 will deal in depth with these secondary sources, it is appropriate here to mention a few specific sources that can be of particular help to the researcher.

While a large number of legal periodicals carry articles on the Supreme Court, several are of special note because of their regular appearance. The *Yearbook of the Supreme Court Historical Society,* published annually by the Society, includes articles, usually in a popular tone, on the history of the Court, its Justices, and the Constitution. The *Supreme Court Review,* published by the University of Chicago, is an annual publication which includes more scholarly articles, usually on important, recent U.S. Supreme Court decisions, many of which deal with constitutional issues. The first issue of each volume of the *Harvard Law Review* usually contains an extensive analysis by its student editors of the activity of the Supreme Court in the preceding term. This survey, always prefaced by a major introductory article written by a noted scholar, is widely read and often cited.

Numerous texts have been devoted to the specific aspects of the Constitution and to the interpretative decisions of the Supreme Court. Among the many historical treatments of the Court and the Constitution, perhaps the most ambitious is the Oliver Wendell Holmes Devise *History of the Supreme Court of the United States,* under the general editorship of Professor Paul Freund.[6] This multi-volume detailed history, with separate authors for each volume, is still in progress, only five of its projected eleven volumes having been issued so far. Each volume covers the major constitutional issues and decisions in its respective period.

Two current texts should be noted for their broad coverage of the Constitution with a focus on current issues. The first is Professor Laurence Tribe's *American Constitutional Law* (Foundation Press, 1978; Supplement 1979). While its analysis has been viewed as controversial by some commentators, the work is probably the most thor-

6. Macmillan, 1971–19__.

SEIZURE OF PROPERTY **FEDERAL**

SEIZURE OF PROPERTY—Cont'd

Remedy, seizure of property as, USCS Rules of Civ Proc, Rule 64

Search and Seizure (this index)

Seizure and confiscation of enemy-owned property. **Trading With the Enemy Act** (this index)

Tax sales: sufficiency of notice of sale of property, under 26 USCS § 6335, seized for failure to pay federal taxes, 26 ALR Fed 381

Vessel, seizure and custody in admiralty proceedings. **Admiralty** (this index)

War (this index)

SELECTION OF FORUM

Conflict of Laws (this index)

SELECTION OF JURY

Grand Jury (this index)

Jury and Jury Trial (this index)

SELECTIONS BOARDS

Navy and Marine Corps, 10 USCS §§ 5701 et seq.

SELECTIVE SERVICE

Armed Forces (this index)

SELF-DEALING

Conflict of Interests (this index)

SELF-DEFENSE

Failure of prosecutor to disclose victim's arrest record to defense in federal murder case and thus allow self-defense argument, effect of, 49 L Ed 2d 342

SELF-EMPLOYMENT

Social Security and Unemployment Compensation (this index)

Tax on. **Income Tax** (this index)

SELF-EMPLOYMENT RETIREMENT PLANS

Generally, see Am Jur 2d New Topic Service, Pension Reform Act §§ 394 et seq.

Federal forms relating to self-employed retirement plans, generally, Am Jur Legal Forms 2d Fed Tax Guide to Legal Forms ¶¶ 134-B et seq.

SELF-HELP REPOSSESSION

Secured Transactions (this index)

SELF-INCRIMINATION

For correlative matters, see topics **Confessions** ; **Interrogations**

Generally, USCS Constitution, Amendment 5; 21 Am Jur 2d Crim L §§ 349 et seq.

Accomplice or codefendant

– due process, confession as violation of, 10 L Ed 2d 215

– reading confession of accomplice who invoked privilege against self-incrimination as violating right of confronting witnesses, 13 L Ed 2d 934

– right to refuse to testify, 6 L Ed 2d 1028

Accused's privilege as violated by extracting evidence from his stomach, 96 L Ed 183

Administrative agency requiring attendance of witnesses and compelling testimony and production of evidence, 2 Am Jur 2d Admin L §§ 268-270

Adverse inference from criminal defendant's election not to take stand, jury's duty not to draw, instruction over defendant's objection concerning, 55 L Ed 2d 319

Alcoholic test. Intoxication, infra

Alibi

– admissibility of testimony of alibi witness named in confession given during police interrogation without advising of right to counsel, 41 L Ed 2d 182

– state requirement of notice as violating privilege, 26 L Ed 2d 446

Aliens (this index)

Answer, incriminatory nature of, 95 L Ed 1118, 1126 (annotation); 99 L Ed 997

Apparel, requiring witness or accused to wear or try on, 18 ALR2d 796

Asking witnesses questions with knowledge that they will invoke privilege against self-incrimination, impropriety of, 10 L Ed 2d 278

Associates of witness, refusal to answer questions as to, 99 L Ed 997

Attorneys

– advice of attorney to disobey court order to produce incriminating evidence as grounds for contempt of court, 42 L Ed 2d 574

– dissolved partnership, self-incrimination privilege as covering financial records of partnership, 40 L Ed 2d 678

– privilege against self-incrimination in disciplinary proceedings against, 6 L Ed 2d 156; 7 Am Jur 2d Attys § 68

550

Illustration I

Sample page from *Federal Quick Index,* showing references to Annotations on the U.S. Constitution.

ough and authoritative one-volume treatment of American constitutional law. The second is Nowack, Rotunda, and Young's *Hornbook on Constitutional Law* (West, 1978—supplemented by pocket parts), an introductory text for students.

Periodical articles are another source of scholarly writing on the Constitution and constitutional issues. In addition to the many relevant articles in law reviews of general coverage, there are several periodicals specializing in this area, e.g., *Civil Rights Research Review, Columbia Human Rights Law Review, Harvard Civil Rights-Civil Liberties Law Review, Hastings Constitutional Law Quarterly, Human Rights,* and the *Supreme Court Review,* noted above.

D. STATE CONSTITUTIONS

1. HISTORICAL RESEARCH ON STATE CONSTITUTIONS

Each of the 50 states has its own constitution. These documents vary considerably in length and scope, many reflecting the earlier prevailing political attitudes of the times at which they were adopted.[7] The amendment process in most states has been used far more frequently and often for quite mundane matters. Many states have had several constitutional conventions and a number of corporate revisions. (Louisiana has done this six times.) For historical information concerning state constitutional conventions or previously enacted state documents, see the following bibliographies and compilations:

C.E. Browne, *State Constitutional Conventions . . . 1776–1959, A Bibliography* (Greenwood Press, 1973), plus Supplements for *1959–1975* by S.R. Yarger (Greenwood Press, 1976) and for *1959–1976*, with *Revisions and Amendments,* by B. Canning (Greenwood Press, 1977).

A.L. Sturm, *A Bibliography on State Constitutions and Constitutional Revision, 1945–1975* (Citizens Conference on State Legislatures, 1975).

W.F. Swindler, *Sources and Documents of United States Constitutions* (Oceana, 1973–1979) 10v. in 11. This is now the most useful historical source for state constitutions.

F.N. Thorpe, *The Federal and State Constitutions, Colonial Charters and Other Organic laws of the States, Territories and Colonies Now or Heretofore Forming the United States of America* (1909) 7 volumes.

State Library of Massachusetts, *Hand-List of Legislative Sessions . . . and Constitutional Conventions* (Boston, 1912).

Selective Bibliography on State Constitution Revision, compiled by B.J. Halevy (National Municipal League, 1963).

7. See, for example, W.P. Adams, *The First American Constitutions: Republican Ideology and the Making of the State Constitutions in the Revolutionary Era* (Univ. of No. Carolina Press, 1980).

2. THE TEXTS OF STATE CONSTITUTIONS

The texts of state constitutions are easily located in any one of several sources. Each state's statutory code contains the text of that state's current constitution, along with earlier constitutions and other organic documents. Most useful, however, are the annotated editions of the state codes, which contain *annotated* texts of the state constitution, similar to those for the U.S. Constitution in *USCA* and *USCS.* These annotated editions usually include references to historical background, Attorney General opinions, and legislative history. The West state annotated codes can also be used for references, by key numbers, to the West digest system. Illustrations J–1 and J–2 consist of sample pages from the Constitution of California, as it appears in *West's Annotated California Codes.* Note the historical references; repealed sections; index to annotations; annotation abstracts of decisions; cross references; and citations to law review articles.

Another source, *Constitutions of the United States, National and State* (2d ed. 1974), published by Oceana Publications for the Legislative Drafting Fund of Columbia University, collects the texts of the constitutions of all 50 states and territories in a looseleaf format that is kept current by supplements. Beginning in 1980, the publisher of *Constitutions of the United States: National and State* began a new indexing service for this set. Rather than indexing the fifty state constitutions in one alphabetical index, as it had previously,[8] it plans to issue a series of separate subject indexes in a looseleaf binder. The first is *Fundamental Liberties and Rights: A 50-State Index* (January 1980), by B.F. Sachs, a sample page of which is shown in Illustration K. When this project is completed it will provide a comprehensive and current subject index to the constitutions of the fifty states.

3. SHEPARDIZING THE STATE CONSTITUTIONS

Each of the Shepard's state citators, in its respective statutory volumes or sections, covers that state's Constitution and provides the usual legislative and judicial history, with citations to secondary sources as well. In addition, proposed amendments to state constitutions are printed in the state session laws, and can also be Shepardized in the Shepard's state citators. Many proposed amendments are not ratified, so it is helpful to be able to check their status in Shepard's.

The *Book of the States,* published biennially with supplements, by the Council of State Governments, also gives information about proposed state constitutional developments and revisions.

8. *Index-Digest of State Constitutions,* 2d ed. (Oceana, 1959), discontinued, but still useful for earlier coverage.

Art. 2, § 1 **CONSTITUTION**

ARTICLE II. VOTING, INITIATIVE AND REFERENDUM, AND RECALL

Former Article 2 was repealed Nov. 7, 1972.

Article 2, Suffrage, was added Nov. 7, 1972. Heading of Article 2 was amended June 8, 1976 to read as it now appears.

TABLE

Showing where the subject matter of the sections of former Article 2 is now covered by sections of new Article 2, as amended in 1976, except as otherwise indicated.

Former Sections	1972 Sections	1976 Sections	Former Sections	1972 Sections	1976 Sections
1	1, 3	2, 4	3, 4	None	None
1½	2	3	5	6	7
2	None	None	6, 7	None	None
2.5, 2½, 2¾	4	5	8	4	5

§ 1. Political power; purpose of government

Section 1. All political power is inherent in the people. Government is instituted for their protection, security, and benefit, and they have the right to alter or reform it when the public good may require.

(Formerly Art. 1, § 26, added Nov. 5, 1974. Renumbered Art. 2, § 1, June 8, 1976.)

Air sovereignty, see Public Utilities Code § 21401.

Former section 1, added Nov. 7, 1972, was renumbered Art. 2, § 2 and amended without change in text on June 8, 1976.

Former section 1 was amended at the primary election held June 6, 1972, to delete voting limitation on naturalized citizens, and was repealed at the general election held Nov. 7, 1972. The subject matter is now covered by this section and Art. 2, § 4.

Amendment of former section 1 proposed by Assembly Const. Amend. No. 5 (1959) was rejected at the general election held on Nov. 8, 1960.

Amendment of former section 1 proposed by Assembly Const. Amend. No. 28 (1965) was rejected by the voters at the general election held on Nov. 8, 1966.

Amendment of former section 1 proposed by Assembly Const. Amend. No. 7 (1969) was rescinded prior to submission to the people by Stats.1970, c. 762, p. 1443, § 3.

1976 Amendment. Renumbered section without change in text.

548

Illustration J–1

California Constitution in *West's Annotated California Codes.*

Law Review Commentaries

Financial disclosure by public officials and public employees—intrusion into right of privacy. (1971) 18 U.C.L.A.Law Rev. 534.

The states and the Supreme Court. Charles H. Davis (1959) 45 A.B.A.J. 233.

Index to Notes

1. Purpose of government

In highly sensitive constitutional area to which First Amendment to Federal Constitution relates, even if compelling state purpose is present, restriction must be drawn with narrow specificity. Fort v. Civil Service Commission of Alameda County (1964) 38 Cal.Rptr. 625, 392 P.2d 385, 61 C.2d 331.

2. Protection, security, and benefit of the people

The Truth in Endorsements Law (Elec. Code § 8600 et seq.), requiring that every advertisement which makes reference to any candidate for nomination in direct primary and contains statement that candidate has been endorsed by organization using as part of its name the name of political party shall bear notice that organization is an unofficial political group does not infringe on freedom of speech and of press as guaranteed by federal and state Constitutions. California Democratic Council v. Arnebergh (1965) 43 Cal.Rptr. 531, 233 C.A.2d 425, appeal dismissed 85 S.Ct. 395, 382 U.S. 202, 15 L.Ed.2d 269.

Provision of Civ.C. § 108 requiring proof of confinement under Welf. & Inst. C. §§ 5000–5189 as part of proof necessary to obtain a divorce on ground of incurable insanity is not unconstitutional for unreasonable classification of insane persons thereby denying equal protection; nor violative of provision of this section that government is for the protection of the people; provision of Const. art. 1, § 21 (repealed; see, now, Art. 1, § 7) that special privileges shall not be granted nor provisions of Const. art. 4, § 1 respecting legislative department. Riggins v. Riggins (1956) 294 P.2d 751, 139 C.A.2d 712.

§ 1½. Repealed. Nov. 7, 1972

The repealed section, added Nov. 4, 1958, authorized state residents of at least 54 days but less than one year to vote in presidential election. See, now, Art. 2, § 2.

New residents, qualifications, registration, etc., see Elections Code § 750 et seq.

§ 2. Voters; qualifications

Sec. 2. A United States citizen 18 years of age and resident in this state may vote.

(Formerly Art. 2, § 1, added by Nov. 7, 1972. Renumbered Art. 2, § 2, June 8, 1976.)

Former section 2 was repealed Nov. 7, 1972.

1976 Amendment. Renumbered section without change in text.

Former section 2, added Nov. 7, 1972, was renumbered Art. 2, § 3, and amended without change in text on June 8, 1976.

Law Review Commentaries

Architecture, aesthetic zoning and First Amendment. (1975) 28 Stan.L.R. 179.

Durational residency requirements for voting violative of equal protection clause. (1972) 13 Santa Clara L. 334.

Electoral process and the power of the states. Donald M. Wilkinson, Jr. (1961) 47 A.B.A.J. 251.

Extraterritorials denied the right to vote. (1980) 68 C.L.R. 126.

Federal remedies for voteless Negroes. Ira Michael Heyman (1960) 48 C.L.R. 190.

Infamous crime as applied to voter disqualification. (1967) 14 U.C.L.A.Law R. 699.

Method for analyzing discriminatory effects under equal protection clause. Gary J. Simson (1977) 29 Stan.L.R. 663.

Need for reform in California civil commitment procedure. (1967) 19 Stan.L.R. 992.

New rights for California's linguistic minorities. (1974) 5 Pacific L.J. 648.

Regulation of campaign financing in California. William B. McKesson and John W. Dickey (1961) 34 So.Cal.L.R. 165.

Suffrage; construction of "convicted": effect of probation. (1954) 27 So.Cal.L.R. 327

The ex-convict's right to vote. (1967) 40 So.Cal.L.R. 148.

Voting Rights Act of 1965. Warren M. Christopher (1965) 18 Stan.L.R. 1.

Who is supreme: people, court or legislature? George M. Vetter, Jr. (1959) 45 A.B.A.J. 1051.

Library references

Literacy tests for voting. Reports of Assembly Interim Committee on Elections and Reapportionment, 1961–62, vol. 7, No. 6, p. 43. Vol. 1 of Appendix to Journal of the Assembly, Reg.Sess., 1963.

Minimum voting age and the age of majority. Report of Assembly Interim Committee on Elections and Constitutional Amendments, Vol. 27, No. 7. Vol. 1 of Appendix to Journal of the Assembly, Reg. Sess., 1970.

For basic development of Notes of Decision, see section 1 of this Article in Main Volume.

Supplementary Index to Notes

I. GENERALLY

¼. Validity

United States constitution does not prohibit state, in this section, from requiring state voters to be United States citizens

Illustration J–2

California's Constitution in *West's Annotated California Codes,* continued.

EVIDENCE (Cont.)

INCRIMINATING EVIDENCE

Model I 1.04
Ala I 6
Alas I 9
Ariz II 10
Ariz II 19
Ark II 8
Cal I 15
Colo II 18
Conn I 8
Del I 7
Fla I 9
Ga I Sec I 13
H I 8
Ida I 13
Ill I 10
Ind I 14
Kan BR 10
Ky BR 11
La I 13
La I 16
Me I 6
Md DR 22
Mass DR 12
Mich I 17
Minn I 7
Miss III 26
Mo I 19
Mont II 25
Nebr I 12
Nev I 8
NH I 15
NM II 15
NY I 6
NC I 23
ND I 13
Ohio I 10
Okla II 21
Okla II 27
Ore I 12
Pa I 9
RI I 13
SC I 12
SD VI 9
Tenn I 9
Tex I 10
Utah I 12
Vt I 10
Va I 8
Wash I 9
W Va III 5
Wis I 8
Wyo I 11

WITNESSES

See WITNESSES

EX POST FACTO LAWS

See also RETROSPECTIVE LAWS

Ala I 7
Ala I 22
Alas I 15
Ariz II 25
Ark II 17
Cal I 9
Colo II 11
Fla I 10
Ga I Sec I 7
Ida I 16
Ill I 16
Ind I 24
Iowa I 21
Ky BR 19
La I 23
Me I 11
Md DR 17
Mass DR 24
Mich I 10
Minn I 11
Miss III 16
Mo I 13
Mont II 31
Nebr I 16
Nev I 15
NH I 23
NJ IV Sec VII 3
NM II 19
NC I 16
ND I 16
Okla II 15
Ore I 21
Pa I 17
RI I 12
SC I 4
SD VI 12
Tenn I 11
Tex I 16
Utah I 18
Va I 9
Wash I 23
W Va III 4
W Va III 11
Wis I 12
Wyo I 35

EXEMPTIONS FROM FORCED SALE

IN GENERAL..............................38
WHO EXEMPTED............................38
WHAT EXEMPTED
In General..............................38
Personal Property.......................38

37

Illustration K

A sample page of *Fundamental Liberties and Rights—a 50-State Index* (Oceana Publications, Jan. 1980).

E. SUMMARY

The impact of judicial interpretation and application of constitutional provisions has had and continues to have significant effect on the development of law in the United States. It is therefore important that research problems be closely examined for possible constitutional issues. The extensive literature and research apparatus described above provides easy access to the text of the federal and state constitutions, as well to annotations to relevant judicial decisions under each constitutional provision. In coping with the bewildering multiplicity of sources, these research tools and secondary sources can be used to locate further analysis and interpretation.

F. ADDITIONAL READING

C. Black, *People and the Court: Judicial Review in a Democracy* (Macmillan, 1960; reprinted Greenwood Press, 1977).

G. Folsom, *Legislative History, Research for the Interpretation of Laws* (University Press of Virginia 1972; reprinted, Fred B. Rothman, 1979) Chapter VI, "Sources for Constitutional Provisions."

J.E. Nowack, R.D. Rotunda & N.J. Young, *Hornbook on Constitutional Law* (West, 1978; with pocket part supplementation).

F.N. Thorpe, *Constitutional History of the United States 1765–1895* (Callaghan, 1901; reprinted, DaCapo, 1970) 3v.

L.H. Tribe, *American Constitutional Law* (Foundation Press, 1979; with supplementation).

C. Warren, *The Making of the Constitution, 1783–1789* (rev.ed., Little, Brown, 1937).

J.S. Williams, *Constitutional Analysis in a Nutshell* (West, 1979).

Chapter 7

STATUTES AND RELATED MATERIALS

A. Introduction.
B. Pattern of Statutory Publication.
   1. Slip Laws.
   2. Session Laws.
   3. Statutory Compilations or Codes.
   4. Annotated Codes.
   5. Summary.
C. Federal Statutory Materials.
   1. Federal Legislative Process.
   2. Federal Slip Laws.
   3. U.S. *Statutes at Large.*
   4. *Revised Statutes.*
   5. *U.S. Code.*
   6. Unofficial Publications of the *U.S. Code.*
      a. *U.S. Code Annotated.*
      b. *U.S. Code Service.*
      c. *U.S.C.C.A.N.*
   7. Other Forms of Federal Legislation.
      a. U.S. Constitution.
      b. Treaties.
      c. Interstate Compacts.
      d. Reorganization Plans.
D. State Statutory Materials.
   1. Slip Laws; Session Laws; Codes.
   2. Legislative Services.
   3. Uniform Laws and Model Acts.
E. Other Statutory Sources.
   1. Looseleaf Services.
   2. Subject Collections.
F. Research in Statutory Law.
   1. Historical Indexes.
      a. Federal Law Indexes.
      b. State Law Indexes.
   2. Subject Access to Codes.
   3. Access to Session Laws.
      a. Volume Indexes.
      b. From Code Provisions.
   4. Popular Name Tables.
   5. Updating the Search.
      a. Supplementation and Legislative Services.
      b. Shepard's Citations.
      c. Looseleaf Services.
   6. Statutory Research by Computer.

A. INTRODUCTION

Statutes and other legislative forms constitute the second category of primary legal sources. Because of the focus on appellate decisions in American legal education, and on cases in the popular conception of the lawyer's work, the role of statutory law in legal research tends to be underemphasized. In practice, however, statutory law is central to many legal issues, and the initial step in approaching most research problems is to ascertain whether there is a governing statute, rather than immediately searching for judicial precedents. Indeed, the vast majority of appellate decisions today involve the application or interpretation of statutes,[1] rather than merely consideration of common law principles.

The United States remains a common law jurisdiction, but the sharp distinction between common and civil law has eroded somewhat in recent years. Civil law jurisdictions are no longer totally oriented by their codes, and common law jurisdictions are governed more directly and pervasively by legislation than by case law. This trend is discussed further in Chapter 20, below. In any event, it is clear that an understanding of the forms and use of statutory law is essential for effective legal research.

The term "legislation" can be broadly construed to include constitutions, statutes, treaties, municipal charters and ordinances, interstate compacts and reorganization plans. Because administrative regulations and court rules are considered "delegated legislation," they are often discussed with statutory materials.[2]

As in the previous consideration of *case* law, the federal nature of our government and legal system is important in understanding legislation. The U.S. Congress and the legislatures of the fifty states each have their own structures and procedures for the initiation and

1. An interesting study of the impact on the courts of this growth of legislation is to be found in Professor Guido Calabresi's Oliver Wendell Holmes lectures, recently published as *A Common Law for the Age of Statutes* (Harvard University Press, 1982).

2. In this work, however, court rules and administrative regulations are treated separately, in Chapters 8 and 11, respectively.

passsage of legislation. Similarly, the forms of publication of statutory materials vary from jurisdiction to jurisdiction although by and large they share similar features.

B. PATTERN OF STATUTORY PUBLICATION

The texts of enacted legislation for the various jurisdictions of the United States are issued successively in a series of forms which constitute a common pattern. The names of each form may differ among the jurisdictions but the generic equivalent always exists. The following diagram illustrates this pattern of statutory publication:

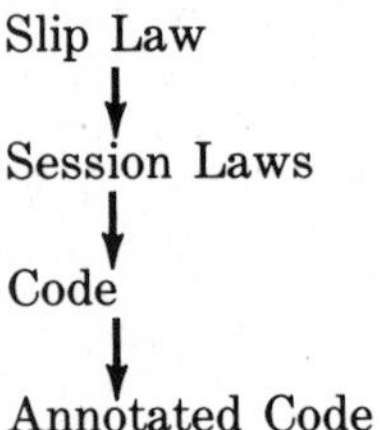

1. SLIP LAWS

"Slip Laws" are separately issued pamphlets, each of which contains the text of a single act. Typically, they are individually paginated, designated by a chapter or law number, and are issued officially by the state. Slip laws for most states are not widely distributed and are received only in the larger research law libraries. Many lawyers rarely see statutes in that initial form, but slip laws are usually the first official text of laws to be published.

2. SESSION LAWS

The term "session laws" refers to the permanent publication in chronological sequence of the "slip laws," as passed by the jurisdiction's legislature and approved by the President or Governor, or passed over the executive's veto. The federal government and each of the fifty states publish some form of session laws, usually in bound volumes issued after considerable delay, following the close of each legislative session. The names of these publications vary from state to state (e.g., Acts and Resolves of Massachusetts, Laws of New York, Alaska Session Laws, California Statutes, etc.) In most states, the session laws constitute the "positive law" form of legislation, *i.e.*, the authoritative, binding text of the laws, and the determinative version if questions arise from textual variations in subsequent printed versions.[3]

Most state session law publications share several common characteristics, including non-cumulative subject indexes and, frequently, a table which indicates which existing laws have been modified or re-

3. Other forms (e.g. Codes, in most states) are only *prima facie* evidence of the statutory language, unless they have been designated as "positive law" by the legislature.

pealed by the laws contained in the volume. These features facilitate subject access within an individual volume of the session laws, but, unfortunately, access to the individual session law volume is inadequate for most research. Since statutory research generally focuses on a particular issue or topic and requires the current text of all law in force on that problem, the session laws alone are of little help. One cannot effectively search every session law volume for laws on a specific topic, and then adjust for the successive amendments or repeals reflected therein. If, for example, one wished to find all federal enactments on the subject of hijacking, searching the subject index of each volume of the session laws for the United States (i.e., the U.S. *Statutes at Large*) then synthesizing provisions enacted over many years, and keeping track of those amended or repealed, would be virtually impossible. It would require in effect a separate and complete codification of the law on each topic being researched. Changes in terminology and major revisions of legislation would further complicate the process. Fortunately, this process is not necessary. Subject arrangements of statutes, usually called codes, are now available for federal statutes and for the statutory law of each of the states. These compilations provide the necessary synthesis and are updated by at least annual supplementation. They form the third level of the diagram shown above.

3. STATUTORY COMPILATIONS OR CODES

As used in this Chapter, the term "code" refers to a publication of the *public*,[4] *general and permanent* statutes of a jurisdiction in a fixed subject arrangement. These codes are fundamentally different in form and purpose from the codes of civil law countries. The codes of the civil law system are original statutory texts designed to summarize the fundamental precepts of a field of law in concise, general prose.[5] American statutory codes preserve the original language of the session laws more or less intact, and merely rearrange and group them together in broad subject categories which are separately designated as *titles* or *parts* of the code. In some states, such as California, the individual subject groupings are each called a code, e.g., Civil Code, Education Code, Labor Code, Penal Code, etc.

In this process of rearranging the individual statutes, amendments are incorporated, repealed laws are deleted, and minor adjustments are made in the language and text of the laws to fit them into a functional and coherent compilation. The subject structure used to organize the statutes varies from state to state. It can consist of a limited number of very general topics (e.g. twenty eight in the California Codes, or fifty in the federal *United States Code*) or a larger number of more specific headings (Maryland, for example, has one hundred and twelve titles).

4. For the difference between *public* and *private* laws, see Section C.1, at page 185 below.

5. This distinction is amplified in Chapter 20, Foreign and Comparative Law.

The proliferation of legislation is usually preserved in these compilations, along with their prolixity and redundancy. Obsolete laws are retained as well. When new legislation must be incorporated, only the necessary grammatical changes are made to facilitate their "codification." The result of this process is that the codes tend to be unwieldy and cumbersome, requiring many cross-references, and frequent use of phrases like "unless otherwise hereinafter prohibited," "other provisions to the contrary notwithstanding," and similar potential ambiguities which often must be resolved in costly litigation.

The unofficial, commercial editions of the Codes are generally provided with detailed indexing, and kept up to date by some form of supplementation. Because of the frequency of legislative change, prompt supplementation is, of course, essential in all statutory compilations.

A particular edition of a code may or may not be "official," depending on whether or not it is published by the state, or otherwise so sanctioned by the legislature. In some states, the code appears in both an official and an unofficial edition, with the unofficial form issued by a commercial publisher, with annotations to relevant court decisions. Some jurisdictions issue new codes on a periodic schedule. The federal government, for example, issues a new edition of the *United States Code* every six years, with annual supplements cumulating in each interim year. Many states rarely revise or reissue their codes, so they become obsolete, and only of historical interest.[6] A very few states reissue their codes in an official edition annually or biennially. In most states, however, the subject arrangement of an earlier official code is retained by a commercial publisher in its modern, supplemented edition which becomes the only effective statutory compilation in that state.

Frequently, even if there is an official code (and *always*, when there is not one), the session law represents the "positive law" text of statutes, all other texts or codes being only *prima facie* evidence of the law (i.e. subject to rebuttal by reference to the session laws).[7]

The names of the session laws and the current codes for each state are listed in Appendix B at the end of this volume. Illustrations A1 to A3 show a sample session law for the state of Washington, and its subject index entry. Illustrations B1 to B3 show that law in its official code form, with its index entry in that compilation.

Despite their convenience as research tools, there are still certain shortcomings in the official codes. As already noted, many judicial decisions involve issues of statutory construction and interpretation. Since legislation often involves compromises between opposing legislative forces, the statutory language that results from that legislative compromise is often ambiguous. Judicial interpretation of statutes

6. For example, the *Consolidated Laws of New York* have not been officially reissued since 1909, and the *General Laws of Massachusetts*, not since 1933.

7. This distinction is discussed further in sections C.3 to C.5, below, with specific reference to the relative authority of the various forms of *federal* statutes.

1969

SESSION LAWS

OF THE

STATE OF WASHINGTON

REGULAR SESSION, FORTY-FIRST LEGISLATURE
Convened January 13, 1969. Adjourned March 13, 1969.

FIRST EXTRAORDINARY SESSION,
FORTY-FIRST LEGISLATURE
Convened March 14, 1969. Adjourned May 12, 1969.

VOLUME NO. 1

Containing All Chapters of the Regular Session, and Chapters 1 through 222, First Extraordinary Session

Published at Olympia by the Statute Law Committee pursuant to Chapter 6, Laws of 1969.

RICHARD O. WHITE
Code Reviser

[*i*]

Illustration A-1

Title page of *1969 Session Laws of . . . Washington.*

WASHINGTON LAWS, 1969 1st Ex. Sess. Ch. 108, 109

~~(4)--Belt-manlifts-are-installed-and-used-exclusively-by--persons-enumerated-by-or-governed-by-Title-51-RCW-and-which-are-subject-to-inspection-as-required-by-RCW-49.16.120.~~))

Passed the House March 24, 1969
Passed the Senate April 9, 1969
Approved by the Governor April 17, 1969
Filed in office of Secretary of State April 17, 1969

CHAPTER 109
[Senate Bill No. 414]
COMPULSORY SCHOOL ATTENDANCE

AN ACT Relating to education; amending section 1, page 364, Laws of 1909 and RCW 28.27.010; amending section 28A.27.010, chapter ...., Laws of 1969 (HB 58) and RCW 28A.27.010; providing sections to effect the correlative and pari materia construction of this act with the provisions of Title 28 RCW, or of Titles 28A and 28B RCW if such titles shall be enacted; and declaring an emergency.

BE IT ENACTED BY THE LEGISLATURE OF THE STATE OF WASHINGTON:

Part I. Sections affecting current law.

Section 1. Section 1, page 364, Laws of 1909 and RCW 28.27-.010 are each amended to read as follows:

All parents, guardians and other persons in this state having or who may hereafter have immediate custody of any child between eight and fifteen years of age (being between the eighth and fifteenth birthdays), or of any child between fifteen and sixteen years of age (being between the fifteenth and sixteenth birthdays) not regularly and lawfully engaged in some useful and remunerative occupation, shall cause such child to attend the public school of the district, in which the child resides, for the full time when such school may be in session or to attend a private school for the same time, unless the superintendent of the schools of the district in which the child resides, if there be such a superintendent, and in all other cases the county superintendents of common schools, shall have excused such child from such attendance because the child is physically or mentally unable to attend school or has already attained a reasonable profi-

[821]

Illustration A–2

Sample law in 1969 Session Law volume of Washington.

SUBJECT INDEX 1969 Reg. and 1st Extra. Sessions

*Denotes Extraordinary Session

2873

Illustration A–3

Index entries in 1969 Session Law volume of Washington.

(1) If a student requires special education, care or guidance, he may be assigned and transported to the school offering courses and facilities for such special education, care or guidance;

(2) If there are health or safety hazards, either natural or man made, or physical barriers or obstacles, either natural or man made, between the student's place of residence and the nearest or next nearest school; or

(3) If the school nearest or next nearest to his place of residence is unfit or inadequate because of overcrowding, unsafe conditions or lack of physical facilities. [1979 c 4 § 1 (Initiative Measure No. 350).]

28A.26.020 Application of next geographically nearest rule. In every such instance where a student is assigned and transported to a school other than the one nearest his place of residence, he shall be assigned and transported to the next geographically nearest school with the necessary and applicable courses and facilities within the school district of his or her residence. [1979 c 4 § 2 (Initiative Measure No. 350).]

28A.26.030 Explanation of phrase as used in RCW 28A.26.010. For purposes of RCW 28A.26.010, "indirectly require any student to attend a school other than the school which is geographically nearest or next nearest the student's place of residence within the school district of his or her residence and which offers the course of study pursued by such student" includes, but is not limited to, implementing, continuing, pursuing, maintaining or operating any plan involving (1) the redefining of attendance zones; (2) feeder schools; (3) the reorganization of the grade structure of the schools; (4) the pairing of schools; (5) the merging of schools; (6) the clustering of schools; or (7) any other combination of grade restructuring, pairing, merging or clustering: *Provided*, That nothing in this chapter shall limit the authority of any school district to close school facilities. [1979 c 4 § 3 (Initiative Measure No. 350).]

28A.26.040 Explanation of "special education, care or guidance" as used in RCW 28A.26.010. For the purposes of RCW 28A.26.010 "special education, care or guidance" includes the education, care or guidance of students who are physically, mentally or emotionally handicapped. [1979 c 4 § 4 (Initiative Measure No. 350).]

28A.26.050 Voluntary options not precluded. The prohibitions of this chapter shall not preclude the establishment of schools offering specialized or enriched educational programs which students may voluntarily choose to attend, or of any other voluntary option offered to students. [1979 c 4 § 5 (Initiative Measure No. 350).]

28A.26.060 Adjudication of constitutional issues not precluded. This chapter shall not prevent any court of competent jurisdiction from adjudicating constitutional issues relating to the public schools. [1979 c 4 § 6 (Initiative Measure No. 350).]

28A.26.900 Severability——1979 c 4. If any provision of this chapter, or its application to any person or circumstance is held invalid, the remainder of the chapter, or the application of the provision to other persons or circumstances is not affected. [1979 c 4 § 8 (Initiative Measure No. 350).]

Reviser's note: This chapter for purposes of RCW 28A.26.900 [1979 c 4] means RCW 28A.26.010, 28A.26.020, 28A.26.030, 28A.26.040, 28A.26.050 and 28A.26.060.

Chapter 28A.27
COMPULSORY SCHOOL ATTENDANCE

Sections

Rules and regulations accepting national guard high school career training: RCW 28A.04.133.

28A.27.010 Attendance mandatory——Age——Persons having custody shall cause child to attend public school unless excused——Excused temporary absences. All parents, guardians and the persons in this state having custody of any child eight years of age and under fifteen years of age shall cause such child to attend the public school of the district in which the child resides for the full time when such school may be in session or to attend a private school for the same time unless the school district superintendent of the district in which the child resides shall have excused such child from attendance because the child is physically or mentally unable to attend school, is attending a residential school operated by the department of social and health services, or has been excused upon the request of his or her parents, guardians, or persons in this state having custody of any such child, for purposes agreed upon by the school authorities and the parent, guardian or custodian: *Provided*, That such excused absences shall not be permitted

Illustration B-1

Statutory section in the official *Revised Code of Washington.*

Compulsory School Attendance

if deemed to cause a serious adverse effect upon the student's educational progress: *Provided further,* That students excused for such temporary absences may be claimed as full time equivalent students to the extent they would otherwise have been so claimed for the purposes of RCW 28A.41.130 and 28A.41.140, as now or hereafter amended, and shall not affect school district compliance with the provisions of RCW 28A.58.754, as now or hereafter amended.

All parents, guardians and other persons in this state having custody of any child fifteen years of age and under eighteen years of age shall cause such child to attend the public school of the district in which the child resides for the full time when such school may be in session or to attend a private school for the same time excepting when the school district superintendent determines that such child is physically or mentally unable to attend school or has already attained a reasonable proficiency in the branches required by law to be taught in the first nine grades of the public schools of this state, or the child has been temporarily excused in accordance with this section, or the child is regularly and lawfully engaged in a useful or remunerative occupation, or the child is attending a residential school operated by the department of social and health services, or the child has already met graduation requirements in accordance with state board of education rules and regulations, or the child has received a certificate of educational competence under rules and regulations established by the state board of education under RCW 28A.04.135.

An approved private and/or parochial school for the purposes of this section shall be one approved under regulations established by the state board of education pursuant to RCW 28A.04.120 as now or hereafter amended. [1980 c 59 § 1; 1979 ex.s. c 201 § 4; 1973 c 51 § 1; 1972 ex.s. c 10 § 2. Prior: 1971 ex.s. c 215 § 2; 1971 ex.s. c 51 § 1; 1969 ex.s. c 109 § 2; 1969 ex.s. c 223 § 28A.27.010; prior: 1909 p 364 § 1; RRS § 5072; prior: 1907 c 240 § 7; 1907 c 231 § 1; 1905 c 162 § 1; 1903 c 48 § 1; 1901 c 177 § 11; 1899 c 140 § 1; 1897 c 118 § 71. Formerly RCW 28.27.010.]

Severability——1973 c 51: "If any provision of this 1973 amendatory act, or its application to any person or circumstance is held invalid, the remainder of the act, or the application of the provision to other persons or circumstances is not affected." [1973 c 51 § 5.] This applies to RCW 28A.27.010, 28A.04.135, 49.12.123 and the repeal of chapters 28A.06 and 28A.28 RCW.

Private and/or parochial schools now private schools: RCW 28A.04.120(4), 28A.02.201 and 28A.02.220–28A.02.250.

Work permits for minors required: RCW 49.12.123.

28A.27.020 School's duties upon juvenile's failure to attend school——Generally. If a juvenile required to attend school under the laws of the state of Washington fails to attend school without valid justification recurrently or for an extended period of time, the juvenile's school, where appropriate, shall:

(1) Inform the juvenile's custodial parent, parents or guardian by a notice in writing in English and, if different, in the primary language of the custodial parent, parents or guardian and by other means reasonably necessary to achieve notice of the fact that the juvenile has failed to attend school without valid justification recurrently or for an extended period of time;

(2) Schedule a conference or conferences with the custodial parent, parents or guardian and juvenile at a time and place reasonably convenient for all persons included for the purpose of analyzing the causes of the juvenile's absences; and

(3) Take steps to eliminate or reduce the juvenile's absences, including, where appropriate, adjusting the juvenile's school program or school or course assignment or assisting the parent or student to obtain supplementary services that might eliminate or ameliorate the cause or causes for the absence from school. [1979 ex.s. c 201 § 1.]

28A.27.022 Petition to juvenile court to assume jurisdiction——Applicability of chapter. If action taken by a school pursuant to RCW 28A.27.020 is not successful in substantially reducing a student's absences from school, the attendance officer of the school district through its attorney may petition the juvenile court to assume jurisdiction under this chapter for the purpose of alleging a violation of RCW 28A.27.010. If the court assumes jurisdiction in such an instance, the provisions of this chapter, except where otherwise stated, shall apply. [1979 ex.s. c 201 § 2.]

28A.27.030 School district superintendent to provide teacher with census——Report of truants, incorrigibles. It shall be the duty of the school district superintendent, at the beginning of each school year, to provide each teacher with a copy of that portion of the last census of school children taken in his school district which would be pertinent to the grade or grades such teacher is instructing and it shall be the duty of every teacher to report to the proper attendance officer, all cases of truancy or incorrigibility in his school, immediately after the offense or offenses shall have been committed: *Provided,* That if there be a principal the report by the teacher shall be made to him and by him transmitted to the attendance officer: *Provided further,* That if there be a city superintendent, the principal shall transmit such report to said city superintendent, who shall transmit such report to the proper attendance officer of his district. [1969 ex.s. c 223 § 28A.27.030. Prior: 1909 c 97 p 367 § 6; RRS § 5077; prior: 1907 c 231 § 6; 1905 c 162 § 6; 1903 c 48 §§ 2, 3, 4. Formerly RCW 28.27.030.]

28A.27.040 Attendance enforcement officers——Authority——Record and report. To aid in the enforcement of RCW 28A.27.010 through 28A.27.130, attendance officers shall be appointed and employed as follows: In incorporated city districts the board of directors shall annually appoint one or more attendance officers. In all other districts the educational service district superintendent shall appoint one or more attendance officers or may act as such himself.

The compensation of attendance officer in city districts shall be fixed and paid by the board appointing

(1981 Ed.) [Title 28A RCW—p 43]

Illustration B–2

Statutory section in the official *Revised Code of Washington* (cont'd.).

SCHOOLS AND SCHOOL DISTRICTS **SCHOOLS AND SCHOOL DISTRICTS**

SCHOOLS AND SCHOOL DISTRICTS—Cont.
Buildings and plants, state aid—Cont.
manual, information and guidance, published by superintendent of public instruction 28A.47.090
modernization of existing facilities
handicapped, for 28A.47.073
portable buildings or classrooms, funds available 28A.47.075
repairs, portable buildings and classrooms, matching funds authorized 28A.47.075
rules and regulations governing applications for 28A.47.080
securities, deposit of 28A.47.220
state board of education, duties 28A.47.060
statutory authority 28A.47.830
superintendent of public instruction
duty to assist districts and state board of education 28A.47.100
duty to publish information and guidance manual 28A.47.090, 28A.47.690, 28A.47.807
treasurer, state, duties 28A.47.220
Buildings and property
community college facilities
sharing of facilities and services 28B.50.530
transfer to new boards or agencies 28B-.50.300, 28B.50.610
handicapped, provisions for in public building, generally Ch. 70.92
modernization of existing facilities 28A.47.073
handicapped, for 28A.47.073
Buses, See SCHOOLS AND SCHOOL DISTRICTS, subtitle Transportation
Capital improvements, See SCHOOLS AND SCHOOL DISTRICTS, subtitle Buildings and plants, state aid
Census
age four years or over included in 28A.35.030
kindergarten law not to affect 28A.35.020
to include children on United States reservations, national parks 28A.58.215
Certificated employees
deferred compensation plan 28A.58.740
defined 28A.01.130
performing services for superintendent of public instruction or state board of education, reimbursement provisions 28A.41.180
Certification, professional, not required for superintendent of a local district 28A.02.260
Certification of personnel 28A.70.005
Child employment and part time schools
child employment under compulsory attendance law, See SCHOOLS AND SCHOOL DISTRICTS, subtitle Compulsory attendance
Child removed from school grounds during school hours, procedure 28A.58.050
Cities and towns owning public utilities
generating facilities located in another county
notice of loss 35.21.426
payment formulas 35.21.427
reimbursement 35.21.425
Cities with generating facility or school district to provide additional funds 28A.58.220
Claims against
liability for debts and judgments against 28A.58.020
service fee for investment, reinvestment of school funds 28A.58.440
treasurer's expenses in issuing, sale, redemption, of bonds 28A.51.200
Classification of school districts
according to population 28A.57.140
change of, delay authorized 28A.57.145

SCHOOLS AND SCHOOL DISTRICTS—Cont.
Classroom activities
parents access to 28A.58.053
Clerk of districts
deaf, mute, or blind youth in districts, report of 72.40.060
Collective bargaining (See also EDUCATIONAL EMPLOYMENT RELATIONS ACT)
limitations 41.56.960
Commencement exercises, funds for 28A.58.107
Common school construction fund
creation 28A.40.100
federal funds as source of 28A.40.100
permanent common school fund, interest of deposited in after June 30, 1965 28A.40.100
sources 28A.40.100
uses 28A.40.100
Common schools
defined 28A.01.060
qualification for admission 28A.58.190
special legislation affecting management prohibited Const. Art. 2 § 28
superintendent of public instruction to supervise Const. Art. 3 § 22
Commonly-used schoolhouse doors defined 28A.01.110
Community colleges, See COMMUNITY COLLEGES
Community education programs
authorized 28A.58.247
purpose 28A.58.246
restrictions 28A.58.247
study and report on 28A.58.248
Compulsory attendance ←
acquiring custody of truants and further disposition thereof 28A.27.070
age limits 28A.27.010
attendance officers
appointment, compensation, qualifications, authority, records 28A.27.040
petition to juvenile court to assume jurisdiction 28A.27.022
reports of truancy or incorrigibility made to 28A.27.030
child employment and part time schools, See SCHOOLS AND SCHOOL DISTRICTS, subtitle Child employment and part time schools
county prosecuting attorney or school district attorney to act 28A.27.110
court jurisdiction 28A.27.100, 28A.27.120
disposition of fines 28A.27.104
employment during school hours forbidden 28A.27.090
proof of employment as violation 28A.27.090
employment permits, contents, retention by employer 28A.27.090
enforcement of for children on United States reservations 28A.58.210
enforcing officers not liable for costs 28A.27.130
exceptions and excuses from
excused temporary absences 28A.27.010
exemptions and excuses from
part time school students 28A.27.010
physical or mental disability 28A.27.010
proficiency in first nine grades 28A.27.010
regularly, lawfully employed 28A.27.010
Indians, assumption of state jurisdiction 37.12.010
penalties, generally 28A.27.100
suspension of fine, when 28A.27.100
penalty for school officials for nonperformance of duty 28A.27.102
disposition of fines 28A.27.102, 28A.27.104

SCHOOLS AND SCHOOL DISTRICTS—Cont.
Compulsory attendance—Cont.
person having custody shall cause child to attend 28A.27.010
petition to juvenile court to assume jurisdiction 28A.27.022
private and/or parochial school defined for purposes of 28A.27.010
proof of absence as evidence of violation 28A.27.010
reports of compliance with law mandatory, penalty 28A.27.080
reports of truancy or incorrigibility 28A.27.030
residential schools, attendance as compliance 28A.27.010
school's duties upon juveniles failure to attend school, generally 28A.27.020
superintendents annual report on compliance 28A.27.080
violations
defenses 28A.27.100
Condemnation, See EMINENT DOMAIN, subtitle School districts, by
Constitutions, study of required 28A.02.080
Construction of buildings, See SCHOOLS AND SCHOOL DISTRICTS, subtitle Buildings and plants, generally; SCHOOLS AND SCHOOL DISTRICTS, subtitle Buildings and plants, state aid
Contagious or infectious diseases, exclusion of persons having from school premises 28A.31.010
Contracts
awarding of bids 28A.58.135
certificated personnel, supplemental contracts for additional duties, requirement 28A.67.074
conditional sales contracts for acquisition of property or property rights, limitations, joint action 28A.58.550
information and research services, for 28A.58.530
intergovernmental cooperation, authority Ch. 39.34
lease of buildings, security systems, computers, etc., for extended periods, authorized 28A.58.131
made in violation of indebtedness limitations void 39.36.040
superintendent, with 28A.58.137
Conveyances, real property 28A.58.040, 28A.58.045
County auditor, duties concerning
annual report to educational service district superintendent 28A.66.100
auditing accounts for
second class districts 28A.66.030
warrants
annual report to educational service district superintendent 28A.66.100
drawing and issuing for
second class districts 28A.66.040
exceeding budget of district, personal liability of county auditor 28A.66.070
redeemed warrants, check and report 28A.66.090
registration
all districts 28A.66.010
second class districts 28A.66.020
County circulating libraries Ch. 27.16
County committees on school district organization
considerations in implementing powers and duties 28A.57.055
created 28A.57.030
election of members 28A.57.032
expenses of members, reimbursement authorized 28A.57.035
joint districts 28A.57.240

(1981 Ed.) **[RCW Index—p 849]**

Illustration B–3

Entries in the index volume of the *Revised Code of Washington.*

thus becomes an important extrinsic aid to understanding the meaning of a controverted statute. A researcher using only the statutory language in the Code may not, therefore, understand its full implications or the nuances within the wording of the statute. The fourth stage in the pattern of statute publication, the "annotated code," fills this need by providing access to relevant court decisions.

4. ANNOTATED CODES

An annotated code reproduces the official code's subject arrangement, and usually its title, part and section numbering. It also incorporates new legislation, revisions, and amendments within that structure, and deletes repealed laws. Its unique contribution is the inclusion, after each statutory section, of annotations to decisions which have interpreted, construed or merely applied the statutory section. The annotation consists of an abstract or "squib" of the point of law decided by the case, and the name and citation of the case. In annotated codes published by West, these abstracts follow the same format as the West case headnote and digest abstract. Where there are several annotations to a statutory section, a subject index, with appropriate detail, will precede the annotations.

Although a few states publish *official* annotated codes, in most states they are the product of a commercial publisher. West, for example, publishes annotated codes for twenty one states. The commercial annotated codes are usually kept up to date by pocket parts and quarterly pamphlet supplements, which include both statutory changes and new annotations. They are also well indexed and usually accompanied by helpful tables and other finding aids. These annotated codes are invariably the editions most frequently used by lawyers and other serious researchers. The annotated edition of the code will not usually be the "positive law" text, and hence recourse to the session laws may be necessary if there is doubt about the statutory language. Fortunately, this rarely occurs.

Illustrations C–1 to C–4 show the same statute depicted in Illustrations A and B, but here as it appears in West's *Revised Code of Washington Annotated.* Note that, following the statutory text, the publisher has provided references to legislative history, cross references to other related sections, to the two national legal encyclopedias, (*Am.Jur.2d* and *CJS*), to Opinions of the Attorney General, *A.L.R.* Annotations, a West digest topic and key number, and then the annotations or notes to decisions which applied or interpreted the statutory sections. Illustration C–3 shows the updating of the coverage in the annual pocket part supplement. Note there that the statute has been amended and cross references to later material, including annotations, have been added. Illustration C–4 shows the subject index entry to that statutory section in the index of the *Revised Code of Washington Annotated.* These various features of the commercial editions of the annotated codes make them the most effective research sources for statutory material.

CHAPTER 28A.27

COMPULSORY SCHOOL ATTENDANCE

Sections

CROSS REFERENCES

Employment permits: RCWA Chapter 28A.28.
Jurisdiction over Indians: RCWA Chapter 37.12.

28A.27.010 Attendance mandatory—Age—When excused. All parents, guardians and other persons in this state having custody of any child eight years of age and under fifteen years of age, or of any child fifteen years of age and under eighteen years of age not regularly and lawfully engaged in some useful and remunerative occupation or attending part time school in accordance with the provisions of chapter 28A.28 RCW or excused from school attendance thereunder, shall cause such child to attend the public school of the district in which the child resides for the full time when such school may be in session or to attend a private school for the same time, unless the school district superintendent of the district in which the child resides shall have excused such child from such attendance because the child is physically or mentally unable to attend school or has already

T. 27–28A.60 Wash.Code—15 225

Illustration C–1

Statutory section in West's *Revised Code of Washington Annotated.*

28A.27.010 COMMON SCHOOL PROVISIONS

attained a reasonable proficiency in the branches required by law to be taught in the first nine grades of the public schools of this state. Proof of absence from any public or private school shall be prima facie evidence of a violation of this section. Private school for the purposes of this section shall be one approved or accredited under regulations established by the state board of education.

LEGISLATIVE HISTORY

1. Enacted Laws 1st Ex Sess 1969 ch 223 § 28A.27.010 p 1720, effective July 1, 1970. Based on:
(a) Laws 1909 ch 231 § 1 p 364, as amended by Laws 1st Ex Sess 1969 ch 109 § 1.
(b) Laws 1907 ch 231 § 1 p 364.
(c) Laws 1905 ch 162 § 1 p 316.
(d) Laws 1903 ch 48 § 1 p 53.
(e) Laws 1899 ch 140 § 1 p 280, as amended by Laws 1901 ch 177 § 11 p 379.
(f) Laws 1897 ch 118 § 71 p 385, as amended by Laws 1907 ch 240 § 7 p 613.
2. Amended by Laws 1st Ex Sess 1969 ch 109 § 2 p 822, effective July 1, 1970, substituting "nine" for "eight" before "grades" in the first sentence.
See RRS § 5072 and former RCW 28.27.010.

CROSS REFERENCES

Age: RCWA 28A.28.020.

COLLATERAL REFERENCES

Am Jur Schools §§ 156–159.
CJS Schools and School Districts §§ 463–470.

Attorney General's Opinions:

Ops Atty Gen 1921–1922 p 168 (failure to furnish transportation as excuse to parent for noncompliance with statute).

Ops Atty Gen 1921–1922 p 196 (right of children attending public schools to be excused during regular school hours for instruction in church schools for which no credit is given).

Ops Atty Gen 1925–1926 p 99 (necessity for attendance of while family living on Indian reservation which is not part of school district).

Ops Atty Gen 1925–1926 p 109 (authority of district superintendent to excuse children from attendance for reasons which he deems sufficient).

Ops Atty Gen 1927–1928 p 282 (necessity for attendance at high school of elementary pupils possessing diploma of graduation).

Ops Atty Gen 63–64 No. 130 (power to permit students of private or parochial school to attend district schools on part-time basis; computation of average daily attendance).

Annotations:

39 ALR 477, 53 ALR 832 (extent of legislative power with respect to attendance).

226

COMPULSORY SCHOOL ATTENDANCE **28A.27.010**

2 ALR2d 1371 (releasing public school pupils from attendance for purpose of attending religious education classes).

3 ALR2d 1401 (religious beliefs of parents as defense to prosecution for failure to comply with compulsory education law).

14 ALR2d 1369 (what constitutes "private schools" within statute making attendance at such a school compliance with compulsory school attendance law).

Key Number Digest:

Schools and School Districts ⚷160.

NOTES OF DECISIONS

Laws 1907 p 569, providing for compulsory education of children, did not conflict with or impliedly repeal Laws 1905 p 262 § 3 subd 9, providing that successful vaccination should be required as condition precedent to school membership. State ex rel. McFadden v Shorrock (1909) 55 Wn 208, 104 P 214.

Information for violation of this provision is not defective in that it charges neglect to cause children to attend public school or "approved" private school, where gist of offense is in failure to attend any school, public or private, and information clearly charges such offense. State v Counort (1912) 69 Wn 361, 124 P 910.

It was no defense to prosecution for violating former provision that parent was experienced and qualified as teacher and gave private instruction to his own children at his home, such home instruction not being attendance at private school within the meaning of law, where he did not maintain private school at his home as determined by purpose, intent, and character of endeavor. State v Counort (1912) 69 Wn 361, 124 P 910.

Statute making attendance on public or private school compulsory did not show that model training school conducted by state normal school was common school or private school within statute (former RCWA 28.48.010), basing apportionment of current state school funds on total days of attendance. State ex rel. School Dist. No. 3 v Preston (1914) 79 Wn 286, 140 P 350.

Criminal liability of school district director for not sending his children to school is no defense to action to recover money illegally paid to him for hauling the children to school, without which he could not have sent them, since he would not have been criminally liable if there had been any sufficient reason for not doing so. Directors of School Dist. No. 302 v Libby (1925) 135 Wn 233, 237 P 505.

Courts have always been in sympathy with laws requiring children within certain ages to attend school, and school authorities and juvenile courts are required to enforce these laws. State ex rel. Pulakis v Superior Court (1942) 14 Wn 2d 507, 128 P2d 649.

Compulsory school attendance laws were not violated by program under which public school children were released for one hour per week for religious education instruction conducted by religious organizations at locations off school grounds, on written consent of parents of children, since, by such legislation, superintendent of schools is vested with statutory discretion to excuse pupils from

227

Illustration C–2

Continuation of statutory section in West's *Revised Code of Washington Annotated,* with various research aids.

CHAPTER 28A.27—COMPULSORY SCHOOL ATTENDANCE

Rules and regulations accepting national guard high school career training: RCWA 28A.04.133.

28A.27.010 Attendance mandatory—Age—Persons having custody shall cause child to attend public school unless excused—Excused temporary absences

All parents, guardians and the persons in this state having custody of any child eight years of age and under fifteen years of age shall cause such child to attend the public school of the district in which the child resides for the full time when such school may be in session or to attend a private school for the same time unless the school district superintendent of the district in which the child resides shall have excused such child from attendance because the child is physically or mentally unable to attend school, is attending a residential school operated by the department of social and health services, or has been excused upon the request of his or her parents, guardians, or persons in this state having custody of any such child, for purposes agreed upon by the school authorities and the parent, guardian or custodian: *Provided,* That such excused absences shall not be permitted if deemed to cause a serious adverse effect upon the student's educational progress: *Provided further,* That students excused for such temporary absences may be claimed as full time equivalent students to the extent they would otherwise have been so claimed for the purposes of RCW 28A.41.130 and 28A.41.140, as now or hereafter amended, and shall not affect school district compliance with the provisions of RCW 28A.58.754, as now or hereafter amended.

All parents, guardians and other persons in this state having custody of any child fifteen years of age and under eighteen years of age shall cause such child to attend the public school of the district in which the child resides for the full time when such school may be in session or to attend a private school for the same time excepting when the school district superintendent determines that such child is physically or mentally unable to attend school or has already attained a reasonable proficiency in the branches required by law to be taught in the first nine grades of the public schools of this state, or the child has been temporarily excused in accordance with this section, or the child is regularly and lawfully engaged in a useful or remunerative occupation, or the child is attending a residential school operated by the department of social and health services, or the child has already met graduation requirements in accordance with state board of education rules and regulations, or the child has received a certificate of educational competence under rules and regulations established by the state board of education under RCW 28A.04.135.

An approved private and/or parochial school for the purposes of this section shall be one approved under regulations established by the state board of education pursuant to RCW 28A.04.120 as now or hereafter amended.
[Amended by Laws 1st Ex Sess 1971 ch 51 § 1, effective May 5, 1971, ch 215 § 2, effective May 21, 1971; Reenacted Laws 1st Ex Sess 1972 ch 10 § 12, effective February 17, 1972; Amended by Laws 1973 ch 51 § 1; Laws 1st Ex Sess 1979 ch 201 § 4, effective September 1, 1979; Laws 1980 ch 59 § 1.]

Severability—1973 c 51: "If any provision of this 1973 amendatory act, or its application to any person or circumstance is held invalid, the remainder of the act, or the application of the provision to other persons or circumstances is not affected."

[1973 c 51 § 5.] This applies to RCW 28A.27.010, 28A.04.135, 49.12.123 and the repeal of chapters 28A.06 and 28A.28 RCW.

Private and/or parochial schools now private schools: RCWA 28A.04.120(4), 28A.02.201, 28A.02.220 to 28A.02.250.

Work permits for minors required: RCWA 49.12.123.

47 Wn LR 331 (compulsory school attendance as opposed to religious liberty).

Ops Atty Gen 1979 No. 21 (the term "private school" as used in RCWA 28A.27.010 requiring attendance by children between prescribed ages at either the public school of the district in which the child resides or a "private school," still denotes an "approved private school" as defined in the last paragraph of the statute, notwithstanding the amendment contained in § 4, chapter 201, Laws of 1979, 1st Ex.Sess.).

65 ALR3d 1222 (what constitutes a private, parochial, or denominational school within statute making attendance at such school a compliance with compulsory school attendance law).

Wisconsin Compulsory Education Law, punishing parents and guardians who withdraw their children from school before age 16, is unconstitutional as applied to parents of the Amish faith whose children, ages 14 and 15, had completed grammar school and expressed no desire to continue their formal training. Wisconsin v Yoder (1972) 406 US 205, 32 L Ed 2d 15, 92 S Ct 1526.

28A.27.020 School's duties upon juvenile's failure to attend school—Generally

If a juvenile required to attend school under the laws of the state of Washington fails to attend school without valid justification recurrently or for an extended period of time, the juvenile's school, where appropriate, shall:

(1) Inform the juvenile's custodial parent, parents or guardian by a notice in writing in English and, if different, in the primary language of the custodial parent, parents or guardian and by other means reasonably necessary to achieve notice of the fact that the juvenile has failed to attend school without valid justification recurrently or for an extended period of time;

(2) Schedule a conference or conferences with the custodial parent, parents or guardian and juvenile at a time and place reasonably convenient for all persons included for the purpose of analyzing the causes of the juvenile's absences; and

(3) Take steps to eliminate or reduce the juvenile's absences, including, where appropriate, adjusting the juvenile's school program or school or course assignment or assisting the parent or student to obtain supplementary services that might eliminate or ameliorate the cause or causes for the absence from school.

[Added by Laws 1st Ex Sess 1979 ch 201 § 1, effective September 1, 1979.]

CJS Schools and School Districts §§ 471 to 474.

Key Number Digests: Schools and School Districts ⟹161.

28A.27.022 Petition to juvenile court to assume jurisdiction—Applicability of chapter

If action taken by a school pursuant to RCW 28A.27.020 is not successful in substantially reducing a student's absences from school, the attendance officer of the school district through its attorney may petition the juvenile court to assume jurisdiction under this chapter for the purpose of alleging a violation of RCW 28A.27.010. If the court assumes jurisdiction in such an instance, the provisions of this chapter, except where otherwise stated, shall apply.

[Added by Laws 1st Ex Sess 1979 ch 201 § 2, effective September 1, 1979.]

Illustration C–3

Updating of statutory section in pocket part supplement to *Revised Code of Washington Annotated.*

SCHOOLS

496

Illustration C–4

Subject index entry to statutory section in *Revised Code of Washington Annotated.*

Similar annotated codes (some of less versatility and quality, however) exist for every state. *Two* competing editions are available for *federal* statutes, and for those of a few states (e.g. California, Massachusetts, New York, etc.).

In addition to the usual pocket part and pamphlet supplementation, several of the codes are also updated by legislative session law services which publish laws in advance sheets, as they are enacted during the legislative session. These services are described in Section D.2 below.

5. SUMMARY

The four stages described above, i.e. slip law, session law, code, and annotated code, exist in some form for federal statutes and statutes for each of the fifty states. As already indicated, the names of the codes will vary from jurisdiction to jurisdiction, and many of the commercial editions of the annotated codes still have the proprietary names of former editors or publishers (e.g. *McKinney's Laws of New York, Vernon's Texas Codes Annotated,* both actually published by West), which have been retained for their local familiarity and good will. The specific designations for each state are set forth in Appendix B, *Primary Legal Sources for the States,* at the end of this volume.

Because of the pervasive impact of *federal* laws and the variety and sophistication of their forms of publication, they will be described in some detail.

C. FEDERAL STATUTORY MATERIALS

1. FEDERAL LEGISLATIVE PROCESS

The various steps in the enactment of a federal law are outlined and documented below in Chapter 10, *Legislative History.* The process is often long and complicated, beginning formally with the introduction of a bill and ending with passage by both houses of Congress of either a bill or a joint resolution, and its approval by the President (or re-passage over a Presidential veto). The Constitution of the United States outlines the procedure in Article 1, Section 7. Under the Constitution and subsequent judicial interpretations, there are only three forms of federal legislation: acts, joint resolutions, and treaties. Simple and concurrent resolutions cannot result directly in laws.

The distinction between acts and joint resolutions is no longer of great significance. Over ninety percent of federal laws are passed as acts, and joint resolutions are used primarily for fiscal measures. Prior to the 77th Congress (i.e. 1941) acts and joint resolutions were numbered in separate chronological series, but now they are issued in one chronological sequence of "Public Laws," without any distinction other than the preliminary designation: "Act" or "Joint Resolution," and the clause of intent: "Be it enacted" or "Resolved."

Each enactment is designated either as a "public law" or a "private law." Generally private laws are passed for the specific benefit of an individual or small group of individuals, whereas public laws are intended to be of general application.[8] The two categories are numbered, as enacted, in *separate* series. Although *private* laws are issued in a slip law form and appear in the federal session law publication (the *Statutes at Large*), most of the other publications discussed herein contain only public laws.

2. FEDERAL SLIP LAWS

The first official form of publication of a federal law is the *slip law*, a separately paginated pamphlet text of each law, with no internal indexing. Each law is designated by a public law number, *e.g.* P.L. 94–279.[9] The first part of the number represents the number of the Congress which enacted the law (i.e. the 94th Congress) and the second part of the number indicates the chronological sequence of its enactment (i.e. the 279th public law enacted by that Congress).

The form of the printing is almost identical to that which appears in the *Statutes at Large*, and in recent years both the slip law and *Statutes at Large* publication include a brief summary of the legislative history of each law after the text (see Illustration D–2, below). Slip laws are published and sold by the U.S. Government Printing Office, and are available on a subscription basis. However, because of the slow distribution of slip laws, most researchers rely on one of the commercial services described below for the text of a recently enacted federal statute.[10]

As shown in Illustration D–1, the slip law and the *Statutes at Large* printing of the Animal Welfare Act Amendments of 1976, both contain a number of citations which are useful for research beyond the text of the law. These include the following, as shown on the Illustration by the number indicated before each: (1) the bill number of the law before it was enacted; [11] (2) the public law number; (3) the citation of the law in its *codified* form, the *U.S.Code;* (4) the date of approval by the President; (5) the statement of purpose; and (6) the short title of the Act (which is in effect the official version of a popular name).

The slip law is the first authoritative official text of the statute and is rebuttable as evidence of the law only by reference to the en-

8. In this century most private laws concern special relief for individuals under the immigration laws. For more on this distinction, see "Private Bills in Congress," 79 *Harvard L.Rev.* 1684 (1966).

9. Although numbers had been assigned to laws since 1901, the term "Public Law" was first used with those numbers in 1941–42. Chapter numbers, which had been the primary designation in the *Statutes at Large* were discontinued in 1957, although they are still used to mark major divisions in titles of the *U.S.Code.*

10. These include West's *U.S.C.C.A.N.*, a session law service for *USCA* (see Section 6.c, below); the *Advance* Service of *USCS;* and looseleaf services in particular subject fields.

11. The bill number is particularly important for researching the legislative history of the law, as will be described below in Chapter 10, *Legislative History.*

rolled Act. When the *Statutes at Large* are published, they supersede the slip law as authority.

3. U.S. STATUTES AT LARGE

The session law publication for federal laws are the U.S. *Statutes at Large.* Since 1936, at the end of each *session* of Congress, the public and private laws enacted in that session are cumulated and published, along with concurrent resolutions, Presidential proclamations, reorganization plans, as the *Statutes at Large* for that session. In recent years, each session's compilation has comprised one, two or three volumes, with overall indexes by subject and individuals' names at the end of the last volume. The several volumes for each session bear one volume number, by which each session's *Statutes at Large* are cited. The volume numbering began in 1846, when the *Statutes at Large* was inaugurated as a publication of Little, Brown & Co., under Congressional authorization.[12] Beginning with volume 18 (1873–75), the *Statutes at Large* have been published by the U.S. Government Printing Office.

The first eight volumes of the *Statutes at Large* covered legislation retrospectively to 1778 and 1789 as follows:

Vols. 1–5: Public Laws of the 1st to 28th Congresses (1789–1845);

Vol. 6: Private Laws of the 1st to 28th Congresses (1789–1845);

Vol. 7: Treaties with Indian Tribes (1778–1845); and

Vol. 8: Treaties with foreign countries (1778–1845).

Then, volume 9 covered three congresses, volumes 10–12 covered two each, volumes 13 to 49 covered one each, and with volume 50 (1936) the present pattern of one numbered volume for each *session* began. Prior to 1936, in addition to the *Statutes at Large* for each Congress, pamphlet or session laws were also published for each *session.* Through 1950–51 (vol. 64) the full text of all treaties approved in the period of that Congress or session were also included in each volume, but that practice was discontinued when the series, *U.S. Treaties and Other International Agreements,* was begun in 1950.

There were two earlier chronological publications of federal laws before the Little, Brown edition of the *Statutes at Large,* both also issued by private publishers with official authorization, under the title, *Laws of the United States.* The first was the Folwell edition[13] in twelve volumes covering the first thirteen Congresses (1789–1815); the second, the Bioren and Duane edition[14] in ten volumes covering the first twenty eight Congresses (1789–1845).

12. By the Joint Resolution of March 3, 1845 (5 *Stat.* 798).

13. Pursuant to the Act of March 3, 1795 (1 *Stat.* 443).

14. Pursuant to the Act of April 18, 1814 (3 *Stat.* 129).

PUBLIC LAW 94–279—APR. 22, 1976 90 STAT. 417

Public Law 94–279
94th Congress

② ④

An Act

To amend the Act of August 24, 1966, as amended, to increase the protection afforded animals in transit and to assure humane treatment of certain animals, and for other purposes. — Apr. 22, 1976 [S. 1941]

⑤ ①

Be it enacted by the Senate and House of Representatives of the United States of America in Congress assembled, That this Act may be cited as the "Animal Welfare Act Amendments of 1976". — **Animal Welfare Act Amendments of 1976.** ⑥

⑥ SEC. 2. Section 1 of the Act of August 24, 1966 (80 Stat. 350, as amended by the Animal Welfare Act of 1970, 84 Stat. 1560; 7 U.S.C. 2131–2155) is amended to read as follows: — 7 USC 2131 note. 7 USC 2131 note. 7 USC 2131. ③

"SECTION 1. (a) This Act may be cited as the 'Animal Welfare Act'.

"(b) The Congress finds that animals and activities which are regulated under this Act are either in interstate or foreign commerce or substantially affect such commerce or the free flow thereof, and that regulation of animals and activities as provided in this Act is necessary to prevent and eliminate burdens upon such commerce and to effectively regulate such commerce, in order—

"(1) to insure that animals intended for use in research facilities or for exhibition purposes or for use as pets are provided humane care and treatment;

"(2) to assure the humane treatment of animals during transportation in commerce; and

"(3) to protect the owners of animals from the theft of their animals by preventing the sale or use of animals which have been stolen.

The Congress further finds that it is essential to regulate, as provided in this Act, the transportation, purchase, sale, housing, care, handling, and treatment of animals by carriers or by persons or organizations engaged in using them for research or experimental purposes or for exhibition purposes or holding them for sale as pets or for any such purpose or use.".

SEC. 3. Section 2 of such Act is amended— — **Definitions.** 7 USC 2132.

(1) by striking out subsection (c) and (d) thereof and inserting lieu thereof the following:

"(c) The term 'commerce' means trade, traffic, transportation, or other commerce—

"(1) between a place in a State and any place outside of such State, or between points within the same State but through any place outside thereof, or within any territory, possession, or the District of Columbia;

"(2) which affects trade, traffic, transportation, or other commerce described in paragraph (1).

"(d) The term 'State' means a State of the United States, the District of Columbia, the Commonwealth of Puerto Rico, the Virgin Islands, Guam, American Samoa, or any other territory or possession of the United States;".

(2) by striking out the term "affecting commerce" in subsections (e) and (f) and inserting in lieu thereof "in commerce";

(3) by revising paragraph (f) thereof to read as follows:

"(f) The term 'dealer' means any person who, in commerce, for compensation or profit, delivers for transportation, or transports,

Illustration D–1

The first page of the law in the *Statutes at Large,* with format similar to the slip law.

PUBLIC LAW 94-279—APR. 22, 1976 90 STAT. 423

"(4) the term 'State' means any State of the United States, the District of Columbia, the Commonwealth of Puerto Rico, and any territory or possession of the United States;

"(5) the term 'animal' means any live bird, or any live dog or other mammal, except man; and

"(6) the conduct by any person of any activity prohibited by this section shall not render such person subject to the other sections of this Act as a dealer, exhibitor, or otherwise.

"(h) (1) The provisions of this Act shall not supersede or otherwise invalidate any such State, local, or municipal legislation or ordinance relating to animal fighting ventures except in case of a direct and irreconcilable conflict between any requirements thereunder and this Act or any rule, regulation, or standard hereunder.

"(2) Section 3001(a) of title 39, United States Code, is amended by adding immediately after the words 'title 18' a comma and the words 'or section 26 of the Animal Welfare Act'.". *Ante*, p. 421.

SEC. 18. Section 23 of such Act is amended by inserting immediately before the period at the end of the third sentence ": *Provided*, That there is authorized to be appropriated to the Secretary of Agriculture for enforcement by the Department of Agriculture of the provisions of section 26 of this Act an amount not to exceed $100,000 for the transition quarter ending September 30, 1976, and not to exceed $400,000 for each fiscal year thereafter". 7 USC 2153. Appropriation authorization.

SEC. 19. Section 14 of such Act is amended by inserting in the first sentence after the term "standards" the phrase "and other requirements". 7 USC 2144.

④ → Approved April 22, 1976.

LEGISLATIVE HISTORY:

HOUSE REPORTS: No. 94-801 accompanying H.R. 5808 (Comm. on Agriculture) and No. 94-976 (Comm. of Conference).

SENATE REPORTS: No. 94-580 (Comm. on Commerce) and No. 94-727 (Comm. of Conference).

CONGRESSIONAL RECORD:

Vol. 121 (1975): Dec. 18, considered and passed Senate.

Vol. 122 (1976): Feb. 9, considered and passed House, amended, in lieu of H.R. 5808.

Apr. 6, House agreed to conference report.

Apr. 7, Senate agreed to conference report.

Illustration D-2

The last page of the law in the *Statutes at Large,* showing legislature history summary at the end.

Although the actual publication of current volumes of the *Statutes at Large* has been slow, usually occurring two or three years after the end of the session covered, they are the authoritative text of the federal statutes, superseding the slip laws. They are the "positive law" form of statutes, and "legal evidence of laws . . . in all the Courts of the United States . . . "[15] The *United States Code* is only *prima facie* evidence of the laws, except for those of its titles which have been reenacted by Congress as positive law.[16]

Illustrations D–1 and D–2, above, show the form of a law as it appears in the *Statutes at Large.*

4. REVISED STATUTES

Because of the difficulty of research in the numerous volumes of the *Statutes at Large* with their non-cumulating separate indexes, it became apparent by the middle of the 19th century that some form of codification or subject arrangement was needed. After much drafting and re-drafting and great legislative effort (and after a few private efforts at publication of subject arrangements), the only *complete* revision of federal laws was enacted on June 22, 1874, under the title, *Revised Statutes of the United States . . . embracing the statutes . . . general and permanent in their nature, in force on* [December 1, 1873] . . . .[17] It did not contain private or temporary acts, or laws otherwise not conceived to be of general, permanent interest.

That first edition of the *Revised Statutes* is variously and confusingly called the *Revised Statutes of 1873* (for the cut-off date of the laws included therein), or "of 1874" (for the date of its enactment), or "of 1875" (for the date of its publication). See Illustration E below for a reproduction of its title page showing those three points of reference. In any case, that historic publication was more than just a topical arrangement of laws into seventy-four subject titles.[18] It was a reenactment as *positive law* of all the laws included in it, and expressly repealed their original *Statutes at Large* texts. Therefore, for all laws in the *Revised Statutes,* it is *the* authoritative text and legal evidence thereof, up to that time, unless they are part of one of the re-enacted "positive law" titles of the *U.S. Code.*

Because of errors in the first edition and some dissatisfaction with it, a second edition of the *Revised Statutes* was published in 1878 (under the Act of March 2, 1877, 19 *Stat.* 268). The second edition, although more frequently used today than the first, was not a reenactment as *positive law* of the laws contained therein, and thus it does not have the same status as the earlier version. Two supple-

15. 1 *U.S.C.* § 112.

16. 1 *U.S.C.* § 204.

17. Published as 18 *Stat.* Part 1 (1875).

18. Although divided into seventy-four titles, with an overall general index, the section numbering of the Revised Statutes is continuous through the work, as distinguished from its successor, the *United States Code,* which begins each title with a new sequence of section numbering.

REVISED STATUTES

OF

THE UNITED STATES,

PASSED AT THE

FIRST SESSION OF THE FORTY-THIRD CONGRESS,

1873-'74;

EMBRACING THE STATUTES OF THE UNITED STATES, GENERAL AND PERMANENT IN THEIR NATURE, IN FORCE ON THE FIRST DAY OF DECEMBER, ONE THOUSAND EIGHT HUNDRED AND SEVENTY-THREE, AS REVISED AND CONSOLIDATED BY COMMISSIONERS APPOINTED UNDER AN ACT OF CONGRESS;

WITH

AN APPENDIX

CONTAINING

"AN ACT TO CORRECT ERRORS AND SUPPLY OMISSIONS."

EDITED, PRINTED, AND PUBLISHED UNDER THE AUTHORITY OF AN ACT OF CONGRESS, AND UNDER THE DIRECTION OF THE SECRETARY OF STATE.

WASHINGTON:
GOVERNMENT PRINTING OFFICE.
1875.

Illustration E

Cover page of the first edition of the *Revised Statutes.*

ments to the *Revised Statutes* were subsequently issued for the periods 1874 to 1891 and 1892 to 1901, respectively, but these also did not have the status of *positive law.* They were chronological arrangements rather than title-by-title supplements to the *Revised Statutes,* although they did contain lists of *Revised Statutes* sections affected by the subsequent legislation.

Twenty five more years of publication of the *Statutes at Large* then ensued before another effort at an official codification of federal laws was undertaken. The resulting repetition of the former chaos and inconvenience in statutory research was somewhat alleviated by privately published subject arrangements, but the need for a new official code was apparent.

5. U.S.CODE

After much legislative travail, a new codification effort resulted in the *United States Code,* approved on June 30, 1926, and "intended to embrace all the laws of the United States, general and permanent in their character, in force on the 7th day of December, 1925." It was published as 44 *Stat.* Part 1 under the official title: *The Code of the Laws of the United States* . . . , etc., but has since been called the *United States Code.* This *Code* was not a "positive law" reenactment and did not repeal the prior *Statutes at Large.* It was *prima facie* evidence of the law, as noted above, and rebuttable by reference to the *Statutes at Large.* However, Congress subsequently began a process of revising the various titles of the *Code* and reenacting them into *positive law,* one by one, as the revision of each is completed. So far, approximately one third of the titles have been so reenacted, and are now legal evidence; for the rest the *Statutes at Large* remain legal evidence and the Code, *prima facie* evidence. The list of titles so reenacted appears in the *Preface* of each volume of the *Code,* and their reenactment is also indicated on a list of the titles of the *Code* which appears in every volume. That list is shown in Illustration F. The distinction is only rarely a matter of concern, but it is of potential legal effect, since in the process of codification the statutory language is sometimes changed slightly and occasional errors have been made.[19]

The official edition is arranged in fifty subject titles with the section numbering of each title beginning anew. The *Code* is reissued in a new edition every six years, with cumulative bound supplements published for each intervening year. The supplements are slow in being issued, and that form of updating is inadequate and cumbersome. Therefore, the two commercial editions of the Code, *USCA*

19. See, for example, at least two cases in which the distinction was an issue: *Stephan v. United States,* 319 U.S. 423 (1943) and *Royer's Inc. v. United States,* 265 F.2d 615 (3d Cir., 1959).

TITLES OF UNITED STATES CODE

- *1. General Provisions.
- 2. The Congress.
- *3. The President.
- *4. Flag and Seal, Seat of Government, and the States.
- *5. Government Organization and Employees.
- *6. Surety Bonds.
- 7. Agriculture.
- 8. Aliens and Nationality.
- *9. Arbitration.
- *10. Armed Forces.
- 11. Bankruptcy.
- 12. Banks and Banking.
- *13. Census.
- *14. Coast Guard.
- 15. Commerce and Trade.
- 16. Conservation.
- *17. Copyrights.
- *18. Crimes and Criminal Procedure.
- 19. Customs Duties.
- 20. Education.
- 21. Food and Drugs.
- 22. Foreign Relations and Intercourse.
- *23. Highways.
- 24. Hospitals and Asylums.
- 25. Indians.
- 26. Internal Revenue Code.
- 27. Intoxicating Liquors.
- *28. Judiciary and Judicial Procedure.
- 29. Labor.
- 30. Mineral Lands and Mining.
- 31. Money and Finance.
- *32. National Guard.
- 33. Navigation and Navigable Waters.
- †34. [Navy.]
- *35. Patents.
- 36. Patriotic Societies and Observances.
- *37. Pay and Allowances of the Uniformed Services.
- *38. Veterans' Benefits.
- *39. Postal Service.
- 40. Public Buildings, Property, and Works.
- 41. Public Contracts.
- 42. The Public Health and Welfare.
- 43. Public Lands.
- *44. Public Printing and Documents.
- 45. Railroads.
- 46. Shipping.
- 47. Telegraphs, Telephones, and Radiotelegraphs.
- 48. Territories and Insular Possessions.
- 49. Transportation.
- 50. War and National Defense; and Appendix.

→ *This title has been enacted as law.
†This title has been eliminated by the enactment of Title 10.

Page III

Illustration F

List of titles in *U.S.Code*, with notice of the reenactment of some.

(West) and *USCS* (Lawyers Co-op), both of which are annotated, are more frequently used than the official version. The *U.S.Code* includes cross references, historical notes after most sections, an overall general index, and a useful volume of tables which provide parallel references between the various forms of statutory publication, and between earlier revisions and later texts, and also lists of various Presidential documents appearing in the *Code*. A popular name table of federal statutes is also located in the Tables volume, and is shown in Illustration G.

Following each statutory section of the *Code*, there is a parenthetical reference to the source of that section in the *Statutes at Large*, including all amendments. This reference enables one to identify and locate the original text which may be its *positive law* form.

Page 15 ACTS CITED BY POPULAR NAME

Animal Welfare Act
Pub. L. 94-279, Apr. 22, 1976, 90 Stat. 417 (Title 7, §§ 2131, 2132, 2134, 2136, 2139-2146, 2149, 2153-2156; Title 39, § 3001)

Animal Welfare Act of 1970
Pub. L. 91-579, Dec. 24, 1970, 84 Stat. 1560 (Title 7, §§ 2131-2147, 2149, 2150, 2155)

Animal Welfare Act Amendments of 1976
Pub. L. 94-279, Apr. 22, 1976, 90 Stat. 417 (Title 7, §§ 2131, 2132, 2134, 2136, 2139-2146, 2149, 2153-2156; Title 39, § 3001)

Annual and Sick Leave Act of 1951
Oct. 30, 1951, ch. 631, title II, §§ 201-209, 65 Stat. 679 (See Title 5, §§ 6301-6305, 6307, 6309-6311)
July 2, 1953, ch. 178, §§ 1, 3, 4(b), 67 Stat. 136 (See Title 5, §§ 5508, 6301, 6302, 6304, 6305, 6308)
Aug. 18, 1959, Pub. L. 86-168, title II, §§ 202(e), 73 Stat. 389 (See Title 5, §§ 6306, 6308)
Sept. 6, 1960, Pub. L. 86-707, title IV, §§ 401, 402, 74 Stat. 799 (See Title 5, §§ 6301, 6303-6305, 6310)
Aug. 19, 1964, Pub. L. 88-448, title II, § 203, 78 Stat. 487 (See Title 5, § 6303)
Aug. 21, 1964, Pub. L. 88-471, § 6(a)-(d), 78 Stat. 583 (See Title 5, §§ 6301, 6307, 6308)

Anthracite Mine Water Control Act
July 15, 1955, ch. 369, 69 Stat. 352 (Title 30, §§ 571-576)
Oct. 15, 1962, Pub. L. 87-818, 76 Stat. 934 (Title 30, §§ 571, 572, 575)

Anthropological Research Act
Apr. 10, 1928, ch. 335, § 1, 45 Stat. 413 (Title 20, §§ 69, 70)
Aug. 22, 1949, ch. 494, § 1, 63 Stat. 623 (Title 20, § 69)

Anti-Assignment Act
July 29, 1846, ch. 66, 9 Stat. 41 (Title 31, § 203)
Feb. 26, 1853, ch. 81, § 1, 10 Stat. 170 (Title 31, § 203)
May 27, 1908, ch. 206, 35 Stat. 411 (Title 31, § 203)
Oct. 9, 1940, ch. 779, § 1, 54 Stat. 1029 (Title 31, § 203)
May 15, 1951, ch. 75, 65 Stat. 41 (Title 31, § 203)

Anti-Beer Act
See National Prohibition Acts

Anti-Deficiency Act
Feb. 27, 1906, ch. 510, § 3, 34 Stat. 49 (Title 31, § 665)
Sept. 6, 1950, ch. 896, ch. XII, § 1211, 64 Stat. 765 (Title 31, § 665)
July 12, 1974, Pub. L. 93-344, title X, § 1002, 88 Stat. 332 (Title 31, § 665)

Anti-Dumping Act, 1921
May 27, 1921, ch. 14, title II, 42 Stat. 11 (Title 19, §§ 160-171)
Sept. 1, 1954, ch. 1213, title III, §§ 301, 302, 68 Stat. 1138 (Title 19, §§ 160, 161)
Aug. 14, 1958, Pub. L. 85-630, 72 Stat. 583 (Title 19, §§ 160, 161, 164, 165, 168, 169, 170a, 171)
June 2, 1970, Pub. L. 91-271, title III, §§ 311-314, 84 Stat. 292, 293 (Title 19, §§ 161, 167-169)
Jan. 3, 1975, Pub. L. 93-618, title III, § 321(a)-(e), 88 Stat. 2043-2048 (Title 19, §§ 160, 162, 163, 164, 170a)

Anti-Gag Law
Aug. 24, 1912, ch. 389, § 6, 37 Stat. 555

Anti-Gambling Act (District of Columbia)
May 16, 1908, ch. 172, 35 Stat. 163

Anti-Heroin Act
June 7, 1924, ch. 352, 43 Stat. 657 (Title 21, § 173)

Anti-Immunity Act (Trusts and Interstate Commerce)
June 30, 1906, ch. 3920, 34 Stat. 798 (Title 49, § 48)

Anti-Injunction Law
Mar. 23, 1932, ch. 90, 47 Stat. 70 (Title 29, §§ 101-115)

Anti-Kickback Acts
June 13, 1934, ch. 482, §§ 1, 2, 48 Stat. 948 (Title 40, §§ 276b, 276c)
Mar. 8, 1946, ch. 80, 60 Stat. 37 (Title 41, §§ 51-54)
Sept. 2, 1960, Pub. L. 86-695, 74 Stat. 740 (Title 41, §§ 51-54)

Anti-Lobbying Act
See, also, Federal Regulation of Lobbying Act
July 11, 1919, ch. 6, § 6, 41 Stat. 68 (See Title 18, § 1913)

Anti-Lottery Act
Sept. 19, 1890, ch. 908, 26 Stat. 465

Anti-Merger Act
Dec. 29, 1950, ch. 1184, 64 Stat. 1125 (Title 15, §§ 18, 21)

Anti-Moiety Act (Informers)
June 22, 1874, ch. 391, 18 Stat. 186 (Title 19, §§ 494, 535, 537)

Anti-Narcotic Act
See Narcotics Acts

Anti-Pass Acts
June 29, 1906, ch. 3591, 34 Stat. 584 (Title 49, § 1)
Apr. 13, 1908, ch. 143, 35 Stat. 60 (Title 49, § 1)
June 18, 1910, ch. 309, 36 Stat. 546 (Title 49, § 1)

Anti-Peonage Act
Mar. 2, 1867, ch. 187, 14 Stat. 546 (Title 42, § 1994. See, also, Title 18, § 1581)

Anti-Polygamy Acts
July 1, 1862, ch. 126, 12 Stat. 501
Mar. 22, 1882, ch. 47, 22 Stat. 30
Mar. 3, 1887, ch. 397, 24 Stat. 635

Anti-Racketeering Act
June 18, 1934, ch. 569, 48 Stat. 979 (See Title 18, § 1951)

Illustration G

Popular name table in *U.S.Code,* official edition.

Illustrations H–1–3, which follow, show pages from the 1976 edition of the *U.S.Code* containing the Animal Welfare Act of 1970 and the 1976 Amendments, shown above in Illustration D–1 and D–2 in their *Statutes at Large* form.

It should be noted that, although statutory provisions are often affected by judicial decisions, there is no indication or reflection in the *U.S.Code* of such interpretations, or even of the fact that a statute may have been declared unconstitutional. Sections of the *Code* are changed only by subsequent legislation, and an unconstitutional provision will remain in place in the *Code* without warning of its status, until it is actually repealed or amended. It is therefore necessary to use either the annotated editions of the *Code* or Shepard's to ascertain what later judicial treatment may have occurred. Most researchers use both of those sources routinely.

6. UNOFFICIAL PUBLICATIONS OF THE U.S.CODE

a. U.S.Code Annotated

Beginning in 1927, the West Publishing Company began publication of its own annotated edition of the *U.S.Code,* entitled *United States Code Annotated,* and known generally as *U.S.C.A.* This edition employs the same title and section numbering, arrangement and designations as in the official version. *USCA* also includes all of the standard research aids of the official version (tables, historical notes, cross references, index, etc.) but here they are expanded, enriched and augmented. The two most significant additional features are the annotations and the varied forms of supplementation.

Following each section of the *Code* in *U.S.C.A.,* West provides abstracts or squibs of each judicial decision published in one of the West reporters, which has applied, interpreted or construed that section. These abstracts include the name of the case and citations to the major reporters. They are the same abstracts that appear in West reporter headnotes and digests. Preceding these annotations, there is usually a simple subject index to the annotations, which assists in locating those on particular aspects or parts of the statutory section.

In addition to the case annotations, West also includes a variety of other research aids and references for each section, as shown in Illustrations I–1 to I–5 below, containing the same Animal Welfare Act which appeared in Illustrations D and H. Both the main volume (Illustrations I–1, 2 and 3) and the pocket part supplement (I–4 and 5) are shown here. The West research aids are indicated on the several parts of Illustration I by the following numbers: (1) source of section, by public law number, date, and *Statutes at Large* citation; (2) historical notes; (3) reference to legislative history in *USCCAN;* (4) reference to a West digest topic and key number; (5) reference to the West encyclopedia, *C.J.S.;* (6) reference to the *Code of Federal Regulations;* and (7) an annotation.

§ 2119. Programs of Commodity Credit Corporation

The Commodity Credit Corporation, in furtherance of its powers and duties under section 714c(e) and (f) of title 15, shall, through the Cotton Board established under this chapter, and upon approval of the Secretary, enter into agreements with the contracting organization specified pursuant to section 2106(g) of this title for the conduct, in domestic and foreign markets, of market development, research or sales promotion programs and programs to aid in the development of new and additional markets, marketing facilities and uses for cotton and cotton products, including programs to facilitate the utilization and commercial application of research findings. Each year the amount available for such agreements shall be 10 million dollars. The Secretary is authorized to deduct from funds available for payments to producers under section 1444 of this title on each of the 1972 through 1977 crops of upland cotton such additional sums for use as specified above (not exceeding $10,000,000 for each such crop) as he determines desirable; and the final rate of payment provided in section 1444 of this title if higher than the rate of the preliminary payment provided in such section shall be reduced to the extent necessary to defray such costs. No funds made available under this section shall be used for the purpose of influencing legislative action or general farm policy with respect to cotton.

(Pub. L. 91-524, title VI, § 610, Nov. 30, 1970, 84 Stat. 1378; Pub. L. 93-86, § 1(23), Aug. 10, 1973, 87 Stat. 235.)

Repeals

Section repealed effective Oct. 1, 1977, by Pub. L. 94-366, § 1, July 14, 1976, 90 Stat. 991.

CODIFICATION

Section was enacted as part of the Agriculture Act of 1970, and not as part of the Cotton Research and Promotion Act which comprises this chapter.

AMENDMENTS

1973—Pub. L. 93-86 substituted provisions authorizing that the amount available each year for agreements be 10 million dollars for provisions authorizing that the amount available each year for agreements be that portion of the funds (not exceeding $10,000,000) authorized to be made available to cooperators under the cotton program for such year but which is not paid to producers because of a statutory limitation on the amounts payable to any producer, and extended the authorization for deductions by the Secretary from 1973 to 1977.

CHAPTER 54—TRANSPORTATION, SALE, AND HANDLING OF CERTAIN ANIMALS

Illustration H-1

Title 7, *U.S.Code*, Chapter 54 (1976 edition).

§ 2131. Congressional statement of policy

The Congress finds that animals and activities which are regulated under this chapter are either in interstate or foreign commerce or substantially affect such commerce or the free flow thereof, and that regulation of animals and activities as provided in this chapter is necessary to prevent and eliminate burdens upon such commerce and to effectively regulate such commerce, in order—

(1) to insure that animals intended for use in research facilities or for exhibition purposes or for use as pets are provided humane care and treatment;

(2) to assure the humane treatment of animals during transportation in commerce; and

(3) to protect the owners of animals from the theft of their animals by preventing the sale or use of animals which have been stolen.

The Congress further finds that it is essential to regulate, as provided in this chapter, the transportation, purchase, sale, housing, care, handling, and treatment of animals by carriers or by persons or organizations engaged in using them for research or experimental purposes or for exhibition purposes or holding them for sale as pets or for any such purpose or use.

(Pub. L. 89-544, § 1(b), formerly § 1, Aug. 24, 1966, 80 Stat. 350; Pub. L. 91-579, § 2, Dec. 24, 1970, 84 Stat. 1560; renumbered and amended Pub. L. 94-279, § 2, Apr. 22, 1976, 90 Stat. 417.)

AMENDMENTS

1976—Pub. L. 94-279 restated and expanded the objectives of this chapter to include regulation of animals and activities in, or substantially affecting, interstate or foreign commerce in order to prevent and eliminate burdens on such commerce and to assure the humane treatment of animals during transportation.

1970—Pub. L. 91-579 restated the objectives to include all animals as defined instead of only cats and dogs and expanded the coverage to regulate animals intended for use for exhibition purposes or for use as pets.

EFFECTIVE DATE OF 1970 AMENDMENT

Section 23 of Pub. L. 91-579 provided that: "The amendments made by this Act [enacting section 2155 of this title, amending this section and sections 2132, 2133, 2134, 2135, 2136, 2137, 2138, 2139, 2140, 2141, 2142, 2143, 2144, 2145, 2146, 2147, 2149, and 2150 of this title, repealing section 2148 of this title, and enacting provisions set out as notes under this section] shall take effect one year after the date of enactment of this Act [Dec. 24, 1970], except for the amendments to sections 16, 17, 19, and 20 of the Act of August 24, 1966 [sections 2146, 2147, 2149, and 2150 of this title], which shall become effective thirty days after the date of enactment of this Act [Dec. 24, 1970]".

SHORT TITLE OF 1976 AMENDMENT

Section 1 of Pub. L. 94-279 provided: "That this Act [enacting section 2156 of this title, amending this section and sections 2132, 2134, 2136, 2139 to 2146, 2149, 2153 to 2155 of this title, and section 3001 of Title 39, repealing section 2150 of this title, and enacting provisions set out as notes under this section] may be cited as the 'Animal Welfare Act Amendments of 1976'."

SHORT TITLE OF 1970 AMENDMENT

Section 1 of Pub. L. 91-579 provided: "That this Act [enacting section 2155 of this title, amending this section and sections 2132, 2133, 2134, 2135, 2136, 2137, 2138, 2139, 2140, 2141, 2142, 2143, 2144, 2145, 2146, 2147, 2149, and 2150 of this title, repealing section 2148 of this title, and enacting provisions set out as notes under this section] may be cited as the 'Animal Welfare Act of 1970'."

SHORT TITLE

Section 1(a) of Pub. L. 89-544, as added by section 2 of Pub. L. 94-279, provided: "That this Act [enacting this chapter] may be cited as the 'Animal Welfare Act'."

§ 2132. Definitions

When used in this chapter—

(a) The term "person" includes any individual, partnership, firm, joint stock company, corporation, association, trust, estate, or other legal entity;

(b) The term "Secretary" means the Secretary of Agriculture of the United States or his representative who shall be an employee of the United States Department of Agriculture;

(c) The term "commerce" means trade, traffic, transportation, or other commerce—

(1) between a place in a State and any place outside of such State, or between points within the same State but through any place outside thereof, or within any territory, possession, or the District of Columbia;

(2) which affects trade, traffic, transportation, or other commerce described in paragraph (1).

(d) The term "State" means a State of the United States, the District of Columbia, the Commonwealth of Puerto Rico, the Virgin Islands, Guam, American Samoa, or any other territory or possession of the United States;

(e) The term "research facility" means any school (except an elementary or secondary school), institution, or organization, or person that uses or intends to use live animals in research, tests, or experiments, and that (1) purchases or transports live animals in commerce, or (2) receives funds under a grant, award, loan, or contract from a department, agency, or instrumentality of the United States for the purpose of carrying out research, tests, or experiments: *Provided*, That the Secretary may exempt, by regulation, any such school, institution, organization, or person that does not use or intend to use live dogs or cats, except those schools, institutions, organizations, or persons, which use substantial numbers (as determined by the Secretary) of live animals the principal function of which schools, institutions, organizations, or persons, is biomedical research or testing, when in the judgment of the Secretary,

Illustration H–2

7 *U.S.C.* §§ 2131 & 2132.

any such exemption does not vitiate the purpose of this chapter;

(f) The term "dealer" means any person who, in commerce, for compensation or profit, delivers for transportation, or transports, except as a carrier, buys, or sells, or negotiates the purchase or sale of, (1) any dog or other animal whether alive or dead for research, teaching, exhibition, or use as a pet, or (2) any dog for hunting, security, or breeding purposes, except that this term does not include—

(i) a retail pet store except such store which sells any animals to a research facility, an exhibitor, or a dealer; or

(ii) any person who does not sell, or negotiate the purchase or sale of any wild animal, dog, or cat, and who derives no more than $500 gross income from the sale of other animals during any calendar year;

(g) The term "animal" means any live or dead dog, cat, monkey (nonhuman primate mammal), guinea pig, hamster, rabbit, or such other warmblooded animal, as the Secretary may determine is being used, or is intended for use, for research, testing, experimentation, or exhibition purposes, or as a pet; but such term excludes horses not used for research purposes and other farm animals, such as, but not limited to livestock or poultry, used or intended for use as food or fiber, or livestock or poultry used or intended for use for improving animal nutrition, breeding, management, or production efficiency, or for improving the quality of food or fiber. With respect to a dog, the term means all dogs including those used for hunting, security, or breeding purposes;

(h) The term "exhibitor" means any person (public or private) exhibiting any animals, which were purchased in commerce or the intended distribution of which affects commerce, or will affect commerce, to the public for compensation, as determined by the Secretary, and such term includes carnivals, circuses, and zoos exhibiting such animals whether operated for profit or not; but such term excludes retail pet stores, organizations sponsoring and all persons participating in State and country fairs, livestock shows, rodeos, purebred dog and cat shows, and any other fairs or exhibitions intended to advance agricultural arts and sciences, as may be determined by the Secretary;

(i) The term "intermediate handler" means any person including a department, agency, or instrumentality of the United States or of any State or local government (other than a dealer, research facility, exhibitor, any person excluded from the definition of a dealer, research facility, or exhibitor, an operator of an auction sale, or a carrier) who is engaged in any business in which he receives custody of animals in connection with their transportation in commerce; and

(j) The term "carrier" means the operator of any airline, railroad, motor carrier, shipping line, or other enterprise, which is engaged in the business of transporting any animals for hire.

(Pub. L. 89-544, § 2, Aug. 24, 1966, 80 Stat. 350; Pub. L. 91-579, § 3, Dec. 24, 1970, 84 Stat. 1560; Pub. L. 94-279, §§ 3, 4, Apr. 22, 1976, 90 Stat. 417, 418.)

AMENDMENTS

1976—Subsec. (c). Pub. L. 94-279, § 3(1), made changes in phraseology, restructured subsection and expanded the definition of the term "commerce" by making it applicable to any activity affecting interstate commerce.

Subsec. (d). Pub. L. 94-279, § 3(1), substituted definition of "State" for definition of "affecting commerce".

Subsec. (e). Pub. L. 94-279, § 3(2), substituted "in commerce" for "affecting commerce".

Subsec. (f). Pub. L. 94-279, § 3(2), (3), made changes in phraseology, restructured subsection and expanded the definition of the term "dealer" to include persons who negotiate the purchase or sale of protected animals.

Subsec. (g). Pub. L. 94-279, § 3(4), expanded the definition of the term "animal" to include dogs used for hunting, security, or breeding purposes.

Subsecs. (i), (j). Pub. L. 94-279, § 4, added subsecs. (i) and (j).

1970—Subsec. (b). Pub. L. 91-579, § 3(1), inserted "of the United States or his representative who shall be an employee of the United States Department of Agriculture" following "Secretary of Agriculture".

Subsec. (c). Pub. L. 91-579, § 3(2), substituted "trade, traffic, commerce, transportation among the several States, or between any State" for "commerce between any State".

Subsec. (d). Pub. L. 91-579, § 3(3), substituted a definition of the term "affecting commerce" for a definition of the term "dog".

Subsec. (e). Pub. L. 91-579, § 3(3), struck out definition of the term "cat" and substituted for it a definition of the term "research facility" formerly set out in subsec. (f), and, in such definition as transferred from former subsec. (f), extended the term's meaning to include those using "animals" rather than only dogs and cats and allowed exemptions of schools, organizations, institutions, or persons which do not use live dogs or cats, with such exemption to be inapplicable in the case of schools, organizations, institutions, and persons in biomedical research using a substantial number of live animals.

Subsec. (f). Pub. L. 91-579, § 3(3), substituted definition of the term "dealer" formerly contained in subsec. (g) for definition of term "research facility" and in such definition of term "dealer" as thus transferred added provisions extending meaning to include live or dead animals rather than only dogs and cats, adding teaching and exhibition purposes or uses as pets, and exempting retail pet stores unless such stores sell animals to a research facility, an exhibitor, or a dealer. Definition of "research facility" transferred to subsec. (e) and amended.

Subsec. (g). Pub. L. 91-579, § 3(3), substituted definition of the term "animal" formerly contained in subsec. (h) for definition of the term "dealer" and in such definition of the term "animal" as thus transferred added the stipulation "live or dead" to the species already covered, and added provisions to include such warm-blooded animals as may be determined by the Secretary but to exclude specific animals used for research, food and fiber, and the improvement of animal breeding, nutrition, management, or production efficiency. Definition of term "dealer" transferred to subsec. (f) and amended.

Subsec. (h). Pub. L. 91-579, § 3(3), substituted definition of the term "exhibitor" for definition of the term "animal". Definition of term "animal" transferred to subsec. (g) and amended.

EFFECTIVE DATE OF 1970 AMENDMENT

Amendment by Pub. L. 91-579 effective one year after Dec. 24, 1970, see section 23 of Pub. L. 91-579, set out as a note under section 2131 of this title.

§ 2133. Licensing of dealers and exhibitors

The Secretary shall issue licenses to dealers and exhibitors upon application therefor in such form and manner as he may prescribe and

Illustration H–3

7 *U.S.C.* § 2132 (cont'd.).

CHAPTER 54.—TRANSPORTATION, SALE, AND HANDLING OF CERTAIN ANIMALS

120

Illustration I–1

Beginning of Chapter in main part of *U.S.C.A.* volume.

Ch. 54 TRANSPORTATION AND SALE 7 § 2132

§ 2131. Congressional statement of policy

In order to protect the owners of animals, from the theft of their animals, to prevent the sale or use of animals which have been stolen, and to insure that certain animals intended for use in research facilities or for exhibition purposes or for use as pets are provided humane care and treatment, it is essential to regulate the transportation, purchase, sale, housing, care, handling, and treatment of such animals by persons or organizations engaged in using them for research or experimental purposes or for exhibition purposes or holding them for sale as pets or in transporting, buying, or selling them for any such purpose or use.

① → Pub.L. 89–544, § 1, Aug. 24, 1966, 80 Stat. 350; Pub.L. 91–579, § 2, Dec. 24, 1970, 84 Stat. 1560.

Historical Note

② → **1970 Amendment.** Pub.L. 91–579 restated the objectives to include all animals as defined instead of only cats and dogs and expanded the coverage to regulate animals intended for use for exhibition purposes or for use as pets.

Effective Date of 1970 Amendment. Section 23 of Pub.L. 91–579 provided that: "The amendments made by this Act [enacting section 2155 of this title, amending this section and sections 2132, 2133, 2134, 2135, 2136, 2137, 2138, 2139, 2140, 2141, 2142, 2143, 2144, 2145, 2146, 2147, 2149, and 2150 of this title, repealing section 2148 of this title, and enacting provisions set out as notes under this section] shall take effect one year after the date of enactment of this Act [Dec. 24, 1970], except for the amendments to sections, 16, 17, 19, and 20 of the Act of August 24, 1966 [sections 2146, 2147, 2149, and 2150 of this title], which shall become effective thirty days after the date of enactment of this Act [Dec. 24, 1970]."

Short Title of 1970 Amendment. Section 1 of Pub.L. 91–579 provided: "That this Act [enacting section 2155 of this title, amending this section and sections 2132, 2133, 2134, 2135, 2136, 2137, 2138, 2139, 2140, 2141, 2142, 2143, 2144, 2145, 2146, 2147, 2149, and 2150 of this title, repealing section 2148 of this title, and enacting provisions set out as notes under this section] may be cited as the 'Animal Welfare Act of 1970'."

Short Title. This chapter is popularly known as the "Federal Laboratory Animal Welfare Act."

Legislative History. For legislative history and purpose of Pub.L. 89–544, see ← ③ 1966 U.S.Code Cong. and Adm.News, p. 2635. See, also, Pub.L. 91–579, 1970 U.S. Code Cong. and Adm.News, p. 5103.

Library References

④ → Animals ⚷40 et seq.

C.J.S. Animals § 67 et seq. ← ⑤

§ 2132. Definitions

When used in this chapter—

(a) The term "person" includes any individual, partnership, firm, joint stock company, corporation, association, trust, estate, or other legal entity;

(b) The term "Secretary" means the Secretary of Agriculture of the United States or his representative who shall be an employee of the United States Department of Agriculture;

(c) The term "commerce" means trade, traffic, commerce, transportation among the several States, or between any State, territory,

121

Illustration I–2

Text of statutory section in main part of *U.S.C.A.* volume.

Ch. 54 **TRANSPORTATION AND SALE** **7 § 2132**

intended distribution of which affects commerce, or will affect commerce, to the public for compensation, as determined by the Secretary, and such term includes carnivals, circuses, and zoos exhibiting such animals whether operated for profit or not; but such term excludes retail pet stores, organizations sponsoring and all persons participating in State and country fairs, livestock shows, rodeos, purebred dog and cat shows, and any other fairs or exhibitions intended to advance agricultural arts and sciences, as may be determined by the Secretary.

① → [Pub.L. 89–544, § 2, Aug. 24, 1966, 80 Stat. 350; Pub.L. 91–579, § 3, Dec. 24, 1970, 84 Stat. 1560.

Historical Note ← ②

1970 Amendment. Subsec. (b). Pub.L. 91–579, § 3(1), inserted "of the United States or his representative who shall be an employee of the United States Department of Agriculture" following "Secretary of Agriculture."

Subsec. (c). Pub.L. 91–579, § 3(2), substituted "trade, traffic, commerce, transportation among the several States, or between any State" for "commerce between any State."

Subsec. (d). Pub.L. 91–579, § 3(3), substituted a definition of the term "affecting commerce" for a definition of the term "dog."

Subsec. (e). Pub.L. 91–579, § 3(3), struck out definition of the term "cat" and substituted for it a definition of the term "research facility" formerly set out in subsec. (f), and, in such definition as transferred from former subsec. (f), extended the term's meaning to include those using "animals" rather than only dogs and cats and allowed exemptions of schools, organizations, institutions, or persons which do not use live dogs or cats, with such exemption to be inapplicable in the case of schools, organizations, institutions, and persons in biomedical research using a substantial number of live animals.

Subsec. (f). Pub.L. 91–579, § 3(3), substituted definition of the term "dealer" formerly contained in subsec. (g) for definition of term "research facility" and in such definition of term "dealer" as thus transferred added provisions extending meaning to include live or dead animals rather than only dogs and cats, adding teaching and exhibition purposes or uses as pets, and exempting retail pet stores unless such stores sell animals to a research facility, an exhibitor, or a dealer. Definition of "research facility" transferred to subsec. (e) and amended.

Subsec. (g). Pub.L. 91–579, § 3(3), substituted definition of the term "animal" formerly contained in subsec. (h) for definition of the term "dealer" and in such definition of the term "animal" as thus transferred added the stipulation "live or dead" to the species already covered, and added provisions to include such warm-blooded animals as may be determined by the Secretary but to exclude specific animals used for research, food and fiber, and the improvement of animal breeding, nutrition, management, or production efficiency. Definition of term "dealer" transferred to subsec. (f) and amended.

Subsec. (h). Pub.L. 91–579, § 3(3), substituted definition of the term "exhibitor" for definition of the term "animal." Definition of term "animal" transferred to subsec. (g) and amended.

Effective Date of 1970 Amendment. Amendment by Pub.L. 91–579 effective one year after Dec. 24, 1970, see section 23 of Pub.L. 91–579, set out as a note under section 2131 of this title.

Legislative History. For legislative history and purpose of Pub.L. 89–544, see 1966 U.S.Code Cong. and Adm.News, p. 2635. See, also, Pub.L. 91–579, 1970 U.S. Code Cong. and Adm.News, p. 5103. ← ③

Library References

④ → Animals ⚷40 et seq.

C.J.S. Animals § 67 et seq. ← ⑤

Code of Federal Regulations

⑥ → Definitions, see 9 CFR 1.1.

123

Illustration I–3

Continuation of statutory section in main part of *U.S.C.A.* volume.

7 § 2106 **AGRICULTURE**

pursuant to section 2107 of this title and for administrative costs incurred by him for supervisory work up to five employee years after an order or an amendment to an order has been issued and made effective, added provisions authorizing assessment of a bale of cotton more than once if called for by a provision in this subsection, and added provisions authorizing the Secretary to amend the rate order to supplement the rate in each marketing year by an additional per bale amount not to exceed 1 per centum of the value of the cotton as determined by the Cotton Board and the Secretary.

Legislative History. For legislative history and purpose of Pub.L. 94-366, see 1976 U.S.Code Cong. and Adm.News, p. 1731.

§ 2119. Repealed. Pub.L. 94-366, § 1, July 14, 1976, 90 Stat. 991

Section, Pub.L. 91-524, Title VI, § 610, Nov. 30, 1970, 84 Stat. 1378; Pub.L. 93-86, § 1(23), Aug. 10, 1973, 87 Stat. 235, related to cotton development programs of the Commodity Credit Corporation, and funding for such programs.

Effective Date of Repeal. Section 1 of Pub.L. 94-366 provided in part that this section is repealed effective Oct. 1, 1977.

CHAPTER 54—TRANSPORTATION, SALE, AND HANDLING OF CERTAIN ANIMALS

§ 2131. Congressional statement of policy

The Congress finds that animals and activities which are regulated under this chapter are either in interstate or foreign commerce or substantially affect such commerce or the free flow thereof, and that regulation of animals and activities as provided in this chapter is necessary to prevent and eliminate burdens upon such commerce and to effectively regulate such commerce, in order—

(1) to insure that animals intended for use in research facilities or for exhibition purposes or for use as pets are provided humane care and treatment;

(2) to assure the humane treatment of animals during transportation in commerce; and

(3) to protect the owners of animals from the theft of their animals by preventing the sale or use of animals which have been stolen.

The Congress further finds that it is essential to regulate, as provided in this chapter, the transportation, purchase, sale, housing, care, handling, and treatment of animals by carriers or by persons or organizations engaged in using them for research or experimental purposes or for exhibition purposes or holding them for sale as pets or for any such purpose or use.

① → Pub.L. 89-544, § 1(b), formerly § 1, Aug. 24, 1966, 80 Stat. 350, amended Pub.L. 91-579, § 2, Dec. 24, 1970, 84 Stat. 1560; renumbered and amended Pub.L. 94-279, § 2, Apr. 22, 1976, 90 Stat. 417.

1976 Amendment. Pub.L. 94-279 restated and expanded the objectives of this chapter to include regulation of animals and activities in, or substantially affecting, interstate or foreign commerce in order to prevent and eliminate burdens on such commerce and to assure the humane treatment of animals during transportation. ← ②

Short Title of 1976 Amendment. Section 1 of Pub.L. 94-279 provided: "That this Act [enacting section 2156 of this title, amending this section and sections 2132, 2134, 2136, 2139 to 2146, 2149, 2153 to 2155 of this title, and section 3001 of Title 39, repealing section 2150 of this title, and enacting provisions set out as notes under this section] may be cited as the 'Animal Welfare Act Amendments of 1976'."

Short Title. Section 1(a) of Pub.L. 89-544, as added by section 2 of Pub.L. 94-279, provided: "That this Act [enacting this chapter] may be cited as the 'Animal Welfare Act'."

Legislative History. For legislative history and purpose of Pub.L. 94-279, see 1976 U.S.Code Cong. and Adm.News, p. 758. ← ③

1. Scope of chapter

Protection of this chapter extends to all warm-blooded animals, including dol- ← ⑦

110

Illustration I-4

Updating of statutory section and insertion of annotation in *U.S.C.A.* pocket part.

⑦ phins, and regulations manifested national policy to protect well-being of laboratory animals such as dolphins taken from laboratory by defendant. State v. Le-Vasseur, Hawaii 1980, 613 P.2d 1328.

§ 2132. Definitions

When used in this chapter—

[*See main volume for text of (a) and (b)*]

(c) The term "commerce" means trade, traffic, transportation, or other commerce—

(1) between a place in a State and any place outside of such State, or between points within the same State but through any place outside thereof, or within any territory, possession, or the District of Columbia;

(2) which affects trade, traffic, transportation, or other commerce described in paragraph (1);

(d) The term "State" means a State of the United States, the District of Columbia, the Commonwealth of Puerto Rico, the Virgin Islands, Guam, American Samoa, or any other territory or possession of the United States;

(e) The term "research facility" means any school (except an elementary or secondary school), institution, organization, or person that uses or intends to use live animals in research, tests, or experiments, and that (1) purchases or transports live animals in commerce, or (2) receives funds under a grant, award, loan, or contract from a department, agency, or instrumentality of the United States for the purpose of carrying out research, tests, or experiments: *Provided*, That the Secretary may exempt, by regulation, any such school, institution, organization, or person that does not use or intend to use live dogs or cats, except those schools, institutions, organizations, or persons, which use substantial numbers (as determined by the Secretary) of live animals the principal function of which schools, institutions, organizations, or persons, is biomedical research or testing, when in the judgment of the Secretary, any such exemption does not vitiate the purpose of this chapter;

(f) The term "dealer" means any person who, in commerce, for compensation or profit, delivers for transportation, or transports, except as a carrier, buys, or sells, or negotiates the purchase or sale of, (1) any dog or other animal whether alive or dead for research, teaching, exhibition, or use as a pet, or (2) any dog for hunting, security, or breeding purposes, except that this term does not include—

(i) a retail pet store except such store which sells any animals to a research facility, an exhibitor, or a dealer; or

(ii) any person who does not sell, or negotiate the purchase or sale of any wild animal, dog, or cat, and who derives no more than $500 gross income from the sale of other animals during any calendar year;

(g) The term "animal" means any live or dead dog, cat, monkey (nonhuman primate mammal), guinea pig, hamster, rabbit, or such other warm-blooded animal, as the Secretary may determine is being used, or is intended for use, for research, testing, experimentation, or exhibition purposes, or as a pet; but such term excludes horses not used for research purposes and other farm animals, such as, but not limited to livestock or poultry, used or intended for use as food or fiber, or livestock or poultry used or intended for use for improving animal nutrition, breeding, management, or production efficiency, or for improving the quality of food or fiber. With respect to a dog, the term means all dogs including those used for hunting, security, or breeding purposes;

(h) The term "exhibitor" means any person (public or private) exhibiting any animals, which were purchased in commerce or the intended distribution of which affects commerce, or will affect commerce, to the public for compensation, as determined by the Secretary, and

111

Illustration I–5

Updating of statutory section and insertion of annotation in *U.S.C.A.* pocket part.

Access to the *U.S.C.A.* is provided by a somewhat more detailed general index to the whole set than that provided in the official edition. The *U.S.C.A.* index now consists of eight volumes, with a popular name table at the end of the last volume. Two volumes of tables, similar to those in the *U.S.Code,* are also included in the set.

Updating of the *U.S.C.A.* is provided in several different ways, and is much more current and effective than that in the official edition. Annual pocket parts inserted in the back of each volume reflect changes in the statutory text, additional annotations to court decisions, and later notes and references to other sources. Quarterly pamphlet supplements provide the same coverage for the whole set between the annual pocket parts. The advance pamphlets of the *U.S. Code Congressional and Administrative News* provide the text of new statutes during each Congressional term on a monthly basis, but do not contain updating annotations to the court decisions. The *U.S. C.C.A.N.* is described more fully in section 6.c below.

b. U.S.Code Service

The other unofficial, commercial edition of the *U.S.Code* is the *U.S.Code Service,* published by Lawyers Co-op/Bancroft-Whitney, and known generally as *U.S.C.S.* It was preceded by a similar compilation, *Federal Code Annotated,*[20] which contained some of the same features as its much improved successor. *U.S.C.S.* retains the title and section numbering of the *U.S.Code,* and it includes many of the research aids found in *U.S.C.A.* (e.g. annual pocket part supplementation; session law updating by monthly pamphlets called *U.S.C.S. Advance Service;* quarterly supplements called "Cumulative Later Case and Statutory Service", covering cases and statutes between pocket parts; annotations to court decisions under each statutory section; cross references to other publications of its own publishers; an over all index to the whole set; tables volumes; procedural and court rules; and a popular name table of federal acts).

The major differences in *U.S.C.S.,* when contrasted with its West competitor,[21] are the following features:

1. *U.S.C.S.* includes fewer annotations than *U.S.C.A.* to most statutory sections, but includes some cases not found in *U.S. C.A.* and provides somewhat longer abstracts of cases deemed particularly relevant or important.
2. *U.S.C.S.* preserves more closely the context and language of the original *Statutes at Large* text, which some view as a preferable approach, and others as a disadvantage because it thus deviates from the official *U.S.Code* text.

20. Bobbs-Merrill, 1937–1972, then acquired by Lawyers Co-op and Bancroft-Whitney, and discontinued shortly thereafter.

21. See J. Benioff, "A Comparison of Annotated U.S.Codes," 2 *Legal Reference Services Q.* 37 (1982), for a fuller study of their respective annotation coverage.

3. *U.S.C.S.* has provided useful references to relevant provisions in the *Code of Federal Regulations* and to administrative agency decisions. West has recently begun adding them to *U.S.C.A.*
4. *U.S.C.S.* includes cross references to a variety of secondary sources and formbooks in the Lawyers Co-op Total Client-Service Library, similar to, but more extensive than, West's cross references in *U.S.C.A.* to *its* other publications.

Illustrations J–1 to J–3 show some of those features of *U.S.C.S.*, in its treatment of the Animal Welfare Act, illustrated above in the other statutory publications.

The competition between these two annotated codes has greatly improved research potential in federal statutory law. They are both excellent compilations, each with its advocates, and, although West's *U.S.C.A.* is still the more popular edition, it is a fortunate researcher who has access to both of them.

c. U.S.C.C.A.N.

West's *United States Code Congressional and Administrative News (U.S.C.C.A.N.)* is a legislative and administrative service which updates *U.S.C.A.* *U.S.C.C.A.N.* first appears in monthly "advance sheet" pamphlets which contain Congressional and Administrative Highlights, the full text of bills that became public laws during that period, important legislative histories consisting of selected committee reports, the text of Executive orders, Proclamations, President's Messages, and Reorganization Plans (when authorized by Congress), and a few administrative rules and regulations (including all tax regulations).

The advance sheets are cumulated into annual bound volumes. For the bound volumes, the following material set out in the advance sheets is deleted: Congressional and Administrative Highlights, President's Messages, and administrative rules and regulations. The tax regulations appearing in the advance sheets are integrated into the special annual bound volumes of the *U.S.C.C.A.N.* containing the text of all tax regulations.

For individuals who do not have access to the official editions of committee reports set out in *U.S.C.C.A.N.*, it is an invaluable aid to Federal statutory research.

7. OTHER FORMS OF FEDERAL LEGISLATION

As discussed above, statutes are not the only form of federal legislation. The following additional legislative materials should be noted in this context.

a. U.S. Constitution

The federal Constitution is the basic, organic legislation of the United States, and appears in a variety of published sources. These publications, and research in constitutional law generally, are discussed in detail in Chapter 6, above.

7 USCS § 2131 **AGRICULTURE**

---

§ 2131. Congressional statement of policy

The Congress finds that animals and activities which are regulated under this Act [7 USCS §§ 2131 et seq.] are either in interstate or foreign commerce or substantially affect such commerce or the free flow thereof, and that regulation of animals and activities as provided in this Act [7 USCS §§ 2131 et seq.] is necessary to prevent and eliminate burdens upon such commerce and to effectively regulate such commerce, in order—

(1) to insure that animals intended for use in research facilities or for exhibition purposes or for use as pets are provided humane care and treatment;

(2) to assure the humane treatment of animals during transportation in commerce; and

(3) to protect the owners of animals from the theft of their animals by preventing the sale or use of animals which have been stolen.

The Congress further finds that it is essential to regulate, as provided in this Act [7 USCS §§ 2131 et seq.], the transportation, purchase, sale, housing, care, handling, and treatment of animals by carriers or by persons or organizations engaged in using them for research or experimental purposes or for exhibition purposes or holding them for sale as pets or for any such purpose or use.

Citations to source of enactment

(Aug. 24, 1966, P. L. 89-544, § 1(b)[1], 80 Stat. 350; Dec. 24, 1970, P. L. 91-579, § 2, 84 Stat. 1560; Apr. 22, 1976, P. L. 94-279, § 2 in part, 90 Stat. 417.)

398

Illustration J–1

U.S.C.S. text of the beginning of the Animal Welfare Act.

ANIMAL TRANSPORT **7 USCS § 2131**

Historical notes

HISTORY; ANCILLARY LAWS AND DIRECTIVES

Amendments:

1970. Act Dec. 24, 1970 (effective one year after Dec. 24, 1970, as provided by § 23 of that Act), substituted "owners of animals," for "owners of dogs and cats"; substituted "theft of their animals" for "theft of such pets"; substituted "use of animals" for "use of dogs and cats"; added "or for exhibition purposes or for use as pets"; added "or for exhibition purposes or holding them for sale as pets"; and substituted "any such purpose or use" for "such use".

1976. Apr. 22, 1976, substituted this section for the former one, which read: "That, in order to protect the owners of animals, from the theft of their animals, to prevent the sale or use of animals which have been stolen, and to insure that certain animals intended for use in research facilities or for exhibition purposes or for use as pets are provided humane care and treatment, it is essential to regulate the transportation, purchase, sale, housing, care, handling, and treatment of such animals by persons or organizations engaged in using them for research or experimental purposes or for exhibition purposes or holding them for sale as pets or in transporting, buying, or selling them for any such purpose or use.".

Redesignation:

This section, formerly § 1 of Act Aug. 24, 1966, was redesignated as § 1(b) of Act Aug. 24, 1966, by § 2 of Act Apr. 22, 1976.

Short titles:

Act Aug. 24, 1966, P. L. 89-544, § 1(a), 80 Stat. 350, as amended by Act Dec. 24, 1970, P. L. 91-579, § 1, 84 Stat. 1560 as amended Apr. 22, 1976, P. L. 94-279, § 2 in part, 90 Stat. 417, provided: "This Act [7 USCS §§ 2131 et seq.] may be cited as the 'Animal Welfare Act'.".

Act Dec. 24, 1970, P. L. 91-579, § 1, 84 Stat 1560, provided that "this Act may be cited as the 'Animal Welfare Act of 1970'.". For full classification of this Act, consult USCS Tables volumes.

Act Apr. 22, 1976, P. L. 94-279, § 1, 90 Stat. 417, provided: "This Act may be cited as the 'Animal Welfare Act Amendments of 1976'.". For full classification of this Act, consult USCS Tables volumes.

Reference to Encyclopedia article

RESEARCH GUIDE

Am Jur:

4 Am Jur 2d, Animals § 20.

Annotations:

Validity, construction, and application of Animal Welfare Act (7 USCS §§ 2131 et seq.)

399

Illustration J–2

Historical notes and references in *U.S.C.C.*

7 USCS § 2131 AGRICULTURE

Annotation to federal decision

Annotation to state decision

INTERPRETIVE NOTES AND DECISIONS

Regulations promulgated pursuant to Animal Welfare Act, 7 USCS §§ 2131 et seq., pertaining to employee skill requirements at zoo, were drawn so as not to require any educational degrees; while some education might be necessary for some requirements, evidence did not establish that high school diploma was related or necessary to job requirements. Padilla v Stringer (1974, DC NM) 395 F Supp 495.

State statute which prohibited importation of pets for resale from states with less stringent licensing laws and regulations for commercial pet dealers was not pre-empted by Animal Welfare Act of 1970, 7 USCS §§ 2131 et seq., given different purposes behind federal statute (preventing pet thievery and inhumane research) and state statute (public health), and clear expressions of Congressional intent to foster co-operation with state interests under Act found in 7 USCS § 2145(d), and therefore there was no Congressional intent to ban remedial state legislation in field of interstate commerce in pets. Winkler v Colorado Dept. of Health (1977, Colo) 564 P2d 107.

§ 2132. Definitions

When used in this Act [7 USCS §§ 2131 et seq.]—

(a) The term "person" includes any individual, partnership, firm, joint stock company, corporation, association, trust, estate, or other legal entity;

(b) The term "Secretary" means the Secretary of Agriculture of the United States or his representative who shall be an employee of the United States Department of Agriculture;

(c) The term "commerce" means trade, traffic, transportation, or other commerce—

(1) between a place in a State and any place outside of such State, or between points within the same State but through any place outside thereof, or within any territory, possession, or the District of Columbia;

(2) which affects trade, traffic, transportation, or other commerce described in paragraph (1).

(d) The term "State" means a State of the United States, the District of Columbia, the Commonwealth of Puerto Rico, the Virgin Islands, Guam, American Samoa, or any other territory or possession of the United States;

(e) The term "research facility" means any school (except an elementary or secondary school), institution, organization, or person that uses or intends to use live animals in research, tests, or experiments, and that (1) purchases or transports live animals in commerce, or (2) receives funds under a grant, award, loan, or contract from a department, agency, or instrumentality of the United States for the purpose of carrying out research, tests, or experiments: Provided, That the Secretary may exempt, by regulation, any such school, institution, organization, or person that does not use or intend to use live dogs or cats, except those schools, institutions, organizations, or persons, which use substantial numbers (as determined by the Secretary) of live animals the principal function of which schools, institutions, organizations, or persons, is biomedical research or testing, when in

400

Illustration J-3

Annotation to federal and state court decisions in *U.S.C.S.*

b. Treaties

Under the U.S. Constitution, treaties are given the same legal authority and force as statutes.[22] Until 1950, they appeared regularly in the *Statutes at Large* volumes covering the period during which they were proclaimed. Beginning in 1950, however, a new, official chronological series was initiated for their publication, *United States Treaties and other International Agreements* (abbreviated as *U.S.T.*). This is similar to a session law publication.

After treaties have been consented to by the Senate and proclaimed by the President, their first official publication is in a slip form, similar to that of federal slip laws. Since 1945, this publication has been called the *Treaties and other International Acts Series* (*T.I.A.S.*), merging two prior series which were then discontinued: the Treaty Series (1908 to 1945) and the Executive Agreement Series (1929 to 1945).[23] The *T.I.A.S.* slip treaties are separately paginated and consecutively numbered pamphlets, each containing the text of the treaty or executive agreement in the languages of all of the parties agreeing to it.

Three preliminary forms of treaty publication should also be noted. Prior to ratification, each treaty is transmitted to the Senate for its consideration in the form of a *Senate Executive Document* (described below in Chapter 10, Legislative History, at Section B.7). Since 1981, *Senate Executive Documents* have been re-named *Senate Treaty Documents. Senate Treaty Documents* also typically contain transmittal messages from the President and the Secretary of State.[24] During their negotiation and their consideration by the Senate, *The Department of State Bulletin* reports on the progress of treaties in a regular feature called "Treaty Information". The text of the treaty often appears, after its signing, in the *Bulletin*. Then, on the date of signing, treaties are also issued in the form of press releases by the Department of State.

The historical forms of treaty publication are varied. As noted above (at p. 186), volume 7 of the *Statutes at Large* contained a retrospective compilation of treaties with Indian tribes from 1778 to 1845,[25] and volume 8 contained a compilation of treaties with foreign countries, also from 1778 to 1845. Thereafter, until 1950, they were published in the volumes of *Statutes at Large*, and then in *U.S. Trea-*

22. Article VI states: "This Constitution, and the Laws of the United States which shall be made in pursuance thereof; *and all treaties made, or which shall be made, under the Authority of the United States*, shall be the supreme Law of the Land . . . "

23. Between 1908 and 1929, the *Treaty Series* included *both* treaties and executive agreements.

24. A useful listing is M.G. Mabry's *Checklist of Senate Executive Documents and Reports . . . 1947–1970* (Tarlton Law Library, Univ. of Texas, 1970).

25. Other notable compilations of Indian treaties are C. Kappler, *Indian Affairs, Laws and Treaties* (U.S. Govt. Printing Office, 1904–1941, reprinted 1976) 5 v.; F.S. Cohen, *Handbook of Federal Indian Law* (U.S. Govt. Printing Office, 1945), revised and reissued as *Federal Indian Law* (1958), revised again (1971) and as *Handbook of Federal Indian Law* (Michie, 1982).

bered volumes of *U.S.T.* contains anywhere from two to four (or more) "Parts" in separate physical volumes, with non-cumulative indexes for each "Part". Access to this chronological series is provided by an annual index published by the Department of State, called *Treaties in Force,* and a new more versatile version, *A Guide to the United States Treaties in Force* by I. I. Karass and A. Sprudzs (Hein, 1982). The use of *Treaties in Force* and other commercial indexes and finding tools, and research procedures for treaties generally, are described in Section C of Chapter 21, *International Law.*

Two other important compilations of treaties, published by the federal government, have not been kept to date: Malloy's *Treaties, Conventions, International Acts, Protocols, and Agreements between the U.S.A. and other Powers* (U.S.G.P.O., 1910–1938) 4 v., and Miller's *Treaties and other International Acts of the U.S.A.* (U.S. G.P.O., 1931–48) 8 v. These collections covering 1776 to 1937, and 1776 to 1863, respectively, were superseded by the now definitive, retrospective set, C.E. Bevans, *Treaties and other International Agreements of the United States of America 1776–1949* (U.S.G.P.O., 1968–1975) in 13 v. with cumulative, analytical indexes. *Bevans* carries the treaty publication up to the period now covered by *U.S.T.*

Treaties which were negotiated but not perfected are published in C. Wiktor, *Unperfected Treaties of the United States of America.*[26] Beginning in 1962, ratified treaties also appear in a bi-monthly compilation of the American Society of International Law, *International Law Materials,* which includes drafts of treaties and related documentation as well. U.S. treaties appear in a number of other *multinational* compilations, which are described in Chapter 21.

c. Interstate Compacts

The Constitution, as interpreted by the courts, authorizes agreements between the states, provided they are first approved by Congress.[27] After the compact is agreed upon by the states, it goes to Congress for authorizing legislation. Thus, when enacted, each compact appears in the U.S. *Statutes at Large* and in the session laws of the respective states which are parties to it. The Council of State Governments has published a description of such compacts in *Interstate Compacts and Agencies: 1979,*[28] which is revised from time to time, and updated between revisions in the Council's biennial publication, the *Book of the States.*

Most interstate compacts also appear in the annotated statutory codes of the states enacting them, and are listed as cited material (by their statutory enactment) in the various Shepard's statutory citators. Thus, by the use of either of those publications, one can locate cases which have applied or interpreted interstate compacts.

26. Oceana Publications, 1976–19__ in progress, projected for five or six volumes, with indexes.

27. Article I, sec. 10: "No state shall, without the Consent of Congress . . . , enter into any Agreement or Compact with another State . . . ." See also F.L. Zimmermann and M. Wendell, *The Law and Use of Interstate Compacts,* 2d. ed. (Council of State Governments, 1976).

28. Lexington, Ky., 1979.

d. Reorganization Plans

Reorganization plans are an unusual hybrid form of legislation. They consist of Presidential proposals to reorganize executive agencies below the departmental level, which are submitted to Congress for approval pursuant to a general authorizing statute.[29] If Congress does not reject the proposed reorganization within sixty days, it then becomes effective and will be published in the *Statutes at Large;* in an Appendix to Title 5 of the *U.S. Code;* in the *Federal Register* and Title 3 of the *Code of Federal Regulations;* and in *U.S.C.C.A.N.* Reorganization plans are also usually published in the *Congressional Record* when they are submitted to Congress. They can also be Shepardized by their separate listing under Title 5 of the *U.S. Code* in Shepard's *United States Citations—Statutes.*

D. STATE STATUTORY MATERIALS

1. SLIP LAWS; SESSION LAWS; CODES

The typical forms of state statutory publication have already been described and illustrated above in Section B, "Pattern of Statutory Publication". State statutes appear in a slip law form in most states, in bound volumes of session laws for every state, in official editions of the state code in some of the states, and in an annotated code in every state. The annotated state codes are almost all commercial editions, with those twenty one published by the West Publishing Company having most of the features described in the *U.S. Code Annotated* (see Section C.6.a, above), and the five published by Lawyers Co-op/Bancroft-Whitney having most of the features described in the *U.S. Code Service* (see Section C.6.b, above). The commercial editions of state annotated codes are usually supplemented by annual pocket parts and pamphlet supplements, which update both the statutory sections and the annotations.

In general, the *session laws* are the authoritative *positive law* text of each state's laws, but there are substantial delays in their publication. For that reason and because of their additional features, most research in state statutory law is done in the annotated codes.

2. LEGISLATIVE SERVICES

To supplement their annotated state codes beyond the methods described above, several publishers (including West and Lawyers Co-op) issue legislative services for most of their codes. These services provide monthly or bi-monthly pamphlets which contain the current laws as they are enacted by the state legislatures. They are similar to West's *U.S.C.C.A.N.* (but without the legislative history component) and to the *U.S.C.S. Advance Service* of Lawyers Co-op.

29. Authorizing statutes usually grant to the President the right to make such proposals for five year periods.

3. UNIFORM LAWS AND MODEL ACTS

For many years, one of the major aspects of the law reform movement in this country has been a drive for the enactment of uniform laws by the several states, in those fields in which it seemed appropriate. To this end, the National Conference of Commissioners on Uniform State Laws was formed in 1912, pursuant to statutory authorization by all of the states. The Conference, consisting of representatives of each of the states, meets annually to draft, promulgate and promote such laws, which the states can then adopt by enactment, or modify, or reject, as they see fit. Over two hundred uniform laws have been approved by the Conference, of which over a hundred have been adopted by at least one state. The *Uniform Commercial Code* has been enacted by every state.

All of the uniform laws which have been adopted by at least one state are compiled and published by the West Publishing Company in an annotated edition called *Uniform Laws Annotated* (Master Edition, 1965–1975), with annual pocket part supplementation. *U.L.A.* includes the Commissioners' notes on each law and annotations (in the usual format of West headnote abstracts) to court decisions of every state which have referred to the laws. These annotations, reflecting as they do the interpretations of the uniform laws in states which have adopted them, are particularly important for research in states which are considering them or have just recently enacted them. References to secondary sources, including legal periodical articles on each law, are also provided.

The *U.L.A.* contains notes indicating the various changes in each uniform law which may have been made by the states adopting it, as well as Tables listing adoptions, and other useful statutory information.

Another important publication on uniform laws is the annual *Handbook of the National Conference of Commissioners on the Uniform State Laws.* The *Handbook* contains current information about new laws under consideration by the Conference, discussions of pending and proposed laws, and is one of the few sources of the texts of uniform laws which have not yet been adopted by any state.

"Model Acts" are also proposed by the National Conference of Commissioners in fields where they are likely to be widely adopted. Such acts have also been drafted and promoted by the American Law Institute, which has collaborated with the National Conference on a few laws (e.g., the Uniform Commercial Code). The most influential of the model acts proposed by the American Law Institute is the Model Penal Code, adopted in part by the State of Illinois and a few other states.

It should be noted that unless actually adopted by some state, neither the uniform laws nor the model acts have any legal effect. When adopted, however, they appear in the session laws and annotated codes of those states which have enacted them. These sources are, of course, most important for research purposes, since only they will contain the actual text *as enacted,* with whatever changes and variations were made in the form proposed by the National Conference.

E. OTHER STATUTORY SOURCES

1. LOOSELEAF SERVICES

Looseleaf services, for the particular subject areas which they cover, invariably include the text of all federal statutes pertaining to that field. Many services also contain state laws relating to that subject. The availability of other legal texts (such as court decisions, administrative rulings and regulations, etc.), weekly supplementation, explanatory discussion, and varied indexing, make these services particularly useful sources for statutory research in specialized subject fields. Looseleaf services are more fully described in Chapter 13 below.

2. SUBJECT COLLECTIONS

Collections of statutes in particular subject fields are published, on occasion, by Congressional committees and government agencies with responsibilities in those fields; by trade associations, public interest groups and labor unions, in their fields of activity; and by commercial publishers. These collections are particularly useful for practitioners or officials working in the areas covered by the collection, particularly those in which there is no looseleaf service. However, such collections are rarely supplemented with adequate regularity and hence are dangerous to use. Always check the publication date of such a compilation and be sure that your search is updated elsewhere. A useful guide to such collections of *state* laws is *Subject Compilations of State Laws, Research Guide and Annotated Bibliography,* by L. Foster and C. Boast.[30] This listing arranges the compilations by subject, provides descriptive annotations to each, and includes an author index and publishers' directory.

F. RESEARCH IN STATUTORY LAW

Because of the different forms of legislative publication, research in statutory law varies considerably from that in case law. Although some of the approaches are similar, there are generally fewer finding tools, and the primary emphasis is on subject indexing and tables. The two computer research services do not yet include substantial state statutory material, but some researching can be done in federal material. This capability will be discussed briefly in Section 6 of this part. The need for extrinsic aids in statutory interpretation (e.g. judicial decisions and legislative history) give an added dimension to statutory research, and these will be covered in Section 7. As with judi-

30. Greenwood Press, 1981. Foster and Boast has been supplemented by an *Update* at 75 *Law Library J.* 121 (1982). See also J. S. Schultz, *Comparative Statutory Sources,* 2d ed. (W. S. Hein Co., 1978).

cial decisions, the research process must include Shepard's citators to verify the current status and authority of statutes and to trace the history of their judicial and legislative treatment. Since research techniques for federal and state law are basically the same, the following discussion will treat them together, differentiating only when specific aids or sources require it.

Statutory research typically begins with a search to determine whether there are statutes applicable to the particular problem or topic under consideration, and then locating the relevant statutory provisions. Sometimes, however, one has a reference to a particular law by number or popular name, and merely needs a table to locate that statute in its code form.

Although statutes can also be located by the broad topical approach described above in Chapter 5 for case finding, this method involves the same disadvantages for statutory research as it did for cases. To select conceptually, from the many titles of a particular code, that title most likely to deal with the problem under study, and then to scan its outline or scope to identify relevant sections is far too uncertain and circuitous. Therefore, unless some identification of a particular statute is available, one generally analyzes the problem into its component issues, reduces those issues to specific catchwords or phrases, and then uses those search words in the subject index to a session law volume (if one is seeking a particular law enacted in that session) or to the annotated code (if, as is usually the case, one is seeking all of the applicable statutory law, currently in force).

1. HISTORICAL INDEXES

There are a few retrospective indexes to federal law which are occasionally useful in historical research. There have also been abortive attempts to index state laws for current use, but these have lapsed and are now rarely used, except for study of the periods they cover.

a. Federal Law Indexes

For retrospective access to an early federal law when its year of enactment is known, one can of course consult the index to the *Statutes at Large* or the state session law volume for that year. For federal laws, however, two cumulative subject indexes are available for the periods indicated in their respective titles: M. G. Beaman and A. K. MacNamara, *Index Analysis of the Federal Statutes, 1789–1873*,[31] and W. H. McClenon and W. C. Gilbert, *Index to the Federal Statutes, 1874–1931*.[32] These include only general, public and permanent laws.

For specific laws contained in the *Revised Statutes* or the early editions of the *U.S. Code*, the indexes and tables of those compila-

31. U.S. Govt. Printing Office, 1911.

32. U.S. Govt. Printing Office, 1933, superseding Scott & Beaman, *Index Analysis of the Federal Statutes, 1873–1907* (U.S. Govt. Printing Office, 1908).

tions can be consulted. For federal statutes *currently* in force, one should use the index to the latest edition of the *U.S. Code,* or preferably the index to one of the two annotated editions of the *Code, U.S.C.A.* or *U.S.C.S.*

b. State Law Indexes

Multi-state statutory searches are not frequently required by practitioners, but they are quite common in scholarly research. The time and effort required to search the indexes to fifty state codes or fifty session law volumes can be frustrating and undoubtedly discourages such research efforts. During the years 1925 to 1948, the Legislative Research Service of the Library of Congress prepared a biennial index of the session laws of all the states. Entries were listed under broad subject headings and then alphabetically by state. For that period, one could survey current enactments of any or all states on a particular topic. Unfortunately, that service was discontinued for lack of funding. Then, from 1963 to 1972, a similar project was undertaken by the Aspen Systems Corporation, which produced by computer a key-word-in-context index of federal and state statutes of general interest, with brief abstracts of each law. This index was issued commercially under several names *(Automated Statutory Reporter, Aspen Computerized Law Index,* and then *Monthly Digest of Current Legislation),* but was discontinued in 1972 for lack of support.

The hope that the present computerized legal research systems would fill this need has so far not been realized. (See Section 6 below.) Current sources for multi-state information on new laws are (1) looseleaf services in those subject fields for which such coverage is available;[33] (2) a limited feature of the Council of State Governments' biennial *Book of the States,* called "Trends in State Legislation"; and (3) the expensive services of Commerce Clearing House, called *CCH Legislative Reporting Service* and *Electronic Legislative Search System (ELSS)* which offer coverage of both legislative history and enactment information for all states, either comprehensively or selectively.

2. SUBJECT ACCESS TO CODES

Most statutory research problems require the use of the subject index to the current code of the relevant jurisdiction. In general, the indexes to the commercial, annotated editions of the various federal and state codes are more detailed and more effective than those in the official edition. In addition, most annotated codes (including *U.S.C.A.* and *U.S.C.S.*) include individual indexes for each title, located at the end of the title. These title indexes are usually more detailed than the coverage of the title in the general index to the code. The

33. Some of these services in fields where state law is particularly significant (e.g. CCH *Insurance Law Reporter* and *State Tax Reporter)* include separate "all state" volumes or sections which provide either texts or abstracts of state statutes.

index volumes of the codes are updated by the same method of supplementation as provided for the other volumes, usually annual pocket parts and quarterly pamphlets. Since new laws or legislative changes may not be reflected in the main part of the index volume, it is, of course, always necessary to consult the supplements to the index.

Some of the code indexes include features which are useful for specific types of research. For example, all three editions of the *U.S. Code* and the annotated editions of many state codes list index entries for statutory definitions together under the heading "Definitions." These definitions are, for most problems (particularly for the definitions of specific *crimes*), of more immediate concern and effect than the judicial definitions contained in the case abstracts of *Words and Phrases.*

Illustrations K to M, which follow, show sample pages from the indexes to the *U.S. Code, U.S. Code Annotated,* and *U.S. Code Service* under "Animals" and the "Animal Welfare Act" illustrated above, both in their main sections and supplements.

3. ACCESS TO SESSION LAWS

a. Volume Indexes

To locate a specific statute, when the session of its enactment is known, one can consult the subject index to that volume of the session laws for the relevant jurisdiction. Illustration N on page 222 shows the subject index of v. 90 of the *Statutes at Large,* which contained the "Animal Welfare Act Amendments of 1976."

b. From Code Provisions

When one has been using a statutory text in its code form and needs access to its original source as enacted in the session laws, a reference is always provided in the code itself. Such references appear either immediately following the text of the section or as a source note just below the section (see Illustrations H, I, and J, above).

If reference is needed from the session law to the code, or from a revision of the title to its earlier text, or from a code section to Executive documents issued under it, the *Tables* volumes of the three editions of the federal code provide parallel reference tables for those purposes. Illustration O–1 (at page 223) shows the list of tables included in the *Tables* volume of the *U.S. Code.* Illustration O–2 (at page 224) shows the table of parallel references in that volume, which takes you from public law number to *Statutes at Large* citations, then to *U.S. Code* section. Similar tables volumes appear in each of the *state* statutory codes.

GENERAL INDEX **Page 236**

Illustration K–1

General Index to the official *U.S. Code,* 1976 edition.

GENERAL INDEX Page 112

Illustration K-2

General Index to the official *U.S. Code,* 1980 Supplement.

Illustration L–1

General Index to the *U.S. Code Annotated*, bound volume.

ANACOSTIA NAVAL ANNEX

176

Illustration L–2

General Index to the *U.S. Code Annotated,* pocket part supplement.

UNITED STATES CODE SERVICE

204

References are to Titles and Sections

Illustration M-1

General Index to the *U.S. Code Service*, bound volume.

UNITED STATES CODE SERVICE

68 *References to the Code are to Titles and Sections*

Illustration M–2

General Index to the *U.S. Code Service,* pocket part supplement.

A6

SUBJECT INDEX

NOTE: Part 1 contains pages 1–1519; Part 2 contains pages 1520–3129.

Illustration N

Subject Index to volume 90 of the *Statutes at Large.*

4. POPULAR NAME TABLES

Some earlier federal statutes and most current enactments have acquired or been given popular names, and are frequently referred to by those names. In recent years, Congress itself has applied descriptive names or short titles to most laws and these are commonly used for popular reference. To convert such a name to its session law and code citations, one uses popular name tables similar to those for cases, which have already been described. As noted above, *Shepard's Acts and Cases by Popular Names—Federal and State* is probably the most versatile of these aids. Since not all such names appear in the Shepard's list, it is worth noting that a popular name table for federal statutes appears in the Tables volume of *U.S. Code* which is now in fact called "Popular Names and Tables." A sample page from that table is shown above in Illustration G at p. 193. Similar Tables appear in the index volumes of *U.S. Code Annotated* and *U.S. Code Service,* and in either the tables or index volumes of most of the annotated editions of the state statutory codes.

CONTENTS

Page v

Illustration O-1

Contents of the *Tables* volume of the official *U.S. Code.*

STATUTES AT LARGE **Page 1308**

94th Cong. 90 Stat.	Pub. L.	Section	Page	U.S.C. Title	U.S.C. Section	Status
1976—Apr. 22	94-278	502(c)	413	21	334 nt	
		601	413	42	201 nt	
		602(a), (b)	413	42	289c-1 nt	
		603(a)(1)	414	42	289a	
		603(a)(2), (3)	414	42	289c-1	
		603(b)	414	42	289c-5	
		603(c)	414	42	289c-6	
		701	414	42	289c-2 nt	
		801(a)	414	42	247d	
		801(b)	415	42	254c	
		901	415	42	234	Rep.
		1001	415	42	217a-1	
		1101	415	42	213	
		1102(a)	415	42	289*l*-1	
		1102(b)	415	42	225a	
		1103	415	42	289*l*-5	
		1104	416	42	295g-23	
		1105(a)	416	42	294*o*	
		1105(b)	416	42	294m	
		1106(a)	416	42	300*l*	
		1106(b)	416	42	300p-3	
		1106(c)	416	42	300s-1	
		1107(a)	416	42	6062	
		1107(b), (c)	416	42	6064	
		1107(d)	416	42	6001 nt	
	94-279	1	417	7	2131 nt	
		2	417	7	2131, 2131 nt	
		3, 4	417	7	2132	
		5	418	7	2134, 2141, 2142	
		6	418	7	2136	
		7	418	7	2139	
		8	418	7	2140	
		9, 10	418	7	2143	
		11	419	7	2145	
		12	420	7	2146	
		13	420	7	2149	
		15	421	7	2154	
		16	421	7	2155	
		17(a)-(h)(1)	421-423	7	2156	
		17(h)(2)	423	39	3001	
		18	423	7	2153	
		19	423	7	2144	
May 5	94-280	101, 102	425	23	101 nts	
		103	425	23	104 nt	
		105(a)(12)	427	23	215 nt	
		105(b)(1)	428	23	104 nt	
		106(b)	429	23	104	
		107(a)	430	23	101	
		107(b)	430	23	104	
		108	431	23	101	
		109, 110	431, 432	23	103	
		111(a)	433	23	103	
		111(b)	433	23	103 nt	
		112, 113(a)	433-435	23	104	
		113(b)	435	23	104 nt	
		114	436	23	106	
		115	436	23	108	
		116	436	23	117	
		117(a)	436	23	118	
		117(b)	437	23	203	
		118(a)	437	23	121	
		119	437	23	125	
		120	438	23	127	
		121	438	23	129	
		122	438	23	131	
		123(a)	439	23	135	
		123(b)	439	23	prec. 101	
		124	440	23	138	
		125	440	23	139	
		126	440	23	140	
		127	440	23	142	
		128(b)	440	23	prec. 101	
		129	440	23	142 nt	
		130	440	23	147	
		131	441	23	152, 153	
		132(a)	441	23	156	
		132(b)	441	23	prec. 101	
		133	441	23	202	
		134	441	23	217	
		135(a)	441	23	219	
		135(b)	442	23	prec. 201	
		135(d)	442	23	prec. 401	
		136(a)	442	23	319	
		136(b)	443	23	319 nt	
		137(a)	443	23	320	
		137(b)	443	23	320 nt	
		139	443	23	prec. 101	
		140(a)-(e)	444	23	130 nt	
		140(f)	444	49	1605 nt	

Illustration O–2

Parallel reference table for different statutory forms in *Tables* volume of the offical *U.S. Code.*

5. UPDATING THE SEARCH

a. Supplementation and Legislative Services

When the relevant statutory sections in a research problem have been located and examined, the next step is to be sure that those provisions have not been changed or that later court decisions interpreting or applying the sections have not been issued. To do so, one must check the appropriate supplements to the statutory code being used. These are usually annual pocket parts and pamphlet supplements, but in a few states the statutory compilations are in a looseleaf format and one must then check to be sure that the latest supplements have been filed.

In those states which have legislative services (described above in Section D.2), one can also use the monthly or bi-monthly pamphlets to determine whether recently enacted laws affect the relevant sections. These services often include convenient tables arranged by code titles and sections which can be scanned quickly to see if the sections have been affected.

b. Shepard's Citations

After checking the code supplementation, the statute should be Shepardized in the statutory unit of Shepard's *United States Citations* or the appropriate state citator. As with decisions, one can trace the history of the primary source itself and also its subsequent treatment by legislation or judicial decisions. Shepard's also includes in the citing materials for statutes Attorney General opinions, articles in selected legal periodicals, and Annotations in *ALR, ALR Federal* or *Lawyers' Edition.* Since Shepard's analyzes the cited provisions by their subsections, one can identify relevant citing sources specifically by those subsections.

The statute should be Shepardized in all citator volumes and supplements from the time of its enactment to the present. Shepard's abbreviations indicate significant judicial *and* legislative actions affecting the statute (e.g. declared constitutional or unconstitutional, amended, repealed, etc.) Shepardizing statutes will be discussed in somewhat more detail in Section E, Chapter 9, Citators.

c. Looseleaf Services

Since most looseleaf services are supplemented weekly, they provide more recent legislative information than any of the updating sources mentioned so far. Therefore, if the statute being researched is in a field covered by a looseleaf service, one should examine the latest supplements to the service for recent changes. Many looseleaf services include finding lists which facilitate checking directly by statutory title and section numbers rather than the more circuitous use of subject indexes.

6. STATUTORY RESEARCH BY COMPUTER

As noted above, state statutes are not well covered by *LEXIS* and *WESTLAW.* Both services, however, do include the *U.S. Code* in their data bases and enable one to search its text with great speed and specificity. They each include specialized data bases in a number of fields of federal law, with the full text of statutes in those fields available for searching (e.g. federal taxation, labor law, securities regulation, anti-trust, etc.) LEXIS has also included the statutes of four states, but seems to be deemphasizing rather than expanding its state statutory content.

As noted above, the CCH *Electronic Legislative Search System* is a recent service providing access to current federal and state legislative history and enactments. Another new development is the availability on-line of several specialized federal law databases from the Bureau of National Affairs, a leading publisher of looseleaf services. These new computer services, which include federal taxation, labor law, and patents, seem to be drawn from the related *B.N.A.* looseleaf services, and are available through Dialog Information Services of Lockheed, a major vendor of on-line data bases.

7. EXTRINSIC AIDS FOR STATUTORY INTERPRETATION

The importance of various external sources for use in statutory interpretation has already been noted. The following four sources, each dealt with in another Chapter of this work, are briefly noted here, with reference to the location of their fuller treatment.

a. Legislative History

To determine the legislative intent behind a statute or statutory provision, one must investigate the various documents of legislative history—bills, hearings, committee reports, debates, etc. These documents, and the finding aids and research procedures for their investigation, are treated in detail in Chapter 10, Legislative History.

b. Judicial Decisions

Previous judicial interpretations and constructions of ambiguous or controverted statutory language are often used to establish the meaning of the statute in question. Such interpretations may have been made in earlier cases dealing with the specific statute, or in cases involving other statutes containing similar provisions or language. There are several means of locating relevant decisions for this purpose: (1) the annotations to cases in the annotated statutory codes (described above in this Chapter, and in Chapter 3, 4 and 5); (2) Shepardizing the statute for judicial treatment (described in Chapter 9 below); and (3) computer searching of the statutory phrase in *LEXIS* and *WESTLAW* (described in Chapter 22, below).

c. Attorney General Opinions

The federal and state Attorneys General are often called upon to render opinions on statutory language of uncertain effect. The frequency of publication and indexing of these opinions are notoriously poor. They are, however, carried as citing material in all of the Shepard's statutory citators and can be identified in that way. Cross references from statutory sections to Attorney General opinions are also provided in the annotated statutory codes issued by West, Lawyers Co-op, and some other publishers. Attorney General opinions are described further in Section H of Chapter 11, Administrative and Executive Publications.

d. Secondary Sources

Significant statutes are often discussed in looseleaf services, legal encyclopedias, treatises and periodical articles. Such discussions may be quite helpful in statutory research and in the preparation of arguments relating to statutes, and may also include references to other primary legal sources. Specialized finding aids of varying quality exist for each of these types of secondary material. They are discussed specifically in the following chapters: Looseleaf Services, Chapter 13; Legal Encyclopedias, Chapter 14; Treatises, Chapter 15; and Periodicals, Chapter 16.

G. LOCAL LAW SOURCES

Legal problems and issues are governed not only by federal and state law, but also by the laws of counties, cities, villages and other local units. Local laws are a form of delegated legislation, based on law-making powers granted by the state legislatures, or, in the case of Washington, D.C. and other federally controlled areas, by the U.S. Congress. Despite the trend toward greater centralization of governmental authority over the last fifty years, local laws remain important in many areas of daily life and economic activity. Housing, transportation, social welfare, municipal services, zoning and environmental conditions are all heavily regulated at this level of government. Local taxation is an ever-increasing area of legal activity. Consequently, there is an extensive literature of municipal charters, local ordinances, codes and regulations which is frequently the subject of very frustrating research. Local law in general is poorly published, inadequately indexed, and infrequently supplemented.

1. MUNICIPAL CHARTERS, CODES AND ORDINANCES

Most of the larger cities in the United States publish collections of their charter and ordinances in a code format. They are usually poorly arranged, not regularly updated, and often not indexed. Annotations to case law in these codes are virtually non-existent. There has been a movement by several small private publishers to prepare codes for smaller cities and towns, particularly in the Northeast, and these have greatly improved access to local law in the communities so served.

In general, however, individual ordinances (if their existence is known and they can be identified) must be obtained from the Clerk's Office of the county, city or town. In larger cities, municipal reference libraries can be very helpful, and some public libraries are useful sources of information on local law.

State digests, state legal encyclopedias and local practice sets include references to court decisions in their respective jurisdictions on particular local law problems and may include local ordinances in point. General legal treatises on municipal law may be helpful for their discussion of broader issues, but are less likely to provide local references.

The practitioner in a particular locale should, of course, become familiar with the sources in that area.

2. ORDINANCE LAW ANNOTATIONS

Shepard's provides a six volume digest of national scope on judicial decisions involving local ordinances, called *Ordinance Law Annotations.* This service provides brief abstracts of such decisions under broad subject headings, which are arranged alphabetically and subdivided by more specific subtopics. It covers ordinances from all states, but only if they are the subject of decisions published in standard reporters. The set is kept up to date by annual pocket parts. Illustrations P–1 and P–2 show sample pages from this service, which should not be confused with the coverage of ordinances in Shepard's state statutory citators.

3. SHEPARDIZING ORDINANCES

Shepard's state statutory citators include coverage of local ordinances of the counties, cities, and towns in their respective states. This coverage lists as citing material, judicial decisions which have applied or interpreted the ordinances. The ordinances themselves are arranged under the name of the local government unit and then alphabetically by subject. In addition, a separate index by subject indicates which units have ordinances on that subject, so that they can then be located under the name of that county, city or town for Shepardizing. These two approaches can be seen in Illustration Q, from the instructional pamphlet, *How to Use Shepard's Citations.*

H. SUMMARY

The variety of published forms of legislation and the multiplicity of their finding aids should not obscure the pivotal importance of statutory law in modern legal research. Most appellate decisions involve the application or interpretation of statutes. Administrative regulations, court rules, and local laws all derive from delegations of

ANIMALS, DOMESTIC

EDITORIAL COMMENT. Animals of various kinds have been domesticated by human beings for thousands of years. Most such animals are used for the production of food or work, but a substantial number are purely for companionship or amusement. In any event, the animal world gets a lot of attention from lawmakers and judges. Some of the finest examples of judicial humor are found in the "dog bite" cases. We do not have space, in a work of this kind, to reproduce such examples, but some very interesting cases are digested here. To cite just one such case, a Tennessee court in 1899 found that a policeman was justified in arresting a disorderly mule found loitering about the streets, with no apparent business and no evidence of ownership. Whether or not the mule was advised of his legal rights does not appear (§39).

Several of the cases digested below arose a good many years ago, but we have included them because they have a certain historical value, and may shed light on modern day traffic and parking problems. Moreover, the horse was once thought to be almost completely replaced by automobiles and tractors, but now we have more horses than ever before. So the horse cases may have some current value.

In this topic we have included only animals having some domestic use. The hunting of animals is covered in HUNTING AND FISHING. And the production from animals kept for food is treated in FOOD, except that dairy product cases will be found in MILK; DAIRIES; DAIRY PRODUCTS. Slaughtering, and related activities, are dealt with in SLAUGHTERHOUSES; RENDERING PLANTS; TANNERIES.

286

Illustration P–1

A sample page from Shepard's *Ordinance Law Annotations,* showing scope of coverage of topic.

ANIMALS, DOMESTIC §1

I. RUNNING AT LARGE

§1. Dogs

For the purpose of imposing civil liability under a city leash ordinance making it unlawful for a person owning or possessing a dog to allow it to be at large upon the streets, a motorcyclist riding on a public street is a member of the group sought to be protected and the harm he suffered when the dog caused his motorcycle to flip over is the kind of harm that the ordinance was designed to prevent. Whether the dog owners' violation of the ordinance was the proximate cause of the injuries is a question for the jury.

Wyo Endresen v Allen (1978) 574 P2d 1219.

Violation of a prohibition against allowing dogs to be at large does not create strict liability. There must be evidence of some degree of knowledge, either actual or constructive. To recover for civil liability it must be established that a person comes within the scope of the ordinance and intentionally or negligently allows the dog to run at large.

Ariz Santanello v Cooper (1970) 106 Ariz 262, 475 P2d 246.

287

Illustration P–2

Continuation of topic in Shepard's *Ordinance Law Annotations,* showing abstracts of two decisions on local ordinances.

CITATIONS TO ORDINANCES

Shepard's compiles citations to ordinances in two ways:

1 — under the name of the city, subdivided thereunder by topics commonly covered in city codes, or

2 — under a general alphabetic list of topics commonly covered in city codes, subdivided by city names.

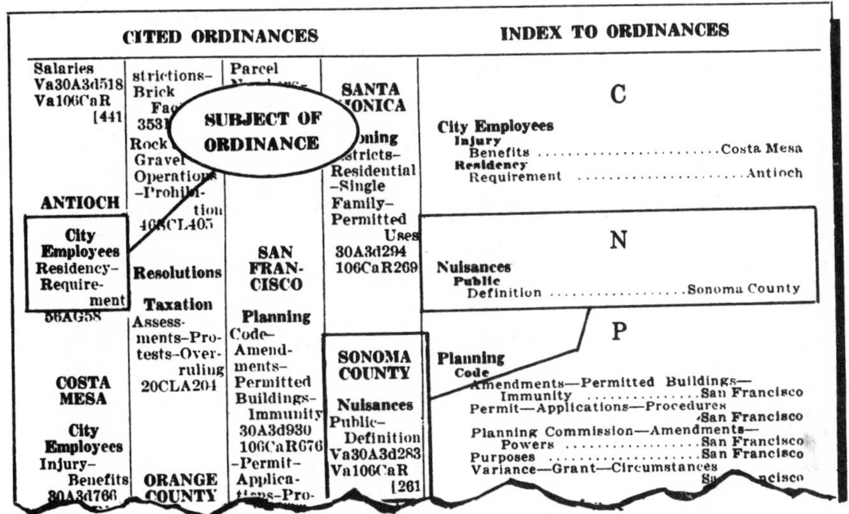

Shepard's Ordinance Section is often the only approach to perplexing "people problems"

State editions of Shepard's Citations show citations to ordinances and charters. Subject matter indices are included to assist in search.

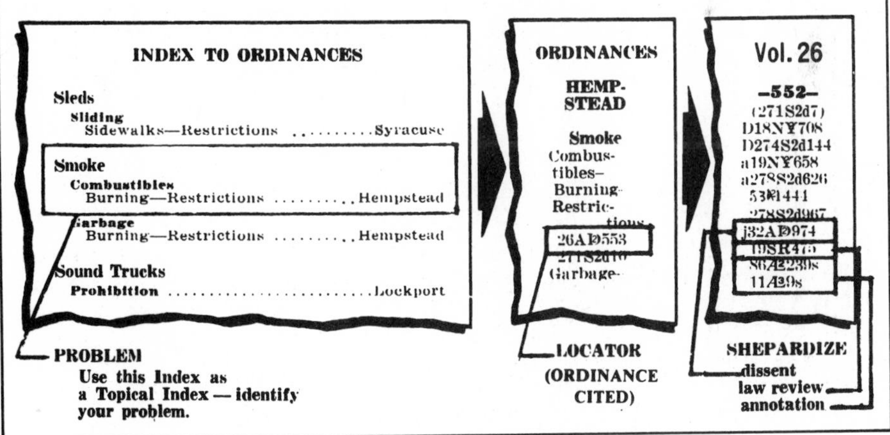

Illustration Q

Shepard's coverage of local ordinances in its various state statutory citators.

power enacted by statutes. The jurisdictions of courts and most executive authority is similarly based on legislative documents, either constitutional or statutory. All legal research must therefore include the question: Is there a statute in point?

This Chapter can perhaps best be summarized by the following questions applicable to every statutory research problem:

1. What statutory materials are available for the applicable jurisdiction and what is their authority?
2. What statutory research approaches are best suited to this issue in the particular jurisdiction?
3. Have I found all possible sources of statutory law on this issue?
4. Is what I have found up to date and does it reflect the latest enactments and the most recent judicial interpretations?
5. What other extrinsic aids to statutory interpretation are available on this problem?

I. ADDITIONAL READING

G. Calabresi, *A Common Law for the Age of Statutes* (Harvard University Press, 1982).

J. Davies, *Legislative Law and Process in a Nutshell* (West Publishing Co., 1975).

R. H. Dwan & E. R. Feidler, "The Federal Statutes—their History and Use," 22 *Minnesota L.Rev.* 1008 (1938).

B. K. Eres, ed., *Legal and Legislative Information Processing* (Greenwood Press, 1980).

J. W. Hurst, *Dealing with Statutes* (Columbia University Press, 1982).

W. P. Statsky and D. Matz, *Legislative Analysis: How to Use Statutes and Regulations* (West Publishing Co., 1975).

J. G. Sutherland and C. D. Sands, *Statutes and Statutory Construction,* 4th ed. (Callaghan, 1972) 6 v. looseleaf.

U.S. Library of Congress. Congressional Research Service. *How to Follow Current Federal Legislation and Regulations* (Report No. 81–197C, 1981).

U.S. Office of the Federal Register, *How to Find U.S. Statutes and U.S. Code Citations,* 3d rev. ed. (U.S. Govt. Printing Office, 1977).

Chapter 8

COURT RULES

A. INTRODUCTION

Court rules are designed to guide and regulate the conduct of business before the courts. They range from purely formal details as the format to be followed in preparing a brief, to matters of substantial importance such as the grounds for appeal, time limitations, and the types of motions and appeals which will be entertained.

Each jurisdiction has its own procedures and requirements for the promulgation of court rules. Some involve action by special conferences of judges constituted for that purpose; others require action or approval by the highest court of the jurisdiction; and some require a combination of judicial action and legislative approval. In general, court rules are considered to be a form of delegated legislation. They constitute an important part of procedural law and, by determining the form of remedies, may affect rights in significant respects.

Court rules, like administrative regulations, are quasi-legislative in nature, and are subject to interpretation by the courts. As judicial construction of statutes may affect the meaning and application of statutes, so also are court rules frequently affected by their judicial interpretation. Thorough research in court rules therefore requires access not only to the rules themselves, but also to court decisions which may have interpreted or construed them.

This chapter will provide a brief survey of the sources that can be used to find the texts of court rules and their judicial interpretation.

B. FEDERAL COURT RULES

1. PRIMARY SOURCES

The U.S. Supreme Court has Congressional authority [1] to promulgate rules that apply to all federal courts, and has issued Rules of Civil and Criminal Procedure for the U.S. District Courts, as well as Rules of Appellate Procedure.[2] These rules are general in application, and separate rules of the individual U.S. District Courts and the U.S. Courts of Appeals, that are not inconsistent with the general rules, are permitted and have also been promulgated by those Courts.

The Supreme Court's rules of a general nature are available in a variety of publications. The *Rules of Civil Procedure* and *Appellate Procedure* are contained in an appendix to Title 28 of the *U.S. Code,* and the *Rules of Criminal Procedure* are found in the *Code* as an appendix to Title 18.

Annotated editions of the rules are available as well. The rules can be found in the volumes following Titles 18 and 28 of *United States Code Annotated,* accompanied by editorial notes, annotations to cases decided on each Rule, and excerpts from the notes of the Advisory Committee for Federal Rules. Updating is provided by annual pocket parts. The *United States Code Service* also includes the rules of civil procedure and criminal procedure, in an annotated form, in a series of unnumbered "Court Rules" volumes. Each rule here also is followed by annotations to relevant decisions, and Advisory Committee notes. It too is kept up to date by annual pocket parts.

Illustrations A–1 to A–3 and B–1 to B–3 show Rule 57 of the Federal Rules of Civil Procedure, with the usual research aids provided, in *USCA* and *USCS,* respectively.

These rules can also be found in the *Rules* volumes of *U.S. Supreme Court Digest, Lawyers' Edition,* published by Lawyers Co-op,[3] and as an adjunct to several of the texts that will be cited below. The *Lawyers' Edition Desk Book* contains a "Table of Federal Laws, Rules, and Regulations Cited and Construed", which provides references to *Lawyers' Edition* decisions and annotations on specific rules. This Table is shown in Illustration C, below.

The following recent survey of federal court rules describes the major sources of these important materials: J. W. Cochran, "Federal Court Rules: A Selective Guide to Resources," 2 *Legal Ref. Services Q.* 65–75 (1982).

1. See 28 U.S.C.A. § 2072, 18 U.S.C.A. §§ 3771–3772.

2. Rules of a more limited nature, such as those related to bankruptcy or admiralty, have also been issued by the Court.

3. This edition of the Rules also contains the major documents of legislative history relating to their adoption and enactment.

to any material fact, the law of case was settled and answer was impotent to revive dispute as to sufficiency of amended complaint or to initiate new one based upon same question of law. Garden City Chamber of Commerce v. Wagner, D.C.N.Y.1952, 104 F.Supp. 235.

District judge's denial of patent licensor's motion for partial summary judgment directing licensee and others to account for royalties did not become "law of the case" so as to preclude another district judge from thereafter reaching his own conclusion on issue whether patent invalidity was a defense to cause of action seeking royalties. Bahamas Paper Co. Ltd. v. Imperial Packaging Corp., D.C.N.Y.1973, 58 F.R.D. 355.

Federal district court was bound by chief judge's prior ruling under which jurisdiction to determine unfair competition claim would survive disposition of claim asserted under letters patent, and federal district court was required to deny defendants' motion for summary judgment, though plaintiff seemed to have been reluctant to proceed to trial, and defendants' argument that there was no possibility of infringement came close to being persuasive. Hirsch v. Scoparino, D.C.N.Y.1950, 10 F.R.D. 205.

A defendant who moves to dismiss a complaint for insufficiency, specifying the ground therefor after his motion is denied, cannot move for summary judgment on the same ground, since decision on first motion would be law of case and he would be estopped from raising the same question again. Michel v. Meier, D.C.Pa.1948, 8 F.R.D. 464. See, also, Munson Line v. Green, D.C.N.Y.1947, 6 F.R.D. 470.

1984. Record

Record on appeal from summary judgment granted plaintiff surety in action for losses allegedly suffered by it as surety on certain indemnity agreements insuring performance of government contracts failed to reveal lack of genuine issue of material fact where there was no contravention of affirmative defense of defendant who had signed certain applications either as owner or contractor or as indemnitor that surety was responsible for loss under one undertaking. Jacobson v. Maryland Cas. Co., C.A.Mo.1964, 336 F.2d 72, certiorari denied 85 S.Ct. 655, 379 U.S. 964, 13 L.Ed.2d 558.

Record on appeal from summary judgment was not deficient, and motion to dismiss appeal would be denied, where all evidence called to attention of district court on motion for summary judgment was included in record. Foley Lumber Industries, Inc. v. Buckeye Cellulose Corp., C.A.Fla.1961, 286 F.2d 697, certiorari denied 81 S.Ct. 1922, 366 U.S. 966, 6 L.Ed.2d 1257.

Rule 57. Declaratory Judgments

Text of Rule

The procedure for obtaining a declaratory judgment pursuant to Title 28, U.S.C., § 2201, shall be in accordance with these rules, and the right to trial by jury may be demanded under the circumstances and in the manner provided in Rules 38 and 39. The existence of another adequate remedy does not preclude a judgment for declaratory relief in cases where it is appropriate. The court may order a speedy hearing of an action for a declaratory judgment and may advance it on the calendar.

(As amended Dec. 29, 1948, eff. Oct. 20, 1949).

Notes of Advisory Committee on Rules

Advisory Committee Notes

The fact that a declaratory judgment may be granted "whether or not further relief is or could be prayed" indicates that declaratory relief is alternative or cumulative and not exclusive or extraordinary. A declaratory judgment is appropriate when it will "terminate the controversy" giving rise to the proceeding. Inasmuch as it often involves only an issue of law on undisputed or relatively undisputed facts, it operates frequently as a summary proceeding, justifying docketing the case for early hearing as on a motion, as provided for in California (Code Civ.Proc. (Deering, 1937) § 1062a), Michigan (3 Comp.Laws (1929) § 13904), and Kentucky (Codes (Carroll, 1932) Civ.Pract. § 639a–3).

The "controversy" must necessarily be "of a justiciable nature, thus excluding an advisory decree upon a hypothetical state of facts." Ashwander v. Tennessee Valley Authority, 1936, 56 S.Ct. 466, 297 U.S. 288, 80 L.Ed. 688. The existence or non-existence of any right, duty, power, liability, privilege, disability, or immunity or of any fact upon which

Illustration A–1

Rule 57 of the Federal Rules of Civil Procedure in the Appendix to Title 28, *U.S.C.A.*

Rule 57 **RULES OF CIVIL PROCEDURE**

such legal relations depend, or of a status, may be declared. The petitioner must have a practical interest in the declaration sought and all parties having an interest therein or adversely affected must be made parties or be cited. A declaration may not be rendered if a special statutory proceeding has been provided for the adjudication of some special type of case, but general ordinary or extraordinary legal remedies, whether regulated by statute or not, are not deemed special statutory proceedings.

When declaratory relief will not be effective in settling the controversy, the court may decline to grant it. But the fact that another remedy would be equally effective affords no ground for declining declaratory relief. The demand for relief shall state with precision the declaratory judgment desired, to which may be joined a demand for coercive relief, cumulatively or in the alternative; but when coercive relief only is sought but is deemed ungrantable, or inappropriate, the court may sua sponte, if it serves a useful purpose, grant instead a declaration of rights. Hasselbring v. Koepke, 1933, 248 N.W. 869, 263 Mich. 466, 93 A.L.R. 1170. Written instruments, including ordinances and statutes, may be construed before or after breach at the petition of a properly interested party, process being served on the private parties or public officials interested. In other respects the Uniform Declaratory Judgment Act affords a guide to the scope and function of the federal act. Compare Aetna Life Insurance Co. v. Haworth, 1937, 57 S.Ct. 461, 300 U.S. 227, 81 L.Ed. 617, 108 A.L.R. 1000; Nashville, Chattanooga & St. Louis Ry. v. Wallace, 1933, 53 S.Ct. 345, 288 U.S. 249, 77 L.Ed. 730, 87 A.L.R. 1191; Gully, Tax Collector v. Interstate Natural Gas Co., 82 F.2d 145 (C.C.A.5, 1936); Ohio Casualty Ins. Co. v. Plummer, Tex.1935, 13 F.Supp. 169; Borchard, Declaratory Judgments (1934), passim.

1948 Amendment

The Amendment effective October 1949, substituted the reference to "Title 28, U.S.C., § 2201" in the first sentence for the reference to "Section 274(d) of the Judicial Code, as amended, U.S.C., Title 28, § 400".

Amendment note

Cross References

Cross References to other rules

Answers to written interrogatories to jury, see rule 49.
Assignment of cases for trial, see rule 40.
Creation of remedy and further relief in declaratory judgment actions, see sections 2201 and 2202 of this title.
Jury trial and advisory jury, see rules 38 and 39.

Federal Practice and Procedure

References to treatise

Applicability of these rules to declaratory judgment actions, see Wright & Miller: Civil § 1616.
Declaratory judgments, see Wright & Miller: Civil § 2751 et seq.
Liberal construction of this rule, see Wright & Miller: Civil § 2755.
Precedence of declaratory judgment actions, see Wright & Miller: Civil § 2351.
Right to jury trial in declaratory judgment actions, see Wright & Miller: Civil § 2313.

West's Federal Forms

References to forms

Complaints, see § 4781 et seq.
Declaratory judgments, particular actions, see §§ 4792, 4792.5.

Library References

Reference to West topic and key number

Declaratory Judgment ⚷1 et seq. C.J.S. Declaratory Judgments § 1 et seq.

Reference to CJS

Notes of Decisions

I. **GENERALLY 1–40**
II. **CONSIDERATIONS GOVERNING RELIEF 41–80**
III. **PRACTICE AND PROCEDURE 81–135**

Generally 1–40
Actions treated as declaratory judgment 8
Adequacy of remedy, existence of other adequate remedy 46

608

Illustration A–2

Cross references following Rule 57 of the Federal Rules of Civil Procedure in the Appendix to Title 28, *U.S.C.A.*

Rule 57 RULES OF CIVIL PROCEDURE

Index to annotations

I. GENERALLY

Subdivision Index

Index to subdivision of annotations

1. Construction

These rules favor declaratory proceedings. Ohio Casualty Ins. Co. v. Richards, D.C.Or. 1939, 27 F.Supp. 18.

2. Construction with statutory provisions

Under this rule governing procedure in suits under Declaratory Judgments Act, former section 400 [now section 2201 et seq.], of this title technicalities of equity practice do not prevail. Tennessee Coal, Iron & R. Co. v. Muscoda Local No. 123, etc., C.C.A.Ala. 1943, 137 F.2d 176, affirmed 64 S.Ct. 698, 321 U.S. 590, 88 L.Ed. 949, 152 A.L.R. 1014, rehearing denied 64 S.Ct. 1257, 322 U.S. 771, 88 L.Ed. 1596.

Beginning of annotations

Former section 400 [now section 2201 et seq.] of this title furnished an additional remedy which was not to be denied because of the pendency of another suit, which view was crystallized in this rule. Dominion Electrical Mfg. Co. v. Edwin L. Wiegand Co., C.C.A. Ohio 1942, 126 F.2d 172.

Under these rules which were applicable to suits under former section 400 [now section 2201 et seq.] of this title, there was but one form of civil action, in which right of trial by jury was recognized and adequately preserved. Hargrove v. American Cent. Ins. Co., C.C.A.Okl.1942, 125 F.2d 225.

Section 2201 of this title and this rule relating to declaratory judgments are not jurisdictional and do not create a case arising under

610

Illustration A–3

Annotations following Rule 57 of the Federal Rules of Civil Procedure in the Appendix to Title 28, *U.S.C.A.*

Partial summary judgment would be granted in favor of defendant telephone company as to plaintiff's claim that defendant invaded his right of privacy in attempting to collect overdue telephone bills where record indicated little evidence would be forthcoming to support such claim, but court would leave open for trial question of alleged wrongful discontinuance of telephone service where allegations and deposition, if true, would give rise to cause of action for plaintiff. Lee v Southern Bell Tel. & Tel. Co. (1967, DC SC) 294 F Supp 1147.

On motion for summary judgment to dismiss petition of vessel owner who sought exoneration from or limitation of liability in boating accident, movant's reliance on depositions and answers to interrogatories to resolve so critical issue as owner's alleged complicity in fault that caused accident was particularly inappropriate. Petition of Klarman (1968, DC Conn) 295 F Supp 1021.

Plaintiff's cross-motion was considered, notwithstanding it was not timely served, and granted, in action for breach of fiduciary duty in operation of labor union pension plan. Morrissey v Curran (1969, DC NY) 302 F Supp 32, affd in part and revd in part on other grounds (CA2 NY) 423 F2d 393, cert den 399 US 928, 26 L Ed 2d 796, 90 S Ct 2245, and cert den 400 US 826, 27 L Ed 2d 56, 91 S Ct 52.

In action by government for failure to comply with order of the secretary of agriculture under Agricultural Marketing Agreement Act of 1937, summary judgment for plaintiff was denied, it appearing that charges that defendant had failed to make reports as required by order were specifically denied in answer. United States v Turner Milk Co. (1941, DC Ill) 1 FRD 643.

Annotations:

Summary judgment procedure in will probate or contest proceedings. 52 ALR2d 1207.

Summary judgment in mandamus or prohibition cases. 3 ALR3d 675.

Rule 57. Declaratory Judgments

Text of Rule

The procedure for obtaining a declaratory judgment pursuant to Title 28, USC, § 2201, shall be in accordance with these rules, and the right to trial by jury may be demanded under the circumstances and in the manner provided in Rules 38 and 39. The existence of another adequate remedy does not preclude a judgment for declaratory relief in cases where it is appropriate. The court may order a speedy hearing of an action for a declaratory judgment and may advance it on the calendar.

NOTES OF ADVISORY COMMITTEE ON RULES

Advisory Committee Notes

The fact that a declaratory judgment may be granted "whether or not further relief is or could be prayed" indicates that declaratory relief is alternative or cumulative and not exclusive or extraordinary. A declaratory judgment is appropriate when it will "terminate the controversy" giving rise to the proceeding. Inasmuch as it often involves only an issue of law on undisputed or relatively undisputed facts, it operates frequently as a summary proceeding, justifying docketing the case for early hearing as on a motion, as provided for in California (Code Civ Proc (Deering, 1937) § 1062a), Michigan (3 Comp Laws (1929) § 13904), and Kentucky (Codes (Carroll, 1932) Civ Pract § 639a-3).

The "controversy" must necessarily be "of a justiciable nature, thus excluding an advisory decree upon a hypothetical state of facts." Ashwander v Tennessee Valley Authority, 297 US 288, 325, 56 S Ct 466, 473, 80 L Ed 688, 699 (1936). The existence or nonexistence of any right, duty, power, liability, privilege, disability, or immunity or of any fact upon which such legal relations depend, or of a status, may be declared. The petitioner must have a practical interest in the declaration sought and all parties having an interest therein or adversely affected must be made parties or be cited. A declaration may not be rendered if a special statutory proceeding has been provided for the adjudication of some special type of case, but general

Illustration B–1

Rule 57 of the Federal Rules of Civil Procedure in the "Court Rules" volumes of *USCS*.

DECLARATORY JUDGMENTS **Rule 57**

ordinary or extraordinary legal remedies, whether regulated by statute or not, are not deemed special statutory proceedings.

When declaratory relief will not be effective in settling the controversy, the court may decline to grant it. But the fact that another remedy would be equally effective affords no ground for declining declaratory relief. The demand for relief shall state with precision the declaratory judgment desired, to which may be joined a demand for coercive relief, cumulatively or in the alternative; but when coercive relief only is sought but is deemed ungrantable or inappropriate, the court may sua sponte, if it serves a useful purpose, grant instead a declaration of rights. Hasselbring v Koepke, 263 Mich 466, 248 NW 869, 93 ALR 1170 (1933). Written instruments, including ordinances and statutes, may be construed before or after breach at the petition of a properly interested party, process being served on the private parties or public officials interested. In other respects the Uniform Declaratory Judgment Act affords a guide to the scope and function of the Federal act. Compare Aetna Life Insurance Co. v Haworth, 300 US 227, 57 S Ct 461, 81 L Ed 617, 108 ALR 1000 (1937); Nashville, Chattanooga & St. Louis Ry. v Wallace, 288 US 249, 53 S Ct 345, 77 L Ed 730, 87 ALR 1191 (1933); Gully, Tax Collector v Interstate Natural Gas Co. 82 F2d 145 (CCA 5th, 1936); Ohio Casualty Ins. Co. v Plummer, 13 F Supp 169 (SD Tex, 1935); Borchard, Declaratory Judgments (1934), passim.

Amendment note

NOTES OF ADVISORY COMMITTEE ON 1949 AMENDMENTS TO RULES

1948—The amendment effective October 1949 substituted the reference to "Title 28, USC, § 2201" in the first sentence for the reference to "Section 274(d) of the Judicial Code, as amended, USC, Title 28, § 400."

Cross References to other rules

CROSS REFERENCES

Jury trial and advisory jury, Rules 38 and 39.
Assignment of cases for trial, Rule 40.
Federal Declaratory Judgment Act, 28 USCS §§ 2201, 2202.

RESEARCH GUIDE

References to *Am Jur 2d*

Am Jur:
22 Am Jur 2d, Declaratory Judgments §§ 14, 96.
32 Am Jur 2d, Federal Practice and Procedure § 423.

References to forms

Forms:
Complaint for interpleader and declaratory relief, Appendix, Form 18.
11 Am Jur Pl & Pr Forms (Rev ed), Federal Practice and Procedure, Forms 1931–1939.

References to *ALR* annotations

Annotations:
Validity, construction, and application of criminal statutes, or ordinances as proper subject for declaratory judgment. 10 ALR3d 727.
Jury trial in action for declaratory relief. 13 ALR2d 777.

Reference to law review article

Law Review Articles:
Right to trial by jury in declaratory judgment actions. 3 Conn L Rev 564.

137

Illustration B–2

Cross references following Rule 57 of the Federal Rules of Civil Procedure in the "Court Rules" volumes of *USCS*.

Rule 57 **RULES OF CIVIL PROCEDURE**

Index to annotations

Annotations

INTERPRETIVE NOTES AND DECISIONS

1. Generally
2. When relief is appropriate
3. —Discretion of court
4. —Existence of controversy
5. —Effectiveness of decree in settling controversy
6. Jurisdiction
7. Parties; who may bring suit
8. —Class actions
9. Availability of other adequate remedies
10. Pendency of other proceedings
11. —Pendency of state court action
12. Coercive or injunctive relief
13. Damages
14. Counterclaim
15. —For declaratory relief
16. Jury trial
17. —Antitrust cases
18. —Insurance cases
19. —Patent cases
20. Speedy hearing; advancement on calendar

1. Generally

An action for declaratory judgment is not an action for equitable relief, but rather a statutory remedy, the procedure under which is fixed by these rules. Mutual Life Ins. Co. v Krejci (1941, CA7 Ill) 123 F2d 594; Hargrove v American Cent. Ins. Co. (1942, CA10 Okla) 125 F2d 225.

Technicalities of equity practice do not prevail in proceedings under Federal Declaratory Judgments Act [28 USCS §§ 2201, 2202]. Tennessee C., I. & R. Co. v Muscoda Local No. 123, etc. (1943, CA5 Ala) 137 F2d 176.

In action by insurer brought in federal district court in Michigan for a declaratory judgment of nonexistence of a claimed automobile liability insurance policy covering an automobile operated by defendant at the time it was involved in an accident with three other defendants and under which some of the defendants had instituted damage actions in Michigan state courts, whether or not declaratory relief could be granted on the complaint was a matter of procedure governed by federal and not state declaratory judgment law; and it was held that such relief could be granted. New Amsterdam Casualty Co. v Berger (1945, DC Mich) 59 F Supp 994.

2. When relief is appropriate

In federal action seeking both declaratory and injunctive relief on ground that state statute is unconstitutional on its face, federal district court has duty to decide appropriateness and merits of the declaratory request irrespective of its conclusion as to propriety of issuance of the injunction. Zwickler v Koota (1967) 389 US 241, 19 L Ed 2d 444, 88 S Ct 391.

Only sentence known to law is sentence appearing on record; therefore, proper remedy where mistake in execution of sentence is made is not mandamus or declaratory judgment, but is petition to court entering sentence for correction. Clark v Memolo (1949) 85 App DC 65, 174 F2d 978.

District court improperly rendered declaratory judgment as to which of two occupants of an airplane was its pilot at the time it crashed, where the action was brought by the liability insurer of the airplane because it was apparently of the view that such determination would also determine which estate of those two persons it was obligated to defend and by the terms of its policy, the insurer was obligated to defend both. Maryland Casualty Co. v Rosen (1971, CA2 Vt) 445 F2d 1012.

An action for declaratory judgment will lie to determine the scope of the matters to be submitted to arbitration pursuant to an arbitration agreement. Lehigh Coal & Nav. Co. v Central R. Co. (1940, DC Pa) 33 F Supp 362.

An action for a declaratory judgment is the proper remedy to be invoked by an insured under a fire policy to determine as to whether insurer had waived its right to examine insured under the provisions of the policy. American Macaroni Mfg. Co. v Niagara Fire Ins. Co. (1942, DC Ala) 43 F Supp 933, affd (CA5 Ala) 164 F2d 878.

Federal district court was competent to adjudicate in a declaratory judgment suit by two railroads against a brotherhood and named individuals the alternative issue that neither of plaintiffs by signing agreements amending or interpreting contract apportioning work at a terminal became liable to individual defendants for the damages which any of them might sustain by reason of the execution of said agreement amending said contract. Texas & P. R. Co. v Brotherhood of R. Trainmen (1945, DC La) 60 F Supp 263.

Where a foreign executor files suit to enforce a sales contract of securities by beneficiary of trust, he would be seeking declaratory judgment although not specially pleaded. Becker v Buder (1949, DC Mo) 88 F Supp 609, affd (CA8 Mo) 185 F2d 311.

3. —Discretion of court

If a multiplicity of suits are undertaken to harass the government or to delay enforcement of a federal regulation, declaratory relief can be denied on this ground alone. Abbott Laborator-

138

Illustration B–3

Annotations following Rule 57 of the Federal Rules of Civil Procedure in the "Court Rules" volumes of *USCS*.

L Ed 2d DESK BOOK

FEDERAL RULES OF CIVIL PROCEDURE

	Vol. and page
Rule 1	3 L Ed 2d 988, 1275; 8 L Ed 2d 510
Rule 2	3 L Ed 2d 988, 1275
Rule 4(d)	11 L Ed 2d 354
Rule 4(d)(1)	14 L Ed 2d 8
Rule 6(a)	15 L Ed 2d 26
Rule 6(b)	4 L Ed 2d 259
Rule 6(c)	1 L Ed 2d 683
Rule 7(c)	8 L Ed 2d 240
Rule 8	1 L Ed 2d 465; 3 L Ed 2d 988
Rule 8(c)	28 L Ed 2d 77, 788; 43 L Ed 2d 482
Rule 8(f)	2 L Ed 2d 80; 20 L Ed 2d 982
Rule 11	8 L Ed 2d 211; 15 L Ed 2d 807
Rule 12(b)(6)	44 L Ed 2d 15
Rule 12(c)	3 L Ed 2d 368
Rule 12(d)	3 L Ed 2d 368
Rule 13(a)	3 L Ed 2d 988; 9 L Ed 2d 31
Rule 15	1 L Ed 2d 1527; 5 L Ed 2d 8
Rule 15(a)	9 L Ed 2d 222; 28 L Ed 2d 77
Rule 15(d)	48 L Ed 2d 478
Rule 16	5 L Ed 2d 8
Rule 17(b)	11 L Ed 2d 945
Rule 18	3 L Ed 2d 988, 1275; 8 L Ed 2d 44
Rule 19	19 L Ed 2d 936
Rule 19(a)	22 L Ed 2d 99
Rule 20(a)	13 L Ed 2d 717
Rule 21	1 L Ed 2d 1525
Rule 22(1)	18 L Ed 2d 270
Rule 23	22 L Ed 2d 319; 42 L Ed 2d 532; 43 L Ed 2d 54, 74; 47 L Ed 2d 444, 810; 48 L Ed 2d 478; 49 L Ed 2d 599
Rule 23(b)	1 L Ed 2d 1221; 15 L Ed 2d 807
Rule 24(a)	15 L Ed 2d 272; 17 L Ed 2d 814; 27 L Ed 2d 580; 30 L Ed 2d 686
Rule 24(a)(2)	6 L Ed 2d 604
Rule 24(b)	15 L Ed 2d 272
Rule 26	4 L Ed 2d 1462
Rule 26(b)	13 L Ed 2d 152
Rule 26(b)(3)	45 L Ed 2d 141
Rule 30(b)	13 L Ed 2d 152
Rule 33	22 L Ed 2d 281; 25 L Ed 2d 1
Rule 34	2 L Ed 2d 1077, 1255
Rule 35	13 L Ed 2d 152
Rule 37	2 L Ed 2d 1255; 48 L Ed 2d 725
Rule 37(a)	8 L Ed 2d 21
Rule 37(b)	2 L Ed 2d 1077; 49 L Ed 2d 747
Rule 38(a)	3 L Ed 2d 988; 8 L Ed 2d 44
Rule 38(b)	3 L Ed 2d 988
Rule 39(a)	3 L Ed 2d 988; 8 L Ed 2d 21
Rule 41(b)	2 L Ed 2d 1255; 5 L Ed 2d 551; 8 L Ed 2d 734; 15 L Ed 2d 807
Rule 42(b)	3 L Ed 2d 988; 24 L Ed 2d 729
Rule 45(e)	13 L Ed 2d 248
Rule 50(c)	18 L Ed 2d 75
Rule 51(d)	12 L Ed 2d 256; 18 L Ed 2d 581
Rule 52(a)	1 L Ed 2d 1057; 3 L Ed 2d 270; 4 L Ed 2d 169, 505, 1218; 5 L Ed 2d 592; 10 L Ed 2d 829; 14 L Ed 2d 640; 16 L Ed 2d 415; 23 L Ed 2d 129; 42 L Ed 2d 498; 43 L Ed 2d 712; 45 L Ed 2d 41
Rule 53	46 L Ed 2d 483
Rule 53(b)	1 L Ed 2d 290; 8 L Ed 2d 44
Rule 53(e)	11 L Ed 2d 629
Rule 54(a)	2 L Ed 2d 721
Rule 54(b)	47 L Ed 2d 435
Rule 54(c)	45 L Ed 2d 280
Rule 54(d)	13 L Ed 2d 248
Rule 56	3 L Ed 2d 368; 4 L Ed 2d 826; 9 L Ed 2d 738; 20 L Ed 2d 569
Rule 56(c)	3 L Ed 2d 368; 8 L Ed 2d 176; 26 L Ed 2d 142
Rule 56(e)	20 L Ed 2d 569; 26 L Ed 2d 142
Rule 56(f)	20 L Ed 2d 569; 26 L Ed 2d 142
Rule 57	13 L Ed 2d 249
Rule 58	2 L Ed 2d 721, 806
Rule 59(e)	9 L Ed 2d 222
Rule 60(a)	3 L Ed 2d 172
Rule 60(b)	5 L Ed 2d 173; 8 L Ed 2d 734; 9 L Ed 2d 222; 18 L Ed 2d 75; 44 L Ed 2d 317; 50 L Ed 2d 21
Rule 61	11 L Ed 2d 4; 12 L Ed 2d 206
Rule 62(d)	17 L Ed 2d 37
Rule 65	49 L Ed 2d 599
Rule 65(d)	43 L Ed 2d 712
Rule 71A	3 L Ed 2d 1163, 1275; 9 L Ed 2d 350
Rule 71A(h)	11 L Ed 2d 629; 25 L Ed 2d 12
Rule 73(a)	2 L Ed 2d 721, 806; 9 L Ed 2d 261; 11 L Ed 2d 389, 636; 15 L Ed 2d 26
Rule 73(d)	17 L Ed 2d 37
Rule 79(a)	2 L Ed 2d 721
Rule 81(a)(1)	4 L Ed 2d 1462
Rule 81(a)(2)	22 L Ed 2d 281; 44 L Ed 2d 317
Rule 83	2 L Ed 2d 496; 8 L Ed 2d 734

174

Illustration C

Table in *Lawyers' Edition Desk Book,* providing references to decisions in *Lawyers' Edition* on the federal rules.

The text of the Rules of Civil Procedure and Appellate Procedure can also be found in the "Finding Aids" volume of Callaghan's *Federal Rules Service,* a very useful source for research on procedural and court rules, and for judicial decisions relating to the rules. This set, now in its second series, provides a *full text* reporting service for all court decisions interpreting the Rules of *Civil* Procedure, and decided since 1938, and decisions interpreting the Rules of *Appellate* Procedure since 1968. Digests of these cases, arranged according to "Findex" numbers based on official rule numbers, and points of editorial analysis, are found in the accompanying *Federal Rules Digest* (2nd ed., covering the years 1938–1954; 3rd ed., 1954–date). Finding aids to the *Digest* include a subject index and table of cases.

This popular set also contains the individual local rules of the various lower federal courts, which will be discussed below.

Another useful source of primary source material relating to federal rules is West's *Federal Rules Decisions (FRD),* which began publication in 1940 as an offshoot of the *Federal Supplement* and the *Federal Reporter.*[4] This unit of the National Reporter System includes the text of U.S. District Court decisions that construe the Rules of Civil and Criminal Procedure, as well as relevant articles, speeches and the proceedings of judicial conferences. Like other West reporters, *FRD* appears first in advance sheets which then cumulate into bound volumes. Both the advance sheets and the bound volumes contain all of the standard finding aids included in other West reporters.

In addition to the Rules of Civil and Criminal Procedure and Appellate Procedure, we should also note here the Federal Rules of Evidence, which were enacted by Congress in 1974, and approved by the President in 1975.[5] The Federal Rules of Evidence were designed as a substitute for the many chaotic and contradictory local rules of evidence, to bring greater uniformity to federal trial procedure. The Rules of Evidence also appear in an appendix to Title 28 of the *U.S. Code,* and, with annotations, as an appendix to Title 28 in both the *USCA* and *USCS.*

As noted above, the lower federal courts are empowered to issue their own rules governing local practice, provided these local rules do not conflict with the pronouncements of the Supreme Court. These local federal court rules are frequently issued as separate pamphlets by the individual courts, but because the pamphlets are not widely distributed and soon become out of date, the single best source of these rules is the "Local Rules" volume of the *Federal Rules Service.* It collects in one place the local rules of all the U.S. Courts of Appeals and District Courts. The looseleaf format of the "Local Rules" volume of the *Federal Rules Service* allows for frequent supplementation.

4. *Federal Rules Decisions* includes cases on the Federal Rules of Civil Procedure decided since 1939, and cases on the Federal Rules of Criminal Procedure decided since 1946.

5. Public Law 93–595, 88 Stat. 1926, 28 U.S.C., Appendix.

2. SECONDARY SOURCES

The technical nature of the various federal rules and their importance in legal practice has led to the development of a number of excellent commentaries on the rules. These include two comprehensive treatises by distinguished scholars in the fields of federal courts and procedure. They are *Moore's Federal Practice* (Matthew Bender), looseleaf, and Wright and Miller, *Federal Practice and Procedure* (West, 1969–1982, with annual pocket part supplements). These multi-volume treatises include commentary on the rules, an analysis of practice under the rules, copious footnotes, forms, detailed indexing and other finding aids. Both sets are kept current by regular supplementation.

When the Federal Rules of Evidence were enacted, one of the principal drafters, Judge Jack B. Weinstein, produced a multi-volume treatise that explained the intent of the various provisions of the Federal Rules of Evidence. Since 1975, this set has been continued under the joint authorship of Weinstein and M. A. Berger, as *Weinstein's Evidence: Commentary on Rules of Evidence for the United States Courts and Magistrates* (M. Bender, 1975–19__). It presently consists of eight looseleaf volumes and includes a table of cases, author/title index, subject index, and table of statutes and rules.

In 1982, the Lawyers Co-op inaugurated a new encyclopedia on procedure. The set, entitled *Federal Procedure, Lawyers' Edition,* is still being issued and, when completed, will consist of eighty chapters. Those volumes issued so far contain discussion of practice under the rules, and extensive topical articles. There are also checklists, synopses of law review articles and the text of related statutes. The set also contains references to its companion set, *Federal Procedural Forms, Lawyers' Edition,* and to other units of the Lawyers Co-op Total Client-Service Library. A general index, tables, and such useful items as a state/federal rules comparator are included as well.

C. STATE COURT RULES

1. PRIMARY SOURCES

The forms of publication of court rules on the state level vary from state to state. The promulgation of state court rules sometimes involves legislative action and, in those instances, rules are issued as part of the state's annotated statutory code. In other instances, when they are promulgated by the judiciary alone, they may be contained only in elusive pamphlets or published in the state reports. Some states which publish codes of administrative regulations include in those codes the court rules in that state.[6]

6. For example, New York's *Official Compilation of Codes, Rules and Regulations,* vol. 22 (looseleaf).

Lower court rules in some states are among the most difficult to locate and sometimes they are only available from the office of the clerk of the court. However, in virtually every state for which West publishes an annotated statutory code, as well as others, they also issue an annual paperback edition of the rules of the state courts and the federal courts sitting in that state.

Although it is now somewhat out of date, the following bibliographic survey of sources of court rules may be helpful in determining the publications in individual states: S. Blau & T. P. Clark, "Sources of Rules of State Courts", 66 *Law Library J.* 37–58 (1973).

2. SECONDARY SOURCES

State practice manuals and procedural aids, containing such material as the text of court rules, commentaries on the rules, annotations of recent court decisions, and model forms keyed to the rules, are separately published in several states. Some of the larger states have two or more competing publications of this kind. The best of these are supplemented regularly, either with looseleaf filings, pocket parts, or complete annual revisions. They provide useful, up-to-date information regarding the local rules of practice, and are essential tools for the lawyer's daily work.

Moller and Horton's *Connecticut Practice—Practice Book Annotated* (West, 2d ed., 1979 & Supp.), for example, is a 3-volume compilation of Connecticut state court rules and forms along with the authors' commentaries and citations to pertinent judicial opinions. The *Connecticut Practice Book* (1979), published by the Commission on Official Legal Publications, is a 2-volume looseleaf set which contains the rules, annotations, and forms. The *New York Standard Civil Practice Service Desk Book* (Lawyers' Co-op, 1982) performs a similar function for N.Y. court rules, annotating the rules with case notes and references to treatises. Also available for that state is the *New York Civil Practice Annual* (Matthew Bender), and the annual *New York CPLR Redbook* (Matthew Bender), which contains the rules of practice along with judicial conference notes and statutory cross references.

D. SHEPARDIZING COURT RULES

1. FEDERAL

The current status and judicial treatment of all federal procedural rules and federal court rules can be ascertained by using *Shepard's United States Citations—Statutes* unit. Shepard's covers the various federal rules shown in Illustration D below, in separate sections of that unit. Each rule is treated in the same manner as are statutes, indicating any amendment to or repeal of the rule itself, as well as any citations to the rule in federal decisions, Annotations in one of the annotated reporters, or in an *American Bar Association Journal* article. See Illustration E. As when Shepardizing a federal statute, the researcher should also check the appropriate Shepard's *state* unit to find state court citations to a federal rule. Citations to the court rule in law reviews and legal periodicals can be found in *Shepard's Federal Law Citations in Selected Law Reviews.*

CITATIONS TO COURT RULES

—— FEDERAL ——

Shepard's compiles citations to the following federal court rules in Shepard's United States Citations – Statutes:

Rules of the Supreme Court of the United States
Rules of Bankruptcy Procedure
Rules of Practice in Admiralty and Maritime Cases
Federal Rules of Appellate Procedure
Rules of the United States Courts of Appeals
Revised General Rules of the Temporary Emergency Court of Appeals
Rules of the Judicial Panel on Multidistrict Litigation
Rules of Procedure for the Trial of Minor Offenses before United States Magistrates
Rules of Civil Procedure for the United States District Courts
Rules of Criminal Procedure for the United States District Courts
Federal Rules of Evidence
Rules of the United States District Courts
Rules of the United States Court of Claims
Rules of the United States Court of Customs and Patent Appeals
Rules of Practice before the United States Tax Court

as cited in

United States Supreme Court Reports
Lawyers' Edition, United States Supreme Court Reports
Supreme Court Reporter
Federal Reporter
Federal Supplement
Federal Rules Decisions
American Bar Association Journal

and in annotations of

Lawyers' Edition, United States Supreme Court Reports
American Law Reports
American Law Reports, Federal

Citations to a federal court rule as cited by state courts may be obtained by referring to the appropriate Shepard state edition.

Additional citations to a federal court rule as cited in law reviews and legal periodicals may be obtained by referring to Shepard's Federal Law Citations in Selected Law Reviews.

Illustration D

Coverage of Federal procedural rules and court rules in *Shepard's U.S. Citations—Statutes,* from *How to Use Shepard's Citations.*

2. STATES

Citations to *state* court rules are found in the statute sections of Shepard's state citator units. Changes in a rule itself as well as citations to it in federal court decisions, state court decisions, state Attorney General opinions, selected law reviews, and *ALR* Annotations are noted. See Illustration F for a typical page in a Shepard's state statutory citator, covering court rules.

RULES OF CIVIL PROCEDURE, UNITED STATES DISTRICT COURTS **Rule 37**

41FRD451
41FRD531
42FRD3
42FRD8
42FRD13
42FRD40
42FRD390
42FRD425
42FRD641
43FRD182
43FRD368
43FRD404
43FRD506
43FRD527
44FRD5
44FRD17
44FRD239
44FRD432
44FRD436
44FRD465
44FRD476
44FRD561
45FRD41
45FRD240
45FRD274
45FRD363
45FRD366
45FRD433
45FRD495
45FRD521
46FRD29
46FRD57
46FRD429
46FRD472
46FRD484
46FRD623
47FRD58
47FRD221
47FRD364
47FRD371
47FRD574
48FRD30
48FRD342
48FRD404
48FRD433
49FRD128
49FRD144
49FRD175
49FRD295
50FRD128
50FRD136
50FRD151
50FRD165
50FRD422
51FRD236
51FRD297
51FRD498
51FRD500
52FRD15
52FRD238
52FRD530
53FRD248
53FRD301
53FRD484
54FRD478
54FRD483
54FRD532
55FRD61
55FRD347
55FRD354
55FRD461
55FRD471
56FRD434
56FRD570

56FRD618
58FRD54
59FRD132
59FRD387
56ABA568
37A21152s
88A2657s
13A3822s
13A3826n
13A31316n
13A31327n
18A3924n
19A31116n
19A31137n
19A31138n
19A31144n
21A3920n
38A31113n
44A3105n
47A3705n
8ARF54n
8ARF76n
13ARF262n

Subd. a

468F2d470
472F2d564
477F2d146
481F2d1204
482F2d825
483F2d303
50FRD82
50FRD151
51FRD245
52FRD112
52FRD508
53FRD247
53FRD320
55FRD338
57FRD475
74A2534s

Subd. b

483F2d303
302FS2
319FS912
336FS310
357FS944
54FRD68
56FRD12
59FRD278
59FRD501

Subd. c

483F2d307
51FRD312
52FRD290
53FRD87
55FRD42
55FRD354
59FRD133
59FRD546
96A2598s

Rule 34

A398US997
372F2d626
373F2d645
374F2d443
379F2d615
380F2d277
388F2d215
388F2d290
392F2d687
398F2d67
402F2d135

403F2d120
404F2d1066
405F2d99
406F2d1086
410F2d188
414F2d119
415F2d777
418F2d148
418F2d633
419F2d956
422F2d470
423F2d490
425F2d24
426F2d223
427F2d578
430F2d221
432F2d697
434F2d70
437F2d703
441F2d577
443F2d257
443F2d912
262FS40
262FS148
264FS573
264FS734
265FS655
266FS35
266FS182
267FS333
268FS769
268FS1011
271FS456
275FS146
277FS319
278FS554
278FS915
283FS1
284FS372
285FS912
287FS375
288FS708
291FS248
291FS282
293FS1230
296FS979
303FS914
304FS1041
308FS400
313FS368
313FS1108
313FS1361
314FS236
319FS715
328FS729
41FRD2
41FRD51
41FRD153
41FRD177
41FRD209
41FRD225
41FRD230
41FRD234
41FRD266
41FRD290
41FRD294
41FRD359
41FRD452
41FRD518
42FRD13
42FRD40
42FRD348
42FRD587
42FRD648
42FRD657

43FRD1
43FRD12
43FRD166
43FRD205
43FRD282
43FRD308
43FRD369
43FRD404
43FRD416
43FRD508
43FRD523
43FRD527
44FRD8
44FRD10
44FRD33
44FRD429
44FRD457
44FRD464
44FRD539
45FRD31
45FRD254
45FRD270
45FRD288
45FRD384
45FRD465
45FRD492
46FRD3
46FRD7
46FRD28
46FRD96
47FRD54
47FRD67
47FRD263
47FRD279
47FRD362
47FRD373
47FRD525
47FRD533
48FRD30
48FRD304
48FRD306
48FRD319
48FRD365
49FRD24
49FRD30
49FRD54
49FRD68
49FRD77
49FRD82
49FRD95
49FRD127
49FRD137
49FRD150
49FRD271
49FRD300
50FRD4
50FRD38
50FRD129
50FRD136
50FRD182
50FRD185
50FRD211
50FRD271
50FRD282
50FRD287
50FRD379
50FRD382
50FRD385
50FRD491
52FRD536
54FRD368
56ABA569
13LE992s
73A212s

98A2241s
13A3826n
19A31137n
19A31141n
20A2764n
38A31113n
44A344n
44A3113n
47A3702n
4ARF514n
7ARF864n
7ARF884n
8ARF54n
8ARF84n
12ARF943n
15ARF448n

Subd. 1

268FS773
50FRD249

Subd. 2

45FRD377

Rule 34

(398US997)
450F2d1000
459F2d303
468F2d469
472F2d47
476F2d1
480F2d624
483F2d1147
321FS2
336FS434
336FS942
348FS1241
349FS129
349FS1402
350FS1297
352FS287
355FS281
355FS543
358FS494
51FRD162
51FRD313
52FRD367
53FRD284
53FRD317
53FRD486
53FRD605
54FRD221
54FRD359
54FRD483
54FRD532
54FRD552
54FRD586
55FRD61
55FRD147
55FRD346
55FRD553
56FRD126
56FRD643
56FRD631
57FRD204
58FRD53
58FRD216
58FRD352
59FRD157
59FRD348
59FRD387
59FRD549
59FRD638
13A3657s
73A312s
74A2876s
83A2302s

95A21061s
97A3770s
47A3682n
47A3687n
13ARF262n
16ARF369n

Subd. a

349FS127
54FRD369
58FRD349

Subd. b

333FS536
353FS614
54FRD528
58FRD97
58FRD349
47A3686n

Rule 35

A398US999
389US105
19LE316
88SC278
372F2d718
430F2d1351
452F2d485
283FS862
309FS1234
331FS1074
41FRD153
41FRD225
41FRD452
42FRD388
42FRD397
42FRD591
43FRD502
43FRD525
46FRD427
47FRD54
47FRD212
50FRD75
53ABA267
54ABA173
13LE992s
46A21000s
86A2138s
95A2320s
18A31438n
21A3912s
33A31014n
46A3547n
15ARF448n

Subd. a

380F2d277
386F2d692
434F2d1195
441F2d1103
361FS961
42FRD387
49FRD308
53FRD590
13LE992s

Subd. b

13LE992s
36A3946s
70A3384s

¶ 1

13LE992s
21A3914n
25A31402n
33A31014n
44A340n

¶ 2

438F2d1317

309FS1234
13LE992s
36A3946s
21A3914n
25A31401s
25A31402n
33A31014n
44A340n

¶ 3

82A21162s

Rule 36

A398US [1000
372F2d626
391F2d903
416F2d1149
417F2d1135
422F2d639
427F2d578
440F2d935
454F2d81
463F2d968
472F2d315
261FS222
261FS790
262FS42
262FS860
270FS534
271FS625
271FS798
311FS753
313FS852
319FS1348
330FS737
333FS727
333FS733
333FS737
349FS437
354FS77
358FS494
360FS123
360FS267
361FS316
41FRD33
41FRD47
42FRD338
43FRD369
44FRD432
45FRD122
45FRD499
45FRD534
48FRD88
49FRD144
49FRD181
52FRD235
53FRD164
54FRD483
55FRD471
56FRD452
56FRD618
57FRD121
58FRD53
58FRD129
36A31192s
93A2757s
20A3756s
2ARF814n

Subd. a

413F2d1391
473F2d1360
261FS239
280FS298
349FS450
55FRD471

57FRD121
36A31192s
93A2757s
20A3757n

¶ 1

49FRD181

Subd. b

427F2d581
473F2d1360
360FS123
42FRD395

Rule 37

A398US [1002
373F2d645
374F2d810
376F2d118
380F2d550
396F2d794
398F2d67
403F2d120
417F2d1135
422F2d470
427F2d1120
438F2d186
441F2d816
443F2d10
446F2d712
449F2d51
450F2d1000
457F2d1307
458F2d395
463F2d968
463F2d973
466F2d254
470F2d778
471F2d521
473F2d333
477F2d819
478F2d720
480F2d294
480F2d624
262FS43
266FS93
278FS887
281FS638
297FS1171
302FS2
303FS517
313FS224
314FS1122
331FS798
339FS942
341FS1154
346FS1357
348FS1187
349FS127
353FS402
357FS802
357FS944
358FS494
362FS1186
41FRD452
42FRD425
43FRD369
43FRD416
45FRD24
45FRD491
49FRD127
49FRD128
50FRD49
50FRD129
50FRD503
Continued

See note on first page of this division. See 1968 Bound Volume for earlier citations 557

Rule amended

Cited by Federal Courts

Cited in *A.B.A. Journal*

Cited in *ALR* Annotations

Illustration E

Shepard's treatment of the Federal Rules of Civil Procedure in its *U.S. Citations—Statutes.*

CONNECTICUT COURT RULES

Form 363
87CBJ 281
Form 364
87CBJ 258
Forms 384 to 386
148Ct 184
169A2d 652
Form 395
155Ct329
231A2d527
4Cir16
224A2d 568
Form 398
152Ct511
208A2d 753
Form 399
25CS120
197A2d 661
Form 402
159Ct427
270A2d546
Form 406
269A2d295
Form 409
153Ct598
219A2d723
Form 426
25CS 255
202A2d 248
Form 434
A June 26, [1972
Form 440
25CS 286
203A2d 85
Form 445
25CS 286
203A2d 85
Form 448
Subd. 5
AdSept.1, [1971
Form 450
27CS404
240A2d574

27CS411
240A2d920
Form 456
A June 3, [1968
27CS404
240A2d574
27CS410
240A2d920
Form 457
148Ct 339
170A2d 732
Form 475
4Cir635
238A2d446
Form 490
A June1, [1970
Form 490A
AdJune1, [1970
Form 493
158Ct374
260A2d596
Form 499
159Ct427
270A2d546
Form 512
155Ct330
231A2d529
156Ct14
238A2d406

Rules for the Supreme Court of Errors
(Practice Book, 1963)
§§ 600 to **729**
45CBJ115
§ 600
151Ct 177
195A2d418
152Ct 168
204A2d837
152Ct 366
207A2d 55
153Ct55
212A2d417
155Ct619
236A2d460
155Ct655
236A2d900
156Ct270
240A2d896
158Ct314
259A2d611
159Ct606
268A2d371
23CS 334
182A2d 922
23CS 477
184A2d 676
24CS 24
186A2d 384
24CS 60
186A2d 562
1Cir225
1Cir325
1Cir363
1Cir396
2Cir 325
198A2d 731
2Cir 635
204A2d 170
3Cir 133
208A2d 762
4Cir187
230A2d619
5Cir14
240A2d220
5Cir201
248A2d588
5Cir334
252A2d141
§ 601
AJune3, [1970
148Ct 222
169A2d 639
149Ct 657

183A2d 276
150Ct 566
192A2d 46
150Ct688
185A2d 475
151Ct92
193A2d 473
152Ct 466
208A2d 541
154Ct634
228A2d134
155Ct593
236A2d910
157Ct401
254A2d571
158Ct488
264A2d576
23CS 403
184A2d 66
28CS465
265A2d718
1Cir269
200FS 915
37CBJ 358
39CBJ251
43CBJ117
§ 602
154Ct634
228A2d134
§ 603
A June3, [1970
A June 26, [1972
154Ct634
228A2d132
155Ct719
231A2d283
160Ct338
278A2d812
4Cir571
237A2d105
5Cir42
241A2d202
37CBJ 358
39CBJ251
§ 604
149Ct 430
180A2d 640
151Ct 261
196A2d597
155Ct692
229A2d548
158Ct257
259A2d598
2Cir 325
198A2d 731
43CBJ117
§ 605
151Ct 287
197A2d69
153Ct55
212A2d417

§ 606
148Ct302
170A2d 269
149Ct548
182A2d 617
149Ct 700
183A2d 604
153Ct453
217A2d692
153Ct496
217A2d713
153Ct696
220A2d274
155Ct726
234A2d449
156Ct109
239A2d479
156Ct506
242A2d706
156Ct511
244A2d386
157Ct46
245A2d568
157Ct460
254A2d871
161Ct580
290A2d326
4Cir605
238A2d436
5Cir243
250A2d347
268A2d683
291A2d736
294A2d549
§ 607
150Ct 382
190A2d 34
150Ct688
185A2d 475
160Ct262
278A2d792
294A2d545
§ 608A
AdJune3, [1969
161Ct605
284A2d131
45CBJ40
§ 609
150Ct346
189A2d 395
151Ct31
193A2d 484
151Ct 409
198A2d 704
151Ct 464
199A2d 698
151Ct 710
200A2d 487
153Ct258
216A2d202
153Ct587
219A2d448
153Ct703
220A2d450

153Ct714
216A2d182
154Ct222
224A2d 547
154Ct248
224A2d 732
154Ct672
228A2d508
155Ct247
230A2d600
155Ct655
236A2d900
156Ct552
244A2d410
160Ct556
274A2d451
4Cir415
233A2d707
5Cir389
254A2d506
294A2d70
321FS415
41CBJ495
§ 611
152Ct698
204A2d410
§ 612
150Ct687
185A2d 475
152Ct704
206A2d482
161Ct521
290A2d351
§ 613 et seq.
321FS415
§ 613
150Ct 243
188A2d 59
159Ct358
269A2d268
24CS 374
190A2d 920
1Cir607
§ 614
154Ct412
226A2d395
155Ct8
229A2d358
§ 615
149Ct 20
175A2d 364
157Ct323
254A2d461
3Cir300
213A2d228
§ 616
159Ct624
264A2d13
159Ct625
264A2d12
160Ct585
273A2d288

See 1962 Bound Volume, Statute Edition for earlier citations

666

Rule amended

Rule cited by State courts

Rule cited in Conn. Bar Journal

Illustration F

Sample page in *Shepard's Connecticut Citations—Statutes,* showing treatment of court rules.

E. SUMMARY

As we have seen, access to court rules, both federal and state, is available in a variety of sources. The most useful forms of publication are those which provide commentary and citations to court decisions interpreting and applying the rules. Some of these publications also include legal forms keyed to their text, or are supplemented by sets of formbooks for use with the rules. Formbooks in general will be discussed in Chapter 15 below, but the importance of forms for use with court rules can be noted here.

The extensive literature of practice books and manuals is also closely related to court rules. Practice books describe the procedure to be followed in litigation and usually include the rules of procedure and court rules for the jurisdiction covered, along with forms and annotations to court decisions. They are an essential component of the working library of every practitioner. These publications will also be discussed in Chapter 15. The particular works available for each state can usually be identified in the state legal research manuals listed in Appendix A at the end of the volume. In addition, the *Law Library Journal* has been publishing a series of detailed surveys of practice books for some states.[7]

F. ADDITIONAL READING

C. A. Korbakes, J. J. Alfini & C. W. Grau, *Judicial Rulemaking in the State Courts: A Compendium* (American Judicature Society, 1978).

J. A. Parness and C. A. Korbakes, *Study of the Procedural Rule-Making Power in the United States* (American Judicature Society, 1973).

J. B. Weinstein, *Reform of Court Rule-Making Procedure* (Ohio State Univ. Press, 1977).

7. Published so far are: R. L. Brown, "An Annotated Bibliography of Current New York State Practice Manuals," 73 *Law Library J.* 28 (1980); K. T. Gruben & L. Philipp, "An Annotated Bibliography of Texas Practice Materials," 74 *Law Library J.* 87 (1981); and B.J. Ochal, "California Current State Practice Materials: An Annotated Bibliography", 75 *Law Library J.* 281 (1981).

Chapter 9

CITATORS

A. Introduction to Shepard's Citations.
B. Organization and Scope of Shepard's Citations.
   1. State Units.
   2. Regional Units.
   3. *Federal Citations.*
   4. U.S. Units.
      a. Cases.
      b. Statutes.
      c. Administrative Decisions.
      d. Patents and Trademarks.
   5. Format and Supplementation.
C. Additional Uses of Shepard's Citators.
   1. Parallel Citations.
   2. References to *A.L.R.*
   3. References to Law Review Articles.
   4. Related Cases.
D. Mechanics of Shepardizing Cases.
   1. State Cases.
      a. Official Unit.
      b. Regional Unit.
   2. *Federal Citations.*
   3. U.S. Supreme Court Cases.
E. Mechanics of Shepardizing Statutes.
F. Additional Shepard's Units.
   1. *Bankruptcy Citations.*
   2. *Code of Federal Regulations Citations.*
   3. *Criminal Justice Citations.*
   4. *Federal Labor Law Citations.*
   5. *Federal Law Citations in Selected Law Reviews.*
   6. *Law Review Citations.*
   7. *Federal Tax Citations.*
   8. *Military Justice Citations.*
   9. *Professional and Judicial Conduct Citations.*
   10. *Restatement Citations.*
   11. Other Shepard's Citators.
   12. Shepard's Publications Other Than Citators.
G. Other Tools Which Function as Citators.
   1. *Federal Register* and *C.F.R.* Lists of Sections Affected.
   2. Citations to the *Restatements of the Law.*
   3. Tables of Statutes Construed.
   4. Annotated Codes.
   5. Looseleaf Services.
   6. Computer-Based Citators.
H. Summary.

A. INTRODUCTION TO SHEPARD'S CITATIONS

As we have emphasized in earlier chapters, constant change is a basic characteristic of our legal system. With courts and legislatures at the federal and state levels producing 50,000 new appellate decisions and many thousands of new statutes every year, the standing and authority of previous cases and laws are always subject to either sudden change or gradual erosion. Decisions may be reversed, overruled, criticized, questioned or distinguished. Similarly, statutes may be repealed, amended, superseded, or declared unconstitutional. The researcher must therefore determine the *current* status of every primary legal source which appears to be relevant to the issue at hand. This function is usually performed by an ingenious series of citators called *Shepard's Citations.* These citators trace the judicial history of every published decision, and the later legislative *and* judicial treatment of every enacted statute.

Having located, read, and established the relevance of a primary authority (whether a decision, a statute or an administrative regulation or ruling), the researcher must then ascertain the current status of that text. This is done by searching the history of the source in a citator. Since the most comprehensive system of citators are *Shepard's Citations,* the process is called *Shepardizing* a case, statute or administrative document. Shepardizing is simply a way of verifying the current authority of the legal source. This research step is an essential consequence of the doctrine of precedent and *stare decisis,* and of the fact that, strictly speaking, decisions and statutes remain in effect, regardless of their age, unless and until they are reversed, overruled, or, in the case of statutes, repealed or judicially declared void.

Shepard's citators facilitate this verification of authority by listing the citation of every published decision, and then following that entry with the citation of every subsequent decision which has mentioned the *cited* decision. If the court in the subsequent decision indicated some specific action or attitude with regard to the earlier case (*e.g.,* reversed or affirmed it, criticized or questioned it, overruled or followed it), that action or attitude is noted by one of a series of alphabetic symbols representing that treatment. The same method is used for statutes. Every federal and state statute is listed in a statutory citator, and followed by citations of subsequent decisions and statutes which have expressly affected the *cited* statute. Again, a series of alphabetic symbols are used to denote the specific action taken or indicated by the *citing* decisions and statutes.

This Chapter will describe the various units of *Shepard's Citations,* explain their use and the several secondary functions they perform, indicate the alphabetic symbols they employ, and mention the use of other research tools as citators.

B. ORGANIZATION AND SCOPE OF SHEPARD'S CITATIONS

The use of a Shepard's citator to verify current authority has become an essential final step in the research process. To neglect this step is to face the embarrassment of basing one's arguments on cases subsequently reversed or statutes already repealed, and thereby failing in one's professional responsibility.

Shepard's Citations, in their various units, provide access to the history and treatment of virtually all published court decisions, statutes, and many items of secondary authority. As will be shown in Sections D and E below, the process of "Shepardizing" is essentially a simple one: The researcher locates an authority (the *cited* source) in the proper unit of Shepard's, and is provided with a list of citations (the *citing* sources) that have in any way mentioned, and therefore potentially affected the validity of, the questioned authority. Shepard's produces and supplements this ever-growing list of subsequent references by continuously examining the major primary sources of American law and some secondary sources, and noting when and how the primary authority has been treated.

Those legal materials which can be *Shepardized* currently within the system as a whole (the *cited* material) and those from which later references to them are drawn (the *citing* material) are set forth below in Illustration A, taken from the publisher's instructional pamphlet, *How to Use Shepard's Citations.*

Locating any of the authorities listed above as *cited* material in one of the Shepard's units is not difficult if one understands the organization of the system, and notes the scope of both *cited* and *citing* source contained in the prefatory listing in each volume.

Shepard's citator system is comprised of state units, regional units, federal units, and an increasing number of specialized citator units. The first three groups of citators are described below; specialized citators will be treated later in Section F.

1. STATE UNITS

A separate unit of Shepard's Citations, covering both cases and statutes, is published for each of the 50 states, unless a separate official or officially sanctioned reporter no longer exists. In that event, only a statutory citator would be published for that state. Beginning in 1968, separate units for the District of Columbia and Puerto Rico have been published as well. Each of these units typically contains, as cited material, official reports of the jurisdiction, state statutes, attorney general opinions, and municipal charters and ordinances. As the scope of coverage for each state may thus vary, it is wise to check the Table of Contents for each unit to determine the exact coverage provided. Each of the state units also contains a section which

THE SCOPE OF SHEPARD'S CITATION BOOKS AND SERVICES

Shepard's citation books and services are essential tools for effective, efficient research at all levels of law.

By applying the techniques outlined in this booklet to your problems, you will be able to LOCATE and EVALUATE authorities quickly. Shepard's bridges the gap between the products of the various publishers - printed or electronic.

A line by line, page by page search and constant quality checks assure completeness and accuracy. The format has been time-tested and universally accepted.

The *CITED* Material Includes

Cases in United States Supreme Court Reports
Cases in federal reports (including administrative agency decisions and orders)
Cases in state reports
Cases in National Reporter System
Opinions of the Attorneys General
United States Constitution
United States Code
United States Statutes at Large
United States Treaties and Other International Agreements
Code of Federal Regulations
Federal Court Rules
State Constitutions
State Codes
State Session Laws
Municipal Charters
Ordinances
State Court Rules
Jury Instructions
Restatement
Legal Periodicals
Standards of Criminal Justice
Patents
Trademarks
Copyrights

The *CITING* Material Includes:

Cases in United States Supreme Court Reports
Cases in federal reports (including administrative agency decisions and orders)
Cases in state reports
Cases in National Reporter System
Opinions of the Attorneys General
Articles in legal periodicals
Annotations in the American Law Reports

Details of the actual scope are fully set out in the preface pages of each Shepard edition. These should be referred to before starting a search in that edition.

Illustration A

List of *cited* material and *citing* material in the Shepard's citators, appearing in *How to Use Shepard's Citations.*

is organized by the regional reporter citations of the reports of that state, so that a case may be Shepardized by its regional reporter citation if only a state unit of Shepard's for cases is available.

2. REGIONAL UNITS

A separate unit of Shepard's is also published for each series in the National Reporter System, including *New York Supplement* and the *California Reporter.* These volumes contain citations to cases arranged by their regional reporter citations. The differences between Shepardizing a case in its state unit and its regional unit will be discussed in Section D below.

3. FEDERAL CITATIONS

Shepard's covers a wide variety of federal sources in a fairly complex arrangement divided into two major units. For lower federal court decisions, the *Federal Citations* unit should be consulted. Here the cited cases include decisions reported in *Federal Reporter, Federal Supplement, Federal Rules Decisions,* and the *U.S. Court of Claims Reports.*

4. U.S. UNITS

The second basic unit for federal materials is *United States Citations.* This unit is further subdivided into four parts:

a. Cases

This unit covers decisions of the U.S. Supreme Court. Although a case may be Shepardized in these volumes by referring to either its official or unofficial citations, the list of citing sources obtained will vary according to which citation is used. The process of evaluating Supreme Court decisions will be explained in Section D–3 at pages 265–266 below.

b. Statutes

The U.S. statutes citators are used to Shepardize the U.S. Constitution, the *U.S. Code,* uncodified U.S. *Statutes at Large* provisions, treaties contained in the U.S. Treaties Series, General Orders in Bankruptcy, and federal court rules.

c. Administrative Decisions

Shepard's Administrative Law Citations provides citations to the decisions of some 29 federal administrative departments, courts, boards, and commissions, such as the Securities and Exchange Commission, Federal Trade Commission, and the U.S. Tax Court. Cross references between the various official and unofficial reporting services are included. A detailed listing of the material which is covered in these volumes can be found in the prefatory material in each volume of this unit.

Although most of Shepard's coverage of federal administrative decisions is found in its *Administrative Law Citations* unit, material relating to a number of specialized fields is now treated by separate citators, described in Section F. For example, administrative decisions in labor law (such as N.L.R.B. decisions) are located in the separate *Federal Labor Law Citations,* to be discussed in Section F below. Federal administrative *regulations* are covered by Shepard's *Code of Federal Regulations Citations,* also discussed in Section F.

d. Patents and Trademarks

This part enables the researcher to Shepardize U.S. patents, trademarks, and copyrights. Also included as *cited* sources are court decisions, administrative decisions, and administrative rules and regulations that relate to these areas of the law. Within the scope of these volumes are decisions reported in *U.S. Patents Quarterly, Decisions of the Commissioner of Patents,* and in the *U.S. Court of Customs and Patents Appeals Reports (Patents).* Cross references between the various series of court reports and administrative decisions are provided.

Earlier in this chapter it was stated that finding the proper unit of Shepard's for any authority is usually not a difficult task, and this is true for the obviously complicated set of federal citators just described. Shepard's provides a table, shown in Illustration B, and found in the preface of the red paper supplement to each volume in the federal series, which lists the part of the series in which each set of reports or decisions can be located. It should be remembered, however, that labor-related materials are arranged in their own separate citator and are omitted from the table.

5. FORMAT AND SUPPLEMENTATION

As the major function of a citator is to evaluate the current authority of any published source, it is especially important that the citator itself be kept current. Every citator must be supplemented regularly, so that it reflects recent changes in, and the latest treatment of, existing law. Shepard's accomplishes this by using the following format, or a slight variation thereof, for each of its units:

One or more bound red volumes exist for each set of citators. These are supplemented by quarterly red pamphlets which serve as cumulative supplements to the bound volumes. White paper advance sheets, which are published six weeks after the red pamphlet and later cumulated into the next red pamphlet, are published for some units. Some sets have annual cumulative supplements as well.

At any point in time, each unit of Shepard's will consist of one or more of the above mentioned items. To make certain that all relevant portions of the unit are consulted, Shepard's prints in a box on the front cover of the latest paper supplement in each series, a list of the volumes and pamphlets to be used. An example of this notice on the cover of a Shepard's advance sheet is shown in Illustration C.

TABLE OF REPORTS IN SHEPARD'S UNITED STATES, UNITED STATES ADMINISTRATIVE, UNITED STATES PATENTS AND TRADEMARKS, FEDERAL AND DISTRICT OF COLUMBIA EDITIONS

Report	Edition
Abstracted Protest Decisions	Administrative
Abstracted Reappraisement Decisions	Administrative
Abstracted Valuation Decisions	Administrative
Abstracts	Administrative
Abstracts, New Series	Administrative
American Maritime Cases	Administrative
Appeal Cases, District of Columbia Reports	District of Columbia
Application for Review Decisions	Administrative
Bankruptcy Reporter	Federal
Black's Reports (66–67 U. S.)	United States
Board of Tax Appeals Reports	Administrative
Court of Claims Reports	Federal
Court of Customs Appeals Reports	Administrative
Court of Customs and Patent Appeals Reports (Customs)	Administrative
Court of Customs and Patent Appeals Reports (Patents)	Patents and Trademarks
Cranch's Reports (5–13 U. S.)	United States
Customs Court Decisions	Administrative
Customs Court Reports	Administrative
Customs Penalty Decisions	Administrative
Customs Rules Decisions	Administrative
Customs Service Decisions	Administrative
Dallas' Reports (1–4 U. S.)	United States
Decisions of the Commissioner of Patents	Patents and Trademarks
Decisions of the Department of the Interior	Administrative
Decisions of the Department of the Interior (Public Lands)	Administrative
Devereux's Reports	Federal
District Court, District of Columbia Reports, New Series	District of Columbia
District of Columbia Reports	District of Columbia
Federal Cases	Federal
Federal Communications Commission Reports	Administrative
Federal Maritime Commission Reports	Administrative
Federal Power Commission Reports	Administrative
Federal Reporter	Federal
Federal Reporter, Second Series	Federal
Federal Rules Decisions	Federal
Federal Supplement	Federal
Federal Trade Commission Decisions	Administrative
Hayward and Hazleton's Reports	District of Columbia
Howard's Reports (42–65 U. S.)	United States
Internal Revenue, Treasury Decisions	Administrative
Interstate Commerce Commission Reports	Administrative
Lawyers' Edition, United States Supreme Court Reports	United States
Motor Carrier Cases	Administrative
Opinions of the Attorneys General of the United States	Administrative
Peters' Reports (26–41 U. S.)	United States
Protest Review Decisions	Administrative
Reappraisement Decisions	Administrative
Securities and Exchange Commission Decisions and Reports	Administrative

10

Illustration B

Left column: Title of report from which cited material comes.
Right column: Shepard's edition citing that cited material.

SEMIANNUAL CUMULATIVE SUPPLEMENT

VOL. 81 JANUARY, 1983 NO. 8

(IN TWO PARTS) PART 2

Shepard's UNITED STATES Citations

(USPS 605470)

STATUTES AND COURT RULES

IMPORTANT NOTICE

Do not destroy the July, 1982 gold paper-covered Semiannual Cumulative Supplement (Parts 2A and 2B) or the November, 1982 issue of Shepard's United States Citations—Statutes until you have received the January, 1983 issue and the 1979-1983 bound volume of Shepard's United States Citations—Statutes to be published January, 1983 and delivered by 2/28/83.

After you have received the 1979-1983 bound volume and the January, 1983 issue, the July, 1982 gold paper-covered Semiannual Cumulative Supplement (Parts 2A and 2B) and the November, 1982 issue of Shepard's United States Citations—Statutes should be destroyed.

FOR YOUR SHEPARD'S REPRESENTATIVE SEE BACK COVER

What Your Library Should Contain

PART 1 CASES	PART 2 STATUTES
1943 Bound Volume(s)	1968 Bound Volume
1943-1971 Bound Volumes	1968-1974 Bound Volume
1971-1976 Bound Volume	1974-1979 Bound Volume
1976-1980 Bound Volume	*1979-1983 Bound Volume
1980-1982 Bound Volume	

Supplemented with

***July, 1982 Semiannual Supplement Vol. 81 No. 2 (Parts 2A and 2B)**

***Nov., 1982 Cumulative Supplement Vol. 81 No. 6 (Part 2)**

Jan., 1983 Semiannual Supplement Vol. 81 No. 8 (Parts 1 and 2)

Destroy All Other Issues

***see IMPORTANT NOTICE above**

SEE TABLE OF CONTENTS ON PAGE THREE

SEE "THIS ISSUE INCLUDES" ON PAGE TWO

Illustration C

Cover of Shepard's pamphlet supplement, showing volumes and supplements to date.

To further supplement its printed citators, Shepard's offers its subscribers the *Federal Law Daily Update Service.* By telephoning or writing Shepard's, the researcher can receive a daily-revised computerized listing of *citing* references to opinions of the U.S. Supreme Court and the lower federal courts, the U.S. Constitution, the *U.S. Code,* and federal court rules. It is also possible to update any citation from any unit in the Shepard's system by contacting the publisher in this way.

C. ADDITIONAL USES OF SHEPARD'S CITATORS

Although Shepard's citators are primarily used to ascertain the current status and treatment of cases and statutes, they can also be helpful in locating additional research leads or other legal information. In the course of checking an authority in a Shepard's citator, in order to determine its current validity, the researcher will find not only sources to be used for that purpose, but may also discover the following information:

1. PARALLEL CITATIONS

The first time a case appears in a Shepard's volume, parallel citations to the same case in another series of reports are provided, in parentheses, as the first citing references. (See Illustrations E and G, below.) If the parallel citations are not available at the time the case is initially listed in Shepard's, they will be provided in the first volumes of the unit that is published after they become available. It is important to remember that, once listed, parallel citation references are not repeated in subsequent volumes of the set.

As Shepard's has units for both official state reporters and regional reporters, it is possible to locate both the unofficial citations of official reports and the official citations of unofficial reports. Shepard's citators may be the best source for this purpose. Note that the *National Reporter Blue Book* and State *Blue and White Books,* discussed above in Chapter 3, which also provide such cross references, are not updated as frequently as Shepards. Similarly, although parallel citations can be found in the tables of cases to the relevant West digests, Shepard's is again updated more frequently and can, therefore, provide more current information.

2. REFERENCES TO A.L.R.

Shepard's state citators include *A.L.R.* annotations among their citing sources, so that the researcher will be alerted to any mention of the authority being researched, in an *A.L.R.* annotation (see Illustration E below).

3. REFERENCES TO LAW REVIEW ARTICLES

In all of its state units, Shepard's also indicates when a case has been cited in any local law review or in any of the twenty national law reviews regularly used as citing references. (A list of these can be found in the prefatory matter in any of the state unit volumes.) It should be remembered that, except for the *American Bar Association Journal,* legal periodical citations to federal cases are not listed in the Shepard's federal units. A separate publication, *Federal Law Citations in Selected Law Reviews,* (discussed below in Section F) can be used for locating such references.

4. RELATED CASES

Shepardizing any case will yield a list of later cases which have in any way mentioned it. Presumably, these subsequent cases will touch upon some or all of the legal issues involved in the original case, so that Shepard's can also function as a related case finder. It should be noted, however, that there is no subject access through the Shepard's system, and a later case that deals with similar issues but does not expressly cite the original case will not be found through *Shepardizing.* Many of the later cases that are found, moreover, may prove upon examination to have made only passing mention to the earlier case. Shepard's provides several ways of indicating what sections or aspects of the cited case has been treated by the later citing case. These are noted below in section D–1.

D. MECHANICS OF SHEPARDIZING CASES

The process of verifying the current authority of cases in Shepard's citators differs slightly depending on the type of reporter, and the particular citator being consulted. There are, however, general instructions for *Shepardizing* decisions which apply to searches undertaken in any of the units. These are set forth in Illustration D, from Shepard's instructional pamphlet.

1. STATE CASES

a. Official Unit

Let us assume that we want to *Shepardize Hortonville Education Association v. Joint School District No. 1,* 66 *Wisconsin 2d* 469. We begin our search by locating *all* volumes and supplements of the *Wisconsin Citations* unit that include our case in their scope. After examining the "This Issue Includes" sections of the volumes, we determine that the 1979 Bound Volume is the first place our case is listed, and we begin our search here. (For the purposes of this example, we will consult not only this volume, but all subsequent pamphlets to complete the citator search.) Using the Table of Contents, we find the section of this volume containing Wisconsin Reports 2d Series, and proceed to locate Volume 66 (shown in the sidehead in the upper left corner on the page) and the first page of our case (shown in boldface type). Illustration E has been marked to indicate the location of these items.

THE MECHANICS

WHAT IS A CITATION?

A reported case is customarily referred to in terms of volume, source (abbreviation) and page. Lawyers often refer to this as the "citation for the case."

In Shepard's the term citation has a more precise meaning. In Shepard terminology a "citation" is a reference *in* a later authority *to* an earlier authority.

The earlier authority is known as the "cited" case, statute, etc. and the later authorities are referred to as the "citing" case, statute, etc. Shepard's is easy to use. Here are some suggestions to follow:

1. Turn to the "TABLE OF CONTENTS." Find the initial page of the division for the material you are "Shepardizing" — check the sources of the citing references listed on that page. (*A word of warning:* Be sure you are in the proper reports series or the proper code year.)
2. Use the numbers shown in the *sideheads* on each page in the division, to speed your search. On the appropriate page, use the *boldface* numbers to find the point you seek.

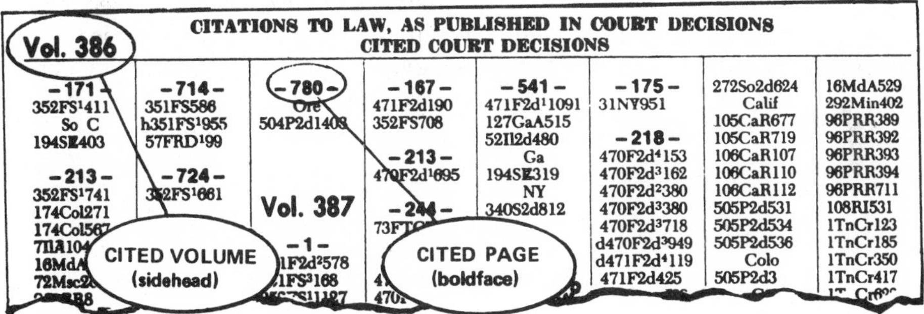

3. At that point you will find:
   —no entry for your text;
   —an entry followed by a reference in parentheses;
   —an entry followed by one or more references not in parentheses.

No entry for your text. You have established that, during the period covered by that part of the Shepard edition, there were no references to your text. **An entry** for your text is followed only by a references in parentheses—you have located another publication of your text.

An entry for your text followed by one or more references *not* in parentheses—you have found *citations* to your text. If a citation begins (at the far left of its line) with a letter or letters, consult the Table of Abbreviations to determine their significance. It is possible to find terminal letters "n" or "s" on a citation line. The "n" indicates that the reference is in an annotation or note. The "s" indicates that the reference is in a supplement to an annotation. If, in between the source name abbreviation and the page in the source, on the citation line, there appears a small elevated number, it indicates the number of the paragraph of the syllabus or headnote of the cited text of a court decision.

(Detailed illustrations of actual usage are fully set out in the preface pages of each Shepard edition.)

Illustration D

General instructions for Shepardizing, from *How to Use Shepard's Citations.*

Under the citation to our case, we find a series of references. The different types of citations are shown in Illustration E, and described below:

1. The first reference, shown in parentheses, represents a parallel citation to the same case as reported in the West Regional Reporter Series.

2. The second group of citations are "history citations," *i.e.*, those which relate to subsequent developments of the same case. Note that history citations are always preceded by an identifying abbreviation assigned by the Shepard's editor. A table explaining these abbreviations is found in the front of the Shepard's volume, and has been reproduced here in the top portion of Illustration F. It is through the use of these notations that the researcher can determine whether or not the case being Shepardized is still good authority. As shown in our example, the case we are evaluating was *reversed* on appeal, and should not be cited as authority.

3. The third set of citations are references to the cited case by Wisconsin state courts and federal courts. The fact that there are thirteen citing references listed in this group does not indicate that our case has been cited in thirteen separate cases. Rather, the citing references are given to each *page* in a decision on which the original case has been mentioned. Consequently, if a court cites our case five separate times on five different pages within the same decision, five distinct citing references will be shown in Shepard's.

Note that the citations in this group may be analyzed by the Shepard's editors to indicate the type of treatment afforded by the citing source. These types of treatment are represented by the abbreviations shown in the *bottom* portion of Illustration F. It is important to note that in assigning these notational symbols, the Shepard's editors rely largely upon the specific language of the citing court. Hence, they will not indicate that, for example, a case has been overruled by a later case if such is not expressly stated, no matter how contrary the holding.

In addition to providing history and treatment symbols, Shepard's employs another notational system, which aids the researcher in narrowing his search to particular points of law. Small elevated numerals, inserted after the abbreviation for the citing source and before the page of the citation, indicate that the citation has particular reference to the point of law in the headnote of the cited case bearing that numeral. As shown in Illustration E, our case has been distinguished at 76 *Wisconsin 2d* 111 with particular reference to headnote # 7, and explained at 429 *F.Supp.* 485 with particular reference to the point of law discussed in headnote # 6.

4. The fourth group of citations are references to Opinions of the Attorney General of Wisconsin which have cited our case.

5. The fifth set of citations are references from articles in law reviews.

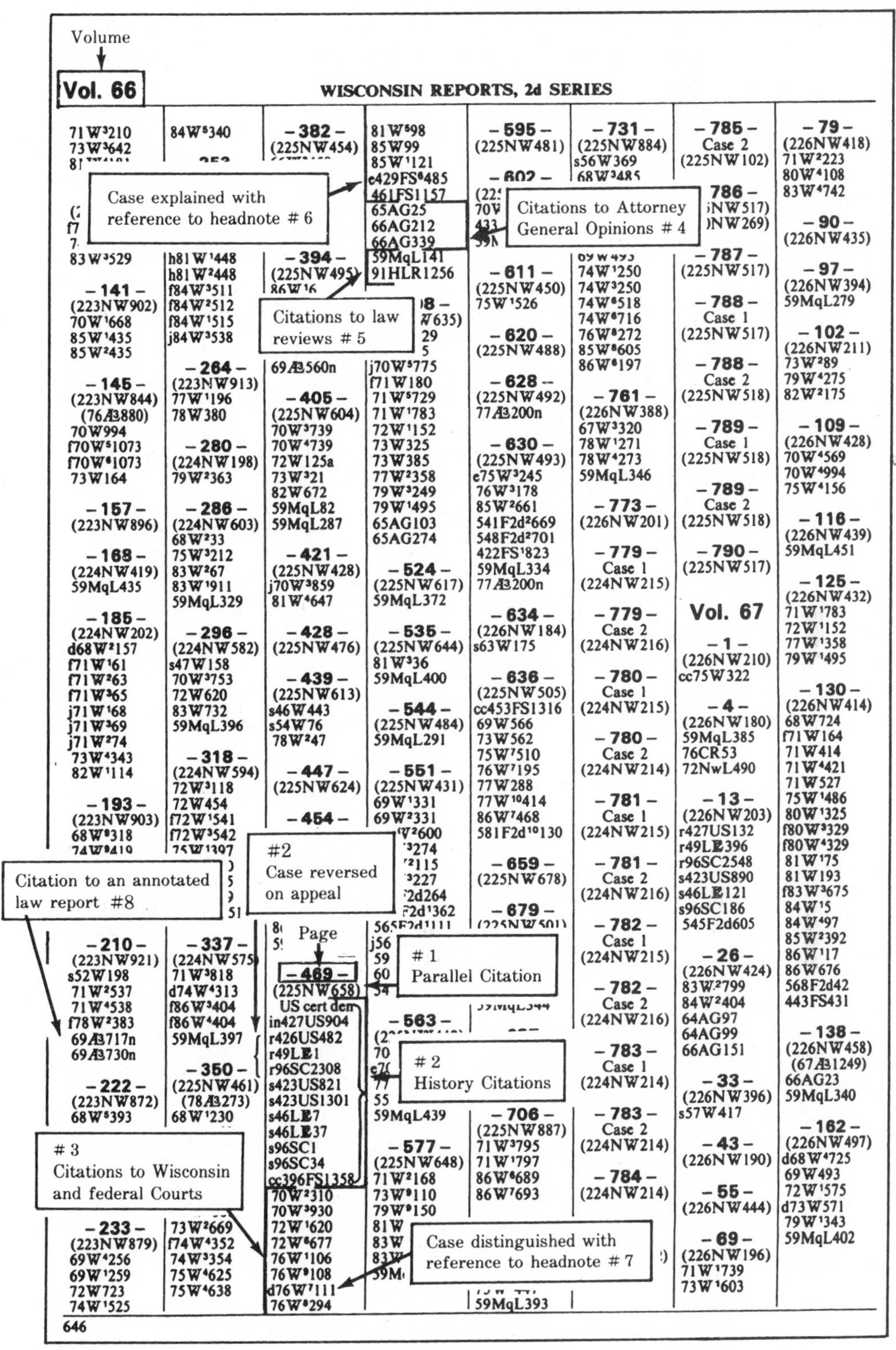

Vol. 66 WISCONSIN REPORTS, 2d SERIES

71W[3]210
73W[3]642
83W[3]529
– 141 –
(223NW902)
70W[1]668
85W[1]435
85W[2]435
– 145 –
(223NW844)
(76A3880)
70W994
f70W[5]1073
f70W[6]1073
73W164
– 157 –
(223NW896)
– 168 –
(224NW419)
59MqL435
– 185 –
(224NW202)
d68W[2]157
f71W[1]61
f71W[2]63
f71W[3]65
j71W[1]68
j71W[3]69
j71W[2]74
73W[4]343
82W[1]114
– 193 –
(223NW903)
68W[6]318
– 210 –
(223NW921)
s52W198
71W[2]537
71W[4]538
f78W[2]383
69A3717n
69A3730n
– 222 –
(223NW872)
68W[5]393
– 233 –
(223NW879)
69W[4]256
69W[1]259
72W723
74W[1]525

84W[5]340
h81W[1]448
h81W[2]448
f84W[3]511
f84W[2]512
f84W[1]515
j84W[3]538
– 264 –
(223NW913)
77W[1]196
78W380
– 280 –
(224NW198)
79W[2]363
– 286 –
(224NW603)
68W[2]33
75W[3]212
83W[2]67
83W[1]911
59MqL329
– 296 –
(224NW582)
s47W158
70W[3]753
72W620
83W732
59MqL396
– 318 –
(224NW594)
72W[3]118
72W454
f72W[1]541
f72W[3]542
– 337 –
(224NW575)
71W[3]818
d74W[4]313
f86W[3]404
f86W[4]404
59MqL397
– 350 –
(225NW461)
(78A3273)
68W[1]230
73W[2]669
f74W[4]352
74W[3]354
75W[4]625
75W[4]638

– 382 –
(225NW454)
– 394 –
(225NW495)
86W[1]6
69A3560n
– 405 –
(225NW604)
70W[3]739
70W[4]739
72W125a
73W[3]21
82W672
59MqL82
59MqL287
– 421 –
(225NW428)
j70W[3]859
81W[4]647
– 428 –
(225NW476)
– 439 –
(225NW613)
s46W443
s54W76
78W[2]47
– 447 –
(225NW624)
– 454 –
– 469 –
(225NW658)
US cert den
in427US904
r426US482
r49LE1
r96SC2308
s423US821
s423US1301
s46LE7
s46LE37
s96SC1
s96SC34
cc396FS1358
70W[2]310
70W[3]930
72W[1]620
72W[6]677
76W[1]106
76W[9]108
d76W[7]111
76W[8]294

81W[5]98
85W99
85W[1]121
e429FS[6]485
461FS1157
65AG25
66AG212
66AG339
59MqL141
91HLR1256
j70W[5]775
f71W180
71W[5]729
71W[1]783
72W[1]152
73W325
73W385
77W[2]358
79W[3]249
79W[1]495
65AG103
65AG274
– 524 –
(225NW617)
59MqL372
– 535 –
(225NW644)
81W[3]36
59MqL400
– 544 –
(225NW484)
59MqL291
– 551 –
(225NW431)
69W[1]331
69W[2]331
– 563 –
55
59MqL439
– 577 –
(225NW648)
71W[2]168
73W[9]110
79W[9]150
81W
83W

– 595 –
(225NW481)
– 602 –
– 611 –
(225NW450)
75W[1]526
– 620 –
(225NW488)
– 628 –
(225NW492)
77A3200n
– 630 –
(225NW493)
e75W[3]245
76W[3]178
85W[2]661
541F2d[2]669
548F2d[2]701
422FS[1]823
59MqL334
77A3200n
– 634 –
(226NW184)
s63W175
– 636 –
(225NW505)
cc453FS1316
69W566
73W562
75W[7]510
76W[7]195
77W288
77W[10]414
86W[7]468
581F2d[10]130
– 659 –
(225NW678)
– 679 –
– 706 –
(225NW887)
71W[3]795
71W[1]797
86W[6]689
86W[7]693
59MqL393

– 731 –
(225NW884)
s56W369
68W[3]485
74W[1]250
74W[3]250
74W[6]518
74W[6]716
76W[8]272
85W[8]605
86W[6]197
– 761 –
(226NW388)
67W[3]320
78W[1]271
78W[4]273
59MqL346
– 773 –
(226NW201)
– 779 –
Case 1
(224NW215)
– 779 –
Case 2
(224NW216)
– 780 –
Case 1
(224NW215)
– 780 –
Case 2
(224NW214)
– 781 –
Case 1
(224NW215)
– 781 –
Case 2
(224NW216)
– 782 –
Case 1
(224NW215)
– 782 –
Case 2
(224NW216)
– 783 –
Case 1
(224NW214)
– 783 –
Case 2
(224NW214)
– 784 –
(224NW214)

– 785 –
Case 2
(225NW102)
– 786 –
– 787 –
(225NW517)
– 788 –
Case 1
(225NW517)
– 788 –
Case 2
(225NW518)
– 789 –
Case 1
(225NW518)
– 789 –
Case 2
(225NW518)
– 790 –
(225NW517)

Vol. 67

– 1 –
(226NW210)
cc75W322
– 4 –
(226NW180)
59MqL385
76CR53
72NwL490
– 13 –
(226NW203)
r427US132
r49LE396
r96SC2548
s423US890
s46LE121
s96SC186
545F2d605
– 26 –
(226NW424)
83W[2]799
84W[2]404
64AG97
64AG99
66AG151
– 33 –
(226NW396)
s57W417
– 43 –
(226NW190)
– 55 –
(226NW444)
– 69 –
(226NW196)
71W[1]739
73W[1]603

– 79 –
(226NW418)
71W[2]223
80W[4]108
83W[4]742
– 90 –
(226NW435)
– 97 –
(226NW394)
59MqL279
– 102 –
(226NW211)
73W[2]89
79W[4]275
82W[2]175
– 109 –
(226NW428)
70W[4]569
70W[4]994
75W[4]156
– 116 –
(226NW439)
59MqL451
– 125 –
(226NW432)
71W[1]783
72W[1]152
77W[1]358
79W[1]495
– 130 –
(226NW414)
68W724
f71W164
71W414
71W[4]421
71W527
75W[1]486
80W[1]325
f80W[3]329
f80W[4]329
81W[1]75
81W193
f83W[3]675
84W[1]5
84W[4]97
85W[2]392
86W[1]17
86W676
568F2d42
443FS431
– 138 –
(226NW458)
(67A31249)
66AG23
59MqL340
– 162 –
(226NW497)
d68W[4]725
69W493
72W[1]575
d73W571
79W[1]343
59MqL402

646

Illustration E

Wisconsin Citations—1979 Bound Volume.

ABBREVIATIONS—ANALYSIS

History of Case	
a (affirmed)	Same case affirmed on appeal.
cc (connected case)	Different case from case cited but arising out of same subject matter or intimately connected therewith.
D (dismissed)	Appeal from same case dismissed.
m (modified)	Same case modified on appeal.
r (reversed)	Same case reversed on appeal.
s (same case)	Same case as case cited.
S (superseded)	Substitution for former opinion.
v (vacated)	Same case vacated.
U S cert den	Certiorari denied by U. S. Supreme Court.
U S cert dis	Certiorari dismissed by U. S. Supreme Court.
U S reh den	Rehearing denied by U. S. Supreme Court.
U S reh dis	Rehearing dismissed by U. S. Supreme Court.
Treatment of Case	
c (criticised)	Soundness of decision or reasoning in cited case criticised for reasons given.
d (distinguished)	Case at bar different either in law or fact from case cited for reasons given.
e (explained)	Statement of import of decision in cited case. Not merely a restatement of the facts.
f (followed)	Cited as controlling.
h (harmonized)	Apparent inconsistency explained and shown not to exist.
j (dissenting opinion)	Citation in dissenting opinion.
L (limited)	Refusal to extend decision of cited case beyond precise issues involved.
o (overruled)	Ruling in cited case expressly overruled.
p (parallel)	Citing case substantially alike or on all fours with cited case in its law or facts.
q (questioned)	Soundness of decision or reasoning in cited case questioned.

Illustration F

Shepard's abbreviations of specific types of treatment of cases.

Also within the scope of Shepard's citing sources for state reports are annotations in annotated law reports. Although our case has not been mentioned in any such annotation during the time period covered by the volume that we are examining, an example of such a citation can be seen in Illustration E at 66 *Wisconsin 2d* 210, at #8.

As mentioned above in Section B, each state unit of Shepard's contains a section which is arranged by the regional reporter citations of the state cases. If we were to locate our case in these pages under its *Northwestern Reporter* citation, we would find only a parallel citation to the official report, a list of references from Wisconsin state cases cited in the regional reporters, and federal cases which have cited the case. Although the scope of citing sources is narrower here than in the official reports section, Shepard's advises one to always check these pages for additional citations. It is possible for a case to be reported in a regional reporter before it appears in an official report, and if a court cites only the regional form, the citation will be listed in Shepard's under the regional form only.

b. Regional Unit

As has been shown above, *Shepardizing* a case in the state unit, under either its official or unofficial citation, will yield references to any home state case or federal case that has affected its authority in any way. As these may be the only cases that can be presented to the court as binding authority, some legal researchers stop *Shepardizing* when they have completed their search in the appropriate state unit. Although decisions from other state courts are not binding on the courts of the home state, they are often useful as persuasive authority. This is particularly true if one is unable to locate relevant decisions within the home state. By using Shepard's regional reporter citators, one can expand a search by tracing the treatment of a state decision in the courts of every state.

To compare the scope of state and regional citator units, we can *Shepardize Hortonville Education Assoc. v. Joint School District No. 1* under its regional reporter citation, 225 *N.W.2d* 658, in *Shepard's Northwestern Reporter Citations.* For the sake of simplicity, we examine the first set of citations listed for the case in the 1979 Bound Volume of the regional citator. This volume covers roughly the same time period as that covered by the volume used in the state citator in Illustration E above.

Illustration G has been marked to indicate the types of citations found. It can be seen that, as in the state unit, the regional citator also provides parallel citations, history citations, and citations from state court opinions (here, however, in their *regional* citation form.) Citations to federal decisions are also provided. Note, however, that the references to Attorney General opinions and law review articles, which were found in the state unit, are not supplied in the regional citator.

In place of these references, two new groups of citing sources are found:

1. Citations to cases decided in states other than the home state, but reported in the same regional reporter, are listed alphabetically by state.
2. Citations to decisions of state courts not within the coverage of the home state's regional reporter unit, are listed in a second alphabetical sequence by state.

2. FEDERAL CITATIONS

Shepard's *Federal Citations* provides citator information for the decisions of the U.S. Courts of Appeals, U.S. District Courts, and the various specialized federal courts, to the extent that the decisions are published in standard federal reporters. As noted above in Illustration B at p. 255, a table is included in the front of federal citators listing which reporters are covered in this unit.

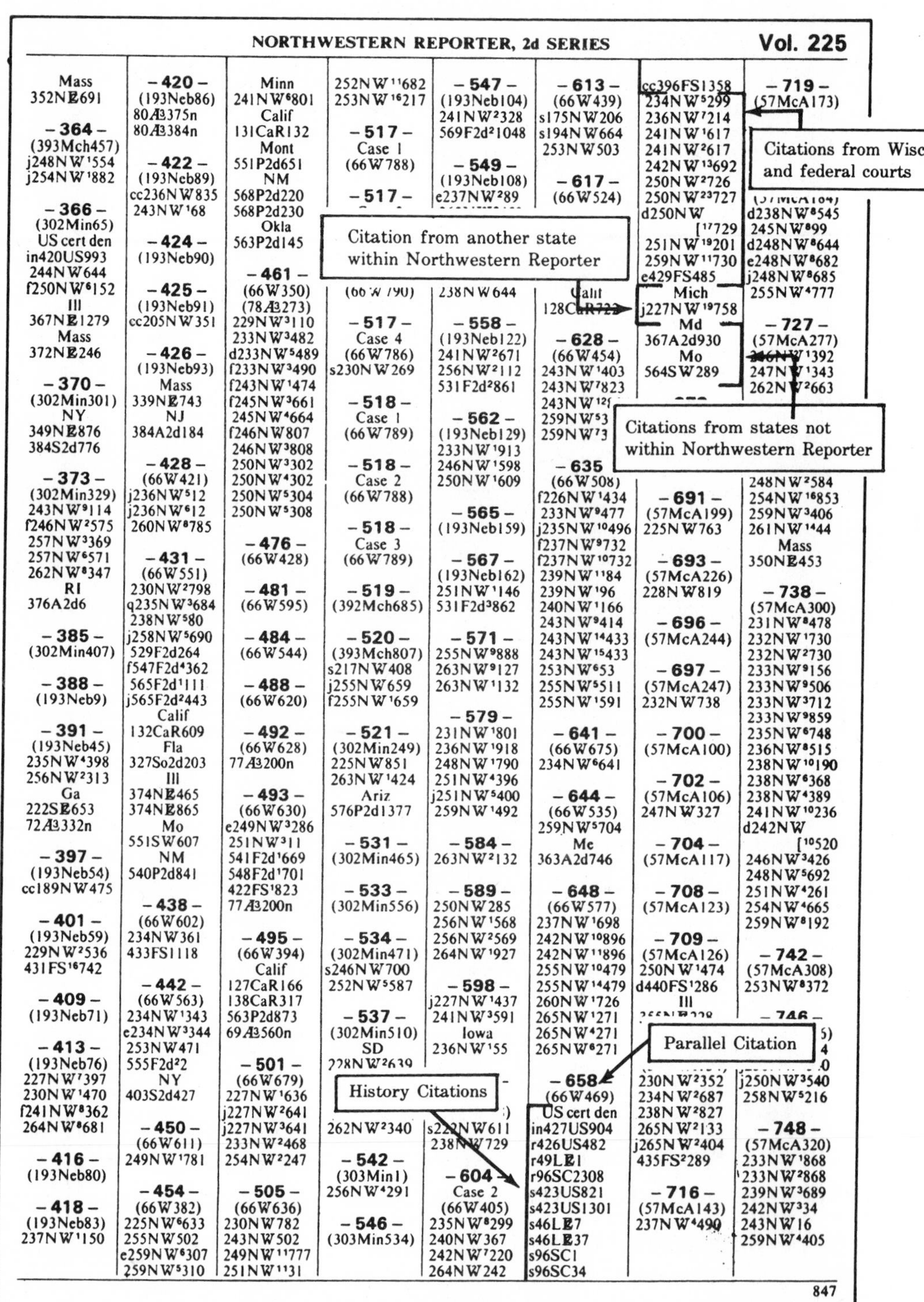

NORTHWESTERN REPORTER, 2d SERIES **Vol. 225**

Mass
352NE691

- 364 -
(393Mch457)
j248NW[1]554
j254NW[1]882

- 366 -
(302Min65)
US cert den
in420US993
244NW644
f250NW[6]152
Ill
367NE1279
Mass
372NE246

- 370 -
(302Min301)
NY
349NE876
384S2d776

- 373 -
(302Min329)
243NW[9]114
f246NW[2]575
257NW[3]369
257NW[6]571
262NW[8]347
RI
376A2d6

- 385 -
(302Min407)

- 388 -
(193Neb9)

- 391 -
(193Neb45)
235NW[4]398
256NW[2]313
Ga
222SE653
72A3332n

- 397 -
(193Neb54)
cc189NW475

- 401 -
(193Neb59)
229NW[2]536
431FS[16]742

- 409 -
(193Neb71)

- 413 -
(193Neb76)
227NW[7]397
230NW[1]470
f241NW[8]362
264NW[8]681

- 416 -
(193Neb80)

- 418 -
(193Neb83)
237NW[1]150

- 420 -
(193Neb86)
80A3375n
80A3384n

- 422 -
(193Neb89)
cc236NW835
243NW[1]68

- 424 -
(193Neb90)

- 425 -
(193Neb91)
cc205NW351

- 426 -
(193Neb93)
Mass
339NE743
NJ
384A2d184

- 428 -
(66W421)
j236NW[5]12
j236NW[6]12
260NW[8]785

- 431 -
(66W551)
230NW[2]798
q235NW[3]684
238NW[5]80
j258NW[5]690
529F2d264
f547F2d[4]362
565F2d[1]111
j565F2d[2]443
Calif
132CaR609
Fla
327So2d203
Ill
374NE465
374NE865
Mo
551SW607
NM
540P2d841

- 438 -
(66W602)
234NW361
433FS1118

- 442 -
(66W563)
234NW[1]343
e234NW[3]344
253NW471
555F2d[2]2
NY
403S2d427

- 450 -
(66W611)
249NW[1]781

- 454 -
(66W382)
225NW[6]633
255NW502
e259NW[6]307
259NW[5]310

Minn
241NW[6]801
Calif
131CaR132
Mont
551P2d651
NM
568P2d220
568P2d230
Okla
563P2d145

- 461 -
(66W350)
(78A3273)
229NW[3]110
233NW[3]482
d233NW[5]489
f233NW[3]490
f243NW[1]474
f245NW[3]661
245NW[4]664
f246NW807
246NW[3]808
250NW[3]302
250NW[4]302
250NW[5]304
250NW[5]308

- 476 -
(66W428)

- 481 -
(66W595)

- 484 -
(66W544)

- 488 -
(66W620)

- 492 -
(66W628)
77A3200n

- 493 -
(66W630)
e249NW[3]286
251NW[3]11
541F2d[1]669
548F2d[1]701
422FS[1]823
77A3200n

- 495 -
(66W394)
Calif
127CaR166
138CaR317
563P2d873
69A3560n

- 501 -
(66W679)
227NW[1]636
j227NW[2]641
j227NW[3]641
233NW[2]468
254NW[2]247

- 505 -
(66W636)
230NW782
243NW502
249NW[11]777
251NW[11]31

252NW[11]682
253NW[16]217

- 517 -
Case 1
(66W788)

- 517 -
[illegible]
(66W790)

- 517 -
Case 4
(66W786)
s230NW269

- 518 -
Case 1
(66W789)

- 518 -
Case 2
(66W788)

- 518 -
Case 3
(66W789)

- 519 -
(392Mch685)

- 520 -
(393Mch807)
s217NW408
j255NW659
f255NW[1]659

- 521 -
(302Min249)
225NW851
263NW[1]424
Ariz
576P2d1377

- 531 -
(302Min465)

- 533 -
(302Min556)

- 534 -
(302Min471)
s246NW700
252NW[5]587

- 537 -
(302Min510)
SD
228NW[2]639
[illegible]
262NW[2]340

- 542 -
(303Min1)
256NW[4]291

- 546 -
(303Min534)

- 547 -
(193Neb104)
241NW[2]328
569F2d[2]1048

- 549 -
(193Neb108)
e237NW[2]89
[illegible]
238NW644

- 558 -
(193Neb122)
241NW[2]671
256NW[2]112
531F2d[2]861

- 562 -
(193Neb129)
233NW[1]913
246NW[1]598
250NW[1]609

- 565 -
(193Neb159)

- 567 -
(193Neb162)
251NW[1]146
531F2d[3]862

- 571 -
255NW[9]888
263NW[9]127
263NW[1]132

- 579 -
231NW[1]801
236NW[1]918
248NW[1]790
251NW[4]396
j251NW[5]400
259NW[1]492

- 584 -
263NW[2]132

- 589 -
250NW285
256NW[1]568
256NW[2]569
264NW[1]927

- 598 -
j227NW[1]437
241NW[3]591
Iowa
236NW[1]55
[illegible]
s222NW611
238NW729

- 604 -
Case 2
(66W405)
235NW[8]299
240NW367
242NW[7]220
264NW242

- 613 -
(66W439)
s175NW206
s194NW664
253NW503

- 617 -
(66W524)
[illegible]
Calif
128CaR723

- 628 -
(66W454)
243NW[1]403
243NW[7]823
243NW[12][illegible]
259NW[5]3
259NW[7]3

- 635 -
(66W508)
f226NW[1]434
233NW[9]477
j235NW[10]496
f237NW[9]732
f237NW[10]732
239NW[11]84
239NW[1]96
240NW[1]166
243NW[9]414
243NW[14]433
243NW[15]433
253NW[6]53
255NW[5]511
255NW[1]591

- 641 -
(66W675)
234NW[6]641

- 644 -
(66W535)
259NW[5]704
Me
363A2d746

- 648 -
(66W577)
237NW[1]698
242NW[10]896
242NW[11]896
255NW[10]479
255NW[14]479
260NW[1]726
265NW[1]271
265NW[4]271
265NW[6]271

- 658 -
(66W469)
US cert den
in427US904
r426US482
r49LE1
r96SC2308
s423US821
s423US1301
s46LE7
s46LE37
s96SC1
s96SC34

cc396FS1358
234NW[5]299
236NW[7]214
241NW[1]617
241NW[2]617
242NW[13]692
250NW[2]726
250NW[23]727
d250NW[17]729
251NW[19]201
259NW[11]730
e429FS485
Mich
j227NW[19]758
Md
367A2d930
Mo
564SW289
[illegible]

- 691 -
(57McA199)
225NW763

- 693 -
(57McA226)
228NW819

- 696 -
(57McA244)

- 697 -
(57McA247)
232NW738

- 700 -
(57McA100)

- 702 -
(57McA106)
247NW327

- 704 -
(57McA117)

- 708 -
(57McA123)

- 709 -
(57McA126)
250NW[1]474
d440FS[1]286
Ill
[illegible]
230NW[2]352
234NW[2]687
238NW[2]827
265NW[2]133
j265NW[2]404
435FS[2]289

- 716 -
(57McA143)
237NW[4]490

- 719 -
(57McA173)
[illegible]
d238NW[8]545
245NW[8]99
d248NW[8]644
e248NW[8]682
j248NW[8]685
255NW[4]777

- 727 -
(57McA277)
246NW[1]392
247NW[1]343
262NW[2]663
[illegible]
248NW[2]584
254NW[16]853
259NW[3]406
261NW[1]44
Mass
350NE453

- 738 -
(57McA300)
231NW[8]478
232NW[1]730
232NW[2]730
233NW[9]156
233NW[9]506
233NW[3]712
233NW[9]859
235NW[6]748
236NW[8]515
238NW[10]190
238NW[6]368
238NW[4]389
241NW[10]236
d242NW[10]520
246NW[3]426
248NW[5]692
251NW[4]261
254NW[4]665
259NW[8]192

- 742 -
(57McA308)
253NW[8]372

- 746 -
[illegible]
j250NW[3]540
258NW[5]216

- 748 -
(57McA320)
233NW[1]868
233NW[2]868
239NW[3]689
242NW[3]34
243NW16
259NW[4]405

847

Illustration G

Shepard's Northwestern Citations, 1979, vol. 2.

The procedure for using this citator is similar to that employed in other case units, as described in Illustration H.

LOWER FEDERAL COURT DECISIONS

Illustrative Case

Federal Reporter, Second Series

Vol. 508

–687–

US cert den
in425US998
v425US987 1
v48LE812
s542F2d8

Cir. D. C.
416FS438
Cir. 3
d538F2d
[1015
544F2d
[[7]1212
f398FS
[[22]1259
L398FS
[[28]1260
e419FS
[[26]627
q419FS
[[26]1048 5
424FS[1]1109
Cir. 4
540F2d
[[29]729
Cir. 5
415FS768
Cir. 6
546F2d
q[[28]689
Cir. 9
q536F2d819
542F2d[3]765
Cir. 10
f412FS
[[29]627

Pa
365A2d659 6

26ALRF125n 7

Citations to the case of Jersey Central Power & Light Co. v. International Brotherhood of Electrical Workers as reported in Volume 508 Federal Reporter, Second Series, at page 687 are shown in the left margin of this page.

Citations to the case of Tape Industries Association of America v. Evelle J. Younger as reported in Volume 316 Federal Supplement at page 340 are shown in the right margin of this page.

Any cross referenes to a cited case reported in Federal Supplement or Federal Reporter as also reported in United States Patents Quarterly, United States Court of Customs and Patent Appeals Reports (Customs or Patents), Decisions of the Commissioner of Patents or the Annotated Reports System are shown enclosed in parentheses immediately following the page number of that case and are not repeated in subsequent volumes.

Citations to each cited case are grouped as follows:

1. citations by federal and state courts analyzed as to the history of the cited case;
2. citations by the United States Supreme Court analyzed as to the treatment accorded the cited case;
3. citations in federal administrative reports;
4. citations in articles in Federal Rules Decisions and the American Bar Association Journal;
5. citations by the federal courts, other than the United States Supreme Court, analyzed as to the treatment accorded the cited case *arranged under their respective circuits;*
6. citations in state reports and units of the National Reporter System arranged under the appropriate state abbreviation; and
7. citations in annotations of Lawyers' Edition, United States Supreme Court Reports and the American Law Reports.

For the purpose of illustration only, this grouping has been indicated by bracketing the citations accordingly.

It will be noted that as yet there are no citations in groups two, three and four in the illustration on the left or in groups three and four in the illustration on the right.

In indicating the history and treatment of a cited case, letter abbreviations shown below are used.

The number of any paragraph of the syllabus or of any headnote of a cited lower federal court case stating a principle of law specifically dealt with in any citing federal court case is indicated by superior figure appearing immediately to the left of the page number of that citing case.

Federal Supplement

Vol. 316

–340–

(166PQ468)

1 D401US902
D27LE801
D91SC880

2 412US[9]549
37LE[9]170
93SC[9]2306

Cir. 2
f362FS[8]868
Cir. 5
494F2d29
344FS[9]50
5 q344FS51
Cir. 7
360FS[9]131
Cir. 8
376FS[5]216
Cir. 9
331FS128

Ill
130IlA433
264NE877
NC
11NCA24
180SE417
NJ
6 124Su327
306A2d495
So C
258SoC476
189SE311
Wis
64Wis2d166
218NW706

7 15LE904s

Illustration H

Instructions for Shepardizing lower federal court decisions, from *How to Use Shepard's Citations.*

3. U.S. SUPREME COURT CASES

The mechanics of *Shepardizing* a U.S. Supreme Court decision are basically similar to those just described for use with state and lower federal court cases. To *Shepardize Dodge v. United States,* 272 *U.S.* 530, for example, we would first assemble all volumes of *Shepard's U.S. Citations—Cases* that contain our case within their scope. The case first appears in the 1943 Case Edition, and Illustration I shows the list of citations found therein when we locate the case under its official citation. Note that the first listings are the parallel citations to the case as reported in unofficial reporters. Next are references to the prior history of the decision, including citations from the U.S. Supreme Court as well as lower federal courts. As can be seen in the Illustration, citations in this edition are listed in groups in both their official and unofficial forms. Following the history references are citations from subsequent Supreme Court and lower federal court opinions, organized according to the point of law to which they refer. A state case which has cited our case is listed next, again in both its official and unofficial citation. The final reference is to an annotated law report.

Each volume of *Shepard's U.S. Citations—Cases* contains sections which are organized according to the unofficial citations for Supreme Court cases. If we *Shepardize* the case by its *Supreme Court Reporter* and *Lawyers' Edition* citations in the 1943 volume which we are examining, the results, shown in Illustration J, are merely references to the case as reported in the official report.

However, if we continue to *Shepardize* the case in the 1943–71 Case Edition Supplement under all three of its citations, the results, shown in Illustration K, are quite different. A close examination of these three lists of sources shows the changes in Shepard's policy.

Note that in all volumes *after 1943,* citations from both the Supreme Court and lower federal courts are given in all three sections. However, parallel citations for the citing sources are no longer grouped together in the official *U.S. Reports* section. Currently, each section lists the source only in the same series as that being *Shepardized.*

Note also that, although the coverage in the unofficial sections has been expanded, it does not duplicate that in the official report section. Only by *Shepardizing* a case under its official citation will you find citations from federal administrative agencies and from state courts.

E. MECHANICS OF SHEPARDIZING STATUTES

Shepard's statutory citators update legislative enactments in much the same way as their case citators update judicial opinions. By locating a statute in the appropriate volume, the researcher can determine if it has been amended, repealed, or judicially interpreted in any way.

Although the mechanics of *Shepardizing* statutes are similar to those for *Shepardizing* cases, there are two basic points to remember when using a Shepard's statute edition:

1. Unlike judicial decisions, which, once reported, always retain the same citation, statutes may appear in different forms at different

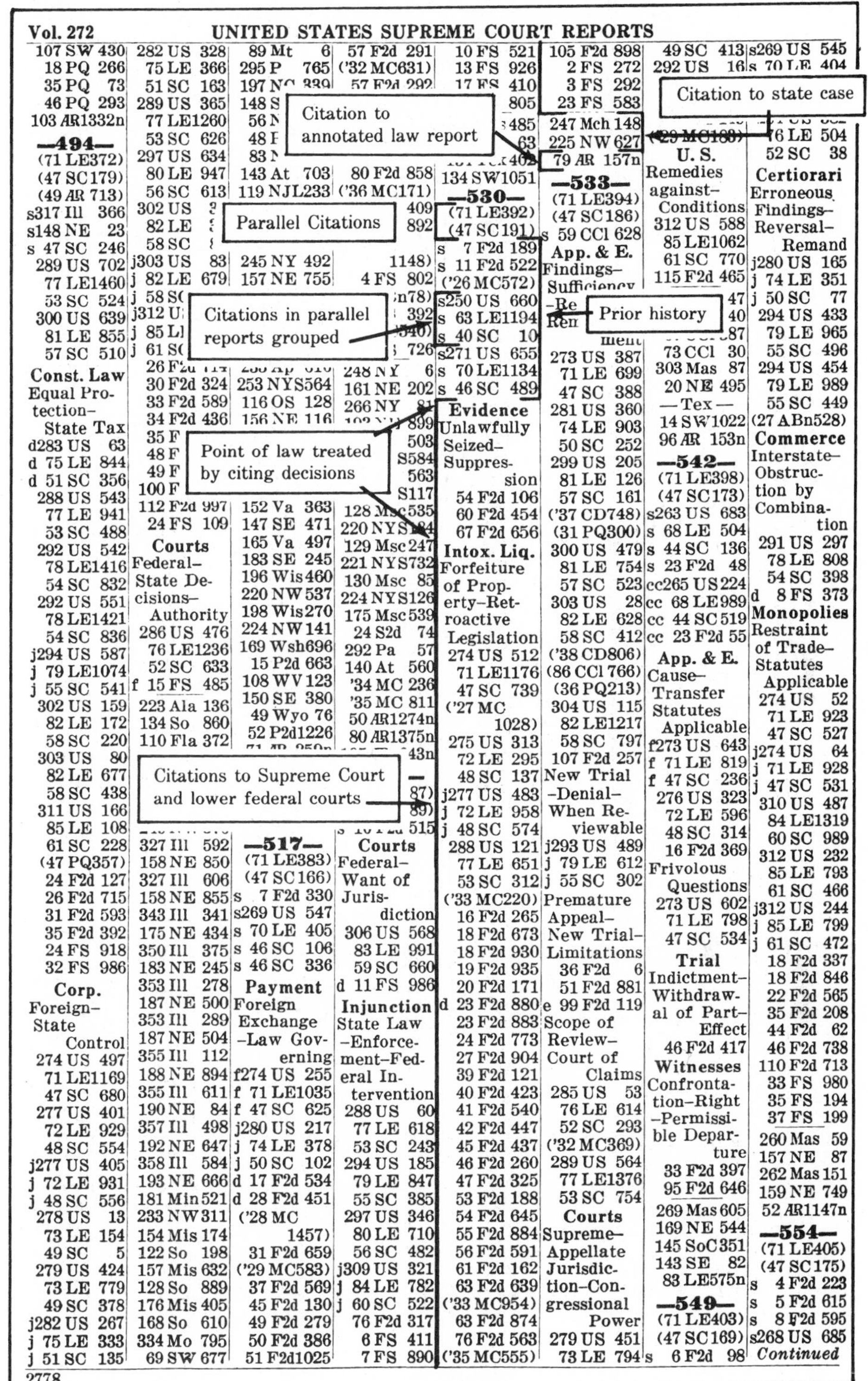

Vol. 272 UNITED STATES SUPREME COURT REPORTS

107 SW 430
18 PQ 266
35 PQ 73
46 PQ 293
103 AR1332n

—494—
(71 LE372)
(47 SC179)
(49 AR 713)
s317 Ill 366
s148 NE 23
s 47 SC 246
289 US 702
77 LE1460
53 SC 524
300 US 639
81 LE 855
57 SC 510
Const. Law
Equal Protection–State Tax
d283 US 63
d 75 LE 844
d 51 SC 356
288 US 543
77 LE 941
53 SC 488
292 US 542
78 LE1416
54 SC 832
292 US 551
78 LE1421
54 SC 836
j294 US 587
j 79 LE1074
j 55 SC 541
302 US 159
82 LE 172
58 SC 220
303 US 80
82 LE 677
58 SC 438
311 US 166
85 LE 108
61 SC 228
(47 PQ357)
24 F2d 127
26 F2d 715
31 F2d 593
35 F2d 392
24 FS 918
32 FS 986
Corp.
Foreign–State Control
274 US 497
71 LE1169
47 SC 680
277 US 401
72 LE 929
48 SC 554
j277 US 405
j 72 LE 931
j 48 SC 556
278 US 13
73 LE 154
49 SC 5
279 US 424
73 LE 779
49 SC 378
j282 US 267
j 75 LE 333
j 51 SC 135

282 US 328
75 LE 366
51 SC 163
289 US 365
77 LE1260
53 SC 626
297 US 634
80 LE 947
56 SC 613
j303 US 83
j 82 LE 679
30 F2d 324
33 F2d 589
34 F2d 436
112 F2d 997
24 FS 109
Courts
Federal–State Decisions–Authority
286 US 476
76 LE1236
52 SC 633
f 15 FS 485
223 Ala 136
134 So 860
110 Fla 372
327 Ill 592
158 NE 850
327 Ill 606
158 NE 855
343 Ill 341
175 NE 434
350 Ill 375
183 NE 245
353 Ill 278
187 NE 500
353 Ill 289
187 NE 504
355 Ill 112
188 NE 894
355 Ill 611
190 NE 84
357 Ill 498
192 NE 647
358 Ill 584
193 NE 666
181 Min 521
233 NW 311
154 Mis 174
122 So 198
157 Mis 632
128 So 889
176 Mis 405
168 So 610
334 Mo 795
69 SW 677

89 Mt 6
295 P 765
143 At 703
119 NJL233
245 NY 492
157 NE 755
253 NYS564
116 OS 128
152 Va 363
147 SE 471
165 Va 497
183 SE 245
196 Wis 460
220 NW 537
198 Wis 270
224 NW 141
169 Wsh 696
15 P2d 663
108 WV 123
150 SE 380
49 Wyo 76
52 P2d1226

—517—
(71 LE383)
(47 SC166)
s 7 F2d 330
s269 US 547
s 70 LE 405
s 46 SC 106
s 46 SC 336
Payment
Foreign Exchange–Law Governing
f274 US 255
f 71 LE1035
f 47 SC 625
j280 US 217
j 74 LE 378
j 50 SC 102
d 17 F2d 534
d 28 F2d 451
('28 MC 1457)
31 F2d 659
('29 MC583)
37 F2d 569
45 F2d 130
49 F2d 279
50 F2d 386
51 F2d1025

57 F2d 291
('32 MC631)
80 F2d 858
('36 MC171)
4 FS 802
248 NY 6
161 NE 202
266 NY 81
128 Msc535
220 NYS184
129 Msc247
221 NYS732
130 Msc 85
224 NYS126
175 Msc539
24 S2d 74
292 Pa 57
140 At 560
'34 MC 236
'35 MC 811
50 AR1274n
80 AR1375n
Courts
Federal–Want of Jurisdiction
306 US 568
83 LE 991
59 SC 660
d 11 FS 986
Injunction
State Law–Enforcement–Federal Intervention
288 US 60
77 LE 618
53 SC 243
294 US 185
79 LE 847
55 SC 385
297 US 346
80 LE 710
56 SC 482
j309 US 321
j 84 LE 782
j 60 SC 522
76 F2d 317
6 FS 411
7 FS 890

10 FS 521
13 FS 926
17 FS 410
134 SW1051

—530—
(71 LE392)
(47 SC191)
s 7 F2d 189
s 11 F2d 522
('26 MC572)
s250 US 660
s 63 LE1194
s 40 SC 10
s271 US 655
s 70 LE1134
s 46 SC 489
Evidence
Unlawfully Seized–Suppression
54 F2d 106
60 F2d 454
67 F2d 656
Intox. Liq.
Forfeiture of Property–Retroactive Legislation
274 US 512
71 LE1176
47 SC 739
('27 MC 1028)
275 US 313
72 LE 295
48 SC 137
j277 US 483
j 72 LE 958
j 48 SC 574
288 US 121
77 LE 651
53 SC 312
('33 MC220)
16 F2d 265
18 F2d 673
18 F2d 930
19 F2d 935
20 F2d 171
d 23 F2d 880
23 F2d 883
24 F2d 773
27 F2d 904
39 F2d 121
40 F2d 423
41 F2d 540
42 F2d 447
45 F2d 437
46 F2d 260
47 F2d 325
53 F2d 188
54 F2d 645
55 F2d 884
56 F2d 591
61 F2d 162
63 F2d 639
('33 MC954)
63 F2d 874
76 F2d 563
('35 MC555)

105 F2d 898
2 FS 272
3 FS 292
23 FS 583
247 Mch 148
225 NW 627
79 AR 157n

—533—
(71 LE394)
(47 SC186)
s 59 CCl 628
App. & E.
Findings–Sufficiency
273 US 387
71 LE 699
47 SC 388
281 US 360
74 LE 903
50 SC 252
299 US 205
81 LE 126
57 SC 161
('37 CD748)
(31 PQ300)
300 US 479
81 LE 754
57 SC 523
303 US 28
82 LE 628
58 SC 412
('38 CD806)
(86 CCl 766)
(36 PQ213)
304 US 115
82 LE1217
58 SC 797
107 F2d 257
New Trial–Denial–When Reviewable
j293 US 489
j 79 LE 612
j 55 SC 302
Premature Appeal–New Trial–Limitations
36 F2d 6
51 F2d 881
e 99 F2d 119
Scope of Review–Court of Claims
285 US 53
76 LE 614
52 SC 293
('32 MC369)
289 US 564
77 LE1376
53 SC 754
Courts
Supreme–Appellate Jurisdiction–Congressional Power
279 US 451
73 LE 794

49 SC 413
292 US 16
U. S.
Remedies against–Conditions
312 US 588
85 LE1062
61 SC 770
115 F2d 465
73 CCl 30
303 Mas 87
20 NE 495
—Tex—
14 SW1022
96 AR 153n

—542—
(71 LE398)
(47 SC173)
s263 US 683
s 68 LE 504
s 44 SC 136
s 23 F2d 48
cc265 US 224
cc 68 LE 989
cc 44 SC 519
cc 23 F2d 55
App. & E.
Cause–Transfer Statutes Applicable
f273 US 643
f 71 LE 819
f 47 SC 236
276 US 323
72 LE 596
48 SC 314
16 F2d 369
Frivolous Questions
273 US 602
71 LE 798
47 SC 534
Trial
Indictment–Withdrawal of Part–Effect
46 F2d 417
Witnesses
Confrontation–Right–Permissible Departure
33 F2d 397
95 F2d 646
269 Mas 605
169 NE 544
145 SoC 351
143 SE 82
83 LE575n

—549—
(71 LE403)
(47 SC169)
s 6 F2d 98

s269 US 545
52 SC 38
Certiorari
Erroneous Findings–Reversal–Remand
j280 US 165
j 74 LE 351
j 50 SC 77
294 US 433
79 LE 965
55 SC 496
294 US 454
79 LE 989
55 SC 449
(27 ABn528)
Commerce
Interstate–Obstruction by Combination
291 US 297
78 LE 808
54 SC 398
d 8 FS 373
Monopolies
Restraint of Trade–Statutes Applicable
274 US 52
71 LE 923
47 SC 527
j274 US 64
j 71 LE 928
j 47 SC 531
310 US 487
84 LE1319
60 SC 989
312 US 232
85 LE 793
61 SC 466
j312 US 244
j 85 LE 799
j 61 SC 472
18 F2d 337
18 F2d 846
22 F2d 565
35 F2d 208
44 F2d 62
46 F2d 738
110 F2d 713
33 FS 980
35 FS 194
37 FS 199
260 Mas 59
157 NE 87
262 Mas 151
159 NE 749
52 AR1147n

—554—
(71 LE405)
(47 SC175)
s 4 F2d 223
s 5 F2d 615
s 8 F2d 595
s268 US 685
Continued

2778

Illustration I

Shepard's *U.S. Citations—Cases,* 1943 Edition.

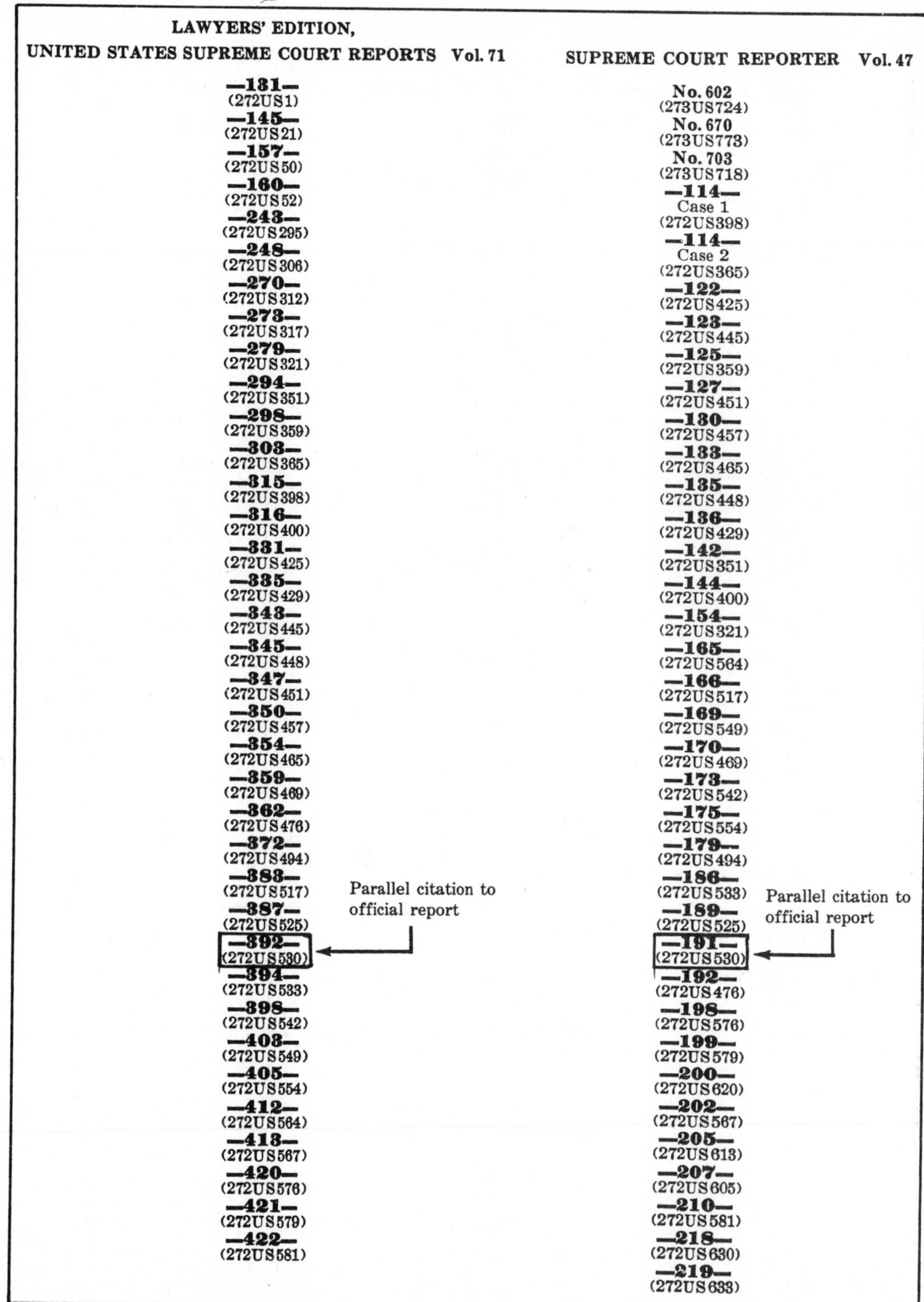

LAWYERS' EDITION,
UNITED STATES SUPREME COURT REPORTS Vol. 71

—131—
(272US1)
—145—
(272US21)
—157—
(272US50)
—160—
(272US52)
—243—
(272US295)
—248—
(272US306)
—270—
(272US312)
—273—
(272US317)
—279—
(272US321)
—294—
(272US351)
—298—
(272US359)
—303—
(272US365)
—315—
(272US398)
—316—
(272US400)
—331—
(272US425)
—335—
(272US429)
—343—
(272US445)
—345—
(272US448)
—347—
(272US451)
—350—
(272US457)
—354—
(272US465)
—359—
(272US469)
—362—
(272US476)
—372—
(272US494)
—383—
(272US517)
—387—
(272US525)
—392—
(272US530)
—394—
(272US533)
—398—
(272US542)
—403—
(272US549)
—405—
(272US554)
—412—
(272US564)
—418—
(272US567)
—420—
(272US576)
—421—
(272US579)
—422—
(272US581)

SUPREME COURT REPORTER Vol. 47

No. 602
(273US724)
No. 670
(273US773)
No. 703
(273US718)
—114—
Case 1
(272US398)
—114—
Case 2
(272US365)
—122—
(272US425)
—123—
(272US445)
—125—
(272US359)
—127—
(272US451)
—130—
(272US457)
—133—
(272US465)
—135—
(272US448)
—136—
(272US429)
—142—
(272US351)
—144—
(272US400)
—154—
(272US321)
—165—
(272US564)
—166—
(272US517)
—169—
(272US549)
—170—
(272US469)
—173—
(272US542)
—175—
(272US554)
—179—
(272US494)
—186—
(272US533)
—189—
(272US525)
—191—
(272US530)
—192—
(272US476)
—198—
(272US576)
—199—
(272US579)
—200—
(272US620)
—202—
(272US567)
—205—
(272US613)
—207—
(272US605)
—210—
(272US581)
—218—
(272US630)
—219—
(272US633)

Illustration J

References under the *Supreme Court Reporter* and *Lawyers' Edition* citations in Shepard's *United States Citations—Cases,* 1943 Edition.

UNITED STATES SUPREME COURT REPORTS

Vol. 272

-530-
h380US[1]700
46F2d[1]260
147F2d[1]83
157F2d[1]793
d182F2d[1]182
187F2d[1]504
f199F2d[1]37
201F2d[1]159
220F2d[1]203
253F2d[1]727
f272F2d[1]494
f303F2d[1]38
326F2d[1]361
d340F2d[1]171
340F2d173
391F2d[1]268
402F2d616
412F2d[1]588
62FS[1]634
65FS898
65FS[1]898
74FS[1]630
88FS[1]96
d101FS[1]495
108FS[1]263
185FS[1]76
f200FS[1]32
210FS[1]52
250FS185
287FS[1]923
TD-44774
TD-45684
TD-51203
7Alk609
243Ark54
218Min519
414Pa544
43PRR824
69PRR408
Ark
418SW619
418SW621
Ky
273SW583
Minn
16NW784
Pa
201A2d430

LAWYERS' EDITION,

Vol. 71

-392-
h14LE[1]174
46F2d[1]260
147F2d[1]83
157F2d[1]793
d182F2d[1]182
187F2d[1]504
f199F2d[1]37
201F2d[1]159
220F2d[1]203
253F2d[1]727
f272F2d[1]494
f303F2d[1]38
326F2d[1]361
d340F2d[1]171
340F2d173
391F2d[1]268
402F2d616
412F2d[1]588
62FS[1]634
65FS898
65FS[1]898
74FS[1]630
88FS[1]96
d101FS[1]495
108FS[1]263
185FS[1]76
f200FS[1]32
210FS[1]52
250FS185
287FS[1]923
8Æ475n

SUPREME COURT REPORTER

Vol. 47

-191-
h85SC[1]1250
46F2d[1]260
147F2d[1]83
157F2d[1]793
d182F2d[1]182
187F2d[1]504
f199F2d[1]37
201F2d[1]159
220F2d[1]203
253F2d[1]727
f272F2d[1]494
f303F2d[1]38
326F2d[1]361
d340F2d[1]171
340F2d173
391F2d[1]268
402F2d616
412F2d[1]588
62FS[1]634
65FS898
74FS[1]630
88FS[1]96
d101FS[1]495
108FS[1]263
185FS[1]76
f200FS[1]32

Illustration K

Shepard's *U.S. Citations—Cases,* 1943–71 Case Supplement.

times. A session law, for example, may become a code section which may then be recodified at a later date. Shepard's has adopted the practice of listing citations to a statute only under its designation at the time of listing. Hence, if a session law has not yet been codified at the time of printing of a Shepard's volume, citations to it in that volume will be found under its session law notation. However, if the law is subsequently incorporated into a code, it must be *Shepardized* under its code section in any succeeding Shepard's volume published after the date of the codification. When preparing cumulations, however, the Shepard's editors do attempt to transfer prior citations listed under an old form of the statute to the current listing under its new form.

2. Courts often cite a number of related statutory provisions in one group, *e.g.*, § 2102 *et seq.*, or § 2102 to § 2105. Because Shepard's mechanically extracts citations from the material it examines, references to such groups of code sections regularly appear in Shepard's statute editions. When *Shepardizing* a particular code section, then, one must be certain to check not only the listings under that particular section, but also the listings under any relevant group of code sections that may include it.

Illustration L shows the citations found when *Shepardizing* § 944.17 of the 1977 Wisconsin Statutes in the 1979 Bound Volume of the statute edition of *Shepard's Wisconsin Citations.* The Table of Abbreviations used in this edition is reproduced in Illustration M, which differs slightly from that for United States statutes.

The types of citing sources found in Illustration L are similar to those in the case editions. The first citation listed indicates subsequent legislative history of the statute. Note that § 944.17 has been amended by Chapter 173 of the *1977 Laws of Wisconsin.* The second group of references are citations from the Supreme Court of Wisconsin and federal courts, which may be analyzed to indicate judicial treatment. It can be seen that our statute has been declared constitutional at 381 *F.Supp.* 988. The next three groups are from a state attorney general's opinion, law review articles, and an *A.L.R.* annotation. The final set of citations are to specific subsections of the law that have been cited.

In addition to references to home state statutes, each Shepard's state statute edition typically provides citations to the U.S. Constitution, the *U.S. Code,* U.S. *Statutes at Large* sections that have not been codified, treaties, and federal court rules. Also included as cited material in Shepard's state statute citators are *uncodified* state session laws, state court rules, and municipal charters and ordinances. Since the coverage for each of the state units varies, one should consult the Table of Contents in each volume to determine its exact scope.

F. ADDITIONAL SHEPARD'S UNITS

In addition to the state and federal units described above, Shepard's publishes a variety of specialized citators. Some of these are

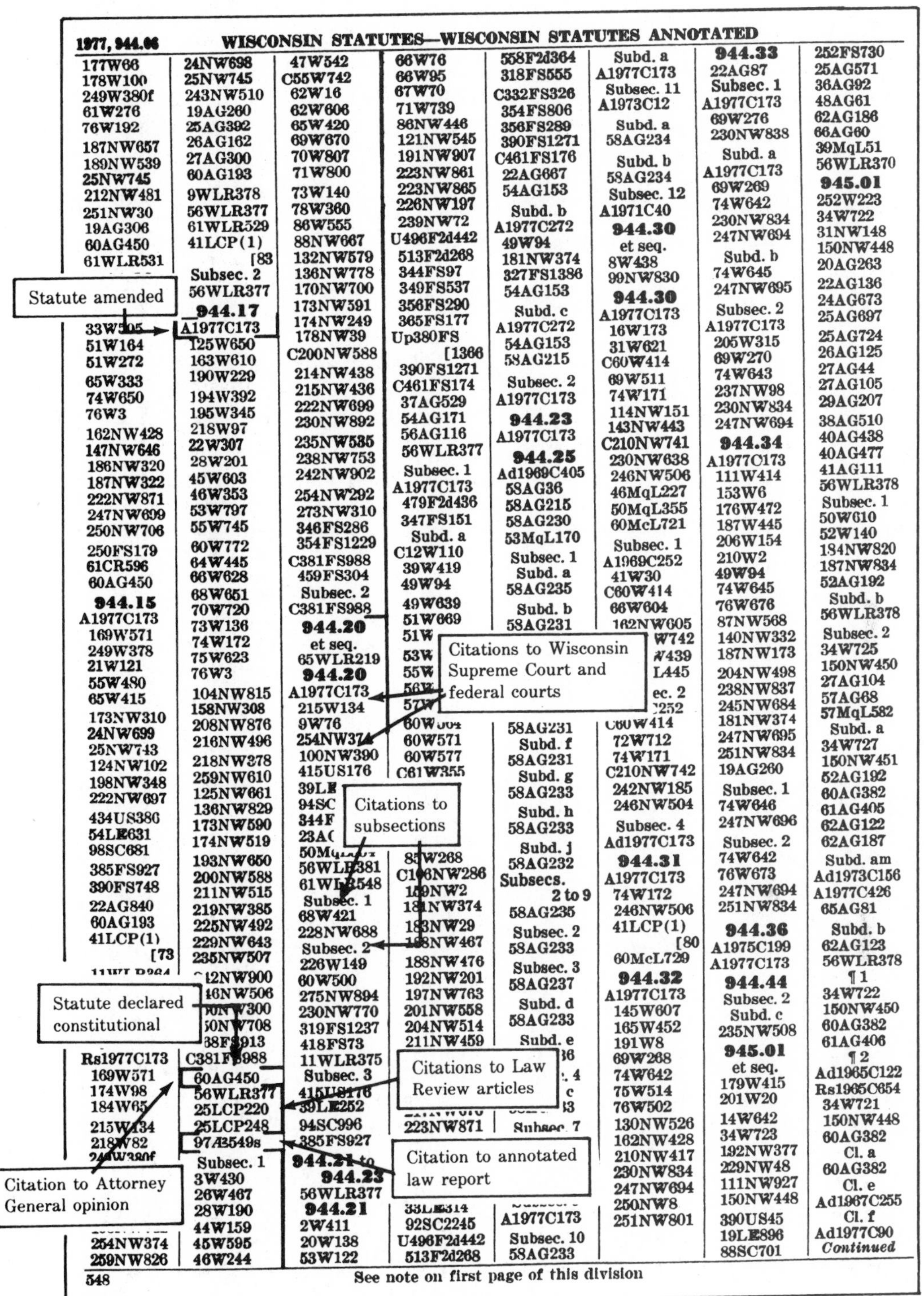
1977, 944.06 WISCONSIN STATUTES—WISCONSIN STATUTES ANNOTATED

177W66 178W100 249W380f 61W276 76W192 187NW657 189NW539 25NW745 212NW481 251NW30 19AG306 60AG450 61WLR531 33W505 51W164 51W272 65W333 74W650 76W3 162NW428 147NW646 186NW320 187NW322 222NW871 247NW699 250NW706 250FS179 61CR596 60AG450 **944.15** A1977C173 169W571 249W378 21W121 55W480 65W415 173NW310 24NW699 25NW743 124NW102 198NW348 222NW697 434US386 54LE631 98SC681 385FS927 390FS748 22AG840 60AG193 41LCP(1) [73 Rs1977C173 169W571 174W98 184W65 215W134 218W82 254NW374 259NW826

24NW698 25NW745 243NW510 19AG260 25AG392 26AG162 27AG300 60AG193 9WLR378 56WLR377 61WLR529 41LCP(1) [83 Subsec. 2 56WLR377 **944.17** A1977C173 125W650 163W610 190W229 194W392 195W345 218W97 22W307 28W201 45W603 46W353 53W797 55W745 60W772 64W445 66W628 68W651 70W720 73W136 74W172 75W623 76W3 104NW815 158NW308 208NW876 216NW496 218NW378 259NW610 125NW661 136NW829 173NW590 174NW519 193NW650 200NW588 211NW515 219NW385 225NW492 229NW643 235NW507 C381FS988 60AG450 56WLR377 25LCP220 25LCP248 97A3549s Subsec. 1 3W430 26W467 28W190 44W159 45W595 46W244

47W542 C55W742 62W16 62W606 65W420 69W670 70W807 71W800 73W140 78W360 86W555 88NW667 132NW579 136NW778 170NW700 173NW591 174NW249 178NW39 C200NW588 214NW438 215NW436 222NW699 230NW892 235NW585 238NW753 242NW902 254NW292 273NW310 346FS286 354FS1229 C381FS988 459FS304 Subsec. 2 C381FS988 **944.20** et seq. 65WLR219 **944.20** A1977C173 215W134 9W76 254NW374 100NW390 415US176 56WLR381 61WLR548 Subsec. 1 68W421 228NW688 Subsec. 2 226W149 60W500 275NW894 230NW770 319FS1237 418FS73 11WLR375 Subsec. 3 415US176 39LE252 94SC996 385FS927 **944.21 to 944.23** 56WLR377 **944.21** 2W411 20W138 53W122

66W76 66W95 67W70 71W739 86NW446 121NW545 191NW907 223NW861 223NW865 226NW197 239NW72 U496F2d442 513F2d268 344FS97 349FS537 356FS290 365FS177 Up380FS [1366 390FS1271 C461FS174 37AG529 54AG171 56AG116 56WLR377 Subsec. 1 A1977C173 479F2d436 347FS151 Subd. a C12W110 39W419 49W94 49W639 51W669 60W571 60W577 C61W355 188NW476 192NW201 197NW763 201NW558 204NW514 211NW459 223NW871 92SC2245 U496F2d442 513F2d268

558F2d364 318FS555 C332FS326 354FS806 356FS289 390FS1271 C461FS176 22AG667 54AG153 Subd. b A1977C272 49W94 181NW374 327FS1386 54AG153 Subd. c A1977C272 54AG153 58AG215 Subsec. 2 A1977C173 **944.23** A1977C173 **944.25** Ad1969C405 58AG36 58AG215 58AG230 53MqL170 Subsec. 1 Subd. a 58AG235 Subd. b 58AG231 58AG231 Subd. f 58AG231 Subd. g 58AG233 Subd. h 58AG233 Subd. j 58AG232 Subsecs. 2 to 9 58AG235 Subsec. 2 58AG233 Subsec. 3 58AG237 Subd. d 58AG233 Subd. e Subsec. 7 A1977C173 Subsec. 10 58AG233

Subd. a A1977C173 Subsec. 11 A1973C12 Subd. a 58AG234 Subd. b 58AG234 Subsec. 12 A1971C40 **944.30** et seq. 8W438 99NW830 **944.30** A1977C173 16W173 31W621 C60W414 69W511 74W171 114NW151 143NW443 C210NW741 230NW638 246NW506 46MqL227 50MqL355 60McL721 Subsec. 1 A1969C252 41W30 C60W414 66W604 162NW605 C60W414 72W712 74W171 C210NW742 242NW185 246NW504 Subsec. 4 Ad1977C173 **944.31** A1977C173 74W172 246NW506 41LCP(1) [80 60McL729 **944.32** A1977C173 145W607 165W452 191W8 69W268 74W642 75W514 76W502 130NW526 162NW428 210NW417 230NW834 247NW694 250NW8 251NW801

944.33 22AG87 Subsec. 1 A1977C173 69W276 230NW838 Subd. a A1977C173 69W269 74W642 230NW834 247NW694 Subd. b 74W645 247NW695 Subsec. 2 A1977C173 205W315 69W270 74W643 237NW98 230NW834 247NW694 **944.34** A1977C173 111W414 153W6 176W472 187W445 206W154 210W2 49W94 74W645 76W676 87NW568 140NW332 187NW173 204NW498 238NW837 245NW684 181NW374 247NW695 251NW834 19AG260 Subsec. 1 74W646 247NW696 Subsec. 2 74W642 76W673 247NW694 251NW834 **944.36** A1975C199 A1977C173 **944.44** Subsec. 2 Subd. c 235NW508 **945.01** et seq. 179W415 201W20 14W642 34W723 192NW377 229NW48 111NW927 150NW448 390US45 19LE896 88SC701

252FS730 25AG571 36AG92 48AG61 62AG186 66AG60 39MqL51 56WLR370 **945.01** 252W223 34W722 31NW148 150NW448 20AG263 22AG136 24AG673 25AG697 25AG724 26AG125 27AG44 27AG105 29AG207 38AG510 40AG438 40AG477 41AG111 56WLR378 Subsec. 1 50W610 52W140 184NW820 187NW834 52AG192 Subd. b 56WLR378 Subsec. 2 34W725 150NW450 27AG104 57AG68 57MqL582 Subd. a 34W727 150NW451 52AG192 60AG382 61AG405 62AG122 62AG187 Subd. am Ad1973C156 A1977C426 65AG81 Subd. b 62AG123 56WLR378 ¶1 34W722 150NW450 60AG382 61AG406 ¶2 Ad1965C122 Rs1965C654 34W721 150NW448 60AG382 Cl. a 60AG382 Cl. e Ad1967C255 Cl. f Ad1977C90 *Continued*

548 See note on first page of this division

Illustration L

Shepard's *Wisconsin Citations—Statutes,* 1979 Bound Volume.

ABBREVIATIONS—ANALYSIS

Form of Statute

Adj.	Adjourned Session	Intro. Par.	Introductory Paragraph	§	Section
Amend.	Amendment	J.R.	Joint Resolution	Sp.	Special Session
Art.	Article	Mem. Ch.	Memorial Chapter	St.	Statutes at Large
Ch. or C	Chapter	No.	Number	Subch.	Subchapter
Cl.	Clause	p	Page	Subd.	Subdivision
Ex. Ord.	Executive Order	¶	Paragraph	Subsec.	Subsection
		P.L.	Public Law	Vet. Reg.	Veterans Regulations

Operation of Statute

Legislative

A	(amended)	Statute amended.
Ad	(added)	New section added.
E	(extended)	Provisions of an existing statute extended in their application to a later statute, or allowance of additional time for performance of duties required by a statute within a limited time.
L	(limited)	Provisions of an existing statute declared not to be extended in their application to a later statute.
R	(repealed)	Abrogation of an existing statute.
Re-en	(re-enacted)	Statute re-enacted.
Rn	(renumbered)	Renumbering of existing sections.
Rp	(repealed in part)	Abrogation of part of an existing statute.
Rs	(repealed and superseded)	Abrogation of an existing statute and substitution of new legislation therefor.
Rv	(revised)	Statute revised.
S	(superseded)	Substitution of new legislation for an existing statute not expressly abrogated.
Sd	(suspended)	Statute suspended.
Sdp	(suspended in part)	Statute suspended in part.
Sg	(supplementing)	New matter added to an existing statute.
Sp	(superseded in part)	Substitution of new legislation for part of an existing statute not expressly abrogated.
Va	(validated)	

Judicial

C	Constitutional.	V	Void or invalid.
U	Unconstitutional.	Va	Valid.
Up	Unconstitutional in part.	Vp	Void or invalid in part.

xii

Illustration M

Abbreviations for statutes, appearing in Shepard's *Wisconsin Citations—Statutes,* 1979 Bound Volume.

devoted to specific legal subjects, while others treat particular types of legal material. The specialized citators presently available include the following:

1. BANKRUPTCY CITATIONS

This service, begun in 1980, provides citations to court decisions and statutes relating to the subject of bankruptcy. It includes as cited sources: bankruptcy decisions as reported in the federal reporters, looseleaf services, and *American Bankruptcy Reports,* as well as federal statutes, and rules and orders relating to bankruptcy.

2. CODE OF FEDERAL REGULATIONS CITATIONS

This unit, which has been published since 1979, lists citations to the *Code of Federal Regulations,* Presidential proclamations, executive orders, and reorganization plans that have appeared in federal court cases (including those reported in the *West Bankruptcy Reporter*), state court cases, annotated law reports, selected law reviews and legal texts, and the *American Bar Association Journal.* Illustration N shows an example of the citations found in this unit.

3. CRIMINAL JUSTICE CITATIONS

Shepard's *Criminal Justice Citations* enables the researcher to locate references in court decisions since 1972, to the American Bar Association's *Standards Relating to the Administration of Criminal Justice.*

4. FEDERAL LABOR LAW CITATIONS

This citator unit, published since 1959, consists of a Case Edition, and a Statute and Cross Reference Edition. The Case Edition lists citations to decisions and orders of the National Labor Relations Board (Illustration O) and to labor cases in both state and federal courts beginning with 1935. The Statute Edition, beginning with 1947, provides citations to those sections of the *U.S. Code* which deal with labor issues, and includes cross references between NLRB decisions and court opinions, and those decisions as reported in the various labor law looseleaf services.

5. FEDERAL LAW CITATIONS IN SELECTED LAW REVIEWS

As noted above in Section C, all Shepard's *state* units provide citations to twenty national law reviews, as well as legal periodicals in that state. To locate law review citations to federal cases and statutes, however, one must use *Federal Law Citations in Selected Law Reviews,* which contains references from eighteen leading law reviews to U.S. Supreme Court and lower federal court decisions, as well as to the U.S. Constitution, *U.S. Code,* and federal court rules. A detailed listing of the specific volumes of each law review that are within the citing scope of this unit can be found in its preface. Illustration P shows an example of references provided in this citator.

TITLE 26 **CODE OF FEDERAL REGULATIONS**

§1.481-2(b)
346FS569 △1972

§1.481-2(c)
346FS569 △1972

§1.481-2(c)(5)(i)
346FS567 △1972

§1.481-2(c)(5)(ii)
346FS568 △1972

§1.481-2(d)
571F2d520 *1974

§1.481-3
280FS241 △1967
346FS566 △1972

§1.481-4(g)(3)
532F2d1355 △1976

§1.481-5
621F2d410 *1959

§1.481-6(b)
322F2d937 △1963

§1.481-6(c)
322F2d937 △1963

§1.482
452F2d139 △1971
452F2d448 △1971

§1.482-1
et seq.
608F2d450 *1968

§1.482-1
410F2d1244 △1969
Va500F2d109 △1974
601F2d902 △1979
215FS597 *1962

§1.482-1(a)(1)
453F2d1152 △1972
530F2d777 *1968
ICT§14.02

§1.482-1(a)(2)
453F2d1152 △1972
530F2d777 *1968
ICT§14.02

§1.482-1(a)(3)
343F2d722 △1965
372F2d419 △1967
407F2d632 *1967
453F2d1152 △1972
598F2d1378 △1979
598F2d1389 *1968
367FS511 △1973
EPFR§11.18
ICT§14.02

§1.482-1(a)(4)
556F2d892 △1977

§1.482-1(a)(6)
405US400 *1971
31LE324 *1971
92SC1089 *1971
362F2d213 △1966
396F2d269 △1968
453F2d1156 △1972

585F2d813 △1978
359FS164 △1973
ICT§14.02

§1.482-1(b)
372F2d419 △1967
417F2d292 △1969
436F2d1195 △1971
453F2d1151 △1972
456F2d1352 △1972
510F2d569 △1975
602F2d279 *1962
617F2d947 △1980
325FS1302 △1971

§1.482-1(b)(1)
405US400 *1971
31LE324 *1971
92SC1090 *1971
362F2d213 △1966
372F2d995 △1967
468F2d807 *1972
498F2d229 △1974
551F2d80 *1976
556F2d891 △1977
598F2d1378 △1979
602F2d279 △1979
608F2d455 △1979
322FS931 △1971
359FS163 △1973
ICT§14.02

Citations to 26 *CFR* § 1.482–1 (b)(1)

361F2d610 △1966
572F2d1048 △1978
602F2d275 *1968
617F2d17 △1980

§1.482-1(c)
361F2d670 △1966
372F2d419 △1967
435F2d58 △1970
436F2d1195 △1971
453F2d1151 △1972
508F2d1102 △1975
510F2d569 △1975
608F2d449 △1979
617F2d947 △1980
ICT§14.04

§1.482-1(d)
602F2d280 △1979

§1.482-1(d)(1)
498F2d227 △1974
359FS165 △1973
ICT§14.05

§1.482-1(d)(2)
498F2d228 △1974
508F2d1102 △1975
Va551F2d80 *1976
572F2d1048 △1978
602F2d272 *1968
359FS162 △1973
397FS927 △1975
ICT§14.05
ICT§14.05
ICT§14.05

§1.482-1(d)(2)(i)
Va551F2d80 *1976

§1.482-1(d)(2)(ii)
Va551F2d80 *1976

§1.482-1(d)(2)(iii)
Va551F2d80 *1976

§1.482-1(d)(2)(iv)
Va551F2d80 *1976

§1.482-1(d)(2)(v)
508F2d1102 △1975
Va551F2d80 *1976

§1.482-1(d)(3)
498F2d230 △1974
602F2d274 *1968
617F2d950 △1980
ICT§14.06

§1.482-1(d)(4)
508F2d1100 △1975
ICT§14.07

§1.482-1(d)(5)
ICT§14.07

§1.482-1(d)(6)
ICT§14.08

§1.482-2
[illegible]d807 *1972
[illegible]d669 △1973
[illegible]2d109 △1974
[illegible]d1101 △1975
585F2d240 △1978
602F2d281 △1979
359FS164 *1968

§1.482-2(a)
Va486F2d3 *1968
508F2d1101 △1975
602F2d276 *1968
359FS163 △1973

§1.482-2(a)(1)
498F2d229 △1974
508F2d1100 △1975
553F2d646 △1977
359FS163 △1973
ICT§14.09

§1.482-2(a)(2)
453F2d1156 △1972
498F2d229 △1974
553F2d647 △1977

§1.482-2(a)(2)(i)
498F2d230 △1974
602F2d281 △1979
ICT§14.09

§1.482-2(a)(2)(ii)
498F2d230 △1974
508F2d1101 △1975
602F2d272 *1968
359FS163 △1973
ICT§14.10

§1.482-2(a)(2)(iii)(A)
ICT§14.11

§1.482-2(a)(2)(iii)(B)
553F2d645 △1977
ICT§14.11

§1.482-2(a)(2)(iv)(A)
ICT§14.12

§1.482-2(a)(2)(iv)(B)
ICT§14.11

§1.482-2(a)(3)
ICT§14.09

§1.482-2(b)
468F2d808 *1972
617F2d947 △1980
304FS634 △1969
ICT§14.20

§1.482-2(b)(1)
ICT§14.14

§1.482-2(b)(2)(i)
ICT§14.14

§1.482-2(b)(2)(ii)
ICT§3.08

§1.482-2(b)(3)
510F2d569 △1975
617F2d947 △1980
304FS634 *1969
ICT§14.14

§1.482-2(b)(4)(i)
ICT§14.14

§1.482-2(b)(4)(ii)
ICT§14.14

§1.482-2(b)(4)(iii)
ICT§14.14

§1.482-2(b)(5)
ICT§14.14

§1.482-2(b)(6)(i)
ICT§14.15

§1.482-2(b)(6)(ii)
ICT§14.15

§1.482-2(b)(6)(iii)
ICT§14.15

§1.482-2(b)(7)
304FS635 *1969
ICT§14.16

§1.482-2(b)(7)(i)
ICT§14.16

§1.482-2(b)(7)(ii)(a)
510F2d569 △1975
ICT§14.17

§1.482-2(b)(7)(ii)(c)
ICT§14.17

§1.482-2(b)(7)(iii)
ICT§14.18

§1.482-2(b)(7)(iv)
ICT§14.19

* followed by a year refers to the CFR edition, if cited. If not cited,
△ followed by a year indicates the date of the citing reference

Illustration N

Shepard's *Code of Federal Regulations Citations,* 1981.

Vol. 192 **Decisions and Orders of the National Labor Relations Board**

s424US507
s47LE196
s96SC1029
s78LC¶11278
s87LRM2289
s91LRM2489
cc133GaA329
Ga
cc210SE821
cc75LC
[¶10375
cc88LRM
[2778
i200Bd1131
No 161
i203Bd269
No 27
i209Bd247
No 47
i222Bd625
No 102
85HLR1361

– 674 –
No 112

m474F2d328
m70LC
[¶13413
m82LRM2651
s212Bd553
No 87
i195Bd31
No 18
i199Bd378
No 64
i199Bd1143
No 159
i204Bd302
No 45
i209Bd172
No 36
i209Bd889
No 140
i211Bd10
No 3
j211Bd463
No 56

– 681 –
No 88

i199Bd427
No 51
i200Bd987
No 146
205Bd1083
No 123
i207[illegible]
i20[illegible]
No 106
212Bd656
No 95
215Bd520
No 95
j219Bd524
No 98
223Bd807
No 120
37BdR46
41BdR44

– 698 –
No 97

196Bd373
No 81
j211Bd250
No 11
d221Bd540
No 121
221Bd1281
No 224
37BdR32
38LCP6

– 705 –
No 99

cc170Bd636
No 84
j192Bd716
No 100
i197Bd1029
No 170
199Bd545
No 113
468F2d256
69LC¶13078
d70LC¶13341
81LRM2468
d82LRM2410
37BdR88
25LLJ620
26ARF162n
26ARF165n
26ARF180n

– 716 –
No 100

i204Bd67
No 17
451F2d798
468F2d256
501F2d168
66LC¶12176
69LC¶13078
d70LC¶13341
75LC¶10352
78LRM2726
81LRM2468
d82LRM2410
87LRM2289
37BdR88
24LLJ200
25LLJ620
26ARF160n
26ARF171n
26ARF181n

Citations to 192 *N.L.R.B.* 716

a70LC¶13341
a82LRM2410
37BdR88
25LLJ620

– 737 –
No 105

a68LC¶12877
a80LRM3163
cc209Bd983
No 151

– 741 –
No 106

r473F2d1079
r70LC¶13429
r82LRM2641
198Bd305
i206Bd951
No 115

– 745 –
No 108

a83LRM2024
s201Bd1028
No 134
i207Bd934
No 142

– 764 –
No 123

194Bd740
No 120
197Bd624
No 57
208Bd808
No 103
214Bd799
No 84
f462F2d193
f68LC¶12776
f80LRM2816
d94LRM2788
37BdR60

– 768 –
No 128

m465F2d1039
m69LC
[¶12977
m81LRM2129
i206Bd941
No 115

– 773 –
No 110

s68LC¶12683
s80LRM2415
i203Bd239
No 55
37BdR115

– 781 –
No 114

[illegible]
200Bd555
No 69
200Bd768
No 93
200Bd956
No 126
203Bd262
No 12

– 785 –
No 115

i206Bd836
No 129

i211Bd706
i220Bd865
No 132
223Bd859
No 105

– 791 –
No 117

s176Bd1025
No 136
s435F2d848
s64LC¶11346
s76LRM2001
198Bd646
No 97
i202Bd175
No 13
i206Bd951
No 115
217Bd42
No 8
i218Bd219
No 10

– 793 –
No 119

a465F2d104
a69LC¶12924
a80LRM3330
i196Bd252
No 41
i201Bd168
No 22
203Bd944
No 147
206Bd275
No 74
i206Bd278
No 74
220Bd560
No 30

– 808 –
No 127

a70LC¶13287
a82LRM2619
i219Bd39
No 9
i220Bd170
No 52
i223Bd1190
No 177
i223Bd1258
No 196

– 816 –
No 135

i195Bd865
No 154
i197Bd15
No 5
i197Bd1178
No 54
i199Bd879
No 118
201Bd803
No 113
i201Bd1042
No 157
i203Bd779
No 116

i205Bd547
No 85
j205Bd711
No 80
i205Bd716
No 80
j208Bd547
No 84
208Bd582
No 82
i208Bd898
No 119
i209Bd8
No 5
i209Bd621
No 92
i209Bd628
No 93
j210Bd635
No 71
i210Bd1032
No 146
d214Bd960
No 142
j214Bd960
No 142
218Bd593
No 73
j218Bd595
No 73
i218Bd602
No 73
i224Bd1258
No 172
d513F2d273
d77LC¶10898
d89LRM2460

– 827 –
No 140

s172Bd1535
No 171
209Bd1167
No 178

– 834 –
No 138

j196Bd1053
No 144
i196Bd1060
No 144
i197Bd485
No 91
i221Bd676
No 105
i221Bd996
No 159
420US253
j420US272
43LE175
j43LE186
95SC962
j95SC970
481F2d1023
485F2d1137
f71LC¶13882
72LC¶14001
76LC¶10662
j76LC¶10662
f83LRM2817
84LRM2436
88LRM2689
j88LRM2689

– 837 –
No 150

s219Bd88
No 18
j194Bd654
No 98
194Bd999
No 170
i194Bd1002
No 170
d195Bd106
No 20
i195Bd246
No 35
195Bd468
No 95
i195Bd470
No 95
f195Bd597
No 113
195Bd621
No 118
i195Bd626
No 118
d195Bd725
No 136
i195Bd731
No 136
i195Bd769
No 141
i195Bd910
No 161
i195Bd998
No 182
i196Bd236
No 38
i196Bd442
No 62
i196Bd838
No 115
196Bd871
No 129
j196Bd872
No 129
i196Bd884
No 131
j196Bd1056
No 144
f196Bd1151
No 165
j196Bd1152
No 165
i196Bd1155
No 165
i196Bd1175
No 172
i197Bd19
No 6
197Bd75
No 14
j197Bd75
No 14
f197Bd147
No 4
j197Bd147
No 4
197Bd282
No 34
197Bd793
No 126
i197Bd794
No 126
f197Bd837
No 121
j197Bd837

No 121
i197Bd942
No 138
197Bd1222
No 150
i197Bd1228
No 150
j198Bd243
No 3
j198Bd337
No 51
i198Bd464
No 86
d198Bd529
No 1
f198Bd529
No 1
j198Bd532
No 1
198Bd543
No 2
f198Bd553
No 4
j198Bd554
No 4
f198Bd561
No 5
j198Bd562
No 5
f198Bd569
No 6
j198Bd571
No 6
f198Bd579
No 7
j198Bd580
No 7
f198Bd695
No 99
j198Bd697
No 99
199Bd168
No 26
i199Bd221
No 29
199Bd326
No 49
i199Bd327
No 49
j199Bd327
No 49
j199Bd344
No 45
i199Bd351
No 45
f199Bd434
No 58
199Bd461
No 44
j199Bd466
No 44
f199Bd570
No 85
i199Bd573
No 85
i199Bd748
No 108
f199Bd804
No 69
j199Bd805
No 69
i199Bd806
No 69
f199Bd841
No 139
j199Bd841

No 139
i199Bd844
No 139
i199Bd1011
No 144
f199Bd1113
No 168
199Bd1161
No 137
j199Bd1162
No 137
f199Bd1225
No 135
j199Bd1225
No 135
200Bd196
No 35
i200Bd197
No 35
200Bd648
No 98
j200Bd648
No 98
i200Bd651
No 98
i200Bd764
No 115
d200Bd861
No 124
i200Bd948
No 100
j200Bd1007
No 140
f200Bd1116
No 156
i200Bd1124
No 156
f200Bd1160
No 165
j201Bd83
No 9
i201Bd84
No 9
f201Bd120
No 5
j201Bd121
No 5
i201Bd128
No 5
i201Bd192
No 27
i201Bd217
No 34
201Bd227
No 29
i201Bd229
No 29
201Bd751
No 99
f201Bd793
No 118
i201Bd798
No 118
i201Bd843
No 125
i201Bd899
No 131
i201Bd973
No 139
f201Bd1020
No 150
i201Bd1022
No 150
j202Bd4
No 1
Continued

648 See note on first page of this division

Illustration O

Shepard's *Federal Labor Law Citations—Cases,* 1959–78, Part 1, Supplement.

UNITED STATES SUPREME COURT REPORTS **Vol. 402**

– 815 –
23CLA437
64Geo1009
91HLR5
60MnL1139

– 847 –
65VaL937

– 1201 –
21CLA59
43LCP(3)21
71NwL426
62VaL927

– 1204 –
79CR691
38LCP6
38LCP91

Vol. 402

– 1 –
65CaL859
66CaL477
67CaL79
67CaL93
67CaL147
69CaL212
69CaL1698
70CaL1211
41ChL724
41ChL768
46ChL784
47ChL226
47ChL433
22CLA356
59Cor817
60Cor54
62Cor540
64Cor12
75CR528
75CR575
78CR739
79CR238
79CR891
81CR737
61Geo963
64Geo850
65Geo881
70Geo15
91HLR50
92HLR1701
93HLR4
82IlLR407
38LCP540
39LCP11
39LCP55
39LCP145
39LCP153
39LCP178
39LCP197
39LCP271
39LCP334
39LCP345
39LCP375
40LCP(2)130
40LCP(4)289
42LCP(4)2
42LCP(4)37
42LCP(4)60
42LCP(4)144
43LCP(3)17
43LCP(3)54
43LCP(2)66
43LCP(3)107
75LF74
75LF504
76LF957
77LF964
74McL1
62MnL1050
67NwL835
69NwL548
70NwL740
71NwL42
72NwL382
72NwL688
74NwL560
50NYL1249
54NYL750
121PaL751
124PaL1293
125PaL576
126PaL717
25StnL547
26StnL279
29StnL897
29StnL1236
30StnL305
30StnL709
34StnL1196
51TxL412
51TxL506
56TxL1255
57TxL184
60VaL59
60VaL928
60VaL960
61VaL956
64VaL529
65VaL91
65VaL209
68VaL324
68VaL411
77WLR989
80WLR1312
81WLR929
82YLJ440
83YLJ483
83YLJ499
85YLJ479
86YLJ1157
86YLJ1596
88YLJ685
88YLJ1434
91YLJ638

– 33 –
62Cor542
61Geo983
93HLR4
39LCP37
39LCP81
39LCP153
39LCP347
42LCP(4)7
42LCP(4)60
75LF502
76LF957
70NwL741
72NwL382
29StnL1236
51TxL449
85YLJ479
91YLJ678

– 39 –
22CLA380
61Geo975
91HLR1244
39LCP37
75LF503
56TxL1259
68VaL370

– 43 –
67CaL104
75CR486
61Geo964
64Geo864
39LCP37
75LF504
72NwL686
27StnL609
60VaL928
82YLJ440

– 47 –
65Cor392
70NwL741
58TxL274
83YLJ488

– 62 –
80CR1257
77McL1648
77McL1727
64MnL579
123PaL114
82YLJ920

– 99 –
94HLR502

– 121 –
62CaL1398
44ChL36
59Cor775
122PaL310
26StnL551
79WLR47
86YLJ1251

– 137 –
67CaL12
41ChL61
43ChL332
21CLA1460
27CLA112
27CLA997
28CLA1040
29CLA592
58Cor57
73CR1257
74CR1428
79CR854
91HLR23
91HLR1375
92HLR8
40LCP(4)258
43LCP(2)8
43LCP(3)53
76LF5
76LF953
77LF963
74McL752
77McL982
58MnL1038
60MnL674
60MnL927
62MnL1060
63MnL608
68NwL653
68NwL722
72NwL696
48NYL98
48NYL603
125PaL585
125PaL809
25StnL372
26StnL272
29StnL702
51TxL478
61VaL948
77WLR331
77WLR398
82YLJ410
86YLJ1166

– 146 –
70CaL634
46ChL351
24CLA479
25CLA1327
65Cor133
91HLR1236
92HLR1217
41LCP(1)18
74McL1555
75McL255
61MnL325
63MnL386
49NYL47
54NYL730
57NYL273
27StnL613
28StnL462
33StnL998
57TxL1416
68VaL385
86YLJ1223
86YLJ1595
88YLJ1394

– 183 –
66CaL484
66CaL966
43ChL334
26CLA757
58Cor1219
75CR829
79CR1288
62Geo9
65Geo1541
66Geo758
68Geo934
91HLR1409
39LCP(3)11
40LCP(3)55
40LCP(4)232
43LCP(4)77
73LF273
73McL119
74McL269
74McL720
75McL1325
78McL854
79McL1034
79McL1339
61MnL401
68NwL837
69NwL687
76NwL8
126PaL995
128PaL806
129PaL3
29StnL902
34StnL768
52TxL709
55TxL247
55TxL283
59TxL845
75WLR351
80WLR473
82YLJ922
88YLJ1426

– 313 –
69CaL1413
44ChL522
45ChL325
49ChL441
62Cor9
65Cor84
66Cor464
66Cor520
74CR204
80CR317
70Geo1080
90HLR350
75McL327
78McL385
78McL1015
79McL443
79McL1512
59MnL96
59MnL982
70NwL860
71NwL526
74NwL749
74NwL772
49NYL1151
50NYL292
52NYL988
32StnL656
53TxL896
60VaL258
61VaL1617
85YLJ650
85YLJ750

– 351 –
27CLA390
62Cor594
76CR1208
79CR1276
43LCP(3)89
60MnL1185
69NwL227
123PaL72
126PaL353
130PaL636
62VaL926
64VaL431
90YLJ527

– 363 –
[illegible]
[illegible]
[illegible]
[illegible]
61Geo1133
62Geo1554
43LCP(3)107
77McL1701
69NwL227
126PaL353
130PaL636
130PaL818
64VaL427
82YLJ1387
86YLJ1649

– 389 –
62CaL786
40ChL10
44ChL28
59Cor775
62Cor1014
78CR285
81CR773
61Geo613
63Geo131
70Geo883
88HLR1722
89HLR845
70NwL149
50NYL602
122PaL310
123PaL1280
124PaL978
126PaL774
127PaL174
26StnL552
27StnL918
27StnL1068
28StnL843
55TxL1326
65VaL291
83YLJ58

– 415 –
68CaL456
70CaL135
44ChL533
25CLA1012
64Cor661
67Cor245
73CR931
80CR1258
63Geo1198
60MnL957
61MnL438
66MnL12
49NYL894
130PaL792
29StnL457
29StnL486
29StnL512
29StnL546
57TxL357
57TxL902
63VaL764
64VaL1231
65VaL1338

– 424 –
66CaL966
22CLA111
27CLA355
62Cor474
77CR77
62Geo102
[illegible]
[illegible]
[illegible]
[illegible]
60MnL415
60MnL726
26StnL56
51TxL1316
56TxL795
62VaL875
63VaL1398
75WLR539
81WLR259

– 479 –
45ChL337
61Geo605
74McL1154
72NwL131

– 515 –
60VaL215

– 530 –
76McL1317
66MnL22
55NYL1045
88YLJ99

– 535 –
62CaL117
64CaL36
40ChL4
42ChL289
44ChL28
44ChL63
62Cor407
62Cor456
62Cor514
73CR757
73CR1609
61Geo592
65Geo3
70Geo862
87HLR1534
88HLR1718
90HLR307
90HLR492
94HLR1522
94HLR1790
39LCP(3)11
76LF1030
78McL105
60MnL482
70NwL154
71NwL596
72NwL149
73NwL4
73NwL904
75NwL1011
54NYL747
123PaL1273
124PaL991
125PaL761
126PaL773
127PaL113
26StnL562
28StnL843
52TxL1278
59TxL1367
59VaL361
60VaL24
60VaL975
61VaL807
63VaL408
66VaL440
[illegible]LR194
[illegible]LR71
[illegible]LR242

– 544 –
62Cor609
63Cor409
82CR264
62VaL925

– 549 –
60Cor635
63Cor872
75CR243
66Geo1434
65VaL959
86YLJ864

– 558 –
86HLR858
74McL1590

– 570 –
44ChL341
68Geo1220
80WLR251

– 600 –
122PaL364
86YLJ1166

– 611 –
70CaL119
44ChL555
25CLA956
28CLA494
62Cor609
63Cor409
67Cor257
73CR1043
93HLR316
60MnL1183
52NYL137
124PaL1237
126PaL106
26StnL323
28StnL456
33StnL661
52TxL272
54TxL45
64VaL1279
68VaL249
83YLJ469

– 622 –
26CLA980
77CR52
62Geo148
69Geo878
91HLR601
73McL155
75McL1573
77McL1388
56TxL174

– 637 –
21CLA419
76CR437
79CR242
60MnL482
48NYL252
49NYL702
56NYL1177
25StnL547
52TxL652
59TxL74

– 673 –
44ChL774
28CLA488
73CR466
80CR1624
50NYL241
123PaL849

– 689 –
73CR1409
61Geo1138
77LF101
64MnL576
52NYL158

Citations to 402 U.S. 389

101

Illustration P

A sample page from the U.S. Supreme Court section of Shepard's *Federal Law Citations in Selected Law Reviews,* for February 1983.

6. LAW REVIEW CITATIONS

Whereas law review articles are contained within the scope of *citing* sources in several Shepard's publications, they are the *cited* sources in Shepard's *Law Review Citations.* This unit enables the researcher to locate citations since 1957 from the U.S. Supreme Court, lower federal courts, state courts, and numerous law reviews to articles in over 180 law reviews. As new periodicals are added to the group of sources cited in this unit, footnotes are provided indicating the year that coverage begins. See Illustration Q for a sample of this citator.

7. FEDERAL TAX CITATIONS

This unit, begun in 1981, is a complete federal tax law citator. *Shepard's Federal Tax Citations* should not be confused with another Shepard's publication, *Federal Tax Locator,* which is not a citator, but rather an *index* to a variety of materials on tax law. *Federal Tax Citations* covers, as *cited* material: decisions of the U.S. Tax Court, U.S. Supreme Court and lower federal courts in tax cases; treasury regulations and decisions; Internal Revenue Service rulings and procedures; and sections of the *U.S. Code* relating to tax matters. Cross references to court decisions also reported in Prentice-Hall's *American Federal Tax Reports* and Commerce Clearing House's *U.S. Tax Cases* are provided. An example of the citations found in this unit is shown in Illustration R.

8. MILITARY JUSTICE CITATIONS

This specialized citator provides the researcher with citations to decisions of the U.S. Court of Military Appeals and the Board and Courts of Military Review, the *Uniform Code of Military Justice,* the *Manual for Courts-Martial,* Military Court rules, and various orders and regulations relating to military law.

9. PROFESSIONAL AND JUDICIAL CONDUCT CITATIONS

Begun in 1980, this citator lists citations to the American Bar Association's Code of Professional Responsibility, Code of Judicial Conduct, and Opinions of the American Bar Association's Committee on Ethics and Professional Responsibility. References from state and federal courts and articles in leading law reviews, as well as citations from the Committee's opinions themselves are provided. See Illustration S for a sample page from *Professional and Judicial Conduct Citations.*

YALE LAW JOURNAL, THE **Vol. 70**

37NYL64
110PaL1095
38SCL5
22SCR690
73YLJ38

– 103 –
328F2d886
446F2d1352
70YLJ1255

– 126 –
52CaL42
53CaL754
41KCR24
17RLR531
37SCL423
9WnL441

– 135 –
14CLA1247
66McL339

– 160 –
61CR579
62WLR598

– 175 –
388US182
401US244
412US75
18LE1129
28LE20
36LE759
87SC2008
91SC616
93SC1957
286F2d79
314F2d903
316F2d450
320F2d275
335F2d344
350F2d1016
384F2d355
388F2d196
393F2d53
407F2d1192
415F2d215
420F2d1166
444F2d722
459F2d1151
525F2d1230
547F2d202
552F2d1029
566F2d746
573F2d554
578F2d385
196FS314
197FS107
203FS295
212FS243
262FS1006
290FS465
300FS1252
389FS911
35FRD7
16Ap2d214
18Ap2d333
53CA3d476
17C3d475
129IlR348
268Min314
35NY19
227Or285
259Or476
16Wis2d372
50Wis2d137
Calif
126CaR503
131CaR95
551P2d415
Ill
264NE49
Minn
129NW346
NY
315NE760
226S2d700
239S2d794
358S2d698
Ore
361P2d1026
486P2d1278
Wis
114NW487
183NW113
20Buf363
53CaL758
17CLA697
71CR584
76CR1320
21CWL212
24CWL139
70DuL1068
29FR277
46FR392
5GaL626
9GaL406
29HLJ108
76HLR985
76HLR1030
76HLR1099
82HLR727
49ILR289
7InLR531
75LF569
22LJ109
22LJ146
34LJ774
61McL1451
51MnL425
51MqL26
13NYF18
43NYL232
43NYL284
122PaL558
27StnL1065
17VLR112
73WLQ484
70YLJ1223
83YLJ277

– 225 –
288F2d147
288F2d397
373F2d459
373F2d471
478F2d668
175Ct109
85Msc2d53
64NJ398
68NJ258
246Or490
Conn
394A2d189
Fla
358So2d195
Me
262A2d363
Mont
593P2d730
NJ
316A2d458
344A2d301
NY
378S2d595
Ore
426P2d449
60ABA1372
24AkL39
38BR3
21Buf725
49BUR33
56BUR315
1Cap13
36ChL759
19CLA299
66CR271
23Cth701
39Dic352
43DLJ18
63DuL408
9Duq220
13Duq770
62Geo25
48ILR70
5JFL140
44JUL459
73LF686
37LJ720
19MB721
19MB736
66McL726
52NbL45
43NDL24
49OLR33
53OLR260
110PaL795
117PaL81
16RLR121
28RLR891
29RLR1060
29RLR1086
51SCL590
26StnL55
35TuL713
56VaL379
15VLR739
11WnL119
13WnL531
18WnL621
70YLJ907
70YLJ930
72YLJ859
86YLJ661

– 240 –
18BCR226
70DLR498
57NwL408
36NYL453

– 259 –
62CR238
32LJ540
57NwL449
36NYL453
55VaL1024

– 298 –
315F2d249

– 308 –
40DCh121
41DCh22
41DCh176
Del
175A2d38
187A2d409
190A2d530
23BL1095
64CR1454
83HLR1497
65McL263
18MiL143
115PaL364
20RLR247
21StnL268
33UCR329
43WsL390

– 322 –
14KLR407
25MiL397
42NDL680
37NYL797

– 345 –
367US808
6LE1183
81SC1819
473F2d474
438FS1131
74AzS43
7BCR191
44BUR480
52CaL2
53C[illegible]
42[illegible]
10[illegible]
11[illegible]
14CM227
63Cor4
62CR423
62CR584
67CR1431
38DLJ582
65DuL231
70DuL1102
34FR220
40FR293
45GW691
26HLJ50
76HLR1057
50ILJ657
50ILR765
56KLJ772
22LJ31
27LR490
61McL1444
15MiL344
49MnL227
61MnL452
37NYL61
110PaL482
20RLR706
48SCL363
50SCL994
16SLJ63
25SLJ675
6StLJ375
14StnL38
47TxL1071
47VaL1364
16VLR554
14VR65
9WFL41
18W&M60
72WLR368
18WnL397
39WsL111
39WsL293
40WsL69
47WsL142

– 376 –
302F2d789
353F2d151
366F2d408
437F2d1047
530F2d454
570F2d913
197FS197
306FS598
345FS13
416FS153
23Ap2d366
355Mas704
Del
296A2d147
Mass
247NE389
NY
260S2d916
7BCR3
32BL1719
44BUR491
79HLR234
26LLR303
48NYL295
28SLJ978
30SLJ1080
18WRL441

Citations to 70 Yale L.J. 376

69DLR355
69DLR374
23LJ111
110PaL941

– 441 –
39DLJ560
70DuL1135
74HLR645
83HLR569
56NwL353
53VaL13
56VaL1435
18VLR134

– 453 –
253FS872
8BCR553
47CLQ503
37GW1038
49ILR716
69McL248
115PaL486
117PaL933
16RLR336
13StnL844
51VaL850
36WsL472
76YLJ933

– 461 –
44BUR185
31FR248

– 469 –
226FS67
44DJ582
57NwL694

– 499 –
303F2d758
363F2d666
385F2d864
398F2d172
453F2d329
498F2d1294
569F2d1206
589F2d1309
276FS528
345FS377
374FS150
413FS1209
24CA3d733
66C2d419
3C3d775
50H216
278Md343
60Msc2d498
15NY468
235Or458
241Or308
[illegible]Su308
Alk
479P2d329
502P2d141
Calif
58CaR139
91CaR757
101CaR329
426P2d539
478P2[illegible]
363A2d958
NJ
296A2d673
NY
209NE82
261S2d28
302S2d698
Ore
385P2d613
405P2d627
23AU833
52ABA639
24AkL270
9AzL179
4BCR325
12BCR255
5Blt61
53BUR354
54CaL1541
54CaL1551
58CaL121
65CaL767
31ChL642
31ChL692
34ChL240
40ChL683
47CK26
12CLA186
18CLA457
22CLA825
51CLQ715
52CLQ237
10CnL116
54Cor671
5Crt27
47CUR156
24CWL492
72DuL909
25EmJ830
26EmJ275
18FLR392
30FLR514
5FSU92
37FR156
40GW366
20HLJ495
78HLR347
78HLR714
78HLR737
80HLR559
80HLR1169
85HLR537
51IBJ711
46ILJ320
51ILJ579
10InLR269
58KLJ37
63KLJ761
64KLJ222
65KLJ331
33LCP429
64LF694
67LF373
39LJ443
22LR391
63McL322
74McL1293
43MLJ164
52MnL630
48MqL293
45NCL997
39NDL517
27OR352
29OR881
115PaL546
27PitL635
18RLR1015
23RLR476
40SCL442
45SCL143
27SCR808
15SDR256
6SeH286
14StLJ201
21StLJ57
13StnL846
16StnL677
18StnL1005
21StnL1505
24StnL463
42TLQ329
47TxL608
53TxL759
38UCR587
46UCR996
68ULR284
51VaL807
53VaL783
53VaL837
53VaL894
53VaL1511
74WLQ552
68WLR155
68WLR1061
69WLR66
23WnL998
24WnL1675
45WsL502
70WVL18
75YLJ220
76YLJ890

– 554 –
304F2d426
498F2d1294
443FS1100
100Az259
41Msc2d659
22NY21
235Or458
439Pa566
Ariz
413P2d737
NY
237NE882
245S2d659
290S2d741
Ore
385P2d613
Pa
267A2d856
28AkL207
4BCR312
15Buf283
16Buf580
49CaL246
49CaL626
54CaL1551
55CaL83
58CaL102
29ChL236
31ChL642
43ChL75
47CK27
12CLA186
25CLA200
48CLQ240
52CLQ237
17CM450
53Cor415
63CR1224
63CR1238
63CR1246
74CR891
24CWL492
63DuL11
9Duq395
9Duq464
18FLR392
37FR156
1Hof126
2Hof583
75HLR493
10JMJ227
56KLJ79
61KLJ381
61KLJ408
28LCP772
69LF306
74McL1293
48MnL301
52MnL631
33MoL42
48MqL293
46NCL510
54NCL595
39NDL518
41NYL269
54OLR299
27OR352
115PaL546
2RCL54
18RLR1015
23RLR475
47SCL833
6SeH286
23SR447
17StLJ471
16StnL682
27StnL780
42TLQ329
68ULR284
Continued

1109

Illustration Q

Shepard's *Law Review Citations*, 1979 volume.

Vol. 31 TAX COURT OF THE UNITED STATES REPORTS

'72TCM#16
'73TCM#203

– 910 –
a279F2d115
a5AF2d1725
a60UTC¶
[9533
619F2d1153
230FS299
454FS439
13AF2d1582
42AF2d5861
64UTC¶9508
78UTC¶9670
35TCt5
35TCt615
36TCt710
37TCt418
37TCt485
37TCt938
42TCt258
47TCt529
48TCt916
51TCt568
54TCt804
54TCt1287
58TCt326
60TCt702
35TCt#1
35TCt#65
36TCt#72
37TCt#44
37TCt#50
37TCt#90
42TCt#13
47TCt#51
48TCt#87
51TCt#54
54TCt#111
54TCt#121
58TCt#28
60TCt#73
'71TCM#155
'72TCM#16
'72TCM#195
'73TCM#203
'73TCM#244
'73TCM#268
'74TCM#264
'75TCM#137
'75TCM#234
'75TCM#251
'75TCM#273
'76TCM#58
'76TCM#299
'77TCM#75
'77TCM#314
d'80TCM#216
'80TCM#347
'80TCM#555
80HLR788
46A2615s
46A2767s

– 916 –
'74TCM#264

– 918 –
r294F2d750
r8AF2d5417
r61UTC¶9644
51TCt1018
51TCt#103

– 934 –
s281F2d419
s6AF2d5357
s60UTC¶9664
41TCt242
41TCt#27

– 938 –
a279F2d657
a5AF2d1553
a60UTC¶
[9596
319F2d478
12AF2d5089
34TCt447
37TCt114
37TCt143
41TCt714
46TCt103
52TCt616
55TCt356
62TCt289
37TCt#14
37TCt#18
41TCt#71
46TCt#8
52TCt#5
55TCt#34
62TCt#34

– 95?
a272
a4AF
a60U
[9106
322F2d748
345F2d906
354F2d413
467F2d49
470F2d1148
481F2d1245
539F2d416
608F2d495
215FS819
c215FS820
11AF2d1301
c11AF2d1301
12AF2d5650
15AF2d880
16AF2d6109
30AF2d5313
31AF2d519
32AF2d5312
38AF2d5834
44AF2d5917
63UTC¶9725
65UTC¶9395
66UTC¶9133
73UTC¶9145
73UTC¶9537
76UTC¶9672
36TCt921
37TCt826
52TCt1057
f53TCt505
d55TCt1119
d60TCt29
63TCt419
63TCt650
e67TCt980
36TCt#93
52TCt#108
f53TCt#48
d55TCt#102
63TCt#37
63TCt#62

e67TCt#80
'73TCM#285
112PaL1113
115PaL184
45VaL676
23A2902s

– 961 –
r281F2d279
r6AF2d5284
r60UTC¶9637
364US92
364US105
e364US116
e364US122
4LE1600
e4LE1613
80SC1418
e80SC1428
5AF2d1780
e5AF2d1780
e5AF2d1786
e5AF2d1795
60UTC¶9554
e60UTC¶
[9554
49TCt344
49TCt#35
36NYL654
46A2615s

Citations to 31 *T.C.* 961

r60UTC¶9686
46TCt569
48TCt549
48TCt652
q48TCt655
50TCt128
65TCt1086
46TCt#57
48TCt#52
48TCt#62
q48TCt#62
50TCt#15
65TCt#91
14StnL551
40TxL75

– 981 –
r277F2d395
r5AF2d1136
r60UTC¶9368
33TCt568
23A2902s

– 986 –
35NYL184
90A2428n

– 990 –
a273F2d867
a5AF2d361
a60UTC¶
[9161
219FS202
31TCt1001
31TCt1009
33TCt1024
34TCt9
34TCt11
34TCt13
34TCt17
34TCt26
35TCt362

37TCt788
39TCt1076
40TCt39
41TCt427
41TCt874
42TCt775
43TCt104
44TCt275
44TCt301
58TCt90
73TCt1194
33TCt#114
34TCt#1
34TCt#2
35TCt#44
37TCt#74
39TCt#109
40TCt#7
41TCt#42
41TCt#81
42TCt#56
43TCt#9
44TCt#28
44TCt#29
58TCt#7
73TCt#93
'70TCM#237
'70TCM#279
'70TCM#332
'79TCM#218
3 –
867
61
a60UTC¶
[9161
301F2d99
33TCt1024
34TCt9
34TCt11
34TCt13
34TCt17
35TCt362
37TCt788
40TCt39
41TCt427
41TCt874
42TCt775
44TCt275
44TCt301
33TCt#114
34TCt#1
35TCt#44
37TCt#74
40TCt#7
41TCt#42
41TCt#81
42TCt#56
44TCt#28
44TCt#29
'70TCM#237
'70TCM#279
'70TCM#332

– 1001 –
335F2d29
14AF2d5144
64UTC¶9614
34TCt9
34TCt11
34TCt13
34TCt17
37TCt788
40TCt39
40TCt427
41TCt874

42TCt775
44TCt277
44TCt301
34TCt#1
37TCt#74
40TCt#7
40TCt#48
41TCt#81
42TCt#56
44TCt#28
44TCt#29
'72TCM#253

– 1009 –
32TCt254
45TCt421
64TCt57
66TCt443
45TCt#39
64TCt#5
66TCt#43

– 1014 –
288F2d652
292F2d639
d354F2d354
367F2d666
7AF2d1000
7AF2d1645
d16AF2d6051
18AF2d5824
61UTC¶9345
61UTC¶9520
d66UTC¶
[9118
33TCt434
33TCt437
35TCt1147
37TCt702
45TCt486
46TCt331
47TCt171
57TCt766
d72TCt1200
33TCt#50
35TCt#119
37TCt#70
45TCt#45
46TCt#31
47TCt#15
57TCt#80
d72TCt#99
'70TCM#178
d173CCL727
112PaL1098
112PaL1103
3A3840n

– 1017 –
342F2d335
221FS35
12AF2d5010
15AF2d246
63UTC¶9631
65UTC¶9200
38TCt178
38TCt#20
61MnL268
19LE1447n
3A3848n

– 1022 –
p208FS385
p10AF2d5529

p62UTC¶
[9716
277F2d615
d331F2d944
j331F2d955
337F2d173
375F2d5
460F2d1018
d175FS366
222FS715
229FS557
d4AF2d5280
5AF2d1345
12AF2d5705
12AF2d5709
d13AF2d1371
19AF2d1051
29AF2d1223
d59UTC¶
[9615
60UTC¶9443
64UTC¶9795
67UTC¶9339
72UTC¶9412
44TCt184
46TCt710
49TCt424
d63TCt394
44TCt#18
46TCt#74
49TCt#44
d63TCt#34
118PaL720
3ARF731n
3ARF748n

– 1031 –
a272F2d709
a4AF2d5972
a60UTC¶
[9125
300F2d39
374FS131
9AF2d883
33AF2d1166
74UTC¶9381
36TCt139
36TCt832
46TCt361
53TCt383
66TCt413
36TCt#11
36TCt#81
46TCt#33
53TCt#37
66TCt#41
'71TCM#105
'77TCM#399
'78TCM#197

– 1041 –
299F2d205
9AF2d733
62UTC¶9271

– 1046 –
308F2d162
10AF2d5523
62UTC¶9713
37TCt399
38TCt381
41TCt643
55TCt14
71TCt1128
38TCt#41
41TCt#63

55TCt#2
71TCt#98
'73TCM#212
'77TCM#422

– 1058 –
33TCt884
36TCt498
36TCt506
42TCt726
52TCt161
54TCt719
33TCt#100
36TCt#49
36TCt#50
42TCt#52
52TCt#19
54TCt#111
'78TCM#414

– 1064 –
s39TCt29
s39TCt341
35TCt896
61TCt622
61TCt#65
30TxR232

– 1072 –
cc14TCt1136
cc14TCt#129

– 1080 –
m281F2d556
m6AF2d5265
m60UTC¶
[9628
s366US964
s6LE1256
s81SC1915
329F2d877
d335F2d80
396F2d834
414F2d985
476F2d1345
e476F2d1347
d232FS148
257FS760
267FS554
434FS92
13AF2d1081
d14AF2d5260
d14AF2d5543
18AF2d5239
19AF2d1126
21AF2d1433
24AF2d5486
31AF2d1095
e31AF2d1095
39AF2d1393
d64UTC¶
[9647
d64UTC¶
[9718
66UTC¶9558
68UTC¶9409
69UTC¶9610
73UTC¶9351
e73UTC¶
[9351
77UTC¶9366
32TCt772
37TCt12
37TCt18
39TCt580
46TCt441

72TCt622
73TCt1162
32TCt#65
37TCt#2
46TCt#40
72TCt#53
73TCt#92
'72TCM#44
201CCL328
275Ala145
Ala
153So2d224
95A2523n

– 1106 –
33TCt210
36TCt993
37TCt313
38TCt897
33TCt#23
36TCt#101
37TCt#32
38TCt#90
'75TCM#247

– 1121 –
d308F2d428
d407F2d535
d10AF2d5641
d23AF2d692
d62UTC¶
[9734
d69UTC¶
[9236
35TCt49
44TCt709
48TCt596
70TCt680
35TCt#7
48TCt#56
70TCt#65
'77TCM#369
25A2633s

– 1126 –
58TCt488
60TCt773
66TCt34
58TCt#49
60TCt#80
66TCt#5
40NYL1068

– 1130 –
r279F2d338
r5AF2d1572
r60UTC¶9493
f281F2d824
f6AF2d5082
f60UTC¶9565
36TCt767
37TCt747
41TCt666
36TCt#76
37TCt#71
41TCt#65
'72TCM#132
'77TCM#174
35NYL707
36NYL664

– 1143 –
46TCt575
f54TCt253
46TCt#58

Continued

150

Illustration R

Shepard's *Federal Tax Citations*, 1981, Part 5.

10. RESTATEMENT CITATIONS

Shepard's initiated this citator in 1976 to enable researchers to obtain citations to the American Law Institute's various *Restatements of the Law* in decisions of the federal courts and state courts and in articles of selected legal periodicals. Illustration T shows a typical listing of citations found in Shepard's *Restatement Citations,* on a page covering the *Restatement of Torts.* Each Restatement is listed in a separate section of this citator.

11. OTHER SHEPARD'S CITATORS

In addition to the specialized citators described above, Shepard's has recently inaugurated several new services, primarily in regulatory and public law areas. They include *Federal Energy Law Citations* (1982), *Federal Occupational and Safety and Health Citations* (1981), *Immigration and Naturalization Citations* (1982), *Partnership Law Citations* (1983), and *Uniform Commercial Code Citations* (1982). The first four of these services follow the same pattern of coverage and arrangement as *Federal Labor Law Citations,* described above in Section F. 4. They include, as *cited* material, federal statutes and regulations, and decisions of the courts and administrative agencies, in their respective subject fields.

Uniform Commercial Code Citations, however, is structured differently. It is arranged by articles and sections of the *U.C.C.,* and lists as *citing* material the decisions of federal and state courts which have applied or interpreted the Code sections, as well as legal periodical articles and some treatises.

12. SHEPARD'S PUBLICATIONS OTHER THAN CITATORS

In addition to the citators described above, Shepard's also publishes a number of research tools which, although technically not citators, are very useful for specific research purposes. These are *Acts and Cases By Popular Names* (discussed above in Chapter 5), *Federal Tax Locator,* (also discussed above in Chapter 5), *New York Code, Rules, and Regulations Citations* (a part citator, part digest covering New York administrative regulations), and *Ordinance Law Annotations* (discussed in Chapter 7).

G. OTHER TOOLS WHICH FUNCTION AS CITATORS

Shepard's citators are not the only services which perform this function. Several other research tools have features which make them useful as citators.

CANON 3 **CODE OF JUDICIAL CONDUCT**

656F2d1165
688F2d1300
471FS1185
498FS1150
507FS717
515FS1084
524FS1117
68FRD273
75FRD115
91FRD519
2MJ18
8MJ800
8MJ826
I#1286
I#1311
I#1477
57Ap2d1016
263Ark508
268Ark590
275Ark496
123Az189
128Az491
170Ct523
22DC3d591
241Ga348
249Ga576
218Kan206
403Mch181
412Mch552
302NC313
113NH54
72NJ160
91NM51
46NY658
293Or185
37OrA753
62OS403
478Pa251
479Pa429
483Pa227
48PaC570
275SoC30
177Su224
182Su243
28WAp197
106Wis2d49
Ariz
598P2d1008
627P2d222
Ark
565SW618
594SW266
628SW573
Conn
368A2d128
Del
412A2d947
Fla
319So2d82
357So2d182
Ga
245SE300
292SE817
Iowa
242NW321
Kan
542P2d684

Ky
610SW615
La
383So2d1014
414So2d671
Mich
267NW914
315NW532
Minn
296NW685
Mo
518SW22
538SW47
568SW256
577SW829
NC
275SE419
ND
261NW884
NH
302A2d822
NJ
369A2d5
426A2d70
440A2d471
NM
570P2d589
NY
389NE800
394S2d490
409S2d970
409S2d1003
416S2d204
Ohio
406NE810
Okla
628P2d374
Ore
588P2d641
645P2d1068
Pa
386A2d918
388A2d730
395A2d1319
411A2d558
So C
267SE87
Tenn
640SW55
Tex
626SW835
Wash
622P2d1294
Wis
315NW712
W Va
246SE99
263SE79
278SE634
279SE188
35AkL250
10Blt229
67IBJ82
15InLR312
51JBK77
35MB296
60MQ141

20NYF126
33OR471
12SMJ728
50StJ448
77ULR399
60WLQ41

Canon 3(A)
579F2d426
498FS1147
22DC3d591
218Kan206
86NJ387
290Or322
Kan
542P2d684
Mass
408NE862
Mo
525SW336
NJ
431A2d840
NY
409S2d1004
409S2d1020
Ore
622P2d308
48JBK240
33OR474
77ULR399
84WVL277

Citations to ABA Canons of Judicial Conduct No. 3(A)

412Mch553
115NH547
75NJ509
85NJ535
47NY473
54OS383
478Pa251
91W2d546
Ala
300So2d434
Fla
402So2d1145
Iowa
244NW233
256NW11
Kan
623P2d1308
La
414So2d671
Me
428A2d861
Mich
315NW532
Minn
296NW657
304NW908
Mo
577SW810
ND
270NW323
NH

345A2d394
NJ
384A2d145
428A2d911
NY
392NE557
418S2d570
Ohio
377NE497
Pa
386A2d918
Tex
581SW251
Wash
588P2d1368
W Va
278SE630
12Pcf4
54TuL400
65VaL77

Canon 3(A)(2)
427FS1249
47Ap2d250
223Kan72
227Kan348
412Mch559
115NH378
75NJ509
85NJ535
37NY582
Ind
437NE957
Kan
572P2d898
607P2d50
Mich
315NW535
NH
341A2d760
NJ
384A2d145
428A2d911
NY
338NE608
366S2d463
376S2d94
48JBK242

Canon 3(A)(3)
505F2d967
542F2d785
427FS1231
13C3d797
134GaA939
137GaA751
4KA2d582
5KA2d399
218Kan198
220Kan177
223Kan72
229Kan196
377Mas367
400Mch716
403Mch193

Continued

172

Illustration S

Shepard's *Professional & Judicial Conduct Citations,*—March 1983.

§ 883

TORTS

41C2d429
Calif
260P2d61

§ 884
et seq.
17FRD405

§§ 884
to 886
37MnL404

§ 884
Comment b
26MnL740

§ 885
377US501
401US345
12LE477
28LE96
84SC1540
91SC809
122F2d752
167F2d613
208F2d428
213F2d796
229F2d418
249F2d6
274F2d693
285F2d753
321F2d893
351F2d929
425F2d1191
451F2d413
453F2d554
60FS562
111FS523
121FS357
135FS675
156FS58
168FS32
179FS42
200FS344
202FS240
215FS797
232FS560
238FS316
259FS362
267FS613
273FS652
278FS271
280FS52
282FS1016
288FS825
308FS200
350FS345
374FS625
18Ap2d384
25Ap2d923
109Az309
19AzA71
134CA2d839
164CA2d768
214CA2d358
13CA3d86
48CA3d392
55C2d861
143Col269
143Col283
168Col75
17CS243

22CS301
142Ct397
152Ct408
124GaA177
35IIA469
332IIA158
337IIA382
349IIA346
308Mch423
224Md120
207Msc1012
14Msc2d971
188Neb422
86Nev354
28NJ370
88OA478
234Or282
410Pa359
72PRR144
8Su467
48Su166
101Su375
157Tex311
191Va310
204Va432
7WAp311
8WAp778
11WAp27
13WAp659
14WAp56
Alk
455P2d892
507P2d766
Ariz
504P2d1294
509P2d202
Calif
13CaR523
29CaR333
91CaR304
122CaR263
286P2d507
331P2d1009
362P2d347
Colo
352P2d92
450P2d64
Conn
114A2d685
170A2d736
207A2d734
Fla
247So2d732
Ga
183SE225
Ill
74NE617
86NE149
110NE697
115NE563
Ky
320SW138
344SW812
409SW310
Md
166A2d897
Mich
14NW52
Mo
349SW3
Nebr
197NW387
Nev
469P2d61
NJ
73A2d293

137A2d39
146A2d675
244A2d351
NY
141S2d812
179S2d87
239S2d610
270S2d94
Ohio
100NE303
Ore
381P2d493
Pa
188A2d724
Tex
165SW779
186SW93
302SW655
341SW221
386SW778
Va
60SE903
132SE464
Wash
499P2d74
508P2d1383
521P2d968
537P2d828
538P2d872
45CLQ7
91PaL510
Comments
b to d
377US501
12LE477
84SC1540
351F2d931
198FS639
259FS362
Comment b
215FS797
278FS271
311FS132
28NJ366
198Or577
NJ
146A2d673
Ore
258P2d139
Comment c
285F2d755
36FS884
215FS798
22CS298
15McA326
Conn
170A2d735
Mich
166NW683
Comment d
218F2d68
249F2d7
238FS312
259FS362
235Min312
242Min128
252Or454
24TnA658
Minn
50NW694
64NW165
Ore
450P2d533
Tenn
148SW54
Tex

386SW769
Comment e
215FS798
69C2d226
33CC925
Calif
70CaR556
444P2d348
Tex
386SW769

§ 886
167F2d613
241F2d458
60FS562
215FS798
232FS762
347FS672
350FS345
225CA2d775
48CA3d392
18CS424
345Mas603
224Md120
251Md37
265Md731
48NJ207
201Or133
253Or50
352Pa549
118Ut458
Calif
37CaR680
122CaR263
Fla
247So2d732
Mass
188NE863
Md
166A2d897
246A2d553
291A2d480
NJ
225A2d12
Ore
253P2d898
453P2d169
Pa
43A2d110
Utah
222P2d593
Comments
a to d
18Ap2d385
NY
239S2d610
Comment a
193F2d455
270NC496
NC
155SE246
Comment b
193F2d456
Comment c
48NJ206
Fla
232So2d40
NJ
225A2d12
Comment d
215FS798

§ 887
et seq.
19CS459
Conn
116A2d919

§§ 887
to 895
91PaL510

§ 887
249FS309
143Col236
393Pa633
404Pa466
417Pa486
149WV713
Colo
353P2d607
Pa
144A2d739
172A2d790
208A2d197
W Va
143SE160
18NYL86
Comment a
272F2d863
249FS309
16IIA300
45IIA353
38McA615
226Md197
Ill
148NE52
195NE424
Md
172A2d514
Mich
196NW869
Comment b
446F2d181
Comment c
218Md273
Md
146A2d28

§ 888
53DC2d443
339Mas423
[illegible]
[illegible]
[illegible]
44A2d266
Wyo
374P2d205
Comment c
262F2d716
17Ap2d10
79Ida383
218Md273
Idaho
318P2d1098
Md
146A2d29
NY
230S2d576
Illustra-
tion 3
66Az133

Ariz
185P2d307

§ 889
221FS145
359Mo879
Mo
224SW88
Okla
530P2d582
Comment b
Mo
417SW8
Comment c
85FS880
321FS1211
36MnL39

§ 890
66Az134
Ariz
185P2d307
Comment c
52FS300
Comment d
139InA699
Ind
220NE279

§ 892
311F2d768
116FS907
176FS810
202FS565
216FS408
216FS806
239Ark743
49H360
Ark
393SW867
Haw
417P2d821
Ky
329SW374
18NYL89
91PaL510
52VaL266
Comment c
446F2d316
58DC626

Citations to Restatement of Torts § 892

234F2d739
240F2d36
256F2d820
404F2d1255
460F2d489
174FS765
116CA2d568
120CA2d107
129CA2d86
131CA2d41
156CA2d262
167CA2d366
187CA2d731
188CA2d153
191CA2d10
192CA2d598
193CA2d203

204CA2d328
213CA2d99
227CA2d777
232CA2d807
26CA3d542
40CA3d41
42C2d162
60C2d272
65C2d244
39CC995
14CS479
85DC218
12DC2d91
246Ia157
361Mch508
178Md186
224Md239
244Md13
246Md175
221Min326
203Msc872
23NJ434
70OA186
77OA186
100OA238
207Or345
222Or501
234Or194
140OS98
356Pa643
160PaS291
73PRR269
76SD156
233SoC25
38Su443
254Wis548
270Wis375
10Wis2d562
60W2d124
66W2d132
Alk
443P2d71
Calif
10CaR187
10CaR342
12CaR423
[illegible]CaR555
13CaR914
22CaR297
28CaR562
32CaR196
39CaR[illegible]23
43CaR27[illegible]
53CaR54[illegible]
[illegible]
[illegible]
[illegible]
265P2d906
276P2d4
280P2d73
308P2d863
319P2d19
334P2d303
383P2d780
418P2d155
Colo
319P2d19
Conn
25A2d46
Iowa
65NW439
Ky
170SW19
249SW137

329SW374
Md
12A2d539
167A2d594
222A2d382
227A2d753
Mich
105NW402
Minn
22NW215
NJ
119A2d168
129A2d441
NY
119S2d521
Ohio
42NE668
66NE241
136NE342
Ore
296P2d498
353P2d256
379P2d1023
Pa
50A2d539
53A2d83
SD
74NW495
So C
103SE397
Tex
315SW615
362SW313
367SW399
371SW377
373SW739
392SW792
401SW142
Wash
372P2d194
401P2d647
Wis
37NW77
71NW295
103NW542
65HLR625
91PaL511
100PaL629
29TxL269
33TxL12
68WLR168
78YLJ186
Comment a
100OA238
45W2d406
Ohio
136NE343
Wash
275P2d435
Comment b
174FS765
77OA186
100OA238
222Or501
45W2d406
Ohio
66NE241
136NE343
Ore
353P2d256
Wash
275P2d435
Illustra-
tion 1

Continued

242

Illustration T

Shepard's *Restatement of the Law Citations,* 1976.

1. FEDERAL REGISTER AND C.F.R. LISTS OF SECTIONS AFFECTED

As discussed above, Shepard's *Code of Federal Regulations Citations* enables one to trace the treatment of administrative rules and regulations in a variety of legal publications. But to discover changes in the rules or regulations themselves, the "List of *CFR* Sections and Parts Affected," appearing in both the *Federal Register* and the *Code of Federal Regulations* must be used. These aids are more fully described in Chapter 11. Monthly publication of the separate *CFR* pamphlet, "Lists of Sections Affected," and similar lists in each issue of the *Federal Register,* aid the researcher in determining whether any changes, additions, or deletions, with regard to a particular CFR section, have been published in the *Federal Register.* The Cumulative "List of Parts Affected", appearing daily in the *Federal Register,* updates the "List of CFR Sections Affected", and should also be used to update the monthly lists in *CFR.*

2. CITATIONS TO THE RESTATEMENTS OF THE LAW

In addition to the Shepard's *Restatement Citations,* described in Section F. 10 above, each section of the various *Restatements of the Law* can also be found through use of the *Restatements in the Courts,* published by West for the American Law Institute. These volumes, formerly issued for all jurisdictions and for many states individually, indicated every reference in a court decision to a section of a *Restatement.* The typical West abstracts of the citing cases were included as well, and irregular supplementation provided.

3. TABLES OF STATUTES CONSTRUED

Each of the West state, regional and federal reporters contains *Tables of Statutes Construed,* which also serve a citator function with regard to statutes. These tables list all statutes which have been cited in any of the cases reported in the particular volume or advance sheet.

4. ANNOTATED CODES

Annotated statutory codes also perform a limited citator function with regard to the statutes contained therein. They contain notations of statutory amendments, and abstracts of decisions which have applied or construed the statutes. These annotations are somewhat less comprehensive then Shepard's, and do not differentiate the specific actions taken by the courts, as indicated by Shepard's abbreviations. It is therefore still necessary to *Shepardize* statutory provisions.

5. LOOSELEAF SERVICES

Most looseleaf services provide a valuable citator function with regard to administrative regulations, cases, and statutes in their particular subject fields. Because these services are updated weekly, they can offer the researcher more current information than even Shepard's, although in a less graphic format. In many instances, the full text of new developments will be printed, and cases, statutes, and regulations on the same topic are often (although not universally) collected in the same section of the service. These features save the researcher much time and effort, as do the varied and detailed indexes in these publications.

The most thorough coverage is found in the tax field,[1] with both Commerce Clearing House and Prentice-Hall offering very complete services. The latter's *Federal Tax Citator*, for example, performs a complete citator function with respect to federal tax decisions and rulings dating from 1796 to present. It should be noted, however, that although looseleaf services can often provide valuable citations to authorities in certain subject areas, they do not attempt to duplicate the comprehensive and sophisticated coverage of the Shepard's services, nor do they exist for every subject area of law. See Chapter 13, below, for fuller treatment of looseleaf services.

6. COMPUTER–BASED CITATORS

Although computerized legal research services are discussed in detail in Chapter 22, the availability of Shepard's citators in both LEXIS and WESTLAW, and access to another more limited citator, AUTOCITE, in LEXIS, are relevant here. AUTOCITE, a service of the Lawyers Cooperative Publishing Co., is another computerized service which performs a citator function limited to parallel citations and the subsequent history of the particular document being searched. West Publishing Company has recently announced the availability of INSTA–CITE, a competitive case validation service. INSTA–CITE provides prior and subsequent case history for cases in the data base. In addition, the use of LEXIS and WESTLAW enable a researcher to retrieve all references to a particular citation, from their extensive data bases. The full text of the decision can also be retrieved, or just that portion of the decision which refers to the cited case, or simply the citations of decisions which mention the case.

1. See J. A. Quattrochi, *Federal Tax Research* (Harcourt Brace Jovanovich, 1982) and G. L. Richmond, "Research Tools for Federal Taxation," 2 *Legal Reference Services Q.* 25 (1982).

H. SUMMARY

Citators are one of the great contributions of law publishing to research in general. They have now been adapted and are being used successfully in other disciplines.[2] The Shepard's firm, now associated with McGraw-Hill, began in 1873 with Frank Shepard's printing of citations to Illinois Cases on gummed paper and selling them to attorneys to paste into the margins of their bound reporters, updating the cases published in those volumes. From the original "Shepard's System of Adhesive Citations" to the use of high speed computers producing long lists of citations to primary and secondary sources, we can trace in microcosm the increasing sophistication of legal research tools.

2. For example, *Social Science Citation Index, Science Citation Index,* etc.

Chapter 10

LEGISLATIVE HISTORY

A. INTRODUCTION

Research in statutory material often deals with the location and study of the legislative histories of particular enactments. Such a search may seek the current status of a proposed law during its pre-enactment consideration by the legislature. It may also concern the determination of the legislature's intent relating to a statute after its passage and involve a search for that intent in a variety of legislative documents. As statutory enactments have proliferated and touched on virtually every aspect of human conduct and endeavor, this type of research has become a regular part of the lawyer's work. Many important appellate decisions turn on questions of legislative history since statutes frequently contain ambiguities which are resolved only through litigation. Lawyers and informed laymen are also increasingly concerned with affecting legislative consideration of pending proposals and this inevitably requires research in these sources.

Justice Felix Frankfurter described this trend over twenty five years ago, as follows:

> As the area of regulation steadily widened, the impact of the legislative process upon the judicial brought into being, and compelled consideration of, all that convincingly illumines an enactment, instead of merely that which is called, with delusive simplicity, "the end result" . . . . Legislative reports were increasingly drawn upon, statements by those in charge of legislation, reports of investigating committees, recommendations of agencies entrusted with the enforcement of laws, etc. etc. When Mr. Justice Holmes came to the Court, the U.S. Reports were practically barren of references to legislative materials. These swarm in current volumes. And let me say in passing that the importance that such materials play in Supreme Court litigation carry far-reaching implications for bench and bar.[1]

B. LEGISLATIVE PROCESS AND SOURCES OF LEGISLATIVE HISTORY

Any discussion of research in legislative history must begin with the legislative process itself—that is, what happens to a bill as it wends its way through the labyrinth of Congress or a state legislature. The documents of legislative history must be viewed in the context of the parliamentary practices which produce them. Congressional procedures are quite complex, however, and the state legislative processes present a wide range of patterns and forms. It is impossible to describe adequately here the variety of possible steps a law may take from its introduction to its passage or defeat, either on the federal or state level. The following brief survey of the stages of Congressional consideration in its simplest form is designed to place the major documents of legislative history in their procedural setting. More detailed information about the federal legislative process can be found in two brief Congressional pamphlets, *How our Laws are Made* [2] and *Enactment of a Law: Procedural Steps in the Legislative Process* [3] Illustrations A–1 and A–2 show the beginning and the end of the text of a federal statute, the Foreign Intelligence Surveillance Act of 1978, as it appears in the *Statutes at Large.* The illustrations that follow in this chapter show various documents and finding tools relating to the legislative history of that law.

1. Frankfurter, "Some Reflections on the Reading of Statutes," 2 *Record of the N.Y.C.B.A.* 213, 233 (1947), reprinted in 47 *Columbia L.Rev.* 527, 542–43 (1947).

2. H. J. Zinn (U.S. Government Printing Office, rev. and updated by E. F. Willett, Jr., 1978).

3. Senate Doc. No. 96–15 (U.S. Government Printing Office, 1979).

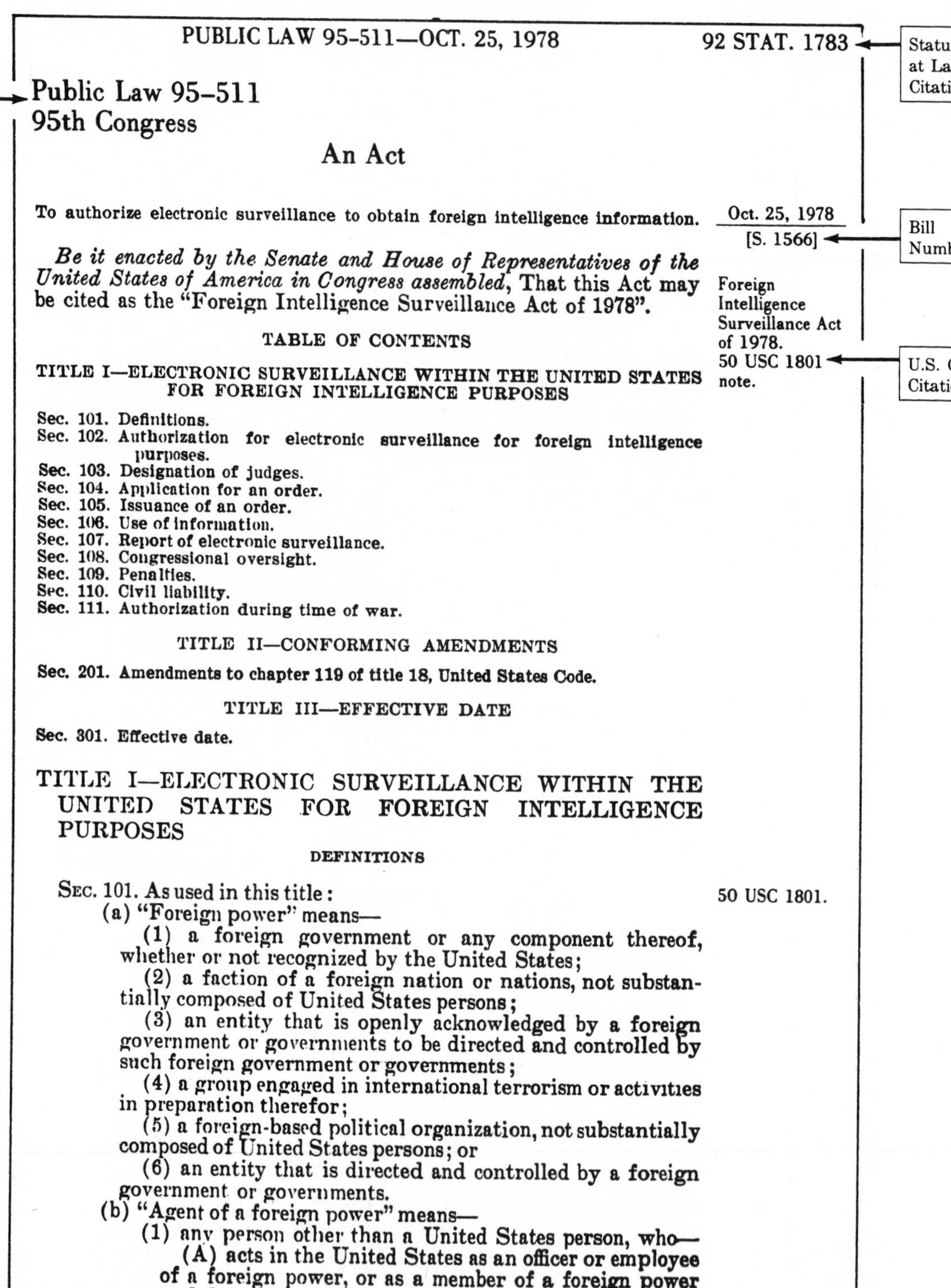

PUBLIC LAW 95-511—OCT. 25, 1978 92 STAT. 1783

Public Law 95-511
95th Congress

An Act

To authorize electronic surveillance to obtain foreign intelligence information.

Oct. 25, 1978
[S. 1566]

Be it enacted by the Senate and House of Representatives of the United States of America in Congress assembled, That this Act may be cited as the "Foreign Intelligence Surveillance Act of 1978".

Foreign Intelligence Surveillance Act of 1978.
50 USC 1801 note.

TABLE OF CONTENTS

TITLE I—ELECTRONIC SURVEILLANCE WITHIN THE UNITED STATES FOR FOREIGN INTELLIGENCE PURPOSES

DEFINITIONS

SEC. 101. As used in this title: 50 USC 1801.

(a) "Foreign power" means—

(1) a foreign government or any component thereof, whether or not recognized by the United States;

(2) a faction of a foreign nation or nations, not substantially composed of United States persons;

(3) an entity that is openly acknowledged by a foreign government or governments to be directed and controlled by such foreign government or governments;

(4) a group engaged in international terrorism or activities in preparation therefor;

(5) a foreign-based political organization, not substantially composed of United States persons; or

(6) an entity that is directed and controlled by a foreign government or governments.

(b) "Agent of a foreign power" means—

(1) any person other than a United States person, who—

(A) acts in the United States as an officer or employee of a foreign power, or as a member of a foreign power as defined in subsection (a)(4);

Illustration A-1

Beginning of the text of the "Foreign Intelligence Surveillance Act of 1978," as it appears in the U.S. *Statutes at Large*.

92 STAT. 1798 PUBLIC LAW 95–511—OCT. 25, 1978

18 USC 2518. (g) Section 2518(10) is amended by striking out "intercepted" and inserting "intercepted pursuant to this chapter" after the first appearance of "communication".

18 USC 2519. (h) Section 2519(3) is amended by inserting "pursuant to this chapter" after "wire or oral communications" and after "granted or denied".

TITLE III—EFFECTIVE DATE

EFFECTIVE DATE

50 USC 1801 note. SEC. 301. The provisions of this Act and the amendments made hereby shall become effective upon the date of enactment of this Act, except that any electronic surveillance approved by the Attorney General to gather foreign intelligence information shall not be deemed unlawful for failure to follow the procedures of this Act, if that surveillance is terminated or an order approving that surveillance is obtained under title I of this Act within ninety days following the designation of the first judge pursuant to section 103 of this Act.

Approved October 25, 1978.

Date of Enactment

Legislative History Summary

LEGISLATIVE HISTORY:

HOUSE REPORTS: No. 95–1283, Pt. I accompanying H.R. 7308 (Comm. on the Judiciary) and (Select Comm. on Intelligence) and No. 95–1720 (Comm. of Conference).
SENATE REPORTS: No. 95–604 and No. 95–604, Pt. II (Comm. on the Judiciary) and No. 95–701 (Select Comm. on Intelligence).
CONGRESSIONAL RECORD, Vol. 124 (1978):
Apr. 20, considered and passed Senate.
Sept. 6, 7, considered and passed House, amended.
Sept. 12, Senate disagreed to House amendments.
Oct. 9, Senate agreed to conference report.
Oct. 12, House agreed to conference report.
WEEKLY COMPILATION OF PRESIDENTIAL DOCUMENTS, Vol. 14, No. 43:
Oct. 25, Presidential statement.

Illustration A–2

End of the text, and legislative history summary, of the "Foreign Intelligence Surveillance Act of 1978," as it appeares in the U.S. *Statutes at Large.*

1. PRELIMINARY CONSIDERATION AND MESSAGES OF RECOMMENDATION

Documents relating to particular enactments may exist even before the proposal is introduced as a bill.

Hearings on a problem of legislative concern may be held prior to the introduction of specific bills to remedy that condition. Such hearings may be held either in a session prior to that which considers the remedial legislation, or in the session that actually passes on it. Sometimes such hearings continue through several sessions. If one's research into the legislative history of a particular law is limited only to the session of its enactment, relevant and important hearings may be overlooked. Discussion of research in hearings follows in Section 3 below.

Many bills introduced in Congress stem from Presidential recommendations and may be accompanied by a Presidential message or a memorandum from an executive agency. These documents describe the purpose of the proposed legislation and reveal the intent of their drafters. As such, they are relevant to the search for legislative history, although they are not strictly direct evidence of legislative intent. The President's annual State of the Union message is an example of an executive document which proposes many legislative enactments in general terms, but there are many other specific messages which in greater detail describe and urge the passage of individual measures. Messages are also frequently issued when the President signs or vetoes particular enactments and these too can shed light on legislative history.

These messages are printed and indexed in the *Congressional Record,* appear in the *Weekly Compilation of Presidential Documents* (see Illustrations B–1 and B–2), the *House* and *Senate Journals,* and separately as *House* and *Senate Documents.* These are further described in Chapter 11 on *Administrative and Executive Publications.*

2. CONGRESSIONAL BILLS—THEIR INTRODUCTION AND REFERRAL TO COMMITTEE

Each bill, when introduced, is printed, assigned a bill number and referred to a committee of the house in which it is presented. The bill may be amended at any stage of its legislative progress and some bills are amended many times. The bill number is the key to tracing legislative actions prior to enactment and to locating many of the documents reflecting such actions. The finding tools for such research are a group of indexes called status tables which usually list bills by number, frequently digest them, describe significant legislative actions taken on the measure and often identify documents relevant to its consideration. These tables are discussed in Section C below.

Variations in the text of the bill as it is introduced, as it appears in its committee print, as amended and as passed, are helpful in deter-

other agency of the Executive Branch. Current statutes provide the Chief Counsel with sufficient authorities to evaluate small business issues and serve as an ombudsman to small business interests.

I am also concerned by the loan pooling provision in this bill that would authorize private dealers to issue a new class of 100 percent federally guaranteed securities which would compete directly with the Treasury and other federally-backed securities in the bond markets.

I look forward to working with the Congress and the small business community who worked on this bill to develop a program to meet the needs of small business. It is my great hope that early in the next Congress an approach will be fashioned to meet the needs of the small business community, with the full involvement of my Administration.

JIMMY CARTER

Foreign Intelligence Surveillance Act of 1978

Statement on Signing S. 1566 Into Law. October 25, 1978

I am pleased to sign into law today the Foreign Intelligence Surveillance Act of 1978. As I said a year and a half ago at the beginning of the process that produced this bill, "one of the most difficult tasks in a free society like our own is the correlation between adequate intelligence to guarantee our Nation's security on the one hand, and the preservation of basic human rights on the other."

This is a difficult balance to strike, but the act I am signing today strikes it. It sacrifices neither our security nor our civil liberties. And it assures that those who serve this country in intelligence positions will have the affirmation of Congress that their activities are lawful.

In working on this bill, the Congress dealt skillfully with sensitive issues. The result shows our country benefits when the legislative and executive branches of Government work together toward a common goal.

The bill requires, for the first time, a prior judicial warrant for *all* electronic surveillance for foreign intelligence or counterintelligence purposes in the United States in which communications of U.S. persons might be intercepted. It clarifies the Executive's authority to gather foreign intelligence by electronic surveillance in the United States. It will remove any doubt about the legality of those surveillances which are conducted to protect our country against espionage and international terrorism. It will assure FBI field agents and others involved in intelligence collection that their acts are authorized by statute and, if a U.S. person's communications are concerned, by a court order. And it will protect the privacy of the American people.

In short, the act helps to solidify the relationship of trust between the American people and their Government. It provides a basis for the trust of the American people in the fact that the activities of their intelligence agencies are both effective and lawful. It provides enough secrecy to ensure that intelligence relating to national security can be securely acquired, while permitting review by the courts and Congress to safeguard the rights of Americans and others.

This legislation is the first long step toward the goal of establishing statutory charters for our intelligence agencies. I am committed to that goal, and my administration will work with the Congress to achieve it.

Illustration B–1

President Carter's statement on signing the "Foreign Intelligence Surveillance Act of 1978" into law, as it appeared in the *Weekly Compilation of Presidential Documents.*

Many people played important roles in securing passage of this bill.

I am convinced that the bill would not have passed without the leadership of Attorney General Bell; the personal commitment of the Director of Central Intelligence, Admiral Turner; and the work of Admiral Inman of the National Security Agency and Directors Webster and Kelley of the FBI. I extend my personal appreciation to these men and their staffs.

My administration's bill was based on some fine work during the Ford administration under the leadership of Attorney General Levi. His contribution to this legislation was substantial, illustrating the bipartisan nature of this process.

There was strong, effective, and bipartisan leadership in the Congress as well. I particularly want to commend Senators Kennedy, Bayh, and Garn for helping to guide this bill to overwhelming approval in the Senate. Chairman Boland and Congressman Morgan Murphy of the House Intelligence Committee and Chairman Rodino and Congressman Kastenmeier of the House Judiciary Committee undertook the hard work of moving the bill through the House. And, once again, I am indebted to the efforts of Speaker O'Neill and Majority Leader Wright.

I wish as well to express my appreciation to the Vice President, who long supported this foreign intelligence reform in the Senate and who assured the wholehearted commitment of the executive branch to this important legislation.

I have said so often, one of the central goals of my administration is to restore the confidence of the American people in their governmental institutions. This act takes us one more step down that road.

NOTE: As enacted, S. 1566 is Public Law 95–511, approved October 25.

Ethics in Government Act of 1978

Remarks on Signing S. 555 Into Law. October 26, 1978

THE PRESIDENT. I'm very pleased this morning to participate in a ceremony that has great significance for our country. During my own campaign for President, I promised the American people that I would do everything in my power to guarantee integrity in the executive branch of Government, and also obviously I have been joined with great enthusiasm by the Members of Congress and members of the judiciary as well.

On May 3 of 1977, shortly after I became President, I proposed legislation to the Congress to meet these commitments. And today I'm pleased to sign into law the Ethics in Government Act of 1978, which gives us added tools to ensure that the Government is open, honest, and is free from conflicts of interest.

I am pleased that no major provision of my own original proposal has been deleted or weakened, and that the Congress, with our support, has actually extended important provisions to the legislative and judicial branches of Government. This is a good indication of cooperation in extending these ethical standards throughout the entire Government of our country.

This bill will provide for mandatory, personal financial disclosures for high officials in the executive branch of Government, for all Members of the Congress, and for all senior members of the judicial branch of Government as well.

The ultimate authority for—or responsibility for endorsing and interpreting the provisions of the act lies in the executive branch of Government. Substantially, it broadens protection against abuses caused by postemployment conflicts of interest, so that people who have been employed in the Government cannot use this employ-

Illustration B–2

President Carter's Statement (concluded).

mining legislative intent. The elimination or insertion of particular language in the text implies a legislative choice and thus illuminates the intent of the legislature. Almost every printing of a bill represents a distinct step in its progress toward enactment and may ultimately be a significant document in its legislative history.

Congressional bills are individually numbered in a separate series for each house and they retain that number through both of the annual sessions of each Congress. At the end of the two year term of Congress, pending bills lose their active status and must be reintroduced if they are to be revived.

Bills are received in many law libraries, usually in microfiche, on a subscription or depository basis. They can also be obtained individually from the clerk of the House or Senate, from the legislators who sponsor them, or from the clerk of the committee considering them. The texts of a few bills also appear in the *Congressional Record,* but that is not the regular form of publication for bills. A private looseleaf service publisher, Commerce Clearing House, through its expensive *Legislative Reporting Services,* may supply subscribers with bills on a particular subject. That CCH service now has a computer-based, on-line bill tracking service, called ELSS (*Electronic Legislative Search System*). Additionally, another publisher, the Congressional Information Service, issues Congressional bills, resolutions, and laws on microfiche, beginning with the 89th Congress.

Illustrations C–1 to C–4 represent the first page of four different stages of the bill, number S.1566, which was to become the Foreign Intelligence Surveillance Act of 1978, as follows: C–1 shows the bill as it was introduced by Senator Kennedy and referred to the Senate Committee on the Judiciary; C–2, the bill after it was reported out by the Judiciary Committee with amendments, and referred to the Select Committee on Intelligence; C–3, a later version of the bill with further amendments and a calendar number assigned; and C–4, the bill as introduced in the House of Representatives, after its passage by the Senate.

3. HEARINGS

Hearings are held by standing and special committees of the House and Senate to investigate particular problems or situations of general concern, and also to elicit the views of persons or groups interested in proposed legislation. Hearings may be designed to air a controversial situation, determine the need for new legislation, or to bring before the Congress information helpful to its preparation, consideration or enactment. Hearings do not *have* to be held and occasionally legislation is enacted for which hearings have not been held in one or both houses. But that is unusual and, even then, relevant hearings may be found on similar or related bills which may aid in interpreting the legislative intent of such an enactment.

The hearings, as published, consist of transcripts of testimony before a particular committee or subcommittee, exhibits submitted by

95TH CONGRESS
1ST SESSION

S. 1566

IN THE SENATE OF THE UNITED STATES

MAY 18 (legislative day, MAY 16), 1977

Mr. KENNEDY (for himself, Mr. BAYH, Mr. EASTLAND, Mr. INOUYE, Mr. MCCLELLAN, Mr. MATHIAS, Mr. NELSON, and Mr. THURMOND) introduced the following bill; which was read twice and referred by unanimous consent to the Committee on the Judiciary, and, if and when reported, then to the Select Committee on Intelligence

A BILL

To amend title 18, United States Code, to authorize applications for a court order approving the use of electronic surveillance to obtain foreign intelligence information.

Be it enacted by the Senate and House of Representatives of the United States of America in Congress assembled, That this Act may be cited as the "Foreign Intelligence Surveillance Act of 1977".

SEC. 2. Title 18, United States Code, is amended by adding a new chapter after chapter 119 as follows:

II

Illustration C–1

Bill as introduced in the Senate and then referred to the Committee on the Judiciary.

95TH CONGRESS
1ST SESSION

S. 1566

[Report No. 95-604]

IN THE SENATE OF THE UNITED STATES

MAY 18 (legislative day, MAY 16), 1977

Mr. KENNEDY (for himself, Mr. BAYH, Mr. EASTLAND, Mr. INOUYE, Mr. McCLELLAN, Mr. MATHIAS, Mr. NELSON, Mr. THURMOND, Mr. HUDDLESTON, and Mr. GARN) introduced the following bill; which was read twice and referred by unanimous consent to the Committee on the Judiciary, and, if and when reported, then to the Select Committee on Intelligence

NOVEMBER 15 (legislative day, NOVEMBER 1), 1977
Reported by Mr. KENNEDY, with amendments

[Omit the part struck through and insert the part printed in italic]

NOVEMBER 15 (legislative day, NOVEMBER 1), 1977
Referred, by unanimous consent, to the Select Committee on Intelligence

---

A BILL

To amend title 18, United States Code, to authorize applications for a court order approving the use of electronic surveillance to obtain foreign intelligence information.

Be it enacted by the Senate and House of Representatives of the United States of America in Congress assembled, That this Act may be cited as the "Foreign Intelligence Surveillance Act of 1977".

SEC. 2. Title 18, United States Code, is amended by adding a new chapter after chapter 119 as follows:

II

Illustration C-2

The bill after being reported out by the Judiciary Committee, with amendments, and referred to the Select Committee on Intelligence.

Calendar No. 643

95TH CONGRESS
2D SESSION

S. 1566

[Report No. 95-604]

[Report No. 95-701]

IN THE SENATE OF THE UNITED STATES

MAY 18 (legislative day, MAY 16), 1977

Mr. KENNEDY (for himself, Mr. BAYH, Mr. EASTLAND, Mr. INOUYE, Mr. McCLELLAN, Mr. MATHIAS, Mr. NELSON, Mr. THURMOND, Mr. HUDDLESTON, and Mr. GARN) introduced the following bill; which was read twice and referred by unanimous consent to the Committee on the Judiciary, and, if and when reported, then to the Select Committee on Intelligence

NOVEMBER 15 (legislative day, NOVEMBER 1), 1977

Reported by Mr. KENNEDY, with amendments

[Omit the part struck through and insert the part printed in italic]

NOVEMBER 15 (legislative day, NOVEMBER 1), 1977

Referred, by unanimous consent, to the Select Committee on Intelligence

MARCH 14 (legislative day, FEBRUARY 6), 1978

Reported by Mr. BAYH, with amendments

[Omit the part in boldface brackets and insert the part in boldface italic]

A BILL

To amend title 18, United States Code, to authorize applications for a court order approving the use of electronic surveillance to obtain foreign intelligence information.

Be it enacted by the Senate and House of Representatives of the United States of America in Congress assembled, That this Act may be cited as the "Foreign Intelligence Surveillance Act of 1977" **[***1978***]**.

SEC. 2. Title 18, United States Code, is amended by adding a new chapter after chapter 119 as follows:

II

Illustration C-3

A later version of the Senate bill, with further amendments and a calendar number assigned.

95TH CONGRESS
2D SESSION

S. 1566

IN THE HOUSE OF REPRESENTATIVES

APRIL 24, 1978

Referred to the Committee on the Judiciary

AN ACT

To amend title 18, United States Code, to authorize applications for a court order approving the use of electronic surveillance to obtain foreign intelligence information.

Be it enacted by the Senate and House of Representatives of the United States of America in Congress assembled, That this Act may be cited as the "Foreign Intelligence Surveillance Act of 1978".

SEC. 2. Title 18, United States Code, is amended by adding a new chapter after chapter 119 as follows:

I

Illustration C–4

Bill as introduced in the House of Representatives after passage by the Senate.

interested individuals or organizations, and sometimes a print of the bill in question. Not every hearing which is held is published. Those that are published are listed in the *Monthly Catalog of U.S. Government Publications* and in some of the status tables and legislative services described in Section C below. For information on hearings, the *Congressional Information Service (CIS Index),* described below, is the most useful of these aids.

As noted above, hearings relevant to the interpretation of a particular enactment may have been held and published by a session of Congress prior to the one which enacted the law in question. Sometimes relevant hearings may extend over several sessions and be published in several parts or volumes. Larger hearings sometimes contain indexes which are helpful in locating specific references.

As evidence of legislative intent, hearings rank below committee reports and the variant texts of bills. The testimony they contain may range from the helpful and objective views of disinterested experts to the most slanted or even mundane comments of partisans. Although careful research can frequently turn up useful material in published hearings, this source must be perused with a critical and discriminating eye.

Hearings are generally identified by the number of the Congress and session in which they are held, the name of the committee which held them, the short title which appears on the cover of the published hearing, the number of the bill being discussed, and the dates covered by the hearing. Hearings are not generally published or numbered in consecutive series. Only a few committees employ a convenient numbering arrangement for their published hearings.

In addition to the *Monthly Catalog of U.S. Government Publications* and its predecessors, the most useful indexes to hearings are in the commercial publication, *Congressional Information Service* (known as *C.I.S.*), which since 1970 has published a comprehensive finding tool for federal legislative history (see Section C.2 below), as well as a microfiche collection of the actual documents of legislative history, including the hearings. Now, *C.I.S.* is in the process of issuing a detailed retrospective index of hearings held from 1833 to 1969 to complete its coverage. This index, in eight parts, provides access to hearings by subject, personal names, bill number, and hearing title. So far, the period from 1953 to 1969 has been published and completion of the set is scheduled for June 1985.

The Library of the United States Senate has published another series of indexes to the hearings of both Houses.[4] These cover the period back to the 41st Congress (1869–1871), but provide less detail and fewer points of access than the *C.I.S.* index described above.

Illustrations D and E, respectively show the cover pages of the Senate hearings on bill no. 1566 for the Foreign Intelligence Surveillance Act of 1978, and House hearings on its own related bills on the same subject.

4. *Cumulative Index of Congressional Committee Hearings* (U.S. Government Printing Office, 1935–19__). With supplements. See Schmeckebier & Eastin, *Government Publications and Their Use* (2nd Revised edition, 1969) pp. 181–182 for a description of the various parts of this index. These indexes now seem to be issued biennially, the sixth and latest supplement covers the 95th Congress, 1977–1978.

FOREIGN INTELLIGENCE SURVEILLANCE ACT OF 1978

HEARINGS

BEFORE THE

SUBCOMMITTEE ON INTELLIGENCE AND THE RIGHTS OF AMERICANS

OF THE

SELECT COMMITTEE ON INTELLIGENCE

OF THE

UNITED STATES SENATE

NINETY-FIFTH CONGRESS

SECOND SESSION

ON

S. 1566

FOREIGN INTELLIGENCE SURVEILLANCE ACT OF 1978

JULY 19, 21, 1977 AND FEBRUARY 8, 24, 27, 1978

Printed for the use of the Select Committee on Intelligence

U.S. GOVERNMENT PRINTING OFFICE

94-628 WASHINGTON : 1978

For sale by the Superintendent of Documents, U.S. Government Printing Office
Washington, D.C. 20402
Stock Number 052-070-04477-2

Illustration D

U.S. Senate hearings on S.1566, for the Foreign Intelligence Surveillance Act of 1978.

FOREIGN INTELLIGENCE ELECTRONIC SURVEILLANCE

HEARINGS

BEFORE THE

SUBCOMMITTEE ON LEGISLATION

OF THE

PERMANENT SELECT COMMITTEE ON INTELLIGENCE HOUSE OF REPRESENTATIVES

NINETY-FIFTH CONGRESS

SECOND SESSION

ON

H.R. 5794, H.R. 9745, H.R. 7308, AND H.R. 5632

THE FOREIGN INTELLIGENCE SURVEILLANCE ACT OF 1977

JANUARY 10, 11, 17, AND FEBRUARY 8, 1978

Printed for the use of the Permanent Select Committee on Intelligence

U.S. GOVERNMENT PRINTING OFFICE

28-615 WASHINGTON : 1978

Illustration E

House of Representatives hearings on various bills related to foreign intelligence surveillance.

4. COMMITTEE REPORTS

The most important documents of legislative history are the reports of the Congressional committees of each house, and the conference committees of both houses. The House and Senate committees issue a report on each bill when it is reported out of committee for consideration and possible legislative action by the whole house. These reports reflect the committee's proposal after the bill has been studied, hearings held, and amendments made. They frequently contain the text of the bill, an analysis of its content and intent, and the committee's rationale for its recommendations. Sometimes the report will also include a minority statement, if there is disagreement among the committee members. Since most bills die in committee and are never reported out for action, one cannot expect to find a committee report on every bill introduced.

If different versions of a proposed enactment have been passed by each house, a conference committee will be convened, including members from each house. The conference committee will reconcile the differences and produce an agreed compromise for return to both houses and final passage. The reports of these conference committees, usually containing the text of the compromise bill, are another very persuasive source of legislative intent.

Committee reports may also be issued on special investigations, studies and hearings not related to the consideration or reporting of a specific bill.

The committee reports of each house are published as single pamphlets in separate numerical series for each session of Congress. They are most easily identified and traced by these report numbers, e.g. House Report No. 95–1283, which refers to a report of the 95th Congress, 2d Session (see Illustration G). The reports are also published, together with House and Senate documents (another form of Congressional publication described below), in a bound series of volumes popularly called the *Serial Set.* In that form, they can also be located by the volume numbers in which they appear. A retrospective index to the Serial Set, covering the period from 1789 to 1969, is published in thirty six volumes by the *Congressional Information Service* under the title, *U.S. Serial Set Index.*

Committee reports are listed and indexed in *Monthly Catalog of U.S. Government Publications* and the *Congressional Information Service.* The reports are available as a series by subscription from the Government Printing Office, or sometimes individually from the clerk of the committee issuing them or from the clerk of the house. Some can be purchased from the Government Printing Office, but supplies are usually exhausted shortly after publication. One or more committee reports on major enactments are reprinted selectively in the *U.S. Code Congressional and Administrative News* (see Illustration I) and a few appear also in the *Congressional Record.*

The following Illustrations show various committee reports on the proposed Foreign Intelligence Surveillance Act of 1978: F, Senate Report; G, House Report; H, House version of Conference Report; I, *USCCAN* publication of Committee Reports selectively.

Another form of Congressional publications are "committee prints", which like the committee reports are issued generally in consecutive series for each House, with the numbering sequence beginning over in each session of Congress. Some committee prints are not numbered at all, however, and some are reissued subsequently as House or Senate reports or documents. Committee prints usually contain material prepared specifically for the use of a committee, such as studies done by the committee staff or outside experts. Others are statements by members of the committee or its subcommittees on a pending bill. Illustration J, on page 307, an example of the latter type, sets forth the views of members of a subcommittee of the House Committee on the Judiciary, on the House version of the proposed Foreign Intelligence Surveillance Act of 1978. The Congressional Information Service has published a comprehensive index to committee prints from the mid-19th century to 1969, *U.S. Congressional Committee Prints Index* (1980, 5 vols.).

5. CONGRESSIONAL DEBATES

Floor debate in Congress relevant to a pending bill can occur at almost any stage of its progress, but typically it takes place after the bill has been reported out by committee. During consideration of the bill, amendments will be proposed and accepted or defeated. Arguments for and against amendments and passage are made, explanations of unclear or controversial provisions are offered, and much of the business of the legislative process is revealed in floor discussion.

The *Congressional Record* (and its predecessors) provide a more or less verbatim transcript of the legislative debates and proceedings, subject, however, to revision of their remarks by the individual legislators. The *Record* is published daily while either house is in session. While the *House* and *Senate Journals* describe the legislative proceedings in brief form, they do not report the details of the debates and discussions of Congress. The *Congressional Record* is therefore the essential source for this form of legislative history.

The chronological record of Congressional debates is contained in these publications: [5]

Annals of Congress, 1789–1824	(1st Congress to 18th Congress, 1st Session)
Register of Debates, 1824–1837	(18th Congress, 2nd Session to 25th Congress, 1st Session)
Congressional Globe, 1833–1873	(25th Congress, 2nd Session to 42nd Congress, 2nd Session)
Congressional Record, 1873–date	(43rd Congress, 1st Session to date)

5. See Schmeckebier & Eastin, Ibid, pp. 134–146, for fuller description.

Calendar No. 643

95TH CONGRESS } SENATE { REPORT
2D SESSION } { No. 95–701

FOREIGN INTELLIGENCE SURVEILLANCE ACT OF 1978

MARCH 14, (legislative day, FEBRUARY 6), 1978.—Ordered to be printed

Mr. BAYH, from the Select Committee on Intelligence, submitted the following

REPORT

together with

ADDITIONAL VIEWS

[To accompany S. 1566]

The Select Committee on Intelligence, to which was referred the bill (S. 1566) to amend title 18, United States Code, to authorize applications for a court order approving the use of electronic surveillance to obtain foreign intelligence information, having considered the same, reports favorably thereon with amendments and recommends that the bill, as amended, do pass.

AMENDMENTS

On page 1, line 4, strike "1977", and insert in lieu thereof "1978".

On page 3, strike out all after line 5 through the end of line 19, and insert in lieu thereof the following:

(A) any person, other than a United States person, who—

(i) acts in the United States as an officer or employee of a foreign power; or

(ii) acts for or on behalf of a foreign power which engages in clandestine intelligence activities contrary to the interests of the United States, when the circumstances of such person's presence in the United States indicate that such person may engage in such activities in the United States, or when such person knowingly aids or abets any person in the conduct of such activities or conspires with any person knowing that such person is engaged in such activities;

Illustration F

Report of the Senate Select Committee on Intelligence on the Foreign Intelligence Surveillance Act of 1978.

95TH CONGRESS } HOUSE OF REPRESENTATIVES { REPORT 95–
2d Session } { 1283, Pt. I

FOREIGN INTELLIGENCE SURVEILLANCE ACT OF 1978

JUNE 8, 1978.—Ordered to be printed

Mr. BOLAND, from the Permanent Select Committee on Intelligence, submitted the following

REPORT

together with

SUPPLEMENTAL, ADDITIONAL, AND DISSENTING VIEWS

[To accompany H.R. 7308 which on November 4, 1977, was referred jointly to the Committee on the Judiciary and the Permanent Select Committee on Intelligence]

The Permanent Select Committee on Intelligence, to whom was referred the bill (H.R. 7308) to amend title 18, United States Code, to authorize applications for a court order approving the use of electronic surveillance to obtain foreign intelligence information, having considered the same, report favorably thereon with amendments and recommend that the bill as amended do pass.

AMENDMENTS

Strike all after the enacting clause and insert in lieu thereof:

That this act may be cited as the "Foreign Intelligence Surveillance Act of 1978".

TABLE OF CONTENTS

29–228

Illustration G

Report of the House Permanent Select Committee on Intelligence on the Foreign Intelligence Surveillance Act of 1978.

95TH CONGRESS } HOUSE OF REPRESENTATIVES { REPORT
2d Session } { No. 95–1720

FOREIGN INTELLIGENCE SURVEILLANCE ACT OF 1978

OCTOBER 5, 1978.—Ordered to be printed

Mr. BOLAND, from the committee of conference, submitted the following

CONFERENCE REPORT

[To accompany S. 1566]

The committee of conference on the disagreeing votes of the two Houses on the amendments of the House to the bill (S. 1566) to authorize electronic surveillance to obtain foreign intelligence information, having met, after full and free conference, have agreed to recommend and do recommend to their respective Houses as follows:

That the Senate recede from its disagreement to the amendment of the House to the text of the Senate bill, and agree to the same with an amendment as follows:

In lieu of the matter proposed to be inserted by the House amendments insert the following:

That this Act may be cited as the "Foreign Intelligence Surveillance Act of 1978".

TABLE OF CONTENTS

Illustration H

House of Representatives Conference Committee Report No. 95–1720 on S.1566.

LEGISLATIVE HISTORY
P.L. 95-511

FOREIGN INTELLIGENCE SURVEILLANCE ACT OF 1978

P.L. 95-511, see page 92 Stat. 1783

Senate Report (Judiciary Committee) No. 95-604 (I and II), Nov. 15, 22, 1977 [To accompany S. 1566]

Senate Report (Intelligence Committee) No. 95-701, Mar. 14, 1978 [To accompany S. 1566]

House Report [Intelligence Committee) No. 95-1283, June 8, 1978 [To accompany H.R. 7308]

House Conference Report No. 95-1720, Oct. 5, 1978 [To accompany S. 1566]

Cong. Record Vol. 124 (1978)

DATES OF CONSIDERATION AND PASSAGE

Senate April 20, October 9, 1978

House September 7, October 12, 1978

The Senate bill was passed in lieu of the House bill. The Senate Reports (this page, p. 3970, p. 3973) and the House Conference Report (p. 4048) are set out.

SENATE REPORT NO. 95-604—PART 1
[page 1]

The Committee on the Judiciary, to which was referred the bill (S. 1566) to amend title 18, United States Code, to authorize applications for a court order approving the use of electronic surveillance to obtain foreign intelligence information, having considered the same, reports favorably thereon with amendments and recommends that the bill, as amended, do pass.

* * * * * * * * *

[page 3]

PURPOSE OF AMENDMENTS

The amendments to S. 1566 are designed to clarify and make more explicit the statutory intent, as well as to provide further safeguards for individuals subjected to electronic surveillance pursuant to this new chapter. Certain amendments are also designed to provide a detailed procedure for challenging such surveillance, and any evidence derived therefrom, during the course of a formal proceeding.

Finally, the reported bill adds an amendment to Chapter 119 of title 18, United States Code (Title III of the Omnibus Crime Control and Safe Streets Act of 1968, Public Law 90-351, section 802). This latter amendment is technical and conforming in nature and is designed to integrate certain provisions of Chapters 119 and 120. A more detailed explanation of the individual amendments is contained in the section-by-section analysis of this report.

3904

Illustration I

USCCAN publication of selections of two of the Committee Reports on the Foreign Intelligence Surveillance Act of 1978.

95th Congress }
2d Session }

COMMITTEE PRINT

No. 19

THE FOREIGN INTELLIGENCE SURVEILLANCE ACT OF 1978
H.R. 7308

SUBCOMMITTEE ON COURTS, CIVIL LIBERTIES, AND THE ADMINISTRATION OF JUSTICE

OF THE

COMMITTEE ON THE JUDICIARY HOUSE OF REPRESENTATIVES

NINETY-FIFTH CONGRESS

SECOND SESSION

JULY 1978

Printed for the use of the Committee on the Judiciary

U.S. GOVERNMENT PRINTING OFFICE

31-388 WASHINGTON: 1978

Illustration J

House of Representatives committee print on the Foreign Intelligence Surveillance Act of 1978.

A bound edition of the *Congressional Record,* in recent years comprising over thirty volumes, is published at the end of each session. Only the daily issues, however, contain the *Appendix* which includes extraneous materials, supplements to floor remarks, exhibits and almost anything a legislator wishes to insert in the *Record.* Prior to the 83rd Congress, 2nd Session, this material was also included in the bound edition. Since the paper on which the daily edition is printed is of poor quality and not usually preserved, many libraries provide access to the appendix on microfilm or microfiche. There are other differences in content and pagination between the daily and bound versions, but for most research, the latter is the standard and generally accepted source.

Illustrations K–1 and K–2 show debates in the *Congressional Record* on the Foreign Intelligence Surveillance Act of 1978, K–2 showing the passage of the Act by the Senate.

An index to the proceedings, by subjects, names of legislators, and titles of legislation, is included in the *Record* every two weeks. These indexes do not cumulate, however, until the bound edition is published at the end of the session. Illustration L shows two sample columns from that index, both relating to the Foreign Intelligence Surveillance Act of 1978—the left hand column under Senator Kennedy's name, and the right hand column under the name of the Act. Both the fortnightly index and the cumulative bound index contain a very useful History of Bills and Resolutions table (See Section C. 4 below and Illustration Q) which lists all bills introduced in that session by their bill number and summarizes their legislative history.

Since the 80th Congress, the daily issues of the *Congressional Record* include the Daily Digest which contains the highlights of the session, summaries of proceedings, actions taken, enactments signed by the President, and useful committee information. The Daily Digests are cumulated in one volume of the bound edition, together with a tabular History of Bills Enacted into Public Law. (See Section C. 5 below and Illustration R.) This useful summary of legislative history of enacted bills is arranged by public law number.

The value of legislative debates as evidence of legislative intent has been greatly diminished by the contradictory nature of the statements they contain and the calculated use of prepared colloquies designed to manufacture evidence of legislative intent. This practice has been widely criticized [6] and courts rely more on committee reports than on legislative debates for aid in statutory interpretation.

6. HOUSE AND SENATE DOCUMENTS

Congress receives many documents as required by law or by special request. These *House* and *Senate Documents* are issued in numerical series which run consecutively through both sessions of each

6. Moorhead, "A Congressman looks at the Planned Colloquy and its Effect in the Interpretation of Statutes," 45 *A.B.A.J.* 1314 (1959); Nutting, "The Planned Colloquy—What Now?" 46 *A.B.A.J.* 93 (1960).

surveillance to obtain foreign intelligence information.

The Senate proceeded to consider the bill, which was reported from the Committee on the Judiciary with amendments; and from the Select Committee on Intelligence with amendments.

The ACTING PRESIDENT pro tempore. Time for debate on this bill is limited to 2 hours, to be equally divided and controlled by the Senator from Massachusetts (Mr. KENNEDY) and the Senator from South Carolina (Mr. THURMOND), with 1 hour on any amendment, with 30 minutes on any debatable motion or appeal, and with 20 minutes on any point of order.

Mr. BAYH. Mr. President, I ask unanimous consent that the following members of my staff and the staff of the Select Committee on Intelligence be granted privilege of the floor during proceedings on S. 1566 and during the vote on the bill and any amendments: Abe Shulsky, Keith Raffel, Stan Taylor, William G. Miller, Earl Eisenhower, Tom Connaughton, Angelo Codevilla, Walter Ricks, Mark Gitenstein, Mike Epstein, Dave Bushong, Tom Crowley, Sam Bouchard, Patrick Norton, Edward Levine, Tom Moore, David Shaw and John Elliff.

The ACTING PRESIDENT pro tempore. Without objection, it is so ordered.

Mr. KENNEDY. Mr. President, I ask unanimous consent that Ken Feinberg, of my staff, be granted privilege of the floor.

The ACTING PRESIDENT pro tempore. Without objection, it is so ordered.

Mr. GARN. Mr. President, I ask unanimous consent that Eric Haltman, of the Judiciary Committee, be granted privilege of the floor during the debate and votes.

The ACTING PRESIDENT pro tempore. Without objection, it is so ordered.

Mr. GARN. I also ask unanimous consent that Bob Heppler, of Senator HEINZ' staff, and Kay Davies, of Senator DOMENICI's staff, be granted privilege of the floor.

The ACTING PRESIDENT pro tempore. Without objection, it is so ordered. Who yields time?

Mr. KENNEDY. Mr. President, I suggest the absence of a quorum and ask unanimous consent that the time not be charged to either side.

The ACTING PRESIDENT pro tempore. Without objection, it is so ordered. The clerk will call the roll.

The assistant legislative clerk proceeded to call the roll.

Mr. KENNEDY. Mr. President, I ask unanimous consent that the order for the quorum call be rescinded.

The ACTING PRESIDENT pro tempore. Without objection, it is so ordered.

Mr. KENNEDY. I yield myself such time as I might use.

Mr. President, today the U.S. Senate writes a new chapter in the ongoing 10-year debate to regulate foreign intelligence electronic surveillance. In considering S. 1566, the Foreign Intelligence Surveillance Act of 1978, the full Senate at long last has the opportunity to place foreign intelligence electronic surveillance under the rule of law. The abuses of recent history sanctioned in the name of national security and documented in detail by the Church committee highlight the need for more effective statutory controls and congressional oversight.

Recent prosecutions in the Humphrey and Trong cases point out the need for this legislation. Without S. 1566 in place serious constitutional issues are raised in those cases: Is the warrantless surveillance constitutional? and, even if it is, may the Government use the evidence obtained in a subsequent criminal prosecution for espionage? or does the Government, in so doing, violate the provisions of title III? S. 1566 resolves these issues and must be dealt with expeditiously.

We have the major responsibility for seeing to it that history does not repeat itself, that civil liberties and the rights of our citizens are not bargained away in the name of national security.

S. 1566 benefits from broad bipartisan support. It has the overwhelming support of both the Senate Judiciary Committee and the Senate Select Committee on Intelligence. My distinguished colleagues, Senator BAYH, Senator THURMOND, and Senator GARN have been particularly instrumental in the development of this legislation. Working together we have fashioned a product which brings to an end the fruitless and unsatisfactory debate of the past.

S. 1566 has been endorsed and supported not only by this administration, but by the Ford administration as well. Both Attorney General Bell and Attorney General Levi have been most cooperative and helpful in the drafting of the bill. The legislation constitutes a major step forward in bringing needed safeguards to the unregulated area of foreign intelligence surveillance. It is designed to strike a balance between the protection of national security and the protection of our human liberties and rights. It is a recognition, long overdue, that the Congress does have a role to play in the area of foreign intelligence surveillance.

S. 1566—building upon S. 3197, legislation drafted in 1976 with the dedicated help of Attorney General Levi—achieves a major breakthrough in the long debate over foreign intelligence electronic surveillance. It is the culmination of past efforts and present hopes. This legislation would, for the first time, substitute carefully prescribed accountability and oversight for the arbitrariness of the past. The bill would require that all foreign intelligence electronic surveillance in the United States—as well as some overseas interceptions—be subject to a judicial warrant requirement based on probable cause. For an American citizen to be surveilled, there must be probable cause that he is an agent of a foreign power—a citizen acting for or on behalf of a foreign power—and engaging in sabotage, terrorism, or clandestine intelligence activities. It is the courts, not the executive, that would ultimately rule on whether the surveillance should occur. The bill would require that, before such surveillance could occur, a named executive branch official—such as the Secretary of Defense—certify in writing and under oath that such surveillance is necessary to obtain foreign intelligence information.

Mr. President, these statutory provisions are the very heart of the legislation. They relegate to the past the wiretapping abuses visited on Joseph Kraft, Martin Luther King, Jr., and Morton Halperin. They prevent the National Security Agency from randomly wiretapping American citizens whose names just happen to be on a list of civil rights or antiwar activists.

The legislation provides the type of accountability which has heretofore not existed. It would for the first time expressly limit whatever inherent power the executive may have to engage in electronic surveillance in the United States. In so doing, the bill ends a decade of debate over the meaning and scope of the "inherent power" disclaimer clause currently found in title III.

S. 1566 would also provide civil and criminal sanctions to those who violate its provisions. It requires that all extraneous information—unrelated to the purposes of the surveillance—be minimized. And it mandates that before any information obtained can be used at a subsequent criminal trial, the trial court must again find that all statutory wiretap procedures have been met.

Most of the concerns expressed by some about various provisions of the bill have been satisfactorily resolved in the Senate committees. I and others in the Congress shared these very concerns over the years; thus, for example, either the Attorney General or the Deputy Attorney General must personally sign off on each application; the application must state whether "physical entry is required to effect the surveillance," thereby notifying the court whether or not a break-in is necessary in order to install the surveillance device; use of the information obtained by the surveillance is further restricted—even in the case of non-American citizens—to "lawful purposes"; any testing of new electronic surveillance equipment, tests which are not covered by this legislation, cannot be directed against specific American citizens without their consent.

Most importantly, Mr. President, the issue of the so-called noncriminal standard has been resolved to the satisfaction of all the parties concerned. Both S. 3197 last year, and the bill introduced this year, retained a narrowly restricted provision allowing for electronic surveillance in the absence of a statutory recognition that the activity is criminal.

This provision, as originally drafted, remained a major stumbling block to prompt passage of the legislation. Many were convinced that S. 1566 would establish an unfortunate precedent if statutory recognition were conferred on electronic surveillance in the absence of a showing of criminal conduct. After long and difficult negotiations this crucial issue has been resolved. A special tribute is owed Senator BAYH, Senator GARN, and the other members of the Senate Intelligence Committee for developing alternate language and providing for a criminal standard. The bill now provides for

Illustration K–1

Debate in the *Congressional Record on S. 1566.*

deserve our thanks and congratulations.●

The PRESIDING OFFICER. Who yields time?

Mr. KENNEDY. Mr. President, I shall ask for the yeas and nays on passage, so I suggest the absence of a quorum, the time to be evenly divided.

The PRESIDING OFFICER. The time will have to come out of the time of the Senator from South Carolina.

Mr. THURMOND. That is fine. I have no objection.

The PRESIDING OFFICER. Without objection, it is so ordered.

The clerk will call the roll.

The assistant legislative clerk proceeded to call the roll.

Mr. KENNEDY. Mr. President, I ask unanimous consent that the order for the quorum call be rescinded.

The PRESIDING OFFICER. Without objection, it is so ordered.

Mr. KENNEDY. Mr. President, I ask for the yeas and nays on passage of the bill.

The PRESIDING OFFICER. Is there a sufficient second? There is a sufficient second.

The yeas and nays were ordered.

Mr. KENNEDY. I ask for third reading, Mr. President.

The PRESIDING OFFICER. If there be no further amendments to be proposed, the question is on the engrossment and third reading of the bill.

The bill was ordered to be engrossed for a third reading and was read the third time.

Mr. KENNEDY. Mr. President, I suggest the absence of a quorum on the time of the Senator from South Carolina.

Mr. THURMOND. I have no objection.

The PRESIDING OFFICER. The clerk will call the roll.

The assistant legislative clerk proceeded to call the roll.

Mr. KENNEDY. Mr. President, I ask unanimous consent that the order for the quorum call be rescinded.

The PRESIDING OFFICER. Without objection, it is so ordered.

Does the Senator from South Carolina yield back his remaining time?

Mr. THURMOND. Mr. President, I yield back my time and suggest we have a vote on the bill.

The PRESIDING OFFICER. The question is, Shall the bill pass? The yeas and nays have been ordered and the clerk will call the roll.

The assistant legislative clerk called the roll.

Mr. CRANSTON. I announce that the Senator from Colorado (Mr. HASKELL), the Senator from New Hampshire (Mr. MCINTYRE), and the Senator from Ohio (Mr. METZENBAUM) are necessarily absent.

I further announce that, if present and voting, the Senator from Ohio (Mr. METZENBAUM) and the Senator from New Hampshire (Mr. MCINTYRE) would each vote "yea."

Mr. STEVENS. I announce that the Senator from Idaho (Mr. MCCLURE) is necessarily absent.

The result was announced—yeas 95, nays 1, as follows:

[Rollcall Vote No. 128 Leg.]

YEAS—95

Abourezk	Glenn	Morgan
Allen	Goldwater	Moynihan
Anderson	Gravel	Muskie
Baker	Griffin	Nelson
Bartlett	Hansen	Nunn
Bayh	Hart	Packwood
Bellmon	Hatch	Pearson
Bentsen	Hatfield,	Pell
Biden	Mark O.	Percy
Brooke	Hatfield,	Proxmire
Bumpers	Paul G.	Randolph
Burdick	Hathaway	Ribicoff
Byrd,	Hayakawa	Riegle
Harry F., Jr.	Heinz	Roth
Byrd, Robert C.	Helms	Sarbanes
Cannon	Hodges	Sasser
Case	Hollings	Schmitt
Chafee	Huddleston	Schweiker
Chiles	Humphrey	Sparkman
Church	Inouye	Stafford
Clark	Jackson	Stennis
Cranston	Javits	Stevens
Culver	Johnston	Stevenson
Curtis	Kennedy	Stone
Danforth	Laxalt	Talmadge
DeConcini	Leahy	Thurmond
Dole	Long	Tower
Domenici	Lugar	Wallop
Durkin	Magnuson	Weicker
Eagleton	Mathias	Williams
Eastland	Matsunaga	Young
Ford	McGovern	Zorinsky
Garn	Melcher	

NAYS—1

Scott

NOT VOTING—4

Haskell	Metzenbaum
McClure	McIntyre

So the bill (S. 1566), as amended, was passed, as follows:

S. 1566

Be it enacted by the Senate and House of Representatives of the United States of America in Congress assembled, That this Act may be cited as the "Foreign Intelligence Surveillance Act of 1978".

SEC. 2. Title 18, United States Code, is amended by adding a new chapter after chapter 119 as follows:

"Chapter 120.—ELECTRONIC SURVEILLANCE WITHIN THE UNITED STATES FOR FOREIGN INTELLIGENCE PURPOSES

"Sec.

"2521. Definitions.

"2522. Authorization for electronic surveillance for foreign intelligence purposes.

"2523. Designation of judges authorized to grant orders for electronic surveillance.

"2524. Application for an order.

"2525. Issuance of an order.

"2526. Use of information.

"2527. Report of electronic surveillance.

"2528. Congressional oversight.

"§ 2521. Definitions

"(a) Except as otherwise provided in this section the definitions of section 2510 of this title shall apply to this chapter.

"(b) As used in this chapter—

"(1) 'Foreign power' means—

"(A) a foreign government or any component thereof, whether or not recognized by the United States;

"(B) a faction of a foreign nation or nations, not substantially composed of United States persons;

"(C) an entity, which is openly acknowledged by a foreign government or governments to be directed and controlled by such foreign government or governments;

"(D) a foreign-based terrorist group;

"(E) a foreign-based political organization, not substantially composed of United States persons; or

"(F) an entity which is directed and controlled by a foreign government or governments.

"(2) 'Agent of a foreign power' means—

"(A) any person, other than a United States person, who—

"(i) acts in the United States as an officer or employee of a foreign power; or

"(ii) acts for or on behalf of a foreign power which engages in clandestine intelligence activities contrary to the interests of the United States, when the circumstances of such person's presence in the United States indicate that such person may engage in such activities in the United States, or when such person knowingly aids or abets any person in the conduct of such activities or conspires with any person knowing that such person is engaged in such activities;

"(B) any person who—

"(i) knowingly engages in clandestine intelligence gathering activities for or on behalf of a foreign power, which activities involve or may involve a violation of the criminal statutes of the United States;

"(ii) pursuant to the direction of an intelligence service or network of a foreign power, knowingly engages in any other clandestine intelligence activities for or on behalf of such foreign power, which activities involve or are about to involve a violation of the criminal statutes of the United States;

"(iii) knowingly engages in sabotage or terrorism, or activities in furtherance thereof, for or on behalf of a foreign power;

"(iv) knowingly aids or abets any person in the conduct of activities described in subparagraph (B) (i) through (iii) above, or conspires with any person knowing that such person is engaged in activities described in subparagraph (B) (i) through (iii) above: *Provided,* That no United States person may be considered an agent of a foreign power solely upon the basis of activities protected by the first amendment to the Constitution of the United States.

"(3) 'Terrorism' means activities which—

"(A) are violent acts or acts dangerous to human life which would be criminal under the laws of the United States or of any State if committed within its jurisdiction; and

"(B) appear to be intended—

"(i) to intimidate or coerce the civilian population,

"(ii) to influence the policy of a government by intimidation or coercion, or

"(iii) to affect the conduct of a government by assassination or kidnaping.

"(4) 'Sabotage' means activities which would be prohibited by title 18, United States Code, chapter 105, if committed against the United States.

"(5) 'Foreign intelligence information' means—

"(A) information which relates to, and if concerning a United States person is necessary to, the ability of the United States to protect itself against actual or potential attack or other grave hostile acts of a foreign power or an agent of a foreign power;

"(B) information with respect to a foreign power or foreign territory which relates to, and if concerning a United States person is necessary to—

"(i) the national defense or the security of the Nation; or

"(ii) the successful conduct of the foreign affairs of the United States; or

"(C) information which relates to, and if concerning a United States person is necessary to, the ability of the United States to protect against—

"(i) sabotage or terrorism by a foreign power or an agent of a foreign power, or

"(ii) the clandestine intelligence activities of an intelligence service or network of a foreign power or an agent of a foreign power.

"(6) 'Electronic surveillance' means—

"(A) the acquisition by an electronic, mechanical, or other surveillance device of

Illustration K–2

Debate and passage of S.1566 in the *Congressional Record.*

Congress. They contain special studies and reports, reprints of Presidential messages, executive agency reports and memoranda, reports of non-governmental organizations, and a great variety of papers ordered to be printed by either house of Congress. They are listed

Illustration L

Congressional Record index, showing references under Senator's name and title of Act.

and indexed in the *Monthly Catalog of U.S. Government Publications*, and since 1970 in the *Congressional Information Service* and are cited by the name of the house issuing the document, the number of the Congress and session, and the document number. *House* and *Senate Documents* also appear in the *Serial Set* and can be cited to that form by volume number. The C.I.S. *U.S. Serial Set Index*, referred to above, now provides access to House and Senate Documents, as well as House and Senate Reports, issued from 1789 to 1969. Their value for legislative history is negligible, but occasionally a document will have some relevance to a pending bill.

7. SENATE EXECUTIVE REPORTS & TREATY DOCUMENTS

The Senate issues two confidential series of publications in connection with their special responsibility for treaty ratification.[7] *Senate Treaty Documents* contain the text of treaties sent to the Senate for their advice and consent, together with related messages or correspondence from the President and Secretary of State. *Senate Executive Reports* are the reports issued by the Senate Foreign Relations Committee after their consideration of the treaty. *Treaty Documents* are designated by letter, while *Executive Reports* are numbered in series. They are cited by Congress, session, and their numerical or alphabetical designations. Neither is published or listed in the *Monthly Catalog of U.S. Government Publications* until they are formally released by order of the Senate.

Senate Treaty Documents and *Executive Reports* are an indispensable part of the legislative history of treaties, but access has frequently been difficult because of the delay in their publication and their omission from the *Serial Set.* Since 1970, however, access to those not kept confidential is available through the *Congressional Information Service* and its microfiche series.

C. FINDING TOOLS

The mass of documents comprising the source material for legislative history would be virtually inaccessible were it not for a number of finding tools which are indispensable for research in this area. No two of them are exactly alike and recourse to several is often necessary to secure adequate information. They are sometimes used to identify and locate a single document, often to establish the current status of a pending bill, and frequently to reconstruct the complete history of a bill or enactment and to identify all of the documents relevant to its interpretation. As in other fields of legal bibliography, it should be noted that some of these tools are official government documents and some are unofficial commercial publications. The lat-

7. For a fuller discussion of the legislative history of treaties, see G. B. Folsom, *Legislative History, Research for the Interpretation of Laws* (University Press of Virginia, 1972; reprinted by Fred B. Rothman, 1979), Chapter VII "Usable Background for Treaty Interpretation." See also M. G. Mabry, *Checklist of Senate Executive Documents and Reports . . . 1947–1970* (Tarlton Law Library, Univ. of Texas, 1970).

ter are often more useful by reason of prompt supplementation, better indexing, or a greater variety of research aids.

As noted above, the bill number of a proposed law (and even an already enacted law) is usually the key to searching its legislative history and identifying the documents of that history. The bill numbers can be found in the *Statutes at Large* and other sources listed below. A new, very useful tool, *Legislative Reference Checklist*, by Eugene Nabors, provides parallel reference tables from public law numbers to their original bill numbers, for the period from 1789 to 1903.[8] Most of the finding tools described below are essentially lists of laws or proposed laws by their bill numbers, with a summary of the provisions, the legislative actions taken from the time of introduction, and the documents issued in connection with consideration. These lists are frequently called *status tables* since they indicate the current status of those bills which are still pending, or the fact of passage for those which have been enacted.

1. CCH CONGRESSIONAL INDEX

The *Congressional Index*, a commercial looseleaf service issued by Commerce Clearing House in two volumes for each Congress, is one of the most popular finding tools for legislative history. In separate sections, it offers these many different approaches: indexes of all public general bills by subject and by sponsor; digests of each bill; a status table of actions taken on bills and resolutions; an index of enactments and vetoes; a table of companion bills; a list of reorganization plans, treaties, and nominations pending; tables of voting records of members of Congress by bill and resolution number; and a weekly report letter on major news and developments in Congress. In its status table section, references to hearings are included, along with the more usual references to committee reports, which is not true of all of the tools described below.

It should be noted that this service does not, however, contain the actual text of bills, debates, reports or laws. *Congressional Index* is only a finding tool, but a most useful one, with weekly supplementation and generally good indexing.

Illustration M shows a typical page of the *Congressional Index's* current status table of Senate bills, with a particularly informative entry for S.1566, the bill which is also the subject of the previous illustrations in this chapter, but which had not been finally passed when this table was issued.

2. CONGRESSIONAL INFORMATION SERVICE/INDEX

This unofficial legislative service, published since 1970, offers indexing and abstracting of the documents of legislative history for each Congressional session. It is supplemented monthly, with quarterly cumulations and annually cumulated bound volumes. There are

8. Fred B. Rothman & Co., 1982.

94 10-25-78

Current Status of Senate Bills **20,507**

See also Status of Senate Bills
For digest, see "Senate Bills" Division.

1487

Reptd., amended, S. Rept. No. 95-962 .... 6/28/78
Amended on S. floor (Voice) 9/29/78
Passed S. as amended (Voice) 9/29/78
Amended to contain text of H. 8853 as passed (Voice) 10/3/78
Passed H. as amended (Voice) 10/3/78
Conferees appointed by H..........10/3/78
H. amends. rejected by S. 10/9/78
Conferees appointed by S. 10/9/78
Conf. Rept. filed, H. Rept. No. 95-1778 ....10/12/78
Agreed to by H. (Roll-call) 10/14/78
Agreed to by S. (Voice) 10/14/78

1493

Hearing in S. 5/10/78
Reptd., amended, S. Rept. No. 95-1412 ....10/14/78

1503

Passed S. as reptd. (Voice) 1/20/78
To H. Committee on Judiciary 1/23/78
Reptd., amended, H. Rept. No. 95-1747 ....10/10/78
H. suspension vote postponed 10/10/78
Passed H. as reptd. (Roll-call).....10/12/78
H. amends. agreed to by S. (Voice) 10/13/78

★1509

Reptd., no amend., H. Rept. No. 95-846 ....1/23/78
Passed H. as reptd. (Voice) 2/6/78
To President 2/8/78
Approved (P.L. 95-232) 2/17/78

1531

Hearing in H. 3/7/78

1537

Indefinitely postponed by S. 4/24/78

1546

Hearing in S. 4/5/78

1547

Amended on S. floor (Voice) 1/31/78
Text of bill incorporated into H. 7442 ....1/31/78
Indefinitely postponed by S. 1/31/78

1556

Hearing in S. 6/15/78

→

1566

Reptd., amended, S. Rept. No. 95-701 ....3/14/78
Amended on S. floor (Voice) 4/20/78
Passed S. as amended (Roll-call) ...4/20/78
To H. Committee on Judiciary 4/24/78
Amended to contain text of H. 7308 as passed (Voice) 9/7/78
Passed H. as amended (Voice) 9/7/78
H. amends. rejected by S. 9/12/78
Conferees appointed by S. 9/26/78
S. amends. rejected by H. (Voice) 9/26/78
Conferees appointed by H. 9/26/78
Conf. Rept. filed, H. Rept. No. 95-1720 ....10/5/78
Agreed to by S. (Voice) 10/9/78
Agreed to by H. (Roll-call) 10/12/78

★1568

Reptd., amended, S. Rept. No. 95-721 ....3/23/78
Passed S. as reptd. (Voice) 4/5/78
To H. Committee on Public Works and Transportation 4/6/78
Passed H. in lieu of H. 10838 ......5/15/78
Approved (P.L. 95-285) 5/25/78

1570

Hearing in S. (Printed) 1/19/78

★1582

Amended to contain text of H. 8009 as amended (Voice) 6/29/78
Passed H. as amended (Voice) 6/29/78
H. amends. agreed to by S. (Voice) 7/13/78
To President 7/17/78
Approved (P.L. 95-328) 7/28/78

★1585

Agreed to by H. (Roll-call) 1/24/78
To President 1/25/78
Approved (P.L. 95-225) 2/7/78

1587

Hearing in S. 3/15/78

1592

Hearing in S. 7/26/78

1613

Reptd., amended, H. Rept. No. 95-1364 ....7/17/78
Amended to contain text of H. 9622 as passed 2/28/78 (Voice) 10/4/78
Passed H. as amended (Voice) 10/4/78
Conferees appointed by H. 10/4/78
Conferees appointed by S. 10/7/78
H. amends. rejected by S. 10/7/78

★1617

Bill title amended (voice) 2/28/78
Passed H. as amended (Voice) 2/28/78

Congressional Index — 1977-1978
014—51

Illustration M

"Current Status of Senate Bills" table in *CCH Congressional Index.* Published and copyrighted by Commerce Clearing House, Inc., Chicago, Il. 60646, and reproduced with their permission.

also two cumulative indexes now covering the periods 1970 to 1974 and 1975 to 1978, and further cumulations may be expected in the future.

The service's main contribution to research in legislative history lies in its excellent coverage of published hearings, reports, committee prints and documents. It offers detailed indexing of these sources, as well as unique abstracts of each hearing, report and document. Illustration N shows the *C.I.S.* index which provides access to the abstracts. The service also includes a status table of pending active bills and, in the annual permanent volumes, cumulative legislative histories of enacted laws (as shown in Illustration O). Note that this summary includes references to bills, hearings, committee reports, debates, Presidential documents, and all legislative actions. It is probably the most complete status table summary of an act's legislative history.

In addition, *C.I.S.* provides a microfiche service from 1970 to date, which offers a microfacsimile edition of all published hearings, reports, committee prints and congressional documents included in the index. This service is issued regularly and offers the full text of the documents themselves in a convenient form. A retrospective microfiche collection of such documents from 1789 to 1969 is also available from *C.I.S.*, accessible through its Indexes to the Serial Set, Hearings, and Committee Prints, described above.

3. DIGEST OF PUBLIC GENERAL BILLS AND RESOLUTIONS

The *Digest of Public General Bills and Resolutions* is the official publication of the Congressional Research Service of the Library of Congress, and is normally published during each session in two cumulative issues with occasional supplements. It is the best source for digests of all bills and resolutions introduced in each session of Congress, with more detailed summaries of those bills which have been reported out of committee. Separate tables are provided for those bills which have been enacted into law (arranged by public law number) and for all other measures receiving action (arranged by bill and resolution number). These tables include citations to committee reports issued on the bill, but not to hearings. Illustrations P–1 and P–2 show the entry for S.1566, when it was enacted as Public Law 95–511. The final issue of the *Digest*, published in two parts after the session is over, cumulates information from the earlier issues and is invaluable for retrospective research.

4. CONGRESSIONAL RECORD—HISTORY OF BILLS AND RESOLUTIONS

The fortnightly index to the *Congressional Record* contains a very useful status table, the *History of Bills and Resolutions*, which is arranged separately for each house by bill and resolution number. It includes a brief digest of each measure, the name of the sponsor,

Illustration N

Index to *Congressional Information Service.*

318 and related

H721-10; H721-14.
:722-2.

H721-5; H721-38;

S721-18;
:6; S721-27.
H722-2; H722-3.
!-14.
;402-5.
No. 95-949); H723-
ice Report).
No. 95-1140);

124 (1978):
ssed House.
ssed Senate,

nference report.
onference report.

TICLES, duty

'8. 95-2. 1 p.
'3 •Item 575.
774.

f June 30, 1981, the
es on certain metal
metal, and other ar-
er purposes."
tures of mashed or
and salt.
2165 and related

No. 95-1361).
No. 95-1243).
124 (1978):
issed House.
issed Senate,

n Senate amend-

:NT OF ENERGY SECURITY AND APPLICATIONS AR ENERGY ATION ACT OF

78. 95-2. 5 p.
/3 •Item 575.
775.

s for the Department
rity programs for fis-
r purposes."
R&D on strategic
:ations of nuclear en-

1686 and related

; H201-25.
.4; S201-19.5;

Io. 95-1108).
nd S313-23 (No.
2693).

Congressional Record Vol. 124 (1978):
May 16, 17, considered and passed House.
Sept. 30, considered and passed Senate, amended, in lieu of S. 2693.
Oct. 11, House concurred in Senate amendment.

PL95–510 SMALL BUSINESS ACT, amendment, volunteer programs, establishment and operation.
Oct. 24, 1978. 95-2. 3 p.
* CIS/MF/3 •Item 575.
92 STAT. 1780.

"To amend the Small Business Act by transferring thereto those provisions of the Domestic Volunteer Service Act of 1973 affecting the operation of volunteer programs to assist small business, to increase the maximum allowable compensation and travel expenses for experts and consultants, and for other purposes."

Transfers statutory authority for SBA-administered Service Corps of Retired Executives and Active Corps of Executives.

Legislative history: (H.R. 13418 and related bills):

1978 CIS/Annual:
House Hearings: H721-27.
House Report: H723-7 (No. 95-1375).

Congressional Record Vol. 124 (1978):
Sept. 25, considered and passed House.
Oct. 11, considered and passed Senate.

PL95–511 FOREIGN INTELLIGENCE SURVEILLANCE ACT OF 1978.
Oct. 25, 1978. 95-2. 16 p.
* CIS/MF/3 •Item 575.
92 STAT. 1783.

"To authorize electronic surveillance to obtain foreign intelligence information."

Establishes judicial warrant requirements for executive branch use of electronic surveillance to obtain foreign intelligence information, and restricts the use of such information.

Legislative history: (S. 1566 and related bills):

1973 CIS/Annual:
Senate Hearings: S521-45.

1974 CIS/Annual:
House Hearings: H521-64.

1975 CIS/Annual:
Senate Hearings: S521-35; S521-60.
Senate Committee Print: S522-6.

1976 CIS/Annual:
House Document: H520-1.
House Hearings: H521-15; H521-16.
Senate Hearings: S521-40.
Senate Reports: S523-32 (No. 94-1035, accompanying S. 3197); S963-8 (No. 94-1161, accompanying S. 3197).

1977 CIS/Annual:
House Hearings: H401-4.4; H521-26.
Senate Hearings: S421-1; S521-52.
Senate Committee Print: S522-2.
Senate Reports: S523-43 (No. 95-604); S523-44 (No. 95-604, pt. 2).

1978 CIS/Annual:
House Hearings: H431-3.
Senate Hearings: S421-3.

House Committee Print: H522-12.
House Reports: H433-3 (No. 95-1283, pt. 1, accompanying H.R. 7308); H433-5 (No. 95-1720, Conference Report).
Senate Report: S423-1 (No. 95-701).

Congressional Record Vol. 124 (1978):
Apr. 20, considered and passed Senate.
Sept. 6, 7, considered and passed House, amended.
Sept. 12, Senate disagreed to House amendments.
Oct. 9, Senate agreed to conference report.
Oct. 12, House agreed to conference report.

Weekly Compilation of Presidential Documents Vol. 14, No. 43 (1978):
Oct. 25, Presidential statement.

PL95–512 COMPTROLLER GENERAL ANNUITY ADJUSTMENT ACT OF 1978.
Oct. 25, 1978. 95-2. 3 p.
* CIS/MF/3 •Item 575.
92 STAT. 1799.

"To provide for cost-of-living adjustments in the annuity of a retired Comptroller General, and for other purposes."

Amends Budget and Accounting Act of 1921.

Legislative history: (S. 3412 and related bill):

1978 CIS/Annual:
House Hearings: H401-31.
Senate Hearings: S401-53.
House Report: H403-10 (No. 95-1241, accompanying H.R. 12196).
Senate Report: S403-54 (No. 95-1267).

Congressional Record Vol. 124 (1978):
July 25, H.R. 12196 considered and passed House.
Oct. 9, considered and passed Senate.
Oct. 11, considered and passed House, in lieu of H.R. 12196.

PL95–513 VIETNAM VETERANS WEEK, designation authorization.
Oct. 25, 1978. 95-2. 1 p.
* CIS/MF/3 •Item 575.
92 STAT. 1802.

"Authorizing and requesting the President to designate the seven-day period beginning on May 28, 1979, as 'Vietnam Veterans Week'."

Legislative history: (H.J. Res. 1147):

Congressional Record Vol. 124 (1978):
Oct. 10, considered and passed House.
Oct. 12, considered and passed Senate.

PL95–514 PUBLIC RANGELANDS IMPROVEMENT ACT OF 1978.
Oct. 25, 1978. 95-2. 8 p.
* CIS/MF/3 •Item 575.
92 STAT. 1803.

"To improve the range conditions of the public rangelands."

Amends Federal Land Policy and Management Act of 1976 to provide for management of public grazing lands under Bureau of Land Management. Includes provisions for grazing fees and control of wild horses and burros.

Legisl
bills):
1976
Senat
Senat
pan
1978
Hous
Hous
H4
Senat
Cong
June
Sept.
am
Oct.
Oct.
Weel
ment
Oct.

PL9!

"To
parin
the s
other
In lie
anism
in Fe
Legis
1976
Hous
Hous
co
1977
Sena
1978
Sena
Hou
co
Sena
Cong
Sept.
Oct.
H
in

PL9

"For
Man
ters.
Also
grap
Legi
bill):
1978
Hou
M
13

JANUARY-DECEMBER 1978 Volume 9, Number 1-12

Illustration O

Cumulative legislative history summary in *C.I.S.*

10-14-78 Measure presented to President
10-24-78 Public Law 95-508

Public Law 95-509 Approved 10/24/78; H.R. 11686.

Department of Energy National Security and Military Applications of Nuclear Energy Authorization Act - *Title I: National Security Programs* - Authorizes the appropriation of funds to the Department of Energy for specified operating expenses, designated plant and capital equipment costs, and for supplemental authorizations for specified previously authorized projects.

Authorizes the appropriation of funds for research and development concerning: inertial confinement fusion; naval reactor development; nuclear materials security and safeguards; weapons activities; special materials production; defense intelligence and arms control; and program direction and management support related to national security programs.

Title II: General Provisions - Prohibits use of any amount appropriated pursuant to this Act for any program: (1) in excess of the amount actually authorized for that particular program by this Act; or (2) which has not been presented to, or requested of, the Congress, unless a specified period has passed after the Secretary of Energy has given Congress notice of the proposed action or unless the appropriate committee has no objection to the proposed action and so notifies the Secretary before such period elapses.

Prohibits the start of specified plant and capital equipment projects if their current estimated cost exceeds by more than 25 percent the amount authorized for such project. Requires the Secretary: (1) to notify Congress whenever such project cost estimates occur; and (2) not proceed with such projects unless and until additional funds are authorized.

Sets certain limits on the costs of general plant projects which the Secretary is authorized to start.

Makes available for use, when necessary, in all national security programs of the Department of Energy amounts appropriated in this Act for policy and management activities, general plant projects, and plant engineering and design.

Authorizes the Secretary to perform construction design services for any construction project of the Department in support of national security programs which have been presented to, or requested of, Congress in specified amounts. Requires the Secretary to notify Congress at least 30 days before any funds are obligated for design services for projects in which the estimated design costs exceed $300,000.

Allows increases in appropriations authorized in this Act for salary, pay, retirement, or other benefits for Federal employees by such amounts as may be necessary for increases in such benefits authorized by law.

Prohibits the use of funds authorized by this Act for the testing, modernization, rebuilding, or replacement of any component of the B43 bomb. Allows use of such funds for quality and reliability testing and for the replacement of limited life components of such bomb.

Provides directions on future authorization requests.

Requires the Secretary to conduct a study and to report to Congress on the status of all Government-owned, contractor-operated, plant, capital equipment, facilities, and utilities which support the nuclear weapons program, including an analysis of measures required to restore the nuclear weapons complex to a satisfactory condition and a plan containing proposed schedules for carrying out and funding any restoration found to be necessary.

Amends the Department of Energy Organization Act by repealing the provision allowing members of the Armed Forces to be detailed for service in the Department by the Secretary concerned pursuant to cooperative agreements.

Stipulates that none of the funds authorized by this or any Act may be expended for the development of a nuclear warhead for the SM-2 standard missile until an arms control impact statement for such warhead has been filed with the Congress.

5-03-78 Reported to House from the Committee on Armed Services, H. Rept. 95-1108
5-16-78 Measure called up by special rule in House
5-16-78 5-17-78, Measure considered in House
5-17-78 Measure passed House, roll call #326 (348-46)
5-22-78 Referred to Senate Committee on Armed Services
9-30-78 Measure called up by committee discharge in Senate
9-30-78 Measure considered in Senate
9-30-78 Measure passed Senate, amended, in lieu of S. 2693, roll call #433 (68-1)
10-11-78 House agreed to Senate amendment
10-13-78 Measure enrolled in House
10-13-78 Measure enrolled in Senate
10-14-78 Measure presented to President
10-24-78 Public Law 95-509

Public Law 95-510 Approved 10/24/78; H.R. 13418.

Amends the Small Business Act and the Domestic Volunteer Service Act of 1973 to transfer to the Small Business Administration the authority to conduct a program of volunteer assistance for small businesses. Includes the transfer of the SCORE (Service Corps of Retired Executives) and ACE (Active Corps of Executives) programs to the Administration from the ACTION Agency.

Increases the maximum allowable compensation and travel expenses for experts and consultants employed by the Administrator of the Small Business Administration to the maximum amounts payable under the executive schedule for Federal employees.

7-19-78 Reported to House from the Select Committee on Small Business, H. Rept. 95-1375
9-25-78 Measure called up under motion to suspend rules and pass in House
9-25-78 Measure considered in House
9-25-78 Measure passed House
10-11-78 Measure called up by unanimous consent in Senate
10-11-78 Measure considered in Senate
10-11-78 Measure passed Senate
10-13-78 Measure enrolled in House
10-13-78 Measure enrolled in Senate
10-14-78 Measure presented to President
10-24-78 Public Law 95-510

Public Law 95-511 Approved 10/25/78; S. 1566.

Foreign Intelligence Surveillance Act - *Title I: Electronic Surveillance within the United States for Foreign Intelligence Purposes* - Permits the President, acting through the Attorney General, to authorize electronic surveillances for foreign intelligence purposes without a court order in certain circumstances. Requires the Attorney General: (1) to certify that the minimization procedures governing these surveillances meet certain standards; and (2) to forward such procedures to the House and Senate intelligence committees at least 30 days prior to their going into effect. Provides for the Attorney General to direct a specified common carrier to render assistance. Directs the Attorney General to transmit a copy of the certification for electronic surveillance to the appropriate court where it is to be maintained under security measures and remain seal, except in certain circumstances.

Requires the Chief Justice of the United States to designate seven district court judges, who shall constitute a special court, each of whom shall have jurisdiction to hear applications for and grant orders approving electronic surveillance anywhere within the United States. Requires the Chief Justice to designate three Federal judges to comprise a special court of appeals which shall have jurisdiction to hear an appeal by the United States from the denial of any application. Grants the United States a further right to appeal an affirmance of denial to the Supreme Court. Provides that such judges shall serve for a maximum of seven years and shall not be eligible for redesignation.

Requires each application for any order approving electronic surveillance for foreign intelligence purposes to be approved by the Attorney General and to include among other information: (1) the identity of the officer making the application; (2) the authority conferred on the Attorney General by the President and the approval of the Attorney General to make the application; (3) the identity, if known,n of the subject of the surveillance; (4) the fact and circumstances justifying belief that the target of surveillance is a foreign power or an agent of a foreign power; (5) a description of the type of information sought and a certification by one of specified Federal officers that such official deems the information sought to be foreign intelligence information, and information which cannot feasibly be obtained by normal investigative techniques; (6) a statement of the period of time for which the surveillance is required; and (7) a statement of procedures to be taken

Illustration P-1

Public Law 95–511 in the *Digest of Public General Bills and Resolutions.*

to minimize intrusion into the privacy of United States persons.

Directs the judge to enter an ex parte order as requested or as modified approving the electronic surveillance if he finds that the criteria specified have been met. Allows issuance of orders to approve surveillance for 90 days or the period necessary to achieve its purposes, whichever is less. Permits extensions of orders upon application for an extension made in the same manner as required for an original application.

Authorizes the Attorney General, upon a reasonable determination that an emergency situation exists, to authorize the emergency employment of electronic surveillance if the appropriate judge is informed by the Attorney General of such authorization at the time it is made and if an application is made as soon as practicable but not more than 24 hours after authorization. Requires, in the absence of a judicial order, that surveillance terminate when the information sought is obtained, when the application for an order is denied, or 24 hours after authorization, whichever is earliest. Directs the Attorney General to retain applications and orders for electronic surveillance for at least ten years.

Prohibits the use or disclosure of any information concerning any United States person acquired from a disapproved emergency surveillance in any manner by Federal officers or employees without the consent of such person. Allows the Government to use such information to protect the life or the physical safety of a person, upon the approval of the Attorney General.

Authorizes electronic surveillance, not targeted against the communications of any particular person, by officers, employees, or agents of the United States in the normal course of their official duties. Specifies that such electronic surveillance shall be solely to: (1) test the capability of electronic equipment; (2) determine the existence and capability of electronic surveillance equipment being used by persons not authorized to conduct such surveillance; and (3) train intelligence personnel.

Allows information acquired from electronic surveillance conducted pursuant to this Act to be used and disclosed only for designated purposes or for the enforcement of the criminal law.

Provides for motions to supress evidence obtained or derived from electronic surveillance. Sets forth the procedure for determining the legality of electronic surveillance.

Requires the Attorney General to submit an annual report to the Administrative Office of the United States Courts and to Congress, including the number of applications made for orders and extensions of orders approving electronic surveillance and the number of such orders and extensions granted, modified, and denied.

Requires the Attorney General to inform the House and Senate Committees on Intelligence semiannually concerning all electronic surveillance under this Title.

Requires the Committees to report annually for five years to the House and Senate concerning the implementation of this Act, with recommendations.

Makes it a criminal offense for officers or employees of the United States to intentionally engage in electronic surveillance under color of law except as specifically authorized or to disclose information through unlawful electronic surveillance. Imposes civil and criminal liability for such violations and authorizes the recovery of actual damages, punitive damages, and reasonable attorney's fees by an aggrieved person other than a foreign power.

Permits the President, through the Attorney General, to authorize electronic surveillance without a court order to acquire foreign intelligence information for up to 15 days during a Congressionally declared war.

Title II: Conforming Amendments - Makes conforming amendments to existing criminal laws.

Title III: Effective Date - States that the provisions of this Act shall become effective upon enactment. Stipulates that any electronic surveillance approved by the Attorney General to gather foreign intelligence information shall not be unlawful if that surveillance is terminated or an order approving that surveillance is obtained within 90 days following the designation of the chief judges pursuant to this Act.

11-15-77 Reported to Senate from the Committee on the Judiciary with amendment, S. Rept. 95-604
11-22-77 Reported to Senate from the Committee on the Judiciary, S. Rept. 95-604 (Part II)
3-14-78 Reported to Senate from the Select Committee on Intelligence with amendment, S. Rept. 95-701
4-20-78 Measure called up by unanimous consent in Senate
4-20-78 Measure considered in Senate
4-20-78 Measure passed Senate, amended, roll call #128 (95-1)
4-24-78 Referred to House Committee on the Judiciary
9-07-78 Measure called up by special rule in House
9-07-78 Measure considered in House
9-07-78 Measure passed House, amended, in lieu of H. R. 7308
9-12-78 Senate disagreed to House amendments
9-26-78 Conference scheduled in House
9-26-78 Conference scheduled in Senate
10-05-78 Conference report filed in House, H. Rept. 95-1720
10-09-78 Senate agreed to conference report
10-12-78 House agreed to conference report, roll call #897 (266-176)
10-12-78 Measure enrolled in House
10-12-78 Measure enrolled in Senate
10-16-78 Measure presented to President
10-25-78 Public Law 95-511

Public Law 95-512 Approved 10/25/78; S. 3412.

Comptroller General Annuity Adjustment Act - Amends the Budget and Accounting Act 1921: (1) to increase the Comptroller General's contribution for a survivorship annuity; (2) to increase the amount of such annuity; (3) to provide for cost-of-living adjustments in such annuity and the Comptroller General's pension; (4) to prohibit the annuity from exceeding the annual rate of compensation of the Comptroller General; and (5) to provide for a lump-sum refund if the Comptroller General is separated from office prior to becoming eligible to receive such annuity.

10-03-78 Reported to Senate from the Committee on Governmental Affairs with amendment, S. Rept. 95-1267
10-09-78 Call of calendar in Senate
10-09-78 Measure considered in Senate
10-09-78 Measure passed Senate, amended
10-11-78 Measure called up by unanimous consent in House
10-11-78 Measure considered in House
10-11-78 Measure passed House
10-14-78 Measure enrolled in House
10-14-78 Measure enrolled in Senate
10-16-78 Measure presented to President
10-25-78 Public Law 95-512

Public Law 95-513 Approved 10/25/78; H.J. Res. 1147.

Authorizes and requests the President to designate the seven-day period beginning on May 28, 1979, as "Vietnam Veterans Week."

10-10-78 Measure called up by committee discharge in House
10-10-78 Measure considered in House
~~10-10-78 Measure passed in House~~
10-12-78 Measure called up by unanimous consent in Senate
10-12-78 Measure considered in Senate
10-12-78 Measure passed Senate
10-12-78 Measure enrolled in House
10-12-78 Measure enrolled in Senate
10-24-78 Measure presented to President
10-25-78 Public Law 95-513

Public Law 95-514 Approved 10/25/78; H.R. 10587.

Public Rangelands Improvement Act - Requires the Secretaries of the Interior and Agriculture to maintain a continuing inventory of rangeland conditions and trends in 16 contiguous western States.

Directs the Secretary of the Interior to manage the public rangelands in accordance with the rangeland management objectives established through the land use planning process prescribed in the Federal Land Policy and Management Act. Continues the policy of protecting wild free-roaming horses and burros, while at the same time facilitating the removal and disposal of excess animals which pose a threat to themselves and their habitat and to other rangeland values.

Requires the Secretary to manage the public rangelands in accordance with the Taylor Grazing Act, the Federal Land Policy

Illustration P–2

Public Law 95–511, continued.

the committee to which it has been referred, as well as references to debates, legislative actions, committee reports, amendments and passage information. Each entry also provides reference to the page number in the *Congressional Record* at which action is reported. Unfortunately, this status table only lists bills and resolutions which were acted upon during the two week period preceding the index and does not cumulate all measures introduced in that session. However, the coverage of each bill listed is complete back to the date of its introduction.

At the end of each session, a completely cumulative *History of Bills and Resolutions* table is published in the *Index* volume of the permanent bound set of the *Congressional Record.* Although it lacks hearing references, this table is the best source for citations to debates and in general is one of the most complete summaries of legislative history of bills and resolutions. The fortnightly index and the permanent cumulative *Index* volume to the *Congressional Record* are invaluable in providing detailed access, by subject and name of legislators, to all congressional proceedings. (See Illustration Q.)

5. CONGRESSIONAL RECORD—DAILY DIGEST

Each issue of the *Congressional Record* contains this daily summary of legislative activity, which includes a short status table of bills acted upon that day. At the end of each session, the *Daily Digest* is cumulated and issued as a separate number of the *Congressional Record.* This cumulation also includes a subject index to the *Daily Digest* and a table called History of Bills Enacted into Public Law. This table lacks the debate entries in the History of Bills and Resolutions, described in section 4 above, but is an otherwise useful summary. The cumulated *Daily Digest,* with the index and table, are subsequently also published as a separate volume in the permanent edition of the *Congressional Record.* Illustration R shows the table, History of Bills Enacted into Public Law.

6. LEGISLATIVE CALENDARS

Calendars issued for each house of Congress and for most committees provide current information on the status of pending bills. Although they are primariy internal publications for the use of the legislators, some are distributed to libraries and, because of their frequency of updating, can be useful sources for the current status of bills listed and particularly for information on hearings.

Perhaps the most important feature of the calendars is the House of Representatives table, *Numerical Order of Bills and Resolutions Which Have Passed Either or Both Houses, and Bills Now Pending on the Calendar.* This table covers bills in both houses, is issued daily and cumulates legislative information for bills on which some action has been taken. It includes several subsidiary tables and a subject index, but does not fully list debates and hearings. The final issue of the Numerical Order table cumulates both sessions at the

SENATE BILLS

From the Committee on the Judiciary. Reported with amendment (S. Rept. 95-696), 6234.

S. 1484—For the relief of Michael Bruce Holland.

From the Committee on the Judiciary. Reported (S. Rept. 95-993), 21149.—Referred to Committee on the Judiciary, 22678.—Reported (H. Rept. 95-1701), 33644.—Passed House, 38216.—Examined and signed, 38775, 38082.—Presented to the President, 38084.—Approved [Private Law 95-81], 38086.

S. 1487—To eliminate racketeering in the sale and distribution of cigarettes, and for other purposes.

Cosponsors added, 6992.—From Committee on the Judiciary. Reported with amendment (S. Rept. 95-962), 19275.—Made special order S. Res. 499, 22181.—Amended and passed Senate, 32562.—Amended and passed House (in lieu of H.R. 8853) title amended. House insisted on its amendment and asked for a conference. Conferees appointed, 33281.—Senate disagreed with House amendment and agreed to a conference. Conferees appointed, 34863.—Conference report (H. Rept. 95-1778), submitted in House, 36510.—Conference report considered and agreed to in House, 38284.—Conference report submitted and agreed to in Senate, 37517.—Examined and signed, 38083, 38776.—Presented to the President, 38085.—Approved [Public Law 95-575], 38086.

S. 1493—To amend the Public Works and Economic Development Act to establish a comprehensive program to provide financial and technical assistance to States, local governments, and Indian tribes to manage impacts caused by energy development, and for other purposes.

From the Committee on Environment and Public Works and the Committee on Governmental Affairs. Reported with amendments (S. Rept. 95-1412), 37654.

S. 1500—To designate certain lands in the State of Alaska as units of the National Park, National Wildlife Refuge, National Wild and Scenic Rivers, and National Wilderness Preservation Systems, and for other purposes.

Cosponsors added, 10948, 16537, 19281, 24157.

S. 1503—To provide for the payment of losses incurred as a result of the ban on the use of chemical Tris in apparel, fabric, yarn, or fiber, and for other purposes.

Amended and passed Senate, 207.—Referred to Committee on the Judiciary, 454.—Reported with amendment (H. Rept. 95-1747), 35194.—Debated, 34906.—Rules suspended. Amended and passed House, 36485.—Senate concurred in House amendment, 36726.—Examined and signed, 38776, omitted in Senate.—Presented to the President, 38085.—Presidential veto, 38087.

S. 1509—To provide for the return to the United States of title to certain lands conveyed to certain Indian Pueblos of New Mexico and for such land to be held in trust by the United States for such tribes.

Reported (H. Rept. 95-846), 455.—Passed House, 2373.—Examined and signed, 2507, 2548.—Presented to the President, 2776.—Approved [Public Law 95-232], 4642.

S. 1537—To amend the Federal Aviation Act to authorize appropriations for the Civil Aeronautics Board, to require the Board to recodify its rules, and for other purposes.

Indefinitely postponed, 11106.

S. 1547—To amend the Communications Act of 1934, as amended, with respect to penalties and forfeitures, and to authorize the Federal Communications Commission to regulate pole attachments, and for other purposes.

Amended and passed Senate, 1595.—Passage vitiated. Indefinitely postponed (H.R. 7442 passed in lieu), 1599.

S. 1556—To amend title 38, United States Code, to authorize a program of assistance to States for the establishment, expansion, improvement, and maintenance of veterans' cemeteries.

Cosponsors added, 5374, 13429.

S. 1559—To provide for the reinstatement of civil service retirement survivor annuities for certain widows and widowers whose remarriages occurred before July 18, 1966, and for other purposes.

Cosponsors added, 5817.

S. 1562—For the relief of Datronics Engineers, Inc.

From Committee on the Judiciary. Reported (S. Rept. 95-944), 18433.—Passed Senate, 19184.—Referred to Committee on the Judiciary, 19431.—Reported (S. Rept. 95-1648), 32467.—Passed over, 33236.—Passed House, 38214.—Examined and signed, 38775, 38082.—Presented to the President, 38084.—Approved [Private Law 95-157], 38086.

S. 1563—For the relief of Do Sook Park.

From the Committee on the Judiciary. Reported (H. Rept. 95-1691), 33644.—Passed House, 38215.—Examined and signed, 38775, 38082.—Presented to the President, 38084.—Approved [Private Law 95-118], 38086.

S. 1564—For the relief of Tomiko Fukuda Eure.

From the Committee on the Judiciary. Reported (S. Rept. 95-994), 21149.—Passed Senate, 22050.—Referred to Committee on the Judiciary, 22350.

S. 1566—To amend title 18, United States Code, to authorize applications for a court order approving the use of electronic surveillance to obtain foreign intelligence information.

From the Committee on Intelligence. Reported with amendments (S. Rept. 95-701), 6800.—Debated, 10886.—Amended and passed Senate, 10906.—Referred to Committee on the Judiciary, 11100.—Amended and passed House (in lieu of H.R. 7308), 28427.—Senate disagreed with House amendments, 28895.—House insisted on its amendments and asked for a conference. Conferees appointed, 31623.—Senate agreed to a conference. Conferees appointed, 31531.—Additional conferees appointed, 31614.—Conference report (H. Rept. 95-1720) submitted in House, 33778.—Conference report submitted in Senate and agreed to, 34844.—Conference report agreed to in House, 36409.—Examined and signed, 38771, 37650.—Presented to the President, 38084.—Approved [Public Law 95-511], 38086.

S. 1568—To name the lake located behind Lower Memorial Lock and Dam, Washington, "Lake Herbert G. West, Senior."

From Committee on Environment and Public Works. Reported with amendment (S. Rept. 95-721), 8266.—Amended and passed Senate, title amended, 8767.—Referred to Committee on Public Works and Transportation, 9142.—Passed House (in lieu of H.R. 10838), 13556.—Examined and signed, 13852, 13946.—Presented to the President, 14054.—Approved [Public Law 95-285], 15564.

S. 1571—To incorporate the National Ski Patrol System, Inc.

Cosponsors added, 628, 4177, 8427, 19892, 36866.

S. 1575—To establish a voluntary program to provide farmers protection against loss of farm production when natural or uncontrollable conditions adversely affect such production.

Cosponsors added, 11457.

S. 1582—Relating to the settlement between the United States and the Ak-Chin Indian community of certain water right claims of such community against the United States.

Committee discharged. Amended and passed House (in lieu of H.R. 8099), 19495.—Senate concurred in House amendment, 20754.—Examined and signed, 21148, 21224.—Presented to the President, 21148.—Approved [Public Law 95-328], 23637.

S. 1585—To amend title 18, United States Code, to make unlawful the use of minors engaged in sexually explicit conduct for the purpose of promoting any film, photograph, negative, slide, book, or magazine.

Conference report agreed to in the House, 525—Examined and signed, 718, 901.—Presented to the President, 718.—Approved [Public Law 95-225], 2548.

S. 1587—To amend the nternal Revenue Code of 1954 to exempt certain State and locai government retirement systems from taxation, and for other purposes.

Cosponsors added, 728, 25122.

S. 1611—To amend the Internal Revenue Code of 1954 to provide for a deduction for additions to a reserve for product liability losses.

Cosponsors added, 12998.

S. 1613—To improve access to the Federal courts by enlarging the civil and criminal jurisdiction of U.S. magistrates, and for other purposes.

From the Committee on the Judiciary. Reported with amendment (S. Rept. 95-1364), 21224.—Made special order, H. Res. 1322, 26522.—Debated, 32899.—Amended and passed House. House insisted on its amendment and asked for a conference. Conferees appointed, 33549.—Senate disagreed with House amendments and asked for a conference. Conferees appointed, 34659.

S. 1617—To establish a program of ocean pollution research and monitoring, and for other purposes.

Rules suspended. Amended and passed House. Title amended, 5000.—Senate concurs in House amendments, 11230.—Examined and signed, 11361, 11434.—Presented to the President, 11572.—Approved [Public Law 95-273], 12870.

S. 1618—For the relief of Sang Yun Yoon.

From the Committee on the Judiciary. Reported (H. Rept. 95-1690), 33644.—Passed House, 38214.—Examined and signed, 38083, 38776.—Presented to the President, 38085—Approved [Private Law 95-119], 38086.

S. 1624—To authorize an additional Assistant Secretary of Commerce.

From the Committee on Governmental Affairs. Reported with amendments (S. Rept. 95-1048), 23273—Amended and passed Senate, 23817.—Referred to Com-

1663

Illustration Q

Congressional Record—History of Bills and Resolutions.

October 14, 1978 **CONGRESSIONAL RECORD—DAILY DIGEST** **D 943**

To declare that the United States holds in trust for the Pueblo of Santa Ana certain public domain lands in New Mexico.	S. 2588 (H.R. 3924)	Feb. 24	IIA	IA	May 25	Aug. 22	95-1219	95-1132	33523	28060	Oct. 4	Sept. 6	Oct. 21	95-498
To declare that the United States holds in trust for the Pueblo of Zia certain public domain lands in New Mexico.	S. 2358 (H.R. 10240)	Dec. 15 1977	IIA	IA	May 25	Aug. 22	95-1220	95-1131	33303	28056	Oct. 3	Sept. 6	Oct. 21	95-499
To make specific tariff provisions for ball or roller bearing pillow block, flange, take-up, cartridge, and hangar units.	H.R. 8755	Aug. 4 1977	WM	Fin	July 14	Sept. 26	95-1356	95-1241	29825	32861	Sept. 18	Sept. 30	Oct. 21	95-500
To strengthen the economy of the United States through increased sales abroad of American agricultural products.	S. 3447 (H.R. 10584)	Aug. 23	Agr IR	Agr.	July 10 Sept. 14	Aug. 23	95-1338	95-1142	31301	28558	Sept. 25	Sept. 8	Oct. 21	95-501
To clarify exemption from political organization taxable income for proceeds from bingo and related games.	H.R. 8533	July 26 1977	WM	....	Sept. 22	....	95-1608	....	31274	35346	Sept. 25	Oct. 10	Oct. 21	95-502
To authorize payment of transportation expenses by U.S. marshals for persons released in one court for appearance in another court.	S. 2411	Jan. 23	Jud	Jud	Sept. 28	Apr. 25 1977	95-1653	95-760	34866	11832	Oct. 10	Apr. 27	Oct. 24	95-503
Air Transportation Regulatory Reform Act of 1978.....	S. 2493 (H.R. 12611)	Feb. 6	PWT	CST	May 19	Feb. 6 1977	95-1211	95-631	30718	10698	Sept. 21	Apr. 19	Oct. 24	95-504
To amend Title XI of the Merchant Marine Act, 1936, to permit the guarantee of obligations for financing Great Lakes vessels in an amount not exceeding 87½% of the actual or depreciated cost of each vessel.	H.R. 11658	Mar. 20	MMF	....	Aug. 25	....	95-1528	....	33253	34461	Oct. 3	Oct. 6	Oct. 24	95-505
To permit the recovery of replacement costs of motor vehicles and other related equipment and supplies.	H.R. 13767	Aug. 7	GO	....	Aug. 25	....	95-1529	....	31190	35373	Sept. 25	Oct. 10	Oct. 24	95-506
To amend and extend programs administered by the Small Business Administration.	H.R. 11318	Mar. 7	SB	SB GA	Mar. 13	Aug. 8 Aug. 23	95-949	95-1070 95-1140	7529	29646	Mar. 20	Sept. 15	Oct. 24	95-507
To extend until the close of June 30, 1981, the existing suspension of duties on certain metal waste and scrap, unwrought metal, and other articles of metal.	H.R. 12165	Apr. 17	WM	Fin	July 14	Sept. 26	95-1361	95-1243	28950	32862	Sept. 12	Sept. 30	Oct. 24	95-508
Authorizing funds for national security programs for the Department of Energy for fiscal year 1979.	H.R. 11686	Mar. 21	AS	....	May 3	....	95-1108	....	14115	32802	May 17	Sept. 30	Oct. 24	95-509
To insert in the Small Business Act those provisions of the Domestic Volunteer Service Act which govern the operation of SBA volunteer counseling programs.	H.R. 13418	July 11	SB	....	July 19	....	95-1375	....	31268	34446	Sept. 25	Oct. 11	Oct. 24	95-510
To establish procedures for electronic surveillance to obtain intelligence information.	S. 1566 (H.R. 7308)	May 18 1977	Jud Intel	Jud Intel	.... July 8	Nov. 15 1977 Mar. 14	 95-1283	95-604 95-701	28432	10906	Sept. 7	Apr. 20	Oct. 25	95-511
To provide cost-of-living adjustments in the annuity of a retired Comptroller General.	S. 3412 (H.R. 12196)	Aug. 15	GO	GA	June 1	Oct. 3	95-1241	95-1267	35708	34846	Oct. 11	Oct. 9	Oct. 25	95-512
Authorizing and requesting the President to designate the seven-day period beginning on May 28, 1979, as "Vietnam Veterans' Week".	H.J. Res. 1147	Oct. 4	....	....	....	....	....	....	34866	36182	Oct. 10	Oct. 12	Oct. 25	95-513
Authorizing funds to improve conditions of the public grazing lands.	H.R. 10587	Jan. 26	IIA	ENR	May 10	July 10	95-1122	95-1237	19507	32820	June 29	Sept. 30	Oct. 25	95-514
To regulate interstate commerce with respect to parimutuel wagering on horseracing.	S. 1185 (H.R. 14089)	Mar. 30 1977	IFC	CST Jud	Oct. 6	Oct. 27 1977	95-1733	95-554 95-1117	34901	31560	Oct. 10	Sept. 26	Oct. 25	95-515
To extend through June 30, 1981, duty-free entry of crude and refined natural graphite, and through June 30, 1980, duty-free entry of assembled freight cars.	H.R. 10161	Nov. 29 1977	WM	Fin	July 14	Aug. 14 Aug. 11	95-1363	95-1114	23674	27407	Aug. 1	Aug. 23	Oct. 25	95-516
Authorizing the Secretary of the Army to return ten paintings to the Navy of the Federal Republic of Germany.	H.R. 11945	Apr. 6	AS	AS	Sept. 18	Oct. 13	95-1575	....	32879	36841	Oct. 2	Oct. 14	Oct. 25	95-517
Designating Gathright Lake on the Jackson River, Virginia, as Lake Moomaw.	H.R. 12112	Apr. 13	PWT	EPW	May 1	Aug. 25	95-1094	95-1165	13556	28061	May 15	Sept. 6	Oct. 25	95-518
To exclude the Librarian of Congress from accruing annual and sick leave.	S. 1626	June 6 1977	POCS	GA	Aug. 16	Aug. 5 1977	95-1496	95-403	29820	28421	Sept. 18	Sept. 9 1977	Oct. 25	95-519
To extend for one year authority to provide benefits to the Philippines for medical care and treatment of elibible veterans.	H.R. 5029	Mar. 14 1977	VA	VA	Mar. 23 1977	May 15	95-111	95-825	10210	15705	Apr. 4 1977	May 26	Oct. 26	95-520

Illustration R

Congressional Record—Daily Digest table.

end of each Congress and is very useful for permanent reference. It is available before the bound edition of the *Congressional Record* is published, but is less complete than the *Record's* History of Bills and Resolutions since it includes only bills on which action was taken.

7. U.S. CODE CONGRESSIONAL AND ADMINISTRATIVE NEWS (WEST PUBLISHING COMPANY)

In addition to its selective inclusion of some committee reports on major legislation, this legislative service also includes a table of the legislative history of enacted laws. Since it does not list pending bills or measures which were not passed and since it is not as thorough as most of the tables described above, this must be considered a secondary tool for tracing legislative history. Illustration S shows the table's entry for Public Law 95–511 and Illustration I, above at p. 306, depicts the summary of information preceding the actual text of the House Committee Report and Conference Committee Report on this legislation. The inclusion in full of those two reports, along with information about other committee reports, is the main value of *U.S. C.C.A.N.* in legislative research.

8. CONGRESSIONAL QUARTERLY

This publication offers weekly reporting of general congressional news, with cumulative indexing and summaries on major legislation. It also provides a final *Almanac* volume covering each session with considerable information of permanent research value on congressional activity during that year. It does not contain the completeness of coverage of the status tables and services previously described, but does include substantial analytical and background discussion of laws and legislative issues which make it popular with political scientists and many general researchers.

9. CONGRESSIONAL MONITOR

This commercial reporting service provides daily coverage of active legislative proposals. It combines some of the features of the *Daily Digest,* with a selective weekly status table of bills acted upon and a weekly list of published hearings, reports and documents. The *Monitor* summarizes daily proceedings in each house and in the major committees, and offers unofficial projections of forthcoming activity. It does not, however provide detailed coverage or analysis in depth, and is primarily useful for lobbyists and others needing quick information on day by day legislative activity.

10. FEDERAL INDEX

Federal Index (published by Capitol Services, Inc.) offers another means of access to the *Congressional Record;* House and Senate bills, reports and hearings; the *Weekly Compilation of Presidential Documents;* the *Federal Register* and the *Code of Federal Regulations;* and many other government-related publications. It is issued monthly, with annual cumulative volumes. Access is provided in

TABLE 4—LEGISLATIVE HISTORY

Public Law		92 Stat. Page	Bill	Report No. 95-		Comm. Reporting		Cong.Rec.Vol.124 (1978) Dates of Consideration and Passage	
No.95-	Date App.		No.	House	Senate	House	Senate	House	Senate
493	Oct. 20	1643	H.R. 11035	1638	none	J	none	Oct. 2	Oct. 5
494	Oct. 21	1648	H.R. 12264	1323	none	IIA	none	Sept. 25	Oct. 9
495	Oct. 21	1649	H.R. 12250	1117 1790	1274 1327	IIA Conf	ENR Conf	June 5, Oct. 15	Oct. 9, 15
496	Oct. 21	1660	S. 1081	1459	1157	IIA (H.R. 11894)	IA	Oct. 3	Sept. 8, Oct. 7
497	Oct. 21	1665	H.R. 12051	1605	none	WM	none	Oct. 3	Oct. 7
498	Oct. 21	1672	S. 2588	1219	1132	IIA (H.R. 3924)	IA	Oct. 4	Sept. 6, Oct. 7
499	Oct. 21	1679	S. 2358	1220	1131	IIA (H.R. 10240)	IA	Oct. 3	Sept. 6, Oct. 7
500	Oct. 21	1683	H.R. 8755	1356	1241	WM	F	Sept. 18, Oct. 10	Sept. 30
501	Oct. 21	1685	S. 3447	1338(I) 1338(II) 1755	1142 1315	Agr IR Conf (H.R. 10584)	ANF Conf	Sept. 25, Oct. 15	Sept. 8, Oct. 11
502	Oct. 21	1693	H.R. 8533	1608	none	WM	none	Sept. 25, Oct. 13	Oct. 10
503	Oct. 24	1704	S. 2411	1653	760	J	J	Oct. 10	Apr. 27
504	Oct. 24	1705	S. 2493	1211 1779	631	PWT Conf (H.R. 12611)	CST	Sept. 21, Oct. 15	Apr. 19, Oct. 14
505	Oct. 24	1755	H.R. 11658	1528	none	MMF	none	Oct. 3	Oct. 6
506	Oct. 24	1756	H.R. 13767	1529	none	GO	none	Sept. 25	Oct. 10
507	Oct. 24	1757	H.R. 11318	949 1714	1070 1140	SB Conf	SB GA	Mar. 20, Oct. 6	Sept. 15, Oct. 10
508	Oct. 24	1774	H.R. 12165	1361	1243	WM	F	Sept. 12, Oct. 10	Sept. 30
509	Oct. 24	1775	H.R. 11686	1108	961	AS	{ AS ENR (S. 2693)	May 17, Oct. 11	Sept. 30
510	Oct. 24	1780	H.R. 13148	1375	none	SB	none	Sept. 25	Oct. 11
511	Oct. 25	1783	S. 1566	1283 1720	604 701	Int Conf (H.R. 7308)	J Int	Sept. 7, Oct. 12	Apr. 20, Oct. 9
512	Oct. 25	1799	S. 3412	1241	1267	GO (H.R. 12196)	GA	July 25, Oct. 11	Oct. 9
513	Oct. 25	1802	H.J.Res. 1147	none	none	none	none	Oct. 10	Oct. 12
514	Oct. 25	1803	H.R. 10587	1122 1737	1237	IIA Conf	ENR	June 29, Oct. 10	Sept. 30, Oct. 11
515	Oct. 25	1811	S. 1185	1733	554 1117	IFC (H.R. 14089)	CST J	Oct. 10	Sept. 26
516	Oct. 25	1816	H.R. 10161	1363	1114	WM	F	Aug. 1, Oct. 10	Aug. 23, Oct. 12
517	Oct. 25	1817	H.R. 11945	1575	none	AS	none	Oct. 2	Oct. 13
518	Oct. 25	1818	H.R. 12112	1094	1165	PWT	EPW	May 15, Oct. 15	Sept. 6
519	Oct. 25	1819	S. 1626	1496	403	POCS	GA	Sept. 18	Sept. 9 * Oct. 10
520	Oct. 26	1820	H.R. 5029	111	825	VA	VA	Apr. 4 * Oct. 13	May 26, Oct. 15

*1977.

10001

Illustration S

Legislative History table in *U.S.C.C.A.N.*, showing Public Law No. 95–511.

three ways: by the government agency involved; by specific governmental functions; and by affected industries, individuals, institutions, and countries. Illustration T, below, shows a sample of its entries.

D. COMPILED LEGISLATIVE HISTORIES

Since the sources of legislative history are scattered among many publications and are published in forms which frequently become unavailable shortly after they are issued, retrospective research is often very difficult. Legislative histories for major legislation, compiled in book form or in microfacsimile, offer a convenient approach to the important documents relating to some laws. At their best, these compilations will include bills, committee reports, hearings, committee prints, debates and executive documents, with detailed indexing. When so done, they can save the researcher many hours of library time in compiling those documents from their disparate sources. Frequently, however, only *some* of the essential documents are included and often indexing is omitted or inadequate.

Compiled legislative histories have been issued by the government agencies concerned with the enforcement of the legislation involved, by commercial publishers, and by trade associations or other private interest groups. In addition to its general microfiche collections of Congressional documents, *C.I.S.* now offers on microfiche its *Legislative History Service* which provides full documentation on all major acts beginning with the 97th Congress (1981).[9] This service includes, in looseleaf format, *Annotated Directories*, which summarize each major law and provide citations to all items in its legislative history, with summary descriptions of the committee reports, hearings, committee prints and documents in each history. It also includes the *Public Law Reporter*, a newsletter listing all laws enacted to date in that session and indicating which are covered by the *C.I.S.* service.

Commerce Clearing House through its *Public Laws—Legislative Histories on Microfiche* series, also issues pertinent documents beginning with enactments of the 96th Congress. Selected legislative histories are published by the American Enterprise Institute, the Congressional Research Service of the Library of Congress, and the U.S. General Accounting Office, as well.

Many law firms compile legislative histories of enactments or proposals which are of interest to their clients. To improve access to these private files, the Law Librarians Society of Washington, D.C. has published the *Union List of Legislative Histories* (4th ed., 1977), which lists legislative histories held by its member libraries and others throughout the country.

9. For retrospective coverage, the Information Handling Service's *Legislative Histories Microfiche Program* included legislative histories on major laws, from the 82nd Congress (1951) to the 95th Congresses (1980). That service is now temporarily discontinued, but will probably be reissued by *C.I.S.* in a new form.

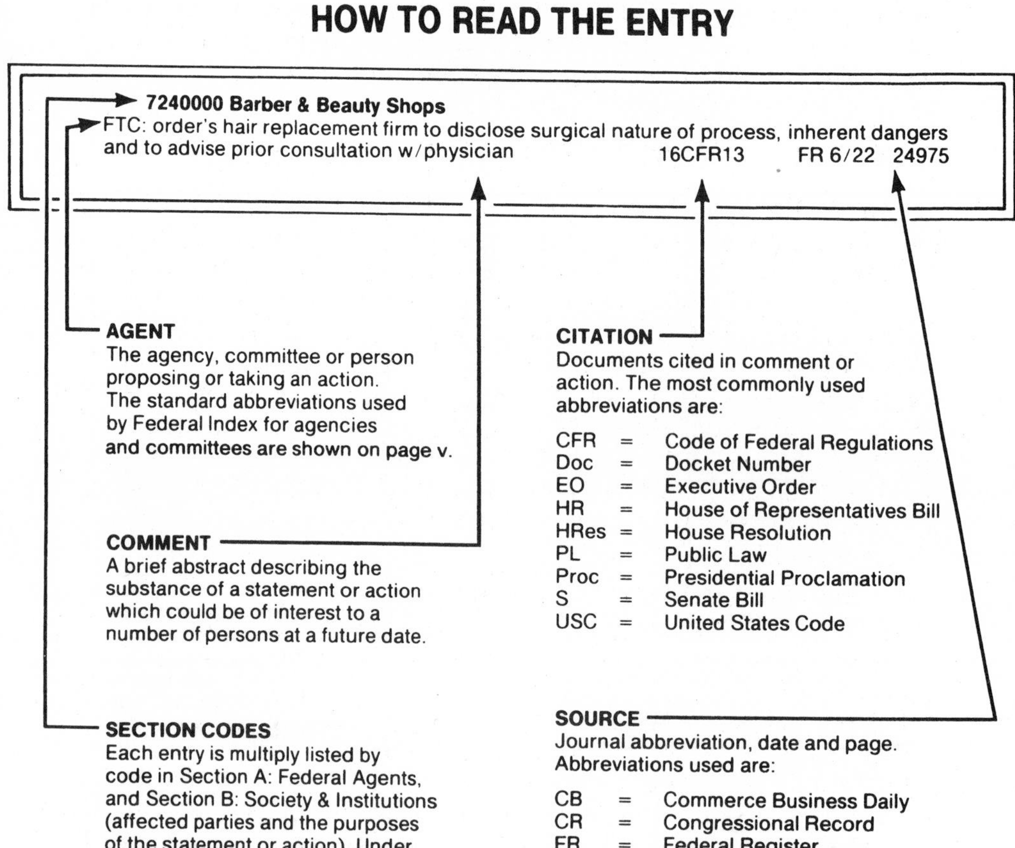

FEDERAL INDEX
HOW TO READ THE ENTRY
7240000 Barber & Beauty Shops
FTC: order's hair replacement firm to disclose surgical nature of process, inherent dangers and to advise prior consultation w/physician 16CFR13 FR 6/22 24975
AGENT
The agency, committee or person proposing or taking an action. The standard abbreviations used by Federal Index for agencies and committees are shown on page v.
COMMENT
A brief abstract describing the substance of a statement or action which could be of interest to a number of persons at a future date.
SECTION CODES
Each entry is multiply listed by code in Section A: Federal Agents, and Section B: Society & Institutions (affected parties and the purposes of the statement or action). Under each code, entries are arranged alphabetically by federal agent.
CITATION
Documents cited in comment or action. The most commonly used abbreviations are:
CFR = Code of Federal Regulations
Doc = Docket Number
EO = Executive Order
HR = House of Representatives Bill
HRes = House Resolution
PL = Public Law
Proc = Presidential Proclamation
S = Senate Bill
USC = United States Code
SOURCE
Journal abbreviation, date and page. Abbreviations used are:
CB = Commerce Business Daily
CR = Congressional Record
FR = Federal Register
PD = Presidential Documents
WP = Washington Post
TWO WAYS TO FIND ENTRIES
(1) Look in Table of Contents for major headers and go there. Then scan down sub-headers to find appropriate entries.
(2) Look up subject in the Alphabetical Guide (see Page No. x) and go directly to code indicated.

Illustration T

Instructions and sample entry, appearing in each volume of *Federal Index.*

Another useful finding tool is Nancy P. Johnson's *Sources of Compiled Legislative Histories.*[10] This source provides a single checklist of all available compiled legislative histories, and is indexed by author, title, and name of the act.

10. American Association of Law Libraries Publication No. 14 (Fred B. Rothman & Co., 1979) with Supplement, 1981.

When searching for a legislative history, it is always wise to consult the reference staff of the nearest large research law library to ascertain whether such a compilation exists on legislation of interest. To overlook such a source could mean many hours of unnecessary work and frequently failure to find documents of significance.

E. STATE LEGISLATIVE HISTORIES

The use of legislative history in the interpretation of state legislation, and in statutory research at the state level generally, is no less important than in the federal area. However, the sources for state legislative history and the available research tools are much less adequate and the process is invariably frustrating. It is virtually impossible to collect the necessary documents for a simple legislative history in most states *outside* of the state capitol or its legislative library. Debates are almost never published, bills are usually available only at the legislature and during the session itself, committee reports are published in only a few states, and hearings even less often. Legislative journals are published for most states, but these rarely contain the actual documents of interest.

A few states are now blessed with commercial legislative services, often including status tables of pending bills, and sometimes with document ordering options—but these services are usually expensive and not widely subscribed to. In several states there are official information services for legislative proceedings, some of which are now using computer facilities.[11] These usually include bill digests, status reports, and sometimes information on legislative documents. For most states, however, there is no convenient method of identifying pending legislation, ascertaining its status, securing copies of documents or abstracts thereof, or tracing legislative proceedings. Recourse must be had to the legislature itself, to the legislative reference library, or in some states to the state library.

A new research tool, *Guide to State Legislative Materials,*[12] by Mary L. Fisher, has vastly improved the process of identifying what documents are available for each state, and from whom they are available. Illustrations U–1 and U–2 show only part of one complete state's listing from the 2d edition, and indicate some of the coverage of this valuable aid to research in state legislative history.

Legal research manuals, describing legislative material, are available for a few states (see Appendix A at the end of this book) and there are articles describing legislative history research in New York and California.[13] Here again the reference staff of a research law library in your state should also be consulted for details as to the local situation.

11. For state-by-state review, see L. Schulte, "A Survey of Computerized Information Systems," 72 *Law Library J.* 99 (1979); and for a fuller, in-depth study, see B. K. Eres, ed., *Legal and Legislative Information Processing* (Greenwood Press, 1980).

12. American Assoc. of Law Libraries Publication No. 15 (Fred B. Rothman & Co., 1979). A second edition is projected for late 1983.

13. For California, B. White, "Sources of Legislative Intent in California," 3 *Pacific L.J.* 63 (1972); and for New York, see Ch. 6, "State Legislative History," in J. J. Marke & R. Sloane, *Legal Research and Law Library Management* (Law Journal Seminars-Press, 1982), pp. 82–96.

CONNECTICUT – 1

BILLS see also Notations

Hard copy ___x___ Microform ___x___ retrospective archival only

Single copy available from Law/Legislative Reference, State Library

Amendment available from Law/Legislative Reference

Sessional subscription not available

Back file dates from 1808

Available from Archives 1808–99; Law/Legislative Reference 1901–

Reproduction and service charge $.25 per page + $1.00 handling

Indexed by: Sponsor ___x___ Bill no. ___x___ Committee ___x___ Subject ___x___ Other

Current bill status from Legislative Workroom, State Library; Bill Room, Capitol

Tel. (203) 566–5736; 566–2326

HEARINGS see also Notations

Officially recorded? yes

Transcription: Hard copy ___x___ Tape ___x___

Deposit copy at Law/Legislative Reference

Copy available from Law/Legislative Reference

Back file dates from early 1900

Indexed by: Bill No. ___x___ Committee ___x___ Subject ___x___

LEGISLATIVE DIGEST (Sponsor or introducer's memo or statement) see also Notations

Prepared by Legislative Commissioner's Office

Deposit copy at Law/Legislative Reference

Copy available from Law/Legislative Reference Cost: see above

Back file dates from 1973

Indexed by: Bill no. ___x___ Committee ______ Subject ___x___ Other Introducer

Illustration U–1

Fisher, *Guide to State Legislative Materials,* 2d ed.

CONNECTICUT - 2

COMMITTEE REPORTS none issued

Special Standing

Recorded?

Deposit copy at

Copy available from Cost

Indexed by: Bill no. ______ Subject ______ Committee ______
Bill no. ______ Subject ______ Committee ______

DEBATES see also Notations

Officially recorded? yes

Deposit copy at Law/Legislative Reference, Univ. of Conn. Law Library

Back file dates from 1980

Indexed by: Bill no. ______ Subject ______ Other ______

JOURNALS AND PROCEEDINGS

Deposit copy at Law/Legislative Reference, Univ. of Conn. Law Library, Yale

Approximate availability date of journal for proceeding recorded

Reproduced pages from Law/Legislative Ref. Cost $.25 per page + $1.00 handling

Back file dates from 1776

Indexed by: Bill no. ______ Committee ______ Subject __x__ Other

LEGISLATOR MANUAL OR DIRECTORY see also Notations

Connecticut Register and Manual Annually in October

Available from Secretary of State

Illustration U–2

Fisher, *Guide to State Legislative Materials*, 2d ed. (cont'd.).

Some of the annotated state statutory compilations offer legislative session services which, like some looseleaf services with state coverage, include the text of laws enacted during the pending legislative session. These services may also provide some legislative history references, but not on a comprehensive or systematic basis. The *Legislative Reporting Services* of Commerce Clearing House, and its computer-based counterpart, ELSS, referred to in Section B.2 above, offer, at considerable cost, custom-tailored information services on proposed legislation in particular subject areas.

Most states now have official or quasi-official agencies devoted to the research and recommendation of new legislation. These include independent law revision commissions, legislatively controlled councils, judicial groups, or academic bodies devoted to legislative study and drafting. The studies and proposals prepared by such agencies frequently result in enactments, although rarely in the exact form proposed. Their publications are an invaluable source of legislative history and may shed considerable light on the legislature's intent with respect to the resulting enactment. Many of these studies are abstracted in the monthly *Legislative Research Checklist* published by the Council of State Governments.

Although the inaccessibility of legislative documents on state legislation is a scandalous impediment to legal research, the astute researcher can frequently find useful material by persistent digging and the resourceful use of local libraries.

F. ADDITIONAL READING

F. R. Dickerson, *Interpretation and Application of Statutes* (Little, Brown, 1975).

G. B. Folsom, *Legislative History: Research for the Interpretation of Laws* (University Press of Virginia, 1972; reprinted, Fred B. Rothman, 1979).

How Federal Laws Are Made (Want Publishing Co., 1982).

L. F. Schmeckebier & R. B. Eastin, *Government Publications and Their Use* (Brookings Institution, 2nd Revised Ed. 1969) Ch. 6, "Congressional Publications."

H. J. Zinn, *How Our Laws Are Made* (E. F. Willett, rev. ed. U.S. Govt. Printing Office, 1978).

Chapter 11

ADMINISTRATIVE AND EXECUTIVE PUBLICATIONS

A. Introduction.
B. Sources of Information About Administrative and Executive Agencies.
    1. *United States Government Manual* and *Federal Regulatory Directory*.
    2. Statute of the Agency.
    3. Regulations of the Agency.
    4. Looseleaf Services.
    5. Miscellaneous Agency Publications.
    6. Secondary Sources.
C. Rules and Regulations of the Federal Administrative Agencies.
    1. The *Federal Register*.
    2. *Code of Federal Regulations*.
    3. Federal Register System Research Procedure.
    4. Special Publications of Agency Regulations.
        a. Official Agency Publications.
        b. Unofficial Sources.
    5. Citators for Rules and Regulations.
D. Decisions of the Federal Administrative Agencies.
    1. Official Reports.
    2. Unofficial Publications.
    3. Citators for Agency Decisions.
    4. Judicial Decisions Relating to Administrative Law.
E. Other Publications of Agencies.
    1. Annual Reports.
    2. Special Reports, Bulletins and Studies.
    3. Indexes and Catalogs.
F. Presidential Documents.
    1. Executive Orders and Proclamations.
    2. Presidential Messages.
    3. Reorganization Plans.
    4. Executive Agreements.
    5. Compilations of Presidential Papers.
G. State Administrative Materials.
    1. General Considerations.
    2. State Administrative Regulations and Decisions.
    3. Checklists and Indexes.
H. Opinions of the Attorneys General.
    1. Opinions of the U.S. Attorneys General.
    2. Opinions of the State Attorneys General.
I. Additional Reading.

A. INTRODUCTION

A great number and variety of documents of legal effect and significance are regularly issued by the President, the various offices of the executive branch, and the many independent administrative agencies which have grown up since the establishment of the Interstate Commerce Commission in 1887. The President has always had a lawmaking function, which is usually exercised through proclamations and executive orders. Similarly, the executive departments and their bureaus have issued regulations and adjudicated matters within their administrative jurisdiction. The independent administrative agencies developed later in response to a need for governmental regulation which could not be met by the established units of government. The existing executive offices were not equipped to handle the administration of new social and economic legislation; the Congress could not foresee, much less legislate, all of the detailed requirements of these complex activities; and the courts could not cope with the mass of adjudication required to enforce and effectuate the legislative standards. Thus new agencies and the expansion of existing agencies provided the expertise and specialization necessary for these tasks, thereby preventing a complete breakdown of the other branches of government. With this development, there grew a large body of administrative and executive publications.

This literature includes materials which resemble the primary sources of judicial and statutory law, such as adjudicative decisions and rulings, and legislative rules and regulations. It also encompasses aids to research, such as digests and indexes to provide access to chronologically published decisions; codes and compilations to impose a subject arrangement on chronologically published regulations; looseleaf services to coordinate and provide current supplementation for collections of relevant documents; citators to verify the current status of regulations and decisions; and a vast secondary literature of treatises, periodicals, monographs, annual and special reports, studies and bulletins.

These publications, while similar to others discussed in the various chapters of this book, are distinguishable in this context, however, by their origin and authorship, their legal effect and functions, and their access tools. They stem from activities which are either within the inherent power of the President or derive from powers delegated by Congress. Since their decisions and rulings result from adjudications which are often called *quasi*-judicial and since their lawmaking is considered *subordinate* or *delegated* legislation, traditionally their legal publications have been accorded less weight and authority than judicial decisions and statutes. Nevertheless, the unique social, economic and legal force of this form of lawmaking and adjudication cannot be doubted. The daily life of every American is affected by these rules and decisions, which are often enforced by penal sanctions and the full power of the state. An understanding of the many volumes, official and unofficial, in which these materials are published and indexed is essential to the legal researcher.

B. SOURCES OF INFORMATION ABOUT ADMINISTRATIVE AND EXECUTIVE AGENCIES

1. UNITED STATES GOVERNMENT MANUAL AND FEDERAL REGULATORY DIRECTORY

In order to work with the administrative and executive publications, it is often necessary to obtain general information about the structure, authority, personnel, and functions of their issuing agencies. The best single source of such information is the *United States Government Manual,* which is an official compendium of descriptive data about the legislative, judicial and executive branches, published annually in paperback form by the Office of the Federal Register. Along with brief coverage of Congress and the Courts, there is up-to-date and encyclopedic detail about every bureau, office, agency, commission and board of the Executive branch. Citations are given to the authorizing legislation; powers and functions are described; personnel are listed; and organization structures set forth. Names, addresses, phone numbers, are among the many useful details available in the *Manual.* One appendix lists executive agencies and functions of the federal government which were abolished, transferred, or terminated since March 4, 1933. A detailed index and a list of names facilitate easy reference. The *Government Manual* is one of the most convenient starting points for any research about executive agencies.

Also useful in this regard is the annual *Federal Regulatory Directory,* published by Congressional Quarterly Inc. since 1979. This reference guide offers detailed descriptions of the larger federal agencies and covers current topics related to their activities.

2. STATUTE OF THE AGENCY

Another helpful source of information is the statute creating the particular administrative unit, since that is usually the primary source of the agency's authority and powers. Citations to that legislation can be obtained from the section in the *U.S. Government Manual* dealing with that agency, or from the various statutory indexes. The text of the statute itself can then be located and examined in the *U.S. Code,* or preferably in the *U.S. Code Annotated* or the *U.S. Code Service.*

3. REGULATIONS OF THE AGENCY

Since the agencies must exercise a legislative function in carrying out their statutory responsibilities, Congress usually expressly delegates to them the power to promulgate rules and regulations. These rules are comparable to statutes and have the full force of law. The relevant statute defines such a rule as: ". . . the whole or any part of any agency statement of general or particular applicability and future effect designed to implement, interpret, or prescribe law or policy describing the organization, procedure, or practice requirements of an agency . . . "[1] After reading the enabling legislation for a particular agency, one can then move on to its rules and regulations to see how the agency has given substance and effect to the general mandate of its statute. These enactments appear first in the daily issues of the *Federal Register,* but are usually examined in the *Code of Federal Regulations* where they are codified by subject very much as the *U.S. Code* arranges the chronologically published enactments of the *Statutes at Large.* The General Index and Finding Aids volume of the *C.F.R.* is revised annually and provides references to the regulations. Research procedures and details of publication of the *Federal Register* and the *Code of Federal Regulations* are discussed in Section C below.

4. LOOSELEAF SERVICES

The statutes and regulations of many agencies, as well as a mass of other general information and documents relating to them or their areas of regulation, can also be found in the many looseleaf services published by commercial publishers like Commerce Clearing House, Prentice-Hall, Pike & Fischer and the Bureau of National Affairs. These compilations of primary and secondary materials are usually issued for specific subject fields rather than for agencies as such, but they invariably provide detailed material on the agency regulating that field (e.g., the Federal Trade Commission in the *CCH Trade Regulation Reporter;* the National Labor Relations Board in B.N.A.'s *Labor Relations Reporter;* the Federal Communications Commission in Pike & Fischer's *Radio Regulation* service; and the Securities and Exchange Commission in the Prentice-Hall *Securities Regulation* service.) Such publications are discussed in detail in Chapter 13, but they are noteworthy here as useful research sources on the various administrative agencies. *B.N.A.*, one of the looseleaf service publishers, now also offers the information in several of its services (federal taxation, labor law, and patents) for on-line computer searching.

5. MISCELLANEOUS AGENCY PUBLICATIONS

The agencies themselves publish pamphlets, monographs and studies describing their own structure and operations. These vary from short, popular descriptions to occasionally quite detailed administrative handbooks. They are noted, as published, in the *Monthly Catalog of Government Publications.* An example of such a survey is *The Work of the Department [of State]* (U.S.G.P.O., 1980). Almost every agency publishes an official literature of this type, descriptive of its organization and work.

1. 80 Stat. 381 (1966), 5 U.S.C. § 551 (1976).

6. SECONDARY SOURCES

There has also been a great deal of descriptive and analytical writing about administrative law and administrative agencies outside of the agencies themselves. Since official statements are often general in nature and primarily devised to enhance the agency's public image, recourse can be had to this vast secondary literature of scholarly and governmental inquiry. This literature takes many forms and includes pioneering procedural monographs such as James Landis, *The Administrative Process* and Walter Gellhorn, *Federal Administrative Proceedings;* analytical studies of particular agencies and areas of regulation such as Louis Loss, *Securities Regulation,* and I. L. Sharfman, *The Interstate Commerce Commission;* and comprehensive academic treatments such as Kenneth Davis, *Administrative Law.* Relevant periodical articles appear in almost all legal journals from time to time and journals like the American Bar Association's *Administrative Law Review* and the *Federal Bar Journal* specialize in this field. Several administrative agencies issue their own periodicals as well.[2]

Contributions to this literature have also been made by governmental inquiries such as the *U.S. Attorney General's Committee on Administrative Procedure,* which in 1940 and 1941 published two series of monographs examining meticulously 27 administrative agencies and in 1941 issued a final report entitled, *Administrative Procedure in Government Agencies,* a landmark study in this field. The Hoover Commission's 1949 *Report on General Management of the Executive Branch,* its 1949 *Task Force Report on Regulatory Commissions,* and its 1955 *Task Force Report on Legal Services and Procedure* also made important contributions to understanding these agencies. From time to time, other government studies and reports are issued to analyze particular problems or develop reforms. Finally, there are bibliographic manuals of government publications which deal directly with the documents themselves; perhaps the best of these is Schmeckebier & Eastin, *Government Publications and Their Use* (2d rev. ed., 1969).

Some of these secondary sources bring to bear the objectivity and critical insight of disinterested scholarship, and others, the often revealing scrutiny of governmental inquiry. Although there is no regularly supplemented, comprehensive bibliography of such works, references can be obtained from law library card catalogs, the *Index to Legal Periodicals, Current Law Index* and *Legal Resources Index,* and the *Monthly Catalog of Government Publications.*

2. E.g., *Federal Reserve Bulletin, Monthly Labor Review* and *Social Security Bulletin,* published by federal agencies. Bar associations specializing in this practice and commercial publishers also publish journals devoted to particular fields, such as *I.C.C. Practitioners' Journal, Journal of the Patent Office Society* and Commerce Clearing House's *Labor Law Journal* and *Food, Drug and Cosmetic Law Journal.*

C. RULES AND REGULATIONS OF THE FEDERAL ADMINISTRATIVE AGENCIES

Although executive and administrative agencies are as old as our government and some were in fact established at its inception, the industrialization of this country at the end of the 19th century brought many new agencies, as well as new functions to existing agencies. The 20th century, with the added impetus of two World Wars and an economic depression, accelerated this development and brought about a tremendous increase in the amount of agency business. Unfortunately, there was no systematic publication of the mass of rules, decisions and administrative actions of this huge bureaucracy and there developed a confusing and unjust "government in ignorance of the law." [3] Hundreds of executive orders, thousands of regulations, and tens of thousands of pages of other documents of legal effect were issued without regular publication. No centralized place of publication existed and in many instances no attempt at public notice was even made. A lawyer who wanted to ascertain the applicable rules and their current status had no recourse for such information. The public dissatisfaction and pressure for reform came to a head in litigation concerning New Deal regulation of the oil industry when it was discovered in cases reaching the Supreme Court [4] that the regulations on which the cases were purportedly based had been revoked without the knowledge of the parties or their attorneys. The resulting furor provided the final impetus for the enactment of remedial legislation in 1935.

1. THE FEDERAL REGISTER

The Federal Register Act of 1935 [5] was designed to end this chaos of uncertainty by establishing a central repository for the publication of federal proclamations, orders, regulations, notices and other documents of general legal applicability. It initiated a new daily publication, the *Federal Register*, in which such documents must be published. The *Federal Register* began publication on March 14, 1936 and ever since has published regularly the following classes of documents, as required by law:

> "(1) Presidential proclamations and executive orders, except those not having general applicability and legal effect . . .
>
> (2) documents or classes of documents that the President may determine from time to time have general applicability and legal effect; and

3. See E. N. Griswold, "Government in Ignorance of Law—A Plea for Better Publications of Executive Legislation," 48 *Harv.L.Rev.* 198 (1934), in which the documentary chaos of the early New Deal is described. This article called for and undoubtedly contributed to the prompt creation of the *Federal Register* and the *Code of Federal Regulations.*

4. U.S. v. Smith, 293 U.S. 633, 55 S.Ct. 65, 79 L.Ed. 718 (1934) (memorandum decision), dismissal of appeal on government motion described in New York Times, October 2, 1934, p. 6; Panama Refining Co. v. Ryan, 293 U.S. 388, 55 S.Ct. 241, 79 L.Ed. 446 (1935).

5. 49 Stat. 500 (1935).

(3) documents or classes of documents that may be required so to be published by Act of the Congress." [6]

For the purposes of this Act, every document or order which prescribes a penalty is deemed to have general applicability and legal effect.[7] Subsequently, the Administrative Committee of the *Federal Register,* which is responsible for its publication, promulgated regulations governing the form and content of the *Register.* These appear in Title 1 of the *Code of Federal Regulations* and among them are the following definitions:

> "Document includes any Presidential proclamation or Executive order, and any rule, regulation, order, certificate, code of fair competition, license, notice, or similar instrument issued, prescribed, or promulgated by an agency;
>
> "Document having general applicability and legal effect" means any document issued under proper authority prescribing a penalty or course of conduct, conferring a right, privilege, authority, or immunity, or imposing an obligation, and relevant or applicable to the general public, members of a class, or persons in a locality, as distinguished from named individuals or organizations.[8]

In addition to the prescribed Presidential, executive and administrative documents, each agency is required to publish in the *Register* proposed rules it wishes to adopt, and to provide an opportunity for interested parties to be heard. Often the agencies also formulate and adopt policies for handling different types of business. These policy statements, if formally adopted for general use, must likewise be published in the *Register.* Policies developed in connection with a particular adjudication, however, do not have to be published.

The current arrangement of material in each issue of the *Register* is as follows:

(1) List of selected subjects covered in the issue

(2) Contents table

(3) List of CFR Parts Affected

(4) Presidential Documents

(5) Rules and Regulations

(6) Proposed Rules

(7) Notices

(8) List of Sunshine Act Meetings

(9) Readers' Aids, which include:

- (a) Telephone numbers for information and assistance.
- (b) A listing of *Federal Register* pages and dates for the month.

6. 44 U.S.C. § 1505 (1976).

7. Ibid.

8. 1 *C.F.R.* § 1.1 (1982).

(c) Cumulative list of *C.F.R.* parts affected, in that month's issues.

(d) A list of agencies which have agreed to publish their documents on designated days of the week.

(e) A list of public bills which have been enacted into law.

The regulations are arranged in the daily *Register* by the title numbers of the *Code of Federal Regulations* into which they will ultimately be codified.

The applicable statutes provide that a person may not be adversely affected by a matter required to be published in the *Federal Register* and not so published, except to the extent that such person has actual and timely notice of that matter.[9] They also stipulate that judicial notice shall be taken of the contents of the *Federal Register.*[10]

Despite the substantial improvements in publication brought about by the Federal Register Act, a feeling remained that the public was still not getting sufficient information concerning the work of these agencies. As a result, further significant improvements were added by the Administrative Procedure Act of 1946,[11] the Freedom of Information Act (1966)[12] and the Government in the Sunshine Act (1976).[13]

The public is now afforded at least formal notice of most of the legally significant actions of these agencies and provided with better access to information and documents relating thereto. Nevertheless criticism has continued both as to the scope and form of the *Federal Register* and as to governmental policies with respect to access to public information.

Each year's output comprises a new volume of the *Federal Register* with continuous pagination throughout the year, but because of its great bulk the issues for each month are usually bound separately. During its first three years of publication a special bound edition was published in two volumes for each year. Unfortunately this arrangement was not continued beyond 1938. There are a small number of rules appearing in the *Register* which are not cumulated in the *Code of Federal Regulations.* For that reason, and since much of the other material in the *Federal Register* is never published elsewhere, it has a permanent reference value and must be retained. For instance, the *C.F.R.* may not contain the following types of documents which appear in the *Federal Register:* descriptive statements on agency organization; proposed rules; agency policy statements in connection with the adoption of certain rules; many rules and regulations which are outside its usual scope; rules which have been repealed; and changes in rules which have been made and then modi-

9. 81 Stat. 54 (1967), 5 U.S.C. § 552 (1976).

10. 82 Stat. 1276 (1968), 44 U.S.C. § 1507 (1976).

11. 60 Stat. 238 (1946).

12. 80 Stat. 250 (1966), codified by 81 Stat. 54 (1967), 5 U.S.C. § 552 (1976), as amended 88 Stat. 1561 (1974), and as limited by Privacy Act of 1974, 88 Stat. 1896.

13. 90 Stat. 1241 (1976), 5 U.S.C. § 552(b), 5 U.S.C. § 552b(e)(3) (1976).

fied before the *C.F.R.* annual revision published the original change. Because of its size and the poor quality of paper used in the *Federal Register,* many libraries are transferring their holdings to microfilm or microfiche editions.

Access to the contents of the *Federal Register* can be obtained by the following means:

(a) The daily table of contents which lists alphabetically the agencies whose regulations appear in that issue, along with page references to where in the *Register* those regulations appear;

(b) The monthly index which cumulates annually, consisting of agency names, and subject entries; and

(c) The *List of CFR Parts Affected,* which indicates changes daily and within each month in the various regulations published in the *Register.*

The *Lists of CFR Parts (or Sections) Affected,* arranged by *C.F.R.* title and section, designate each regulation which has been affected by material in that issue or period of the *Federal Register.* Changes may consist of modifications, new or proposed regulations, or the revocation of a regulation. These guides provide references to each page of the *Register* on which the text of the listed changes actually appears.

A list of changes covering the daily contents appears at the front of each issue of the *Federal Register,* just after the table of contents. The back of each issue also contains another list in the same form which cumulates all changes from the first day of that month to date. Finally, at the end of each month a larger guide is published in a separate monthly pamphlet of the *Code of Federal Regulations,* entitled *List of CFR Sections Affected,* which cumulates all changes back to the last published revision of the title of the *Code.* Now the researcher need consult only these two lists of sections affected—the daily guide in the *Federal Register* which cumulates changes within that month, and the last monthly *List of CFR Sections Affected,* which cumulates changes since the last revision of each title—in order to ascertain changes made in a regulation. These lists of sections affected have developed into a quick and convenient citator. Illustration A shows the daily *List of CFR Parts Affected* and the list which cumulates changes within that month, from issues of the *Federal Register;* Illustration B shows the cumulative *List of CFR Sections Affected,* which appears as a monthly pamphlet of the *CFR* itself, reflecting changes back to the last revision of each title.

Also useful for locating material in the *Federal Register* is the *Federal Index,* published by Capitol Services Inc. which provides *montnly* indexing of the *Federal Register,* the *Congressional Record,* and the *Weekly Compilation of Presidential Papers,* and an annual cumulative volume. Prentice Hall's *Federal Regulatory Week* contains a summary of all significant proposed, interim and final regulations issued during the prior week, as well as rescinded regulations, a list of *CFR* parts affected, a calendar of deadlines for proposed rules, and hearings scheduled for pending rules.

VIII **Federal Register** / Vol. 47, No. 227 / W

CFR PARTS AFFECTED IN THIS ISSUE

A cumulative list of the parts affected this month can be found in the Reader Aids section at the end of this issue.

3 CFR
Executive Orders
12395 52957

7 CFR
905 52959
906 52959
912 52959
982 52960
987 52959
989 52959
1701 52961
Proposed Rules:
442 53025

9 CFR
Proposed Rules:
55 53026
113 53026
201 53027
203 53027

10 CFR
456 53224
Proposed Rules:
2 53028
50 53030
55 53028
458 53236

11 CFR
Proposed Rules:
106 53030
9031–9039 53030

12 CFR
541 52961
561 52961
563 52961

13 CFR
Ch. I 52966
311 52976

14 CFR
204 52977
250 52980
254 52987
291 52991

15 CFR
369 52991

16 CFR
13 52993

17 CFR
Proposed Rules:
170 53031

18 CFR
Proposed Rules:
271 (2 documents) 53032, 53033
385 53034

21 CFR
193 52994
Proposed Rules:
1306 53038

24 CFR
Proposed Rules:
200 53038
203 53038
221 53038
234 53038

27 CFR
9 52996
Proposed Rules:
9 (2 documents) 53048, 53051

30 CFR
Proposed Rules:
915 53053

34 CFR
408 52997
500 52997
520 52997
525 52997
526 52997
527 52997

37 CFR
Proposed Rules:
2 53054

39 CFR
Proposed Rules:
3001 53056

40 CFR
52 53000
162 53003
180 (4 documents) 53004–53006
466 53172
Proposed Rules:
52 53057
61 53059
86 53059
158 53192
180 (2 documents) 53060, 53061

42 CFR
52 53007
52d 53007
52h 53007
55a 53007
86 53007

45 CFR
74 53007
304 53014
1336 53007

47 CFR
73 (6 documents) 53018–53020
74 53021
Proposed Rules:
34 53062
35 53062
68 53063

49 CFR
1002 53291
1045B 53260
1046 53260
1139 53279
1142 53282
1143 53283
1160 53260
1165 53286
1168 53260
1169 53291
Proposed Rules:
1002 53297
1170 53297

i

Federal Register
Vol. 47, No. 19
Thursday, January 28, 1982

CFR PARTS AFFECTED DURING JANUARY

At the end of each month, the Office of the Federal Register publishes separately a list of CFR Sections Affected (LSA), which lists parts and sections affected by documents published since the revision date of each title.

3 CFR
Proclamations:
4707 (Amended by Proc. 4889) 1
4889 1
4890 2855
4891 2977
4892 3339
Executive Orders:
1643 (Revoked by PLO 6101) 769
11157 (Amended by EO 12337) 1367
11476 (See EO 12340) 3071
11835 (See EO 12340) 3071
12018 (See EO 12340) 3071
12171 (Amended by EO 12338) 1369
12198 (See EO 12340) 3071
12233 (See EO 12340) 3071
12251 (Revoked by EO 12341) 3341
12306 (See EO 12340) 3071
12310 (Amended by EO 12339) 2475
12315 (See EO 12340) 3071
12337 1367
12338 1369
12339 2475
12340 3071
12341 3341

5 CFR
Ch. XIV 3343
293 3077
359 2283
410 935
832 2284
1201 936
Proposed Rules:
Ch. I 154
352 956
550 958
610 958
890 961

6 CFR
Ch. VI 2285
Ch. VII 2285

7 CFR
Ch. XII 2981
Subtitle B 745
1a 2073
2 .... 5, 6
68 .... 129, 2074
160 3343
226 3539
282 532
301 1257
319 .... 3082, 3086
425 6
631 130
701 937
800 .... 131, 2254
801 2979
905 589
906 1265
907 .... 746, 2074, 2980, 4039
910 .... 939, 2767, 3082
944 .... 747, 1265
1300 2981
1701 3088
1924 590
1942 590
1980 4039
Proposed Rules:
Ch. I 3126
102 631
360 2874
979 631
1004 2118
1006 814
1007 .... 962, 2122
1011 2999
1012 814
1013 814
1033 814
1036 814
1040 814
1046 2999
1098 2999
1124 814
1125 814
1133 814
1134 .... 778, 814
1135 814
1136 .... 778, 814
1137 .... 778, 814
1139 .... 814, 3361
1250 1105
1701 .... 3126, 3554, 3555
1865 33
1942 2774
1951 33

8 CFR
101 940
204 942
238 .... 131, 3757
264 940
316a 132
Proposed Rules
3 1396

9 CFR
Ch. I 745

Illustration A

Daily and cumulative lists of *CFR* parts affected, appearing in the *Federal Register*.

LSA

List of CFR Sections Affected

September 1982

SAVE THIS ISSUE*

TITLES 1-16
Changes January 4, 1982 through September 30, 1982

TITLES 17-27
Changes April 1, 1982 through September 30, 1982

TITLES 28-41
Changes July 1, 1982 through September 30, 1982

*TITLES 42-50 (ANNUAL)
Changes October 1, 1981 through September 30, 1982

PARALLEL TABLE OF AUTHORITIES AND RULES

CHANGES JANUARY 4 THROUGH SEPTEMBER 30, 1982

Page

TITLE 8—ALIENS AND NATIONALITY

Chapter I—Immigration and Naturalization Service, Department of Justice

3.1 (d)(1-a) and (e) revised.......... 16772
100.4 (c)(2) amended.................... 19672
(b) amended.................................. 25003
(d) amended.................................. 27549
101.3 Revised..................................... 940
101.4 Added.. 941
103.1 (e) corrected.......................... 18122
204.2 (h) revised................................. 942
(c)(7) revised; interim.................. 12131
212.1 (a) revised.............................. 5990
(e) corrected.................................... 8005
212.2 (a) through (i) redesignated as (b) through (j); new (a) added; new (b) through (g) revised; interim.. 12131
212.5 Revised, interim.................... 30045
212.7 (b) revised; interim.............. 12132
212.10 Added; interim.................... 12132
214.2 (j)(2)(ii) and (3) revised; interim.. 12132
223.2 Revised; interim.................... 12132
223.4 Added; interim...................... 12132
235.3 Revised, interim.................... 30046
237.6 Added; interim...................... 12132
238.3 (b) amended............................. 132, 3757, 8759, 12939, 38865
238.4 Amended........ 9982, 20110, 28608
242.1 (a) revised.............................. 38267
(a) correction................................ 40786
242.8 (a) revised; interim.............. 12133
242.17 (d) redesignated as (e); new (d) added; interim............ 12133
245.1 (d) and (e) removed; (f), (g), and (h) redesignated as (d), (e), and (f); (a), (b), (c), and new (d) revised; interim.. 12133
245.3 Revised; interim.................... 12134
248.2 Revised; interim.................... 12134
264.2 Added.. 941
265.1 Revised; interim.................... 12134
274 Revised; interim....................... 19317
316a.2 Amended................................ 132
316a.21 (d) added.......................... 10777
328.2 Revised................................... 10777
328.3 Revised................................... 10778
332.11 Revised................................. 10778
332a.2 Amended.............................. 10778
332a.13 (b) revised; (e) removed.. 10778
332c.1 Revised................................. 38673
334.2 Revised................................... 10778
334.11 Revised................................. 10778
334.21 Revised................................. 10778
335.11 (a) revised............................ 10778
335b Removed.................................. 10779
336.11 Revised................................. 10779
336.16 Removed............................... 10779
336.16a Revised............................... 10779
336.17 Removed............................... 10779
339.1 Revised................................... 10779
344.3 Revised................................... 10779

Title 8—*Proposed Rules:*

1—499 (Ch. I).................................... 18604
3.. 1396, 37556
103...................................... 32952, 37556
204.. 35226
214............ 20147, 23463, 24596, 27565, 29851
248.................. 23463, 24596, 27565, 32952

TITLE 9—ANIMALS AND ANIMAL PRODUCTS

Chapter I—Animal and Plant Health Inspection Service, Department of Agriculture

2.75 Amended...................................... 746
2.76 Amended...................................... 746
2.77 Amended...................................... 746
2.78 Amended...................................... 746
2.79 Amended...................................... 746
2.80 Amended...................................... 746
2.81 Amended...................................... 746
11.21 Amended.................................... 746
53.10 (d) addition confirmed.......... 5996
71.3 (a) revised................................ 7826
72.13 (b)(4) added.......................... 11002
73.7 Amended...................................... 746
79.2 (a)(1) amended...................... 42719
82.1 (q) added; interim.................. 11245
82.3 (c)(1) added............................ 1109
(c)(2) added...................................... 3089
(c)(3) added...................................... 3758
(c)(1)(i) removed............................ 4043
(c)(1)(ii) removed........................... 5701
(c)(3)(i) removed............................ 7390
(c)(2) removed............................... 13322
(c)(1) added.................................... 21238
(c)(1) amended................................ 29648
82.6 Added; interim........................ 11245

Illustration B

Cumulative lists of *CFR* sections affected, appearing in monthly pamphlet of *CFR* and reflecting changes occurring since the last revision of each title.

2. CODE OF FEDERAL REGULATIONS

Ordinarily research into the current regulations of an administrative agency does not begin with the *Federal Register,* but with its companion publication, the *Code of Federal Regulations.* Because of the tremendous mass of chronologically published rules and regulations, it was necessary to provide a convenient text of current rules in force, arranged by subject, which could be kept up-to-date. Although section 11 of the original Federal Register Act required each agency to compile and publish in the *Register* its then current body of regulations,[14] it was not until an amendment to the Act in 1937 [15] that a regular form of codification was established. The first edition of this *Code of Federal Regulations* was published in 1938 and contained regulations in force as of June 1, 1938. It was kept up-to-date with cumbersome bound supplements between 1938 and 1943. Although the 1937 Act called for a new codification every five years, World War II delayed the second edition until 1949 and modified the original plan.[16] The present *Code* is now issued in pamphlet form with each of the fifty titles revised and re-published once a year, containing all of the regulations in force at the time of publication. The publication of the various titles is on a quarterly basis approximately as follows: Titles 1–16 as of January 1; titles 17–27 as of April 1; titles 28–41 as of July 1; and titles 42–50 as of October 1.

The latest statement of which documents are to be included in the *Code* provides that it is "to contain each Federal regulation of general applicability and current or future effect." [17] The *Code* is also *prima facie* evidence of the text of the original document.[18] In addition to the regulations which form the main contents of the *Code,* it also includes, in Title 3, the texts of Presidential proclamations, executive orders, and other Presidential documents, described below in Section F.

The regulations of the *C.F.R.* are codified in a subject arrangement consisting of some fifty titles similar to those employed for federal statutes in the *United States Code,* but with some variations. The various titles collect the current effective texts of the rules and regulations from the *Federal Register* and organize them under such broad areas of regulation as agriculture, highways, labor, etc. Not surprisingly, there is a very close association between most of the individual *C.F.R.* titles and the work and product of a particular federal agency. Each title is divided into *chapters, parts* and *sections.* The section is the basic unit of the *Code,* and section numbers incorporate their respective part numbers, so that § 8.1 is the citation for Part 8, Section 8.1.

Access to the *Code* is now provided by a combined "Index and Finding Aids" volume which contains entries for both agency names

14. 49 Stat. 503 (1935).

15. 50 Stat. 304 (1937).

16. See Kennedy, "The Code of Federal Regulations and the United States Statutes at Large," 44 *Law Lib.J.* 1 (1951), for a summary of these changes.

17. 1 C.F.R. § 8.1(a) (1973).

18. 44 U.S.C. § 1510(e) (1970).

and subjects. See Illustration C for a sample page. This volume is revised annually. Prior to 1977, it was issued as two separate volumes: "Index" and "Finding Aids". Use of the Index is now facilitated by a little-known *Thesaurus of Indexing Terms* which so far appears only in the *Federal Register* (45 *F.R.* 2999, January 15, 1980 and 46 *F.R.* 12617, February 17, 1981). The Thesaurus is prepared by the Administrative Committee of the *Federal Register.* Its reissuance annually and reprints for distribution have been promised by the Office of the Federal Register.

A commercially published annual *Index to the Code of Federal Regulations* is now issued by Congressional Information Service. The 1980 edition in four volumes was originally a publication of Information Handling Service. It provides very detailed indexing of the *C.F.R.* by subject and by geographic locations. See a sample page in Illustration D, below. The *Federal Register* and the *C.F.R.* are now also available for searching by computer, and, in view of the slow publication of the commercially published *Index to the Code of Federal Regulations,* computer access may become increasingly important for the most effective subject searching.

In addition to the lists of sections affected, described above, each revised volume of the *Code* contains such a list, at the end of the volume, cumulating all changes back to January 1, 1973. For the period prior to 1973, there is a separate three volume set for the whole code, entitled "List of CFR Sections Affected, 1949–1963 and 1964–1972." An example of the former list is shown in Illustration E.

Since each daily issue of the *Federal Register* contains changes in many sections of the various titles of the *Code,* the *Register* is in effect a daily supplement to the *Code.* As noted above, these amendments are arranged in the *Register* under the *Code* numbering system and are also listed numerically by *Code* title and section in the *Lists of Sections Affected.* A complete search of federal regulations must therefore use the cumulative *Lists* of the *Federal Register* and the *C.F.R.* to bring up-to-date the various titles of the *Code.*

To further facilitate research in the *Code of Federal Regulations,* the "Index and Finding Aids" volume includes tables with parallel references to related documents outside the *Code.* A discussion of some of the more important of these tables follows.

U.S. Code to C.F.R.: This table lists every section of the *U.S. Code* which has been cited by some agency as authority for its rules. (See Illustration F at page 347.) Opposite those statutory references are citations to the sections of the *C.F.R.* containing the rules which are derived from them and which cite them as authority. This table is updated in the separately published monthly pamphlet of *C.F.R.* entitled, *List of CFR Sections Affected.*

Presidential document to C.F.R.: These tables which were last revised in 1976 and are found in the "Finding Aids" volume for that year, provide parallel references from Presidential proclamations, executive orders and other miscellaneous documents, to the various sec-

Labor Management Services Administration **CFR Index**

Labor Management Services Administration

Labor Management Standards Enforcement Office

360

Illustration C

A sample page from the *CFR* Index in the "Index and Finding Aids" volume.

CFR INDEX, 1980
SUBJECT INDEX

LABOR DISPUTES *(continued)*

RAIL CARRIERS — MEDIATION
Executive Order 12182 Creating an Emergency Board to Investigate a Dispute Between the Long Island Rail Road and Certain of Its Employees
T3 3PR1980: Pg 471
Rules of Procedure
T29B Ch10 Pt1202 29LB1980: Pg 817

RAIL CARRIERS — *NATIONAL MEDIATION BOARD*
Rules of Procedure
T29B Ch10 Pt1202 29LB1980: Pg 817

RAIL CARRIERS — PUBLIC NOTICE
Notices in Re: Railway Labor Act
T29B Ch10 Pt1205 29LB1980: Pg 822

REPORTING REQUIREMENTS — *FEDERAL MEDIATION AND CONCILIATION SERVICE*
Procedures of the Service [Forms]
T29B Ch12 Pt1402 29LB1980: Pg 852

SPECIAL ADJUSTMENT BOARDS — TRANSPORTATION INDUSTRY
Establishment of Special Adjustment Boards
T29B Ch10 Pt1207 29LB1980: Pg 824

SUPPLY CONTRACTS — *FEDERAL SUPPLY SERVICE*
Fixed Price Supply Contracts [Forms]
T41A Ch5–A Pt7–01 41PM1980: Pg 510

TRANSPORTATION INDUSTRY — SPECIAL ADJUSTMENT BOARDS
Establishment of Special Adjustment Boards
T29B Ch10 Pt1207 29LB1980: Pg 824

VESSELS
Protests, Disputes and Offenses
T22 Ch1–I Pt83 22FR1980: Pg 247

LABOR FEDERAL SECURITY AGENCY APPROPRIATION ACT, 1950
Grants, Advances and Audits
T20 Ch5 Pt601–B 20EB1980: Pg 15

LABOR MANAGEMENT RELATIONS
USED FOR: INDUSTRIAL RELATIONS
SEE ALSO:
(RT) COLLECTIVE BARGAINING; FEDERAL LABOR MANAGEMENT RELATIONS PROGRAM; LABOR ORGANIZATIONS; LABOR RELATIONS CONSULTANTS; SPECIAL ADJUSTMENT BOARDS

ADVISORY SERVICES — *FEDERAL LABOR RELATIONS AUTHORITY*
General Statements of Policy or Guidance
T5 Ch14–C Pt2427 5AP1980: Pg 732

CONSTRUCTION CONTRACTS — *DEPARTMENT OF ENERGY*
Labor Relations
T41A Ch9 Pt50–12 41PM1979: Pg 484

CONTRACTORS — *DEFENSE LOGISTICS AGENCY*
Contractor Industrial Labor Relations
T32B Ch12–A Pt1212 32ND1980: Pg 115

CONTRACTORS — *DEPARTMENT OF DEFENSE*
Basic Labor Policies
T32A Ch1–A Pt12–01 32ND1979: Pg 828

CONTRACTORS — *NATIONAL AERONAUTICS AND SPACE ADMINISTRATION*
Basic Labor Policies
T41A Ch18 Pt12–01 41PM1980: Pg 533

CONTRACTS — COST ALLOCATIONS
Contracts With Commercial Organizations
T32A Ch1–A Pt15–02 32ND1979: Pg 954

COST ALLOCATIONS — CONTRACTS
Contracts With Commercial Organizations
T32A Ch1–A Pt15–02 32ND1979: Pg 954

DEPARTMENT OF ENERGY
Security Policies and Practices Relating to Labor-Management Relations
T10 Ch3 Pt706 10EN1980: Pg 469

FEDERAL SERVICE IMPASSES PANEL
General
T5 Ch14–D Pt2470 5AP1980: Pg 741

FOREIGN SERVICE
Employee-Management Relations
T22 Ch1–B Pt14 22FR1980: Pg 83

FOREIGN SERVICE EMPLOYEES
Executive Order 12128. Employee-Management Relations in the Foreign Service
T3 3PR1980: Pg 377

MILITARY INSTALLATIONS — *DEPARTMENT OF THE AIR FORCE*
Industrial Labor Relations Activities
T32A Ch7–A Pt801 32ND1980: Pg 12

PERSONNEL POLICIES AND PRACTICES — *FEDERAL LABOR RELATIONS AUTHORITY*
Processing of Cases Pending as of December 31, 1978, and Cases Filed During the Period of January 1 Through January 10, 1979
T5 Ch14–A Pt2400 5AP1980: Pg 679

POSTAL SERVICE
Procedure Governing Matters Affecting Employment-Management Agreements Under the Postal Reorganization Act
T29B Ch1 Pt102–Q 29LB1980: Pg 807
Groups and Departments
T39 Ch1–D Pt224 39PS1980: Pg 40
Postal Regions
T39 Ch1–D Pt225 39PS1980: Pg 49

LABOR MANAGEMENT RELATIONS *(continued)*

REPORTING REQUIREMENTS — *LABOR MANAGEMENT SERVICES ADMINISTRATION. OFFICE OF LABOR MANAGEMENT STANDARDS ENFORCEMENT*
Labor-Management Reports
T29B Ch4–A 29LB1980: Pg 836

SERVICE CONTRACTS — *DEPARTMENT OF ENERGY*
Labor Relations
T41A Ch9 Pt50–12 41PM1979: Pg 484

LABOR MANAGEMENT REPORTING AND DISCLOSURE ACT OF 1959
Procedure Governing Applications for Certificates of Exemption Under the Labor-Management Reporting and Disclosure Act of 1959, and the Employee Retirement Income Security Act of 1974
T28 Ch1 Pt4 28JA1980: Pg 108
Substantive Requirements Concerning Standards of Conduct
T29B Ch2 Pt208–A 29LB1980: Pg 816
Labor-Management Reports
T29B Ch4–A 29LB1980: Pg 836
Labor Organizations as Defined in the Labor-Management Reporting and Disclosure Act of 1959
T29B Ch4–A Pt451 29LB1980: Pg 861
General Statement Concerning Bonding Requirements of the Labor-Management Reporting and Disclosure Act of 1959
T29B Ch4–A Pt453 29LB1980: Pg 897

LABOR MANAGEMENT SERVICES ADMINISTRATION
USED FOR: DEPARTMENT OF LABOR. LABOR MANAGEMENT SERVICES ADMINISTRATION; LMSA

INFORMATION ACCESS
Special Rules Applicable to Certain Specific Records
T29A Pt70–C 29LB1980: Pg 266

REGIONAL OFFICES AND FACILITIES
Payment of Premiums [Tables]
T29B Ch26 Pt2602 29LB1980: Pg 631

REPORTING REQUIREMENTS — RULINGS
Procedures
T29B Ch4–B Pt462–A 29LB1980: Pg 914

RULINGS — REPORTING REQUIREMENTS
Procedures
T29B Ch4–B Pt462–A 29LB1980: Pg 914

LABOR MANAGEMENT SERVICES ADMINISTRATION. OFFICE OF EMPLOYEE BENEFITS SECURITY
Fiduciary Responsibility Under the Employee Retirement Income Security Act of 1974
T29B Ch25–F 29LB1980: Pg 597

LABOR MANAGEMENT SERVICES ADMINISTRATION. OFFICE OF LABOR MANAGEMENT STANDARDS ENFORCEMENT
USED FOR: DEPARTMENT OF LABOR. OFFICE OF LABOR MANAGEMENT STANDARDS ENFORCEMENT; OFFICE OF LABOR MANAGEMENT STANDARDS ENFORCEMENT

Office of Labor Management Standards Enforcement, Department of Labor
T29B Ch4 29LB1980: Pg 835

LABOR MANAGEMENT RELATIONS — REPORTING REQUIREMENTS
Labor-Management Reports
T29B Ch4–A 29LB1980: Pg 836

ORGANIZATION AND FUNCTIONS
Meaning of Terms Used in This Subchapter
T29B Ch4–A Pt401 29LB1980: Pg 836

LABOR MANAGEMENT SERVICES ADMINISTRATION. OFFICE OF PENSION AND WELFARE BENEFIT PROGRAMS
USED FOR: OFFICE OF PENSION AND WELFARE BENEFIT PROGRAMS

Pension and Welfare Benefit Programs, Department of Labor
T29B Ch25 29LB1980: Pg 473

EMPLOYEE BENEFIT PLANS — REPORTING REQUIREMENTS
Rules and Regulations for Reporting and Disclosure
T29B Ch25–C Pt2520 29LB1980: Pg 499

RULE MAKING
General
T29B Ch25–A 29LB1980: Pg 474

LABOR ORGANIZATION OFFICIALS
SEE ALSO:
(BT) LABOR ORGANIZATION REPRESENTATIVES
(RT) LABOR ORGANIZATIONS

ANNUAL REPORTS
Labor Organization Officers and Employees Report
T29B Ch4–A Pt404 29LB1980: Pg 845

CANDIDATES — ELIGIBILITY
Candidacy for Office; Reasonable Qualifications
T29B Ch4–A Pt452–E 29LB1980: Pg 874

CRIMINAL OFFENDERS
Other Provisions of the Act Affecting Title IV
T29B Ch4–A Pt452–B 29LB1980: Pg 868

Illustration D

A sample page from the Subject Index of the 1980 edition of the C.I.S. *Index to the Code of Federal Regulations* (4 vols.).

List of CFR Sections Affected

All changes in this volume of the Code of Federal Regulations which were made by documents published in the Federal Register since January 1, 1973, are enumerated in the following list. Entries indicate the nature of the changes effected. Page numbers refer to Federal Register pages. The user should consult the entries for chapters and parts as well as sections for revisions.

For the period before January 1, 1973, see the "List of Sections Affected, 1949-1963 and 1964-1972," published in three separate volumes.

1973

8 CFR — 38 FR Page

Chapter I

1.1 (l) added.... 8590
100.4 (c)(3) amended.... 5996
(a) revised; (d) amended.... 16632
(a), (b), and (c) (2) and (3) amended.... 16855, 16856
(c)(2) amended.... 17713, 29877
(c)(2) corrected.... 19907
Republished.... 34183
103.1 (e)(12a) added.... 8237
Effective date extended.... 14261
(c) revised.... 8590
(e)(12) revised.... 19812
(e-1) added.... 34188
Revised.... 35294
103.2 (b)(1) amended.... 8590
103.7 revised.... 6806
(b)(1) amended.... 8238, 19812
Effective date extended.... 14261
Revised.... 35296
103.10 Revised.... 6806
204.1 (a) and (c)(1) amended.... 7791
204.2 (d)(1) amended.... 3187
(e-1) added.... 7791
204.4 (a) and (b) revised.... 7791
204.5 (a)(1) and (b) revised.... 7791
205.1 (a) and (b) revised.... 7792
211.1 (b)(2) amended.... 8238
Effective date extended.... 14261
211.3 Heading revised; text amended.... 8238
Effective date extended.... 14261
212.1 (a) and (e)(1) revised.... 18868
(e)(1) corrected.... 21172
212.7 (b)(2)(i) revised.... 16632
212.8 (b)(4) revised.... 1380, 8590

8 CFR—Continued — 38 FR Page

Chapter I—Continued

214.2 (h)(7) revised; (h)(8) redesignated as (h)(12); new (h)(8), (9), (10), and (11) added.... 8591
(c)(1) revised.... 14962, 24891
(c)(1) amended.... 17198, 18631
(c)(1) corrected.... 26354
Revised.... 35425
214.4 (a) revised.... 8591
223.2 Revised.... 19812
223a Added.... 8238
Effective date extended.... 14261
234 Revised.... 33061
234.1 Corrected.... 34315
235.10 Revised.... 16856
236.3 (e) added.... 8239
Effective date extended.... 14261
238.3 (b) amended.... 16632, 19812, 24891, 33062
238.4 Amended.... 3188, 33062, 34188
245.1 (g)(1) revised.... 18361
245.2 (a)(1) CFR correction.... 11340
(a)(2) revised.... 18361
(a)(3) revised.... 33062
245.6 Revised.... 33062
264.1 (b) amended; (f) revised.... 8591
265 Revised.... 33062
299.1 Table amended.... 1380, 3188, 8239, 8592, 14261, 19813, 29877
Table corrected.... 30735
299.3 Revised.... 21995
Effective date extended to March 1, 1974.... 34727
312.3 Revised.... 8592
316a.2 Amended.... 3188, 16632, 29878
316a.3 Amended.... 29878
316a.4 Amended.... 16633

Illustration E

List of CFR Sections Affected in *CFR* Title 8, "Aliens and Nationality", cumulating changes since January 1, 1973.

tions of the *C.F.R.* which incorporate or cite them. They list the executive documents by date, number and *Federal Register* citation, indicate their subject, provide the relevant *C.F.R.* reference, and then add a comment indicating whether the document has been cited, codified, amended, quoted, interpreted or applied in the *Code* section. This arrangement can be seen in the table covering executive orders (Illustration G).

Table I—Authorities

33 U.S.C.—Continued	CFR
	40 Parts 6, 15, 30, 33, 35, 104, 108, 110, 112, 116, 117, 122-125, 129, 133, 136, 403, 435
1251	40 Parts 25, 35, 113, 116, 117, 124, 125, 401, 405-412, 414-428, 430-434, 436, 439, 443, 446, 447, 454, 457-460
	46 Part 542
1251 note	40 Parts 133, 136
1254	40 Parts 12, 40, 45, 46
1255	40 Part 40
1256	40 Part 35
1257—1258	40 Part 40
1259—1260	40 Part 45
1261	40 Parts 45, 401
1263	40 Part 40
1281 et seq	40 Part 39
1288	7 Part 634
	40 Part 35
1311	40 Parts 401, 405-432, 434, 436, 439, 440, 443, 446, 447, 454, 455, 457-460
1313	40 Part 120
1314	40 Parts 401, 405-432, 434, 436, 439, 440, 443, 446, 447, 454, 455, 457-460
1316	40 Parts 401, 405-412, 414-425, 427-432, 439, 443, 446, 447, 454, 457-460
1317	40 Parts 128, 401, 405-432, 443, 446, 447, 454, 457, 458, 460
1318	40 Parts 2, 413
1319	40 Part 413
1320	40 Part 414
1321	33 Parts 25, 153, 154, 156
	40 Parts 112, 114, 1510
	43 Part 29
	46 Parts 542, 543
1322	33 Parts 1, 159
	40 Parts 140, 413
1325	40 Part 413
1326	40 Parts 401, 409
1341	40 Part 413
1342	40 Part 133
1344	33 Parts 221, 320, 323, 325-327
	40 Parts 230, 231
1345	40 Parts 133, 257
1361	40 Parts 2, 35, 100, 112, 114, 133, 230, 423, 429
1365	40 Part 135
1367	29 Part 24
1369	40 Parts 2, 100
1372	29 Parts 1, 5
1412	40 Parts 220-225, 227-229
1413	33 Parts 320, 324-327
1414	40 Parts 2, 223
1415	40 Part 22
1417	40 Part 223
1418	40 Parts 2, 220-229
1504	33 Part 148
1509	33 Parts 148-150

33 U.S.C.—Continued	CFR
	46 Parts 54, 56, 110, 197
1520	49 Part 106
1601—1608	32 Part 706
1605	32 Parts 701, 720, 722, 728, 730, 737, 750, 755, 757
1606	33 Part 707
1607	33 Part 80
1655	33 Part 66
2071	33 Parts 84, 85
34 U.S.C.	
App. 1123d	46 Part 310
35 U.S.C.	
6	15 Parts 370, 379
	37 Parts 1-5
10	37 Parts 1, 2
23	37 Part 1
25	37 Parts 1, 2
26	37 Part 1
31—32	37 Parts 1, 2
41—42	37 Parts 1, 2
111—119	37 Part 1
121	37 Part 1
122	37 Part 3
131—134	37 Part 1
135	37 Parts 1, 3
141—142	37 Part 1
145—146	37 Part 1
151	37 Part 1
161—162	37 Part 1
164	37 Part 1
171	37 Part 1
181—188	15 Parts 370, 379
	37 Part 5
183	10 Parts 780, 782
207	14 Part 1245
208	14 Part 1245
251	37 Part 1
254	37 Part 1
256	37 Part 1
261	37 Part 1
266	38 Part 1
36 U.S.C.	
121	32 Part 536
123—125	36 Part 401
123	36 Parts 402, 403
124	45 Part 2101
138b	32 Part 536
201—208	32 Part 842
37 U.S.C.	
101	32 Part 733
209	32 Part 110
251 et seq	32 Part 59
351—354	33 Part 49
401	32 Part 733
403	32 Part 733
551—558	32 Part 718
	38 Part 17
601—604	32 Parts 725, 726
701 et seq	32 Part 59
701—706	32 Part 59
704	37 Part 201

Illustration F

Table showing *U.S. Code* sections as authority for federal regulations, in *CFR* "Index and Finding Aids" volume for Jan. 1, 1982.

Finding Aids — **Table II—Presidential Documents**

E. O. No.	Date	F.R. Citation	Subject	Reference	Comment
	1975 (Con.)	**39 F.R.**			
11834	Jan. 15	2971	Energy Research and Development Administration and Nuclear Regulatory Commission; activation.	41 CFR 9-9 App. A	Cited in text.
11838	Feb. 6	5743	Labor-management relations in the Federal service; amending E.O. 11491 as amended by E.O.s 11616 and 11636.	5 CFR Part 2411	Cited as authority and in text.
				Part 2413	Cited as authority.
				Part 2471	Cited as authority.
				29 CFR Parts 201–206	Cited as authority.
				Part 201	Cited in text.
11839	Feb. 15	7351	Career service; amending Civil Service rules to except certain positions in Regional offices.	5 CFR 6, 8, 9.11	Codified.
11846	Mar. 27	14291	Trade Agreements Program administration	15 CFR Ch. XX, App. A	Cited in text.
				Part 1300	Cited as authority.
				Parts 2001–2003	Cited as authority and in text.
				Parts 2006–2007	Cited as authority.
11856	May 7	20259	Career service; amending the Civil Service rules to except certain positions.	5 CFR 9.11	Codified.
11887	Nov. 4	51411	Amending the Civil Service rules to except certain positions from the career service.	5 CFR 6.8	Codified.

Illustration G

Presidential Documents cited as authority for *CFR* sections, Table in Finding Aids volume of *CFR*, as of Jan. 1, 1976.

U.S. Statutes to Presidential Documents: It is often very important to establish the relationships between particular Presidential documents and the statutes which are cited as their authority. Through 1970 the five-year cumulations of Title 3 of the *Code of Federal Regulations* contained a series of tables entitled "Statutes Cited as Authority for Presidential Documents" which provided these parallel references both from the *Statutes at Large* and the *U.S. Code.* These tables listed citations to all such statutes opposite the appropriate executive orders, proclamations, or other executive texts which cited them as authority. Although these tables did not appear in the annual cumulations from 1971 to 1973, they were reinstated in 1974 and now appear in current cumulations of Title 3 of the *C.F.R.* See Illustrations H and I for sample pages of these tables.

The reverse process, *Presidential Documents to U.S. Code,* that is, from the Presidential documents which implement particular federal statutes to their statutory source in the *U.S. Code,* is provided in Table VI to VIII of the *U.S. Code.*[19] See Illustration J for a sample of Table VI, covering Executive Orders.

C.F.R. to U.S. Statute: Although tables are not available for these important cross references, the same purpose is served by *Authority* notes throughout the *Code of Federal Regulations,* which indicate the statutory sources for each section of regulations. These notes appear either as footnotes following each section or as an introductory note before a series of related sections.

3. FEDERAL REGISTER SYSTEM RESEARCH PROCEDURE

A search in the *Federal Register* and *Code of Federal Regulations* for the latest administrative regulations on a particular topic would ordinarily cover the following steps:

(a) Use of the general index to the *Code of Federal Regulations* or the commercial C.I.S. publication, *Index to the Code of Federal Regulations,* referred to above, in order to ascertain the appropriate title and sections of the *Code* for that subject. One might refer to the *Thesaurus of Indexing Terms,* described on page 343 above, to be sure that the most appropriate search words were used.

(b) Examination of the text of the designated regulations in the last revised volumes of *Code* titles.

(c) Inspection of the last monthly pamphlet of the *List of CFR Sections Affected* to determine whether the relevant sections have been affected by later changes. These pamphlets cumulate changes back to the last published volume of each *C.F.R.* title.

19. Table VI—Executive Orders; Table VII—Proclamations; and Table VIII—Reorganization Plans.

Table 5—STATUTES CITED AS AUTHORITY FOR PRESIDENTIAL DOCUMENTS

EDITORIAL NOTE: Statutes which were cited as authority for the issuance of Presidential documents signed during 1981 and published in the Federal Register are listed under one or both of these headings:

United States Statutes at Large
United States Code

Most citations have been set forth in the style in which they appear in the documents and without change; however, where the reference was to the public law only, available citations to volumes of the Statutes and Code have been added. Since the form of the citation varies from document to document, users of this table should search under both headings for pertinent references.

United States Statutes at Large

Date	Citation	Title of Act	Document
1878			
....	Sec. 202, Revised Statutes.	Foreign Service	EO 12293.
1928			
May 18........	45 Stat. 617, amended by 73 Stat. 627.	Child Health Day	Proc. 4862.
1933			
May 12........	48 Stat. 31, sec. 22; added by 49 Stat 773.	Agricultural Adjustment Act.	Procs. 4835, 4887.
1945			
July 31.........	Sec. 2(b)2, 82 Stat. 48......	Export-Import Bank Act of 1945.	Memorandums of May 20 and Sept. 4, 1981.
Aug. 11........	59 Stat. 530, amended by 84 Stat. 914.	National Employ the Handicapped Week.	Proc. 4868.
1946			
Aug. 13........	60 Stat. 999, sec. 805; added by 90 Stat. 835.	Foreign Service Act of 1946.	EO 12272.
1947			
July 26.........	61 Stat. 495, as amended.	National Security Act of 1947.	EO 12333.
1948			
June 30........	62 Stat. 1155, sec. 313; added by 86 Stat. 875.	Federal Water Pollution Control Act.	EO 12327.

295

Illustration H

Statutes at Large cited as authority for Presidential Documents, Table in Title 3 of *C.F.R.*, as of January 1, 1982.

United States Code

Title and Section No.	Document
3 U.S.C. 301	Proc. 4887; EO's 12263, 12268, 12276, 12277, 12278, 12279, 12280, 12281, 12282, 12283, 12284, 12293, 12294, 12297, 12318, 12321, 12328.
5 U.S.C. app	EO's 12307, 12308, 12310, 12318.
5 U.S.C. 3301	EO 12300.
5 U.S.C. 3302	EO 12300.
5 U.S.C. 5561 note	EO's 12268, 12313.
7 U.S.C. 624	Procs. 4835, 4887.
7 U.S.C. 1736f-1	EO 12266.
8 U.S.C. 1157	Memorandum of Oct. 10, 1981.
8 U.S.C. 1182(f)	Proc. 4865; EO 12324.
8 U.S.C. 1185(a)(1)	Proc. 4865; EO 12324.
10 U.S.C. ch. 47	EO's 12306, 12315.
12 U.S.C. 635(2)(b)(2)	Memorandums of May 20 and Sept. 4, 1981.
12 U.S.C. 1904 note	EO 12288.
15 U.S.C. 751 et seq	EO 12287.
18 U.S.C. 437(b)	EO 12328.
19 U.S.C. 1821	Proc. 4888.
19 U.S.C. 2101 et seq	Memorandum of June 2, 1981.
19 U.S.C. 2134	Proc. 4889.
19 U.S.C. 2135	Procs. 4817, 4876.
19 U.S.C. 2461 et seq	EO's 12267, 12302, 12311.
19 U.S.C. 2462	EO 12302.
19 U.S.C. 2483	Procs. 4817, 4876, 4889; EO's 12267, 12302, 12311.
22 U.S.C. 1065	EO 12272.
22 U.S.C. 1732	EO's 12276, 12277, 12278, 12279, 12280, 12281, 12282, 12283, 12284, 12294.
22 U.S.C. 2151 et seq	Memorandums of Apr. 14, July 8, and Sept. 28, 1981.
22 U.S.C. 2318	Memorandums of Jan. 16 and Mar. 5, 1981.
22 U.S.C. 2321i(f)	EO 12321.
22 U.S.C. 2364	Memorandums of May 13 and June 9, 1981.
22 U.S.C. 2656	EO 12293.
22 U.S.C. 2753(a)(1)	Memorandums of Feb. 27 and Nov. 23, 1981.
22 U.S.C. 2769	EO 12321.
22 U.S.C. 3901 et seq	EO's 12292, 12293.
22 U.S.C. 4067	EO 12289.
31 U.S.C. 581c	EO 12318.
33 U.S.C. 1323	EO 12327.
36 U.S.C. 142a	Proc. 4845.
36 U.S.C. 153	Proc. 4858.
36 U.S.C. 161	Proc. 4847.
36 U.S.C. 163	Proc. 4874.
36 U.S.C. 169c	Proc. 4871.
36 U.S.C. 169d	Proc. 4863.
36 U.S.C. 169g	Proc. 4842.
36 U.S.C. 143	Proc. 4862.
36 U.S.C. 155	Proc. 4868.
36 U.S.C. 159	Proc. 4858.
36 U.S.C. 160	Proc. 4839.
36 U.S.C. 162	Proc. 4836.
36 U.S.C. 165	Proc. 4824.
36 U.S.C. 166	Proc. 4839.

Illustration I

U.S. Code cited as authority for Presidential Documents, Table in Title 3 *C.F.R.*, as of January 1, 1982.

TABLE VI—EXECUTIVE ORDERS

This Table lists the Executive Orders that implement general and permanent law as contained in the United States Code.

Exec. Ord.		U.S.C.		
Date	No.	Title	Sec.	Status
1943				
Oct. 4	9384	31	21 nt	Elim.
1951				
May 8	10242	50 App.	2253 nt	Elim.
1953				
Aug. 14	10480	50 App.	2153 nt	
Oct. 15	10494	50 App.	2101 nt	Elim.
1954				
Apr. 23	10529	50 App.	2251 nt	Elim.
June 9	10536	49	1723 nt	Elim.
29	10540	5	6301 nt	Elim.
Sept. 13	10560	7	1691 nt	Elim.
14	10561	5	1302 nt	Elim.
1955				
June 22	10616	10	5751 nt	Elim.
Aug. 31	10634	50 App.	2092 nt	Elim.
1956				
Oct. 29	10685	7	1691 nt	Elim.
1957				
Apr. 17	10705	47	606 nt	Elim.
June 27	10718	22	4219 nt	
1958				
July 1	10773	47	606 nt	Elim.
		50 App.	2092 nt	Elim.
			2101 nt	
			2253 nt	
			2271 nt	Elim.
Aug. 20	10779	42	7401 nt	Elim.
Sept. 6	10782	47	606 nt	Elim.
		50 App.	2092 nt	Elim.
			2101 nt	
			2253 nt	
			2271 nt	Elim.
1960				
Feb. 20	10866	22	288 nt	Elim.
Nov. 28	10893	22	2382 nt	Elim.
1961				
Jan. 5	10900	7	1691 nt	Elim.
May 19	10943	22	288 nt	Elim.
July 20	10952	50 App.	2271 nt	Elim.
Nov. 6	10973	22	2381 nt	Elim.
1962				
Jan. 18	10988	5	7101 nt	Elim.
Sept. 27	11051	50 App.	2271 nt	Elim.
1963				
Nov. 1	11126	42	2000e nt	Elim.
1964				
Apr. 8	11151	10	5770 nt	Elim.
Nov. 23	11189	5	5317 nt	Elim.
1965				
Jan. 4	11191	47	721 nt	Elim.
30	11195	5	5317 nt	Elim.
Mar. 25	11209	40 App.	101 nt	Elim.
May 6	11221	42	2000e nt	Elim.
1966				
May 26	11282	42	7418 nt	Elim.
Aug. 10	11296	33	701 nt	Elim.
Oct. 14	11312	22	2459 nt	Elim.
1967				
Jan. 5	11322	22	287c	Elim.
Mar. 5	11330	42	nt prec. 2711.	
Nov. 28	11382	23	313 nt	Elim.
		33	981 nt, 1051 nt	Elim.
		49	1723 nt	Elim.
		50	401 nt	Elim.
1968				
June 24	11415	50 App.	454 nt	Elim.
July 29	11419	22	287c nt	Elim.
Dec. 2	11437	10	5751 nt	Elim.
1969				
Jan. 17	11449	19	1356h nt	Elim.
19	11451	5	4103 nt	Elim.
Mar. 20	11460	50	403 nt	Elim.
Sept. 22	11482	29	171 nt	Elim.
Oct. 28	11490	50 App.	2251 nt	
29	11491	5	7101 nt	
1970				
Feb. 4	11507	42	7401, 7418 nts	Elim.
27	11512	40	490 nt	Elim.
June 4	11533	50 App.	2403 nt	Elim.
	11534	18	nt prec. 1	Elim.
Aug. 29	11554	10	5707 nt	Elim.
Sept. 4	11556	47	305, 606, 721 nts	Elim.
Dec. 31	11557	42	nt prec. 4411.	Elim.
1971				
Feb. 24	11583	20	2982 nt	
May 26	11595	20	2982 nt	
June 30	11603	22	2501 nt	Elim.
Aug. 26	11616	5	7101 nt	
Dec. 17	11636	5	7101 nt	

Illustration J

Table VI—Executive Orders to *U.S. Code* sections in Tables volumes of *U.S. Code.*

(d) Examination of the cumulated *List of CFR Parts Affected* in the most recent issue of the *Federal Register.* This list indicates changes during the current month and updates the monthly *C.F.R.* pamphlet referred to in step (c) above.

(e) Using the *Federal Register* citations found through the searches in steps (c) and (d), the relevant changes must then be checked in the issue of the *Federal Register* itself to assure the accuracy of the references and to evaluate the substance of the changes.

(f) Using Shepard's *Code of Federal Regulations Citations,* verify the current status of the regulation.

Alternatively, one might shortcut this somewhat cumbersome process by using a commercial looseleaf service covering the field dealt with by the regulation, after it was identified. One might also make the search in a computerized legal research service. If either of those procedures were used, however, it would still be advisable to follow steps (d), (e) and (f) to be sure that the looseleaf or computer service had been currently updated.

4. SPECIAL PUBLICATIONS OF AGENCY REGULATIONS

a. Official Agency Publications

Although the *Federal Register* and the *Code of Federal Regulations* are the primary official sources, many agencies also issue their own texts of their rules and regulations. Some are designed solely for agency use, but many are published and distributed directly, or through the Government Printing Office. These compilations are designed to provide a convenient and inexpensive text of the agency's regulations, without the necessity of using the cumbersome *Federal Register* system. They are sometimes supplemented by relevant statutes and other documents which may not be in the *Register.* However, these publications can be used as reliable substitutes for the *Register* and the *C.F.R.* only if they are promptly updated. Although some appear in looseleaf format and are supplemented by regular transmittal sheets, none of them actually reflect changes as fast as they appear in the *Federal Register.* One of the best of these compilations is the Internal Revenue Service's *Regulations* which have been issued in five comprehensive series since 1961. Unfortunately, transmittal sheets for such services are generally issued at least two weeks *after* the appearance of the changes in the *Federal Register,* which, therefore, must still be checked to obtain the latest information. The Securities and Exchange Commission has published biennial revisions of its rules and regulations, but they are not kept up-to-date during the year. Information as to the availability of these editions can be obtained from the *Monthly Catalog of Government Publications.*

b. Unofficial Sources

As indicated above, commercially published looseleaf services offer one of the best sources of agency rules and regulations. These publications, are usually issued for particular areas of regulation (e.g., labor relations, securities, taxation, etc.), and invariably focus on the work of the particular administrative agency regulating that field. They provide currently supplemented and well annotated texts of both the substantive regulations and the rules of practice and procedure of that agency. More detailed coverage of these tools is provided in Chapter 13, and Appendix D, at the end of this volume, contains a list of sources of federal regulatory agency rules, regulations and adjudications, indicating both official and unofficial sources for the regulations and decisions of major agencies. These sources include *CFR* locations, official agency reports, computer data bases, and looseleaf services which incorporate both regulations and decisions.

Pike and Fischer's *Administrative Law Service* (2nd Series, 1951–date)[20] collects materials on the procedural aspects of administrative practice before the government agencies. In addition to publishing many decisions on agency procedures, the service also compiles the current rules of practice of nine federal agencies. It does not include, however, their substantive regulations.

The *U.S. Code Congressional and Administrative News* [21] is a useful compendium of current statutes, legislative documents and related news. It also includes a small selection of important administrative rules and regulations, Presidential proclamations and executive orders and reorganization plans.

Legal Times and *U.S. Law Week* also publish selections of important regulations.

5. CITATORS FOR RULES AND REGULATIONS

In order to ascertain the current status of regulations and their treatment in the courts, the use of citators is an important part of research in these documents. Since 1979, Shepard's has published a separate citator expressly for this purpose. Shepard's *Code of Federal Regulations Citations* currently traces the judicial treatment of *CFR* sections, as well as of Presidential proclamations, executive orders and reorganization plans that have been cited by the Courts. That citator does not, however, indicate when regulations have been amended or repealed by the agency. Illustration K shows a typical page from *Shepard's CFR Citations* and Illustration L shows the abbreviations used to describe particular actions in that citator. In addition, other topical Shepard's citators list agency regulations as *cited* material and thus enable one to Shepardize them. These include Shepard's *Federal Tax Citations, Bankruptcy Citations, Federal*

20. Matthew Bender & Co., 1951 to 1953; Pike & Fischer, Inc., 1954 to date.

21. West Publishing Co., 1939 to date.

Energy Law Citations, Immigration and Naturalization Citations, Occupational Safety and Health Citations, and *United States Patents and Trademarks Citations.*

There are also several other ways of accomplishing some of the functions of a citator, which should be noted: (a) The *Lists of CFR Sections Affected* of the *Federal Register* and the *Code of Federal Regulations,* as shown above, offer a citator service for recent changes in the text of the regulations themselves. (b) If the regulation or Presidential document in question has been cited directly with a related federal statute, the statute can be Shepardized under its *U.S. Code* or *Statutes at Large* citation in Shepard's Citations. (c) Looseleaf services covering enactments of particular agencies will indicate current changes in the text and form of their regulations and often cite decisions of courts and administrative tribunals which have applied or construed them. See Appendix D for list of relevant looseleaf services. (d) *Tables of Statutes Construed* appearing in the volumes and advance sheets of the National Reporter System list those judicial decisions which have construed Presidential documents and administrative regulations.

D. DECISIONS OF THE FEDERAL ADMINISTRATIVE AGENCIES

1. OFFICIAL REPORTS

Among the functions of every administrative agency is the exercise of judicial power in determining cases and questions arising under its statutes and regulations. These adjudications usually involve a fact finding process and the application of the law as contained in the agency's statute and regulations to the particular situation or problem. Agency decisions may follow lengthy formal hearings or consist of direct rulings on submitted inquiries. During the 1930's and 1940's these tribunals and their hearings were under strong attack from many quarters as to their fairness, efficiency and procedural rules. There was also a feeling that many agencies which were not then preparing or publishing their decisions should do so in order to inform the public and the bar of their policies, standards and authorities.[22] The resulting pressure for legislative reform culminated in the Administrative Procedure Act of 1946 and the Freedom of Information Act, both cited above.[23] The former Act strengthened procedural safeguards, established minimum standards to assure fairer hearings and added to the required legal publications of the agencies. The latter improved public access to information and documents.

22. Final Report of the Attorney General's Committee on Administrative Procedure (1941) at pp. 29–30.

23. Op. cit., supra notes 11 and 12. For background and analysis of the former Act, see Administrative Procedure Act, Legislative History, Sen.Doc. 248, 79th Congress (1946) and the Attorney General's Manual on the Administrative Procedure Act (1947). On the latter, see Attorney General's Memorandum on the Public Information Section of the Administrative Procedure Act (U.S. Dept. of Justice, June 1967).

TITLE 13 **CODE OF FEDERAL REGULATIONS**

§316.7(a)(1)(ii)(B)
429FS1090 *1976
429FS1099 *1976

§316.8(b)
429FS1100 *1976
435FS1054 *1976

§316.8(c)
429FS1100 *1976

§316.9(a)
429FS1091 *1976

§316.9(b)
429FS1091 *1976

§316.9(c)
435FS1059 *1976

§316.9(f)
429FS1091 *1976

§316.10
428FS1168 *1976

§316.10(a)
429FS1100 *1976

§316.10(a)(1)
431FS120 *1977

§316.10(a)(1)(i)(C)
Va435FS1057 *1976

§316.10(a)(2)
431FS120 *1977

§316.10(a)(2)(i)
429FS1100 *1976
435FS1054 *1976

§316.10(a)(2)(i)(A)
428FS1168 *1976
431FS120 *1977
435FS1060 *1976

§316.10(a)(2)(i)(B)
428FS1168 *1976
429FS1091 *1976
431FS120 *1977
435FS1060 *1976

§316.10(a)(2)(i)(C)
428FS1168 *1976
429FS1101 *1976
431FS120 *1977

§316.10(a)(2)(i)(D)
428FS1168 *1976
429FS1103 *1976
431FS120 *1977

§316.10(a)(2)(ii)
428FS1168 *1976
429FS1100 △1977
431FS120 *1977

§316.10(a)(2)(ii)(A)
429FS1102 *1976
431FS120 *1977

§316.10(a)(2)(ii)(B)
431FS120 *1977

§316.10(a)(2)(ii)(C)
431FS120 *1977

§316.10(a)(2)(ii)(D)
429FS1103 *1976
431FS120 *1977

§316.10(a)(2)(iii)
431FS120 *1977

§316.10(a)(3)
431FS121 *1977
C435FS1058 *1976

§316.10(a)(3)(i)
429FS1100 *1976

§316.10(a)(3)(ii)
429FS1100 *1976

§316.10(a)(3)(iii)
429FS1100 *1976
431FS121 *1977

§316.10(b)
435FS1060 *1976

§316.14
435FS1059 *1976

§316.14(b)
435FS1059 *1976

Part 317
65LE909 *1978
100SC2762 *1978
441FS958 △1977
468FS885 *1978
489FS602 △1980
64Ap2d758 *1978
81Il2d303 *1978
Ill
410NE46 *1978
NY
407S2d448 *1978

§317.1
et seq.
570F2d116 *1977

§317.15(e)
Va578F2d559 *1977

§317.17(b)
441FS967 △1977

§317.19
65LE918 *1978
100SC2770 *1978
439FS854 △1977
441FS969 △1977

§317.19(b)
C441FS941 △1977
U441FS958 △1977
442FS396 △1977
443FS256 *1978
444FS1031 *1978
444FS1173 *1978
450FS345 *1978
C452FS1018 *1978

§317.19(b)(1)
U441FS961 △1977

§317.19(b)(2)
U441FS960 △1977
450FS359 *1978

§317.31(a)
571F2d1321 *1977

§317.53(d)
578F2d563 *1977

§317.55(e)
571F2d1319 *1977
578F2d563 *1977

§317.55(f)
571F2d1319 *1977
578F2d563 *1977

§317.99
450FS358 *1978

§375.26
NY
408S2d832 △1978

TITLE 14

132FS876 △1955
268FS601 △1967
271FS793 △1964
349FS305 △1972
205Neb122 △1979
Nebr
286NW442 △1979

Part 1
et seq.
635F2d146 △1980

§1.0
et seq.
346F2d143 *1961

Parts 1 to 399
Tex
545SW759 *1976

Parts 1 to 199
490FS909 △1980
27ARF157n △1976

Parts 1 to 171
26C3d94 △1979
Calif
160CaR736 △1979
603P2d1332 △1979

Part 1
361F2d918 △1966

§1.1
et seq.
261FS510 △1966
417FS483 △1975

§1.1
416F2d121 △1969
489F2d796 △1973
497F2d372 △1974
500F2d292 △1974
502F2d800 △1974
512F2d1310 △1975
540F2d384 △1976
543F2d494 *1976
297FS209 △1968
318FS918 △1970
377FS206 △1974
378FS1150 △1974
420FS1346 △1976
422FS1173 △1975
429FS845 △1977
455FS226 *1975
Fla
382So2d353 △1980
Tex
545SW759 *1976
595SW561 *1978
27ARF158n △1976
Commercial
operator
C635F2d148 △1980
Colo
623P2d377 △1981
Maintenance
46OrA20 △1980
Ore
610P2d306 △1980
Operate
623F2d626 △1980
Rating
Tex
545SW759 *1976

§1.2
416F2d121 △1969

§1.68
361F2d918 △1966

§§2.31 to 2.35
547F2d955 *1974

§3.74
251FS396 △1965

§3.75
251FS396 △1965

§3.76
251FS397 △1965

§4b.300
264FS677 △1967

§4b.409
264FS677 *1959

Part 8
361F2d918 △1966

§8.32
361F2d918 △1966

§8.33
361F2d918 △1966

* followed by a year refers to the CFR edition, if cited. If not cited,
△ followed by a year indicates the date of the citing reference

110

Illustration K

A typical page in Shepard's *Code of Federal Regulations Citations.*

ABBREVIATIONS—ANALYSIS

C.F.R., Executive Orders, Proclamations, Reorganization Plans

App.	Appendix	St.	Statute at Large
C	Constitutional	U	Unconstitutional
Ch.	Chapter	Up	Unconstitutional in part
No.	Number	V	Void or invalid
p.	page	Va	Valid
P.L.	Public Law	Vp	Void or invalid in part
§	Section		

Proclamations, Reorganization Plans

A	(amended)	Provision amended.
Ad	(added)	New section added.
E	(extended)	Existing provision extended in its application to a later provision or allowance of additional time for performance of duties required by a provision within a limited time.
L	(limited)	Existing provision declared not to be extended in their application to a later provision.
R	(repealed)	Abrogation of an existing provision.
Re-en	(re-enacted)	Provision re-enacted.
Rn	(renumbered)	Renumbering of existing sections.
Rp	(repealed in part)	Abrogation of part of an existing provision.
Rs	(repealed and superseded)	Abrogation of an existing provision and substitution of new legislation therefor.
Rv	(revised)	Provision revised.
S	(superseded)	Substitution of new provision for an existing provision not expressly abrogated.
Sd	(suspended)	Provision suspended.
Sdp	(suspended in part)	Provision suspended in part.
Sg	(supplementing)	New matter added to an existing provision.
Sp	(superseded in part)	Substitution of new legislation for part of an existing provision not expressly abrogated.

Illustration L

List of abbreviations and symbols used in Shepard's *Code of Federal Regulations Citations.*

Most federal agencies write formal opinions to justify or explain their decisions and these are often published in both official and unofficial editions. These opinions are very much like those issued by courts, both in form and method of publication. Many of the agencies publish official reports in various preliminary forms such as releases, printed slip decisions and advance pamphlets. These are then cumulated, usually after a considerable time lag, as permanent bound volumes in numbered series. They often contain indexes, digests and tables.

Although most of the agencies do not consider themselves strictly bound by their prior decisions under the doctrine of stare decisis, the decisions do have considerable precedential value within an agency and for attorneys practicing before it. The Attorney General's Committee on Administrative Procedure in 1941 found that many agencies felt they were following the usual practice of appellate courts in this regard.[24] Reports of agencies' decisions thus are an important and often cited area of legal bibliography. Over thirty federal agencies, including all of the major regulatory commissions, publish official reports of their decisions and many issue preliminary texts as well. For information about the availability of these publications, see the *Monthly Catalog of Government Publications.* Appendix D, as noted above, lists most of the official reports.

2. UNOFFICIAL PUBLICATIONS

In addition to the various official reports, the decisions of many agencies are also published regularly by commercial publishers, either in looseleaf services or in numbered series of bound volumes. There are probably as many unofficial reporters of agency decisions as there are official editions. Examples of such looseleaf services are the B.N.A. *Labor Relations Reference Manual,* the C.C.H. *Trade Regulation Reporter,* and the tax reporters issued by Commerce Clearing House and Prentice-Hall. Looseleaf editions have several advantages over the official report—they are issued to subscribers more quickly, better indexed, often supplemented by editorial discussion and other relevant source material, and many include a citator service. Announcements of the various publishers are the best source of information as to what services are available currently, and see Appendix D below for a listing as of this time. Chapter 13 offers a fuller discussion of these services and a subject list.

Pike and Fischer's *Administrative Law Service* also publishes a very comprehensive collection of the decisions of many agencies and courts relating to administrative practice. These decisions appear chronologically, first in looseleaf form and then in bound volumes.

There are a number of special subject or topical reporters primarily devoted to court decisions in particular subject areas. The central focus of these reporters, as with the looseleaf services, is usually an industry or area of law subject to federal regulation by an administrative agency. Therefore, a number of these reporters also regularly publish the decisions of the administrative agency or tribunal in that field, e.g. *Public Utilities Reports*[25] which includes, for example, Federal Energy Regulatory Commission decisions and Nuclear Regulatory Commission decisions, and the *U.S. Patents Quarterly*[26] which includes, among others, decisions of the Commissioner of Patents and the Patent Office Board of Appeals. These reporters are

24. Final Report, pp. 466–474.

25. Public Utilities Reports, Inc., 4th Series, 1974 to date.

26. Bureau of National Affairs, Inc., 1929 to date.

chronologically arranged and usually issue both advance parts and bound volumes.

3. CITATORS FOR AGENCY DECISIONS

Although citators are discussed in detail in Chapter 9 above, it should be noted here that some citators are available for decisions and rulings of the major administrative agencies. The most important of these is *Shepard's United States Administrative Citations*, which began in 1967, and offers a compilation of citations to decisions and orders of a number of federal administrative departments, courts, boards, and commissions. *Shepard's United States Citations; Patents and Trademarks* includes, as *cited* material, the *Reports of the Court of Customs and Patent Appeals*, the *Decisions of the Commissioner of Patents, U.S. Patents Quarterly* and litigated patents, copyrights, and trade-marks themselves. Since 1959, the *Decisions and Orders of the National Labor Relations Board* have appeared in the specialized *Shepard's Federal Labor Law Citations.*

In recent years, Shepard's has added several other new citators in special subject fields. As noted above in Section F of Chapter 9, these include *Shepard's Federal Energy Law Citations, Federal Occupational Safety and Health Citations, Federal Tax Citations, Immigration and Naturalization Citations*, and *Military Justice Citations.* Each of these citators includes as *cited* materials decisions and rulings of the administrative agencies and tribunals in its subject area. For example, *Federal Tax Citations* enables the researcher to *Shepardize* decisions of the U.S. Treasury and rulings of the Internal Revenue Service, as shown in Illustrations M and N respectively. Somewhat modified lists of abbreviations and symbols are used to signal specific actions by the citing material, as set forth in Illustrations O and P from that citator. The effectiveness of this coverage will be enhanced by their availability in the computerized legal research services, when that occurs.

In addition to Shepard's publications, some of the looseleaf services discussed above also perform a citator function for their administrative decisions. Among the best of these are the citators provided with the C.C.H. *Standard Federal Tax Reporter* and the Prentice-Hall *Federal Taxes.*

4. JUDICIAL DECISIONS RELATING TO ADMINISTRATIVE LAW

Since many of the actions and decisions of the federal administrative agencies are appealed to the federal courts or otherwise become the subject of litigation, a considerable amount of case law has developed around them. These decisions are of interest to researchers in this field since the courts may directly review agency actions, set legal standards, and determine policies and limitations on administrative activity. The court decisions are published in the law reports

No.2639 TREASURY DECISIONS, INTERNAL REVENUE

Sg IR2680
Sg IR2703
IR2718

2642
qIR2845

2646
sIR2590
IR2795

2649
sIR2744
IR2740

2650
48F2d457
9AF1144

2654
fIR2926

2655
IR2788

2659
285F409
287F926
2AF1788
2AF1890
IR2678
IR2700
IR2734
IR2736
IR2740
IR2763
IR3420

2661
(249F27)
IR2763
IR3420

2684
(251F49)
(1AF986)
sIR2448

2685
269US443
269US457
70LE356
46SC155
5AF5681
1UTC¶153
IR3249
IR3678

2686
(248F688)
(1AF918)
sIR2441

2688
E IR2871
L IR2926
IR2991

2689
R IR3848

2690
144FS625
50AF417
56UTC¶9606
337Mas212
Mass
148NE653
44TxL267

2706
IR2733
IR2755

2710
(250F1)
(1AF949)
IR3799

2713
sIR2257
350US383
350US390
100LE448
76SC421
25F2d562
106F2d179
319F2d170
6AF7555
23AF332
48AF693
11AF2d2054
1UTC¶305
39UTC¶9687
56UTC¶9319
63UTC¶
[15507

2716
A IR2759

2717
IR2788

2719
283US570
283US574
75LE1280
51SC602

2723
(247US179)
(62LE1054)
(38SC467)
(3AF2979)
(1UTC¶17)
IR2724
IR2725
IR2740
IR2744
IR3562
IR3881
IR3883
IR4258

2724
(247US189)
(62LE1061)
(38SC470)
(3AF2982)
IR2725
IR2740
IR3173
IR3667
IR3883
IR4165

2725
(247US195)
(62LE1064)
(38SC472)
(3AF2984)
IR2740
IR3173

2726
(247US165)
(62LE1049)
(38SC432)
(3AF2971)
IR3344
IR3420
dIR3461
fIR3609
IR3881
IR3883

2731
(247US339)
(62LE1149)
(38SC543)
(3AF2992)
(1UTC¶20)
IR2732
IR2740
IR3420
IR4217

2732
(247US347)
(62LE1152)
(38SC546)
(3AF2995)
(1UTC¶21)
IR2740
fIR3006
IR3052
IR3270

2733
IR2755

2734
j68F2d843
j13AF605
j4UTC¶1230

2735
91F2d218
19AF1097

2750
283US242
283US248
75LE1010
51SC402
9AF1425
2UTC¶705

2752
264F614
292F1011
94FS119
1AF1178
4AF3622
39AF1372
1UTC¶31
50UTC¶9509
IR3014

2752
¶ 1
264F614
1AF1178
1UTC¶31

2757
(252F758)

2760
A IR2767
IR2788

2763
287F926
2AF1890

2764
mIR2774

2765

2783
(248US71)
(63LE133)
(39SC35)
(3AF2997)
(1UTC¶23)
fIR3270
dIR3461
fIR3609

2788
251US279
271US358
281US619
64LE265
70LE976
74LE1075
40SC142
46SC533
50SC418
IR2827
IR2881
IR2888
IR2940
IR2946
Rp IR3583

2788
¶ 10
Subd. g
mIR2854

2788
¶ 12
mIR2912

2788
¶ 14
Subd. b
251US279
293US186
293US187
79LE268
79LE278
55SC130
55SC134
49F2d233
f51F2d428
52F2d349
69F2d854
9AF1310
f10AF260
10AF429
13AF885
14AF688
14AF694
35UTC¶9003
35UTC¶9005
IR2931
IR3146

2798
IR2799
IR2801

2800
A IR3156

2802
S IR3144
IR2878
IR2898
IR2905
IR3145
IR3227

2803
(256F964)
IR3507

Illustration M

Treasury Decisions as *cited* matter in Shepard's *Federal Tax Citations*, 1981 volume.

#73-270 REVENUE RULINGS

#73-270
R 78-2CuB
[266

#73-286
S 75-1CuB161

#73-305
m79-2CuB83

#73-310
e79-1CuB356

#73-333
d74-1CuB160

#73-339
e76-2CuB53

#73-342
S 78-2CuB259

#73-343
S 78-1CuB342

#73-350
R 75-2CuB
[289

#73-373
S 74-1CuB237

#73-400
S 74-2CuB361

#73-555
d76-1CuB125

#73-565
d77-2CuB82

#73-584
S 74-2CuB153

#73-593
d76-1CuB337

#73-599
m77-1CuB41

#74-21
m74-2CuB22

#74-23
m74-2CuB22

#74-33
m77-2CuB368

#74-38
e76-1CuB170
d79-2CuB238

#74-47
e77-1CuB329

#74-48
S 74-2CuB361

#74-346
m75-1CuB348
m75-2CuB434
m75-2CuB435

#74-407
e78-1CuB41

#74-433
m77-2CuB85

#74-464
m77-1CuB43
e74-2CuB380

#74-471
m74-2CuB200
e75-1CuB195

#74-485
m78-2CuB101

#74-486
e75-1CuB62

#74-499
e76-1CuB382

#74-535
S 78-1CuB450

#74-553
d76-2CuB150

#75-92
R 79-2CuB95

#75-120
e77-1CuB37

#75-121
e76-1CuB52

#75-152
S 79-2CuB210

#75-157
e76-1CuB129

#75-161
d79-2CuB145

#75-195
e77-2CuB67

#75-223
d77-2CuB106
e77-2CuB107

#75-239
R 78-1CuB
[292

#75-266
R 75-2CuB
[410

#75-273

#75-501
e76-1CuB52

#75-535
e77-1CuB344

#75-536
S 79-2CuB391

#75-545
d75-2CuB428

#75-557
e76-1CuB12

#75-561
m78-2CuB152
e78-2CuB146

#75-564
e79-1CuB262

#76-13
S 78-2CuB142

#76-25
d76-2CuB360

#76-28
m76-1CuB107

#76-42
d78-2CuB149

#76-214
d79-1CuB264

#76-215
e78-2CuB347

#76-242
m77-1CuB136
R 79-1CuB
[184

#76-264
d78-1CuB365
e79-1CuB363

#76-318
S 77-1CuB122

#76-323
e77-2CuB26

#76-334
d78-2CuB149

#76-352
e78-1CuB304

#76-423
m77-2CuB372

#76-468
e78-2CuB93

#76-488

#77-184
R 78-1CuB
[447

#77-185
e78-2CuB213

#77-189
R 78-2CuB
[266

#77-223
S 78-1CuB302

#77-232
e78-1CuB67

#77-290
e79-1CuB62

#77-294
e79-1CuB179

#77-301
d79-2CuB372

#77-316
d78-2CuB107

#77-363
m79-2CuB18

#77-405

#78-302
e78-2CuB96

#78-363
S 79-1CuB293

#78-371
d79-1CuB448

#79
S 76-1CuB54

#79-28
e79-2CuB279

#79-112
d79-2CuB379

#108
S 75-2CuB343

#130
S 72-1CuB45

#138
S 73-2CuB341

#147
S 75-2CuB402

#165
R 76-2CuB
[334

Illustration N

Revenue Rulings as *cited* matter in Shepard's *Federal Tax Citations*, 1981 volume.

ABBREVIATIONS—ANALYSIS

History of Case

a (affirmed)	Same case affirmed or enforced.
cc (connected case)	Different case from case cited but arising out of same subject matter or intimately connected therewith.
D (dismissed)	Same case or appeal therefrom dismissed.
m (modified)	Same case modified.
r (reversed)	Same case reversed or enforcement denied.
s (same case)	Same case as case cited.
S (superseded)	Substitution for former opinion.
v (vacated)	Same case vacated.
US cert den	Certiorari denied by U. S. Supreme Court.
US cert dis	Certiorari dismissed by U. S. Supreme Court.
US reh den	Rehearing denied by U. S. Supreme Court.
US reh dis	Rehearing dismissed by U. S. Supreme Court.

Treatment of Case

c (criticised)	Soundness of decision or reasoning in cited case criticised for reasons given.
d (distinguished)	Case at bar different either in law or fact from case cited for reasons given.
e (explained)	Statement of import of decision in cited case. Not merely a restatement of the facts.
f (followed)	Cited as controlling.
h (harmonized)	Apparent inconsistency explained and shown not to exist.
j (dissenting opinion)	Citation in dissenting opinion.
L (limited)	Refusal to extend decision of cited case beyond precise issues involved.
o (overruled)	Ruling in cited case expressly overruled.
p (parallel)	Citing case substantially alike or on all fours with cited case in its law or facts.
q (questioned)	Soundness of decision or reasoning in cited case questioned.

Form of Statute

Amend.	Amendment	Proc.	Proclamation
App.	Appendix	Pt.	Part
Art.	Article	Res.	Resolution
Ch.	Chapter	§	Section
Cl.	Clause	St.	Statutes at Large
Ex. Ord.	Executive Order	Subch.	Subchapter
H.C.R.	House Concurrent Resolution	Subcl.	Subclause
		Subd.	Subdivision
No.	Number	Sub ¶	Subparagraph
p	Page	Subsec.	Subsection
¶	Paragraph	T.	Title
P.L.	Public Law	Vet. Reg.	Veterans' Regulations
Pr.L.	Private Law		

xii

Illustration O

Abbreviations for case materials and form of statute, from Shepard's *Federal Tax Citations*, 1981 volume.

ABBREVIATIONS—ANALYSIS

Operation of Regulation or Order

A	(amended)	Regulation or order amended.
E	(extended)	Provisions of an existing regulation or order extended or amplified in scope.
L	(limited)	Provisions of a regulation or order declared not to be extended.
m	(modified)	Regulation or order modified.
R	(revoked or rescinded)	Existing regulation or order abrogated.
Rein	(reinstated)	Regulation or order reinstated.
Rn	(renumbered)	Existing article renumbered.
Rp	(revoked or rescinded in part)	Existing regulation or order abrogated in part.
Rv	(revised)	Regulation or order revised.
S	(superseded)	New regulation or order substituted for an existing one.
Sd	(suspended)	Regulation or order suspended.
Sdp	(suspended in part)	Regulation or order suspended in part.
Sg	(supplementing)	New matter added to an existing regulation or order.
Sp	(superseded in part)	New matter substituted for part of an existing regulation or order.

Operation of Statute

Legislative

A	(amended)	Statute amended.
Ad	(added)	New section added.
E	(extended)	Provisions of an existing statute extended in their application to a later statute, or allowance of additional time for performance of duties required by a statute within a limited time.
L	(limited)	Provisions of an existing statute declared not to be extended in their application to a later statute.
R	(repealed)	Abrogation of an existing statute.
Re-en	(re-enacted)	Statute re-enacted.
Rn	(renumbered)	Renumbering of existing sections.
Rp	(repealed in part)	Abrogation of part of an existing statute.
Rs	(repealed and superseded)	Abrogation of an existing statute and substitution of new legislation therefor.
Rv	(revised)	Statute revised.
S	(superseded)	Substitution of new legislation for an existing statute not expressly abrogated.
Sd	(suspended)	Statute suspended.
Sdp	(suspended in part)	Statute suspended in part.
Sg	(supplementing)	New matter added to an existing statute.
Sp	(superseded in part)	Substitution of new legislation for part of an existing statute not expressly abrogated.
Va	(validated)	

Judicial

C	Constitutional.	V	Void or invalid.
U	Unconstitutional.	Va	Valid.
Up	Unconstitutional in part.	Vp	Void or invalid in part.

xiii

Illustration P

Abbreviations for operation of regulations and statutes, from Shepard's *Federal Tax Citations*, 1981 volume.

discussed in Chapters 3 and 4 and are retrievable through the various finding tools described in Chapter 5. They also appear and are often digested in the special subject and topical reporters and looseleaf services described above.

Since work with administrative documents invariably leads into judicial case law on related topics, its may be helpful to refer again to the basic finding tools for this material. Bear in mind that, unless otherwise indicated, these case-finders do not usually refer to the decisions of administrative agencies, but only those of courts. The West Publishing Company's American Digest System began using the topic "Administrative Law and Procedure" in its 5th Decennial Digest and currently indexes and digests many judicial decisions under it. The other West digests have also incorporated this main title. The current digests to *American Law Reports* use the main topic "Administrative Law" for this purpose.

Each of the two leading legal encyclopedias has an extensive article on this subject: *Corpus Juris Secundum* under the title, "Public Administrative Bodies and Procedures" and *American Jurisprudence 2nd* under "Administrative Law". Both contain citations to many of the leading cases in the footnotes to their respective articles.

Some of the special subject reporters and topical services like Pike and Fischer's *Administrative Law Service* and *U.S. Patents Quarterly* report both court and agency decisions. Others like *American Maritime Cases* [27] contain only court decisions, although many of these relate to the law and practice of regulatory agencies in their fields.

Finally, we note again the new method of access to court decisions provided by the two computerized legal research services, LEXIS and WESTLAW, both of which now offer specialized data bases in fields of administrative law.

E. OTHER PUBLICATIONS OF AGENCIES

1. ANNUAL REPORTS

We have noted above some of the publications of administrative agencies related to law, particularly regulations and decisions. All of the agencies also issue annual reports which contain a great deal of information relating to their legal business. These may describe important litigations and list statistics concerning cases handled, prosecutions, settlements and dispositions. They often discuss or announce new enforcement policies, interpretations of agency statutes or proposed amendments. Investigations and decisions may be summarized and organizational changes noted. Reports of the regulatory agencies are also frequently helpful in their coverage of important developments in their respective fields or industries.[28] Occasionally

27. American Maritime Cases, Inc., 1923 to date.

28. E.g., The Annual Reports of the Civil Rights Commission have contained

an agency may use its annual report as the vehicle for a special review or history of its work.

2. SPECIAL REPORTS, BULLETINS AND STUDIES

In addition to publishing periodicals of general interest in their areas of activity,[29] many of the bureaus, commissions and other units, also issue special studies, reports and monographs on major problems. Sometimes these include compiled legislative histories of statutes which are to be enforced by the particular agency.[30] Two of the bureaus of the Department of Labor have regularly issued excellent bulletins and monographs in series [31] which often prove useful to lawyers and labor specialists.

3. INDEXES AND CATALOGS

The most comprehensive bibliographic listing of recent agency publications is the *Monthly Catalog of United States Government Publications.* Its annual indexes are still the best sources of information for government publications, including those in this field.[32] (See Illustration Q for a typical page from a monthly issue.) Many Departments and Bureaus distribute their own catalogs and lists from time to time. There are also many retrospective and historical indexes and catalogs of the older material.[33]

Access to many important government reports by their popular name is facilitated by the Library of Congress listing, *Popular Names of U.S. Government Reports* (3rd ed., 1976). A sample entry from this helpful popular name table is shown in Illustration R.

There are a variety of commercially published bibliographies and guides to government documents which provide access to administrative and executive publications by agency and subject, and often contain information on serial publications of existing agencies and on the often-elusive publications of now defunct agencies. Particularly useful among these are:

John L. Andriot, *Guide to U.S. Government Serials and Periodicals, 1959–72* (Documents Index, 1959–72).

major surveys of the state of civil liberties throughout the country.

29. See e.g., those listed in footnote 2 above at page 335.

30. The National Labor Relations Board has issued compilations of the legislative histories of the National Labor Relations Act of 1935 (1949), the Labor Management Relations Act of 1947 (1948), and the Labor Management Reporting and Disclosure Act of 1959 (1959), each in 2 volumes, which are classics of this type.

31. See, e.g., the safety bulletins and state law studies of the Bureau of Labor Standards; and the area wage surveys and the reports on "Labor Law and Practice" in various foreign countries, issued by the Bureau of Labor Statistics.

32. There are also decennial cumulative indexes for 1941–1950 and 1951–1960, and an index for 1971–1976.

33. See Schmeckebier & Eastin, *Government Publications and Their Use,* Chapter 1.

Federal Mediation and Conciliation Service

82-23386

FEM 1.209:720000-16

Flood insurance study : Rio Culebrinas Basin, Puerto Rico. — [Washington, D.C.?] : Federal Emergency Management Agency, 1982. ii, 20 p., 14 folded leaves of plates : ill., 1 map ; 28 cm. Cover title. "March 16, 1982." Includes bibliographical references. "Community number — 720000." ●Item 594-C-42 (microfiche) 1. Insurance, Flood — Puerto Rico. I. United States. Federal Emergency Management Agency. II. Title: Rio Culebrinas Basin, Puerto Rico. OCLC 08717645

82-23387

FEM 1.209:720000-17

Flood insurance study : Rio Blanco Basin, Puerto Rico. — [Washington, D.C.?] : Federal Emergency Management Agency, 1982. ii, 20 p., 12 folded leaves of plates : ill., 1 map ; 28 cm. Cover title. "March 16, 1982." Includes bibliographical references. "Community number — 720000." ●Item 594-C-42 (microfiche) 1. Insurance, Flood — Puerto Rico. I. United States. Federal Emergency Management Agency. II. Title: Rio Blanco Basin, Puerto Rico. OCLC 08722780

82-23388

FEM 1.209:300001, 300088, 300117

Flood insurance study : city of Dillon, town of Lima, unincorporated areas of Beaverhead County, Montana. — [Washington, D.C.?] : Federal Emergency Management Agency, [1982] ii, 30 p., 28 folded leaves of plates : ill., 1 map ; 28 cm. Cover title. "January 5, 1982." Includes bibliographical references. "300088, 300117, 300001." ●Item 594-C-29 (microfiche) 1. Insurance, Flood — Montana — Beaverhead County. I. United States. Federal Emergency Management Agency. II. Title: City of Dillon, town of Lima, unincorporated areas of Beaverhead County, Montana. OCLC 08694261

FEDERAL MEDIATION AND CONCILIATION SERVICE
Washington, DC 20427

82-23389

FM 1.1:979

United States. Federal Mediation and Conciliation Service.

Annual report / Federal Mediation and Conciliation Service. Washington, D.C. : The Service : For sale by the Supt. of Docs., U.S. G.P.O., Federal Mediation and Conciliation Service, 2100 K St., NW, Washington, D.C. 20427 v. : ill, ports. ; 24 cm. x 21 x 26 cm. Annual $4.50 Began with

FEDERAL MARITIME COMMISSION
Washington, DC 20573

82-23390

FMC 1.11:980

Approved conference, rate, interconference, pooling and joint service agreements and selective major cooperative working and charter agreements of steamship lines in the foreign commerce of the United States. Washington, D.C. : Federal Maritime Commission : [Supt. of Docs., U.S. G.P.O., distributor, 1980- Supt. of Docs., U.S. Govt. Print. Off., Washington, D.C. 20402 v. ; 23 cm. Annual $7.00 Sept. 1, 1980- Spine title: Approved service agreements 1980- Title from cover. Sept. 1, 1980. ●Item 432-L S/N 014-000-00071-2 Continues: Approved conference, rate, interconference, pooling and joint service agreements and selective major cooperative working arrangements of steamship lines in the foreign commerce of the United States ISSN 0276-1750 1. Shipping conferences — Periodicals. I. United States. Federal Maritime Commission. OCLC 08717466

FEDERAL TRADE COMMISSION
Washington, DC 20580

82-23391

FT 1.2:M 54/3/978-2

Statistical report on mergers and acquisitions / Bureau of Economics, Federal Trade Commission. [Washington, D.C.] : The Bureau : For sale by the Supt. of Docs., U.S. G.P.O., Supt. of Docs., U.S. Govt. Print. Off., Washington, D.C. 20402 v. ; 28 cm. Annual $8.00 Title from cover. 1978 report issued Aug. 1980. Description based on: 1979. ●Item 535 S/N 018-000-00280-9 ISSN 0731-0692 Continues: F.T.C. statistical report on mergers and acquisitions ISSN 0094-1662 1. Consolidation and merger of corporations — United States — Statistics — Periodicals. I. United States. Federal Trade Commission. Bureau of Economics. HD2775.F92c 82-640399 338.8/3/0973 OCLC 04055476

82-23392

FT 1.11:97

United States. Federal Trade Commission.

Federal Trade Commission decisions / compiled by Editorial/Publishing Services Branch of the Office of the Secretary. Washington, D.C. : The Commission : For sale by the Supt. of Docs., U.S. G.P.O., Supt. of Docs., U.S. Govt. Print. Off., Washington, D.C. 20402 v. ; 24 cm. Semiannual $16.00 Began with Mar. 16, 1915/June 30, 1919. Vol. 97, Jan. 1, 1981 to June 30, 1981. Description based on: Vol. 94 (July 1, 1979 to Dec. 31, 1979). ●Item 534 S/N 018-000-00286-8 1. Competition — United States — Periodicals. 2. Competition, Unfair — United States — Periodicals. I. United States. Federal Trade Commission. Editorial/Publishing Services Branch. II. Title. OCLC 01768407

Illustration Q

A typical page listing agency publications from the *Monthly Catalog of U.S. Government Publications,* for October 1982.

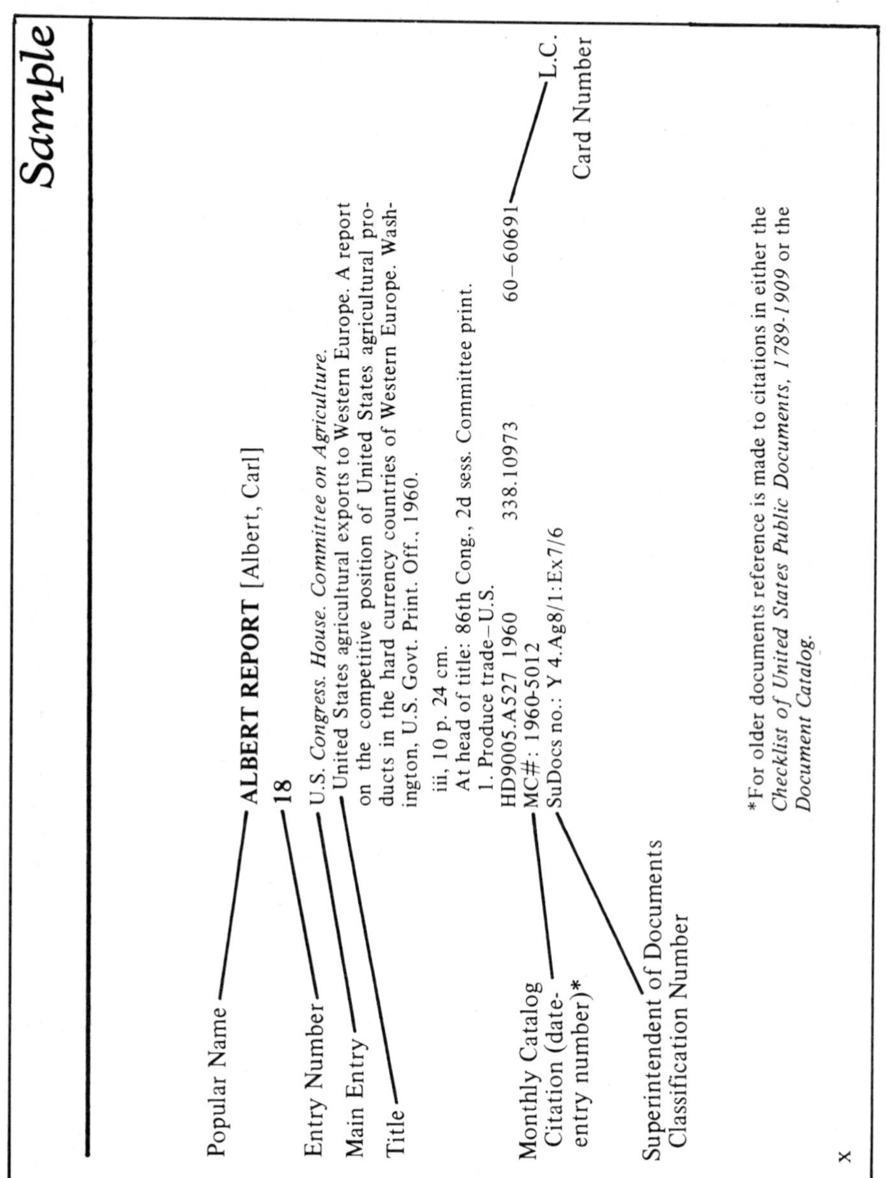

Illustration R

A Sample Entry from *Popular Names of U.S. Government Reports* (3d ed., 1976).

John L. Andriot, *Guide to U.S. Government Publications, 1973–19__* (Documents Index, 1973–19__). Looseleaf, with quarterly updating.

John L. Andriot, *Checklist of Major U.S. Government Series* (Documents Index, 1972–19__).

As noted above, the Freedom of Information Act of 1966 expanded considerably access to internal records and documents of executive and administrative agencies. Although there has been increasing governmental resistance to applications and suits under these Acts, they have been quite effective in opening new areas for fact-finding for those involved in legal research.[34]

F. PRESIDENTIAL DOCUMENTS

The President has specific authority and responsibility over a wide range of governmental matters and national concerns, serving as the administrative head of the executive branch, the agent of foreign relations, military commander, and a law maker of considerable importance. In fulfilling these roles and functions, the President issues executive orders, proclamations and other documents of legal effect which are published officially and unofficially in several forms.

The best current source for all Presidential documents is the *Weekly Compilation of Presidential Documents* which has been published by the Government Printing Office since 1965. In addition to executive orders, proclamations and other legally significant documents, it also includes speeches, press conferences, etc. All of the documents described in the next four numbered sections, except Executive Agreements, appear in the *Weekly Compilation.*

1. EXECUTIVE ORDERS AND PROCLAMATIONS

These two forms of executive fiat are used to perform Presidential functions pursuant to statutory authority or inherent powers. Although proclamations are commonly associated with formal announcements of policy, and orders with a more direct exercise of authority, in actuality both have been used for executive actions and have the same legal effect. Most orders and proclamations must be published in the *Federal Register* and they are the first documents appearing in each issue. Those that lack general applicability or legal effect, or proclaim treaties or other international agreements are not included.[35]

Executive orders and proclamations are also cumulated and published in Title 3 of the *Code of Federal Regulations*. When issued under the specific authority of a statute, some of them are also published in full text in the *U. S. Code* (and its annotated editions, *U. S. Code Annotated* and *U. S. Code Service*), with the authorizing statu-

34. See, for example, Evan Hendricks, *Former Secrets: Government Records Made Public Through the Freedom of Information Act* (Washington, D.C.: Campaign for Political Rights, 1982).

35. 44 U.S.C. §§ 1505 and 1511 (1976).

tory section. Proclamations appear regularly in the volumes of the *U. S. Statutes at Large*, but executive orders do not. Most executive orders and proclamations are also published in the *U. S. Code Congressional and Administrative News* and in the supplements to the *U. S. Code Service*. In order to locate specific documents, references can be found in appropriate indexes and tables in these publications. Retrospective and historical indexes and tables are described in the *first* edition of Price & Bitner, *Effective Legal Research*.[36]

Also useful in this regard is the *Codification of Presidential Proclamations and Executive Orders*, published in 1981 by the Office of the Federal Register. Arranged by fifty titles similar to those of the *Code of Federal Regulations*, this codification brings together *by subject* all proclamations and executive orders from January 20, 1961, to January 20, 1981, and also includes amendments to those orders and proclamations. Annual revision and updating of the codification is promised.

For citator purposes, proclamations and executive orders are carried as *cited* material in Shepard's *Code of Federal Regulations Citations*, described above, and in the tables of the reporter volumes of the National Reporter System which list cases construing statutes and related material.

2. PRESIDENTIAL MESSAGES

Communications to Congress by the President are typically made in the form of Presidential messages. They may propose new legislation, explain Presidential vetoes, transmit reports or other documents to Congress, or convey information about the state of national affairs or some matter of concern. Most messages are printed as Congressional documents and as such are listed in the *Monthly Catalog of U. S. Government Publications*. They are also printed and indexed in the *Congressional Record* and in the *House and Senate Journals*. A few important ones also appear in the *U. S. Code Congressional and Administrative News*. Although, for research purposes, these documents are most significant in developing legislative histories of particular statutes, they are also of general interest as part of the literature of the Presidency.

3. REORGANIZATION PLANS

In recent years, reorganization plans have become a frequently used form of executive action. They consist of Presidential proposals for changes in the form of agencies of the executive branch and are sent to Congress in the form of executive orders. A reorganization plan can abolish, transfer, or reorganize agencies and becomes law automatically unless, within a stated period, Congress disapproves the specific plan. This unusual form of joint lawmaking was established in general terms by an Act of June 30, 1932,[37] and later extend-

36. Little, Brown & Co., 1st ed., 1953, at pp. 143–148; reprinted by Fred B. Rothman & Co., 1969.

37. 47 Stat. 413–414 (1932).

ed to permit reorganization plans as a specific form of action by the Reorganization Act of 1939.[38] When submitted to Congress, the plans are printed in the *Congressional Record* and in the House and Senate documents series. These are the best sources for plans which have been disapproved by Congress. Those plans which become effective by Congressional acquiescence are then published in the *Federal Register*, in Title 3 of the *Code of Federal Regulations* (along with other Presidential documents collected there), in the *Statutes at Large* and unofficially in the *U. S. Code Congressional and Administrative News*. All of the effective plans also appear in Title 5 of the *U. S. Code* following the particular Reorganization Act under which they were authorized. This collection, in proximity to the basic statute, includes also helpful notes, Presidential messages, and executive orders relating to the plans. It is, therefore, the most useful research source for these documents. Like proclamations and executive orders, reorganization plans can be traced in Shepard's *Code of Federal Regulations Citations*, Shepard's *United States Citations* under their *Statutes at Large* source; they are also listed in the "Statutes Construed" tables of the various reporters in the National Reporter System.

4. EXECUTIVE AGREEMENTS

Executive agreements are made by the President with other countries, under the authority to conduct foreign affairs. Unlike treaties, they do not require the advice and consent of the Senate and are usually based on the President's constitutional powers, authorizing legislation, or the provisions of a treaty. In recent years, more and more diplomatic arrangements have been made through this convenient device. Although consideration of executive agreements belongs more properly with treaties, brief mention can be made here of the current sources of their publication.

Since 1945 these agreements have been published officially in a slip or pamphlet form in the *Treaties and Other International Acts* series. In 1950 the official bound edition of that series began publication as *U. S. Treaties and Other International Agreements* and since that time has included executive agreements. These are roughly chronologically arranged collections which have indexes in each volume. There are also two cumulative indexes covering 1776 to 1949 and 1950 to 1970, (with a *Supplement* covering 1971–1975), respectively, which provide access by document number, country, subject and date to the executive agreements in the *Statutes at Large* prior to 1950 and the *U. S. T.* since 1950.[39] One seeking access by subject or country to a particular agreement can also use *Treaties in Force*, an annual index to treaties and agreements actually in force, which is prepared by the Department of State.

38. 53 Stat. 561–565 (1939).

39. Kavass & Michael, *United States Treaties and Other International Agreements, Cumulative Index 1776–1949* (1975) 4 v. Kavass & Sprudzs, *UST Cumulative Index*, 1950–1970 (1973) 4 v., and *Supplement, 1971–1975* (1977).

Executive agreements appear in the *United Nations Treaty Series* and appeared as well in its predecessor, the *League of Nations Treaty Series.* Executive agreements can be *Shepardized,* along with treaties, under their *U. S. Treaties and Other International Agreements* citations in the *Shepard's United States Citations* and in the state Shepard's as well.

The bibliographic development and available sources of executive agreements prior to 1950 are varied and complex. Between 1908 and 1929, they usually appeared in slip form in the *Treaty Series;* from 1929 to 1945 they appeared in its successor, *Executive Agreement Series;* and from 1931 to 1949 most also appeared in the *Statutes at Large.*

5. COMPILATIONS OF PRESIDENTIAL PAPERS

Over the years there have been numerous official and unofficial compilations of the public papers of many of the Presidents. The most comprehensive is the 10 volume set by James D. Richardson, *A Compilation of the Messages and Papers of the Presidents, 1789–1897.*[40] Later editions of Richardson, which were numerous, supplemented it down to 1929. Since then, unofficial compilations of the papers of Presidents Hoover[41] and Franklin Roosevelt[42] have been published. In 1958 the Federal Register Division began publishing a series of annual bound volumes called *Public Papers of the Presidents of the United States,* which contain the formal and informal Presidential documents of recent administrations. There are annual indexes to these documents and a commercially published series of cumulative indexes to each recent President's entire administration, called *Cumulative Indexes to the Public Papers of the Presidents of the United States.*[43] The Library of Congress now has underway a mammoth project of microfilming all of its historic files of *Presidential Papers* for public distribution. These will also include detailed indexes prepared for each set.

All of these compilations include, in varying degrees, executive documents of legal significance which are often difficult to locate in standard sources. They are quite helpful in retrospective or historical research and may contain documents which do not appear in any other published form.

G. STATE ADMINISTRATIVE MATERIALS

1. GENERAL CONSIDERATIONS

The executive and administrative agencies of the 50 states and their localities have undergone an expansion in recent years at least

40. Washington, D. C., 1896–1899; also published as House Misc.Doc. 210, 53rd Congress, 2nd Session.

41. Myers, W. S., ed., *The State Papers and Other Public Writings of Herbert Hoover,* 2 vols. (1934).

42. Rosenman, S. I., ed., *The Public Papers and Addresses of Franklin D. Roosevelt,* 13 vols. (1938–1950).

43. K. T. O. Press, 1977–19__.

equal to that of the federal government. When multiplied by the number of units involved, the outpouring of regulations, decisions and rulings is staggering. Although they are less in public view than the national bureaucracy, the regulatory bodies of the various states affect their citizens no less profoundly. They set and enforce public health and housing standards, fix and regulate utility rates and practices, govern labor and business activities, and perform many other functions.

Unfortunately the bibliographic problems of publication, access and control in this area are enormous and, with a few exceptions, are not being met with sufficient interest, resources or imagination. In most of the states the requirements of public information and notice are at almost the same primitive level as in the federal government before 1935. Although each state and its resources, tools and problems, must be faced individually, some general comments can be made.

Virtually all of the states publish state manuals of some kind which provide basic information about their government, its agencies, functions and officials. Although their quality varies widely, they have somewhat the same utility for research in state administrative law, as the *U. S. Government Manual* does on the federal level. The titles of these manuals are different from state to state, e.g., Redbook, Legislative Manual, Register, etc. Although they usually have to be supplemented by relevant statutes, regulations and publications of particular agencies, they can provide the basic information about which agency regulates what field, with what powers, and under whose direction.

For a survey of the officers, agencies, functions, practices, and statistics in all the states, *The Book of the States*, published by the Council of State Governments is very helpful. It is revised and supplemented regularly and is the best reference tool on the governmental operations of the various states.

2. STATE ADMINISTRATIVE REGULATIONS AND DECISIONS

The publication and availability of state rules and regulations has improved considerably in recent years, but in about a third of the states remains quite chaotic. In those states, the publication of regulations is often left to the discretion of the particular agency and hence they are issued quite rarely. Approximately thirty-eight states, however, now publish modern looseleaf or bound editions of their regulations, with regular supplementation.[44] Appendix B, at the end of this volume, indicates such publications under each state.

44. For sources of fuller information on such publications, see Tseng & Pederson, "Acquisition of state administrative rules and regulations—update 1979," 31 *Administrative L.Rev.* 405 (1979) National Association of Secretaries of State, *Administrative Codes and Registers: 1982 State/Federal Survey* (1982); M. L. Fisher, *Guide to State Legislative Materials* (Fred B. Rothman & Co., 1979; 2d ed. projected for late 1983); and E.H. Fox, "Status of State of Administrative Codes and Registers," 2 *Legal Ref. Services Q.* 77–93 (1982).

In approximately twenty of those states, the compilation is supplemented by monthly or weekly legal newspapers or gazettes, such as the *California Administrative Register*, the *Connecticut Law Journal*, etc.

For states which do not have such compilations, the Secretary of State or the agencies themselves may be contacted to ascertain what sources are available. A few commercial looseleaf services also contain state administrative regulations in the particular subject fields covered by the service.

Some state agencies publish official reports of their decisions, similar to those of the federal bodies. The most common are the reports of the various state tax commissions, public utilities commissions, banking commissions, insurance commissions, and labor agencies. Advance sheets are quite rare, although some agencies issue their decisions only in a separate slip form. Occasionally state administrative decisions can be found in the special subject reporters and looseleaf services, which may publish both court and agency decisions, as well as provide cumulative indexing, digesting and relevant secondary material.

3. CHECKLISTS AND INDEXES

Although no state issues an equivalent of the *Monthly Catalog of U. S. Government Publications*, there are some finding tools which should be noted. The Library of Congress publishes the *Monthly Checklist of State Publications*, which is a very useful record of state documents received at the Library. Publications are listed alphabetically by state and agency and an annual index is also prepared. Since most administrative and executive materials are listed, it is a useful bibliographic guide in this field. A few states issue their own periodic lists of recent publications and some issue annual catalogs, but the *Monthly Checklist of State Publications* is more complete than many of them. Also helpful in this regard is the *Guide to State Legislative Materials*, edited by Mary L. Fisher,[45] which includes selected state administrative materials in a state by state listing, with addresses of issuing officers or publishers.

The determined researcher can also get assistance from the State Library or the Secretary of State in most of the states. The location and acquisition of state materials, however, requires persistence, imagination and often patience.

H. OPINIONS OF THE ATTORNEYS GENERAL

1. OPINIONS OF THE U. S. ATTORNEYS GENERAL

Falling between the categories of primary and secondary authority, attorney general opinions have a significant value in legal research. They are usually written in response to specific inquiries

45. Ibid.

from government officials and may construe statutes, interpret case law and give legal counsel. Although only advisory in nature, they are usually accepted and are often quite persuasive on courts faced with similar problems of interpretation.

The *Opinions of the Attorneys General of the United States* is the official series of these documents. The opinions appear first in slip form and are cumulated into volumes very slowly; some are kept secret for many years. Each volume is separately indexed and some cumulative indexing is provided. Citations to these opinions appear in *Shepard's United States Citations, U. S. Administrative Citations,* and *Federal Citations,* as well as in the annotations of some federal and state statutory compilations.

2. OPINIONS OF THE STATE ATTORNEYS GENERAL

The attorneys general of the various states issue opinions very similar in form and purpose to those of the U. S. Attorney General. Every state publishes its own opinions and for the years 1937 through 1969 the Council of State Governments has published a regular digest of all of the states' attorney general opinions, which was indexed annually. Unfortunately, no other service has replaced it. The individual volumes for each state usually contain their own separate indexes and some states issue cumulative digests from time to time.

These opinions are used as citing material in many of the Shepard's citators for the states and in some of the states' annotated codes. A checklist of all published attorney general opinions has been published with looseleaf supplementation under the auspices of the American Association of Law Libraries.[46]

Fisher's *Guide to State Legislative Materials*[47] also includes current publication information on the opinions of the Attorneys General of each of the states. The annual proceedings of the National Association of Attorneys General are another source of material on the work of these officials and on legal trends and problems in the states in general.

I. ADDITIONAL READING

K. C. Davis, *Administrative Law Treatise* (2d ed., 1978–19__), Vol. I, Chs. 5 and 6; Vol. II, Ch. 7.

E. N. Griswold, "Government in Ignorance of Law—A Plea for Better Publications of Executive Legislation", 48 *Harv.L.Rev.* 198 (1934).

Note, "The Federal Register and the Code of Federal Regulations—A Reappraisal", 80 *Harv.L.Rev.* 439 (1966).

46. Pimsleur, *Checklists of Basic American Legal Publications* (Fred B. Rothman, 1962–19__), Section III, Attorneys General, now edited by M. Zubrow.

47. Op. cit. footnote 44.

Schmeckebier and Eastin, *Government Publications and Their Use* (2nd Revised Edition, 1969), Chs. 11, 12 and 14.

U. S. Office of the Federal Register, *The Federal Register: What it is and How to Use it; A Guide for the User of the Federal Register, Code of Federal Regulations System* (U.S.G.P.O., 1980).

Chapter 12

RESEARCH APPROACHES AND STRATEGIES

A. INTRODUCTION TO RESEARCH SYSTEMS

As the first chapter indicated, legal literature is a broad field, including many published forms of primary legal sources, a large number of secondary materials, and a wide range of sophisticated finding tools. An individual conducting legal research is less likely to be confronted by the problem of not finding any sources, but rather by the necessity of having to winnow through a multiplicity of available materials for those which are most relevant and useful for the research problem. Therefore, it is important to conceptualize one's research, and discern a systematic structure underlying the profusion of primary and secondary sources.

In dealing with primary sources, the materials are largely self-organizing, by chronological order of publication (as with court reports and session laws) or by subject (as with statutory codes). The chapters on case law, statutory law and administrative law provided some paradigms of the structures of those areas of bibliography. To some extent, the actual pattern of publication shapes one's research in the primary sources or leads to specific finding tools designed for those sources. Secondary sources are somewhat more difficult to explore. Here it is necessary to identify and distinguish patterns and strategies in the profusion of publications and publishing systems. This chapter will attempt to suggest some research approaches. By working with these sources and their finding aids, researchers become more knowledgeable and sophisticated in the materials of particular fields, and can formulate their own strategies and approaches. An overview of alternative systems and research options is offered here, but it is hoped (and assumed) that individuals will develop their own preferences through experience, and reach a higher level of research skill by devising and testing their own approaches to particular types of problems.

This "systematic approach" is suggested to bring some order out of the chaos of varied legal forms and details encountered by students of legal research. Although most American law schools offer some formalized instruction in research methods and materials in the first year curriculum, these programs have been subject to widespread criticism.[1] One of the major difficulties is the limited amount of time and attention allotted by most law schools to the legal research program. In addition, the frequent concentration of such instruction in the short and hectic first semester forces the student to learn many legal sources and publications in such a dizzying array that individual titles make little or no lasting impression.

Perhaps the more dangerous problem, however, is the communication of misleading information or emphases. Because the student often associates each research tool with its *primary* function (e.g., the use of Shepard's citators to verify the status of a case), one assumes that the indicated function is the only one offered by the publication, or that it is the *only* tool serving that purpose. For example, the student may assume that the only use of Shepard's is to verify the status of a case, or that the use of a Shepard's citator is the only way to perform that function. Learning these bits and pieces of bibliographic information without fitting them into an integrated pattern is a poor introduction to the complexities of real legal research. One of the most common laments of law firms is that new Associates arrive without a *systematic* understanding of how to carry on legal research.

By mastering general research patterns and fitting particular sources and finding tools into a systematic approach, one can save enormous amounts of time and effort in future research. Rather than grappling with a random collection of source materials, the researcher can approach a problem in an orderly fashion and move by internal references from one tool to another. By utilizing the links between publications and exploiting the cross-references provided by

1. Two of the numerous articles on this problem are C. Brock, "The Legal Research Problem," 24 *DePaul L.Rev.* 827 (1974), and R. Mills, "Legal Research Instruction in Law Schools, the State of the Art, or: Why Law School Graduates Do Not Know How to Find the Law," 70 *Law Library J.* 343 (1977).

their publishers, the researcher can make faster, more efficient, and more thorough searches.

This chapter is also intended to serve as a bridge between the primary sources, which were the main focus of the preceding chapters, and the secondary materials which are the subject of the second half of the book.

B. THE RESEARCH SPECTRUM

All of the materials of legal research can be viewed in a simple spectrum as shown in Illustration A.

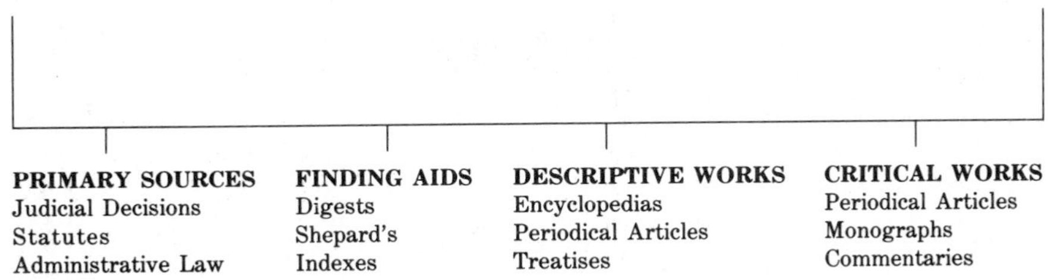

Illustration A

On the left-hand side of this spectrum are the primary source materials. These cases, statutes, and administrative rules and decisions form the actual body of law to be searched. Although there can be argument over the correct interpretation of a statute, or dispute as to the meaning of a particular judicial decision, the black letter rule of that statute or decision can usually be found. Once the primary source material is located, the individual interpretive powers of the researcher come into play. Once the relevant decision is found and analyzed, the researcher can fit it into a framework of argument for use as binding or persuasive authority.

The process of legal research should be viewed as an attempt to move to the left-hand side of the spectrum, *from* the descriptive materials or the finding tools *to* the rules of law embodied in decisions and statutes. Once the rules are identified, the creative powers of the researcher can be brought to bear in analyzing, distinguishing, analogizing, and otherwise utilizing them for the purposes of the problem or issue under consideration. All of the material to the right of the legal research spectrum—the case finders, the digests, the encyclopedias, the periodicals, monographs, etc.—are based on the primary sources. The commentaries, analyses and explanations found in the secondary sources can be used effectively as persuasive authority in an argument, or can help one understand the primary rules. The essential point, however, is that the secondary sources build upon the primary sources and are subordinate to them.

In doing research one must always consider where in the spectrum of authority the particular tool or text belongs. A headnote is in fact a secondary source, and the seemingly authoritative interpretation found in an encyclopedia, a periodical article or a monograph, is really the interpretation of a scholar or editor, and not a primary source. Imposing this "pattern" on all research tools will help the legal researcher to keep perspective on the relative weight of these texts. The legal research spectrum can be used to evaluate the various materials described throughout this book.

C. WORKING FROM PRIMARY SOURCES

Because all secondary materials are built upon primary sources, a useful method for locating substantial amounts of useful information is to work from one relevant primary source. Once the researcher locates a relevant decision or statute covering the issue of law in question, or a relevant administrative decision or regulation, one can use that source to broaden the search and discover additional primary sources and helpful secondary material. Although it is not the *only* approach, the use of a single relevant primary source is often the most efficient opening step in research. Consulting the subject indexes which accompany most finding tools and secondary sources is usually slower and less certain than working from a primary source which is clearly relevant to the issue at hand. Even if that decision or statute is not ultimately dispositive of the problem, it often provides the most direct access to a wide range of useful materials.

1. WORKING FROM A KNOWN CASE

A. West Digest System

Perhaps the most familiar way of using a known case to locate other potentially relevant decisions is by identifying the West digest topic and key number assigned to the relevant headnote of that decision, and then searching under that key number in the appropriate West digest for other similar decisions. Depending on the jurisdiction and time period most appropriate to the issue being researched, one can select one or more West state digests, a regional digest, the federal digests, West's *U. S. Supreme Court Digest*, or the *Decennial Digests* and the *General Digest*. If only the most recent cases in a specific jurisdiction are being sought, the search can even be limited to the mini-digests found in the last volume and advance sheets of the West reporter for that jurisdiction.

The advantage of this approach, as described in Chapter 5 on case finding, is that one can move freely through the full range of West digests, covering all published cases in all jurisdictions from the most recent months, back to the 17th century. The key to the most efficient use of this method is to limit one's search to the most relevant time periods and jurisdictions, and to refine and revise the topics and key numbers being used, as the search progresses. The usual problem with the "key number system" is that it yields too many decisions, some of which may not be relevant. Careful reading of the abstracts *and*, more important, reading the decisions themselves, is necessary to select those which are most relevant and persuasive.

b. Shepard's Citations

Similarly, a known decision can be *Shepardized* in the appropriate case citator, and additional *later* decisions found in the citing material. These will be relevant to the cited decision in *some* respect since the opinion mentioned that case, but the reference may not have been on an issue similar to that being researched. Thus, this method of expanding one's search is not precise and often produces false leads. In many of its citators, however, Shepard's does indicate the headnote number of the *cited* case to which the subsequent case referred. That enables the researcher to select from the many citations listed, those which relate to the specific issue under consideration. In other citators, Shepard's uses legal phrases as headings above groups of citations to indicate their particular focus. The decisions found in this way must, of course, be read and evaluated. As with West headnotes, one cannot rely on the Shepard's listing to establish the relevancy of the later decisions.

If a subsequent decision is found to be relevant, however, it can then be *Shepardized* to locate other decisions which have cited that case, and so on, in a continuous expansion of the search from the original decision.

In addition to later cases, the Shepard's citators for the official state reporters provide citations to articles in legal periodicals and Attorney General opinions, and many of the citators provide references to Annotations in *ALR, ALR Federal* and *Lawyers' Edition*. These references enable one to extend the range of research opportunities into new areas.

c. Computer Services

LEXIS and *WESTLAW* can also be used to expand the research from the known decision. Shepard's citators are now available in those services and can be used in the same process as described above in Section (b). *WESTLAW*, however, also offers the capability of searching by West topic and key number, as described in Section (a), and thereby provides access to all of the West digests with the speed of computer searching.

Since LEXIS contains many cases not published in either official or West reporters, a search in that system by the name or citation of the known case may turn up *other* cases which have referred to that case. These otherwise unpublished decisions might not have appeared in Shepard's or in the West digest system. It should be recalled, however, that, as noted above in Chapters 3 and 5, some courts have imposed restrictions on the use of these decisions.

In addition, the computer services can be searched by using significant words or phrases derived from the opinion in the known case. This is the typical form of computer searching and permits widening or narrowing the scope of the search through changes in the search words used, the time period, or the jurisdictions covered.

d. Looseleaf Services

Some of the looseleaf services, described below in Chapter 13, can also be used to expand a search from a known case. One of the advantages of looseleaf services is their integration of varied legal forms (decisions, statutes, administrative regulations and rulings, etc.) in one subject field. Some of these services actually arrange their contents topically, so that each statutory provision is followed by abstracts of the judicial decisions, regulations and rulings which relate to that statute. By locating the known case through the tables of cases which appear in each looseleaf service, one may find that case in proximity to the other related legal sources. The researcher can then move from a single case to a variety of documents, including other decisions on the same topic, statutes, regulations and rulings. In addition, an explanatory discussion of that topic (another feature of these services) may elucidate the issue and provide still more leads.

2. WORKING FROM A KNOWN STATUTE

If a statutory provision is known to be applicable to the issue being researched, that provision can also be used in several ways to enlarge one's search. This process is basically the same as that described above for a known *case.* One could use any of the following finding aids for this purpose.

a. Annotations to Statutory Sections

As described above in Chapter 7, there are annotated editions for the *U. S. Code* (*U. S. Code Annotated* and *U. S. Code Service*) and for the codes of each of the fifty states and the District of Columbia. These codes include annotations in the form of case abstracts for each statutory section. If the known statute can be located in an annotated code, the researcher will have direct access to virtually every judicial decision which has applied, interpreted or construed each of its sections. Many of the codes, as shown in Chapter 7, also contain references under each section to legal encylcopedias, West digest topics and key numbers, Attorney General opinions, periodical articles, and *ALR* and *ALR Federal* Annotations. These will provide a variety of additional leads to such finding tools and secondary sources and may enable one to expand the search even further.

b. Shepard's Citations

The known statute can also be Shepardized to find later legislative changes, interpretive decisions, and selected secondary sources. The process of *Shepardizing* statutes is described in Chapter 9, Section E.

c. Computer Services

Although *WESTLAW* and *LEXIS* have limited statutory data bases (see Chapter 7, Section F.6), any statutory name or citation can be used as a search phrase to find, in their other data bases, judicial decisions or administrative materials which have referred to that statute. This can also be done by actually *Shepardizing* the statute in *WESTLAW* or *LEXIS* with slightly different results. Through either procedure, the new sources which cited the relevant statute can then be used to enlarge the search.

d. Looseleaf Services

As with known cases (see Section 1.d above), the known statute can be located in a looseleaf service which covers that subject field. The service may, at that point, refer to cases, regulations, rulings, etc. which derive from, or interpret, the statutory provision. These sources can then be researched individually and the research thus advanced.

D. ALTERNATIVE RESEARCH APPROACHES

If a known case or statute is not apparent at the beginning of one's research, the following alternative approaches are suggested. No one of these procedures is best for every problem—they are simply possible research models to consider. Each can be modified to meet the needs of a particular problem, or they can be used in various combinations.

1. SPECIFIC FINDING TOOLS

One method of locating that first relevant primary source is through the use of one of the finding tools specifically designed for access to primary sources. These include the "Descriptive Word Index" to the West Digest System, the "Quick Indexes" to *ALR* and *ALR Federal*, the general indexes to the annotated statutory codes and administrative codes. Indexes to a looseleaf service (if one is published in the subject field of the problem being researched) and computer searches in *WESTLAW* and *LEXIS* are also possible options.

2. SECONDARY SOURCES

Another alternative is to search first in secondary sources, such as encyclopedias, treatises and periodical articles. Access to these materials will be described in the following Chapters which are specifically devoted to each of them. Aside from their sources, these narrative texts may offer helpful introductions to the subject matter of the problem being studied, a synthesis of the decisions and statutes which govern that field, analysis of trends and historical background. Many researchers prefer this approach in order to first gain a general familiarity with the concepts, issues and rules in the field. After reading the relevant text, one can then use the footnote citations and other documentation to locate leading decisions and applicable statutes, moving from right to left on the research spectrum.

As will be described in Chapter 16 below (Legal Periodicals), the major indexes to legal periodicals (*Index to Legal Periodicals, Current Law Index* and *Legal Resources Index*) contain tables of cases and statutes which can be used to locate articles discussing particular cases or statutes. They thus provide another means of working from a known primary source to scholarly treatment of that text, or its subject matter, in the periodical literature.

3. PUBLISHERS' SYSTEMS

As we have seen in the earlier Chapters, the two major law publishers, West Publishing Company and Lawyers Co-op, provide cross references in all of their respective publications which facilitate research movement between different types of legal material and their finding tools. By working within one of these research systems and fully exploiting its cross references, one can save considerable time and effort. After all avenues in one system have been exhausted, the same procedure can be followed in the other system. This is much more efficient than skipping randomly from set to set, back and forth between the two systems. The instructional pamphlets issued by these publishers [2] describe the interrelationships among their respective publications, but they will be briefly restated here.

a. The West Publishing Company

The West system of publications extend to almost every type of legal publication except looseleaf services. It includes court reports, statutes, court rules, encyclopedias, digests, phrasebooks, dictionaries, treatises, formbooks, and practice manuals. Through the WESTLAW terminal one can also reach Shepard's citators, and the databases of Dialog Information Services which include legal periodical indexes, and vast amounts of economic and social science data.

Among the most frequent links between West publications are the references to West digest topic and key numbers and *Corpus Juris Secundum* in virtually every West product. West's *U. S. Code Annotated* and its annotated state codes provide case annotations, as well as a variety of other cross references. By branching out from the West set to many others, a researcher can be led quickly through the wide range of primary and secondary sources. These also include sources not published by West, such as annotated reporters, periodical articles, Attorney General opinions and administrative regulations in *C.F.R.*

The following diagram, illustrating some of these relationships, can be rearranged into almost any configuration depending on where one's research is begun. A third dimension to the diagram can be

2. *West's Law Finder, a Legal Research Manual* (West Publishing Company, 1983) and *The Living Law, A Guide to Modern Legal Research* (Lawyers Co-op/Bancroft-Whitney, 1982–1983).

projected with WESTLAW at *its* center to accurately visualize its access potential to most of the same sources.

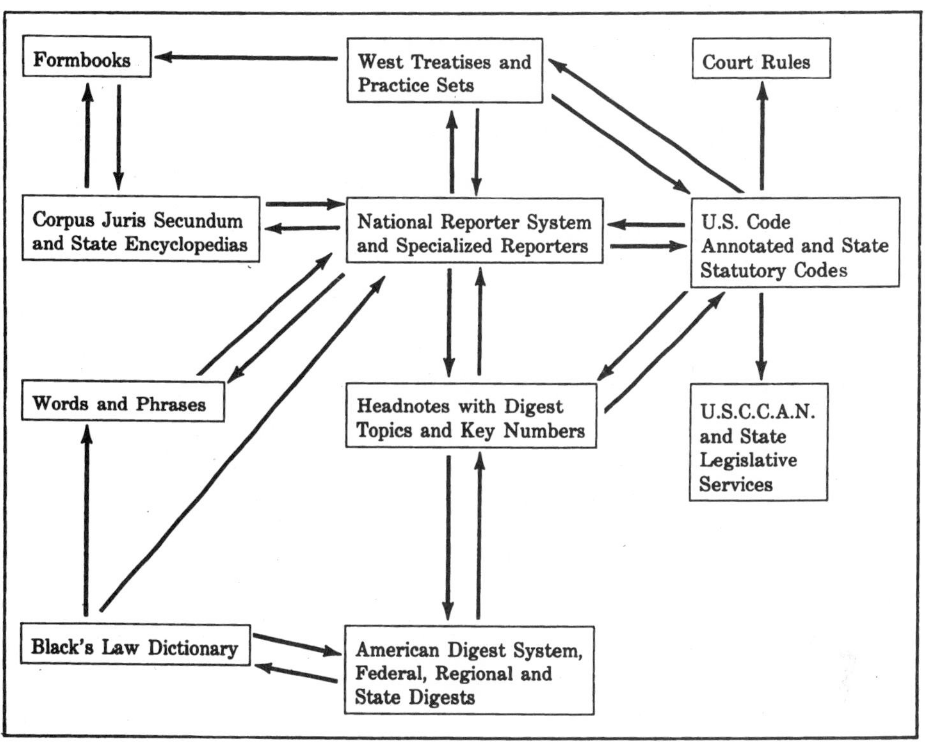

Illustration B

Diagram of the West Publishing Company's system of publications.

b. Lawyers Co-op and Its Total Client-Service Library

The Lawyers Co-op/Bancroft Whitney system organizes its various publications under the marketing name, *Total Client-Service Library,* and provides cross references between them and to some legal materials not published by these firms. At the heart of this system are the annotated reporters, *ALR, ALR Federal* and *Lawyers' Edition*; the legal encyclopedia, *Am.Jur.2d*; and several state encyclopedias. The *Library* also includes *U. S. Code Service*; the *Lawyers' Edition Digest*; several annotated state codes; state reporters; a large number of specialized practice and procedure sets, formbooks, and treatises; two regulatory services; and related finding tools. Within this structure, varied cross references and tables serve as links, and significant legal sources of other publishers are cited as well.

The following diagram provides one possible view of the Total Client-Service Library, but, like the West diagram above, does not include all of its publications. *Auto-Cite,* the Lawyers Co-op computerized citator service (not shown here, but described below in Chapter 22), provides another dimension to this system.

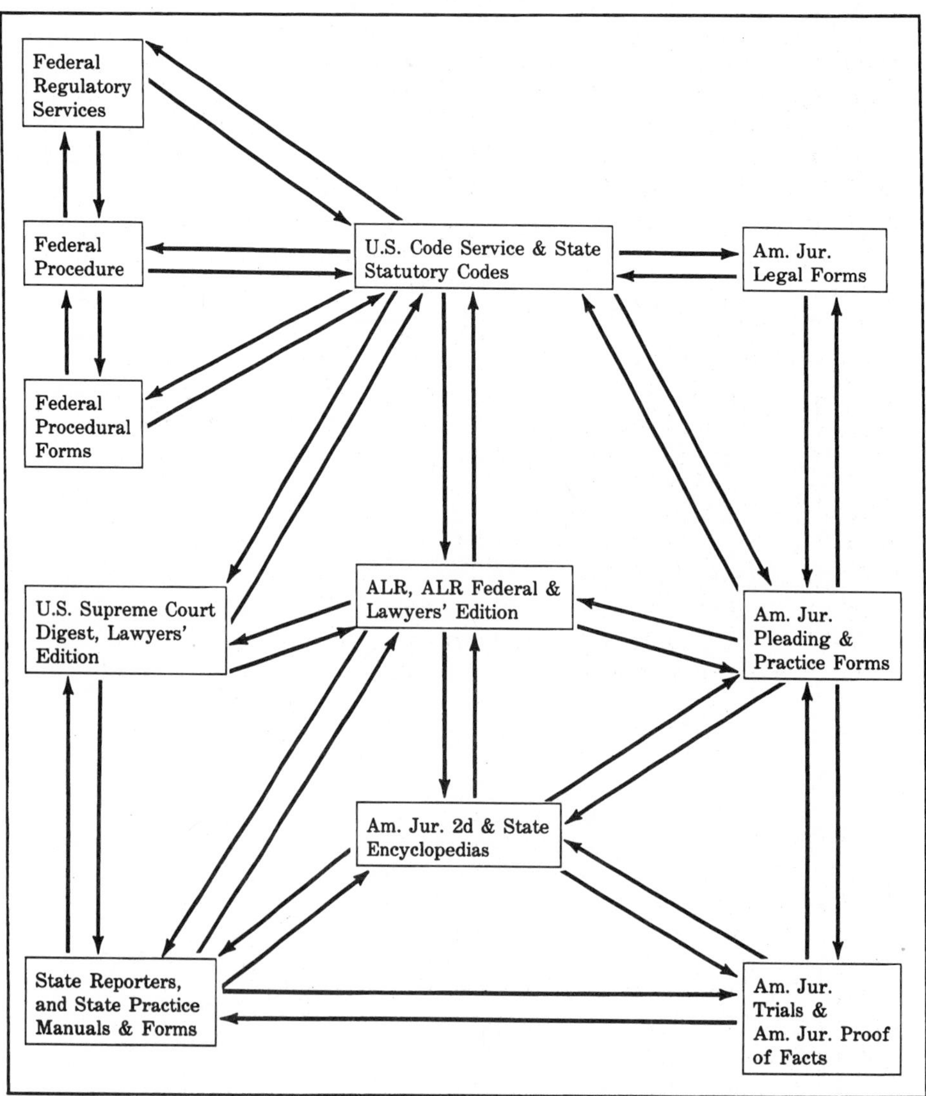

Illustration C

The *Total Client-Service Library* of Lawyers Co-op/Bancroft-Whitney.

c. Looseleaf Services and Computer Research Systems

The various looseleaf services (described in Chapter 13) and the two major computer research systems, WESTLAW and LEXIS (described above, and fully treated in Chapter 22), offer additional approaches to many research problems.

The looseleaf services, for those subject fields which they cover, provide integrated indexing and explanatory text to a variety of legal forms. Their frequent supplementation allows faster updating than most of the publications previously described. Perhaps their main research advantage, however, is the coverage of administrative law in most regulatory fields. In addition to statutes and judicial decisions, the looseleaf services afford access to administrative regulations, rulings and decisions, all of which are integrated into a functional unit, with explanatory text and indexing. The traditional case finding and statutory aids cover this increasingly important administrative law area only secondarily. The inclusion of regulatory and administrative data bases in WESTLAW and LEXIS, and the growing movement of two looseleaf service publishers (Bureau of National Affairs and Commerce Clearing House) into computerized data bases may signal a change in access to this material.

Although both LEXIS and WESTLAW began as computer programs for access to case law and have steadily widened that coverage, they are now expanding into administrative law and secondary sources. Each system is also offering some foreign legal materials and their respective terminals can be used to reach many non-legal data bases. These developments are discussed in detail in Chapter 22, but are noted here since the two services are now quite versatile and can be used effectively either to initiate research or to expand a search from sources already identified. The one striking weakness of both systems is their lack of state statutory coverage.

E. DEVELOPING ONE'S OWN RESEARCH STRATEGY

In beginning research on any legal problem one should plan at least the initial phases of the inquiry. A systematic approach will usually save time and effort. The planning procedure should include the following steps:

(1) Careful analysis of the problem, reducing it to the component legal issues;

(2) Review of the issues to determine whether particular legal sources (e.g., a constitutional provision, a statute, administrative regulation, etc.) are likely to be applicable;

(3) Consideration of whether a definition or interpretation of a word or phrase is involved;

(4) Consideration of whether the problem is within the coverage of a looseleaf service;

(5) Preparation of a list of significant search words and phrases, drawn from the facts and legal issues;

(6) Preparation of a checklist of sources to be searched (grouping them within each of the major research systems);

(7) If an introduction to the field is needed, that should be sought in an encyclopedia article, one of the restatements, a treatise, or periodical article.

With such a research plan, including lists of sources to be consulted, finding tools to be used, and search words and phrases to be employed, one can then begin the actual research. As each source and research tool is examined, it is checked off the list and the results noted. Thus, crucial omissions can be prevented and the retracing of steps avoided. At each point, supplements and other forms of updating are used, and significant findings are Shepardized to minimize the danger of being misled by decisions or statutes which have been changed or otherwise rendered obsolete.

As the results of these steps become apparent, the plan can be modified or redirected. One need not be bound by the initial strategy, or locked into an unproductive approach. The original checklist should be revised and enlarged, as necessary, but records of all steps taken should be retained. Full notes of relevant citations should be made to avoid the hectic scrambling to complete citations while the brief or memorandum is being written.

Legal research can be both organized *and* creative. Imagination, serendipity and the flash of seemingly spontaneous insight are more likely to occur in the course of systematic research than in the random consultation of unrelated sources.

Chapter 13

LOOSELEAF SERVICES

A. INTRODUCTION: CONCEPT OF A LOOSELEAF SERVICE

The looseleaf service, in its many manifestations, is simply a lawbook, or set of lawbooks, that continues to grow after its initial publication. It is an ingenious publishing response to the constant change inherent in our legal system. Through the periodic insertion of new material and the removal of superseded pages, the looseleaf service is continuously being reedited to reflect the current state of the law. Since the looseleaf service contains all relevant sources of law in its subject area, it is in effect a mini-library in one field of law. The varied legal sources in that field (statutes, decisions, regulations, rulings, etc.) are unified by explanatory text, several types of indexes, and a method of organization approriate to the subject being covered.

Although the proliferation of these services is the result of increasing governmental regulation of economic activity beginning in the 1930's, the first looseleaf service followed immediately on the federal income tax in 1913.[1] Because of the frequency of new regulations from the many administrative agencies created since 1930 and the inadequacy of traditional forms of publication to provide access to rapidly changing law issued in a variety of forms, looseleaf publications have achieved great success in virtually all public law fields and in some private law subjects as well. Although tax law services are the most sophisticated and widely used of these publications, there are now over three hundred different services covering almost a hundred different subjects.

Looseleaf services are published in a variety of different sizes, shapes and configurations. They are largely issued by commercial publishers, but also by government agencies, public interest organizations, and a few academic groups. Because of their varied schemes of arrangement, it is difficult to offer a general description or a single research model, valid for all services. Instead, we will attempt to provide an overview of the field, describe (in Section B) the basic types, (in Section C) their common features, and (in Section D) a generalized research procedure. In Section E, some suggestions for locating relevant services will be offered, together with a selective list of available services arranged by subject. Although the birth rate for new services is still surprisingly high, the death rate is quite low, and it is hoped that this list will have some utility during the life of this edition.

B. TYPES OF LOOSELEAF SERVICES

Looseleaf services, as the term is generally used, are issued in one of two different formats, which for the purposes of this discussion, we will call *cumulating services* and *interfiling services*. A few statutory codes, administrative codes, formbooks, and treatises are also published in looseleaf format—usually with *annual* supplementation by interfiled pages—but these are not looseleaf services. The true looseleaf services are distinguished by the frequency of their updating, usually weekly, but occasionally bi-weekly or monthly.

1. CUMULATING SERVICES

The cumulating looseleaf service utilizes packets of new material to be filed as a unit or a series of units, supplementing rather than displacing previous filings. These units or releases can be read through as a single publication and thereby serve a "current awareness" function. Typical of this form are most of the Bureau of National Affairs services, e.g. B.N.A.'s *Criminal Law Reporter* or *Labor Relations Reporter*. They are easily distinguishable from the

1. For a brief history of this form of legal publication, see P. R. Neal, "Looseleaf Reporting Service," 62 *Law Library J.* 153–156 (1969). For services in looseleaf binders in the years just before 1913, see also F. C. Hicks, *Materials and Methods of Legal Research*, 3d rev.ed. (Lawyers Co-op, 1942) at pp. 308-311.

interfiling services, in which individual pages are filed *in place of* superseded pages, the latter then being discarded. The releases of a cumulating service are not interfiled, but are merely added to the accumulation of previous releases.

A typical release may contain new court decisions, administrative agency decisions, statutory changes, new regulations, and commentary covering both those documents and recent developments in the subject field of the service. The weekly or monthly release can be read as an issue of a periodical, and then filed in the service and become accessible through regularly revised or updated indexes. At the end of the year, the cumulating service may remain in its binders for permanent reference, accessible through a master index and supplementary indexes, or may receive a superseding annual index. That part of the cumulating service which has substantial, permanent research value (e.g., the text of decisions) may, however, be replaced at the end of the year by bound volumes which become topical reporters (i.e., specialized reports of judicial and administrative decisions in that subject field). These spin-off reporters are becoming increasingly common and have a permanent viability beyond that of the more transitory looseleaf service from which they came.

Illustration A shows a typical page from the current developments section of a cumulating service; Illustration B shows the title-page of the spin-off bound reporter from the same service.

2. INTERFILING SERVICES

Looseleaf services that are updated by interfiling separate pages and removing superseded pages (called here "Interfiling Services") are perhaps the most common and familiar type. These are the services from which the name "looseleaf" came to be used. The new pages, which usually arrive weekly, not only replace existing pages, but may add entirely new sections to the service.

The weekly releases often include, as a regular component, a "report letter" or similar bulletin that describes the new developments in the subject field, and contains instructions for filing the new pages. In some services, these reports are actually filed into the binders; in others, they are separate leaflets which are usually routed to individuals in the law office, and then returned to the library for temporary retention, but ultimately discarded. The filing instructions should be retained in the binders and each entry checked off by the filer, so that users of the service can be certain that the set has been properly filed and is up to date.

The retention of those sections of "interfiling services" which have permanent reference value (usually court decisions or decisions of administrative agencies) are sometimes provided by transfer binders into which they can be placed to make room in the service for later additions. Other services meet the same need by issuing bound spin-off topical reporters similar to those described above in the "cu-

ENVIRONMENT REPORTER Current Developments

A weekly review of pollution control and related environmental management

Volume 13, Number 36 THE BUREAU OF NATIONAL AFFAIRS, INC **January 7, 1983**

HIGHLIGHTS

CLEAN AIR ACT SANCTIONS will be proposed by the Environmental Protection Agency by the end of January for approximately 145 counties that failed to meet the Act's deadlines, agency staff members say. According to EPA's final policy on the sanctions, the agency will proceed against those non-attainment areas that fail to qualify for redesignation to attainment or to meet the conditions of a state implementation plan (p. 1499).

AN EPA DRAFT POLICY would require publicly owned treatment works to comply with Clean Water Act effluent limitations even in the absence of federal sewage treatment construction funds. Several cities complain to the agency that the proposal would impose a "significant financial burden" on municipal governments (p. 1500) ... Full Texts (pp. 1562, 1566).

TWO ATTORNEYS HIRED BY EPA to assist in defending Administrator Anne M. Gorsuch against contempt of Congress charges are employed by a law firm that represents the owner of a major hazardous waste site, according to EPA officials. Rep. Elliot H. Levitas (D-Ga), chairman of the House panel that subpoenaed enforcement documents from Gorsuch, questions whether the lawyers had access to the documents and whether a conflict of interest exists (p. 1501).

REFINERY FUGITIVE EMISSIONS would be restricted under new source performance standards proposed by EPA. The proposed regulations would require leak detection and repair programs to reduce the emissions from pumps and valves (p. 1504) ... Full Text (p. 1542).

HIGH-LEVEL NUCLEAR WASTES such as spent reactor fuels would be regulated based on radionuclide concentration levels under disposal and management standards proposed by EPA (p. 1506) ... Full Text (p. 1527) ... The agency also indicates in an advance notice of proposed rulemaking that it is contemplating the need for regulating uranium mill tailings at low-priority sites (p. 1505) ... Full Text (p. 1567).

HAZARDOUS WASTE GENERATORS would be allowed to accumulate up to 55 gallons of the substances at various locations on facility sites without obtaining a Resource Conservation and Recovery Act permit, according to an EPA proposed regulation (p. 1506) ... Full Text (p. 1523).

418 HIGH-PRIORITY SITES would be added to the superfund program's National Contingency Plan by an EPA proposal. The action would make the hazardous waste sites eligible for federal cleanup aid (p. 1507) ... Full Text (p. 1537).

AMONG THE STATES: A ban on surface mining near Utah's Bryce Canyon National Park is upheld by a federal district court (p. 1511) ... New York's request for $20 million to clean up polychlorinated biphenyls in the Hudson River is rejected by EPA (p. 1512) ... Florida and New Hampshire apply to EPA to obtain authorization for portions of their Phase II hazardous waste management programs (p. 1516).

IN INDUSTRY: Olin Corp. and several other parties settle lawsuits stemming from the firm's manufacture of DDT in Alabama (p. 1500) ... U.S. Steel Corp. and EPA agree to a delay on installing about $14 million worth of pollution control equipment, but the agency denies a similar request by Jones & Laughlin Steel Corp. (p. 1503) ... Pollution control costs "were alleged to be a factor" in the closing of 154 plants employing over 32,000 people between January 1971 and June 1982, according to EPA statistics (p. 1510).

THE OUTLOOK IN CONGRESS for revision and reauthorization in 1983 of most major environmental laws, including the Clean Water Act, Clean Air Act, and Resource Conservation and Recovery Act, is examined in a Special Report in this week's issue (p. 1518).

This week's supplement to Environment Reporter reference file binders includes amended consolidated permit rules and new source performance standards for metal furniture, metal coils, and publication rotogravure presses.

Section 1

0013-9211/83/$00.50

Illustration A

Sample page from "Current Developments" in B.N.A. *Environment Reporter* (copyright 1983 by The Bureau of National Affairs, Inc., Washington, D.C.).

ENVIRONMENT REPORTER—CASES

Volume 16

Opinions of Federal and State Courts and Administrative Agencies in the Field of Environmental Law, with a Topical Index, Classification Guide, Index Digest, Table of Cases, and Table of Cases by Jurisdiction.

To be cited: 16 ERC ——

Published 1982 by THE BUREAU OF NATIONAL AFFAIRS, INC.
Washington, D.C.

Title page of permanent topical reporter from B.N.A. *Environment Reporter* (copyright by The Bureau of National Affairs, Inc., Washington, D.C.).

mulating services". The CCH *Federal Tax Reporter* and *Labor Law Reporter* are typical of "interfiling services" with bound topical reporters.

Most interfiling services utilize the same binders from year to year, with new material filling the space left by the removal of decision sections when the bound topical reporter volumes are published. A few services, like the major tax services, issue a complete set of new binders each year because of the large amount of new material being published continuously in those fields. Although many law firms discard the superseded sets, more and more libraries, realizing their permanent reference value, are now retaining them.

Illustration C shows the filing checklist which accompanies each weekly release in a typical interfiling service.

3. VARIED METHODS OF ORGANIZATION

Looseleaf services can also be distinguished one from another by the different organizational schemes they employ in the arrangement of their contents. These include arrangement by the sections of a large statute (as in the CCH and Prentice-Hall federal tax services); by the several statutes which regulate a particular subject field (as in the BNA and CCH labor law services); or by the topics or functional components of a common law field or a mixed common law and statutory field (as in the BNA *Family Law Reporter* and the Prentice-Hall *Wills, Estates and Trusts* service).

Regardless of the method of organization used, access to the different parts of the service is facilitated by a variety of finding aids. Among these aids are volume titles visible on the back of each binder, divider tabs designating each section of every binder, tables of contents for the whole service and for individual binders, and several different indexes covering the entire service.

4. LEADING PUBLISHERS

The final distinguishing characteristic of these services are their respective publishers, who tend to employ common research aids, indexing schemes, numbering patterns, and even colors, in their various publications.

C. COMMON FEATURES

As noted above, looseleaf services vary greatly in approach, format, and method of organization. They generally share a number of common advantages over most other legal publications, however, including the following features.

1. MULTIPLICITY OF PRIMARY SOURCES

Most of the publications described in earlier Chapters contain one primary legal source, with possible references to one or more other sources. The annotated statutory codes, for example, are quite versatile, but contain the full text of only legislative provisions, with brief abstracts of decisions, and citation references to secondary sources. Looseleaf services are unique in providing a multiplicity of primary sources in full text, and others by at least abstracts. These include statutes, judicial *and* administrative agency decisions, rulings, and administrative regulations. With the added advantage of frequent supplementation, the looseleaf services are often the *first*

CONTENTS

New Matters

	Pages Not Required	Pages in This Report
Current Table of Cases • Cumulative Index		
Current Cumulative Index.	36,875—36,879	36,875—36,880
Food and Drug Decisions		
New decisions beginning at ¶ 38,197.	39,089—39,090	39,089—39,096
New Developments		
New items beginning at ¶ 42,374.	42,749—42,750	42,749—42,754
Proposed Regulations		
Status Table.	45,003—45,006 45,031—45,033 45,051—45,057	45,003—45,006 45,031—45,033 45,051—45,057
Superseded proposals.	46,193—46,214 46,295—46,302 46,381—46,388	46,193—46,200 46,295—46,296 46,381—46,383
New proposal at ¶ 45,402.	46,759	46,759—46,765

Drugs • Cosmetics 1

	Pages Not Required	Pages in This Report
Drugs • General		
New § 201.63.	70,633	70,633
OTC Drugs		
New § 330.2.	72,253—72,254	72,253—72,254
Antibiotics • Human • Insulin		
Amended § 430.5.	73,089—73,090 73,093—73,094	73,089—73,090 73,093—73,094
Amended § 430.6.	73,095-3—73,096	73,095-3—73,096
Official correction at ¶ 73,175.	73,187—73,188	73,187—73,188
New § 436.336.	73,217-21—73,218	73,217-21—73,218
New § 440.1a.	73,275—73,276	73,275—73,276
New § 440.201.	73,383—73,384	73,383—73,384
Amended § 444.220.	73,541—73,541-2	73,541—73,541-2

Drugs • Cosmetics 2

	Pages Not Required	Pages in This Report
Veterinary Drugs		
Amended § 520.580.	75,187-3—75,188	75,187-3—75,188
Amended § 520.1805.	75,205-3—75,206	75,205-3—75,206
Amended § 522.540.	75,247-3—75,249-2	75,247-3—75,249-2

Illustration C

Weekly filing checklist from CCH *Food Drug Cosmetic Law Reports*. Published and copyrighted by Commerce Clearing House, Inc., Chicago, Il. 60646, and reproduced with their permission.

available sources of these documents. As noted above, bound topical reporters reissue the decisional literature for permanent retention, thereby allowing space for new current material.

2. EXPLANATORY TEXT

In addition to the primary sources of law, the services also provide descriptive and explanatory sections to aid the researcher in understanding the primary sources and their legal effect, in integrating and synthesizing them, and in using them in practice. The length, arrangement and location of the text varies from service to service. Although not written by well known scholars, it is usually competently and accurately done. This material is not, however, authoritative, and is generally not quoted or cited in briefs or arguments to courts. Like the other features of the looseleaf service, the editorial text is updated and supplemented, as necessary. Since the subject matter of particular services often require variations in treatment, the publishers do not attempt total uniformity in these features. Although there are now about twenty significant publishers of legal looseleaf services, three firms continue to dominate the field—Bureau of National Affairs, Commerce Clearing House, and Prentice-Hall.[2]

The three publishers compete in a number of fields, particularly energy regulation, labor law and taxation, in which each offers a service. The quality of their respective publications vary from field to field, as do user preferences. Despite the similarity of approach used by each publisher in their own services, cross referencing between services is not a significant factor in looseleaf publishing and the researcher can feel free to select from among the available services in any field based on individual experience. The several services on any particular subject do not overlap completely, and cases not found in one, may well appear in another. Similarly, the quality of indexing and editorial treatment varies from service to service.

Because of the intense competition between the various publishers, each offers special services which are often not widely known or fully exploited by users. For example, one or another of these publishers may replace missing pages or even replace a hopelessly misfiled volume, offer telephone service for late developments, or mail to subscribers the full text of documents which are abstracted or referred to in their publications. These auxiliary services can often be quite helpful when a particularly elusive decision or ruling is needed, yet they are rarely used by most subscribers.

3. VARIATIONS IN INDEXING

Another major advantage of these services is the variety and multiplicity of the indexes which are provided for access to their contents. This can best be described by examining the several different

2. The publishing activities of the Corporation Trust Company, which started the first real service in 1913, merged with CCH in 1927. Bureau of National Affairs began publishing in 1933, and Prentice-Hall, organized in 1913, issued its first looseleaf service about 1919.

approaches employed in their indexing. The specific names of these indexes will vary from publisher to publisher, but the generic forms can be found in most services. It should be noted that many looseleaf services, particularly those published by Commerce Clearing House and Prentice-Hall, provide references in their indexes and finding aids to paragraph numbers, rather than pages. This practice is sometimes confusing to users, but does simplify access and avoids the necessity of frequently revising all indexes to reflect the constant change inherent in most regulatory fields.

a. By Time of Issuance

Because of their frequency of supplementation and the expense of revising an entire index weekly or monthly in order to give access to both older and more recent material, most looseleaf services use "layered indexing" for subject access. That approach utilizes several indexes covering the whole service, but with different intensity of detail and frequency of revision. The primary access is through a very detailed general index, (sometimes called a "master index" or "topical index") which is not frequently revised, or is revised only in those parts rendered obsolete by extensive changes.

The general index is then supplemented by a less detailed, but frequently revised, *updating* index called "current index", "latest additions", or "late developments index". This updating index does not purport to cover the whole service in detail, but rather provides access to material issued *since* the last revision of the general index. Some services offer two updating indexes—a current index *and* a later developments index—but many researchers find the necessity of consulting three subject indexes more of a nuisance than an advantage. Needless to say, the use of a subject approach to any looseleaf service should include each of the several indexes provided, in order to assure sufficient detail and the *latest* coverage of the contents.

Four typical indexes, differentiated by their time of issuance and their detail, are shown below, in Illustrations D, E, F and G, from the CCH *Employment Practices Guide.* Those illustrations will also be used in Section D–2 to describe the procedures for using a looseleaf service.

b. By Intensity

As noted above, the three chronologically differentiated indexes described in Section (a) also vary in their detail and intensity. For example, note the differences in detail between Illustrations D, E, F and G below, under the entry "Physical fitness requirements" in each.

Many looseleaf services also provide a *very* general index which has only a few broad entries, but directs the user to the sections of the service where particular large topics begin. In CCH services this is called the "Rapid Finder Index." (See Illustration D below, for an

176 8-82 **Rapid Finder Index** **13-7**

Employment Practices **QUA**
014—62

Illustration D

"Rapid Finder Index," in CCH *Employment Practices Guide.* Published and copyrighted by Commerce Clearing House, Inc., Chicago, Il. 60646, and reproduced with their permission.

29-4

Topical Index

References are to paragraph (¶) numbers.
See also Topical Index at page 2851.

PER

033—74

Illustration E

"Topical Index", the main subject index to the CCH *Employment Practices Guide*. Published and copyrighted by Commerce Clearing House, Inc., Chicago, Il. 60646, and reproduced with their permission.

186 1-83

Current Items **2765**

References are to paragraph (¶) numbers.
See also Topical Indexes at pages 17, 2801 and 2851.

Employment Practices
016—74 **PRO**

Illustration F

"Current Items", the *first supplement* to the Topical Index in the CCH *Employment Practices Guide.* Published and copyrighted by Commerce Clearing House, Inc., Chicago, Il. 60646, and reproduced with their permission.

2812 162 3-82

Latest Additions

References are to paragraph (¶) numbers.
See also Topical Indexes at pages 17 and 2851.

NEW

Illustration G

"Latest Additions", the *second supplement* to the Topical Index in the CCH *Employment Practices Guide.* Published and copyrighted by Commerce Clearing House, Inc., Chicago, Il. 60646, and reproduced with their permission.

example.) The use of a Rapid Finder Index is similar to approaching a digest by its component topics, while the use of the Topical or General Index is like approaching a digest by its "Descriptive Word Index".

c. Type of Material

Most looseleaf services also include specific indexes for each particular type of legal material they contain. These "finding aids," as they are often called, enable one to locate a known document directly in the service, without the necessity of consulting the subject indexes. Because of the integrated nature of many services, finding a known document may also lead to other related documents. These aids include the familiar table of cases which is often supplemented by an updating table. See Illustration H below for such a supplementary table (called "Latest Additions to Case Table") in the CCH *Employment Practices Guide.*

Other finding aids provide access to statutes (by name or citation), regulations, rulings, agency directives, and similar documents of legal effect. See Illustrations L, M, N, P and Q, below for examples of such lists appearing in the CCH *Employment Practices Guide.* In a few services, these lists also include a citator component which indicates changes in the document or refers to later documents which have affected it, but most services provide that feature only for cases. Information describing what finding lists are included and their specific coverage can be found in the "How to Use" section of that service.

4. PROMPT SUPPLEMENTATION

The frequent supplementation of looseleaf services makes these publications the first available source of most legal documents. They appear long before the official and other commercial editions of statutes and both judicial and administrative decisions. Administrative regulations, however, are available even faster in the daily *Federal Register* and some court decisions may be retrievable in LEXIS shortly before they are issued in a looseleaf service.

The major CCH, BNA and Prentice-Hall services include weekly releases, and occasionally distribute special releases to cover a particularly important development between regular issues. Other services are issued bi-weekly or monthly, and some on a quarterly basis. A publication which is supplemented only annually lacks the essential element of frequency for designation as a looseleaf service. Because of their filing schemes and layered indexing, the new material is usually easily accessible as soon as it is filed.

5. INSTRUCTIONS SECTION

Every looseleaf service includes an instructional section, located either in the first binder or in the index binder, and usually called "How to Use This Service." These brief guides describe the contents

149-10 176 8-82

Latest Additions to Case Table
See also Case Tables at pages 111 and 151.

Small v. United Airlines, Inc.
(DC NJ 1981) .... 27 EPD ¶ 32,232

Smallwood v. United Air Lines, Inc.
(CA-4 1981) 661 F2d 303 .... 27 EPD ¶ 32,130
—cert den (US SCt 1982) .... 29 EPD ¶ 32,733

Smith (Bell); Paralyzed Veterans of America v. (see Paralyzed Veterans of America v. Smith (Bell))

Smith (Civiletti); Segar v. (see Segar v. Smith (Civiletti))

Smith v. Dow Chemical Co.
(DC Tex 1981) .... 26 EPD ¶ 32,075

Smith v. Lubbers
(DC DofC 1982) .... 29 EPD ¶ 32,816

Smith (Civiletti); Stewart v. (see Stewart v. Smith (Civiletti))

Smith; Valentine v. (see Valentine v. Smith)

Snipes v. U.S. Postal Service
(CA-4 1982) .... 28 EPD ¶ 32,684

Sobel v. Yeshiva University
(DC NY 1980) 85 FRD 322 .... 22 EPD ¶ 30,653
—ruling on counsel interviews (DC NY 1981) .... 28 EPD ¶ 32,479

Solomon; Roberts v. (see Roberts v. Solomon)

Sommers aka Cornish v. Budget Marketing, Inc.
(CA-8 1982) 667 F2d 748 .... 27 EPD ¶ 32,318

Southeast Neighborhood House; Ali v. (see Ali v. Southeast Neighborhood House)

Southern Baptist Hospital v. EEOC
(DC La 1982) .... 28 EPD ¶ 32,585

Southern College of Optometry; Dacus v. (see Dacus v. Southern College of Optometry)

Southern Imperial Coatings Corp. v. EEOC
(DC La 1981) .... 29 EPD ¶ 32,741

Southern Oil Co. of New York; Klausner v. (see Klausner v. Southern Oil Co. of New York)

Southern Pacific Transportation Co.; Willey v. (see Willey v. Southern Pacific Transportation Co.)

Southwestern Baptist Theological Seminary; EEOC v.
(CA-5 1981) 651 F2d 277 .... 26 EPD ¶ 32,017
—cert den (US SCt 1982) .... 28 EPD ¶ 32,548

Southwestern Bell Telephone Co.; Spearmon v. (see Spearmon v. Southwestern Bell Telephone Co.)

Southwestern Bell Telephone Co.; Wood v. (see Wood v. Southwestern Bell Telephone Co.)

Spagnuolo v. Whirlpool Corp.
(DC NC 1979) 467 FSupp 364 .... 19 EPD ¶ 9195
—aff'd in part, rev'd in part and rem'd (CA-4 1981) .... 25 EPD ¶ 31,596
—cert den (US SCt 1981) .... 27 EPD ¶ 32,145

Spaulding v. University of Washington
(CA-9 1982) .... 28 EPD ¶ 32,683

Spearmon v. Southwestern Bell Telephone Co.
(CA-8 1981) 662 F2d 509 .... 27 EPD ¶ 32,226

Spencer Turbine Co.; Hague v. (see Hague v. Spencer Turbine Co.)

Sperry Rand Corp.; Elliott v. (see Elliott v. Sperry Rand Corp.)

Spiess v. C. Itoh & Co., Inc.
(DC Tex 1979) 469 FSupp 1 .... 19 EPD ¶ 9022
—rev'd and rem'd (CA-5 1981) 643 F2d 353 .... 25 EPD ¶ 31,768
—reh'g *en banc* granted (CA-5 1981) ...... 27 EPD ¶ 32,210
—vac'd (CA-5 1981) .... 28 EPD ¶ 32,407
—vac'd and rem'd (US SCt 1982) ...... 29 EPD ¶ 32,822

Spirides v. Reinhardt
(DC DofC 1980) 485 FSupp 685 .... 22 EPD ¶ 30,740
—aff'd (CA DofC 1981) .... 27 EPD ¶ 32,267

Spirt v. Teachers Insurance and Annuity Assn.
(DC NY 1979) 475 FSupp 1298 .... 21 EPD ¶ 30,455
—rulings on intervention (DC NY 1982) .... 29 EPD ¶ 32,732

Spivey v. Lucky Mc Uranium Corp.
(Wyo SCt 1981) 636 P2d 518 .... 28 EPD ¶ 32,532

Spokane Concrete Products, Inc.; EEOC v.
(DC Wash 1982) .... 28 EPD ¶ 32,624

Staats; Lawrence v. (see Lawrence v. Staats)

Stacy v. Michigan Employment Security Com.
(DC Mich 1980) .... 26 EPD ¶ 32,007

Standard Oil Co. of California; Wiltshire v. (see Wiltshire v. Standard Oil Co. of California)

State Board for Community Colleges and Occupational Education; Rivas v. (see Rivas v. State Board for Community Colleges and Occupational Education)

State Board of Education; Perkins v. (see Perkins v. State Board of Education)

State Farm Mutual Automobile Insurance Co. v. EEOC
(DC Cal 1981) .... 27 EPD ¶ 32,331

State Farm Mutual Automobile Insurance Co.; EEOC v.
(DC Cal 1982) .... 28 EPD ¶ 32,587

State Farm Mutual Insurance Co.; Rubin v. (see Rubin v. State Farm Mutual Insurance Co.)

State Teachers' Retirement System; Probe v. (see Probe v. State Teachers' Retirement System)

State University of New York at Albany v. New York State Human Rights Appeal Board
(NY SCt AppDiv 1981) .... 26 EPD ¶ 32,056
—aff'd (NY CtApp 1982) .... 28 EPD ¶ 32,620

Stauffer Chemical Co.; Guyette v. (see Guyette v. Stauffer Chemical Co.)

Steelworkers (USA); Anness v. (see Anness v. Steelworkers (USA))

Steelworkers (USA); Carroll v. (see Carroll v. Steelworkers (USA))

Steelworkers (USA), Local 8141 v. Tooley (see Tooley v. Martin-Marietta Corp.)

Steelworkers (USA) v. Swint
(US SCt 1982) .... 28 EPD ¶ 32,619

Sterling Transit Co. v. California Fair Employment Practice Com.
(Cal CtApp 1981) .... 28 EPD ¶ 32,543

Stetson; Mackey v. (see Mackey v. Stetson)

Stewart v. CPC International, Inc.
(CA-7 1982) .... 29 EPD ¶ 32,702

Stewart v. Campbell Soup Co.
(DC Ohio 1981) .... 27 EPD ¶ 32,340

Stewart v. Hannon
(DC Ill 1979) 469 FSupp 1142 .... 20 EPD ¶ 30,223
—denial of attys' fees aff'd (CA-7 1982) 675 F2d 846 .... 28 EPD ¶ 32,582

Stewart v. Smith (Civiletti)
(DC DofC 1979) .... 21 EPD ¶ 30,508
—aff'd (CA DofC 1982) .... 28 EPD ¶ 32,509

Stewart v. Thomas
(DC DofC 1982) .... 29 EPD ¶ 32,860

Stock v. Horsman Dolls, Inc.
(DC SC 1981) .... 27 EPD ¶ 32,275

Stoller v. Marsh
(CA DofC 1982) .... 29 EPD ¶ 32,847

Stone; Middleson-Keirn v. (see Middleson-Keirn v. Stone)

Stone v. Xerox Corp.
(DC Ga 1981) .... 28 EPD ¶ 32,643

Stotts v. Memphis Fire Department
(CA-6 1982) .... 28 EPD ¶ 32,678

SMA

Illustration H

"Latest Additions to Case Table", showing reference to decision in *EEOC v. Spokane Concrete Products, Inc.* Published and copyrighted by Commerce Clearing House, Inc., Chicago, Il. 60646, and reproduced with their permission.

of the service, the various means of access, and any special features it may contain. Many users neglect this important aid and consequently lose much time and efficiency in using the service, and are unaware of many useful features. A few minutes with these instructions will inevitably repay itself by far more time saved in the use of the service. A major advantage of looseleaf services lies in their organizational schemes, which cannot always be learned by a superficial scanning of the contents. No two services are exactly the same and unless one has already learned the structure, access methods, and contents of a service by frequent use, the "How to Use" section is the best place to begin one's approach to the publication. In addition this section often provides references to other services issued by the same publisher which relate to the same subject field.

D. PROCEDURES FOR USE

This section will describe the actual use of a looseleaf service. It will repeat some of the foregoing material, but in a more functional context. We will focus on a specific legal problem in the CCH *Employment Practices Guide* and use illustrations from that service to portray graphically a typical looseleaf research inquiry.

1. VARIETY OF APPROACHES

There are several different approaches for retrieving information from a looseleaf service. These include a variety of subject indexes, tables of cases, finding lists for statutes, regulations, and other administrative documents.

Let us assume that a woman has been denied employment for a physically strenuous job, without being given a test of her ability to perform the tasks involved. She has been told that she was not hired because of the physical requirements of the job, but she suspects that there was sex discrimination underlying her rejection, and now seeks relief. After analysis of the problem stated and selection of search words and phrases, you decide to begin research of the question in the CCH *Employment Practices Guide*, having ascertained that it covers sex discrimination in employment. By checking under "Fair Employment" in the selective list of looseleaf services in Section E.2, beginning at p. 420, below, you will see that there are several other publications covering this field.

To simplify this presentation, we will assume that our problem is governed solely by federal law. In fact, some states have applicable laws and the research might include state sources as well. The CCH service which we are examining here contains extensive coverage of state law on this topic.

2. SUBJECT INDEXES

By consulting the "How to Use the Reporter" section in volume 1, we discover that there are the following subject indexes: (a) "Rapid

Finder Index" which, under very general subject headings, refers to the major topical divisions of the service (see Illustration D); (b) "Topical Index" which includes, under many, quite specific headings, references to the particular paragraphs and subdivisions dealing with those subjects (see Illustration E) and a "Cumulative Index" which provides references from paragraphs in the main part of the service to related material in the "New Development" paragraphs; (c) Separate supplements to the "Cumulative Index" and the "Topical Index", called respectively, *Current Items to Cumulative Index* and *Current Items to Topical Index,* which provide access to material issued since the last revision of those indexes (see Illustration F for the latter); and (d) Separate "Latest Additions" supplements to both the "Cumulative Index" and the "Topical Index", which include even later material (see Illustration G for "Latest Additions to Topical Index"). Note that the entries in each of these indexes lead to paragraph numbers in the service, not page numbers.

In using these indexes to locate material on our problem, one of the likely search words and phrases would be "physical fitness requirements". Note that the "Rapid Finder Index" (in Illustration D at page 396) leads to paragraph 441, where an extensive explanatory text by the CCH editorial staff summarizes the applicable law on the topic "Physical Fitness" with references to subparagraphs in the service where various aspects of that topic are treated.

The "Topical Index" (Illustration E at page 397), however, also provides many direct references to decisions on that topic and, under the subtopic "Strenuous jobs/exclusion of women", refers to a subsection of paragraph 441, i.e., ¶ 441.60. Illustration I–1 shows that subsection with its references to two federal cases that seem to be relevant. Illustration I–2 shows several other subsections of ¶ 441 which also list apparently related cases. The names and citations of these cases should be noted. Before reading them, however, we check the supplementing indexes for later decisions which may be closer to our problem, and find in "Current Items" (Illustration F at page 398) a reference to ¶ 23,624 under the heading "Strenuous jobs/female truck driver applicant."

Another updating technique in this service is the "Cumulative Indexes" which reflect material in the "New Developments" section of the service. Listings in these indexes are *from* paragraph numbers. Although neither the "Cumulative Index", nor the "Current Cumulative Index" list anything under ¶ 441.60, the "Latest Additions to Cumulative Index" (Illustration J) does show two more recent decisions under ¶ 441.60 including another reference to the truck driver case in ¶ 32,624. This listing gives a fuller description and indicates that the woman was "rejected due to assumption about strength."

Turning now to paragraph 32,624, we find that it is not in the looseleaf binder, but in bound volume 28 of CCH *Employment Practices Decisions* (28 *EPD* ¶ 32,624) a topical reporter deriving from the

overweight Caucasians or used weight requirement in racially biased manner.

EEOC Decision, No. 74-14, August 1, 1973.
EEOC Decision, No. 76-47, October 8, 1975.

.32 Difference in body frames.—Evidence indicating that weight limitations for male flight attendants took into account large body frames while those for female attendants did not was not adequate for purposes of establishing unlawful sex discrimination.

Comstock v. Eastern Air Lines, Inc. (DC Va 1975) 10 EPD ¶ 10,392.

.35 Disparate treatment.—Trucking company committed racial discrimination by applying its height and weight requirements for truck drivers most strictly when considering Negro applicants while applying same standards loosely and granting exceptions when considering white applicants.

U.S. v. Lee ay Motor Freight, Inc. (DC Ok 1973) 7 EPD ¶ 9066.
EEOC Decision, No. 70-140, September 9, 1969.

.36 Exclusion short women.—Height requirement for city police department was not shown to be rationally related to position of police officer, nor fairly and substantially related to performance of duties of position.

Vanguard Justice Society, Inc. v. Hughes; Gumpman v. Hughes; Bosworth v. Hughes (DC Md 1979) 20 EPD ¶ 30,077, 471 FSupp 670.

.40 Pregnancy-caused discharge.—Discharge of female police officer based on presumption that she was unable to perform her job because of pregnancy was unlawful sex discrimination where she was denied opportunity to prove otherwise.

U.S. City of Philadelphia; U.S. v. Fraternal Order of Police (CA-3 1978) 16 EPD ¶ 8177, 573 F2d 802; cert den (1978) 17 EPD ¶ 8604A, 439 US 830, 99 SCt 105.

.50 Physical fitness.—Discharge of Negro employee soon after he was hired as railroad fireman was not due to racial considerations where employer had acted upon advice of its chief surgeon who disqualified employee from further employment after x-ray revealed curvature of spine, which prevented employee from meeting physical requirements consistently adhered to by employer.

Roberts v. St. Louis Southwestern Ry. Co. (DC Ar 1971) 3 EPD ¶ 8344, 329 FSupp 973.
EEOC Decision, No. 70-694, April 13, 1970.
EEOC Decision, No. 70-840, May 25, 1970.

.501 Even though evidence showed rejected job applicant was physically qualified, he was rejected by company pursuant to advice, however erroneous, given by its examining physician that complainant was physically disqualified.

Weaden v. American Cyanamid Co. (DC ND Fl 1976) 14 EPD ¶ 7557.

.502 Where other females had been hired for position and male and female applicants faced same qualifying standards, employer was not guilty of sex discrimination for refusing to hire claimant for heavy lifting position on strength of doctor's report that she was unfit for job.

EEOC Decision, No. 75-064, November 4, 1974.

.503 It is improper to conclude that every individual above specified age limit is physically unable to perform certain vigorous work. However, differentiation among employees is justified if based on reasonable factors other than age, such as physical fitness requirements.

W&H Opinion Letter, August 30, 1968.
W&H Opinion Letter, September 24, 1968.
W&H Opinion Letter, July 11, 1968.

.504 Employer unlawfully refused to hire Negro applicant with 10 years' experience not, as applicant was told, because his blood pressure was too high to do mining work, but because of race.

EEOC Decision, No. 70-134, September 5, 1969.

.52 Informal examination.—Fact that employer's doctor reached his conclusion as to physical disability of Negro applicant upon informal examination rather than upon medical examination under employer's auspices did not violate applicant's rights since doctor was acquainted with and had treated various members of applicant's family.

Dorcus v. Westvaco Corp. (DC Va 1972) 5 EPD ¶ 8086, 345 FSupp 1173.

.54 Non-competitive examination.—Use of only qualifying examination, rather than competitive physical examination, for fire department applicants, plus written exam which was not shown to be job-related, amounted altogether as proof that hiring process for firemen was unconstitutionally discriminatory against minority applicants.

Vulcan Society v. Civil Service Commission (CA-2 1973) 6 EPD ¶ 8974, 490 F2d 387.

.56 Disparate physical examinations.—Giving male production employees physical examinations which included back x-rays at time they were hired, while not giving back x-rays to female employees until they sought assignment to job that required lifting of weights was sex bias.

EEOC Decision, No. 71-1332, March 2, 1971.

.58 Frequency of physical examinations.—Requiring more frequent examinations for bus drivers over 50 years of age than for younger drivers does not violate statutory ban on age discrimination if health standards are applied uniformly to persons of all ages.

W&H Opinion Letter (WH-137), June 24, 1971.

.60 Strenuous work.—Employer failed to prove that particular requirements of switchman job justified excluding women from consideration, since it introduced no evidence that duties of job were so strenuous that all or most women would be unable to perform them.

Weeks v. Southern Bell Telephone & Telegraph Co. (CA-5 1969) 1 EPD ¶ 9970, 408 F2d 228.
Rosenfeld v. Southern Pacific Co. (CA-9 1971) 3 EPD ¶ 8247, 444 F2d 1219.

.601 Employer, who admitted to preference for workers under 40 years of age in filling positions in

Illustration I–1

Decisions listed under ¶ 441 in CCH *Employment Practices Guide.* Published and copyrighted by Commerce Clearing House, Inc., Chicago, Il. 60646, and reproduced with their permission.

its production department, could not properly claim RFOA (reasonable factors other than age) exception in defending its preference. Although employer argued that applicants 40 years of age and older as class lacked strength and stamina to perform economically, productively, and safely, RFOA defense cannot be based on age and must be applied on individual, and not on class or group, basis.

Marshall v. Goodyear Tire & Rubber Co. (DC WD Tn 1979) 19 EPD ¶ 8973; referral to magistrate (DC Tn 1980) 22 EPD ¶ 30,709.

.602 Where there was no evidence that female airline employee could not perform duties required in job involving weight lifting, employer was found to have used stereotypical and culturally based concepts of sex in refusing to transfer her to job.

Pond v. Braniff Airways, Inc. (DC Tx 1976) 12 EPD ¶ 11,274.

.603 Failure to judge female applicant for weight lifting position on basis of her individual capacity to perform job rather than on basis of preconceived opinions as to capacities of women as class was unlawful sex bias.

EEOC Decision, No. 75-115, December 16, 1974.

.61 "Heavy" and "light" jobs.—Switch from classifying jobs as "male" and "female" to "heavy" and "light" was not continuation of improper sex discrimination where company made adequate analysis of requirements of each job and then reviewed capabilities of each female employee to see if any of them could, as individuals, perform "heavy" jobs.

Taylor v. Goodyear Tire and Rubber Co. (DC Al 1972) 5 EPD ¶ 8545.

.65 Lifting.—Employer could not be viewed as having acted reasonably and in interest of safety of female employees in imposing limit of 35 pounds as maximum weight which female employees could lift in their work.

Bowe v. Colgate-Palmolive Co (CA-7 1969) 2 EPD ¶ 10,090, 416 F2d 711.

Long v. Sapp (CA-5 1974) 8 EPD ¶ 9712, 502 F2d 34.

EEOC Decision, No. 77-32, August 16, 1977.

.66 Heavy lifting in initial assignment.—Job assignment practices discriminated against females on the basis of sex where females were effectively barred from material handling jobs by heavy physical requirements of intial assignments given to material handlers, even though majority of material handling work required little heavy lifting. Employer was required to attempt to remedy sex-biased effects of assignment practices.

Payne v. Travenol Laboratories, Inc. (DC Ms 1976) 11 EPD ¶ 10,784; aff'd on this issue (CA-5 1978) 15 EPD ¶ 8039, 565 F2d 895; reh'g den (CA-5 1978) 17 EPD ¶ 8383; cert den (CA-5 1978) 17 EPD ¶ 8604A; 439 US 835, 99 SCt 118.

.67 Sampling of lifting ability.—Employer's use of only few females as small sampling of ability of all women to perform work was insufficient to establish that women were not qualified for jobs.

EEOC Decision, No. 71-1868, April 22, 1971.

.68 Alternative to heavy lifting.—Where duties of utility position involved carrying 100-pound bundle of laundry, an alternative was available by making up laundry in bundles of less than 100 pounds, and accordingly, designation of utility positions as "male jobs" on basis of having to lift heavy garbage cans and bundles of laundry was unlawful.

McLean v. State of Alaska (Ak SCt 1978) 18 EPD ¶ 8787, 583 P2d 867.

.69 State ban on lifting.—State protective laws excluding women from work involving lifting of objects weighing in excess of twenty-five pounds are invalid in that they require employment practices amounting to unlawful sex discrimination under federal law.

Manning v. General Motors Corp. (DC Oh 1971) 3 EPD ¶ 8325; aff'd sub nom *Manning v. Automobile Workers (UAW)* (CA-6 1972) 5 EPD ¶ 7964, 466 F2d 812; cert den sub nom *Manning v. General Motors Corp.* (1973) 5 EPD ¶ 8463, — U.S. —.

General Electric Co. v. Hughes (DC Oh 1971) 3 EPD ¶ 8245; aff'd per curiam (CA-6 1972) 4 EPD ¶ 7658.

EEOC Decision, No. 72-1008, February 3, 1972.

EEOC Decision, No. 72-1919, June 6, 1972.

EEOC Decision, Case No. Ch 68-2-539 E, May 7, 1969.

.70 Physically demanding jobs.—Savings and loan institution engaged in age discrimination with regard to hiring of tellers within protected age bracket, but not in rejecting 47-year-old complainant who admitted that teller's job would be too physically demanding for him.

Hodgson v. First Federal Savings & Loan Assn. of Broward Co. (DC Fl 1970) 3 EPD ¶ 8066; aff'd (CA-5 1972) 4 EPD ¶ 7629, 455 F2d 818.

.80 Sickle cell anemia.—Discharge of Negro employee after x-rays revealed bone degeneration in his spinal region was not considered racial discrimination even though degeneration may have resulted from sickle cell anemia, disease common to Americans of African heritage. It was condition of his back, not his blood, that disqualified employee from further employment as laborer. The discharge did not have to be justified by business necessity since business necessity can be presumed where physical requirement is so directly related to job peformance as good back is to manual labor.

Smith v. Olin Chemical Corp. (DC La 1974) 9 EPD ¶ 9876; aff'd (CA-5 1977) 14 EPD ¶ 7702.

.90 Transsexual operation.—Discharge of teacher who had undergone sex-change operation from male to female was proper where it was found that her effect on students would have been disturbing. Such effect, when shown by competent testimony of psychiatric experts, amounted to just cause to dismiss even though her ability to teach subject matter of courses was unimpaired.

Grossman v. Bernards Township Board of Education (DC NJ 1975) 11 EPD ¶ 10,686; aff'd (CA-3 1976) 12 EPD ¶ 11,241.

Illustration I–2

Continuation of decisions under ¶ 441, with reference to a relevant E.E.O.C. decision shown.

2554 **Latest Additions to Cumulative Index** 175 7-82

See also Cumulative Index at page 2601.

From Compilation Paragraph No.			To New Development Paragraph No.
	.50	Trauma associated with earlier injury disqualifies machine operator (DC La) 28 EPD ¶ 32,480.—Aff'd (CA-5) 28 EPD ¶ 32,481.—Cert den (US SCt)	**32,838**
	.60	Female truck applicant rejected due to assumption about strength (DC Wash)	**32,624**
	.60	Rejection of disabled applicant for park technician job justified (DC Ga)	**32,560**
443	.034	Unreasonable to accommodate park job to disabled applicant (DC Ga)	**32,560**
445		Ex-policeman's rejection as bus driver on basis of conviction for acceptance of bribe unlawful (EEOC)	**6804**
		Failure to consider job relatedness to applicant's conviction improper (EEOC)	**6811**
		Possession of weapon conviction not job related (EEOC)	**6822**
	.18	Lack of high school diploma and conviction record do not justify refusal to hire (EEOC)	**6807**
	.50	Serious offenses warranted disapproval for security guard position (EEOC)	**6825**
	.58	Rehabilitation record warrants forger's hiring as photographer (EEOC)	**6808**
	.58	Shoplifting conviction involving inexpensive merchandise improper basis for refusal to hire (EEOC)	**6791**
	.58	Unrelated-to-job drunkenness convictions did not warrant dismissal (EEOC)	**6805**
	.75	Coworkers' preferences do not justify felon employee's dismissal (EEOC)	**6810**
	.75	Position unjustifiedly denied on basis of murder conviction not threatening coworkers' safety (EEOC)	**6809**
449	.455	*Mahroom v. Marsh (Alexander) (Hook)* (DC Cal).—Aff'd (CA-9) 27 EPD ¶ 32,326.—Cert den (US SCt)	**32,562**
451	.20	Hard hat preferred over turban for safety (EEOC)	**6817**
	.35	Respirator does not facilitate wearing of beard (EEOC)	**6817**
461		Ability tests for handicapped persons inadequate, study shows	**5056**
462	.101	*EEOC v. American National Bank* (DC Va).—Aff'd in part and rev'd in part (CA-4) 26 EPD ¶ 31,920.—Rehearing denied (CA-4)	**32,720**
466	.10	No remedial promotional exam for provisional city employees (DC NY)	**32,649**
	.12	Auditor test has disparate impact on Spanish-surnamed applicants (CA-9) 25 EPD ¶ 31,728.—Amended opinion issued (CA-9) 27 EPD ¶ 32,182.—Cert den (US SCt)	**32,534**
	.12	Senior accountant job test has no disparate impact (CA-9) 25 EPD ¶ 31,728.—Amended opinion issued (CA-9) 27 EPD ¶ 32,182.—Cert den (US SCt)	**32,534**
	.155	Hiring preference given to veterans in state employment allowed under state law (EEOC)	**6812**
	.20	Discriminatory component is violative despite non-discriminatory final result (CA-2) 25 EPD ¶ 31,702.—Aff'd and rem'd (US SCt)	**32,820**
	.201	*Stewart v. Hannon* (DC Ill).—Attorneys' fee denial aff'd (CA-7)	**32,582**
470	.10	Test with disparate impact has sufficient correlation with work elements (CA-9) 25 EPD ¶ 31,728.—Amended opinion issued (CA-9) 27 EPD ¶ 32,182.—Cert den (US SCt)	**32,534**
480	.38	*Stewart v. Hannon* (DC Ill).—Attorneys' fee denial aff'd (CA-7)	**32,582**
496	.105	*Williams v. New Orleans Steamship Assn.* (DC La).—Aff'd in part, rev'd and rem'd in part (CA-5)	**32,677**
	.132	*Swint v. Pullman-Standard* (CA-5).—Rev'd and rem'd (US SCt)	**32,619**
	.20	Denying job to qualified Hispanic national origin bias (DC NM) 24 EPD ¶ 31,200.—Consent decree approved (DC NM)	**32,472**
	.30	Class fails to demonstrate bias in initial assignments (CA-5)	**32,647**
	.32	*Williams v. New Orleans Steamship Assn.* (DC La).—Aff'd in part, rev'd and rem'd in part (CA-5)	**32,677**
	.404	*Williams v. New Orleans Steamship Assn.* (DC La).—Aff'd in part, rev'd and rem'd in part (CA-5)	**32,677**
	.80	Isolated physically arduous position is not sex biased (CA-5)	**32,647**
	.93	Sex bias in bar to females in male unit of detention center (EEOC)	**6819**
498	.35	Provisional state employee had no expanded rights under consent decree (DC NY)	**32,849**
502	.405	*Williams v. New Orleans Steamship Assn.* (DC La).—Aff'd in part, rev'd and rem'd in part (CA-5)	**32,677**
512	.30	Traditional industry classification no defense to Equal Pay claim (CA DofC)	**32,668**
	.302	*EEOC v. Pacific Press Publishing Assn.* (DC Cal).—Aff'd (CA-9)	**32,817**
	.50	*Electrical Workers (IUE) v. Westinghouse Electric Corp.* (CA-3).—Settlement tentatively approved (DC NJ)	**32,645**
	.50	Public health nurses, public health sanitarians perform comparable work (DC Wis)	**32,721**
	.51	Library director not comparable to other municipal directors (DC Ala)	**32,648**
514	.16	No pay bias shown where others not similarly situated (DC Tex)	**32,724**
518	.08	Bookbinders and specific bindery worker jobs substantially equal (CA DofC)	**32,668**
	.08	Pursers, flight attendants did not have similar working conditions (DC NY)	**32,689**
	.102	*Thompson v. (Boyle) Sawyer* (DC DofC).—Aff'd on this issue (CA DofC)	**32,668**
519	.43	Male co-director's higher salary justified by education and experience (DC ND)	**32,497**
	.43	Need to compete in marketplace explains pay differences between public health nurses and public health sanitarians (DC Wis)	**32,721**
526	.10	Pursers had greater responsibility than flight attendants (DC NY)	**32,689**
528	.15	Professors' salary differentials based on merit/seniority system (DC Ohio)	**32,783**
	.15	Statistical shortcomings defuse assertions of merit pay system bias (CA-5)	**32,647**

Illustration J

"Latest Additions to Cumulative Index" (the second of three *Cumulative Indexes*) showing a relevant decision under 441.60. Published and copyrighted by Commerce Clearing House, Inc., Chicago, Il. 60646, and reproduced with their permission.

decisions in this service. The decision is a recent one, *E.E.O.C. v. Spokane Concrete Products, Inc.*, decided by the U. S. District Court, Eastern District of Washington, in March, 1982. Illustrations K–1 and K–2 show the beginning of the decision and its apparent relevance to our problem. No citation is given to Federal Supplement, but the case *was* in fact reported by West at 524 *Fed.Supp.* 518 (1982). CCH usually provides West citations, if available, but the West report may not have been published when CCH issued its publication of the decision. The West topics and key numbers in *its* head notes to the *Federal Supplement* can be used to locate other cases on the same subject in the West digests.

Since the *Spokane Case* applies Title VII of the Civil Rights Act of 1964, we should turn to that statute. That can be done quickly by consulting a finding list in the same service.

3. DOCUMENTARY FINDING AIDS

As described above in Section C.3.c, looseleaf services usually contain documentary finding aids, including tables of cases and finding lists of other legal sources. If we had a reference to the *Spokane Case* earlier in our research, we might have located it in this service through a case table. (See Illustration H, above.) The "back reference" to ¶ 441.60, as shown following the first headnote of the decision in Illustration K–1 above, would have referred back to the original section of the service and possibly to other relevant cases.

To locate Title VII of the Civil Rights Act of 1964, we turn to a Section of the service called "Federal Laws—Regulations—Orders." The table of contents of that section, the beginning of which is shown in Illustration L, lists a number of provisions of the U. S. Constitution and many federal statutes applicable to the subject matter of the service. Each is designated by the paragraph number where its text can be found.

Among the statutes listed is the *Fair Employment Practices Law*, consisting of several titles of the *Civil Rights Act of 1964*, including Title VII. Its location in this service is given as paragraph 3005. At that paragraph number, we find that the statutory text is preceded by a table of contents specifically analyzing that Act (Illustrations M–1 and M–2). Note that the table of contents converts sections of the Public Law to sections of the *U.S. Code*, and that in scanning the contents, we find a reference to 42 *U.S.C.* 2000e–12a which gives the enforcement agency created by the Act (the Equal Employment Opportunity Commission) the "right to issue regulations."

The E.E.O.C. regulations would actually have been referred to at several other places in our use of this service. For example, had we continued scanning the "Federal Laws—Regulations—Orders" finding list, we would come to "Regulations and Rules" and under that section, "Equal Employment Opportunity Commission", as shown in

168 5-82 **Cases Cited "28 EPD ¶ ...."** **24,781**

EEOC v. Spokane Concrete Products, Inc.

13. The defendant was justified in concluding that the plaintiff had insubordinatley refused to do work as assigned by his supervisor. It is not an employee's perception of events which is pertinent, but "[i]t is the perception of the decision maker which is relevant." *Smith v. Flax,* [22 EPD ¶ 30,823] 618 F.2d 1062, 1067 (4th Cir. 1980). An employee may not keep to himself reasons for not performing work and expect his employer to excuse non-performance which on its face appears to be insubordination. *See also Martinez v. Bethlehem Steel Corp.,* 496 F.Supp. 1002, 1004 (E.D.Pa. 1979).

14. It is not necessary for this court to find, or for the defendant to prove, that plaintiff did, in fact, refuse to perform an assignment as directed by his supervisor. "It is sufficient only that there be a good faith belief of infraction of a disciplinary rule, even if it is later determined that the belief was mistaken." *Hicks v. Sears, Roebuck and Co., Inc.,* [25 EPD ¶ 31,619] 503 F.Supp. 930, 938 (E.D.Pa. 1980). *See also Jefferies v. Harris County Community Action Association,* [22 EPD ¶ 30,858] 615 F.2d 1025, 1036 (5th Cir. 1980). Furthermore, the plaintiff has not stated a factual basis warranting a determination that defendant's belief of plaintiff's refusal was mistaken. The plaintiff's own testimony has established that he refused to perform the assignment as directed.

15. The only "relevant inquiries" for this court are whether or not the defendant "reasonably and in good faith believed" that the plaintiff refused to perform assigned work and "given such a belief, whether or not the defendant treated plaintiff differently from others committing the same infraction." *Rivers v. Westinghouse Electric Corp.,* 451 F.Supp. 44, 49 (E.D.Pa. 1978). The court has determined both that the defendant's belief was in good faith and that the defendant treated the plaintiff identically to others committing the same infraction.

16. The defendant's discharge of the plaintiff was authorized by the defendant's handbook and did not constitute a breach of any contractual rights of the plaintiff.

17. The plaintiff has not presented any evidence of racial discrimination in his job assignments or in his termination, and defendant should therefore be awarded summary judgment. "It is clear that Title VII actions cannot be successfully maintained on the basis of conjectural and speculative evidence." *Harper v. Transworld Airlines, Inc.,* [10 EPD ¶ 10,498] 525 F.2d 409, 414 (8th Cir. 1975). "When, in fact, nothing remains to be tried, a defendant has the right to judgment without the expense of the trial. The courts must protect defendants from oppression and meritless litigation." *Reich v. New York Hospital,* [26 EPD ¶ 31,865] 513 F.Supp. 854, 863 (S.D.N.Y. 1981). Accordingly, defendant is entitled to summary judgment as to all of the plaintiff's claims.

The court will enter a judgment in keeping with this memorandum opinion.

[¶ 32,624] Equal Employment Opportunity Commission, Plaintiff v. Spokane Concrete Products, Inc., Defendant.

United States District Court, Eastern District of Washington. Civil Action No. C-79-253. March 12, 1982.

Title VII—Civil Rights Act of 1964

Physical Fitness Requirements—Strenuous Jobs—Female Truck Driver Applicant.—A trucking company failed to overcome a case of sexually disparate treatment made by a qualified female applicant for a truck driver job who was rejected after a perfunctory interview and a visual evaluation of her strength by an employee who later testified that one reason the claimant was rejected was that she was a woman. The hiring of a male applicant instead of the claimant because he appeared to be strong was not justified as a professionally acceptable testing method or as a business necessity. Male sex was not a good faith occupational qualification for the job. The employer was not entitled to use untested assumptions about the physical differences between men and women as a hiring criterion.

Back reference.—¶ 441.60.

Employment Practices **¶ 32,624**
023 45

Illustration K-1

Beginning of U. S. District Court decision in *E.E.O.C. v. Spokane Concrete Products, Inc.,* appearing in v. 28 of CCH *Employment Practices Decisions.*

Back Pay—Entitlement—Hiring "But for" Bias.—A female applicant rejected for a truck driving job because of her sex was entitled to injunctive relief and to an award of back pay. Once the claimant established that she was rejected due to bias, the employer was required to show by clear and convincing evidence that she would not have been selected absent discrimination. Use of subjective hiring criteria did not establish that the claimant would not have been hired. The back pay award was computed for a period ending when the claimant accepted alternate equivalent employment that she would likely have taken even if she had been hired by the defendant in view of the high turnover of the job involved.

Back reference.—¶ 2605.11.

Michael Reiss, Sheila F. McKinnon and Lutecia Gonzalez-Quintanilla, Equal Employment Opportunity Commission, Seattle, Washington, for Plaintiff.

Lawrence Small, Spokane, Washington, for Defendant.

QUACKENBUSH, D.J.: This is a sex discrimination case brought by the Equal Employment Opportunity Commission (hereinafter the "EEOC") pursuant to Title VII of the Civil Rights Act of 1964, 42 U.S.C. § 2000(e), *et seq.* The EEOC action was brought on behalf of Beatrice Sellers-McKenna, a female applicant for a position as truck driver with Spokane Concrete Products, Inc., defendant, (hereinafter referred to as "Spokane Concrete"). Plaintiff contends that the defendant intentionally engaged in unlawful employment practices in violation of Title VII by failing to consider and hire Beatrice Sellers-McKenna. A bench trial was held on October 27 and 28, 1981, with both sides presenting witnesses and exhibits. The post-bench-trial supplemental briefing schedule was completed on January 13, 1982.

Spokane Concrete is a Washington corporation, doing business in the State of Washington, engaged in the manufacture, sale and distribution of concrete pipe and related concrete products. At all times pertinent to this action, Spokane Concrete has employed more than fifteen (15) employees. The acts alleged in plaintiff's complaint were committed within the state and the Eastern District of Washington. All conditions precedent to the filing of this action have been fulfilled. On May 12, 1977, Beatrice Sellers (Beatrice Sellers-McKenna since July, 1981), filed a charge with the Commission against Spokane Concrete alleging that Spokane Concrete had discriminated against her in employment because of her sex.

On May 9, 1977, a vacancy for a truck driver position existed at Spokane Concrete. Spokane Concrete called the Spokane office of the Washington State Employment Security Department on or about May 9, 1977, requesting applicants for the position of truck driver. The job order which the Department issued in response to Spokane Concrete's request for applicants stated:

> Need person who is qualified to drive combination diesel rigs, semi- and tractor-trailer rigs. Will haul concrete pipe products in and out of town. Will return home every night. Will have to load and unload own rig. Must have or be able to obtain combination license. 8-5 M-F . . .

Beatrice Sellers-McKenna was sent to Spokane Concrete by Margaret Burns Pirie, her WIN counselor at the Washington State Employment Security Department, as an applicant for the truck driver position. Ms. Sellers-McKenna filled out an application for the truck driver position at Spokane Concrete on May 9, 1977. At that time, she had a combination license, she had worked as a truck driver for a salvage business since 1974 whenever the company needed a truck driver, and held a full-time position as a truck driver between 1975 and 1977 for a carrier company where she was responsible for loading and unloading heavy items from the truck. Before she applied at Spokane Concrete, Ms. Sellers-McKenna also attended a mechanical training and manuvering course in 1975, had received a truck driving training certificate in 1977 and was finishing a course in traffic management. Defendant's application form did not ask about the applicant's strength or physical abilities.

After filling out the application form, Ms. Sellers-McKenna was interviewed for approximately five to ten minutes on May 9, 1977, by Leland R. Hubenthal. Ms. Sellers-McKenna testified that approximately one minute of the interview was spent in actual verbal exchange. She further testified that she was not asked about previous experience, whether she had any health problems, or how much weight she could lift. She recalled her interviewer saying to

Illustration K-2

Continuation of Decision in *E.E.O.C. v. Spokane Concrete Products, Inc.* at 28 *E.P.D.* ¶ 32,624. Published and copyrighted by Commerce Clearing House, Inc., Chicago, Il. 60646, and reproduced with their permission.

187 1-83 **2001**

Federal Laws—Regulations—Orders

¶ 3000

Table of Contents

Paragraph

United States Constitution

Federal Laws

Employment Practices

Illustration L

Table of Contents of "Federal Laws—Regulations—Orders" in CCH *Employment Practices Guide.* Published and copyrighted by Commerce Clearing House, Inc., Chicago, Il. 60646, and reproduced with their permission.

65 3-79 **2007**

Federal Laws

Civil Rights Act of 1964, As Amended

—Fair Employment Practices Law—

¶ 3005

Table of Contents

Employment Practices **¶ 3005**

Illustration M–1

Table of Contents of the Fair Employment Practices Law in the *Employment Practices Guide.* Published and copyrighted by Commerce Clearing House, Inc., Chicago, Il. 60646, and reproduced with their permission.

2008 **Table of Contents—FEP Law** 65 3-79

¶ 3005

Illustration M–2

Continuation of the table of contents of the Fair Employment Practices Law, showing authority of E.E.O.C. to issue regulations. Published and copyrighted by Commerce Clearing House, Inc., Chicago, Il. 60646, and reproduced with their permission.

Illustration N–1. Then in the listing of various categories of E.E. O.C. regulations, we see the "Sex Discrimination Guidelines", listed in Illustration N–2, with references to their *Code of Federal Regulations* citation and to their location in this service at paragraph 3950.

At paragraph 3950 (see Illustration O), the E.E.O.C. Sex Discrimination Guidelines are set forth, preceded by a brief historical note and a table of contents. Section 1604.2, subdiv. (1)(ii), seems to relate to our problem. If a *C.F.R.* reference to the Guidelines had been found elsewhere, without a citation to their location in this service, one could locate them here by using the Finding List under "Code of Federal Regulations", as shown in Illustration P, at page 417.

If we refer back to paragraph 441.60 in Illustration I–1, we recall two federal court decisions listed there with both their *Federal Reporter 2d* and *E.P.D.* citations. There were no E.E.O.C. decisions cited under that paragraph number, but a little further on, under ¶ 441.603, as shown in Illustration I–2 at page 405, there was a reference to E.E.O.C. decision no. 75–115, which seemed relevant to our problem. No location was given there, but by using the Finding List again, this time under "Departmental Decisions" and then at Decision # 75–115, we see in Illustration Q, at p. 418, several paragraph references for that decision. Upon examination, we find that the reference to ¶ 6533 is to the text of that decision in the "E.E.O.C. Decisions" section of the service. Illustration R, at p. 419, shows ¶ 6533 and the beginning of that decision. The several CCH headnotes summarize different aspects of the decision with back references for each issue. The second headnote seems to relate to our problem, but perhaps not as closely as the *Spokane Case.* Both decisions will, of course, have to be read and evaluated more carefully than we can from their headnotes.

4. FOLLOW–UP PROCEDURES

The looseleaf service in a very short time has provided a number of useful primary sources and research leads for further exploration. We have a relevant statute, administrative guidelines, several judicial decisions, and at least one E.E.O.C. decision. Actually there are other approaches available in this service, and other sources to be found there. We focused on these to illustrate the main procedures for using a looseleaf service.

If, after checking for later developments in this service, nothing further was found, one could use these leads to continue the research in other sources and tools. The statutes could be checked in *U. S. Code Annotated* or *U. S. Code Service* for annotations to other decisions and for cross references to legislative history and to secondary sources. West digest topics and key numbers obtained from the decisions in West reporters could be used for digest searching. The statute, the *CFR* Guidelines, and the decisions found here and in other sources, should all be *Shepardized* to determine their current authori-

2002 **Table of Contents** 187 1-83

Illustration N–1

List of *Regulations and Rules* in Table of Contents of "Federal Laws—Regulations—Orders". Published and copyrighted by Commerce Clearing House, Inc., Chicago, Il. 60646, and reproduced with their permission.

187 1-83 **Table of Contents** **2003**

Paragraph

Regulations and Rules—Continued

Illustration N-2

Continuation of E.E.O.C. Regulations and Rules, showing listing of *Sex Discrimination Guidelines.* Published and copyrighted by Commerce Clearing House, Inc., Chicago, Il. 60646, and reproduced with their permission.

100 3-80 **2213**

Equal Employment Opportunity Commission

Sex Discrimination Guidelines

¶ 3950

Originally issued by the Equal Employment Opportunity Commission, November 22, 1965, the Guidelines on Discrimination Because of Sex were reaffirmed by the Commission on February 21, 1968 (33 F. R. 3344), amended on August 19, 1969 (34 F. R. 13367), and last amended and reissued on March 30, 1972 (37 F. R. 6835), effective on April 5, 1972. The Guidelines are codified as Title 29 CFR, Chapter XIV, Part 1604, Sections 1604.1 to 1604.11, as amended.[1]

Table of Contents

[¶ 3950.01]

Section 1604.1 General Principles.—(a) References to "employer" or "employers" in this Part 1604 state principles that are applicable not only to employers but also to labor organizations and to employment agencies insofar as their action or inaction may adversely affect employment opportunities.

(b) To the extent that the views expressed in prior Commission pronouncements are inconsistent with the views expressed herein, such prior views are hereby overruled.

(c) The Commission will continue to consider particular problems relating to sex discrimination on a case-by-case basis.

[¶ 3950.02]

Sec. 1604.2 Sex as a Bona Fide Occupational Qualification.—(a) The Commission believes that the bona fide occupational qualification exception as to sex should be interpreted narrowly. Labels—"men's jobs" and "women's jobs"—tend to deny employment opportunities unnecessarily to one sex or the other.

(1) The Commission will find that the following situations do not warrant the application of the bona fide occupational qualification exception:

(i) The refusal to hire a woman because of her sex based on assumptions of the comparative employment characteristics of women in general. For example, the assumption that the turnover rate among women is higher than among men.

(ii) The refusal to hire an individual based on stereotyped characterizations of the sexes. Such stereotypes include, for example, that men are less capable of assembling intricate equipment; that women are less capable of aggressive salesmanship. The principle of non-discrimination requires that individuals be considered on the basis of individual capacities and not on the basis of any characteristics generally attributed to the group.

(iii) The refusal to hire an individual because of the preferences of co-workers, the employer, clients or customers except as covered specifically in subparagraph (2) of this paragraph.

(2) Where it is necessary for the purpose of authenticity or genuineness, the Commission will consider sex to be a bona fide occupational qualification, e.g., an actor or actress.

(b) Effect of sex-oriented State employment legislation. (1) Many States have enacted laws or promulgated administrative regulations with respect to the employment of females. Among these laws are those which prohibit or limit the employment of

[1] **Authority.**—The provisions of this Part 1604 issued under Section 713(b), 78 Stat. 265, 42 U. S. C. 2000e-12.

Illustration O

E.E.O.C. *Sex Discrimination Guidelines* in paragraph 3950 of the CCH *Employment Practices Guide.* Published and copyrighted by Commerce Clearing House, Inc., Chicago, Il. 60646, and reproduced with their permission.

174 7-82 **Finding Lists** **45-5**

29 CFR

Sec.	Par. (¶)
1602.51	3940.51
1602.52	3940.52
1602.53	3940.53
1602.54	3940.54
1602.55	3940.55
PART 1604	
1604.1	3950.01
1604.2	3950.02
1604.3	3950.03
1604.4	3950.04
1604.5	3950.05
1604.6	3950.06
1604.7	3950.07
1604.8	3950.08
1604.9	3950.09
1604.10	3950.10
1604.11	3950.11
Appendix	3951
PART 1605	
1605.1	3970.01
1605.2	3970.02
1605.3	3970.03
Appendix A	3970.04
PART 1606	
1606.1	3990.01
1606.2	3990.02
1606.3	3990.03
1606.4	3990.04
1606.5	3990.05
1606.6	3990.06
1606.7	3990.07
1606.8	3990.08
PART 1607	
1607	4010; 4010.18
PART 1608	
1608.1	4012.01
1608.2	4012.02
1608.3	4012.03
1608.4	4012.04
1608.5	4012.05
1608.6	4012.06
1608.7	4012.07
1608.8	4012.08
1608.9	4012.09
1608.10	4012.10
1608.11	4012.11
1608.12	4012.12
PART 1610	
1610.1	4110.01
1610.2	4110.02
1610.3	4110.03
1610.4	4110.04
1610.5	4110.05
1610.6	4110.06
1610.7	4110.07
1610.8	4110.08
1610.9	4110.09
1610.10	4110.10
1610.11	4110.11
1610.13	4110.13
1610.14	4110.14
1610.15	4110.15
1610.16	4110.16
1610.17	4110.17
1610.18	4110.18

29 CFR

Sec.	Par. (¶)
1610.19	4110.19
1610.20	4110.20
1610.21	4110.21
1610.30	4110.30
1610.32	4110.32
1610.34	4110.34
1610.36	4110.36
PART 1611	
1611.1	4111.01
1611.2	4111.02
1611.3	4111.03
1611.4	4111.04
1611.5	4111.05
1611.6	4111.06
1611.7	4111.07
1611.8	4111.08
1611.9	4111.09
1611.10	4111.10
1611.11	4111.11
1611.12	4111.12
1611.13	4111.13
1611.14	4111.14
PART 1612	
1612.1	4113.01
1612.2	4113.02
1612.3	4113.03
1612.4	4113.04
1612.5	4113.05
1612.6	4113.06
1612.7	4113.07
1612.8	4113.08
1612.9	4113.09
1612.10	4113.10
1612.11	4113.11
1612.12	4131.12
1612.13	4113.13
1612.14	4113.14
PART 1613	
1613.201	4114.201
1613.202	4114.202
1613.203	4114.203
1613.204	4114.204
1613.205	4114.205
1613.211	4114.211
1613.212	4114.212
1613.213	4114.213
1613.214	4114.214
1613.215	4114.215
1613.216	4114.216
1613.217	4114.217
1613.218	4114.218
1613.219	4114.219
1613.220	4114.220
1613.221	4114.221
1613.222	4114.222
1613.231	4114.231
1613.232	4114.232
1613.233	4114.233
1613.234	4114.234
1613.235	4114.235
1613.241	4114.241
1613.251	4114.251
1613.261	4114.261
1613.262	4114.262
1613.271	4114.271
1613.281	4114.281
1613.282	4114.282
1613.283	4114.283

29 CFR

Sec.	Par. (¶)
1613.301	4114.301
1613.302	4114.302
1613.414	4114.414
1613.415	4114.415
1613.416	4114.416
1613.417	4114.417
1613.501	4114.501
1613.502	4114.502
1613.511	4114.511
1613.512	4114.512
1613.513	4114.513
1613.514	4114.514
1613.521	4114.521
1613.601	4114.601
1613.602	4114.602
1613.603	4114.603
1613.604	4114.604
1613.605	4114.605
1613.606	4114.606
1613.607	4114.607
1613.608	4114.608
1613.609	4114.609
1613.610	4114.610
1613.611	4114.611
1613.612	4114.612
1613.613	4114.613
1613.614	4114.614
1613.631	4114.631
1613.632	4114.632
1613.641	4114.641
1613.642	4114.642
1613.643	4114.643
1613.701	4114.701
1613.702	4114.702
1613.703	4114.703
1613.704	4114.704
1613.705	4114.705
1613.706	4114.706
1613.707	4114.707
1613.708	4114.708
1613.709	4114.709
1613.801	4114.801
1613.802	4114.802
1613.803	4114.803
1613.804	4114.804
1613.805	4114.805
1613.806	4114.806
PART 1620	
1620.19	4121.19
1620.20	4121.20
1620.21	4121.21
1620.22	4121.22
1620.23	4121.23
PART 1625	
1625.1	4758.01
1625.2	4758.02
1625.3	4758.03
1625.4	4758.04
1625.5	4758.05
1625.6	4758.06
1625.7	4758.07
1625.8	4758.08
1625.9	4758.09
1625.10	4758.10
1625.11	4758.11
1625.12	4758.12
1625.13	4758.13

Employment Practices
033—103 **¶ 135**

Illustration P

Finding List for *Code of Federal Regulations* sections, with reference to paragraphs in CCH *Employment Practices Guide*.

52 **Finding Lists** 142 7-81

Decision Number	Date 1974	Par. (¶)
75-080	Nov. 14	546.152; 6525
75-082	Nov. 14	245.095; 6501
75-084	Nov. 14	310.305; 6526
75-086	Nov. 14	518.084; 6527
75-091	Nov. 19	596.40; 6528
75-095	Nov. 18	310.50; 582.20; 583.501; 600.15; 600.17; 600.211; 6444
75-098	Nov. 19	618.10; 6502
75-099	Nov. 19	614.102; 6503
75-100	Nov. 19	2194.251; 6504
75-103	Nov. 12	455.151; 6529
75-104	Dec. 16	604.152; 6530
75-111	Dec. 16	848.16; 6531
75-112	Dec. 16	482.20; 618.371; 792.12; 6532
75-115	Dec. 16	437.11; 441.305; 447.33; 6533
75-117	Dec. 16	360.13; 6534
75-119	Dec. 16	306.101; 6535
75-120	Dec. 16	360.755; 6536

Decision Number	Date 1975	Par. (¶)
75-125	Jan. 9	439.131; 6537
75-128	Jan. 9	721.12; 6538
75-129	Jan. 9	616.12; 6539
75-137	Jan. 9	457.101; 6540
75-147	Jan. 13	582.10; 6447
75-148	Jan. 13	496.106; 562.102; 598.201; 618.96; 746.18; 6541
75-164	Jan. 30	618.082; 6542
75-165	Jan. 30	554.502; 564.552; 6543
75-166	Jan. 30	618.935; 6544
75-167	Jan. 30	618.935; 6545
75-168	Jan. 30	494.256; 494.45; 622.8231; 6546
75-169	Jan. 30	445.165; 6547
75-172	Feb. 12	457.101; 6548
75-174	Feb. 12	842.37; 6549
75-175	Feb. 12	457.305; 6550
75-176	Feb. 12	1014.204; 6551

Decision Number	Date 1975	Par. (¶)
75-177	Feb. 12	618.29; 6552
75-186	Feb. 21	753.09; 6553
75-192	Feb. 21	306.101; 6554
75-199	Feb. 27	445.505; 6555
75-215	Mar. 10	542.62; 6449
75-225	Mar. 17	6491
75-239	Apr. 15	6492
75-249	May 6	260.16; 310.25; 360.41; 437.78; 464.35; 464.655; 6457
75-251	May 8	604.107; 6448
75-256	May 18	580.10; 580.921; 600.175; 6462
75-257	May 18	422.68; 466.185; 6458
75-268	May 30	245.051; 792.17; 794.15; 1354.101; 1354.60; 6452
75-269	May 30	445.16; 6453
75-271	June 3	518.191; 1039.11; 1045.25; 6451
75-273	June 9	310.26; 1008.30; 6456
75-274	June 9	420.32; 622.5551; 6454
75-281	June 10	414.10; 6455
75-S-6	Aug. 7	1960.46; 1964.25; 6510
75-S-47	Mar. 17	1960.291; 1962.47; 6515
75-S-87	May 13	1960.11; 1960.652; 6517
76-01	July 11	544.322; 618.101; 6596
76-02	July 11	546.10; 618.1035; 6597
76-03	July 14	422.201; 6598
76-04	July 21	594.101; 2326; 452; 6599
76-05	July 25	496.48; 580.25; 845.122; 6600
76-06	July 25	494.25; 512.355; 542.30; 616.13; 6601
76-07	July 25	6602
76-08	July 28	1039.075; 6603
76-09	Aug. 7	498.151; 564.101; 618.10; 6604
76-10	Aug. 14	360.13; 6605
76-11	Aug. 14	360.13; 600.855; 6606
76-12	Aug. 15	420.12; 566.356; 6607
76-13	Aug. 15	422.401; 6608

Decision Number	Date 1975	Par. (¶)
76-14	Aug. 18	445.507; 542.731; 761.20; 6609
76-15	Aug. 18	422.35; 6610
76-16	Aug. 18	445.506; 6611
76-17	Aug. 21	420.12; 502.48; 512.35; 6612
76-19	Aug. 25	542.2054; 6613
76-20	Aug. 25	2326.452; 6614
76-21	Aug. 25	466.77; 580.281; 6615
76-23	Aug. 25	566.35; 6616
76-24	Aug. 25	496.581; 518.103; 6617
76-25	Aug. 25	447.61; 6618
76-26	Aug. 25	542.103; 622.10; 6619
76-27	Aug. 25	618.365; 6620
76-28	Aug. 25	1935.205; 6621
76-29	Aug. 25	548.201; 849.1054; 6622
76-30	Aug. 25	542.622; 622.961; 6623
76-31	Sept. 10	441.205; 6624
76-32	Sept. 10	1039.076; 6625
76-33	Sept. 11	662.8231; 1039.074; 6626
76-36	Sept. 24	574.506; 6627
76-37	Sept. 30	451.625; 6628
76-38	Sept. 30	1165.305; 6629
76-39	Sept. 30	445.30; 6630
76-40	Sept. 30	1008.60; 6631
76-41	Oct. 8	542.204; 542.5011; 564.402; 622.205; 6632
76-42	Oct. 8	622.6351; 6633
76-45	Oct. 8	441.152; 6634
76-47	Oct. 8	441.312; 6635
76-50	Oct. 14	1010.75; 6636
76-51	Nov. 5	1039.075; 6637
76-52	Nov. 5	1089.512; 6506
76-53	Nov. 24	422.233; 6638
76-54	Oct. 25	422.21; 441.12; 6639
76-55	Oct. 24	604.251; 6640
76-56	Oct. 24	1135.2552; 1135.301; 6641
76-57	Oct. 24	422.57; 6642

¶ 140

Illustration Q

Finding List for Departmental Decisions, providing paragraph references for E.E.O.C. decisions. Published and copyrighted by Commerce Clearing House, Inc., Chicago, Il. 60646, and reproduced with their permission.

4332 **EEOC Decisions** 18 5-77

Decision

Respondent No. 2:

Charging Party No. 1:

There is not reasonable cause to believe that Respondent Employment Agency violated Title VII of the Civil Rights Act of 1964, by denying Charging Party employment opportunities because of her race, as alleged.

There is reasonable cause to believe that Respondent Employment Agency is violating Title VII of the Civil Rights Act of 1964 by administering generalized pre-employment tests which have a disparate effect upon minority group applicants, because of their race.

Charging Party No. 2:

There is reasonable cause to believe that Respondent Employment Agency violated Title VII of the Civil Rights Act of 1964, as alleged.

Charging Party No. 4:

There is not reasonable cause to believe that Respondent Employment Agency violated Title VII of the Civil Rights Act of 1964, as alleged.

Charging Party No. 1:

There is reasonable cause to believe that Respondent Employer violated Title VII of the Civil Rights Act of 1964, by refusing to hire Charging Party because of her race, as alleged, and by utilizing a racially discriminatory testing program.

Charging Party No. 3:

There is reasonable cause to believe that Respondent Employer violated Title VII of the Civil Rights Act of 1964 by discharging Charging Party because of his race, as alleged.

Charging Party No. 4:

There is not reasonable cause to believe that Respondent Employer violated Title VII of the Civil Rights Act of 1964 by refusing to hire Charging Party because of his race, as alleged.

Respondent No. 4:

Charging Party No. 4:

There is not reasonable cause to believe that Respondent Employer violated Title VII of the Civil Rights Act of 1964 by refusing to hire Charging Party because of his race, as alleged.

[¶ 6533] QUESTIONED PERFORMANCE BASED UPON OUT-OF-STATE SPOUSE, SEX BIAS

Decision of the Equal Employment Opportunity Commission, Decision No. 75-115, December 16, 1974.

Title VII—Civil Rights Act of 1964

Educational Requirements—Sex Discrimination—Disparate Impact on Females.—There was no evidence that an employer's educational requirements had a significantly adverse impact upon the employment opportunities of females because of their sex nor that the requirements were not applied equally to both male and female job applicants. Therefore, there was no evidence that educational requirements had a disparate impact on females which constituted sex discrimination.

Back reference.—¶ 447.

Weight Lifting Requirements—Sex Discrimination—Females.—An employer's failure to judge a female applicant for a weight lifting position on the basis of her individual capacity to perform the job rather than on the basis of preconceived opinions as to the capacities of women as a class was unlawful sex bias.

Back reference.—¶ 441.65.

Height Requirements—Equal Application—Disparate Impact of Females.—Since women can be shown to be shorter than men, an employer's height requirements, even though applied equally to both men and women, had the effect of excluding a disproportionate number of females and, therefore, constituted unlawful sex discrimination.

Back reference.—¶ 441.20.

Hiring—Questions of Permanency—Out-of-State Spouse.—An employer's assertion that it could not hire claimant because of her questionable permanence on the job with a spouse in another state, when the same factor was not considered with men, constituted sex bias.

Back reference.—¶ 447.

¶ 6533

Illustration R

The beginning of E.E.O.C. Decision 75–115 and its headnotes in the CCH *Employment Practices Guide*. Published and copyrighted by Commerce Clearing House, Inc., Chicago, Il. 60646, and reproduced with their permission.

ty and perhaps obtain later cases which have cited them. A variety of secondary sources (encyclopedias, *ALR Federal* Annotations, treatises, periodical articles, etc.) could be explored. The looseleaf service has provided an excellent start, but the research is not over.

E. FINDING LOOSELEAF SERVICES BY SUBJECT

1. BIBLIOGRAPHIC AIDS

There are several ways of discovering what looseleaf services may be available in any particular subject field. Published lists of looseleaf services, like the one set forth below, soon become out-of-date unless they are supplemented regularly. Services are discontinued from time to time, and new ones are constantly being issued. The following sources of information are suggested:

(a) *Legal Looseleaf in Print 1982*, compiled by Arlene L. Stern (New York, Infosources Publishing, 1982). Revised annually.

(b) R. C. Berring & V. Wedin, "Looseleaf Services: A Subject Bibliography," 1 *Legal Reference Service Q.* 51 (Winter 1981).

(c) Pamphlets issued by the major looseleaf publishers which list their respective services and frequently include general instructions for use (e.g., B.N.A.'s *Reporter Services and their Use,* 1980).

(c) The card catalog of any law library. Many libraries use the form heading "Looseleaf Services" which will bring together entries for all services held by that library. Otherwise, the subject heading for the field of interest should be checked.

(f) The following selected list of looseleaf services.

2. LIST OF SERVICES BY SUBJECT

The following is a selection of the major looseleaf services available as of February 1, 1983:

Abbreviation	**Publisher**
Bender	Matthew Bender & Co.
BNA	Bureau of National Affairs
Callaghan	Callaghan & Company
CCH	Commerce Clearing House
CIS	Congressional Information Service
ELI	Environmental Law Institute
FPAS	Federal Programs Advisory Service
IBFD	International Bureau of Fiscal Documentation
IBP	Institute for Business Planning
L C	Lawyers Co-op
L-M	Legal-Medical Studies, Inc.
NCCD	National College for Criminal Defense, University of Houston
Oceana	Oceana Publications
P & F	Pike & Fischer
P-H	Prentice-Hall
PLEI	Public Law Education Institute

Abbreviation	Publisher
PLR	Professional Liability Reporter (San Francisco)
RIA	Research Institute of America
UPA	University Publications of America
WSB	Washington Service Bureau

Selected Looseleafs by Subject

ABORTION, see HUMAN REPRODUCTION

ACCOUNTING and AUDITING

Accountancy Law Reports (CCH)

Accounting Articles (CCH)

Cost Accounting Standards Guide (CCH)

Federal Audit Guides (CCH)

SEC Accounting Rules (CCH)

ADMINISTRATIVE LAW

Pike & Fischer Administrative Law (P & F)

Federal Regulatory Week (P-H)

ADMIRALTY

Shipping Regulation (P & F)

AFFIRMATIVE ACTION, see FAIR EMPLOYMENT

AMERICAN INDIANS, see NATIVE AMERICANS

ANTITRUST, see TRADE REGULATION

ARBITRATION, see LABOR AND EMPLOYMENT RELATIONS

ATTORNEYS, see also ETHICS

Manual for Managing the Law Office (P-H)

National Reporter on Legal Ethics and Professional Responsibility (UPA)

Reporter on the Legal Profession (L-M)

AVIATION

Aviation Law Reporter (CCH)

BANKING

Banking (Control of Banking; Federal Aids to Financing) (P-H)

Federal Banking Law Reports (CCH)

Washington Financial Reports (BNA)

BANKRUPTCY

Bankruptcy Law Reports (CCH)

Bankruptcy Services, Lawyer's Edition (L C)

BIOETHICS, see ETHICS

CARRIERS

Federal Carrier Reports (CCH)

Federal and State Carrier Reports (CCH) *

State Motor Carrier Guide (CCH)

CHARITIES, see EDUCATION, FOUNDATIONS AND CHARITIES

CHEMICAL AND TOXIC SUBSTANCES, see ENVIRONMENT

COLLECTIVE BARGAINING, see LABOR AND EMPLOYMENT RELATIONS

COLLEGES AND UNIVERSITIES, see EDUCATION AND FOUNDATIONS

COMMERCIAL LAW AND CONSUMERISM, see also PRODUCTS LIABILITY

Consumer and Commercial Credit—Credit Union Guide (P-H)

Consumer and Commercial Credit—Installment Sales Service (P-H)

Consumer Credit Guide (CCH)

Secured Transactions Guide (CCH)

Uniform Commercial Code Reporting Service (Callaghan)

COMMON MARKET, see TRADE, INTERNATIONAL

COMMUNICATIONS

Communications Service (P-H)

Media Law Reporter (BNA)

Radio Regulation (P & F)

COMPUTER LAW

Computer Law Reporter (Computer Law Reporter, Inc.)

COPYRIGHT, see PATENT AND COPYRIGHT

CORPORATIONS

Business Franchise Guide (CCH)

Capital Changes Reporter (CCH)

Corporate Practice Series (BNA)

Corporation Management Edition (P-H)

Corporation Law Guide (CCH)

Corporation Service (P-H)

Professional Corporation Guide (P-H)

Professional Corporation Handbook (CCH)

CRIMINAL LAW

Criminal Law Monthly (NCCD)

Criminal Law Reporter (BNA)

* This service combines *Federal Carrier Reports* and *State Motor Carrier Guide.*

CUSTOMS LAW, see TRADE, INTERNATIONAL

DIVORCE TAXATION, see FAMILY LAW and TAXATION

EDUCATION, FOUNDATIONS AND CHARITIES

Charitable Giving and Solicitation (P-H)

College and University Reporter (CCH)

Exempt Organizations (CCH)

ELECTIONS

Federal Election Campaign Financing Guide (CCH)

ENERGY

Economic Regulation Administration Enforcement Manual . . . DOE (CCH)

Energy Controls (P-H)

Energy Management and Federal Energy Guidelines (CCH)

Energy Users Report (BNA)

Federal Energy Regulatory Commission Reports (CCH)

Federal Power Service (Bender)

Natural Gas Policy Act Information Service (FPAS)

Nuclear Regulation Reporter (CCH)

Oil & Gas Reporter (Bender)

ENVIRONMENT

Chemical Regulation Reporter (BNA)

Environment Reporter (BNA)

Environmental Law Reporter (ELI)

Noise Regulation Reporter (BNA)

Pollution Control Guide (CCH)

Water Pollution Control (BNA)

ENVIRONMENT, INTERNATIONAL

International Environment Reporter (BNA)

EQUAL OPPORTUNITY, see FAIR EMPLOYMENT

ESTATES—WILLS—TRUSTS, also see TAXATION, ESTATE AND GIFT

Estate Planning (IBP)

Estate Planning Review (CCH)

Financial and Estate Planning (CCH)

Successful Estate Planning Ideas and Methods (P-H)

Wills Estates and Trusts (P-H)

ETHICS, see also MALPRACTICE

Bioethics Reporter (UPA)

Ethics in Government (WSB)

National Reporter on Legal Ethics and Professional Responsibility (UPA)

Reporter on the Legal Profession (L-M)

EXECUTIVES, see also TAXATION

Executive Action Report (P-H)

FAIR EMPLOYMENT, see also LABOR AND EMPLOYMENT RELATIONS

Affirmative Action Compliance Manual for Federal Contractors (BNA)

EEOC Compliance Manual (P-H)

EEOC Compliance Manual (BNA)

EEOC Compliance Manual (CCH)

Employment Practices Guide (CCH)

Equal Employment Compliance Manual (Callaghan)

Fair Employment Practice Series (BNA)

FAMILY LAW, see also TAXATION

Family Law Reporter (BNA)

FARM TAXATION, see TAXATION

FEDERAL CONTRACTS, see GOVERNMENT CONTRACTS

FOOD, DRUG AND MEDICAL

Food, Drug, Cosmetic Law Reporter (CCH)

Medical Devices Reporter (CCH)

FOREIGN TAXATION, see TAXATION, INTERNATIONAL AND FOREIGN

FOUNDATIONS, see EDUCATION, FOUNDATIONS AND CHARITIES

FRANCHISES

Business Franchise Guide (CCH)

GOVERNMENT CONTRACTS

Contract Appeals Decision (CCH)

Federal Contracts Reports (BNA)

Government Contracts Reporter (CCH)

OFCCP Federal Contract Compliance Manual (CCH)

GOVERNMENT INFORMATION, see also ADMINISTRATIVE LAW

Government Disclosure (P-H)

HEALTH AND SAFETY, see OCCUPATIONAL SAFETY AND HEALTH

HOUSING, see URBAN PROBLEMS

HUMAN REPRODUCTION, see also ETHICS

Bioethics Reporter (UPA)

Family Law Reporter (BNA)

Human Reproduction Reporter (L-M)

IMMIGRATION

Federal Immigration Law Reporter (WSB)

INSURANCE, see also MEDICARE AND MEDICAID

Automobile Law Reports (CCH)

Benefits Review Board Service (Bender)

Fire & Casualty Insurance Law Reports (CCH)

Insurance Guide (P-H)

Insurance Law Reporter (CCH) *

Life, Health & Accident Law Reports (CCH)

Loss Prevention & Control (BNA)

Workmen's Compensation Law Reporter (CCH)

INTERNATIONAL TAXATION, see TAXATION, INTERNATIONAL AND FOREIGN

INTERNATIONAL TRADE, see TRADE, INTERNATIONAL

LABOR AND EMPLOYMENT RELATIONS, see also FAIR EMPLOYMENT; INSURANCE; OCCUPATIONAL SAFETY AND HEALTH; PENSIONS

Collective Bargaining Negotiations and Contracts (BNA)

Compensation (P-H)

Construction Labor Report (BNA)

Daily Labor Report (BNA)

Employment and Training Reporter (BNA)

Employment Practices Guide (CCH)

Federal Regulation of Employment Service (L C)

Government Employee Relations Report (BNA)

Human Resources Management (CCH)

Industrial Relations Guide (P-H)

Labor Arbitration Awards (CCH)

Labor Arbitration Reports (BNA)

Labor Law Reporter—Labor Relations—Wages—Hours (CCH)

Labor Relations Guide (P-H)

Labor Relations Reporter (BNA)

Labor-Management Relations

State Laws

Fair Employment Practice

Wages and Hours

Labor Arbitration

* This service combines *Automobile Law Reports* (CCH); *Fire & Casualty Insurance Law Reports* (CCH); and *Life, Health & Accident Law Reports* (CCH).

NLRB Case Handling Manual (CCH)

Personnel Policies and Practices (P-H)

Public Employee Bargaining (CCH)

Public Personnel Administration—Labor-Management Relations (P-H)

Retail/Services Labor Report (BNA)

Union Labor Report (BNA)

Wage-Hour Guide (P-H)

White Collar Report (BNA)

LEGAL PROFESSION, see ETHICS and ATTORNEYS

LEGISLATION

Advance Session Law Reporter (CCH)

Congressional Index (CCH)

Congressional Information Service/Index (CIS)

Congressional Legislative Reporting (CCH)

State Legislative Reporting Service (CCH) *

LIQUOR CONTROL LAW REPORTER (CCH)

Liquor Control Law Reporter (CCH)

MALPRACTICE

Professional Liability Reporter: Malpractice Decisions & Developments (PLR)

MEDICARE AND MEDICAID

Medicare and Medicaid Guide (CCH)

MILITARY LAW

Military Law Reporter (PLEI)

NATIVE AMERICANS

Indian Law Reporter (Amer. Indian Lawyer Training Program, Inc.)

NATURAL RESOURCES, see ENVIRONMENT

OCCUPATIONAL SAFETY AND HEALTH

Employment Safety and Health Guide (CCH)

Job Safety and Health (BNA)

Job Safety and Health Reporter (Business Publishers, Inc.)

Labor Relations Guide: Occupational Safety and Health (P-H)

Mine Safety and Health Reporter (BNA)

OSHA Compliance Guide (CCH)

Occupational Safety and Health Reporter (BNA)

* CCH publishes a guide to each state individually.

PATENT AND COPYRIGHT

Copyright Law Reporter (CCH)

Patent, Trademark & Copyright Journal (BNA)

United States Patent Quarterly (BNA)

PENSIONS AND COMPENSATION

ERISA Update (WSB)

Compliance Guide for Plan Administrators (CCH)

Individual Retirement Plans Guide (CCH)

Pay Planning Program (IBP)

Payroll Guides (P-H)

Payroll Management Guide (CCH)

Pension and Profit Sharing (P-H)

Pension and Annuity Withholding Service (RIA)

Pension Plan Guide (CCH)

Pension Reporter (BNA)

Plan Administrator's Compliance Manual (P-H)

POLLUTION, see ENVIRONMENT

PRODUCTS LIABILITY

Consumer Product Safety Guide (CCH)

Product Safety and Liability Reporter (BNA)

Products Liability Reporter (CCH)

PROFIT SHARING, see PENSIONS AND COMPENSATION

PUBLIC EMPLOYMENT, see LABOR AND EMPLOYMENT RELATIONS

PUBLIC UTILITIES

Federal Power Service (Bender)

Utilities Law Reporter (CCH)

REAL PROPERTY

Real Estate Guide (P-H)

SAFETY, see OCCUPATIONAL SAFETY AND HEALTH

SECURITIES, also see ACCOUNTING

American Stock Exchange Guide (CCH)

Blue Sky Law Reporter (CCH)

Commodity Futures Law Reports (CCH) *

Corporate Capital Transactions Coordinator (RIA)

Executive Disclosure Guide—SEC Compliance (CCH)

Federal Securities Law Reporter (CCH)

MSRB Manual (CCH)

Mutual Funds Guide (CCH)

* CCH also publishes *Chicago Board Options Exchange Guide, New York Futures Exchange Guide*, and *Coffee, Sugar, and Cocoa Exchange, Inc., Guide.*

NASD Manual (CCH)
New York Exchange Guide (CCH) **
SEC Compliance—Financial Reporting and Forms (P-H)
SEC Docket (CCH)
SEC Enforcement Reporter (WSB)
SEC No-Action Letters—Index and Summaries (WSB)
SEC Today (WSB)
Securities Regulation and Law Report (BNA)
Securities Regulation Service and Guide (P-H)
Significant SEC Filings (WSB)
Stock Transfer Guide (CCH)

SOCIAL SECURITY

Unemployment Insurance—Social Security Reporter (CCH)

SUPREME COURT

U. S. Supreme Court Bulletin (CCH)
United States Law Week (BNA)

TAXATION

American Federal Tax Reports (P-H)
Capital Adjustments (P-H)
Code and Regulations (CCH)
Cumulative Changes (P-H)
Divorce Taxation (P-H)
Executive Tax Review (CCH)
Farmers Tax Watch (CCH)
Federal Income Tax Regulations (CCH)
Federal Tax Articles (CCH)
Federal Tax Compliance Reporter (CCH)
Federal Tax Guide (CCH)
Federal Tax Guide (P-H)
Federal Tax Guide Reports—Control Ed. (CCH)
Federal Taxes Citator (P-H)
Federal Tax Coordinator (RIA)
Federal Taxes—IRS Letter Rulings (CCH)
Federal Taxes—Private Letter Rulings (P-H)
Federal Taxes Service (P-H)
Interest Dividend—Withholding—Information Returns (CCH)
IRS Positions Reports (CCH)
IRS Publications (CCH)

** CCH also publishes *Boston, Philadelphia, Midwest,* and *Pacific Stock Exchange Guides* and the *California Eligible Securities List.*

Internal Revenue Manual (CCH)
Oil and Gas—Natural Resources Taxes (P-H)
Publications of the IRS (P-H)
Standard Federal Tax Reports (CCH)
Tax Court Decisions Reports (CCH)
Tax Court Reports (CCH)
Tax Court Service (P-H)
Tax-Exempt Organizations (P-H)
Tax Guide (RIA)
Tax Ideas (P-H)
Tax Management (BNA)
- U. S. Income
- Primary Sources

Tax Planning (IBP)
Tax Planning Review (CCH)

TAXATION, ESTATE AND GIFT

Estate Planning (IBP)
Estate Planning Review (CCH)
Financial and Estate Planning (CCH)
Inheritance, Estate and Gift Tax Reports (CCH)
Inheritance Taxes (P-H)
Successful Estate Planning Ideas and Methods (P-H)
Tax-Management—Estates, Gifts, and Trusts (BNA)
Wills, Estates and Trusts (P-H)

TAXATION, EXCISE

Excise Taxes (P-H)
Federal Excise Tax Reports (CCH)

TAXATION, INTERNATIONAL AND FOREIGN

African Tax Systems (IBFD)
Corporate Taxation in Latin America (IBFD)
European Taxation (IBFD)
Foreign Tax and Trade Briefs, edited by Walter Diamond (Bender)
Guides to European Taxation (IBFD)
- Taxation of Patent Royalties, Dividends, Interest in Europe
- Taxation of Companies in Europe
- Corporate Taxation in the Common Market
- Taxation of Private Investment Income
- Value Added Taxation in Europe

Tax Havens of the World, edited by Walter Diamond (Bender)
Tax Management—Foreign Income (BNA)

Tax Treaties (CCH)

Tax Treaties (P-H)

U. S. Taxation of International Operations (P-H)

TAXATION, PROPERTY

Property Tax Service (P-H)

Real Estate Federal Tax Guide (P-H)

TAXATION, STATE

All-State Sales Tax Reports (CCH)

All-States Tax Guide (P-H)

Sales Taxes Service (P-H)

State and Local Taxes (P-H)

State Income Taxes (P-H)

State Tax Cases Reports (CCH)

State Tax Guide (CCH)

State Tax Reports (CCH)

TELECOMMUNICATIONS, see COMMUNICATIONS

TRADE, INTERNATIONAL

Common Market Reporter (CCH)

Digest of Commercial Law of the World (Oceana)

Encyclopedia of European Community Law (Sweet & Maxwell; Bender)

United Kingdom Sources

European Community Treaties

International Trade Reporter's Export Shipping Manual (BNA)

International Trade Reporter's U. S. Export Weekly (BNA)

International Trade Reporter's U. S. Import Weekly (BNA)

Investment Laws of the World: the Developing Nations (Oceana)

TRADE REGULATION

Antitrust and Trade Regulation Reporter (BNA)

Trade Regulation Reporter (CCH)

TRADEMARKS, see PATENT AND COPYRIGHT

TRUST, see ESTATES—WILLS—TRUSTS

UNEMPLOYMENT COMPENSATION, see SOCIAL SECURITY

UNFAIR COMPETITION, see TRADE REGULATION

URBAN PROBLEMS

Equal Opportunity in Housing (P-H)

Housing and Development Reporter (BNA)

Urban Affairs Reporter (CCH)

UTILITIES, see PUBLIC UTILITIES

WILLS, see ESTATES—WILLS—TRUSTS

WOMEN AND THE LAW

Women's Rights Law Reporter (Rutgers Law School)

WORKERS' COMPENSATION, see INSURANCE

F. CONCLUSION

The looseleaf service is still the most versatile form of legal publication, combining a variety of primary legal sources, secondary editorial analysis and explanation, frequent supplementation, and a number of indexing approaches. These publications frequently include both federal *and* state law, and, although not available on every subject, their number increases and the range of topics they cover expands steadily. Their auxiliary services, such as bound topical reporters, telephone hotlines for updating information, and full-text document transmittals, add to their utility.

Although looseleaf services remain very popular among practitioners and scholars, one cannot but wonder about their future, as computerized research becomes more widespread. The special advantages of the looseleaf service are almost identical to those of computer research systems, except for the area of state statutes which the computer services do not provide.[3] As noted in Chapter 12, both BNA and CCH, two of the leading looseleaf publishers, are now moving rapidly into on-line computer data bases, while still maintaining their looseleaf services. At the same time, both WESTLAW and LEXIS are offering more and more specialized data bases in many of the fields in which looseleaf services have been most effective (e.g., taxation, labor law, anti-trust, securities regulation, etc.). The lower costs of the looseleaf services may assure their survival for many years, but the bibliographic revolution which they brought to legal research now seems to be duplicated by their electronic descendants—the computer services.

3. Except for those of four states available in LEXIS.

Chapter 14

LEGAL ENCYCLOPEDIAS AND RELATED RESEARCH TOOLS

A. INTRODUCTION TO SECONDARY MATERIALS AND LEGAL ENCYCLOPEDIAS

In the previous Chapters, we have described the *primary* legal sources (cases, statutes and administrative law) and the basic finding tools for those sources. We now turn to those descriptive or explanatory materials which are commonly designated as "secondary" sources. Although several features of the primary sources in their published forms (*e.g.,* the headnotes preceding a reported case and the case annotations following each section of an annotated code) are secondary in nature, they relate to the primary sources themselves and therefore were treated as part of those sources. Now we move further from the primary sources, and deal with materials that are *entirely* secondary, with only citations to, analysis of, or quotations from, the primary sources.

It is important to note that secondary source materials have two functions. They *provide citations to primary source material.* By using secondary sources as finding tools, one can locate references to decisions and statutes that may open fruitful lines of research. The second and usually the primary function, at least from their authors' point of view, is to *describe, explain, or analyze issues of law, or legal developments.* For one unfamiliar with a particular area of law, secondary sources, such as encyclopedias, treatises, or periodical articles, can be most helpful for their narrative introductions to the basic concepts, terminology and rules of the field, or for their synthesis and summary of numerous, sometimes contradicting, primary sources.

This narrative simplicity may, however, carry disadvantages. Encyclopedias and hornbooks, by seeking to provide a clear and concise statement of law, often over-simplify complicated concepts and describe as settled and fixed a body of law which is in fact unsettled and changing. Text writers are more comfortable with order and certainty, while the law is in reality often disordered and uncertain. For this reason the researcher is cautioned to use secondary sources for what they can provide, but to beware of their dangers. Secondary materials also lack the authority of primary sources of law. The quality of the work or the author's reputation may give a particular text considerable persuasive authority, but that is quite different from the authority that is carried by the primary legal sources.

This chapter and the several which follow explore a number of the most commonly used secondary sources, beginning with legal encyclopedias.

Through a series of individual articles on specific concepts and areas of law, legal encyclopedias attempt to describe systematically the entire field of American law. Legal encyclopedias focus primarily on case law, however, and tend to neglect the large body of statutory law, which is, of course, central to our legal system. Legal encyclopedias are organized much like most general encyclopedias, employing an alphabetic arrangement of broad topics, with access provided by detailed subject indexes and a comprehensive general index.

Legal encyclopedias are among the most maligned of research tools, and law students today are frequently warned against citing to, or quoting from them. At one time they were viewed as serious and reliable statements of law, and were frequently cited by the courts.[1] In recent decades however, the legal encyclopedias have come to be viewed primarily as research tools, useful for case-finding and as introductions to research, but not as independent authority. The two national encyclopedias, *Corpus Juris Secundum* and *American Jurisprudence 2d*, provide in their footnotes numerous citations to primary source material, while offering simplified, somewhat bland, summaries of most legal topics. Each is part of its respective publisher's total research system and, by cross references, is linked to other sets issued by its publisher.

1. For an historical discussion of legal encyclopedias, see F. C. Hicks, *Materials and Methods of Legal Research*, 3d ed. (Lawyers Co-op, 1942) pp. 259–275. For a more critical view, see J. H. Merryman, "The Authority of Authority," 6 *Stanford L.Rev.* 613 (1954) at pp. 634–646.

B. CORPUS JURIS SECUNDUM

Corpus Juris Secundum, which began publication in 1936, is part of the West Publishing Company's inter-related system of publications. The previous edition of *C.J.S., Corpus Juris* (1911–1936), is still referred to occasionally in checking citations or quotations from earlier sources, but is now rarely consulted for its own text. The footnote citations in *Corpus Juris,* however, are by and large not repeated in *C.J.S.,* so the older set is still useful for historical research. Currently, *C.J.S.* consists of 101 numbered volumes, contained in 148 physical volumes, with various supplements. Both the text volumes and the General Index volumes are updated annually by pocket parts inserted in each volume. When the amount of material in the pocket part requires it, the volume will be revised and sometimes expanded into two volumes, incorporating the accumulated supplementary material.

The grand concept of *Corpus Juris Secundum* is described in the Preface to Volume 1, which was published in 1936, and is still part of the set:

> *Corpus Juris Secundum* (cited *C.J.S.*) is a complete restatement of the entire body of American law, mainly in the language of the courts, based upon the authority of all the reported cases from 1658 to date.[2]

Corpus Juris Secundum thus claims to reflect all published case law in its discussions of legal topics. In this, it carries forward the West Company's philosophy of "comprehensiveness." Many pages of *C.J.S.* contain more material in their footnotes than in the text. Illustration A shows a typical page of *Corpus Juris Secundum.*

C.J.S. contains 433 topical articles in an alphabetical arrangement, ranging from "Abandonment" to "Zoning." Within each article, the subject is presented in a logical sequence, with a scope note at the beginning outlining the contents. Numerous case citations in the footnotes provide references to the primary sources supporting the statements in the text. Because the encyclopedias attempt to cover all American jurisdictions, and because they are designed for a wide range of readers, the text tends to be overly general and simplistic in its analysis. To reflect the real complexity of each topic would require that the encyclopedia be of an unmanageable size and be supplemented more frequently than the annual pocket parts allow. The simplified text, however, can provide an introduction to an area that is unfamiliar to the researcher, and can explain the basic concepts and terminology that underlie a new field.

Access to *Corpus Juris Secundum* can be achieved initially either by going directly to one of the topics (a list of all topics is printed at the beginning of the set) and scanning the scope note for that topic, or, preferably, by use of the General Index to locate the relevant top-

2. 1 *Corpus Juris Secundum,* p. vii (1936).

§§ 5–6 CONSTITUTIONAL LAW 16 C. J. S.

tion.[46] As discussed in States § 22, federal sanction is necessary to the admission of a new state. The people of a territory of the United States cannot adopt a constitution without the assenting action of congress,[47] and compliance must be had with the fundamental conditions prescribed by congress in giving such consent.[48] Where new states have been formed out of territory of existing states, as in the case of Vermont, Kentucky, West Virginia, and Maine, the consent of the parent state has also been necessary to the adoption of a constitution establishing the new state. The separation of territory from a state for the formation of new state is considered in the C.J.S. title States § 11.

Where the enabling act requires the constitution to be submitted for adoption or rejection, the submission must be made to those designated in the enabling act.[49] When submission to "the people" is required, this means to the electors only.[50] Where the enabling act requires for adoption a "majority of the legal votes cast," it is sufficient if the constitution or articles therewith submitted receive a majority of the votes cast on the question of adoption, although that number may be less than a majority of the votes cast for candidates voted for at the same election.[51] In some states, the approval and adoption by the constitutional convention of everything in the constitution was necessary, and matter contained therein which was not so approved and adopted by the convention was a nullity regardless of the fact that it was submitted and apparently ratified by the people.[51.5] Irregularities in the process of adoption are cured by subsequent acceptance and recognition of the instrument by the state.[52] Congress is the ultimate judge of the due original adoption of the constitution of a new state.[53]

§ 6. Amendment and Revision of Federal Constitution

The federal Constitution expressly provides the manner in which it may be amended, and amendments must be made in such manner.

Amendments to the federal Constitution may be made only in the manner therein provided in Article 5,[54] and the only limitation now existing on the power of amendment under Article 5 is that "no State, without its Consent, shall be deprived of its equal Suffrage in the Senate."[55] The provisions of the federal Constitution as to amendments have the same meaning today as they had when adopted,[56] and the people of any one of the several states cannot impose any limitations on the amending power established by the federal Constitution.[57] As discussed in States § 7, the people may, if they choose, take away from the powers reserved to the states and bestow the incidents of sovereignty thus withdrawn on the United States through the process of amendment. Accordingly, various matters have been held to be proper subjects for

46. Neb.—Brittle v. People, 2 Neb. 98.
12 C.J. p 680 note 58.

47. U.S.—Scott v. Jones, Mich., 5 How. 343, 12 L.Ed. 181.
Ohio.—Myers v. Manhattan Bank, 20 Ohio 283.
12 C.J. p 681 note 61.

48. Neb.—Brittle v. People, 2 Neb. 198.

49. U.S.—Marsh v. Burroughs, C.C. Ga., 16 F.Cas.No.9,112, 1 Woods 463.

50. Mo.—Blair v. Ridgely, 41 Mo. 63, 177, 97 Am.D. 248.

51. N.D.—State v. Barnes, 55 N.W. 883, 3 N.D. 319.

51.5 Idaho.—Higer v. Hansen, 170 P. 2d 411, 67 Idaho 45.

Compensation of judicial officers

Where constitutional convention rejected inclusion of judicial officers in provision that increases in compensation should not affect compensation of officers then in office, but provision inadvertently included judicial officers and was apparently ratified by the people, such inclusion was a nullity.
Idaho.—Higer v. Hansen, supra.

52. Minn.—Secombe v. Kittelson, 12 N.W. 519, 29 Minn. 555.
Neb.—Brittle v. People, 2 Neb. 198.
Pa.—Wells v. Bain, 75 Pa. 39, 15 Am. R. 563.
Va.—Kamper v. Hawkins, 1 Va.Cas. 21.

Every reasonable presumption of law and fact must be indulged in favor of the validity of a constitution attacked after the ratification thereof by the people.
Ga.—Wheeler v. Board of Trustees of Fargo Consol. School Dist., 37 S.E.2d 322, 200 Ga. 323.

53. Neb.—Brittle v. People, 2 Neb. 198, 217.
12 C.J. p 681 note 68.

54. Cal.—Barlotti v. Lyons, 189 P. 282, 182 Cal. 575.
Mich.—Decher v. Vaughan, 177 N.W. 388, 209 Mich. 565.
Ohio.—Switzer v. State, 133 N.E. 552, 103 Ohio St. 306.

Within the legal and technical definition of the term is included any amendment which adds to or in any manner changes the powers granted in the original Constitution.
U.S.—Ex parte Dillon, D.C.Cal., 262 F. 563, affirmed Dillon v. Gloss, 41 S. Ct. 510, 256 U.S. 368, 65 L.Ed. 994.

Legislative amendment

Congress having after full consideration and with acquiescence, and long practice of all branches of government, established construction of Constitution, it cannot subsequently by mere legislation reverse such construction since it is not given power by itself thus to amend the Constitution.
U.S.—Myers v. U. S., Ct.Cl., 47 S.Ct. 21, 272 U.S. 52, 71 L.Ed. 160.

55. **Prior to 1808,** there were two other limitations on the power of amendment. Under U.S.Const. art. V it was provided that, prior to 1808, no amendment should be made in any manner affecting the first and fourth clauses of the ninth section of the first article, relating to migration or importation of persons, and capitation and direct taxes.

56. Cal.—Barlotti v. Lyons, 189 P. 282, 182 Cal. 575.

57. Cal.—Barlotti v. Lyons, supra.
Md.—Leser v. Garnett, 114 A. 840, 139 Md. 46, affirmed 42 S.Ct. 217, 258 U.S. 130, 66 L.Ed. 505.

28

Illustration A

A typical page in *Corpus Juris Secundum.*

ic and then by use of the individual index to that article. *C.J.S.* has both a five-volume General Index at the end of the alphabetical arrangement of topics, and individual indexes in every volume which cover separately each topic discussed in that volume. The indexes are detailed, clear, and easy to use. The General Index was completely revised and re-issued in 1981, and will be supplemented annually by pocket parts until another revision is needed.

When a topic is located on the subject desired, either from the list of topics at the beginning of the set or from the General Index, one can go directly to that topic, and consult either the detailed scope note, or table of contents, preceding the text of the article, or the index of the article, at the end of the volume.

Because *C.J.S.* is a West publication, it shares not only West's "comprehensive" approach, but also provides lateral citations to other West publications. If there is a West digest "key number" covering a topic that the encyclopedia is discussing, that key number will be cited. The researcher may therefore find in *C.J.S.* not only footnote citations directly to relevant cases, but also a key number that can be used in any of the West digests to locate more cases on the same issue. If other West publications are relevant to the topic, they will be cited as well. It is essential in using encyclopedias that the pocket part be checked for later citations and for text supplementation. As will be discussed below, many *C.J.S.* volumes are quite dated, and as the insertion of some of these finding aids to other West publications is a recent phenomenon, some may be found only in the pocket parts. Illustration B shows a typical page from the General Index of *C.J.S.*

C.J.S. also provides definitions of important legal terms and phrases and is particularly useful for its definitions of legal maxims, which are listed in the regular alphabetical sequence of articles, and defined with citations to case authority. In addition, there is an alphabetic list of "words and phrases defined" in the back of each volume of *C.J.S.*, covering the words and phrases defined in that volume.

One difficulty with using *C.J.S.* is the fact that a considerable number of titles have not been recompiled in recent years. Therefore, a researcher is advised to check the currency of the bound volume and to make careful use of the title's latest pocket part supplementation. For a detailed analysis of *C.J.S.* bound volume publication dates see Berring and Wedin's Study.[3]

The publisher of *C.J.S.* issues annual pocket parts, from time to time, replaces some volumes entirely, and occasionally issues special supplementary volumes designed to up-date is contents. Unfortunately, while pocket parts can supplement the text and add citations to new cases, one must constantly refer from the text to the pocket part to bring narrative and references up to date. To further compli-

3. R. C. Berring and V. Wedin, "Corpus Juris Secundum," 1 *Legal Reference Services Q.* 67–93 (1981).

Illustration B

A sample page from the *C.J.S.* General Index.

cate the use of *C.J.S.*, the frequency of issuance of new volumes and supplements has been somewhat irregular. It is hoped that there will be a continuing effort by West to bring the set up to date, since the publisher has indicated that it will not be replaced by another total revision. *C.J.S.* is an important resource, but at present it must be used with care.

C. AMERICAN JURISPRUDENCE 2d

American Jurisprudence 2d, popularly known as *Am.Jur.2d,* is the general legal encyclopedia published by the Lawyers Cooperative Publishing Company. It supersedes *American Jurisprudence* (1936–1940), which had in turn superseded *its* predecessor, *Ruling Case Law* (1914–1921). *Am.Jur.2d* differs from *Corpus Juris Secundum* in several respects. It contains some 82 volumes, as opposed to the almost 150 volumes of *C.J.S.* Part of this difference in size relates to the rationale of the encyclopedia itself. Much like the approach of Lawyers Co-op's other publications, *A.L.R.* and *A.L.R. Federal, Am.Jur.2d* takes a more "selective" approach to the use of footnote references. Whereas *C.J.S.* claimed to provide citations to *every* relevant case, *Am.Jur.2d* provides a more modest number of citations, with heavy emphasis on the cases appearing in the annotated reporters, *A.L.R.* and *A.L.R.Federal.* This method is designed to give broad coverage by referring the researcher to any relevant annotation that has been prepared as part of one of the several *A.L.R.* series. If, therefore, an *A.L.R.* annotation covers the topic being discussed in the encyclopedia, the encyclopedia will offer a citation to that annotation. This more selective approach keeps the footnotes from over-powering the text. Note the difference in the make-up of a page of *Am.Jur.2d* in Illustration C, as compared to the same topic in *C.J.S.*, shown in Illustration A above.

In providing access to their articles by topic or subject, *C.J.S.* and *Am.Jur.2d* are quite similar. *Am.Jur.2d* has an eight volume General Index at the end of the set that leads the researcher to specific topics. In addition, as in *C.J.S.*, each individual volume has its own indexes for the articles in that volume. Even the number of topics covered by *Am.Jur.2d,* 430, is almost the same as in *C.J.S.* Illustration D presents a sample page of the *Am.Jur.2d* General Index, similar to that of *C.J.S.*, as shown in Illustration B above.

There *are* several other notable differences between *C.J.S.* and *Am.Jur.2d.* One is the *New Topic Service* binder in *Am.Jur.2d,* which allows the publisher to introduce new topics into the encyclopedia, without having to reissue an entire volume. Through the *New Topic Service, Am.Jur.2d* reacts more quickly to changes in the law and to newly developing legal fields. The *New Topic Service* supplements the whole set, and should always be checked. In addition to the looseleaf binder, the *New Topic Service* also currently includes two bound volumes, representing substantial new topics, entitled "Federal Rules of Evidence" and "Pension Reform Act."

powers of the state legislature as involving a disregard of the provisions of Article V of the Federal Constitution as to the mode in which amendments may be proposed and adopted; the court proceeded on the theory that an elector's expression of opinion on such a question was an exercise of the right to petition guaranteed by the constitutions, state and federal.[35]

Any question as to whether the amendment procedure stated in Article V has been properly followed is a federal question which necessarily must ultimately be decided by the United States Supreme Court, and state and federal courts are bound by decisions of the Supreme Court as to the validity of amendments to the Constitution.[36]

A federal constitutional amendment which is duly ratified by three-fourths of the states is effective as against all of the states. For example, it was held that there was nothing in the character of the proposed Nineteenth Amendment to the Federal Constitution, extending suffrage to women, which prevented its adoption in the exercise of the power of amendment conferred by the Constitution, even as against a state which refused to ratify it.[37]

The term "amendment" has different meanings, which are determined by the connection in which it is used. When used in connection with the Constitution it has obviously a dual meaning, the particular one to be determined by its relationship. An amendment to the Constitution, which is made by the addition of a provision on a new and independent subject, is a complete thing in itself, and may be wholly disconnected with other provisions of the Constitution—such amendments, for instance, as the first 10 amendments of the Constitution of the United States. These were therein referred to as "articles in addition to, and amendment of" the Constitution.[38]

§ 20. Proposal of amendments; by Congress.

Congress, in proposing an amendment to the Federal Constitution, is not acting strictly in the exercise of ordinary legislative power,[39] and a congressional resolution proposing an amendment does not require the approval of the President,[40] nor is it affected by a Presidential veto.[41]

There is no limit to what Congress can propose in the way of an amendment to the Constitution, except that found in the final clause of Article V—no state can be stripped of equal suffrage in the Senate without its consent. The Supreme Court has thus remarked that an examination of Article V discloses that it is intended to invest Congress with a wide range of power in proposing

35. Spriggs v Clark, 45 **Wyo** 62, 14 P2d 667, 83 ALR 1364.

36. Keogh v Neely (CA7 Ill) 50 **F2d** 685, app dismd 284 US 583, 76 L Ed 504, 52 S Ct 39.

37. Leser v Garnett, 258 **US** 130, 66 L Ed 505, 42 S Ct 217.

38. State ex rel. Greenlund v Fulton, 99 **Ohio** St 168, 124 NE 172.

39. Re Opinion of Justices, 118 **Me** 544, 107 A 673, 5 ALR 1412.

40. Hawke v Smith, 253 **US** 221, 64 L Ed 871, 40 S Ct 495, 10 ALR 1504; Hollingsworth v Virginia, 3 **US** 378, 1 L Ed 644; State v American Sugar Refining Co., 137 **La** 407, 68 So 742; Re Opinion of Justices, 118 **Me** 544, 107 A 673, 5 ALR 1412; Warfield v Vandiver, 101 **Md** 78, 60 A 538; State ex rel. Wineman v Dahl, 6 **ND** 81, 68 NW 418; Commonwealth ex rel. Atty. Gen. v Griest, 196 **Pa** 396, 46 A 505.

41. The negative of the President applies only to the ordinary cases of legislation; he has nothing to do with the proposition or adoption of amendments to the constitution. Hollingsworth v Virginia, 3 **US** 378, 1 L Ed 644.

Illustration C

A typical page in *Am.Jur.2d.*

GENERAL INDEX

447

Illustration D

A sample page from the General Index to *Am.Jur.2d.*

Am.Jur.2d offers comprehensive statutory coverage. Examples of this include the extensive statutory coverage reflected in the *New Topic Service*, the use of three volumes (33, 34 and 34A) for Federal Taxation, and the *Tables of Statutes and Rules Construed* which appear in every *Am.Jur.2d* volume.

Am.Jur.2d is part of the Lawyers Co-op research system, the *Total Client-Service Library*. As such, it provides citations not only to the *A.L.R.* annotated case series, but to a variety of other Lawyers Co-op research tools as well, some of which are described below in Section G of this Chapter. The two legal encyclopedias illustrate the general tendency of their publishers to provide extensive references to other parts of their respective systems. These cross-references often make it desirable for the researcher to stay within a single publisher's system in a small library, at least in the initial stages of research.

D. USING THE NATIONAL ENCYCLOPEDIAS

In using general legal encyclopedias like *C.J.S.* and *Am.Jur.2d*, it is necessary to remember their relative place in the spectrum of authority. The text of an encyclopedia is entirely secondary authority, and has relatively little weight in persuading a court to accept a particular proposition of law. The authors of encyclopedia articles are not well-known scholars or jurists. Encyclopedias are best considered as functionally analogous to case digests, but instead of providing only a subject arrangement of case abstracts, they offer a convenient narrative text which synthesizes the case law of each topic.

Therefore, *C.J.S.* and *Am.Jur.2d* are best used as starting points for research in unfamiliar areas of law. If the researcher lacks a relevant decision or statutory citation, and is unable to start with primary source material and work outward in a search pattern, the encyclopedia, by its general indexing, can often help focus on a relevant topic. Through the use of West's references to the key number system, and *Am.Jur.2d*'s references to the *A.L.R.* annotations, one can be led to a wide range of primary sources and to other secondary materials. By exploiting fully the cross-references provided, as well as the citations given in footnotes, the researcher can often gain an effective start on a research project. In addition, the text of the encyclopedia can be used to clarify an unfamiliar area and explain the terminology and basic concepts of that field of law.

Encyclopedias should not be used as authoritative statements of law, nor should they be relied upon without reading and *Shepardizing* the cases cited in them. Because of the infrequent revision of the volumes of these encyclopedias, it is important to check the copyright date on the volume being used. Pocket parts, although essential in supplementing both case annotations and text, cannot provide the thorough revision sometimes required in areas of rapid change. Nor do legal encyclopedias provide the detailed coverage, the subtle distinctions, or the predictive analysis, of a good law review article.

E. STATE ENCYCLOPEDIAS

Jurisdictionally specialized legal encyclopedias have also been published for a few individual states. These state encyclopedias are arranged much like the national legal encyclopedias, but emphasize the case law, and to a less extent the statutory law, of that state. Published either by West or Lawyers Co-op, these encyclopedias tend to follow the pattern set by their respective publisher's national encyclopedia. Often disparaged by legal researchers, the state encyclopedias can actually be quite useful in their treatment of jurisdictionally specific concepts, *e.g.*, community property, oil and gas law, etc. A researcher unfamiliar with the domestic law of another jurisdiction can locate quickly within that state's encyclopedia locally accepted interpretations. The state encyclopedias published by West or Lawyers Co-op, as might be expected, also provide cross-references to other tools of their respective publisher. Thus, the state encyclopedias are an integral part of their publisher's research system. The following are the state encyclopedias published as of January 1, 1983:

California Jurisprudence 3d (Lawyers Co-op)

Florida Jurisprudence 2d (Lawyers Co-op)

Illinois Law and Practice (West)

Maryland Law and Practice (West)

Michigan Law and Practice (West)

New York Jurisprudence 2d (Lawyers Co-op)

Ohio Jurisprudence 3d (Lawyers Co-op)

Pennsylvania Law Encyclopedia (West)

Texas Jurisprudence 2d (Lawyers Co-op)

F. OTHER STATE RESEARCH TOOLS

In addition to the major state encyclopedias, several law publishers issue related research tools which focus on the law of particular states. The following examples are useful supplements to the encyclopedias and digests for the states they cover.

1. STATE LAW SUMMARIES

Lawyers Co-op has published outlines of the law for several states which are more limited than their state encyclopedias. These include *Summary of California Law* and *Summary of Mississippi Law*, both supplemented by annual pocket parts. Another such publication, *Summary of Pennsylvania Jurisprudence*, has been discontinued.

2. STATE PRACTICE SERIES

West and several other publishers offer another form of state law coverage with multi-volume sets on practice in various states. Some of these series are almost encyclopedic in coverage, but do not purport to be comprehensive encyclopedias. Typically, they consist of individual subject treatises, with legal forms, procedural checklists, and other practice-oriented features, published in a uniform format. These practice sets do not usually include a general index, but rather each treatise in the series contains its own index. Supplementation is provided by annual pocket parts, and occasional revision and expansion of individual volumes. For example, West currently issues the following substantial series: *California Practice, Massachusetts Practice Series, New Jersey Practice,* and the *Louisiana Civil Law Treatise Series.* West also publishes practice volumes or sets of forms for about twenty other states. These, however, do not offer the comprehensive scope of encyclopedias, and therefore will be treated in Chapter 15 under Treatises or Formbooks.

3. STATE LAW FINDERS

Several publishers have issued law finders which provide consolidated subject indexing and access to a wide range of primary legal sources *and* secondary materials for individual states, focusing particularly on the publications of that publisher. Although these indexes have not been highly publicized outside of the state covered, they do offer an interesting alternative research tool for the few jurisdictions covered. Examples are West's *Illinois Law Finder, Massachusetts Law Finder, Missouri Law Finder* (in preparation), *New York Law Finder, Pennsylvania Law Finder* and *Texas Law Finder.* Each of these is issued in a new edition annually and each covers Federal law as well as the law of the designated state. Lawyers Co-op issues a similar finding tool for North Carolina, called *Strong's North Carolina Index 3d* (1976, with annual pocket part supplementation), and Shepard's publishes a comparable tool, called the *Texas Law Locator.* Illustration E shows a sample page from West's *New York Law Finder,* a typical example of these indexes.

G. SPECIAL ADJUNCTS TO AM.JUR.2d

Lawyers Co-op publishes several research tools that are keyed to, and often associated with, *American Jurisprudence 2d.* Although they are not legal encyclopedias, they are described here because of their relationship to *Am.Jur.2d.*[4]

1. AM. JUR. DESKBOOK

This general reference volume offers a vast array of information about the legal system and often saves considerable time in locating such data. It is divided into seven parts, and contains historical legal

4. These publications are more fully described in the Lawyers Co-op promotional pamphlet, *The Living Law* (1982).

CONTINUANCE

United States district courts
West's Federal Forms § 1541 et seq.

CONTRABAND

Correctional institutions
McK Consol.Laws, Penal §§ 205.20, 205.25.

Gambling vehicles
McK Consol.Laws, Penal § 415.00.

CONTRACTORS

Generally
C.J.S. Public Contracts § 1 et seq.

Bonds
C.J.S. Public Contracts § 1 et seq.

Independent contractors, see, generally, Independent Contractors

Materials and supplies, surety bonds
Corbin on Contracts § 798.

Trusts and trustees, liens
McK Consol.Laws, Lien § 70 et seq.

CONTRACTS

Generally
McK Consol.Laws, Exec § 162 et seq.
McK Consol.Laws, Gen Obl § 1–101 et seq.
N.Y.Encyc.Contracts Law § 101 et seq.
C.J.S. Contracts § 1 et seq.
Contracts 🔑1 et seq.
Public Contracts 🔑1 et seq.
Secured Transactions 🔑1 et seq.
Corbin on Contracts.
Restatement of the Law, Second, Contracts.

Abandonment
C.J.S. Contracts.
Contracts 🔑249 et seq.

Acceptance
C.J.S. Contracts.
Contracts 🔑11 et seq.
Corbin on Contracts § 22 et seq.
N.Y.Encyc.Contracts Law § 201 et seq.

Accord and satisfaction
McK Consol.Laws, Gen Obl §§ 15–501, 15–503.

Accord executory
Corbin on Contracts § 1268 et seq.

214

Illustration E

A sample page from West's *New York Law Finder*.

documents, information on the federal and state codes, the legal profession, the court systems, prisons, statistical data, uniform laws, tables of law reports, and much other useful reference material. The contents page of the *Deskbook* shown in Illustration F demonstrates the range of its coverage.

2. AM. JUR. TRIALS

This is a set designed to acquaint the lawyer with court room techniques, by approaching litigation from two different perspectives. The first six volumes of *Am. Jur. Trials* constitute an extensive treatise on the various general aspects of trial preparation and procedure. This segment also contains useful citations to both primary sources and background material in its cross-references and footnotes, and includes a separate index.

Following the six volume treatise, are a series of volumes which form the *Model Trials* segment. These are devoted to a detailed analysis of a variety of civil and criminal trials, through signed articles by individual lawyers, who describe the unique aspects of these types of litigation, in which they specialize. In addition, this part contains numerous checklists, and citations to other parts of the Lawyers Co-op *Total Client-Service Library.* Its contents are indexed in the *Federal Quick Index* described in Chapter 4, Annotated Law Reports.

3. AM. JUR. PROOF OF FACTS

This set, now in its second series, is described by Lawyers Co-op as a "synthesis of substantive law, elements of damages, elements of proof, and sample testimony designed to assist in the preparation for, and the proving of facts that may be at issue in judicial or administrative proceedings." [5] *Proof of Facts,* consisting of signed articles by individual authors, describes the elements of proof required for establishing particular facts in judicial proceedings, and outlines useful procedures for making that proof. As with all *Total Client-Service Library* products, these articles are accompanied by numerous checklists and cross-references. The set is also indexed in the *Federal Quick Index.*

4. AM. JUR. FORMBOOKS

Am. Jur. Forms and *Am. Jur. Pleading and Practice Forms, Revised* are multi-volume sets of forms which are cross-referenced to *Am.Jur.2d* and often sold with that encyclopedia. Although they will be treated in Chapter 15, with other formbooks, they are noted here

5. *The Living Law,* supra, p. 121.

CONTENTS

ix

Illustration F

Contents page of the *Am. Jur. Deskbook.*

because of their relationship to *Am.Jur.2d.* Like other general collections of forms, these sets lack jurisdictional specificity for the requirements of individual states, but that disadvantage is somewhat alleviated by references to state statutes and procedural rules. As part of the Lawyers Co-op *Total Client-Service Library,* they provide cross-references to other Lawyers Co-op research tools and can be used effectively with *Am.Jur.2d.* Both formbooks are supplemented by cumulative pocket parts.

H. CONCLUSION

In addition to the various encyclopedias and related publications described in this Chapter, there are a number of single-subject treatises which are so extensive in scope and size as to be considered encyclopedic in nature. Examples of these include such classics as *Corbin on Contracts, Williston on Contracts,* and *Wigmore on Evidence,* and more modern sets like Wright and Miller on *Federal Practice and Procedure,* Blashfield's *Automobile Law and Practice,* and Frumer and Friedman, *Products Liability.* Since these works focus on one subject, however, and are generally the product of one or two authors, they are substantially different than the traditional legal encyclopedias and will therefore be treated in the next chapter under Treatises.

Chapter 15

TREATISES, RESTATEMENTS, DICTIONARIES, ETC.

A. Treatises.
  1. Types of Treatises.
    a. The Encyclopedic Treatise.
    b. Scholarly Monographs.
    c. Hornbooks and Student Texts.
    d. Practice Guides.
    e. Law for the General Public.
  2. Finding Treatises by Subject.
    a. The Card Catalog.
    b. *Law Books Recommended.*
    c. *Law Books in Print.*
    d. Other Bibliographies.
  3. Evaluation of Treatises.
  4. Using Treatises Effectively.
    a. Indexes, Tables and Footnotes.
    b. Supplementation.
    c. Computer Access.

B. Restatements of the Law.
  1. History and Purpose.
  2. Coverage and Format.
  3. Access to the Restatements.
  4. Court Treatment and Shepardizing.

C. Legal Dictionaries.
  1. Major Works.
    a. *Black's Law Dictionary.*
    b. *Ballentine's Law Dictionary.*
  2. Other Dictionaries.
  3. Judicial Dictionaries.
  4. Legal Maxims.
  5. Legal Abbreviations.

D. C.L.E. Materials.
  1. Practising Law Institute (P.L.I.) and California Continuing Education of the Bar (C.E.B.).
  2. Other State Programs.
  3. Formats.

E. Directories.
  1. *Martindale-Hubbell Law Directory.*
  2. Specialized Directories.
  3. Jurisdictional Directories.
  4. Judicial Directories.

F. Formbooks.
  1. General Encyclopedias of Forms.
  2. Specialized Subject Formbooks.

F. Formbooks—Continued
   3. State Practice and Statutory Forms.
   4. Computer-Assisted Drafting.
G. Records and Briefs.
   1. U. S. Supreme Court.
   2. U. S. Court of Appeals.
   3. State Courts.
H. Conclusion.

A. TREATISES

From the earliest periods of English law, text-writers produced commentaries, guides and summaries of the developing case law and legislation. The *Tractatus de Legibus et Consuetudinibus Angliae* (Treatise on the Laws and Customs of England), attributed to Ranulph de Glanvill and completed between 1187 and 1189, and Henry de Bracton's work of the same title, dating from about 1250, are two of the most ambitious attempts to present the law of that time.[1] Treatises have continued to be an important part of the literature of our legal system, although they have never achieved the authoritative status of the civil law commentaries. Legal texts, by restating and synthesizing the myriad of decisions and statutes, seek to impose order on the chaos of individual precedents. They also summarize historical developments, analyze and explain apparent discrepancies and inconsistencies, predict future changes, and provide practical guides to the conduct of legal business for the lay public and the legal profession. The treatise literature, from the first printed lawbooks in the 15th century to the multitude of volumes pouring from the presses today, has been characterized by a wide range of quality, style and purposes.

As distinguished from the increasingly sophisticated forms used for primary sources and finding tools, the basic structure of the treatise has remained surprisingly constant—a narrative text, following the main areas of the subject in a more or less logical sequence; documentation by footnote citations to relevant cases or other primary sources, supporting the principles stated; occasionally, an appendix of illustrative primary sources; and finally an index. When designed for the *practical* guidance of either the general public or the bar, the treatise may also include model forms for particular legal transactions of procedures. Although the several components of the treatise have changed relatively little, the breadth of coverage of individual works has narrowed considerably in recent years. The comprehensive, almost encyclopedic scope of works like Sir William Blackstone's

1. This early period of legal writing has been described by a number of legal historians. See, for example, T. F. T. Plucknett, *Early English Legal Literature* (Cambridge University Press, 1958); P. H. Winfield, *The Chief Sources of English Legal History* (Harvard University Press, 1925); and W. S. Holdsworth, *Sources and Literature of English Law* (Oxford, Clarendon Press, 1925). The introductions to the scholarly editions and translations of many early English treatises, published by the Selden Society, are often the best source for the history and significance of those works.

Commentaries on the Laws of England [2] and its American counterpart, James Kent's *Commentaries on American Law* [3] has not been duplicated in modern times, and such broad treatments are unlikely to be attempted again. The texts of the 19th and 20th centuries have been devoted to single subjects, and, even there, extensive multi-volume treatments of one field like *Wigmore on Evidence,*[4] *Williston on Contracts,*[5] *Corbin on Contracts,*[6] and *Scott on Trusts* [7] seem to be a disappearing form.[8] With a few exceptions, scholarly treatises are now focusing on increasingly narrow areas of the law.

Treatises can be very helpful in legal research and are widely used by practitioners, scholars and students for different purposes. Some treatises synthesize complex legal developments and provide a relatively clear statement of the law in a difficult or changing field. Others serve primarily as pragmatic reference guides for practicing lawyers in specialized areas. Another increasingly popular type of treatise provides a general introduction to a legal subject for the student, in a form typified by the West Publishing Company's hornbook and nutshell series.

1. TYPES OF TREATISES

Despite the foregoing generalizations on the trend toward more specific or simplified texts, we can still see a considerable variety of forms among legal treatises today. Their quality, extent of documentation, and detail vary widely, depending on the audience for which the work is designed, the capacity of the author, and the standards of the publisher. The following examples are typical of current publications.

a. The Encyclopedic Treatise

Multi-volume texts covering a single field exhaustively are still occasionally being written, either as a long-term project by one or two distinguished scholars, or as collaborative efforts by groups of writers. Typical of this genre are those referred to earlier—*Wigmore on Evidence,* Corbin and Williston's works on *Contracts,* and *Scott on Trusts.* More recent examples are four different treatises covering the same field comprehensively: Professor James W. Moore's *Feder-*

2. Oxford, Clarendon Press, 1765–1769, 4v. For a comprehensive bibliography of the many editions of the *Commentaries* and Blackstone's other works, see C. S. Eller, *The William Blackstone Collection in the Yale Law Library, A Bibliographical Catalogue* (Yale University Press, 1938).

3. New York, O. Halsted, 1826–1830, 4v. Revised and reissued in many subsequent editions.

4. 3d ed., Boston, Little, Brown, 1940, 10v.; eight volumes revised by J. H. Chadbourn, 1961–1979.

5. 3d ed. Little, Brown, 1967. 6v. with supplements.

6. West Publishing Co., 1950–1964. 8v. in 12, with supplements.

7. 3d ed. by W. H. E. Jaeger. Baker, Voorhis, 1957–1978. 18v., with supplements.

8. For a discussion of this trend, see A. W. B. Simpson, "The Rise and Fall of the Legal Treatise: Legal Principles and the Forms of Legal Literature", 48 *U. of Chicago L.Rev.* 632 (1981).

al Practice;[9] *Federal Practice and Procedure,*[10] by Professors Arthur R. Miller and Charles A. Wright; West's *Federal Practice Manual,* 2d ed.;[11] and Lawyers Co-op's *Federal Procedure.*[12] The last two sets are prepared by their respective publisher's editorial staffs, and each is supplemented by multi-volume sets of federal procedure forms.

These massive treatises are usually kept current by annual pocket parts, and are designed for scholars, students, and practicing lawyers. They have some of the characteristics of legal encyclopedias, and because of their obvious appeal to practitioners, are often supplemented by forms, court rules, and other aids to practice.

Some encyclopedic treatises are issued in a looseleaf format to facilitate supplementation. The Matthew Bender Company is probably the major publisher of this form, although Callaghan, Clark Boardman, and Oceana also use it extensively. Although they are usually supplemented only annually or biennially, they are often advertised as if they were looseleaf services, and are frequently purchased on that assumption.

b. Scholarly Monographs

As a group, scholarly monographs tend to be narrow in scope and usually one volume in length, although many of the encyclopedic multi-volume treatises described above can certainly be considered scholarly in approach *and* in authority. Typically, scholarly monographs are critical texts, examining the law analytically rather than just descriptively. They are rarely supplemented, but occasionally revised and published in several successive editions. Although issued by many publishers, they come most often from University presses or academic institutes. These treatises tend to focus heavily on the historical background, underlying causes and policies, and future directions of particular legal subjects.

c. Hornbooks and Student Texts

Student texts are designed to convey the fundamentals of a legal field and to serve as an introduction to its terminology, concepts and the present state of the law. The best of this class, however, go beyond the "black letter" rules, and offer some historical background, critical analysis of recent developments, and prediction of future trends. Supplementation is uncommon in this genre, but the more popular texts are frequently revised and reissued in new editions.

d. Practice Guides

Many treatises are designed primarily for practitioners in particular fields of law, and the most widely used of this type are the practice and procedure guides and manuals issued commercially for par-

9. 2d ed. (Bender, 1948–1964) 13v. in 29, with supplements.

10. West Publishing Company, 1969–1982, 27v., with annual supplements.

11. West Publishing Company, 1970–1980, 11v. in 12, with annual supplements.

12. Lawyers Co-op, 1982, in progress.

ticular jurisdictions. Some of these have already been described above in Sections C.2 and E of Chapter 8, Court Rules.[13] Supplementation is important in these publications, and is furnished by looseleaf inserts, pocket parts, or new editions every year. Model forms are provided, either in the text itself or in supplementary volumes. Court rules and civil practice acts are also frequently included.

Both the West Publishing Company and Lawyers Co-op issue multi-volume sets of practice books for many states, often including both procedural and substantive law. Some of the substantive law volumes in these series are major subject treatises, but with a single-jurisdiction emphasis. West is probably the largest publisher in this format and offers such sets for some 22 states.

e. Law for the General Public

Among the oldest forms of legal texts are handbooks of law for the layperson. These were published in England in the first century of printing and have continued in popularity. New versions still appear almost every year. Justice of the Peace manuals and similar guides for peace officers and town officials, most of whom did not have formal legal training, were common in England and America. Many such works for the general public have been published under the title, *Every Man His Own Lawyer*, and at least one *Every Woman Her Own Lawyer* has appeared in this country.[14] These texts tend to be general introductions to the law and often include simplified instructions for conducting legal business, with model forms for specific transactions.

In recent years, there has been an increasing emphasis in this form on self-lawyering, particularly in organizing a business, writing a will, avoiding probate, collecting a debt, getting a divorce, etc. Many of these guides suffer from over-simplification, lack of supplementation, and failure to reflect variation in the requirements of different jurisdictions. The organized bar, as might be expected, has opposed and widely criticized those publications which are claimed to involve the unauthorized practice of law, and in a few instances have brought legal actions against them.[15]

2. FINDING TREATISES BY SUBJECT

There are several different approaches to locating treatises on a particular subject. Recommendations from colleagues, instructors

13. See footnote 7 in Chapter 8, at p. 248, for recent bibliographies of state practice books in California, New York and Texas.

14. By George Bishop (New York, Dick & Fitzgerald, 1858). Because of their legal disabilities and distinct status, many handbooks and treatises on the law relating to women have been published over the centuries. The womens' rights movement and rising concerns of women with their legal status generally have stimulated many new books of this kind in recent years.

15. See, for example, *Grievance Committee of the Bar of Fairfield County, Dacey et al.*, 154 Conn. 129, 222 A.2d 339, appeal dismissed 386 U.S. 683 (1967); *Dacey et al. v. N. Y. County Lawyers Assoc.*, 290 F.Supp. 835, aff. 423 F.2d 188, cert. denied 398 U.S. 929 (1970); *Dacey v. Florida Bar, Inc., et al.*, 414 F.2d 195, cert. denied 397 U.S. 909 (1970).

and reference librarians are obvious sources. The following bibliographic tools are suggested for more detailed inquiries.

a. The Card Catalog

Because most legal materials are self-organizing serials, law libraries were slow in developing sophisticated card catalogs, and law was the last of the major disciplines to utilize classification schemes for book arrangement. The most widely used law classification, that of the Library of Congress, has not yet been completed today and a number of large research law libraries are still using local schemes. For many years, most law libraries were arranged by form of publication and then within each form, alphabetically by jurisdiction (i.e. court reports, session laws, codes, etc. alphabetically by state name, in separate units, with Federal materials sometimes shelved all together, or each Federal type of material preceding the alphabet of state materials of that type). Periodicals were shelved alphabetically by title, and treatises alphabetically by author's name. As collections grew, catalogs became necessary as a versatile record of holdings, and classification became desirable as a more rational arrangement scheme for browsing and retrieval, and as an identification device for the location and retrieval of increasingly varied and complex materials.

Today most law libraries have adopted the near universal cataloging format and rules used by virtually all research libraries. As card catalogs have grown more and more expensive to maintain and cumbersome to use, many libraries are now exploring (and some are already adopting) microform and computer alternatives. Catalog cards in most large libraries, including those in law schools, are now being generated by cooperative, computer-based library networks. Although card catalogs in research libraries may be replaced in the near future by on-line computer systems, a brief reminder of the main features of the card catalog may still be useful here. For most of us, it will remain the primary search tool for legal treatises—at least until the next edition of *How to Find the Law.*

The card catalog is an alphabetical index of all books and materials in a particular library, providing access by author, subject, titles and occasionally also by specialized forms (e.g. looseleaf services, legislative histories, trials, etc.). Some catalogs have *one* alphabetical arrangement for author, title and subject, while others are divided, with authors and titles in one section, and subjects in another.

Author entries (generally called by libraries "main entries") usually represent the named individuals who are primarily responsible for the particular work, but the names of editors, compilers, revisors, joint authors, annotators, and translators are often included as well, as "added entries". Many books issued in the name of corporate bodies are listed by the name of that body (e.g., bar associations, law schools, institutes, corporations, etc.). Conference proceedings are frequently listed under the name of the conference.

Title entries are omitted by some libraries when the title is not distinctive or is identical to its subject (e.g., a treatise simply called "Contracts" might not have an added title entry, and some libraries omit titles when they begin with very common words like "Treatise on the law of . . . " or "Cases and Materials on . . . ").

Subject entries are used for each of the subjects covered *generally* in the book, but not usually for the individual subjects of particular chapters of sections of the book. For collections of essays, or books with distinct divisions by different authors, some libraries make what are called "analytic" entries, which bring out the authors, titles and subjects of those discrete parts. To facilitate specific subject searching in the catalog, most libraries subdivide their subject headings by jurisdiction (e.g., Criminal law—U.S.; Criminal law—New York; Criminal law—France) and by form (e.g., Criminal law—Bibliographies; Criminal law—Periodicals; Criminal law—Statistics), and by combinations of both (e.g., Criminal law—U.S.—Cases).

Two types of cross references are also widely used for subject headings—"see" references, from a heading that is *not* used, to the heading for the subject that *is* used (e.g., Death penalty, *see* Capital punishment), and "see also" references, from one heading that *is* used to another related heading that may also be of interest (e.g., Capital punishment, *see also* Hanging).

Among other useful features of standard catalog cards are the following: *Series notes*, indicating that a book is one of a particular named series (e.g., "West Nutshell Series"; "A.A.L.L. Publications Series No. 18"; "Legal Almanac Series No. 12"); and *Contents notes*, indicating that the work includes specific features, such as a Bibliography, or an Appendix of legal forms (pagination is usually indicated so that one can determine the length and location of that feature). A separate card for the book is usually added to the catalog under the name of the series so that it can also be found under that heading.

Illustration A shows a sample "author" catalog card with the main features identified. Illustration B shows a set of "added entry" cards, based on that in Illustration A, with the various entries identified.

Several large law libraries also have published printed book catalogs of their holdings.[16] Those issued in recent years include subject entries and are therefore helpful in identifying treatises on particular subjects (see section (d) below), as well as providing location information for inter-library loans. These book catalogs are not regularly supplemented and hence are only useful for books published up to their closing dates. Printed book catalogs were quite common

16. For a listing of these, see B. W. Taylor, "American Law Library Book Catalogs," 69 *Law Library J.* 347 (1976). Professor Taylor's bibliography became the basis of a microform edition of these catalogs issued by Trans-Media.

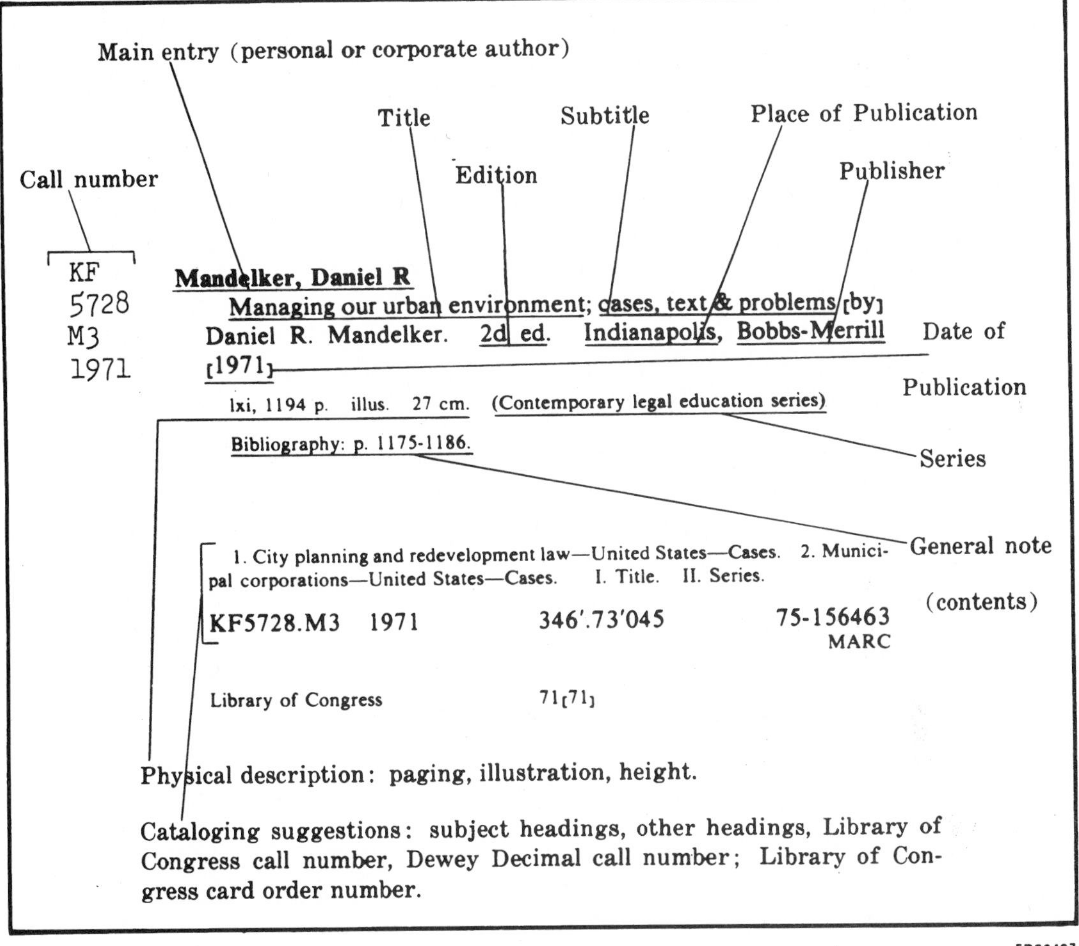

Illustration A

Sample catalog card issued by the U. S. Library of Congress, with call number added.

Contemporary legal education series

KF 5728 M3 1971

Mandelker, Daniel R

Managing our urban environment; cases, text & problems [by] Daniel R. Mandelker. 2d ed. Indianapolis, Bobbs-Merrill [1971]

series card

Managing our urban environment

KF 5728 M3 1971

Mandelker, Daniel R

Managing our urban environment; cases, text & problems [by] Daniel R. Mandelker. 2d ed. Indianapolis, Bobbs-Merrill [1971]

title card

MUNICIPAL CORPORATIONS - UNITED STATES - CASES

KF 5728 M3 1971

Mandelker, Daniel R

Managing our urban environment; cases, text & problems [by] Daniel R. Mandelker. 2d ed. Indianapolis, Bobbs-Merrill [1971]

subject card

CITY PLANNING AND REDEVELOPMENT LAW - UNITED STATES - CASES

KF 5728 M3 1971

Mandelker, Daniel R

Managing our urban environment; cases, text & problems [by] Daniel R. Mandelker. 2d ed. Indianapolis, Bobbs-Merrill [1971]

subject card

KF 5728 M3 1971

Mandelker, Daniel R

Managing our urban environment; cases, text & problems [by] Daniel R. Mandelker. 2d ed. Indianapolis, Bobbs-Merrill [1971]

lxi, 1194 p. illus. 27 cm. (Contemporary legal education series)

Bibliography: p. 1175-1186.

1. City planning and redevelopment law—United States—Cases. 2. Municipal corporations—United States—Cases. I. Title. II. Series.

KF5728.M3 1971 346'.73'045 75-156463

MARC

Library of Congress 71[71]

main entry (author) card

[B3293]

Illustration B

Sample set of cards with headings typed, ready to file in card catalog.

among law libraries in the 19th and early 20th centuries, and the best of these are still valuable for historical and bibliographic research.[17]

Today, however, the most comprehensive sources for both bibliographic study and inter-library loan locations are the *National Union Catalog, Pre-1956 Imprints,*[18] and the two computerized cataloging network systems, OCLC and RLIN, both of which give library locations for each title listed and contain extensive records of legal materials held by law libraries *and* general libraries. These systems, accessible by terminals in the subscribing libraries, have greatly simplified inter-library lending procedures.

b. Law Books Recommended

A useful bibliographic tool for finding older treatises by subject is *Law Books Recommended for Libraries,*[19] a looseleaf collection of forty-six subject bibliographies prepared under the auspices of the Association of American Law Schools. Although the primary purpose of the set was to help law school libraries develop their treatise collections, it is one of the best analytic bibliographies of legal treatises. Unfortunately, the bibliographies have not been updated since their 1974–75 supplement and so do not cover later publications.

There are two evaluative features in these bibliographies which add to their value. Most of the lists contain brief critical annotations to each title listed. These comments, and many of the bibliographies themselves, were prepared by leading scholars in the subject field. In addition, the works listed in each bibliography are graded A, B, or C, designating their relative importance for libraries of different sizes.

In addition to bibliographies on most subject fields in Anglo-American law, *Law Books Recommended* also includes lists on Comparative Law, Foreign Law, International Law, and the law of several other specific areas and legal systems (African, Chinese, Islamic, Latin American, Roman and Russian-Soviet law).

c. Law Books in Print

Legal treatises which are currently in print are listed separately by author, title, subject, and publisher in *Law Books in Print,*[20] a five volume set now in its 4th edition. The listings do not include evaluation, but the subject section enables one to compile a substantial bibliography of relatively recent monographs on specific topics. Jurisdictional breakdown of each subject is provided so that titles can be identified by their state or country emphasis. New editions of *Law Books in Print* have been issued in the past approximately every five or six years, and are supplemented by *Law Books Pub-*

17. See particularly, Harvard Law School, *Catalogue of the Library* . . . (1909) 2v., reprinted, Dennis & Co., 1967.

18. Mansell, 1968–1980, 685v.; with Supplement, 1980–1981, 69v.

19. Fred B. Rothman & Co., 1967–70, 6v. looseleaf; with 4v. Supplement, 1974–75.

20. Compiled by Robert Buckwalter (Glanville Publishers, 1982).

lished, which is currently planned for several issues each year, the last being an annual cumulation.

d. Other Bibliographies

In addition to the foregoing sources, another useful retrospective bibliography of legal treatises, monographs, and collected works, is *Law Books, 1876–1981, Books and Serials on Law and its Related Subjects.*[21] This compilation provides access to a vast array of legal literature by author, title and subject.

As noted above, a number of law libraries have published catalogs of their collections in book form. Among them, the following modern lists include *subject* access to their entries, and, at least up to their dates of publication, are useful for finding treatises on particular subjects:

Combined Catalog Anglo-American Law Collections: University of California Law Libraries, Berkeley and Davis . . ., by M. Schwartz and D. Henke, 10v. (1970).

Dictionary Catalog of the Columbia University of Law Library, 28v. (1969) with Suppl. 7v. (1973).

New York University Law Center. *A Catalogue of the Law Collections . . .,* by J. J. Marke (1953).

Legal bibliographies are published frequently in a variety of formats, many of substantial size with annotations, others in pamphlet form or in legal periodicals. These are often useful for identifying or collecting secondary sources in particular fields, but they are rarely updated on a regular basis. Many have been referred to in other Chapters of this book. Those appearing as separate publications can be identified by their subject in all of the retrieval sources discussed above. Those which appear in periodicals can be located by the periodical indexes described below in Chapter 16, Periodical Literature. In addition, two helpful bibliographies of bibliographies have been published in the past, but unfortunately, neither has been kept up to date. They are, however, still useful for their retrospective coverage: W. L. Friend, *Anglo-American Legal Bibliographies, An Annotated Guide* (Library of Congress, 1944; reprinted 1966), and M. Howell, *A Bibliography of Bibliographies of Legal Material* (N.J.Appellate Print, 1969) 2v.; Supplement, 1969–1971 (1972). Fortunately, current coverage of legal bibliographies in books and periodicals is now provided by subject in L. E. Dickson & W. S. Chiang, *Legal Bibliography Index,* published annually since 1979 by the Louisiana State Univ. Law Center.

3. EVALUATION OF TREATISES

Legal treatises can be evaluated by a combination of the following criteria:

(a) The reputation and stature of the author, including the critical reception given to his or her past work, the degree of experi-

21. 4v. (N.Y., R. R. Bowker, 1981).

ence and expertise in the subject field, the clarity and style of the writing. (Legal prose does *not* have to be dull.)

(b) The general reputation of the publisher, including the quality, reliability and accuracy of previous publications (e.g. beware of misleading advertising, of the reprint which omits the original date of publication, and the "new" edition of a work by a long-deceased author, when its editor or revisor is not named).

(c) The purpose and originality of the work—is it a new effort or a rehash of previous writing? what is the scope and depth of its analysis, the extent of its documentation? is it a work of serious scholarship or a slapdash effort to capitalize on sudden interest in a new field?

(d) The research aids and scholarly apparatus provided (index, footnotes, appendices, tables, bibliography, etc.).

(e) The adequacy and frequency of supplementation if the book purports to describe the current state of the law.

Many of these criteria must inevitably be subjective in application, but the advice of those we respect (other recognized scholars in the field, literate colleagues, trustworthy librarians, etc.) can always be sought. Book reviews of new legal treatises, alas, are not always reliable. They appear slowly and many significant publications are never adequately reviewed.[22]

4. USING TREATISES EFFECTIVELY

a. Indexes, Tables and Footnotes

As noted above, treatises are not only to be read and studied; many can also be used as research aids and as references to primary legal sources. This depends on the quality of their scholarly apparatus—indexes to find the relevant discussions; tables of contents, tables of cases cited, and tables of statutes construed; and footnotes to document the assertions, arguments and conclusions stated in the text. These finding aids and references can be used effectively to further one's research, after the author's analysis and discussion of the legal topic has been read and evaluated. Grabbing footnote citations without reading the relevant text to see why the authority was cited can be time-wasting and misleading.

b. Supplementation

Treatises on current law must always be supplemented. This can be done by pocket parts, looseleaf inserts, separate pamphlets or bound supplements, but the frequency of updating is important. Treatises are rarely supplemented more frequently than annually. Many are not even kept that current. In rapidly changing fields, the text must be supplemented by the researcher directly in the primary sources themselves. In using a treatise one should always check the

22. For additional comments on book reviews in legal periodicals, see Section B.1 of Chapter 16, Legal Periodicals, at p. 490–491 below.

date of publication, although the date of the actual completion of the work may pre-date publication by several years. A comparison of the date of the preface and the date of publication is often a clue to such delays.

c. Computer Access

Although WESTLAW and LEXIS are still largely retrieval systems of primary legal sources, there are growing indications of their movement into secondary sources, including treatises. LEXIS has already contracted with the Matthew Bender Company, a major publisher of legal treatises in looseleaf format, and is offering a computer searching capability of a limited number of Bender treatises. WESTLAW now includes in its databases *Black's Law Dictionary* and will undoubtedly be adding some of its treatises in the near future. It is perhaps too early to determine how useful computer searching of legal treatises will be, but it may add a new dimension to their research value by enabling one to search for specific words and phrases which would not appear as entries in a treatise's index.

B. RESTATEMENTS OF THE LAW

1. HISTORY AND PURPOSE

Over the last fifty years, the *Restatements of the Law*, prepared under the auspices of the American Law Institute, have become one of the most frequently cited, widely respected, and yet controversial secondary legal authorities. They are a unique form of legal literature and cover only ten specific fields of law—agency, conflict of laws, contracts, foreign relations law, judgments, property, restitution, security, torts, and trusts. All of the Restatements, except those on restitution and security, have been issued in second editions. The original plan of the Restatements, as stated by the American Law Institute was as follows:

> "To present an orderly restatement of the general common law of the United States, including in that term not only the law developed solely by judicial decision, but also law that has grown from the application by the courts of statutes that were generally enacted and were in force for many years."

One of the hopes of some members of the Institute was that the Restatements would achieve such authority as to provide relief from the burden of research in the numerous volumes of court reports. For many reasons that hope was never realized. In fact, the considerable authority achieved by the first series of Restatements has been decreasing.[23]

23. See in that regard, J. H. Merryman, "Toward a Theory of Citations: an Empirical Study . . . ," 50 *So.Calif.L.Rev.* 381 (1977) at p. 405 & ff.

The first series of Restatements required over twenty years to complete,[24] and, after thirty years of effort, the second series is still unfinished.[25] The process of preparing a Restatement involves an initial draft by the Reporter, an outstanding scholar in that subject field. The draft is reviewed by a committee of Advisors, who are also noted specialists on that subject, and the resulting text is then reviewed by the Council of the American Law Institute, and further revised. The next version, the *Tentative Draft*, is distributed to all of the members of the Institute, considered, debated and often further amended at their annual meetings. The text may be returned to the Reporter for revision or redrafting, and the final version ultimately adopted. The Tentative Drafts are often treated as a form of legislative history of the Restatements, and are frequently cited to explain, support or attack particular Restatement rules.

The members of the Institute are among the most distinguished lawyers, judges and scholars in the country. Although the Restatements have no official legal status, and their reception and acceptance has varied from field to field, they have been remarkably successful on the whole and have had considerable influence on the courts. While often criticized for stating what the law *ought to be*, rather than what it *is*, the Restatements have had an impact in bringing about needed changes in the law. A Director of the American Law Institute has defended the Restatements' frequent adoption of the "best" rule rather than a majority rule, by arguing that the Institute was "not obliged to govern its appraisals by a count of jurisdictions." [26]

2. COVERAGE AND FORMAT

The field of law covered by each Restatement is divided into a logical arrangement of numbered Chapters, each Chapter containing a major topic of that field. The Chapters are then divided into numbered sections, each of which deals with a general principle of law in that topic. The section numbering is continuous throughout each Restatement, so the Chapter numbers are not included in a citation to a Restatement, e.g., *Restatement (Second) of Torts* § 48 (1965). Each section begins with a statement of the principle of law of that section, printed in bold face type (thus often called the "black letter" rule or principle). If a caveat to the rule is necessary, it follows the statement of the rule. Then, an explanatory comment is set forth, with one or more illustrations of the rule in the form of hypothetical applications. Illustrations C–1, C–2 and C–3 show these components in Section 48 of the *Restatement (Second) of Torts*.

24. Work was begun in 1923, and the last volume was issued in 1944. The final texts of both series are published by the West Publishing Company.

25. The second series began in 1952, and two Restatements 2d, as noted above, have not yet been published in full.

26. H. Wechsler, "The course of the Restatements," 55 *A.B.A.J.* 147 (1969) at p. 150. That article also contains a short history of the A.L.I. and the Restatements.

coverable. In many instances there may be recovery for emotional distress as an additional, or "parasitic" element of damages in an action for such a tort. Reference should be made to Chapter 47.

§ 48. Special Liability of Public Utility for Insults by Servants

A common carrier or other public utility is subject to liability to patrons utilizing its facilities for gross insults which reasonably offend them, inflicted by the utility's servants while otherwise acting within the scope of their employment.

See Reporter's Notes.

Caveat:

The Institute expresses no opinion as to whether the rule stated in this Section may also be applicable to possessors of land whose premises are held open to the public for a business or other purpose.

Comment:

a. The rule stated in this Section is based on the public interest in freedom from insult on the part of those who undertake the obligations of a public utility. The chief value of the rule lies in the incentive which it provides for the selection of employees who will not be grossly discourteous to those who must come in contact with them, and for the making of proper rules and supervision to enforce them.

The earliest cases involved insults to passengers by the hands of employees of common carriers. The rule was then extended to innkeepers, who always have been regarded as analogous to carriers; and in the later decisions it has been further extended to other public utilities. Any such utility is subject to liability to patrons who are making use of its facilities. The earlier cases found an "implied contract" not to insult the patron; but the later decisions have based the liability on the public duty, and have found it even where there is as yet no contract. It is not necessary that the insult be offered on the utility's own premises.

Illustrations:

1. A, intending to buy a ticket on a train, enters the waiting room of the B Railroad, and sets her parcels on

See Appendix for Reporter's Notes, Court Citations, and Cross References

Illustration C-1

Restatement (Second) of Torts § 48 (1965), showing components of a typical Restatement section.

one of the seats. An employee of the railroad removes the parcels. When A protests, he abuses her with profane language, calls her a woman of low character, and accuses her of indecent conduct. B Company is subject to liability to A.

2. A messenger employed by the A Telegraph Company delivers a telegram to B at her home. While she is signing the receipt he makes an indecent proposal to her. A Company is subject to liability to B.

b. Patrons. The rule stated in this Section applies only to insults to patrons who are utilizing the facilities of the carrier or other public utility, for the purpose for which they are offered to the public. If an insult is offered to any other person, it does not fall within this Section, and he must recover, if at all, under the rule stated in § 46.

Illustration:

3. A enters B's hotel for the purpose of meeting her brother, who is not a guest of the hotel. While A is waiting in the lobby the hotel detective orders her to leave, and uses insulting language to her. B Company is not liable to A.

c. Gross insults. Any public utility may of course be liable for the infliction of severe emotional distress by extreme and outrageous conduct, under the rule stated in § 46. The rule stated in this Section goes further and makes such a defendant liable for conduct which falls short of extreme outrage, but is merely insulting. At the same time the rule of this Section does not extend to mere trivialities. Even at the hands of public servants the public must be expected and required to be hardened to a certain amount of rudeness or minor insolence, which any reasonable man would consider offensive but harmless and unimportant. Even profanity may not be grossly insulting, where it obviously amounts to nothing more than mere emphasis or a habit of speech, or where it is so customary in the particular community that it may be said to be generally tolerated. An unduly sensitive plaintiff, even though he may be badly upset and suffer illness as a result, cannot found a cause of action upon mere hurt feelings at conduct which is essentially trivial. No passenger on a railroad can mulct the carrier in damages merely because he is told to "Hurry up! We haven't got all night!"

The obvious condition of the plaintiff must, however, be taken into account in determining whether the conduct is grossly

See Appendix for Reporter's Notes, Court Citations, and Cross References

Illustration C–2

Restatement (Second) of Torts § 48, continued.

insulting; and language addressed to a pregnant or a sick woman may be actionable where the same words would not be if they were addressed to a United States Marine. The defendant is never liable for doing more than he is privileged to do, even though his manner of doing it may be lacking in the politeness which would be desirable.

Illustrations:

4. A is riding on a train of the B Railroad with the wrong ticket. B's conductor tells A in a rough and rude tone of voice that she must leave the train at the next station, and requires her to do so. B Company is not liable to A.

5. A, a mature man, and B, his ten year old daughter, are in the waiting room of the station of C Railroad, waiting for their train. Employees of C in the adjoining station agent's office use vulgar and profane language, knowing that it will be overheard in the waiting room, and that the passengers are there. A is accustomed to such language and is in the habit of using it himself; B is not. C Company is subject to liability to B, but not to A.

d. Scope of Employment. The rule stated in this Section does not make any defendant liable for insults offered by its employees while they are not acting within the scope of their employment. Whether the employee is so acting is determined by the rules stated in §§ 228–237 of the Restatement of Agency, Second.

Comment on Caveat:

e. A possessor of land who holds his premises open to the public for business or other purposes may be liable, as in the case of any other person, for the intentional infliction of emotional disturbance by conduct which is extreme and outrageous, under the rule stated in § 46. In a few cases, however, the rule stated in this Section has been extended beyond carriers and other public utilities, and owners of business premises have been held liable to patrons for conduct which apparently amounted to no more than gross insult. As many other cases have rejected the liability. The law is apparently still developing. For the present, in the absence of sufficient decisions to permit a conclusion, the Institute expresses no opinion as to whether the rule of this Section should be so extended.

See Appendix for Reporter's Notes, Court Citations, and Cross References

Illustration C–3

Restatement (Second) of Torts § 48, concluded.

The assertions, counter-assertions, and cautions embodied in the Restatements have been parodied in the following hypothetical Restatement of the law on the power to regulate interstate commerce:[27]

> "Black letter text: Congress has power to regulate interstate commerce.
>
> Comment: The states may also regulate interstate commerce, but not too much.
>
> Caveat: How much is too much is beyond the scope of this Restatement."

The *second* series of Restatements include appendices at the end of each Restatement, which contain the following aids not present in the *first* series: (a) Reporter's Notes, citing court decisions, statutes, and periodical articles, both supporting and contrary to the stated rule; (b) Citations in court decisions to the first series of the Restatements and to the tentative drafts; and (c) Cross references to relevant West digest topics and key numbers, and to *A.L.R.* Annotations. Illustrations D–1, D–2 and D–3 show parts of these several added features from the Appendix to the *Restatement (Second) of Torts.*

3. ACCESS TO THE RESTATEMENTS

The *first* series of Restatements had a General Index volume covering the contents of all volumes, and each of the individual Restatements has its own index, but a general index for the whole second series has not yet been prepared. In addition, the tables of contents of each Restatement in *both* series can be used for a topical approach, but as with digests and statutory codes this tends to be a less satisfactory means of access.

The Restatements have also been the subject of frequent comment in periodical articles, and such articles are often of interest for research involving the Restatements. Both the annual *Proceedings* and the *Annual Reports* of the American Law Institute include bibliographies of articles published during the preceding year on the various Restatements. The major periodical indexes (described below in Chapter 16) also provide access to such articles. *The Index to Legal Periodicals* lists them under the heading, "American Law Institute", while *Current Law Index* and *Legal Resources Index* list them both under "American Law Institute" and under the names of the individual Restatements.

The *Proceedings* of the Institute also include transcripts of the discussions of the A.L.I. drafts of the Restatements. These, like the tentative drafts themselves, provide additional insights into the texts of the various Restatements, and the rationale for the formulation of their rules, as adopted.

27. Quoted in J. H. Merryman, "The Authority of Authority . . .," 6 *Stanford L.Rev.* 613 (1954) at p. 634, ft. 62. Merryman's article also contains an extensive discussion and critique of the *Restatements.*

Recovery by tenant for mental anguish occasioned by wrongful eviction. 17 A.L.R.2d 936.

§ 48. Special Liability of Public Utility for Insults by Servants.

REPORTER'S NOTES

See, as to this Section generally, Wade, Tort Liability for Abusive and Insulting Language, 4 Vand. L. Rev. 63 (1950); Prosser, Insult and Outrage, 44 Calif. L. Rev. 40 (1956).

The rule stated frequently has been applied to common carriers. See for example Birmingham Ry. L. & P. Co. v. Glenn, 179 Ala. 263, 60 So. 111 (1912); Bleecker v. Colorado & Southern R. Co., 50 Colo. 140, 114 P. 481, 33 L.R.A. N.S. 386 (1911); Louisville & Nashville R. Co. v. Bell, 166 Ky. 400, 179 S.W. 400 (1915); Haile v. New Orleans Ry. & Light Co., 135 La. 229, 65 So. 225, 51 L.R.A. N.S. 1171, Ann. Cas. 1916C 1233 (1914); Humphrey v. Michigan United R. Co., 166 Mich. 645, 132 N.W. 447 (1911); Barbknecht v. Great Northern R. Co., 55 N.D. 104, 212 N.W. 776 (1927); Gillespie v. Brooklyn Heights R. Co., 178 N.Y. 347, 70 N.E. 857, 66 L.R.A. 618, 102 Am. St. Rep. 503 (1904); Lipman v. Atlantic Coast Line R. Co., 108 S.C. 151, 93 S.E. 714, L.R.A.1918A 596 (1917); Knoxville Traction Co. v. Lane, 103 Tenn. 376, 53 S.W. 557, 46 L.R.A. 549 (1899).

It has also been applied to innkeepers. Milner Hotels, Inc. v. Dougherty, 195 Miss. 718, 15 So. 2d 358 (1943); Boyce v. Greeley Square Hotel Co., 228 N.Y. 106, 126 N.E. 647 (1920). Many of the cases have involved conduct which was extreme and outrageous, such as breaking into a room and accusing the occupants of being unmarried, which might well fall under § 46; but the decisions have relied chiefly upon the innkeeper's special responsibility. Emmke v. De Silva, 293 F. 17 (8 Cir. 1923); Dixon v. Hotel Tutweiler Operating Co., 214 Ala. 396, 108 So. 26 (1926); Moody v. Kenny, 153 La. 1007, 97 So. 21, 29 A.L.R. 474 (1923); Frewen v. Page, 238 Mass. 499, 131 N.E. 475, 17 A.L.R. 134 (1921); DeWolf v. Ford, 193 N.Y. 397, 86 N.E. 527, 21 L.R.A. N.S. 860, 127 Am. St. Rep. 969 (1908).

The extension to other public utilities is supported by Dunn v. Western Union Tel. Co., 2 Ga. App. 845, 59 S.E. 189 (1907); Magouirk v. Western Union Tel. Co., 79 Miss. 632, 31 So. 206, 89 Am. St. Rep. 663 (1901); Western Union Tel. Co. v. Watson, 82 Miss. 101, 33 So. 76 (1903); Butler v. Western Union Tel. Co., 62 S.C. 222, 40 S.E. 162 (1901); Buchanan v. Western Union Tel. Co., 115 S.C. 433, 106 S.E. 159, 18 A.L.R. 1414 (1921).

Illustration 1 is taken from Texas & Pacific R. Co. v. Jones, 39 S.W. 124 (Tex. Civ. App. 1897), refused, no reversible error. See also St. Louis-San Francisco R. Co. v. Clark, 104 Okl. 24, 229 P. 779 (1924); Jones v. Atlantic Coast Line R. Co., 108 S.C. 217, 94 S.E. 490 (1916); cf. Moody v. Kenny, 153 La. 1007,

See also cases under division, chapter, topic, title, and subtitle that includes section under examination.

Illustration D-1

Reporter's Notes to Section 48 in Appendix to *Restatement (Second) of Torts.*

97 So. 21, 29 A.L.R. 474 (1923), hotel guest not yet registered.

Illustration 2 is taken from Buchanan v. Western Union Telegraph Co., 115 S.C. 433, 106 S.E. 159, 18 A.L.R. 1414 (1921).

Illustration 3 is taken from Jenkins v. Kentucky Hotel, 261 Ky. 419, 87 S.W.2d 951 (1935). Cf. Wallace v. Shoreham Hotel Corp., 49 A.2d 81 (Mun. Ct. App. D.C. 1946).

Illustration 4 is taken from New York, Lake Erie & Western Ry. Co. v. Benett, 50 F 496 (6 Cir. 1892). See also Crutcher v. Cleveland, Chicago, Cincinnati & St. Louis Ry. Co., 132 Mo. App. 311, 111 S.W. 891 (1908); Daniels v. Florida Central & Penninsular Ry. Co., 62 S.C. 1, 39 S.E. 762 (1901).

Illustration 5 is taken from Fort Worth & Rio Grande Ry. Co. v. Bryant, 210 S.W. 556 (Tex. Civ. App. 1919), error refused.

Caveat: In several cases theaters and other places of amusement have been held liable for gross insults to patrons, which apparently amounted to extreme outrage falling within the rule stated in § 46. See Interstate Amusement Co. v. Martin, 8 Ala. App. 481, 62 So. 404 (1913); Saenger Theatres Corp. v. Herndon, 180 Miss. 791, 178 So. 86 (1938); Boswell v. Barnum & Bailey, 135 Tenn. 35, 185 S.W. 692, L.R.A.1916E 912 (1916). In other cases the facts involved expulsion from the premises and a clear breach of contract, or some other tort. Weber-Stair Co. v. Fisher, 119 S.W. 195 (Ky. 1909); Planchard v. Klaw & Erlanger New Orleans Theatres Co., 166 La. 235, 117 So. 132, 60 A.L.R. 1086 (1928); Aaron v. Ward, 203 N.Y. 351, 96 N.E. 736, 38 L.R.A. N.S. 204 (1911); Smith v. Leo, 92 Hun 242, 36 N.Y.Supp. 949 (Sup. Ct. 1895); Kral v. Philadelphia Quick Lunch, 47 Dauph. Co. Rep. (Pa.) 279 (1939).

The extension of the rule to other business premises is supported by Malczewski v. New Orleans Ry. & Light Co., 156 La. 830, 101 So. 213, 35 A.L.R. 553 (1924); O'Connor v. Dallas Cotton Exchange, 153 S.W.2d 266 (Tex. Civ. App. 1941); Davis v. Tacoma R. & Power Co., 35 Wash. 203, 77 P. 209, 66 L.R.A. 802 (1904).

Such extension was rejected in Republic Iron & Steel Co. v. Self, 192 Ala. 403, 68 So. 328, L.R.A. 1915F 516 (1915); Wallace v. Shoreham Hotel Corp., 49 A.2d 81 (Mun. Ct. App. Dist. Col. 1946); Flowers v. Price, 190 S.C. 392, 3 S.E.2d 38 (1939); Slocum v. Food Fair Stores of Florida, Inc., 100 So. 2d 396 (Fla. 1958); Stavnezer v. Sage-Allen & Co., 146 Conn. 460, 152 A.2d 312 (1959). Compare, in connection with other torts, Mann v. Roosevelt Shop, Inc., 41 So. 2d 894 (Fla. 1949); Larson v. R. B. Wrigley Co., 183 Minn. 28, 235 N.W. 393 (1931); Nance v. Mayflower Tavern, 106 Utah 517, 150 P.2d 773 (1944).

COURT CITATIONS TO FIRST RESTATEMENT

D.C.Munic.App. 1946. Caveat cited. A casual patron of hotel cocktail lounge who was not a registered guest of hotel had no cause of action against hotel owner for humiliation and embarrassment resulting from insulting words of waiter because of a dispute as to the correct amount

Cit.—cited; fol.—followed; quot.—quoted; sup.—support.
A complete list of abbreviations faces page 1.

Illustration D–2

Reporter's Notes (cont'd) and Court Citations to First Restatement in Appendix to *Restatement (Second) of Torts.*

of change due the plaintiff upon payment of the bill. Wallace v. Shoreham Hotel Corp., 49 A.2d 81, 83.

E.D.S.C. 1956. Citation in Restatement sec. quot. in dictum. Allegations that over a period of several months defendant's agents made frequent phone calls at all hours to plaintiff's home using abusive language in order to harass and annoy her were sufficient to state a claim for damages arising out of the emotional disturbance caused thereby. Wiggins v. Moskins Credit Clothing Store, Inc., 137 F.Supp. 764, 765.

Cal. 1952. Com. c cit. in disc. Where person made financial settlement after threats of physical violence for failure to settle, cause of action was established for physical injuries resulting from emotional distress, though threats all related to future actions and no immediate physical harm was threatened. State Rubbish Collectors Ass'n v. Siliznoff, 38 Cal.2d 330, 240 P.2d 282, 285.

Fla. 1958. Cit. in disc. In action for damages for mental suffering or emotional distress and ensuing heart attack caused by insulting language of store employee to customer, complaint failed to state cause of action against proprietor absent allegation showing special knowledge or notice or that language was intended to have real meaning or serious effect upon customer. Slocum v. Food Fair Stores of Florida, Inc., 100 So.2d 396, 398.

N.J.Super. 1957. Cit. in dictum. In a case tried on the basis of a common carrier's refusal to carry the plaintiff, it was not error for the trial court to fail to charge the jury that the defendant could recover for humiliation and embarrassment inflicted upon her by the actions of the drivers even though not denied passage. Gebhardt v. Public Serv. Coordinated Transport, 48 N. J. Super. 173, 137 A.2d 48, 53.

Pa.Super. 1947. Cit. in sup. Theatre patron was guilty of contributory negligence as matter of law where she was struck by door controlled by pneumatic check but had done nothing to protect herself and had not been reasonably vigilant. Armstrong v. Warner Bros. Theatre, 161 Pa.Super. 385, 54 A.2d 831, 832.

Pa.Com.Pl. 1939. Cit. in analogy. A restaurateur who grabs a cup of coffee from the hands of a patron and who threatens to strike the patron is liable for his acts even though the person of the patron was not touched. Kral v. Phila. Quick Lunch, 47 Dauphin Co. Rep. 279, 283.

Cross References to

1. **Digest System Key Numbers**
   Carriers ⚷283(3, 4)
   Innkeepers ⚷10.2
   Master and Servant ⚷306

2. **A.L.R. Annotation**
   Civil liability of carrier, innkeeper, owner of business premises, etc. to patron or customer for insulting or abusive language not amounting to defamation. 15 A.L.R.2d 108, 132 et seq.
   Refusing admission to, or ejecting from, place of amusement. 60 A.L.R. 1089.
   Liability for misconduct or negligence of messenger not directly related to the service. 18 A.L.R. 1416.
   Liability of innkeeper for interference with guest. 17 A.L.R. 139.
   Liability of innkeeper for indignity to one occupying room without being registered. 29 A.L.R. 481.

See also cases under division, chapter, topic, title, and subtitle that includes section under examination.

Illustration D–3

Court citations (cont'd) and Cross References under Section 48 in Appendix to *Restatement (Second) of Torts.*

Beginning in 1976, a full bibliography of the various drafts and other documentation for the several Restatements was added to the *Checklists of Basic American Legal Publications.*[28]

4. COURT TREATMENT AND SHEPARDIZING

References to judicial decisions which have cited specific Restatement sections can be found in several sources. Prior to 1976, many of the Shepard's state citators included a section in which the various Restatements were listed as cited entries, followed by citations to the decisions of the courts of that state which had referred to particular sections of the Restatement. Since 1976, Shepard's has issued a separate citator for this purpose, *Restatement of the Law Citations.* The citing material includes federal and state court decisions, and articles in selected legal periodicals. Illustration E shows a page in this citator listing section 48 of the *Restatement (Second) of Torts.*

In addition to the inclusion of citations to the first series of Restatements in the Appendices of the units of the second series, the American Law Institute has also prepared separate volumes, called *Restatements in the Courts,* for this purpose, for both series. These contain abstracts, in the usual West Publishing Company headnote format, of decisions which have cited Restatement sections, and citations to periodical articles. A "Permanent Edition" of the *Restatement in the Courts,* covered the period from 1932 to 1944, and included a glossary of terms defined in the Restatements, a history of the Restatements and of the American Law Institute. This was followed by a series of supplementary volumes containing similar citations for the period 1945 to 1975. Since 1976 this material is included in pocket parts to each of the Restatement volumes. Individual volumes of state court annotations for some of the Restatements, in the same format as the *Restatement in the Courts,* were also issued for a number of states, but neither for all of the states, nor for all of the Restatements. These have not been kept up to date.

The American Law Institute has an almost obsessive concern with the extent to which the Restatements have been cited by the courts, as reflected in the foregoing research aids. Tables in their Annual Reports summarize the statistics of such citations every year and they are a focus of all A.L.I. publicity for the Restatements. This concern is part of a continuing effort to elevate the authority of the Restatements and has been the subject of some criticism and friendly humor.[29] The Restatements remain, however, a *secondary* authority, but one still accorded unusual respect and attention by the courts and the bar.

C. LEGAL DICTIONARIES

The complexity of legal terminology and the necessity for accuracy and precision in the use of words and phrases of legal significance

28. American Association of Law Library Publication No. 4 (Fred B. Rothman, 1976).

29. See articles by J. H. Merryman, footnotes 23 and 27, above.

TORTS, SECOND **§ 77**

86CaR90
89CaR95
97CaR582
468P2d218
Fla
285So2d662
Kan
529P2d109
NY
330S2d667
Ore
453P2d687
Wash
530P2d295
Comment f
470F2d4
20CA3d303
2C3d498
35CC726
215Kan820
359Mas254
85W2d59
Calif
86CaR90
97CaR582
468P2d218
Kan
529P2d109
Mass
268NE921
Wash
530P2d295
Comment g
9CA3d395
10CA3d394
40CA3d850
85W2d59
Ariz
540P2d196
Calif
88CaR562
89CaR88
99CaR403
115CaR587
Wash
530P2d295
Illustra-
tion 14
10CA3d395
Calif
89CaR89
Comment h
10AzA562
20CA3d308
2C3d499
35CC727
50DC2d49
215Kan824
216Kan210
217Ten481
28U2d401
Ariz
460P2d668
540P2d196
Calif
86CaR91
97CaR586
468P2d219
Colo
536P2d841
Kan
529P2d113
531P2d8
Okla
518P2d62
Tenn

398SW275
Utah
503P2d450
Comment i
245CA2d530
20CA3d311
50DC2d49
215Va341
Calif
54CaR85
97CaR588
Va
210SE147
62CaL1493
Comment j
10CA3d396
20CA3d311
50DC2d50
52H171
359Mas255
80NM410
259Or63
262Or420
85W2d59
Ariz
540P2d196
Calif
89CaR90
97CaR588
Haw
472P2d519
Mass
268NE921
NM
456P2d884
Okla
518P2d62
Ore
485P2d32
495P2d1196
Wash
530P2d295
Comment k
259Or64
Ore
485P2d32
Comment l
85W2d60
Wash
530P2d295

§ 47
35Ap2d113
54C2d338
139Ct308
51H52
149OS321
399Pa26
Calif
5CaR692
353P2d300
Conn
93A2d295
Haw
451P2d820
NY
313S2d35
Ohio
78NE744
Pa
159A2d218
49HLR1050
52HLR845
22MnL1032
Comment a

66McL452
Comment b
54C2d338
52H170
117NJL96
110Su314
Calif
5CaR692
353P2d300
Haw
472P2d519
NJ
186At588
265A2d413

§ 48
455F2d861
10CA3d403
161PaS388
48Su181
54W2d447
Calif
89CaR95
Mo
396SW569
447SW266
NJ
137A2d53
Pa
54A2d832
Wash
341P2d864
44CaL41
44CaL59
44CaL60
49HLR1052
22MnL1031
90PaL812
Caveat
22MnL1033

§ 49
et seq.
43WLR190

§§ 49
to 62
20TxL775

§ 49
64NwL637
103PaL31

§§ 50
to 59
15TxL214

§ 50
340Pa310
Pa
16A2d17
43WLR193
Comment b
242CA2d552
31IlA215
Calif
51CaR588
Ill
334NE260
Illustra-

tion 4
242CA2d552
Calif
51CaR588
Illustra-
tion 5
242CA2d552
Calif
51CaR588
Illustra-
tion 6
242CA2d552
Calif
51CaR588

§ 51
et seq.
Mo
263SW736

§ 53
5WAp221
69W2d105
Wash
417P2d367
486P2d340
64NwL643
Comment a
Illustra-
tion 4
69W2d105
Wash
417P2d367

§§ 55
to 58
464F2d783

§ 55
2AzA368
Ariz
409P2d84
49HLR1002
23MnL521
15TxL255

§ 56
142Col582
Colo
351P2d812

§ 57
2AzA368
142Col582
Ariz
409P2d84
Colo
351P2d812
Comment a
Illustra-
tion 1
23MnL521
Illustra-
tion 3
251CA2d314
Calif
59CaR470
23MnL521
Comment b
142Col582

Colo
351P2d813

§ 58
142Col582
227Min156
Colo
351P2d812
Minn
34NW701

§ 59
58DC626
78DC281
20McA763
227Min157
166OS25
Mich
174NW634
Minn
34NW702
Ohio
139NE33
15CLA390
75HLR495
41MnL385
20TxL775
41WLR120
43WLR194
Comment a
Illustra-
tion 1
270NC604
NC
155SE113

§ 60
125CA2d631
141Kan325
227Min168
Calif
271P2d143
Kan
41P2d991
Minn
34NW708
49HLR1053
33MnL551
100PaL637
15TxL214
33TxL13
41WLR121
43WLR190
62WLR562
Comment a
Illustra-
tion 1
62YLJ709
Illustra-
tion 4
125CA2d631
Calif
271P2d143

§ 61
288FS459
119GaA317
Ga
167SE369
Tex
408SW583
63HLR175

32MnL118
33MnL553
15TxL214
43WLR190
62WLR563

§ 62
2AzA370
Ariz
409P2d86
Ky
254SW476
La
139So2d66

§ 63
36NJ71
219PaS84
221PaS434
66Su381
Mo
410SW542
NJ
169A2d175
174A2d885
Pa
280A2d601
292A2d478
Comment b
66Su381
NJ
169A2d175
Comment c
130Ct155
Conn
32A2d648
Comment f
1CLA134
Comment h
130Ct155
Conn
32A2d648
Illustra-
tion 5
1CLA134
Comment i
130Ct155
66Su382
Conn
32A2d648
NJ
169A2d176
1CLA135
Comment j
1CLA135

§ 64
1CLA136

§ 65
502F2d1275
513F2d81
64Su200
66Su381
Fla
241So2d189
298So2d464
La
28So2d283
Mass
318NE916
Mo

419SW950
NJ
165A2d541
169A2d176
1CLA136
1CLA151
98PaL593
102PaL675
Comment c
Illustra-
tion 1
1CLA136
Comment e
66Su382
NJ
169A2d176
Comment g
280Min524
64Su200
Minn
160NW243
NJ
165A2d541
Comment h
96NH40
NH
69A2d854
Comment i
133Neb766
Nebr
277NW74
1CLA144

§ 68
91NH353
NH
19A2d433

§ 69
86Nev393
51W2d755
Nev
469P2d401
Wash
321P2d896
Comment a
5W2d265
Wash
105P2d23

§ 70
513F2d81
NJ
270A2d280
1CLA133
1CLA134
Comment b
502F2d1276
57NJ157
NJ
270A2d280
Comment c
502F2d1277

§ 71
502F2d1278
513F2d81
10Wis2d545
Wis
103NW564
Comment b
502F2d1278

§ 73
103IlA142
Ill
242NE478

§ 75
502F2d1277
103IlA144
56Il2d98
260Min133
Ill
242NE479
306NE41
Ind
312NE497
Minn
109NW265
Tex
281SW772
Comment a
502F2d1277
Comment b
502F2d1278

§ 76
513F2d81
261Ia570
Iowa
154NW119
168NW924
Ky
333SW524
Mo
410SW542
419SW949
20MnL439
21MnL266
Comment e
Mo
410SW542
Comment f
Mo
410SW542

§§ 77
to 80
348Mo703
Mo
155SW77

§ 77
52GaA733
243Md370
253Min229
110NH457
349Pa479
Calif
73CaR111
Ga
184SE639
La
28So2d283
77So2d231
Md
221A2d358
Minn
91NW767
Mo
399SW440
NH

Continued

251

Illustration E

Entries for *Restatement (Second) of Torts* § 48 in Shepard's *Restatement of the Law Citations.*

have made law dictionaries an important tool of the lawyer's craft. The nuances, subtleties and ambiguities of legal language have been a source of humor, anger, and misunderstanding on the part of the general public, and have often created great animosity toward the legal profession. The language of the law is itself a fascinating field of study, but one beyond the scope of this work. For those interested, there are many excellent studies.[30]

Our concern here, however, is with the law dictionary, an essential aid to legal research. The late Professor Karl Llewellyn described its importance for the law student as follows:

> ". . . It is a pity, but you must learn to *read*. To read each word. To understand *each* word. You are outlanders in this country of the law. You do not know the speech. It must be learned. Like any other foreign tongue, it must be learned: by seeing words, by using them until they are familiar; meantime, by constant reference to the dictionary. What dictionary? Tort, trespass, trover, plea, assumpsit, nisi prius, venire de novo, demurrer, joinder, traverse, abatement, general issue, tender, mandamus, certiorari, adverse possession, dependent relative revocation, and the rest. Law Latin, law French, aye, or law English—what do these strange terms mean to you? Can you rely upon the crumbs of language that remain from school? Does *cattle levant and couchant* mean *cows getting up and lying down?* Does *nisi prius* mean *unless before?* Or *traverse* mean an upper gallery in a church? I fear a dictionary is your only hope—a law dictionary—the one-volume kind you can keep ready on your desk. Can you trust the dictionary, is it accurate, does it give you what you want? Of course not. No dictionary does. The life of words is in the using of them, in the wide network of their long associations, in the intangible something we denominate their feel. But the bare bones to work with the dictionary offers; and without those bare bones you may be sure the feel will never come." [31]

There are many American law dictionaries currently available, and they vary widely in approach, size and quality. The first published in this country was an edition of John and William Rastell's *Les Termes de la Ley*,[32] a successor to the oldest English law dictionary, first published in 1527 by the older John Rastell. For almost a hundred years, the numerous editions of John Bouvier's *A Law Dictionary* [33] were most popular among American lawyers. Today, the leading American law dictionaries are *Black's Law Dictionary*, 5th ed. (West

30. See, for example, the following: D. Mellinkoff, *The Language of the Law* (Little, Brown, 1963); J. B. White, *The Legal Imagination, Studies in the Nature of Legal Thought and Expression* (Little, Brown, 1973); F. A. Philbrick, *Language and the Law* (Macmillan, 1949); M. M. Bryant, *English in the Law Courts* (Frederick Unger, 1930, 1962). Mellinkoff's book contains an extensive bibliography on this field, at pages 455–478.

31. *The Bramble Bush* (Oceana, 1951) at p. 41.

32. Portland, Me., 1812, based on the London edition of 1721.

33. First published in Philadelphia, 1839, it went through many editions until the last, the 3d revision, 8th ed., 1914 (West Publishing Company), 3v., which is still often used by older lawyers and some scholars.

Res ipsa loquitur /ríyz ípsə lówkwədər/. The thing speaks for itself. Rebuttable presumption or inference that defendant was negligent, which arises upon proof that instrumentality causing injury was in defendant's exclusive control, and that the accident was one which ordinarily does not happen in absence of negligence. Res ipsa loquitur is rule of evidence whereby negligence of alleged wrongdoer may be inferred from mere fact that accident happened provided character of accident and circumstances attending it lead reasonably to belief that in absence of negligence it would not have occurred and that thing which caused injury is shown to have been under management and control of alleged wrongdoer. Hillen v. Hooker Const. Co., Tex.Civ.App., 484 S.W.2d 113, 115. Under doctrine of "res ipsa loquitur" the happening of an injury permits an inference of negligence where plaintiff produces substantial evidence that injury was caused by an agency or instrumentality under exclusive control and management of defendant, and that the occurrence was such that in the ordinary course of things would not happen if reasonable care had been used.

Black's Law Dictionary, 5th ed. (1979) p. 1173.

res ipsa loquitur (rēz ip'sa lo'qui-ter). The thing speaks for itself. The rule that proof that the thing which caused the injury to the plaintiff was under the control and management of the defendant, and that the occurrence was such as in the ordinary course of things would not have happened if those who had its control or management had used proper care, affords sufficient evidence, or, as sometimes stated by the courts, reasonable evidence, in the absence of explanation by the defendant, that the injury arose from, or was caused by, the defendant's want of care. 38 Am J1st Negl § 295.

The three essential elements of the doctrine of res ipsa loquitur are: (1) the instrumentality must be under the control or management of the defendant; (2) the circumstances, according to common knowledge and experience, must create a clear inference that the accident would not have happened if the defendant had not been negligent; and (3) the plaintiff's injury must have resulted from the accident. Lewis v Wolk, 312 Ky 536, 228 SW2d 432, 16 ALR2d 974.

The term means "the thing speaks for itself," and that means the thing or instrumentality involved speaks for itself. It clearly does not mean the accident speaks for itself. It means that when the initial fact, namely what thing or instrumentality caused the accident has been shown then, and not before, an inference arises that the injury or damage occurred by reason of the negligence of the party who had it under his exclusive control. The inference of negligence arising from the initially established fact compels the defendant, in order to relieve himself of liability, to move forward with his proof to rebut the inference of negligence. Travelers Ins. Co. v Hulme, 168 Kan 483, 213 P2d 645, 16 ALR2d 793.

Ballentine's Law Dictionary, 3d ed. (1969) pp. 1104–5.

Illustration F

Res ipsa loquitur in *Black's* and *Ballentine's* law dictionaries.

Publishing, 1979) and *Ballentine's Law Dictionary,* 3d ed. (Lawyers Co-op/Bancroft-Whitney, 1969).[34] They will be described first, and then a number of other dictionaries and related works will be treated briefly. Illustrations F and G show comparative treatment of the Latin term, *res ipsa loquitur,* in *Black's, Ballentine's,* and several other dictionaries referred to in section 2, below. General dictionaries, which can also be very important in legal research and writing, are dealt with in Section C.4 of Chapter 17, General Research and Reference Sources.

1. MAJOR WORKS

a. Black's Law Dictionary

The fifth and latest edition of *Black's Law Dictionary* incorporates many improvements over the preceding editions and for now at least gives it an edge over its competitors. According to the publish-

34. The competition between *Black's* and *Ballentine's* is quite keen, and new editions of either produce comparative reviews. See, for example, a review of *Black's,* 5th edition, by R. Sloane, 11 *U. of Toledo L.Rev.* 322 (1980).

RES IPSA LOQUITUR *(rās ēp'-sȧ lō'-kwĭ-tûr)*—Lat: the thing speaks for itself; "a rule of evidence whereby **negligence** of the alleged wrongdoer may be inferred from the mere fact that the accident happened, provided: (1) the character of the accident and the circumstances attending it lead reasonably to the belief that in the absence of negligence it would not have occurred, and (2) the thing which caused the injury is shown to have been under the [exclusive] management of the alleged wrongdoer." 484 S.W. 113, 115. The rule may not apply when direct evidence of negligence exists. See 270 So. 2d 900, 904. "The gist of it, and the key to it, is the inference, or process of reasoning by which the conclusion is reached. This must be based upon the evidence given, together with a sufficient background of human experience to justify the conclusion. It is not enough that plaintiff's counsel can suggest a possibility of negligence. The evidence must sustain the **burden of proof** by making it appear more likely than not." Prosser, Torts 212 (4th ed. 1971). The procedural effect of successful invocation of the doctrine is to shift the **burden** of going forward with the evidence, which normally attaches to the plaintiff, to the defendant, who is thereby charged with introducing evidence to refute the presumption of negligence which has been created.

S.H. Gifis, *Law Dictionary* (Barron's, 1975) p. 180.

RES IPSA LOQUITUR (Latin—the thing speaks for itself). A doctrine of tort law which allows the plaintiff to rely on circumstantial evidence to raise an inference of negligence. If he cannot come forward with proof of negligence, the plaintiff may avoid a directed verdict for the defendant by showing that (1) the injury in question generally results from negligence, and (2) the defendant was in sole control of the instrumentality which caused the injury. Although Res Ipsa establishes a Prima Facie case for negligence, the jury may still find for the defendant.

K.R. Redden & E.L. Veron, *Modern Legal Glossary* (Michie, 1980) p. 445.

Res ipsa loquitur. (Latin) "The thing speaks for itself"; a **rebuttable presumption** (a conclusion that can be changed if contrary facts are brought out) that a person is **negligent** if the thing causing an accident was in his or her control only and that type of accident does not usually happen without negligence. It is often abbreviated "res ipsa" or "R.I.L."

D. Oran, *Oran's Dictionary of the Law* (West, 1982) p. 365.

Illustration G

Res ipsa loquitur in three other law dictionaries.

er, this edition includes ten thousand revised or new entries (e.g. brain death, ombudsman, palimony and environmental impact statement). For the first time, it offers pronunciation aids for foreign and difficult words and phrases, and it still includes many Latin, Norman French, Saxon, and other ancient legal terms, and many legal maxims. Many definitions are from judicial decisions, and the citations to those cases are given. References are also provided to the *Restatements of the Law*; the Uniform Commercial Code, the Internal Revenue Code and other statutes; and to federal court rules. It includes a table of abbreviations, covering law reports, legal periodicals and other legal publications, and has several other Appendices which are useful for research purposes. As noted earlier, *Black's Law Dictionary* can also be searched by computer on WESTLAW.

b. Ballentine's Law Dictionary

Ballentine's Law Dictionary is an excellent comprehensive dictionary, although slightly smaller than *Black's*. It contains many of the same features as *Black's*, e.g., pronunciation aids; legal maxims; citations to decisions, statutes and other legal sources; and a somewhat shorter table of abbreviations. *Ballentine* cites frequently to *A.L.R.* annotations and to the Lawyers Co-op encyclopedias, *American Jurisprudence* and *American Jurisprudence 2d*. Until the new, fifth edition of *Black's*, many felt that *Ballentine's* definitions and citations were more current than *Black's*, but now the comparison is much more difficult. Both still contain some outdated references, and each has some recent words and phrases lacking in the other. For example, *Ballentine* does not include *brain death, ombudsman, palimony,* and *environmental impact statement,* which are in *Black's* 5th edition. But *Ballentine* includes some words and phrases which are not in *Black's*, e.g., air pollution, radiation and water pollution. Both dictionaries include popular names of cases and statutes, but not always the same ones.

2. OTHER DICTIONARIES

There are many other law dictionaries, which are considerably shorter than the two major dictionaries described above. There are also useful dictionaries in several fields related to law (e.g., criminology, economics, finance, and political science) which often contain words and phrases not likely to be found in law dictionaries. Among the other law dictionaries, a few will be noted briefly here.

The *Modern Legal Glossary* [35] is a substantial modern dictionary, devoted exclusively to the definition of *legal terms, phrases and concepts,* rather than *words*. It also includes the names of professional associations, government agencies and international organizations; foreign phrases; famous trials; popular names of cases and statutes; biographical notes on important legal figures; and bibliographic entries. It is not a substitute for a word dictionary, but is quite well done and is a useful supplementary reference book to *Black's* or *Ballentine's*. As the authors indicate in their preface: ". . . you'll even enjoy browsing through the pages on a rainy day as a valuable compendium of useful information presented in an interesting fashion."

Of the numerous, smaller paperback dictionaries now available, the best in the opinion of many is S. H. Gifis, *Law Dictionary* (Barron's, 1975). Although quite limited in coverage, compared to those described above, its selection is careful and astute, and it contains a high percentage of the most important older legal words and phrases and the most frequently used modern terminology. Its definitions are clear and concise, and its case citations are often more recent

35. By K. R. Redden & E. L. Veron (Michie, 1980).

than those in the two major dictionaries. It also includes reference to treatises and periodical articles.

D. Oran, *Law Dictionary for Non-Lawyers* (West, 1983) is a good small dictionary for the general public. Others of similar size and approach include the following:

E. J. Bander, *Dictionary of Selected Legal Terms and Maxims*, 2d ed. (Oceana, 1979).

G. C. Coughlin, *Dictionary of Law* (Harper & Row, 1982).

P. J. Dorman, *Running Press Dictionary of Law* (Running Press, 1976).

W. Gilmer, *The Law Dictionary* (Scribner, 1981).

C. F. and P. Hemphill, *The Dictionary of Practical Law* (Prentice-Hall, 1979).

Law Dictionary for Laymen (Citizens Law, 1980).

R. E. Rothenberg, *The Plain Language Law Dictionary* (Viking, 1981).

R. Z. Volkell, *Quick Legal Terminology* (Wiley, 1979).

Although it is not a dictionary, another related research aid deserves attention here. There has long been a need for a legal thesaurus to provide variants and alternatives for words commonly used in legal writing and argument. In 1980, the first modern *legal* equivalent of Roget's popular *Thesaurus* was published: W. C. Burton, *Legal Thesaurus* (Macmillan, 1980). It is in two parts, like Roget's. The first part lists the main words alphabetically, with the form indicated (noun, verb, adjective or adverb), followed by their synonyms and alternatives, and a helpful listing of associated concepts, and foreign phrases. The second part is an index which provides references from the secondary words to the main words in the first part.

3. JUDICIAL DICTIONARIES

Judicial dictionaries base their definitions of words and phrases on judicial decisions. To some extent, *Black's Law Dictionary, Ballentine's*, and other good law dictionaries are judicial dictionaries. *Bouvier's Law Dictionary* in its later editions carried that approach to much greater lengths than modern dictionaries. Its treatment of *res ipsa loquitur*, for example, contained over three columns in small type, largely devoted to case abstracts.

Words and Phrases, the West Publishing Company's encyclopedic collection of abstracts of cases which have interpreted or defined words and phrases is a form of judicial dictionary, and probably the most comprehensive example of that genre. Some, however, would consider it more like a case digest than a dictionary, and, with that view, it has been treated above in Chapter 5 on Case Finding, rather than here.

4. LEGAL MAXIMS

Legal maxims in English, Latin, and a few in Norman French, are still significant in legal writing and research. With the decline in the general knowledge of Latin, many maxims are now impenetrable to most researchers, without assistance. Both *Black's* and *Ballentine's* law dictionaries (and most of the older substantial law dictionaries, like *Bouvier's*), give good coverage to maxims, with translations, definitions, and pronunciations. The maxims are listed alphabetically, by their *first* word, in the main listing of words in each dictionary, usually with no reference from any other word in the maxim. This is often confusing when the first word is insignificant and not within the researcher's recollection.

There are a few other sources of maxims. Perhaps, the most comprehensive and detailed is H. Broom, *A Selection of Legal Maxims, Classified and Illustrated,*[36] based on English law. *Latin for Lawyers*[37] also contains a list of Latin maxims with their definitions or translations.

The two major legal encyclopedias, *Corpus Juris Secundum* and *American Jurisprudence 2d,* include treatment of maxims, by different approaches. *C.J.S.* lists them in its regular alphabetical sequence of topics and translates or defines them there, either in text or footnotes. *Am.Jur.2d* lists them in its *General Index* and refers to specific articles of that encyclopedia in which they are discussed. For convenience in locating maxims, the *C.J.S.* approach seems preferable, although in some instances, the explanation of a maxim is fuller in *Am.Jur.2d.*

5. LEGAL ABBREVIATIONS

Because of the extensive abbreviation of legal publications in citations, there is often need for tables of abbreviations to identify the source cited. As noted above, both of the two major law dictionaries, *Ballentine's* and *Black's,* contain tables of abbreviations. *A Uniform System of Citation* (the "Bluebook") also contains several lists of abbreviations, but none as comprehensive as those in the dictionaries, or those listed below.

A new citation guide giving abbreviated forms for 2100 legal citations has recently been published under the title: *Current American Legal Citations with 2100 Examples,* by D. M. Bieber (William S. Hein, 1983).

The following recent, separate volumes, each devoted exclusively to abbreviations, are now the most current and comprehensive sources for interpreting abbreviations:

D. M. Bieber, *Dictionary of Legal Abbreviations Used in American Law Books* (William S. Hein, 1960; paperback reprint, 1979);

36. 10th ed. by R. H. Kersley (London, Sweet & Maxwell, 1939).

37. 3d ed. (London, Sweet & Maxwell, 1960).

M. D. Powers, *The Legal Citation Directory* (Franas Press 1971); and

D. Raistrick, *Index to Legal Citations and Abbreviations* (Abingdon, England, Professional Books, 1981).

Many law books include their own tables of abbreviations, for works cited therein. Before using extrinsic aids such as those described above, it may save time and needless confusion to check the front of the volume in which a citation is found, for the full designation of the abbreviated reference. Many abbreviations have multiple sources,[38] and the interpretive table in the work using an abbreviation is more likely to give the source actually referred to in that citation. This is particularly important in Shepard's various citators, which occasionally use somewhat unique abbreviations and often use the same abbreviation for different reporters in different citator units.

D. C.L.E. MATERIALS

The growing movement for continuing legal education of the bar produces a substantial literature of instructional materials. Some states now require participation in C.L.E. courses as a condition of membership in the bar, and others are considering such action. Many of the publications generated by these sources are similar to the various treatises described above in Section A.1, particularly the practice guides of subsection (d) thereof. The two major sponsors of such programs on a *national* basis, and consequently, the leading national publishers of C.L.E. materials are the Practising Law Institute and the Joint Committee on Continuing Legal Education of the American Law Institute and the American Bar Association.

Most states now have their own programs and publications as well, often under the sponsorship of the state bar association. These, of course, tend to focus on the law of the particular state, but many of the publications of some state groups (e.g. those of California, Illinois, and Michigan) have achieved national distribution and interest.

There are two periodicals which cover this field regularly: the *CLE Register* and *The Practical Lawyer,* both published monthly by the A.L.I.—A.B.A. Committee on Continuing Professional Education. The *CLE Register* lists courses of this kind offered throughout the country.

C.L.E. courses usually consist of a series of lectures and discussions, with practitioners, judges, and scholars presenting recent developments in specialized areas of the law or instruction on particular legal skills. Written materials are provided to the participants, and, in most cases, these materials are also available for sale separately.

C.L.E. publications range widely in quality. At their best, they will present cogent summaries on specific topics, written by experts in the field, and usually keyed to the law of the specific jurisdiction.

38. "C.L.R.", for example, has eleven different references in both *Bieber* and *Raistrick,* cited above.

At their worst, they are bare outlines, or collections of materials already published elsewhere.

Two leading series of C.L.E. materials are described below, followed by a general note on state sources, and a brief description of special formats used for some C.L.E. materials.

1. PRACTISING LAW INSTITUTE (P.L.I.) AND CALIFORNIA CONTINUING EDUCATION OF THE BAR (C.E.B.)

The Practising Law Institute, based in New York City, has been conducting C.L.E. programs around the country for decades. P.L.I. seminars attract outstanding speakers and generally focus on current legal issues. P.L.I. distributes materials from its programs in several subject series, including: Commercial Law and Practice; Corporate Law and Practice; Criminal Law and Urban Problems; Tax Law and Estate Planning; Patents, Copyright, Trademarks and Literary Property; Litigation and Administrative Practice; Tax Law and Practice; and Real Estate Law and Practice. In 1981, P.L.I. published the one-volume *Index to Course Handbooks*, which aids in the location of specific titles, or titles on particular subjects.

California Continuing Education of the Bar was established by the State Bar of California and is operated in conjunction with the University of California Extension. Practice books, which are often substantial treatises, are written for its programs. These monographs are based on the law of California, but because of their high quality and the influence of California law in other jurisdictions, they are popular throughout the country and are found in the law libraries of many other states.

2. OTHER STATE PROGRAMS

Many of the C.L.E. programs in other states have developed their own publication series. Often in looseleaf format, they are sometimes the best guides to current practice for their state. One can locate C.L.E. publications for any particular jurisdiction in the card catalogs of local law libraries, in *Law Books in Print*, and the other finding tools for legal treatises described in section A.2. Legal newspapers, such as the *National Law Journal*, and the *CLE Register*, as noted above, regularly list the courses themselves.

3. FORMATS

A number of C.L.E. organizations and some commercial publishers, now issue audio tapes of C.L.E. programs or outstanding lecture series. Video tapes of such programs are now also being issued for later use. The video materials have the advantage of being able to demonstrate arguments and other skills visually. Some law school libraries collect these materials for student use, but their expense has tended to limit availability.

E. DIRECTORIES

Directories of lawyers are published for individual states, or for particular areas of specialization. Several comprehensive, national directories, which are revised and issued in new editions annually, are also available. These directories are important reference tools for a variety of purposes, from job-hunting to the referral of legal matters to another jurisdiction or to a specialist.

Since 1937, the American Bar Association has maintained standards for law lists, and an approval procedure for certification of such lists and directories. A listing of the approved directories appears regularly in the *Annual Reports* of the A.B.A. and from time to time in the *American Bar Association Journal.*

There are a number of annual bar directories which are national in coverage. Of these, the *Martindale-Hubbell Law Directory* is the largest, best known and most widely used. It is described below in some detail. The other leading directories of this kind include *The Lawyers' List* (Danbury, Ct., *annual*); *The Bar Register* (Summit, N. J., *annual*); *The Lawyers Directory* (Charlottesville, Va., *annual*); and *The American Bar* (Reginald Bishop Forster & Associates, *annual*). The publishers of *The American Bar* also issue annually *The Canadian Bar* and *The International Bar.* Other directories with international scope are *The International List, International Lawyers,* and *Kime's International Law Directory.*

For current biographical information on leading American lawyers, judges, and legal scholars, the best source is probably *Who's Who in American Law.*[39] In 1977, the Ford Foundation sponsored the publication of the *Directory of Women Attorneys in the United States,* 5 vols., which unfortunately has not been updated. Another directory of legal interest is the *Directory of Law Teachers,* issued annually by the Association of American Law Schools. It includes biographies of faculty members at all of the accredited law schools in this country, preceded by a list of those schools, with addresses, phone numbers, and rosters of their respective faculties. *The Directory of Law Libraries* is published biennially by the American Association of Law Libraries.

1. MARTINDALE-HUBBELL LAW DIRECTORY

This multi-volume directory is by far the most extensive and widely-used source of information on American attorneys, with more selective coverage of Canadian and other foreign lawyers. The set is divided into two parts: the first provides information on individual attorneys and law firms; while the second (in the last volume) contains a potpourri of helpful information on a variety of legal topics. Published annually, the 1983 edition is in seven volumes.

39. 2d ed. (Marquis Publications, 1979). 3d ed. in preparation.

The first section is an alphabetic arrangement of the fifty states. For each state there are two sources of information. In the front of each volume there is the *Bar Roster*, an alphabetical list, by city, of practicing attorneys in the State. These entries include the date of birth, date of admission to the Bar, and the college and law school attended by each attorney. These latter items are provided by a code number—one must consult a table at the front of the volume to convert the number. If the attorney is a member of a firm, that will be indicated, and if the firm is listed in the second half of the volume, that will be noted as well.

The second part of the set, called the *Biographical Section*, consists of display advertisements which law firms purchase. As a result it is far more limited than the list at the front, but arranged also by city, and then alphabetically by firm name. The display advertisements list areas of specialty, provide references and include biographical information concerning members of the firm. Since the information provided is drawn from questionnaires prepared by the attorneys, it is not always completely objective.

The last volume of Martindale-Hubbell is a general legal reference book, containing information on the American Bar Association, on Uniform Laws, and the text of the Code of Professional Responsibility. It also incorporates abstracts of the law of all fifty states and many foreign countries on selected topics. These abstracts cannot be relied upon as official or definitive, but most include citations to primary sources, and are handy guides for superficial inquiries. The abstracts are prepared by reputable attorneys in the individual states and countries, and are usually reliable, although obviously too limited for serious research. Illustration H shows a typical page from this section of law digests.

Martindale-Hubbell also contains separate lists of government attorneys, patent and trademark attorneys, Canadian lawyers, and other foreign lawyers.

2. SPECIALIZED DIRECTORIES

With the increasing specialization of law practice, directories of lawyers practising in particular fields of law have become important for the referral of legal matters. Such directories are published both by specialized bar associations or, in some cases, by commercial organizations. They vary in scope and detail, but are almost always based on information supplied by the listed individuals and firms. Some sections of the American Bar Association also publish rosters of their members, and these are often used as specialized directories. The following are a few examples representing several different types of specialized directories:

Markham's Negligence Counsel, Annual Directory of Attorneys and Firms Active in Negligence Law (Stamford, CT., Markham Publishing Corp., 1982).

to interplead and litigate their claims. (C.C.P. 386). Action of interpleader may be maintained although claims have not common origin but are adverse to and independent of one another. (C.C.P. 386). Separate provisions relating to particular claims found in Com'l. C. 7603 (consigned goods); C.C.P. 1197.1(d) (public improvements); Rev. & Tax C. 4988 (conflicting property assessments); and 26133 (conflicting tax liens).

Joinder of Causes of Action.—Plaintiff who alleges cause of action against one or more defendants may unite with such cause any other causes which he has alone or with any co-plaintiffs against any such defendants. (C.C.P. 427.10).

Person filing cross-complaint may unite with cause of action asserted in cross-complaint any other causes he has against any of cross-defendants (other than plaintiff in eminent domain proceeding) whether or not such cross-defendant already is a party to action. (C.C.P. 428.30). Must file cross-complaint for indemnity to pursue right under case law adoption of concepts of comparative indemnity. (20 C.3d 578; 578 P.2d 899).

Consolidation or Severance.—Court may consolidate actions involving common question of law or fact and, to further convenience, expedition and economy or avoid prejudice, may order a separate trial of any cause of action or issue, preserving right of jury trial. (C.C.P. 1048).

Abatement of pending action will not be caused by death of party, disability, or transfer of interest, if cause of action survive. (C.C.P. 385).

Survival.—No cause of action is lost by reason of death of any person, but may be maintained by or against his executor or administrator, except exemplary damages may not be awarded when it is person against whom cause of action is asserted to exist who dies. When person having cause of action dies before judgment, damages recoverable by his personal representatives are limited to damages sustained by decedent before death, including exemplary damages, but excluding damages for pain, suffering or disfigurement. (Prob. C. 573).

Small Claims.—See topic Courts.

Prohibited Actions.—No cause of actions arises for criminal conversation, seduction of a person over the age of consent, alienation of affections or breach of promise to marry. (C.C. 43.5).

Fraudulent promise to marry or to cohabit after marriage does not give rise to cause of action for damages. (C.C. 43.4).

Certificate of Meritorious Malpractice Action.—In most malpractice actions against physicians, dentists, architects, professional engineers or land surveyors, condition precedent to filing of action is filing of certificate under oath by plaintiff's attorney that he has reviewed case, has consulted with knowledgeable member of profession involved and has concluded that there is reasonable and meritorious cause for filing of action. (C.C.P. 411.30 and 411.35). Failure to file is ground for demurrer. (C.C.P. 430.10).

Limitation of.—See topic Limitation of Actions.

Administration.—See topic Executors and Administrators.

Direct Actions Against Insurer.—See topic Motor Vehicles, subhead Direct Actions.

ADMINISTRATION:

See topic Executors and Administrators.

ADOPTION:

Any adult may adopt any minor child if former is at least ten years older, and if in best interest of both, court may approve adoption by stepparent or certain classes of relatives without regard to relative ages. (C.C. 221-2). Any adult may adopt any younger adult person, except adopter's spouse. (C.C. 221, 227p).

Consents Required.—Of child's parents, including presumed father, if living; in certain cases, consent of single parent having sole custody, after other spouse has been given notice in manner provided for service of summons in civil action. Parent's consent is unnecessary where parent is judicially deprived of child's custody by court, or has deserted child without provision for its identification, or has signed and acknowledged statement relinquishing child for adoption. (C.C. 224, 7017). Consent to adoption, once given, can only be withdrawn by natural parent if court approves. (C. C. 226a). Consent of child necessary if it is over 12 (C. C. 225), as is consent of spouse of adult or married minor adoptee (C. C. 227p). Where not lawfully separated from spouse, married person cannot (a) adopt another adult without consent of adopter's spouse or (b) be adopted without consent of adoptee's spouse. (C. C. 227p). Regarding other cases and participation by Dept. of Health or licensed agancy, see C. C. 226-27.

Illegitimates.—Uniform Parentage Act adopted, providing procedures to establish parent-child relationship without regard to distinctions based on legitimacy. (C. C. 7000 et seq.). Such relationship can exist between child and natural or adoptive parents. (C. C. 7001, 7003).

Venue.—Petition to be filed in superior court of county in which petitioner resides. (C. C. 226).

Proceedings.—Delineated by C. C. 226-7 for agency, stepparent and direct adoptions and by C. C. 227p for adult and married minor adoptions.

Name.—Adoptee may take family name of adopter. (C. C. 228).

Effect of Adoption.—Adopter and adoptee sustain legal relation of parent and child with all its rights and duties. (C. C. 228). Natural parents of adoptee are relieved of all parental duties and responsibilities and have no rights. (C. C. 229). Adoptee deemed descendant of adopter as though natural child, for all purposes of succession. Adopted child does not succeed to estate of natural parent or relative, and neither natural parent nor relative inherits from child adopted by another. (Prob. C. 257).

Setting Aside Adoption.—Within five years from decree of adoption, adoption parents may petition to set aside adoption of minor child because of mental deficiency or mental illness of which adopting parents had no notice. (C. C. 227b).

ADVANCEMENTS:

See topic Descent and Distribution.

ADVERSE POSSESSION:

Character of Possession.—When occupant claims under judgment or written instrument possession deemed adverse and possession of part of a single plot or piece deemed possession of the whole except where tract divided into lots. (C. C. P. 322-23). Where there is no judgment or written instrument the land must have been protected by a substantial inclosure or usually cultivated or improved. (C. C. P. 325). Occupant claiming adverse possession must pay all taxes for five years. (C. C. P. 325).

Duration of Possession.—Land must be continuously occupied and claimed for period of five years. (C. C. P. 325).

Easements.—Necessary elements same as for title except need to pay taxes. (1 C.3d 679, 463 P.2d 711).

Disabilities.—If person against whom adverse title is asserted is either under age of majority, insane or imprisoned at time he acquires title, time during which such disability continues, not to exceed 20 years, may not be included in five-year period required for acquiring title by adverse possession. (C. C. P. 328). No adverse possession possible of state or public entity land or land dedicated to public use. (C. C. 1007).

Easements may be acquired by prescriptive user for five years. (C. C. 1007; 1 Cal. 3d 679, 463 P.2d 711).

AFFIDAVITS:

Within the state, affidavits may be taken before any officer authorized to administer oaths, who are judges, justices, clerks of court, and notaries public. (C. C. P. 2012, 2093). Fee of notary public for administering oath or affirmation to one person and executing jurat is $2. (Govt. C. 8211). Fee of county clerk for taking affidavit, except criminal case or adoption proceedings where no fee is charged, is $1. (Govt. C. 26853 and 26857).

Without the state but within the United States, affidavits may be taken before commissioner appointed by Governor of this state, notaries public, or any judge or clerk of court of record having a seal. (C. C. P. 2013).

Without the United States, affidavits may be taken before ambassador, minister, consul, vice-consul, or consular agent of U. S., or judge of court of record having a seal. (C. C. P. 2014).

Affidavits of Persons in U. S. Armed Forces.—See topics Acknowledgments; Notaries Public.

General Requirement as to Administration.—Although no restriction upon taking affidavit by notary public who also is affiant's attorney, such practice not recommended. (56 Cal. 588).

General Requirement of Jurat.—Absence of seal is not fatal to affidavit's validity. (160 Cal. 695, 117 P. 905). Notary public seal must show expiration date of commission. (Govt. C. 8207).

Authentication.—Authentication required, in case of affidavits taken before judge of court outside state, by certificate of clerk of court under seal thereof, verifying genuineness of signature of judge, existence of court and fact that such judge was at the time a member thereof. (C. C. P. 2015).

Authentication of signatures, when instruments are to be used without the state, is made by county clerk whose fee is $1. (Govt. C. 26852).

Use.—Affidavit may be used to verify pleading or paper in special proceeding; to prove service of summons, notice, or other paper in action or special proceeding; to obtain provisional remedy, examination of witness, or stay of proceedings; in uncontested proceedings to establish record of birth; or upon motion, and in any other case expressly permitted by statute. (C. C. P. 2009).

Publication of document or notice in newspaper may be proved by affidavit of printer, his foreman or principal clerk. (C. C. P. 2010).

Form

No particular form required, the following is usual: State of . . . ., County of . . . .—ss.: . . . ., being first duly sworn, deposes and says: (Here state fully and clearly, but in ordinary language, matters necessary to be shown).

. . . .

Subscribed and sworn to before me this . . . . day of . . . ..
(Signature and full official designation of officer)

Alternative to Affidavit.—Whenever, under any law, rule, regulation, order or requirement of this State or any other State, any matter is required or permitted to be supported, evidenced, established, or proved by affidavit, such matter may with like force and effect be supported, evidenced, established or proved by unsworn statement in writing of person, stating date and place of execution, and subscribed by him and certified or declared to be true "under penalty of perjury." Certification or declaration may be as follows: "I certify (or declare) under penalty of perjury that the foregoing is true and correct." (C. C. P. 2015.5, operative Jan. 1, 1977).

See Topical Index in front part of this volume.

Illustration H

"Law Digest" section of *Martindale-Hubbell Law Directory.*

National Directory of Criminal Lawyers, edited by Barry Tarlow (University Publishers, 1979).

Association of Trial Lawyers of America, 1981–1982 Directory.

1981 Directory of Legal Aid and Defender Offices (National Legal Aid and Defender Association, 1980). Includes listings of attorneys in each office, and a separate section arranged by subject specialty.

Directory of Corporate Counsel, 1980–1981 (Law & Business, 1980).

Directory of Patent Attorneys and Agents (Pergamon, 1980).

Probate Counsel (Probate Counsel, Inc., *annual*).

3. JURISDICTIONAL DIRECTORIES

A variety of state and regional directories of lawyers provide information on practitioners in specific geographical areas. Over two dozen are published by the Legal Directories Publishing Company, Inc. of Los Angeles. These include directories for individual states (e.g., *Illinois Legal Directory*) and for regions (e.g., the *New England Legal Directory*). Because of their pale blue covers, they are often called the "Bluebook" directories. Each of the directories in this series contains listings of federal and state officials in that jurisdiction; names and addresses of federal, state and local courts, judges, and court officers; a listing of lawyers and law firms, by county and city; and advertisements for specialized support services offered to the legal profession. The "Bluebooks" include the names of some practitioners who are not listed in *Martindale-Hubbell.*

There are also bar directories issued by other commercial publishers and by bar associations for many states.

4. JUDICIAL DIRECTORIES

Although judges are listed in most of the national and jurisdictional directories described above, there are a number of directories and biographical works, focusing specifically on the judiciary. These include the following:

The American Bench, 2d ed. (Reginald Bishop Forster & Associates, 1979).

Biographical Dictionary of the Federal Judiciary (Gale Research, 1974).

Federal Court Directory (Washington, D. C., Want Publishing, *annual*).

Justices and Judges of the United States Courts (Administrative Office of the United States Courts, *restricted to official use*).

National Roster of Women Judges (American Judicature Society, 1980).

Register of the U. S. Department of Justice and the Federal Courts (U. S. Govt. Printing Office, *irregular*; latest edition, 52d, 1980).

United States Court Directory (Legal Reporters Associates, *annual*).

F. FORMBOOKS

Because of the repetitive nature of many legal transactions, the use of model forms has always been common among lawyers in all times and places. Single printed forms for a variety of transactions have been prepared and sold by legal stationers in this country since the 18th century. Individual practitioners and law firms retain, revise and re-use forms prepared in the course of their practice. It would be an enormous waste of time and effort (and probably a dangerous practice) to draft every form anew, without regard to the standard forms available, which incorporate the experience of others, legal precedents and statutory requirements. On the other hand, simple copying of standard forms, without the modifications necessary for the specific facts and circumstances of each transaction, would be a gross violation of professional responsibility.

Modern law publishing has developed standard forms into a major segment of legal literature. Legal forms are still published and sold singly and in pads, but the publication of formbooks in separate volumes, in sets, and in massive encyclopedias now offers a sophisticated and often bewildering array of selections to the drafter. Formbooks are annotated; the tax consequences of particular forms are noted and explained; they are issued for particular subjects and specific jurisdictions, and keyed to applicable statutes. As with other legal publications, formbooks must be supplemented frequently to reflect changes in the legal requirements on which they are based. The latest technological development in legal drafting are computer-produced forms, which can be custom-designed for specific transactions.

Each of these developments is described briefly in the following sections.

1. GENERAL ENCYCLOPEDIAS OF FORMS

Several large multi-volume sets of legal forms are published for the two principle purposes which forms generally serve. These two categories can be described, as follows: (a) forms of instruments, designed to effectuate specific legal transactions, such as contracts, leases, wills, deeds, etc.; and (b) practice forms, designed to conduct litigation or other business before courts and administrative agencies. The distinction can be clearly seen in the two largest sets of forms, those published by Lawyers Co-op/Bancroft-Whitney: *Am.Jur. Legal Forms* 2d, 24 vols. (1971–74, with pocket part supplementation) and *Am.Jur. Pleading and Practice Forms, Revised*, 28 vols. (1966–67, with annual pocket parts). Both sets have extensive general indexes, annotations to cases, statutes and other primary sources, notes on tax consequences, and cross references to other publications in the Lawyers Co-op *Total Client-Service Library.*

The West Publishing Company's *Modern Legal Forms,* 19 vols. (1950–72, with pocket part supplementation) includes both practice forms and instruments, but will be superseded by a new West series, *West Legal Forms,* 2d ed., the first volumes of which, *Business Organizations, with Tax Analysis,* by Paul Lieberman were published in 1981.

Other sets of comparable scope and coverage are Rabkin & Johnson's *Current Legal Forms with Tax Analysis,* 22 vols. (Matthew Bender, 1968, with looseleaf supplementation) and *Nichols Cyclopedia of Legal Forms Annotated,* 18 vols. (Callaghan, 1973, with looseleaf supplementation).

There are several multi-volume collections of forms specifically designed for *federal* practice. These include West's *Federal Forms,* 10 vols. (1964–82); *Federal Procedural Forms, Lawyer's Edition,* 18 vols. (Lawyers Co-op, 1975–date); and *Moore's Manual/Federal Practice Forms,* 4 vols. (Matthew Bender, 1964, with looseleaf supplementation).

2. SPECIALIZED SUBJECT FORMBOOKS

Many formbooks are issued for specialized practice or for the drafting of instruments in specific subject fields. Among the most common of this type are those for real estate transactions, corporate practice, wills and estates, matrimonial practice, and, more recently, for practice under the Uniform Commercial Code. The *U.C.C.* has already stimulated publication of at least three multi-volume formbooks geared specifically to its articles and sections.

Forms in specialized fields of practice appear also, of course, in the large encyclopedic sets described in section 1 above, and in many practice-oriented treatises for their area, e.g., H. B. Newberg, *Class Actions,* 8 vols. (Shepard's, 1977) contains forms for a variety of class actions. Similarly, most treatises on bankruptcy law, include extensive sections of practice forms or separate volumes of forms, keyed to the text of the treatises. Some formbooks are designed for specific procedural steps, such as Bender's *Forms of Discovery,* 10 vols. (Matthew Bender, 1963, with annual looseleaf supplementation).

Formbooks can be located by subject and/or jurisdiction in the card catalogs of law libraries, in the standard bibliographic sources described above in section A.2, or upon the advice of a reference librarian.

3. STATE PRACTICE AND STATUTORY FORMS

As noted above in section A.1(d), legal forms are an essential part of most state practice guides. Such forms are often published in separate volumes and coordinated with the text of the practice guide, or directly to the sections of state's practice acts and court rules.

Similar to the multi-volume state practice formbooks are sets of statutory forms, usually published with, and keyed to, annotated state codes. These forms relate both to substantive and procedural matters, and are designed to meet the specific statutory requirements.

Both the West Publishing Company and Lawyers Co-op publish practice formbooks and statutory forms for many states.

4. COMPUTER-ASSISTED DRAFTING

From the inception of word-processing equipment, lawyers have used that technology to store and retrieve complete legal forms and individual provisions for particular instruments. Legal composition and drafting is greatly expedited by this method and its use has become widespread.

The American Bar Foundation since 1978 has been experimenting with computerized drafting of legal documents, beyond the simple storage and retrieval of forms and clauses in word processors.[40] In a series of pilot projects under the direction of James Sprowl, this research has developed programs which store statutes and regulations governing particular transactions, along with the clauses and provisions of related forms. By applying those data bases to the specific facts and requirements of particular situations, the computer can be used to design forms which reflect both the applicable law and the needs of the instant transaction. This project may produce a far more sophisticated drafting procedure than that offered by current word-processing technology.

G. RECORDS AND BRIEFS

At the appellate level of litigation, attorneys present their arguments in written briefs and, in most cases, orally. In addition, counsel for the *appellant* prepares, serves on the opposing attorney, and files with the court, a full record of the proceedings below, including the trial transcript and pre-trial documents. The briefs contain counsels' arguments on the points of law at issue, with citations to the primary sources and secondary authorities selected to support the arguments. Since oral arguments are not held in every case, and, when held, are usually less extensive than the brief, the latter affords the best opportunity to persuade the court. In some cases, amicus curiae briefs are also filed with the permission of the court, by persons or groups interested in the outcome of the case.

Some of the copies of the records and briefs filed with the court are distributed on a regular basis to selected law libraries. These documents are of substantial research value. The court's decision is based on the arguments presented, and its opinion is written in response to specific arguments made in the briefs. Appellate decisions

40. J. A. Sprowl, "Automating the legal reasoning process: a computer that uses regulations and statutes to draft legal documents," *American Bar Foundation Research Journal* (Winter 1979) 1–81.

can therefore be best understood in the light of the briefs, and the record of the case below. The briefs can be used to develop arguments or obtain research leads in similar cases. They can also be used to study the appellate process in general or specific aspects of appellate advocacy. The trial transcript and pre-trial proceedings, contained in the record, can similarly be used to study the earlier phases of litigation.

1. U. S. SUPREME COURT

Copies of the records and briefs of the Supreme Court of the United States are distributed to approximately twenty five law libraries throughout the country on a regular basis, but many of those sets are incomplete when they reach the libraries and they often arrive long after the end of the Court's term. Their availability has been greatly improved by the commercial publication of two competing microfiche editions of complete sets of the Supreme Court's records and briefs. Over a hundred libraries now receive them in that format, within a few weeks after the oral argument. In addition, a microfilm edition of the Supreme Court's records and briefs from 1832 to 1925, with hardcopy indexes, is available commercially.

Complete oral arguments before the U. S. Supreme Court since the 1969 term are available on microfiche from University Publications of America. That publisher also issued briefs and oral arguments on a very selective basis in the field of constitutional law and antitrust law *in book form* under the title, *Landmark Briefs and Arguments* . . .. Tape recordings of oral arguments have been available from the National Archives since 1955, with several limitations. They are available only three years after decision of the case, only for scholarly or instructional purposes, and only with permission upon application to the Marshal of the Supreme Court.

2. U. S. COURT OF APPEALS

The records and briefs of the various circuits of the U. S. Court of Appeals are also distributed to a few law libraries in each of their respective regions, and to the Law Library of Congress and the Center for Research Libraries in Chicago. Microfiche editions for the Second Circuit and the District of Columbia Circuit have expanded the distribution of their records and briefs considerably. It is hoped that other circuits of the Court of Appeals will make similar arrangements.

3. STATE COURTS

The records and briefs of the high court in most states, and of the intermediate appellate courts in a few states, are available at several libraries in each of the states. Inquiry can be made to each court to determine where its briefs are deposited. Microfilm or microfiche editions are also available for the records and briefs of the high courts of a very few states.

H. CONCLUSION

The use of the various secondary materials described above is a regular part of American legal research and practice today. Their authority and persuasiveness vary widely, and many are primarily useful as research aids and finding tools rather than for the originality or brilliance of their analysis. Some, however, do offer new insights and can improve the quality of one's general understanding of the law and of specific legal issues.

The study of the relative authority of particular secondary sources has attracted some scholarly attention in recent years,[41] and is still a fruitful area for investigation. As with many of the publications described in earlier Chapters, their full research potential is often not realized. The most creative aspects of a lawyer's work can be enhanced by the effective use of these secondary sources.

41. See, for example, the two articles by Professor Merryman cited in footnotes 23 and 27 above.

Chapter 16

LEGAL PERIODICALS

A. INTRODUCTION

Among the various secondary resources available to the researcher, legal periodicals hold a special place. Although general American periodicals in the 18th century gave considerable coverage to legal developments, it was not until 1808 that the first exclusively legal journal was issued in the United States—the *American Law Journal and Miscellaneous Repertory*, published in Philadelphia from 1808 to 1817. As the major reflection of legal thinking today, the best modern legal periodicals provide the researcher with sophisticated analysis of current legal issues, historical research, the results of empirical studies, inter-disciplinary treatment of legal problems, and a wealth of citations to other primary and secondary sources. The nature and quality of the periodical literature range, however, from the theoretical essays and serious scholarship found in academic law reviews to the practical "how to do it" articles in bar journals. Legal periodicals have become controversial in a number of respects—for their alleged baleful influence on the judiciary, for their elitist role in legal education, and for their proliferation, prolixity, and redundancy.

Some of this controversy is reflected in the Additional Readings suggested at the end of this chapter.

Because of the importance of legal periodicals in advocacy, research, and the life of the law generally, this separate chapter will be devoted to a discussion of legal periodicals and their indexing.

B. TYPES OF LEGAL PERIODICALS

By their nature, purpose and format, legal periodicals fall into several different categories. The differences are so marked that the several major types will be described in some detail.

1. ACADEMIC LAW REVIEWS

The most serious and highly reputed legal periodicals are those produced at the major American law schools.[1] The most thorough presentation of new legal developments and issues, and the most serious analysis of important decisions, and statutes, are to be found in the law school reviews. These journals are cited extensively by the courts,[2] by each other and by scholars,[3] and they provide a wealth of primary citations for legal researchers.

Among scholarly periodicals, law school reviews are unique in serving an important educational function, as well as providing the major forum for publication of scholarship and research. The field of law is unusual in having its most prestigious and advanced journals edited by students who have not yet even attained their first professional degree. They are so well accepted for pedagogical purposes that virtually every accredited law school in the United States publishes at least one review, despite the fact that most require substantial subsidy. The faculty and administration of every law school is concerned about the quality of its periodical, since the reputation of the school will be judged in part on the respect accorded to it.

The "law review experience" is considered a superb learning opportunity for student editors and contributors.[4] The student role in editing the reviews is not merely nominal. At most schools, they exercise complete control over the acceptance of articles, and rigorously maintain editorial standards, often ruffling professorial feathers by

1. The controversy over which is the oldest review still being published is of no great moment, but the contenders are the *Harvard Law Review*, founded in 1887, and continuously published under that name, and the *University of Pennsylvania Law Review* which dates its inception from that of its predecessor, the *American Law Register*, a periodical which began in 1852.

2. See D. B. Maggs, "Concerning the Extent to Which the Law Review Contributes to the Development of the Law," 3 *So.Calif.L.Rev.* 181 (1930).

3. See O. Maru, "Measuring the Impact of Legal Periodicals," 1976 *American Bar Foundation Research Journal* 227. Note that one can find articles cited in subsequent articles by using *Shepards's Law Review Citations* (discussed below in Section C–6).

4. A more jaundiced view of law review service is offered by Kenney "The Law Review Priesthood," 1 *Learning and the Law* 60 (1975). For critical view of the strains of working on a law review, see B. Cane, "Role of the Law Review in Legal Education," 31 *J. of Legal Education* 215 (1981).

insisting upon the restructuring or rewriting of submissions. The student response to the prestige and educational benefit engendered by this role has been to seek more opportunities for that experience. As a result, more and more schools have supported the creation of additional journals, usually focusing on specific subject areas.[5] This development has allowed a greater number of students to participate in that activity, but has also raised concerns about the proliferation of legal periodicals and the maintenance of their quality.

Another interesting characteristic of the law school law reviews is their uniformity of format. Typically, these journals consist of three sections. The first part contains "lead articles," normally written by scholars or practitioners, and usually consisting of an extensive exploration of a somewhat narrow legal issue. They are marked by extensive footnoting, sometimes with hundreds of citations,[6] the checking of which is part of the drudgery of candidacy for editorship. Those footnotes, however, give the law reviews great value as case finding aids for legal research. In addition, the text of the article can provide useful analysis which can be cited as persuasive authority, if it supports one's particular argument or thesis. Occasionally, new concepts or theories appear first in the periodical literature, are debated and developed there, and later adopted by the courts.[7]

The second component of most law reviews is the Note and Comment section, which normally contains student writing. Comments, generally preceding the Notes, are longer and more ambitious and are often similar to law review articles in style and purpose, although narrower in focus. They usually have the same extensive footnoting as articles, and thus can be used just as easily for primary source finding. As secondary authority, they lose some impact because they are the work of students and often appear without author attribution. Notes, following the Comments, tend to be shorter, and are usually written by candidates for the review or junior editors. They are frequently devoted to analysis of a single new case or statute.

A few law school journals are entirely intramural in nature, publishing only student work. These lack the prestige of those containing outside articles, but do provide a forum and an incentive for student writing. Obviously, they are less likely to be cited as persuasive authority.

The third section is usually devoted to the book reviews, but unfortunately in most journals this component has declined in length and importance. Because of the long delay in the appearance of reviews after the publication of the book, their impact is diminished, and sometimes the review is so late that the book has already gone

5. For example, the Harvard Law School currently publishes: *Harvard Law Review, Harvard Civil Rights—Civil Liberties Law Review, The Harvard Environmental Law Review, Harvard International Law Journal, Harvard Journal of Law & Public Policy, Harvard Journal on Legislation,* and *Harvard Women's Law Journal.*

6. A recent article in the *Columbia Law Review* contained more than 550 footnotes. See Linzer, "The Meaning of Certiorari Denials," 79 *Col.L.Rev.* 1227 (1979).

7. The classic example is Brandeis & Warren, "The Right to Privacy," 4 *Harvard L.Rev.* 193 (1890).

out of print. It is occasionally possible, however, to find stimulating exchanges through the medium of the book review section,[8] but the likelihood is reduced by the reluctance of most journals to publish correspondence responding to previous articles or reviews. The *University of Michigan Law Review* has in recent years introduced the practice of devoting one issue of each volume to reviews of current legal literature. This is a promising development in a field where book reviews have been plagued by the extremes of excessive and uncritical praise or self-promoting sophistry.

An increasingly common departure from the traditional review format are "symposium" issues. In these issues, the law review chooses a topic of special or current interest and solicits articles from scholars and practitioners who specialize in that field.[9] At least one prominent review, *Law and Contemporary Problems,* is exclusively devoted to symposia issues.

Some law school reviews publish annual surveys of legal developments in their states. Individual subjects are assigned to different authors, either to scholars or practitioners specializing in that field, or to students. The *Annual Survey of American Law,* for example, began as part of the *New York University Law Review,* but since 1963 has been issued as a separate annual publication. Although national in coverage, it has served as a model for similar state surveys.[10]

The development of multiple reviews at many law schools has increased the number of subject-specialized journals. Perhaps the most popular subject for these single-theme journals has been international law and related issues. At least seventeen law schools now publish journals in this field.

There are also some, usually subject-specialized, academic journals which are not student-edited, or on which students play only a secondary role. These include the *American Journal of Legal History* at Temple Law School, *Tax Law Review* at N.Y.U. Law School, and at least four at the University of Chicago Law School.[11]

Before leaving the topic of law school reviews, one must say a word concerning their critics. Some commentators find that the courts give academic views in law journals too great a weight in the formulation of legal policy. While this argument has been waning,

8. An outstanding example is Berger's "Soifer to the Rescue of History," 32 *So.Carol.L.Rev.* 427 (1981) which is a reply to a book review by Professor Soifer at 54 *N.Y.U.L.Rev.* 651 (1979). It includes comments like "So gross and reckless are his many misrepresentations that one might attribute them to malice but for his inability to weigh evidence, to comprehend what he reads." (p. 428).

9. Examples include a two-issue "Copyright Symposium" on the Copyright Act of 1976 in 22 *N. Y. Law School L.Rev.* Nos. 2 & 3 (1976–77); "Symposium on Legal Education" in *N.Y.U.L.Rev.* Nos. 2–3 (1978); and a symposium on legal writing in 44 *Albany L.Rev.* No. 2 (1980).

10. For a recent listing of such annual surveys of federal courts and state law, see C. A. Roehrenbeck, "A Checklist of Annual Surveys of State and Federal Laws," 73 *Law Lib.J.* 17 (1980).

11. *Crime and Justice, an Annual Review of Research; Journal of Law and Economics; Journal of Legal Studies;* and *Supreme Court Review.*

some have attacked the proliferation of law school journals on other grounds, contending that the increasing number of law reviews and the publish-or-perish system of promotion and tenure for law professors have produced an outpouring of "unnecessary" literature. Many of these critics also assail the often dry and ponderous style of the review prose. See, for example, this widely quoted comment:

> There are two things wrong with almost all legal writing. One is its style. The other is its content. That, I think, about covers the ground. And though it is in the law reviews that the most highly regarded legal literature . . . is regularly embalmed, it is in the law reviews that a pennyworth of content is most frequently concealed beneath a pound of so-called style.[12]

2. BAR ASSOCIATION PERIODICALS

Most national and state bar associations and many local and specialized bar groups publish journals. Although they primarily focus on the interests of their membership, some have achieved a broader audience and even a national reputation. Although in the past, bar journals were considered well outside the scholarly literature, many of those devoted to particular types of practice have attained a respect equal to that of the specialized academic journals. The locally-oriented bar journals have generally remained of interest only to practitioners in those areas, or to researchers interested in a specific issue or problem of that jurisdiction.

The publications of the American Bar Association are the most numerous and important of the bar journals. The *American Bar Association Journal* publishes some articles on substantive legal topics, usually shorter and of a more popular nature than the law reviews, and contains much news about the Association, the legal profession generally, and national legal developments. Even more diverse are the various publications of American Bar Association sections. Most of the sections issue their own publications, either in newsletter format,[13] law review style,[14] or in the form of glossy magazines.[15] State, county and city bar journals occasionally contain useful coverage of legal developments in their area, but, with a few exceptions, are of only local interest. Most notable is the *Record of the Association of the Bar of the City of New York,* which contains not only useful re-

12. F. Rodell, "Goodbye to Law Reviews," 23 *U. of Va.L.Rev.* 38 (1936).

13. For example, *Syllabus,* published by the A.B.A. Section of Legal Education and Admission to the Bar.

14. These are perhaps the most important and respected of the A.B.A. periodicals, and include *Administrative Law Review* (Section of Administrative Law), *American Criminal Law Review* (Section of Criminal Justice), *Antitrust Law Journal* (Section of Antitrust Law), *Business Lawyer* (Section of Corporation, Banking and Business Law), *Family Law Quarterly* (Section of Family Law), *Human Rights* (Section of Individual Rights & Responsibilities), *International Lawyer* (Section of International & Comparative Law), *Jurimetics* (Section on Science and Technology), *Natural Resources Lawyer* (Section of Natural Resources Law), *Public Contract Law Journal* (Section of Public Contract Law), *Real Property, Probate & Trust Journal* (Section of Real Property, Probate & Trust Law), *The Tax Lawyer* (Section of Taxation), and *The Urban Lawyer* (Section of Local Government Law).

15. For example, *Litigation,* published by the Section of Litigation.

search articles and important bar addresses, but also a well-prepared, monthly bibliography of source material on topics of current interest.

Some of the periodicals of specialized bar associations, like the journals of the Sections of the American Bar Association, often provide significant sources of information on legal developments in their subject field.[16] While typically less scholarly in tone than the specialized law reviews, they can offer help to a researcher whose problem falls into an area of their particular expertise.

3. COMMERCIALLY PUBLISHED JOURNALS

In the nineteenth century most major legal periodicals were commercially published.[17] By the turn of the century, however, academic law journals had become dominant, and commercial publications became limited to a relatively few topical journals and fell into lower esteem. Several commercial periodicals, particularly those published by Commerce Clearing House,[18] have survived as subject specialized journals, although without great distinction.

A more recent development in commercially published periodicals are the numerous topical newsletters, usually of short length and high price. As the number of specialized lawyers has increased, and specialities multiplied, commercial publishers have risen to the market. Many of them now publish journals for these narrow, highly technical practice areas. Often these publications appear in the form of newsletters or current awareness services. Some are published by public interest groups, without commercial motives. Issued weekly or monthly to subscribers, they focus on the most recent developments in a specific subject area, often only briefly abstracting judicial, administrative or legislative developments. These publications serve primarily as a source of current information, and because of their brevity, transitory interest, and lack of serious analysis, tend to have little or no permanent research value. They can be useful, however, for the busy practitioner and sometimes are the most important source on new, relatively limited topics (*e.g.*, Swine flu vaccine, asbestos poisoning, solar law, etc.).

4. LEGAL NEWSPAPERS

Although local legal newspapers have been in existence for a long time,[19] the most interesting recent development in the field of commercial periodicals has been the development of national legal newspapers. Recognizing the size and affluence of the market represented by the legal profession in this country, commercial publishers have issued three national legal news journals, two of which are weekly

16. For example, the *I.C.C. Practitioners' Journal* and the *Journal of the Patent Office Society.*

17. For a brief survey of legal periodical publishing, see Chapter 1 of Mersky, et al. *Author's Guide to Journals in Law, Criminal Justice and Criminology* (Haworth Press, 1979).

18. For example, *Food, Drug Cosmetic Law Journal, Insurance Law Journal* and *Labor Law Journal.*

19. The *Legal Intelligencer,* published in Philadelphia for the bench and bar of that City since 1843, is the oldest continuously published legal newspaper in the country.

newspapers: the *National Law Journal* and the *Legal Times.* Both have attracted considerable advertising and a substantial audience. The first of the three, the *National Law Journal,* originated by the publishers of the highly successful daily, the *New York Law Journal,* offers national coverage of both the legal profession and legal issues generally. It features articles on prominent attorneys, noteworthy trends in litigation, professional controversies, and developments in both substantive and procedural law. Regular, continuing features keep readers posted on certain subject specialites, current periodical literature, and professional gossip. Special supplements also cover various aspects of the economics and technology of law practice.

The Legal Times (formerly, *Legal Times of Washington*) focuses on developments in Washington, D.C. It reports on administrative agencies, their regulatory activities, and important rulings and regulations. It also covers legislative and judicial news, and is perhaps the most serious in tone of these three new periodicals.

The third national legal journal is the *American Lawyer.* This monthly publication tends to concentrate on personalities, and has been called the *People Magazine* of legal publishing. By concentrating on personalities and lighter issues, it has attracted a wide readership. One of its most popular features is its annual issue rating law firms that employ law students as summer clerks.

Local legal newspapers continue to serve the bench and bar of the larger metropolitan areas, focusing primarily on publication of dockets, calendars and local court announcements. Some also include court orders, dispositions of motions, and decisions of lower courts which may not be reported elsewhere. They are heavily supported by legal advertisements which are required by statutes or court rules to be published in local newspapers. The legal articles and essays published by a few of these newspapers have long been elusive, because they have not been covered by the *Index to Legal Periodicals.* They are now accessible in a new index, however, which will be described below.

The following bibliography of legal newspapers published throughout the United States lists them by state and city: A.R. Ashmore, "Checklist of Legal Newspapers in the United States", 74 *Law Library J.* 543 (1981).

C. PERIODICAL INDEXING

1. INDEX TO LEGAL PERIODICALS

The most widely used access tool to legal periodicals is the *Index to Legal Periodicals,* which began in 1908 and assumed its present frequency in 1926. This publication of the H. W. Wilson Company indexes approximately four hundred legal periodicals in a format similar to its publisher's other standard indexes, such as *Readers Guide to Periodical Literature* and *Social Science Index.* It is issued in monthly pamphlets (except for September) and then cumulates its issues in annual and three year volumes. It was preceded by the *Jones-Chipman Index to Legal Periodicals,* which covered American legal periodical literature from the early 19th century to 1937, in six volumes published between 1888 and 1939. Since the later volumes of the Jones-Chipman Index and the early volumes of the *I.L.P.* overlap, the former is used today primarily for its coverage up to 1908.

The *Index to Legal Periodicals* includes four different indexing categories. The first and most important is its subject-author index. A list of the subject headings used in this index, as well as a list of the periodicals covered, are included in each issue and volume of the index.

Full bibliographic information on each article appears only under its listing in the subject index. The author entry provides only a cross reference to the relevant subject heading and the first letter of the title of the article. Articles are listed alphabetically by title under each subject heading. Illustration A shows an author entry from the *Index to Legal Periodicals* and Illustration B shows the full bibliographic entry under the subject heading. Note also the Symposium entry in Illustration B.

After the Subject and Author Index, the *I.L.P.* provides a *table of cases commented upon.* This table lists judicial decisions that have been the subject of articles, comments or notes in legal periodicals. The listing is arranged alphabetically by the name of the case in which the decision was rendered. If one is using a decision as authority and needs clarification of its meaning or impact, this index may provide useful references to periodical writing on the decision. Illustration C contains a sample page from this part of the *I.L.P.*

The *Index's* third feature is a *table of statutes commented upon,* similar in structure and function to the case table, described above. This table lists statutes that have been discussed in indexed articles, comments and notes, and provides references to the relevant periodicals. A sample page from this table is shown in Illustration D.

As described in Chapter 9, many units of *Shepard's Citations* include references to periodical articles which discuss decisions or statutes, thereby providing another approach to this information. The references in Shepard's, however, cover a much smaller number of periodicals so these tables in the periodical indexes are a far more useful source for such citations.

The final section indexes book reviews. Book reviews that appear in the journals covered by the *Index* are listed by the name of the author of the book reviewed. Illustration E shows a sample page from the Book Review Section.

For decades, the *Index to Legal Periodicals* was the standard index used by legal researchers, and provided the only effective access tool to most of the legal periodicals. However, user complaints about the format, subject headings, and coverage of the *Index* accumulated over the years. There were objections to the lack of new subject

SUBJECT AND AUTHOR INDEX

Illustration A

Author entries in the *Index to Legal Periodicals,* showing cross references to the subject entries.

SUBJECT AND AUTHOR INDEX

BEST, Franklin L., Jr
Gifts (T)
Med juris (T)

BETTAUER, Raija H.
Antitrust law: sp industries, etc (J)
Banks and banking (J)

BETTWY, Samuel W.
Recognition (U)
US: for relat (U)
Vatican City (U)

BEVAN, John S.
Suretyship and guaranty (F)

BEVAN, V. T.
Search and seizure (T)
Taxation: prac and proc—Gt Brit (T)

BEVAN, Vaughan
Eavesdropping (I)

BEYTAGH, Francis X.
Biog (Young)

BHARDWAJ, Vijay K.
Alimony and maintenance (D)
Social welfare (D)

BIANCAMANO, John J.
Corporations (C)

BIANCHESI, John J.
Attorneys (I)
Insurance (I)

BIBLE, Jon
Schools and sch dist (B)
Teachers and teaching (B)

BIBLIOGRAPHY
See also
Annotations and citations
Legal research
Periodicals

Administrative conference of the United States: a selected bibliography 1968-1980. S. J. Boley. Ad L Rev 33:235-53 Spr '81
Annual bibliography. J Comp Corporate L & Securities Reg 2:339-49 D '79
Appendix A: Judge Wright's non-judicial writings. Hastings Const L Q 7:969-70 Summ '80
Bankruptcy reform act bibliography. C. F. Miller, jr. Com L J 85:373-7 O '80
Bibliografia sobre el terrorismo internacional. Rev D P 18:109-12 Jl/D '78
Bibliography. Bull Cr Soc 27:389-418 Je; 441-78 Ag; 28:70-110 O; 204-36 D '80; 316-50 F '81
Bibliography. Clearinghouse Rev 14:402-4 Jl; 509-12 Ag/S; 609-11 O; 804-6 N; 896-9 D '80; 217-21 Mr; 1320-3 Ap; 15:103-7 My '81
Bibliography. L. A. Schulte. Computer/Law J 2:787-803 Summ '80
Bibliography on arbitration and litigation in East Asian-United States transactions. M. G. Goldman, E. C. Routh. Int Law 15:149-60 Wint '81
Bibliography to legal periodicals dealing with historic preservation and aesthetic regulation. NC Central L J 11:384-93 Spr '80
Books and articles on jurisprudence and related areas published in Germany, Switzerland, Austria, France and Italy, 1979. Am J Juris 25:189-229 '80
Criminal law—white-collar crime: a topical bibliography. Temp L Q 53:1191-201 '80
Current literature. UCC LJ 13:282-7 Wint; 379-82 Spr '81
Current literature in law/science: policy and intellectual and industrial property. T. M. Steele, J. G. Norcross. IDEA 22:95-102 '81
Current literature on aerospace law. T. M. Steele, D. W. Martin. J Air L 45:1141-6 Summ; 46:229-35 Fall '80; 567-72 Wint '81
Enforceability of due-on-sale clauses—a bibliography. J. A. Gose. ALI-ABA Course Materials J 5:109-18 F '81
European commercial arbitration practice. M. Domke. NYU J Int L & Pol 13:397-401 Fall '80
Federal agencies: information can make the difference. E. M. Ricci. Trial 16:36-7+ N '80
Foreign law in English. Am J Comp L 29:176-213 Wint '81
Gerontology and the law: a selected bibliography. J. Mubarak, D. Sapienza, R. Shimane. L Lib J 73:255-335 Spr '80
Guide to real estate law resources for the practicing attorney. D. M. Tuke. Ill B J 69:104-8 O '80
Human rights bibliography. Introduction. I. I. Kavass; Human rights research in periodicals: a bibliographic note. H. A. Hood; Human rights and the Helsinki conference on security and cooperation in Europe: an annotated bibliography of United States government documents. J. P. Granier. Vand J Transnat L 13:513-73 Spr/Summ '80
Index and fourteenth selected bibliography on computers and the law (July 1979 through October 1980) Rutgers J Computers Tech & L 8:155-72 '80
Index to selected bibliography of articles relating to labor law. L. T. Gardiner. L Notes 15:41-4 Spr '79
James Willad Hurst: a bibliography. Wis L Rev 1980:1131-3 '80
Juror sums up: a bibliography. G. F. DuPre, C. F. Myers. Litigation 7:41-2 Fall '80
Latin America, Africa, and the third United Nations conference on the law of the sea: annotated bibliography. M. A. Morris, P. S. Ferreira. Ocean Devel & Int L 9:101-86 '81
Law and literature: a comment and bibliography of secondary works. D. R. Papke. L Lib J 73:421-37 Spr '80
Lawyer's 1981 midsummer night's reading. J. S. Marsh. Prac Law 27:71-9 Je '81
Legal bibliography on the proposed federal criminal code. J Crim L 72:631-6 Summ '81
Legal futurology: the field and its literature. D. A. Funk. L Lib J 73:625-33 Summ '80
Legal writings of Hiram H. Lesar. So Ill U L J 1980:26-8 Mr '80
Legalized gambling: a selectively annotated bibliography from 1970-1980. N. Triffin. Conn L Rev 12:920-47 Summ '80
Michigan practice materials: a selective, annotated bibliography. B. S. Johnson. L Lib J 73:672-82 Summ '80
Paperbacks for the bar. Record 35:598-623 D '80
Products liability bibliography: a comprehensive subject categorization of law journal articles from January 1975 to August 1980. D. Vetri. Tr Law Guide 25:1-63 Spr '81
Raw materials of international law. L. C. Green. Int & Comp L Q 29:187-205 Ap/Jl '80
Recent acquisitions. Record 36:148-58 Mr '81
Recent literature. Bus Law 36:545-67 Ja; 1415-37 Ap '81
Recent publications. J Space L 8:91-101 Spr; 214-19 Fall '80
Review of legal and social science journals. J System J 5:313-23 Spr '80
Reviewing the codes: a student primer. S. A. Cohen. McGill L J 26:129-33 '80
Samuel Mermin: a bibliography. Wis L Rev 1980:XIII-XVI '80
Select international law bibliography of the Arab-Israeli conflict. S. R. Silverburg. Suffolk Transnat L J 4:47-88 '80
Selected bibliography—Massachusetts constitution of 1780. Suffolk U L Rev 14:1007-10 Summ '80
Selected checklist on six-member juries. Record 35:276-80 Ap '80
Selected checklist on small claims court. Record 35:145-9 Mr '80
Selected legislative history of the federal income, estate and gift tax laws since 1913. I. Lang. L Lib J 73:382-420 Spr '80
Selected materials on antidumping. Record 35:518-23 N '80
Selected materials on attorney-corporate client privilege. Record 35:360-3 My/Je '80
Selected materials on child custody. Record 36:337-45 My/Je '81
Selected materials on "plain English". Record 36:249-52 Ap '81
Selected materials on the foreign corrupt practices act. Record 36:65-70 Ja/F '81
Selected readings in the area of foreign and international law. E. Weisbaum. Int Law 14:731-45 Fall '80
Selective bibliography. NC J Int L & Com Reg 5:165-7 Wint '80
Significant probate and trust literature. Real Prop Pro & Trust J 15:460-71 Summ '80
Significant real property literature. Real Prop Pro & Trust J 15:472-99 Summ '80
Sixty year annotated index of coal related articles in the West Virginia law review. W Va L Rev 82:1347-60 '80
Sources of medical information. M. E. Ehrhardt, W. B. Wheeler. Federation Ins Coun Q 30:347-74 Summ '80
Subject index for Canadian federal statutes: a proposal based on the new index to the U.S. code of federal regulations. J. Fraser. L Lib J 73:634-71 Summ '80
Theatrical motion pictures and the law: a comprehensive bibliography of law-related materials. F. G. Houdek. Comm/Ent 3:117-59 Fall '80
Uniform commercial code bibliography. A. M. Squillante. Com L J 85:321-4 Ag/S '80; 86:22-7 Ja '81
Update on Ohio judicial reporting. P. Richert. Ohio St L J 41:675-82 '80

Subject

Symposium issue

Illustration B

Subject entries in the *Index to Legal Periodicals*.

TABLE OF CASES COMMENTED UPON

AARON v. SEC, 100 S Ct 1945
ABA J 66:1436 N '80
Harv L Rev 94:270-9 N '80
New England L Rev 16:899-915 '80/'81
St Mary L J 12:754-69 '81
U Cin L Rev 49:937-49 '80
ABO Petroleum Corp. v. Amstutz (NM) 600 P 2d 278
New Mexico L Rev 10:471-9 Summ '80
ADAMS v. Texas, 100 S Ct 2521
ABA J 66:1280+ O '80
J Crim L 71:538-46 Wint '80
ADAMSON; ex parte W.A. Natl. Football League, In re (1979) 53 A L J R 273
Mel U L Rev 12:567-74 D '80
ADDINGTON v. Texas, 99 S Ct 1804
U Det J Urb L 57:651-70 Spr '80
ADOPTION of R.P.R. In re (Wis) 291 N W 2d 591
J Family L 19:350-4 Mr '81
ADVISORY Opinion on the Interpretation of the Agreement of 25 March 1951 between the WHO and Egypt [1980] I C J 73
Harv Int L J 22:429-36 Spr '81
AETNA Cas. & Surety Insur. Co. v. Greene, 606 F 2d 123
Kan L Rev 29:143-52 Fall '80
AFL-CIO v. Kahn, 618 F 2d 784
Brigham Young U L Rev 1980:431-49 '80
Calif L Rev 68:1044-69 S '80
Colum L Rev 80:1535-51 N '80
Iowa L Rev 66:425-37 Ja '81
Wash L Rev 55:717-32 Je '80
AFL-CIO v. Kahn, 472 F Supp 88
Albany L Rev 44:959-77 Jl '80
A.G. of B.C. v. The Canadian Trust Co [1980] 5 W W R 591
Can B Rev 59:161-5 Mr '81
AGEE v. Muskie, 629 F 2d 80
Harv Int L J 22:187-94 Wint '81
AGENT Orange Product Liab. Litigation, In re, No. 80-7079 (2d Cir. Nov. 24, 1980)
Am J L & Med 7:46-9 Spr '81
AGINS v. City of Tiburon, 100 S Ct 2138
ABA J 66:1289 O '80
Am J Tr Adv 4:836-43 Spr '81
Conn L Rev 13:167-201 Fall '80
Det Coll L Rev 1981:179-201 Spr '81
Environ L 11:755-67 Spr '81
Natural Resources J 21:169-75 Ja '81
Pepperdine L Rev 8:839-59 Mr '81
AGINS v. City of Tiburon (Cal) 598 P 2d 25
Calif L Rev 68:822-8 Jl '80
Loyola U L Rev (LA) 13:157-77 D '79
ALABAMA Power Co. v. Costle, No. 78-1006 (D.C. Cir. Dec. 14, 1979)
BC Environ Aff L Rev 9:13-61 '80/'81
Environ L 10:585-642 Spr '80
Stan L Rev 32:943-75 My '80
ALAMEDA v. Secretary of HEW, 622 F 2d 1044
Notre Dame Law 56:333-43 D '80
ALASKA Bulk Carriers, Inc. v. Kreps, 595 F 2d 814
Suffolk Transnat L J 4:225-36 '80
ALBERNAZ v. U.S. 101 S Ct 1137
ABA J 67:633 My '81
ALCOA Steamship Co. v. M/V Nordic Regent, 453 F Supp 10
J Maritime L 12:123-37 O '80
Nw J Int L & Bus 1:700-18 Aut '79
ALDANA v. Holub (Fla) 381 S 2d 231
Am J Tr Adv 4:816-20 Spr '81
ALESNA v. Legrue (Alaska) 614 P 2d 1387
UCLA-Alaska L Rev 9:229-34 Spr '80
ALLEN v. Gulf Oil Refining Ltd [1980] Q B 156
L Q Rev 97:203-6 Ap '81
ALLEN v. McCurry, 101 S Ct 411
ABA J 67:208-9 F '81
ALLEN Oil Co. v. C I R 614 F 2d 336
Va L Rev 67:751-65 My '81
ALLIED Int. Inc. v. International Longshoremen's Ass'n, AFL-CIO, 640 F 2d 1368
Harv Int L J 21:763-9 Fall '80
ALLIED Structural Steel v. Spannaus, 98 S Ct 2716
Colum J L & Soc Prob 16:119-28 '80
ALLSTATE Insur. Co. v. Elkins (Ill) 396 N E 2d 528
Chi-Kent L Rev 57:297-321 Wint '81
ALLSTATE Insur. Co. v. Hague, 101 S Ct 633
ABA J 67:490 Ap '81
ALLSTATE Insur. Co. v. Ivie (Utah) 606 P 2d 1197
Utah L Rev 1981:379-91 '81
ALMA Soc., Inc. v. Mellon, 601 F 2d 1225
Brooklyn L Rev 46:717-45 Summ '80
Nw U L Rev 75:316-44 Ap '80
ALVEZ v. American Export Lines (NY) 389 N E 2d 461
Brooklyn L Rev 46:321-44 Wint '80
AMADOR Valley Joint Union High School Dist. v. State Bd. of Equalization (Cal) 583 P 2d 1281
Calif L Rev 68:856-61 Jl '80
So Calif L Rev 53:173-222 N '79
AMBACH v. Norwick, 99 S Ct 1589
Colum Human Rights L Rev 11:227-44 Fall/Wint '79/'80
Duquesne L Rev 18:957-68 Summ '80
Hastings L J 32:163-99 S '80
Seton Hall L Rev 10:870-86 '80
So Ill U L J 1980:107-24 Mr '80
Stetson L Rev 10:171-89 Fall '80
Tex Int L J 15:203-10 Wint '80
AMCA Int. Corp. v. Krouse, 482 F Supp 929
Capital U L Rev 10:129-57 Fall '80
AMCHEM Products Co. v. Costle, Civ. No. 76-2913 (S.D.N.Y. filed July 9, 1978)
BC Environ Aff L Rev 8:593-639 '80
AMERICAN Airlines, Inc. v. National Mediation Bd. 588 F 2d 863
Brooklyn L Rev 46:1017-41 Summ '80
AMERICAN Bell Int. Inc. v. Islamic Republic of Iran, 474 F Supp 420
Colum J Transnat L 19:301-32 '81
AMERICAN Export Lines, Inc. v. Alvez, 100 S Ct 1673
ABA J 66:1002-3 Ag '80
Maritime Law 5:117-25 Spr '80
Suffolk Transnat L J 5:105-14 '80
AMERICAN Petroleum Institute v. OSHA, 581 F 2d 493
Environ L 10:664-75 Spr '80
U Richmond L Rev 14:623-37 Spr '80
AMERICAN Security Council Educ. Foundation v. FCC, 607 F 2d 438
Am U L Rev 29:181-204 Fall '79
West New England L Rev 2:775-92 Spr '80
AMERICAN Tel. & Tel. Co. v. Merry, 592 F 2d 118
Brooklyn L Rev 46:961-92 Summ '80
AMERICANS United for Separation of Church and State, Inc. v. HEW, 619 F 2d 252
Hastings L J 32:975-1012 Mr '81
AMMINISTRAZIONE delle Finanze dello Stato v. Simmenthal S.p.A., Preliminary Ruling [1978] E Comm Ct J Rep 629,23 Comm Mkt L R 263 (1978)
Tex Int L J 15:139-61 Wint '80
AMOCO Production Co. v. Alexander (Tex) 594 S W 2d 467
St Mary L J 12:600-10 '80
AMODIO v. Cunningham, No. 9955 (Conn. Aug. 12, 1980)
Am J L & Med 6:505-7 Wint '81
ANDREWS v. Andrews, 425 N Y S 2d 120
Am J Tr Adv 4:486-8 Fall '80
ANDRUS v. Glover Constr. Co. 100 S Ct 1905
ABA J 66:1278+ O '80
ANDRUS v. Shell Oil Co. 100 S Ct 1932
ABA J 66:1288 O '80
Environ L 11:721-54 Spr '81
ANDRUS v. Sierra Club, 99 S Ct 2335
BC Environ Aff L Rev 9:205-43 '80/'81
NY LS L Rev 26:385-404 '81
Va L Rev 66:843-77 My '80
ANDRUS v. Utah, 100 S Ct 1803
ABA J 66:901 Jl '80
Utah L Rev 1981:409-29 '81
ANSETT Transp. Industries (Operations) Pty Ltd v. Wardley [1980] 28 ALR 449
UNSW L J 3:426-33 O '80
ANTHONY H., In re, 166 Cal Rptr 607
New England J Prison L 7:230-2 Wint '81
ARCTIC Structures, Inc. v. Wedmore (Alaska) 605 P 2d 426
UCLA-Alaska L Rev 9:219-27 Spr '80
ARETZ v. U.S. 604 F 2d 417
Mercer L Rev 31:1095-102 Summ '80
ARIZONA v. Manypenny, 101 S Ct 1657
ABA J 67:910-11 Jl '81
ARIZONA v Maricopa County Med. Soc [1980-1] Trade Cas. (CCH) ¶63,239 (9th Cir.)
Wash U L Q 58:1065-74 '80
ARIZONA Pub. Serv. Co. v. Snead, 99 S Ct 1629
W Va L Rev 83:79-98 Fall '80
ARKANSAS v. Sanders, 99 S Ct 2586
Fordham Urban L J 9:185-214 '80-'81
NY LS L Rev 26:366-84 '81
Seton Hall L Rev 11:121-35 '80
Wash L Rev 55:871-83 N '80
ARMSTRONG v. McAlpin, 625 F 2d 433
Det Coll L Rev 1981:151-78 Spr '81
ARNOLD v. Arnold (NJ) 401 A 2d 261
West New England L Rev 3:127-43 Summ '80

Illustration C

A sample page from the "Table of Cases Commented Upon" in the *Index to Legal Periodicals.*

TABLE OF STATUTES COMMENTED UPON

UNITED STATES

Federal

Administrative procedure act of 1976—Pub L 94-409, Sept. 13, 1976; 90 Stat 1247; 5 USC §§ 551-706
Duke L J 1981:116-40 F '81
U Chi L Rev 48:201-62 Spr '81

Adoption assistance and child welfare act of 1980—Pub L 96-272, June 17, 1980; 94 Stat 500; scattered sections of 42 USC
So Calif L Rev 54:633-765 My '81

Age discrimination in employment act amendments of 1978—Pub L 95-256, Apr. 6, 1978; 92 Stat 189; 29 USC §§ 621-634
Brigham Young U L Rev 1980:569-97 '80
Drake L Rev 30:617-33 '80/'81
Ill B J 69:280-7 Ja '81
Indus Rel L J 4:90-111 '80

Agricultural foreign investment disclosure act of 1978—Pub L 95-460, Oct. 14, 1978, 92 Stat 1263, 7 USC §§ 3501-3508
Case W Res J Int L 12:231-47 Wint '80
Tex Int L J 15:287-315 Spr '80
Washburn L J 20:514-34 Spr '81

Agricultural trade act of 1978—Pub L 95-501, Oct 21, 1978; 92 Stat 1685; 5 USC § 5314, 7 USC §§ 612c-3, 1707a-d, 1761, 1762, 1764-1766c, 1769, 2211a, 19 USC § 2431
NC J Int L & Com Reg 5:263-77 Spr '80

Airline deregulation act of 1978—Pub L 95-504, Oct. 24, 1978; 92 Stat 1705 (to be codified in scattered sections of 49 USC)
J Air L 45:961-1000; 1001-26; 1029-57 Summ; 46:71-100 Fall '80; 329-45 Wint '81
Nw J Int L & Bus 1:299-317 Spr '79

American fisheries promotion act of 1980—Pub L 96-561, tit. II, pt. C, Dec. 22, 1980; 94 Stat 3296 (to be codified in scattered section of 16 USC)
Harv Int L J 22:485-91 Spr '81

American Indian religious freedom act—Pub L 95-341, Aug 11, 1978; 92 Stat 469; 42 USC § 1996
Am Indian L Rev 7:125-54 '79

Archaeological resources protection act of 1979 Pub L 96-95, Oct. 31, 1979; 93 Stat 721; 16 USC §§ 470aa-470ll
Am Indian L Rev 7:125-54 '79
Ariz L Rev 22:675-751 '80

Aviation safety and noise abatement act of 1979 —Pub L 96-193, Feb. 5, 1980, 94 Stat 50 (to be codified in scattered sections of 49 USC)
J Air L 45:921-60 Summ '80

Bankruptcy reform act of 1978—Pub L 95-598, Nov. 6, 1978; 92 Stat 2549; 11 USC §§ 101 et seq
Am Bankr L J 54:299-337 O '80; 55:177-90 Ap '81
Bus Law 36:79-97 N '80; 721-6 Mr '81 (Sp issue)
Case W Res L Rev 30:631-75 Summ '80
Catholic U L Rev 29:843-66 Summ '80
Colum L Rev 80:560-96 Ap '80
Com L J 85:542-57 D '80
Emory L J 28:581-783 Summ '79
Fed B J 39:62-88 Summ '80
Forum 15:778-89 Summ '80
Houston L Rev 17:217-370 Ja '80
Ill B J 68:782-92 Ag '80
Ind L Rev 13:761-97 Ap '80
J Family L 19:1-26 N '80
La B J 27:151-3+ D '79
Litigation 6:8-11+ Spr '80
Memphis St U L Rev 10:177-278 Wint '80
NC L Rev 58:667-853 Ap; 881-996 Je '80
Pacific L J 12:163-88 Ja '81
San Diego L Rev 17:1113-35 Ag '80
SD L Rev 25:509-27 Summ '80
Securities Reg L J 9:140-70 Summ '81
Tenn L Rev 47:501-99 Spr '80
U Ark Little Rock L J 3:13-73 '80
U San Francisco L Rev 14:341-73 Spr '80
UCLA L Rev 27:722-56 F '80
W&M L Rev 21:575-699 Spr/Summ '80
Wash & Lee L Rev 36:977-1025 Fall '79

Bankruptcy reform act of 1978—Pub L 95-598, Nov. 6, 1978; 92 Stat 2564; 11 USC §§ 330, 331 (Compensation of officers, Interim compensation)
Com L J 86:79-89 Mr '81

Bankruptcy reform act of 1978—Pub L 95-598, Nov. 6, 1978; 92 Stat 2570; 2602; 11 USC § 362 (Automatic stay) 11 USC § 553 (Setoff)
ALI-ABA Course Materials J 5:5-14 D '80

Bankruptcy reform act of 1978—Pub L 95-598, Nov. 6, 1978; 92 Stat 2549; 11 USC §§ 363 (Use, sale, or lease of property) 522 (Exemptions) 541 (Property of the estate)
W&M L Rev 21:701-29 Spr/Summ '80

Bankruptcy reform act of 1978—Pub L 95-598, Nov 6, 1978; 92 Stat 2549; 11 USC §§ 363h (Use, sale or lease of property) 522 (Exemptions)
NY SB J 53:272-5+ Je '81

Bankruptcy reform act of 1978—Pub L 95-598, Nov. 6, 1978; 92 Stat 2549; 11 USC § 522 (Exemptions)
Am Bankr L J 54:339-54 O '80
Fordham L Rev 49:615-41 Mr '81
Houston L Rev 17:373-98 Ja '80
Rutgers L Rev 33:70-103 Fall '80
U Cin L Rev 49:791-813 '80

Bankruptcy reform act of 1978—Pub L 95-598, Nov. 6, 1978; 92 Stat 2549; 11 USC § 523(a) (5) (Exceptions to discharge. Alimony, maintenance, or support)
Harv Women L J 4:177-92 Spr '81

Bankruptcy reform act of 1978—Pub L 95-598, Nov. 6, 1978; 92 Stat 2549; 11 USC § 522(b)(d)(e) (Exemptions)
Tex B J 44:145-51 F '81

Bankruptcy reform act of 1978—Pub L 95-598, Nov. 6, 1978; 92 Stat 2549; 11 USC §522(d) (Property which may be exempted) §522(f) (Debtor may avoid the fixing of a lien)
Akron L Rev 14:632-47 Spr '81
Harv L Rev 94:1616-36 My '81

Bankruptcy reform act of 1978—Pub L 95-598, Nov. 6, 1978; 92 Stat 2594, 2598, 2605; 11 USC §§ 541, 542(a), 704 (Property of the estate)
U Tol L Rev 12:305-45 Wint '81

Bankruptcy reform act of 1978—Pub L 95-598, Nov. 6, 1978; 92 Stat 2596; 11 USC §§ 544-548, 550, 551, 553 (avoidance powers of trustees)
Real Prop Pro & Trust J 15:588-605 Fall '80

Bankruptcy reform act of 1978—Pub L 95-598, Nov. 6, 1978; 92 Stat 2549; 11 USC § 545 (Statutory liens) § 546 (Limitations on avoiding powers)
Am Bankr L J 55:1-42 Wint '81
Ark L Rev 34:252-75 '80
La L Rev 41:1159-76 Summ '81

Bankruptcy reform act of 1978—Pub L 95-598, Nov. 6, 1978; 92 Stat 2597; 11 USC § 547 (preferences)
Houston L Rev 17:289-329 Ja '80
Marq L Rev 63:447-88 Spr '80
Va L Rev 67:249-73 Mr '81
Wake Forest L Rev 16:959-74 D '80

Bankruptcy reform act of 1978—Pub L 95-598, Nov 6, 1978; 92 Stat 2549; 11 USC §§ 705, 1102-, 1103, 151102 (Creditor committees)
Am Bankr L J 55:43-62 Wint '81

Bankruptcy reform act of 1978—chapter 7 (liquidation) chapter 11 (reorganization) chapter 13 (consumer rehabilitation)—Pub L 95-598, Nov. 6, 1978; 92 Stat 2549; 11 USC §§ 101 et seq
UCC L J 13:291-316 Spr '81

Bankruptcy reform act of 1978 (chapter 11)—Pub L 95-598, Nov. 6, 1978; 92 Stat 2549; 11 USC §§ 1101-1174 (Reorganization)
Com L J 86:51-6 F '81
Harv L Rev 94:1808-28 Je '81
J Coll & U L 8:2-19 '81/'82
So Calif L Rev 53:1527-62 Jl '80
U Ill L Forum 1980:251-76 '80
U Mich J L Ref 14:347-69 Wint '81

Bankruptcy reform act of 1978 (chapter 11)—Pub L 95-598, Nov. 6, 1978; 92 Stat 2549; 11 USC §§ 1111 (b), 1129 (b)
Ill B J 69:498-501 Ap '81

Bankruptcy reform act of 1978 (chapter 13)—Pub L 95-598, Nov. 6, 1978; 92 Stat 2549; 11 USC §§ 1301-1330 (adjustment of debts of an individual with regular income)
Am Bankr L J 55:143-75 Ap '81
Hofstra L Rev 9:593-624 Wint '81
Ky L J 69:327-58 '80/'81
Minn L Rev 65:659-84 Ap '81
NYU L Rev 55:941-70 N '80
U Mich J L Ref 14:321-45 Wint '81
Washburn L J 20:1-19 Fall '80
Wis B Bull 53:18-23 Ag '80

Bankruptcy reform act of 1978—Pub L 95-598, Nov. 6, 1978; 92 Stat 2672; 11 USC, § 101 et seq. scattered sections of 28 USC (Bankruptcy courts) (Jurisdiction)
Am Bankr L J 55:63-91 Wint '81

Bankruptcy reform act of 1978—Pub L 95-598, Nov. 6, 1978; 92 Stat 2549; 11 USC §§101-1330
Banking L J 98:525-66 Je/Jl '81

Bankruptcy tax act of 1980—Pub L 96-589, Dec. 24, 1980; 94 Stat 3389; scattered sections of IRC
ALI-ABA Course Materials J 5:7-34 Je '81
NYU Inst Fed Taxation 39:41.1-.20, 57.1-.161 '81
Prac Law 27:11-18 Je '81
Tax Adviser 12:68-78 F; 147-51 Mr; 277-85 My '81

Illustration D

A sample page from the "Table of Statutes Commented Upon" in the *Index to Legal Periodicals.*

BOOK REVIEW INDEX

AAZPA manual of federal wildlife regulations. comp. and ed. by C. A. Hill and others. 1979
Ecology L Q 9:241-2 '80

ABA real property, probate and trust law section. Title insurance and you: what every lawyer should know. 1979
Loyola U L J (Chicago) 12:201-8 Wint '81. C. G. Cooper

Abecassis, D. W. Law and practice relating to oil pollution from ships. 1978
J Soc Pub TL 15:129-30 Mr '80. D. W. Bowett

Abi-Saab, G. United Nations operation in the Congo, 1960-1964. 1978
Int Law 14:194-5 Wint '80. L. P. Wragg, jr

Abrahamson, M. W. Engineering law and the I.C.E. contracts, 4th ed. 1979
Irish Jur 14:389-90 Wint '79. R. W. Clark

Abuse on Wall Street: conflicts of interest in the securities markets. 1980
ABA J 67:618+ My '81. R. T. Howell, jr

Ackerman, B. Private property and the constitution. 1977
Wake Forest L Rev 16:875-82 O '80. D. A. Nance

Ackerman, B. A. Social justice in the liberal state. 1980
ABF Res J 1981:231-49 Wint '81. R. A. Posner
Minn L Rev 65:685-700 Ap '81. A. Weale

A.C.T. supplement to legal resources book (N.S.W.); ed. by N. Seddon. 1979
Aust L J 54:375 Je '80

Adams and Richardson's law of estate and gift duties. 5th ed. by I. L. M. Richardson and R. L. Congreve. 1978
NZ U L Rev 9:96-100 Je '80. J. Prebble

Adams, W. ed. Structure of American industry. 5th ed. 1977
Antitrust Bull 25:861-89 Wint '80. J. J. Siegfried, K. D. James and K. E. Maddox

Adewoye, O. Judicial system in southern Nigeria, 1854-1954: law and justice in a dependency. 1977
Am J Comp L 28:517-20 Summ '80. A. Sawyerr

Agid, S. Fair employment litigation: proving and defending a title VII case. 1979
Houston L Rev 17:661-85 Mr '80. L. M. Schooler

Aguda, T. A. Law and practice relating to evidence in Nigeria. 1980
L Q Rev 96:637 O '80. A. C. Hutchinson

Akehurst, M. Modern introduction to international law. 3d ed. 1977
Brit Year Book Int L 49:221-2 '78. J. C. Woodliffe

Albu, I. and Ursa, V. Ráspunderea civilá pentru daunele morale [Civil responsibility for moral damages] 1979
Int & Comp L Q 29:535-6 Ap/Jl '80. H. Smith

Alder, J. Development control. 1979
Can B Rev 59:223-30 Mr '81. J. M. Evans
Modern L Rev 43:601-2 S '80. C. Crawford
No Ire L Q 31:201-3 Summ '80. B. Thompson

Aldridge, T. M. Your home and the law. n.d.
New L J 130:458 Je 12 '80. F. G. Glover

Alexander, E. R. Family and the law of torts. 1979
Man L J 10:491-2 '80
UBC L Rev 14:405-6 '80. K. F. Nordlinger

Alexander, Y. and others. eds. Terrorism: theory and practice. 1979
Am J Int L 74:711-16 Jl '80. J. F. Murphy

Alix, E. K. Ransom kidnapping in America, 1874-1974—the creation of a capital crime. 1978
J Crim L 71:654-7 Wint '80. N. N. Kittrie

Allen, D. K. and others. eds. Accident compensation after Pearson. 1979
Cambrian L Rev 11:126-7 '80. R. Kidner

Allen, F. A. Law, intellect, and education. 1979
ABA J 66·1096 S '80. J. E. Cribbet
Minn L Rev 65:319-30 Ja '81. D. P. Bryden
Tex L Rev 58:861-74 Ap '80. J. C. Dougherty
U Tol L Rev 11:1072-80 Summ '80. A. B. Johnson

Allen, S. and Craven, J. P. eds. Alternatives in deepsea mining. 1979
Int Law 14:757-8 Fall '80. A. D. Chrisopoulos

Altshuler, A. ed. Current issues in transportation policy. 1979
J Air L 45:1137-9 Summ '80. D. M. Kirstein

American international law cases, v20; ed. by F. Deak and others. 1978
Int Law 14:189-90 Wint '80. N. R. Thorpe

Amnesty international. Death penalty. 1979
Ariz St L J 1980:815-25 '80. D. Kader

Amory, C. Trouble with nowadays: a curmudgeon strikes back. 1979
ABA J 67:600+ My '81. A. C. Bowman

Andemicael, B. ed. Regionalism and the United Nations. 1979
Am J Int L 74:707-8 Jl '80. H. K. Jacobson
UBC L Rev 14:394-6 '80. L. C. Green

Anderman, S. D. Law of unfair dismissal. 1978
L Q Rev 96:294-5 Ap '80. A. D. Hughes

Anderson, J. Confessions of a muckraker: the inside story of life in Washington during the Truman, Eisenhower, Kennedy and Johnson years. 1979
ABA J 67:322 Mr '81. H. C. Streibich

Anderson, N. Liberty, law and justice. 1978
No Ire L Q 31:312 Aut '80. S. Guest

Anderson, R. La prensa en Puerto Rico. 1977
Rev Jur U PR 47:324-30 '78

Andrew, W. J. and others. Criminal law and practice of Papua New Guinea. 1979
Crim L J 4:259-60 Ag '80. E. P. Aughterson
Int & Comp L Q 29:781-2 O '80. H. H. Marshall
U Queens L J 11:209-10 D '80. R. G. Kenny

Andrews, L. B. Birth of a salesman: lawyer advertising and solicitation. 1980
ABA J 67:458 Ap '81. J. L. Allison

Annual review of medicine: selected topics in the clinical sciences, v31; ed. by W. P. Creger and others. 1980
Am J L & Med 6:69 Spr '80

Annual survey of Commonwealth law 1977. ed. by J. M. Finnis and C. H. Beatson. 1979
Camb L J 39:398-9 N '80. R. Munday

Anthoine, R. ed. Tax incentives for private investment in developing countries. 1979
Int Law 14:195-6 Wint '80. L. A. Freeman

Appenzeller, H. and Appenzeller, T. Sports and the courts. 1980
ABA J 67:458+ Ap '81. H. C. Streibich

Arangio-Ruiz, G. L'Etat dans le sens du droit des gens et la notion du droit international. 1975
Brit Year Book Int L 49:222-3 '78. J. Crawford

Arangio-Ruiz, G. UN declaration on friendly relations and the system of the sources of international law. 1979
Dalhousie L J 6:397-401 N '80. L. C. Green

Archbold, J. F. Archbold: pleading, evidence & practice in criminal cases. 4th ed. by S. Mitchell. 1979
Modern L Rev 43:485-6 Jl '80. F. O'Donoghue

Areeda, P. and Turner, D. F. Antitrust law. 4v. 1978, 1980
Antitrust Bull 25:891-901 Wint '80. M. J. Adelman
Ga L Rev 15:530-8 Wint '81. T. W. Rhodes

Arizona. State bar. Appellate handbook committee. Arizona appellate handbook. v2-3. 1980
Ariz St L J 1980:827-9 '80. F. X. Gordon, jr

Arntz, J. Der begriff der friedensbedrohung in satzung und praxis der vereinten nationen. 1975
Brit Year Book Int L 49:223-30 '78. L. Gross

Aronstam, P. Consumer protection, freedom of contract and the law. 1979
L Q Rev 96:283-6 Ap '80. J. K. Macleod

Atiyah, P. S. From principles to pragmatism. 1978
J Soc Pub TL 15:81-2 Mr '80. O. Kahn-Freund

Atiyah, P. S. Rise and fall of freedom of contract. 1979
Camb L J 39:396-7 N '80. C. Turpin
Jurid Rev 1980:234-6 D '80 D. M. Walker
Modern L Rev 43:467-9 Jl '80. J. H. Baker
No Ire L Q 31:308-10 Aut '80. B. Dickson
SD L Rev 26:152-3 Wint '81. J. F. Hagemann
Yale L J 90:216-31 N '80. C. M. Gray

Attwooll, E. ed. Perspectives in jurisprudence. 1977
Jurid Rev 1979:229-31 D '79. I. D. Willock

Auchincloss, L. House of the prophet. 1980
ABA J 67:599 My '81. D. S. Machlowitz

Audier, J. Les droits patrimoniaux a caractere personnel. 1978
RJT 14:357-8 '79/'80. J.-L. Baudouin

Audretsch, H. A. H. Supervision in European community law. 1978
Brit Year Book Int L 49:230-1 '78. M. Akehurst

Australia. Law reform commission. Child welfare: child abuse and day care. Discussion paper 12. 1980
Crim L J 4:256-8 Ag '80. L. Foreman

Australia. Law reform commission. Child welfare: children in trouble. Discussion paper 9. 1979
Crim L J 4:256-8 Ag '80. L. Foreman

Australian criminal reports, v 1, no 1. 1980
Mon L Rev 7:116-17 D '80. R. G. Fox

Australian yearbook of international law, 1970-3. ed. by R. H. Miller. 1975
Can Yearbook Int L 17:451-2 '79. L. C. Green

Illustration E

A sample page from the "Book Review Index" in the *Index to Legal Periodicals.*

headings, to the limited number of journals and articles covered (for a long time most bar association periodicals were not covered, and articles under five pages in length were not indexed), to the policy of putting the full bibliographic entry only under the subject entry, to the print-size, and to the quality and intensity of the indexing itself. The American Association of Law Libraries, which originally published the *Index* and had later sold it to the H.W. Wilson Company, maintained an advisory board that worked closely with the editors of the *Index to Legal Periodicals* to preserve and improve its quality. Because of the complaints described above, the American Association of Law Libraries withdrew this endorsement.[20] The H.W. Wilson Company continued its publication of the *Index*, and formed its own board of distinguished law librarians as advisors. In response to some of the criticisms, new subject headings were created, the number of journals covered was expanded, the "Table of Statutes Construed" added, and the quality of the indexing improved. The *Index to Legal Periodicals* will undoubtedly survive and continue to be an important research tool, but it now has imaginative competition from the new indexes described below.

2. CURRENT LAW INDEX AND LEGAL RESOURCES INDEX

The newest development in legal periodical indexing are two companion indexes, developed by Information Access Corporation in collaboration with a group of law librarians who had become frustrated by the conservative policies of the *Index to Legal Periodicals.* The *Current Law Index,* which began in January 1980, provides access to over six hundred legal and law-related periodicals. Full bibliographic information is supplied under both author and subject, and the very detailed Library of Congress subject headings are used. The additional number of journals covered, the more detailed indexing available through Library of Congress headings, and the companion microfilm format, described below, led the American Association of Law Libraries to endorse the new publication. A committee of members of the American Association of Law Libraries now oversees *Current Law Index* as it once advised the *Index to Legal Periodicals.*[21] Its subject headings, cross references, and the journals covered are augmented by their recommendations.

The structure of *Current Law Index* is similar to that of the *Index to Legal Periodicals,* but includes separate subject and author-title indexes, both of which provide full bibliographic entries. It contains case and statute tables that function like their counterparts in the *I.L.P.*, but book reviews appear under both the author and title of the book reviewed in the regular Author-Title Index, not in a separate section. One added feature of its book review coverage is the assign-

20. This controversy is described in the 1979 proceedings of the American Association of Law Libraries, at 72 *Law Library J.* 567 (1979).

21. For a comparison of the two indexes, see T. Steele, "The Index to Legal Periodicals and Current Law Index—A Comparison," 1 *Legal Reference Services Q.* 43 (1981).

ment of "grades" based on the degree of favor expressed in the review.

Illustrations F to I, inclusive, show the standard features of *Current Law Index.*

Legal Resources Index is a companion publication to *Current Law Index* and is also issued by the Information Access Corporation. It provides the same information as *Current Law Index* but in a microfilm format, loaded into a motorized reader. An updated microfilm reel is distributed each month so that the researcher need only check one place to find all cumulated references. The publisher has also announced that the service may eventually incorporate Library of Congress cataloging tapes, so that access to monographs can be included. Some federal government documents are already being added. *Legal Resources Index,* like *Current Law Index* is not useful for pre–1980 searches and, because of its high cost, is not as widely used as the standard printed indexes.

3. INDEX TO FOREIGN LEGAL PERIODICALS

Although the *Index to Legal Periodicals, Current Law Index,* and *Legal Resources Index* cover many British, Canadian and Commonwealth legal periodicals, they do not cite those of other countries which appear in languages other than English. For these periodicals, the *Index to Foreign Legal Periodicals,* published under the auspices of the American Association of Law Libraries, offers comprehensive access to over 330 periodicals, primarily from countries outside of the common law system. This *Index* is published quarterly, with triennial cumulative bound volumes. It is divided into four sections, as follows: (1) subject index, (2) geographical index, (3) book review index, and (4) author index. A new list of subject headings was published in 1980 as a guide for researchers.[22] Illustration J shows entries in its author index and Illustration K, entries in its subject index.

The *Index to Foreign Legal Periodicals* has been criticized for the limited number of journals being indexed. Because of the wide range of international and foreign journals published and the variety of languages involved, only a small percentage can be included. The *Index* is currently evaluating major changes in format and is considering a substantial expansion in the number of journals covered.

4. INDEX TO PERIODICAL ARTICLES RELATED TO LAW

To fill the gap created by the limited coverage of the *Index to Legal Periodicals,* another index was begun in 1958 to cover legal periodicals not being indexed in *I.L.P.,* and a wide range of non-legal periodicals carrying articles of interest to lawyers and others engaged in legal research. The *Index to Periodical Articles Related to Law* (Glanville Publishers), was created for this purpose, and cur-

22. *Index to Foreign Legal Periodicals,* Special Number, 1980.

FOOD ADULTERATION AND INSPECTION — SUBJECT INDEX

Inspection policy. (planning company policy) by John F. Schaefer
36 Food Drug Cosm. L.J. 493-500 Sept '81
FDA investigator: from his office to yours. (description of FDA inspection procedure) by Marc M. Feinberg
36 Food Drug Cosm. L.J. 486-492 Sept '81
Judgment of the Supreme Court in State of Tamil Nadu v. S. Shanmugham Chettiar and another. (India - food adulteration) by T.S. Parthasarathy
87 Crim. L.J. 41-42 Aug '81
Regulatory implementation of dietary recommendations. by Peter Barton Hutt
36 Food Drug Cosm. L.J. 66-89 Feb '81
FDA seizure and injunction actions: judicial means of protecting the public health. by David F. Weeda
35 Food Drug Cosm. L.J. 112-121 Feb '80
see also
Food contamination
Meat inspection

FOOD aid programs *see*
Food relief

FOOD containers
see also
Aluminum cans

FOOD contamination
Problems in the control of pesticide residue on imported foods. by Jeffrey H. Nicholas
36 Food Drug Cosm. L.J. 573-595 Nov '81
Food safety and chemical residues. by Ronald E. Engel *36 Food Drug Cosm. L.J. 33-38 Jan '81*
FDA regulation of environmental contaminants of food. by Richard A. Merrill and Michael Schewel
66 Va. L. Rev. 1357-1441 Dec '80

FOOD control *see*
Food supply

FOOD, Convenience *see*
Convenience foods

FOOD crops
see also
Grain

FOOD industry and trade
Problems in the control of pesticide residue on imported foods. by Jeffrey H. Nicholas
36 Food Drug Cosm. L.J. 573-595 Nov '81
The DFDA inspection: what you need to know to protect your company. by Stephen H. McNamara
36 Food Drug Cosm. L.J. 245-257 May '81
Food processors - V: 1979 corporate federal tax burden. *12 Tax Notes 936 April 27 '81*
Food processors - IV: 1979 corporate federal tax burden. *12 Tax Notes 607 March 16 '81*
Food processors - I, II, III: 1979 corporate federal tax burden. *12 Tax Notes 6-8 Jan 5 '81*
Food retailers: 1979 corporate federal tax burden.
11 Tax Notes 1301 Dec 29 '80
What corporations have done to our food. by Joan Gussow *Bus. & Soc'y Rev. 19-25 Fall '80*
The FTC's breakfast cereal case: procedural history. by Anthony Low Joseph
12 Antitrust L. & Econ. Rev. 9(9) Summ '80
Output per unit of labor input in the retail food store industry. by John L. Carey and Phyllis Flohr Otto *v100 Monthly Labor Review p42(6) Jan '77*
see also
Farm produce
Food additives
Food prices
Food supply

FOOD inspection *see*
Food adulteration and inspection

FOOD, Junk
What corporations have done to our food. by Joan Gussow *Bus. & Soc'y Rev. 19-25 Fall '80*

FOOD law and legislation
EEC directives on the approximation of member states' legislation relating to foodstuffs. by Alain Gerard
36 Food Drug Cosm. L.J. 543-549 Oct '81
Criminal liability under the Federal Food, Drug, and Cosmetic Act - the large corporation perspective. by Jonathan S. Kahan
36 Food Drug Cosm. L.J. 314-331 June '81
Food laws and regulation: the impact on food research. by Theodore P. Labuza
36 Food Drug Cosm. L.J. 293-302 June '81
Food safety and regulations - A Canadian perspective. by Ron O. Read
36 Food Drug Cosm. L.J. 120-128 March '81
Sale of 'food' declaring it as not for human consumption. (India) by Yetukuri Venkateswara
86 Crim. L.J. 54-55 Dec '80
Federal food and drug violations. (White-collar crime: a survey of law) by Robert B. Fiske Jr.
18 Am. Crim. L. Rev. 336-344 Fall '80
Mandatory food and drug recalls - An analysis of a developing FDA enforcement tool. by Blake Muir Harper *Utah L. Rev. 809-828 Fall '80*

FOOD poisoning
see also
Salmonellosis

FOOD policy *see*
Nutrition policy

FOOD prices
Documenting food expense in the financial affidavit. by Mary Jane Cox
10 Colo. Law. 2279-2282 Sept '81
Inflation cross-currents: energy, food, and homeownership. by David Callahan, Andrew Clem and John Wetmore
v104 Monthly Labor Review p14(8) June '81
The monopoly component of inflation in food prices. by Neal Smith
14 U. Mich. J.L. Ref. 149-172 Wntr '81
Inflation rate high in the second quarter, but prices of raw materials declined. by Toshiko Nakayama and Craig Howell
v100 Monthly Labor Review p29(5) Sept '77
Productivity and new technology in eating and drinking places. by Richard B. Carnes and Horst Brand
v100 Monthly Labor Review p9(7) Sept '77
Anatomy of price change - the sharp first-quarter rise. by Craig Howell, Paul Monson and William Thomas
v100 Monthly Labor Review p3(6) June '77

FOOD processing plants
see also
Quaker Oats Co.

FOOD relief
The impact of food aid on world malnutrition. by James N. Schubert *35 Int'l Org. 329-354 Spr '81*

FOOD research
Food laws and regulation: the impact on food research. by Theodore P. Labuza
36 Food Drug Cosm. L.J. 293-302 June '81

FOOD Research and Action Center
Food Research and Action Center.
15 Clearinghouse Rev. 70-72 May '81

FOOD service
see also
Caterers and catering
waiters

FOOD stamp program
Food stamps for residents of shelters for battered women and children.
15 Clearinghouse Rev. 144 June '81
Food stamp fraud hearings..
14 Clearinghouse Rev. 1263-1265 April '81
Controlling food stamp fraud investigations.
14 Clearinghouse Rev. 1159-1160 March '81

-cases
Administrative law - the Food Stamp Act - scope of judicial review of administrative sanctions under 7 U.S.C. 2023. (case note) Studt v. United States 607 F.2d 1216 (8th Cir. 1979) by Alice L. Gallaher
10 Memphis St. U.L. Rev. 782-792 Summ '80

FOOD supply
Global future: time to act. Report to the president on global resources, environment and population. (by Council on Environmental Quality)
9 B.C. Envt'l Aff. L. Rev. 261-283 Spr '81
The Global 2000 report to the president. by Gus Speth *8 B.C. Envt'l Aff. L. Rev. 695-703 Fall '80*
A new food regime: necessary but impossible. (critique of special issue on food, Int'l Org., Summ '78) by Helge Ole Bergesen
34 Int'l Org. 285-302 Spr '80

FOODS, Contaminated *see*
Food contamination

FOOTBALL
A critique of the National Football League's blackout exemption from the antitrust laws. by Cori Jan Ching *8 J. Legis. 104-120 Wntr '81*
see also
Australian football
Rugby football

FOOTBALL clubs
Eligibility requirements for young athletes. (players' rights) by Marvin A. Demoff
4 L.A. Law. 34(7) June '81

FOOTBALL clubs, Professional *see*
Football clubs

FOOTBALL players
Sport in court: the legality of professional football's system of reserve and compensation. by Steven M. Strauss *28 U.C.L.A.L. Rev. 252-290 Dec '80*
The battle of the superstars: Player restraints in professional team sports. by Leslie Michele Lava
32 U. Fla. L. Rev. 669-700 Summ '80

-cases
Torts - civil liability of athletes - professional football player may have tort claim for injuries intentionally inflicted during football game. (case note) Hackbart v. Cincinnati Bengals, Inc. 601 F.2d 516 (10th Cir. 1979)
84 Dick. L. Rev. 753-768 Summ '80
On finding civil liability between professional football players. (case note) Hackbart v. Cincinnati Bengals, Inc. 100 S. Ct. 275 (1979) by Peter R. Nadel
15 New Eng. L. Rev. 741-764 Summ '79-80

FOOTWEAR *see*
Boots and shoes

FORCE (Law) *see*
Violence (Law)

FORCE majeure *see*
Vis major (Civil law)

FORCED heirs *see*
Legitime

FORCIBLE entry and detainer
Swales v. Cox: the Englishman's castle. by Alan Wharam *131 New L.J. 673-674 June 25 '81*
Forcible entry and detainer. (survey of Ohio Supreme Court decisions 1979-1980)
7 Ohio N.U.L. Rev. 577 July '80

FORD automobile
Ford transmissions: the illusory park problem. by Donald M. Gilberg *16 Trial 10-11 May '80*

FORD Motor Co.
Two automakers resume merit pay increases. (developments in industrial relations) by George Ruben
v104 Monthly Labor Review p47(1) July '81
Steelworkers at Ford accept cut in hourly pay.
v104 Monthly Labor Review p60(1) May '81

FORD Motor Com. *fix*
Ford Motor Co.

FORD Motor Corp. *fix*
Ford Motor Co.

FORD Pinto
Corporate homicide: definitional processes in the creation of deviance. by Victoria Lynn Swigert and Ronald A. Farrell
15 Law & Soc'y Rev. 161-182 Fall '80-81

FORD, Harold E.
Who's who on the House Ways and Means Committee. (short profile of each member)
12 Tax Notes 1311-1318 June 8 '81

FORECASTING
2100, and all that. (Great Britain - fantasy about the future) by Simon Chalton
125 Solicitor's J. 646(3) Sept 25 '81
What to ask about management's forecast: 17 tough questions. by J. Scott Armstrong
6 Direct. & Boards 20-26 Summ '81
Legal futurology: The field and its literature. by David A. Funk *73 Law Lib. J. 625-633 Summ '80*
see also
Social prediction

FORECASTING, Business *see*
Business forecasting

FORECASTING, Economic *see*
Economic forecasting

FORECASTING, Employment *see*
Employment forecasting

FORECASTING theory *see*
Prediction theory

FORECASTING, Weather *see*
Weather forecasting

FORECLOSURE
see also
Tax-sales

-analysis
The tax consequences of defaulting on a mortgage. (ALI-ABA syllabus) by Theodore Z. Geltz
5 ALI-ABA Course Mat. J. 7-34 June '81

-cases
Landlord and tenant - mortgages - New Jersey's Anti-Eviction Act, N.J. Stat. Ann. 2A:18-61.1 to -61.12 (West Cum. Supp. 1980-1981) prohibits removal of residential tenants by foreclosure mortgagee upon default of landlord-tenant mortgagor absent good cause. (case note) Guttenberg Savings & Loan Association v. Rivera 409 A.2d 816 (N.J. App. Div. 1979) by Harold N. Hensel
11 Seton Hall L. Rev. 311-329 Wint '80
Landlord and tenant - mortgages - New Jersey's Anti-Eviction Act, N.J. Stat. Ann. 2A:18-61.1 to -61.12 (West Cum. Supp. 1980-1981) prohibits removal of residential tenants by foreclosure mortgagee upon default of landlord-tenant mortgagor absent good cause. (case note) Guttenberg Savings & Loan Association v. Rivera 409 A.2d 816 (N.J. App. Div. 1979) by Harold N. Hensel
11 Seton Hall L. Rev. 311-329 Wint '80

-costs
Allocation of expenses of preservation and sale of liened property. by Chauncey H. Levy and Lawrence C. Gottlieb
86 Com. L.J. 356-358 Oct '81

-law and legislation
Sidewalks in the woods: evolution of in rem tax foreclosure. (New Jersey) by Alvin B. Lebar
N.J.L. 14-18 Nov '81
Enforcing mortgage securities. (Australia) by E.L.G. Tyler *55 Austl. L.J. 559-581 Aug '81*
Pre-sale judicial intervention in public trustee foreclosures. by Patrick F. Kenney and Christina Neslund *10 Colo. Law. 1631-1635 July '81*
New developments in real estate financing. (Symposium: Real estate finance - An emphasis on Texas law)- by Jesse B. Heath Jr.
12 St. Mary's L.J. 811-887 Summ '81
ULTA and non-judicial mortgage foreclosure in Texas. (Symposium: Real estate finance - An emphasis on Texas law) by Patricia E. Rant
12 St. Mary's L.J. 1104-1129 Summ '81
Compensating the receiver in foreclosure actions. by Bruce J. Bergman
53 N.Y. St. B.J. 276(9) June '81
Selected problems of real estate in bankruptcy. by Nancy D. Miller *10 Colo. Law. 1363(6) June '81*
Selling mortgaged property. (Great Britain) by Henry E. Markson
125 Solicitor's J. 249-251 April 10 '81
The effect of Certified Realty on mortgage foreclosure in Colorado. by Kathy Eaton Cranmer
52 U. Colo. L. Rev. 301-312 Wntr '81
Mortgage Foreclosure in Pennsylvania.
2685 Dick. L. Rev. 275-287 Wntr '81
La clause de transport de loyers et la vente en justice. (Quebec) by Jacques Auger
40 Rev. Barreau Que. 831-840 Nov-Dec '80
Mechanic's liens in Iowa. by Roger W. Stone
30 Drake L. Rev. 39-121 Fall '80-'81
The land sale contract. (Survey of Tennessee property law) by Beverly A. Rowlett
48 Tenn. L. Rev. 72-86 Fall '80
Subsidized rental projects in default: rights and remedies. by Alan S. Ganz and Marc A. Primack
29 De Paul L. Rev. 1025-1062 Summ '80

-litigation
Guarantor's liability after mortgage foreclosure sale: issue resolved. by John P. Roberts
52 Okla. B.J. 723-725 March 28 '81
Dation en paiement - Retroactivite - Radiation des enregistrements posterieurs au titre du creancier. (Quebec) by Roger Comtois
83 Rev. Notariat 504-5006 March-April '81

248

Illustration F

A sample page from the "Subject Index" of *Current Law Index.*

AUTHOR/TITLE INDEX

FULCO, Lawrence J.
Productivity drops, output and hours rise during fourth quarter. (productivity reports) by Lawrence J. Fulco
v104 Monthly Labor Review p40(4) June '81
Long nonfarm productivity slide ends during third quarter. by Lawrence J. Fulco
v104 Monthly Labor Review p66(2) March '81
Sixth consecutive productivity drop recorded during the second quarter. by Lawrence J. Fulco
v103 Monthly Labor Review p52(3) Dec '80
Productivity and costs in the second quarter. by John R. Norsworthy and Lawrence J. Fulco
v100 Monthly Labor Review p34(5) Nov '77
Productivity and costs in the private economy, 1976. by John R. Norsworthy and Lawrence J. Fulco
v100 Monthly Labor Review p3(6) Sept '77
Productivity and costs in the first quarter, 1977. by John R. Norsworthy and Lawrence J. Fulco
v100 Monthly Labor Review p38(3) Aug '77
Productivity and costs in the fourth quarter. by John R. Norsworthy and Lawrence J. Fulco
v100 Monthly Labor Review p68(4) April '77
Productivity and costs in the third quarter, 1976. by John R. Norsworthy and Lawrence J. Fulco
v100 Monthly Labor Review p75(5) Feb '77

FULD, James J.
Dear board of directors - a legal opinion in the year 2000. (Symposium: the role of professionals in corporate governance) by James J. Fuld
56 Notre Dame Law. 869-872 June '81

FULER, N.A.
The measurement of breath alcohol. by V.J. Emerson, R. Holleyhead, M.D.J. Isaacs, N.A. Fuler and D.J. Hunt rev by H.J. Walls grade B
Crim. L. Rev. 434-435 June '81

FULGENCY, Robert J.
Dramatization: pricing and promotional decisions. (proceedings of National Institute on Antitrust Counseling and the Marketing Process, Chicago, June 12-13, 1980) (transcript) by Herbert M. Liss, Bernat Rosner, James F. Rill and Robert J. Fulgency *49 Antitrust L.J. 497-526 June '80*

The full employment alternative.
by Andrew Levison rev by Rose M. Rubin grade B
v104 Monthly Labor Review p51(1) July '81

FULLAM, John P.
A judicial talk show - more conversations on patent and trademark litigation from both sides of the bench. (7th Ann. Judicial Conf. of U.S. Court of Customs and Patent Appeals) (transcript) by Howard T. Markey, John P. Fullam, Frank J. McGarr, Tom Arnold and C. Frederick Leydig
88 F.R.D. 379-413 March '81

FULLER, C. Andrew
Exclusion of evidence of subsequent repairs in drug products liability actions - an unnecessary resurrection of an obsolete rule. by C. Andrew Fuller and A. Leroy Toliver
31 Mercer L. Rev. 801-814 Spr '80

FULLER, C.W.F. Baden
Economic issues relating to property rights in trademarks: export bans, differential pricing, restrictions on resale and repackaging. by C.W.F. Baden Fuller *6 European L. Rev. 162-179 June '81*

FULLER, David S.
Should you invest in precious metals? by David S. Fuller *130 New L.J. 1078(2) Nov 13 '80*

FULLER, Graham
En garde - it can happen to you. (preventing legal malpractice)(Australia) by Graham Fuller
55 Law Inst. J. 561 Sept '81
En garde - it can happen to you. (Victoria) by Graham Fuller *55 Law Inst. J. 488-489 Aug '81*
Professional indemnity insurance certificates are portable. (Victoria) by Graham Fuller
55 Law Inst. J. 487 Aug '81
Go manual in the 80's. (written office procedures) by Graham Fuller *55 Law Inst. J. 169 April '81*

FULLER, Jamie L.
Multimember electoral systems and the discriminatory-purpose standard. (case note) by Jamie L. Fuller
12 Tex. Tech. L. Rev. 743-763 May '81

FULLER, N.A.
The measurement of breath alcohol. by V.J. Emerson, R. Holleyhead, M.D.J. Isaacs, N.A. Fuller and D.J. Hunt rev by Soren Felby grade B
18 For. Sci. Int'l 99-100 July-Aug '81

FULLER, Stephen H.
Becoming the organization of the future. (Symposium of revitalizing human resources) by Stephen H. Fuller *7 Empl. Rel. L.J. 77-84 Summ '81*

FULLERTON, Don
Income tax incentives to promote saving. (Public finance in the 1980s: illusions and realities: NTA-TIA symposium, May 1980) by Charles Becker and Don Fullerton *33 Nat'l Tax J. 331-351 Sept '80*

FULLERTON, Howard N., Jr.
The 1995 labor force: a first look. by Howard N. Fullerton Jr.
v103 Monthly Labor Review p11(11) Dec '80

FULLINWIDER, Robert K.
The reverse discrimination controversy. by Robert K. Fullinwider rev by Alan H. Goldman grade C
65 Minn. L. Rev. 718-727 April '81

FULTON, Colin Scott Cole
Constitutional law - double jeopardy - prosecution of related offenses in separate trials. (case note) by Colin Scott Cole Fulton
32 S.C.L. Rev. 585-597 March '81

FULTON, Joy D.
Sixth Amendment - Massiah revitalized. (case note) by Joy D. Fulton
71 J. Crim. L. & Criminology 601-609 Wntr '80

The functioning and effectiveness of selected United Nations system programs.
by David A. Kay rev by Lawrence S. Finkelstein grade B- *75 Am. J. Int'l L. 1014-1015 Oct '81*

Fundamental duties.
by D. Lasok, D.L. Perrott and Christina Sachs grade B *26 J.L. Soc'y Scot. 150(2) April '81*

Fundamentals of criminal investigation: 5th ed.
by C.E. O'Hara and G.L. O'Hara rev by T.A. Johnson grade D *26 J. For. Sci. 612-613 July '81*

Fundamentals of radio broadcasting.
by John Hasling rev by Paul Hemenway grade B
24 J. Broadcast. 561-562 Fall '80

Fundamentals of trial techniques.
by Thomas A. Mauet rev by Richard P. Glovka grade B *7 Litigation 45(3) Spr '81*

FUNK, David A.
Legal futurology: The field and its literature. by David A. Funk *73 Law Lib. J. 625-633 Summ '80*

FUQUA, David
Justice Harry A. Blackmun: the abortion decisions. by David Fuqua
34 Ark. L. Rev. 276-296 Wint '80

FUQUA, J.B.
What CEO's expect of their corporate lawyers. (Proceedings of Corporate Law Department Forum) by J.B. Fuqua, Daniel J. Haughton and Sidney Topol *36 Bus. Law. 605-616 March '81*

FUQUA, Laura D.
United Nations principles on remote sensing: report on developments, 1970-1980. by Gerald J. Mossinghoff and Laura D. Fuqua
8 J. Space L. 103-155 Fall '80

FUQUA, William G.
Closing criminal trials. (a report of the Kentucky Circuit Judges' Association's Committee) by Thomas B. Spain, William G. Fuqua, Benjamin F. Shobe and E.N. Venters
45 Ky. Bench & B. 20(2) Jan '81

FURET, Marie-Francoise
La guerre et le droit. (book reviews) by Marie-Francoise Furet, Jean-Claude Martinez and Henri Dorandeu rev by Dietrich Schindler grade B
74 Am. J. Int'l L. 986-987 Oct '80

FURKIN, David Scott
Constitutional law - State's general interest in preservation of life held insufficient to warrant judicial intervention in temporary guardian's decision to terminate life-sustaining medical treatment of terminally ill, mentally incompetent ward. (case note) by David Scott Furkin
19 J. Fam. L. 158-162 Nov '80

FURLOW, Terrance
Polygraph decides outcome of medical malpractice case. by Terrance Furlow
9 Legal Aspects Med. Prac. 7-8 Nov '81

FURMAN, Ellen B.
Criminal law and procedure: explicit waiver of Miranda rights mandatory. (Pa. S. Ct. review, 1979) (case note) by Ellen B. Furman
53 Temp. L.Q. 698-711 Wint '80
Torts - New Jersey recognizes parent's cause of action for emotional damages for wrongful birth but denies infant's cause of action for wrongful life. (case note) by Ellen B. Furman
53 Temp. L.Q. 176-192 Wntr '80

FURR, David M.
Constitutional law - right to speedy trial in civilian prosecution denied by delay following dismissal of military charges. (case note) by David M. Furr
17 Wake Forest L. Rev. 89-119 Feb '81

FURUSETH, Owen J.
Update on Oregon's agricultural protection program: A land use perspective. by Owen J. Furuseth
21 Nat. Resources J. 57-70 Jan '81
The Oregon agricultural protection program: a review and assessment. by Owen J. Furuseth
20 Nat. Resources J. 603-614 July '80

FURZE, A.S.
Calculating the minimum statutory deposit with the Law Institute. (Australia) by A.S. Furze
55 Law Inst. J. 124-125 March '81

FUSTER, Jaime B.
Una nueva estrategia: la participacion del ciudadano en la lucha contra el crimen. by Jaime B. Fuster
42 Rev. C. Abo P.R. 101-112 May '81

Future coal prospects.
by Robert P. Greene and J. Michael Gallagher rev by J.G. Polach grade B
21 Nat. Resources J. 675-679 July '81

Future developments in telecommunications.
by James Martin rev by Brian Winston grade C-
25 J. Broadcast. 88-92 Wntr '81

The future of business regulation.
by Murray L. Weidenbaum rev by Melvin J. Dubnick grade B-
41 Pub. Ad. Rev. 287-288 March-April '81

The future of labor arbitration in America.
by Benjamin Aaron rev by Paul Staudohar grade A
v100 Monthly Labor Review p51(1) Sept '77

The future of the Inter-American system.
by Tom J. Farer rev by A.J. Thomas Jr. grade B-
75 Am. J. Int'l L. 1016-1017 Oct '81

The future of the prison system.
by Roy D. King, Rod Morgan, J.P. Martin and J.E. Thomas rev by David Downes grade B
21 Brit. J. Criminology 384-388 Oct '81
by Roy D. King, Rod Morgan, J.P. Martin and J.E. Thomas rev by B. Tahourdin grade B-
25 Int'l J. Offend. Ther. & Comp. Criminology 189-191 Sept '81
by Roy D. King, Rod Morgan, J.P. Martin and J.E. Thomas grade B *125 Solicitor's J. 254 April 10 '81*

The future of the workplace.
by Paul Dickson rev by Louis E. Davis grade B
v100 Monthly Labor Review p87(1) April '77

The future of United States naval power.
by James A. Nathan and James K. Oliver rev by Miles A. Libbey III grade B-
5 Fletcher F. 184-186 Wntr '81

FYFE, James J.
Obvservations on police deadly force. by James J. Fyfe *27 Crime & Delinquency 376-389 July '81*
The court and the cops. by James J. Fyfe
5 Update 6(6) Wntr '81

GAAR, James R.
Clifford trust for oil and gas property. by James R. Gaar *12 Tax Adviser 36-37 Jan '81*

GAASHOLT, Oystein
In the wake of the Boldt decision: a sociological study. (fishing rights controversy) by Oystein Gaasholt and Fay Cohen
6 Am. Indian J. 9-17 Nov '80

GABAY, Amnon
Chemical reagents for the development of latent fingerprints. III: Visualization of latent fingerprints by fluorescent reagents in vapor phase. by Joseph Almog and Amnon Gabay
25 J. For. Sci. 408(3) April '80

GABEL, Peter
A critical anatomy of the legal opinion. by Peter Gabel *5 ALSA F. 4-11 Fall '80*

GABIN, Sanford Byron
Judicial review and the reasonable doubt test. by Sanford Byron Gabin rev by Herbert Hovekamp grade B *8 Hastings Const. L.Q. 432-438 Wntr '81*

GABLE, Carl I., Jr.
Standby letters of credit: nomenclature has confounded analysis. by Carl I. Gable Jr.
12 Law & Pol'y Int'l Bus. 903-945 Fall '80

GABOR, Francis A.
A socialist approach to codification of private international law in Hungary: comments and translation. (includes text of code) by Francis A. Gabor *55 Tul. L. Rev. 63-113 Dec '80*

GABOR, Thomas
The crime displacement hypothesis: An empirical examination. by Thomas Gabor
27 Crime & Delinquency 390-404 July '81

GABRIEL, Jack E.
Tax-free step-up in basis for complex trust beneficiary (revisited). (response to Paul Galvin article in Mar. 1981 issue) by Jack E. Gabriel
12 Tax Adviser 224 April '81

GABRIEL, James H.
Domestic relations - Application of the parental preference rule. (case note) by James H. Gabriel
2 Miss. C.L. Rev. 73-84 June '80

GABRIELLI, William F., Jr.
EEG as a predictor of antisocial behavior. by Sarnoff A. Mednick, Jan Volavka, William F. Gabrielli Jr. and Turan M. Itil
19 Criminology 219-229 Aug '81

GABRIELSKI, Robert C.
The sale of almost patented property to a related person will no longer be taxed at capital gains rates in the Ninth Circuit. (Ninth Circuit Survey) by Robert C. Gabrielski
11 Golden Gate U.L. Rev. 417-431 Spr '81
Employment-related expenditures may lead to deductions or exclusions in the Ninth Circuit. (Ninth Circuit Survey) by Robert C. Gabrielski
11 Golden Gate U.L. Rev. 383-417 Spr '81

GABRIELSSON, T.
Income tax practices maintained by France: report of the panel. (for GATT) by L.J. Mariadason, W. Falconer, F. Forte, T. Gabrielsson and A.R. Prest
13 Tax Notes 1258-1264 Nov 23 '81

GACEK, Stanley A.
The employer's duty to bargain on termination of unit work. (part 1) by Stanley A. Gacek
32 Lab. L.J. 659-678 Oct '81

GADBAW, Michael
Multilateral trade negotiations: dispute settlement. (transcript) by Robert E. Hudec, Thomas R. Graham, John H. Jackson, Donald E. DeKieffer and Michael Gadbaw
Am. Soc. Int'l L. Proc. 129-145 Ann '80

GAEBLER, David B.
Union political activity or collective bargaining? First Amendment limitations on the uses of union shop funds. (Symposium on labor law) by David B. Gaebler *14 U.C.D.L. Rev. 591-619 Spr '81*

798

Illustration G

A sample page from the "Author-Title Index" of *Current Law Index.*

TABLE OF CASES

A.A. Store Fixture Company, Inc. v. Kouzoukas,
410 N.E. 2d 131 (Ill. 1980) Judgment revival ... notice requirement. *86 Com. L.J. 59 Feb '81*

A. Agar v. The Queen,
(1980) C.T.C. 397 Payment to services company for services rendered by taxpayer - arrangement held to constitute a sham. (Canada)
28 Can. Tax J. 790-791 Nov-Dec '80

A and M Consolidated Independent School District, Marshall v,
605 F.2d 186 (5th Cir. 1979) Employment discrimination. (1979 Fifth Circuit survey)
31 Mercer L. Rev. 921-950 Summ '80

A.B. v. Lewis,
No.M. 13740 (August 21, 1979) Get behind me Satan; or some recent decisions on the Administrative Law Act 1978. (Australia)
12 Melb. U.L. Rev. 417-424 June '80

A.C. Williams v. Hart,
No. 16328 (Boston Hous. Ct. July 29, 1980) The Massachusetts Consumer Protection Act, Chapter 93A - A look at provisions for double and treble damages, the written demand for relief, and reasonable attorney's fees.
16 New Eng. L. Rev. 449-480 Summ '81

A.E. and R.R. v. Mitchell,
No. C-78-466 (D. Utah June 16, 1980) Utah federal court reviews right to refuse treatment in a different light.
5 Mental Disab. L. Rep. 154-155 May-June '81

A.E. Nelson and Co. v. Haggett's Sport Shop,
418 A.2d 1273 (N.H. 1980) Secured transactions ... after-acquired inventory. *86 Com. L.J. 59 Feb '81*

A.F.E. Industries, Inc., Shanks v,
403 N.E.2d 849 (Ind. Ct. App. 1980) Foreword: products liability. (survey of Indiana law)
14 Ind. L. Rev. 1-64 Jan '81

A.F. Stoddard and Co. Ltd. v. Dann,
195 U.S.P.Q. 97 (D.C. Cir. 1977) Stoddard v. Dann revisited. *62 J. Pat. Off. Soc'y 575-579 Sept '80*

A.F. Stoddard and Company, Ltd. v. Dann,
195 U.S.P.Q. (BNA) 97 (1977) A tale of two applicants or how declaration and inventorship requirements raise

A.H. Robins Co. v. Medicine Chest Corp.,
206 U.S.P.Q. 1015 (E.D. Mo. 1980) U.S. courts in some cases hold that colors of drugs are protectable under principles of unfair competition and common law trademark. *79 Pat. & T.M. Rev. 15-17 Jan 81*

A-S Awilco v. Fabria S.p.A.,
(1981) 1 W.L.R. 314 Banking. (Great Britain)
J. Bus. L. 295-296 July '81

A-S Rosshavet, International Produce, Inc. v,
638 F.2d 548 (2d Cir. 1981) Arbitration: Appearance of bias is not a basis for vacating an award.
12 J. Mar. L. & Com. 407-410 April '81

A.V.C.O. Financial Services Ltd., Federal Commissioner of Taxation v,
(1980) 11 A.T.R. 401 Exchange gains: Borrowings by financiers and money-lenders. (Australia)
10 Austl. Tax Rev. 91-95 June '81

A.V.G. Management Science Ltd. v. Barwell Developments Ltd.,
(1979) 2 S.C.R. 43 Developments in property law: The 1978-79 and 1979-80 terms. (Canada)
2 Sup. Ct. L. Rev. 279-324 ann '81

A. v. Liverpool City Council,
(1981) 2 All E.R. 385 (House of Lords) Care order under Children and Young Persons Act 1969 - mother's access to child reduced - whether mother can invoke wardship jurisdiction to challenge local authority's decision. (Great Britain)
J. Soc. Welfare L. 300-302 Sept '81
(1981) 2 W.L.R. 948 Wardship and children in care. (Great Britain) *L.A.G. Bull. 190-191 Aug '81*

A., W. v,
(1981) 2 W.L.R. 124 Change of child's name. (Great Britain) *97 Law Q. Rev. 197-200 April '81*

AARON, SEC v,
605 F.2d 612 (2d Cir. 1979) Obscuring the standard for aiding and abetting liability. (Second Circuit review: 1979-80 term) (case note)
46 Brooklyn L. Rev. 1071-1101 Summ '80

AARON v. SEC,
100 S. Ct. 1945 (1980) Aaron v. SEC: the scienter requirement in SEC injunctive actions.
58 Den. L.J. 493-521 Spr '81
Injunctive relief under the antifraud provisions of the securities acts. (Supreme Court, 1979 term)
94 Harv. L. Rev. 270-279 Nov '80
Securities ... civil enforcement.
66 A.B.A.J. 1436 Nov '80
Securities - fraud - injunctions - the Securities and Exchange Commission must establish scienter in a civil enforcement action to enjoin violations of section 17(a)(1) of the Securities Act of 1933, section 10(B) of the Securities Exchange Act of 1934, and Rule 10b-5. (case note)
49 U. Cin. L. Rev. 937-949 Fall '80
446 U.S. 680 (1980) Aaron: the demise of equitable fraud under Section 10(b). (Symposium: securities law) *30 Emory L.J. 305-342 Wint '81*
Securities regulation: scienter means less protective power for the Securities and Exchange Commission. (case note) *46 Mod. L. Rev. 686-694 Summ '81*
Implication under Section 17(a) of the Securities Act of 1933 - The effect of Aaron v. SEC.
49 Fordham L. Rev. 1161-1177 May '81
The trend toward a strict construction of rule 10b-5. (case note) *13 Conn. L. Rev. 549-593 Spr '81*
A scienter requirement for SEC injunctions under section 10(b) - investor protection under the securities laws is further restricted. (case note)
22 B.C.L. Rev. 595-630 March '81

ABBEY v. Control Data Corp.,
603 F.2d 724 (8th Cir. 1979) The business judgment rule: Burks v. Lasker and other recent developments.
6 J. Corp. L. 453-480 Spr '81
The business judgment rule: A review of its application to the problem of illegal foreign payments. *6 J. Corp. L. 481-510 Spr '81*

ABBOTT Laboratories, Payton v,
83 F.R.D. 382 (D. Mass. 1979) Diethylstilbestrol: extension of federal class action procedures to generic drug litigation. *14 U.S.F.L. Rev. 461-493 Spr '80*

ABBOTT Laboratories, Sindell v,
26 Cal.3d 588 (1980) Manufacturers' liability based on a

Illustration H

"Table of Cases" in *Current Law Index.*

TABLE OF STATUTES

A.B.A. Code of Judicial Conduct
Judicial ethics: removal from office for political activity. (Missouri) (case note)
46 Mod. L. Rev. 676-685 Summ '81

A.B.A. Code of Professional Responsibility
The lawyer's obligation to be trustworthy when dealing with opposing parties.
33 S.C.L. Rev. 181-196 Dec '81

The continuing story of Code v. Kutak: a comparison that uncovers the trouble spots.
16 Docket Call 3(4) Fall '81

Former corporate counsel and client confidences in a derivative action.
23 Corp. Prac. Comment. 200-228 Summ '81

Developments in the law: conflicts of interest in the legal profession.
94 Harv. L. Rev. 1244-1503 April '81

Access to the disqualified attorney's work product: a plea for a strict prophylactic rule. (case note)
52 U. Colo. L. Rev. 465-487 Spr '81

Disclosure of incriminating physical evidence received from a client: the defense attorney's dilemma. *52 U. Colo. L. Rev. 419-463 Spr '81*

Lawyer solicitation today and under the proposed Model Rules of Professional Conduct.
52 U. Colo. L. Rev. 393-408 Spr '81

Teaching ethical considerations in the clinical setting: professional, personal and systemic.
52 U. Colo. L. Rev. 409-418 Spr '81

Professional responsibility issues in international law practice. *29 Am. J. Comp. L. 1-58 Wntr '81*

The representation of multiple insureds - defense counsel's perspective. (open forum: the insurance defense counsel on trial: outline)
48 Ins. Counsel J. 136-138 Jan '81

Competence and the professionally responsible lawyer. *29 Emory L.J. 971-995 Fall '80*

The rules of professional conduct in an era of change. (address to Bar Association of Boston in celebration of Boston's 350th anniversary)
29 Emory L.J. 889-908 Fall '80

Disqualifying counsel in corporate representation - eroding standards in changing times.
34 U. Miami L. Rev. 995-1042 July '80

Canon 9 The appearance of impropriety under Canon 9: a study of the federal judicial process applied to lawyers. *65 Minn. L. Rev. 243-265 Jan '81*

D.R. 2-102(e) The dual practitioner - DR 2-102(e).
5 J. Legal Prof. 191-207 ann '80

D.R. 5 Disciplinary Rules under canon V of the Code of Professional Responsibility.
51 Okla. B.J. 3089 Dec 31 '80

D.R. 7-107 Restrictions on attorneys' extrajudicial comments on pending litigation - the constitutionality of disciplinary rule 7-107. (case note)
41 Ohio St. L.J. 771-800 Summ '80

ADMINISTRATIVE Procedure Act
Constitutional issues in administrative practice.
55 Fla. B.J. 840-843 Dec '81

A unified corps of ALJs: a proposal to test the idea at the federal level. *65 Judicature 266-276 Nov '81*

Strict scrutiny: new rules, old games. (Regulatory Reform Act) *3 Am. Law. 61-62 Oct '81*

Counter revolution in the federal courts of appeal - the aftermath of Vermont Yankee. (case note)
15 U. Rich. L. Rev. 723-739 Spr '81

A French view of Vermont Yankee. (Vermont Yankee symposium)
55 Tul. L. Rev. 465-481 Feb '81

A British view of Vermont Yankee. (Vermont Yankee symposium)
55 Tul. L. Rev. 435-464 Feb '81

Judicial review of the Commodity Futures Trading Commission. (case note)
60 Neb. L. Rev. 152-168 Wntr '81

The judicial standard for review of environmental impact statement threshold decisions.
9 B.C. Envt'l Aff. L. Rev. 63-101 Wint '80-'81

Deference makes a difference: a study of impacts of the Bumpers Judicial Review Amendment.
49 U. Cin. L. Rev. 739-790 Fall '80

5 U.S.C. 500 Judicial review of informal rulemaking: waiting for Vermont Yankee II. (Vermont Yankee symposium) *55 Tul. L. Rev. 418-427 Feb '81*

5 U.S.C. 551 A Japanese view of Vermont Yankee. (Vermont Yankee symposium)
55 Tul. L. Rev. 482-489 Feb '81

5 U.S.C. 551-559 Administrative investigation - preventing agency disclosure of confidential business information. *28 U. Kan. L. Rev. 467-486 Spr '80*

5 U.S.C. 551-706 Rethinking regulation: negotiation as an alternative to traditional rulemaking.
94 Harv. L. Rev. 1871-1891 June '81

A right of rebuttal in informal rulemaking: may courts impose procedures to ensure rebuttal of ex parte communications and information derived from

Illustration I

"Table of Statutes" in *Current Law Index.*

AUTHOR INDEX 103

Hüffer, U.
Corporations – Germany, Western(Z)
Hülsen, H.-V. von
Products liability – USA(P)
Hulsman, L.H.C.
Criminal law: general – Netherlands(Z)
Hutchison, D.
Contracts – South Africa (Republic)(D)
Negligence – South Africa (Republic)(D)
Hutzelman, M.L.
Evidence – (I)
International judicial & legal assistance – (I)
Witnesses – (I)
Iakubov, A.E.
Penology – USSR(O)
Iampol'skaia, Ts.A.
Communism & socialism – USSR(D)
Trade unions – USSR(D)
Ianovski, B.
Hypothecary law – Bulgaria(R)
Legal history – (R)
Ideliovich, L.L.
Labour law – USSR(R)
Ijjas, J.
History – Hungary(C)
Iliasov, S.G.
Crime prevention – USSR(O)
Iliescu, N.
Criminal law: general – Roumania(U)
Ingelse, P.
Judgments – Netherlands(W)
Ionescu, N.
Arrest, detention & bail – Roumania(L)
Iorgovan, A.
Agriculture – Roumania(N)
Ipsen, H.P.
Arts – Germany, Western(M)
Labour management relations – Germany, Western(M)
Science – Germany, Western(M)
Isabirye, D.M.
Treaties – Kenya(S)
Isaev, I.A.
Legal history – USSR(K)
Ishanov, A.I.
History – USSR(P)
Iudica, G.
Inheritance & succession – Italy(D)
Iudin, V.Ia.
Economic activities & the state – USSR(P)
Iukov, M.K.
Civil procedure – USSR(D)
Iumashev, Iu.M.
International trade – European Communities(V)
Ivanashchenko, L.A.
Book Review (Vysotsiĭ)
Ivanov, I.V.
International organisations – Socialist Countries(P)
Ivanov, S.N.
Treaties – (V)
Ivanova, S.A.
Civil procedure – USSR(O)
Izdebski, H.
Civil rights – Poland(E)
Legal history – Poland(E)
Jackson, B.S.
Jewish law – (J)
Jäckle, W.
Debtors & creditors – Germany, Western(S)

Jäckle, W. -cont.

Hypothecary law – Germany, Western(S)
Jain, N.P.
International trade – Developing Countries(A)
Jain, S.N.
Water & watercourses – India(L)
Janse de Jonge, J.A.
Criminal law: general – Netherlands(P)
Jansen, G.J.
Administrative law & procedure – Netherlands(S)
Government immunity & liability – Netherlands(S)
Human rights (international law) – Europe(S)
Jappur, J.
Jurisprudence (philosophy of law) – Brazil(C)
Jarass, H.D.
Administrative law & procedure – France(B)
Administrative law & procedure – Germany, Western(B)
Public enterprises – France(S)
Jardim, T.L.
Administration of justice – Brazil(C)
Administration of justice – USA(C)
Courts & tribunals – USA(C)
Jayagovind, A.
Foreign aid – Developing Countries(T)
International trade – Developing Countries(T)
Investment, foreign – Developing Countries(T)
Patents – Developing Countries(I)
Jeammaud, A.
Labour law – France(D)
Labour management relations – France(D)
Jelačić, A.
Experts, expert witnesses & scientific evidence – Yugoslavia(S)
Medical jurisprudence – Yugoslavia(S)
Jelowik, L.
Biography: individual – (L)
Criminal law: general – Germany(K)
Legal history – Germany(K)
Jenkins, D.
Legal history – UK(M)
Jessup, P.C.
International adjudication – (I)
Jessurun d'oliveira, H.U.
Citizenship & nationality – Netherlands(H)
Divorce, separation & annulment – Netherlands(E)
Jestaz, P.
Legal history – France(P)
Jobbágyi, G.
Euthanasia – Hungary(E)
Johnston &
International law – (A)
Pollution & protection of the environment – (A)
Joko Smart, H.M.
African traditional law – Sierra Leone(P)
Islamic law – Sierra Leone(P)
Marriage – Sierra Leone(P)
Jong, H.M. de
Jurisprudence (philosophy of law) – (R)

Joutsamo, K.
Administration of justice – European Communities(S)
Jurisprudence (philosophy of law) – European Communities(S)
Precedents – European Communities(S)
Jović, L.
Public administration – Yugoslavia(O)
Joyner, C.C.
Maritime law (international) – (E)
Sovereignty – Antarctica(E)
Juenger, F.K.
Private international law: contracts – European Communities(P)
Private international law: general & principles – Europe(A)
Private international law: general & principles – USA(A)
Juglart, M. de
Liability (incl. culpa & dolus) – France(V)
Maritime law (commercial) – France(V)
Juncadella, S.
Corporations, foreign – America, Central(B)
Multinational corporations – America, Central(B)
Junger-Tas, J.
Sociology – Netherlands(J)
Jurgens, S.J.F.M.
Book Review (Bocken)
Kaasen, K.
Administrative law & procedure – Norway(N)
Continental shelf – Norway(N)
Oil & gas – Norway(N)
Kahale,III., G.
Arbitration: commerce, incl. foreign – USA(A)
Government immunity & liability – USA(A)
Private international law: choice of law & forum – USA(A)
Kahn, E.
Biography: individual – (B)
Judges – South Africa (Republic)(T)
Legal history – South Africa (Republic)(T)
Kahn, P.
Private international law: commercial law – (C)
Sales – (C)
Kahn-Freund, O.
Book Review (Morse)
Kandić, Z.
Criminal complicity – Yugoslavia(P)
Kanowitz, L.
Book Review ()
Kapor-Stanulović, N.
Legal history – Yugoslavia(Z)
Karl, F.
Damages & indemnity – Germany, Western(W)
Personal injuries – Germany, Western(W)
Karlov, A.A.
Economic activities & the state – USSR(P)
Karneeva, L.M.
Evidence: criminal law – USSR(D)
Karnell, G.
Copyright – Nordic Countries(A)
Kastner, K.
Defamation – Germany, Western(F)

Illustration J

A sample page from the "Author Index" of the *Index to Foreign Legal Periodicals.*

SUBJECT INDEX

Periodicals: *Titles:* The periodicals referred to are those listed on pages i-vii. Thus, for example, A115 refers to "Archiv des öffentlichen Rechts" and D55 to "Droit Social".

References: The symbol for the periodical is followed by an indication of the volume (or year) and the pages on which the article, etc., begins and ends, *e.g.,* 29:331-340 means "volume (year) 29, pages 331-340."

Date or coverage of publication: The abbreviation for the volume (year) and pages is followed by a reference to the time period for which the issue was published; *e.g.,* Mr '66 means "March 1966".

Ja	January	Jy	July
F	February	Ag	August
Mr	March	S	September
Ap	April	O	October
My	May	N	November
Je	June	D	December

Form of title: This is normally given as published, *transliterated* according to the Library of Congress rules for those languages not using the Roman alphabet. *Initial articles* are omitted where possible. Where an article is *printed in two (or more) languages,* the first or main language of the title is used followed by, *e.g.* [In French and German]. Where an article has a title in a *more widely understood language* (e.g. a Polish article having a title in English), the title would be given in that language, with a note indicating the language of the article (e.g. [In Polish]). Where the translation of a title has been supplied by the indexer, it is enclosed in square brackets. *Summaries* of articles in other languages are shown as, *e.g.* [Summ. in French]. Articles published in a *series* are shown as [I] [II], etc.

Arrangement: Under each subject heading, any general articles on that subject are given first. These are followed by sub-divisions for countries or special aspects of a subject where appropriate. Titles under main headings and those in sub-divisions are arranged in separate alphabetical sequences according to the initial letter of the first main word of the title (initial articles being omitted or disregarded). The only exception to this arrangement is for entries under Biography: Individual, which are sorted by the surname of the person written about, and this name, in square brackets, precedes the entry.

ABORTION

Derecho a la vida y delito de aborto.
J.M. Martínez Val. *E15 38:449-471 S '79*

France

Evolución de la legislación francesa sobre el aborto y la ley de 17 de enero de 1975 "relativa a la interrupción voluntaria del embarazo".
M. Lions. *B40 14:1199-1244 S-D '81*

South Africa (Republic)

Can a foetus be protected from its mother?
S. Bedil. *S50 98:462-466 N '81*

ACCESSION & ACCRETION

Yugoslavia

Stjecanje prava vlasništva preradom, sjedinjenjem, izgradnjom zgrade i odvajanjem plodova. [Summ. in German.]
N. Gavella. *Z3 31:39-79 '81*

ACCOUNTING & AUDITING

Belgium

Boekhoudrecht en boekhoudtheorie. [Summ. in French, English & German.]
S. van Crombrugge. *T20 18:973-1021 O-D '81*

Italy

Questione delle divergenze tra normativa di diritto commerciale e tributario sul reddito d'impresa.
G. Falsitta. *R385 26:870-920 Jy-O '81*

ACTIONS & DEFENCES

Prix de la nature.
M. Rémond-Gouilloud. *R30 33-36 F '82*

Netherlands

Voorontwerp van een wet gelijke behandeling en class actions.
J.W.J. van den Oord. *N5 57:394-404 Mr '82*

ADMINISTRATION OF JUSTICE

Justice: restaurer la confiance.
M. Storme. *J40 101:133-136 F '82*

"Poder judicial: implicaciones políticas de la función jurisdiccional".
E. Liberati. *B25 44:163-174 Ja-D '80*

Belgium

Onverenigbaarheid van het ambt van onderzoeksrechter met dat van rechter in eerste aanleg of appelrechter en het recht van de beklaagde op een onpartijdige rechtbank.
B. Maes. *R25 45:1857-1870 Mr '82*

Brazil

Congestionamento do Supremo Tribunal Federal e da Suprema Corte Americana.
T.L. Jardim. *R155 77:93-99 Ja-Mr '81*

Cameroon

Abiding influence of English and French criminal law in one African country: some remarks regarding the machinery of criminal justice in Cameroon.
P. Bringer. *J50 25:1-13 '81*

European Communities

Contribution du pouvoir judiciaire à l'intégration de la Communauté économique européenne.
W. van Gerven. *J40 101:244-248 F '82*

Some aspects of the impact of the Court of Justice on integration in the European Communities.
K. Joutsamo. *N55 50:75-84 '81*

Italy

Sull'amministrazione della giustizia nell'anno 1981.
S. Borghese. *F25 105:21-28 Ja '82*

Nicaragua

Strategie revolutionärer Justizentwicklung in Nikaragua.
K.-H. Schöneburg. *S80 30:1107-1117 '81*

Illustration K

A sample page from the "Subject Index" of the *Index to Foreign Legal Periodicals.*

rently consists of three bound cumulative volumes covering the years 1958–68, 1969–73, and 1974–78. Since 1978, it has been supplemented by quarterly issues. Each volume contains a list of subjects under which articles are indexed and a list of the authors of articles. The advent of *Current Law Index* and *Legal Resources Index,* which include many of the same periodicals, has cast some doubt on the continuance of *Index to Periodical Articles Related to Law,* but is still being issued at the time of this publication. Illustration L illustrates a page from the *Index to Periodical Articles Related to Law.*

5. OTHER INDEXING SOURCES

In addition to the coverage of Commonwealth legal periodicals in the standard indexes described above, there are several other indexes which include many more periodicals for the specific areas indicated:

(a) *Index to Canadian Legal Literature* (3 vols., 1981, with quarterly supplements). Includes monographs and periodical articles.

(b) *Index to Canadian Legal Periodicals* (1965 – date, three quarterly issues, cumulated with the fourth quarter in an annual volume).

(c) *Index to Commonwealth Index Periodicals* (1982 cumulation covers Sept. 1978–Aug. 1981; previously published bi-monthly since Sept. 1974).

(d) *Current Australian and New Zealand Legal Literature Index* (quarterly, non-cumulating index, since 1973; there is some doubt about its current status).

(e) *Index to Indian Legal Literature* (1963–date, semi-annual, with annual cumulations).

Another important index of secondary legal materials was the *Current Legal Bibliography/Annual Legal Bibliography,* published by the Harvard Law Library from 1961 to 1981. This index provided only subject access by broad topical headings, but covered a very wide range of publications. All periodicals and all monographs acquired and cataloged by the Harvard Law School Library were included—not only American sources, but foreign and international law as well. Thus, almost two thousand periodicals in law and related fields were indexed, more than twice the number covered by *I.L.P.* and *I.F.L.P.* combined. It was also the only regular indexing tool for texts *and* monographs during that period. *Current Legal Bibliography* appeared monthly for nine months of the year, and then cumulated into the much-expanded *Annual Legal Bibliography.* Each issue and volume included separate sections for common law and civil law jurisdictions, and for public international law, and an overall subject index aided the reader. *ALB/CLB* was perhaps the most ambitious universal index to domestic, foreign and international secondary legal sources ever attempted. Its termination in 1981 left a major gap in the apparatus of legal research, but the Harvard Law Library is now exploring new means of providing comparable coverage.

INFORMED CONSENT (Cont'd.)

Informed consent in California. Latent liability without 'negligence'. A. Fine. Western Journal of Medicine. 127:158-163. Aug., 1977.

Informed consent to medical treatment. Gene R. Beaty and Thomas Knapp. The Air Force Law Review. 19:63-75. Spring, 1977.

Some observations on informed consent in non-therapeutic research. J.C. Garnham. Journal of Medical Ethics. 1:138-145. Sept., 1975.

Tests of competency to consent to treatment. L.H. Roth, A. Meisel, and C.W. Lidz. American Journal of Psychiatry. 134:279-284. Mar., 1977.

Toward a model of the legal doctrine of informed consent. A. Meisel, L.H. Roth, and C.W. Lidz. American Journal of Psychiatry. 134:285-289. Mar., 1977.

INSANITY
(See also: Criminal Law and Procedure, Medical Jurisprudence)

Anglo-American criminal insanity: an historical perspective. Jacques M. Quen. The Bulletin of the American Academy of Psychiatry and the Law. 11:115-123. June, 1974; 10:313-323. July, 1974.

The determination of criminal insanity in western Nigeria. Leigh Bienen. Journal of Modern African Studies. 14:219-246. June, 1976.

The insanity defense: a juridical anachronism. Abraham L. Halpern. Psychiatric Annals. 7:41-65. Aug., 1977.

Insanity defense in Canada. J. Arboleda-Florez. Canadian Psychiatric Association Journal. 23:23-27. Feb., 1978.

The New Jersey insanity defense: present and proposed. Howard A. Cohen. Criminal Justice Quarterly. 2:38-53. Winter, 1974.

The policy implications of predictive decision-making: "likelihood" and "dangerousness" in civil commitment proceedings. A. Fagin. Public Policy. 24:491-528. Fall, 1976.

Punishing the not guilty: hospitalization of persons acquitted by reason of insanity. J.R. German, A.C. Singer. Psychiatric Quarterly. 49:238-254. Fall, 1977.

Sex and race as factors affecting the attribution of insanity in a murder trial. R.P. McGlynn, J.C: Megas, and D.H. Benson. Journal of Psychology. 93:93-99. May, 1976.

INSURANCE
(See also: Automobile Insurance)

The insurer's liability for judgments in excess of policy limits and the movement toward strict liability: an assessment. Donald A. Orlovsky. Nova Law Journal. 1:31-46. Spring, 1977.

109

Illustration L

A sample page from the *Index to Periodical Articles Related to Law (Glanville Publishers).*

For researchers who prefer scanning the recent issues of periodicals to detailed subject indexing, there are current contents services available. These services are compendia of the actual contents lists of current legal periodicals and enable the reader to know what is being published (at least by author and title) in the numerous issues of legal periodicals that appear each month. Many law school libraries produce such services by photocopying contents pages for the use of their own faculty and staff, and several are published at the national level. One of the most prominent is *Legal Contents* (formerly called *Contents of Current Legal Periodicals*), published by the Corporation Service Company. Since 1972, this service reproduces and distributes in a pamphlet format facsimile copies of the tables of contents of recently published legal periodicals on a monthly basis. A recent competitor offering a similar *weekly* service is *Law Review Ink*, published in Concord, Mass.

To fill the gap created by the time lag in the publication of the *Index to Legal Periodicals*, the Marian G. Gallagher Law Library of the University of Washington issues its weekly, *Current Index to Legal Periodicals.* This popular service arranges citations to articles in the major law reviews received during the preceding week into a convenient subject order. Illustration M shows a sample page from the *Current Index.*

It should also be noted that many standard legal research tools which are primarily designed for other purposes carry references, where relevant, to periodical articles as well. Among these are some looseleaf services and a number of West publications, including *Corpus Juris Secundum*, case digests, and annotated codes.

With the expansion of legal research into many interdisciplinary areas, indexes from related fields have become increasingly important to lawyers and other users of legal materials; for example, the *Public Affairs Information Service, Social Science Index, Social Science Citation Index*, and similar indexing and abstracting services.

The field of taxation is particularly well covered by a variety of specialized periodical services and access tools. These include the following publications:

(a) *Monthly Digest of Tax Articles*—a monthly magazine containing condensed versions of recent periodical articles on taxation.

(b) *CCH Federal Tax Articles*—a looseleaf reporter, issued in monthly installments, containing abstracts of tax articles and conference papers, arranged by sections of the Internal Revenue Code.

(c) *Index to Federal Tax Articles* (Warren, Gorham & Lamont, 1975)—a comprehensive index, by author and subject, of periodical articles and other publications in all fields of taxation, with quarterly supplements.

For those busy readers who are willing to peruse condensed versions of arbitrarily selected articles in a variety of legal fields, there are two publications available—*Law Review Digest* (bi-monthly) and the *Monthly Digest of Legal Articles.* A similar compilation, established in 1979, is the *National Law Review Reporter* (published in New York City by The Reporter) which reprints a selection of complete articles six times a year. Hardly useful for research purposes,

CURRENT INDEX TO LEGAL PERIODICALS

M. G. Gallagher Law Library

University of Washington School of Law

Key to Citations ---- October 22, 1982

Amer.U.	31 American University Law Review, No. 4, Summer,
DeP.	30 DePaul Law Review, No. 3, Spring, 1981.
Env.	12 Environmental Law, No. 4, Summer, 1982.
*Gold.	12 Golden Gate University Law Review, No. 3, Summer,
J.Marsh.	15 John Marshall Law Review, No. 3, Summer, 1982.
Nat.Res.	22 Natural Resources Journal, No. 3, July, 1982.
O.D.	11 Ocean Development and International Law, Nos. 3/4, Pp. 149-320, 1982.
S.T.	23 South Texas Law Journal, No. 1, Pp. 1-257, 1982.
S.Cal.	55 Southern California Law Review, No. 6, September, 1982.
Tenn.	49 Tennessee Law Review, No. 3, Spring, 1982.
U.Ill.	1982 University of Illinois Law Review, No. 1, Pp. 1-384, 1982.
Vermont	7 Vermont Law Review, No. 1, Spring, 1982.
**Wayne	28 Wayne Law Review, No. 2, Winter, 1982.
***W.Va.	84 West Virginia Law Review, No. 3, April, 1982.

* A portion of this issue comprises a Survey: Women and California Law.

** This entire issue comprises the 1981 Annual Survey of Michigan Law.

*** A portion of this issue comprises a Survey of Developments in the Fourth Circuit: 1981.

ADMINISTRATIVE LAW

Hand, J. Douglas. Survey. 28 Wayne 517-552.

EPA administrator has broad discretion in SDWA aquifer designation. (*Montgomery County Maryland v. Environmental Protection Agency*, 16 Envir. Rep., BNA, 1541, 1981.) 22 Nat.Res. 707-709.

ARTS

Unraveling the choreographer's copyright dilemma. 49 Tenn. 594-621.

ATOMIC ENERGY

Ninth Circuit upholds nuclear power moratorium provision. (*Pacific Legal Foundation v. State Energy Resources Conservation & Development Commission*, 659 F.2d 903, 9th Cir. 1981.) 22 Nat.Res. 689-698.

BANKRUPTCY

Bankruptcy after divorce: rights and liabilities of former spouses in Texas. 23 S.T. 173-186.

Bankruptcy Symposium. 84 W.Va. 573-702.

Bankruptcy preference concerns in industrial development bond financing. . . . . . .C. Edward Dobbs, & . . . . .Margaret M. Joslin 573

An enhanced conception of the bankruptcy judge: from case administrator to unbiased adjudicator. . . . . Richard L. Levine 637

Attorney fees: handling bankruptcies without getting there yourself. . . . . .Edwin F. Flowers 669

Bankruptcy reform and the Constitution: retroactive application of Section 522(f)(2) "takes" private property. . .James B. Craven III, & . . . . Pamela A. Bates-Smith 687

CIVIL RIGHTS

Feiger, Lynn D., and Leslie M. Lawson. Evaluation of an employment discrimination case: the plaintiff's perspective. 15 J.Marsh. 621-631.

Hill, Marvin F., Jr., and Curtiss K. Behrens. Love in the office: a guide for dealing with sexual harassment under Title VII of the Civil Rights Act of 1964. 30 DeP. 581-622.

The application of Section 1983 to the violation of federal statutory rights. (*Maine v. Thiboutot*, 448 U.S. 1, 1980.) 30 DeP. 651-667.

Coerced resignation creates Fifth Amendment *Bivens* remedy. (*Sonntag v. Dooley*, 650 F.2d 904, 7th Cir. 1981.) 15 J.Marsh. 693-705.

Conference: The American Red Cross--Washington College of Law Conference: International Humanitarian Law. 31 Amer.U. 805-1029.

Introduction. . . Thomas Buergenthal, .Jerome H. Holland, & Alexandre Hay 805

Illustration M

A sample page from the *Current Index to Legal Periodicals.*

these current surveys of selected articles apparently attract a sufficient audience to justify their existence.

6. SHEPARD'S LAW REVIEW CITATIONS

Beginning in 1957, Shepard's has offered a unique citator service for periodical articles in its *Shepard's Law Review Citations.* This unusual citator lists as *cited* matter, periodical articles, comments, and notes since 1947, by reference to their volume and page citations. It then gives for each citation subsequent references to the piece, appearing in other articles or in any reported federal or state court decision since 1957. This enables the researcher who is interested in a particular article, its author, or a position taken therein, to locate other periodical articles or judicial decisions which have discussed or cited that article. Illustration N shows a sample page from that citator.

As noted above in Chapter 9, Citators, Shepard's also includes, as *citing* material in all of its state citators, articles from selected periodicals which have dealt with the primary legal sources listed there. These periodicals generally include the legal periodicals published in the state covered by the citator and twenty major law reviews. Since 1974, Shepard's has provided similar periodical coverage for federal court decisions and federal statutory material in its service, *Federal Law Citations in Selected Law Reviews.* The citing references are from nineteen major law reviews and journals. Illustration O shows a sample page from that citator.

D. SUMMARY

Legal periodicals comprise one of the most important secondary source materials. Because of their number and variety, they offer assistance in almost every research situation. They can serve as sources of persuasive authority or as repositories of citations to other materials. Long accessible through traditional indexing, the recent competition stimulated by new indexes and citators has improved access considerably. The use of legal periodicals and their indexes should be a regular part of the sophisticated lawyer's research strategy.

E. ADDITIONAL READING

H.C. Havighurst, "Law Reviews and Legal Education," 51 *Northwestern L.Rev.* 24 (1956).

"The Law Review—Is it Meeting the Needs of the Legal Community?" 44 *Denver L.J.* 426 (1967).

Vol. 63 AMERICAN JOURNAL OF INTERNATIONAL LAW

Vol. 63

– 1 –
73WLR75

– 47 –
51OLR797
14SDL607

– 86 –
62KLJ336
8SDL463
9SDL474
16SDL492

– 197 –
20DeP599

– 211 –
15SDL415

– 224 –
27AU215

– 237 –
70FRD157
24AU929
19Buf35
60Cor263
21DeP275
21DeP308
6Hof859
53ILJ625
71LF10
24MiL387
72NwL263
24NYF201
51TLQ449
51TuL225
81YLJ602

– 272 –
56ABA72
7GaL81

– 284 –
17CLA89
121PaL3
50TxL894

– 415 –
26AU265
20DeP355
59KLJ687
19KLR379
31PitL217
19SDR259
44StJ392
44StJ472
22StLJ610

– 444 –
61CaL145
20DeP583
20DeP677
10LoyL22
53TuL519

– 490 –
54BUR710
7SDL442
16SDL492
73WLR123
14WML204

– 504 –
51OLR794

– 514 –
49CK20
22HLJ634
23HLJ1354
71LF206
41UCR539

– 521 –
21SR409

– 536 –
16NYF337

– 544 –
14StLJ413

– 591 –
25FLR475
69McL6

– 695 –
16AzL701
19DeP218
16NYF543
9SwR101

– 711 –
14AzL671
65NwL771
56VaL587

– 875 –
351FS707
61CaL117
70McL885
18NYF372

Vol. 64

– 19 –
18CLA342
53ILJ638

– 42 –
24HLJ67
18HWL371
51OLR794
7SDL394
16SDL638

– 62 –
51OLR794
7SDL394

– 64 –
10Duq164

– 73 –
26AU265
19KLR379
19SDR259
44StJ392

– 152 –
16NYF337
51OLR809

– 211 –
59KLJ673
59KLJ682

– 229 –
18HWL366
16NYF327
14SDL565

– 270 –
19KLR386
19SDR259

– 277 –
49CK27

– 310 –
58Cor552
64IBJ419
9JMJ8
9JMJ169
46StJ717
8Val587

– 344 –
19KLR424
81YLJ653

– 349 –
71CR71
16NYF345

– 398 –
69McL16

– 471 –
69McL16
70McL508
50OLR523

– 481 –
69McL16
70McL508

– 495 –
71CR42
24DeP844
23KLR242
65NwL767
25SCR558
73WLR78

– 562 –
14SDL565

– 809 –
49DJ65
19KLR389
47NDL69

– 853 –
14AzL674
61MqL257
58VaL430

– 905 –
8SDL492

Vol. 65

– 1 –
10Duq156
81YLJ601

– 38 –
57Cor745
10Duq159

– 84 –
4AlkR279
25FLR491
24HLJ91
59KLJ674
33LJ83
7LWR391
70McL470
11SDL638

– 131 –
25FLR489
40FR553
24HLJ78
33LJ86
7LWR394
50OLR490

– 253 –
27AU228
24HLJ105

– 327 –
9SwR9
83YLJ916

– 459 –
27Buf709
75DCL81
7Val86
12Val297
32W&L49
32W&L69
81YLJ638

– 476 –
24AU1010

– 532 –
14BCR79

– 544 –
49DJ66

– 713 –
26AU271
7Akr419
6InLR207
32W&L70

– 757 –
24HLJ90
7LWR410
37PitL506
11SDL544
11SDL646
29StnL1139
51TuL1123
73WLR131

Vol. 66

– 1 –
26AU270
7Akr401
7Akr407
50TxL851

– 60 –
23WnL1046

– 82 –
406US773
32LE485
92SC1816
44CUR173
52ILJ610
3ONU120
9SwR1

– 255 –
14AzL671
60ILR1105

– 290 –
4EnL94
24HLJ86

– 321 –
12Crt778
75DCL85

– 337 –
24AU1016
61CaL119
12Crt776
75DCL81
63MnL43
24NYF68

– 509 –
25StnL698

– 537 –
23AU323

– 763 –
23AU301
78AzS199
33BL1805
10CFW33
78CR1623
27Mer514
49NDL321
48TuL482

– 795 –
49NYL390
53NYL114

Vol. 67

– 1 –
73WLR68

– 63 –
37LCP422
37LCP548
38LCP265
48TuL545

– 84 –
25SCR559

– 275 –
24AU1055
12Crt776
75DCL87
22StLJ608

– 465 –
75AzS271

– 641 –
16Duq296
8RCL214

– 693 –
75AzS271

– 711 –
52ILJ610

Vol. 68

– 1 –
18HWL384
74LF253
45MLJ1099
17SAC531
12SDL637
15SDL495
28StnL1114
29StnL1135
9SwR662
52WsL203

– 33 –
9SwR646

– 69 –
26AU222
12Crt747
63IBJ452
72NwL239
23NYF207
5ONU441

– 217 –
10CnL414

– 221 –
33MiL414

– 258 –
15SDL502

– 391 –
24CLA1126

– 410 –
24AU1111
7Akr400
7Akr417
60Cor231
54TxL1356
33W&L346

– 475 –
26AU48
8LoyC472
27Mer497

– 591 –
24AU1111
54TxL1357

46

Illustration N

A sample page from *Shepard's Law Review Citations.*

UNITED STATES SUPREME COURT REPORTS **Vol. 328**

52TxL837
53TxL1188
54TxL211
55TxL46
55TxL85
57TxL712
61VaL526
61VaL1403
63VaL778
65VaL803
66VaL900
82WLR57
84YLJ270
91YLJ256

– 88 –
75CR483
79CR253
68Geo6
71McL891
76McL105
68VaL370
90YLJ744

– 99 –
20CLA688
66Cor571
82CR24
62Geo104
70Geo909
87HLR696
91HLR357
91HLR1254
92HLR1005
80LF983
78McL315
78McL886
60MnL103
74NwL783
49NYL397
56NYL1256
122PaL601
122PaL1084
122PaL1202
128PaL72
129PaL295
30StnL109
32StnL665
55TxL399
55TxL1165
57TxL194
84YLJ25
85YLJ754

– 120 –
69CaL356
75CR89
68Geo58
55NYL1061
28StnL1145
55TxL282
75WLR368
83YLJ1575
88YLJ1343

– 135 –
75LF560
74McL519
75McL1581
57MnL70
72NwL25
83YLJ45

– 207 –
25StnL346
91YLJ451

– 224 –
73McL487
88YLJ54

– 236 –
80CR936

– 265 –
59Cor1000
61VaL20

– 271 –
58Cor1089
64Geo819

– 287 –
26CLA272
122PaL349

– 310 –
69CaL254
70CaL686
45ChL610
49ChL463
26CLA450
61Cor190
62Cor96
62Cor152
66Cor415
66Cor566
73CR765
78CR1591
81CR961
81CR1016
81CR1047
62Geo162
69Geo1188
69Geo1350
91HLR375
92HLR1005
82IlLR115
41LCP(3)147
73LF243
72McL479
78McL872
78McL1083
60MnL102
66MnL335
66MnL736
68NwL24
70NwL395
70NwL495
74NwL717
74NwL742
75NwL366
75NwL1112
53NYL34
53NYL104
25StnL551
25StnL672
27StnL616
28StnL721
29StnL502
30StnL848
34StnL397
58TxL520
59VaL367
75WLR590
82WLR347
90YLJ107

– 327 –
43ChL755
44ChL47
48ChL241
64Cor817

75CR784
78CR282
40LCP(4)255
65MnL67
72NwL139
74NwL886
52TxL1293
55TxL75
59TxL910
59VaL1171
61VaL486
64VaL238
64VaL1322
77WLR649
82YLJ1601
83YLJ458

– 340 –
25CLA484
64Geo1013
67Geo1139
94HLR500
76LF665
122PaL349
125PaL1300
27StnL1405
51TxL877
59TxL57
76WLR1146

– 367 –
122PaL349

– 371 –
65Geo1510
60VaL44
83YLJ64

– 376 –
21CLA157
81CR500
73NwL17
122PaL358

– 404 –
73McL75
130PaL346
86YLJ859

– 432 –
86HLR657

– 438 –
64Cor357
66Cor427
73CR793
76CR935
67Geo1108
69Geo978
87HLR720
91HLR344
57MnL831
60MnL99
74NwL713
122PaL1250
28StnL433

– 446 –
63CaL634
61Cor964

– 455 –
25CLA1037
88HLR1085

– 465 –
122PaL336
122PaL922
55TxL646

– 480 –
122PaL336
58TxL10

– 490 –
69CaL381
30StnL1124

– 496 –
63MnL616

– 501 –
43ChL41
43ChL276
26CLA518
28CLA537
62Cor455
63Cor4
66Cor637
73CR222
78CR1030
79CR1279
61Geo1126
65Geo778
69Geo757
91HLR35
38LCP537
43LCP(3)74
75LF89
75McL28
76McL99
76McL261
77McL1009
60MnL1133
61MnL434
64MnL504
70NwL160
122PaL962
126PaL622
26StnL835
34StnL1008
52TxL268
52TxL663
52TxL850
59TxL1360
59VaL377
60VaL19
60VaL757
65VaL843
77WLR7
82WLR191
90YLJ780
91YLJ245

– 521 –
81IlLR580
122PaL336
85YLJ862

– 561 –
60Cor93

– 572 –
44ChL291
48ChL837
25CLA1341
61Cor930
78CR1036
79CR886
89HLR712
41LCP(3)162

44LCP(3)258
71NwL349
74NwL422
49NYL56
54NYL724
53TxL955
62VaL538
66VaL1079
76WLR1146
86YLJ1166
86YLJ1224
86YLJ1558

– 599 –
122PaL336

– 620 –
65CaL833
92HLR1702
72NwL164

– 630 –
76LF691
76LF707
122PaL260

Vol. 327

– 1 –
68Geo10
37LCP174
64MnL598
83YLJ725

– 92 –
25CLA1337
73NwL21
49NYL55
68VaL448
76WLR1146
86YLJ1166
86YLJ1257

– 114 –
44ChL796
64Geo854
72NwL130
27StnL910
83YLJ459

– 146 –
74CR385
76CR1222
44LCP(4)46
49NYL60
123PaL55
127PaL90
55TxL71
63VaL749
63VaL1256
90YLJ529

– 161 –
88HLR1385
57MnL459

– 173 –
66Cor214

– 178 –
61VaL1403

– 186 –
75CR873
61Geo12

61Geo605
65Geo756
69Geo69
76LF1088
74McL230
58MnL451
60MnL416
64MnL76
127PaL1492
129PaL633
52TxL837
63VaL760
75WLR306
91YLJ253

– 220 –
81CR1053
65Geo19
66MnL755
75NwL385

– 251 –
70CaL901
41ChL88
24CLA484
77CR709
60MnL1236
64MnL756
73NwL759
51NYL383
86YLJ500
86YLJ809

– 280 –
67Cor70
122PaL350

– 293 –
67Cor70
122PaL350

– 304 –
26CLA15
37LCP176
40LCP(3)57
42LCP(2)198
58MnL242
62MnL806
121PaL3
59TxL861
61VaL1213
82YLJ1419

– 358 –
82CR934
122PaL309

– 385 –
70CaL561
122PaL358

– 392 –
70CaL535
78CR1416
78CR1488
87HLR737
78McL313
49NYL1111
52NYL1310
55TxL400
65VaL646

– 404 –
122PaL336

– 416 –
20CLA750
65MnL1056

– 512 –
122PaL350

– 515 –
61Geo614
59TxL1183
65VaL282

– 546 –
75CR490
75McL256
52TxL224

– 558 –
89HLR705

– 573 –
49ChL701
62Cor277
126PaL517
126PaL1222
66VaL1090

– 582 –
65CaL838
46ChL646
49NYL830
122PaL1172
55TxL1162

– 608 –
59Cor511
68Geo758
90HLR695
57MnL231
61MnL711
64VaL299

– 645 –
43LCP(4)38
64MnL482

– 661 –
61CaL680
65Cor62

– 678 –
61CaL692
62CaL1159
67CaL1258
69CaL226
69CaL382
29CLA52
79CR213
65Geo1538
89HLR347
40LCP(2)131
41LCP(3)153
59MnL1007
68NwL58
70NwL274
70NwL771
71NwL734
72NwL543
55NYL561
55TxL600
59TxL850
67VaL566
75WLR527
86YLJ848

– 686 –
83YLJ704

– 711 –
63Cor95

– 726 –
88HLR1379
79McL1513
70NwL879
85YLJ750

– 742 –
79CR1245

Vol. 328

– 1 –
53TxL1412
55TxL977

– 12 –
122PaL591

– 25 –
122PaL338

– 61 –
61Geo1134
62Geo1295
40LCP(3)76

– 80 –
57MnL32

– 85 –
77McL1271
53TxL1412
55TxL977
60VaL1234

– 108 –
75WLR311
91YLJ503

– 123 –
58MnL508

– 134 –
58MnL523
64MnL366

– 152 –
62Cor251
76CR448
68Geo58
37LCP14
40LCP(1)86
75McL255
28StnL1125

– 204 –
41LCP(2)121
54NYL727
56NYL1251
122PaL601

– 217 –
65CaL778
69CaL74
41LCP(1)206
43LCP(4)144
76McL1045
27StnL553
67VaL917

53

Illustration O

A sample page from Shepards *Federal Law Citations in Selected Law Reviews.*

D.B. Maggs, "Concerning the Extent to Which the Law Review Contributes to the Development of the Law," 3 *So.Calif.L.Rev.* 181 (1930).

O. Maru, "Measuring the Impact of Legal Periodicals," 1976 *American Bar Foundation Research Journal* 227.

R.M. Mersky, R.C. Berring, & J.K. McCue, editors, *Author's Guide to Journals in Law, Criminal Justice and Criminology* (Haworth Press, 1979) Chapter 1.

F. Rodell, "Goodbye to Law Reviews," 23 *U. of Va.L.Rev.* 38 (1936).

Chapter 17

GENERAL RESEARCH AND REFERENCE SOURCES

A. INTRODUCTION

The inclusion of a chapter on general reference materials in a book devoted to legal research may require explanation. Why would a legal researcher, immersed in a sea of legal materials, need guidance in the use of tools designed to provide access to facts and figures of a non-legal nature?

Most of a lawyer's routine work involves factual questions rather than great abstract issues of law. Lawyers are generally far less involved in litigation than in counselling, drafting, negotiation, informal dispute resolution—that is, in the prevention or avoidance of litigation. All of these functions require the ability to find and use facts effectively.

Even in litigation, the trial level focuses on fact finding and the proof of factual issues. Appellate litigation, which is largely concerned with legal issues, often requires access to non-legal data to understand those legal issues. Advocacy of any kind can be enhanced by a thorough grasp of the underlying (and often non-legal) basis of the issues being contested. In more poetic terms, Henry Finch, a late sixteenth century English lawyer, noted that "the sparks of all sciences in the world are raked up in the ashes of the law . . . "[1]

Most readers of this text, being law students, have already acquired general research skills in their undergraduate work. Those skills should include familiarity with the workings of a research library and the ability to do effective research in the literature of other academic disciplines. Because this chapter cannot provide a complete introduction to all areas of general research, a basic level of expertise must be assumed. Several standard guides to general research skills are included in Section 1.b of the bibliography at the end of this chapter to provide that basic introduction for the insecure. Perhaps the best short treatment available is Alden Todd's *Finding Facts Fast.*[2] It provides a brief introduction to the principles of good research, and citations to a wide range of current references sources.

This chapter will offer some general suggestions on how to locate and use non-legal information sources quickly and effectively. The problem will be approached in three ways in the three sections to follow. The first of these sections provides guidance on how to find and use the resources of non-legal library collections. The next section offers a general description of ten different categories of reference material.[3] The last of these sections consists of selective bibliographies of specific titles for research and reference in the areas covered by this chapter.

A caveat of personal preference should be noted. There are many reference sources in the areas described below, with much duplication and overlapping. What follows is a subjective treatment, with the listed sources chosen on the basis of the authors' own preferences. Other researchers might choose other, equally satisfactory titles. What is offered here is only a sampling of the rich universe of reference tools.[4] The most comprehensive listing of standard reference books in all fields is Eugene Sheehy's *Guide to Reference Books,*[5] described below.

B. FINDING AND USING LIBRARY RESOURCES

1. FINDING THE APPROPRIATE LIBRARY

Most of the basic reference tools, described in Section C and listed in Section D, contain general information and can be found in the reference collection of any large research library. Frequently, however, the information needed will not be general in nature, but rather quite

1. *Law, or a Discourse thereof* (London, 1678 edition) p. 6.

2. 2d ed. Berkeley, Ca., Ten Speed Press, 1979.

3. Chapter 18, which follows, focuses specifically and in greater detail on one particular area of concern, Social Science Literature.

4. For another view of general reference titles that may be of use to legal researchers, see W.L. Peat, "Non-legal Reference Books for Law Libraries," *1 Legal Reference Services Quarterly* 13–31 (1981). See also G. Finnigan, *Effective Factual Research for Lawyers* (Information Store, 1981).

5. 9th ed. (American Library Association, 1976), with occasional supplements.

specialized, and the researcher may require a library collection that is particularly strong in that subject field. If your own librarian cannot recommend an appropriate specialized library, two standard library directories may help.

The *American Library Directory,* published annually by R.R. Bowker, lists more than 30,000 libraries in the United States. Entries are arranged geographically by state and city, and addresses, telephone numbers, hours of opening, size, special services, and subject areas of concentration are provided for each library. Using this Directory, one can find library resources in specific fields, in virtually every area of the country. Illustration A shows several sample entries from the *American Library Directory.*

Another R.R. Bowker guide of this kind is *Subject Collections,*[6] but it is revised less frequently. This work is arranged by subject (rather than location), and includes not only libraries that concentrate on a particular subject, but also special subject collections that are contained in larger libraries. Within each subject area, the libraries and collections are arranged geographically. Information similar to that provided in the *American Library Directory* can be found in each entry, but with less detail. Illustration B shows sample entries from *Subject Collections,* in one subject field.

Most private libraries will provide access to serious researchers, although a letter of introduction from your local institution (law school, bar association, law firm, etc.) may be required. Preliminary inquiry by phone as to such requirements is desirable.

In addition to their extensive collections, such specialized libraries are likely to have experienced reference personnel trained to give help in their particular subject fields, and a wide range of indexes, research aids, and bibliographic services, to facilitate access to their holdings.

2. USING THE LIBRARY EFFECTIVELY

Libraries, at their best, are organized as service institutions, as well as repositories of information, and try to provide as much assistance to their users as possible. Yet many people find libraries intimidating and confusing, and today many research libraries do not have sufficient staff to meet their users' needs. Ironically, the sources that often appear to be most difficult to use are the indexes and finding tools that are designed to aid the researcher. The reference staff in most libraries are willing and able to help the reader, if they are consulted. The following additional suggestions may also assist one in an unfamiliar library.

a. The User's Guide

Most libraries have printed guides for users of their collections. Some larger libraries even have separate guides for their various spe-

6. By Lee Ash, 5th ed. (R.R. Bowker, 1978).

WORCESTER — 161,799. Area code 617

S AMERICAN ANTIQUARIAN SOCIETY LIBRARY, 185 Salisbury St, 01609. SAN 307-8191. Tel 617-755-5221. *Dir* Marcus McCorison; *Assoc Librn* Frederick E Bauer Jr. Staff 40 (prof 16, nonprof 24)
Founded 1812. Open to qualified adult researchers
1981-82 Inc $757,618. Exp Bks $84,360, Per $5000, Bd $24,367; Sal $500,000
1982-83 Projected Inc $775,000. Projected Exp $120,000
Library Holdings: Bk titles 605,000, vols 628,895; Per sub 550, vols bd 33,500; Doc bd 31,000; Micro — Cards 90,000, fiche 9100, reels 2775; AV — Rec, Slides, Maps, Art repro. VF 1500
Subject Interests: American hist, culture & life through 1876
Special Collections: Americana (Early American Imprints), almanacs, bks, directories & micro; Cookery; Graphic Arts, maps & prints; Music (Songsters & Psalmody), sheet music; Newspapers through 1876, per & broadsides
Publications: Proceedings, bibliographies, source materials
Partic in New England Libr Info Network; Res Librs Group Inc; Worcester Area Coop Librs

MEIKLEJOHN CIVIL LIBERTIES INSTITUTE LIBRARY, 1715 Francisco St, Box 673, 94701. SAN 300-6158. Tel 415-848-0599. *Dir* Ann Fagan Ginger; *Librn* David Christiano
Founded 1965
1982 Inc $67,589
1983 Projected Inc $69,500
Library Holdings: 150 Hollinger boxes of archival mat. VF 100 (incl legal case mat)
Subject Interests: Civil liberties & civil rights law, Cold War era & anti-Vietnam War, econ & soc rights law, hist of civil rights movement
Publications: Alexander Meiklejohn: Teacher of Freedom; The Ford Hunger March; The Human Rights Docket; Human Rights Organizations & Periodicals Directory, 5th ed (fall, 1982)

NATIONAL HOUSING & ECONOMIC DEVELOPMENT LAW LIBRARY, 2150 Shattuck Ave, Suite 300, 94704. SAN 300-6166. Tel 415-548-2600, Ext 504. *Librn* Katherine Parkes. Staff 3 (prof 1, nonprof 2)
Founded 1969. Ref libr
Library Holdings: Bk vols 10,000; Per sub 150; AV — V-tapes, Slides 500, Maps. VF 15
Subject Interests: Commun econ develop, health servs to poor & elderly, landlord-tenant, pub housing, rural develop

M NEW YORK ACADEMY OF MEDICINE LIBRARY, 2 East 103rd St, 10029. SAN 311-9327. Tel 212-876-8200. TWX 710-581-6131. *Librn* Brett A Kirkpatrick; *Assoc Librn* Lynn Kasner; *Asst Librn* Anne M Pascarelli; *Cat* Mira Myhre; *Ref* Judy Consales; *Hist of Med & Rare Bks* Salli Morgenstern; *Serials & Acq* Helen Plachta; *Circ* Kathy Finch; *ILL* Donald Clyde. Staff 51 (prof 20, nonprof 31)
Founded 1847
1981 Inc $1,129,663. Exp $313,273, Bks $108,454, Per & Doc $185,704, Bd $19,115; Sal $648,619
1982 Projected Exp $320,000
Library Holdings: Bk vols & doc bd 464,168; Per vols bd 4012; Illustrations 25,412; Incunabula 139; Pamphlets 180,981; Portraits 250, 043; Micro — Cards 34, reels 494
Subject Interests: Hist of med, med & allied subjects
Special Collections: Rare Medical Works (Friends of Rare Book Room), bk, mss; Medical Americana By & About J & W Hunter (Beekman Coll); Francesco Redi & Contemporaries (Cole Coll); Plague (Neinken Coll), bks, broadsides; Medical Theses-16th-18th Century (Gamble-Cranefield), pamphlets; Cardiology (Levy Coll), bks, mss; Engravings of Medical Men (Ladd Coll), prints; 16-19th Century Medals (Greenwald Coll), medals; German Psychology & Psychiatry (Harms Coll); Anatomy & Surgery (Lambert Coll); Medical Economics (Michael Davis Coll), VF; Foods & Cookery (Wilson Coll)
Publications: Author Catalog of the Library & first supplement; History of Medicine Series; Illustration Catalog of the Library; Catalog of Biographies in the Library; Newsletter & Selected Acquisitions List (monthly, on request); Subject Catalog of the Library & first supplement
Partic in Bibliog Retrieval Servs, Inc; Nat Libr of Med; NY & NJ Regional Med Libr; NY State ILL Network, OCLC, Inc

Illustration A

Listings for four specialized libraries in *American Library Directory*, 1982, reprinted with permission of the R.R. Bowker Company.

New England Historic Genealogical Society. James B. Bell, Dir. & Libn.; James Green, Cur., Rare Books. 101 Newbury St., Boston, **Mass.** 02116
Vols. (250,000) Mss. Maps Microforms Pix.
Notes: New England genealogy. Especially strong Massachusetts, Maine, and New Hampshire, although all states are well represented, as are the relevancies of each subject listed in this volume with regard to British antecedent and contemporary history. Special strengths in local history and biography, obituaries, etc., incl. parish registers, censuses, British and American. 3125 linear ft. of mss.

Harvard University Library, Widener Library. F. Nathaniel Bunker, Charles Warren Bibliographer in American History. Cambridge, **Mass.** 02138
Cat.
Notes: Published shelflist volumes (*Widener Library Shelflist*, Nos. 9-13) list 125,591 volumes as of 1967. See *Harvard Library Bulletin*, XV (1967): pp. 376-400 for account of the collection, which is strong in nearly all subdivisions except genealogy.

John F. Kennedy Library. Dan H. Fenn, Jr., Dir. 380 Trapelo Rd., Waltham, **Mass.** 02154
Vols. 20,000 Cat. Mss. Maps Pix. Slides Phonorecords Audiotapes Videotapes 16mm Films Microforms
Notes: *The* major collection about JFK, his life, family and administration. It contains personal papers, audiovisual materials, books, oral history interviews. Collection is described in "Historical Materials in the John F. Kennedy Library." "The Kennedy Collection," a subject guide to the book collection, is available for sale.

American Antiquarian Society, Library. Marcus A. McCorison, Dir. & Libn. 185 Salisbury St., Worcester, **Mass.** 01609
Cat. Mss. Maps Pix. Slides Microforms
Notes: Over half a million manuscript pieces; extensive collection of contemporary imprints before 1850 (with supplementary supporting studies); over 10,000 maps (weak for 15th–17th centuries; excellent for 18th, strongest in 19th century, especially maps of local nature). Also a good collection of portraits of early New Englanders; paintings, engravings, and miniatures. Further, the largest collection of regional, state, county, and local histories. Sixty percent of the total of books and pamphlets known to have been printed in the United States before 1821. Source of Readex Microprint Corp. project called *Early American Imprints, 1639–1800*, a Microprint edition of every extant book, pamphlet, and broadside printed in what is now the United States. Keyed to Evans *American Bibliography* it reprints in full the texts of nearly 50,000 titles and includes all of Shipton's revision of Evans. A second series, keyed to Shaw and Shoemaker's *American Bibliography* will bring these Microprint reproductions up to 1820. One of the great strengths of the collection is its broadsides and American newspapers—the best anywhere. From it

Illustration B

Partial listing under one subject in L. Ash, *Subject Collections*, 5th ed., reprinted with permission of the R.R. Bowker Company. Copyright © 1978 by Xerox Corporation.

cial collections. In addition to very practical matters like the hours of opening, requirements for access, photocopying facilities, and rules of use, such guides may also describe peculiarities of the library's catalogs and classification, physical arrangement of its collections, and special services and facilities that are available (e.g., computer search terminals, microform materials, archival holdings, dictating equipment, etc.) Some large libraries are forced to store part of their holdings at remote locations. With that knowledge, researchers can arrange beforehand to have needed materials retrieved for use and available at the time of their visit. A quick preliminary perusal of such a guide will solve many initial problems and may save considerable time in the actual use of the library.

b. The Library Catalog

Library catalogs are simply large indexes, providing access to the library's collection by author, title and subject. The card catalog has been described above in Section A.2.a. of Chapter 15, pp. 453–457. While there are widely accepted rules for the listing of authors' names, the subject headings used in many specialized fields differ from library to library. Even where the subject headings are based on a standard list (the most widely used being the very detailed subject heading list of the Library of Congress) many libraries have developed local variations. Since researchers working in an unfamiliar field usually search the catalog by subject, it is often desirable to ask a reference librarian for the subject entries likely to be used for the topic being searched.

Some libraries divide their card catalog into separate files, with author and title in one section, and subjects in another. Although catalogs are usually clearly marked if so divided, many users waste considerable time searching in the wrong file. One should always check the catalog's arrangement before consulting it. The *User's Guide,* described above, will indicate the basic characteristics of the library catalog and any unusual features.

More and more research libraries today use the Library of Congress classification system. The main categories of that scheme are as follows:

Outline of the Library of Congress Classification

A—General Works

B—Philosophy—Religion

C—History—Auxiliary Science
    (Including CT: Biography)

D—History and Topography
    (except America)

E—F—America

G—Geography—Anthropology

H—Social Science
    (Including HB to HJ: Economics
                    HM to HX: Sociology)

J—Political Science
    (Including JX: International Law)

K—Law
    (Including KF: U.S. Law)

L—Education

M—Music

N—Fine Arts

P—Language and Literature

Q—Science

R—Medicine

S—Agriculture—Plant and Animal Industry

T—Technology

U—Military Science

V—Naval Science

Z—Bibliography and Library Science

Some libraries now use microfiche or microfilm adjuncts to update or, in a few instances, replace their card catalog. These microform catalogs simply use a different medium to present the same information as a card catalog. When using such catalogs, one should determine whether it replaces or simply supplements the existing card catalog. Some libraries are in a transition stage between card catalogs and an on-line system, and thus have temporary files, which may require checking in two or three different places to get complete coverage.

c. Getting Help

No matter how thorough the guide for users or how straightforward the catalog, every library has its own idiosyncrasies. Some maintain special files, some have computerized information systems, and some offer facilities that may be unfamiliar. Before embarking on a research project in a new library, therefore, one should consult its reference staff for a general orientation.

3. USING ONE LIBRARY TO REACH OTHERS

If after searching your own library's collection, you find that it lacks materials that you need and have already identified, they may be obtainable *without* going to another library. Many libraries are now linked by computer terminals and can search each other's catalogs. The needed item may be in another collection and may be borrowed by interlibrary loan. Even if your library lacks a computer link to other collections, the *National Union Catalog,* or regional union catalogs can be used to find lending locations. Many large research libraries are now part of extensive library networks and can provide access to thousands of other libraries and their collections. Reference librarians can provide information about such services.

C. SPECIFIC TOOLS

The various subdivisions of this section contain brief discussions and selective suggestions of sources in ten different reference areas. Social science research sources will be treated separately in more detail in Chapter 18 below. Most of these sources will be in the reference collections of any large public or academic library, and will be in the reference collections of large law libraries.

1. GENERAL INFORMATION

a. Encyclopedias

The standard legal encyclopedias have already been described above in Chapter 14. Two other law-related encyclopedias which are most popular in approach merit attention here. The one-volume *Oxford Companion to Law* (1980) and the new *West's Guide to American Law* are designed primarily for general reference purposes rather than for intensive legal research.

The *Oxford Companion to Law* contains over 1,300 pages, in a two column format, and thousands of relatively short articles on legal institutions, events, individuals, cases and statutes. It focuses primarily on English law, but offers a wide range of information on American subjects and longer survey articles on the law of some other countries, particularly those in the common law system and Western Europe. Many of the articles provide citations to other sources for further research on that subject. Its breadth of coverage, lively style, and conciseness make it very useful for quick reference, particularly on historical topics. Its wit and an occasionally iconoclastic tone make it a delight for browsing.

The West Publishing Company's new publication, entitled *West's Guide to American Law: Everyone's Legal Encyclopedia,* is projected for publication in twelve volumes late in 1983. It has a similar focus to the *Oxford Companion,* but offers more extensive coverage of most topics and generally reflects an American point of view. This encyclopedia is designed for a varied audience, both lay and professional, but should be a valuable reference tool to law and related subjects. Although it includes articles on legal concepts and terms, it will probably be most helpful for the cultural and historical aspects of law.

General encyclopedias such as the *Encyclopedia Americana, Encyclopedia Britannica, Encyclopedia International,* and *World Book Encyclopedia,* are primarily designed for a mass audience, including high school students. They can be useful, however, in legal research as introductions to unfamiliar fields or for specific information on well-settled topics. Access by the traditional alphabetical arrangement of articles is supplemented by detailed general indexes. Most are updated by annual yearbooks, but these become cumbersome to use as their number increases. The unusual format of the current edition of the *Encyclopedia Britannica* [7] disturbs some users who prefer the traditional approach of the still highly regarded,

7. 15th ed. (1974) 30v., consisting of the single *Propaedia* volume (outlining all human knowledge), the ten volume *Micropaedia* (containing over one hundred thousand short "ready-reference" articles) and the nineteen volume *Macropaedia* of over four thousand longer articles, many of which include selective bibliographies.

but considerably outdated, 9th (25v., 1875–1889) and 11th (29v., 1911) editions.

One-volume encyclopedias, providing a similar level of sophistication, are particularly helpful for quick reference. One of the best of these is *The New Columbia Encyclopedia,* 4th ed. (1975).

The growth of specialized subject encyclopedias, most of which are more scholarly than the general encyclopedias, has created a new reference literature of more utility to legal researchers. *The Encyclopedia of the Social Sciences,* 15v. (1930–1935) and the *International Encyclopedia of the Social Sciences,* 17v. (1968) are described below in Chapter 18. Other examples include the *Encyclopedia of Philosophy,* 8v. (1967), *Dictionary of the History of Ideas,* 4v. (1973–1974), *Encyclopedia of Education,* 10v. (1971), *Encyclopedia of Urban Planning* (1974), *Encyclopedia of Psychology,* 3v. (1972), and *Worldmark Encyclopedia of the Nations,* 4th ed., 5v. (1971).

The articles in many of these specialized encyclopedias are signed by recognized scholars in their fields. Bibliographies are usually provided, and detailed indexing enhances access to specific information beyond the basic alphabetic arrangement of articles. If they are available, these reference works are usually preferable to the general encyclopedias.

b. Almanacs

There are a number of annually published fact books or almanacs providing a wide range of facts, figures and data on politics, sports, awards, current events, weather, and virtually every field of general interest. These reference tools provide quick answers to simple factual questions, and their effectiveness is dependent on the quality of indexing and the arrangement of information. The most popular annual almanacs include the following:

The World Almanac and Book of Facts

Information Please Almanac

Readers Digest Almanac

The Official Associated Press Almanac

The Hammond Almanac

c. Other Factual Sourcebooks

There are several factbooks designed specifically for lawyers and those engaged in legal research. The *Am.Jur.2d Deskbook* (described above in Section G of Chapter 14) is a general compendium of information on the legal profession, the courts, other legal agencies and institutions, and a variety of data useful to the bar. It is supplemented by annual pocket parts.

The Lawyer's Almanac 1982–83, a Cornucopia of Information about Law, Lawyers, and the Legal Profession is a new sourcebook, similar in content and purpose to the *Am.Jur.2d Deskbook.* If revised annually, it may become a popular almanac-type reference book for law. It includes sections on the legal profession, legal education, the judiciary, government agencies, statutes, statutory practice, and commonly used abbreviations.

The Law and Legal Information Directory, 2d ed. (Gale Research, 1983) includes sections on the legal profession; legal education; the judiciary; government departments and agencies; statutory summaries and checklists; texts of selected statutes and codes; and commonly used abbreviations. All three of these factbooks draw their material from standard sources, often simply providing photocopies of data available elsewhere in most law libraries.

General factual compendia are published for many specialized fields, by government agencies, trade associations and commercial publishers. Examples include *Aerospace Facts and Figures, Insurance Fact Book, Labor Fact Book, Yearbook of Agriculture,* and deskbooks published for a variety of professions.

Facts on File, a weekly digest of world news, with annual bound cumulations, arranges summaries of current developments under broad subject areas. Two similar British services are *Keesing's Contempory Archives,* a weekly diary of world events, and the *Annual Register of World Events.*

The *Information Age Source Book,* edited by S. Osborn and J. Weiss (1982) is a collection of "how-to-do-it" information assembled from publications of government agencies, universities, trade associations, and professional societies.

The *Worldwide Government Directory with Inter-Governmental Organizations* (1983) identifies officials of 168 nations and describes the major intergovernmental organizations of the world. The governmental structure of individual countries is outlined, with addresses, telephone, telex and cable numbers for major national offices and agencies, as well as for international and regional organizations. If updated regularly, it will be a valuable source for this practical information.

2. INFORMATION ABOUT PEOPLE

Directories and biographical sources for lawyers and judges have already been described in Section E of Chapter 15. Most other professions have similar reference tools, and the following additional sources provide general coverage of prominent individuals in *all* fields of activity.

Some caution must be used with respect to biographical directories generally—most are based on information supplied by the subjects themselves, and some are essentially vanity publications designed only to enrich the publisher and please the described individuals. There are very few contemporary sources which utilize disinterested scholarly contributors, as do such major historical works of collective biography as the *Dictionary of National Biography, Dictionary of American Biography,* and *Notable American Women,* described below in subsection c.

In addition to the following sources, two indexes to biographies should be noted: *Biography Index* (H.W. Wilson, 1946 to date) provides references to biographical material appearing in approximately 2400 periodicals. It appears monthly and cumulates in annual and three-year volumes. Gale's *Biographical Index Series,* 8 vols. (1980), with 4 vol. Supplement (1982) provides access to over four million entries in a variety of biographical directories published by the Gale Research Company.

a. Who's Who Series

Who's Who in America, published biennially, is the most widely used and respected compendium of contemporary American biographies. It is based on data submitted by the subjects, but is reasonably accurate and carefully compiled. The same publisher, Marquis Publishing Company, also provides four regional collections in the same format and frequency, each containing many entries not in the national version—*Who's Who in the East, Who's Who in the South and Southwest, Who's Who in the Midwest,* and *Who's Who in the West.*

In addition to *Who's Who in American Law,* Marquis also publishes *Who's Who in Finance and Industry* (frequency irregular) and *Who's Who of American Women* (biennial). R.R. Bowker publishes *American Men and Women of Science* and *Directory of American Scholars,* both revised irregularly. Similar collections for religious, ethnic, and professional groups are issued by other publishers, usually without a regular pattern of revision.

Biographical dictionaries are published on a more or less regular basis for many foreign countries by individual publishers in each country, e.g. *Who's Who* (annual, primarily British), *Wer ist Wer, Das Deutsche Who's Who* and *Who's Who in Germany* (both issued irregularly), *Who's Who in France* (biennial), *Who's Who in Japan* (annual), etc. *International Who's Who* (London, annual) offers world-wide coverage.

The *Guide to American Directories* (McGraw-Hill, revised irregularly; last ed., the 10th, 1979) and *The Directory of Directories,* 2d ed. (Gale Research, 1983) are useful finding tools for directories in particular subject fields. The latter also includes reference to directories from nearly eighty foreign countries. Sheehy, *Guide to Reference Books,* described above, and local reference librarians can be consulted for other sources.

b. Current Biography

Biographies of contemporary figures of prominence in many fields are provided in the *monthly* publication, *Current Biography* (H.W. Wilson Co.) with annual cumulative volumes. The number of individuals covered is relatively small (approximately 350 each year) and it tends to emphasize entertainment and cultural areas. A cumulative index covers 1940 to 1970, and each subsequent annual volume contains an index which cumulates all entries thereafter.

c. Biographies of Deceased Individuals

There are several sources for biographical information on deceased individuals. For figures of historical importance, two classic biographical encyclopedias are considered most authoritative. For Americans, there is the *Dictionary of American Biography,* 20v. (1982–1937), with supplements, and its abridgment, *Concise Dictionary of American Biography* (1964). For English subjects the leading source is *The Dictionary of National Biography,* 22v. (1912–1959), also with supplements, and *The Concise Dictionary,* 2v. (revised and reprinted, 1953–1961). *Notable American Women 1607–1950,* 3 vols. (1971), modelled after *D.A.B.,* is an excellent retrospective biographical encyclopedia, of distinguished American women. A one-volume supplement, *The Modern Period* (1980) has now also been published.

The Marquis publication, *Who was Who in America,* consisting of an *Historical Volume 1607–1896* (1963) and seven supplementary volumes to date, covering the period from 1897 to 1981, is another useful source for data on some 105,000 deceased Americans. The entries in the seven later volumes are largely based on the original entries for each individual, as they appeared in *Who's Who in America.* A cumulative index volume (1981) covers the period 1607 to 1981. A similar *English* reference source is *Who was Who . . . a Companion to Who's Who* (1929–1980) 7v., covering the years 1897 to 1970, with further supplements expected.

The New York Times Obituary Index, which so far covers the period from 1858 to 1978 in two vols. (1970, 1980), provides access to obituaries appearing in that newspaper. Accounts of the life and work of both prominent and less-known individuals can be located through that source.

Other retrospective biographical works exist for many states, countries, and professions, and can be identified through the reference sources described above.

d. Finding Information on Non-celebrities

Lawyers frequently need information on people who are not prominent enough to be included in standard reference tools. Tracking down such data is often difficult. Local newspaper files and indexes are often good sources of information about non-celebrities. Magazines and newsletters published for particular trades, professions and even companies may be helpful if the person's work history is known.

Another set of useful tools are the city directories published by the R.L. Polk Co. Polk compiles and publishes more than 1,400 separate city directories. They record information on all businesses and on individuals over the age of 18, in the various locales covered. A few American cities are so large that Polk has abandoned its coverage of them, but for most U.S. cities, these directories, often held by large public libraries, can be useful for tracing firms or individuals.

3. INFORMATION ON INSTITUTIONS

Information about specific institutions, associations, and corporations is provided by a number of special reference guides. Those few listed here are notable for their breadth of coverage and general acceptance, but there are many others available.[8]

a. Encyclopedia of Associations

This multi-volume guide is issued biennially by the Gale Research Company, and contains information on many associations and organizations. Tens of thousands of entries are arranged by broad subject categories, with geographic and executive indexes included. The entries include the name of the director, address, phone number, size, meeting information, organizational purpose, and publications. Illustration C shows a typical page from this encyclopedia.

b. Other Association Directories

There are many other directories for particular types of associations and organizations. The following are but a few examples of the many which may be helpful to those engaged in law-related research:

Foundation Directory (irregular; latest ed. is 8th, 1981), arranged by state and then alphabetically by name of foundation. Separate indexes provide access by foundation name; names of donors, trustees and administrators; and field of interest. This directory also includes extensive statistical information on foundation assets, grants, funding, etc. It is updated by the bi-monthly *Foundation News.*

Directory of Consumer Protection and Environmental Agencies (1973), arranged by state in two lists, for *Consumer Protection* and *Environmental Protection,* with separate indexes by organization names, personnel, publications, and subjects.

The National Directory of State Agencies 1982–1983 (biennial), arranged in two sections, by state and by function, with an appendix of associations of state government officials.

National Trade and Professional Associations of the United States (annual since 1966), arranged alphabetically by association name, with separate indexes by subject, state and city, and size of budget. Illustration D shows a sample page.

8. Both the *Guide to American Directories* and *The Directory of Directories,* noted above in Section 2, are comprehensive guides to directories of this kind.

by the Society's Board of Review and Development, consider such topics as the role of international law in civil wars, the law of treaties, international telecommunications, the new international economic order, self-determination, science and international law, and terrorism. Grants awards and helps coordinate the Philip C. Jessup International Law Moot Competition (see separate entry). Maintains specialized library on international legal affairs. **Publications:** (1) International Legal Materials, bimonthly; (2) Newsletter, bimonthly; (3) American Journal of International Law, quarterly; (4) Proceedings, annual; also publishes Studies in Transnational Legal Policy. **Convention/Meeting:** annual - always April, Washington, DC.

★4333★ ASSOCIATION OF STUDENT **INTERNATIONAL LAW** SOCIETIES (ASILS)
2223 Massachusetts Ave., N.W. Phone: (202) 387-8467
Washington, DC 20008 Richard W. Nelson, Exec.Sec.
Founded: 1961. **Members:** 117. **Staff:** 2. International law societies at law schools throughout the U.S. and the world; interns and associate members. To promote interest in international legal problems through cooperative development of programs. Conducts annual Philip C. Jessup International Law Moot Court Competition (see separate entry), open to all international law societies, both domestic and foreign. Bestows Francis Deak and Dean Rusk Awards for student writing in student international law journals. Serves as clearinghouse for international legal authorities visiting the U.S. and who are interested in speaking engagements at member societies. Provides research opportunities to undergraduate, graduate and law students in field of international law. Maintains library of 22,000 items. **Publications:** (1) Newsletter, quarterly; (2) Directory of Student International Law Journals, annual; (3) International Law Journal, annual; (4) Jessup Moot Court Materials, annual; also publishes Handbook for Student International Law Societies. **Convention/Meeting:** annual - always April, Washington, DC, with American Society of International Law.

★4334★ BRITISH INSTITUTE OF **INTERNATIONAL** AND COMPARATIVE **LAW** (BRICLAW)
Charles Clore House
17 Russell Sq.
London WC1B 5DR, England Prof. K. R. Simmonds, Hon.Dir.
Founded: 1958. **Members:** 2500. **Staff:** 9. Practicing lawyers, academics, and those interested in international affairs. International center for studying the practical application to current problems of public international law, private international law and comparative law (the last with particular reference to Commonwealth law and the legal problems of the European communities). Conducts and promotes research; organizes a wide range of lecture meetings, seminars and conferences; offers an advisory legal service for governments of commonwealth countries; maintains library of 10,000 volumes. **Publications:** (1) Bulletin of Legal Developments, biweekly; (2) International and Comparative Law Quarterly; (3) Annual Report; also publishes three or four books a year on a wide variety of legal topics. **Formed by Merger of:** The Grotius Society, and Society of Comparative Legislation and International Law. **Convention/Meeting:** annual.

★4335★ COMMISSION FOR **INTERNATIONAL** DUE PROCESS OF **LAW** (CIDPL)
105 W. Adams St. Phone: (312) 782-1946
Chicago, IL 60603 Luis Kutner, Chm.
Founded: 1931. **Members:** 2000. Heads of state, chief justices, associate justices, judges, delegates, professors. Advocates world habeas corpus as a procedure to implement human rights principles in all international documents, conventions, charters and protocols. Initiates litigation for political prisoners and minority groups. Is promoting a program whereby the Universal Declaration of Human Rights, now only morally binding, would become legally binding world-wide. Maintains extensive library and numerous committees. Publishes law journals, periodicals and directory. **Convention/Meeting:** annual.

★4336★ CONSULAR LAW SOCIETY **(International Law)** (CLS)
460 Park Ave. Phone: (212) 751-2660
New York, NY 10022 Michael Alexander, Exec. Officer
Founded: 1940. **Members:** 100. Membership by invitation. Attorneys representing consulates and/or embassies, or otherwise specializing in international matters. Publishes occasional papers; bestows awards. **Committees:** Diplomatic and Consular Practice; Governments in Exile; Human Rights; Immigration and Nationality; Immunities; International Companies; International and Comparative Law; International Copyright Relations; International Double Taxation; International Law in U.S. Courts; Neutrality; Private Claims Against Governments; Recognition of States; Treaties. **Convention/Meeting:** annual - always first Wednesday in June.

★4337★ FOUNDATION FOR THE ESTABLISHMENT OF AN INTERNATIONAL CRIMINAL COURT **(International Law)** (FEICC)
P.O. Box 12 Phone: (617) 969-4482
Auburndale, MA 02166 A. N. F. Ballester, Exec.Dir.
Founded: 1970. **Regional Groups:** 3. International consultants (representing 30 countries) who are experts in the fields of international, criminal and humanitarian law; United Nations affiliates. Seeks to establish international uniformity of criminal codes and to expand the jurisdictions of international courts for offenses such as kidnapping and hijacking which have become international in scope. Conducts educational seminars for U.N. diplomats, students and academic and government experts. Maintains library of related documents and relevant publications in the fields of international criminal law and humanitarian law. Bestows awards; maintains charitable program. **Committees:** Awards. **Publications:** Establishment of an International Criminal Court, biennial. **Convention/Meeting:** annual.

★4338★ HAGUE CONFERENCE ON PRIVATE **INTERNATIONAL LAW** (CODIP)
2 C, Javastraat
NL-2585 AM The Hague, Netherlands G. A. L. Droz, Sec.Gen.
Members: 29 states. **Staff:** 11. Intergovernmental organization not open to individuals. Objective is to work for the progressive unification of the rules of private international law. Permanent Bureau conducts research on new subjects and furnishes scientific and secretarial assistance to commissions and reporters. **Publications:** Actes et Documents des Sessions de la Conference, quadrennial. **Convention/Meeting:** quadrennial.

3

★4339★ INSTITUTE OF **INTERNATIONAL LAW** (IIL)
22 Avenue William-Farre
CH-1207 Geneva, Switzerland Nicolas Valticos, Sec.Gen.
Founded: 1873. **Members:** 132. Members are chosen by co-optation for contributions to international law in theory and practice, associates and honorary members. The Commission's main areas of interest are: problems of the law in maintaining international order; effect of war on international treaties; sources of international law; unfair competition and conflict of law; extradition and multilateral treaties; creation of artifical islands; self-defense. Presents James Brown Scott Prize biennially. **Publications:** Annuaire, biennial. **Convention/Meeting:** biennial - next 1983 September, Cambridge, England.

★4340★ **INTERNATIONAL LAW** ASSOCIATION (ILA)
Three Paper Buildings, Temple
London EC4Y 7EU, England John Churchill, Sec.
Founded: 1873. **Members:** 4000. **Staff:** 2. Branches: 46. Individuals and organizations interested in "the study, elucidation and advancement of international law, public and private; the study of comparative law; the making of proposals for the solution of conflicts of law, and for the unification of law." Maintains 15 committees including: International Criminal Law; International Commercial Arbitrations; and Space Law. **Publications:** (1) Conference Bulletin, biennial; (2) Conference Reports, biennial; also published The Effect of Independence on Treaties, The Present State of International Law and an Index of Conference Reports (1873-1972). **Formerly:** (1899) Association for the Reform and Codification of the Law of Nations. **Convention/Meeting:** biennial conference - 1982 Aug. 29-Sept. 4, Montreal, PQ, Canada.

★4341★ **INTERNATIONAL LAW** INSTITUTE (ILI)
Georgetown University Law Center
600 New Jersey Ave., N.W. Phone: (202) 624-8330
Washington, DC 20001 Prof. Don Wallace, Jr., Dir.
Founded: 1955. **Staff:** 16. Offers a combination of research and training programs that focus on the legal aspect of international business transactions. Sponsors international conferences, exchange fellowships and service programs for foreign students and lawyers. Publishes conference proceedings, reports and articles on the results of Institute projects. **Divisions:** Foreign and Domestic Student Programs; Investment Negotiation Center; Orientation in U.S. Legal System; Research and Publications. **Formerly:** (1979) Institute for International and Foreign Trade Law. **Convention/Meeting:** annual.

★4342★ INTERNATIONAL THIRD WORLD LEGAL STUDIES ASSOCIATION **(International Law)** (INTWORLSA)
c/o Intl. Center for Law in Development
777 United Nations Plaza Phone: (212) 687-0036
New York, NY 10017 James Paul, Sec.Treas.
Founded: 1981. **Members:** 120. Law-oriented scholars interested in encouraging the comparative study of law and social change in Africa, Asia, Latin America and the Caribbean. Plans to produce publications, hold annual meetings, and cosponsor seminars with other international groups. **Supersedes:** African Law Association in America (founded 1965).

★4343★ PHILIP C. JESSUP **INTERNATIONAL LAW** MOOT COURT COMPETITION (PJILMCC)
Assn. of Student Intl. Law Societies
2223 Massachusetts Ave., N.W. Phone: (202) 387-8467
Washington, DC 20008 Richard W. Nelson, Intl.Admin.
Founded: 1961. **Members:** 180. **Staff:** 2. **Regional Groups:** 36. Law schools throughout the world whose students participate in annual competition in the field of international law. Sponsored by the Association of Student International Law Societies and the American Society of International Law (see separate entries); named for Judge Philip C. Jessup, retired from the International Court of Justice. Objectives are: to improve international legal facilities among law schools; to create an interest in international legal

Illustration C

Sample entries from the *Encyclopedia of Associations,* edited by Denise S. Akey (copyright © 1959–1982, by Gale Research Company; reprinted by permission of the publisher), seventeenth edition, 1983, p. 371. Reduced in size here.

AMERICAN ASS'N ON MENTAL DEFICIENCY **ASSOCIATION INDEX**

Monograph Series. irreg.
Annual Meetings:
1982-Boston(Sheraton)/May 31-June 4/2,500
1983-Dallas/May 30-June 4/2,500
1984-Minneapolis(Hyatt Regency)/May 28-June 1/2,500
1985-Philadelphia/2,500

American Astronautical Federation
Hist. Note: Recorded in 1978 as being inactive or defunct.

American Astronautical Soc. (1953)
Key Towers, 6060 Duke St., Alexandria VA 22304
Exec. Secretary: George Cranston
Members: 600-625 *Staff:* 2-5
Annual Budget: $25-50,000 *Tel:* (703) 751-7323
Hist. Note: Founded at the American Museum of Natural History in New York in November 1953 by a small group of engineers, scientists and others who wished to initiate an American activity similar to the British Interplanetary Society as spokesman for a substantive space program. Incorporated in the State of New York in 1954. Membership: $30/yr.
Publications:
AAS Newsletter. bi-m. $10/yr. 750 circ.
Journal of the Astronautical Sciences. q. $45/yr. 1,000 circ.
Annual Meetings: Fall

American Astronomical Soc. (1899)
1816 Jefferson Place, N.W., Washington DC 20036
Exec. Officer: Dr. Peter B. Boyce
Members: 3,800 *Staff:* 2-5
Annual Budget: $1-2,000,000 *Tel:* (202) 659-0134
Hist. Note: Organized September 6, 1899 at the Yerkes Observatory, Green Bay, Wisconsin as the Astronomical and Astrophysical Soc. of America. Name changed to American Astronomical Soc. in 1914. Incorporated in Illinois in 1928. A member of the American Institute of Physics.
Publications:
Astronomical Journal. m.
Astrophysical Journal. semi-m.
Bulletin of the American Astronomical Society. 4/yr.
Semi-annual meetings: Summer and Winter
1982-Boulder, CO(U. Col.)/Jan. 10-13/800
1982-Troy, NY(RPI Campus)/June/600
1983-Boston(Park Plaza)Jan. 9-12/800
1983-Baltimore(Johns Hopkins)/June/800

American Auto Racing Writers and Broadcasters Ass'n (1955)
922 North Pass Ave., Burbank CA 91505
Exec. Director: Miss Norma 'Dusty' Brandel
Members: 500-550 *Staff:* 1
Annual Budget: under $10,000 *Tel:* (213) 842-7005
Hist. Note: Established in Indianapolis in 1955 with 17 charter members.
Publication:
Newsletter. m. adv. 500 circ.
Annual Meetings: May, in Indianapolis

American Automatic Control Council (1957)
Box 12277, 67 Alexander Dr., Research Triangle Park NC 27709
Secretary: Sharon Vonney
Members: 6 societies *Staff:* 1
Annual Budget: $10-25,000 *Tel:* (919) 549-0600
Hist. Note: Founded in Chicago March 1957 as the North American Control Council, but became the American Automatic Control Council in October of that Year. A federation of sponsoring societies-American Institute of Aeronautics and Astronautics, American Institute of Chemical Engineers, American Soc. of Mechanical Engineers, Institute of Electrical and Electronic Engineers, Instrument Soc. of America, Soc. of Manufacturing Engineers. Affiliated with The Internat'l Federation of Automatic Control.
Annual Meetings: Joint Automatic Control Conference

American Automotive Leasing Ass'n (1955)
Heritage Park, 8330 North Teutonia Ave., Milwaukee WI 53209
Admin. Secretary: Sidney R. Rose
Members: 175 companies *Staff:* 2-5
Annual Budget: $100-250,000 *Tel:* (414) 355-8379
Hist. Note: Formed in late 1955 by 19 charter auto leasing companies in response to an effort by the IRS to deny leasing companies capital gains treatment on the sale of their used vehicles.
Publication:
Newsletter. m. 600 circ.
Annual Meetings:
1982-Miami(Doral)/Jan. 30-Feb. 3/300
1982-Miami/January
1984-Boca Raton(Hotel & Club)/300
1984-Scottsdale/January

American Award Manufacturers Ass'n (1976)
Hist. Note: Manufacturers of awards and trophies. Ceased effective operations in 1980.

American Bakers Ass'n (1897)
Suite 850, 2020 K St., N.W., Washington DC 20006
President: Robert J. Wager
Members: 325 companies *Staff:* 11-15
Annual Budget: $500-1,000,000 *Tel:* (202) 296-5800
Hist. Note: Formed at a meeting in Walter Baker & Co.'s room in the Mechanics' Building, Boston, October 20, 1897 at which eleven states and two Canadian provinces were represented. Known originally as the National Association of Master Bakers and then the American Association of the Baking Industry, it has operated under its present name since 1921. Incorporated in Illinois in 1917. Supports the BREAD Political Action Committee.
Annual Meetings: Fall
1982-New Orleans/Oct. 8-13/750

American Bandmasters Ass'n (1929)
2019 Bradford Dr., Arlington TX 76010
Secy.-Treas.: Jack H. Mahan
Members: 300-350 *Staff:* 1
Annual Budget: under $10,000 *Tel:* (817) 261-8629
Hist. Note: Formed at a meeting on July 5, 1929 at the Hotel Pennsylvania in New York City. Incorporated March 13, 1930 in the State of New York.
Publication:
Journal of Band Research. semi-a. $5/yr.
Annual Meetings:
1982-Indianapolis/March 3-6

American Bankers Ass'n (1875)
1120 Connecticut Ave., N.W., Washington DC 20036
Exec. V. President: Willis W. Alexander
Members: 13,200-13,400 *Staff:* 340
Annual Budget: over $5,000,000 *Tel:* (202) 467-4000
Hist. Note: Organized in Saratoga, NY, July 20-22, 1875. Absorbed the Charge Account Bankers Ass'n and the Foundation for Full Service Banks in 1972. The association now has a budget of more than twenty million dollars and represents about 93% of the nation's banks. Affiliated with BankPac, its political action committee, and other groups throughtout the country which contribute to the political campaigns of selected state and national candidates who favor the interests of commercial banking.
Publications:
ABA Bank Card Letter. m.
ABA Bank Installment Lender Report. m.
ABA Banking Journal. m. adv.
Agricultural Banker. m.
Bank Insurance & Protection Bulletin. m.
Bank Marketing Newsletter. m.
Bank Personnel News. m.
Branch Administrator. m.
Capital Newsletter. w.
Leaders Letter. m.
Thruput. m.
Trust Letter. m.
Trust Management Update. m.
Urban and Community Economic Development. m.
Annual Meetings: Fall
1982-Atlanta/Oct. 16-20/12,000
1983-Honolulu(Waikiki)/Oct. 8-12/12,000
1984-New York City/Oct. 20-24/12,000

American Baptist Education Ass'n
Hist. Note: Recorded in 1978 as being inactive or defunct.

American Bar Ass'n (1878)
1155 East 60th St., Chicago IL 60637
Exec. Director: Thomas H. Gonser
Members: 260,000 *Staff:* 500
Annual Budget: over $5,000,000 *Tel:* (312) 947-4000
Hist. Note: Represents more than 50% of practising lawyers in the U.S. Federally approved accrediting agency for law schools. Maintains the nationally-honored Code of Professional Responsibility. Operates the Center for Professional Discipline, and an information center for the bar admission and bar disciplinary agencies. Has an annual budget of $30,000,000.
Publications:
American Bar Association Journal. m.
Barrister. q. adv.
Student Lawyer. 9/yr. adv.
Annual Meetings: August
1982-San Francisco/Aug. 4-11/15,000
1983-Atlanta/July 27-Aug. 3/15,000

American Barter Trade Export Ass'n
600 American Federal Bldg., c/o Conrad and Associates, Tacoma WA 98402
Exec. Director:
Tel: (206) 383-3816
Hist. Note: A Webb-Pomerene Act trade association. Membership includes a large number of individuals and agricultural cooperatives.

American Basketball Ass'n (1967)
Hist. Note: Absorbed by the Nat'l Basketball Ass'n June 17, 1976.

American Beefalo Ass'n (1975)
116 Executive Park, Louisville KY 40207
Exec. Director: George E. O'Connor
Members: 900-1,000 breeders *Staff:* 2-5
Annual Budget: $50-100,000 *Tel:* (502) 897-1650
Hist. Note: Members are North American breeders of a cross between a buffalo and a cow.
Publication:
Beefalo Nickel. bi.m. adv. $10/yr. 1,500 circ.
Annual Meetings: Louisville, in November(Hyatt Regency)/300

American Beekeeping Federation (1943)
13637 N.W. 39th Ave., Gainesville FL 32601
Secy.-Treas.: Frank Robinson
Members: 1,800-1,900 *Staff:* 2-5
Annual Budget: $50-100,000 *Tel:* (904) 375-0012
Hist. Note: Formerly Nat'l Federation of Beekeepers Ass'ns. Members are honey producers, packers, shippers and suppliers.
Publication:
Federation Newsletter. bi-m. adv.
Annual Meetings: January, and odd years with The Apiary Inspectors of America.
1982-Savannah/Jan. 18-23/750
1983-Honolulu/Jan. 17-21/750

American Berkshire Ass'n (1875)
601 West Monroe St., Springfield IL 62704
Secretary: Jack W. Wall
Members: 5-600 *Staff:* 6-10
Annual Budget: $50-100,000 *Tel:* (217) 523-2123
Hist. Note: Breeders and fanciers of Berkshire swine. Member of the National Society of Livestock Record Associations.
Publication:
Berkshire News. m. adv.
Annual Meetings: Summer

American Bio-Environmental Ass'n (1977)
Hist. Note: Became the International Bio-Environmental Foundation in 1978.

American Blasting Ass'n (1969)
Hist. Note: Established as the New England Blasting Association, it became the American Blasting Association in 1970 and the New England chapter of the Society of Explosive Engineers in 1979.

American Bleached Shellac Manufacturers Ass'n (1924)
c/o William Zinnser Co., 39 Belmont Dr., Somerville NJ 08873
President: Gardner R. Cunningham
Members: 5-10 companies *Staff:* 1
Annual Budget: under $10,000 *Tel:* (201) 469-8100

American Blonde D'Aquitaine Ass'n (1973)
Grand View Farms, Grand View ID 83624
Exec. Officer: Gerald Cunningham
Members: 300 cattle breeders *Staff:* 1
Annual Budget: under $10,000 *Tel:* (208) 834-2244
Annual Meetings: January in Denver

American Blood Resources Ass'n (1972)
Box 3346, Annapolis MD 21403
Exec. Director: Robert W. Reilly
Members: 90-100 companies *Staff:* 2-5
Annual Budget: $100-250,000 *Tel:* (202) 261-2204
Hist. Note: Members are commerical blood processors.
Annual Meetings: Fall

American Blue Cheese Ass'n (1954)
Hist. Note: A division of the Nat'l Cheese Institute.

American Board of Medical Specialties (1933)
1603 Orrington Ave., Evanston IL 60201
Exec. V. President: Dr. Donald G. Langsley
Members: 25-30 organizations *Staff:* 6-10
Annual Budget: $500-1,000,000 *Tel:* (312) 491-9091
Hist. Note: Established in 1933 as the Advisory Board for Medical Specialties. Became the American Board of Medical Specialties in 1970.
Semi annual meetings: Spring and Fall

American Board Products Ass'n (1976)
Hist. Note: Became the American Hardboard Ass'n in 1978.

American Boarding Kennels Ass'n (1977)
311 N. Union, Colorado Springs CO 80909
Exec. Director: James J. Krack
Members: 1,000 kennels *Staff:* 2-5
Annual Budget: $100-250,000 *Tel:* (303) 635-7082
Publications:
Boarderline. bi-m.
Boarding Kennel Proprieter. m. adv. $12.50/yr. 7,500 circ.
Annual Meetings: Fall
1982-New Orleans/Sept. 19-22/900
1983-California/Sept. 25-28/950
1984-Hershey/Sept. 23-26/1,000
1985-Denver/Sept. 15-18/1,200

American Boat and Yacht Council (1954)
Box 806, Amityville NY 11701
Exec. Director: G. James Lippmann
Members: 1,000 individuals, 40-50 companies *Staff:* 6-10
Annual Budget: $100-250,000 *Tel:* (516) 598-0550
Hist. Note: Members are individuals concerned with the design, construction, and maintenance of recreational boats and related equipment. Membership: $45/year.
Publication:
American Boat and Yacht Council News. irreg.
Annual Meetings: January, in New York City
1982-New York(Coliseum)/Jan. 14/100

American Boat Builders and Repairers Ass'n (1943)
715 Boylston St., Boston MA 02116
Exec. Secretary: Richard S. Guild, CAE
Members: 135-140 *Staff:* 1
Annual Budget: under $10,000 *Tel:* (617) 266-6800

38

Illustration D

Sample entries from National Trade and Professional Associations of the U.S., reprinted by permission of the publisher, Columbia Books, Inc., Washington, D.C. Reduced in size here.

Social Science Organizations and Agencies Directory (1982), arranged by broad subject categories, with indexes by organization names and subject key-words. It includes both public and private organizations.

c. Information on Corporate Enterprises

A wide variety of tools provide information on corporations and companies. Perhaps the best known are the *Moody's Manuals.* These annual publications, with their weekly updates, give information on the assets and operations of companies whose stock is publicly traded. Much the same is done in the manuals published by *Standard and Poor's. Poor's Register of Directors and Executives* (annual) focuses specifically on the officers and directors of business enterprises.

An irreverent look at some larger corporations can be found in *Everybody's Business Almanac* (1982) which contains profiles on a selective list of American corporations.

If the researcher is interested in locating information on a specific product, *Thomas' Register of American Manufacturers* (annual) can be used. The *Register* provides listings of leading manufacturers, trade names, and commercial organizations such as boards of trade and chambers of commerce.

The following additional sources are of a more specialized nature:

H. Frank, *ERC Closely-Held Corporation Guide* (1981).

How to Find Information About Companies (1979).

F.A. Lovejoy, *The Princeton Mergers & Acquisitions Reporter & Directory,* 5v., looseleaf (1981).

Directory of Corporate Affiliations (1982) and *International Directory of Corporate Affiliations* (1982).

4. INFORMATION ABOUT WORDS AND MEANINGS

Given the large amount of both reading and writing inherent in the practice of law, the legal researcher often needs reference tools to aid in the understanding and use of language. Some of the more helpful of these sources are outlined below, and many more can be identified by use of a comprehensive bibliography of such sources, *Dictionaries, Encyclopedias and Other Word-Related Books,* edited by A.M. Brewer, 3 vols. (3d ed., 1982).

a. Dictionaries

In addition to the *legal* dictionaries previously described in Chapter 15, the following general language dictionaries are valuable reference tools and are readily available in most libraries.[9]

9. Foreign language dictionaries are described below in Section E.4 of Chapter 20, Foreign and Comparative Law.

Webster's New International Dictionary of the English Language (first published, 1934, and popularly known as Webster's *Second* edition) is perhaps the most commonly found unabridged dictionary in American libraries. It contains approximately 600,000 vocabulary entries, including proper names, abbreviations, proverbs, and some foreign phrases. The standard dictionary type information is provided for each entry: spelling, pronunciation, syllabication, and definitions, presented here in historical sequence. Additionally, this work includes an appendix including abbreviations, signs and symbols, forms of address, a pronouncing gazetteer and a biographical dictionary.

Webster's Third New International Dictionary of the English Language (first published, 1961) is also found in many libraries, but it is not merely an updated version of the earlier Webster edition. This is a different work in both design and scope, and includes approximately 100,000 new entries, many of which are considered to be slang or colloquial. However, many rare and obsolete words have been omitted, dropping the total vocabulary to 450,000, and the geographical and biographical appendixes have not been included.

The researcher interested in the origin and history of English words should consult the *Oxford English Dictionary,* available in several different editions and formats, with current supplements. This historical dictionary offers encyclopedic treatment of more than 400,000 words. For each entry, the editors present the history of its usage, and numerous quotations from authors of all relevant historical periods.

There are many specialized subject dictionaries that may be of use to the legal researcher confronted with a problem in an unfamiliar or technical area. A few examples include the following: *Schmidt's Attorneys' Dictionary of Medicine and Word Finder* (1962, plus annual looseleaf supp.); A. Gilpin, *Dictionary of Economic Terms,* 4th ed. (1977); *Banking Terminology* (1981); D.D. Runes, et al., *Dictionary of Philosophy* (1962); L.E. Davids, *Dictionary of Insurance* (1977); G.A. Theodorson & A.G. Theodorson, *A Modern Dictionary of Sociology* (1969); W. Laqueur, *A Dictionary of Politics* (rev.ed., 1974); McGraw-Hill *Dictionary of Scientific and Technical Terms* (1976); and *Dictionary of Criminal Justice Data Terminology* (2nd ed., 1981). Subject dictionaries are also listed in Sheehy's *Guide to Reference Books,* and can be located with the help of a reference Librarian.

b. Thesauri and Synonyms

Roget's Thesaurus, available in a variety of editions, is the classic synonym/antonym dictionary of the English language. Roget sought to classify human thought according to specific categories, and this work is arranged by approximately a thousand classifications corresponding to the idea or significance of individual words. Since individual words are not presented alphabetically, one must use the index to locate the category within which a specific word is listed.

Webster's New Dictionary of Synonyms (1968) is easier to use, as its entries are arranged in standard alphabetical order. For each word, a list of synonyms and antonyms is presented, and analogous and contrasted words are included as well. Within each entry, nuances of meaning are explained and illustrative quotations from both classical and popular literature are provided.

c. Acronyms and Abbreviations

Reference tools for *legal* abbreviations have been described above in Section C.5 of Chapter 15. For identifying non-legal acronyms and abbreviations, the most comprehensive sources are the following two publications of the Gale Research Company:

Abbreviations, Acronyms, Ciphers and Signs, edited by A.M. Brewer (1981), arranged by subject, with an index to the full names.

Acronyms, Initialisms, and Abbreviations Dictionary, 8th ed., by E.T. Crowley, 3 vols. (1982).

R. DeSola's *Abbreviations Dictionary* (5th ed., 1978) is another useful tool of this kind.

d. Semantics

The intricacies of legal terminology, and the use (and perhaps misuse) by lawyers of the English language, has stimulated a number of interesting studies. Several of these are listed above in Footnote 30 to Chapter 15, at p. 471.

e. Style Guides and Legal Writing Texts

There are now many fine style guides and texts on legal writing for law students and lawyers. The following are some examples:

Legal Writing Style, 2d ed. (1980) by Henry Weihofen is a handbook primarily intended for law students who seek to improve the style of their written work, and includes a useful chapter on writing law school and bar examinations. The stylistic aspects of composing letters, memoranda, and briefs are also discussed in this work, as are general principles of organization. Another helpful style book is Gertrude Block's *Effective Legal Writing,* 2d ed. (1983). This source includes Chapters on grammar and meaning, legal style, and expository and argumentative techniques.

Reed Dickerson's *The Fundamentals of Legal Drafting* (1965) and his several later works concentrate on principles specifically relating to the drafting of legal instruments such as legislative bills, contracts, and wills. Also useful as style guides pertaining to legislation are the legislative bill drafting manuals prepared by many state legislatures.

The Grammatical Lawyer (1979) by Morton S. Freeman is in large part a collection of articles previously published in the American Law Institute-American Bar Association periodical, *The Practical*

Lawyer. The articles are concerned with the standards of English writing for lawyers.

These additional recent titles may also be helpful as aids to improving one's writing ability:

J.C. Dernbach & R.V. Singleton II, *A Practical Guide to Legal Writing and Legal Method* (1981).

R.L. Goldfarb & J.C. Raymond, *Clear Understandings, a Guide to Legal Writing* (1982).

G.D. Gopen, *Writing from a Legal Perspective* (1981).

D. Mellinkoff, *Legal Writing: Sense and Nonsense* (1982).

L.B. Squires & M.D. Rombauer, *Legal Writing in a Nutshell* (1982).

R.C. Wydick, *Plain English for Lawyers* (1979).

A wide variety of general style manuals, ranging from Strunk & White's little classic, *The Elements of Style* (3d ed., 1978) to the detailed University of Chicago *A Manual of Style* (13th ed., 1982), are recommended and available in most libraries.

5. INFORMATION ABOUT PLACES AND GEOGRAPHY

The researcher in need of geographical information will find two types of reference sources particularly helpful: atlases, and gazetteers or geographical dictionaries. Major selections are indicated below. For other titles, see one of the following bibliographies in this field: *Bibliographic Guide to Maps and Atlases* (G.K. Hall, *annual*); G.L. Alexander, *Guide to Atlases* (Scarecrow, 1971); J.P. Walsh, *General World Atlases in Print*, 4th ed. (Bowker, 1973).

a. Atlases

The *Times Atlas of the World* (1955–59), produced by the London *Times*, is considered by many to be the best world atlas for general reference use. Each of its five volumes is devoted to a different geographical region and is individually indexed. Since 1967, the London *Times* has also published *The Times Atlas of the World* in regularly revised one volume editions (6th ed., 1980). These are based on the maps of the multi-volume work, but reflect the latest status of political boundaries and place names.

For geographical information regarding the United States, the *Rand McNally Commercial Atlas and Marketing Guide* is probably the most useful tool. Revised annually, it is a source of current statistical data pertaining to the country as a whole as well as to individual states. Although its primary focus is on the United States, a smaller section provides maps of foreign countries. As its title suggests, emphasis in this work is placed on commercial aspects of the areas covered and much information on business, agriculture, and manufacturing is included with the maps.

Other atlases of varying size, scope and format are published regularly by Hammond, Inc., the National Geographic Society, and Rand McNally.

b. Gazetteers

A gazetteer is essentially a dictionary of geographical names, and is a convenient reference tool for locating basic information regarding cities, towns, mountains, lakes, rivers and other points of geographical interest. Typically, an entry for a place in a gazetteer will include its pronunciation, location, and physical description. Population statistics, economic data, and historical material, where relevant, are included as well.

The two most popular American Gazetteers are the *Columbia Lippincott Gazetteer of the World* (1962) and *Webster's New Geographical Dictionary,* rev. ed. (1980). The former is the more comprehensive work of the two, with regard to both number of entries and amount of information provided, but the latter is more current. The London *Times Index-Gazetteer of the World* (1966) describes many more places, and gives latitudes and longitudes for each. Probably the most comprehensive for research purposes is the *Gazetteer* series (1955–date) originally issued by the U.S. Board on Geographic Names in the Department of the Interior, but now put out by the Defense Mapping Agency. It includes separate guides to most countries in the world, and consists of approximately 150 such studies.

Countries of the World and Their Leaders Yearbook, 1982 (Gale Research, 1982) 2v. with 6 month *Supplement,* is a sourcebook of geographic, political, economic, and related information on many countries. Its data is largely drawn from State Department publications and other governmental sources.

6. PERIODICALS AND NEWSPAPERS

Legal periodicals and newspapers, and their indexes, have been described above in Chapter 16. Non-legal periodicals and their contents, however, have become increasingly important in legal research. This section will therefore describe a few of the major directories for identifying such publications, and some of the periodical indexes which are available for access to their contents. Similar guides and indexes for social science periodicals will be treated separately in Chapter 18 below. For the rest, this discussion must necessarily be brief, but further information can be obtained from *Indexes, Abstracts and Digests* (Gale Research, 1982), a guide to some 6,000 aids for searching the contents of books, periodicals, and documents; Sheehy's *Guide to Reference Books* and many of the bibliographies of periodicals listed therein; and your local reference librarians.

The following directories are the most comprehensive and widely used sources for information on periodicals:

Standard Periodical Directory (biennial) is probably the most complete guide to U.S. & Canadian periodicals, describing over

68,000 titles in an alphabetical subject arrangement, with indexing by title and subject.

Ulrich's International Periodicals Directory (biennial) is also arranged by subject, with indexing by title and subject. Although less extensive than *Standard,* it also includes foreign periodicals, which are not covered by *Standard.* It indicates which indexing and abstracting sources cover each title listed and which periodicals have ceased publication since the last edition of the directory.

Ayer's Directory of Publications (annual) is particularly useful for its coverage of newspapers. It also lists magazines, but on a more selective basis than the two directories described above. *Ayer's* covers publications in the U.S., Canada, Puerto Rico, The Virgin Islands, Bermuda, the Bahamas, Panama and the Philippines. It lists trade publications and those designed for particular religious, racial and ethnic groups.

Irregular Serials and Annuals, an International Directory (annual) is a companion to *Ulrich's,* with the same format, coverage and features, but it focuses on yearbooks, transactions, proceedings, and many other irregularly published serials.

a. Reader's Guide to Periodical Literature and The Magazine Index

The *Reader's Guide* is the H.W. Wilson Company's index to over 180 popular periodicals of general interest. It is issued bi-monthly, with annual cumulations, and provides author and subject indexing. It is probably the most widely used periodical index in the world.

Since 1976, *The Magazine Index* has been published on microfilm by Information Access Corp., on the same basis as that publisher's *Legal Resources Index,* described above in Chapter 16, *Legal Periodicals.* It indexes about four hundred magazines, twice the number covered by the *Reader's Guide,* and provides more points of access to their contents than its traditional competitor. The microfilm is revised and updated monthly and permanent microfiche cumulations are issued to permit reduction of the main microfilm index. *The Magazine Index* is also available on-line for computer searching through DIALOG.

b. The New York Times Index

The *New York Times* has a unique research value as the most comprehensive newspaper of record in this country, and its index is frequently used by lawyers to locate information on individuals, institutions, or events. *The New York Times Index* has been published with varying frequency since 1913, and is now issued semimonthly, with annual cumulations. Its "Prior Series" from 1851 to 1912 was originally an in-house index at the *Times.* Most of the "Prior Series" volumes are available on microfilm from Microfilming Corporation of

America, and have also been issued in book form by R.R. Bowker. For computer access, see below in subsection d.

The *Personal Name Index to the "New York Times Index" 1851–1974*, projected for 22 vols. (Roxbury Data Interface, 1976—in progress) will be another means of access to the *N.Y. Times*, by individual names.

c. Other Indexes of General Interest

Public Affairs Information Service (PAIS) indexes over one thousand periodicals published in English throughout the world, and selective books, documents and pamphlets. Its focus is primarily on political science, economics, government, legislation, and other social sciences. The Bulletin of *PAIS* is issued weekly, with five cumulations per year, the fifth cumulation being an annual bound volume. Since 1972, *PAIS* has also issued a *Foreign Language Index*, on a quarterly basis, for French, German, Italian, Spanish and Portugese periodicals in the fields of economics and public affairs.

The H.W. Wilson Company publishes a number of other periodical indexes in a format similar to that of the *Reader's Guide* and the *Index to Legal Periodicals*. The following are of interest here: *Social Sciences Index* and *Humanities Index*, both published since 1974, continuing the earlier combined *Social Sciences and Humanities Index* (1916–1974); the *Business Periodicals Index* (1958–date), covering approximately 270 journals in a variety of commercial fields; and the *Applied Science & Technology Index* (1958–date), covering about 225 journals in English. From 1913 to 1957, the *Industrial Arts Index* included the fields covered by both the *Applied Science and Technology Index* and the *Business Periodicals Index*.

National Newspaper Index (Information Access Corp., 1979–date) is a monthly microfilm index, similar in format and frequency to the same publisher's *Magazine Index*. It covers the *Christian Science Monitor*, the *New York Times*, and the *Wall Street Journal*, as is also available for on-line searching through DIALOG.

Newspaper Index (Bell & Howell, 1972–date) provides access to the contents of the *Chicago Tribune*, the *Los Angeles Times, The New Orleans Times-Picayune*, the *Washington Post*, and (since 1976) to four other metropolitan newspapers. Each newspaper is covered by a separate monthly index, which is cumulated annually.

There are three other periodical indexes covering popular, regional, and alternative magazines not indexed in the *Readers Guide to Periodical Literature:*

Access: The Supplementary Index to Periodicals (Gaylord, 1975–date) three times a year, the last issue being an annual cumulation; covers about 130 popular and regional magazines.

Alternative Press Index (Alternative Press Center, 1970–date) quarterly, covers about 150 offbeat, liberal and radical newspapers, magazines and journals.

Popular Periodical Index (1973–date) covers about 36 special interest and regional magazines.

d. Computer Indexes to Periodicals

An increasing number of specialized indexes are now available through commercial vendors of computerized data bases. Some will be described below in Chapter 22, New Media in Legal Research, and some have been mentioned in earlier chapters. Those offered by the major vendors, such as Lockheed's DIALOG services, are accessible through many personal home computers and the multi-purpose computers used in many law offices.

Among the most important periodical indexes which are available on-line is the *Legal Resources Index,* described above in Section C.2 of Chapter 16, Periodical Literature. *Legal Resources Index* is available for on-line searching through Lockheed's DIALOG services, which are accessible through LEXIS and most WESTLAW terminals.

The *New York Times Information Service* (successor to *The Information Bank*) indexes and digests the contents of *New York Times* and about sixty other newspapers and magazines, from 1974 to date. Although business, scientific, current affairs and international periodicals are included, most are of a general rather than technical nature. Although formerly available through the *N.Y. Times* itself, this service is now available on-line *exclusively* from Mead Data Central, as an addition to its NEXIS service. The service includes full-text searching of the *N.Y. Times* from June 1, 1980.

NEXIS, a computerized news service available from Mead Data Central through its LEXIS research system, is a full-text data base of some forty general interest, business, and technological newspapers, magazines, wire services, newsletters, and also includes many government publications. Most of the contents is retrospective to the mid-1970's and its coverage is both domestic and foreign.

The following directories offer information on a wide range of data bases available in these and other fields:

Directory of Online Databases (Cuadra Associates, 1979–date) quarterly.

Directory of Online Information Resources (CSG Press, 1978–date) Projected for semi-annual updating.

Computer Readable Bibliographic Data Bases: a Directory and Sourcebook (Knowledge Industr., 1979–date) Projected for biennial editions.

Online Bibliographic Databases, 2d ed. (Gale Research, 1981).

All of these on-line data bases are commercial products and searching on them can be quite expensive. A good understanding of their respective search strategies is necessary to minimize charges. One should consult the reference librarians in the libraries offering these services, for information about the data bases, their contents, and their most effective use. This area will be explored further in Chapter 22, New Media in Legal Research.

7. GOVERNMENT PUBLICATIONS

The United States Government is probably the largest publisher in the world, and certainly one of the largest publishers of legal and law-related materials. Previous chapters have discussed a number of the government's legal publications, especially those in the fields of primary sources, legislative history, and administrative law. Since many other publications of the federal and state governments are also of significance in legal research, this section is devoted to such materials. Three types of publications will be described: (a) sources of information *about* the federal government and its officers; (b) directories and indexes of federal government publications; and (c) state government publications.

a. Information About the Government

The *United States Government Manual,* an annual publication, is an excellent *official* guide to the numerous agencies of the federal government, providing background, names, addresses, and phone numbers of offices, and includes lists of activities and major publications of each agency. It is well indexed and relatively easy to use.

Washington Information Directory, (Congressional Quarterly, *annual*) is a compendium on the federal government, containing subject oriented chapters (e.g., "Energy," "Housing & Urban Affairs," etc.) designed to assist users in getting information in those subjects. Each chapter lists sources of information for that field, divided into three categories: (1) agencies of the executive branch; (2) Congress; and (3) private or "non-governmental" organizations. The subject index is detailed and extensive, and an index to agencies and organizations is also provided. The annual revision of *Washington Information Directory* keeps its contents relatively current. Among other directories of similar coverage are the following sources, each of which focuses more specifically on the government sectors indicated in its title:

Federal Regulatory Directory (Congressional Quarterly, 1979–date) annual.

Official Congressional Directory (U.S. Govt. Printing Office, 1809–date) annual.

Encyclopedia of Governmental Advisory Organizations, 3d ed. (Gale Research, 1980) irregular revisions, but updated by *New Governmental Advisory Organizations,* looseleaf with irregular supplements.

Commercial publications dealing primarily with federal government officials include the following:

Congressional Staff Directory (1959–date) annual.

Congressional Yellow Book . . . (Washington Monitor) annual.

Federal Yellow Book, a looseleaf directory of the federal departments and agencies (Washington Monitor) annual.

Congressional Quarterly, Inc., publisher of *Congressional Quarterly,* described above in Chapter 10, and the *Washington Information Directory,* also issues a number of handbooks on the federal government. Although popular in approach, they are of good quality and are often useful for background information in legal research. They are revised with irregular frequency and include *Guide to the Congress, Guide to the U.S. Supreme Court, Guide to Current American Government,* and *Guide to the U.S. Elections.*

b. Information About Government Publications

Because of the large number and importance of government publications, various catalogs, guides and indexes to such documents are available, and several deserve mention here.

The *Monthly Catalog of U. S. Government Publications* is the sales catalog of U.S. Government Printing Office and the most comprehensive guide and index to federal government documents. Each issue contains over a thousand entries, and some over two thousand. There are detailed annual indexes, and several decennial and quinquennial indexes as well. More and more government documents are being issued on microfiche, particularly to depository libraries, and that format will undoubtedly become increasingly important for access to these materials in most research libraries. The Government Printing Office has been experimenting with other forms of catalogs, pricelists, notices of new publications and any depository library can provide copies of the latest versions.

Among the many commercially published guides to government publications, the following selection may be useful:

J. Morehead, *Introduction to United States Public Documents,* 2d ed. (Libraries Unlimited, 1978).

J. Andriot, *Guide to U. S. Government Serials and Periodicals* (Documents Index) irregular frequency.

J. Andriot, *Guide to U. S. Government Publications* (Documents Index, 1973–date) looseleaf updating.

c. Information About the States

Publications of state governments are somewhat more elusive than those of the federal government, but there are a number of reliable sources which can be consulted.

The *Book of the States* (Council of State Governments, 1935–date) is an extremely useful biennial compendium of varied information on state governments. It includes legal, political and statistical information from all states, which would otherwise require much effort to collect from governmental sources in the fifty states.

The *Municipal Year Book* (International City Management Ass'n, 1934–date), annual, and the *County Year Book* (International City

Management Ass'n, 1975–date), provide similar information for those levels of government.

Official state directories, often called "Blue Books" and sometimes "Red Books" are published annually or biennially by most states. Their contents are similar to that of the *U. S. Government Manual,* but focusing of course on the state government which issued them. The Council of State Governments has published a bibliography of these manuals: *State Blue Books and Reference Publications* (1972).

For state publications generally, the *Monthly Checklist of State Publications* (Library of Congress, 1910–date), monthly, is the most comprehensive source but is far from complete. A retrospective guide is S.A. Mac Manus, *Selective Bibliography on State Government, 1973–1978* (Council of State Governments, 1979) which updates a previous edition covering 1959–1972. It is hoped that this useful work will continue to be supplemented.

Other helpful works on state governments include the following:

S. Lukowski & C.T. Grayson, *State Information Book* (Potomac Books, 1980).

National Directory of State Agencies (Information Resources Press, 1974–date) biennial.

Index to Current Urban Documents (Greenwood Press, 1972–date) quarterly with annual cumulations.

8. STATISTICAL INFORMATION

The use of statistical data of varying kinds is substantial in modern litigation and legal research. There are many sources of statistics and most derive from the work of the U.S. Bureau of the Census, the Bureau of Labor Statistics, and other government agencies. Full information on the many publications of this material can be found in E. Sheehy's *Guide to Reference Books* and the documentary bibliographies cited above. The following sources are among the most widely used, and many others are available in computer data bases.

a. Statistical Abstract of the United States

The *Statistical Abstract,* an annual publication of the Bureau of the Census since 1879, is the most versatile compendium of statistics on political, economic, social and demographic subjects. It is well indexed and gives sources for all of its tables and summaries.

b. Historical Statistics of the United States

A retrospective survey, drawn from the Census Bureau's past data is the *Historical Statistics of the United States, Colonial Times to 1970,* 2 vols. (U.S. Govt. Printing Office, 1975). Its twenty six chapters cover broad subject areas, accessible also by detailed subject and time period indexes.

c. Other Statistics Sources

American Statistics Index . . . a comprehensive guide and index to the statistical publications of the U.S. government (Congressional Information Service, 1973–date) monthly, with annual cumulations.

Index to International Statistics (Congressional Information Service, 1983–date) monthly, with annual cumulations. Covers statistics from international organizations.

Statistical Reference Index (Congressional Information Service, 1980–date) monthly, with annual cumulations. Covers statistics from sources other than the U. S. government.

J. Andriot, *Guide to U.S. Government Statistics,* 4th ed. (Documents Index, 1973).

Statistics Sources, edited by P. Wasserman, 4th ed. (Gale Research, 1974).

Statistical Yearbook (United Nations, 1949–date) annual.

Demographic Yearbook (United Nations, 1949–date) annual.

Vital Statistics of the United States (U.S. Govt. Printing Office, 1939–date) annual.

International Encyclopedia of Statistics, edited by W.H. Kruskal & J.M. Tanur (Free Press, 1978) 2v.

N. Johnson, "Legal Statistics", 1 *Legal Reference Service Q.* 3–16 (1981).

Statistics-America, edited by Joan M. Harvey, 2d ed. (Gale Research, 1980).

Statistics-Europe, edited by Joan M. Harvey, 4th ed. (Gale Research, 1981).

Subject Index to Sources of Comparative International Statistics, comp., by F.C. Pieper (Gale Research, 1978).

9. QUOTATION BOOKS

There are a variety of legal and non-legal quotation books to aid the researcher in finding famous or interesting statements relating to the law or to particular legal issues. These compilations differ from the collections of legal maxims, described above in Section C.4 of Chapter 15. Legal maxims summarize generally accepted legal principles in a concise form. Quotations are gathered from a wide range of legal and non-legal sources, and are usually arranged by subject with cross-references provided through indexes to authors and key words. Although these quotations are not legally authoritative in any sense, they can be of considerable rhetorical value. A quotation containing a well-turned phrase or illustration often makes a point more clearly and succinctly than numerous or lengthy citations to more weighty authority.

Among the non-legal quotation books, the following may be of use: *Barlett's Familiar Quotations* (15th ed., 1980), arranged *chronologically* by author, with separate author and word indexes; Evans, *Dictionary of Quotations* (1968), arranged by subject, with topical and author indexes; Jones, *Dictionary of Foreign Phrases and Classical Quotations* (1977); Magill's *Quotations in Context,* 2d series (1969), arranged alphabetically by first word of quotation, with author and word indexes; Mencken, *A New Dictionary of Quotations* (1942), arranged by subject; Murphy, *Crown Treasury of Relevant Quotations* (1978), arranged topically, with separate author and subject indexes; *Oxford Dictionary of Quotations* (3rd ed., 1979), arranged by author, with key word index; Palmer, *Quotations in History: A Dictionary of Historical Quotations c. 800 A.D. to the Present* (1976), arranged by author, with index of key words and key words in foreign languages; Cohen, *Penguin Dictionary of Quotations* (1977), arranged by author, with word index; W. Safire and L. Safir, *Good Advice* (1982), arranged by subject, with general index; Seldes, *The Great Quotations* (1966), arranged by author, with subject index; Simpson, *Contemporary Quotations* (1964), arranged by subject with source (author) and subject indexes; J. Green, *Morrow's International Dictionary of Contemporary Quotations* (1982), arranged by broad subject categories, with author and word indexes; and Stevenson, *The Home Book of Quotations* (1967), arranged by subject, with author and word indexes.

Redden and Veron, *Modern Legal Glossary,* described above in Section C.2 of Chapter 15, Treatises, etc., includes many *legal* quotations. The following compilations also focus specifically on legal quotations: Clark, *Great Sayings of the Lawyers* (1926); Cook, *Treasury of Legal Quotations* (1961), arranged by author, with subject index; Gerhart, *Quote It! Memorable Legal Quotations* (1969); Jackson, *The Wisdom of the Supreme Court* (1973), arranged by subject with appendixes containing parallel references and court terms and brief biographies of the justices; Jones, *A Translation of all the Greek, Latin, Italian, and French quotations which occur in Blackstone's Commentaries on the Laws of England* (1889), following volume and page number of Blackstone's *Commentaries;* Kornblitt, *Dictionary of Persuasive Phrases for Lawyers* (1962); McNamara, *2,000 Famous Legal Quotations* (1967), arranged by subject, with separate subject and author indexes; Mead, *Manual of Forensic Quotations* (1968); and Norton-Kyshe, *Dictionary of Legal Quotations* (1968).

10. COMPUTER DATA BASES

Many of the reference areas covered in this chapter are now substantially augmented by computer data bases. Commercial vendors of data bases and some government agencies make available a wide variety of new sources for on-line access by computer terminals. As noted above, most of these services are expensive to use, but with preparation and assistance sophisticated searchers can minimize their costs. Four directories of on-line data bases are listed in section 6.d above, and many others will undoubtedly be published during the life of this book. Reference librarians can suggest the latest sources of information on new data bases and can assist in choosing those most useful for particular searches and in preparing for their use.

More information on law-related computer research can be found in Chapter 22, New Media in Legal Research.

D. LISTS OF SOURCES: TITLES REFERRED TO IN THIS CHAPTER

1. GENERAL INFORMATION

a. Legal Reference Tools

Am.Jur.2d Desk Book, 2d ed. (Lawyers Co-op/Bancroft-Whitney, 1979).

Effective Factual Research For Lawyers, by Georgia Finnigan (Information Store, 1981).

Law and Legal Information Directory, 2d ed. (Gale Research, 1983).

Lawyer's Almanac: A Cornucopia of Information About Law, Lawyers, and the Legal Profession, annual (Law & Business, 1982–date).

b. General Reference Tools and Guides to Library Research

Finding Facts Fast, by Alden Todd, 2d ed. (Ten Speed Press, 1979).

Guide to Reference Books, by Eugene P. Sheehy, 9th ed. (American Library Association, 1976); 2d *Supplement,* 1982.

Guide to the Use of Books and Libraries, by Jean K. Gates, 4th ed. (McGraw-Hill, 1979).

The Modern Researcher, by Jacques P. Barzun and Henry F. Graff, 3d ed. (Harcourt, Brace & World, 1977).

The New Library Key, by Margaret G. Cook, 3d ed. (H.W. Wilson Co., 1975).

Reference Books: A Brief Guide, by Marion V. Bell and Eleanor A. Surdan, 8th ed., revised irregularly (Baltimore: Enoch Pratt Free Library, 1978).

c. Encyclopedias

Dictionary of the History of Ideas (Scribner's 1973–74), 5v.

Encyclopedia Americana (Grolier Ed. Corp., 1982), 30v.

Encyclopedia Britannica, 15th ed. (Ency. Brittanica, 1980), 30v.

Encyclopedia International (Grolier Ed. Corp., 1982), 20v.

Encyclopedia of American Economic History (Scribner's 1980), 3v.

Encyclopedia of Education (Macmillan Co. & The Free Press, 1971), 10v.

Encyclopedia of Philosophy (Macmillan Co. & The Free Press, 1973) 4v.

Encyclopedia of Psychology, 2d ed. (Continuum, 1979)

Encyclopedia of the Social Sciences (Macmillan, 1930–1935) 15v.

Encyclopedia of Urban Planning, (Krieger, 1980)

Guide to American Law: Everyone's Legal Encyclopedia (West Publishing Co., 1983), 12v. (in progress)

International Encyclopedia of the Social Sciences (Free Press, 1977), 8v. plus supplement (1979).

New Columbia Encyclopedia, 4th ed. (Columbia Univ. Press 1975).

Oxford Companion to Law (Oxford Univ. Press, 1980).

Palgrave's Dictionary of Political Economy (Macmillan and Co., 1925), 13v.

World Book Encyclopedia, (World Book-Childcraft, 1982), 22v.

Worldmark Encyclopedia of the Nations, 4th ed. (Harper & Row, 1971), 5v.

d. Almanacs

The Hammond Almanac, annual (Hammond Almanac, Inc., 1979–date).

Information Please Almanac, annual (Macmillan, 1947–date).

The Official Associated Press Almanac, annual (Almanac Publishing Co., 1973–date).

Reader's Digest Almanac, annual (Reader's Digest Assoc., 1966–date).

The World Almanac and Book of Facts, annual (Newspaper Enterprise Assoc., 1868–date).

e. Other Factual Sourcebooks

Aerospace Yearbook (American Aviation Publ., 1919–date).

Annual Register: A Record of World Events, annual (Gale, 1982).

Facts on File, weekly, with annual bound cumulations (Facts on File, 1940–date).

Information Age Sourcebook (Pantheon, 1982).

Keesing's Contemporary Archives, weekly (Keesing's, 1931–date).

Labor Fact Book, biennial (irregular) (Internat., 1930–65), 17v.

Life Insurance Fact Book, annual (Institute of Life Insurance, 1946–date).

Worldwide Government Directory with Inter-Governmental Organizations, with bimonthly update (Lambert Publications, 1983).

Yearbook of Agriculture (Arno, 1976).

2. INFORMATION ABOUT PEOPLE

American Men and Women of Science, 14th ed. (R.R. Bowker, 1979).

Biographical Index Series (Gale Research Co., 1980), 8v. plus 4v. *Supplement* (1982).

Biography Index, monthly with annual and three-year cumulations (H.W. Wilson, 1946–date).

Current Biography, monthly with annual cumulative Yearbooks (H.W. Wilson 1940–date).

Current Biography Cumulated Index 1940–70 (H.W. Wilson, 1973).

Dictionary of American Biography (Scribner's, 1882–1937), 20v., with supplements, and its abridgment, *Concise Dictionary of American Biography* (1964).

Dictionary of National Biography (Oxford Univ. Press, 1912–1959), 22v., with supplements, and its abridgment, the *Concise Dictionary,* 2v., (1953–61).

Directory of American Scholars, 8th ed. (R.R. Bowker, 1982), 4v.

Directory of Directories, 2d ed. (Gale Research, 1983).

Guide to American Directories, 10th ed., revised irregularly (McGraw-Hill, 1979).

International Who's Who, annual, 46th ed. (Internat'l. Pubs. Service, 1982).

New York Times Obituaries Index (Microfilming Corp., 1970, 1980) covering 1858–1978, 2 vols.

Notable American Women 1607–1950 (Harvard University Press, 1971) 3v., plus *The Modern Period* (1980) 1v. supplement.

Wer Ist Wer, 21st ed., published irregularly (Internat'l. Pubs. Service, 1981).

Who Was Who in America (Marquis, 1963–81), 9v. with cumulative index. Includes *Historical Volume 1607–1896,* with 7 supp. volumes.

Who Was Who . . . A Companion to Who's Who (1929–1980), 7v. with supplements.

Who's Who, 133d ed., annual (St. Martin, 1981).

Who's Who in America, 42d ed., biennial (Marquis, 1982), 2v.

Who's Who in American Law, 3d ed. (Marquis, 1983).

Who's Who in Canada, 70th ed. (Internat'l. Pubs. Serv. 1980).

Who's Who in Canadian Law, 2d ed. (Trans-Canada Press, 1982).

Who's Who in Finance and Industry, 22d ed., published irregularly (Marquis, 1981).

Who's Who in France, 7th ed., biennial (Internat'l. Pubs. Service, 1980), 2v.

Who's Who in Germany, 4th ed., irregular (Oldenbourg, 1955–date).

Who's Who in the East, 18th ed. (Marquis, 1981).

Who's Who in the Midwest, 18th ed. (Marquis, 1982).

Who's Who in the South and Southwest, 18th ed. (Marquis, 1982).

Who's Who in the West, 18th ed. (Marquis, 1982).

Who's Who of American Women, 13th ed., biennial (Marquis, 1983).

3. INFORMATION ON INSTITUTIONS

Directory of Consumer Protection and Environmental Agencies (Academic Media, 1973).

Directory of Corporate Affiliations of Major National Advertisers, annual (National Register, 1982).

Encyclopedia of Associations, 17th ed. (Gale Research, 1982), 3v.

ERC Closely-Held Corporation Guide (Exec. Reports, 1981).

Everybody's Business Almanac (Harper & Row, 1982).

Foundation Directory, 8th ed., irregular (Foundation Center, 1981), updated by the bimonthly publication, *Foundation News.*

How to Find Information About Companies (B. Klein Publications, 1979).

International Directory of Corporate Affiliations (National Register, 1982).

Moody's Manuals, multi-volumed (Moody's Investor's Service, 1982).

National Directory of State Agencies, biennial (Information Resources, 1974–date).

National Trade and Professional Associations of the United States, 17th ed. annual (Columbia Books, 1972–date).

Poor's Register of Corporations, Directors and Executives, annual (Standard & Poor's, 1962–date), 3v.

The Princeton Mergers and Acquisitions Reporter and Directory, looseleaf (Princeton Research Inst., 1981), 5v.

Social Science Organizations and Agencies Directory (Gale Research, 1982).

Standard and Poor's Register (Standard and Poor's, 1983), 3v.

Thomas' Register of American Manufacturers, annual (Thomas Publ. Co., 190?–date).

4. INFORMATION ABOUT WORDS AND MEANINGS

a. Dictionaries

Banking Terminology (American Bankers Association, 1981).

Dictionaries, Encyclopedias, and Other Word-Related Books, 3d ed. (Gale Research, 1982), 3v.

Dictionary of Criminal Justice (Holbrook Press, 1977).

Dictionary of Criminal Justice Data Terminology, 2d ed. (U.S. Dept. of Justice, 1981).

Dictionary of Criminal Justice Terms (Gould, 1982).

Dictionary of Economics, 5th ed. (Barnes & Noble, 1971).

Dictionary of Economic Terms, 2d ed. (Butterworths, 1970).

Dictionary of Insurance, 5th ed. (Littlefield, 1977).

Dictionary of Philosophy (Philosophical Library, 1982).

Dictionary of Politics (Free Press, 1974).

Dictionary of Scientific and Technical Terms (McGraw-Hill, 1976).

McGraw-Hill Dictionary of Modern Economics, 2d ed. (McGraw-Hill, 1973).

A Modern Dictionary of Sociology (Crowell, 1969).

Oxford English Dictionary (Oxford Univ. Press, available in several editions and formats).

Schmidt's Attorneys' Dictionary of Medicine and Word Finder (Bender, 1962) 3v., plus annual looseleaf supplement.

Webster's New International Dictionary of the English Language, 2d ed. (first published, 1934).

Webster's Third New International Dictionary of the English Language (Merriam, 1981).

Webster's New World Dictionary of The American Language (Popular Library, 1982).

b. Thesauri and Synonyms

Roget's II: The New Thesaurus (Houghton Mifflin, 1980), plus many other publishers' editions.

Webster's Collegiate Thesaurus (Merriam, 1976).

Webster's New Dictionary of Synonyms (Merriam, 1978).

c. Acronyms and Abbreviations

Abbreviations, Acronyms, Ciphers, and Signs (Gale Research, 1981).

Abbreviations Dictionary, 6th ed. (Elsevier, 1981).

Acronyms, Initialisms, and Abbreviations Dictionary, 8th ed. (Gale Research, 1982).

d. Style Guides

The Chicago Manual of Style, 13th ed. (Univ. of Chicago Press, 1982).

Clear Understandings, A Guide to Legal Writing, by R.L. Goldfarb & J.C. Raymond (Random House, 1982).

Effective Legal Writing, by Gertrude Block 2d ed. (Foundation Press, 1983).

Elements of Style, 3d ed., by William Strunk and E.B. White (Macmillan, 1978).

The Fundamentals of Legal Drafting, by Reed Dickerson (Little, Brown, 1965).

The Grammatical Lawyer, by Morton S. Freeman (American Law Institute/ABA, 1979).

Legal Writing in a Nutshell, by L.B. Squires and M.D. Rombauer (West Publishing Co., 1982).

Legal Writing: Sense and Nonsense, by D. Mellinkoff (West, 1982).

Legal Writing Style, 2d ed., by Henry Weihofen (West Publishing Co., 1980).

Plain English for Lawyers, by R.C. Wydick (Carolina Academic Press, 1979).

A Practical Guide to Legal Writing and Legal Method, by J.C. Dernbach and R.V. Singleton II (Fred B. Rothman, 1981).

The Practical Lawyer's Manual on Legal Research, Writing, and Indexing (American Law Institute/ABA, 1979).

Writing From a Legal Perspective, by G.D. Gopen (West Publishing Co., 1981).

5. INFORMATION ABOUT PLACES AND GEOGRAPHY

a. Atlases

Bibliographic Guide to Maps and Atlases, annual (G.K. Hall, 1979–date).

General World Atlases in Print, 4th ed. (Bowker, 1973).

Guide to Atlases (Scarecrow, 1971).

Rand McNally Commercial Atlas and Marketing Guide, annual (Rand McNally, 1876–date).

Times Atlas of the World (1955–1959), 5v.; and "Comprehensive" edition, 6th ed. (Times Publ. Co., 1980) 1 vol.

b. Gazetteers

Columbia Lippincott Gazetteer of the World (Columbia Univ. Press, 1962).

Countries of the World and Their Leaders Yearbook (Gale Research, 1982), 2v., with six-month Supplement.

Times Index-Gazetteer of the World (London Times, 1966).

Webster's New Geographical Dictionary, rev. ed. (Merriam, 1980).

6. PERIODICALS AND NEWSPAPERS

Access: The Supplementary Index to Periodicals, annual (Gaylord, 1976–date).

Alternative Press Index, quarterly (Alternative Press Center, 1970–date).

Applied Science and Technology Index, monthly, with annual cumulations (H.W. Wilson, 1958–date).

Ayer Directory of Publications, annual (Ayer Press, 1981).

Business Periodical Index, monthly, with annual cumulations (H.W. Wilson, 1958–date).

Computer-Readable Bibliographic Data Bases: A Directory & Data Sourcebook (Knowledge Industry, 1982).

Directory of Online Databases, quarterly (Cuadra Associates, 1979–date).

Directory of Online Information Resources, semi-annual (CSG Press, 1978–date).

Humanities Index, quarterly, with annual cumulations (H.W. Wilson, 1974–date).

Industrial Arts Index (H.W. Wilson, 1913–1957).

Irregular Serials and Annuals, an International Directory, annual, 8th ed. (Bowker, 1982).

The Magazine Index, monthly microfilm (Information Access Corp., 1976–date).

National Newspaper Index, monthly microfilm (Information Access Corp., 1979–date).

New York Times Information Service (1974–date).

Newspaper Index (Bell and Howell, 1972–date).

Online Bibliographic Databases, 2d ed. (Gale Research, 1981).

Personal Name Index to the "New York Times Index" 1851–1974 (Roxbury Data Interface, 1976–date), 22v., in progress.

Public Affairs Information Service (PAIS), weekly, with five cumulations per year and annual bound volume (PAIS, 1915–date). PAIS also publishes *Foreign Language Index,* quarterly, with annual cumulations (PAIS, 1972–date).

Social Sciences and Humanities Index (H.W. Wilson, 1916–1974).

Social Sciences Index, quarterly with annual cumulations (H.W. Wilson, 1974–date).

7. GOVERNMENT PUBLICATIONS

Book of the States, biennial (Council of State Governments, 1935–date).

Congressional Quarterly's Guide to Current American Government (1962–date).

Congressional Quarterly's Guide to the Congress, 3d ed. (1982).

Congressional Quarterly's Guide to U.S. Elections (1975).

Congressional Quarterly's Guide to the U.S. Supreme Court (1979).

Congressional Staff Directory, annual (Cong. Staff Directory, 1959–date).

Congressional Yellow Book, annual (Washington Monitor).

County Year Book (International City Management Assn., 1975–date).

Encyclopedia of Governmental Advisory Organizations, 3d ed., irregular revisions (Gale Research, 1980), updated by *Governmental Advisory Organizations* (1979–date).

Federal Regulatory Directory (Congressional Quarterly, 1979–date).

Federal Yellow Book, annual (Washington Monitor).

Guide to U.S. Government Publications, by J.L. Andriot, ed., looseleaf, with quarterly update (Documents Index, 1973–date).

Guide to U.S. Government Serials and Periodicals, by J.L. Andriot, ed., irregular frequency (Documents Index, 1959–1977).

Index to Current Urban Documents, quarterly with annual cumulations (Greenwood Press, 1972–date).

Introduction to United States Public Documents, 2d ed. (Libraries Unlimited, 1978).

Monthly Catalog of U.S. Government Publications (U.S.G.P.O., 1895–date).

Monthly Checklist of State Publications (Library of Congress, 1910–date).

Municipal Year Book, annual (International City Management Association, 1934–date).

National Directory of State Agencies, biennial (Information Resources Press, 1974–date).

Official Congressional Directory, irregular revisions (U.S.G.P.O., 1809–date).

Selective Bibliography on State Government, 1973–1978 (Council of State Governments, 1979).

State Blue Books and Reference Publications (Council of State Governments, 1972).

United States Government Manual, annual (1935–date).

Washington Information Directory, annual (Congressional Quarterly).

8. STATISTICAL INFORMATION

American Statistics Index. . . ., monthly, with annual cumulations (Congressional Information Service, 1973–date).

Demographic Yearbook, annual (United Nations, 1949–date).

Guide to Reference Books, by E.P. Sheehy (American Library Assoc., 1976), with supplements.

Guide to U.S. Government Statistics, by J.L. Andriot, 4th ed. (Documents Index, 1973).

Historical Statistics of the United States, Colonial Times to 1970 (U.S.G.P.O., 1970), 2v.

Index to International Statistics, monthly, with annual cumulations (Congressional Information Service, 1983–date).

International Encyclopedia of Statistics (Free Press, 1978), 2v.

Johnson, N., "Legal Statistics," 1 *Legal Reference Service Q.* 3–16 (1981).

The Statistical Abstract, annual (Bureau of the Census, 1879–date).

Statistical Reference Service, monthly, with annual cumulations (Congressional Information Service, 1980–date).

Statistical Yearbook, annual (United Nations, 1949–date).

Statistics—America, 2d ed. (Gale Research, 1980).

Statistics—Europe, 4th ed. (Gale Research, 1981).

Statistics Sources, edited by P. Wasserman, 4th ed. (Gale Research, 1974).

Subject Index to Sources of Comparative International Statistics (Gale Research, 1978).

Vital Statistics of the United States, annual (U.S.G.P.O., 1939–date).

9. QUOTATION BOOKS

Bartlett's Familiar Quotations, 15th ed. (Little, Brown, 1980).

Contemporary Quotations (Crowell, 1964).

Crown Treasury of Relevant Quotations (Crown, 1978).

Dictionary of Foreign Phrases and Classical Quotations (Longwood Press, 1977).

Dictionary of Legal Quotations (Gale Research, 1968).

Dictionary of Quotations (Larousee, 1981).

Dictionary of Persuasive Phrases for Lawyers (Marby Publications, 1962).

Good Advice (Times Books, 1982).

The Great Quotations (Lyle Stuart, 1966).

Great Sayings by Great Lawyers, by G.J. Clark (Vernon Lawbook, 1926).

Home Book of Quotations, 10th ed. (Dodd, 1967).

Magill's Quotations in Context (Harper & Row, 1969).

Manual of Forensic Quotations (Gale Research, 1968).

Modern Legal Glossary (Michie Co., 1980).

Morrow's International Dictionary of Contemporary Quotations (William Morrow, 1982).

New Dictionary of Quotations (Knopf, 1942).

Oxford Dictionary of Quotations, 3d ed. (Oxford Univ. Press, 1979).

Quotations in History: A Dictionary of Historical Quotations c. 800 A.D. To The Present (Barnes & Noble, 1976).

Quote It! Memorable Legal Quotations (Clark Boardman, 1969).

Penguin Dictionary of Quotations (Penguin, 1977).

A Translation of all the Greek, Latin, Italian, and French Quotations Which Occur in Blackstone's Commentaries (T. and J.W. Johnson, 1889).

Treasury of Legal Quotations (Vantage Press, 1961).

2000 Famous Legal Quotations (Aqueduct Books, 1967).

The Wisdom of the Supreme Court (Greenwood Press, 1973).

Chapter 18

RESEARCH IN THE SOCIAL SCIENCES *

A. THE GROWING ACCEPTANCE OF SOCIAL SCIENCE IN LAW

For those even slightly familiar with the contemporary practice of law, it may come as a surprise that legal uses of social science analysis are a recent development. When Holmes began *The Common Law* with the observation, "The life of law has not been logic: it has been experience" (p. 1), he was not stating the self-evident; rather, he was making the point that the development of law was not so much governed by the play of formal rules as by the largely private understandings of social issues which individual judges and attorneys brought to particular cases.

In each of their professional roles, lawyers serve as intermediaries between the official agencies of the legal system and individuals or groups. Whether functioning as counselor, advocate, judge, legisla-

* The authors acknowledge with thanks the assistance of Scott Burson, Esq., of the Marian G. Gallagher Law Library, University of Washington School of Law, in the preparation of this Chapter.

tor, or legal scholar, a lawyer can mould the law or influence the legal system to achieve a more rational or just solution to the issue at hand. In that effort, knowledge and use of the social sciences are a valuable, if not essential aid.

The systematic application of social science to legal issues has largely developed in this century. Although there may be earlier instances of detailed presentations of the findings of social scientists to courts, Louis D. Brandeis's brief in *Muller v. Oregon* is generally recognized to be the first extensive, successful use of social science research before the United States Supreme Court. In its decision of *Muller v. Oregon,* 208 U.S. 412 at 421 (1907), the Court opened the door to the future use of social science research in litigation by applying the concept of judicial notice. The Court stated: "We take judicial cognizance of all matters of general knowledge."

If, however, the use of social science data were limited to instances where judicial notice is appropriate, this category of research would be far less significant in the law than in fact it is. Judicial notice is generally appropriate only where the facts to be noticed are not subject to dispute. Frequently, social science data and the conclusions drawn from them are subject to dispute; in many cases such data is now presented to courts by social scientists testifying as expert witnesses, subject to cross examination and rebuttal. Perhaps the most dramatic instance of this use of social science culminated in the Supreme Court's unanimous decision in *Brown v. Board of Education,* 347 U.S. 483 (1953). There the Court found that "separate educational facilities are inherently unequal," in part because racial separation was demonstrated to the Court's satisfaction to have a detrimental effect on black children in segregated schools. The Court in footnote 11 (at 347 U.S. 494–95) limited its references to *published* materials, to illustrate this effect of segregated educational facilities. The plaintiffs, however, presented expert testimony at the trial of these issues to prove the harmful effect of segregated schools.[1]

The Court's reliance on social science analysis in *Brown* may have seemed extensive in 1953; today such reliance is commonplace. Much constitutional litigation under the Fourteenth Amendment's Equal Protection Clause must turn upon social science and statistical data because there is no other method of demonstrating that racially neutral categories or ostensibly innocent actions are in fact discriminatory in effect. Additional examples should make clear that the use of social science in law is not an isolated phenomenon. Psychological and psychiatric testimony is often necessary to resolve key issues of sanity, capacity, competency, and custody in criminal law and family

1. The use of social science research in the school segregation cases has been the subject of many publications. See, for example two symposia: 42 *Law & Contemporary Problems* Nos. 3 & 4 (Summer 1978 & Autumn 1978). The arguments, briefs and decisions in the Brown Case were set forth in L. Friedman, ed., *Argument* (Chelsea House, 1969) and the case was put in historical perspective in R. Kluger, *Simple Justice* (Knopf, 1976; paperback reprint, Vintage, 1977).

law; economic analysis is crucial in many phases of antitrust litigation, in the determination of damages in torts and contract actions, and as a means of analyzing legal rules and the legal system; systems analysis and management theory have been applied to evaluate court performance, to help streamline court procedures, and to make law firms more efficient; pollsters have helped trial lawyers construct profiles of sympathetic jurors to aid in jury selection. The list of examples could be multiplied endlessly.[2]

Because lawyers and judges are pragmatic in their use of information, generalizations about social science analysis in law are ultimately futile. Additional applications and novel uses will certainly appear in the future. Nevertheless, the following categories may be helpful in suggesting possible applications for social science analysis, so long as these categories are recognized as tentative, not exclusive, and not exhaustive: (i) Social science data may directly support or challenge a legal rule (as was done in the *Brown* Case); (ii) data may generate inferential support for factual premises necessary to a litigant's position (for instance, plaintiffs in actions under Title VII of the Civil Rights Act of 1964, 42 *U.S.C.* sec. 2000e, et seq., often rely on statistical evidence to establish a prima facie case of discrimination); (iii) data may buttress policy arguments which favor a particular interpretation of a statute or legal rules; and (iv) data may be used in straightforward, instrumental ways (for instance, to suggest improvements in the operation of a court system or in the delivery of legal services).

This much is clear: the law has become increasingly reliant on social science, and properly so. Society and its members only benefit if legal rules are formulated and interpreted in light of their real effects on people and institutions.

B. PURPOSE AND SCOPE OF CHAPTER

This chapter will describe in general terms some approaches to research in social sciences, and suggest a general research strategy. It will also outline a small selection of the many materials which are available for law-related research in the social sciences, and offer a short list of additional readings. Although particular books or periodicals are mentioned in the text, for the most part such references are merely examples; there are undoubtedly many publications not mentioned here which will be appropriate to a particular research problem. The focus of this chapter is to suggest ways to locate sources of relevant information, rather than to catalog and evaluate all of the sources. A knowledge of at least the basic approaches and

2. P.L. Rosen, *The Supreme Court and Social Science* (University of Illinois Press, 1972) describes the use of social science data by the U.S. Supreme Court in a variety of cases. Two broader surveys, which deal with applications at the *trial* level as well, are J.W. Loewen, *Social Science in the Courtroom* (Lexington Books, 1982) and M.J. Saks & C.H. Baron, editors, *The Use/Nonuse/Misuse of Applied Social Research in the Courts* (Abt Books, 1980).

sources in these fields is becoming part of the literacy of competent lawyers.

C. A GENERAL RESEARCH STRATEGY

The problem most legal researchers face in attempting to identify relevant social science information is how to penetrate a vast and sophisticated maze of largely unfamiliar materials. Although there is no single research method or approach that is effective and efficient for all of the social sciences and in all situations, following a general strategy of research will increase one's efficiency, save time, and make it more likely that the most relevant information will be found.

A broad outline of such a strategy includes the following steps:

1. Think through the problem at the outset. What propositions are to be established or what questions are to be answered? What kind of information is necessary for those purposes? Where is that information most likely to be found? A researcher can save vast amounts of time by taking a few moments at an early stage of research and determining a rational approach by answering those introductory questions.

2. Do not overlook the law library. Few law libraries are equipped to support in-depth research in the social sciences. Nevertheless, most law library collections reflect the increasing use of the social sciences in law. The legal periodical indexes described in Chapter 16 will provide appropriate references to articles in both scholarly and practice-oriented journals. Although most social science articles in legal periodicals lack the methodological sophistication or depth to be authoritative, these articles have the twin virtues of both explicitly applying social science data to particular *legal* issues and of being written so as to be comprehensible to lawyers. Such articles will usually provide references to "hard" research, which may be consulted if more depth is required. Finally, judges and attorneys may be more comfortable with analyses drawn from legal journals precisely because they are familiar sources.

Check the law library's subject card catalog before going to a college, university, or major public library. Your problem or similar problems may have arisen in the legal community before and the library may have already acquired relevant sources. Though selective, a law library's collection may contain sufficient material to provide a sound beginning to research.

3. Seek professional assistance. A major research library may be unfamiliar terrain to many law students and attorneys. New bibliographic tools and sources of information are constantly being developed. Reference librarians at major research libraries are information specialists who are knowledgeable with respect to materials within their collection and beyond it.

4. Expand the research from the law library to the sources and finding tools of the discipline relevant to the instant problem. These may require use of other libraries, or of computer data bases accessi-

ble in your own library. Suggestions on using another library are set forth above in Section B of Chapter 17, General Reference Works.

5. Be sensitive to the adversarial context in which social science analysis will be used. A consensus of experts on many issues may not exist within particular disciplines of social science. Disputes about basic methodology as well as about the conclusion to be drawn from particular observations may not necessarily invalidate social science data offered as evidence. In an adversarial system, however, opposing litigants will raise such issues in an attempt to persuade the court to ignore or discount such evidence. Such challenges must be anticipated and countered, or the value of the social science evidence will be greatly diminished.

6. As with legal materials, social science research must be updated to reflect the latest findings and publications.

D. SOURCES OF INFORMATION

This section discusses some of the major sources of bibliographic information in the social sciences. The suggestions here are selective and not intended to be comprehensive. If the social science materials within a law library prove inadequate for a researcher's needs, the following discussion should facilitate entry into the more complex and unfamiliar collections of research libraries.

1. BASIC SOURCES

a. Encyclopedias

Encyclopedias are primarily useful to a researcher with little or no background in a subject. Although seldom authoritative, an encyclopedia can provide a researcher with sufficient background on a subject so that sensible decisions about additional research may be made. The *International Encyclopedia of the Social Sciences* (Macmillan and the Free Press, 1968) 17v., covers anthropology, economics, geography, history, law, political science, psychiatry, psychology, sociology, and statistics. Topics are arranged alphabetically and the articles are signed by experts in each field. The articles provide clear expositions of basic concepts and include selected bibliographies of sources. These lists of references can assist in discovering quickly authoritative works on a subject. An index to the entire set helps locate discussion of subtopics and related topics. The earlier *Encyclopedia of the Social Sciences* (Macmillan, 1930–35) 15v., also provides signed articles by leading scholars and is not completely superseded by the *International Encyclopedia.* Unfortunately, neither of these encyclopedias is updated in any way. Both are more scholarly than the legal encyclopedias discussed above in Chapter 14, but like all encyclopedias, they are by necessity limited in their coverage of particular topics.

A number of specialized encyclopedias for particular disciplines are also available.[3] These, too, may provide a useful starting point for research. By their nature, encyclopedias cannot be relied upon for the most recent developments, nor are they always effective in providing introductions to cross-disciplinary and multi-disciplinary approaches to problems. However, the *Encyclopedia of Bioethics* (Free Press, 1978) 4v., is an example of a multi-disciplinary encyclopedia focusing on one area involving several social sciences. In general, indexing and abstracting services, bibliographies issued serially, and computerized literature searching provide access to the latest materials treating these issues.

b. Guides to the Literature

A guide to the literature provides a systematic introduction to the literature of a field. Through organized presentations and evaluative annotations of particular materials, such guides assist the researcher in selecting titles relevant to a particular problem. They impose order on the vast array of material available in social sciences.

The best and most comprehensive guide to the social sciences is still *Sources of Information in the Social Sciences,* edited by Carl M. White[4] (hereafter referred to as White), although it is badly in need of updating. This guide provides references to treatises, sources of statistics and empirical data, specialized dictionaries, handbooks, the principal journals in each field, and indexing and abstracting services. It first treats the literature relating to the social sciences generally and then gives detailed coverage to the literatures of economics and business administration, sociology, psychology, political science, history, anthropology, education, and geography. White breaks down the broad social science disciplines into appropriate subtopics. In addition, it has a very detailed index to help find related materials in more than one discipline, an important aid because of the increasingly interdisciplinary nature of so many access tools and information sources.

An unusual compendium of social science information was prepared specifically for lawyers by the Legal Action Support Project of the Bureau of Social Science Research, Inc. in a looseleaf format, entitled *Sources and Uses of Social and Economic Data: A Manual for Lawyers* (National Social Science and Law Center, 1973). Although funding problems have prevented updating, this guide focuses on those social science data sources which are most useful to lawyers. It covers both public and private sources, and includes separate chapters on evaluating data, conducting surveys, and

3. See, for example, the variety of encyclopedias in the fields of psychology and psychiatry: *Encyclopedia of Mental Health* (Watts, 1963) 6v.; *Encyclopedia of Psychoanalysis* (Free Press, 1968); *Encyclopedia of Psychology,* 2d ed. (Continuum, 1979); *Encyclopedia of Human Behavior; Psychology, Psychiatry, and Mental Health* (Doubleday, 1970) 2v.; *American Handbook of Psychiatry,* 2d ed. (Basic Books, 1974–1981) 7v.

4. 2d ed. (American Library Association, 1973).

describing methods of using data in specific types of litigation. The manual is illustrated and has a detailed subject index.

Although less comprehensive than White and *Sources and Uses of Social and Economic Data,* the following guides also provide useful introductions to social science resources:

F.L. Holler, *The Information Sources of Political Science,* 3d ed. (ABC—Clio, 1981). Despite its title, this work provides an organized approach to the literature of the social sciences, covering political science, history, anthropology, sociology, psychology, economics, and geography. References are annotated.

T.C. Li, *Social Science Reference Sources—a Practical Guide* (Greenwood Press, 1980).

J.B. Mason, *Research Resources: Annotated Guide to the Social Sciences,* (ABC–Clio, 1968–71) 2v.

B. Mausner, *A Citizens Guide to the Social Sciences* (Nelson Hall, 1979).

Social Science Researching: Twentieth Century Guide to the Literature (Social Science & Sociological Resources, 1981).

R.E. Stevens & D. Davis, *Reference Books in the Social Sciences* (Stipes, 1977).

Guides are also available for particular disciplines and should be consulted before attempting extensive research in any discipline. To locate such guides, check the library's card catalog using the subject heading "name of discipline—bibliography," or consult E.P. Sheehy, *Guide to Reference Books,* and its supplements. A few varied examples of guides to particular disciplines and subject areas include the following:

P. Bart & L. Frankel, *The Student Sociologist's Handbook,* 3d ed. (Scott, Foresman, 1981). Includes research and resource information, and lists governmental and private data sources.

B.C. Field & C.E. Willis, ed., *Environmental Economics: A Guide to Information Sources* (Gale Research, 1979).

F. Freidel & R.K. Showman, ed., *Harvard Guide to American History,* revised edition (Harvard Univ. Press, 1974). This guide provides both topical and chronological arrangements of references to materials and tools deemed most useful to researchers in American political, social, constitutional and economic history.

B. Greenberg, *How to Find Out in Psychiatry* (Pergamon, 1978). A guide to basic information sources relating to mental health.

E.C. Porpa, *Guide to Basic Information Sources in Anthropology* (J. Norton Publications, 1981).

U.S. Library of Congress, *Guide to the Study of the United States* (U.S. Govt. Printing Office, 1960, with 1978 suppl.). A comprehensive annotated guide to all aspects of American studies.

P. Wasserman & J. Morgan, *Ethnic Information Sources of the U.S.*, 2d ed. (Gale Research, 1983).

Unfortunately, these guides do not always refer researchers directly to the most current information in a field. Other sources (see Section 2 below) must be consulted to find such material.

c. Dictionaries

A variety of dictionaries cover the terminology of the social sciences generally, as well as particular disciplines. In addition to providing definitions of specialized terms, some of these dictionaries include additional directory material or background information about that discipline. The three leading dictionaries for the social sciences generally are J. Gould & W.L. Kolb, *UNESCO Dictionary of the Social Sciences* (Free Press, 1964); G.D. Mitchell, *A New Dictionary of the Social Sciences* (Aldine, 1979), and B.B. Wolman, *Dictionary of Behavior Science* (Van Nostrand Reinhold, 1973; paperback reprint, 1979).

To locate other dictionaries in specific fields, consult a guide to the literature of the particular discipline; Sheehy's *Guide to Reference Books;* A.M. Brewer, *Dictionaries, Encyclopedias and Other Word-Related Books* (Gale Research, 1982), 3d ed., 3v.; or a reference librarian.

d. Directories

Directories provide names, addresses, and additional information about individuals or organizations active in particular fields. There are many directories focusing on the social sciences, some of which are listed above in Sections C.2 & 3 of Chapter 17. Particularly helpful in locating relevant directories are *The Directory of Directories*, 2d ed. (Gale Research, 1983) and *Guide to American Directories*, 10th ed. (McGraw-Hill, 1979), revised irregularly.

Specific directories worth noting here are *A Directory of Information Resources in the United States: Social Sciences*, rev. ed. (Library of Congress, National Referral Center; 1973); *Research Centers Directory*, 7th ed. (Gale Research, 1982); and the *World Directory of Social Science Institutions* (Unipub, 1980). In addition, the two Library directories, *American Library Directory* and *Subject Collections*, described above in Section B.1 of Chapter 17, are useful in identifying libraries which specialize in one or another of the social sciences.

2. SOURCES OF CURRENT INFORMATION

Because of the frequency of new developments in the social sciences, it is important to have access to the *latest* publications and findings. Guides to literature provide detailed references to many of the bibliographic sources for *current* information. These sources are of five basic types: indexes, abstracts, citators, bibliographies, and periodicals that review new literature. Publications and services designed for this purpose generally fall into one of three categories: those covering several disciplines; those focusing on a particular discipline; and those which are oriented toward a specific problem or subject. Because the use of social science data in legal research does not usually fall within a single discipline, it is desirable for a researcher to concentrate on multi-disciplinary sources or, if available, on one that deals with the specific problem being investigated.

a. Indexes and Abstracts

Indexes usually provide author, title, and subject access to periodical articles in a particular field. Occasionally, indexes will also cover collections of essays and government documents, and a few provide access to monographs and treatises as well. Each index should be checked to ascertain its exact coverage.

Abstracting services provide brief summaries of articles and/or books. They are therefore more informative than simple indexes, but usually are not available as promptly.

1. Tools Covering Several Disciplines

The *Social Sciences Index* (H.W. Wilson, 1974–date), formerly published together with *Humanities Index* as the *Social Sciences and Humanities Index* (1916–1974), covers approximately 270 leading scholarly journals in economics, anthropology, geography, history, political science, and sociology. An H.W. Wilson publication, similar in format to the *Index to Legal Periodicals,* it indexes only material in journals and its entries are not annotated. It is issued quarterly with annual bound cumulations. Because *Social Science Index* is limited, covering only *journals* and only *some* of the social sciences, other indexes must be consulted to supplement it.

One of these is the selective *Public Affairs Information Service* (popularly known as *PAIS*) which is described above in Section C.6(c) of Chapter 17. *PAIS* indexes books, pamphlets, government documents, periodical articles, and emphasizes materials relating to economics, public affairs, and social science topics of general interest.

Although *PAIS* includes references to government documents and reports, it is selective, and will not cover all of the documents or reports needed in legal research. To search more thoroughly for government documents, one can use the *Monthly Catalog of Government Publications,* the *Congressional Information Service Index,* and the *Monthly Checklist of State Publications,* each of which has been described in earlier chapters of this book.

The *Index to Current Urban Documents* (Greenwood Press, 1972–date) indexes many documents issued by the largest cities and counties in the United States, as well as documents issued by other local government agencies and organizations. Published quarterly, with an annual cumulated volume, this index provides access by subject and also by the name of the issuing city, county, or other agency.

It provides references to publications and reports on many of the important social problems affecting the urban scene.

Many of the earliest published reports of social science research are issued in government reports. These reports are indexed in the bimonthly *Government Reports Announcements & Index* (referred to hereafter as *GRA & I*; 1975–date), which was published under several other titles from 1946 to 1974. *GRA & I* provides access by author and subject. Cumulated annual index volumes, covering *GRA & I* and its predecessors, are available from 1968 to date. These publications are issued by the National Technical Information Service (NTIS) of the U.S. Department of Commerce. Research reports relating to the social sciences are listed in *GRA & I* in a section designated "Field 5, Behavioral and Social Science."

Other indexing and abstracting services covering the social sciences generally include the following:

Index to Social Sciences and Humanities Proceedings (Institute for Scientific Information, 1979–date). Quarterly, with annual cumulations, it covers published proceedings whether appearing in books, reports or journals, and provides seven different indexing approaches.

Recent Publications in the Social and Behavioral Sciences (American Behavioral Scientist, 1966–date). Annual. All entries are annotated; arrangement is by author or other main entry, with separate title and subject indexes.

For information about other indexing and abstracting publications and services of this kind, as well as those covering particular disciplines or specific subjects or issues, see *Indexes, Abstracts, and Digests,* edited by A.M. Brewer (Gale Research, 1982). That compilation is being updated by a new service, *Abstracting and Indexing Services Directory* (Gale Research, 1982–date).

2. Tools Covering Particular Disciplines

There are many specialized indexing and abstracting services and publications covering current writing and developments in *particular* disciplines. One of the best known is *Psychological Abstracts* (American Psychological Association, 1927–date), but there are similar services in virtually every other social science discipline, some of which are also available for on-line computer searching. A complete listing of such research tools would be beyond the scope of this book, but the following few examples illustrate the variety of coverage:

Abstracts on Criminology and Penology, formerly *Excerpta Criminologica* (1961–date), bi-monthly, international in scope.

Anthropological Literature: An Index to Periodical Articles and Essays (Redgrave Publ. Co., 1979–date), quarterly, international in scope.

Historical Abstracts . . . ; Bibliography of the World's Periodical Literature (ABC—Clio, 1955–date), with periodic cumulative indexes.

Index Medicus (National Library of Medicine, 1960–date), monthly, now based on a partial printout from the computer-based MEDLARS service.

Index of Economic Articles in Journals and Collective Volumes (R.D. Irwin, 1961–date).

International Political Science Abstracts (Blackwell, 1951–date), quarterly, international in scope, with abstracts in English or French.

Sociological Abstracts (1952–date) six issues a year, the last being an annual cumulation.

3. Subject Oriented Index Tools

The proliferation of indexing and abstracting publications has extended these useful research aids into specific subject and problems areas, many of which are interdisciplinary in scope and involve substantial legal issues. Examples of such fields which are frequently the subject of legal research are environmental control, housing, mental health, poverty, and transportation. Since studies in these subjects often draw on sources in several social sciences and on the natural or physical sciences as well, they do not fall within the framework of one traditional discipline, and hence are not well covered by traditional single-discipline research tools. New research tools, however are being published which provide convenient access to the growing literature and research in such fields. These include indexing and abstracting services which permit rapid searches of a vast body of published material, some of it not otherwise readily accessible.

An example of such a tool is *Environment Abstracts,* (EIC/Intelligence, 1971–date), formerly called *Environment Information Access.* It is issued monthly, and contains abstracts of new books, periodical articles and reports, as well as a variety of other source material. The same publisher provides *Environment Index* (1971–date), an annual volume cumulating the monthly indexes of its companion service, but containing additional features as well. They also provide microfiche documentation, under the title, *Envirofiche,* and an on-line searching service called *Enviroline.* These microfiche and computer services offer full-text access to a wide variety of federal and state documents, both legal and technical, in the environmental protection field.

b. Social Sciences Citation Index

Since 1973, research in the social sciences has been much improved by the *Social Sciences Citation Index* ®, referred to hereafter as *SSCI* (Institute for Scientific Information ®, 1973–date, with retrospective coverage to 1966). Functionally similar in part to a Shepard's citator, *SSCI* allows a researcher to identify publications which refer to previously published books and articles in the social sciences. In addition, *SSCI* lists the books and periodical articles cited in particular articles, provides a "permuted" title, key word list which can be used as a subject index, and offers several other search approaches. *SSCI* fully indexes articles and other significant material in over a thousand journals covering every field of social science, including many legal periodicals. It also provides *selective* coverage for over 2,000 additional journals and important monographs.

SSCI is a complex, computer-produced service and requires some patience to learn. It does not evaluate or describe its references, and hence often frustrates one with numerous marginal leads. The frequent necessity of referring to more than one part of the index to find all of the desired information can also be time-consuming. However, *SSCI* does offer access to many sources on law-related issues which are not available through the legal indexes described in Chapter 16, Periodical Literature.

Illustration A shows a series of author entries in *SSCI,* including references under "Calabresi, G." to articles and reviews commenting on that author's book, *Tragic Choices.* Some of those citations would not be found in the standard indexes to legal periodicals. Illustration B displays entries from the key word section of *SSCI* under the terms *Prison, Prisoners,* and *Privacy,* with references to authors whose writings contain those terms in their titles. Those authors can be searched in another section of the Index for full citations to their books or articles.

Social Scisearch ®, the corresponding on-line data base, contains over a million records beginning with 1972.

c. Sources of Statistical Data

Statistical data are used frequently by lawyers in connection with their research in social science materials, and for many other purposes as well. Although much of it is derived from governmental sources, its secondary forms of publication are often more accessible. These publications are varied and tend to be less familiar to non-specialists. Fortunately there are numerous finding aids available for locating relevant statistics on almost any subject. Several are described in Section C.8 of Chapter 17 above, General Reference Materials. For an overview of access tools published by the government, see J.W. Duncan, "Accessing Social Statistics," 30 *Library Trends* 363 (1982).

Three statistical indexes published by the Congressional Information Service now provide the most comprehensive and versatile coverage of statistical sources. They are:

American Statistics Index (1973–date, with retrospective coverage to the early 1960's). Issued monthly, with an annual cumulation volume, *ASI* covers statistical publications of the United States government and is also available for on-line computer searching.

CALABRESI			VOL	PG	YR
ORLAND L	AM CRIM LAW		17	501	80
POLINSKY AM	AM ECON REV		70	363	80
WALTHALL HP	BUS LAWYER	R	35	659	80
WILSON DK	GEORGE WASH		48	83	79
61 YALE LAW J 70 519					
ORLAND L	AM CRIM LAW		17	501	80
61 YALE LAW J 70 547					
HENDERSO EJ	FORDHAM LAW		48	1165	80
61 YALE LAW J 70 548					
KOEHN SB	RUTGERS LAW		32	342	79
65 HARVARD LAW REV 78 713					
BOBBITT P	TEX LAW REV		58	695	80
67 U ILL LF 600					
67 U ILL LF 610					
OCONNELL J	UNIV IL LAW		1979	591	79
68 CRISIS CAR INSURANCE 240					
OCONNELL J	INS LAW J		1980	206	80
68 JL EC 11 67					
BOBBITT P	TEX LAW REV		58	695	80
INGBER S	VA LAW REV		65	785	79
LEVIN L	SYRAC LAW R		30	741	79
68 LAW CONT PROB 33 429					
68 LAW CONT PROB 33 435					
INGBER S	VA LAW REV		65	785	79
72 HARVARD LAW REV 85 1089					
	HARV LAW RE		93	966	80
BLUMSTEIJF	LAW CONT PR		43	5	79
BREYER S	BK# 15099		1980	206	80
COLEMAN JL	CALIF LAW R		68	221	80
CONYBEARJA	INT ORGAN		34	307	80
ELLICKSO RC	S CAL LAW R		52	1627	79
ENGEL DI	STANF LAW R		32	1	79
FUNG KK	BEHAV SCI		25	197	80
GETZ M	LAW CONT PR		43	197	79
INGBER S	VA LAW REV		65	785	79
LAYCOCK D	TEX LAW REV	B	57	1065	79
MARCY DE	S CAL LAW R		52	1581	79
OVERDORF JS	TRIAL		16	96	80
POLINSKY AM	ECON INQ		18	233	80
"	J LEG STUD		8	1	79
ROGERS CP	HARV LAW RE	B	93	1039	80
YOUNG OR	OCEAN DEV I		8	183	80
"	WORLD POLIT		32	331	80
72 HARVARD LAW REV 85 1092					
	HARV LAW RE		93	966	80
BLUMSTEIJF	LAW CONT PR		43	5	79
GETZ M	"		43	197	79
INGBER S	VA LAW REV		65	785	79
72 HARVARD LAW REV 85 1094					
MARCY DE	S CAL LAW R		52	1581	79
72 HARVARD LAW REV 85 1105					
LAYCOCK D	TEX LAW REV	B	57	1065	79
72 HARVARD LAW REV 85 1106					
ELLICKSO RC	S CAL LAW R		52	1627	79
72 HARVARD LAW REV 85 1115					
GETZ M	LAW CONT PR		43	197	79
72 HARVARD LAW REV 85 1125					
ENGEL DI	STANF LAW R		32	1	79
72 YALE LAW J 81 1055					
	MINN LAW R		64	949	80
BIRNBAUM SI	VANDER LAW		33	593	80
ELLICKSO RC	S CAL LAW R		52	1627	79
FINKELST JM	J BANK FIN		4	249	80
HANDL G	AM J INT LA		74	525	80
OWEN DG	VANDER LAW		33	681	80
RIPER J	STANF LAW R		32	391	80
VARGO JF	TRIAL		15	48	79
WALKOWIA VS	VANDER LAW		33	651	80
72 YALE LAW J 81 1060					
ELLICKSO RC	S CAL LAW R		52	1627	79
HANDL G	AM J INT LA		74	525	80
72 YALE LAW J 81 1071					
WALKOWIA VS	VANDER LAW		33	651	80
75 ALTRUISM MORALITY EC 57					
ENGEL DI	STANF LAW R		32	1	79
75 U CHICAGO LAW REV 43 69					
75 U CHICAGO LAW REV 43 71					
PEARSON RN	LA LAW REV		40	343	80
75 YALE LAW J 84 656					
BIRNBAUM SI	VANDER LAW		33	593	80
BREYER S	BK# 15099		1980	206	80
OWEN DG	VANDER LAW		33	681	80
RATNER LG	NORTHW U LA		75	363	80
77 U TORONTO LJ 27 131					
KOEHN SB	RUTGERS LAW		32	342	79
78 NY TIMES 0706 19					
LEEDES GC	TEX LAW REV		57	1361	79
78 NEW PERSPECTIVES COM 291					
CAPPELLE M	S CAL LAW R		53	409	80
78 TRAGIC CHOICES 73					
PALMER LI	COLUMB HUM		11	1	79
79 CATH U L REV 28 427					
BOBBITT P	TEX LAW REV		58	695	80
STANTOIN TJ	CATH U L R		29	535	80
79 VT L REV 4 247					
BOBBITT P	TEX LAW REV		58	695	80
OCONNELL J	INS LAW J		1980	206	80
"	UNIV IL LAW		1979	591	79
80 COMMUNICATION 0308					
BURT RA	SUPR COURT		1979	329	79
CALABRESI G					
*** COMMON LAW FUNCTION*					
BOBBITT P	TEX LAW REV		58	695	80
*** UNPUBLISHED*					
BREST P	BOSTON U LR		60	204	80
OCONNELL J	INS LAW J		1980	206	80
65 HARVARD LAW REV 78 713					
HEYDEBRA W	BK# 11831	R	2	29	79
68 J LAW EC APR					
TEECE DJ	J ECON BEH		1	223	80
70 COST ACCIDENTS					
CORRIGAN JC	BOSTON U LR	B	60	801	80
FINKELST JM	J BANK FIN		4	249	80
MUSGRAVE RA	PUBL FINAN		35	1	80
70 COST ACCIDENTS LEGAL					
HEYDEBRA W	BK# 11831	R	2	29	79
70 COSTS ACCIDENTS					
	HARV LAW RE		93	1761	80
BOBBITT P	TEX LAW REV		58	695	80
ROGERS CP	HARV LAW RE	B	93	1039	80
70 COSTS ACCIDENTS LEGA					
BLUMSTEIJF	J HEALTH P		4	382	79
BREYER S	BK# 15099		1980	206	80
COLEMAN JL	CALIF LAW R		68	221	80
HADDEN SG	POLICY ST J		9	109	80
HIRSHLEIJ	J ECON LIT	R	17	1375	79
LLOYDBOS SM	INS LAW J		1980	331	80
OWEN DG	VANDER LAW		33	681	80
SHULMAN D	J OCCUP BEH		1	119	80
70 COST ACCIDENTS 6					
RIZZO MJ	BK# 13679		1979	71	79
70 COSTS ACCIDENTS 9					
THORNE JF	NORTHW U LA		75	147	80
70 COSTS ACCIDENTS 21					
ROTHFELD CA	UNIV CHIC L		46	935	79
70 COSTS ACCIDENTS LEGA 24					
HANDL G	AM J INT LA		74	525	80
70 COST ACCIDENTS 25					
LINDGREN JS	BUFF LAW R		28	711	79
70 COSTS ACCIDENTS LEGA 26					
INGBER S	VA LAW REV		65	785	79
MARCY DE	S CAL LAW R		52	1581	79
MCLEAN RA	POLICY ST J		8	392	79
OCONNELL J	INS LAW J		1980	206	80
"	UNIV IL LAW		1979	591	79
70 COSTS ACCIDENTS 39					
70 COSTS ACCIDENTS 40					
COFFEE JC	AM CRIM LAW		17	419	80
70 COST ACCIDENTS 55					
WHITFORD WC	WI LAW REV		1979	1047	79
70 COSTS ACCIDENTS 56					
	HARV LAW RE		93	1816	80
70 COSTS ACCIDENTS 86					
HENDERSO JA	U PA LAW RE		128	1036	80
70 COSTS ACCIDENTS 135					
ELLICKSO RC	S CAL LAW R		52	1627	79
SCHWARTZ A	YALE LAW J		89	271	79
70 COSTS ACCIDENTS 150					
EPSTEIN RA	J LEG STUD		8	49	79
70 COST ACCIDENTS LEGAL 314					
HAMADA K	JPN ECON ST		8	67	80
70 COST ACCIDENTS CH 6					
CANE P	J PROD LIAB		3	215	79
72 HARVARD LAW REV 85					
MUSGRAVE RA	PUBL FINAN		35	1	80
74 ETHICS HLTH 46					
BLUMSTEIJF	J HEALTH P		4	382	79
75 ALTRUISM MORALITY EC 59					
KENNETT DA	AM J ECON S		39	337	80
77 COMMON LAW FUNCTION					
ABRAHAM KS	RUTGERS LAW		32	676	79
77 TRAGIC CHOICES					
KAYE D	UNIV CHIC L		47	34	79
78 TRAGIC CHOICES					
ATIYAH PS	INS LAW J		1980	625	80
CAVANAGH R	LAW SOC REV		14	371	80
CLAASSEN A	SOCIAL PROB		27	526	80
COLEMAN JL	CALIF LAW R	B	67	1379	79
DELGADO R	MINN LAW R		64	467	80
EDNEY JJ	AM PSYCHOL		35	131	80
HADDEN SG	POLICY ST J		9	109	80
KARST KL	YALE LAW J		89	624	80
MOORE JH	PUBL CHOICE	B	34	241	79

2014

CALABRESI G			VOL	PG	YR
TEMIN P	J ECON BEH		1	175	80
WRIGHT EE	AM J MED G	E	5	391	80
78 TRAGIC CHOICES 24					
SPITZER ML	UNIV CHIC L		47	647	80
78 TRAGIC CHOICES 26					
BOBBITT P	TEX LAW REV		58	695	80
78 TRAGIC CHOICES 31					
COLEMAN JL	CALIF LAW R	B	67	1379	79
78 TRAGIC CHOICES 57					
KAYE D	CALIF LAW R		68	1004	80
78 TRAGIC CHOICES 74					
THORNE JF	NORTHW U LA		75	147	80
79 VT L REV 4 35					
OCONNELL J	UNIV IL LAW		1979	591	79
CALABRESI P					
76 PHARMACOLOGIC BASIS 1248					
PETERSON LG	PSYCHOSOMAT	R	21	141	80
CALABY JH					
66 CSIRO10 DIV WILDL RE					
SEE SCI FOR 3 ADDITIONAL CITATIONS					
KITCHENE DJ	BIOL CONSER		18	179	80
67 AUSTR J SCI 29 473					
CALABY J	BK# 14835		1980	321	80
71 ABORIGINAL MAN ENV A 80					
ABBOTT I	OECOLOGIA		44	347	80
71 ABORIGINAL MAN ENV A 81					
GRAYSON DK	BK# 15416		3	357	80
71 AUST ZOOL 16 17					
SEE SCI FOR 1 ADDITIONAL CITATION					
ABBOTT I	OECOLOGIA		44	347	80
73 ALLIGATOR RIVERS REG 1					
CALABY J	BK# 14835		1980	321	80
74 FAUNA SURVEY PORT ES 7					
JONES R	BK# 14835		1980	107	80
74 FAUNA SURVEY PORT ES 179					
SEE SCI FOR 3 ADDITIONAL CITATIONS					
CALABY J	BK# 14835		1980	321	80
76 ORIGIN AUSTR 23					
ABBOTT I	OECOLOGIA		44	347	80
77 MANKIND 11 150					
CALABY J	BK# 14835		1980	321	80
CALAFELL RC					
79 3RD WORLD TEL FOR 2					
CAWKELL AE	ANN R INFOR	R	15	37	80
CALAHAN D					
69 6 RUTG CTR ALC STUD					
BANKS E	PSYCHOL REP		46	571	80
SHEEHAN DV	BR J ALC		14	234	79
74 PROBLEM DRINKING AM					
DEMBO R	AM J DRUG A		6	313	79
77 SCIS 17 16					
SCHMIDT MT	PUBL HEAL R	R	8	107	79
CALAHAN DA					
73 11TH P ANN ALL C CIR 729					
74 BASIC QUESTIONS DESI					
76 94 U MICH SYST ENG L					
SEE SCI FOR 1 ADDITIONAL CITATION					
WING O	IEEE COMPUT		29	632	80
CALAHAN HA					
44 WHAT MAKES WAR END					
WITTMAN D	J CONFL RES		23	743	79
CALAHANLEVY CM					
79 J PERS SOC PSYCHOL 37 433					
GREENBERJ	J PERS SOC		38	579	80
CALAM J					
71 PARSONS PEDAGOGUES S					
HINER NR	SOCIETAS		8	89	78
71 PARSONS PEDAGOGUES 55					
ROPER D	SOCIAL ST		71	90	80
CALAMANDREI P					
*** OPERE GIURIDICHE 7*					
SHAPIRO M	LAW SOC REV		14	629	80
46 EULOGY JUDGES 72					
WARD OP	NORTHW U LA	I	74	702	79
54 PROCESSO DEMOCRAZIA					
FROSINI V	LAH V PARET		18	127	80
56 PROCEDURE DEMOCRACY 72					
CARRINGT PD	J LEG STUD		8	303	79
76 OPERE GIURIDICHE 6					
SHAPIRO M	LAW SOC REV		14	629	80
CALAMARI					
74 FORDHAM L REV 43 341					
GEDICKS FM	S CAL LAW R		52	1513	79
77 LAW CONTRACTS 700					
BEANE C	UNIF C CODE		13	135	80
CALAMARI D					
68 J NURSING ED 7 11					
WONG S	J ADV NURS		5	531	80
CALAMARI J					
70 CONTRACTS 430					
SCHWARTZ A	YALE LAW J		89	271	79
77 CONTRACTS					
LEATHERB WC	RUTGERS LAW		32	431	79
NAAR BR	"		32	520	79
77 CONTRACTS 47					
WARREN A	YALE LAW J		89	1081	80
77 CONTRACTS 136					
	HARV LAW RE		93	1816	80
77 CONTRACTS 146					
HILLMAN RA	IA LAW REV		65	343	80
77 CONTRACTS 308					
	VA LAW REV		66	217	80
77 CONTRACTS 581					
FRIEDMAN D	COLUMB LAW		80	504	80
77 CONTRACTS 640					
GIRAUDO JP	BANK LAW J		97	806	80
77 HDB LAW CONTRACTS 279					
STEINER IA	FORDHAM LAW		48	471	80
77 LAW CONTRACTS					
GOSFIELD GG	TEMPLE LAW		52	552	79
HOLMES EM	CORNELL L R		65	330	80
KLARE KE	NY U LAW RE	B	54	876	79
MARGUET S	INDIANA LAW		55	563	80
ORELUP EA	IA LAW REV		65	209	79
SIMONS KW	GEORGET LAW		68	919	80
77 LAW CONTRACTS 15					
YANKOWIT BJ	S CAL LAW R		52	1917	79
77 LAW CONTRACTS 22					
HOLMES EM	CORNELL L R		65	330	80
77 LAW CONTRACTS 230					
77 LAW CONTRACTS 235					
FOYE PJ	FORDHAM LAW	N	49	81	80
77 LAW CONTRACTS 448					
GEDICKS FM	S CAL LAW R		52	1513	79
77 LAW CONTRACTS 498					
NOVAK RS	BOSTON U LR	N	59	950	79
77 LAW CONTRACTS 518					
BOLTEN JB	STANF LAW R		32	409	80
77 LAW CONTRACTS 525					
SCHIRO R	S CAL LAW R		52	1727	79
CALAME A					
72 SCHWEIZ MED WSCHR 102 65					
SEE SCI FOR 1 ADDITIONAL CITATION					
HANSEN H	BK# 12349	R	11	21	80
LEE KS	AM J PUB HE		70	15	80
76 HELV PAEDIAT ACTA 31 287					
SEE SCI FOR 3 ADDITIONAL CITATIONS					
BUCHER H	HELV PAED A		35	489	80
DRILLIEN CM	DEVELOP MED		22	26	80
CALAME GP					
73 AM J PHYS 41 184					
FREEDMAN RA	AM J PHYS		48	548	80
CALAMEGRIAULE G					
65 ETHNOLOGIE LANGAGE P 373					
THOMAS LV	REV FR PSYC		43	441	79
77 LANGAGE CULTURE AFRI					
RAPHAEL F	ANNALES-ESC		35	127	80
CALANCA A					
76 MED HYG 43 231					
SAAMELI W	THER UMSCH		37	23	80
CALANCHINI P					
71 LEARNING DISORDERS C					
SCHERE RA	J ABN C PSY		8	5	80
CALANCHINI PR					
71 LEARNING DISORDERS C					
SABATINO DA	J CLIN CHIL		8	188	79
CALANDRA A					
72 J COLLEGE SCI TEACH 1 35					
HAYES AB	AM BIOL TEA		42	84	80
CALANTONE R					
77 CONT MARKETING THOUG 492					
DILLON WR	MANAG SCI		25	1184	79
CALANTONE RJ					
78 J MARKETING RES 15 395					
MAHAJAN V	J MARKET		44	71	80
CALARESU FR					
75 BRAIN RESEARCH 87 335					
SEE SCI FOR 1 ADDITIONAL CITATION					
BELOVA TI	B EXP B MED		88	975	79
75 PROGR NEUROBIOL 5 1					
SEE SCI FOR 15 ADDITIONAL CITATIONS					
JENNINGS JR	PHYSL PSYCH		8	130	80
CALAS A					
74 NATURE 250 241					
SEE SCI FOR 8 ADDITIONAL CITATIONS					

2015

Illustration A

Author entries in *Social Sciences Citation Index,* 1980 Annual (Reprinted with permission of the Institute for Scientific Information ®, Inc. from the *Social Science Citation Index* ®. Copyright 1981, by ISI ®).

PRISON

PRISON (CONT)

AGED	♦WOODEN WS
AGGRESSION	ROUNDTRE GA
ALABAMA	♦CONLEY JA+
AMENDMENT	♦PLEVIN MD
ANDERSONVI	♦TUCKER GA
APOLOGIES	♦BR MED J■
APPLICATIO	♦WALLE EL
ATTITUDES	♦CROUCH BM
BAD	♦BERNSTEI PW
BARRIOS	♦COHEN S+
	♦MARTINEZ T+
	♦SIEGAL HA+
BEDFORD	♦KUHLICKE FW+
BEHAVIOR	♦GEARING ML
	♦LUTZ U+
	♦NOWLIS S
	♦PRICE ET
BETA	♦PANTON JH
BIRTH	♦BOWKER LH+
	♦GREENBER DF+
BOARDS	♦FOWLER GW
BOUND	CONLEY JA+
BUCKEBURG	♦KRIMINALIST■
BUDGET	♦TRIAL■
CARE	♦CORDEN J
CAREER	BERNSTEI PW
CENTURIES	♦KRIMINALIST+■
CHANGING	♦RUTHERFO A
CHAPLAIN	♦BENTHALL J
CHAPLAINS	♦GLAZER P
CHAU PHAN	♦KERKVLIE BJ+
CLINICAL	WALLE EL
COED	♦SMYKLA JO
COLLEGE	♦MORROW R
COMPARISON	♦DAX EC
	PANTON JH
COMPONENTS	CROUCH BM
CONDITIONS	♦FLETCHER GP
CONTRIBUTI	DOUGLAS C
CORRECTION	WHITE RB
COURSES	LUTZ U+
CRIMINAL	" +
CRIMINAL-J	CROUCH BM
CRIMINAL-L	LUTZ U+
CRISIS	♦FITZGERA M+
CURRENTLY	DAX EC
CUTTING	♦WRIGHT M
CYNICISM	♦POOLE ED
DETERMINAN	♦WITTE AD
DIARY	KERKVLIE BJ+
DIFFERENTI	GEARING ML
DIMENSIONS	♦STRICKLI AB
DISTRIBUTI	PANTON JH
DISTURBANC	DOUGLAS C
DOCTORS	BR MED J■
DOCUMENTS	LUTZ U+
DRUG-ABUSE	♦KRIMINALIST■
DRUG-ADDIC	♦KINDERMA W
	♦LEDUCSAO A
DRUGS	COHEN S+
	MARTINEZ T+
	SIEGAL HA+
DUTIES	♦WATSON JRH
EDITION	PANTON JH
EDITORS	PLEVIN MD
EDUCATIONAL	LUTZ U+
EDUCATIONA	ROUNDTRE GA
EFFECTIVEN	♦GLASER D
EFFECTS	♦GOODSTEI L
	NOWLIS S
	PRICE ET
EMPLOYMENT	♦POTUTO JR
	♦THARNISH DM
END	BOWKER LH+
	♦TAYLOR L
ENFORCEMENT	TRIAL■
ENVIRONMENT	♦BERNHEIM J
	WOODEN WS
ENVIRONMEN	NOWLIS S
	PRICE ET
ERA	BOWKER LH+
ESCAPE	FLETCHER GP
ETHICAL	♦KASLOW FW
ETHICS	BERNHEIM J
EXAMINATION	PANTON JH
EXCUSE	FLETCHER GP
EXPERIMENT	TAYLOR L
EXPERIMENT.	NOWLIS S
	PRICE ET
EXPLODING	♦FITZGERA M+
EXPLORATION	WITTE AD
FACTORY	♦GREENBER DF+
FAMILIES	DAX EC
FAVORS	TRIAL■
FEASIBLE	LEDUCSAO A
FEDERAL	ROBBINS IP
	WHITE RB
FEMALE	ROUNDTRE GA
	STRICKLI AB
FUNDING	♦VITALE AT
FUTURE	ROBBINS IP
GANGS	COHEN S+
	MARTINEZ T+
	SIEGAL HA+
GATES	VITALE AT
GENERATE	FLETCHER GP
GERMAN	KRIMINALIST+■
GOVERNMENT	VITALE AT
GREAT-BRIT	WRIGHT M
GUARDS	CROUCH BM
	♦POOLE ED@
HOME	♦HITCHENS C+
HOMICIDE	♦WHIDDON MF+
ILLNESS	WATSON JRH
IMAGERY	STRICKLI AB
IMPACT	ROUNDTRE GA
IMPOSSIBLE	♦HISTOIRE+■
INQUIRY	♦RUTHERFO A
INTERVENTI	ROBBINS IP
INTOLERABLE	FLETCHER GP
JUDICIAL	ROBBINS IP
JUDICIAL-R	JONES S
JUSTICE	TRIAL■
JUSTIFICAT	FLETCHER GP
LABOR-MARK	WITTE AD
LAW-LIBRARY	♦KELLY ES
LAWS	♦KRIMINALIST+■
LEVELS	STRICKLI AB
LIBRARY	MORROW R
LIVING	♦SKEIST L+
LOS-ANGELES	COHEN S+
	MARTINEZ T+
	SIEGAL HA+
MANAGED	♦BRYDENSH HH
MAXIMUM	♦POLICE CHIE+■
MEDICAL-SE	BR MED J■
MEDICINE	BERNHEIM J
	♦OWEN T
MEN	WOODEN WS
MENTAL-HEA	♦CARTER JH
METHODS	♦KRIMINALIST@
	LUTZ U+
MINH HO CHI	KERKVLIE BJ+
MMPI	GEARING ML
NEO-NAZI	KRIMINALIST■
NEWSPAPER	PLEVIN MD
NON-CONVICT	NOWLIS S
	PRICE ET
NORTH-CARO	CARTER JH
NORWAY	♦BJORNSEN B
NOTEBOOKS	♦PARIS R+
NOTES	KERKVLIE BJ+
	♦PAO F
OBSTACLES	BJORNSEN B
OFFENCES	♦ZELLICK G
OPERATIONAL	POTUTO JR
OVERCROWDI	WRIGHT M
PAROLE	GLASER D
PPRFORMANCE	WITTE AD
PERSONALITY	STRICKLI AB
PLAN	POTUTO JR
POLICY	RUTHERFO A
POOR	♦HEWITT JD+
	♦MIHANOVI CS+
	♦PECK DL+
	♦RUSTIGAN MA+

7603

PRISON (CONT)

POPULATION	BRYDENSH HH
	♦FARAWAY MJ
	♦LOUGHRAN L
	PANTON JH
	ROUNDTRE GA
	STRICKLI AB
	WHITE RB
PREDICTABI	GOODSTEI L
PREDICTION	♦SMITH JQ
	WHITE RB
PREDICTOR	GEARING ML
PRIMARY	"
PRISONERS	LUTZ U+
PROBLEM	DAX EC
PROBLEMS	KASLOW FW
PROGRAMS	CARTER JH
	TRIAL■
PSYCHOLOGI	GOODSTEI L
	WATSON JRH
PSYCHOLOGY	KASLOW FW
RE-SOCIALI	KRIMINALIST+■
REALISTIC	POTUTO JR
RECENT	♦DELGODA JP
RECIDIVISTS	DAX EC
REDUCE	BRYDENSH HH
REFORM	BJORNSEN B
	♦MULLERDI H
	♦VANGRONI J
REFORMS	DELGODA JP
RELATIONS	POOLE ED
RELEASE	GOODSTEI L
RELEASES	WITTE AD
REPORT	RUTHERFO A
REVISED	PANTON JH
RICH	HEWITT JD+
	MIHANOVI CS+
	PECK DL+
	RUSTIGAN MA+
RICHER	HEWITT JD+
	MIHANOVI CS+
	PECK DL+
	RUSTIGAN MA+
RIGHT	VITALE AT
RIGHTS	PLEVIN MD
RIOTS	SMITH JQ
RULE	ROUNDTRE GA
SCORE	PANTON JH
SECURITY	POLICE CHIE+■
SENTENCES	KRIMINALIST■
SENTENCING	FARAWAY MJ
SERVICE	KELLY ES
SERVICES	RUTHERFO A
SETTING	WALLE EL
SEX-DISCRI	THARNISH DM
SEXOLOGY	♦MONEY J
SIDE	VANGRONI J
SMASH	♦BHABHA J+
	♦JEFFERY P+
SRI-LANKA	DELGODA JP
STATE	PANTON JH
STUDY	♦CHEN TH
	♦HISTOIRE+■
	POOLE ED
STYLE	♦CLEMENTS CB
SUBJECTS	NOWLIS S
	PRICE ET
SYSTEM	CONLEY JA+
	CROUCH BM
	GLASER D
	HISTOIRE+■
TASMANIAN	DAX EC
TEACHING	POLICE CHIE+■
TREATMENT	♦KRIMINALIST■
	LEDUCSAO A
TRIAL	KRIMINALIST■
UNITED-KIN	RUTHERFO A
VIOLATIONS	ROUNDTRE GA
VOL	PARIS R+
VOLUNTARY	CORDEN J
VOLUNTEER	NOWLIS S
	PRICE ET
WALLS	♦BRODSKY SL+
WELFARE	CORDEN J
WILL	BHABHA J+
	JEFFERY P+
WOMEN	♦SOBEL SB
WORK	LUTZ U+
	POOLE ED
	SMYKLA JO
WORLD	BENTHALL J
YEARS	CONLEY JA+
1ST	PANTON JH
	PLEVIN MD
19TH-CENTU	HISTOIRE+■
2ND	PANTON JH

PRISON-DIARY

CHAU PHAN	♦LONG NV+
MINH HO CHI	" +
PRISON-NOT	" +

PRISON-INMATES

AMENDMENT	♦SANSOUCY A
APPLYING	"
ATTITUDES	♦HARTNETT J
ETHICAL	"
FORCE	SANSOUCY A
MATURITY	HARTNETT J
MORAL	"
OPERATORS	♦TAHASH GJ
PSYCHIATRI	♦EDINGER JD
REGRESSED	"
THERAPEUTI	"
TRAINING	TAHASH GJ
TREATING	EDINGER JD
USE	SANSOUCY A
WELDING	TAHASH GJ
8TH	SANSOUCY A

PRISON-NOTES

CHAU PHAN	♦LONG NV+
MINH HO CHI	" +
PRISON-DIA	" +

PRISONER

AMERICAN	♦BARTOL CR
BURMA	♦VANDERSC A
CIRCUMSTAN	♦SMITH PB
DILEMMA	♦HUSSY W
ENGLAND	♦RADZINOW L
EX-POW	VANDERSC A
EXPERIENCE	♦JADRESIC A
	♦PETERSON RW
EXPERIENCES	VANDERSC A
FACILITATOR	SMITH PB
GAME	HUSSY W
GROUP	SMITH PB
INFORMATION	HUSSY W
JANUARY	VANDERSC A
JAPANESE	"
MAGISTRATES	PETERSON RW
MEXICAN	"
MODIFIED	HUSSY W
NEED	"
POLITICAL	RADZINOW L
POPULATION	BARTOL CR
PROGRAM	PETERSON RW
PSYCHIATRY	♦HALLECK SL
RAILROAD	VANDERSC A
RECONSIDER	♦BURTCH BE
REDRESS	♦HEPBURN JR
STATUS	RADZINOW L
SUICIDE	♦HANKOFF LD
SUICIDES	BURTCH BE
TEST	BARTOL CR
TRANSFER	PETERSON RW
UNITED-STA	"
VETERINARY	VANDERSC A
WAR	"

PRISONERS

ACCESS	♦BRIAN R
ACCOUNT	♦BROGAN H+
ADOLESCENTS	♦FREYBERG H+
AMERICA	♦SPIDLE JW+

7604

PRISONERS

PRISONERS (CONT)

ANNOTATED-	♦CURTIN JJ+
	♦TAYLOR PJ+
ANXIOUS	♦ANDREWS DA
ARMED	♦BURGER JA+
AUSTRALIAN	♦WARDLAW G
AUSTRIAN	♦BENDA R
	♦KRIMINALIST■
BEHAVIOR	♦LUTZ U+
BEHAVIOR-1	♦BARTHOLO AA
BLACK	♦MOORE RD
BONAFIDE	♦THARNISH DM
CARE	♦PINTER F+
CHILDREN	FREYBERG H+
CODE	♦HARTNAGE TF
COMMITTEE	♦HASSIN Y
COMPARED	♦KOLLER KM
COMPENDIUM	♦CHASET A+
COMPUTER	HASSIN Y
CONCENTRAT	FREYBERG H+
	♦LUCHTERH E
CONFLICT	BURGER JA+
	♦KEEHN RJ
CONSEQUENC	FREYBERG H+
COUNSELING	♦RILDER HP
COURSES	LUTZ U+
CRIMINAL	+
CRIMINAL-L	+
DAY	♦BALKIN S
DISCHARGED	♦HARROLD S+
DISEASE	♦GIBBERD FB
DISEASES	♦GILL GV
DOCUMENTS	LUTZ U+
EARLY	HASSIN Y
EDUCATIONAL	LUTZ U+
ENGLAND	♦PETRIE G+
ENVIRONMENT	♦BRAND C
EVALUATIONS	♦CAHILL TJ
EX-FAR-EAST	GIBBERD FB
EXAMINATIO	FREYBERG H+
EXPERIENCES	HARROLD S+
FAMILIES	KOLLER KM
FAR-EAST	♦LANCET■
FEMALE	HARTNAGE TF
FOLLOW-UP	KEEHN RJ
FORMER	FREYBERG H+
	♦GILL GV@
	LANCET■
FUNCTIONING	ANDREWS DA
GROUP-COUN	"
HEALTH	LANCET■
HEPATITIS-B	GILL GV
HIGH	ANDREWS DA
IMPROVING	♦JAMES JF
INFECTION	GILL GV
INMATE	HARTNAGE TF
INQUIRY	CURTIN JJ+
	TAYLOR PJ+
INTERNATIO	BURGER JA+
INTERPERSO	♦DAIGLEZI WJ
JAPANESE	GILL GV@
KOREAN	KEEHN RJ
LATER	FREYBERG H+
LAW	CHASET A+
LEGAL	BRIAN R
LEGAL-RIGH	♦BOWKER LH+
	♦MORSE BW+
LIFE	♦TENNENT TG+
LISJ	♦ANTONIUS S
LONG-TERM	PINTER F+
	WARDLAW G
LOW	ANDREWS DA
MANAGEMENT	WARDLAW G
MATERIALS	BRIAN R
MEDICAL	FREYBERG H+
MEDICAL-CA	♦DUBLER NN
	♦EVERS FL
METHODS	LUTZ U+
MOVEMENT	♦HUFF CR+
NAZI	FREYBERG H+
	SPIDLE JW+
NEUROLOGIC	GIBBERD FB
NON-ANXIOUS	ANDREWS DA
OCCUPATION	THARNISH DM
PALESTINE	♦ANTONIUS S
PAST	KOLLER KM
PERSECUTION	FREYBERG H+
PERSISTING	GILL GV
POLITICAL	ANTONIUS S
	MOORE RD
POST-RELEA	HARROLD S+
PREDICTION	♦SAPSFORD RJ
PREFERENCES	CAHILL TJ
PRISON	LUTZ U+
PRISONS	WARDLAW G
PRIVACY	THARNISH DM
PROBLEM	♦HAESLER WT+
	WARDLAW G
PSYCHIATRI	JAMES JF
PSYCHIATRY	BENDA R
PUBLICITY	♦KOTZIA S+
QUALIFICAT	THARNISH DM
RATIONAL	KRIMINALIST■
RE-OFFENDI	SAPSFORD RJ
REAL-ESTATE	♦GLASSMAN JK
REGIME	FREYBERG H+
RELEASE	HASSIN Y
RELEASED	SAPSFORD RJ
REPATRIATED	♦JONES DR
RIGHTS	BARTHOLO AA
	CHASET A+
	♦MORSE BW+
	THARNISH DM
RISE	HUFF CR+
SENTENCE	TENNENT TG+
SEXUALITY	HAESLER WT+
SILENCE	♦MERTZ MP+
SKILL	DAIGLEZI WJ
SOCIAL-BEH	LUCHTERH E
SOVIET	♦CECIL R+
	♦KREKER J+
STUDIES	KEEHN RJ
STUDY	HARROLD S+
SUICIDE	CURTIN JJ+
	TAYLOR PJ+
TEXAN	BROGAN H+
THEMSELVES	JONES DR
TIME	KOLLER KM
TOO	♦CRIM LAW R■
TRAINING	DAIGLEZI WJ
TREATMENT	BENDA R
	HAESLER WT+
	KOTZIA S+
	KRIMINALIST■
TROPICAL	GILL GV
UNITED-STA	MOORE RD
VICTIMS	FREYBERG H+
VOLUNTEERS	ANDREWS DA
WAR	BURGER JA+
	CECIL R+
	GIBBERD FB
	GILL GV
	JONES DR
	♦KAUFFMAN F
	KREKER J+
	LANCET■
	SPIDLE JW+
WEHRMACHT	CECIL R+
	KREKER J+
WOMEN	ANTONIUS S
WORK	LUTZ U+
WORLD-WAR-	KEEHN RJ
WROTE	JONES DR
YOUNG-ADULT	DAIGLEZI WJ
1ST	KOLLER KM
2ND-WORLD-	FREYBERG H+

PRISONERS-DILEMMA

	♦BENORE P
	♦CHAPMAN S
ASSOCIATED	♦SMALE S
BEHAVIOR	♦KNIGHT GP
	♦LONGSHOR D
BEHAVIORAL	KNIGHT GP
CHOICE	♦AXELROD R@
COMPOSITION	KNIGHT GP
CONFEDERATE	"

7605

PRISONERS-DILEMMA (CONT)

CONNOTATIVE	♦MISRA S
DETERMINAN	KNIGHT GP
DYAD	"
DYNAMICAL-	SMALE S
EFFECT	MISRA S
EFFECTIVE	AXELROD R@
GAME	KNIGHT GP
GAMES	SMALE S
INFLATION	♦MAITAL S
INTER-RACI	LONGSHOR D
INTERPERSO	KNIGHT GP
JUDGMENTS	"
MEANING	MISRA S
NON-COOPER	SMALE S
SEX	KNIGHT GP
SIMILARITY	"
SOCIOLOGY	♦STINCHCO AL
STRATEGY	KNIGHT GP
TRIANGLE	MISRA S
TRUST	"
TRUSTWORTH	♦LINDSKOL S
VARIATIONS	"
VULNERABIL	"

PRISONERS-OF-WAR

AUSTRALIAN	♦GROVE DI
SOUTHEAST-	"
STRONGYLOI	"

PRISONIA

VIEW	♦NAGEL WG

PRISONIZATION

EFFECTS	♦FELD BC+
	♦LIDZ CW+
FRIENDSHIP	♦MILOVANO D+
	♦TAYLOR S+
	♦VANDENAS B+
JUVENILE	FELD BC+
	LIDZ CW+
LEADERSHIP	MILOVANO D+
	TAYLOR S+
	VANDENAS B+
REPORT	FELD BC+
	LIDZ CW+
SENTENCING	FELD BC+
	LIDZ CW+

PRISONS

	♦WALKER N+
ACT	♦ROBERTSO G
ADULT	♦CRIM JUST B■
ALTERNATIV	♦UMBREIT M
AMERICA	♦PRICE RR+
AUSTRALIAN	♦WARDLAW G
BARRIOS	♦KLEIN MW+
BEHAVIOR	♦SUEDFELD P
CARE	♦KAUFMAN E
CHURCH	♦RIEDER HP
COLLECTIVE	♦FLYNN EE
COMMUNITY	UMBREIT M
CONFINEMENT	♦WALKER B
CONTROLLING	FLYNN EE
COUNSELING	♦SHOWALTE D
COURTS	PRICE RR+
CRIME	♦MOSELEY LG
CRIMINALS	PRICE RR+
DANISH	UMBREIT M
DRUGS	KLEIN MW+
ENVIRONMEN	SUEDFELD P
FAMILY	SHOWALTE D
FEDERAL	♦SPENCER WJ
FUTURE	♦JEPSON N+
GANGS	KLEIN MW+
HEALTH	WALKER B
HIGH-DENSI	"
JAILS	CRIM JUST B■
	WALKER B
LESSONS	SPENCER WJ
LOCAL	ROBERTSO G
LONG-TERM	WARDLAW G
LOS-ANGELES	KLEIN MW+
MANAGEMENT	WARDLAW G
MARITAL	SHOWALTE D
MENTAL-HEA	ROBERTSO G
MENTAL-HOS	♦MILIT LAW R+
MILITARY	" +■
MORBIDITY	♦JAMES JF
OPEN	♦BOWKER LH+
	♦MCCABE WF+
PAST	JEPSON N+
POLICE	PRICE RR+
POSSIBLE	♦FRIEDENB EZ+
PRESENT	" +
PRISONERS	WARDLAW G
PROBLEM	"
PSYCHIATRIC	JAMES JF
	KAUFMAN E
PSYCHIATRI	ROBERTSO G
PSYCHOLOGY	CRIM JUST B■
RESOCIALIZ	♦DEIMLING G
SCHOOLS	MILIT LAW R+
SECTION	ROBERTSO G
SERVICE	RIEDER HP
SERVICES	CRIM JUST B■
SPORTS	♦NICKOLAI W
STANDARDS	CRIM JUST B■
	KAUFMAN E
TRANSFERS	ROBERTSO G
TURMOIL	♦MCWHORTE WL
USE	MOSELEY LG
	UMBREIT M
VIOLATION	KAUFMAN E
VIOLENCE	FLYNN EE
VIOLENT	SUEDFELD P
WORLD	♦GUERRERO AM+
	♦ZELLER LJ+

→*PRIVACY*

	♦BROTMAN SN+
	♦COPE D+
	♦GREGORY SW+
	♦LINOWES DF+
	♦MARSHALL G+
	♦NEISSER E+
	♦WHITE P
ACT	♦GREGURAS FM
	♦HANCOCK G
	♦SMITH ME
ACTS	♦RICHARDS DA
AFFECTING	♦FUSILIER MR
ASA	♦AM STATISTN■
AUTOMOBILE	♦J CRIM LAW■
BANKS	♦LAUDON KC
BASIC	♦BING J
	♦KIRBY MD
BONAFIDE	♦THARNISH DM
BROADCASTS	♦GLASSER TL
BUGS	♦OSHINSKY WS
CALIFORNIAS	HANCOCK G
CENSUSES	♦OBRIEN J+
CIVIL-LAW	♦GINSBURG G+
	♦JOURN Q+■
COMMERCIAL	♦KAPLAN MR
COMMITTEE	AM STATISTN■
COMMUNALITY	♦RAPOPORT A+
COMMUNITY	♦VICTOR JS
COMPARATIVE	BING J
COMPUTER	♦WONG K
COMPUTER-A	♦ISAACSON WJ
COMPUTERS	♦LINDOP N
CONCEPT	BING J
	♦FODDY WH
CONCERNS	♦SNELLING HE+
CONFIDENTI	AM STATISTN■
	♦COUSINS B@
	♦EVERSTIN L
	♦NYE SG
	♦SCI TECHNOL+■
CONGRESSIO	OSHINSKY WS
CONSTITUTI	♦RICHARDS DA@
CONTROL	♦IWATA O
COPYRIGHT	GINSBURG G+
	JOURN Q+■

7606

PRIVACY

LEGEND

- ♦ UNIQUE ARTICLE INDICATOR
- @ AUTHOR OF MORE THAN ONE ARTICLE WITH SAME PRIMARY AND CO-TERM
- + BOOK REVIEW
- ■ SEE ANONYMOUS SOURCE SECTION

PRIVACY (CONT)

CORRECTIONS	♦SMITH DE
CROWDING	IWATA O
DATA	♦HONDIUS FW
	KIRBY MD
	LAUDON KC
	♦SALTON G
DATA-PROCE	♦TURN R
DEFAMATION	GINSBURG G+
	JOURN Q+■
DELEGE-LAT	GINSBURG G+
DESIGN	RAPOPORT A+
DETERMINAN	IWATA O
EFT	GREGURAS FM
EMPLOYEE	ISAACSON WJ
	♦SWARTS W
EMPLOYEES	♦KRIMINALIST■
ENTRIES	OSHINSKY WS
ETHICS	♦BULMER M+
	♦DINGWALL R+
EXPECTATIO	J CRIM LAW■
EXPERIENCES	♦TAYLOR RB
FACTORS	SCI TECHNOL+■
FEDERAL	KRIMINALIST■
	LAUDON KC
FINANCIAL	♦SMITH ME@
FINDINGS	AM STATISTN■
FLOWS	KIRBY MD
FREE-FLOW	SNELLING HE+
FREEDOM	♦RELYEA HC
FRENCH	VICTOR JS
FUTURE	♦KRIMINALIST■
GUIDELINES	♦SCHRIER CJ
HOME	♦WOODS P
HOMOSEXUAL	RICHARDS DA
HOMOSEXUAL.	"
IMAGINARY	♦APPLETON SF
IMPLICATIO	♦JOHNSEN K
	♦SKIPPER H
	♦SWARTS WB
	♦TURN R
	WONG K
INDECENT	GLASSER TL
INDIVIDUALS	SMITH ME
INFORMATION	♦FELDMAN AR
	♦INF PRIVACY■
	RELYEA HC
	SALTON G
	SKIPPER H
	SNELLING HE+
	SWARTS WB
INFORMATIO	♦GREGURAS FM
INSTALL	OSHINSKY WS
INSURANCE	♦SEILER RS
INSURERS	SKIPPER H
	SWARTS WB
INTERESTS	OSHINSKY WS
INTIMACY	VICTOR JS
INTRODUCTI	SMITH ME
INVASION	FUSILIER MR
	♦LIEBMAN HR
	♦STEVENS GE
ISSUES	GREGURAS FM
→JUVENILES	WOODS P
LAW	♦GAVISON R
	♦GENOVESE MA+
	♦ISAACSON WJ
	♦NAYLOR DT+
LAWS	SCHRIER CJ
LAWSUIT	APPLETON SF
LEGISLATION	BING J
	INF PRIVACY■
	JOHNSEN K
	KRIMINALIST■
LIMITS	APPLETON SF
	GAVISON R
LINKING	TAYLOR RB
LISTENERS	GLASSER TL
LOCUS	IWATA O
OCCUPATION	THARNISH DM
OFFICE	KRIMINALIST■
OFFICIAL	RELYEA HC
OPEN-ACCESS	SCHRIER CJ
ORDER	ISAACSON WJ
ORIENTATION	IWATA O
PATIENT	NYE SG
PEN	♦FISHMAN CS
PERCEPTION	IWATA O
PERCEPTIONS	FUSILIER MR
PERSONAL	FELDMAN AR
	ISAACSON WJ
PERSONNEL	SWARTS W
PERSONNEL-	FUSILIER MR
PERSPECTIVE	BING J
	FODDY WH
PITFALLS	♦BELAIR RR
PRACTICES	SKIPPER H
	SWARTS WB
PRISONERS	THARNISH DM
PROGRESS	SALTON G
PROTECTING	♦BINDRIM P
PROTECTION	♦POSNER RA
	SNELLING HE+
	TURN R@
PSYCHOTHER	EVERSTIN L
PUBLIC-INT	♦MARTIN BA
PUBLIC-POL	GENOVESE MA+
QUALIFICAT	THARNISH DM
REASONABLE	J CRIM LAW■
RECOMMENDA	AM STATISTN■
RECORD-KEE	SCHRIER CJ
RECORDKEEP	SWARTS W
REFLECTIONS	APPLETON SF
REGISTERS	FISHMAN CS
REPORT	SALTON G
REPORTING	FELDMAN AR
REPRODUCTI	APPLETON SF
REQUIREMEN	TURN R
RESPONSE	SCI TECHNOL+■
RIGHT	GLASSER TL
	KAPLAN MR
	KRIMINALIST■
	MARTIN BA
	♦MCCLOSKE HJ
	RICHARDS DA@
	SMITH ME
→	WOODS P
RIGHTS	KRIMINALIST■
	THARNISH DM
RULES	KIRBY MD
SEARCHES	J CRIM LAW■
SECRECY	RELYEA HC
	♦WARREN C
SECURITY	♦COVVEY HD
	SALTON G
	TURN R
	WONG K
SHAME	VICTOR JS
SILENCE	OSHINSKY WS
SITUATION	FUSILIER MR
SOCIAL-SCI	BULMER M+
	DINGWALL R+
SOLIDARITY	♦FIRESTON IJ
SOVIET	GINSBURG G+
	JOURN Q+■
SPECIAL	KRIMINALIST■
SPEECH	KAPLAN MR
STUDENT	STEVENS GE
SUPREME-CO	POSNER RA
SURVEY	SCI TECHNOL+■
SURVEYS	OBRIEN J+
SYMBOLIC-I	FODDY WH
SYSTEM	JOHNSEN K
SYSTEMS	TURN R

7607

PRIVACY (CONT)

TECHNICAL	TURN R
TERRITORIA	IWATA O
	TAYLOR RB
THREAT	♦LANGAN KJ
TRANSBORDER	KIRBY MD
TRANSNATIO	TURN R
UNCERTAIN	APPLETON SF
	POSNER RA
UNITED-STA	GREGURAS FM
UPDATE	SWARTS W
USA	GREGURAS FM
VARIABLES	FUSILIER MR
WAKE	OSHINSKY WS
WORK	♦SUNDSTRO E
YIELD	OSHINSKY WS
1980S	WONG K

PRIVATE

ABROAD	♦GRAHAM PA+
ACCESS	♦BACH L
ACCESSIBIL	"
ACCIDENTAL	♦HANDL G
ACCOUNT	♦CREEL R
ACCOUNTS	♦JOHNSON JM+
ACCUMULATI	♦MATTHEWS K
	♦SOBOL MG
ACT	♦FRANKHAU MM
ACTION	♦PAOLICEL DM
	♦REDLICH DN
	♦ROSS AM
	♦SMITH M
ACTIONS	FRANKHAU MM
	♦HARV LAW RE■
	♦MILLER R
	♦RIV INT EC■
ACTOR-OBSE	♦THORNTON B
ACTORS	♦PINCUS AJ
ADAMS	♦NEILSON MS
ADJUDICATI	♦CARRINGT PD
	♦HAZARD GC
	♦LANDES WM
ADMITTING	♦KALAI E
ADULT	♦KOSS MP
AFFAIRS	♦MASSING M
AFFIRMATIV	♦SOBLE RS
AGENCIES	♦KRIMINALIST■
AGRARIAN	♦KATO F
AGRICULTUR	♦RUOZI R
AID	♦DOERR E
ALTERNATIVE	♦KELLY TJ
	REDLICH DN
ALTERNATIV.	♦GOLDBERG VP
	KALAI E
	♦MANNE HG
	♦STEINHAU MB
AMENDMENT	SOBLE RS
AMERICAN	♦BARBER JP+
	♦DUNNE M+
	♦EDGINGTO SW+
	♦GARNHAM D+
	♦GELFAND LE+
	♦REESE WLM
	♦SMITH TC+
	♦STONE WF+
AMERICAN-C	♦WILLIAMS PM+
ANALYSIS	♦EVE RA
	♦OHLSON JA@
	♦STROBEL CD
	♦TAYLOR D
ANTITRUST	HARV LAW RE■
	♦SNELL RK
API	OHLSON JA@
APPROACH	♦MCNEILL DN
APPROPRIAT	♦HOUSTON DA
APPROXIMATE	♦BALACHAN KR
ARGUMENT	♦CANDLISH S
ARREST	♦KELDER G
ARROW	KALAI E
ASSET	MATTHEWS K
	♦WHITMORE HW
ASSETS	♦LANOFF ID
	♦SMIRLOCK M
ASSISTANT	♦BRUNE LH+
ATTACKING	♦HARV LAW RE■
ATTITUDE	♦UNGAR S
ATTRIBUTION	♦QUADLAND MC
ATTRIBUTIO	THORNTON B
AUTOMATION	♦MAREK K
AVIATION	♦WILSON LIB+■
BAHAMAS	♦AGOR WH
BAR	♦BRAKEL SJ
BARS	♦J TAXATION■
BASED	BACH L
BASIS	♦ANDERSON DL
BEHALF	RIV INT EC■
BEHAVIOR	UNGAR S
BEHAVIORAL	♦FROMING WJ
BEHAVIORS	EVE RA
BELIEFS	♦SCHEIER MF
BENEFITS	♦BOSWORTH DL
	♦CHO DW
BIBLIOGRAP	♦LANSKY R+
BIG	♦THOMPSON D
BLACK	♦BRACY R
BOON	♦KADENS MG
BRAZIL	♦TRINDADE SC
BRIDGMAN P	♦ALLEN HJ
BRITAIN	♦GRAY C
BUDGETS	WHITMORE HW
BUILDING	♦HAUPT HG+
	♦NICHOLSO RJ
	♦SAUTENKO V
BURGER	♦GERSTEIN RS
CANADA	♦STENNING PC
CANAL	HAUPT HG+
CAPITAL	" +
	RIV INT EC■
	SOBOL MG
CARE	♦ANNAS GJ
	♦BLOMQVIS A
	♦HOSPITALS+■
	♦MOFFET D+
	♦SPORTY L
CASE	♦FINKIN MW
	TRINDADE SC
CENTERS	♦ETTORRE EM+
CETA	♦BERNICK MS+
	♦KAZIS R
CHANGE	♦SCHEIER MF
CHARACTERI	♦DAVIS OA
	KOSS MP
CHARACTERI.	KALAI E
CHARITY	♦KENNETT DA
	♦RIPLEY A
CHICAGOS	THOMPSON D
CHILD	KOSS MP
CHOICE	♦AM J LAW M+
	♦BERNSTEI S+
	♦BLOOM HS
	♦BULMER M+
	♦GRAY JN+
	♦IMBER JB+
	♦LOVIN RW+
	♦MEIKLEJO D+
	♦PUKA B+
	♦STEVENSO I+
	♦THAYER FC+
	♦WILLIAMS B+
CITY	♦BERLIN B+
CLIENTS	KOSS MP
CLINIC	♦JOST A
CLINICAL	♦SOKOLOFF KA
CLINICS	♦WILLIAMS AJ

7608

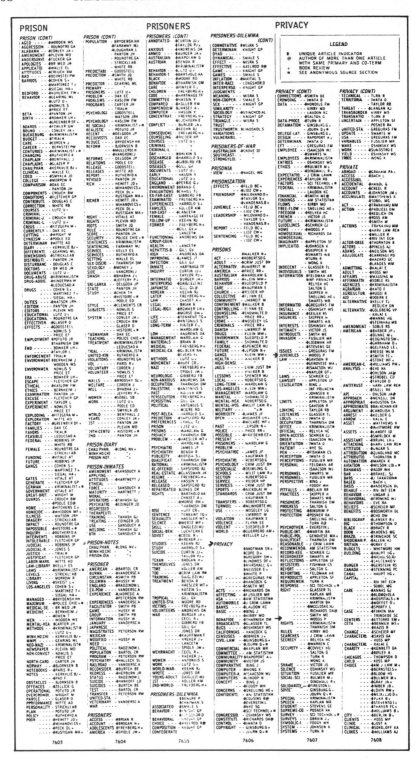

Illustration B

Subject entries in *Social Sciences Citation Index*, 1980 Annual (Reprinted with permission of the Institute for Scientific Information ®, Inc. from the *Social Science Citation Index* ®. Copyright 1981, by ISI ®).

Index to International Statistics (1983–date). Issued monthly, with an annual cumulation volume, *IIS* covers statistical publications of *international intergovernmental organizations.*

Statistical Reference Index (1980–date). Issued monthly, with an annual cumulation volume. *SRI* covers statistical publications from sources *other than* the U.S. Government (i.e. private, foreign, etc.).

All three of these indexes are supplemented by microfiche libraries of the actual publications referred to by each index.

Beginning in March 1981, two agencies within the U.S. Department of Commerce have published *A Directory of Federal Statistical Data Files.* This directory was developed to assist users in accessing machine-readable data files, but its indexing (by subject matter keyword, and by agency) and abstracts should be useful in identifying relevant data in conventional format as well.

d. Current Bibliographies

Many bibliographies of varying scope, coverage and detail, with or without annotations and evaluations, are published on every discipline and subject field in the social sciences. Most are not updated and hence become of decreasing value as time passes after their publication. Those which are issued periodically or supplemented regularly are particularly useful for following the literature in particular fields or on specific problems.

The *International Bibliography of the Social Sciences,* prepared by the International Committee for Social Science Documentation (UNESCO) in four sections is perhaps the most comprehensive social science bibliography of books, periodical articles, government publications, and pamphlets in many languages. Each of its four subject series (listed below) is issued in annual volumes, with indexes by author and subject in English and French:

International Bibliography of Economics (Aldine, 1955–date).

International Bibliography of Political Science (Aldine, 1953–date).

International Bibliography of Social and Cultural Anthropology (Aldine, 1955–date).

International Bibliography of Sociology (Aldine, 1952–date).

There is unfortunately a one or two year delay in the publication of the annual volumes of these series, but their breadth of coverage nevertheless makes them particularly useful.

Other bibliographies listed in Sheehy's *Guide to Reference Books,* Brewer's *Abstracting and Indexing Services Directory,* and the H.W. Wilson Company's *Bibliographic Index* will offer coverage of specific subjects and more current references.

e. Periodicals and Annuals Covering Law and Social Sciences

As noted above in Chapter 16, Legal Periodicals, there are a number of periodicals and annuals dealing specifically with law and the social sciences. These include the following titles:

American Behavioral Scientist (Sage Publications, 1957–date) 6 issues per year.

Columbia Journal of Law and Social Problems (Columbia Univ. Law School, 1965–date) quarterly.

International Journal of Law and Psychiatry (Pergamon Press, 1977–date) quarterly.

International Journal of the Sociology of Law (Academic Press, 1973–date; formerly the *International Journal of Criminology and Penology*) quarterly.

Journal of Law and Economics (University of Chicago Law School, 1958–date) semiannual.

Journal of Legal Studies (University of Chicago Law School, 1972–date) three issues per year.

Law and Behavior (Research Press, 1976–date) quarterly.

Law and Contemporary Problems (Duke University Law School, 1933–date) quarterly.

Law and Housing Journal (Case Western Reserve Law School, 197?–date).

Law and Human Behavior (Plenum, 1977–date) quarterly.

Law and Policy Quarterly (Sage, 1979–date) quarterly.

Law and Psychology Review (University of Alabama, 1975–date).

Law and Social Work Quarterly (Haworth, 1980–date) quarterly.

Law and Society Review (Law and Society Association, 1966–date) quarterly.

New York University Review of Law and Social Change (N.Y.U. Law School, 1971–date) semi-annual.

Yale Law & Policy Review (Yale Law School, 1982–date) semi-annual.

Some of these periodicals include book reviews and literature surveys of the fields they cover, and can thereby be used to follow publications and developments outside of the particular journal.

Jai Press, Inc. issues four annual inter-disciplinary publications which contain articles largely focused on research in fields of social sciences related to law. These annuals are *Advances in Law and Child Development* (1982–date); *Research in Law and Economics* (1979–date); *Research in Law and Sociology* (1978–date); and *Research in Law, Deviance and Social Control* (1978–date).

Two other quite different periodicals are useful for their evaluations of new publications in the social sciences. The *Annals of the American Academy of Political and Social Science* (1890–date), a quarterly journal, contains book reviews of a wide range of social science monographs. *Choice* (Association of College and Research Libraries, 1964–date), is a monthly library book selection guide which lists new scholarly publications in all fields, with a heavy emphasis on the social sciences. Each listing includes a critical annotation of the book. Books are listed and evaluated in *Choice* long before they are reviewed in the specialized journals of their respective disciplines. It also includes annual cumulated indexing of its contents, by author and subject.

3. COMPUTERIZED LITERATURE SEARCHING

Most of the indexing and abstracting materials referred to in this chapter are now compiled and produced with the aid of computers, and many are also available to researchers for direct searching by computer.

The delay in traditional forms of publication is greatly reduced when the material is entered into a computer data base and made available for on-line searching. Computerized literature searches therefore tend to yield more recent citations than printed volumes, and there is no need to wait for a new edition or supplement to be compiled, printed, distributed and processed by the recipient. Computer searches can usually be performed more quickly than locating and using the printed source, and often provide more varied and sophisticated approaches to the data. Computerized literature searching, however, is typically available only on a fee basis.

Law students and attorneys may be familiar with full-text computer assisted legal research in systems such as LEXIS and WESTLAW. Most computer services available for social science materials do not employ full-text searching, however. Instead, these services make available citations to these materials in fixed formats—the researcher must use these citations to locate and then inspect the actual article or report. Unlike WESTLAW and LEXIS, the major computerized literature search services require substantial training in their operation, and researchers who use them only occasionally should seek the assistance of trained library staff in performing searches.

The use of non-legal computer data bases will be dealt with further in Chapter 22, New Media in Legal Research.

E. ADDITIONAL READING

Any selection of additional reading on the legal uses of social science research and analysis will necessarily be arbitrary. The following list of books is representative of recently published material available. No periodical articles are listed, although many of considerable interest have been published. The real purpose of this section of the chapter is to suggest a beginning for further study.

G.P. Calabresi & P.C. Bobbitt, *Tragic Choices* (Norton, 1978).

P.L. Dubois, *Analysis of Judicial Reform* (D.C. Heath, 1982).

L.M. Friedman & S. Macauley, editors, *Law and the Behavioral Sciences* (Bobbs–Merrill, 1977).

J. Katzer, K.H. Cook & W.W. Crouch, *Evaluating Information, A Guide for Users of Social Science Research*, 2d ed. (Addison-Wesley, 1982).

J.W. Loewen, *Social Science in the Courtroom* (Lexington Books, 1982).

L.C. Parker, Jr., *Legal Psychology* (Thomas, 1980).

H. Kalven, Jr. and H. Zeisel, *The American Jury* (Little, Brown, 1966).

R.A. Posner, *Economic Analysis of Law,* 2d ed. (Little, Brown, 1977) and *The Economics of Justice* (Harvard Univ. Press, 1981).

P.L. Rosen, *The Supreme Court and Social Science* (Univ. of Illinois Press, 1972).

M.J. Saks and C.H. Baron, eds., *The Use/Nonuse/Misuse of Applied Social Research in the Courts* (Abt Books, 1980).

Chapter 19

ENGLISH AND CANADIAN MATERIALS *

A. INTRODUCTION

English law is the ancestral model for the American legal system, as it is for the common law provinces of Canada. English and Canadian cases are therefore used as persuasive authority in many U.S. courts when issues arise on which there is little American precedent. Similarly, decisions from other common law countries are occasionally

* The authors wish to acknowledge the substantial assistance of Kathy E. Shimpock, then Librarian and Assistant Professor of Law, University of Bridgeport Law School, and Diane Teeple of the Ontario Legislative Library, in the preparation of this chapter.

used in such situations. This chapter will focus, however, only on English and Canadian materials.

Research in English and Canadian law is usually not very difficult, but it is useful to keep in mind the differences between the two systems. Britain (though including England, Scotland and Wales) is a unitary state without a written constitution, and the validity of acts passed by its sovereign Parliament cannot by questioned by the courts.[1] In addition, constitutional change can be brought about by a simple act of the United Kingdom Parliament, amending those laws, customs and conventions which constitute the unwritten constitution.

Canada, on the other hand, is a federation consisting of ten provinces. There are, in addition, two Territories for which the federal government has direct authority, although power to legislate in certain areas has been delegated to the Territorial Councils. In Canada, both the federal Parliament and the provincial legislatures derive their powers from the Constitution, in particular from sections 91 and 92 of what was formerly the *British North American Act,* and is now part of the *Constitution Acts, 1867–1982,* proclaimed in force April 17, 1982. These provisions grant the federal Parliament authority to legislate in respect of matters under sec. 91, and give the provincial legislatures power to legislate with respect to matters listed under sec. 92. Residual powers not specifically enumerated are left to the federal authority. Canadian courts can be called upon to determine the validity of legislation which appears to exceed the limits of legislative authority granted. A more detailed description of the new Canadian Constitution follows at pp. [592, 594].

B. THE BRITISH CONSTITUTIONAL BACKGROUND

While a full discussion of British Constitutional law is beyond the scope of this chapter, it is useful to remember the following. English law generally refers to the municipal law of England and Wales, and other parts of the British Isles are not automatically subject to it. Great Britain, consisting of England, Wales and Scotland, has had a unified Parliament since the Treaty of Union in 1707. The United Kingdom, which is the body recognized for international purposes, is comprised of Great Britain and Northern Ireland. Legislative authority was vested in the Parliament of the United Kingdom of Great Britain and Ireland from the Act of Union in 1880 to the partition of Ireland in 1922. At that time, Southern Ireland became the Republic of Ireland and separated from the British Crown. Power to legislate over Northern Ireland was divided between the United Kingdom Parliament and the Northern Ireland Parliament at Stormont until direct rule was imposed in 1972. There have been continuing efforts to create separate Assemblies in Scotland, Wales and Northern Ireland,

1. For a concise overview, see D.C.M. Yardley, *Introduction to British Constitutional Law* (5th ed. 1978). A useful introduction to Canadian law and legal institutions is provided by G.L. Gall, *The Canadian Legal System* (1977), although it predates the constitutional changes of 1982.

with a division of legislative powers between the local Assembly and the Parliament at Westminster, but so far these have been without success.[2]

Finally, the researcher should also consider the fact that the United Kingdom became a member of the European Community on January 1, 1973. By the terms of the Treaty of Accession, European Community law, consisting of the treaties and secondary legislation of the Community, is binding in the U.K., and British courts must follow precedents laid down by the European Court of Justice when questions of European law are in issue. Therefore, in certain important trade and economic matters, legislative power resides with the Community and precedents based on Continental legal concepts must be followed by the courts. This background is essential for understanding the following outline of English legal materials, most of which can be found in the larger U.S. law libraries. Because English citations may be confusing to the American researcher, Donald Raistrick's *Index to Legal Citations and Abbreviations* (Professional Books, 1981) may be helpful.

C. ENGLISH STATUTES

1. EARLY ENGLISH STATUTES

Early English statutes, dating from the 13th century, were published in different editions, and often varied as to year and chapter number. Until 1962, the statutes were officially cited by regnal year, not by calendar year, making statutory research somewhat confusing.

Most research law libraries have one or more of the various editions of the *Statutes at Large* which include acts published from 1225–1869. A discussion of these series can be found in *Sweet & Maxwell's Guide to Law Reports and Statutes* (4th ed. 1962). The most authoritative edition of early English statutes is called the *Statutes of the Realm* which is comprised of all statutes enacted from 1235 to 1713.[3] However, acts passed during the Interregnum are not included in any of the above collections; for these, see *Acts and Ordinances of the Interregnum, 1642–1660* (1911), 3 vols.

2. CURRENT STATUTES

Since 1831, the Public General Acts have been published yearly in a chronological arrangement similar to the U.S. session laws. The bound volumes for each year contain alphabetical and chronological tables of acts, a table of derivations and destinations, and an index. A list of Local and Personal Acts passed during the year is also

2. See the *Scotland Act, 1978,* 1978 c. 51 (U.K.); *the Wales Act 1978,* 1978, c. 52 (U.K.); *the Northern Ireland Assembly Act 1973,* 1973, c. 17 (U.K.); *the Northern Ireland Constitution Act, 1973,* 1973, c. 36 (U.K.); and *the Northern Ireland Act, 1974,* 1974, c. 28 (U.K.).

3. Published in 9 vols., 1810–1825, with an alphabetical index (1824) and a chronological index (1828).

printed, but the text of these acts is published separately. An identical but unofficial edition is published as part of the *Law Reports* series, described below in Section E. The acts are first issued in advance sheets, usually almost a year after enactment. A more current source of the text of individual acts is the official Queen's Printer copy published by Her Majesty's Stationery Office (the U.K. government publications agency, known as *HMSO*), within a few days of the act receiving Royal Assent.

3. STATUTES IN FORCE

Three editions of the *Statutes Revised* have been published between 1870 and 1950, reprinting all public acts in force at the date of publication. These sets are essentially a republication in chronological order of the statutes in force, with no consolidation of amended legislation, or renumbering of chapters. They have been replaced by a new edition entitled *Statutes in Force: Official Revised Edition,* which began publication in 1972, in loose-leaf format to provide for continuous updating. Each act is published in a separate booklet incorporating amendments to date and will be replaced when amended extensively or repealed. These can be filed in any manner, but are generally arranged by subject groups and then the individual acts placed chronologically within each subject. The work includes Public General Acts in force throughout the United Kingdom, but a subscription may also be limited to a particular area. There are both alphabetical and chronological lists of all acts published in the series, and a general index will be issued when the set is complete. (See Illustration A.) Publication of the *Statutes Revised* has been quite slow and it is much less convenient to use than American statutory compilations. Most researchers therefore prefer the annotated, commercial editions described below. A microfiche edition of *Statutes in Force* is now available from Unifo Publishers.

4. ANNOTATED EDITIONS OF STATUTES

Halsbury's Statutes of England (Butterworth, 3d ed., 1968–1975) is an unofficial, but widely used compilation of statutes in force. (See Illustration B.) The statutes are arranged alphabetically in broad subject headings, with annotations following each section. Its volumes are updated by annual bound continuation volumes, annual cumulative supplements, and two loose-leaf volumes, *Current Statutes Service* and *Noter-Up.* There is also a volume entitled *European Continuation Vol. 1, 1952–1972,* which contains the treaties and secondary legislation of the European Community.

The *Cumulative Supplement* updates the main volumes, the continuation volumes and the European continuation volume, and is arranged by corresponding subject titles. Cross-referencing between the volumes and the *Supplement* is by title and page number. For changes made too late for mention in the *Supplement,* a "Noter-up" is supplied as part of the *Current Statutes Service.* That shows the

EQUAL PAY ACT 1970 (c. 41)

S.1

*An Act to prevent discrimination, as regards terms and conditions of employment, between men and women.
[29th May 1970]

**This Act is printed in the form in which it is set out in Sex Discrimination Act 1975 (c. 65), Sch. 1 Pt. II, with subsequent amendments*

1.—(1) If the terms of a contract under which a woman is employed at an establishment in Great Britain do not include (directly or by reference to a collective agreement or otherwise) an equality clause they shall be deemed to include one.

(2) An equality clause is a provision which relates to terms (whether concerned with pay or not) of a contract under which a woman is employed (the "woman's contract"), and has the effect that—

(a) where the woman is employed on like work with a man in the same employment—

(i) if (apart from the equality clause) any term of the woman's contract is or becomes less favourable to the woman than a term of a similar kind in the contract under which that man is employed, that term of the woman's contract shall be treated as so modified as not to be less favourable, and

(ii) if (apart from the equality clause) at any time the woman's contract does not include a term corresponding to a term benefiting that man included in the contract under which he is employed, the woman's contract shall be treated as including such a term;

(b) where the woman is employed on work rated as equivalent with that of a man in the same employment—

(i) if (apart from the equality clause) any term of the woman's contract determined by the rating of the work is or becomes less favourable to the woman than a term of a similar kind in the contract under which that man is employed, that term of the woman's contract shall be treated as so modified as not to be less favourable, and

(ii) if (apart from the equality clause) at any time the woman's contract does not include a term corresponding to a term benefiting that man included in the contract under which he is employed and determined by the rating of the work, the woman's contract shall be treated as including such a term.

(3) An equality clause shall not operate in relation to a variation between the woman's contract and the man's contract if the employer

Illustration A

A sample act from the *Statutes in Force,* (H.M.S.O., 1980).

THE EQUAL PAY ACT 1970

(1970 c. 41)

PRELIMINARY NOTE

The object of this Act, which received the Royal Assent on 29th May 1970, is to eliminate discrimination on grounds of sex in remuneration and other terms and conditions of employment. S. 9, *post*, provides for the Act to come into force on 29th December 1975 and enables the Secretary of State to provide by Order for an intermediate stage coming into effect on 31st December 1973 at which date women would become entitled to receive treatment which amounted as respects pay to nine-tenths of that of the corresponding men. The Act does not extend to Northern Ireland (see s. 11 (3), *post*).

S. 1, *post*, provides for equal treatment as between men and women where they are engaged on the same or broadly similar work, or where a woman's job has been rated as equivalent to a man's job, though of a different nature from her own, as a result of a job evaluation exercise.

S. 2, *post*, provides for industrial tribunals to deal with disputes arising in connection with the provisions of s. 1, *post*. References to the tribunal may be made by a party to the dispute or by the Secretary of State. Sub-s. (6) places the onus of proof on employers to show that differences in pay between women and men result from a material difference (other than the difference of sex) between their cases.

S. 3, *post*, provides for the removal of specific discrimination between men and women in collective agreements. Parties to an agreement or the Secretary of State may refer it to the Industrial Arbitration Board for a declaration of the amendments necessary to be made to the agreement for the removal of discrimination. The extent of the amendments to be made by the Board is defined in sub-s. (4) of that section. Sub-s. (6) extends the operation of the section to employers' pay structures.

In line with the provision in s. 3, *post*, provision is made in ss. 4 and 5, *post*, to remove discrimination between men and women in Wages Regulations Orders and Agricultural Wages Orders respectively.

S. 6, *post*, makes certain exclusions from the Act including terms and conditions related to retirement, marriage or death. S. 7, *post*, makes provision with regard to the pay of the armed forces (including women's services); and s. 8, *post*, makes similar provision with regard to the police.

S. 10, *post*, deals with preliminary references to the Industrial Arbitration Board before the commencement of the Act.

The Act, so far as material, is extended to civil servants by s. 1 (8) and s. 3 (7), *post*.

ARRANGEMENT OF SECTIONS

Illustration B

Halsbury's Statutes of England (Butterworth, 3d ed.), Continuation volume, 1968–70.

effect of new legislation and case law on the published volumes, with a separate table for the European continuation volume. Also included is the text of new acts with annotations, and a list of statutes and appointed day orders.

There is a Table of Statutes and an Index for volumes 1–45 which provides subject access to the set, and also includes an alphabetical title and chronological list of statutes, and an index of words and phrases. The alphabetical and chronological lists are updated by listings at the front of the *Cumulative Supplement.* While generally preferred to the *Statutes in Force* for statutory research because of its superior finding aids and historical annotations, one disadvantage in using *Halsbury's Statutes* is that acts dealing with more than one subject will be divided between the several subject categories. In addition to *Halsbury's Statutes,* there are two annotated session law services which may be available in some libraries: *Current Law Statutes Annotated,* (1948–date) and *Butterworth's Annotated Legislation Service* (1939–date).

D. ENGLISH ADMINISTRATIVE LAW

Parliament may grant to a Minister, board, or local authority the power to make rules and regulations in an area covered generally by an act of Parliament. These rules have the same force of law as the enabling statute, provided they do not exceed the limits of the powers granted, but they can be easily altered without first obtaining Parliamentary approval. In addition, this delegated or subordinate legislation may take the form of *orders in council,* made by the Queen in Council, in which case authority for their creation may stem from the Royal Prerogative, as well as from Parliament. In published form, English administrative regulations are known as *Statutory Instruments,* or *Statutory Rules and Orders* before 1948.

Since 1949, the official source for subordinate legislation is the *Statutory Instruments* volumes, formerly called *Statutory Rules and Orders.* (See Illustration C). First published individually in slip form, the instruments are incorporated into bound volumes which give the full text of all general statutory instruments issued during the year. The annual volumes are comprised of three parts, each covering four months, with a cumulative index at the end of each part. Each section is designated by year and number (e.g., S.I. 1980/1104) and appears in numerical order within the bound volumes.

A Table of Governmental Orders is issued yearly and lists numerically all general rules, orders, and statutory instruments still in force, and also gives the history of those orders, etc., affected by subsequent legislation. Entries in bold type are still fully or partially in force; those in italics are not. The *Index to Government Orders* is a subject index to the orders, rules and statutory instruments in force. This index is published biannually with a supplement issued in alternating years. For the most recent instruments, there is in addition the monthly *List of Statutory Instruments* containing a numerical and subject listing of those instruments.

STATUTORY INSTRUMENTS

1975 No. 1938 (C. 55)

TERMS AND CONDITIONS OF EMPLOYMENT

The Employment Protection Act 1975 (Commencement No. 1) Order 1975

Made - - - *25th November* 1975

The Secretary of State, in exercise of the powers conferred on him by section 129 of the Employment Protection Act 1975 **(a)** and of all other powers enabling him in that behalf, hereby makes the following Order:—

Citation

1.—This Order may be cited as the Employment Protection Act 1975 (Commencement No. 1) Order 1975.

Commencement

2.—The provisions of the Employment Protection Act 1975 specified in the Schedules hereto shall come into operation:—

(*a*) in the case of the provisions mentioned in Schedule 1, on 1st January 1976,

(*b*) in the case of the provisions mentioned in Schedule 2, on 1st February 1976,

(*c*) in the case of the provisions mentioned in Schedule 3, on 1st March 1976.

Transitional provisions

3.—(1) The repeal of the Conciliation Act 1896 **(b)** or any repeal of the Industrial Courts Act 1919 **(c)** brought into operation by this Order shall not affect the validity of anything done before the coming into operation of this Order by or in relation to the Secretary of State in pursuance of any of the repealed provisions of those Acts; and anything which at the time of the said coming into operation is in the process of being done by or in relation to or on the reference of the Secretary of State, shall be treated as if done and be continued by or in relation to or on the reference of the Advisory, Conciliation and Arbitration Service, and in the case of a reference to a person or persons to whom any matter has been referred by the Secretary of State in pursuance of any of the repealed provisions of those Acts, that person or those persons shall be deemed to be a person or persons appointed under section 2 or 3 of the Employment Protection Act 1975, as appropriate.

(2) Any matter which immediately before the commencement of section 10(2) of the said 1975 Act stood referred to the Industrial Arbitration Board under any enactment, statutory instrument or other document shall be treated as if it had been referred to the Central Arbitration Committee.

(a) 1975 c. 71. **(b)** 1896 c. 30.
(c) 1919 c. 69.

Illustration C

Statutory Instruments (H.M.S.O., 1975) (Part III. Section 3).

A more convenient, *unofficial* compilation, *Halsbury's Statutory Instruments* (Butterworth, 1978–date), can be found in many U.S. law libraries. It is arranged by subject in a manner similar to the *Code of Federal Regulations,* and includes the full text or summaries of statutory instruments in force. Bound volumes are occasionally replaced for updating, and there is a one volume loose-leaf supplement, containing a chronological list of instruments. (See Illustration D). The looseleaf volume also contains an updating service in the form of an *Annual Cumulative Supplement and Quarterly Survey.* Subject access is also provided by a general index to the set, updated by pocket part supplementation.

E. ENGLISH LAW REPORTS

The earliest reports of English cases can be found in *Year Books,* published from 1272–1535 and written primarily in "Law French." Today these reports are primarily of interest to legal historians. A series of privately published reports, called the *Nominative Reports* (since they were ordinarily referred to by the compiler's name), followed the *Year Books.*[4] These reports varied in accuracy, quality, and reliability, and the authority of a case often depended upon the reputation of its reporter. In 1785, the courts designated the first *authorized* case reports; yet unauthorized series were still published, usually in advance of the official reports.

Most of the *Nominative Reports* were later reprinted in the *English Reports: Full Reprint* (1900–1932). Containing 176 volumes and two volumes of case indexes, this series is the most comprehensive reprint of early English case law, covering about 100,000 cases from 1220 to 1865. Access to the set is also facilitated by a wall chart, which some libraries bind, listing abbreviations of the original *Nominative Reports.* Most law libraries contain this series even though they may not have the original reports. Cases should be cited to both the original report and to the *English Reports.* It should be noted that the *Revised Reports* (published in 149 volumes, 1891–1917) also contain selected reprints of cases decided from 1785 to 1866, including some cases not found in the *English Reports.*

Since 1865, the Incorporated Council of Law Reporting began publishing reports of decisions before the English superior courts in an effort to organize the reporting system in England. Although these reports, known as the *Law Reports,*[5] are semi-official publications, they are the preferred series for court reporting. Originally issued in eleven series, they have now been reduced to four, as a result of restructuring of the court system. These are: Appeal Cases (cases from the House of Lords and the Judicial Committee of the Privy Council); Queen's Bench; Chancery; and Family Divisions (formerly,

4. This period of transition is described in L.W. Abbott, *Law Reporting in England 1485–1585* (Athlone Press, 1973).

5. For a history of the *Law Reports,* see W.T.S. Daniel, *The History and Origin of the Law Reports* . . . (1884, reprinted Wildy & Sons, 1969).

1965 is now contained in s. 149 (1) (*a*) of the Employment Protection (Consolidation) Act 1978; see further the note " General " *infra*.

Commencement.—1st September 1973.

General.—This order excluded certain employments as a merchant seaman from the operation of s. 1 of the Redundancy Payments Act 1965 which had made general provision regarding the right to redundancy payment. The Act of 1965 has now been largely repealed by the Employment Protection (Consolidation) Act 1978, and it is replaced by provisions mainly contained in Part VI of that Act.

Certain provisions of the Employment Protection (Consolidation) Act 1978 are now excluded in relation to merchant seamen by s. 144 of the Act; and under s. 149 (1) there is a general power (corresponding to that under which the present order was made) enabling the Secretary of State by order to provide that any enactment in the Act is not to apply to any employment of a class specified in such an order.

The present order also revoked the Redundancy Payments Exclusion of Merchant Seamen Order 1968, S.I. 1968 No. 1201.

THE EMPLOYMENT PROTECTION ACT 1975 (COMMENCEMENT No. 1) ORDER 1975

S.I. 1975 No. 1938

NOTE.—**Authority.**—This order was made on the 25th November 1975 by the Secretary of State under s. 129 of the Employment Protection Act 1975, 45 Halsbury's Statutes (3rd Edn.) 397.

General.—It is to be noted that many of the provisions of the Employment Protection Act 1975 have now been repealed by the Employment Protection (Consolidation) Act 1978 and are replaced by the corresponding provisions therein enacted. The repeals mainly affect Part II (ss. 22–88) of the Act of 1975, which dealt with the rights of employees. The whole of that Part (except s. 40) is repealed by the Act of 1978.

Summary.—This order brought into operation the provisions of the Employment Protection Act 1975 specified below, as follows:—

(*a*) *on the 1st January* 1976:—ss. 1, 2, 3 (except as to the Central Arbitration Committee), 4–6, 89–91, 92 (except as to the said Committee), 93–97, 109, 112, 114, 115, 116 (part), 118, 121–123; s. 124 (1), (2) (*b*), (5) and (6); s. 125 (1), (2) and (3) as to certain amendments, transitional provisions and repeals; ss. 126 (1) (part), (2), (8) and (9), 127 and 129; Sch. 1, Parts I and III, so far as they relate to the Advisory, Conciliation and Arbitration Service and its Council; Schs. 7–10, 13 and 14; and certain provisions of Schs. 15, 16, 17 and 18;

(*b*) *on the 1st February* 1976:—ss. 3 (so far as not already in operation), 7–16, 92 (so far as not already in operation); s. 125 (1), (2) and (3) as to certain amendments, transitional provisions and repeals; ss. 126 (1) (part) and (4) and 128; Sch. 1 (so far as not already in operation); and certain provisions of Schs. 16, 17 and 18;

(*c*) *on the 1st March* 1976:—s. 116 (so far as not already in operation); s. 125 (3) (part); Sch. 15 (so far as not already in operation); and Sch. 18 (part).

Further orders.—At the issue date of this volume eight further " commencement orders " had been made under s. 129 of the Employment Protection Act 1975; all are listed at pp. 129, 130, *ante*. The provisions of the Act so brought into operation are specified in the following table.

TABLE

Commencement order	Provisions of the Act brought into operation
S.I. 1976 No. 144	On the 8th March 1976:—ss. 85 (1) (so far as it relates to the purposes of s. 102); 99 to 108; 110 (so far as it relates to ss. 99 to 107); 113 (in part); 117 (so far as it relates to any offence under s. 105); 119 (so far as it relates to ss. 99 and 100); 126 (1) (in part); Sch. 4 (so far as it relates to the purposes of s. 102); and Sch. 12 (so far as it relates to ss. 99 to 107). The order also brought into operation the following provisions of the Act on the 20th April 1976:—ss. 63 (1) and (2) (*d*); 64 (in part); 65 to 69; 110 (so far as it relates to ss. 63 to 69); 119 (so far as it relates to ss. 64 and 65); 125 (2) (so far as it relates to para. 8 of Sch. 17); Sch. 12 (so far as it relates to ss. 63 to 69); and Sch. 17, para. 8.

Illustration D

Halsbury's Statutory Instruments (Butterworth, 1978)
(Vol. 7, 4th Re-issue).

the Probate, Divorce, and Admiralty Division). (See Illustration E). *The Weekly Law Reports* (1953–date) is also published by the Incorporated Council of Law Reporting and provides a weekly updating of the *Law Reports.* Bound yearly in three volumes, the first volume contains cases which will not be republished later in the *Law Reports.*

Many private reports continued publication even after the *Law Reports* were issued. The most common of these include the *Law Journal Reports* (1822–1949); the *Times Law Reports* (1884–1952); and the *Law Times Reports* (1859–1947). *The Law Journal Reports* are difficult to use, because of the duplicate numbering and pagination of the bound volumes. For most of this set's history, two volumes were published yearly with the same volume number and duplicate pagination, one containing cases heard in the common law courts, the other containing equity cases. The *All England Law Reports* (Butterworth, 1936–date) is the only current, privately published *general* set of reports. This set incorporated both the *Law Journal Reports* and the *Law Times Reports.* The content is not always the same as the *Law Reports,* and the headnotes, which take the form of lengthy annotations, are often found to be more helpful. (See Illustration F). There is also the *All England Law Reports Reprint, 1558–1935,* which contains about 5,000 older cases.

Finally, several specialized subject reporters are published currently, containing decisions relevant to particular areas of law and often not reported elsewhere.

F. ENGLISH DIGESTS

The *English and Empire Digest,* 3d ed. (Butterworth, 1971–date), recently re-named *The Digest,* is the best and most comprehensive summary of English case law from the *Nominative Reports* to date. The *Digest* is intended to cover the whole of the reported case law of England, together with a considerable body of cases from the courts of Scotland, Ireland, Canada, Australia, New Zealand, and other Commonwealth countries. Each case summary is followed by "annotations," giving the subsequent cases in which judicial opinions have been rendered in the English courts.

From 1950–1970, the second edition of this set was published in blue banded volumes. These are now being replaced by the green banded volumes of the third edition, which began publication in 1971. Cases are arranged topically, following as far as possible the arrangement of titles in *Halsbury's Laws of England.* Cross references are given to *Halsbury's Laws,* and also to *Halsbury's Statutes.* Each topic is preceded by a detailed outline and an index is found at the end of each volume. (See Illustration G). Every digested case receives a paragraph number and cases on the same topic are arranged chronologically. Scottish, Irish and Commonwealth cases are included within the topic as well, but are printed in italics and receive

132

[1979]

[COURT OF APPEAL] A

NATIONAL VULCAN ENGINEERING INSURANCE GROUP LTD. *v.* WADE

1978 Jan. 26, 27

Lord Denning M.R., Ormrod and Geoffrey Lane L.JJ. B

Discrimination—Sex—Equal pay—Variation due to material difference—Woman clerk paid less than male clerk doing " like work "—Wages fixed according to employers' grading scheme based on ability and performance—Whether variation in pay due to material difference other than sex—Burden of proof—Equal Pay Act 1970 (*c.* 41), *s.* 1 (3) (*as amended by Sex Discrimination Act* 1975 (*c.* 65), *s.* 8 (1)) C

An insurance company graded its clerks in accordance with their experience, capacity, skill and application. All the clerks, male and female, in the company's policy department were employed in " like work," but were paid according to their grade. A woman clerk applied to the industrial tribunal for equality of pay on the ground that she was doing the same work as male clerks who, being in higher grades, D were paid more than she was. The industrial tribunal, awarding the applicant equality of pay, held that the company had failed to establish that the variation between the applicant's contract and that of a higher-graded male clerk was genuinely due to a material difference in their cases pursuant to section 1 (3) of the Equal Pay Act 1970.[1] The tribunal's decision was upheld by the Employment Appeal Tribunal.

On appeal by the company:— E

Held, allowing the appeal, that a grading scheme such as that operated by the company was not contrary to the Equal Pay Act 1970 so long as it was genuinely applied irrespective of sex (post, pp. 140D–E, 141B–C, 143E–G); that the burden of proof required of an employer by section 1 (3) of the Act was no higher than the civil standard of proof on the balance of probabilities (post, pp. 139H—140A, 141A–B, 142D–E); and that on the evidence the company had plainly discharged that F burden and established that the variation between the applicant's contract and that of her male colleague was genuinely due to a material difference in their skill and capacity (post, pp. 140B, 141H, 143C).

Decision of the Employment Appeal Tribunal [1977] I.C.R. 455; [1977] 3 All E.R. 634 reversed.

The following cases are referred to in the judgments: G

Clay Cross (Quarry Services) Ltd. v. *Fletcher* [1977] I.C.R. 868, E.A.T.

Electrolux Ltd. v. *Hutchinson* [1977] I.C.R. 252, E.A.T.

Hornal v. *Neuberger Products Ltd.* [1957] 1 Q.B. 247; [1956] 3 W.L.R. 1034; [1956] 3 All E.R. 970, C.A.

Navy, Army and Air Force Institutes v. *Varley* [1977] 1 W.L.R. 149; [1977] I.C.R. 11; [1977] 1 All E.R. 840, E.A.T.

Snoxell v. *Vauxhall Motors Ltd.* [1978] Q.B. 11; [1977] I.C.R. 700; [1977] H 3 W.L.R. 189; [1977] 3 All E.R. 770, E.A.T.

[1] Equal Pay Act 1970, s. 1 (3) as amended: see post, p. 138F–G.

Illustration E

A decision in the quasi-official *Law Reports* (1979).

QBD Marcel Beller Ltd v Hayden (Judge Edgar Fay QC) 121

the offences of dangerous driving and driving while under the influence of drink are
a sufficiently serious to qualify. In my judgment wherever the line is to be drawn these offences are on the exemptive side of it. As counsel pointed out, the Court of Appeal has held that in a breathalyser case where the alcohol count was 289 milligrammes per 100 millilitres a sentence of imprisonment was ordinarily proper: *R v Tupa*[1]. These are serious offences and cannot be excluded from the insured person's own criminal acts which afford the underwriters a defence to the claim. I must accordingly and on this ground give
b judgment for the defendant.

Judgment for the defendant.

Solicitors: *L A Reefe & Co* (for the plaintiffs); *Reynolds, Porter, Chamberlain & Co* (for the defendant).

c

Janet Harding Barrister.

National Vulcan Engineering Insurance Group Ltd v Wade

d COURT OF APPEAL, CIVIL DIVISION
LORD DENNING MR, ORMROD AND GEOFFREY LANE LJJ
26th, 27th JANUARY 1978

Employment – Equality of treatment between men and women – Variation between woman's and man's contract due to material difference other than sex – Burden of proof – Grading according to
e *skill and capacity – Woman in like work with man in same employment paid less than man – Burden of proof on employer civil burden that on balance of probabilities variation due to difference other than sex – Employer operating grading scheme according to personal assessment and performance of employee – Employer proving that scheme applied genuinely and sex irrelevant – Employer also proving variation in pay due to different grading of woman and man according to skill and capacity – Whether employer discharging burden of proof – Equal Pay Act 1970, s 1(3).*

f

The employers, an insurance company, paid their employees in accordance with a grading system whereby employees were placed in a grade and given a 'performance rating' within that grade on the basis of the employers' personal assessment of them and their performance. The sex of an employee was not a factor in grading and men and women in the same grade received, according to their performance ratings within the grade, equal
g pay. The applicant, a woman employee, worked in a department with 17 other employees, some of whom were men. All the employees in the department did the same work. One of the men in the department, because of the employers' assessment of his skill and ability, was placed in a higher grade than the applicant and therefore received more pay than she did. The applicant applied to an industrial tribunal under s 1(2)(*a*)[a] of the Equal Pay Act 1970 for equal pay with the man on the ground that they were both employed on like
h work. The employers claimed that the variation between their pay was genuinely attributable to a material difference between them other than sex, within s 1(3)[b] of the 1970 Act, since it was due to different grading according to the difference in their skill and capacity. The tribunal and, on appeal, the appeal tribunal[c] rejected the employers' claim on the ground that merely by establishing that the difference in pay was attributable to a grading scheme they had not discharged the burden on them of proving that s 1(3)
j applied. The employers appealed.

1 [1974] RTR 153
a Section 1(2), so far as material, is set at p 124 *e f* post
b Section 1(3) is set out at p 124 *j* post
c [1977] 3 All ER 634

Illustration F

All England Law Reports (Butterworth, 1978).

Part I.—Definitions

SECT. 1. **" TRADE "**

LAW. *See* HALSBURY'S LAWS (3rd Edn.), Vol. 38, pp. 8 *et seq.*

CROSS-REFERENCES. *See* Nos. 21 *et seq.*, *post* (who are traders); INCOME TAX, Vol. 28 (Repl.), Nos. 78 *et seq.* (for purposes of income tax).

1. Operations of a commercial character.]—We may reasonably say that it [the word " trade "] was intended to embrace a great variety of different operations, though all of a commercial character, something therefore like a warehouse, like a shop, like a counting house (KELLY, C.B.).

It was never the intention of the legislature so to limit the meaning of the word " trade " [to the business of buying & selling] (KELLY, C.B.).

No doubt the word " trade " was originally there [in the Bkpcy. Acts] intended as applying only to persons who either bought or sold, or whose business was immediately cognate to the buying or selling of goods, but even then we find from time to time the words used in a much wider sense (POLLOCK, B.).—CHARTERED MERCANTILE BANK OF INDIA, LONDON & CHINA *v.* WILSON (1877), 3 Ex. D. 108; 47 L. J. Q. B. 153; 38 L. T. 254; 1 Tax Cas. 179.

2. Whether limited to buying & selling.]—DOE d. WETHERELL *v.* BIRD, No. 13, *post.*

3. ——.]—HARRIS *v.* AMERY, No. 24, *post.*

4. ——.]—CHARTERED MERCANTILE BANK OF INDIA, LONDON & CHINA *v.* WILSON, No. 1, *ante.*

5. ——.]—[A tradesman denotes] " a person carrying on a trade, buying & selling, & a barber does not come within that description (CHANNELL, J.).—PALMER *v.* SNOW, [1900] 1 Q. B. 725; 69 L. J. Q. B. 356; 82 L. T. 199; 64 J. P. 342; 48 W. R. 351; 16 T. L. R. 168; 44 Sol. Jo. 211; 19 Cox, C. C. 475, D. C.

Annotation:—**Apld.** Gregory *v.* Fearn, [1953] 2 All E. R. 559.

6. ——.]—A trading business is one which involves the purchase & the sale of goods (LUSH, J.).—HIGGINS *v.* BEAUCHAMP, [1914] 3 K. B. 1192; [1914–15] All E. R. Rep. 937; 84 L. J. K. B. 631; 111 L. T. 1103; 30 T. L. R. 687, D. C.

7. —— **With view to profit.**]—The definition of the mere word " trade " does not necessarily mean something by which a profit is made (LORD COLERIDGE, C.J.). — *Re* DUTY ON ESTATE OF INCORPORATED COUNCIL OF LAW REPORTING FOR ENGLAND & WALES (1888), 22 Q. B. D. 279; 58 L. J. Q. B. 90; 60 L. T. 505; *sub nom.* I. R. COMRS. *v.* INCORPORATED COUNCIL OF LAW REPORTING, 3 Tax Cas. 105, D. C.

Annotations:—**Consd.** Griffiths *v.* J. P. Harrison, Ltd., [1962] 1 All E. R. 909. **Refd.** British Institute of Preventive Medicine *v.* Styles (1895), 11 T. L. R. 432; Brighton College *v.* Marriott (No. 1), [1926] A. C. 192; Skinner *v.* Breach, [1927] 2 K. B. 220.

8. —— ——.]—There can be no definition of the words " exercising a trade." It is only another mode of expressing " carrying on a business "; but it certainly carries with it the meaning that the business or trade must be habitually or systematically exercised, & that it cannot apply to isolated transactions (LORD MORRIS).

How does a wine merchant exercise his trade? I take it, by making or buying wine & selling it again, with a view to profit (LORD HERSCHELL).—GRAINGER & SON *v.* GOUGH, [1896] A. C. 325; 65 L. J. Q. B. 410; 74 L. T. 435; 60 J. P. 692; 44 W. R. 561; 12 T. L. R. 364; 3 Tax Cas. 462, H. L.

Annotations:—**Consd.** Crookston *v.* Furtado (1910), 5 Tax Cas. 602; Smith *v.* Greenwood, [1921] 3 K. B. 583. **Refd.** La Bourgogne (1898), 68 L. J. P. 9; Taxation Comrs. *v.* Kirk, [1900] A. C. 588; Badische Anilin und Soda Fabrik *v.* Thompson (1902), 88 L. T. 492, n.; Scott *v.* Solomon, [1905] 1 K. B. 577; Kirkwood *v.* Gadd, [1910] A. C. 422;

Illustration G

The Digest, formerly the *English and Empire Digest,* 2d ed., Vol. 45 (Butterworth, 1965).

a separate sequence of paragraph numbers. References to the paragraph numbers of these cases are identified by an asterisk in the index and table of cases of the "green-band" reissue edition. The set is updated by Annual Cumulative Supplements which eventually become Continuation Volumes. Volumes 52–54 of the blue banded second edition are the *Consolidated Table of Cases* and include cases to the end of 1966. The *Annual Cumulative Supplement* includes a table of cases reported after 1966.

Access to the set is provided by volumes 55–56 of the second edition in the *Consolidated Index.* However, when using the *Consolidated Index,* it must be remembered that the volume listed may have been replaced after its inclusion in the index. Therefore, after the correct volume number is found, the "Reference Adaptor" table in the third edition volume must be consulted to convert the *case number* in the "blue band" edition to the *case number* in the "green band" edition. Note that a source of difficulty in using the set is the change in references from page numbers in the "blue band" edition, to references to the case numbers in the "green band" edition, including the *Cumulative Supplement* and *Continuation Volume E.* The *Consolidated Index* includes references to both.

From 1865–1949 the *Law Reports Digest* was published by the Incorporated Council of Law Reporting. The original coverage was extended in 1911 to include other contemporaneous English law reports. From 1951, the Digest was replaced by a *Consolidated Index.* In addition to an index of subject matter, this contains a table of cases, and case and statute citators. There are annual and ten-year cumulations. Cases for the current year are included in the "pink" index, issued in pamphlet form several times during the year. Many law libraries receive this publication rather than *The Digest* (formerly the *English and Empire Digest*), as it is part of their subscription to the *Law Reports.*

From 1947, the *Current Law* service (Sweet & Maxwell) also digests all English law, from cases, statutes, and statutory instruments, to legal treatises and periodical articles. There is a *Current Law Consolidation,* 1947–1951, supplemented by *Year Books* which are supplemented in turn by monthly digests for the current year. Summaries of cases are arranged alphabetically by topic and legal issue. In addition to the digest, the *Current Law* service includes case and statute citators (described below in Section H) and *Current Law Statutes Annotated.*

G. ENGLISH LEGAL ENCYCLOPEDIAS

The best known and most comprehensive legal encyclopedia in England today is *Halsbury's Laws of England,* 4th ed. (Butterworth, 1973–date). The fourth edition began publication in 1973, and until it is completed, the third edition must also be consulted. The encyclopedia covers both statutory and case law and is arranged alphabetically by broad legal headings which are subdivided into more specific concepts and issues. Each concept has a paragraph number making the material easier to access. Every volume has its own table of cases, statutes and statutory instruments, and subject index. There is also a two volume general subject index for the third edition and a paper bound index to volumes one to twenty in the fourth edition. The set is updated by annual *Cumulative Supplements* and the *Current Service.* This is a loose-leaf volume which includes the "Monthly Review", summarizing current developments, and the "Noter-up", citing recent changes. The "Index Key" found in the *Cumulative Supplement* to the fourth edition shows where material from replaced volumes can be located in the new edition. The material in the "Monthly Review" has been republished in the form of "Annual Abridgments" since 1974.

There are also many loose-leaf subject encyclopedias published in England. These generally give a brief explanation of the law while including pertinent statutes, statutory instruments, etc. An example of these can be found in Sweet & Maxwell's *Encyclopedia of Capital Taxation,* the *Encyclopedia of Labor Relations Law* or the *Encyclopedia of Planning Law and Practice.*

H. ENGLISH CITATORS

The *Chronological Table of Statutes* (HMSO) acts as a statute citator for English law. Statutes from 1235 are listed with reference to all amendments or repeals. The *Index to Statutes in Force* (HMSO) provides a subject listing of all public statutes in force at the date of publication. A difficulty with using these official publications is that they are usually published a few years out of date, however. Statute citators can also be found in *Halsbury's Statutes of England* and the *All England Law Reports.*

The easiest way to locate the history of a statute or case, however, is to consult the *Current Law Service's* case or statute citator. The *Current Law Case Citator,* 1947 to 1976, gives an alphabetical listing of cases with references to subsequent case citations (See Illustration H, which highlights the *Vulcan Case* shown in Illustrations E and F, above). The *Current Law Statute Citator,* 1947 to 1971, lists cases decided after 1947 which may have cited even earlier statutes (statutes from 1235 are included). (See Illustration I, which highlights the *Equal Pay Act,* shown in Illustrations A and B, above). Updating is provided monthly in *Current Law,* and annually by the statute and case citator sections of the *Current Law Citator,* which also includes Statutory Instruments affected, 1947–81. Many libraries receive the Scottish version of this publication, *Scottish Current Law Service,* which contains citations to *both* English and Scottish law.

The *English and Empire Digest* (now, *The Digest*) can also be used as a case citator. Each case is assigned a case number which can later be updated by consulting the latest cumulative supplement. The "annotation" section found after each digest lists subsequent references to

NAT CASE CITATOR 1977–81

National Union of Gold, Silver and Allied Trades *v.* Albury Bros. [1979] I.C.R. 84; (1978) 122 S.J. 662; [1978] I.R.L.R. 504, C.A.; affirming [1978] I.C.R. 62; (1977) 12 I.T.R. 413; [1977] 173, E.A.T. .... *Digested*, 79/**2713**
Referred to, 78/1131

National Union of Mineworkers (Kent Area) *v.* Gormley, *The Times*, October 20, 1977, C.A. .... *Digested*, 77/**3078**
National Union of Mineworkers (Yorkshire Area) *v.* Gormley, *The Times*, December 22, 1977 .... *Digested*, 77/**3086**
National Union of Tailors & Garment Workers *v.* Ingram (Charles) & Co. [1977] I.C.R. 530; [1978] 1 All E.R. 1271; (1977) 12 I.T.R. 285; [1977] I.R.L.R. 147, E.A.T. .... *Digested*, 77/**3086**: *Approved*, 79/2713
National Union of Teachers *v.* Avon County Council [1978] I.C.R. 626; (1977) 76 L.G.R. 403; [1978] I.R.L.R. 55, E.A.T. .... *Digested*, 78/**994**
National Vulcan Engineering Insurance Group *v.* Wade [1979] Q.B. 132; [1978] I.C.R. 800; [1978] 3 W.L.R. 214; (1978) 122 S.J. 470; [1978] 3 All E.R. 121; [1978] I.R.L.R. 225; (1978) 13 I.T.R. 212, C.A.; reversing [1977] I.C.R. 455; [1977] 121 S.J. 221; [1977] 3 All E.R. 634; (1977) 12 I.T.R. 220; [1977] I.R.L.R. 109, E.A.T. .... *Digested*, 78/**939**: *Followed*, 81/848
National Water Council *v.* Customs and Excise Commissioners (1978) 122 S.J. 627; [1979] S.T.C. 157; [1978] T.R. 307 .... *Digested*, 78/**3031**
National Westminster Bank *v.* BSC Footwear (1981) 42 P. & C.R. 90; (1980) 257 E.G. 277, C.A. .... *Digested*, 81/**1548**: *Followed*, 81/1570
—— *v.* Gordon. *See* Gordon's Will Trusts, *Re*.
—— *v.* Halesowen Presswork and Assemblies [1972] .... *Applied*, 79/160
—— *v.* Stockman [1981] 1 W.L.R. 67; (1980) 124 S.J. 810; [1981] 1 All E.R. 800; *sub nom.* National Westminster Bank *v.* Stockton, *The Times*, August 19, 1980 .... *Digested*, 81/**2457**
—— *v.* Stockton. *See* National Westminster Bank *v.* Stockman.
National Westminster Bank Corp. *v.* Greenless Wennards .... *Followed*, 81/1570
Nationwide Building Society *v.* Bateman [1978] 1 W.L.R. 394; (1977) 122 S.J. 179; [1978] 1 All E.R. 999 .... *Digested*, 78/**1416**
Native Guano Co. *v.* Sewage Manure Co. (1889) 8 R.P.C. 125 .... *Distinguished*, 79/2690
Nautamix B.V. *v.* Jenkins of Retford [1977] F.S.R. 379, C.A. .... *Digested*, 75/**2486**
Naviera de Canarias S.A. *v.* Nacional Hispanica Aseguradora S.A.; Playa de la Nieves, The [1978] A.C. 853; [1977] 2 W.L.R. 442; (1977) 121 S.J. 186; [1977] 1 All E.R. 625; [1977] 1 Lloyd's Rep. 457, H.L.; reversing [1976] 3 W.L.R. 45; [1976] 3 All E.R. 167, C.A. .... *Digested*, 77/**2762**
Navone *v.* Shimco (U.K.). *See* Montecchi *v.* Shimco (U.K.); Navone *v.* Same.
Navy, Army & Air Force Institutes *v.* Varley [1977] I.C.R. 11; [1977] 1 W.L.R. 149; (1976) S.J. 84; [1977] 1 All E.R. 840; [1976] I.R.L.R. 408; (1976) 11 I.T.R. 328, E.A.T. .... *Digested*, 77/**973**
Nawala, The. *See* N.W.L. *v.* Woods; N.W.L. *v.* Nelson.
Naz *v.* Kaleem, July 8, 1980, Bow County Ct. .... *Digested*, 80/**409**
Nea Agrex S.A. *v.* Baltic Shipping Co. [1976] ......*Applied*, 78/101: *Considered*, 77/119:
Referred to, 77/117
Nea Karteria Maritime Co. *v.* Atlantic and Great Lakes Steamship Corp. and Cape Breton Development Corp. (No. 1) [1981] Com.L.R. 132 .... *Digested*, 81/**2489**
—— *v.* —— (No. 2) [1981] Com.L.R. 138 .... *Digested*, 81/**1191**
Nea Tyhi Maritime Co. of Piraeus *v.* Compagnie Graniere S.A. of Zurich. *See* Finix, The.
Neal *v.* Gribble (1978) 68 Cr.App.R. 9; [1978] R.T.R. 409; [1978] Crim.L.R. 500, D.C. .... *Digested*, 78/**638**
Neapolis II, The. *See* Alberta Shipping *v.* Briton Ferry Stevedoring Co.; Neapolis II, The.
Neath Rural District Council *v.* Williams (1951) .... *Considered*, 78/2201:
Not followed, 78/2201
Needham (Bert) Automotive Co. Pty. *v.* Commissioner of Taxation of the Commonwealth of Australia (1975) 26 F.L.R. 108, Sup.Ct. of New South Wales .... *Digested*, 77/**1594**
Negocios del Mar S.A. *v.* Doric Shipping Corp. S.A.; Assios, The [1979] 1 Lloyd's Rep. 331, C.A. .... *Digested*, 79/**2144**
Neilson *v.* Laugharne [1981] 1 Q.B. 736; [1981] 2 W.L.R. 537; (1980) 125 S.J. 202; [1981] 1 All E.R. 829, C.A. .... *Digested*, 81/**2142**
Nelmes *v.* Rhys Howells Transport [1977] R.T.R. 266; [1977] Crim. L.R. 227, D.C. .... *Digested*, 77/**2629**

184

Illustration H

Current Law Case Citator (Sweet & Maxwell, 1980).

STATUTE CITATOR 1972–81 **1970**

CAP.

1970—cont.

41. *Equal Pay Act 1970—cont.*
W.L.R. 26; *Navy, Army and Air Force Institutes* v. *Varley* [1977] I.C.R. 11; [1977] 1 W.L.R. 149; *Green* v. *Broxtowe District Council* [1977] 1 All E.R. 694; *Snoxell and Davies* v. *Vauxhall Motors; Charles Early & Marriott (Witney)* v. *Smith and Ball* [1977] I.R.L.R. 121; *Murray* v. *Lothian Regional Council*, December 8, 1976, E.A.T.; *Electrolux* v. *Hutchison* [1977] I.C.R. 252, E.A.T.; *Waddington* v. *Leicester Council for Voluntary Service* [1977] I.C.R. 266; [1977] 1 W.L.R. 544, E.A.T.; *Eaton* v. *Nuttall* [1977] I.C.R. 272, E.A.T.; *Ainsworth* v. *Glass Tubes and Components* [1977] I.C.R. 347, E.A.T.; *Redland Roof Tiles* v. *Harper* [1977] I.C.R. 349, E.A.T.; *Kerr* v. *Lister* [1977] I.R.L.R. 259, E.A.T.; *Edmonds* v. *Computer Services (South-West)* [1977] I.R.L.R. 359, E.A.T.; *A. R. W. Transformers* v. *Cupples* (1977) 12 I.T.R. 355, E.A.T.; *United Biscuits* v. *Young* [1978] I.R.L.R. 15, E.A.T.; *MacCarthys* v. *Smith* [1978] I.R.L.R. 10, E.A.T.; *England* v. *Bromley London Borough Council* [1978] I.C.R. 1, E.A.T.; *British Leyland* v. *Powell* [1978] I.R.L.R. 57, E.A.T.; *National Vulcan Engineering Insurance Group* v. *Wade* [1978] 3 W.L.R. 214, C.A.; *Outlook Supplies* v. *Parry* [1978] I.C.R. 388, E.A.T.; *Hebbes* v. *Rank Precision Industries (Trading as Rank Hilger)* [1978] I.C.R. 489, E.A.T.; *Sun Alliance and London Insurance* v. *Dudman* [1978] I.C.R. 551, E.A.T.; *De Brito* v. *Standard Chartered Bank* [1978] I.C.R. 650, E.A.T.; *National Coal Board* v. *Sherwin* [1978] I.C.R. 700, E.A.T.; *O'Brien* v. *Sim-Chem* [1979] I.C.R. 13, E.A.T.; *Shields* v. *E. Coomes (Holdings)* [1978] 1 W.L.R. 1408, C.A.; *Clay Cross (Quarry Services)* v. *Fletcher* [1979] 1 All E.R. 474, C.A.; *Handley* v. *H. Mono* [1979] I.C.R. 147, E.A.T.; *Maidment* v. *Cooper & Co. (Birmingham)* [1978] I.C.R. 1094, E.A.T.; *Methven* v. *Cow Industrial Polymers* [1979] I.C.R. 613, E.A.T.; *Jankins* v. *Kingsgate (Clothing Productions), The Times*, November 15, 1979, E.A.T.; *Durrant* v. *North Yorkshire Area Authority and Secretary of State for Social Services* [1979] I.R.L.R. 401, E.A.T.; *Capper Pass* v. *Alcan* [1980] I.C.R. 194, E.A.T.; *O'Brien* v. *Sim-Chem* [1980] 1 W.L.R. 1011, H.L.; *Methven* v. *Cow Industrial Polymers* [1980] I.C.R. 463, C.A.; *Noble* v. *David Gold & Son (Holdings)* [1980] I.C.R. 543, C.A.; *Ministry of Defence* v. *Farthing* [1980] I.C.R. 705, C.A.;

CAP.

1970—cont.

41. *Equal Pay Act 1970—cont.*
Avon and Somerset Police Authority v. *Emery* [1981] I.C.R. 229, E.A.T.; *Albion Shipping Agency* v. *Arnold, The Times*, October 24, 1981, E.A.T.; *Jenkins* v. *Kingsgate (Clothing Productions)* [1981] I.C.R. 715, E.A.T.
ss. 1, 7, repealed in pt.: 1981,c.55,sch.5.
ss. 1, 6, amended: **1975,c.65,s.8,sch.1.**
s. 2, repealed: **1978,c.44,sch.17.**
s. 3, see *R.* v. *Central Arbitration Committee, ex p. Hy-Mac* [1979] I.R.L.R. 461, D.C.
ss. 3, 4, 5, 7, 10, amended: **1975,c.71, sch.16.**
s. 4, amended: 1979,c.12,sch.6; repealed in pt.: 1975,c.71,sch.18.
s. 6, see *Worringham* v. *Lloyds Bank* [1979] I.R.L.R. 440, C.A.
s. 8, repealed: 1975,c.65,sch.1.
ss. 9, 10, repealed in pt.: *ibid.*

42. Local Authority Social Services Act 1970.
ss. 2, 3, amended: 1973,c.32,schs.4,5.
s. 3, substituted: 1980,c.65,s.183.
s. 3A, added: *ibid.*
s. 6, repealed in pt.: *ibid.*,sch.34.
ss. 8, 10, repealed: **1972,c.70,sch.30; ss. 1, 5–7, sch. 2, amended: *ibid.*, s. 195, schs. 29, 30.**
s. 12, order 80/328.
ss. 13, 15, repealed in pt.: **1980,c.65, sch.34.**
s. 15, amended: **1973,c.36,sch.6.**
sch. 1, amended: 1973,c.18,sch.3; c.32, schs.4,5; 1975,c.37,sch.1; c.72,schs.3, 4; 1976,c.36,sch.3; c.71,sch.7; 1977,c. 48,s.20; c.49,sch.15; 1978,c.22,sch.2; 1980,c.5,sch.5; c.6,sch.2; c.7,sch.1; c. 30;sch.4; repealed in pt.: 1975,c.72, schs.3,4; 1976,c.36,sch.4; c.71,sch.8; 1977,c.49,sch.16; 1978,c.22,schs.2,3; S.L.R. 1978; 1980,c.5,sch.6; c.6,schs. 2, 3.
sch. 2, repealed in pt.: 1980,c.5,sch.6.

43. Trees Act 1970.
s. 1, repealed: 1972,c.52,sch.23.

44. Chronically Sick and Disabled Persons Act 1970.
s. 1, order 72/1420.
ss. 2, 21, amended: 1972,c.70,sch.30.
s. 3, amended: 1980,c.51,sch.25; repealed in pt.: *ibid.*,sch.26.
s. 4, amended: 1976,c.49,s.1.
ss. 4–6, amended: 1981,c.28,s.37; c.43, s.6.
ss. 5, 21, amended: 1973,c.65,s.141,sch. 14.
s. 6, amended: 1976,c.57,s.20; repealed in pt.: *ibid.*,sch.2.
s. 7, substituted: 1981,c.43,s.5.
s. 8, amended: 1976,c.49,s.2.
s. 8A, amended: 1981,c.23,s.37;c.43,s.6.
s. 8B, added: *ibid.*,s.7.

643

Illustration I

Current Law Statute Citator (Sweet & Maxwell, 1980).

the original case and indicates whether the case has been approved, followed, distinguished, overruled, etc.

I. ENGLISH PERIODICAL INDEXES

Most English periodicals are indexed in the *Index to Legal Periodicals* or the *Legal Resources Index.* Journals from the United Kingdom are also included in the *Index to Commonwealth Legal Periodicals.* The *Current Law Year Book* includes an index to articles at the back of each volume, which can be supplemented by the list of articles appearing in the monthly issues under the appropriate topic.

J. ENGLISH DICTIONARIES, ETC.

Since common law jurisdictions have relatively similar terminology, American legal dictionaries list most English words and phrases. There is sufficient divergence in many areas, however, to necessitate checking for a specific definition in an English law dictionary. The most comprehensive, *Jowitt's Dictionary of English Law,* 2d ed. (Sweet & Maxwell, 1977), is updated with paper supplements. Others include *Mozley & Whiteley's Law Dictionary,* 9th ed. (Butterworth Canada, 1977) and *Osborn's Concise Law Dictionary,* 6th ed. (Sweet & Maxwell, 1976).

There are two sets which deal specifically with *judicial* definitions in England. The first is *Stroud's Judicial Dictionary of Words and Phrases,* 4th ed. (Sweet & Maxwell, 1971–1974). Besides giving references to cases and statutes, this five volume set includes quotations from legal treatises. Paperbound supplements provide the updating. The second series, *Words and Phrases Legally Defined,* 2d ed. (Butterworths, 1969–1970), includes predominantly judicial interpretations, but also gives selections from textbooks and statutes. Cumulative supplement pamphlets are published annually. In addition, references to *Halsbury's Law of England* makes this a companion volume to that set. Both collections of words and phrases contain references to sources from other Commonwealth jurisdictions.

K. ENGLISH LEGAL BIBLIOGRAPHIES

A Legal Bibliography of the British Commonwealth of Nations, 2d ed. (Sweet & Maxwell, 1955–64) is a seven-volume set of which the first two volumes contain listings of publications on English law: Volume One covers English law to 1800, and Volume Two from 1801 to 1954. Treatises are arranged by author, and each volume has a subject index.

A Bibliographical Guide to the Law of the United Kingdom, the Channel Islands and the Isle of Man, edited by A.G. Chloros, 2d ed. (University of London, Institute of Advanced Legal Studies, 1973) was prepared to introduce English law to foreign attorneys, and can be a valuable place to begin legal research. Each chapter covers a broad subject area and the bibliography is preceded by a brief introduction to the law.

The most recent bibliography to date is Donald Raistrick and John Rees's *Lawyers' Law Books: A Practical Index to Legal Literature* (Professional Books, 1977). This bibliography, covers a wide range of legal materials on the United Kingdom, European Community, Commonwealth and some Common Law countries. There is a list of subject headings and an author/title index. The bibliography is arranged by subject and includes cross references to basic English legal materials (e.g., *Halsbury's Law of England*).

Where to Look for Your Law, by C.W. Ringrose, 14th ed. (Sweet & Maxwell, 1962) is a selected bibliography of law books which are arranged by subject and author. This volume also includes a list of Command Papers, a table of abbreviations and a table of the regnal years of English sovereigns.

How to Use a Law Library, by J. Dane and P.A. Thomas (Sweet & Maxwell, 1979) is the standard research guide for English law students.

L. THE CANADIAN CONSTITUTIONAL BACKGROUND

On April 17, 1982, the *Constitution Act, 1982* was enacted,[6] providing Canada with a written Constitution, containing an amending formula which eliminated the role of the Parliament of the United Kingdom. Prior to 1982, the Canadian constitutional framework was derived from both written and unwritten sources, the main written element being a British statute entitled the *British North America Act, 1867*, and subsequent amendments. This statute provided for the establishment of both federal and provincial executives and legislative bodies. It included provisions relating to courts and the appointment of judges; and, primarily in sections 91 and 92, set out the distribution of legislative powers. By an act of the United Kingdom Parliament entitled the *Canada Act, 1982*,[7] the BNA Act and amend-

6. 1982, c. 11 (U.K.); proclaimed in force in Canada (1982) *Canada Gazette* (Part 1) 2927, also published as Extra No. 20, April 17, 1982. Section 15, the equality rights provision, does not take effect for three years, by s. 32 (2), in order that appropriate structural and legislative changes can be made.

7. For an outline of the events leading up to referral of the proposed constitutional amendments to the Supreme Court of Canada and an analysis of that decision, see Comment, "Reference re Amendment of the Constitution of Canada (1981)," (1982) 50 *C.B.R.* 307–334. For hearings concerning the draft of the Charter which was adopted by the House of Commons on April 23, 1981, and by the Senate on April 24, 1981, and referred to the Supreme Court, see "Minutes of Proceedings of the Special Joint Committee of the Senate and House of Commons on the Constitution of Canada," Nos. 1–57, November 6, 1980 to February 13, 1981. For the text of the final version adopted by the House on December 2, 1981, see Canada, Parliament, House of Commons, *Debates* 32 Parl., 1st sess. (1981) 13632–13663. See also Gt. Britain, House of Commons, Foreign Affairs Committee, *British North America Acts:* the *Role of Parliament. First Report*, Session 1980–81, January 30th, 1981; *Second Report*, April 15, 1981; *Third Report*, January 18, 1982, for treatment of the role of the United Kingdom Parliament.

ments, renamed the Constitution Acts, 1867–1982, the legislation embodying the terms of union with the other provinces and territories, and the *Statute of Westminster, 1931,* were incorporated into the *Constitution Act, 1982.* In addition, the power of the United Kingdom Parliament to legislate for Canada was relinquished (the "patriation" of the constitution), and an amending formula defining the role of the federal and provincial governments in future amendments was added. For the first time, an entrenched Charter of Rights protecting various civil liberties and denying the federal Parliament or the legislatures the power to limit them, was added. An important change was made to the distribution of legislative powers in the *Constitution Act, 1867,* by adding s. 92A, expanding provincial power to tax and control natural resources. Finally, provisions were included which recognized aboriginal rights and promoted equalization of regional disparities.

The effect of the new Constitution, and in particular the *Canadian Charter of Rights and Freedoms* on the legal system, is potentially very great. Until now, the British concept of Parliamentary sovereignty was modified in Canada only to the extent that legislative power was divided between the federal and provincial legislative bodies, and the courts assumed the power to declare a statute invalid if found to be outside the powers of the enacting body. The Charter embodies the principle of limiting legislative powers, with the role of the courts becoming more like those of the U.S. in balancing fundamental rights against the powers of the state, and in having the power to declare acts of an elected legislature invalid.[8]

Since few precedents exist, and since terminology in certain Charter provisions is similar to that of the *Bill of Rights* of the United States Constitution, considerable reliance upon U.S. precedents is anticipated. Reference is also expected to be made to the European Convention on Human Rights and the U.N. International Covenant on Civil and Political Rights. Also still of interest are decisions interpreting the *Canadian Bill of Rights,*[9] which, in accordance with s. 26, co-exists with the Charter. Therefore certain rights, such as the right not to be deprived of property except by due process of law are preserved in the *Bill of Rights,* although they are not duplicated in the Charter.

In addition to numerous texts and articles on the Charter, the following have been published:

The Constitution Act, 1982 (Ottawa, Supply and Services, 1982). Official text of the Constitution as proclaimed in force in Canada.

The Canadian Constitution, 1981 (Ottawa, Supply and Services, c. 1981). Text of the Resolution respecting the Constitution of Canada adopted by the House of Commons on December 2, 1981, and by the Senate on December 8, 1981.

8. See s. 1 (the limitations clause); s. 24 (the enforcement clause); and s. 32 (the application clause).

9. R.S.C. 1970, App. III.

Canada Act 1982 Annotated, by P.W. Hogg (Carswell, 1982). Provides a legislative history and explanation of the 1982 Constitutional Amendments, with analysis of each provision and its effect on pre-existing law.

The Charter of Rights and Freedoms: A Guide for Canadians (Ottawa, Supply and Services, c. 1982). Text of the Charter, with explanatory notes.

Constitutions of Canada: Federal & Provincial, by C. Wiktor & G. Tanguay (Oceana Publications, 1978 to date). Potentially useful, this compilation is intended to contain the texts of all Canadian constitutions, federal and provincial. At present, however, it includes only the text of the Constitutional Resolution of December 1981.

The Canadian Charter of Rights Annotated, edited by John B. Laskin et al. (Canada Law Book, 1982–date). A looseleaf citator service which includes a section by section analysis of the Charter with judicial interpretations, and the text of the *Canadian Bill of Rights* and the U.S. *Bill of Rights.* In addition to summarizing significant Canadian decisions involving Charter issues, the service includes relevant U.S. Supreme Court decisions.

Canadian Rights Reporter (Toronto, Butterworths, 1982–date). This law report series contains the text of decisions from all courts decided under the new Charter. Annotations are provided with some decisions, and relevant articles and notes of American decisions. Also includes Native Peoples' legislation, with Canadian and U.K. judgments.

Another source of Charter decisions is the *Reasons for Judgment of Unreported Cases*, distributed weekly by the Canadian Law Information Council, Ottawa. QL Systems Limited, a computerized research service, is developing a data base for the federal Justice Department on the Charter of Rights and Freedoms, which will be available as well to subscribers to the QL data bases.

Canadian Human Rights Reporter (1980–date), contains the text of human rights legislation and regulations for all jurisdictions, including the Charter of Rights, and relevant court and administrative decisions of the tribunals administering the legislation.

Charter of Rights Decisions (Western Legal Publications, 1982–date). Provides digests of decisions relating to the Charter of Rights and the Canadian Bill of Rights; issued bi-weekly.

M. CANADIAN STATUTES

To locate a current Canadian statute it is necessary to first check the latest edition of the federal or relevant provincial *Revised Statutes.* These contain the statutes in force at the date of the revision, arranged alphabetically by title. Hence, there is no codification of Canadian law as found in the *U.S. Code.* Every 10 to 15 years, a new revision is published in most Canadian jurisdictions, incorporating amendments into the parent acts, which are rewritten as necessary (although the substance is not changed), and consolidates them with any new acts passed. The revision then repeals and replaces the former *Revised Statutes* and subsequent legislation, to the extent shown in an accompanying schedule. Not all acts omitted are automatically repealed by the revision, and certain acts can be identified by reference to a history and disposal table as unconsolidated and unrepealed. Essentially a table of derivations and destinations, it is useful for tracing a reference to earlier legislation, since it lists statutes which have been examined for inclusion in the revision, and where they may be located in it. Some jurisdictions include a table of unconsolidated statutes with the *Revised Statutes* as well.

The present revision, the *Revised Statutes of Canada 1970,* is comprised of 11 volumes; 7 volumes in the main set, 2 supplements, an appendix, and an index. Volumes 1–7 consolidate statutes to December 31, 1969 and provide the first bilingual arrangement of statutes in Canada. The First Supplement contains amendments to acts passed during the 2d session of the 28th Parliament (1969–70), while the Second Supplement includes amendments to the R.S.C. 1970 or the First Supplement enacted during the 3d session of the 28th Parliament (1970–71–72). The Second Supplement contains the following tables, which supersede those found in the First Supplement and in the Appendix: Schedule A, showing acts repealed and replaced by R.S.C. 1970, and the extent of the repeal; a table showing this history and disposal of acts; a Table of Public Statutes showing the location of acts in the R.S.C. 1970 and its Supplements (updated by a table found in the *Canada Gazette,* Part III), and a table of unconsolidated acts. The Appendix includes the text of certain constitutional documents then in effect, and the *Canadian Bill of Rights.*

More recent acts are found in bound sessional volumes, also known as *Annuals.* Therefore, except for those unconsolidated statutes, the body of statute law in force is found in the most recent revision together with annual statute volumes to date. For the current year, the *Canada Gazette,* Part III publishes the text of federal acts, after Royal Assent, in paperbound supplements.

To update an act, the "Table of Public Statutes" included in the *Canada Gazette,* Part III, should be consulted. (See Illustration J). This table lists all acts and amendments subsequent to the latest revision. It acts, in essence, as a citator. For more information on updating both federal and provincial statutes, consult *How to Update a Statute for All Canadian Jurisdictions* (G. Dykstra, ed. 1980). In addition to the official sources, *Canadian Current Law* contains a section entitled "Statutes Amended, Repealed or Proclaimed in Force" which lists statutes of the Federal Parliament and of the provincial and territorial legislatures. Once Royal Assent is received, all federal and selected provincial statutes are digested.

For pending federal legislation, the Canadian Law Information Council publishes a *Status of Bills Report* which is prepared by the Library of Parliament. The Report lists bills in numerical order and traces the progression of current bills. The "Progress of Bills" section in the *Canadian Current Law* also provides selective information on the status of proposed legislation.

TABLE OF PUBLIC STATUTES 1907 TO FEBRUARY, 1982

SHOWING ALL THE CHAPTERS OF THE REVISED STATUTES, 1970, WITH AMENDMENTS THERETO, AND CERTAIN OTHER PUBLIC ACTS AND AMENDMENTS THERETO FROM 1907 TO FEBRUARY, 1982.*

[**Note:** (1) Acts in the following categories are listed alphabetically thereunder: **Agreements**—Income Tax, Estate Tax, Succession Duty, and related tax matters, **Agreements**—Trade, Commerce and related matters, **Bridges, Electoral Districts, Provincial Boundaries,** and **Treaties of Peace.**

(2) References in bold face in the 3rd Column opposite an Act indicate the provisions of that Act have been amended or added.

(3) The term SOR or SI is a reference to Statutory Orders and Regulations or Statutory Instruments as published in the *Canada Gazette* Part II. CIF refers to the date of coming into force. (E) indicates the English version only is amended and (F) indicates the French version only is amended.]

Subject	R.S., 1970 Chap.	Amendments, new Acts from 1 January, 1970, and unconsolidated Acts from 1907 to 1982
A		
Adjustments of Accounts		1980-81-82, c. 17
		s. 21, 1980-81-82, c. 47, s. 2
		Schedule III, 1980-81-82, c. 47, s. 2
		CIF 31.03.81 *see* s. 34
Admiralty		R.S., c. A-1 repealed, c. 10(2nd Supp.), s. 64(1) (*see* Federal Court)
Adult Occupational Training	A-2	**s. 2,** 1976-77, c. 54, s. 74
		s. 3, 1972, c. 14, s. 1
		s. 4, 1972, c. 14, s. 2; 1976-77, c. 54, s. 74
		s. 5, 1972, c. 14, s. 3; 1976-77, c. 54, s. 74
		s. 6, 1972, c. 14, s. 4
		s. 7, 1972, c. 14, s. 4; 1976-77, c. 3, s. 2, c. 54, s. 74
		s. 8, 1972, c. 14, s. 5; 1976-77, c. 22, Sch. (M&I) vote 10; 1976-77, c. 3, s. 2
		s. 9, 1972, c. 14, s. 6
		s. 12, 1972, c. 14, s. 7
		ss. 17-20, repealed, c. 33(2nd Supp.), s. 1
		s. 22, 1976-77, c. 54, s. 74
		General, 1976-77, c. 54, s. 74
Advance Payments for Crops (*see* Crops, Advance Payments)		
Aeronautics	A-3	**s. 1.1,** added, 1976-77, c. 26, s. 1
		ss. 3, 4, 1976-77, c. 28, s. 49(F)
		s. 5.1, added, 1973-74, c. 20, s. 1; 1974-75-76, c. 100, s. 1
		s. 6, c. 16(1st Supp.), s. 43; 1976-77, c. 28, ss. 2, 49(F)
		s. 7, 1976-77, c. 28, s. 49(F)
		s. 14, 1976-77, c. 26, s. 2
		s. 15.1, added, 1976-77, c. 26, s. 3

*There are a certain number of Acts, passed before January 1, 1970, that were not consolidated in the Revised Statutes of Canada, 1927, 1952 or 1970. As those Acts are still in force, they are included in this Table. There are also a number of sections (or parts thereof) in Acts passed before January 1, 1970, that were not consolidated in the Revised Statutes of Canada, 1927, 1952 or 1970. With respect to these provisions, see the footnote on page 569 of the 2nd Supplement to the Revised Statutes of Canada, 1970.

Illustration J

Canada Gazette, Part III. Table of Public Statutes.

The Province of Quebec differs from the other provinces, in that private law is essentially governed by two civil codes, the Civil Code of Quebec and the Code of Civil Procedure. These are enacted as part of the statute law of the province. A new Civil Code is currently being enacted, beginning with the reform of family law.[10] There are

10. S.Q. 1980, c. 39 established Book Two, a new Civil Code to reform family law. Sections and articles as set out by Proclamation, *la Gazette Officielle du Québec* (partie 2) 1565, which came into force on April 2, 1981.

currently four editions of the Civil Code published in a bilingual format, the one considered most authoritative being *Les Codes Civils: The Civil Codes, édition critique,* by Paul-André Crepeau and John E.C. Brierley, published by SOQUIJ (2nd ed. 1982). They have also prepared *Code Civil: Civil Code, 1866–1980, An Historical and Critical Edition* (1981), which provides a legislative history of each article, giving the text of every provision as it stood on August 1, 1866, and the text of successive legislative amendments. Annual cumulative supplements are planned until the new Civil Code is completely enacted. Two loose-leaf editions of the Codes currently in force are available as well. The first, by Saintonge-Poitevin, is published by Wilson et Lafleur Ltée, and includes in addition to the text of the Code with annotations, an alphabetical index to subject matter, and an index citing cases dealing with the Code from all reports and reviews since 1964. The text of sections of the new Code in force is also included, and the text of sections of the old Code which have been repealed is omitted, with a note of the repeal.

The second, published by Kingsland Publications, also contains, in addition to the Code, an index of subject matter and an index citing cases dealing with the Code from 1954. The text of certain provincial and federal statutes also relevant to private law matters is included as well. All sections of the new Code are incorporated, together with the text of the Proclamation indicating which are in force. Sections of the old Code which have been repealed are omitted. In addition to the above, there is also an edition prepared by Baudouin and Renaud and published by Judico (4th ed. 1980). Both Wilson et Lafleur and Kingsland Publications issue loose-leaf editions of the Code of Civil Procedure as well.

N. CANADIAN ADMINISTRATIVE LAW

1. FEDERAL REGULATIONS

Regulations in force and of general application as of December 31, 1977 are included in a 19 volume consolidation entitled the *Consolidated Regulations of Canada, 1978.* The instruments are arranged alphabetically by the enabling statute, and each is designated by an individual chapter number and is cited "C.R.C.c.", with the chapter number added. There is no index, although there is a table of contents. A small number of regulations which have been made under other than statutory authority are listed under that heading.

Regulations published during 1978 which amend or revoke the consolidation have been published in a special two volume issue of the *Canada Gazette, Part II.* However, regulations adopted after 1978 are contained in the biweekly issues of the *Canada Gazette, Part II.*

"Regulations" as defined by the *Statutory Instruments Act*[11] are designated *S.O.R.* and numbered chronologically by year. The other classes of statutory instruments such as proclamations, which are required to be published by the Act, are designated *S.I.*, and are numbered in a separate chronological sequence.

In order to update a Canadian regulation published after the 1978 consolidation, it is necessary to first check the "Consolidated Index" to the *Canada Gazette, Part II.* (See Illustration K.) This is issued quarterly as part of the *Gazette* and lists regulations in the consolidation or made subsequent to it which were in force at any time during the calendar year.

2. PROVINCIAL REGULATIONS

Regulations made by authority of provincial legislation are published in the official provincial Gazettes, usually following the arrangement of the *Canada Gazette, Part II.* Ontario publishes an official consolidation of regulations as companion volumes to its revised statutes. There are also loose-leaf commercial publications available for many provinces (e.g., Alberta, Ontario, Quebec).

3. ADMINISTRATIVE DECISIONS AND RULINGS

The reporting of Canadian administrative decisions is not consistent, since many tribunals do not make their decisions available other than to the parties, unless provided for in the enabling statute of the board. However, commercial publishers often issue reports containing the decisions of various provincial boards on a specific topic. An example of this is Butterworths' *Canadian Labour Relations Boards Reports* and CCH's *Dominion Tax Cases,* containing the decisions of the federal Tax Review Board, as well as court decisions on tax matters.

Although now somewhat dated, a helpful guide to administrative decisions in Canada can be found in Alice Janisch's *Publication of Administrative Board Decisions in Canada: A Report* (London, Ont.: Canadian Association of Law Libraries, 1971).

O. CANADIAN REPORTS

The Canadian court system is comprised of both federal and provincial courts, although it is not a dual court system, as in the United States. There are two courts constituted under federal statutes with judges federally appointed: the Supreme Court of Canada and the Federal Court. The Supreme Court is the final court of appeal for

11. S.C. 1970–71–72, c. 38. Certain regulations and classes of regulations are exempted from publication by s. 14 of the *Statutory Instruments Regulations* made pursuant to s. 27. Other statutory instruments not defined as regulations by the Act may be included in the *Canada Gazette,* Part I, if required to be published by the enabling act.

47

II–TABLE OF REGULATIONS, STATUTORY INSTRUMENTS (OTHER THAN REGULATIONS) AND OTHER DOCUMENTS ARRANGED BY STATUTE

SEPTEMBER 30, 1982

This Table provides a reference to regulations, statutory instruments (other than regulations), and other documents that were in force at any time in the current calendar year. For instruments in force in any previous year that were published in the *Canada Gazette* Part II, reference should be made to the Table of Statutory Orders and Regulations of December 31st of the year in question.

The instruments included in this Table are listed alphabetically according to their short title under the name of the statute pursuant to which they were made, and the statutes are listed alphabetically. For instruments published in the *Canada Gazette* Part II, reference is made to the publication in which they may be found. The Table also shows the citation of the amendments that have been made to each instrument. The abbreviation in the "Comments" column indicates whether the instrument is new, a revision or revocation of a previous instrument, became spent in the current year, is superseded by another instrument or is an erratum to a previous instrument. Where no abbreviation appears in the "Comments" column, the instrument was amended by the citation shown. The date on which instruments were made, and the date on which they were registered, is shown only with respect to instruments made after January 1, 1972, the date on which the *Statutory Instruments Act* came into force.

The reference to a section number following the title of the regulations indicates the section number of the Act in which the authority for making the regulations is found. This reference is being added to the Index in respect of regulations published in the Consolidated Regulations of Canada, that have been amended since January 1, 1980. Subsequent issues of the Index will contain this reference in respect of regulations amended since January 1, 1978.

A blank space in the publication column indicates that the document was not published in the *Canada Gazette* Part II. Such documents may be inspected or purchased at the office of the Registrar of Statutory Instruments, Room 300, Blackburn Building, 85 Sparks Street, Ottawa, Canada.

Abbreviations

No. —Registration Number for Instruments made after January 1, 1972
—*Canada Gazette* Citation for Instruments made before January 1, 1972

Com—Comments
e—Erratum
n—New
r—Revises
s—Spent
w—Superseded
x—Revokes

C55—1955 Consolidation

CRC—Consolidated Regulations of Canada

STATUTES Regulations and other documents	Date made	No.	Date Registered	1955 Consolidation or Canada Gazette Part II Date	Page	Com
ADULT OCCUPATIONAL TRAINING ACT, *RSC 1970, c. A-2*						
Adult Occupational Training Regulations (s. 12)	CRC, Vol. I, c. 1, p. 1					
	27/ 9/78	SOR/78-743	28/ 9/78	11/10/78	3716	
	17/ 5/79	SOR/79-435	22/ 5/79	13/ 6/79	2242	
	5/ 9/80	SOR/80-730	8/ 9/80	24/ 9/80	3177	
	18/ 8/82	SOR/82-776	18/ 8/82	8/ 9/82	2824	x
ADVANCE PAYMENTS FOR CROPS ACT, *1976-77, c. 12*						
Advance Payments for Crops Regulations (s. 10 & 14)	CRC, Vol. V, c. 446, p. 3263					
	6/ 9/78	SOR/78-707	11/ 9/78	27/ 9/78	3640	
	25/10/79	SOR/79-773	26/10/79	14/11/79	4005	
	9/10/80	SOR/80-786	10/10/80	22/10/80	3293	
	5/11/81	SOR/81-905	9/11/81	25/11/81	3389	
	3/ 9/82	SOR/82-817	7/ 9/82	22/ 9/82	3004	
AERONAUTICS ACT, *RSC 1970, c. A-3*						
Air Carrier Regulations (s. 14)	CRC, Vol. I, c. 3, p. 45					
	8/ 3/78	SOR/78-224	9/ 3/78	22/ 3/78	1003	
	25/ 8/78	SOR/78-687	29/ 8/78	13/ 9/78	3590	
	25/ 8/78	SOR/78-688	29/ 8/78	13/ 9/78	3591	
	25/ 8/78	SOR/78-689	29/ 8/78	13/ 9/78	3592	
	25/ 8/78	SOR/78-690	30/ 8/78	13/ 9/78	3593	
	25/ 8/78	SOR/78-691	30/ 8/78	13/ 9/78	3594	
	21/12/78	SOR/79-16	22/12/78	10/ 1/79	26	
	21/12/78	SOR/79-17	22/12/78	10/ 1/79	27	
	21/12/78	SOR/79-18	22/12/78	10/ 1/79	30	
	21/12/78	SOR/79-19	22/12/78	10/ 1/79	31	
	21/12/78	SOR/79-20	22/12/78	10/ 1/79	35	

Illustration K

Canada Gazette, Part II, Consolidated Index II—Table of Regulations.

both federal and provincial courts, and also has jurisdiction to give opinions on constitutional and other matters. The Federal Court, which was created in 1971, also has federally appointed judges, and consists of two divisions, the Appeal Division and the Trial Division. This court took over the jurisdiction formerly exercised by the Exchequer Court in matters such as copyright, patents, and claims against the Crown. It was also given a new function consisting of judicial review jurisdiction over virtually all federal statutory authorities.

Courts constituted under provincial statutes vary in names and structures. Very generally, they consist of courts of superior jurisdiction with judges federally appointed, governed by provisions set out in sections 96 to 100 of the Constitution Act, 1867. These are an upper tier consisting of the Supreme Court of a province, including both appellate and trial divisions, although in some provinces, the two divisions are constituted as separate courts; and the county or district courts of a province, which form a middle tier. Provincial courts constituted under provincial statutes with judges provincially appointed comprise the lowest tier. Provincial courts do not deal exclusively with matters falling within provincial legislative competence, however. For most purposes, both federal and provincial matters will be tried in the same courts.

Decisions of the Supreme Court of Canada are binding upon all courts; decisions of the highest provincial appellate courts are binding upon all lower courts of that jurisdiction, and judgments of courts of co-ordinate jurisdiction are generally followed in the absence of strong reasons to the contrary. Canadian courts were bound to follow decisions of the Judicial Committee of the Privy Council before appeals to that body were abolished (in 1933 for criminal cases and in 1949 for civil cases).

It should be noted that there is no systematic reporting of cases such as that found in the West Publishing Company's National Reporter System. The Canadian reporting system contains much duplication of coverage, and there is little cooperation among the publishers. Another difficulty with Canadian law reports is their time of publication. Many cases go unreported for four to ten months after a decision is rendered.

The reports of the Supreme Court of Canada began publication in 1876. Now known as the *Canada Supreme Court Reports,* they contain virtually all decisions rendered by the Supreme Court; including the decisions of civil and criminal cases on appeal from the provincial courts, and the cases on appeal from the Federal Court. These reports are bilingual and are issued monthly, cumulating in bound volumes. From 1923–1967, the set was combined with the *Reports of the Exchequer Court of Canada* and issued as the *Canada Law Reports,* consisting of two separate series: the *Supreme Court Reports* and the *Exchequer Court Reports.*

The *Reports of the Exchequer Court of Canada* began publication in 1875 and reported cases involving claims against the Crown, or issues of patents, copyrights and admiralty. In 1923, it became part of the *Canada Law Reports: Exchequer Court;* and by 1971, it was known as the *Canada: Federal Court Reports,* including selected cases from the Trial Division and all cases decided by the Appeal Division.

Since 1974, there has also been an unofficial reporter containing federal decisions: the *National Reporter,* which includes all judgments of the Supreme Court of Canada, and the Federal Court, Appeal Division. Selected judgments of the Trial Division are included as well. The publisher, Maritime Law Book Company, has initiated a key number digest system similar to that found in West's *National Reporter System.*

The *Dominion Law Reports,* which began publication in 1912 and started its 3d series in 1969, contains both federal and provincial decisions. It issues a weekly series of cases reported in all the courts, particularly at the Supreme Court and provincial Superior Court levels. There is a cumulative table of cases for the 2d series and an annotation service for each of the series. This service gives the disposition of all appeals and lists all times when a case has been judicially considered in any Canadian jurisdiction. A table of cases for the 3d series is included as well.

While all provinces have had official or quasi-official law reports, only the following are published currently: *Ontario Reports,* second series (1974–date); and *Recueils de jurisprudence du Quebec,* at present published in three series, *Cour d'appel* (1970–date); *Cour superieure* (1967–date); and a combined series entitled *Cour provinciale, Cour des sessions de la paix, and Tribunal de la jeunesse* (1980–date). In addition, there are the following commercially published provincial reports being issued currently: *Alberta Reports* (1977–date); *Alberta Law Reports,* second series, (1976–date); *British Columbia Law Reports* (1976–date); *Manitoba Reports,* second series, (1979–date); *New Brunswick Reports,* second series, (1969–date); *Nova Scotia Reports,* second series, (1970–date); *Newfoundland and Prince Edward Island Reports* (1971–date); and *Saskatchewan Reports,* (1979–date). The *Atlantic Provinces Reports* (1975–date) covers cases from the provinces of New Brunswick, Nova Scotia, Prince Edward Island, and Newfoundland; while the *Western Weekly Reports* (1912–date) includes cases from the Western provinces and territories, and appeals therefrom to the Supreme and Federal Courts.

Also, as in the United States, Canada has many subject case reporters covering such diversified areas as criminal law, torts, bankruptcy, and motor vehicle law, from various jurisdictions.

P. CANADIAN DIGESTS

Canada has no one digest as comprehensive as West's *American Digest System.* The *Canadian Abridgment,* (Carswell), however, digests all reported decisions from both federal and provincial courts. The second edition began publication in 1966 and is comprised of 38 bound volumes of substantive law and three procedure volumes. The First Permanent Supplement (1975) was published in three volumes and covers reports up to December 31, 1974. The Second Permanent Supplement (1980) consists of five volumes covering reports from January 1, 1975 to December 31, 1979. There is also a two volume loose-leaf cumulative supplement.

Access to this classification system of 120 subject titles is provided by the *Key* volume which also gives instructions on using the tables found in the Abridgment. The finding aids include a three volume *General Index,* arranged alphabetically by subject, plus a fourth volume covering 1975–1979; a two volume *Consolidated Table of Cases;* a four volume *Table of Cases Judicially Considered* (See Illustration N), updated by a first (1974–1978) and a second (1979–1980) permanent supplement; a two volume *Table of Statutes Judicially Considered,* with a third volume covering 1975–1980; and a *Words and Phrases* volume. A loose-leaf appendix updates the tables in the finding aids and the *Index to Canadian Legal Literature,* described below in Section S. The *Western Weekly Reports, British Columbia Law Reports,* and *Alberta Law Reports,* all provide references to the *Canadian Abridgment's* classification system. Carswell plans to expand this feature to other of its reports in the future.

Canadian Current Law (Carswell) is the monthly supplement to the *Canadian Abridgment* (2d ed.). Digested cases are arranged according to the Abridgment's classification system. Each *Canadian Current Law* also contains a "Table of Cases", "Cases Judicially Considered", "Statutes Judicially Considered", "Words and Phrases" and an index, plus a number of tables designed to alert the lawyer to new developments. The digests found therein are eventually cumulated in the *Canadian Abridgment* (2d).

There are many other digests published in Canada, some exclusive to individual jurisdictions. The *Supreme Court of Canada Reports Service* (Butterworth, 2d ed.) is a three volume loose-leaf set with two current service volumes which indexes all reports of the Canadian Supreme Court from 1876 to date. (See Illustration L). Arranged alphabetically by subject, the set also includes a cumulative index and a table of cases. The case annotations are extremely brief, however, and the set is more like an index than a digest; but the Current Service volumes contain longer digests of judgments released during the year.

The *Dominion Reports Service* (CCH Canadian Ltd.) consists of a loose-leaf current service with monthly releases which are refiled in transfer binders or replaced by annual bound volumes. Reported and selected unreported decisions from all Canadian courts are digested and arranged into thirteen subject areas. There is a useful topical index with many subheadings.

A number of provincial digests are published currently as well. *Butterworth's Ontario Digest* is a twelve volume loose-leaf encyclopedic digest, the final volume being a *Key Word Index.* The set is arranged by subject and summarizes every Ontario case reported since 1901. The *Canadian Weekly Law Sheets* serve as a companion service, and provide cross references to the appropriate *B.O.D.* key number where cases on point are digested. The Maritime Law Book Company also publishes consolidated index and digest volumes for the law reports series that it issues.

Finally, a relatively recent development has been the publishing of digests of unreported cases for the Supreme and Federal Court, Ap-

Member of—Contesting election of mayor. *Paulin* v. *Poirier*, [1970] S.C.R. 576.

COURT

Constitutional Law—County court judge rendering decisions in criminal proceedings after resigning. *Ritcey* v. *The Queen* (1980), 30 N.R. 442, 37 N.S.R. (2d) 68, 67 A.P.R. 68, 50 C.C.C. (2d) 481, 106 D.L.R. (3d) 1, [1980] 1 S.C.R. 1077; revg 29 N.S.R. (2d) 50, 45 A.P.R. 50, 5 C.R. (3d) 270, 43 C.C.C. (2d) 510, 92 D.L.R. (3d) 324 (N.S.C.A.); affg 32 C.C.C. (2d) 354 (N.S.Co.Ct.), Current Service 2, 1980, Dig. 706.

Federal Court jurisdiction—Claim made by federal Crown on advance payment default made under Prairie Grain Advance Payments Act, 1957-58 (Can.), c. 2. *Rhine* v. *The Queen* (1980), 34 N.R. 290, 116 D.L.R. (3d) 385, affg 98 D.L.R. (3d) 496, [1979] 2 F.C. 651, 26 N.R. 526, revg 75 D.L.R. (3d) 730, [1978] 1 F.C. 356; affg 99 D.L.R. (3d) 91, [1979]2 F.C. 516, 28 N.R. 226, revg 76 D.L.R. (3d) 142, [1978] 1 F.C. 198, Current Service 2, 1980, Dig. 766.

Federal Court jurisdiction—Subrogation claim made by federal Crown on Canada student loan default. *Prytula* v. *The Queen* (1980), 34 N.R. 290, 116 D.L.R. (3d) 385, affg 98 D.L.R. (3d) 496, [1979] 2 F.C. 651, 26 N.R. 526, revg 75 D.L.R. (3d) 730, [1978] 1 F.C. 356; affg 99 D.L.R. (3d) 91, [1979] 2 F.C. 516, 28 N.R. 226, revg 76 D.L.R. (3d) 142, [1978] 1 F.C. 198, Current Service 2, 1980, Dig. 765.

COVENANT

Restrictive—Lease providing no other hairdresser would be permitted in shopping centre—Adjoining store rented to wigmaker. *Russo* v. *Field*, [1973] S.C.R. 466, 34 D.L.R. (3d) 704, Current Service, 1973, Dig. 115.

Restrictive—Sale of all shares of company—Covenant not to compete—Valid. *Hecke* v. *La Compagnie de Gestion Maskoutaine Ltée. and La Compagnie de Gestion Cayouette Ltée.*, [1972] S.C.R. 22, 5 C.P.R. (2d) 195, Current Service, 1971, Dig. 2.

Restrictive—Sale of business—Agreement not to compete. *Cochrane* v. *Trudeau*, Current Service, 1976, Dig. 361.

Restrictive—Sale of business and employment contract with covenant as to competition—Breach—Quantum of damages. *Elsley* v. *J.G. Collins Insurance Agencies Ltd.*, Current Service, 1978, Dig. 517.

CRIMINAL CODE

Construction of s. 170—Nudity in public place. *The Queen* v. *Verrette*, Current Service, 1978, Dig. 534.

Construction of s. 213(d)—Murder—Defence of drunkenness. *Swietlinski* v. *The Queen* (1980), 18 C.R. (3d) 231, 34 N.R. 569, 55 C.C.C. (2d) 481; affg 5 C.R. (3d) 324, 44 C.C.C. (2d) 267, 22 O.R. (2d) 604, 94 D.L.R. (3d) 218 (C.A), Current Service 2, 1980, Dig. 773.

Construction of s. 237(1)—Admissibility of breathalyzer certificate—Expert evi-

Illustration L

Sample page in the *Supreme Court of Canada Reports Service* (Butterworth).

peal Division and all the common law provinces except the Maritimes, by Western Legal Publications, supplemented by a photocopy service supplying the full text of the reasons for judgment on request. Canada Law Book also provides a similar service for all jurisdictions in its *All-Canada Weekly Summaries* and *Weekly Criminal Bulletin.* Thus, the problems of slow and selective reporting in the law reports are overcome to a degree by these services providing summaries of cases soon after they are decided on a comprehensive basis for all but the lower level provincial courts. The Canadian Law Information Council also provides digests of unreported decisions of the federal courts.

For more information on Canadian digests, consult Mary Burbidge Helleiner, *Case Law Indexing in Canada* (1980).

Q. CANADIAN ENCYCLOPEDIAS

The *Canadian Encyclopedic Digest* (Carswell) is published in two editions, an Ontario edition covering Ontario law, and a Western edition covering the laws of the Western provinces, with some emphasis on federal law. The *Canadian Encyclopedic Digest* (Ontario, 3d ed.) began publication in 1973, in loose-leaf volumes, to provide a complete statement of Ontario law. Volumes have been issued yearly, and the set is now near completion. Indexed by one hundred fifty subject headings, each topic has a complete "Key Word Index" and a "Table of Cases." Access to the set is by the *Key,* which lists titles from both the 2d and 3d editions and shows any changes occurring to date. The *Key* is comprised of four indexes, covering contents, statutes, title key, and "key words". Use of the last index necessitates a two-step process, first locating the appropriate volume and title number, then checking the index to that title to locate the appropriate paragraph number.

The final bound *Key* volume will be published simultaneously with the last volume of the set, but interim keys are published annually. The set is updated on a continuing basis by coloured supplement pages at the front of the volumes, and eventually by replacement parts. Updating material appears in the supplement under the same title and paragraph number. A one-volume table of concordance was published in 1982, converting references to the earlier *Revised Statutes of Ontario, 1970,* in the titles to the appropriate *R.S.O.* 1980 citations.

The *Canadian Encyclopedic Digest (Western, 3d ed.)* is also a loose-leaf service emphasizing the federal law and provincial law of Alberta, British Columbia, Manitoba, Saskatchewan, and two territories, patterned after the *C.E.D.* (Ont. 3d). Four to five volumes are published yearly in an attempt to replace the 2d edition. Published titles are supplemented regularly, and each article contains both a key word index and a table of cases and statutes.

The *Laws of Canada* (Butterworths, in preparation) is scheduled for publication in 1983. Intended to be a statement of all the laws of common law Canada, there are fifty-one proposed topics in this set which will replace the *Halsbury's Laws of England, Canadian Converter* (3d ed.).

R. CANADIAN CITATORS

There is no comprehensive set of case or statute citators in Canada. Several commercial publishers, however, issue citators for specific jurisdictions either individually, or as part of other services. For statutes, there are the following. The *Canada Statute Citator* (Canada Law Book Ltd.) is comprised of two loose-leaf volumes which alphabetically list every act found in the 1970 revision (See Illustration M). All amendments, repeals, and reenactments of statutes are cited, and the text of the amendments is given, along with summaries of relevant court decisions. The one volume *Canada Statute Annotation* compiles cases from 1941–71 under the appropriate statute, and provides a history of the legislation.

As noted above, an official table of public statutes is issued as part of the *Canada Gazette, Part III* which lists all new acts and amendments from the time of the last revision. If a statute or section of a statute has been declared *ultra vires,* then the citation will be given; otherwise, no references to cases are included.

There are loose-leaf statute citators issued for many of the provinces (e.g., Alberta, British Columbia, Manitoba, Ontario and Saskatchewan). Most print the text of amendments and statutory repeals, and provide summaries, or give references to, cases interpreting the legislation. A two-volume statute citator updated by a bound supplement and a table in the appendix volume, which is in turn updated by issues of *Canadian Current Law,* is included as part of the *Canadian Abridgment.* A statute citator function is also performed by the "Index to Statutes Judicially Noticed" included in the index-digests published in conjunction with the reports covering the Maritime Provinces by the Maritime Law Book Company. Finally, an official table of public statutes listing new acts and amendments from the time of the last revision appears in each provincial annual statute volume, and also in the federal statutes.

For cases, the most comprehensive citator is the table of "Cases Judicially Considered" which is published as part of the *Canadian Abridgment.* The four main volumes of this table include cases judicially considered until 1973, and also case history and treatment until that date. They are supplemented by bound volumes covering 1974–1980, by the table in the appendix volume, and by *Canadian Current Law.* There are also citators for individual provinces such as *Index Gagnon* for Quebec, and the annotations included in *Butterworths Ontario Digest,* described above. Case citator features are also included as part of certain law reports series. Examples are the *Dominion Law Reports Annotation Service,* covering the second and third series of the D.L.R.s. and the "Index to Cases Judicially Noticed" found in the Maritime Law Book Digests.

THE CANADA STATUTE CITATOR 43—1

COLD STORAGE ACT

R.S.C. 1970, Chap. C-22

Administered by the Dept. of Agriculture

(No cases and no amendments)

COMBINES INVESTIGATION ACT

R.S.C. 1970, Chap. C-23

Amended R.S.C. 1970, c. 10 (1st Supp.), s. 34

Amended R.S.C. 1970, c. 10 (2nd Supp.), s. 65; proclaimed in force August 1, 1972

Amended 1974-75-76, c. 76; proclaimed in force, except s. 14(1), January 1, 1976, s. 14(1) proclaimed in force July 1, 1976, but see s. 31(2) printed under "Generally" below

Amended 1976-77, c. 28, s. 9; in force June 29, 1977

Administered by the Dept. of Consumer and Corporate Affairs

Generally

For cases 1941 to 1971, see *Canada Statute Annotations,* R.S.C. 1970 edition.

1974-75-76, c. 76, s. 30 (proclaimed in force January 1, 1976) repeals 1966-67, c. 23 (unconsolidated and unrepealed).

1974-75-76, c. 76, s. 31(2) provides as follows:

(2) For the purpose of applying section 32 of the *Combines Investigation Act,* as amended by this Act, to conspiracies, combinations, agreements and arrangements related to services to which that section does not now apply at a day that is later than the day fixed by a proclamation issued under subsection (1), any provision or provisions of this Act that are specified in a proclamation issued under this subsection, and any provision or provisions of the *Combines Investigation Act* enacted or amended by this Act and specified in such proclamation shall come into force on a day fixed by a proclamation issued under this subsection.

R. v. K.C. Irving Ltd. and three other Corporations; R. v. K.C. Irving Ltd. (1974), 45 D.L.R. (3d) 45, 16 C.C.C. (2d) 49, 13 C.P.R. (2d) 115, 7 N.B.R. (2d) 360 (N.B.Q.B.).

The acquisition of ownership of the five newspapers within a relevant market also involves the acquisition of control over their business notwithstanding that the editors thereof are allowed to pursue completely independent editorial policies. Thus a combine, merger, trust or monopoly exists, and a monopoly has been formed within the meaning of this Act. Once a complete monoply has been established, detriment to the public within the meaning of the Act is also established and evidence of economic advantages cannot be considered.

Jabour v. Law Society of British Columbia et al. (1979), 98 D.L.R. (3d) 442 (B.C.S.C.).

The Act, as amended to include suppliers of services and the professions, applies to the Law Society of British Columbia and its members and is *intra vires* the Parliament of Canada. In the Legal Professions Act (B.C.) the Legislature does not give the Benchers the specific authority to fix prices or to set the number of lawyers who may practice. In the absence of such specific powers, if the Benchers were to engage in marketing activities

DEC. 1980

Illustration M

Canada Statute Citator (Canada Law Book Ltd., 1970).

S. CANADIAN PERIODICAL INDEXES

Most leading Canadian legal periodicals are indexed in the *Index to Legal Periodicals* and the *Legal Resource Index.* However, for more complete coverage the following indexes should be consulted.

Since it started in 1964, the *Index to Canadian Legal Periodical Literature* has indexed both legal periodicals and articles related to law found in non-legal Canadian journals. The index is divided into four sections: Subject, Author-Title, Table of Cases, and Book Review Index; with all entries giving full citations. Although the policy is to publish the index quarterly, with the fourth issue becoming the annual bound volume, in practice it is frequently a year behind.

The *Canadian Abridgment's Index to Canadian Legal Literature* (1981) purports to index all law books and articles published in Canada to 1981. The entries in this three volume set are arranged alphabetically by author under *Abridgment* subject headings. Updated quarterly by a table in the appendix, it contains entries first appearing in *Canadian Current Law.*

The *Index to Commonwealth Legal Periodicals* has been published bi-monthly since 1974, indexing Canadian and other Commonwealth periodicals. It provides a broad coverage of Canadian Journals, using most of the subject headings found in the *Index to Legal Periodicals.* A 1982 cumulation covers the period from Sept. 1978 to Aug. 1981.

T. CANADIAN DICTIONARIES, ETC.

The *Canadian Law Dictionary,* edited by R.S. Vasan (Law & Business, 1980) and *A Handbook of Canadian Legal Terminology,* by W.J. Flynn, rev. ed. (General Publishing Co., 1981) are two dictionaries to interpret and define Canadian legal terminology.

The *Encyclopedia of Words and Phrases, Legal Maxims, Canada, 1825–1978,* 3d ed. (De Boo, 1979) is the only comprehensive service covering Canadian words and phrases exclusively. This four volume set is alphabetically arranged.

It should be noted, however, that many of the Canadian digests and encyclopedias have a words and phrases volume. These include the *Canadian Abridgment, 2d,* the *Canadian Encyclopedic Digest* (Western, 2d ed.), and the *Canadian Current Law.*

U. CANADIAN LEGAL BIBLIOGRAPHIES AND RESEARCH MANUALS

The most recent Canadian legal bibliography is *A Bibliography of Canadian Law,* New Edition, (Canadian Law Information Council, 1977; First Supplement, 1982), by Reynald Boult. This edition lists over eleven thousand selected periodical articles and treatises by broad bilingual subject headings; the First Supplement adds over four thousand more references.

In 1974–1975, the National Library of Canada with the cooperation of the Canadian Association of Law Libraries surveyed the collections of law libraries in Canada. As a result of this survey the *Checklist of Law Reports and Statutes in Canada Law Libraries* (1977–1980) was published. This four volume set is both a bibliography and a union list. The arrangement for reports and administrative decisions is by subject and jurisdiction.

Volume three of *A Legal Bibliography of the British Commonwealth of Nations,* entitled *Canadian and British-American Colonial Law,* lists all Canadian law books issued prior to 1957. It is arranged alphabetically by province and subdivided by type of material.

The best guide to Canadian legal research has been Margaret A. Banks' *Using a Law Library,* 3d ed. (Carswell, 1980). This comprehensive manual covers both Canadian and English materials, describing in detail the steps necessary to solve any Canadian legal research problem. Another text, recently published, is D.T. MacEllven, *Legal Research Handbook* (Butterworth, 1983). *Canadian Legal Research Guide (with Special Reference to Ontario Law),* by P.T. Murphy (University of Windsor Faculty of Law, Community Law Program, 1976), is a handy pamphlet guide, but now somewhat out of date.

For information on the proper form of Canadian legal citations, see J.W. Samuels' *Legal Citation for Lawyers* (Butterworth, 1968), although the "Bluebook", *A Uniform System of Citation* (13th ed., 1981) does include brief coverage of Canadian sources.

V. RESEARCH BY COMPUTER IN CANADIAN LAW

QL Systems, which originated under the name QUIC/LAW at Queens University in Kingston, Ontario, is the most comprehensive computerized legal research system for Canadian law. It includes summaries or headnotes of decisions from the federal courts and the common law provinces; the Revised Statutes of Canada and statutes of several common law provinces; and federal regulations. This and other Canadian computer services are described in Margaret Banks' *Using a Law Library,* at pp. 178–184. Two systems designed for Quebec law, *DATUM* and *MODUL,* are not now operational, but the SOQUIJ (Société Québecoise d'Information Juridique) is planning to offer a computer service for Quebec law in the near future.

Chapter 20

FOREIGN AND COMPARATIVE LAW *

A. INTRODUCTION

The expansion of trade, tourism, labor mobility, and cultural activities between people, companies, and countries has been greatly accelerated by improved communication and transportation. The growth of such external relationships and the frequency of contact resulting from them have given rise to many problems involving the law of other countries. It has also increased our awareness of and interest in foreign law developments. This Chapter focuses on comparative law research and on research in foreign law, primarily the law of those jurisdictions which comprise the civil law system.

* The authors acknowledge their indebtedness in the preparation of this Chapter to Judge Mario P. Goderich and Dr. Jan Stepan. This revision is based in part on their work in the 7th edition of *How to Find the Law*. Needless to say, they are not responsible for any errors of omission or commission herein.

For the purposes of this work, foreign law can be defined as the domestic law of any country other than the United States. In that sense, Chapter 19 dealing with English and Canadian legal materials covered foreign law. However, because of their similarities and common source, we will not be treating *common law* jurisdictions in this Chapter, but, as noted above, will focus on *civil law jurisdictions.* The domestic law of any country is the *internal* law governing all matters within that particular country, and in some situations governing also activities, transactions, or events occurring abroad which derive from relationships in that country.

Comparative law can be defined as the study of the similarities and differences between the laws of two or more countries, or between two or more legal systems. As such, comparative law is not itself a system of law or a body of rules, but rather a method or approach to legal inquiry. It is both an academic discipline and a practical tool for understanding the operation of legal systems or particular laws by comparing two or more different systems or the laws of different countries.

The importance of foreign and comparative law to the citizens, lawyers, judges, and legal scholars of the United States can be seen in the extent to which the law of other countries is the subject of legal advice and drafting, negotiation and contractual obligation, litigation and judicial decisions, and legal research and scholarly writing. Foreign and comparative law are taught in many of our law schools, and, in their published forms, are collected by most of the larger law libraries in this country. In the course of their practices, many American lawyers may have to become familiar with the law of other countries. Although foreign legal experts are frequently retained in important matters, [1] some knowledge of another legal system and its rules is essential to work effectively with that counsel and to fulfill one's own responsibilities.

B. MAJOR LEGAL SYSTEMS OF THE WORLD

Most of the countries of the world can be divided between two large legal systems. The common law system is the basis of the law of the United States, England and those countries which have been influenced by them. The civil law system forms the basis of law in the countries of continental Western Europe, most of Latin America, and parts of Asia and Africa.

The law of the socialist countries of the world, most of which have traditionally been part of the civil law system, has been developing

1. A New York Court of Appeals decision has, in dictum, defined the responsibility of a lawyer in that State in regard to foreign law as follows:

"Where counsel who are admitted to the Bar of this State are retained in a matter involving foreign law, they are responsible to the client for the proper conduct of the matter, and may not claim that they are not required to know the law of the foreign State". Matter of New York County Lawyers Ass'n (Roel), 3 N.Y.2d 224, 165 N.Y.S.2d 31, 144 N.E.2d 24, app. dismissed, 355 U.S. 605 (1958).

into a third legal system. That system, which is now operative in many countries, still reflects substantially the civil law heritage of most of the socialist states. There is, however, considerable variation in some of its details, from country to country. Many scholars consider socialist law to be merely a branch of the civil law system, with its own unique characteristics, and it is clear that most socialist countries have retained the essential features and bibliographic forms of the civil law.

There is yet another group of countries whose legal traditions do not fall within either the common law, civil law or socialist systems. These include countries whose law is based in whole or part on modern adaptations of customary law, Roman law, and the religious traditions of Hindu, Jewish and Moslem law.

A useful scholarly introduction to all of these legal systems is *Major Legal Systems in the World Today,* by R. David and J.E.C. Brierley, 2d ed. (Free Press, 1978). The *International Encyclopedia of Comparative Law* (J.C.B. Mohr, 1971–date) is probably the single most comprehensive and detailed survey in English of the law of many countries of the world. Described below in Section D.2(a), at pages 620–621, this massive work is still in process of publication, with new segments being issued periodically.

C. CONTRAST BETWEEN THE COMMON LAW AND CIVIL LAW SYSTEMS

In the past, the common law and civil law systems were viewed as two monolithic and opposite approaches to legal control, uniformly different in form and content. The reality today is far less simple. The variations between particular countries within each system have been increasing, and the essential differences between the two systems have been decreasing. Each has been incorporating features of the other, and individual countries have moved away in varying degrees from the traditional patterns of their respective models. These changes are in part developmental, but may also stem in part from more realistic perceptions of how law functions in the constituent countries of each system. The variations have been shaped by the history, geography, economy, and culture of particular countries and are reflected in differences between the national versions of the larger systems. We can still accurately generalize to some extent, however, about basic differences between the two approaches.

One of the major distinctions between the common law and civil law systems is the primacy of legislation and the relative deemphasis on case law in civil law countries. Legislation, in this sense, is the legal norm and includes constitutions, statutes, decrees, subordinate legislation, and even administrative regulations. Judicial decisions are not treated as primary sources and are clearly less important than in common law countries. Judges can interpret the law, and this may be very important, but their decisions are, as a rule, only persuasive, non-binding authority. Under the civil law system, the practical effects of judicial precedent and *stare decisis* are weaker, although their existence is increasingly apparent.

This general characterization does not apply equally, however, to all civil law countries. In France, for example, decisions of high courts are very important, and since the 19th century there has been some controversy among scholars over the actual status of jurisprudence (i.e. case law) as a formal source of law in various civil law countries. There are also some large subject areas in which the law has been historically created by a constant flow of decisions of high courts rather than by statutes, e.g. French administrative law, or Austrian administrative process.

The civil law was usually seen as a codified statutory system, while the common law was considered uncodified and based mainly on judicial decisions. This unqualified distinction has ceased to be valid today. The State of California has more codes than some civil law nations. The unanimous adoption of the *Uniform Commercial Code* by all states in the United States [2] further evidences the change in this common law country. There are similar tendencies toward such comprehensive legislation in some fields in Great Britain.

However, most codes in the United States are not comparable to codes of the civil law system. Typically, our codes are only compilations, or alphabetical subject arrangements, of previously enacted laws. The codes of the civil law system, on the other hand, are original statutes. They contain a comprehensive and systematic statement of the law on the subject covered. In addition to the classic codes (civil, criminal, commercial, civil procedure, and criminal procedure), statutory compilations in other fields have been designated as "codes" in many civil law countries. These include codes of family law, taxation, labor, and even motor vehicle traffic, which lack the conciseness and linguistic purity of the classic Napoleonic codes. Stendahl who was reputed to read the French Civil Code as a stylistic model while writing *The Red and the Black,* can hardly be suspected of using a tax code for the same purpose.

In any case, there is no significant legal distinction between a code and other statutes. Ordinary legislation can amend or even repeal codes, and this is done regularly in most civil law countries.

Courts in civil law countries are assumed to know the law, and civil lawyers therefore do not have to prove the law by citing and arguing from soures. In France and Italy, decisions are not cited as precedents by the high courts. In Italy, such use is expressly forbidden by the Code of Civil Procedure. On the other hand, in Germany, Austria and Eastern Europe, high court decisions are frequently cited—not as mandatory authority, but as highly persuasive.

2. The *U.C.C.* has been adopted by all states with the partial exception of Louisiana. Louisiana is a state that is highly influenced by the *Code Napoleon* and, therefore, for a long time has had a commercial code of its own. However, in 1974 even Louisiana adopted Articles 1, 3, 4 and 5 of the Code, and in 1978 adopted Articles 7 and 8, with some modification.

Although in the civil law countries ordinary statutes cannot violate constitutional provisions, the distinction between a constitution and other legislation is less significant than in common law countries. This results in part from the lack of a strong tradition of judicial review of legislation. Constitutions do not directly influence the life of the law in those countries, since individual litigants as a rule cannot raise the question of the constitutionality of an ordinary law. (Such a possibility, however, exists in Mexico under the Latin American concept of the *amparo.*) The situation varies from country to country. Thus in France once a law has been published, courts cannot declare its provisions unconstitutional. In Western Germany or in Italy, if a court comes to the conclusion that a statutory provision violates the constitution, the court itself can request a decision of the *constitutional* courts on this issue.

In those civil law countries which have a *federal* government structure, the distinction between federal and state law is less important than in the United States. The main fields of law in Austria and West Germany, both of which have federal systems, are governed by federal law. The relationships are more complex, however, in Switzerland, the U.S.S.R. and Yugoslavia.

Under the common law, the task of adapting the law to changing social and economic conditions is shared by the courts and the legislatures. Judicial law-making has been a long accepted feature of the common law system, with courts developing and modifying the law on a case by case basis. In the civil law system much of this function is performed by legal scholars working from hypothetical cases and systematically developing new concepts and approaches in their teaching and writing. To the extent that the *Restatements of Law* of the American Law Institute have influenced legal change in this country, that process has followed the civil law model. Thus, in civil law countries, the writing of scholars is a recognized source of law called *doctrine,* and has a much greater authoritative role than under the common law, where judicial law-making performs that function, and scholarly writing is at most a persuasive *secondary* source.

In statutory interpretation, scholarly commentaries on the codes are viewed as prime authority in the civil law system, particularly in the Germanic countries. In France, that direct influence of scholarly writing on the courts is also strong, but the decisions of the *Cour de Cassation* and the *Conseil d' Etat* have great authority. In general, however, civil law judges, in distinction with those of comon law countries, have a lower status in the legal profession and do not ordinarily produce rules of general scope and effect. In the ideal view under the common law, judges are lawyers of distinction who are elevated to the bench. Under the civil law, judges are civil servants who are usually trained for that role from the beginning of their legal careers.

There has been another distinction between the two systems in regard to their respective treatment of public and private law issues. In civil law countries, public law and private law were more clearly differentiated, with the former largely handled in administrative agencies and the latter in the courts. Although in the twentieth century England and the United States have come much closer to that pattern, the distinction is still not as marked. Today under the common law, courts still have a major role in public law matters, but the growth of administrative agencies has moved us toward the civil law separation. In *some* civil law countries, on the other hand, the courts have now come to exercise a more significant part in resolving public law disputes.

This is necessarily only a very superficial view of the many differences between the civil and common law systems. Although the two systems have come to borrow from each other and thus diminish the sharp dichotomies of the past, distinctions of history, philosophy, terminology and procedure remain strong. The professional roles of the lawyer, judge, jury and prosecutor in each system, for example, still differ quite markedly and dramatically color their functional appearance—certainly in literature [3] and the cinema. For purpose of research in the civil law, these differences will still be striking—particularly in language, forms of material and their respective authority, and in the purposes and procedures of research.[4]

D. ENGLISH LANGUAGE MATERIALS

Research in foreign law is aided today by the extensive translation of foreign law sources into English, and the growth of scholarly interest in comparative law. There is now a vast literature of the primary sources of foreign law in English translation, although much of it is uneven in quality and accuracy. There are also many books and articles describing, analyzing or summarizing the law of foreign countries, and comparing the law on particular subjects in various civil and socialist law countries with our own or with each other.

However, serious research in foreign and comparative law, whether for scholarly purposes or legal practice, requires consideration and analysis of the legal materials of the subject jurisdiction in their original language. Research which is limited to translations, secondary descriptions, digests or summaries may be useful for some purposes, and has produced interesting studies. However, it cannot be a substitute for the study of original legal texts and is not likely to produce a reliable and complete understanding of the applicable law. If a significant foreign law problem is to be handled adequately, it will

3. For literary views of civil law inquisitorial procedure, one thinks of Kafka's *The Trial* (which seems less surrealistic today), Camus' *The Stranger,* and Dostoyevskii's *The Brothers Karamazov.* A little known, but candid account of French trial procedure is Andre Gide's personal memoir, *Recollections of the Assize Court,* edited by P. A. Wilkins (Hutchinson, n.d.). Sybille Bedford's *The Faces of Justice* (Simon & Schuster, 1961) is a fascinating comparison of English, German, Austrian, Swiss and French court proceedings.

4. In addition to the readings suggested at the end of this Chapter, two others focus on these differences: J. Dainow, ed., *The Role of Judicial Decisions and Doctrine in Civil Law and in Mixed Jurisdictions* (Louisiana State Univ. Press, 1974) and F. H. Lawson, *The Comparison* (North-Holland Publ. Co., 1977).

usually require the assistance of a trained specialist in the law of that jurisdiction.

Practically, American lawyers frequently require a general sense of the foreign law applicable to a particular problem. Even if a lawyer lacks the necessary language skills and does not have access to an expert in that law, preliminary study is still possible and can be quite helpful, provided the limitations of such inquiry are understood, and reliance on such research is qualified accordingly. The following brief survey illustrates some of the materials which are available for that study. More and more English language publications on foreign law are being published. Although there are relatively few substantial foreign law libraries in this country, many law school libraries and some of the larger bar libraries have good collections of foreign law materials in English.[5]

The materials described in this section are arranged roughly in the order of their recommended use by an American researcher, although the nature of the research and the time and materials actually available may dictate another order or shortcuts. A model approach for research limited to English language materials might begin with a bibliographic guide for a survey of the country's legal materials; then use of an encyclopedia or treatise for a general understanding of the legal concepts involved; an examination of digests or summaries for a brief statement of the law governing the problem involved; followed by a more careful study of actual legal sources in translation; and finally to periodical articles for more detailed discussions and later developments.

1. BIBLIOGRAPHIC GUIDES

Research in the law of a country other than one's own should begin with an introduction to the legal materials available for that jurisdiction. This information can be found in comprehensive bibliographies or bibliographic guides to foreign law generally, or, preferably, in more detailed guides to the law of particular countries. The general bibliographies or guides are primarily useful as leads to particular books or articles on specific topics, whereas bibliographic surveys of individual countries can also provide a full description of the forms of law of that jurisdiction and their major legal publications. Many of these tools and sources are now available in English.

a. General

Perhaps the best comprehensive bibliography of foreign law is *A Bibliography on Foreign and Comparative Law,* compiled by Charles Szladits (Oceana, 1955–1982, with supplements), and includ-

5. In addition to Charles Szladits' comprehensive *Bibliography on Foreign and Comparative Law,* which is described below, each issue of two invaluable periodicals contain references to current foreign and comparative law sources, many of which are in English. These journals are the *American Journal of Comparative Law* and the *International Journal of Legal Information* (formerly the *International Journal of Law Libraries*).

ing books and articles in English. This work, now consists of nine volumes covering the period from 1790 to 1978. It is to continue with annual supplements and five year cumulations. The bibliography is arranged by subject with geographical and author indexes. There is a time lag of approximately three or four years in the publication of its supplements, but the work is also updated annually in the *American Journal of Comparative Law.*

Law Books Recommended for Libraries, described above in Chapter 15, is a compilation of annotated bibliographies on various fields of law. It includes as Volume 5 a useful bibliography of foreign law, also prepared by Charles Szladits, which contains sources in English and other languages. Several of the individual subject bibliographies in other volumes of this publication also include foreign law sources and several are devoted to particular foreign countries and systems.

The *International Encyclopedia of Comparative Law,* described below in Section 2, contains (in its *National Reports*) bibliographies on selective subjects in the law of each country covered.

Law Books in Print, also cited above in Chapter 15, lists law books, currently in print, in English on all subjects. As such, it includes many useful titles on foreign and comparative law. It is updated quarterly, with annual cumulations, by *Law Books Published.* Access is provided by author, title and subject.

Register of Legal Documentation in the World, 2nd ed. (1957), published by UNESCO, is a survey of the major legal sources of the countries of the world (as of that date). It contains still useful, although somewhat antiquated, information on codes, law reports, legal periodicals, bibliographies, and legal research centers for the countries listed. Regretfully, it has not been kept up to date and must be supplemented elsewhere. The *Register,* if revised regularly, would have been an invaluable research tool in foreign law.

Harvard Current and *Annual Legal Bibliography,* discussed above in Chapter 16, Legal Periodicals, indexed books and articles on law from all countries, from 1961 to 1981. Its annual volumes for that period contain separate sections on common law countries and civil law countries. The arrangement was by subject, with separate subdivisions thereunder by individual country. It was an excellent source for current publications on foreign law, but unfortunately has been discontinued.

Introduction Bibliographique a L'Histoire Du Droit et a L'Ethnologie Juridique/Bibliographical Introduction to Legal History and Ethnology (1963–in progress), edited by John Gilissen and being published in Brussels by the Institute Solvay in nine looseleaf volumes, is the most comprehensive series of *historical* bibliographies on individual countries and systems. Since its references are to the original language of publication and only a few of the sections are in English, its utility for most American researchers may be limited.

b. By Region

A few bibliographic guides or bibliographies have been prepared for particular regions or groups of countries. Where those areas or groupings share common problems, histories or legal forms, such guides are particularly useful. In some instances, they include the best available bibliographic coverage for a particular country. The following are quite varied examples of this form:

Africa

W.K. Oni & O.O. Gbinigie, *Sources of African Law—a Preliminary Checklist of African Legal Materials* (1975).

J. Vanderlinden, *African Law Bibliography* (1972–1981), covering 1947 to 1980 in 3v.

Developing Countries

R. Lansky, *Handbook of Bibliographies on Law in the Developing Countries* (1981).

W. Twining & J. Uglow, ed., *Legal Literature in Small Jurisdictions (1981).*

Europe (Eastern)

P.M. Leideritz, *Key to the Study of East European Law* (1978).

G. Walker, ed., *Official Publications of the Soviet Union and Eastern Europe, 1945–1980, a Selected Annotated Bibliography* (1982).

Europe (Western)

Council of Europe, *Bibliography of Translations of Codes and Other Laws of Private Law* (1975).

C.M. Germain, "European Community Law—A Selective Bibliography . . . " at 8 *Internatl. J. of Legal Information* 239–281 (1980).

P. Graulich, et al., *Guide to Foreign Legal Materials: Belgium, Luxembourg, Netherlands* (1968).

J. Jeffries, *A Guide to the Official Publications of the European Communities,* 2d ed. (1981).

C. Szladits, *Guide to Foreign Legal Materials: French, German, Swiss* (1959).

Latin America

S.A. Bayitch, *Latin American and the Caribbean, Bibliographic Guide to Works in English* (1967).

K. Wallach, *Union List of Basic Latin American Legal Materials* (1971).

Scandinavia

R.B. Ginsburg, *A Selective Survey of English Language Studies on Scandinavian Law* (1970).

Iuul, Malmstrom and Sondergaard, *Scandinavian Legal Bibliography* (1961).

c. By Country

A complete listing of all bibliographic guides to the law of individual countries in English would be impossible here. They exist in a variety of forms. The following is an illustrative selection of some works on a few countries of particular interest to American lawyers. Two series of guides are also noted, for Eastern Europe and Latin America. The Graulich, et al. and Szladits *Guides to Foreign Legal Materials,* noted above, are excellent for the several important countries covered in each of those regional works.

China	F. Lin, *Chinese Law Past and Present, A Bibliography of Enactments and Commentaries in English Text* (1966).
Denmark	J. Sondergaard, *Bibliography of Danish Law, 1950–1971* (1973).
Eastern Europe	Mid-European Law Project, *Legal Sources and Bibliography of . . .* (various East European countries). (1956–1964).
Ethiopia	J. Vanderlinden, *An Introduction to the Sources of Ethiopian Law* (1966).
Germany	German Association of Comparative Law, *Bibliography of German Law in English and German* (1964) with Suppl. 1964–1973, in 2v. (1969, 1975).
	R. Lansky, *English Books on the Law of the Federal Republic of Germany . . .* (1979).
Indonesia	J. Ball, *Bibliography of Materials on Indonesian Law in the English Language,* 3d ed. (1981).
Israel	J.R. Wegner, *A Bibliography of Israel Law in English and other European Languages* (1972).
Italy	A. Grisoli, *Guide to Foreign Legal Materials: Italian* (1965).
Japan	R. Coleman and J.O. Haley, *An Index to Japanese Law: A Bibliography of Western Language Materials 1967–1973* (1975), kept current in *Law in Japan: an Annual* (1967–date).
Latin America	U.S. Library of Congress, *Guide(s) to the Law and Literature of . . .* (various Latin American countries). (1917–1948). Although some-

what dated now, many of these *Guides* are still helpful.

Mexico — H. Clagett & D.M. Valderrama, *A Revised Guide to the Law and Literature of Mexico* (1973).

Nigeria — Harvard Law School Library, *Nigerian Legal Bibliography,* compiled by O. Jegede (1975).

Philippines — F.B. Moreno, *Philippine Legal Bibliography,* 2nd ed. (1962).

Spain — T.W. Palmer, *Guide to the Law and Literature of Spain* (1915, reprinted 1979).

J.T. Vance, *The Background of Hispanic-American Law: Legal Sources and Juridical Literature of Spain* (1937, reprinted 1979).

U.S.S.R. — Harvard Law School Library, *Soviet Legal Bibliography,* edited by V. Mostecky and W. E. Butler (1965).

d. By Subject

There are also useful bibliographic guides to law on particular subjects, which cover the law of individual countries on a world-wide or regional basis. Again, their number precludes a complete listing here, but the following examples indicate the types of coverage:

Air Law — W.P. Heere, *International Bibliography of Air Law 1900–1971* (1972), with *Supplement, 1972–1976* (1976).

L.C. Morris, *Bibliography of Air and Space Law Materials* (Southeast Publications, 1978).

Commercial Law — T.H. Reynolds, "Foreign Commercial Legislation in English", 69 *Law Library Journal* 41–59 (1976).

Corporations — E. Browndorf, *Bibliography of Multinational Corporations and Foreign Direct Investment,* 2v. looseleaf (1979–date).

Copyright — Paul T. Huang, *Bibliography on Copyright* (2nd ed., 1972).

F.J. Kase, *Copyright Thought in Continental Europe . . . a Selected and Annotated Bibliography* (1967).

Criminal Law — R. Rank, *The Criminal Justice Systems of Latin American Nations. A Bibliography of the Primary and Secondary Literature* (1974).

Environmental Law — F.L. Grieves, *International Law, Organization, and the Environment: A Bibliography and Research Guide* (1974).

Jurisprudence	R.W.M. Dias, *A Bibliography of Jurisprudence,* 2d ed. (1970).
Medical Jurisprudence	R.P. Brittain, *Bibliography of Medico-Legal Works in English* (1962).
Mergers	R. Sperry, *Mergers and Acquisitions, a Comprehensive Bibliography* (1972).
Patents	F.J. Kase, *Foreign Patents. A Guide to Official Patent Literature* (1972).
Taxation	R.M. Bird, *Bibliography on Taxation in Developing Countries* (1968).
	E.A. Owens, *Bibliography on Taxation of Foreign Operations and Foreigners* (1968) and Supplementary volume, 1968–1975 (1976).
Trademarks	F.J. Kase, *Trademarks. A Guide to Official Trademark Literature* (1974).

The most comprehensive listings of bibliographic guides and bibliographies on foreign law in both books and articles—whether general, or by region, country or subject—can be found in the various volumes and supplements of Szladits, *A Bibliography of Foreign and Comparative Law.* Local availability of particular titles can be determined in individual law library catalogs.

2. ENCYCLOPEDIAS AND TREATISES

a. General

Encyclopedias and treatises are invaluable sources of foreign legal bibliography. Their value stems from the inherent importance of *doctrine* in the civil law system and has considerable influence on actual legal research procedures. Although really effective research requires access to encyclopedias and treatises in the language of the country whose law is being studied, English language materials and English translations of vernacular works can be quite helpful for introductory research. These writings can again be divided into those of a general scope, those dealing with a region or group of countries, and those covering individual countries.

The *International Encyclopedia of Comparative Law* is the most comprehensive scholarly survey in English of the law of many countries and systems. It is projected to include seventeen volumes (many to be issued in several parts) and is arranged as follows:

Volume	
I	National Reports
II	The Legal Systems of the World/Their Comparison and Unification

Volume	
III	Private International Law
IV	Persons and Family
V	Succession
VI	Property and Trust
VII	Contracts in General
VIII	Specific Contracts
IX	Commercial Transactions and Institutions
X	Quasi-Contracts
XI	Torts
XII	The Law of Transport
XIII	Business and Private Organizations
XIV	Copyright and Industrial Property
XV	Labor Law
XVI	Civil Procedure
XVII	State and Economy

Note that it does *not* cover several large areas of public law, e.g. criminal law, social security, taxation, etc.

The *National Reports* volume, issued in many parts, includes coverage of most countries of the world, with material on the following ten topics: Constitutional System; Sources of Law; Historical Evolution of Private and Commercial Law; Private Law; Commercial Law; State Direction of Trade; Industrial Property Rights and Copyrights; Principles of Judicial Procedure in Civil and Commercial Cases; Private International Law and International Law of Procedure; and Selective Bibliography. Thus, when completed, this part alone will, in size and coverage, constitute a concise but very useful survey of the legal system and legal bibliography of every country, with brief lists of primary sources.

Among the useful general treatises of foreign law are David and Brierley, *Major Legal Systems in the World Today,* 2d ed. (1978), Merryman, *The Civil Law Tradition* (1969) and A. Watson, *The Making of Civil Law* (1981). Casebooks like Von Mehren's *The Civil Law System: Cases and Materials for the Comparative Study of Law,* 2d ed. (1977) and Schlesinger's *Comparative Law: Cases-Text-Materials* (4th ed., 1980) are also helpful introductions. For historical purposes, the excellent (but now outdated) studies of the *Continental Legal History Series* (10 vols., 1912–1928) are still quite helpful. The series was sponsored by the Association of American Law Schools and its authors were primarily distinguished European scholars. The individual volumes in the series cover a variety of topics, focusing largely on France, Germany and Italy.

b. By Region

The following publications covering specific regions and groups of countries can also be noted, as well as several series of monographs devoted to a particular region:

Africa

Two extensive series of monographs on specific legal topics in various Sub-Saharan African countries:

Law in Africa Series (1961–date)—not to be confused with the Butterworth's *African Law Series*, a competitive project which may now have lapsed.

Restatement of African Law, edited by E. Cotran (1968–date).

T.O. Elias. *Nature of African Customary Law* (1956). *Readings in African Law*, ed. by N. Rubin and E. Cotran (2 vols., 1970).

Eastern Europe

Leyden University. Documentation Office for East European Law. *Law in Eastern Europe*, ed. by Z. Szirmai (1958–date); now edited by F.J.M. Feldbrugge. An irregularly published series of monographs on specific legal topics in East European socialist countries.

Latin America

H.P. DeVries. *The Law of the Americas* (1965).

Middle East and Islam

J.N.D. Anderson. *Islamic Law in the Modern World* (1959, reprinted 1975).

N.J. Coulson. *A History of Islamic Law* (1978).

M. Khadduri and H.J. Liebensy. *Origin and Development of Islamic Law* (1955). Vol. 1 in series, *Law in the Middle East.*

D. Pearl. *A Textbook on Muslim Law* (1979).

J. Schacht. *An Introduction to Islamic Law* (1964).

Scandinavia

L.B. Orfield. *The Growth of Scandinavian Law* (1953).

Danish Committee on Comparative Law. *Danish and Norwegian Law. A General Survey* (1963); updated in part by *Danish Law: a General Survey* (1982).

c. By Country

Naturally, the most numerous category of treatises is that comprising works which deal with the law or legal system of a particular country. The following are but a few examples for countries of major interest:

France R. David. *French Law, its Structure, Sources and Methodology* (1972).

O. Kahn-Freund, et al. *A Source-book on French Law*, 2d ed. (1979).

F. H. Lawson, et al. *Amos and Walton's Introduction to French Law* (3rd ed., 1967).

Germany E.J. Cohn, ed. *Manual of German Law* (2 vols., 2nd ed., 1968).

Italy M. Cappelletti, J.H. Merryman and Joseph M. Perillo. *The Italian Legal System, An Introduction* (1967).

Japan A. von Mehren. *Law in Japan. The Legal Order in a Changing Society* (1963).

Sweden S. Stromholm, ed. *An Introduction To Swedish Law* (1981) 2v.

U.S.S.R. H.J. Berman. *Justice in the U.S.S.R.* (rev. ed., 1963).

G.D. Cameron III. *The Soviet Lawyer and his System, an Historical and Bibliographical Study* (1978).

J.N. Hazard, W.E. Butler and P.B. Maggs. *The Soviet Legal System; Fundamental Principles and Historical Commentary,* 3d ed. (1977).

F.J.M. Feldbrugge, ed. *Encyclopedia of Soviet Law* (2 vols., 1973).

G.C. Guins. *Soviet Law and Soviet Society* (1979).

3. DIGESTS, SUMMARIES AND TRANSLATIONS

After the introductory phase of foreign law research, the next step of the American lawyer or law student, when faced with a specific problem, may be to check digests, summaries or translations of laws on the subject and country involved. There are many such aids available in English—some are general in scope, some focus on a specific subject area. Their quality will depend on the care and expertise of the editors, on the accuracy of translation, on their thoroughness and—as with all legal materials—on whether they are revised and supplemented regularly to reflect the latest legal developments. With those caveats, the following is a small sampling of such publications.

a. General

Martindale-Hubbell Law Directory (annual revision), the last volume for each edition includes "Digests of the Laws of Foreign Countries"—contains summaries of law on selected topics, arranged by country and then by subject, with citations to primary sources. In 1981 and 1982, it was in Vol. 8, but in 1983, it is in Vol. 7.

World Peace Through Law Center. *Law and Judicial Systems of Nations* (looseleaf, 1965). Really a directory of lawyers, bar associations, judges, courts and law schools of many countries, with brief coverage of the legal system of each.

Arthur Andersen and Co. *Tax and Trade Guides.*

Deloitte, Haskins & Sells, *International Tax and Business Service.*

Ernst and Ernst. *International Business Series.*

Peat, Marwick, Mitchell and Company. *International Tax and Business Guides.*

Price, Waterhouse and Co. *Information Guide(s) for Doing Business in . . .* (various countries).

These last five large accounting firms issue (primarily for their larger clients, but with some distribution to libraries) a series of pamphlets on the laws of selected countries relating to taxation, trade and business operations. Their coverage and frequency of revision varies, but they can be useful and informative summaries. The Price, Waterhouse series covers the most countries, but the Andersen guides are generally the most comprehensive.

Organization of American States. *A Statement of the Law of . . .* (various Latin American countries) *in Matters Affecting Business.* A series of country studies, revised periodically, each covering a wide range of legal topics. Previously issued by the Pan American Union.

b. By Subject

This is a selective list of publications and services. Titles, formats and publishing practices change frequently, so current bibliographic sources should be checked for changes and new publications.

Commercial Law

National Association of Credit Management, *Digest of Commercial Laws of the World* (looseleaf, 8 vols., 1966–19__).

Foreign Tax Law Association, *Commercial Laws of the World* (looseleaf, 1956–19__).

H.L. Pinner, *World Unfair Competition Law* (looseleaf, 4 vols., 1978–19__).

World Law of Competition, edited by J.O. Von Kalinowski (looseleaf, 9 vols., 1979–19__).

Constitutional Law

A.P. Blaustein and G.H. Flanz, ed., *Constitutions of the Countries of the World* (looseleaf, 14 vols., projected, 1971–19__).

A.P. Blaustein and E.B. Blaustein, eds., *Constitutions of Dependencies and Special Sovereignties* (looseleaf, 3 vols. 1975–19__). Complements the above collection.

A.J. Peaslee, *Constitutions of Nations* (Vol. 1, rev. 4th ed., 1974; Vols. 2–4, rev. 3rd ed., 1965–1970).

	W.B. Simons, ed., *The Constitutions of the Communist World* (1980).
Copyright	UNESCO and WIPO, *Copyright Laws and Treaties of the World* (looseleaf, 3 vols., 1956–19__).
Criminal Law	N.Y.U. School of Law, Comparative Criminal Law Project. *The American Series of Foreign Penal Codes* (1960–19__). Individual volumes of translations of penal codes for many countries.
Environmental Law	*International Protection of the Environment; Treaties and Related Documents,* ed. by B. Rüster and B. Simma (26 vols., as of 1981, looseleaf, 1975–19__).
Food & Agriculture	Food and Agriculture Organization, *Food and Agricultural Legislation* (semi-annual).
Health Law	World Health Organization, *International Digest of Health Legislation* (Quarterly).
Industrial Property	World Intellectual Property Organization, *Industrial Property Laws and Treaties* (4 vols., looseleaf, 1976–19__).
Investment Law	International Center for Settlement of Investment Disputes. *Investment Laws of the World. The Developing Nations.* (looseleaf, 10 vols., 1972–19__).
	R. Blanpain, ed., *International Encyclopedia for Labour Law and Industrial Relations* (5 vols., looseleaf, 1977–19__).
Labor Law	International Labour Office, *Legislative Series* (bi-monthly).
	U.S. Dept. of Labor, *Labor Law and Practice in . . .* (various countries). Individual country studies, revised irregularly.
Licensing	L.J. Eckstrom, *Eckstrom's Licensing in Foreign and Domestic Operations . . . ,* by R. Goldscheider (2 vols., looseleaf, 1978–19__).
	G. M. Pollzien and E. Lange, *International Licensing Agreements* (2nd ed., 1973).
Patents	*Digest of Commercial Laws of the World: Patents and Trademarks,* ed. by G. Kohlik (2 vols., looseleaf, 1968–19__).
	W. Lang, *Foreign Patent Laws with Comparative Analysis* (looseleaf, 1968–19__).

J. W. Baxter & J. P. Sinnott, *World Patent Law and Practice* (3 vols., looseleaf, 1968–19__).

W. W. White and B. G. Ravenscroft, *Patents Throughout the World*, edited by A. M. Greene (2d ed., looseleaf, 1978–19__).

Population

Law and Population Monograph Series (1971–1977). Issued by the Law and Population Programme, Fletcher School of Law and Diplomacy, Tufts University. 45 vols.

Resources

Petroleum Legislation. *Middle East Basic Oil Laws and Concession Contracts.* (many vols., rev. with supplements, 1969–19__).

U.S. Bureau of Mines, *Summary of Mining and Petroleum Laws of the World*, by N. Ely, (1971–1974) 3 vols.

Taxation

Foreign Tax Law Association, a private publisher, issues two series of translations in looseleaf format for many countries: *Tax Laws of . . .* (various countries) and *Income Tax Service*. These are revised irregularly.

Great Britain. Board of Inland Revenue, *Income Taxes Outside of the United Kingdom* (multi-volume survey by countries; 5 vols., looseleaf, 1976).

Harvard Law School, International Tax Program, *World Tax Series. Taxation in . . .* (various countries). Comprehensive studies of taxation in individual countries.

Deloitte, Haskins and Sells, *International Tax and Business Service* (5 vols., looseleaf).

International Bureau of Fiscal Documentation. This organization publishes a variety of looseleaf services covering different forms of taxation in many countries. Among their current services are *African Tax Systems* (2 vols., looseleaf); *Guides to European Taxation* (4 vols., looseleaf); and *Corporate Taxation in Latin America* (2 vols., looseleaf).

Trade Law

Bureau of National Affairs, *International Trade Reporter* (2 vols., looseleaf, 1974–19__). Legal and business data arranged by topic and country.

Trademarks	A. M. Greene, ed., *Trademarks Throughout the World* (3d ed., looseleaf, 1979–19__).
Trade Secrets	A. N. Wise, *Trade Secrets and Know-How Throughout the World* (4 vols., looseleaf, 1974–19__).
Transportation	D. Hill & M. Evans, ed., *Transport Laws of the World* (4 vols., looseleaf, 1977–19__).

In addition to the foregoing publications, many individual codes, collections of laws and separate statutes of foreign countries have been translated into English and published.[6] They are listed in the various volumes and supplements of Szladits' *Bibliography on Foreign and Comparative Law* in Part II, Section 6, "Translations of Codes and Commentaries, Laws and Decrees." There are a few serial publications of such translations, e.g., *Collection of Yugoslav Laws* (Institute of Comparative Law, Belgrad); *Bulletin of Czechoslovak Law* (Union of Lawyers of the Czechoslovak Socialist Republic, 1960–19__); and *Law and Legislation in the German Democratic Republic* (Association of German Democratic Lawyers, East Germany, 1959–19__). Several periodicals are devoted to such translations (see Section 4 below).

Indexes in English to foreign legislation for particular regions or countries can also be helpful to the American researcher, even if the legislation itself hasn't been translated. See, for example: U.S. Library of Congress, *Index to Latin American Legislation 1950–1960,* 2 vols., *First Supplement 1961–1965,* 2 vols., *Second Supplement 1966–1970,* 2 vols., *Third Supplement, 1971–1975;* and the *African Law Digest* (annual, 1965–19__) which indexes legislation and regulations of various African countries.

4. PERIODICALS

Periodical articles are a valuable source of current information on foreign law in general, on the laws of individual countries, and on specific legal problems. Such writings are frequently by scholarly authors, often focus in detail on particular issues, and have the added value of reflecting the latest developments. The standard indexes to legal periodicals, described in Chapter 16, above, provide access to this extensive literature. The most useful sources today are the *Index to Foreign Legal Periodicals* and Szladits', *Bibliography on Foreign and Comparative Law.* Since many articles appear in the general American law journals, the *Index to Legal Periodicals, Legal Resources Index* and *Current Law Index* are also helpful.

There is also a useful guide to foreign legal periodicals (most of which are not in English) with information about country of origin,

6. Among recent translations of important civil codes, note I. S. Forrester's *The German Civil Code, as Amended to January 1, 1975* (1975) and M. Beltramo et al., *The Italian Civil Code* (1969). Somewhat surprisingly, no current English translation of the French Civil Code is available. However, in 1959 the Louisiana State Law Institute translated the famous work of M. Planiol, *Treatise on Civil Law* (6 vols., from the 12th ed. of 1939).

language of publication, subject coverage, etc. This aid is A. Blaustein, *Manual on Foreign Legal Periodicals and Their Index* (1962).

Among the leading English language periodicals specializing in foreign and comparative law are the *American Journal of Comparative Law* (quarterly) and the *International and Comparative Quarterly* (published by the British Institute of International and Comparative Law). There are also numerous journals and annuals in English which focus on the law of particular regions or countries, such as *African Law Studies* (annual, 1969–19__), *Annual Survey of African Law* 1967–19__), *Scandinavian Studies in Law* (annual, 1957–19__), *Inter-American Law Review* (semi-annual, 1959–19__), *Comparative Juridical Review* (annual, 1964–19__), *Journal of African Law* (quarterly, 1956–19__), *Journal of Islamic and Comparative Law* (irregular, 1966–19__), and *Lawasia* (1970–19__). A few journals are devoted entirely to translations from foreign law sources, e.g., *Chinese Law and Government* (quarterly, 1968–19__), *Law in Japan* (annual, 1967–19__), *Review of Socialist Law* (quarterly, 1975–19__), *Soviet Law and Government* (quarterly, 1962–19__), *Soviet Statutes and Decisions* (quarterly, 1964–19__), and for West Germany, *Law and State* (semi-annual, 1970–19__), *Yugoslav Law* (1979–19__).

Research law libraries in the United States subscribe to many foreign periodicals and local law libraries frequently request photocopies of less accessible journal articles from larger libraries, if the basic bibliographic information has been accurately obtained by the reader from the periodical indexes or bibliographies. Various union lists of the foreign periodical holdings of law libraries have been published to facilitate this process.[7]

E. RESEARCH IN ORIGINAL FOREIGN LANGUAGE SOURCES

It must be repeated that no research, even within a broad meaning of the word, can be undertaken in foreign law without using sources in their original language, and that literature available in English cannot supply more than a basic, though useful, informative orientation.[8] However, those law students who undertake research in a problem of foreign law, or a comparative study, are usually able to work with the language of at least one foreign country and can select

7. See, for example, Schwerin and Kavass, "Foreign Legal Periodicals in American Law Libraries 1973 Union List," 67 *Law Library Journal* 120–144 (1974) and Kavass, "Selected Soviet and Eastern European Periodicals of Special Interest to Lawyers . . . ", 10 *International J. of Legal Information* 102 (1982).

8. A British view: "The Committee does not believe that any study of the law of any country other than the most superficial one which would be well below any academic standard could be undertaken without literature which is available only in the language of the country concerned." Society of Public Teachers of Law, Committee on Libraries, in 13 *Journal of the Society of Public Teachers of Law*, New Series, 113 (1974).

such a jurisdiction as the field of their work. The following section is written for such researchers.

1. TERMINOLOGY

Even if acquainted with the language of the foreign law system to be studied, an American student or lawyer will have to adjust to some differences in the terminology. For example, one may find even "civil law" to be a rather confusing term, as it has at least three connotations. "Civil law" is used in English in distinction to common law, to represent the legal system described above. It is also used in this country to express the dichotomy between the areas of civil and criminal law, procedure, courts, etc. Finally, civil law (*droit civil* in French, *Zivilrecht* in German) is the continental term for private law. It has been explained above that a "code" is nothing more and nothing less than a statute comprehensively covering a field of law. "Jurisprudence" in countries of Latin culture means judicial decisions, not theory of law. The term "paragraph" generally in German law denotes an "article" of a statute, generally referred to as a section in the U.S.A.[9]

2. BASIC MATERIALS

The basic primary sources of law in civil law countries are (a) the serial "collections of laws" (i.e. of statutes, orders, etc.) and (b) collections of judicial decisions. As to the first category, there are two distinct patterns of collections of laws, one predominantly used in the countries of Latin culture, the other in the rest of Europe. A prototype of the first group of both publications, that of comprehensive official gazettes, is the *Journal Officiel de la Rèpublique Francaise* (its first series, *"Lois et dècrets"*). It contains laws, decrees, and various kinds of orders and ordinances of ministries and other agencies.[10] In addition, in many countries such gazettes carry various official announcements, appointments to certain positions, etc. They may be voluminous, as they often appear daily. The French and Italian versions have one volume a month; there are no cumulative indexes for long periods of time. (The French *Journal Officiel* has annual indexes, both by subject and chronology.) In other European

9. As an illustrative example of problems arising out of terminological issues in comparative research, see H. J. Berman "A Linguistic Approach to the Soviet Codification of Criminal Law and Procedure" in Barry, Feldbrugge, Lasok, eds., *Codification in the Communist World,* Leiden, 1975, pp. 39–52.

10. In a footnote to a title of a newly published law, in the *Journal Officiel,* the main materials showing the legislative history of the law are listed. These include texts of governmental drafts, reports of parliamentary committees, and verbatim reports on the parliamentary discussions. There are different views in Europe as to the importance of legislative history for the interpretation of a statute. Where the wording of the law is clear, legislative history cannot be used to show that the legislation actually intended to enact something different. Otherwise, the interpretation of a statute operates with governmental drafts and their successive changes, with governmental reports and explanatory remarks, with the *exposès* of ministers, etc. On the other hand, what individual members of the legislature had said during the discussion, is seldom taken into account when the legislative intent is reconstructed.

countries (including the Socialist countries, but not the U.S.S.R.), there is one central publication, in which only laws and secondary legal norms appear, such as orders and decrees of the governments, generally binding orders and regulation of the ministries, etc. This type is represented by the *Bundesgesetzblatt* in West Germany and in Austria. Instructions of ministries for internal use only, or official announcements and similar materials, are published in other official publications. The advantage of this system is the concentration of the most important laws and regulations in one easily accessible collection, usually a volume a year. There are cumulative indexes for periods of several years, so that locating an item of legislation may not be too difficult.

There exist incomparably fewer reported court decisions in civil law countries than there are in the United States; accordingly, there are fewer reporters. It may seem surprising that in the U.S.S.R., for example, on the federal level only one small collection of selected judicial decisions, published by the Supreme Court, exists. (In addition, selected arbitration decisions are reported.) On the other hand, there is an abundance of commercially published reporters both in West Germany and Italy.[11]

As to the standard citation of judicial decisions, the French practice uses, as a rule, citation to the three legal periodicals mentioned below, most often to the *Recueil Dalloz Sirey*. (Even the decisions of the *Cour de cassation* are usually not cited to the official reporter.) In West Germany, the decisions of the high courts are cited to the official collections, by the standard abbreviation of the court, the volume of the collection (not, however, year) and page: *BGHZ* 19,153 or *BGHSt* 20,296 for civil or criminal decisions of the *Bundesgerichtshof* (Federal Supreme Court); *BVerfGE* 7,377 of the *Bundesverfassungsgericht* (Federal Constitutional Court), or *BVerwGE* 19,339 of the *Bundesverwaltungsgericht* (Federal Administrative Tribunal). Most usually, decisions of the appeals courts of West Germany are reported in, and cited to, the leading German law review, the weekly *Neue Juristische Wochenschrift*.

3. RESEARCH APPROACH

Two works deal in depth with research into French law, both with the scholarly approach (Kahn-Freund, *A Source-book on French Law*, 2d ed.) and with that of the practising lawyer (de Vries, *Civil Law and the Anglo-American Lawyer*). For discussion of the extensive sources of West German law, Cohn's *Manual of German Law* has been already mentioned.

11. It should be noted that the distinction of official as opposed to unofficial reporters of judicial decisions is unimportant, if not meaningless, in civil law countries. In Italy, for example, no official set of reported decisions exists; in France the decisions of the *Cour de cassation* are published in the official *Bulletins des Arrêts* . . . (one for civil matters and another for criminal) whereas another high court, the *Conseil d'Etat's* decisions, together with the decisions of the *Tribunal des Conflicts*, appear in the unofficial *Collection Lebon*.

Where a foreign lawyer or student has to look for an answer to a problem in French law, one can probably start by perusing one of the large French legal encyclopedias, either the looseleaf services of the *Juris-Classeurs* [12] or in the *Répertoires* published by Dalloz. Both works are arranged by broad subjects. Although they are only guides to the material rather than authority to be cited, both encyclopedias have a high level of accuracy, are published under direction of law school professors or judges of high reputation, with articles now signed by their authors. The Dalloz encyclopedias,[13] which are currently updated by large supplements (*Mise à jour*), will be available in more of the large American law libraries than the huge system of the *Juris-Classeurs.*

As a further step, the researcher will probably want to use either some comprehensive treatise, or one of the three standard French periodicals, traditionally divided into several parts, which contain legislative texts, judicial decisions, and doctrinal articles. These now include the following (since the *Recueil Sirey,* was absorbed by *Recueil Dalloz* in 1965):

(a) *Recueil Dalloz Sirey* (cited, since 1945,[14] by the abbreviation D., year, and page (e.g., D.1975, 135).

(b) *La Semaine Juridique* (with a sub-title *Juris-classeur périodique*) the items of which are cited not by pages, but by consecutive numbers. The citation is by the abbreviation *J.C.P.*, year, part, and number of item (e.g. *J.C.P.* 1975, II. 139).

(c) Somewhat less frequently the *Gazette du Palais* is used, cited by the abbreviation *Gaz.Pal.*, year, the half-year (as the issues are published in two volumes a year) and page (e.g. *Gaz.Pal.* 1975, I. 78).

For French administrative law, the part "Droit administratif" of the periodical, *Actualités juridiques,* may be very useful in locating materials, including the decisions of administrative tribunals (citation *A.J.D.A.*).

The weight of judicial decisions in French legal practice (greater, perhaps, than in many other civil law countries) has been mentioned. However, the reading of the decisions of French courts (other than the *Conseil d'Etat,* the supreme administrative tribunal), and especially of the *Cour de cassation,* is difficult for a foreign lawyer. Each judgment, in the traditional French format, is in one long sentence, broken only by many "whereases". The language of the West

12. See description in Szladits' *Guide to Foreign Legal Materials: French etc.* (p. 396 above) at 81ff.

13. There is, first the general encyclopedia of French law, Dalloz *Nouveau Répertoire de droit,* containing in a not too concise form ample references to sources. The voluminous encyclopedias of individual fields include the following: *Répertoire de droit civil, Répertoire de droit pénal et de procédure pénale, Répertoire de procédure civile et commerciale, Répertoire de droit commercial, Répertoire de droit public et administratif, Répertoire de droit social et du travail,* and *Répertoire notarial.*

14. Previous to 1945 several different forms of citation have been used consecutively, as the *Recueil* has changed its format; for those older forms see Szladits' *Guide . . . French,* supra, on p. 71.

German courts, as well as of the courts in other parts of Europe, is in narrative form and opinions clearly given.

Now to the usual steps by which a German, Austrian, or Czechoslovak attorney or judge proceeds when confronted with a question of law he or she is unable to answer offhand. The first step of a lawyer in those countries is usually to reach for the much used edition of a code (or a cumulative index to statutory law, if the problem may not be governed by a code). These tools are used to find the basic statutory provision or provisions, which may, for example, be a short section of a code. The country's systematically arranged legal rules should permit easy locating of such basic provisions as may serve as a starting point for further detailed examination of legal problems. From this, one proceeds to a large commentary, i.e., a heavily annotated edition of the code.[15] Here one can find a condensed—or, sometimes, a quite extensive—comment on the provision which has been found; reference to other statutory provisions or to secondary legislation and other secondary regulation; citation of cases and extensive citation of treatises and articles in periodicals.

The next step may be to inspect two or three major treatises, to use as authority for the position to be taken, and also to see the existing problems and ramifications of the issue researched. Finally, with this background, the lawyer will search for cases dealing with the problem. As there are no publications similar to *Shepards Citations* (again, the main reason being that judicial decisions are not "primary" law), the decisions found may be checked and updated through indexes to the collections of decisions, or through some digests (if available),[16] or with the aid of the most recent treatises or articles dealing with the subject.

The above description of how to start research into the law of two of the most important European jurisdictions was but a sample demonstration of one possible approach. Similar techniques for many other jurisdictions would be beyond the scope of this chapter. For some countries, it is not too difficult for a foreign lawyer to begin looking for information in the original language, because a general collection of the most important primary material has been compiled and is available as a springboard for more thorough research. Those acquainted with the respective languages may find, for example, the initial approach to Danish law to be relatively easy (as there exists an excellent, regularly updated commercial compilation of Danish law, *Karnovs Lovsamling*) or to the law of Belgium (where *Les Codes Larcier* are an annotated compilation of that country's law). Compilations of statutes and secondary legislation have been published in large looseleaf services in Austria, where there is also a very helpful

15. This sort of publication, frequent in West Germany, Austria, or Switzerland, is essentially a voluminous treatise, the contents of which are arranged in the order of the "paragraphs" of the code.

16. In a few countries there exist, mostly on a yearly basis, indexes of both judicial decisions and legal writings which make an easy check possible. In West Germany, such are the various sets of the *Fundhefte*, each for a broad subject area of law.

index of the appellate decisions and legal literature, *(Index der Rechtsmittelentscheidungen und des Schrifttums*, compiled by R. Stohanzl et al.). Similar services exist for Switzerland, in either French or German. In other countries, such compilations may not exist and the researcher must then decide on the best approach—most often starting with a treatise or textbook relevant to the problem at hand. This is true even for such an immense jurisdiction as the U.S.S.R.; here, however, the abundance of literature in English may be a substantial help.

Frequently, the *International Encyclopedia of Comparative Law* can supply the researcher with much needed information as to the basic sources for that country. The sections, "Sources of Law" and "Selective Bibliography" for individual countries in the excellent introductory volumes of *National Reports* are useful for this purpose—if a report has already been published on the country in question.

4. DICTIONARIES AND ABBREVIATIONS

For American lawyers working with foreign legal texts or even with books and articles in English on foreign law (which frequently use terms in the original language, if they do not have an accurate English equivalent), foreign language dictionaries are essential. *Legal* dictionaries or glossaries which convert from the foreign language to English are also important aids to effective research. Fortunately, there are available a variety of multilingual and bilingual law dictionaries which include English, and, of course, many more bilingual *general* dictionaries to choose from.

The following multilingual legal dictionaries can be noted:

R. Herbst, *Dictionary of Commercial, Financial and Legal Terms*, 3 vols. (Zug Translegal, 1968–1975). Includes English, German and French.

L.D. Egbert & F. Morales-Macedo, *Multilingual Law Dictionary* (Oceana, 1978). Includes English, Dutch, French and Spanish.

E. LeDocte, *Legal Dictionary in Four Languages*, 2d ed. (Fred B. Rothman, 1978). Includes English, Dutch and German equivalents for French legal terms and provides indexes for each of the languages covered.

Bilingual legal dictionaries include the following:

Afrikaans:	V.G. Hiemstra & H.L. Gonin, *English/Afrikaans Legal Dictionary*, 2d ed. (Juta, 1963).
	C. Marais, *Marais' Juridical Dictionary: Afrikaans-English, English-Afrikaans* 2d ed. (Hennop, 1980).
Arabic:	J. Szentendrey, *Arabic-English Legal Glossary* (Harvard Law School Library, 1973).
	I.I. Wahab, *Law Dictionary; English-Arabic . . . ,* 2d ed. (Librairie du Liban, 1972).

Chinese: P.R. Bilancia, *Dictionary of Chinese Law and Government: Chinese-English* (Stanford, 1981).

Danish: F. Nielsen, *Anglo-Amerikansk/Dansk Retsordbog* (Nordisk Forlag, 1975).

French: See multilingual dictionaries above, and R. Aghion, *Dictionaire Juridique, Anglais-Francais . . .* (Brentano's, 1947).

A. Chandesaigues-Deysine, *Dictionaire anglais-francais et lexique francais-anglais des termes politiques, juridiques et economiques* (Flammarion, 1978).

Dictionnaire Juridique: Nouveau Dictionnaire Th. A. Quemner: Francais-Anglais . . . (Editions de Navarre, 1977).

German: See multilingual dictionaries above, and D.H. Beseler & B. Jacobs, *Law Dictionary: Technical Dictionary of the Anglo-American Legal Terminology, English-German*, 3d ed. (de Gruyter, 1976).

E.A. Geissler, *Juristisches Worterbuch, Englisch-Deutsch* (Verlag, Enzyklopedie, 1980).

H.P. Kniepkamp, *Legal Dictionary: English-German and German-English* (Oceana, 1954).

Greek: G.A. Perris, *Greek-English Dictionary of Legal Terms* (Kivotos, 1980).

Latin: R.S. Vasan, *Latin Words and Phrases for Lawyers* (Law & Business, 1980).

Russian: N. Prischepenko, *Russian-English Law Dictionary* (Praeger, 1969).

Spanish: L.A. Robb, *Dictionary of Legal Terms: Spanish-English and English-Spanish* (Wiley, 1955).

G.N. Vanson, *Spanish—English Legal Terminlogy* (South-Western Publ. Co., 1982).

Swedish: T. Backe, et al., *Concise Swedish-English, Glossary of Legal Terms* (Fred B. Rothman, 1971).

Welsh: R. Lewis, *Welsh Legal Terms* (Gomerian, 1972).

Zulu: J.C. Bekker, *Zulu Legal Terminology* (Qualitas, 1978).

The foregoing sampling is intended only to indicate the range of languages covered by such legal glossaries. Many more are available on these and other languages, and in particular subject fields. A few examples of such specialized legal dictionaries include the following:

S.F. Al-'Adah, *Dictionary of Diplomacy and International Affairs, English-French-Arabic,* (Librairie Liban, 1974).

European Communities Glossary, French-English, 7th ed. (Office of Official Publications of the European Communities, 1979).

F.J. Kase, *Dictionary of Industrial Property, Legal and Related Terms: English, Spanish, French and German* (Sythoff & Noordhoff, 1980).

WIPO Glossary of Terms of the Law of Copyright and Neighboring Rights, English-French-Spanish (World Intellectual Property Organization, 1980).

For locating legal and non-legal dictionaries of foreign languages, one can use the reference sources noted above in Section C.4.a of Chapter 17, General Research and Reference Sources. Most helpful is A.M. Brewer, ed., *Dictionaries, Encyclopedias, and Other Word-Related Books,* 3d ed. (Gale Research, 1981).

The extensive and confusing use of abbreviations in foreign law is alleviated somewhat by the availability of several guides to abbreviations. These include:

Benelux: A. Sprudzs, *Benelux Abbreviations and Symbols: Law and Related Subjects* (1971).

French: G. Leistner, *Abbreviations, Guide to French Forms in Justice and Administration,* 2d ed. (1975).

A. Sprudzs, *Foreign Law Abbreviations: French* (1967).

German: H. Kirchner, *Abkuerzungsverzeichnis der Rechtsprache,* 2d ed. (1968).

Italian: A. Sprudzs, *Italian Abbreviations and Symbols: Law and Related Subjects* (1969).

In addition to those for specific languages, the two general abbreviation guides described above also include some foreign abbreviations: D.M. Bieber, *Dictionary of Legal Abbreviations Used in American Law Books* (1979) and M.D. Powers, *The Legal Citation Directory* (1971). The *Uniform System of Citation,* 13th ed. (1981), the "Bluebook", also contains a section on foreign citations and abbreviations.

Translators and translation services are often needed by lawyers, both in litigation and for routine interpretation of foreign language documents and texts. Many individuals and firms offer such services to the legal profession and their advertisements appear regularly in legal newspapers and practitioner-oriented periodicals such as the *American Bar Association Journal.* In addition, the following guide is one of several which are helpful in locating suitable specialists: S. Congrat-Butlar, *Translation and Translators: An International Directory and Guide* (R.R. Bowker, 1979).

F. RESEARCH BY COMPUTER IN FOREIGN AND COMPARATIVE LAW

Some foreign law is now, or soon will be, available through the same on-line data retrieval systems which are used to access American legal material.

WESTLAW has recently added EUROLEX, a data base currently in use in England. Designed by the London-based European Law Centre, EUROLEX provides coverage of English, Scottish and Continental European legal materials in English. Some of the "libraries" available in EUROLEX correspond to printed publications of the European Law Centre, such as *Common Market Law Reports, European Commercial Cases, European Human Rights Reports,* and *European Law Digest.* Most of the rest of the data base focuses on British primary legal sources.

WESTLAW's American competitor, LEXIS, is already making available the decisions of the European Court of Justice, and is planning to offer four data bases on the law of France (in French). These will cover French public and private law, and are stated to include fifteen or more years of reported and unreported court decisions; statutes; decrees; and regulations.

Computerized legal research systems are being developed or are operational on a limited basis, in several European and Latin American countries.

For information on European data bases, a useful guide is now available: *Databases in Europe, 1982* (Commission of the European Communities, 1982).

If problems of communication and system inter-face can be solved and the inevitable political and copyright issues resolved, it is conceivable that today's modest beginnings toward a world network for the exchange of legal information may become a reality.

G. ADDITIONAL READING

H. Berman, *Justice in the USSR,* rev. ed. (Harvard Univ. Press, 1963). A popular, but now dated introduction to the Soviet legal system.

R. David and J.E.C. Brierley, *Major Legal Systems in the World Today,* 2d ed. (Free Press, 1978). A broad view of the common law, civil law, socialist, religious and traditional legal systems.

J.P. Dawson, *The Oracles of the Law* (University of Michigan Law School, 1968). A superb comparative analysis of the role of case law in English, Roman, French and German legal development.

H.P. De Vries, *Civil Law and the Anglo-American Lawyer* (Oceana, 1976). Although based on French law, a useful and current introduction to the civil law system, designed for American lawyers.

H.P. De Vries and J. Rodriguez-Novas, *The Law of the Americas* (Oceana, 1965). An introduction to the legal systems of the American republics.

M.A. Glendon, M.W. Gordon & C. Osakwe, *Comparative Law Traditions in a Nutshell* (West Publishing Co., 1982).

F.H. Lawson, *A Common Lawyer Looks at the Civil Law* (University of Michigan Law School, 1955). The "form and sources of the civil law" in an excellent and readable treatment.

J.H. Merryman, *The Civil Law Tradition* (Stanford University Press, 1969). Coverage of the basic sources of civil law and the use of such materials in interpretation and research.

A.T. Von Mehren, *The Civil Law System: An Introduction to the Comparative Study of Law* (Little, Brown, 2d ed., 1977). Provides insight into the workings of the civil law as typified by the French and German legal systems.

A. Watson, *The Making of Civil Law* (Harvard Univ. Press, 1981). A comparative study of the civil law in Western European and Latin American countries, with the view that differences between civil and common law systems are more rooted in legal history than in social, economic, or political developments.

Chapter 21

INTERNATIONAL LAW *

A. INTRODUCTION

According to its traditional definition, international law consists of a body of rules governing the relations between states. Its historical function, which many still consider its primary purpose, was the preservation of peace. Its many failures to accomplish this objective has led some writers to question its usefulness and at times its very existence as a branch of law.

International law is indeed inextricably related to foreign policy, economic relationships and power balance. Furthermore, it has no legislative body, no executive, no enforceable sanctions. The publicity given to its failures, such as breaches of treaties, only contributes to its poor public image.

* This Chapter has been prepared by Emeritus Professor Vaclav Mostecky, University of California Law School, Berkeley, and is based on revision and updating of his Chapter on this subject in the 7th edition.

Yet a great lawyer, John Bassett Moore, stated that "International law is on the whole as well observed as municipal law." In fact, it would be impossible to mail a letter overseas, place a telephone call to Paris, conduct trade with foreign countries, exchange currencies, travel beyond one's border, or maintain diplomatic offices in foreign capitals, without international law. Self-interest and reciprocity are the most effective guarantees of observation. Its existence is rarely denied by governments: at the height of the Vietnam conflict, for example, all parties constantly invoked the rules of international law although some were not signatories to the treaties governing military operations.

The pressure of the world public opinion is another effective way of enforcing international law. The seizure of the American Embassy personnel by Iran was clearly illegal. The United States Government carried its complaint through the proper United Nations organs, including the General Assembly, the Security Council, and finally the International Court of Justice. The first vote of the Court was unanimously against Iran; the second—since the crisis in Afghanistan intervened—with one dissenting vote. Not long thereafter, Iran was forced to bring its own complaint before the U.N., against the Iraqi invasion. The Iranian delegates found themselves so hopelessly isolated in the United Nations headquarters that the Iranian Government felt compelled to seek an end to the hostage crisis. Through the good offices first of Germany, then later and successfully of Algeria, the hostages were released and a basic rule of international law was restored.

In recent years, the concept and scope of international law have been considerably broadened. For several centuries, at least since the publication of Hugo Grotius' *Of the Law of War and Peace* in 1625, the object of international law was to establish rules of warfare and to supply a system of principles which would govern inter-state relations in times of peace. Oppenheim's *International Law* treatise which was published three hundred years later in 1905 and remained the basic textbook for half a century, continued to reflect the traditional approach and treat in two separate volumes the law of peace and the law of war. While the preoccupation with the preservation of peace has not been abandoned by contemporary authors, there is more concern with economic, social, cultural and trade relations between countries, in the firm belief that increased trade, communications, and reduction of economic and social disparities will ultimately serve the cause of peace more effectively.

A parallel development can be seen in the work of international organizations. While newspapers concentrate their reporting on the political organs of the United Nations such as the Security Council and the General Assembly, much of the useful and successful activity of the Economic and Social Council and of the specialized agencies of the U.N. remains virtually unknown to the general public.

International law is traditionally divided into two branches, public and private. The former regulates the relations of states among themselves and with each other's nationals. The latter is concerned with questions of choice of law in private litigation when the laws of two or more jurisdictions might apply to a given transaction, and to the enforcement of foreign judgments. In this country, private international law is better known as conflict of laws and is often considered a part of domestic law. The basic rules of conflict of laws and private international law are identical. The division of the law into public and private is a characteristic of the continental civil law system with which international law has had close ties throughout its history.

The hierarchy of sources of international law as established by the Statute of the International Court of Justice also somewhat resembles the hierarchy of sources of law in a civil law system.

Sources of International Law

a. International conventions, whether general or particular, establishing rules expressly recognized by the signatories;

b. International custom, as evidence of general practice accepted as law;

c. The general principles of law recognized by all or most nations;

d. . . . judicial decisions and the teachings of the most highly qualified publicists of the various nations, as subsidiary means for the determination of rules of law.[1]

This hierarchy of sources can serve as a guide to research in international law. In approaching a problem, the researcher will first consult a treatise for general information and for help in accurately analyzing the issues. One will then determine whether there is a treaty covering the problem. If a treaty provision is found, it will be useful to trace its legislative history in the U.S. Senate and the preparatory work leading to the signing of the treaty. The next step is to find judicial cases interpreting the pertinent provisions of the treaty. Finally, the researcher will check scholarly writings for concurring or opposing views. If there was no treaty provision covering the issue, one will turn to "international custom" and "general principles of law." To find how these apply, the same process will be followed as in interpreting a treaty provision. One will look for cases and scholarly works dealing with the problem, but will also determine whether there is an established United States practice in the matter.

The following pages will deal with each of these approaches in some detail. Much of the pertinent American material has already been covered in previous chapters. While some repetition will be unavoidable, most of the following discussion will be focused on books specifically dealing with international law and those published by international organizations. The treatment of foreign law sources, although very important in international law research, will be limited to a few examples selected from the major foreign jurisdictions. The

1. Article 38 of the Statute of the I.C.J. (June 26, 1945).

preceding Chapter on Foreign and Comparative Law, may offer further helpful leads.

B. GENERAL TEXTS, REFERENCE WORKS, AND BIBLIOGRAPHIES

1. GENERAL TEXTS

The special importance of doctrine—as the French refer to treatises—has been stated earlier. Because of the relative lack of reference materials in the field and because of its vastness, even an experienced international lawyer will keep a basic text at hand, and often refer to it. For many years, Oppenheim's treatise cited earlier and Hyde's three-volume *International Law Chiefly as Interpreted and Applied by the United States* (1922; 2d ed., 1945) were standard texts used in most international law courses.

A shorter survey, *The Law of Nations* by J.L. Brierly, first published in 1928 (latest edition 1963), remains very useful as an authoritative introductory text. Brownlie's *Principles of Public International Law* (3d. ed., 1979) has a similar scope but is more up-to-date. Among the modern general treatises, Schwarzenberger's two volume *International Law* (Vol. 1, 3d. ed., 1957, Vol. 2, 1968) relies heavily on decisions of international courts in its systematic treatment of the whole field of international law. Other leading works include: Schwarzenberger's shorter *Manual of International Law,* (6th ed., 1976), Asbeck's *International Society in Search of a Transnational Legal Order* (1976) with an extensive bibliography, and Lissitzyn's *International Law Today and Tomorrow* (1965).

Phillip C. Jessup who was a Judge at the International Court of Justice is probably the first author to combine public and private international law and apply it to such varied issues as copyright, taxes, inheritance, and air lanes in his *Lectures on International Law* (1956). He was followed by Katz and Brewster in their *Law of International Transactions and Relations* (1960), by Chayes, Ehrlich and Lowenfeld in *International Legal Process* (1968), and by Steiner and Vagts in their *Transnational Legal Problems* (2d ed., 1976). These in many respects pioneer works preserve a broad scope and treat a wide range of issues affecting states, individuals, and their inter-relationships. In the 1970's the number of books combining all branches of international law with national law has increased at a fast rate and has also become more specialized, dealing primarily with trade and economic relations.

In criminal law, only two books with a similar subject matter will be listed: Evans & Murphy's *Legal Aspects of International Terrorism* (1978) and Bassiouni's *International Criminal Law* (1981) which both deal with skyjacking, taking of hostages and other aspects of terrorism.

In the last decade, a brand new medium made its appearance: audio and audio-visual cassettes. Among the first cassettes in international law are *Reflection on Trends in International Law,* by the late R.R. Baxter, Professor and Judge on the International Court of Justice (1977); and Professor McDougal's *Reflections on American Perspectives on International Law,* (1976).

For private international law, perhaps the best of the many available treatises is *Dicey and Morris on Conflict of Laws* (10th ed., 1980). In addition, volume 3 of the *International Encyclopedia of Comparative Law* covers "Private International Law." Chapter 2 of that volume, "Sources," is a useful survey of both international and national publications in this field.

2. REFERENCE WORKS

Since the only special dictionary in international law is available in French, one must rely for an explanation of terms on general legal dictionaries. In 1938, the International Federation of National Academies of Arts and Sciences agreed to sponsor the publication of a dictionary of terminology of international law. Delayed by the war, it was finally published in 1960 under the French title *Dictionnaire de la Terminologie du Droit International.* Each term is accompanied by explanations and examples supported by citations to sources. The tables at the end of the volume are bilingual from English, German, Italian and Spanish to French, enabling the user to find the French equivalent of a term and refer to the text for its meaning and usage. The text itself, however, is only in French.

Much useful information on international and regional organizations and problems can be found in the extensive annual editions of Europa Publications, Ltd., London. These include: *The Europa Yearbook; A World Survey; The Far East and Australasia; The Middle East and North Africa;* and *Africa South of the Sahara.*

In 1981, the leading German research center, Max Planck Institute for Comparative Public Law and for International Law, began publication of an *Encyclopedia of Public International Law.*[2] Although it is too early to review the work, the sponsor's name is a sufficient guarantee of its scholarly quality. In spite of the German publisher, the signed articles are in English. The French have had an encyclopedia of international law for some time (Dalloz *Répertoire de Droit International,* 1968–69, 2 vols., supplements) and the Germans for two decades (*Wörterbuch des Völkerrechts,* 1960–62, 3 vols., ed. by Karl Strupp; rev. 2d ed. by H.J. Schlochauer). Both contain signed articles, well selected bibliographies, and give special attention to diplomatic law and to judicial opinions. The new *Encyclopedia of Public International Law* in English will undoubtedly quickly become an important reference source in this field.

Some biographic information is available in the specialized *Who's Who in the United Nations and Related Agencies* (1975) and the annual *International Who's Who* is also helpful. J. Robinson's *In-*

2. Projected for 5 vols. (North-Holland Publishing Co., 1981–19__).

ternational Law and Organization (1967) contains over twelve hundred names of international lawyers and authors with reference to their writings. It will be found useful for the identification of contemporary writers, diplomats and lawyers, although it is also retrospective. The names of American diplomatic personnel currently assigned overseas appear in *Foreign Service List,* published three times a year by the Department of State. Foreign diplomats accredited to the United States are listed in the parallel *Diplomatic List.* Similar directories are made available by foreign countries and by the major international organizations, such as the United Nations. Other biographical data may be found in many periodicals and yearbooks in the field.

3. BIBLIOGRAPHIES

Although there is no comprehensive bibliography on international law, several recent publications have partially filled that need. J. Robinson, *International Law and Organization, General Sources of Information* (1967) is a good bibliographic survey of the field, but will need updating. J. G. Merrills' *Current Bibliography of International Law* (1978) covers a selection of books and articles from 1960–1977. It is strong in traditional subjects, but weak on documents and newer topics. See also I. Delupis, *Bibliography of International Law* (Bowker, 1975). In 1976, the Max Planck Institute in Heidelberg began publication of a new and scholarly series, *Public International Law: A Current Bibliography of Articles on Public International Law* (2 vols. per year). The semi-annual volumes supplement the basic work *Public International Law; a Bibliography of Articles* (1975).

One still has to rely on general services such as the standard legal periodical indexes for articles (see Chapter 16 above) and *Law Books in Print,* 4th ed. in 5 v. (Glanville Publishers, 1982) for books. Current lists, however, appear in many journals. The *American Journal of International Law* contains a bibliographic section and is known for its authoritative book reviews; articles are arranged by journal rather than by subject. An annotated list, *Foreign Affairs Bibliography* issued in ten year cumulations (the volume covering 1962–1972, published in 1976, is the latest available), has a section on international law. A *Fifty-Year Index,* of vols. 1–50, 1922–1972, compiled by R. J. Palmer (N.Y., Bowker, 1973) is also available. An annotated selection of over two thousand titles has been published as *The Foreign Affairs 50-Year Bibliography; New Evaluations of Significant Books on International Relations 1920–1970,* edited by B. Dexter (1972).

There are also lists of books received by the two United Nations Libraries in New York and Geneva. From 1960 to 1981, the Harvard Law School Library issued its *Annual Legal Bibliography,* supplemented by the monthly *Current Legal Bibliography,* which contained separate sections on public and private international law and included books as well as selected articles in periodicals and collections of essays. This useful bibliography is no longer published.

Most major treatises on international law can be used as bibliographic sources. Schwarzenberger's *Manual of International Law* (6th ed., London, 1976) devoted more than two hundred pages to a systematic listing of books and articles in the field. It also contains a short glossary of terms and a list of abbreviations. Volume 6, International Law, of *Law Books Recommended for Libraries,* compiled by the Association of American Law Schools and published in 1968, is a basic list of the more important international law documents, serials, and treatises, with brief annotations.

The most comprehensive retrospective listing can be found in the published catalogs of libraries with large holdings in international law: the Peace Palace Library at the Hague; Cambridge University Squire Law Library; Columbia University Law Library; and Harvard Law School Library's *Catalog of International Law and Relations.* The latter appeared in twenty volumes in 1965–66 and is a photo-reproduction of the card catalog with entries under authors, titles and subjects in a single alphabetical sequence. It contains close to one hundred thousand titles in all languages and is uniquely helpful in the identification of documents of international conferences and organizations.

There are some useful bibliographies in specific fields of international law such as air law, law of the sea, etc., but their large number and specialized topics are beyond the scope of this general survey. An excellent recent example of such a bibliography (actually an annotated bibliography of bibliographies) focusing on one area is *Peace and War, A Guide to Bibliographies,* by B.A. Carroll, C.F. Fink & J.E. Mohraz (ABC-Clio, 1983).

C. TREATIES

The research problems relating to treaties may be grouped into three broad categories: (1) Locating the text of the treaty; (2) Determining whether a particular treaty is in force, for what parties and with what reservations; and (3) Interpreting the text of the treaty.

1. LOCATING THE TEXT

Treaties are usually cited by their title which indicates their general subject content. Lists of treaties are often arranged by the date of their signature (as opposed to the date of entry into force, which usually follows the exchange of ratification instruments as provided for in the final clause of the treaty). Since there is no provision for registration of draft treaties and no draft treaty service is available, it is not easy to locate the text of a treaty before it has been ratified and entered into force. The time which may elapse between the signing and the ratification may be months or years. Drafts prepared by international conferences appear in their proceedings; other texts may be found in the periodical literature (see below); U.S. draft agreements appear as Senate documents by session and letter (Senate Executive Document A, B, C, etc.).

The official text of a treaty which has been ratified and is now in force is published in the official gazettes issued by the countries of the continental legal system, in their statutory series, or in separate treaty series.

Since treaties are functionally part of the statutory law of the United States, their forms of publication are dealt with in detail in Section 7b of Chapter 7, Statutes and Related Materials, above. Research aids for locating and using treaties will, however, be described below.

A researcher interested in treaties to which the United States is not a party, in agreements which have not yet entered into force, or in those which have been terminated, will have to use either foreign sources or publications of international organizations. The most comprehensive current collection of treaties is the *United Nations Treaty Series* which has been published by the United Nations Secretariat since 1946 and which continues a similar publication, the *League of Nations Treaty Series,* going back to 1919. Over one-thousand volumes of UNTS have appeared so far at the rate of some thirty to forty a year.

Still the series is by no means complete. The registration and publication of treaties was prescribed by Art. 102 of the United Nations Charter which reads:

1. Every treaty and every international agreement entered into by any Member of the United Nations after the present Charter comes into force shall as soon as possible be registered with the Secretariat and published by it.
2. No party to any such treaty or international agreement which has not been registered in accordance with the provisions of paragraph 1 of this Article may invoke that treaty or agreement before any organ of the United Nations.

Although the text of Art. 102 appears to allow for no exception to treaty registration, it has been interpreted as being limited to agreements registered with the UN Secretariat on the initiative of one of its parties and to treaties to which the United Nations is a party or at least official depository.

Because of the relative vagueness of these provisions and the lack of sanctions (except that no party to an unregistered treaty may invoke it before any organ of the U.N.), a considerable number of treaties never find their way into the series. It has been estimated, for example, that less than one out of five treaties which appear in the French *Journal Official* can be found in *UNTS.* Recently France has increased significantly the number of its registrations.

Another problem which constantly plagues researchers in this field is the delay with which treaties appear in the UN series. This is due not only to the fact that the Secretariat has to wait for the initiative of one of the signatories for registration, but also to the necessity for translating into English and French the treaties in another official language.

The *UNTS* carries the texts of treaties in their entirety, first in their official language, followed by English and French translations as needed. At the end of each volume there is a section listing the deposit of instruments of ratification by various countries.

Indexes were originally published for every one hundred volumes of *UNTS,* and more recently they have been issued for every fifty volumes. The indexes consist of the following three sections: (1) a chronological index, where treaties are listed in the order of the date on which they were signed; (2) a separate chronological list of multilateral agreements; and (3) an alphabetical index by country and subject. The indexes use only broad subject headings and do not attempt to analyze individual provisions of the treaties. Their publication has been very slow and it is often necessary to check dozens of still unindexed volumes to find a particular treaty.

In the past several years, great efforts have been made to improve the arrangement of older treaties and their accessibility. United States treaties appeared in the *Statutes at Large,* together with other legislative documents. Since 1950, they were published separately in *U.S. Treaties and International Agreements.* In order to facilitate access to earlier treaties scattered through *Statutes at Large,* I. I. Kavass and M. A. Michael brought out a *Cumulative Index, 1776–1949, U.S. Treaties and Other International Agreements* (Hein, 1975), 4 vols. Then, Kavass & Sprudzs issued *U.S.T. Cumulative Index, 1950–1970,* (Hein, 1973), 4 vols., with *Supplement, 1971–1975* (Hein, 1977); the *U.S.T. Cumulative Indexing Service 1976–1978* (Hein, 1978) looseleaf; and more recently, for later U.S. treaties, the *Current Treaty Index 1982* (Hein, 1982). With Blake as co-author, Kavass also compiled a parallel index of statutory texts dealing with international law and affairs entitled *United States Legislation on Foreign Relations and International Commerce; A Chronological and Subject Index of The Laws and Resolutions of the Congress* (Hein, 1976), 3 vols.

One of the most ambitious projects of treaty analysis resulted in *World Treaty Index* by Peter H. Rohn (ABC-Clio Press, 1974), 5 vols., followed by a supplement, *Treaty Profiles* (1976). The *Index* provides multiple access to the *League of Nations Treaty Series,* the *U.N. Treaty Series,* and about 6,000 other treaties in 42 national collections from 1920 to 1972. The treaties are accessible from a multitude of points, including citation, serial number, title, by each party to the treaty, and by the date of signature. For U.N. and L.N. treaties, indexing extends even farther: entry into force, official languages, registrants, amendments, and reservations. The last two volumes are a subject analysis: vol. 4 is restricted to *UNTS* topics, whereas vol. 5 uses the author's 68 main topics and 530 concepts. The result of a number of years of toil has proved useful not only in international law, but also to several sociological studies based on treaty profiles. Illustration A shows the structure of a typical entry in the *World Treaty Index.* A new edition has been announced to extend the coverage to 1980 and it will include references to many more national collections, especially for treaties not registered with the United Nations. That forthcoming 2d edition is said to include citations to some 44,000 twentieth century treaties, doubling the coverage of the 1st edition.

5. Structure

The structure of this INDEX is largely self-explanatory to users familiar with legal reference materials, especially with treaty collections and treaty indexes, but a few introductory comments may be helpful even to seasoned treaty experts.

There is a basic difference between the "Main Entry Section" and the other "specialized sections." The Main Entry Section contains *all* the information the INDEX offers for *any* treaty. Each specialized section is fully independent of the others and semi-independent of the Main Entry Section. Each specialized section rotates the same basic information: (1) Date of Signature, (2) Party One, (3) Party Two, (4) Topic, (5) Citation and (6) Treaty Number. The only basic difference among the specialized sections is in the *order* in which the information is arranged to provide access by date of signature, by parties, by topics, and so forth.

a. MAIN ENTRY SECTION

All treaties in this Section are arranged in order of treaty number, see paragraph (1) below. The following sample entry illustrates the Main Entry Section. Subsequent comments give examples and clarify doubtful points and borderline cases.

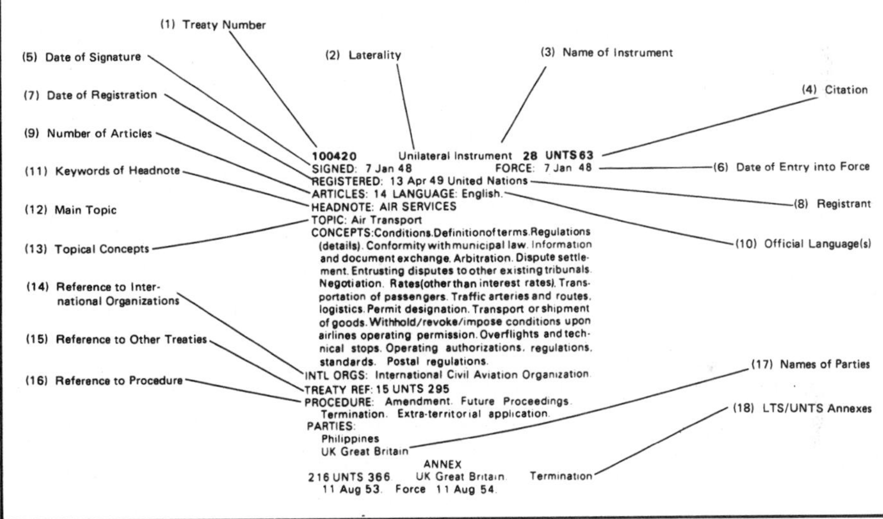

Illustration A

A description of the entry structure in *World Treaty Index,* v. 1, Introduction. (The forthcoming 2nd Edition will have a revised entry format.)

None of these tools are of much help in the location of treaties before their ratification. Newsworthy agreements may find their way into the *New York Times* or other newspapers, and others may appear in journals, such as the Dutch official gazette which alone includes the text of a treaty soon after its signature.

Since 1961, the American Society of International Law has been publishing the bi-monthly *International Legal Materials* and including in it the text of many significant treaties and other documents soon after their appearance, often in draft stage. These are either too recent to be available in other collections at the time of publication or reproduced and translated from foreign gazettes not readily accessible to general research. The Department of State files, its *Bulletin,* and United Nations documents are among the most frequent sources from which the selection is made. The ratification data from the *Department of State Bulletin* under "Treaty Information" are also reproduced in each issue.

International Legal Materials expands and supplements the *American Journal of International Law,* which continues to publish similar documents of permanent value.

In practice, when a researcher is trying to determine whether a particular treaty has entered into force, one can consult *Treaties in Force,* an annual publication of the Department of State, listing separately all bilateral and multilateral treaties to which the U.S. is a party and which have not expired, been revoked, or in any other way lost their validity. Illustration B shows a sample page from the bilateral section of *Treaties in Force* and Illustration C shows a sample page from the multilateral section. Illustration D is a listing of the abbreviations used for various series in *Treaties in Force.*

A new commercial variation of the official *Treaties in Force* has been published under the title, *A Guide to the United States Treaties in Force,* edited by I. I. Kavass, A. Sprudzs (Hein, 1982). The first part of the *Guide* includes numerical lists of both treaties and executive agreements in force as of Jan. 1, 1982, and a unique combined subject index to bilateral and multilateral treaties. This service is already a substantial improvement over *Treaties in Force* and includes many features not offered by the official publication. If annual publication can be maintained, as projected, it will be *the* major access tool for U.S. Treaties.

If the treaty is not listed, one must go through the Treaty Information section of each issue of the Department of State *Bulletin,* which keeps *Treaties in Force* up to date until the next edition is published.

Some of the reasons for leaving a properly concluded, possibly even signed, treaty unratified and thus not allowing it to enter into force can be found in a list of such treaties for the U.S., *Unperfected Treaties of the United States of America, 1776–1976,* edited by C. L. Wiktor (Oceana, 1976–19__). Because of the obvious painstaking search through 200 years of Congressional documents, this work can be classed among the more original bibliographic contributions to the ratification process.

The United Kingdom and most countries of the Commonwealth have their own treaty series in which the text of current international agreements is printed. The British *Treaty Series* is issued as part of the *Command Papers.* Other countries publish the text of their treaties in their official gazettes, either in a simple chronological arrangement with their statutes (as used to be case with the U.S. *Statutes at Large*) or in a separate annex or treaty series similar to the present *United States Treaties.* Multilateral treaties concluded among countries of the Western Hemisphere are published in the *Organization of American States Treaty Series.*

TREATIES IN FORCE

CANADA (Cont'd)

Agreement relating to channel improvement work in Pelee Passage area of Lake Erie. Exchange of notes at Ottawa June 8, 1959 and October 17, 1961; entered into force October 17, 1961.
12 UST 1669; TIAS 4883; 424 UNTS 101.

Treaty relating to cooperative development of the water resources of the Columbia River Basin. Signed at Washington January 17, 1961; entered into force September 16, 1964, with related agreements effected by exchanges of notes at Washington January 22, 1964, and at Ottawa September 16, 1964.
15 UST 1555; TIAS 5638; 542 UNTS 244.

Agreement implementing sec. (4) of art. XV of the treaty of January 17, 1961 relating to cooperative development of the water resources of the Columbia River Basin. Exchange of notes at Washington October 4, 1965; entered into force October 4, 1965.
16 UST 1263; TIAS 5877; 592 UNTS 272.

Agreement relating to an interpretation of art. IV of the treaty of February 27, 1950 relating to uses of the waters of the Niagara River. Exchange of notes at Washington April 17, 1973; entered into force April 17, 1973.
24 UST 895; TIAS 7599.

Agreement governing the operation of pilotage on the Great Lakes. Exchange of notes at Ottawa August 23, 1978 and March 29, 1979; entered into force March 29, 1979; effective January 18, 1977.
TIAS 9445.

NOTES:

[1] Paragraphs 3, 4, and 5 of art. V terminated October 10, 1950 upon the entry into force of the treaty relating to uses of waters of the Niagara River, signed February 27, 1950 (1 UST 694; TIAS 2130; 132 UNTS 223).

[2] See also agreement of April 17, 1973 (TIAS 7599).

CAMPOBELLO

Agreement relating to the establishment of the Roosevelt Campobello International Park. Signed at Washington January 22, 1964; entered into force August 14, 1964.
15 UST 1504; TIAS 5631; 530 UNTS 89.

CLAIMS

Convention for the establishment of a tribunal to decide questions of indemnity arising from the operation of the smelter at Trail, British Columbia. Signed at Ottawa April 15, 1935; entered into force August 3, 1935.
49 Stat. 3245; TS 893; 6 Bevans 60; 162 LNTS 73.

Agreement supplementary to the convention signed April 15, 1935 for the establishment of a tribunal to decide questions of indemnity and future regime arising from the operation of the smelter at Trail, British Columbia. Exchange of notes at Washington November 17, 1949 and January 24, 1950; entered into force January 24, 1950.
3 UST 539; TIAS 2412; 151 UNTS 171.

Agreement relating to claims arising out of traffic accidents involving vehicles of the armed forces of the United States and Canada. Exchange of notes at Ottawa March 1 and 23, 1944; entered into force March 23, 1944.
60 Stat. 1948; TIAS 1581; 6 Bevans 345; 125 UNTS 345.

Agreement relating to waiver of certain claims involving government vessels. Exchange of notes at Washington September 28 and November 13 and 15, 1946; entered into force November 15, 1946.
61 Stat. 2520; TIAS 1582; 6 Bevans 422; 7 UNTS 141.

Agreement relating to the settlement of certain war accounts and claims. Exchange of notes at Washington March 14, 1949; entered into force March 14, 1949.
63 Stat. 2432; TIAS 1925; 6 Bevans 482; 82 UNTS 3.

CONSERVATION

Arrangement prohibiting the importation of raccoon dogs. Exchange of letters at Ottawa and Washington September 1 and 4, 1981; entered into force September 4, 1981.
TIAS

Convention for the protection of migratory birds in the United States and Canada. Signed at Washington August 16, 1916; entered into force December 7, 1916.
39 Stat. 1702; TS 628; 12 Bevans 375.

CONSULS

Convention to regulate commerce (art. IV) between the United States and the United Kingdom. Signed at London July 3, 1815; effective July 3, 1815.
8 Stat. 228; TS 110; 12 Bevans 49.

Arrangement relating to visits of consular officers to citizens of their own country serving sentences in penal institutions. Exchange of notes at Ottawa July 29 and September 19, 1935; entered into force September 19, 1935.
Foreign Relations, 1935, Vol. II, p. 57; 6 Bevans 65.

COPYRIGHT (See APPENDIX)

CUSTOMS

Agreement relating to importation privileges for government officials and employees. Exchanges of notes at Ottawa July 21, October 29, and November 9, 1942; entered into force November 9, 1942.
57 Stat. 1379; EAS 383; 6 Bevans 289; 101 UNTS 233.

DEFENSE

Declaration by the Prime Minister of Canada and the President of the United States of America regarding the establishing of a Permanent Joint Board on Defense. Made at Ogdensburg, New York, August 18, 1940.
Department of State *Bulletin*, Vol. III, No. 61, August 24, 1940, p. 154; 6 Bevans 189; Canada Treaty Series, 1940, No. 14.

Illustration B

Entries under Canada from the bilateral treaty section of *Treaties in Force*, 1982.

216 TREATIES IN FORCE

CONSERVATION (See also FISHERIES; POLAR BEARS; SEALS; WHALING; WORLD HERITAGE)

Convention on nature protection and wildlife preservation in the Western Hemisphere, with annex. Done at the Pan American Union, Washington, October 12, 1940; entered into force for the United States April 30, 1942.
56 Stat. 1354; TS 981; 3 Bevans 630; 161 UNTS 193.
States which are parties:
Argentina[1]
Brazil
Chile
Costa Rica
Dominican Rep.
Ecuador
El Salvador
Guatemala
Haiti
Mexico
Nicaragua
Panama
Peru
Trinidad & Tobago
United States
Uruguay
Venezuela

NOTES:
[1] With reservation.

Convention on international trade in endangered species of wild fauna and flora, with appendices. Done at Washington March 3, 1973; entered into force for the United States July 1, 1975.
27 UST 1087; TIAS 8249.
States which are parties:
Argentina[1]
Australia
Bahamas, The
Bangladesh*
Bolivia
Botswana[1]
Brazil
Cameroon
Canada[1]
Central African Rep.
Chile
China
Colombia
Costa Rica
Cyprus
Denmark[2]
Ecuador
Egypt
Finland
France[1]
Gambia, The
German Dem. Rep.
Germany, Fed. Rep.[3]
Ghana
Guatemala
Guinea
Guyana
India
Iran
Israel
Italy[1]
Japan[1]
Liberia
Liechtenstein
Madagascar
Malaysia
Mauritius
Monaco
Morocco
Mozambique
Nepal
Nicaragua
Niger
Nigeria
Norway
Pakistan
Panama
Papua New Guinea
Paraguay
Peru
Philippines
Rwanda
Senegal
Seychelles
South Africa[1]
Sri Lanka
Suriname[1]
Sweden
Switzerland
Tanzania
Tunisia
Union of Soviet Socialist Reps.[1]
United Arab Emirates
United Kingdom[4]
United States
Uruguay
Venezuela
Zaire
Zambia[1]
Zimbabwe

NOTES:
* Effective February 18, 1982.
[1] With reservation.
[2] Extended to Greenland and the Faroe Islands. However, application as regards the Faroe Islands will only be accomplished at the time the authorities of the Faroe Islands will have enacted the appropriate legislation.
[3] Applicable to West Berlin.
[4] Applicable to Hong Kong, the Bailiwick of Guernsey, the Bailiwick of Jersey, the Isle of Man, Bermuda, British Indian Ocean Territory, British Virgin Islands, Falkland Islands, Gibraltar, Montserrat, Pitcairn, St. Helena and Dependencies (Tristan da Cunha, Ascension Islands), Cayman Islands. Also extended to Belize; continued application not yet determined.

Convention on the conservation of Antarctic marine living resources, with annex for an arbitral tribunal.* Done at Canberra May 20, 1980; enters into force for the United States April 7, 1982.
TIAS 10240.
States which are parties:
Australia
Chile
German Dem. Rep.
Japan
New Zealand
South Africa
Union of Soviet Socialist Reps.
United Kingdom
United States

NOTES:
* Enters into force April 7, 1982.

CONSULS

Convention relating to the duties, rights, prerogatives, and immunities of consular agents. Signed at Habana February 20, 1928; entered into force for the United States February 8, 1932.
47 Stat. 1976; TS 843; 2 Bevans 714; 155 LNTS 291.
States which are parties:
Brazil
Colombia
Cuba
Dominican Rep.[1]
Ecuador
El Salvador
Haiti
Mexico
Nicaragua
Panama
Peru
United States
Uruguay

NOTES:
[1] With a statement.

Convention on consular relations. Done at Vienna April 24, 1963; entered into force for the United States December 24, 1969.
21 UST 77; TIAS 6820; 596 UNTS 261.
States which are parties:
Algeria
Antigua & Barbuda[1]
Argentina
Australia
Austria
Bahamas, The
Bangladesh
Belgium
Benin
Bhutan
Bolivia
Brazil
Cameroon
Canada
Cape Verde
Chile
China
Colombia
Costa Rica
Cuba[2]
Cyprus
Czechoslovakia
Denmark[2, 3]
Djibouti
Dominican Rep.
Ecuador
Egypt
El Salvador
Equatorial Guinea
Fiji[2]
Finland[2, 3]
France[3]
Gabon
Germany, Fed. Rep.[3, 4]
Ghana
Greece
Grenada[1]
Guatemala
Guyana
Haiti
Holy See
Honduras
Iceland
India
Iran
Iraq

Illustration C

A sample entry from the multilateral treaty section of *Treaties in Force,* 1982.

References

Stat.	United States Statutes at Large.
UST	United States Treaties and Other International Agreements (volumes published on a calendar-year basis beginning as of January 1, 1950).
TS	Treaty Series, issued singly in pamphlets by the Department of State (until replaced in 1945 by the TIAS).
EAS	Executive Agreement Series, issued singly in pamphlets by the Department of State (until replaced in 1945 by the TIAS).
TIAS	Treaties and Other International Acts Series, issued singly in pamphlets by the Department of State.
Miller	Treaties and other International Acts of the United States of America, edited by Hunter Miller.
Bevans	Treaties and Other International Agreements of the United States of America 1776–1949, compiled under the direction of Charles I. Bevans.
Foreign Relations	Foreign relations of the United States.
F.R.	Federal Register.
LNTS	League of Nations Treaty Series.
UNTS	United Nations Treaty Series.

Illustration D

Reference abbreviations to various treaty sources used in *Treaties in Force.*

Treaties among the members of the Council of Europe and the European Communities appear in the *European Treaty Series.* They are also published (often earlier) in the *European Yearbook* which may be more readily available in libraries than individual numbers of the treaty series. A valuable compilation of European treaties has been issued by the Council of Europe: *European Conventions and Agreements,* Vol. I, 1949–1961; Vol. II, 1961–1970 with index volume; Vol. III, 1972–1974.

For historical research purposes, it may be necessary to locate texts of treaties no longer in force and concluded before the League of Nations series began publication. Two guides to treaty collections are available: Myers' *Manual of Collections of Treaties and of Collections Relating to Treaties* (Harvard University Press, 1922) which lists 3,468 items divided into general collections, then by country, and finally by subject matter. The *United Nations List of Treaty Collections* (New York, 1956) is more selective, containing 698 entries divided in the same three sections as the Myers list. There are also a number of lists of treaties for individual countries covering varying time periods.[3]

3. For example, R. M. Slusser & G. Ginsburgs, *Calendar of Soviet Treaties, 1958–1973* (Sijthoff, 1980) and C.L. Wiktor, *Canadian Treaty Calendar/Répertoire des Traités du Canada,* 2 vols. (Oceana, 1982).

The two most extensive sets reproducing older treaties are those edited by Martens which goes back to 1760 and was continued in several editions and three series until 1938; and by Dumont, published in the early part of the eighteenth century and going back to 800 A.D. Because both Martens and Dumont have been long out-of-print and therefore not accessible except in the large and long established libraries, a photographic reprint of older treaties, under the editorship of Clive Parry, is now being published as the *Consolidated Treaty Series* (Oceana Publications, 1969–date). As of 1983, 231 vols. have been issued. The coverage of the work goes back to 1648 and is scheduled to tie into the *League of Nations Treaty Series* thus producing an uninterrupted sequence of treaty sources from the end of the Thirty Years War, generally regarded as the time of the foundation of the modern system of states, to the present. The arrangement is strictly chronological, the text in the original language along with translations into English or French provided they could be found in an existing source. Summaries are supplied for those treaties for which no translation is available. Subsequent modifications or terminations of a treaty are noted by the editor. In 1979, C. Parry and P. Irwin published an *Index-Guide to Treaties* (Oceana) based on the *Consolidated Treaty Series* and all other series being utilized.

The first effort to supplement the index to the *UNTS* from national statutory sources was the *Index to Multilaterial Treaties* published by the Harvard Law School Library in 1965 and supplemented for three years thereafter. The *Index* is a chronological list of multiparty international agreements from 1596 to 1963. Its format is based on the *Catalogue of Treaties* compiled by the Department of State in 1919.

A very useful guide for research in treaties generally is A. Sprudzs, *Treaty Sources in Legal and Political Research* (Univ. of Arizona Press, 1971). A recent work explaining the very important Vienna Convention on Treaties (1969) on the basis of its legislative history is Elias, *The Modern Law of Treaties* (1974).

2. DETERMINING WHETHER THE TREATY IS IN FORCE

The determination of the precise status of a treaty as of a particular time remains difficult, except for treaties of the United States and Germany which alone publish an authoritative "treaties-in-force" services (for a description of the U.S. service, see page 648, above).

The United Nations issues a monthly *Statement of Treaties and International Agreements* for documents registered, filed and recorded with the Secretariat, which contains much relevant information, but because of its dependence on the initiative of the signatory states cannot be relied upon for completeness. In addition, the lack of an index forces the user to search through dozens of monthly pamphlets to find treaties of interest.

The United Nations Secretariat now publishes the annual *Multilateral Treaties in Respect of Which the Secretary-General Performs Depository Functions,* which summarizes the information scattered through the issues of the monthly *Statement.* Originally issued in looseleaf format, this list now appears annually and is in many respects similar to the U.S. *Treaties in Force.* However, the service is restricted not only to multilateral treaties as its title indicates, but also to conventions for which the Secretary-General acts as depository (i.e. those which had been designated as such in their text and those concluded under the auspices of the United Nations and its affiliated organizations).

The annual is arranged in 24 broad subject categories and lists all pertinent conventions chronologically by date of their signature or adoption by the General Assembly. For each treaty, it then gives the date of the entry into force, a reference to the text in the *UNTS,* and a list of signatories with the date of receipt by the United Nations of their instrument of accession, as well as the text of any accompanying declaration or reservation.

For its own treaties, the Organization of American States publishes an annual *Status of Inter-American Treaties and Conventions* in an easy-to-use tabular form. Similar tables can be found in the *European Yearbook* for the treaties of the Council of Europe and European Communities. The Council of Europe also publishes a separate list under the title, *Chart Showing Signatures and Ratifications of Council of Europe Conventions and Agreements* (Council of Europe, Directorate of Legal Affairs).

3. INTERPRETING THE TEXT

In interpreting the text of a treaty, the researcher will need access to its legislative history, its application by the executive and the judiciary, and its analysis by international law writers.

Legislative history of treaties consists of documents prepared within government agencies of each of the parties, exchanges of notes between countries, proceedings of the conference which led to the conclusion of the treaty, documents of international organizations dealing with the subject matter, and the parliamentary documents relating to ratification in each country.

Foreign offices of some countries release the documents contained in their files for public use. The Historical Office of the Department of State issues an official record of foreign policy in the series, *Foreign Relations of the United States.* With the exception of documents which remain restricted because of security considerations, the series (published twenty or more years after the date of the documents) is designed to give a comprehensive record of the major foreign policy decisions, together with their background. The set includes a considerable number of declassified secret materials. On a current basis, the Department publishes the annual *American Foreign Policy: Current Documents* which began in 1956 following the publication of *A Decade of American Foreign Policy: Basic Documents, 1941–1949.* A recent unofficial reference tool is the *Guide to American Foreign Relations Since 1700,* edited by R. D. Burns for the Society for Historians of American Foreign Relations (ABC-Clio, Inc., 1983).

In addition to its "papers-by-command," the United Kingdom publishes a series similar to the U.S. *Foreign Relations* under the title of *British and Foreign State Papers,* also issued about twenty years after the date of the documents.

Based on published as well as unpublished sources, the Department of State has been issuing a series, *Digest of International Law,* which discusses the issues of foreign policy, diplomacy and general international law, including matters relating to treaties, in a systematic manner. The result in many respects is similar to a voluminous treatise. The forerunner of the series was an early *Digest* published in 1877 and prepared by John L. Cadwalader.[4] The second *Digest* which set the pattern for the rest of the series in that it was based primarily on the files of the Department of State rather than judicial materials, came out in three volumes in 1886 and was prepared by Francis Wharton. The third was John Bassett Moore's *International Law Digest* published in eight volumes in 1906. The fourth was Hackworth's *Digest* in the 1940's in eight volumes. The present set, *Digest of International Law* (1963–1973), complete in 15 volumes, was compiled by Marjorie M. Whiteman. The various editions of the Digest are not cumulative so that Whiteman, for example, does not supercede Hackworth. Whiteman, however, is an invaluable current sourcebook on U.S. practice.

The Whiteman Digest is supplemented by a new series of annual volumes, *Digest of United States Practice in International Law.* Volumes have been published by the Department of State annually from 1973 to 1978 and future annual volumes are projected. The latest is by M. L. Nash (1978).

A parallel *British Digest of International Law* compiled by Clive Parry from the Archives of the Foreign Office is currently being issued in London and scheduled to cover the period of 1860–1914 in ten volumes and the years 1914–1960 in an additional five. For Canada, *International Law, Chiefly as Interpreted and Applied in Canada,* was compiled by Castel and published in its 3rd edition in 1976. A seven-volume French digest edited by A. C. Kiss was completed by a detailed index volume in 1972.[5]

The American and British practice digests are kept up-to-date respectively by articles in the *American Journal of International Law* and by supplements to the *International Comparative Law Quarterly.*

4. Cadwalader's *Digest* included the relevant opinions of the Attorneys-General and the leading decisions of the federal courts in matters relating to international law and treaties. It consisted of a single volume of less than three hundred pages.

5. *Repértoire de la pratique Française en Matière de droit international public* (1962–72). The index consists of subject and author parts and also includes a chronological listing of the French Foreign Ministers, a table of cases, a table of statutes, and a list of treaties.

Two *Restatements of the Law* published by the American Law Institute are in many respects a summary of the United States practice in international law and can thus be used as an unofficial condensation of the Digest series: the one-volume *Foreign Relations of the United States, 2d* (1965) deals with public international law [6] and the *Restatement on Conflict of Laws 2d,* 4 vols. (1971, 1980) with private international law.

For legislative history of U.S. treaties in the strict sense, Senate Executive documents, reports and debates in the *Congressional Record* are the basic sources.[7]

The proceedings and documents of international conferences are very frequently available in convenient book form, as for example the records of the Intellectual Property Conference in Stockholm, published in two volumes in 1972. Such materials may also appear as part of the documentation of the United Nations General Assembly, its Economic and Social Council, or other related agencies.

Unfortunately, documents of many conferences remain unpublished and are distributed in a limited number of copies among the delegates and signatories only. For example, the enormous documentation of the International Institute for the Unification of Private Law, which has been drafting conventions to achieve legislative uniformity, consists of over sixty volumes of typescript and has only recently been made available on microfilm.

The complexity of the judicial interpretation of treaty texts, particularly if the official version is in a foreign language is well illustrated by *Berner v. British Commonwealth Pacific Airlines, Ltd.* 219 F.Supp. 289 (1963). One of the issues was the interpretation of the French words "faute" and "dol," which appear in the official French text of the Warsaw International Aviation Convention of 1929 for which there is no official text in English. The Court found it necessary to study the usage of the terms not only in decisions of international courts but also in the French domestic negligence cases, and the opinion runs over 100 pages, with long footnote citations to French authors.

Shortly after World War II, the Department of State made an attempt to compile, for each treaty, references to their legislative history and their judicial applications. The resulting *United States Treaty Developments* came out in five volumes in 1947–1950 but, for reasons of economy, has never been continued.

In order to collect at least some of the data, one has to resort today to such standard legal research aids as West's several *Federal Digests* and *Shepard Citations.*[8] Only in the field of taxation is it

6. Three tentative drafts for a revised edition have been issued (1980–1982).

7. For further discussion, see Chapter 10, Legislative History, above; G. B. Folsom, *Legislative History, Research for the Interpretation of Laws* (1972), Part VII "Usable Background for Treaty Interpretation; and M. McDougal, *The Interpretation of Agreements and World Public Order* (1967).

8. Treaties can be found in separate sections of *Shepard's United States Citations-Statutes Edition* and in the statutes part of the various Shepard's state citators.

easy to find not only the English text of treaties and executive agreements (e.g., in the United Nations *International Tax Agreements,* nine volumes, currently published as looseleaf), but also the related rulings of the Internal Revenue Service and in some cases its foreign counterparts, in two parallel looseleaf services on tax treaties published by Commerce Clearing House and Prentice-Hall.

Research in the treaty area generally involves difficulties caused by the vastness of the materials, its multilingual character, and the almost insurmountable restrictions of traditional indexing techniques. For several years, the federal government, the United Nations and public and private research organizations have been attempting to apply to the field the versatility of electronic retrieval systems. The two operational systems, LEXIS and WESTLAW, do not specialize in international law, but can be used for locating judicial decisions in the field. It is in this direction that a significant breakthrough in treaty control may be expected.

D. ADJUDICATIONS

As in domestic law, most disputes arising among states are settled by direct negotiation. If an agreement cannot be reached through diplomatic procedures, disputes can be submitted to courts, arbitration, or special commissions established for that purpose.

Among the recent writings on international courts and other means of settlement of disputes, the following selection will be found helpful: C. Rhyne's *Law and Judicial System of Nations* (collection of essays, 1977); L. Gross' *The Future of the International Court of Justice* (2v., 1976); Schwarzenberger's *International Law as Applied by International Courts and Tribunals* (Vol. III, United Nations; Vol. IV, International Judicial Law, 1976); Sandifer's *Evidence Before International Tribunals* (1975); Keith's *Extent of the Advisory Jurisdiction of the International Court of Justice* (1977); McWhinney's *World Court and the Contemporary International Law-making Process* (1978) and Bar-Yaacov's *Handling of International Disputes by Means of Inquiry* (1974).

The International Court of Justice, created by the Charter of the United Nations as one of the organization's principal organs, is the only truly world-wide tribunal, its jurisdiction extending to all states whether or not they are members of the United Nations; non-members can be parties before the court if they accept its jurisdiction. Like any other court, however, it can only consider the issues submitted to it by parties to a dispute; judging strictly from its case load, it would appear to be one of the very few courts not plagued by congestion and overwork.[9]

9. The Court consists of fifteen members elected for nine years, with the right to re-election. The judges are elected by an absolute majority of the votes of the General Assembly and the Security Council of the United Nations. The jurisdiction of the Court includes all cases which the parties refer to it and all matters specifically provided for in the Charter or in existing treaties. The parties can also recognize as compulsory the jurisdiction of the Court in all legal dis-

The Court's decisions are based on general principles of international law, international conventions, and international custom. In line with the continental legal tradition, judicial precedents serve as "subsidiary means for the determination of the rules of law." (Art. 38 of the Statute). The decisions issued by the Court have no binding force except between the parties and only with respect to the question before the Court.

The Court publishes its decision first in advance sheet form, later in the annual collection, *Report of Judgments, Advisory Opinions and Orders.* See Illustration E for a typical judgment in the *I.C.J. Reports.* A second published series, *Pleadings, Oral Arguments and Documents,* is in many respects similar to the briefs and records made available by American appellate courts. The *Yearbook* of the Court contains valuable information on the developments in the Court's jurisdiction, of its organization, its administration, its finances, extensive biographical data on the judges, and a bibliographic list of all cases before the Court.

The rules of the Court are published as Series D, which is somewhat confusing since there are no series A, B, or C. Actually, the designation of the rules as Series D is a carryover from the Court's predecessor, the Permanent Court of International Justice. The latter was organized by the Peace conferences following World War I and was affiliated with the League of Nations. Its documentation appeared in six series as follows: (1) Series A, judgments; (2) Series B, advisory opinions (in 1931 these two series were consolidated as A/B); (3) Series C, pleadings, oral statements and documents; (4) Series D, rules and organization documents; (5) Series E, annual report; and (6) Series F, Index.

An annotated unofficial compilation of the reports of the Permanent Court for the period of 1922 to 1942 was published in four volumes under the title, *World Court Reports,* by Manley O. Hudson, who was for many years one of the Court's judges. Since the United States had not ratified the League of Nations Covenant, there always loomed the danger that it might withdraw from the Court, too. Professor Hudson was an eloquent defender of the Court's role in world affairs in Washington, in his scholarly writings and dozens of newspaper articles directed to the general public (cf. G. Strait. *Bibliography of Judge Manley O. Hudson,* Harvard Law Library, 1962).

Decisions of the present International Court of Justice are analyzed, arranged by topic and digested in Edvard Hambro's *Case Law of the International Court.* This series was begun in 1961 and has

putes concerning treaty interpretation, any question of international law, any potential breach of an international obligation and the nature and extent of the reparation to be made for such a breach (International Court of Justice Statute, Art. 36). Although only a minority of the members of the United Nations have accepted the compulsory jurisdiction of the Court, several major countries are among them, in particular France, Japan, the United Kingdom and most of the Commonwealth, and the United States. However, no countries of the Socialist bloc will be found on this list.

3

1980
24 May
General List
No. 64

INTERNATIONAL COURT OF JUSTICE

YEAR 1980

24 May 1980

CASE CONCERNING UNITED STATES DIPLOMATIC AND CONSULAR STAFF IN TEHRAN

(UNITED STATES OF AMERICA *v.* IRAN)

Article 53 of the Statute – Proof of Facts – Admissibility of Proceedings – Existence of wider political dispute no bar to legal proceedings – Security Council proceedings no restriction on functioning of the Court – Fact-finding commission established by Secretary-General.

Jurisdiction of the Court – Optional Protocols to Vienna Conventions of 1961 and 1963 on Diplomatic and Consular Relations – 1955 Treaty of Amity, Economic Relations and Consular Rights (USA / Iran) – Provision for recourse to Court unless parties agree to "settlement by some other pacific means" – Right to file unilateral Application – Whether counter-measures a bar to invoking Treaty of Amity.

State responsibility for violations of Vienna Conventions of 1961 and 1963 on Diplomatic and Consular Relations – Action by persons not acting on behalf of State – Non-imputability thereof to State – Breach by State of obligation of protection – Subsequent decision to maintain situation so created on behalf of State – Use of situation as means of coercion.

Question of special circumstances as possible justification of conduct of State – Remedies provided for by diplomatic law for abuses.

Cumulative effect of successive breaches of international obligations – Fundamental character of international diplomatic and consular law.

JUDGMENT

Present : *President* Sir Humphrey WALDOCK ; *Vice-President* ELIAS ; *Judges* FORSTER, GROS, LACHS, MOROZOV, NAGENDRA SINGH, RUDA, MOSLER, TARAZI, ODA, AGO, EL-ERIAN, SETTE-CAMARA, BAXTER ; *Registrar* AQUARONE.

3

1980
24 mai
Rôle général
n° 64

COUR INTERNATIONALE DE JUSTICE

ANNÉE 1980

24 mai 1980

AFFAIRE RELATIVE AU PERSONNEL DIPLOMATIQUE ET CONSULAIRE DES ÉTATS-UNIS À TÉHÉRAN

(ÉTATS-UNIS D'AMÉRIQUE c. IRAN)

Article 53 du Statut – Preuve des faits – Recevabilité de l'instance – L'existence d'un différend politique plus large ne fait pas obstacle à l'instance judiciaire – La procédure devant le Conseil de sécurité n'a pas d'effet restrictif pour la Cour – Commission d'établissement des faits instituée par le Secrétaire général.

Compétence de la Cour – Protocoles de signature facultative aux conventions de Vienne de 1961 et 1963 sur les relations diplomatiques et consulaires – Traité d'amitié, de commerce et de droits consulaires de 1955 (Etats-Unis/Iran) – Disposition permettant de saisir la Cour du différend à moins que les parties ne conviennent « de le régler par d'autres moyens pacifiques » – Droit d'introduire une requête unilatérale – Les contre-mesures empêchent-elles d'invoquer le traité d'amitié ?

Responsabilité de l'Etat pour violation des conventions de 1961 et 1963 sur les relations diplomatiques et consulaires – Faits de personnes n'agissant pas pour le compte de l'Etat – Ces faits ne sont pas imputables à l'Etat – Manquement à l'obligation de protéger commis par l'Etat – Décision ultérieure de perpétuer, au nom de l'Etat, la situation ainsi créée – Utilisation de la situation comme moyen de contrainte.

Problème de la justification possible du comportement de l'Etat du fait de circonstances spéciales – Remèdes en cas d'abus prévus par le droit diplomatique.

Effet cumulatif de violations successives d'obligations internationales – Caractère fondamental du droit diplomatique et consulaire.

ARRÊT

Présents : Sir Humphrey WALDOCK, *Président* ; M. ELIAS, *Vice-Président* ; MM. FORSTER, GROS, LACHS, MOROZOV, NAGENDRA SINGH, RUDA, MOSLER, TARAZI, ODA, AGO, EL-ERIAN, SETTE-CAMARA, BAXTER, *juges* ; M. AQUARONE, *Greffier*.

4

Illustration E

A Judgment in I.C.J. *Report of Judgments, Advisory Opinions and Orders* (1980).

continued with the collaboration of Arthur W. Rovine. Another useful retrospective compilation is *A Digest of the Decisions of the International Court,* 2 vols., edited by K. Marek (Vol. 1, published in 1974, includes summaries of cases brought before the Permanent Court of International Justice; Vol. 2, covers the I.C.J.). A more up-to-date collection is *Documents of the International Court of Justice,* 2d ed., compiled by S. Rosenne (Oceana Publications, 1979). A critical review of the law governing the Court can be found in Rosenne's *The Law and Practice of the International Court* (Leyden, 1965).

The usefulness of the Court is seriously limited by two factors. First, not all conflicts of interest can be resolved by judicial techniques. Second, although judgments of the Court are final without appeal, there is no machinery for enforcing compliance. The United Nations Charter provides, in Article 94, that the Security Council may recommend or decide upon measures to be taken to give effect to the judgment but it is not under a duty to do so. The decisions of the Security Council are furthermore subject to the veto of any one of the five permanent members: United States, USSR, United Kingdom, France, and China. In fact, neither the League of Nations Council nor the United Nations Security Council has ever been asked to enforce a judgment of the Court. The Charter appears to assume voluntary compliance, particularly since it forbids the threat or use of force and thus self-help.

The Court of Justice of the European Communities is an example of a tribunal of a regional organization with full international jurisdiction. Its decisions are published officially in several languages, including English, as *Reports of Cases Before the Court.* The European Court of Human Rights publishes its decisions in two series: Series A: *Judgments and Decisions;* Series B: *Pleadings, Oral Arguments, Documents.*

A much larger body of judicial decisions dealing with international law can be found in the national court reports of individual countries. A careful selection of such decisions on a worldwide scale is published in English in *International Law Reports* (now published by Grotius Publications, Inc.) and its predecessor, *Annual Digest and Report of Public International Law Cases* which goes back to 1919. In 1969, the long time editor of the series, E. Lauterpacht, prepared a two volume consolidated index to the first thirty-five volumes of the reports, analyzing their contents by country and subject and including a table of treaties as well as a table of cases (see Illustration F).

Although its primary contribution lies in the reprinting of selected decisions of national courts of almost every country in the world, *International Law Reports* also includes decisions of such international courts as the Administrative Tribunals of the International Labor Organization, the League of Nations and the United Nations, decisions of selected claims, conciliation and arbitration commissions, the Court of Justice of the European Communities, the European Commission and Court of Human Rights, as well as the Permanent Court

TABLE OF CASES REPORTED

[ARRANGED ACCORDING TO COURTS AND TRIBUNALS (INTERNATIONAL CASES) AND COUNTRIES (MUNICIPAL CASES).]

(The figures in heavier type indicate the page numbers of the actual reports. The ordinary type indicates pages containing notes or relevant cross-references.)

I. DECISIONS OF INTERNATIONAL TRIBUNALS

European Court of Human Rights

1980

International Court of Justice

1979

1980

1981

II. DECISIONS OF MUNICIPAL COURTS

England

1975

1976

Germany, Federal Republic of

1968

xxvii

Illustration F

"Table of Cases Reported" in Lauterpacht's *International Law Reports* (v. 61, 1981).

of International Justice and the International Court of Justice. Illustrations G–1 and 2 show the opening of a typical case in the *International Law Reports.*

American cases can be located through general research aids, particularly the digests and the citators. A photo-reprint edition of reports dealing with international law began publication under the editorship of the late Francis Deak as *American International Law Cases, 1783–1968.* The collection covers both federal and state courts, and individual opinions are arranged in a systematic subject breakdown. A consolidated table of contents has been announced for the last volume of the series. Cases dealing with several subjects appear under one and are cross referenced from the others. A current survey of judicial decisions is a regular feature of the *American Journal of International Law,* contributed until her untimely death in 1980 by Alona E. Evans. The survey articles contain summaries and notes concerning each case, but not its text.

British International Law Cases is a summary collection of decisions of United Kingdom courts on points of international law. The basic set was completed in 1967 in six volumes; a consolidated index by subject is appended to the last volume. Supplementary volumes carry the series up to date. Clive Parry, the editor of this series, with J. A. Hopkins has recently started a more extensive collection of decisions, *Commonwealth International Law Cases.*

The decisions of the German high courts for the period of 1879–1960 were published in *Fontes Juris Gentium, Series A/II.* The text is in German and a subject digest in German, English, French. Since World War II, the scope of international judicial activity increased with the first application of international criminal law at Nuremberg and Tokyo. These war crimes trials resulted in an extensive and historic literature of international adjudication.[10]

E. ARBITRATIONS

The Hague International Peace Conference of 1907 established the Permanent Court of Arbitration and encouraged states to submit

10. The documentation of the post-World War II trials is readily available in English in the following collections: *Trials of the Major War Criminals before the International Military Tribunal,* published by the Tribunal itself in 1947–49 in forty-two volumes;

Nazi Conspiracy and Aggression published in nine volumes by the U.S. Government Printing Office in 1946–47;

Trials of War Criminals before the Nuernberg Military Tribunal under Control Law No. 10, published in fifteen volumes by the U.S. Government;

Law Reports of the Trials of War Criminals, prepared by the United Nations War Crimes Commission and published in London by H.M.S.O. in 1947–49; and

The Judgment of the International Military Tribunal for the Far East, published in 1948 in ten volumes.

CASE CONCERNING UNITED STATES DIPLOMATIC AND CONSULAR STAFF IN TEHRAN (UNITED STATES OF AMERICA *v.* IRAN)

International Court of Justice

(Sir Humphrey Waldock, *President*; Elias, *Vice-President*; Forster, Gros, Lachs, Morozov, Nagendra Singh, Ruda, Mosler, Tarazi, Oda, Ago, El-Erian, Sette-Camara and Baxter, *Judges*)

Request for the Indication of Provisional Measures. 15 *December* 1979

Order Fixing Time-Limits. 24 *December* 1979

Judgment. 24 *May* 1980

Order Relating to Discontinuance. 12 *May* 1981

SUMMARY:[1] *The facts*[2]:—On 4 November 1979 a large demonstration took place outside the United States Embassy in Tehran. The demonstrators were protesting against the United States Government's decision to allow the former Shah of Iran into the United States and against alleged United States intervention in Iran during the Shah's reign. Several hundred armed demonstrators (the militants) invaded the Embassy and seized everyone present. Shortly afterwards, demonstrators occupied the United States Consulates in Tabriz and Shiraz. The Iranian security forces made no apparent attempts to prevent the invasions or to secure the release of the captives. Instead, in the days following the invasions, statements were made by various members of the Iranian Government expressing approval of the actions of the militants. In addition, the United States Chargé d'Affaires and two members of his staff, who had been at the Iranian Foreign Ministry when the Embassy was attacked, were apparently detained in the Ministry.[3] The militants accused members of the Embassy staff of espionage and announced that they would be held unless the former Shah was returned to Iran to stand trial for crimes allegedly committed during his reign and his wealth was returned to Iran. The possibility of trying some of the hostages for espionage was also discussed. Iranian Government statements endorsed the militants' demands. Although some of the hostages were released on the orders of the Iranian Government, 50 were still being held at the end of November 1979. Of these, 28 were members of the diplomatic staff and 20 members of the technical and administrative staff within the terms of the Vienna Convention on Diplomatic Relations, 1961, while two, both United States nationals, were private individuals. In addition, the Chargé d'Affaires and his two companions continued to be confined in the Foreign Ministry. The militants ransacked the Embassy archives and published documents, allegedly found in the Embassy, which they claimed proved the Embassy staff had been involved in subversive activities.

[1] Prepared by Mr C. J. Greenwood.
[2] For an account of the final settlement of the dispute see p. 592 below.
[3] The circumstances of this detention are not clear. See pp. 538-41.

Illustration G-1

Opening of typical case in Lauterpacht's *International Law Reports* (v. 61, 1981).

530 DIPLOMATIC INTERCOURSE AND PRIVILEGES

JUDGMENT

In the case concerning United States Diplomatic and Consular Staff in Tehran, [4]

between

the United States of America,

represented by

The Honorable Roberts B. Owen, Legal Adviser, Department of State,

as Agent,

H.E. Mrs. Geri Joseph, Ambassador of the United States of America to the Netherlands,

as Deputy Agent,

Mr. Stephen M. Schwebel, Deputy Legal Adviser, Department of State,

as Deputy Agent and Counsel,

Mr. Thomas J. Dunnigan, Counsellor, Embassy of the United States of America,

as Deputy Agent,

assisted by

Mr. David H. Small, Assistant Legal Adviser, Department of State,
Mr. Ted L. Stein, Attorney-Adviser, Department of State,
Mr. Hugh V. Simon, Jr., Second Secretary, Embassy of the United States of America,

as Advisers,

and

the Islamic Republic of Iran,

THE COURT,

composed as above,

delivers the following Judgment :

1. On 29 November 1979, the Legal Adviser of the Department of State of the United States of America handed to the Registrar an Application instituting proceedings against the Islamic Republic of Iran in respect of a dispute concerning the seizure and holding as hostages of members of the United States diplomatic and consular staff and certain other United States nationals.

2. Pursuant to Article 40, paragraph 2, of the Statute and Article 38, paragraph 4, of the Rules of Court, the Application was at once communicated to the Government of Iran. In accordance with Article 40, paragraph 3, of the Statute and Article 42 of the Rules of Court, the Secretary-General of the United Nations, the Members of the United Nations, and other States entitled to appear before the Court were notified of the Application.

3. On 29 November 1979, the same day as the Application was filed, the

Illustration G–2

Continuation of case in Lauterpacht's *International Law Reports* (v. 61, 1981).

their disputes to it in the interest of peaceful settlement.[11] The same conference also created an International Commission of Inquiry to settle differences of opinion on points of fact rather than law by means of an impartial investigation.

Awards of the Court and the Commission were collected and published by James B. Scott as the *Hague Court Reports* (1st series, 1916; 2d series 1932). In 1948 the United Nations began its collection, *Reports of International Arbitral Awards,* which continues the Scott volumes. The set goes back to World War I and is being carried on by supplements. Currently the awards are published in English or French according to the language of the original; headnotes are in both languages. These reports include mediation and conciliation agreements as well as arbitral awards rendered by a tribunal or an individual selected by the parties. They are, however, limited to cases involving states as parties.

There is a large and growing body of arbitration proceedings and awards in international law matters between private parties, such as business entities. No systematic collection of these documents is in existence, although its value to research is beyond dispute. A few have appeared in *International Legal Materials* or other periodical literature but most remain inaccessible. One of the reasons is that the parties may prefer to keep such agreements confidential.

There are three standard older collections of arbitration cases: La Fontaine's of 1902, de Lapradelle's and Politis' of 1905–1923, and for the U.S., J. B. Moore's *International Arbitrations* (1898) in six volumes. Among the more recently issued, compiled or reprinted digests are A. M. Stuyt's *Survey of International Arbitrations, 1794–1970* (1972); Wetter's *The International Arbitral Process: public and private* (5 vols., 1979); Schmitthoff's *International Commercial Arbitratrion* (2 vols., 1974–76); and Lew's *Choice of Applicable Law in International Commercial Arbitration* (1978).

Territorial changes, wars and, most recently, nationalizations often violate the rights of individual citizens and give rise to claims for compensation and reparation of damages. Ever since 1794, the United States has been engaged in settling such disputes by means of specially organized claims commissions.[12]

No comprehensive collection of the awards of international claims commissions is available, not even an exhaustive index. An impres-

11. The creation of a real court was a significant step forward from the time of the first Hague Peace Conference in 1899 which had organized an international bureau at the Hague to maintain a list of persons, from which nations could select five members to form a temporary tribunal.

12. The 1794 commission settled a controversy arising out of the interpretation of the Treaty of Peace of 1783 between the United States and Great Britain. The Alabama Claims Commission of 1795 was set up to consider liability for damages inflicted upon American shipping during the war between Spain and France. Another important Mixed Claims Commission Tribunal was established under an 1868 treaty by the United States and Mexico. Mixed Claims Commissions with Germany after World War I and various East European countries after World War II are but a few examples of different types of settlement of disputed claims.

sive listing of documents in this area can be found in the *Catalog of International Law and Relations* of the Harvard Law School Library, described above. The decisions dealing with claims under the International Claims Settlement Act of 1959 with the Soviet Union and other East European countries can be located by means of the *Index-Digest: Decisions, 1949–1962,* which was issued by the United States Foreign Claims Settlement Commission. Borchard's *The Diplomatic Protection of Citizens Abroad* (N.Y., 1927) remains helpful as a general treatise on the law of international claims. Wormser's *Collection of International War Damage Claims* (N.Y., 1944) discusses the kinds of such claims, the methods of their presentation, proof and determination, with special reference to those which were likely to arise out of World War II. The now prevalent settlement of International claims by lump-sum agreements has been covered by R. B. Lillich's *International Claims: Postwar British Practice* (Syracuse, 1971) and Lillich & Weston's *International Claims: Their Settlement by Lump Sum Agreements,* 2 vols., (Charlottesville, 1975) and their *International Claims: Contemporary European Practice* (Charlottesville, 1982).

F. PERIODICALS AND YEARBOOKS

The periodical literature in international law is covered by the *Index to Foreign Legal Periodicals,* and the Max Planck Institute's *Public International Law: A Current Bibliography . . . ,* published twice a year. The *I.F.L.P.* covers all articles (notes excluded) in a wide selection of international law periodicals. Their arrangement is alphabetical, but the subject breakdown for public international law topics is restricted to broad categories without sufficient detail. International and domestic legal subjects are mixed in a single alphabet. The Max Planck Institute bibliography is devoted solely to international law and arranged in a classified topical scheme, with separate author and subject indexes. The scope of both publications is worldwide and materials in all languages are included.

1. PERIODICALS

The *American Journal of International Law* is the most prestigious publication of its type in the world. In addition to substantive articles, each issue of the *Journal* contains a summary of the United States practice relating to international law, notes on judicial decisions involving questions of international law, scholarly book reviews and book notes, which, together with the listing of books received, provide a reliable current bibliography of the whole field, and a selection of documents, particularly treaties and important resolutions of international organizations. Until the publication of *International Legal Materials,* which began in 1962, the documentary section has been issued in a supplemental volume. *International Legal Materials* concentrates on the more current documentation before it becomes available in permanent collections or on material of somewhat ephemeral value, whereas the documents included in the issues of the *Journal* itself are selected for their permanent value.

The leading British journal in the field, the *International and Comparative Law Quarterly,* is frequently supplemented by documentary material in pamphlet form.

In public international law, the best French journal is the *Revue génèrale de droit international public.* The *Journal du droit international* concentrates on private international law and unification of law, and is very useful for its survey of judicial decisions of the major countries of Europe as well as those of the European organizations. The more recent *Revue critique de droit international privé* is devoted entirely to private international law and includes, in its documentary section, the text of the most important French treaties as well as references to related statutory texts.

The two leading German journals are *Zeitschrift für ausländisches öffentliches Recht und Völkerrecht* and *Rabels Zeitschrift für ausländisches und internationales Privatrecht,* both published under the sponsorship of the Max Planck Institutes. The first one deals with public international law, the second with private; both also cover comparative law. While the majority of articles are in German, an increasing number appear in English or are provided with an English summary. The *Netherlands International Law Review* and the *Nordisk tidsskrift for international ret* also contain much material in English. Specialized journals of international law appear in many other countries.

Starting in 1951 in Virginia, law students have organized their own societies of international law for the purpose of promoting interest in the subject, holding regional conferences and participating in the national Jessup Moot Court Competition. Among the more significant contributions of these societies has been the publication of student periodicals devoted to international law.[13]

The student journals carry articles written by their editors as well as outside authors, book reviews, case comments, and generally follow the policies of the general law reviews.

2. YEARBOOKS

Among the many yearbooks published in the field of international law, three separate types can be distinguished: (1) Annually published collections of articles or documents which differ from the journals only by their frequency; (2) Proceedings and reports of conferences and conventions containing papers presented to and read at the conference, resolutions adopted, and directory-like biographical information; (3) Annually published almanacs or manuals which contain

13. There are now many such journals, including for example: *Columbia Journal of Transnational Law,* the *Cornell International Law Journal,* the *Harvard International Law, The Virginia Journal of International Law,* the *Yale Journal of World Public Order,* and those of approximately thirty other law schools. For a recent list, see 11 *Internat'l. J. of Legal Information* 26–28 (1983).

factual data regarding the activity of a specific organization or the achievements in a specific field in a given year, as well as the listing of officers and the documentation of the publishing organization.

The *British Yearbook of International Law* is the most prominent example of the first category. It contains substantive articles by leading British specialists, a survey of British court decisions in public and private international law, and book reviews.[14]

The *Japan Annual of International Law* has been appearing in English since 1957. In addition to articles, it carries the text of decisions of Japanese courts, a chronological listing of treaties concluded by Japan in the year preceding the year of publication, and the text of the majority of these treaties.[15]

Among *foreign language* yearbooks of the first type, the following may be mentioned:

The French *Annuaire* includes articles, selected decisions of international courts, surveys of developments in international organizations, a listing of the French treaties concluded during the year with references to the *Journal Officiel,* a review of the French court and diplomatic practice, a chronology of events of major importance to international law, and an extensive bibliography;

The West German *Jahrbuch für Internationales Recht* contains, in addition to articles of general interest, summaries of activities of international organizations, texts of important multilateral conventions (English text often included), literature surveys, and a listing of German treaties for the year with data concerning their ratification status. The last part of this publication is thus, in many respects, similar to the U.S. *Treaties in Force;*

The Swiss *Jahrbuch* is divided into public and private international law sections and is mostly devoted to documentary information, including a list of treaties entered into by Switzerland, surveys of Swiss court decisions, and book reviews:

The *Soviet Yearbook of International Law* which started with the year 1958, contains, like the others, articles (with English summaries), a news section covering the Soviet treaty developments as well as a digest of Soviet legislation in foreign relations, book reviews,

14. In the 1960's the *British Yearbook* was joined by two sister publications, the *Canadian* and *Australian Yearbooks.* The *Yearbook of World Affairs,* published since 1947 by the Institute of World Affairs (London), contains articles on international relations, international law and international organizations, as well as useful summaries of current literature in those fields.

15. Since 1970, the *Netherlands Yearbook of International Law* contains, in English, articles and documents, yearly reports on Dutch practice of international law, Netherlands' treaties and judicial decisions. The *Italian Yearbook of International Law* started publication in 1975. The only yearbook of the first type published in socialist countries in English is the *Polish Yearbook of International Law* (published since 1966–67). Other yearbooks are now available from South Africa (since 1976), and Nigeria (since 1979).

and a very extensive bibliography of Soviet writings (books and periodicals) in international law for the year.

The second type of yearbooks can best be exemplified by the *Proceedings* of the American Society of International Law, which during 1970–1973 was published as part of the *American Journal of International Law.* In 1974, the previous practice of separate publication was resumed. The *Reports of the Conferences of the International Law Association* contain the discussions at the annual meeting, as well as a worldwide membership list, often very useful as a directory of international lawyers. The *Annuaire* of the International Law Institute reports on the annual meeting of the Institute and contains the text of the resolutions adopted, often in the form of draft multilateral conventions.

Finally, the collected lectures of the Hague Academy of International Law (*Recueil des Cours)* now comprise a library of some 150 volumes reflecting the development of international law in the last fifty years. The *Recueil* prints the text of the lectures offered by the Academy at the Peace Palace of the Hague by international legal authorities from various countries. The annual sessions of the Academy last about six weeks and are divided into two periods, one devoted to private, the other to public international law.

The *United Nations Yearbook* and the *Yearbook of International Organizations* serve as examples of the third category; because of their subject matter, they will be discussed in the next section.

G. INTERNATIONAL ORGANIZATIONS

The number of international organizations in existence at present cannot be determined with accuracy but it is certainly well over 10,000. The quarterly lists of scheduled international meetings, circulated by the Department of State, the Library of Congress and the United Nations showed, for example, 4,021 conferences to be held within a three month period in 1980. The large majority of these organizations, however, are of a private nature, or, in United Nations terminology, non-governmental. Public or governmental organizations must be created by a treaty between states. As almost any multilateral convention establishes a Secretariat or a mechanism for the settlement of disputes, there may well be almost as many international organizations as there are treaties. Not all of these, however, are active and only a limited number produce documents of legal interest.

A few very useful surveys of the law of international organizations are D. W. Bowett, *The Law of International Institutions* (4th ed., 1982); Schermers, *International Institutional Law* (3 vols., 1972–1974; v. 1 & 2 revised and consolidated in 1 v., 1980); Van Asbeck, *International Society in Search of an International Legal Order (1970)*; and Kirgis, *International Organizations in their Legal Setting: Documents, Comments and Questions* (1977).

The *Yearbook of International Organizations* contains over four thousand entries in its latest edition (19th ed., 1981). For each, it gives the name of the organization in its official languages, address, date of establishment, purpose, organizational structure, the list of serial publications, and membership. Indexes provide access to various organizations by their name in English, by broad subject (e.g., sixty are listed under Law, Administration), by geographical location, initials, and alphabetically by specific subject. The main periodical publications of each organization are listed. Supplementary sections also include the membership of the United Nations and its affiliated agencies, statistics on international organizations in general and detailed directorial information. The large majority of the organizations listed in the Yearbook are non-governmental.

There are two comprehensive compilations of documents on international organizations:

International Governmental Organizations; Constitutional Documents, compiled by Amos F. Peaslee, 3d rev. ed., 5 vols. (1974–1977).

International Organization and Integration, Annotated Basic Documents and Descriptive Directory of International Organizations and Arrangements, edited by P.J.G. Kapteyn and others., 2d rev. ed., 3 vols. (1981–1982).

Although many international law journals and many of the yearbooks contain articles and documents dealing with international agencies, the quarterly *International Organization* is devoted in its entirety to the legal and political aspects of the subject.

1. THE UNITED NATIONS

The creation of the League of Nations after World War I and particularly the establishment of the United Nations in 1945 have greatly expanded the traditional function of international law by giving it a visible focal point, an effective organizational structure, and a legislative center.[16] Moreover, the major subject oriented organizations of the past, as well as the various regional organizations, have been

16. The League of Nations was by no means the first international organization in history. It was preceded by numerous alliances and agencies specializing in one or several subject areas. The League was to be, however, the first universal organization of its kind. The failure of the ratification of its Covenant by the United States and its unfortunate history in the 1930's made it ineffective and finally contributed to its dissolution. The dream of a world government—although without full sovereignty—has been transferred to the United Nations whose membership is indeed very close to universal.

The United Nations Headquarters are in New York City, with additional offices in the Palais des Nations in Geneva and in Vienna, with field offices scattered throughout the world. U.N. grounds and buildings are protected by the same exterritorial rights as are embassies. The higher officials and the delegates to U.N. conferences enjoy the privileges and immunities of the diplomatic corps. The New York, Geneva, and Vienna U.N. Postal Administration has the right to issue postage stamps, accepted in all countries as long as cancelled in a U.N. Post Office. Since 1980, for example, the U.N.P.A. of New York has been issuing sheets of stamps depicting the flags of the entire membership. The program is scheduled for completion by 1990.

brought into a legal relationship with the United Nations by its Charter.

The United Nations Charter was drafted at the San Francisco Conference and signed there on June 26, 1945. It came into force on October 24, 1945 when ratified by the five major powers (China, France, USSR, United Kingdom and the United States) and the majority of the forty-six other participants. Thus, the United Nations has fifty-one original charter members. Since the San Francisco Conference, membership has been steadily increasing and as of Fall, 1983, is more than three times as high as in 1945 (the 1981 admission of Belize and Vanuatu brought the membership to 157). The official languages of the United Nations are English, French, Russian, Spanish and Chinese. Every member state has the right to send ten delegates and ten alternates to the General Assembly and to U.N.-sponsored conferences. Each, however, has but one vote (except for the Soviet Union which actually has three since Byelorussia and the Ukraine are members of the U.N. in addition to the USSR itself). The Security Council has five permanent members ("major powers") with the right of veto, and ten additional members elected for two-year terms.

Several treatises are available describing in detail the history of the United Nations and analyzing its functions and legal status. Two of these are considered standard texts: Goodrich, Hambro and Simons, *Charter of the United Nations; commentaries and documents* (3d ed., N.Y., 1969) and Kelsen, *The Law of the United Nations; a critical analysis of its fundamental problems* (N.Y., 1950). The basic casebook is Sohn, *Cases on United Nations Law*, supplemented by *Basic Documents of the United Nations* and, with Singh, by *International Organization: a classified bibliography* (all frequently updated).

Surveys of United Nations activities can be found in *Everyman's United Nations* (U.N. Office of Public Information). The basic volume, covering the period from 1945 to 1965 in its cumulative 1968 edition, is supplemented every five years by companion volumes. Directed primarily to lay readers, this handbook deals with political and security questions, economic and social issues, human rights developments, nonself-governing territories, administrative and budgetary questions, and activities of intergovernmental agencies related to the United Nations. It serves as an easy-to-read introduction to U.N. organization and activities, although it will not satisfy a serious researcher.

The *Yearbook of the United Nations* describes the proceedings and activities of the organization for every twelve-month period and gives an account of the major aspects of the work of the specialized agencies for each year. It is divided into the same sections as the preceding item but is much more comprehensive. Particularly helpful are references to official documentation at the end of each chapter. Membership lists of the United Nations and its specialized agencies appear in every volume. Although the *Yearbook* has often suffered from long delays (as much as three years) in publication, it is frequently the best place to begin research on a problem of international law handled by or relating to the United Nations.

The *United Nations Juridical Yearbook*, published since 1965 (for 1963), contains selected texts concerning the legal status of organizations in the United Nations system, legal activities of these organizations, and judicial decisions by international and national tribunals. The last chapter is a legal bibliography of books and articles dealing with the United Nations and international organizations in general.

The *United Nations Chronicle* reports on the activities of the organization on a current basis.[17]

Approximately 40,000 documents are distributed annually by the United Nations. To bring this mass under control, the U.N. has developed an elaborate but easy to understand system of codes which closely parallels the structure of the organization itself. Every document is provided with a symbol composed of capital letters and numerals. The components of the symbol are separated by a slash (/). Most documents are published first in near-print form. Those which are subsequently printed are assigned, in addition to their document symbol, a sales number.

The *Organizational Chart of the United Nations*, shown in Illustration H, is reproduced from *Basic Facts About the United Nations* (U.N. Office of Public Information, 1980) pp. 72–73, where it is followed by more detailed charts of individual U.N. agencies.

As the document symbols give a good idea of the United Nations organization and the range of its activities, and as U.N. documents will be found in most libraries arranged by these symbols, it may be useful to list the principal ones and explain briefly their meaning. Most symbols begin with a letter corresponding to one of the five major organs of the United Nations:

A/–	General Assembly
S/–	Security Council
E/–	Economic and Social Council
T/–	Trusteeship Council
ST/–	Secretariat

Documentary series for specific specialized organs begin with the following letter combinations:

AEC/–	Atomic Energy Commission
AT/–	UN Administrative Tribunal

17. In addition to those publications issued by the United Nations, brief factual information together with the text of the major United Nations constitutional documents can be found in *A Chronology and Factbook of the United Nations, 1941–1979*, 6th ed. by Hovet, (1979). The *Annual Review of United Nations Affairs* consisting mainly of reprints of parts of the Annual Report of the Secretary-General, statements of United Nations officials, and key documents of the year, has been published since 1949.

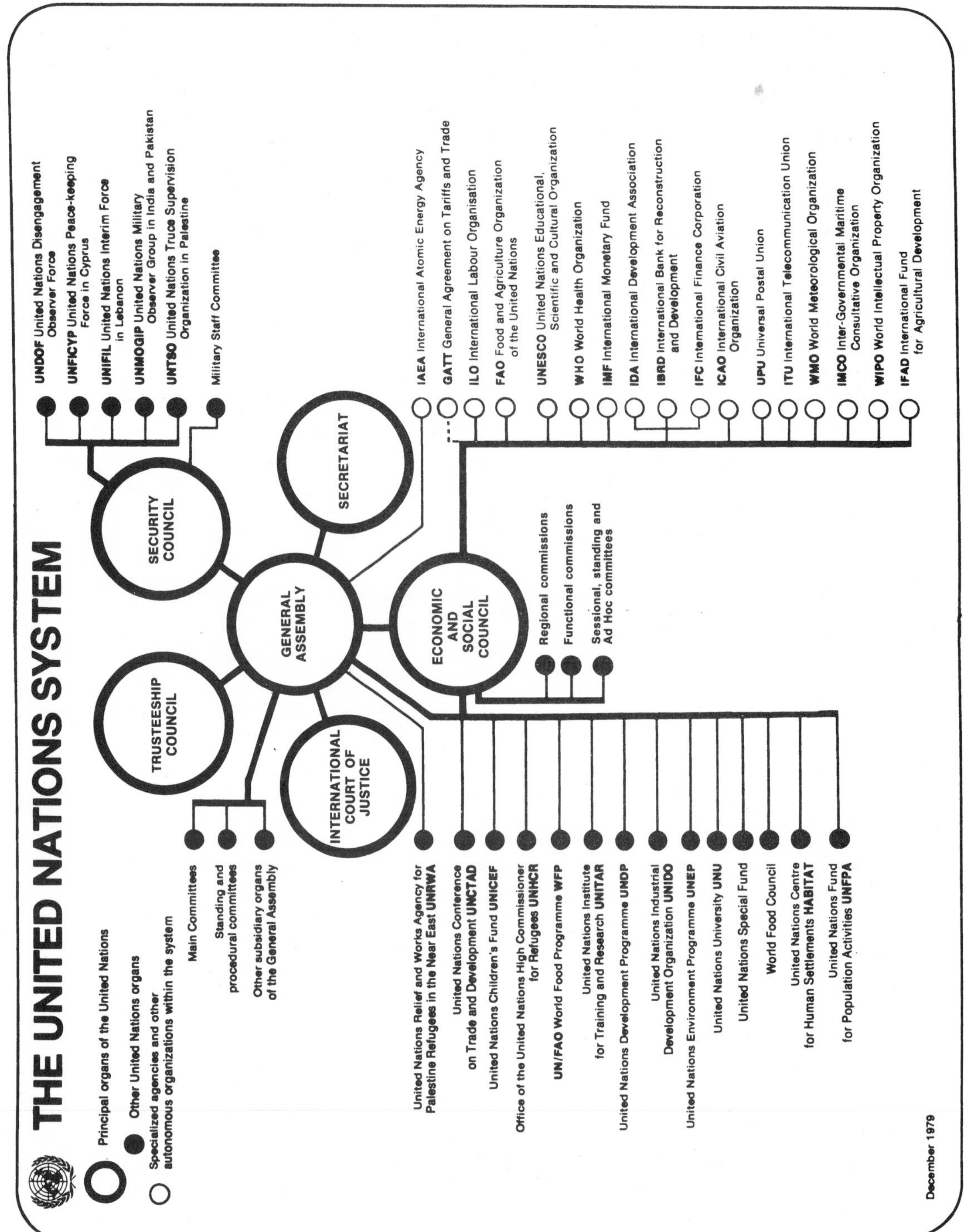

Illustration H

Organizational Chart of the United Nations, from *Basic Facts About the United Nations* (U.N. Office of Public Information, 1980).

CB/–	Inter-Agency Consultative Board
CERD/–	International Conference on the Elimination of All Forms of Racial Discrimination
DC/–	Disarmament Commission
DP/–	UN Development Program
ID/–	UN Industrial Development Organization
MSC/–	Military Staff Committee
SF/–	United Nations Special Fund
TD/–	UN Conference of Trade and Development

For documents of the parent body, the second part of a symbol consists of a chronological number of the document (e.g. A/1235). Documents of the committees and other subsidiary organs, are provided by one or several of the following additional elements:

–/C/–	Standing, permanent, main committee
–/AC./–	Ad hoc committee
–/DC./–	Drafting Committee
–/SC./–	Sub-committeee
–/WG./–	Working group
–/WP./–	Working Party
–/PC./–	Preparatory committee
–/CN./–	Commission
–/SP./–	State parties
–/Sub./–	Sub-commission
–/CONF./–	Conference

The series of subsidiary organs are then numbered in the order of their establishment, e.g.: A/C.1 through A/C.6 stands for the six committees of the General Assembly; E/CONF.6/– stands for the UN Conference on Freedom of Information held under the auspices of the Economic and Social Council in Geneva in 1948.

Additional materials dealing with the subject of an earlier document are indicated by the suffix –/Add.; a new edition of a document containing corrections and revisions is designated by –/Corr. and –/Rev.

Most U.N. documents are widely distributed to depository libraries and, as long as the supply lasts, on demand. Some, however, get only limited distribution or are restricted for security reasons. Limited distribution is indicated by the letter "L" appearing before the consecutive number at the end of the symbol; they usually are documents of a provisional nature such as draft resolutions or amendments. The letter "R" denotes restricted documents withheld from public circulation. The records of meetings are either verbatim (VR) or summary (SR), for example E/CONF.6/SR.3. Most of these are available in near-print form, but official records of the four principal organs, including those of the main committees of the General Assembly, are printed. Their symbols are GAOR (General Assembly

Official Records); ESCOR (Economic and Social Council Official Records); SCOR (Security Council Official Records); and, TCOR (Trusteeship Council Official Records).[18]

A complete *List of United Nations Documents Series Symbols* is available from the United Nations. Detailed handbooks to UN documents were published as *A Guide to the Use of United Nations Documents,* by Brenda Brimmer, et al. (1962) and *Publications of the United Nations System,* compiled by Harry Winton (1972). Similar manuals for the League of Nations documents, much less voluminous than those of the UN, are: *Guide to League of Nations Publications,* by H. Aufricht (1951) and *International Organizations, 1918–1945; A Guide to Research and Research Materials,* by G. W. Baer (Scholarly Resources, Inc., 1981).

Two more comprehensive and useful guides for the later period are *World Bibliography of International Documentation,* 2 vols., edited by T. D. Dimitrov (UNIFO Publishers, 1981) and *The Complete Reference Guide to U.N. Sales Publications 1946–78,* 2 vols., edited by M. E. Birchfield & J. Coolman (UNIFO Publishers, 1981).

Both printed documents and other U.N. publications are listed by sales numbers, consisting of date, a broad subject classification (in Roman numerals) and a consecutive number. For example, 66.II.F.12 stands for Publication No. 12 in the series dealing with Far Eastern and Asian economy (II.F) published in 1966. Sales numbers identify individual documents in the *Catalog of UN Publications,* distributed by the Sales Section, from which they can be ordered.

There are two types of indexes to United Nations documents: a general index and indexes of the main bodies.

Prior to 1973, documents were listed in the *United Nations Documents Index.* That index was issued monthly and cumulated annually. The annual cumulation consisted of two parts issued separately. Part One was simply a consolidation of the twelve monthly subject indexes. Part Two consisted of the following sections: (a) a consolidated list by symbol of all documents of the United Nations and the International Court of Justice received by the United Nations Library during that year; (b) a consolidated list of mimeographed documents re-published in the official records or elsewhere; (c) a list of sales publications; (d) an updating of the document series symbols; and, (e) a worldwide list of libraries and United Nations information centers receiving UN materials.

Although the arrangement of the *United Nations Documents Index* was gradually simplified, particularly by permitting direct access to documents by means of symbols, the lack of cumulative indexes beyond the annual volume and subject indexing from title without more detailed analysis, remained a serious limitation to research. Therefore the *Cumulated Index, Volumes 1–13, 1950–1962,* to the

18. That part of the Official Records of the General Assembly which contains records of the sessions of the Assembly and speeches delivered there usually appears a few years after the sessions. Before that, provisional records of the sessions can be found in the near-print series, A/PV. . . .

UN Documents Index, which was published in four volumes in 1974, is of substantial help. A successive cumulation covering volumes 14 to 24 (1963–1973) is an alphabetically arranged author and subject index.[19]

In January 1974, the Index was replaced by UNDEX, *United Nations Documents Index*, compiled by electronic means and published in three series, each issued ten times a year. Series A was a subject index; Series B listed the documents by the countries to which they refer; Series C was a listing and bibliographic description of all UN documents and publications except restricted material and internal papers.

Then in 1979, UNDEX was in turn replaced by a similar index called UNDOC which continues to provide access to UN documents today. No longer in three series, UNDOC includes in each of its issues a "Checklist of Documents and Publications" (with bibliographic citations, arranged by UN series symbols), and author, title and subject indexes. The annual cumulation of UNDOC is in three parts and includes a cumulative "Checklist," subject and author-title volumes.

Illustrations I and J, which follow, show sample entries for various UN documents, as they appear in the "Checklist" and the indexes of each UNDOC issue.

Separate indexes are available for each session of the General Assembly under the title *Index to Proceedings of the General Assembly.* They consist of the following parts: (a) list of the session officers and schedule of meetings; (b) agenda; (c) alphabetical subject index to the issues discussed and disposition of each item; (d) index to speeches in alphabetical order by country, subdivided by subject and by name of speaker; and, (e) numerical list of documents arranged by document symbol. There are similar indexes to the proceedings of the Security Council and the Economic and Social Council. The Trusteeship Council has been inactive in recent years since most countries under trusteeship have gained their independence, with the notable exception of Namibia.

In addition to the official records and reference works discussed earlier, the following series are of special interest to legal research:

(a) *Resolutions of the General Assembly* and other major organs of the United Nations, published in separate supplemental volumes for each session. For example, A/RES/2139 (XXI) refers to resolution no. 2139 of the 21st session of the General Assembly. In 1972, an official *Index to the Resolutions of the General Assembly, 1946–1970* was published; its Part 2 is an impor-

19. Familiarity with the jurisdiction of the various organs and knowledge of the period in which a particular issue was treated will permit the researcher to locate the information by consulting the documents of the relevant organ directly without going through the *Index.* This method will have its reward in the satisfaction that all documents, including the most recent items, issued by a particular organ have been reviewed. It may not even be more time-consuming.

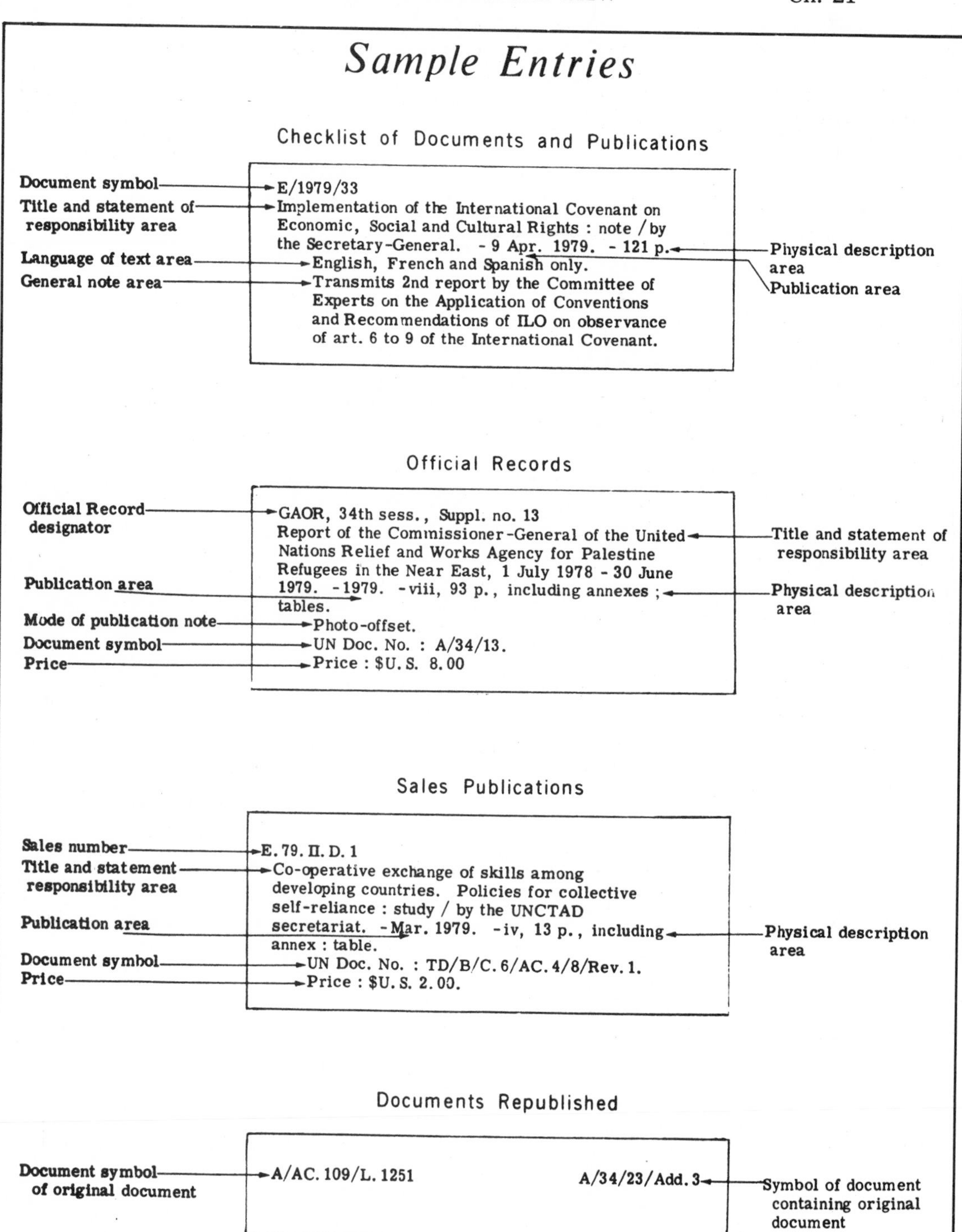

Sample Entries

Checklist of Documents and Publications

E/1979/33
Implementation of the International Covenant on Economic, Social and Cultural Rights : note / by the Secretary-General. - 9 Apr. 1979. - 121 p.
English, French and Spanish only.
Transmits 2nd report by the Committee of Experts on the Application of Conventions and Recommendations of ILO on observance of art. 6 to 9 of the International Covenant.

Official Records

GAOR, 34th sess., Suppl. no. 13
Report of the Commissioner-General of the United Nations Relief and Works Agency for Palestine Refugees in the Near East, 1 July 1978 - 30 June 1979. -1979. -viii, 93 p., including annexes ; tables.
Photo-offset.
UN Doc. No. : A/34/13.
Price : $U.S. 8.00

Sales Publications

E.79.II.D.1
Co-operative exchange of skills among developing countries. Policies for collective self-reliance : study / by the UNCTAD secretariat. -Mar. 1979. -iv, 13 p., including annex : table.
UN Doc. No. : TD/B/C.6/AC.4/8/Rev.1.
Price : $U.S. 2.00.

Documents Republished

A/AC.109/L.1251 A/34/23/Add.3

xvii

Illustration I

Sample document entries in UNDOC.

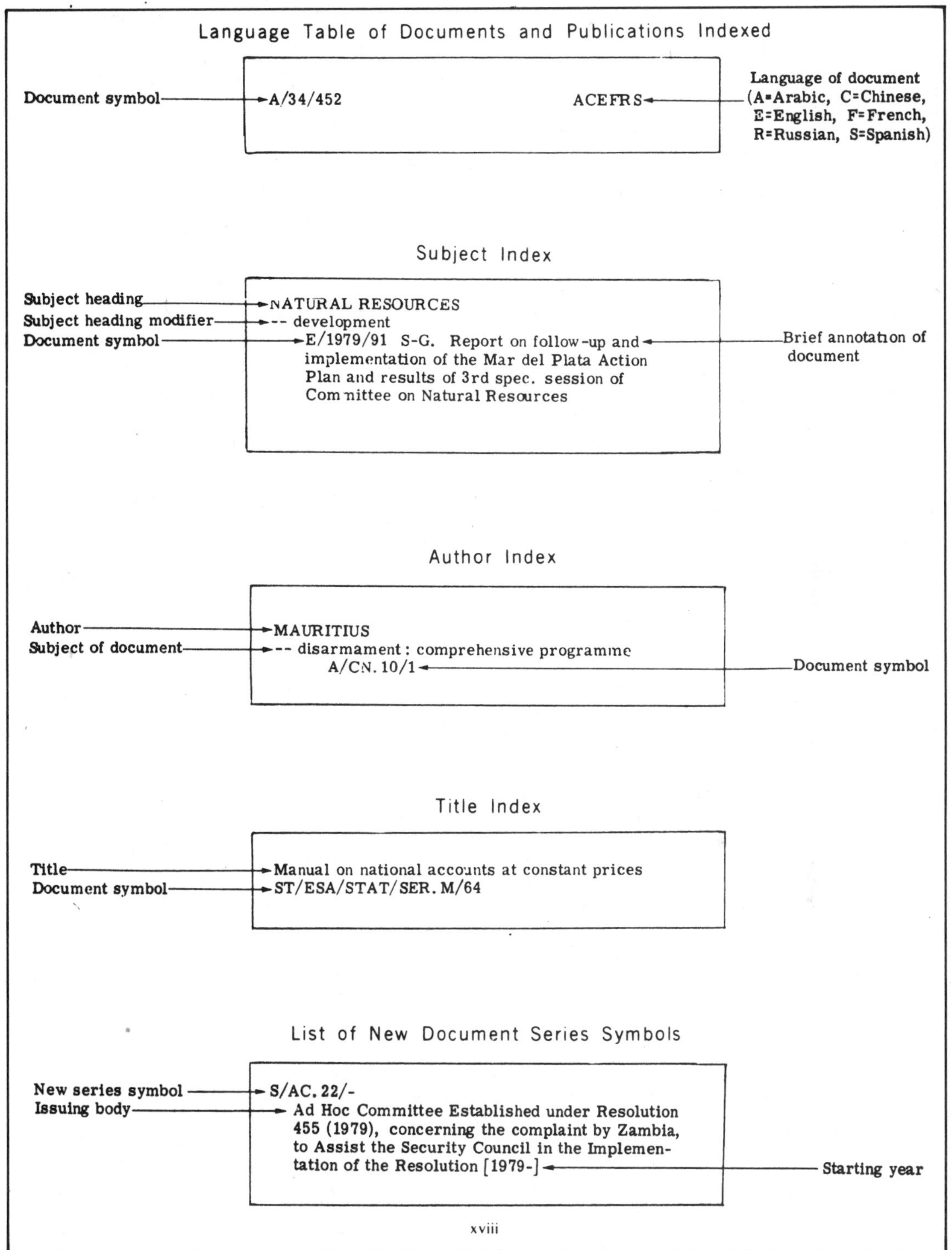

Illustration J

Sample index entries in UNDOC.

tant subject index. There is also an *Index to Resolutions of the Security Council, 1946–1970.* Oceana Publications is issuing a series of reprints of *United Nations Resolutions* in chronological order, compiled by D. J. Djonovich in four sub-series, one each for the General Assembly, the Security Council, the Economic and Social Council, and the Trusteeship Council. The United Nations issues the resolutions as a part of the *Official Records* of each of the three organs annually.

(b) *Repertory of Practice of United Nations Organs,* issued since 1955 in response to the General Assembly Resolution A/RES/796(VIII) of 1953.

(c) *Judgments of the United Nations Administrative Tribunal.* (Symbol AT/DEC/–.)

(d) *Yearbook of the International Law Commission* containing the summary records and documents of the Commission's sessions and its reports to the General Assembly. (Symbol A/CN.-4/SER.A/–.).

(e) *United Nations Legislative Series* which publishes the text of national legislation and treaty provisions concerning topics which are on the agenda of the International Law Commission in order to facilitate its work. (Symbol ST/LEG/SER.B/–.) [20]

The work of the United Nations in many fields is carried on by separate international organizations affiliated to the UN by agreements based on Article 57 of the Charter. These organizations, referred to in the Charter as "specialized agencies," submit reports to the Economic and Social Council which in turn presents them to the General Assembly. No indexing or bibliographic service is available covering the publications of all these organizations. As of the present time, the list of UN associated organizations includes the following fifteen:

1. *The International Atomic Energy Agency (IAEA),* while not technically a "specialized agency", was established by the UN in 1957 and is related to the UN by treaty. It issues its own annual catalog and a bimonthly *Bulletin.* Its activities are analyzed in Szasz, *The Law and Practice of the International Atomic Energy Agency* (1970).

2. *The International Labor Organization (ILO)* established in 1919 and associated with the UN since 1946. An annual catalog of its publications as well as a bi-weekly computerized *International Labor Documentation* (since 1965) are available. ILO also publishes a quarterly *Official Bulletin* since 1920, *Minutes* of the Governing Body, and sessional documents of international labor conferences. Since 1919, the ILO has prepared more than 120 conventions extending the benefits achieved by organized labor in

20. To the above should be added among others, documents issued by the Sixth Committee (Legal) of the General Assembly (A/C.6/–), those of the Commission on Human Rights (E/CN.4/–), on the Status of Women (E/CN.6/–) and on Narcotic Drugs (E/CN.7/–) of the Economic and Social Council, as well as its Committee on Crime Prevention and Control (E/CN.5/C.1/–).

the industrialized countries throughout the world. These have been compiled and published in *International Labour Conventions and Recommendations, 1919–1981,* in a subject arrangement. The I.L.O. *Legislative Series* which is a selection of the more important texts in the field of national labor and social security legislation in three parallel editions in English, French and Spanish.

3. *The Food and Agricultural Organization (FAO),* established in 1945, issues, since 1967, a *Current Index* to its documents. In addition to reports of its annual conferences, the FAO also publishes a digest of agricultural legislation of its member states, entitled *Food and Agricultural Legislation.* In 1970, a collection of the FAO *Basic Texts* appeared in two volumes.

4. *United Nations Educational, Scientific, and Cultural Organization (UNESCO)* adopted its constitution in 1945 and was affiliated with the UN in 1946. A *General Catalogue* of its publications is kept up to date by bi-monthly supplements. The most important documentary series is the *Record* of the General Conference which includes resolutions, committee reports, and proceedings. A recent publication, *Guide to UNESCO,* by P.I. Hajnal (Oceana Publications, 1983) describes the organization's structure and functions and includes an extensive bibliography and a number of documentary appendices.

5. *The World Health Organization's (WHO)* constitution was ratified in 1948. It publishes the monthly WHO *Chronicle,* the annual *Official Records,* and a bibliography of its publications every five years. A selection of brief summaries of national health legislation of significance appears in its quarterly *International Digest of Health Legislation.*

6. *International Bank for Reconstruction and Development* (World Bank, *IBRD*), established in 1945, is active in the promotion of private foreign investments by loans, particularly to developing countries. Its publication program includes annual reports and summaries of proceedings of its Governing Board, and since 1964, a quarterly periodical *Finance and Development.*

7. *The International Finance Corporation (IFC)* has been in existence since 1956 for the purpose of assisting less developed countries in their economic growth.

8. *The International Development Association (IDA)* provides, since 1960, financing of economic projects in developing countries.

9. *The International Monetary Fund (IMF),* established in 1945 engages in foreign exchange and gold transactions in order to promote a balanced expansion of trade and support for weak currencies. Its publication program includes the annual summary proceedings of the meetings of the Board of Governors (since 1946), selected decisions of the Executive Directors (since 1970), a *Catalogue of Publications,* 1946–1972, and a periodical, *Staff Pa-*

pers, issued three times a year jointly with the World Bank. The combined library of the Bank and Fund prepares an index to economic and financial literature, as well as issues dealing with developing countries. *International Monetary Relations,* by Yeager (1976) is an analysis of the role of the Bank, the Fund, and other selected agencies in international finance.[21]

10. *The International Civil Aviation Organization (ICAO),* founded in Chicago in 1944 and affiliated with the UN since 1945, has an annual cumulative index of publications since 1951 with weekly supplements, annual reports of the Council to the Assembly, sessional Assembly reports, resolutions, and minutes, and a monthly *Bulletin.* Its activities have been analyzed by Thomas Buergenthal in *Law-Making in the International Civil Aviation Organization* (Syracuse, 1969).

11. *The Universal Postal Union (UPU),* established in 1874, promotes international cooperation in postal services. It distributes a report on its activities, the documents of postal congresses, the sessional documents, resolutions, and decisions of its Executive Council, and a monthly periodical, *Union Postale.*

12. *The International Telecommunications Union (ITU),* established in 1865, parallels the work of the postal union in telecommunications. It publishes an annual *Report of Activities,* the *Final Acts* of its Administrative Conference, *Resolutions and Decisions* of its Administrative Council (since 1965 in looseleaf form), documents of its Plenary Assembly, and a monthly *Telecommunications Journal.*

13. *The World Meteorological Organization (WMO)* was established in 1947. A catalog of its publications is available. The WMO issues sessionally abridged final reports and resolutions of its Congresses and meetings of its Executive Committee.

14. *The Intergovernmental Maritime Consultative Organization (IMCO),* established in 1948, issues a documents index in looseleaf form since 1966. Other publications include a three-volume set of its *Basic Documents* (1968–1969), Assembly resolutions since 1959, a biennial Report of the Council to the Assembly, and a semi-annual *Bulletin.*

15. *The International Trade Organization and General Agreement on Tariffs and Trade (GATT):* The Agreement, drafted in 1947 and modified in 1955 and 1965, is a multilateral convention embodying reciprocal rights and obligations of member countries in international trade. *Basic Instruments and Selected Documents* are issued annually since 1952, an annual activity re-

21. The Bank and the Fund were established by the Bretton Woods Agreement which provided for a gold standard for the U.S. dollar, with all other major currencies pegged to it. The exchange system thus created succeeded in maintaining a relative stability of world currencies for almost thirty years. Without being expressly repealed, it was in fact abandoned when the United States quit the gold standard in the early 1970's, letting the dollar float against gold and foreign currencies.

port since 1952, and an *Analytical Index* of articles of GATT appeared in a fourth edition in 1980.

The *World Intellectual Property Organization (WIPO)*, dealing with copyright, patents, and related topics, was established in the late 1960's and is, in its activities, very similar to a specialized agency.

The Economic and Social Council maintains four regional commissions to cooperate with the locally established regional organizations: The Economic Commission for Europe *(ECE)*, Asia and the Far East *(ECAFE)*, Latin America *(ECLA)*, and Africa *(ECAF)*. Each publishes its own very informative *Bulletin*.

2. REGIONAL ORGANIZATIONS

Article 71 of the United Nations Charter acknowledges the existence of regional organizations with objectives often very similar to those of the UN itself. A handy general collection of the basic documents of the most regional organizations was compiled by Ruth C. Lawson, *International Regional Organizations* (N.Y., 1962). A more recent text was published in 1978 by the U.N. Institute for Training and Research under the title *Regional International Organizations and the United Nations*. The documentation of the more active regional organizations will be briefly surveyed in this section.

a. Organization of American States

The Organization of American States is the oldest regional organization, having been established in 1890 at the First International Conference of American States. It has its own General Assembly, a Meeting of Consultation of Ministers of Foreign Affairs, a Permanent Council, and an Economic and Social Council, as well as a number of specialized committees. Information about its current activities can be found in the quarterly *OAS Chronology* published in English and Spanish. Official documents of the organization are issued in nineteen series designated by letters of the alphabet.[22]

Unfortunately, a large number of OAS documents are of limited distribution and, although listed in the Documents Series, are very difficult to obtain. In addition, much of the documentation is available only in Spanish.

A good though older bibliography of the OAS can be found in the standard treatise by Charles G. Fenwick, *The Organization of American States* (Washington, 1963).

Of the four Latin American organizations aiming at economic cooperation and ultimately integration,[23] the Andean Program is the

22. Series A, B and M, for example, contain the text of treaties; Series C consists of final acts of inter-American conferences: Series D through L print the documents of the various organs of the organization and Series Z is a general index. Of particular interest are the documents of the Inter-American Juridical Committee (Series Q) which is engaged in the preparation and drafting of multilateral conventions in a way similar to the work of the United Nations International Law Commission.

23. More recently efforts to promote trade among Latin American countries

most active while the others, especially the two most ambitious ones (LAFTA and CACM), suffer from political instability and wide economic differences among member countries and are almost inactive at this time. The Andean Program, on the other hand, is presently engaged in exciting development projects, such as a cooperative automobile production and assembly and particularly the construction of a powerful hydro-electric plant on the Upper Amazon (with Brazil). Garcia-Amador, the Secretary General of the OAS, analyzed the legal aspects of the Program in *The Andean Legal Order; A New Community Law* (Oceana, 1978).

b. Organization of African Unity

The Organization of African Unity (since 1963) superseded an array of regional groupings created shortly after the former African colonies had gained independence. The principal organs of the OAU include the Assembly of Heads of States, the Council of Foreign Ministers, and a Secretariat. OAU basic documents, as well as those of its predecessors and its related organizations, have been collected by Louis B. Sohn in *Basic Documents of African Regional Organizations* (3 vols. 1971–72). A textual treatment of Africa's efforts at cooperation are described in *African International Legal History* published by the U.N. Institute for Training and Research in 1975.[24]

c. Council of Europe

The Council of Europe, established in 1959, aims at achieving a greater unity among its members, mostly by drafting conventions in a large variety of fields (e.g. human rights, social security, university studies and reciprocity of academic diplomas, patents, criminal matters, and television frequencies). Close to 100 such agreements have been signed so far. Their texts appear in the *European Treaty Series.* The Council's structure consists of a Committee of Ministers and a Consultative Assembly. The most important documentation of the Council of Europe is issued in several Consultative Assembly series of pamphlets. These include speeches and discussions before the Assembly as well as its resolutions, orders, draft conventions and their official interpretation. The documents of the Committee of Ministers are confidential and only available to member governments.

The structure, functions, and achievements of the Council have been described in Robertson's *The Council of Europe* (2d ed., 1961),

and eliminate restrictions affecting imports led to the establishment of the Latin American Free Trade Association (LAFTA, established in 1961). Among other Latin American organizations are the Organization of Central American States (1951); the Central American Common Market (CACM, organized in 1958); and the Andean Program (1969). The basic documents of these and other organizations with similar goals have been collected in *Instruments Relating to the Economic Integration of Latin America*, published by the Inter-American Institute of International Legal Studies (N.Y., 1968). In 1973, twelve Caribbean Commonwealth countries established the Caribbean Community.

24. Documents related to the network of Asian organizations have been compiled in *Basic Documents of Asian Regional Organizations*, edited by M. Haas (4 vols, 1974).

in his *European Institutions, Cooperation: Integration: Unification* (3rd ed., 1973), and in *The Manual of the Council of Europe* (1980).

A system of international protection of human rights was established among the member countries of the Council of Europe by the European Convention of Human Rights and Fundamental Freedoms of November 4, 1950. Its unique feature is that it enables individuals to seek redress against their own governments before international bodies (the European Human Rights Commission and the European Court of Human Rights). A considerable literature has developed on and from this system. The *Reports* of the court, the *European Yearbook of Human Rights* and the many writings of K. Vasak, the Head of the Human Rights Division, are the most important research sources. A useful, although irregularly published periodical on legal activities in the Council is the *Information Bulletin on Legal Activities Within the Council of Europe and in Member States* (June 1978–date).

d. European Communities

The European Communities comprise the European Coal and Steel Community (from 1952), European Economic Community (established 1958) and the European Atomic Energy Community (1958). In 1967, the principal executive organs of the three communities were merged and the name European Communities adopted. These organs are the Commission, a permanent body responsible for implementing the basic Treaty, and the Council of Ministers. The Commission reports annually to the European Parliament which may compel it to resign by a vote of no confidence. The meetings of the Commission and the Council of Ministers are private but those of the European Parliament are open to the public. The judicial organ of the Communities is the Court of Justice which interprets and applies the basic Treaty. Originally, the Council of Ministers was to be the top executive agency to protect the special interests of the member states. Because of its continuity and a large Secretariat, the Commission gradually increased its authority and the consent of the Council has become largely a formality.

The original membership of the three communities consisted of Belgium, France, West Germany, Italy, Luxembourg and the Netherlands. Greece, Turkey and several African countries were associated to the Community by special conventions. As of January 1, 1973, Denmark, Eire, and the United Kingdom joined the European Communities. Greece was admitted January 1, 1981, bringing the total membership to ten. Applications for admission by Turkey, Portugal and Spain are before the organization.

A handy official collection of basic documents relating to the group is *Treaties Establishing the European Communities* (1973). A small but useful pamphlet by E. Noel, *How the European Community's Institutions Work*, has appeared in several editions, the last in 1978. Among the introductory treatises on the Community are Lasok and Bridge, *An Introduction to the Law and Institutions of the European Communities* (1973), Robertson, *European Institutions* (3rd ed., 1973), cited above, and Kapteyn and van Themaat, *Introduction of the Law of the European Communities after the Accession of New Member States* (1973). The communities themselves published an appraisal of their external relations in *European Community, International Organizations, and Multilateral Agreements* (1978).

Until 1972, the official languages of the European Communities were French, German, Italian and Dutch, although many unofficial publications were also available in English. As of 1973, the official languages include also English. Retrospective publication in English of some basic documents (e.g. parts of the *Official Journal* and the reports of the Court of Justice) is now completed.[25]

The major publication of the Communities is the *Official Journal* of the European Communities, issued in two parts: *Legislation,* which includes among other material, the regulations of the Commission and the Council; and *Information and Notices.* The *Debates of the European Parliament* are published as an Annex to the *Journal.* Reports and other documents relating to the Parliament appear as its *Working Documents.*

The Secretariat of the Commission issues a monthly *Bulletin of the European Communities* in English, which reprints selected documents and surveys the activity of the organization. It also lists all items published in the *Official Journal* and gives the docket of the Court of Justice. In a concluding part, it contains a listing of other Community publications including those of limited distribution. General reports for each of the three Communities are published annually.

The European Parliament publishes a *Yearbook* which contains biographical information about its members, the text of the adopted documents for the year and a listing of the session and committee reports issued during the year.

Biographical information can also be found in *Who's Who: European Communities and Other European Organizations, 1981–1982,* 2d ed. (Editions Delta, distrib. by Unipub, 1981).

Current information about developments in European integration appears in the quarterly *European Documentation,* issued by the Parliament.

Since 1973 the Court of Justice makes its decisions public in English, in its *Reports of Cases Before the Court.* Beginning in 1954, they were published in French as the *Recueil de la Jurisprudence* and in the other three official languages of the Communities. The decisions of the first ten years have been digested and evaluated in

25. Official texts of all secondary legislation in force on January 1, 1973, in English, chronologically arranged, are contained in the "Special Edition" of the *Official Journal,* 17 volumes, 1972–73. This material has been also published under a subject arrangement in 42 volumes, as *European Communities, Secondary Legislation,* in London, 1973–74.

Dix ans de Jurisprudence de la Cour de Justice des Communautés Europeennes (Cologne, 1965). A detailed index-digest of decisions of the European Court as well as national courts interpreting the basic treaties of the Communities is published annually as *Repertoire de al jurisprudence relative aux traites instituant les Communautes Europeennes.*

The Court's decisions also appear in English in the unofficial *Common Market Law Reports* (European Law Centre, Ltd., 1962–date). The scope of this publication is broader than its title indicates as it also includes selected decisions of national courts.

For the American researcher, the Commerce Clearing House *Common Market Reporter* (4 vols. looseleaf) is a most valuable source of current information in English. The scope of the looseleaf service includes primarily the European Communities, but incidentally also the regional organizations of Latin America, the League of Arab States and the Council for Mutual Economic Assistance. Volumes 1 and 2 include the Community treaties and selected regulations. Volume 3 contains court decisions, new developments, biographies and bibliographies. Volume 4, "Doing Business in Europe" is a summary of national legislation of European countries in business-related matters, in particular corporate structure, taxation, labor law, and patents. Illustrations K, L, M and N show the finding of a regulation and a clarification of that regulation in the CCH *Common Market Reporter.*

In 1973, another looseleaf service started publication in London, the *Encyclopedia of European Economic Community Law,* 11 vols. (London, Sweet & Maxwell). Series A contains United Kingdom sources, Series B the Community Treaties, and Series C the Community Secondary Legislation.

Common Market Law, by A. Campbell (3 vols., 1969–1973, with annual supplements) is a valuable reference work on the law of the Community, covering legislation, case law and treaties.

The *European Law Digest* (European Law Centre, Ltd., 1973–date), published monthly in London, is an analytical summary of the major published decisions of the courts of West European countries relating to the European Communities treaties.

A useful commentary on the E.E.C. Treaty is H. Smit & P. E. Herzog, *The Law of the European Economic Community,* 6 vols. (Matthew Bender, 1976, with annual supplements).

There are now a number of journals, both general and specialized, covering legal developments in the European Community. These include the following selected examples:

Common Market Law Review (British Institute of International and Comparative Law, 1964–date, *quarterly*).

EURODOC, a Monthly Review of European Community Documents and Related Publications (Euroinformation, Ltd., 1982–date, 11 times a year).

(¶ 1-3299 are in Volume 1; ¶ 3300-7999 are in Volume 2.)

References are to paragraph (¶) numbers

Illustration K

"Topical Index" to CCH *Common Market Reporter*, v. 1, showing entry for description of wine.

(This and the following four Illustrations are reproduced from *Common Market Reporter*, published and copyrighted by Commerce Clearing House, Inc., Chicago, Ill. 60646).

Chapter I. Description of Products Originating Within the Community

Section A. Description of Table Wines

I. Labeling

• ***Regulation No. 355/79***

[¶ 523B] Article 2. **[Description on labels]**

1. In the case of table wines, the description on the labeling shall include the following information:

(a) the words "table wine";

(b) the nominal volume of the table wine in accordance with the provisions of Directive 75/106/EEC [see ¶ 3381.51];

(c) in the case of:

—containers with a nominal volume of not more than 60 liters; the name or business name of the bottler and the local administrative area or part thereof in which his head office is situated,

—other containers; the name or business name of the consignor and the local administrative area or part thereof in which his head office is situated.

Where wine is bottled in or consigned from a local administrative area or part thereof other than that mentioned above or a neighboring local administrative area, the information referred to in the first and second indents of (c) shall include an indication of the local administrative area or part thereof where the operation took place;

(d) in the case of:

(i) consignment to another Member State or export: the Member State in whose territory the grapes were harvested and turned into wine, provided that both these operations took place in the same Member State;

(ii) table wine which was made in a Member State other than that in which the grapes were harvested: the words "wine made in . . . from grapes harvested in . . ." completed by the indication of the respective Member States;

(iii) table wine:

—resulting from a mixture of grapes or from coupage of products originating in more than one Member State, or

—resulting from coupage of a table wine referred to in the first indent, with a table wine referred to in (ii):

the words "blend of wines from different countries of the European Community."

(e) in the case of the table wines referred to in the third indent of point 11 of Annex II to Regulation (EEC) No. 337/79: the word "retsina."

2. In the case of table wines, the description on the labeling may be supplemented by the following information:

(a) a statement as to whether the wine is red, rosé or white;

(b) a brand name, in accordance with the conditions laid down in Article 8;

Illustration L–1

Regulation on description of wine in CCH *Common Market Reporter,* v. 1.

(c) the names or business names of the natural or legal persons or group of persons involved in the distribution of the table wine in question, and the local administrative area or part thereof in which their head offices are situated;

(d) a distinction awarded to one of the persons or to the group of persons referred to in (c) by an official body or a body officially recognized for the purpose, where this is likely to enhance the reputation of the table wine concerned and provided that such distinction is governed by implementing rules or, failing this, by provisions of the Member State concerned;

(e) where the table wine is not consigned to another Member State or exported and if the conditions laid down in paragraph 1(d)(ii) and (iii) are not fulfilled, the Member State in whose territory the grapes were harvested and turned into wine;

(f) the actual and/or total alcoholic strength by volume and other analytical data, in so far as such information is governed by implementing rules.

(g) a recommendation to the consumer as to the use of the wine;

(h) details as to:

—the type of product,

—the particular color of the table wine,

(i) the lower-case letter "e," indicating that the prepackages satisfy the conditions laid down in Directive 75/106/EEC as regards filling.

in so far as this information is governed by implementing rules or, failing this, by provisions of the Member State concerned. However, the use of this information may be confined to the table wines referred to in paragraph 3.

3. In the case of table wines described in accordance with Article 54(2) and (3) of Regulation (EEC) No. 337/79, the description may be further supplemented by the following information:

(a) the name of a geographical unit which is smaller than the Member State, in accordance with the conditions laid down in Article 4;

(b) the name of one or two vine varieties, in accordance with the conditions laid down in Article 5;

(c) the vintage year in accordance with the conditions laid down in Article 6;

(d) details regarding the method of production of the table wine as described on a list to be adopted. This list may include only those descriptions which are governed, as to the conditions for their use, by provisions of the producer Member States;

(e) an award granted by an official body or a body recognized for the purpose to a specified quantity of table wine, provided that the information is accompanied by a statement of the vintage year and the award can be proved by an appropriate document.

The Member States shall notify the Commission on any awards that may be granted to table wines in their territory and of the rules that are applied in this connection;

(f) a statement that the wines were bottled:

Illustration L–2

Continuation of regulation in CCH *Common Market Reporter*, v. 1.

469 3-1-83 **Current Topical Index** **6949**

[The next page is 6957.]

Illustration M

"Current Topical Index" showing entry for later ruling on wine labelling in CCH *Common Market Reporter*, v. 3.

in the interests of the Community that such possibilities exist?

3. What obstacles does the Commission see to issuing decisions, albeit of a limited period of validity, in cases where its present practice is to send undertakings comfort letters?

Answer:

1. The practice of issuing "comfort letters" informing the firms concerned that a case has been closed is applied only where the Commission has no objections to put forward, and would therefore have no reason to take part in infringement proceedings.

2. The Commission is not so far aware of any case in which the national courts have applied Community competition law or stricter domestic competition law, after a comfort letter of this kind has been sent.

If a national court has doubts about the applicability of Article 85 of the EEC Treaty in a case where a comfort letter has been sent, it is entitled to seek the Commission's opinion, particularly if it should find that the Commission was not informed of all the facts. This would certainly help to limit the possibility of contradictory rulings. On the other point, the Commission sees no threat to the Community interest in the exercise of national powers under stricter laws after the Commission has held that a case is not caught by the EEC Treaty competition rules.

3. The Commission sees no obstacles to this step; it simply thinks that it would protract the proceedings.

The Commission would also refer the Honorable Member to its answer to Written Question No. 813/82, by Mr. Prout.[1]

[¶ 10,433] Labeling of Wines to Indicate Alcoholic Strength to Be Proposed.

Written Question No. 420/82, submitted by Mr. Diana, Member of the European Parliament, to the Commission of the European Communities. Official Journal No. C287, November 4, 1982, page 3.

Back reference: ¶ 525.41.

Subject: Labeling of wines.

Under existing Community rules indication of alcoholic strength on wine labels is optional. In Italy, for example, the law requires that such information be given, while in France and Germany there is no such obligation.

Does the Commission consider that it would be advisable to make it compulsory in the Community to indicate the alcoholic strength of wines on the label in order to provide the consumer with more information?

Answer:

Regulation (EEC) No. 355/79,[1a] as last amended by Regulation (EEC) No. 3685/81,[2] makes it optional for the alcoholic strength to be shown on wine labels. For the period up to August 31, 1983, however, the Member States may make it compulsory for the actual alcoholic strength to be shown in the case of wines distributed in their territories. The 1978 directive on labeling[3] also provides that particulars of the alcoholic strength may be required by law. The Commission

[1] Official Journal No. C275, October 18, 1982, page 15 [¶ 10,427].

[1a] Official Journal No. L54, March 5, 1979, page 99 [¶ 521, 525.41].

[2] Official Journal No. L369, December 24, 1981, page 1.

[3] Official Journal No. L33, February 8, 1979, page 1 [¶ 3341.13, 3353].

Illustration N

Answer to Question on wine labelling in CCH *Common Market Reporter,* v. 3.

European Competition Law Review (ESC Publishing Ltd., 1980–date, *quarterly*).

European Law Review (Sweet & Maxwell, 1975–date, *bimonthly*).

Excellent bibliographies on the law of the European Communities include G. Dahlmanns, "European Communities Law," in vol. 3 of the *International Journal of Law Libraries* (1975);[26] C. M. Germain, "European Community Law–A Selective Bibliography . . . ," 8 *International Journal of Law Libraries* 239 (1980); and J. Jeffries, *A Guide to the Official Publications of the European Communities*, 2d ed. (Mansell Publishing, 1981).

e. Council for Mutual Assistance

The Council for Mutual Economic Assistance was established in 1949 as an eastern counterpart to the then planned European Economic Community. It has ten members, nine from Eastern Europe and Mongolia. Its activities can be followed from its annual reports. Since the documentation is in Russian and other East European languages, an American scholar will welcome two very thorough works on the Council: Szawlowski's *System of International Organization of the Communist Countries* (1976) and a 110-page compilation of documents and references by W. Butler, *Source Book on Socialist International Organization* (1978).

H. CONCLUSION

In recent years, the perennial international law interests in national sovereignty, collective security, and disarmament have been eclipsed by new topics, some of obvious global scope such as space exploration, nuclear energy, and the law of the sea, and some traditionally reserved to individual nations, in particular human rights. Substantial literatures have grown up on each of these topics, but to review them would be beyond the scope of this work. The researcher in international law, however, should be aware of the existence of large collections of material on these specialized problems. These may include official documents, commercial publications as well as periodicals and looseleaf services. Each major topic of modern international law may, in a sense, offer a bibliographic microcosm of the larger literature of the field as a whole.

Research in international law is now also being enhanced by computer access. EUROLEX, a European research system, includes coverage of European Communities and Council of Europe materials, English law, and other European sources. This service has recently become available through WESTLAW. Some European Communities materials (including the Court of Justice decisions) are contained in the United Kingdom data base recently added to LEXIS.

26. Now the *International Journal of Legal Information.*

Chapter 22

NEW MEDIA IN LEGAL RESEARCH

A. INTRODUCTION

This chapter examines the use of new media in legal research and law practice. However, most of what will be described here is no longer strictly "new". Microforms (a composite term which encompasses microfilm, microfiche, and other forms of miniaturized texts), for example, have been in use for decades. What *is* new is the growing use of these materials and their integration into the process of legal research. A legal researcher of thirty years ago would be quite surprised by a visit to a law library today. The use of computerized legal research systems and microforms for access to legal materials has become commonplace. These media are no longer experimental in nature, but are proven and accepted research tools.

Still, these materials do differ in format and technique from the standard printed sources, and justify an introduction to their use. What follows is necessarily brief. The Additional Readings, suggested at the end of the chapter, will provide more detailed treatments of the topics covered.

B. COMPUTERIZED LEGAL RESEARCH

In tracing the history of modern legal research methods, one can see three major technological advances which fundamentally changed access to legal information. The first was clearly the invention of printing in the middle of the fifteenth century. The second was the almost simultaneous development, at the end of the nineteenth and the beginning of the twentieth centuries, of several new forms of legal publication: West's key number digest system, annotated statutes, the annotated reports of Lawyers Co-op, Shepard's citations, and the looseleaf services initiated by Prentice-Hall and CCH. The third of these bibliographic revolutions was the adaptation of the computer for full-text searching of legal sources. The two major examples of this last development in this country are the competing commercial services, *LEXIS* and *WESTLAW.*

1. LEXIS

a. Scope

LEXIS, a service of Mead Data Central, was the first commercially successful computerized legal research system. The LEXIS data base includes the full text of all current federal and state appellate court decisions. Retrospective coverage varies from jurisdiction to jurisdiction, but is growing. LEXIS includes within its data base many lower federal court slip opinions that are not published in any printed source. Although LEXIS began primarily as a case retrieval system, it now includes the *U.S. Code,* statutes from four states, material on several administrative and regulatory fields, and some secondary sources. It also provides access to a large number of nonlegal data bases.

The material in the LEXIS data base is broadly organized, by subject or jurisdiction, into "libraries", which are further subdivided into appropriate "files". For example, one of the federal libraries available is the "general federal", which includes such files as the decisions of the federal courts, the *U.S. Code, the Federal Register* beginning with 1980, Supreme Court briefs in argued cases beginning with 1979, and certain titles of the *CFR.* Separate libraries are also available in taxation; securities; trade regulation; bankruptcy; patents, trademarks, and copyrights; communications; labor; energy; public contracts; and professional responsibility.

Libraries of state law with the full text of appellate court decisions exist for each of the fifty states, but at present statute files are available for only Kansas, Missouri, New York, and Ohio. Mead has begun adding state attorney general opinions. A separate Delaware Corporation Law library is also available. Foreign libraries for the United Kingdom, France, and the European Community have recently been added. As the competition between LEXIS and WESTLAW continues, more libraries are likely to be added to each system.

b. Search Procedure

A detailed explanation of the search procedure employed in the LEXIS system is beyond the scope of this chapter. The reader's attention in this regard is directed to the very helpful *LEXIS Handbook* available from Mead Data Central. It should be noted also that training sessions and films are provided to subscribers, and many law schools now offer their students instruction in the use of the LEXIS service. The basic features of the system and a brief summary of the search and retrieval methods used are set forth below.

Conducting legal research on the LEXIS computer involves asking the computer to find and display documents in its data base, which contain words or phrases in particular configurations as specified by the searcher. The researcher communicates with the computer through the use of a typewriter-like keyboard device on which commands are typed. Items which meet the criteria set out in the search request are displayed on the screen of a CRT (cathode ray tube) terminal. A printer is available which enables the researcher to obtain copies of the documents displayed. The LEXIS system was designed for simplicity of operation. Many of the commands that the researcher will use are allocated special keys on the terminal's keyboard which can activate procedures directly at a single touch. Those unique features have, however, limited access to LEXIS from other multi-purpose terminals, but LEXIS has recently announced that it will soon be accessible from some other standard terminals.

After logging on to the computer and choosing the desired *library* and *file,* the user must then type in the search request. Because the documents in the LEXIS data base have not been indexed or subject-categorized in any way, the user is limited to asking the computer to locate documents in which specific words or phrases appear. For example, the researcher interested in finding cases on the products liability of furniture manufacturers can request all cases containing the phrase "products liability" and the word "furniture". Such a request will produce all documents in the relevant *library* that contain these specific terms, but will not retrieve any items that deal with specific types of furniture, e.g., "sofabeds," where the word "furniture" does not actually appear. In other words, the system (with very few exceptions) will not locate synonyms, antonyms, or other forms of the words used in the search.

Because of the strictly literal nature of the LEXIS research process, efficient use of the system presupposes the user's familiarity with legal terminology. It is also essential that the researcher formulate the search request in such a way as to compensate for synonymous representation of concepts. The word "automobile", for example, might also be expressed as "vehicle" or "car". A search for "attorney" will not automatically retrieve "lawyer", "counsel", or any other synonym.

Search requests in LEXIS are based on the principles of Boolean logic. Connectors such as "and", "or", and "and not" are used to appropriately tie together all the words and phrases which the researcher deems relevant to the problem at hand. They can be used to expand or contract one's search. For example, the search request for the products liability problem discussed above might read "products liability and furniture", which would retrieve only those documents containing *both* terms. Alternatively, the request "products liability or furniture" would retrieve any document in which *either* phrase appears. It is also possible to specify that the system retrieve only those cases which contain two terms within a certain number of words of each other. This is accomplished by means of the proximity connector "w/n". In our example, the searcher could enter "products liability w/6 furniture" to retrieve the cases in which the phrase "products liability" appears within *six* words of "furniture". The connectors can be used to structure creatively any search.

In addition to the above type of search, LEXIS can perform several specialized searches, called "segment" searches. One can use a segment search on LEXIS to find the decisions of a particular court—opinions written by a particular judge, cases decided on, before, after, or between certain dates, and cases in which a particular party is a named litigant. It is also possible to search for a case by its citation. These specialized searches can be combined with word phrase searches and/or with other segment searches.

Once LEXIS has processed the search request, the total number of documents found is displayed. The user then has the option of modifying the request, if necessary, in order to retrieve a smaller or greater number of documents. Once an acceptable number of documents has been retrieved, the user can display them in a variety of formats. These are: (1) FULL (full text); (2) KWIC (key word in context) in which the search word plus 25 words on either side of the search word are displayed); (3) VARKWIC (in which the number of words on either side of the search word can be increased or decreased); (4) CITE (citations only) and (5) SEGMTS (segments), in which only chosen portions of the case, such as headnotes, are provided. Regardless of the format chosen, the search words within the displayed text are highlighted on the screen, and documents are displayed in a *reverse* chronological order with decisions of highest courts displayed *first.*

c. Additional LEXIS ® Services

In addition to its regular features, LEXIS provides a number of other services to subscribers. (LEXIS is a registered trademark of Mead Data Central.) Some of these are described below.

(1) *Autocite* ®

Autocite is a service of Lawyers Co-op and its affiliate, Bancroft Whitney. (Autocite is a registered trademark of Lawyer's Co-operative Publishing Company.) It was designed to help Lawyer's Co-op editors confirm the accuracy of citations. It verifies the accuracy of case-law citations, provides parallel citations, and cites any subsequent decision that directly affects the status of the case in question. It is a useful mechanism for checking the accuracy and validity of citations. Although less comprehensive than *Shepardizing* a case, it is usually faster and less expensive.

(2) *Shepard's Citations*

LEXIS presently offers most of the federal, state, and regional case law citations in the Shepard's series. The dates of coverage vary from one set to another. The availability of Shepard's *on-line* greatly augments the system's utility. Now both location and verification of cases can be done on the same system.

(3) *Additional Data Bases*

Mead Data Central has recently announced arrangements with Lockheed to make the DIALOG data bases available through LEXIS terminals. This will enable its subscribers to reach all of the DIALOG information services which are already accessible through WESTLAW terminals.

LEXIS has also added a substantial United Kingdom data base, including a variety of English reporters most of which begin in 1945; statutes and statutory instruments; and specialized libraries on taxation, industrial relations, intellectual property and local government. European Community materials have also been incorporated in the LEXIS system, and a French law library, as described above in Section F of Chapter 20, *Foreign and Comparative Law,* will also be included.

(4) *Secondary Sources*

LEXIS has incorporated a small selection of the treatises published by the Matthew Bender Co. into its data base. This allows the researcher, using Boolean search strategy, to search the full text of these books. Mead Data is also planning to add to the LEXIS data base a certain number of major law reviews. The eventual availability of these secondary sources could greatly enhance the scope of legal research by computer.

LEXIS is now also adding all briefs in *argued* cases before the Supreme Court of the United States from 1979 on. The *records* of those cases are not included in the data base, however, and cases which are not argued will not be included.

NEXIS ® is a library containing the full text of many general and business news publications, including major wire services. (NEXIS is a registered trademark of Mead Data Central.) Newspapers such as the *American Banker* and the *Washington Post* and such journals as *Business Week, Newsweek* and *U.S. News and World Report* are among those included. Mead has recently announced their purchase of the *New York Times Information Service,* which suggests that the full text of the *Times* will be searchable through *NEXIS.* The NEXIS system allows one to perform sophisticated general reference searching on-line by the same Boolean search strategy described above.

A major portion of the latest edition of the *Encyclopedia Britannica* (15th ed., 1974) is now available on LEXIS. Although this may seem like a trivial addition, the complex structure of this new edition of the *Britannica* (see Section C.1.a. of Chapter 17) makes computer searching of its text potentially quite useful. *Britannica* contains considerable general reference information of help in legal research, and some of its articles relating to law are of significant scholarly value. See, for example, the article on *Civil Law* (*Macropaedia,* v. 4, p. 665-667).

An *Accounting Information* data base contains annual reports of selected corporations listed on the N.Y. and American Stock Exchanges and quoted over the counter; extracts from proxy statements; secondary literature relating to the accounting field; and statements of auditing standards issued by the AICPA, and other professional information. LEXIS also offers the *DISCLO* library which includes abstracts and extracts of reports filed with the SEC by over 10,000 companies.

(5) *The Future*

LEXIS has continued to grow and expand its various data bases and those offerings will undoubtedly increase in the future. Access to non-legal data bases and specialized law libraries in regulatory fields had given it a strong lead over WESTLAW initially. But now WESTLAW is also adding to its data bases and competition can be expected to intensify, to the advantage of those consumers of legal information who can afford either or both of the services.

One can follow changes in the coverage of LEXIS from its newsletter, *LEXIS Brief,* its regional representatives, and advertisements in the legal newspapers.

2. WESTLAW ®

a. Scope

WESTLAW is the computerized legal research service of West Publishing Company. (WESTLAW is a registered trademark of West Publishing Company.) It began in the early 1970's as an automated version of the West digest system, with a data base consisting solely of the headnotes of the cases as reported in its National Reporter System. An early decision was made to add a full text component, however, and now full text, as well as headnote searching of recent cases is possible. The scope of coverage varies from jurisdiction to jurisdiction, and from court to court.

Although originally less comprehensive than LEXIS, WESTLAW's data base has been expanded and the two systems are now close in their coverage. As with LEXIS, retrospective material is being added continually to the existing WESTLAW data bases, and new data bases incorporated into the service. WESTLAW has also expanded significantly its subject area coverage and now has special libraries in the fields of taxation; securities; antitrust and business regulation; labor; government contracts; patent, trademark and copyright; communications; admiralty; and energy. As with LEXIS, these libraries contain a mix of primary sources. The *U.S. Code,* C.F.R., the *Federal Register*, and West's *Bankruptcy Reporter* and *Military Justice Reporter,* are also included, and a "quick opinion" service covers some opinions before their regular publication. INSTA–CITE and Shepards also assist users in validating their research.

Many of the basic search techniques and procedures are common to both LEXIS and WESTLAW, so they will not be repeated. A basic summary highlighting the differences in the systems appears below.

The equipment used by WESTLAW is similar to that used in LEXIS, with a keyboard and CRT terminal. An important difference is that WESTLAW has been designed to be accessible over a number of multi-purpose terminals, including such standard ones as the TRS–80 and the IBM personal computer. This allows the researcher to be much more flexible in setup and use. It also means that one can use WESTLAW without purchasing special equipment, which can result in significant savings. Access to WESTLAW may also be gained through a number of compatible word processing terminals and micro-computers that already exist in many law firms. The corollary of this flexibility is that the keyboard is a bit more complicated to operate than that of LEXIS. Commands must be formulated in symbols instead of simply pushing a special key. This is not a major problem as the system is still quite easy to use and the resultant flexibility is beneficial.

Recently, WESTLAW has offered a custom terminal, WALT, West's Automatic Law Terminal, with function keys that further simplify the search process. Researchers now have the option of either a general terminal that meets compatibility criteria or the custom terminal.

b. Search Procedure

WESTLAW affords the researcher a choice of approaches in formulating search requests. After choosing the appropriate *library* and *file*, the user can search for cases by full-text, headnotes, key number topics, or combinations of these alternatives.

The search strategies for using WESTLAW are best taught by a WESTLAW account representative. As with LEXIS, WESTLAW is taught in a growing number of law schools. One extra feature of WESTLAW is its on-line computer-assisted instruction program which allows self-training in the use of the system. What follows is a brief summary of the system's searching capability.

In WESTLAW literal key word or phrase queries can be formulated according to the principles of Boolean logic. The researcher can combine relevant words and phrases by using the ampersand for "and," and a space between words for "or." The searches for "furniture" and "products liability" described in the section on LEXIS could also be run on WESTLAW. A similar array of "connectors" and the same search flexibility are offered by the WESTLAW system. In addition, WESTLAW offers the capability of searching by a West Digest Topic and Key Number. This allows the user to search more quickly for widely-accepted legal concepts that may lack unique or specific terminology.

Other searches possible with WESTLAW are similar to the LEXIS segment searches. Called "field searches," they include limitations by court, judge's name, case citation, and name of case. It is also possible to limit a search by date, and to specify proximity by requiring that two words or phrases appear in the same sentence.

Documents can be displayed in a variety of formats such as full text, headnotes only, or citations. The computer also will indicate the total number of documents found, and the user may modify his/her request if necessary. Documents in the WESTLAW system are displayed in order of their relevancy to the particular search request or by age. Relevancy is determined by the computer on the basis of the frequency of the occurrence of the search terms used in the request. If age ranking is desired, documents are displayed in reverse chronological order.

In early 1983 WESTLAW announced a number of improvements designed to simplify the formulation of searches and increased the number of options available to users.

c. Additional WESTLAW Services

The following is a selected list of additional features available with the WESTLAW system.

(1) INSTA-CITE

INSTA-CITE is the case history and case validation service offered by West Publishing Company. This service provides instant cite verification and complete appellate history. Both subsequent case history, and prior case history, if appropriate, are furnished.

(2) Shepard's Citations

The WESTLAW data base now contains the federal and regional units of the *Shepard's Citations* system. This allows one to move freely into Shepard's while searching in WESTLAW, and then to retrieve easily a particular citing case.

(3) Additional Data Bases

Subscribers to the WESTLAW system can also gain access to multi-disciplinary commercial data bases on their WESTLAW terminals. Among these are System Development Corporation's ORBIT data base, and all of Lockheed's DIALOG information services. These additional data bases now contain many sources which are useful to legal researchers, such as the *Legal Resources Index, Congressional Information Service, Social Sciences Citation Index, Public Affairs Information Service,* U.S. Census records, medical data bases, and abstracts from the *Federal Register,* and *Congressional Record.* The future expansion of DIALOG will, of course, extend both LEXIS and WESTLAW's capability for reaching additional legal and non-legal sources.

WESTLAW has added the EUROLEX data base, an English service covering both U.K. and European legal sources. Its contents are described above in Section F of Chapter 20, Foreign and Comparative Law.

(4) Secondary Sources

WESTLAW has recently added several secondary sources and has indicated that further development in this area is likely. Among these developments will be an expansion in the area of legal periodicals. These data bases, some of which are accessible through DIALOG, include:

Accountant's Index, providing access to monographic and periodical literature in a variety of fields of interest to accountants, many of which are also useful in law-related research.

Black's Law Dictionary.

Disclosure, extracts from S.E.C. Filings by over 10,000 companies.

Dow Jones News/Retrieval Services, containing *Dow Jones News Service, Wall Street Journal, Barron's National Business and Financial Weekly,* and price quotations for over 6,000 stocks and securities.

Forensic Services Directory, listing consultants and experts, laboratories, translators and investigators in forensic areas useful for litigation support services.

Legal Resources Index, periodical indexing in law and related fields, as described above in Chapter 16, Legal Periodicals.

WPI, Comprehensive World Patent Index, containing documents relating to patents.

(5) The Future

WESTLAW has undergone significant expansion in recent months and is continuing to enlarge its scope. It is therefore difficult to predict the extent of its data bases at the time this book will be published. Nevertheless, it seems likely that the growth of its coverage will continue, in part as a result of its competition with LEXIS, and in part through the capacity of its terminals to access large systems like DIALOG.

Information about expansion and improvements in WESTLAW can be obtained from its monthly newsletter, *WESTLAW UPDATE*, from its representatives, and from advertisements appearing regularly in the *American Bar Association Journal, National Law Journal, Legal Times* and other legal periodicals.

3. LEXIS AND WESTLAW: A COMPARATIVE WORD

The relevant literature contains many comparisons between LEXIS and WESTLAW.[1] At this point both systems are growing in size and striving to simplify their use. Both LEXIS, with its "user friendly" keyboard and its small UBIQ terminals, and WESTLAW, with its multi-access data bases, custom terminal option, and its search strategy enhancements, are improving constantly. Law students, as part of their legal education, should be trained on at least one of the systems—and, if possible, on both systems.

With the rapid change in technical features and data base coverage, it is difficult to make a fair comparative evaluation of the two systems. Several studies undertaken in the past have little validity today because of subsequent improvements in both systems. The definitive study has not yet been made and probably cannot occur until the systems settle into fixed patterns—a development that is hard to foresee at the present time. Even then, subjective user preferences will remain, as with traditional legal finding tools in book form.

C. OTHER COMPUTERIZED SYSTEMS

1. JURIS

In 1970, the U.S. Department of Justice began developing its own full text computer system for the retrieval of legal information. JURIS (Justice Retrieval and Inquiry System) is the result of that effort and now has about 150 terminals in offices of the Department

1. See, for example, the following recent comparisons: A. J. Onove, "A Comparison of the LEXIS and WESTLAW Databases," 9 *Legal Economics* 27 (March/April 1983) and several articles in the two-part "Forum on Computerized Legal Research," 2 *Legal Reference Services Q.* Nos. 2 & 3 (Summer & Fall 1982).

of Justice, offices of U.S. Attorneys throughout the country, the U.S. Supreme Court, the Library of Congress, the Department of Defense, and other federal agencies.

Its data bases contain about 150,000 federal court decisions in full-text, with West headnotes, about 400,000 state court decisions, the *U.S. Code, Shepard's Citations,* and a substantial amount of internal documentation of the Department of Justice and related governmental offices and services.

2. FLITE

The first governmental legal retrieval system, and one of the first under any sponsorship, was the FLITE system (Federal Legal Information Through Electronics) of the U.S. Air Force, begun in the early 1960's. This pioneering program provided much of the groundwork for JURIS and for the development of WESTLAW. Still operational, it is primarily a retrieval system for the Air Force and for Congress. FLITE includes a broad range of federal court decisions, the *U.S. Code, Decisions of the Comptroller General,* and various legislative history and administrative law sources, as well as internal data bases of the Air Force.

3. OTHER LAW DATA BASES

Several other legal data bases offered primarily by looseleaf publishers have been mentioned in earlier chapters, particularly Chapters 10 (*Legislative History*), 11 (*Administrative and Executive Publications*), 13 (*Looseleaf Services*) and 16 (*Legal Periodicals*). They will therefore be mentioned only briefly here.

Bureau of National Affairs (*BNA*) now provides four legal computer services, largely based on their traditional looseleaf services in the fields covered. The first three of these services are accessible through Lockheed's DIALOG information systems, which can now be reached either through LEXIS or WESTLAW. The four *BNA* data bases are:

LABORLAW, containing virtually all of the decisions in *BNA*'s *Labor Relations Reports* and related labor services (*Fair Employment Practice Service, Occupational Safety & Health Reporter, Labor Arbitration Reports, Mine Safety & Health Reporter,* etc.).

CHEMLAW, containing decisions and regulations from *BNA*'s *Chemical Regulation Reporter* and *Chemical Substances Control* and other material from various government agencies active in the regulation of chemical substances.

PATLAW, containing patent, trademark, copyright and unfair competition decisions from *BNA*'s U.S. Patents Quarterly and its *Patent, Trademark & Copyright Journal.*

ADVANCELINE, containing *daily* information on taxation and securities in two services, *Daily Tax Advance* and *Daily Se-*

curities Advance, drawn in part from its regular services, *Daily Report for Executives, Daily Tax Report* and *Securities Regulation & Law Report.*

Congressional Information Service *(CIS)* has mounted a large legislative history data base, with monthly updating, based on its indexes to Congressional publications. This service is also available through DIALOG.

Commerce Clearing House *(CCH)* now offers its *Electronic Legislative Search System (ELSS)* which provides current legislative status information from all fifty states and the U.S. Congress.

The latest issue of DIALOG's *Database Catalog* lists a variety of other law-related services, some of which have been mentioned earlier in this book (e.g., *Disclosure, Federal Index, Legal Resource Index, PAIS International, Social Scisearch,* etc.). Among those not previously referred to are the following: *Child Abuse and Neglect* (from U.S. Children's Bureau, National Center for Child Abuse and Neglect); *Claims/Citation,* a patent search service from Search Check Inc.; *Criminal Justice Periodical Index* from University Microfilms International); *Environline,* a data base of primary and secondary sources in the area of environmental protection, from the Environment Information Center; *Environmental Bibliography,* indexing over 300 periodicals in environmental science and protection, from Environmental Studies Institute; *Mental Health Abstracts,* which abstracts material from 12,000 domestic and foreign journals in that field, plus relevant books, conference proceedings and technical reports; *Medline,* the National Library of Medicine's comprehensive data base of medical and health science literature; and *U.S. Political Science Documents* from the University of Pittsburgh which covers 120 American journals in the field of political and policy sciences.

D. LITIGATION SUPPORT SYSTEMS

In recent years, computers have been receiving increased attention not only for their research capability, but also as systems for the control and retrieval of the massive documentation generated in large and complicated litigation. Computerized litigation support systems have achieved a wide acceptance, primarily in very extensive, protracted litigation where the amount of data and the number of documents becomes unmanageable by manual retrieval.

For fuller discussion of these systems, see S. L. Haynes, *Computers and Litigation Support* (Law & Business, Inc., 1981), E. H. Kinney, *Litigation Support Systems, An Attorney's Guide* (Callaghan, 1980), and J. H. Young, et al., ed., *Use of Computers in Litigation* (American Bar Association, 1979). The Section on Litigation and the Section on Science and Technology of the American Bar Association are major sources of information in this field. The national legal newspapers periodically contain lists of vendors and consultants, and news of current developments.

The terminals of both the major computerized legal research services—LEXIS and WESTLAW—can be used for litigation support, but as *separate* services, not part of their regular research systems.

There are three different ways in which computers are being used in support of litigation:

1. EVIDENTIARY MANAGEMENT SYSTEMS

These are the most commonly known litigation support services, storing and retrieving in *full text* the voluminous documents, depositions, trial testimony and exhibits in large lawsuits. These materials handled manually require extensive storage space, and it is very difficult to identify and locate single documents or specific items of testimony from such files.

An attorney or law firm, usually in consultation with a technical consultant, decides which aspects of the documents are likely to be chosen as access points in future searches, and the documents (or abstracts of the documents) are appropriately coded so that they can be identified when needed. The computer can thus identify all documents signed on a given date, for example, or produce a list of all material written by a certain person—in considerably less time than manual searching would require.

There are a variety of advantages to computerized storage and retrieval of pretrial documents, trial testimony and exhibits—ease of storage, access by a variety of means (e.g., by date, personal name, subjects, author, recipient, witness, etc.), and speed of searching. The justification for using computers in support of litigation rests largely on *improving access* to large amounts of materials, that is, getting more information faster from the same documents. Lowering costs of storage and retrieval is rarely an inducement for using these systems. Generally, such computer use is justified only in cases involving at least 10,000 documents.

2. ANALYTICAL SYSTEMS

These systems are not research tools, but are designed to analyze and manipulate computer-stored data in large cases to produce correlations, frequency distributions, marketing studies, models for estimating damages, and other mathematical and statistical analyses. Such programs can produce new evidence, or studies which can be used to support or refute existing evidence.

While the computer has no cognitive abilities, it can, if correctly programmed, perform sophisticated analytical functions. Because of the specialized expertise needed for these systems, such operations are usually contracted to an outside firm, several of which now offer these services to the legal profession.

3. CASE MANAGEMENT SYSTEMS

A variety of data processing and retrieval systems are now being used by both federal and state courts to improve the efficiency of routine administrative operations. Similar programs adapted for practitioners are also being employed in law firms and offices throughout the country to control pending cases, regularize the firm's dockets, calendars, and court appearances. They also provide for allocation of staff resources, keeping time records, and handling financial aspects of particular litigation. These systems are primarily housekeeping devices enabling the firm to control its own administrative functions in the management of cases.

E. FOREIGN AND INTERNATIONAL SYSTEMS

The new media of legal research are now moving into the fields of foreign and international law. Both LEXIS and WESTLAW are now offering or will soon be offering significant data bases of British and European legal materials. These are described above in Section F of Chapter 20, *Foreign and Comparative Law,* and in the earlier sections on LEXIS and WESTLAW in this Chapter.

Virtually all of the major countries are developing their own information systems for legal sources, and the International Telecommunications Union has been working to standardize technology to facilitate better international exchange of such information. The Section of Science and Technology of the American Bar Association has been working with similar professional and governmental groups abroad to the same end.

F. MICROFORMS

1. INTRODUCTION

The use of microforms (i.e. miniaturized photographs of printed material in cartridges or on reels of microfilm, or in a cut-form called microfiche) is increasing in almost all law libraries. There are several reasons for the growth of this new medium. The advantage most-often cited is the enormous space saving produced by storing information in microforms. Recent technological developments have made possible reduction ratios as high as 90:1, which means that a printed page, can be reduced to $^{1}/_{90}$ of its original size in a photographic image. Thus, a 1500 page volume of West's National Reporter System, which is available on a microform called ultrafiche (see below), with a 75:1 reduction ratio, is reproduced and stored on a single 4″ x 6″ piece of film. The information that would have been stored in several ranges of books can be held in a few file drawers. For information that is not frequently needed but which a library must hold for occassional use, this format is ideal.

The second advantage is that microforms make possible the preservation of printed legal materials whose pages are deteriorating. Many books that are disintegrating from use, age or the acidity of their paper, can be acquired, stored and used on microfilm or microfiche.

The third advantage is access to out-of-print volumes which cannot be obtained easily in the market, as well as to large compilations of materials (such as Congressional documents or state administrative materials or appellate records and briefs), all of which are too voluminous for storage and control in many libraries and offices. It also includes new packaging of materials on a particular subject which would be difficult to collect in book form. An example of this possibility is a currently offered commercial service of environmental legal material including statutes, regulations, administrative documents, decisions, and legislative history. These compilations often bring together far more material than can be collected in a loose-leaf service, but the approach and rationale are similar to that of the looseleaf service.

The attractiveness of these advantages, the increased *availability* of legal materials in microform, and improvements in the quality of equipment for reading microforms and printing paper copy from them, have stimulated a growing use of these new formats.

2. TYPES OF MICROFORMS

a. Microfilm

Microfilm was the earliest type of microform and is still widely used today, particularly for newspapers, periodicals, and other long continuous series. Originally rolls of microfilm were stored on reels, but they are now available in the form of cassettes and cartridges as well. These protect the film, and are much easier to handle by eliminating the inconvenience of threading the reel into the film-reader.

Traditionally, reels of microfilm have been produced by photographing individual pages of documents in a continuous series, but microfilm can now also be produced directly from computer tapes. Called computer output microfilm (*com*), this medium is gaining in popularity as more information is being generated by and stored in computer files. It is a less expensive process for producing film and allows for greater flexibility.

A microfilm reader, a device capable of magnifying the microfilmed image back to readable size, is used to read the material. Another version, called *reader/printers,* have the added capability of producing on paper standard-size photocopies of the images on the screen.

b. Microfiche

Microfiche is a sheet of cut film, on which photographic images of pages, greatly reduced in size, are placed. Although available in several sizes, the most common microfiche are 4″ x 6″ and employ a 24:1

reduction ratio, thereby making it possible to provide up to 98 pages of text on a single sheet. Microfiche is generally preferred to microfilm due to its relative ease of use. Supplementation of microfiche publications is also less expensive, and more convenient for filing and reading.

Many microfilm readers and reader/printers can be adapted to accommodate microfiche, and separate fiche readers are available as well. Inexpensive, portable microfiche readers are also available for office or home use. Some libraries have fiche to fiche duplicators available which allow one to make a copy of the fiche to keep.

c. Ultrafiche

Ultrafiche is a form of microfiche, with a significantly higher reduction ratio. As noted above, a reduction ratio of 90:1 is possible, with over 1500 pages being reproduced on one sheet of ultrafiche. Highly specialized equipment is needed for both the reading and printing of this medium, and this has limited its use. However, many libraries are now acquiring the first series and increasing parts of the second series of West's National Reporter System in this format, and a CCH tax library on ultrafiche has advantages for small law offices.

d. Micro-opaques

This medium utilizes opaque cards rather than transparent film to store the photographic images. Special readers are necessary, and the quality of the magnified image is generally not as clear as that produced with either microfiche or ultrafiche. This early microform technology has become obsolete except for a few publications which are only available in that medium.

3. MATERIAL AVAILABLE IN MICROFORM

A diverse and ever expanding body of legal materials is presently available in microform. A comprehensive bibliography of such materials, H. Tseng's *Complete Guide to Legal Materials in Microform* was published in 1976 and lists 15,000 entries as of 1975. By 1981, three large supplements had already been issued. The scope of materials is obviously too large to be listed here, but a brief summary can indicate the variety of available publications.

a. Primary Sources

Among the primary legal sources which are available, in addition to the early West Reports on ultrafiche, are microform editions of all of the official state reports prior to the National Reporter system, and many current state reports. There are also session laws from all of the states, attorney generals' opinions, the *Federal Register, Code of Federal Regulations,* federal legislative histories and congressional documents, and the very popular collection of Records and Briefs of the Supreme Court of the United States. The Records and Briefs of the District of Columbia and 2nd Circuits of the U.S. Court of Appeals are now issued in microfiche, as are those of the California and Massachusetts Supreme Courts.

b. Secondary Materials

There is now a wide variety of treatises, monographs and leading American legal periodicals available in microform. The new periodical index, *Legal Resource Index* is on microfilm, as described above. Important trial proceedings, back runs of legal newspapers, and even collections of rare legal manuscripts are available on microforms.

G. FACSIMILE TRANSMISSION

Another important development of great potential significance in legal research is *facsimile transmission,* the electronic transmission of research materials by page images from larger libraries to smaller libraries or law offices. This technology is now widely marketed by several vendors, for use by commercial, financial, and industrial firms, and is already used extensively by large law firms for communication with substantial clients. Electronic equipment transmits printed pages over telephone lines for varying distances, rapidly and at relatively low cost. Xerox, Burroughs, Canon, Rapicom, and other firms offer a variety of machines, with transmission speeds ranging from six minutes to less than thirty seconds per page. The distances which can be reached by these machines also vary considerably but some offer the capability of transmission overseas and wherever telephone connections exist. Presently, the images are transmitted over regular telephone lines, but communications satellites are already being used for the same purpose, and laser beams may also have great potential in this area.

So far, there has not been significant use of this equipment for linking libraries directly to readers, but commercial uses have been quite extensive, and use between large libraries or library systems is beginning. There may, of course, be copyright problems relating to such use, but the transmission of a single copy of protected work for research purposes should fall within the *fair use* doctrine. Of course, many public documents needed in legal research are outside of copyright protection.

Facsimile transmission can make the resources of the largest research law libraries (like the Law Library of Congress; the Harvard, Berkeley, Columbia, Michigan, and Yale Law School Libraries; and the larger bar and public law libraries like the Association of the Bar of the City of New York and the Los Angeles County Law Library) accessible to lawyers who cannot otherwise reach those collections. Inter-library loan cannot adequately serve that function since it involves the loss of use of the book from the owning library for long periods of time. Both inter-library loan and its modern substitute, library photocopying in lieu of loan, are quite slow and for that reason often do not meet the practitioner's needs. Facsimile transmission offers a relatively fast, efficient means of disseminating legal information, at least in small quantities. The equipment and communication costs will, of course be a major limiting factor in its use.

The fullest use of facsimile transmission for this purpose is going to require a national network of law libraries, coordinated through some central bibliographic facility, as well as smaller regional networks to service routine local needs. Such networks have been formed by general libraries—including both public *and* academic libraries—on national, regional, state, and local bases. Many law libraries are now part of these large networks. The links are still expensive, however, and although widely used for cooperative cataloging and inter-library lending, they have not been used for facsimile transmission. Most of the law libraries in these networks do not yet have the equipment for such transmission, but the capability is there, and the advantages are clear.

H. CONCLUSION

There will undoubtedly be more technological changes in legal research in the years to come. In that regard, a caveat may be in order here.

A newspaper article back in *1967,* dealing with the impact of computers on legal research, reported that, "The computer will soon achieve such universal use in law research as to revolutionize the practice of law and the process of legal systems." The article referred to a computer in Geneva which would store and retrieve the statutory law of every nation in the world and provide indexes to the high court decisions of all nations. It was suggested that "any user who wants to know the law in other countries about party committees, human rights, transfer of real estate, or other problems, will only have to submit a coded number and the computer will find the texts he wants and give him photographed copies." The article also referred to a law research service which allegedly *then* had *(in 1967)* in its computer *three million* federal and state decisions. None of that existed in 1967 and it seems little closer today. Perhaps the most accurate part of that dispatch was the statement that, "the method of financing has not yet been worked out."

The acceptance of new techniques in legal research has been hampered in the past by *over-sell* on the part of some entrepreneurs and lawyers. The road to that progress which has been made in this field is cluttered with the debris of broken promises, unrealistic and premature claims, and shattered hopes. Although the legal profession has been over-conservative in its reception of new research techniques, lawyers *should* properly evaluate the new services being offered with a critical eye. When convinced of their value, these tools should be acquired and used—but used properly, with adequate training and full knowledge of what they can do. The bar presently wastes huge sums each year on law books which are not used, or are not used to their *full* potential. The new technology is much more expensive than traditional lawbooks, and can only be justified by skilled use and maximum employment.

The most promising achievements of information science and new technology in law, as elsewhere, will involve a combination of machines and human effort. Legal research will continue to be a human activity, dependent on our own developed skills and intellect, but aided by the searching speed of machines. Computerization in law libraries will not eliminate the intellectual skills of reading, analysis, synthesis and advocacy, but rather should improve our capacity to do them better.

The late Norbert Wiener, who was perhaps the philosophic godfather of computer technology, summed up some guideposts for the legal profession in the coming years when he said in his last book: [2]

> "Render unto man the things which are man's and unto the computer the things which are the computer's. This would seem the intelligent policy to adopt when we employ men and computers together in common undertakings. It is a policy as far removed from that of the gadget worshipper as it is from the man who sees only blasphemy and degradation of man in the use of any mechanical adjuvants whatever to thoughts. What we now need is an independent study of systems involving both human and mechnical elements. This system should not be prejudiced by a mechanical or an anti-mechanical bias . . . "

I. ADDITIONAL READING

J. Bing & T. Harvold, *Legal Decisions and Information Systems* (Oslo, Universitetsforlag, 1977).

E. H. Kinney, *Litigation Support Systems* (Callaghan, 1980).

J. E. Leininger & B. Gilchrist, *Computers, Society and Law: The Role of Legal Education* (AFIPS Press, 1973).

T. B. Marvell, *Appellate Courts and Lawyers, Information Gathering in the Adversary System* (Greenwood Press, 1978).

B. Niblett, ed., *Computer Science and Law* (Cambridge University Press, 1980).

J. A. Sprowl, *A Manual for Computer-Assisted Legal Research* (American Bar Foundation, 1976).

Teaching Law With Computers: a Collection of Essays (Westview Press, for EDUCOM, 1979).

D. S. Yen & M. D. Scott, *Computer Law Bibliography* (Center for Computer Law, 1979).

---

2. *God and Golem Inc.* (M.I.T. Press, 1964) at p. 73.

In addition, information about new developments and publications in these fields can be obtained in the following specialized periodicals:

Computer/Law Journal, quarterly (Los Angeles, Center for Computer Law).

Jurimetrics Journal, quarterly (Chicago, American Bar Association).

The Justice System Journal, 3 times a year (Denver, Institute for Court Management).

Law and Computer Technology, quarterly (Washington, D.C., World Peace Through Law Center).

Rutgers Journal of Computers and the Law, semi-annual (Newark, N.J., Rutgers Law School).

*

Appendix A

LEGAL BIBLIOGRAPHY IN THE STATES

Legal research in the materials of the several states is complicated by variations in the history and forms of their publications. A general treatise, such as this one, cannot fully treat the many special characteristics of legal materials in each state. There are, however, an increasing number of bibliographical and instructional manuals available on state legal research, and more are undoubtedly on the way to publication. The following guides of varying scope and purpose are currently available and recommended for local orientation:

California	Myron Fink, *Research in California Law* (Dennis, 2d ed., 1964).
	Ron Granberg, *Introduction to California Law Finding* (Why Not Creations, 1977).
	Dan F. Henke, *California Law Guide* (Parker & Son, 2d ed., 1976).
District of Columbia	*Carolyn Ahearn, et al., *Selected Information Sources for the District of Columbia* (American Association of Law Libraries, 1981).
Florida	Richard L. Brown, *Guide to Florida Legal Research* (Florida Bar, Continuing Legal Education, 1980).
	Harriet French, *Research in Florida Law* (Oceana, 2d ed., 1965).
Georgia	Leah Chanin, *Reference Guide to Georgia Legal History and Legal Research* (Michie, 1980).
Illinois	Bernita J. Davies, *Research in Illinois Law* (Oceana, 1954).
	Roger F. Jacobs, et al., *Illinois Legal Research Sourcebook* (Illinois Institute for Continuing Legal Education, 1977).
Indiana	*Linda K. Fariss & Keith A. Buckley, *An Introduction to Indiana State Publications for the Law Librarian* (American Association of Law Libraries, 1982).
Louisiana	Kate Wallach, *Louisiana Legal Research Manual* (LSU Law School, Institute of Continuing Legal Education, 1972).
Maryland	*Lynda C. Davis, *An Introduction to Maryland State Publications for the Law Librarian* (American Association of Law Libraries, 1981).

* Prepared for the Government Documents, S.I.S., American Association of Law Libraries, 75th Annual Meeting, 1982.

Massachusetts	Margot Botsford & Ruth G. Matz, *Handbook of Legal Research in Massachusetts* (Massachusetts Continuing Legal Education, 1982), looseleaf.
Michigan	Richard L. Beer, *An Annotated Guide to the Legal Literature of Michigan* (Fitzsimmons Sales, 1973).
	*Stuart D. Yoak & Margaret A. Heinen, *Michigan Legal Documents: An Annotated Bibliography* (American Association of Law Libraries, 1982).
Missouri	*Patricia Aldrich, et al., *A Law Librarian's Introduction to Missouri State Publications* (American Association of Law Libraries, 1980).
New Jersey	New Jersey State Law and Legislative Reference Bureau, *Legal Research Guide for the New Jersey State Library* (1957).
New Mexico	Arie Poldervaart, *Manual for Effective New Mexico Legal Research* (University of New Mexico Press, 1955).
North Carolina	Igor Kavass & Bruce Christensen, *Guide to North Carolina Legal Research* (Hein, 1973).
Pennsylvania	Erwin Surrency, *Research in Pennsylvania Law* (Oceana, 2d ed., 1965).
South Carolina	Robin Mills & Jon Schultz, *South Carolina Legal Research Methods* (Hein, 1973).
Tennessee	Lewis Laska, *Tennessee Legal Research Handbook* (Hein, 1977).
Texas	Marian Boner, *A Reference Guide to Texas Law and Legal History: Sources and Documentation* (University of Texas Press, 1976).
Virginia	*Margaret Aycock, et al., *A Law Librarian's Introduction to Virginia State Publications* (American Association of Law Libraries, 1981).
Washington	*Legal Research Guide* (University of Washington Law School, 1980).
Wisconsin	Richard Danner, *Legal Research in Wisconsin* (University of Wisconsin Ext., Law Dept., 1980).
	William Knudson, *Wisconsin Legal Research Guide* (University of Wisconsin—Extension Department of Law, 2d ed., 1972).

Appendix B

PRIMARY LEGAL SOURCES FOR THE STATES[1]

Model:

Reporters: (years generally indicate periods of coverage, not imprint dates):

1. Major reporter first (whether or not discontinued)
2. Current official reporter (if different from # 1)
3. Regional reporter
4. Nominative and other reports (Number of volumes indicated in parenthesis)

* indicates official status

Session Laws:

Statutory Compilation:

Administrative Code:

Administrative Register: (with frequency of publication in parenthesis)

ALABAMA

- **Reporters:**

Supreme Court

*Alabama Reports	1840–1976	Disc. with v.295 (1976)
Alabama Appellate Reporter	–date	Advance sheet
*West's Alabama Reporter	1976–date	Official since 1976
*Southern Reporter	1886–date	Official since 1976
Minor	1820–1826	(1v.)
Smith's Condensed Reports	1820–1879	(10v.)
Stewart	1827–1831	(3v.)
Stewart & Porter	1831–1834	(5v.)
Porter	1834–1839	(9v.)
Shepard's Select Cases	1861–1863	(1v.)

1. For a recent survey of these state materials, see L.F. Chanin, "Developing a State Law Collection: Part I (and Part II)", 2 *Legal Ref. Services Q.* 47–94 (No. 3) and 3–63 (No. 4) (1982).

Court of Civil Appeals and Court of Criminal Appeals

*Alabama Appellate Court Reports	1910–1976	Disc. with v.57 (1976)
Alabama Appellate Reporter	–date	Advance Sheet
*Southern Reporter	1911–date	Official since 1976
*West Alabama Reporter	1976–date	Official since 1976

- **Session Laws:**

  Acts of Alabama

- **Statutory Compilation:**

  Code of Alabama

- **Administrative Code:**

  ——

- **Administrative Register:**

  ——

ALASKA

- **Reporters:**

Supreme Court

*Pacific Reporter	1960–date	(Begins with v.348 P.2d) Official since 1960
*West's Alaska Reporter	1960–date	Official since 1960

District Court of Alaska

*Alaska Reports	1867–1959	Disc. with v.17 (1958)
Alaska Federal Reports	1869–1937	(5v.)
Alaska Terr. Reports	1869–1940	(14v.)
Federal Reporter	1884–1932	
Federal Supplement	1932–1959	

U.S. District Courts for California, Oregon, and District of Washington
(had jurisdiction over Alaska until 1884)

Federal Reporter	1880–1884
Federal Cases	1867–1880

- **Session Laws:**

  Alaska Session Laws

- **Statutory Compilation:**

  Alaska Statutes

- **Administrative Code:**

  Alaska Administrative Code

- **Administrative Register:**

  Register (quarterly)

ARIZONA

• **Reporters:**

Supreme Court		
*Arizona Reports	1866–date	Published by West since v.64 (1945).
Pacific Reporter	1886–date	
Court of Appeals		
*Arizona Appeals Reports	1965–1976	(27v.) Published by West since v.1 (1965).
*Arizona Reports	1976–date	
Pacific Reporter	1965–date	

• **Session Laws:**

Sessions Laws, Arizona

Arizona Legislative Service (West)

• **Statutory Compilation:**

Arizona Revised Statutes Annotated (West)

• **Administrative Code:**

Official Compilation of Administrative Rules and Regulations

• **Administrative Register:**

Administrative Digest (Monthly)

ARKANSAS

• **Reporters:**

Supreme Court		
*Arkansas Reports	1837–date	
Southwestern Reporter	1886–date	
Arkansas Cases (West)	1886–date	
Arkansas Territorial Reports		
Martin's Decisions in Equity (1st Chancery District)	1895–1900	(1v.)
Arkansas Law Reporter	1911–1916	(17v.)
The Law Reporter	1919–1937	(63v.)
Court of Appeals		
*Arkansas Appellate Reports	1979–date	Bound with Ark. Reports
Southwestern Reporter	1979–date	
Arkansas Cases (West)	1979–date	
(Hempstead)-*Superior Court*	1820–1836	(1v.)

• **Session Laws:**

General Acts of Arkansas

• **Statutory Compilation:**

Arkansas Statutes Annotated

• **Administrative Code:**

—

- **Administrative Register:**

  Arkansas Register (Monthly)

CALIFORNIA

- **Reporters:**

Supreme Court

*California Reports 1st series ..	1850–1934	(220v.)
2nd series ..	1934–1969	(71v.)
3rd series ..	1969–date	
*California Decisions	1890–1940	(100v.)
*Advance California Reports ...	1940–1969	
California Official Reports	1969–date	Advance Sheet
Pacific Reporter	1883–date	
West's California Reporter	1959–date †	
California Unreported Cases ...	1855–1910	(7v.)
Late Political Decisions of the Supreme Court ("State Journal Office, Sacramento)	1855	(1v.)
Unwritten Decisions (Ragland)	1878–1879	(1v.)

Court of Appeals

*California Appellate Reports ..	1905–date	
*California Appellate Decisions	1905–1940	(103v.)
*California Appellate Decisions Supplement	1929–1940	(3v.)
*Advance California Appellate Reports	1940–1969	
*California Official Reports	1969–date	
Pacific Reporter	1905–1959	
West's California Reporter	1959–date	

Appellate Departments of the Superior Court

*California Appellate Reports Supplement	1929–date
West's California Reporter	1959–date
Pacific Reporter	1929–1959

- **Session Laws:**

  Statutes of California

  California Legislative Service (West)

  California Advance Legislative Service (Deering)

- **Statutory Compilation:**

  West's Annotated California Code

  Deering's Annotated California Code

- **Administrative Code:**

  California Administrative Code

- **Administrative Register:**

  California Administrative Register

† Also extended retrospectively to 1883 with *Pacific Reporter* numbering.

COLORADO

• **Reporters:**

Supreme Court		
*Colorado Reports	1864–1980	Disc. with v.200 (1980)
*Pacific Reporter	1883–date	Official since 1980
*Colorado Reporter (West)	1883–date	Official since 1980
Colorado Law Reporter	1880–1884	(4v.)
Colorado Decisions (Annotated)	1900–1902	(4v.)
Court of Appeals		
*Colorado Court of Appeals Reports	1891–1905	
	1912–1915	
	1970–1980	Disc. with v.44 (1980)
*Pacific Reporter	1891–1905	
	1912–1915	
	1970–date	
*Colorado Reporter (West)	1891–date	
Colorado Decisions (Annotated)	1900–1902	(4v.)

• **Session Laws:**

Session Laws of Colorado

• **Statutory Compilation:**

Colorado Revised Statutes

• **Administrative Code:**

Code of Colorado Regulations

• **Administrative Register:**

Colorado Register (Monthly)

CONNECTICUT

• **Reporters:**

Supreme Court		
*Connecticut Reports...........	1814–date	
*Connecticut Law Journal	1935–date	Advance Sheet
Atlantic Reporter	1885–date	
Connecticut Reporter (West)...	1885–date	
Kirby........................	1785–1788	(1v.)
Root.........................	1789–1798	(2v.)
Day	1802–1813	(5v.)
Superior Court		
*Connecticut Supplement	1935–date	
*Connecticut Law Journal	1935–date	Advance Sheet
Atlantic Reporter	1954–date	
Connecticut Reporter (West)...	1954–date	
Circuit Court		
*Connecticut Circuit Court Reports	1961–1974	(6v.)
Atlantic Reporter	1961–1974	
Connecticut Reporter (West)...	1961–1974	

• **Session Laws:**

Connecticut Public & Special Acts	1971–date	
Connecticut Public Acts	1650–1971	
Connecticut Special Acts (published under various titles)	1789–1971	
Connecticut Legislative Service (West)		

• **Statutory Compilations:**

General Statutes of Connecticut (1977)

Connecticut General Statutes Annotated

• **Administrative Code:**

Regulations of Connecticut State Agencies

• **Administrative Register:**

Connecticut Law Journal (Weekly)

DELAWARE

• **Reporters:**

Supreme Court		
*Delaware Reports	1832–1966	Disc. with v.59 (1966)
*Atlantic Reporter	1884–date	Official since 1966
*Delaware Reporter (West)	1966–date	Official since 1966
Delaware Cases	1792–1830	(3v.)
Harrington	1832–1855	(5v.) (1–5 Del.)
Houston	1885–1893	(9v.) (6–14 Del.)
Marvel	1893–1897	(2v.) (15–16 Del.)
Pennewill	1897–1909	(7v.) (17–23 Del.)
Boyce	1909–1919	(7v.) (24–30 Del.)
W.W. Harrington	1919–1939	(9v.) (31–39 Del.)
Terry	1939–1958	(11v.) (40–50 Del.)
Storey	1958–1966	(9v.) (51–59 Del.)
Court of Chancery		
*Delaware Chancery Reports	1814–1968	Disc. with v.43 (1968)
*Atlantic Reporter	1886–date	Official since 1968
*Delaware Reporter (West)	1966–date	Official since 1968
Superior Court and Other Courts		
Atlantic Reporter	1951–date	
Houston's Criminal Reports—Delaware Criminal Cases	1856–1879	(1v.)
Family Court		
Atlantic Reporter	1977–date	

• **Session Laws:**

Laws of Delaware

• **Statutory Compilation:**

Delaware Code Annotated

- **Administrative Code:**

    Register of Regulations

- **Administrative Register:**

    ——

FLORIDA

- **Reporters:**

Supreme Court		
*Florida Reports	1846–1948	Disc. with v.160 (1948)
*Southern Reporter	1886–date	
*Florida Cases (West)	1941–date	Official since 1948
Florida Law Weekly	1976–date	Advance Sheet
District Court of Appeal		
*Southern Reporter	1957–date	
*Florida Cases (West)	1957–date	
Florida Law Weekly	1976–date	
Circuit Court, County Court, Public Service Commission		
*Florida Supplement	1950–date	

- **Session Laws:**

    Laws of Florida

    Florida Session Law Service (West)

- **Statutory Compilation:**

    Florida Statutes

    Florida Statutes Annotated (West)

    Florida Statutes Annotated (Harrison)

- **Administrative Code:**

    Florida Administrative Code

- **Administrative Register:**

    Florida Administrative Weekly (Weekly)

GEORGIA

- **Reporters:**

Supreme Court		
*Georgia Reports	1846–date	
Georgia Appellate Reporter Advance Decisions	1980–date	
Southeastern Reports	1887–date	
Georgia Cases (West)	1939–date	
Gault, Joseph	1820–1846	(1v.)
Dudley	1830–1833	(1v.)
Georgia Law Reporter	1885–1886	(1v.)

Court of Appeals

*Georgia Appeals Reports	1907–date	
Georgia Appellate Reporter	1930–date	
Southeastern Reporter	1907–date	
Georgia Cases (West)	1939–date	

- **Session Laws:**

  Georgia Laws

- **Statutory Compilations:**

  Code of Georgia

  Code of Georgia Annotated (Michie)

  Georgia Code Annotated (Harrison)

- **Administrative Code:**

  Official Compilation of Rules & Regulations of the State of Georgia

- **Administrative Register:**

  ——

HAWAII

- **Reporters:**

Supreme Court

*Hawaii Reports	1847–date	
Pacific Reporter	1959–date	
Ke Alakei o Ki Kanaka Hawaii (Poepoe)	1849–1889	(1v.)

Intermediate Court of Appeals

Pacific Reporter	1980–date	
Hawaii Appeals	1980–date	

Federal

U.S. District Court of Hawaii	1900–1917	(4v.)

- **Session Laws:**

  Session Laws of Hawaii

- **Statutory Compilation:**

  Hawaii Revised Statutes

- **Administrative Code:**

  ——

- **Administrative Register:**

  ——

IDAHO

- **Reporters:**

Supreme Court

*Idaho Reports	1866–date	Published by West since v.67 (1946)

Pacific Reporter	1881–date	
Cummins	1866–1867	(1v.)

- **Session Laws:**

  Sessions Laws, Idaho

- **Statutory Compilation:**

  Idaho Code [Annotated]

- **Administrative Code:**

  ——

- **Administrative Register:**

  ——

ILLINOIS

- **Reporters:**

Supreme Court

*Illinois Reports	1819–date	
Northeastern Reporter	1885–date	
Illinois Decisions (West)	1976–date	
Breese	1819–1831	(1v.) (1 Ill.)
Blackwell	1819–1841	(1v.)
Reports (no reporter)	Dec. term 1832	(1v.)
Forman	1832–1838	(in 1 Scammon)
Scammon	1832–1844	(4v.) (2–5 Ill.)
Gilman	1844–1849	(5v.) (6–10 Ill.)

Appellate Court

*Illinois Appellate Court Reports	1877–date	
Northeastern Reporter	1936–date	
Illinois Decisions (West)	1976–date	

Court of Claims

*Illinois Court of Claims Reports	1889–date	

- **Session Laws:**

  Laws of Illinois

  Illinois Legislative Service (West)

- **Statutory Compilation:**

  Illinois Revised Statutes

  Smith-Hurd Illinois Annotated Statutes (West)

- **Administrative Code:**

  (Administrative Code not expected until 1984 or 1985)

- **Administrative Register:**

  Illinois Register (Weekly)

INDIANA

• **Reporters:**

Supreme Court

*Indiana Reports	1848–date	
Northeastern Reporter	1885–date	
Indiana Cases (West)	1885–date	
Indiana Supreme Court Reports	1816–1846	
Blackford	1817–1847	(8v.)
Smith's Supreme Court	1848	(1v.)
Indiana Courts Bulletin	1980–1982	

Court of Appeals

*Indiana Court of Appeals Reports (prior to 1972, Indiana Appellate Court Reports)	1890–date	
Northeastern Reporter	1891–date	
Indiana Cases (West)	1936–date	

Superior Court

Wilson's Superior Court	1871–1874	(1v.)

• **Session Laws:**

Acts, Indiana

• **Statutory Compilation:**

Indiana Code

Burns Indiana Statutes Annotated Code Edition

West's Annotated Indiana Code

• **Administrative Code:**

Burns Indiana Administrative Rules and Regulations

Indiana Administrative Code

• **Administrative Register:**

Indiana Register (Monthly)

IOWA

• **Reporters:**

Supreme Court

*Iowa Reports	1855–1968	Disc. with v.261 (1968)
*Northwestern Reporter	1878–date	
Bradford	1938–1841	(3v. in 1) (1–3 Iowa)
Morris	1839–1846	(1v.) (4 Iowa)
Greene	1847–1854	(4v.) (5–8 Iowa)

Court of Appeals

Iowa Court of Appeals Reports	1977–date	
*Northwestern Reporter	1977–date	

- **Session Laws:**

  Acts & Joint Resolutions of the State of Iowa

  Iowa Legislative Service (West)

- **Statutory Compilation:**

  Iowa Code Annotated (West)

  Code of Iowa

- **Administrative Code:**

  Iowa Administrative Code

- **Administrative Register:**

  The Iowa Administrative Bulletin (Bi-weekly)

KANSAS

- **Reporters:**

Supreme Court

*Kansas Reports	1862–date	
Pacific Reporter	1883–date	
Kansas Cases (West)	1968–date	
McCahon	1858–1868	(1v.)
Dassler	1862–1868	(1v.)

Court of Appeals

Kansas Appellate Reporter		
1st series	1895–1901	(10v.)
2nd series	1977–date	
Pacific Reporter	1895–1901	
	1977–date	
Kansas Cases (West)	1977–date	
Randolph	1895–1896	(2v.)
Dewey	1895–1896	(2v.)
Clemens	1896–1897	(2v.)
Dewey	1897–1901	(4v.)

- **Session Laws:**

  Sessions Laws of Kansas

- **Statutory Compilation:**

  Kansas Statutes Annotated (Official)

  Kansas Statutes Annotated (Vernon)

- **Administrative Code:**

  Kansas Administrative Regulations (1978)

- **Administrative Register:**

  Kansas Register (Weekly)

KENTUCKY

- **Reporters:**

Supreme Court (Court of Appeals, prior to 1976)		
*Kentucky Reports	1785–1951	Disc. with v.314 (1951)
*Southwestern Reporter	1886–date	Official since 1973
*Kentucky Decisions	1886–date	Official since 1973
Hughes	1785–1801	(1v.) (1 Ky.)
Lithell's Selected Cases	1795–1821	(1v.) (16 Ky.)
(Sneed) Kentucky Decisions	1801–1805	(1v.) (2 Ky.)
Hardin	1805–1808	(1v.) (3 Ky.)
Bibb	1808–1817	(4v.) (4–7 Ky.)
Marshall, A.K.	1817–1821	(3v.) (8–10 Ky.)
Littell	1822–1824	(5v.) (11–15 Ky.)
Monroe, T.B.	1824–1828	(7v.) (17–23 Ky.)
Marshall, J.J.	1829–1832	(7v.) (24–30 Ky.)
Dana	1833–1840	(9v.) (31–39 Ky.)
Monroe, Ben	1840–1857	(18v.) (40–57 Ky.)
Metcalf	1858–1863	(4v.) (58–61 Ky.)
Duvall	1863–1866	(2v.) (62–63 Ky.)
Bush	1866–1879	(14v.) (64–77 Ky.)
Kentucky Law Reporter	1880–1908	(33v.)
Court of Appeals		
*Southwestern Reporter	1976–date	
*Kentucky Decisions (West)	1976–date	
Kentucky Opinions (Unreported Cases)	1864–1886	(15v.)

- **Session Laws:**

  Kentucky Acts

  Kentucky Revised Statutes & Rules Service (Baldwin)

- **Statutory Compilation:**

  Kentucky Revised Statutes

  Baldwin's Kentucky Revised Statutes Annotated

  Kentucky Revised Statutes Annotated (Michie; formerly Bobbs-Merrill)

- **Administrative Code:**

  Kentucky Administrative Regulations Service

- **Administrative Register:**

  Administrative Register (Monthly)

LOUISIANA

- **Reporters:**

Supreme Court		
Louisiana Reports	1900–1972	(160v.), (104–263) † Published by West since

† following earlier reporters

		v.109 (1902) Disc. with vol. 263 (1972). No current official reporter.
Southern Reporter	1887–date	
West's Louisiana Cases	1966–date	
Louisiana Reports & Nominative	1809–1896	(100v. in 55 Books)
Annotated		(1 Martin–48 La.Ann.)
Martin Louisiana Term Report Old Series	1809–1823	(12v.)
Orleans Term Reports	1809–1812	(2v.)
Louisiana Term Reports	1812–1823	(10v., 3–12)
Martin Louisiana Term Reports New Series	1823–1830	(8v.)
Harrison Condensed Reports	1809–1830	(4v.)
Louisiana Reports (Miller)	1830–1833	(5v.)
Louisiana Reports (Curry)	1833–1841	(14v., 6–19)
Robinson	1841–1846	(12v.)
Louisiana Annual	1846–1900	(52v.)
Mannings Unreported Cases	1877–1880	(1v.)
Court of Appeals		
Louisiana Courts of Appeal Reports	1924–1932	(19v.)
Southern Reporter	1928–date	
West's Louisiana Cases	1966–date	
McGloin's Louisiana Courts of Appeal Reports	1881–1884	(2v.)
Gunby's Reports (Circuit Court of App.)	1885–	(1v.)
Teisser's Court of Appeal, Parish of Orleans Reports	1903–1917	(14v.)
Peltier's Decisions, Court of Appeal, Parish of Orleans	1917–1923	

- **Session Laws:**

  State of Louisiana: Acts of the Legislature

  Louisiana Session Law Service (West)

- **Statutory Compilation:**

  West's Louisiana Revised Statutes Annotated

  West's Louisiana Civil Code Annotated

  West's Louisiana Code of Civil Procedure Annotated

  West's Louisiana Code of Criminal Procedure

- **Administrative Code:**

  ——

- **Administrative Register:**

  Louisiana Register (Monthly)

MAINE

- **Reporters:**

Supreme Judicial Court		
*Maine Reports	1820–1965	
*Atlantic Reports	1885–date	Official since 1966
*Maine Reporter (West)	1966–date	Official since 1966
Greenleaf	1820–1832	(9v.) (1–9 Me.)
Fairfield	1833–1835	(3v.) (10–12 Me.)

- **Session Laws:**

  Laws of the State of Maine

  Acts, Resolves & Constitutional Resolutions of the State of Maine

  Maine Legislative Service

- **Statutory Compilation:**

  Maine Revised Statutes Annotated (West)

- **Administrative Code:**

  (*Code of Maine Rules* is now discontinued)

- **Administrative Register:**

  ——

MARYLAND

- **Reporters:**

Court of Appeals		
*Maryland Reports	1851–date	
Atlantic Reporter	1885–date	
Maryland Reporter (West)	1968–date	
Harris and McHenry	1658–1799	(4v.)
Harris and Johnson	1800–1826	(7v.)
Harris and Gill	1826–1829	(2v.)
Gill and Johnson	1829–1842	(12v.)
Gill (v. 8 and 9 completed by Miller.)	1843–1851	(9v.)
Court of Special Appeals		
*Maryland Appellate Reports	1962–date	
Atlantic Reporter	1967–date	
Maryland Reporter (West)	1968–date	
Court of Chancery		
Bland (High Court of Chancery)	1811–1832	(3v.)
Maryland Chancery Decisions	1847–1854	(4v.)

- **Session Laws:**

  Laws of Maryland

- **Statutory Compilation:**

  Annotated Code of Maryland

- **Administrative Code:**

  Code of Maryland Regulations

- **Administrative Register:**

  Maryland Register (Bi-weekly)

MASSACHUSETTS

- **Reporters:**

Supreme Judicial Court		
*Massachusetts Reports	1804–date	
*Massachusetts S.J.C. Advance Sheets	? –date	
Northeastern Reporter	1884–date	
Massachusetts Decisions (West)	1884–date	
Williams	1804–1805	(1v.) (1 Mass.)
Tyng	1806–1820	(16v.) (2–17 Mass.)
Pickering	1820–1839	(24v.) (18–41 Mass.)
Metcalf	1840–1847	(13v.) (42–54 Mass.)
Cushing	1848–1853	(12v.) (55–66 Mass.)
Gray	1854–1860	(16v.) (67–82 Mass.)
Allen	1861–1867	(14v.) (83–96 Mass.)
Department Reports . . . " affecting business with Supreme Court decisions in full	1915–1920	(9v.)
Appeals Court		
*Massachusetts Appeals Court Reports	1972–date	
Massachusetts Appeals Court	? –date	Advance Sheet
Northeastern Reporter	1972–date	
Massachusetts Decisions (West)	1972–date	
District Court		
*Appellate Decisions	1941–date	
Appellate Decisions Reports	1936–1950	(15v.)

- **Session Laws:**

  Acts & Resolves of Massachusetts

  Massachusetts Advance Legislative Service (Lawyers Co-op)

- **Statutory Compilation:**

  Massachusetts General Laws Annotated (West)

  Annotated Laws of Massachusetts (Lawyers Co-op)

- **Administrative Code:**

  Code of Massachusetts Regulations

- **Administrative Register:**

  Massachusetts Register (Weekly)

MICHIGAN

- **Reporters:**

Supreme Court

*Michigan Reports	1847–date	
Northwestern Reporter	1879–date	
West's Michigan Reporter	1941–date	
Blume Supreme Court Transaction	1805–1836	(6v.)
Blume Unreported Opinion	1836–1843	(1v.)
Douglass	1843–1847	(2v.)
Fuller's Practice Reports (S.C.)	1896	(1v.)
Fisk's Overruled Cases (S.C.)	1925	(1v.)

Court of Appeals

*Michigan Appeals Reports	1965–date
Northwestern Reporter	1965–date
West's Michigan Reporter	1965–date

Court of Claims

Michigan Court of Claims Reports	1938–1942

Other Courts

Harrington's Chancery	1838–1842	(1v.)
Walker's Chancery	1842–1845	(1v.)
Brown's Nisi Prius Reports	1869–1871	(2v.)

- **Session Laws:**

  Public and Local Acts of the Legislature of the State of Michigan

  Michigan Legislative Service (West)

- **Statutory Compilation:**

  Michigan Compiled Laws (1970)

  Michigan Compiled Laws Annotated

  Michigan Statutes Annotated (Callaghan)

  Michigan Court Rules Annotated (West)

- **Administrative Code:**

  Michigan Administrative Code (1979) (updated by supplements, quarterly and annually)

- **Administrative Register:**

  ——

MINNESOTA

- **Reporters:**

Supreme Court

*Minnesota Reports	1851–1977	Disc. with v.312
*Northwestern Reporter	1879–date	Official since 1978
*Minnesota Reporter (West)	1978–date	Official since 1978

- **Session Laws:**

  Laws of Minnesota

  Minnesota Session Law Service (West)

- **Statutory Compilation:**

  Minnesota Statutes (even-numbered years & Supp. odd-numbered years)

  Minnesota Statutes Annotated (West)

- **Administrative Code:**

  Minnesota Code of Agency Rules

- **Administrative Register:**

  Minnesota State Register (Weekly)

MISSISSIPPI

- **Reporters:**

Supreme Court		
*Mississippi Reports	1818–1966	Disc. with v.254 (1966)
*Southern Reporter	1886–date	Official since 1966
*Mississippi Cases (West)	1966–date	Official since 1966
Walker	1818–1832	(1v.) (1 Miss.)
Howard	1834–1843	(7v.) (2–8 Miss.)
Smedes and Marshall	1943–1850	(14v.) (9–22 Miss.)
Chancery Court		
Freeman's Chancery	1839–1843	(1v.)
Smede's & Marshall's Chancery	1840–1843	(1v.)

- **Session Laws:**

  General Laws of Mississippi

- **Statutory Compilation:**

  Mississippi Code Annotated

- **Administrative Code:**

  ——

- **Administrative Register:**

  Mississippi Register (Monthly)

MISSOURI

- **Reporters:**

Supreme Court		
*Missouri Reports	1821–1956	Disc. with v.365 (1956)
*Southwestern Reporter	1886–date	Official since 1956
*Missouri Decisions (West)	1886–date	Official since 1956
Court of Appeals		
*Missouri Appeal Reports	1876–1952	Disc. with v.241 (1952)
*Southwestern Reporter	1902–date	Official since 1952
*Missouri Decisions (West)	1902–date	Official since 1952

- **Session Laws:**

  Laws of Missouri

  Missouri Legislative Service

- **Statutory Compilation:**

  Missouri Revised Statutes

  Vernon's Annotated Missouri Statutes (West)

- **Administrative Code:**

  Missouri Code of State Regulations

- **Administrative Register:**

  Missouri Register (Monthly)

MONTANA

- **Reporters:**

Supreme Court

*Montana Reports	1868–date
*State Reporter (mimeographed advance sheets)	1947–date
Pacific Reporter	1882–date

- **Session Laws:**

  Laws of Montana

- **Statutory Compilation:**

  Montana Code Annotated

- **Administrative Code:**

  Administrative Rules of Montana

- **Administrative Register:**

  Montana Administrative Register (Bi-weekly)

NEBRASKA

- **Reporters:**

Supreme Court

*Nebraska Reports.............	1860–date	
Northwestern Reporter	1879–date	
Nebraska Unofficial...........	1901–1904	(5v.)

- **Session Laws:**

  Laws of Nebraska

- **Statutory Compilation:**

  Revised Statutes of Nebraska

- **Administrative Code:**

  Nebraska Administrative Code

- **Administrative Register:**

  ——

NEVADA

- **Reporters:**

Supreme Court

*Nevada Reports	1865–date	
Pacific Reporter	1882–date	

- **Session Laws:**

  Statutes of Nevada

- **Statutory Compilation:**

  Nevada Revised Statutes

- **Administrative Code:**

  (Code in preparation)

- **Administrative Register:**

  ——

NEW HAMPSHIRE

- **Reporters:**

Supreme Court

*New Hampshire Reports	1816–date	
Atlantic Reporter	1886–date	
New Hampshire Reports (Smith)	1796–1816	(1v.)
New Hampshire Law Reporter	1897	(1v.)

- **Session Laws:**

  Laws of the State of New Hampshire

- **Statutory Compilation:**

  New Hampshire Revised Statutes Annotated

- **Administrative Code:**

  ——

- **Administrative Register:**

  ——

NEW JERSEY

- **Reporters:**

Supreme Court

*New Jersey Law Reports	1790–1948	(137v.)
*New Jersey Equity Reports	1830–1948	(142v.)
*New Jersey Reports	1948–date	Published by West since v.53 (1968)
Atlantic Reporter	1885–date	
Coxe	1790–1795	(1v.) (1 N.J.Law)
Pennington	1806–1813	(2v.) (2–3 N.J.Law)
Southard	1816–1820	(2v.) (4–5 N.J.Law)

Halsted	1796–1804	
	1821–1831	(7v.) (6–12 N.J.Law)
Saxton	1830–1832	(1v.) (1 N.J.Eq.)
Greene, J.S.	1831–1836	(3v.) (13–15 N.J.Law)
Green	1834–1845	(3v.) (2–4 N.J.Eq.)
Harrison	1837–1842	(4v.) (16–19 N.J.Law)
Spencer	1842–1846	(1v.) (20 N.J.Law)
Halsted	1845–1853	(4v.) (5–8 N.J.Eq.)
Zabriskie	1847–1855	(4v.) (21–24 N.J.Law)
Stockton	1852–1858	(3v.) (9–11 N.J.Eq.)
Dutcher	1855–1862	(5v.) (25–29 N.J.Law)
Beasley	1856–1861	(2v.) (11–12 N.J.Eq.)
McCarter	1861–1863	(2v.) (14–15 N.J.Eq.)
Vroom, P.D.	1862–1872	(6v.) (30–35 N.J.Law)
Green, C.E.	1862–1876	(12v.) (16–27 N.J.Eq.)
Vroom, G.D.W.	1872–1914	(50v.) (36–85 N.J.Law)
Stewart	1877–1889	(18v.) (28–45 N.J.Eq.)
Dickinson	1889–1904	(21v.) (46–66 N.J.Eq.)
Robbins	1904–1905	(4v.) (67–70 N.J.Eq.)
Buchanan	1906–1916	(15v.) (71–85 N.J.Eq.)
Gummere	1914–1940	(41v.) (86–125 N.J.Law)
Stockton	1916–1927	(16v.) (86–101 N.J.Eq.)
New Jersey Miscellaneous	1923–1949	(26v.)
Supreme Court		
Backes	1926–1948	(41v.) (102–142 N.J.Eq.)
Abbott	1940–1948	(10v.) (126–137 N.J.Law)
Superior Court		
*New Jersey Law Reports	1790–1948	(137v.)
*New Jersey Equity Reports	1830–1948	(142v.)
*New Jersey Superior Court Reports	1948–date	Published by West since volume 103 (1968)
Atlantic Reporter	1885–date	
New Jersey Miscellaneous Reports	1923–1949	(26v.)
Tax Court		
*New Jersey Tax Court Reports	1979–date	Published by West since 1979

- **Session Laws:**

  Laws of New Jersey

  New Jersey Session Law Service (West)

- **Statutory Compilation:**

  New Jersey Revised Statutes (1937)

  New Jersey Statutes Annotated (West)

- **Administrative Code:**

  New Jersey Administrative Code

- **Administrative Register:**

  New Jersey Register (Bi-weekly)

NEW MEXICO

- **Reporters:**

Supreme Court		
*New Mexico Reports	1852–date	Published by West since v.36 (1933)
Pacific Reporter	1883–date	
Gildersleeve Reports, E.W.S. ed.	1852–1889	(4v.) (1–4 N.M.)
Court of Appeal		
*New Mexico Reports	1967–date	
Pacific Reporter	1967–date	

- **Session Laws:**

  Laws of New Mexico

- **Statutory Compilation:**

  New Mexico Statutes Annotated

- **Administrative Code:**

  ——

- **Administrative Register:**

  ——

NEW YORK

- **Reporters:**

Court of Appeals		
*New York Reports	1847–date	
Northeastern Reporter	1885–date	
West's New York Supplement		
(1st series)	1888–1938	(300v.)
(2nd series)	1938–date	
Howard's Appeal Cases	1847–1848	(1v.)
Cornstock	1847–1851	(4v.) (1–4 N.Y.)
Abbot	1850–1869	(4v.)
Selden	1851–1854	(6v.) (5–10 N.Y.)
Kernan	1854–1856	(4v.) (11–14 N.Y.)
Keyes	1863–1868	(4v.) (Unofficial; cited as 40–43 N.Y.)
Tiffany, Transcript Appeals	1867–1868	(7v.)
New York Condensed Reports	1881–1882	(1v.)
Silvernail	1886–1892	(4v.)
Supreme Court, Appellate Division		
*Appellate Division Reports	1896–date	
West's New York Supplement	1896–date	
Barbour's Supreme Court Reports	1847–1877	(67v.)
Lansing's Reports	1869–1873	(7v.)

Supreme Court Reports (Thompson & Cook)	1873–1875	(6v.)
Supreme Court Reports (Hun)	1874–1895	(12v.)

Other Lower Courts (e.g., N.Y. App.Term., N.Y.Sup.Ct., N.Y. Ct.Cl., N.Y.Civ.Ct., N.Y.Crim. Ct., N.Y.Fam.Ct.): Cite to Misc. or Misc.2d and to N.Y.S. or N.Y.S.2d.

*New York Miscellaneous Reports	1892–date	
West's New York Supplement	1888–date	

Court for the Correction of Errors (N.Y. Supreme Court of Judicature and N.Y.Sup. Ct.): Cite to one of the following reporters.

Coleman's Cases	1791–1800	(1v.)
Coleman & Caines' Cases	1794–1805	(1v.)
Caines' Cases in Error	1796–1805	(2v.)
Johnson's Cases	1799–1803	(3v.)
Lockwood's Reversed Cases	1799–1857	(1v.)
Caines' Reports	1803–1805	(3v.)
Johnson's Reports	1806–1823	(20v.)
Anthon's Nisi Prius	1807–1851	(1v.)
Yates Select Cases	1809	(1v.)
Cowen's Reports	1823–1829	(9v.)
Wendell's Reports	1828–1841	(26v.)
Edmund's Select Cases	1834–1853	(2v.)
Hill's Reports	1841–1844	(7v.)
Hill and Denio Supplement (Lalor)	1842–1844	(1v.)
Denio's Reports	1845–1848	(5v.)

Court of Chancery

Johnson's Chancery Reports	1814–1823	(7v.)
Hopkins' Chancery Reports	1823–1826	(1v.)
Paige's Chancery Reports	1828–1845	(11v.)
Edwards' Chancery Reports	1831–1850	(4v.)
Hoffman's Chancery Reports	1838–1840	(1v.)
Clarke's Chancery Reports	1839–1841	(1v.)
Saratoga Chancery Sentinel	1841–1847	(6 in 1v.)
Sanford's Chancery Reports	1843–1847	(4v.)
Barbour's Chancery Reports	1845–1848	(3v.)

Other Lower Courts before 1888

Howard's Practice Reports	1844–1886	(70v.)
Abbott's Practice Cases	1854–1875	(35v.)
Abbott's New Cases	1876–1894	(32v.)

- **Session Laws:**

  Laws of New York

  McKinney's Session Laws

West Annual

Lawyers Co-op Annual

N.Y. Consolidated Laws Service

Legislative Bill Drafting Committee

- **Statutory Compilation:**

McKinney's Consolidated Laws (West)

Consolidated Laws Service (Lawyers Co-op)

- **Administrative Code:**

Official Compilation of Codes, Rules and Regulations of the State of New York

- **Administrative Register:**

New York State Register (Weekly)

NORTH CAROLINA

- **Reporters:**

Supreme Court

*North Carolina Reports	1778–date	
Southeastern Reporter	1887–date	
New Carolina Reporter (West)	1939–date	
Martin	1778–1797	(1v.) (1 N.C.)
Taylor	1798–1802	(1v.) (1 N.C.)
Conference by Cameron & Norwood	1800–1804	(1v.) (1 N.C.)
Haywood	1789–1806	(2v.) (2–3 N.C.)
Carolina Law Repository	1813–1816	(2v.) (4 N.C.)
Taylor's North Carolina Term Reports	1816–1818	(1v.) (4 N.C.)
Murphey	1804–1813 1818–1819	(3v.) (5–7 N.C.)
Hawks	1820–1826	(4v.) (8–11 N.C.)
Devereux's Law	1826–1834	(4v.) (12–15 N.C.)
Devereux's Equity	1826–1834	(2v.) (16–17 N.C.)
Devereux & Battle's Law	1834–1839	(4v.) (18–20 N.C.) (v.3, 4 are N.C. v.20)
Devereux & Battle's Equity (21–22)	1834–1839	(2v.) (21–22 N.C.)
Iredell's Law (23–35)	1840–1852	(13v.) (23–35 N.C.)
Iredell's Equity (36–43)	1840–1852	(8v.) (36–43 N.C.)
Busbee's Law	1852–1853	(1v.) (44 N.C.)
Busbee's Equity	1852–1853	(1v.) (45 N.C.)
Jones' Law	1853–1862	(8v.) (46–53 N.C.)
Jones' Equity	1853–1863	(6v.) (54–59 N.C.)
Winston	1863–1864	(2v.) (60 N.C.)
Phillips' Law	1866–1868	(1v.) (61 N.C.)
Phillips' Equity	1866–1868	(1v.) (62 N.C.)

Court of Appeals

*North Carolina Court of Appeals Reports	1968–date	
Southeastern Reporter	1968–date	
North Carolina Reporter (West)	1968–date	

- **Session Laws:**

  Session Laws of North Carolina

  Advance Legislative Service to the General Statutes of North Carolina

- **Statutory Compilation:**

  General Statutes of North Carolina (Michie)

- **Administrative Code:**

  North Carolina Administrative Code

- **Administrative Register:**

  ——

NORTH DAKOTA

- **Reporters:**

Supreme Court

*North Dakota Reports	1890–1953	Disc. with v.79 (1953)
*Northwestern Reporter	1890–date	Designated official reporter (in 1980), back to 1953

Supreme Court of Dakota

Dakota Reports	1867–1889	(6v.)
Northwestern Reporter	1867–1889	

- **Session Laws:**

  Laws of North Dakota

- **Statutory Compilation:**

  North Dakota Century Code

- **Administrative Code:**

  North Dakota Administrative Code

- **Administrative Register:**

  ——

OHIO

- **Reporters:**

Supreme Court

*Ohio Official Reports, New Series	1982–date	
*Ohio Reports	1821–1851	(20v.)
*Ohio State Reports	1852–date	

Northeastern Reporter	1885–date	
Ohio Cases (West)	1933–date	
Wilcox's Condensed Reports (Reprint of 1–7 Ohio Reports)	1821–1831	(5v.)
Hammond's Condensed Reports (Reprint 1–2 Ohio Reports)........................	1821	(1v.)
Wright	1831–1834	(1v.)
Ohio Unreported Cases........	1889–1899	(1v.)
Ohio State Bar Association Reports	1927–date	
Court of Appeals		
*Ohio Official Reports, New Series..........................	1982–date	
*Ohio Appellate Reports	1913–date	
Northeastern Reporter	1921–date	
Ohio Cases (West)	1943–date	
Ohio Law Reporter	1903–1934	(40v.) (v.21–40 continuation of Ohio Court of Appeals Reports.)
Ohio Court of Appeals Reports	1915–1922	(6v., 27–32)
Other Law Courts		
*Ohio Official Reporter, New Series	1982–date	
*Ohio Miscellaneous............	1965–date	
Ohio Opinions.................	1934–date	
Ohio Decisions, Reprint	1840–1893	(5v.)
Dayton Reports, 3 Ohio Misc. Decisions (Gotschall)	1865–1873	(1v.)
Goebel's Probate Reports	1885–1890	(1v.)
Ohio Circuit Court Reports (Jahn)	1885–1901	(22v.)
Ohio Circuit Decisions.........	1885–1901	(12v.)
Ohio Decisions	1894–1920	(31v.)
Ohio Decisions (Ohio Lower Decisions).....................	1894–1896	(3v.)
Ohio Nisi Prius Reports	1894–1934	(40v.)
Idding's Term Reports	1899–1900	(1v.)
Ohio Circuit Court Decisions ..	1902–1923	(22v.)

- **Session Laws:**

  State of Ohio: Legislative Acts Passed and Joint Resolutions Adopted

  Ohio Legislative Bulletin (Anderson)

  Baldwin's Ohio Legislative Service

- **Statutory Compilation:**

  Ohio Revised Code Annotated (Page)

  Ohio Revised Code Annotated (Baldwin)

- **Administrative Code:**

  Ohio Administrative Code (official compilation published by Banks-Baldwin).... 1977–date

- **Administrative and Executive Registers:**

Ohio Monthly Record (Banks-Baldwin)	1977–date	(Monthly)
Ohio Government Reports	1965–date	
Ohio Department Reports	1914–1964	

OKLAHOMA

- **Reporters:**

Supreme Court		
*Oklahoma Reports	1890–1953	Disc. with v.208 (1953)
*Pacific Reporter	1890–date	Official since 1953
*Oklahoma Decisions (West)	1931–date	Official since 1953
Court of Appeals of Indian Territory		
Indian Territory Reports	1896–1907	
Southwestern Reporter	1896–1907	
Court of Criminal Appeals		
*Oklahoma Criminal Reports	1908–1953	Disc. with v.97 (1953)
*Pacific Reporter	1908–date	Official since 1953
*Oklahoma Decisions (West)	1931–date	Official since 1953
Court of Appeals		
*Pacific Reporter	1969–date	Official since 1969
*Oklahoma Decisions (West)	1969–date	Official since 1969

- **Session Laws:**

  Oklahoma Session Laws

- **Statutory Compilation:**

  Oklahoma Statutes (1971 & Supp.1978)

  Oklahoma Statutes Annotated (West)

- **Administrative Code:**

  ——

- **Administrative Register:**

  Oklahoma Gazette (Bi-weekly)

OREGON

- **Reporters:**

Supreme Court	
*Oregon Reports	1853–date
Pacific Reporter	1883–date
Oregon Cases (West)	1966–date
Court of Appeals	
*Oregon Reports, Court of Appeals	1969–date
Pacific Report	1969–date
Oregon Cases (West)	1969–date

Tax Court

*Oregon Tax Reporter	1962–date	

- **Session Laws:**
  Oregon Laws and Resolutions
- **Statutory Compilation:**
  Oregon Revised Statutes
- **Administrative Code:**
  Oregon Administrative Rules
- **Administrative Register:**
  Administrative Rules Bulletin (Bi-weekly)

PENNSYLVANIA

- **Reporters:**

Supreme Court

*Pennsylvania State Reports	1845–date	Published by West since v.459 (1974)
Atlantic Reporter	1885–date	
Pennsylvania Reporter (West)	1939–date	
Dallas	1754–1806	(4v.)
Yeates	1791–1808	(4v.)
Addison	1793–1799	(1v.)
Binney	1799–1814	(6v.)
Sergeant and Rawle	1814–1828	(17v.)
Rawle	1828–1835	(5v.)
Penrose and Watts	1829–1832	(3v.)
Watts	1832–1840	(10v.)
Wharton	1835–1841	(6v.)
Watts and Sergeant	1841–1845	(9v.)
Walker	1855–1885	(4v.)
Pennypacker	1881–1884	(4v.)
Sadler	1885–1888	(10v.)
Monaghan	1888–1890	(2v.)

Superior Court

*Pennsylvania Superior Court Reports	1895–date	Published by West since v.241 (1976)
Atlantic Reporter	1931–date	
Pennsylvania Reporter (West)	1939–date	

Commonwealth Court

*Pennsylvania Commonwealth Court Reports	1970–date	
Atlantic Reporter	1970–date	
Pennsylvania Reporter (West)	1970–date	

Other Lower Courts

*Pennsylvania District and County Reports	1921–date	
Pennsylvania Fiduciary Reporter	1951–date	

Pennsylvania County Court Reports......................	1885–1921	(50v.)
Pennsylvania District Reports	1892–1921	(30v.)

- **Session Laws:**

  Laws of the General Assembly of the Commonwealth of Pennsylvania

  Pennsylvania Legislative Service (Purdon)

- **Statutory Compilation:**

  Pennsylvania Consolidated Statutes

  Pennsylvania Consolidated Statutes Annotated (Purdon)

  Purdon's Pennsylvania Statutes Annotated (West)

- **Administrative Code:**

  Pennsylvania Code

  Pennsylvania Code Reporter (Monthly)

- **Administrative Register:**

  Pennsylvania Bulletin (Weekly)

RHODE ISLAND

- **Reporters:**

Supreme Court

*Rhode Island Reports	1828–date	
Atlantic Reporter	1885–date	

Superior Court

Rhode Island Superior Court Rescripts	1917–1919	(2v.)
Rhode Island Decisions........	1924–1935	(12v.)

- **Session Laws:**

  Public Laws of Rhode Island

- **Statutory Compilation:**

  General Laws of Rhode Island

  Rhode Island Current Laws

- **Administrative Code:**

  None, but an *index* is published under the title, *Compilation of Rules of State Agencies* (latest ed., 1981, with revision every 2 years.). Quarterly supplement has become less regular.

- **Administrative Register:**

  ——

SOUTH CAROLINA

- **Reporters:**

Supreme Court After 1868

*South Carolina Reports	1868–date
Southeastern Reporter	1886–date

Court of Law Before 1868:
Cite to S.C.L.

South Carolina Law Reports		
(Nominatives, as listed below)	1783–1868	(49v.)
Bay	1783–1804	(2v.) (1–2 S.C.L.)
Brevard	1793–1816	(3v.) (3–5 S.C.L.)
Treadway..................	1812–1816	(2v.) (6–7 S.C.L.)
Mill's Constitutional Court		
Reports.....................	1817–1818	(2v.) (8–9 S.C.L.)
Nott and McCord	1817–1820	(2v.) (10–11 S.C.L.)
McCord.....................	1821–1828	(4v.) (12–15 S.C.L.)
Harper	1823–1828	(1v.) (16 S.C.L.)
	1830–1831	
Bailey	1828–1832	(2v.) (17–18 S.C.L.)
Richardson	1832	(1v.) (18 S.C.L.)
Hill.........................	1833–1837	(3v.) (19–21 S.C.L.)
Riley	1836–1837	(1v.) (22 S.C.L.)
Dudley	1837–1838	(1v.) (23 S.C.L.)
Rice	1838–1839	(1v.) (24 S.C.L.)
Cheves	1839–1840	(1v.) (25 S.C.L.)
McMullan....................	1840–1842	(2v.) (26–27 S.C.L.)
Speers......................	1842–1844	(2v.) (28–29 S.C.L.)
Richardson	1844–1846	(2v.) (30–31 S.C.L.)
Strobhart...................	1846–1850	(5v.) (32–38 S.C.L.)
Richardson	1850–1868	(13v.) (37–49 S.C.L.)

Court of Equity Before 1869

South Carolina Equity Reports		
(Nominatives, as listed below)	1784–1868	(35v.)
Desaussure's Equity	1784–1816	(4v.) (1–4 S.C.Eq.)
Harper's Equity	1824	(1v.) (5 S.C.Eq.)
McCord's Chancery	1825–1827	(2v.) (6–7 S.C.Eq.)
Bailey's Equity	1830–1831	(1v.) (8 S.C.Eq.)
Richardson's Cases	1831–1832	(1v.) (9 S.C.Eq.)
Hill's Chancery	1833–1837	(2v.) (10–11 S.C.Eq.)
Riley's Chancery............	1836–1837	(1v.) (12 S.C.Eq.)
Dudley's Equity	1837–1838	(1v.) (13 S.C.Eq.)
Rice's Equity	1838–1839	(1v.) (14 S.C.Eq.)
Cheves' Equity	1839–1840	(1v.) (15 S.C.Eq.)
McMullan's Equity..........	1840–1842	(1v.) (16 S.C.Eq.)
Speers' Equity..............	1842–1844	(1v.) (17 S.C.Eq.)
Richardson's Equity.........	1844–1846	(2v.) (18–19 S.C.Eq.)
Strobhart's Equity	1846–1850	(4v.) (20–23 S.C.Eq.)
Richardson's Equity.........	1850–1868	(12v.) (24–35 S.C.Eq.)

- **Session Laws:**

  Acts and Joint Resolutions, South Carolina

- **Statutory Compilation:**

  Code of Laws of South Carolina, 1976, Annotated (Lawyers Co-op)

- **Administrative Code:**

  South Carolina Code of Regulations

• **Administrative Register:**

South Carolina State Register (Monthly, Legislative Council)

SOUTH DAKOTA

• **Reporters:**

Supreme Court

*South Dakota Reports	1890–1976	Disc. with v.90 (1976)
*Northwestern Reporter	1890–date	Official since 1976

Supreme Court of Dakota

Dakota Reports	1867–1889	
Northwestern Reporter	1867–1889	

• **Session Laws:**

Laws of South Dakota

• **Statutory Compilation:**

South Dakota Codified Laws Annotated

• **Administrative Code:**

South Dakota Administrative Rules

• **Administrative Register:**

South Dakota Register (Weekly)

TENNESSEE

• **Reporters:**

Supreme Court

*Tennessee Reports	1791–1972	Disc. with v.225 (1972)
*Southwestern Reporter	1886–date	Official since 1972
*Tennessee Decisions (West)	1886–date	Official since 1972
Overton	1791–1816	(2v.) (1–2 Tenn.)
Cooke	1811–1814	(3, 3a Tenn.)
Haywood	1816–1818	(3v.) (4–6 Tenn.)
Peck	1821–1824	(1v.) (7 Tenn.)
Martin & Yerger	1825–1828	(1v.) (8 Tenn.)
Yerger	1828–1837	(10v.) (9–18 Tenn.)
Meigs	1838–1839	(1v.) (19 Tenn.)
Humphreys	1839–1851	(11v.) (20–30 Tenn.)
Swan	1851–1853	(2v.) (31–32 Tenn.)
Sneed	1853–1858	(5v.) (33–37 Tenn.)
Head	1858–1859	(3v.) (38–40 Tenn.)
Coldwell	1860–1870	(7v.) (41–47 Tenn.)
Heiskell	1870–1874	(12v.) (48–59 Tenn.)
Baxter	1872–1878	(9v.) (60–68 Tenn.)
Legal Reporter (Supreme Court) N.S.	1877–1879	(3v.)
Lea	1878–1886	(16v.) (69–84 Tenn.)
Pickle	1886–1902	(24v.) (85–108 Tenn.)
Cates	1902–1913	(19v.) (109–127 Tenn.)
Thompson	1913–1926	(26v.) (128–153 Tenn.)
Smith	1925–1932	(11v.) (154–164 Tenn.)

Court of Appeals		
*Tennessee Appeals	1925–1972	Disc. with v.63 (1972)
*Southwestern Reporter	1932–date	Official since 1972
*Tennessee Decisions (West)	1932–date	Official since 1972
Tennessee Civil Appeals (Higgins)	1910–1918	(8v.)
Court of Chancery Appeals, Court of Criminal Appeals		
*Tennessee Criminal Appeals Reports	1967–1971	Disc. with v.4 (1971)
*Southwestern Reporter	1967–date	
*Tennessee Decisions (West)	1967–date	
Tennessee Chancery (Cooper)	1872–1878	(3v.)
Tennessee Chancery Appeals (Wright)	1901–1904	(2v.)
Tennessee Chancery Appeals Decisions (Reprint)	1895–1907	(7v.)

lc3]• Session Laws:

Public Acts of the State of Tennessee

Private Acts of the State of Tennessee

- **Statutory Compilation:**

Tennessee Code Annotated

- **Administrative Code:**

Official Compilation—Rules & Regulations of the State of Tennessee

- **Administrative Register:**

Tennessee Administrative Register (Monthly)

TEXAS

- **Reporters:**

Supreme Court		
*Texas Reports	1846–1961	Disc. with v.163 (1961)
Southwestern Reporter	1886–date	No Current Official Reporter
Texas Cases (West)	1886–date	
Dallam's Opinions	1840–1844	
Court of Civil Appeals		
*Texas Civil Appeals Reports	1892–1911	Disc. with v.63 (1911)
Southwestern Reporter	1932–date	No Current Official Reporter
Texas cases (West)	1892–date	
Texas Court of Appeals Decisions, Civil Cases (White & Wilson)	1876–1892	

Court of Criminal Appeals

*Texas Criminal Reports (Texas Court of Appeals Reports)	1876–1963	Disc. with v.172 (1963) No current official reporter
Southwestern Reporter	1892–date	
Texas Cases (West)	1892–date	

Texas Court of Appeals

Texas Appeals Reports	1873–1892	
Southwestern Reporter	1886–1892	

- **Session Laws:**

  General and Special Laws of the State of Texas

  Texas Session Law Service (Vernon)

- **Statutory Compilation:**

  Texas Codes Annotated (Vernon)

  West's Texas Statutes and Codes

  Texas Rules Annotated Civil (West)

- **Administrative Code:**

  Texas Administrative Code

- **Administrative Register:**

  Texas Register (Twice Weekly)

UTAH

- **Reporters:**

Supreme Court

*Utah Reporters (1st series)	1855–1953	(123v.)
(2nd series) ...	1953–1974	Disc. with v.30, 2d series (1974). West published v.1, 2d–v.30, 2d.
*Pacific Reporter	1881–date	Official since 1974
*Utah Reporter (West)	1974–date	Official since 1974

- **Session Laws:**

  Laws of Utah

- **Statutory Compilation:**

  Utah Code Annotated

- **Administrative Code:**

  Administrative Rules of the State of Utah

- **Administrative Register:**

  State of Utah Bulletin (Bi-weekly)

VERMONT

- **Reporters:**

Supreme Court

*Vermont Reports	1826–date	

Atlantic Reporter	1885–date	
Chipman, N.	1789–1791	(1v.)
Chipman, D.	1789–1824	(2v.)
Tyler	1800–1803	(2v.)
Brayton	1815–1819	(1v.)
Aikens	1825–1828	(2v.)

- **Session Laws:**

  Laws of Vermont

- **Statutory Compilation:**

  Vermont Statutes Annotated

- **Administrative Code:**

  Vermont Administrative Procedures Compilation

  (Suspended 1982; issuance in new format expected, but not yet available)

- **Administrative Register:**

  Vermont Administrative Procedures Bulletin (Quarterly–Office of Secretary of State)

VIRGINIA

- **Reporters:**

Supreme Court

*Virginia Reports	1790–date	
Southeastern Reporter	1887–date	
Virginia Reports, Annotated, from Jefferson to 33 Grattan	1730–1880	(26v.)
Washington	1790–1796	(2v.) (1–2 Va.)
Virginia Cases, Criminal	1789–1826	(2v.) (3–4 Va.)
Call	1797–1825	(6v.) (5–10 Va.)
Henning & Munford	1806–1810	(4v.) (11–14 Va.)
Munford	1810–1820	(6v.) (15–20 Va.)
Gilmer	1820–1821	(1v.) (21 Va.)
Randolph	1821–1828	(6v.) (22–27 Va.)
Leigh	1829–1842	(12v.) (28–39 Va.)
Robinson	1842–1843	(2v.) (40–41 Va.)
Grattan	1844–1880	(33v.) (42–74 Va.)

- **Session Laws:**

  Acts of the General Assembly of the Commonwealth of Virginia

- **Statutory Compilation:**

  Code of Virginia

- **Administrative Code:**

  ——

- **Administrative Register:**

  Register of Regulations of Agencies of the Commonwealth (Annual)

WASHINGTON

- **Reporters:**

Supreme Court		
*Washington Reports		
(1st Series)	1889–1939	(200v.)
(2nd Series)	1939–date	
*Washington Territory Reports	1854–1888	
Pacific Reporter	1880–date	
Washington Reporter (West) ..	1955–date	
Court of Appeals		
*Washington Appellate Reports	1969–date	
Pacific Reporter	1969–date	
Washington Reporter (West) ..	1969–date	

- **Session Laws:**

  Laws of Washington

  Washington Legislative Service (West)

- **Statutory Compilation:**

  Revised Code of Washington (1974)

  Revised Code of Washington Annotated (West)

- **Administrative Code:**

  Washington Administrative Code

- **Administrative Register:**

  Washington State Register (Monthly)

WEST VIRGINIA

- **Reporters:**

Supreme Court of Appeals		
*West Virginia Reports	1863–date	Not officially Disc., but last is vol. 157 (1973–1974)
Southeastern Reporter	1886–date	
Court of Claims		
*West Virginia Court of Claims Report........................	1942–date	Last vol. publ. is vol. 12 (1977–1979)

- **Session Laws:**

  Acts of the Legislature of West Virginia

- **Statutory Compilation:**

  West Virginia Code

- **Administrative Code:**

  State Register

- **Administrative Register:**

  ——

WISCONSIN

- **Reporters:**

Supreme Court

*Wisconsin Reports	1853–date	
Northwestern Reporter	1879–date	
*Wisconsin Reporter (West)	1941–date	Co-official since 1975
Pinney	1839–1852	(3v.)
Burnett (bound with session laws for Dec. 1841)	1841	(1v.)
Burnett	1842–1843	(1v.)
Chandler	1849–1852	(4v.)
Dixon and Ryan Supreme Court Selected Opinions (Roe)	1859–1878	(1v.)

Court of Appeals

Wisconsin Reports	1978–date
Northwestern Reporter	1978–date
Wisconsin Reporter (West)	1978–date

- **Session Laws:**

  Laws of Wisconsin

  Wisconsin Legislative Service (West)

- **Statutory Compilation:**

  Wisconsin Statutes (1975 and biannually)

  West's Wisconsin Statutes Annotated

- **Administrative Code:**

  Wisconsin Administrative Code

- **Administrative Register:**

  Wisconsin Administrative Register (Monthly)

WYOMING

- **Reporters:**

Supreme Court

*Wyoming Reports	1870–1959	Disc. with v.80 (1959)
*Pacific Reporter	1883–date	Official since 1959
*Wyoming Reporter (West)	1959–date	Official since 1959

- **Session Laws:**

  Session Laws of Wyoming

- **Statutory Compilation:**

  Wyoming Statutes

- **Administrative Code:**

  State Register

- **Administrative Register:**

  ——

Appendix C

WEST REGIONAL REPORTERS AND THEIR STATE COVERAGE

Atlantic Reporter (1886 to date): Includes decisions beginning with the designated volumes of the following major state reports: 53 Connecticut; 12 Delaware (7 Houston); 6 Delaware Chancery; 77 Maine; 63 Maryland; 63 New Hampshire; 47 New Jersey Law; 40 New Jersey Equity; 108 Pennsylvania State; 102 Pennsylvania Superior; 15 Rhode Island; 58 Vermont.

North Eastern Reporter (1885 to date): 112 Illinois; 284 Illinois Appellate; 102 Indiana; 1 Indiana Appellate; 139 Massachusetts; 99 New York; 43 Ohio State; 20 Ohio Appellate.

North Western Reporter (1879 to date): 1 Dakota; 51 Iowa; 41 Michigan; 26 Minnesota; 8 Nebraska; 1 North Dakota; 1 South Dakota; 46 Wisconsin.

Pacific Reporter (1884 to date): 1 Arizona; 64 California; 1 California Appellate; 7 Colorado; 1 Colorado Appellate; 2 Idaho; 30 Kansas; 1 Kansas Appellate; 4 Montana; 17 Nevada; 3 New Mexico; 1 Oklahoma; 1 Oklahoma Criminal Appeals; 11 Oregon; 3 Utah; 1 Washington; 2 Washington Territory; 3 Wyoming.

South Eastern Reporter (1887 to date): 77 Georgia; 1 Georgia Appellate; 96 North Carolina; 25 South Carolina; 82 Virginia; 29 West Virginia.

South Western Reporter (1887 to date): 47 Arkansas; 84 Kentucky; 8 Kentucky Law Reporter; 1 Kentucky Decisions; 89 Missouri; 93 Missouri Appellate; 85 Tennessee; 16 Tennessee Appellate; 66 Texas; 21 Texas Appellate; 1 Texas Civil Appeals; 31 Texas Criminal Reports.

Southern Reporter (1887 to date): 80 Alabama; 1 Alabama Appellate; 22 Florida; 104 Louisiana; 39 Louisiana Annotated; 9 Louisiana Appellate; 64 Mississippi.

California Reporter (1960 to date): 53 California 2d; 176 California Appellate 2d.

New York Supplement (1888 to date): 1 New York (1 Comstock); 1 Appellate Division; 1 Miscellaneous; and containing many other now discontinued lower court reporters, plus numerous decisions, not otherwise reported. Since February 1963, however, coverage is virtually the same as that of the three official reporters, *New York, Appellate Division* and *Miscellaneous Reports.*

Appendix D

SOURCES OF FEDERAL REGULATORY AGENCY RULES, REGULATIONS AND ADJUDICATIONS (IN BOTH OFFICIAL AND COMMERCIAL PUBLICATIONS).[1]

1. Prepared by Terry Swanlund, Reference Librarian, Harvard Law School library, to whom our thanks are acknowledged.

Sources of Federal Regulatory Agency Rules, Regulations and Adjudications

AGENCY	RULES AND REGULATIONS		ADJUDICATIONS	
	CFR Location	Commercial Sources	Official	Commercial
Civil Aeronautics Board	14 CFR, pts. 200–399	CCH Aviation Law Reporter	Civil Aeronautics Board Reports	CCH Aviation Law Reporter (includes National Transportation Safety Board)
Commodity Futures Trading Commission	17 CFR, Ch. I	CCH Commodity Future Law Reporter; and WESTLAW.		CCH Commodity Futures Law Reporter
Consumer Product Safety Commission	16 CFR, pts. 1000–end	CCH Consumer Product Safety Guide Reams & Ferguson. Fed'l Consumer Protection: Laws, Rules & Regulations; and WESTLAW.	Available on written request from Commission	CCH Consumer Product Safety Guide (digests)
Economic Regulatory Administration (DOE)	10 CFR, pts. 1–260	CCH Energy Management (selected)		CCH Energy Management Vol. 6
Energy Department	10 CFR, pts. 200–end	CCH Energy Management	Available for inspection & photocopying at DOE Public Docket Room, Washington, D.C.	Office of Hearings and Appeals decisions and orders (full texts and digests) in Energy Management, Vol. 7

Sources of Federal Regulatory Agency Rules, Regulations and Adjudications—Continued

AGENCY	RULES AND REGULATIONS		ADJUDICATIONS	
	CFR Location	Commercial Sources	Official	Commercial
Environmental Protection Agency	40 CFR, pts. 1–762	BNA Chemical Regulation Reporter (selected) BNA Environment Reporter ELI Environmental Law Reporter (selected)	Formal adjudications in federal district	Chemical Regulation Reporter, Environment Reporter, ELI Environmental Law Reporter
Equal Employment Opportunity Commission	29 CFR pts. 1600–1612	CCH Employment Practices Guide		CCH Employment Practices Guide; CCH EEOC Decisions (1968–73); Fair Employment Practice Service of BNA Labor Relations Reporter (digests)
Federal Aviation Administration	14 CFR, pts. 1–199	CCH Aviation Law Reporter (selected)		
Federal Communications Commission	47 CFR, Ch. 1	Pike & Fischer Radio Regulation; and WESTLAW.	Federal Communications Commission Reports	Pike & Fischer Radio Regulation; WESTLAW 1975–date; LEXIS, 1965–date.
Federal Election Commission	11 CFR, pts. 1–146	CCH Federal Election Campaign Financing Guide US	Available from Public Records Office of the Commission; Federal Election Commission Record (advisory opinions digests) vertical file	CCH Federal Election Campaign Financing Guide (advisory opinions)

Sources of Federal Regulatory Agency Rules, Regulations and Adjudications—Continued

AGENCY	RULES AND REGULATIONS		ADJUDICATIONS	
	CFR Location	Commercial Sources	Official	Commercial
Federal Energy Regulatory Commission	18 CFR, pts. 1–260	CCH Utilities Law Reporter; CCH Federal Energy Regulatory Commission Reports (selected)	Federal Power Commission Reports (predecessor agency)	CCH Utilities Law Reports; LEXIS, 1977–date.
Federal Labor Relations Authority	5 CFR, pts. 2400–2471		Decisions of the Fed'l Labor Relations Authority	
Federal Reserve System	12 CFR, pts. 201–294 and 32A, pt. 1505	CCH Federal Banking Law Reporter; LEXIS, G, T, U and X final and proposed regulations.	Federal Reserve Bulletin; Fed'l Reserve Regulatory Service	CCH Federal Banking Law Reporter
Federal Service Impasses Panel (FLRA)	5 CFR, pt. 2471		Federal Service Impasses Panel Releases	
Federal Trade Commission	16 CFR, pts. 0–800	CCH Trade Regulation Reporter; LEXIS and WESTLAW.	FTC Decisions	CCH Trade Regulation Reporter; LEXIS and WESTLAW.
Food and Drug Administration	21 CFR, pts. 1–1299	CCH Medical Devices Reporter (selected); CCH Food, Drug, Cosmetic Reporter (selected)		CCH Medical Devices Reporter; Food, Drug, Cosmetic Reporter
Health Care Financing Administration (H.H.S.)	42 CFR, pts. 430–489	CCH Medicare & Medicaid Guide, Vol. 4		

Sources of Federal Regulatory Agency Rules, Regulations and Adjudications—Continued

AGENCY	RULES AND REGULATIONS		ADJUDICATIONS	
	CFR Location	Commercial Sources	Official	Commercial
Immigration and Naturalization Service	8 CFR, pts. 1–499	American Council for Nationalities Service Interpreter Releases (selected)	Administrative Decisions under Immigration & Nationality Laws of the United States	American Council for Nationalities Service Interpreter Releases (selected digests)
Interstate Commerce Commission	49 CFR, pts. 1000–1199	CCH Federal Carriers Reporter	ICC Reports	Federal Carriers Reporter, digests or full text (selected). Older cases cumulated in CCH Federal Carrier Cases
Mine Safety & Health Administration (Dept. of Labor)	30 CFR, pts. 1–100		Federal Mine Safety & Health Review Commission (an independent adjudicatory agency) Decisions 1979–date.	
National Labor Relations Board	29 CFR, pts. 100–103	CCH Labor Law Reporter, Vol. 1	Decisions and Orders of the NLRB	CCH Labor Law Reporter, Vol. 5 (digests); Labor Management Relations binder (#2 of BNA Labor Relations Reporter) (digests or full text); WESTLAW and LEXIS, 1972–date. Older decisions cumulated in Labor Relations Ref. Manual

Sources of Federal Regulatory Agency Rules, Regulations and Adjudications—Continued

AGENCY	**RULES AND REGULATIONS**		**ADJUDICATIONS**	
	CFR Location	Commercial Sources	Official	Commercial
Nuclear Regulatory Commission	10 CFR, pts. 0–199	CCH Nuclear Regulation Reporter	AEC Reports; Nuclear Regulatory Commission Issuances	CCH Nuclear Regulation Reporter; LEXIS, beginning 1983.
Occupational Safety and Health Administration	29 CFR, pts. 1900–end	CCH Employment Safety & Health Guide	Citations issued by OSHA. Appellate review by Occupational Safety and Health Review Commission. Administrative Law Judge and Comm. Decisions 1971–date.	CCH Employment Safety and Health Guide (selected full texts or digests, current) CCH Occupational Safety & Health Decisions, 1971–date. WESTLAW, 1971–date.
Securities and Exchange Commission	17 CFR, Ch. II	CCH Federal Securities Law Reporter; P–H Securities Regulations Guide; WESTLAW and LEXIS.	SEC Decisions and Reports	CCH Federal Securities Law Reporter; P–H Securities Regulation Guide, digest or full text (selected), WESTLAW and LEXIS (selected) 1933–date.
Social Security Administration (H.H.S.)	20 CFR, pts. 401–450	CCH Medicare & Medicaid Guide (selected Medicare), Vol. 3	Social Security Rulings: On Federal Old-Age, Survivors Disability, Supplemental Security Income and Black Lung Benefits	

NAME INDEX

By
Laura Praglin

References are to Pages

References are to Pages

References are to Pages

References are to Pages

SUBJECT INDEX

By
Sara Robbins

References are to Pages

†